HALSBURY'S
Laws of England

FIFTH EDITION
2014

Volume 39

This is volume 39 of the Fifth Edition of Halsbury's Laws of England, containing the first part of the title EMPLOYMENT.

The title EMPLOYMENT replaces the EMPLOYMENT title contained in volumes 39 (2009), 40 (2009), 41 (2009).

Volumes 39 (2009), 40 (2009), 41 (2009) may now be archived.

For a full list of volumes comprised in a current set of Halsbury's Laws of England please see overleaf.

Fifth Edition volumes:

1 (2008), 2 (2008), 3 (2011), 4 (2011), 5 (2013), 6 (2011), 7 (2008), 8 (2010), 9 (2012), 10 (2012), 11 (2009), 12 (2009), 13 (2009), 14 (2009), 15 (2009), 16 (2011), 17 (2011), 18 (2009), 19 (2011), 20 (2014), 21 (2011), 22 (2012), 23 (2013), 24 (2010), 25 (2010), 26 (2010), 27 (2010), 28 (2010), 30 (2012), 31 (2012), 32 (2012), 33 (2013), 34 (2011), 35 (2011), 36 (2011), 37 (2013), 38 (2013), 38A (2013), 39 (2014), 40 (2014), 41 (2014), 41A (2014), 42 (2011), 43 (2011), 44 (2011), 45 (2010), 46 (2010), 47 (2014), 47A (2014), 48 (2008), 49 (2008), 50 (2008), 51 (2013), 52 (2014), 53 (2014), 54 (2008), 55 (2012), 56 (2011), 57 (2012), 58 (2014), 58A (2014), 59 (2014), 59A (2014), 60 (2011), 61 (2010), 62 (2012), 63 (2012), 64 (2012), 65 (2008), 66 (2009), 67 (2008), 68 (2008), 69 (2009), 70 (2012), 71 (2013), 72 (2009), 73 (2009), 74 (2011), 75 (2013), 76 (2013), 77 (2010), 78 (2010), 79 (2014), 80 (2013), 81 (2010), 82 (2010), 83 (2010), 84 (2013), 84A (2013), 85 (2012), 86 (2013), 87 (2012), 88 (2012), 88A (2013), 89 (2011), 90 (2011), 91 (2012), 92 (2010), 93 (2008), 94 (2008), 95 (2013), 96 (2012), 97 (2010), 97A (2014), 98 (2013), 99 (2012), 100 (2009), 101 (2009), 102 (2010), 103 (2010), 104 (2014)

Fourth Edition volumes (bold figures represent reissues):

12(1)

Additional Materials:

Sentencing and Disposition of Offenders (*Release and Recall of Prisoners*) containing vol **92** (2010) paras 761–820; *Tort* (*Conversion and Wrongful Interference with Goods*) containing vol **45(2)** (Reissue) paras 542–686

Fourth and Fifth Edition volumes:

2014 Consolidated Index (A–E), 2014 Consolidated Index (F–O), 2014 Consolidated Index (P–Z), 2015 Consolidated Table of Statutes, 2015 Consolidated Table of Statutory Instruments, etc, 2014 Consolidated Table of Cases (A–G), 2014 Consolidated Table of Cases (H–Q), 2014 Consolidated Table of Cases (R–Z, ECJ Cases)

Updating and ancillary materials:

2014 Annual Cumulative Supplement; Monthly Current Service; Annual Abridgments 1974–2013

November 2014

HALSBURY'S
Laws of England

Volume 39

2014

Members of the LexisNexis Group worldwide

United Kingdom	LexisNexis, a Division of Reed Elsevier (UK) Ltd, Lexis House, 30 Farringdon Street, LONDON, EC4A 4HH, and 9–10, St Andrew Square, EDINBURGH, EH2 2AF
Australia	LexisNexis Butterworths, Chatswood, New South Wales
Austria	LexisNexis Verlag ARD Orac GmbH & Co KG, Vienna
Benelux	LexisNexis Benelux, Amsterdam
Canada	LexisNexis Canada, Markham, Ontario
China	LexisNexis China, Beijing and Shanghai
France	LexisNexis SA, Paris
Germany	LexisNexis GmbH, Dusseldorf
Hong Kong	LexisNexis Hong Kong, Hong Kong
India	LexisNexis India, New Delhi
Italy	Giuffrè Editore, Milan
Japan	LexisNexis Japan, Tokyo
Malaysia	Malayan Law Journal Sdn Bhd, Kuala Lumpur
New Zealand	LexisNexis NZ Ltd, Wellington
Singapore	LexisNexis Singapore, Singapore
South Africa	LexisNexis Butterworths, Durban
USA	LexisNexis, Dayton, Ohio

FIRST EDITION	*Published in 31 volumes between 1907 and 1917*
SECOND EDITION	*Published in 37 volumes between 1931 and 1942*
THIRD EDITION	*Published in 43 volumes between 1952 and 1964*
FOURTH EDITION	*Published in 56 volumes between 1973 and 1987, with reissues between 1988 and 2008*
FIFTH EDITION	*Published between 2008 and 2014, with reissues from 2014*

© Reed Elsevier (UK) Ltd 2014

A CIP Catalogue record for this book is available from the British Library.

ISBN 13 (complete set, standard binding): 9781405734394

ISBN 13: 9781405780605

ISBN 978-1-4057-8060-5

9 781405 780605

Typeset by Letterpart Limited, Caterham on the Hill, Surrey CR3 5XL
Printed and bound by CPI Group (UK) Ltd, Croydon, CR0 4YY
Visit LexisNexis at www.lexisnexis.co.uk

EMPLOYMENT

Consultant Editor
IAN SMITH, LLB, MA,
of Gray's Inn, Barrister;
Emeritus Professor of Employment Law,
School of Law, University of East Anglia

The law stated in this volume is in general that in force on 1 October 2014,
although subsequent changes have been included wherever possible.

Any future updating material will be found in the Current Service and annual
Cumulative Supplement to Halsbury's Laws of England.

TABLE OF CONTENTS

Volume 39

EMPLOYMENT

Volume 40

Volume 41

HOW TO USE HALSBURY'S LAWS
OF ENGLAND

Volumes

Each text volume of Halsbury's Laws of England contains the law on the titles contained in it as at a date stated at the front of the volume (the operative date).

Information contained in Halsbury's Laws of England may be accessed in several ways.

First, by using the tables of contents.

Each volume contains both a general Table of Contents, and a specific Table of Contents for each title contained in it. From these tables you will be directed to the relevant part of the work.

Readers should note that the current arrangement of titles can be found in the Current Service.

Secondly, by using tables of statutes, statutory instruments, cases or other materials.

If you know the name of the Act, statutory instrument or case with which your research is concerned, you should consult the Consolidated Tables of statutes, cases and so on (published as separate volumes) which will direct you to the relevant volume and paragraph. The Consolidated Tables will indicate if the volume referred to is a Fifth Edition volume.

(Each individual text volume also includes tables of those materials used as authority in that volume.)

Thirdly, by using the indexes.

If you are uncertain of the general subject area of your research, you should go to the Consolidated Index (published as separate volumes) for reference to the relevant volume(s) and paragraph(s). The Consolidated Index will indicate if the volume referred to is a Fifth Edition volume.

(Each individual text volume also includes an index to the material contained therein.)

Additional Materials

The reorganisation of the title scheme of Halsbury's Laws for the Fifth Edition means that from time to time Fourth Edition volumes will be *partially* replaced by Fifth Edition volumes.

In certain instances an Additional Materials softbound book will be issued, in which will be reproduced material which has not yet been replaced by a Fifth Edition title. This will enable users to remove specific Fourth Edition volumes from the shelf and save valuable space pending the replacement of that material in the Fifth Edition. These softbound books are supplied to volumes subscribers free of charge. They continue to form part of the set of Halsbury's Laws Fourth Edition Reissue, and will be updated by the annual Cumulative Supplement and monthly Noter-Up in the usual way.

Updating publications

The text volumes of Halsbury's Laws should be used in conjunction with the annual Cumulative Supplement and the monthly Noter-Up.

The annual Cumulative Supplement

The Supplement gives details of all changes between the operative date of the text volume and the operative date of the Supplement. It is arranged in the same volume, title and paragraph order as the text volumes. Developments affecting particular points of law are noted to the relevant paragraph(s) of the text volumes. As from the commencement of the Fifth Edition, the Supplement will clearly distinguish between Fourth and Fifth Edition titles.

For narrative treatment of material noted in the Cumulative Supplement, go to the Annual Abridgment volume for the relevant year.

Destination Tables

In certain titles in the annual *Cumulative Supplement*, reference is made to Destination Tables showing the destination of consolidated legislation. Those Destination Tables are to be found either at the end of the titles within the annual *Cumulative Supplement*, or in a separate *Destination Tables* booklet provided from time to time with the *Cumulative Supplement*.

The Noter-Up

The Noter-Up is contained in the Current Service Noter-Up booklet, issued monthly and noting changes since the publication of the annual Cumulative Supplement. Also arranged in the same volume, title and paragraph order as the text volumes, the Noter-Up follows the style of the Cumulative Supplement. As from the commencement of the Fifth Edition, the Noter-Up will clearly distinguish between Fourth and Fifth Edition titles.

For narrative treatment of material noted in the Noter-Up, go to the relevant Monthly Review.

REFERENCES AND ABBREVIATIONS

ACT	Australian Capital Territory
A-G	Attorney General
Admin	Administrative Court
Admlty	Admiralty Court
Adv-Gen	Advocate General
affd	affirmed
affg	affirming
Alta	Alberta
App	Appendix
art	article
Aust	Australia
B	Baron
BC	British Columbia
C	Command Paper (of a series published before 1900)
c	chapter number of an Act
CA	Court of Appeal
CAC	Central Arbitration Committee
CA in Ch	Court of Appeal in Chancery
CB	Chief Baron
CCA	Court of Criminal Appeal
CCR	County Court Rules 1981 (as subsequently amended)
CCR	Court for Crown Cases Reserved
C-MAC	Courts-Martial Appeal Court
CO	Crown Office
COD	Crown Office Digest
CPR	Civil Procedure Rules
Can	Canada
Cd	Command Paper (of the series published 1900–18)
Cf	compare
Ch	Chancery Division
ch	chapter
cl	clause
Cm	Command Paper (of the series published 1986 to date)

Cmd	Command Paper (of the series published 1919–56)
Cmnd	Command Paper (of the series published 1956–86)
Comm	Commercial Court
Comr	Commissioner
Court Forms (2nd Edn)	Atkin's Encyclopaedia of Court Forms in Civil Proceedings, 2nd Edn. See note 2 post.
CrimPR	Criminal Procedure Rules
DC.......................................	Divisional Court
DPP	Director of Public Prosecutions
EAT	Employment Appeal Tribunal
EC	European Community
ECJ......................................	Court of Justice of the European Community
EComHR..............................	European Commission of Human Rights
ECSC....................................	European Coal and Steel Community
ECtHR Rules of Court...........	Rules of Court of the European Court of Human Rights
EEC......................................	European Economic Community
EFTA	European Free Trade Association
EWCA Civ	Official neutral citation for judgments of the Court of Appeal (Civil Division)
EWCA Crim..........................	Official neutral citation for judgments of the Court of Appeal (Criminal Division)
EWHC...................................	Official neutral citation for judgments of the High Court
Edn......................................	Edition
Euratom	European Atomic Energy Community
Ex Ch...................................	Court of Exchequer Chamber
ex p	ex parte
Fam	Family Division
Fed	Federal
Forms & Precedents (5th Edn).....................................	Encyclopaedia of Forms and Precedents other than Court Forms, 5th Edn. See note 2 post.
GLC	Greater London Council
HC	High Court
HC	House of Commons
HK	Hong Kong
HL..	House of Lords
IAT.......................................	Immigration Appeal Tribunal
ILM......................................	International Legal Materials
INLR.....................................	Immigration and Nationality Law Reports
IRC.......................................	Inland Revenue Commissioners
Ind.......................................	India

Int Rels	International Relations
Ir	Ireland
J	Justice
JA	Judge of Appeal
Kan	Kansas
LA	Lord Advocate
LC	Lord Chancellor
LCC	London County Council
LCJ	Lord Chief Justice
LJ	Lord Justice of Appeal
LoN	League of Nations
MR	Master of the Rolls
Man	Manitoba
n	note
NB	New Brunswick
NI	Northern Ireland
NS	Nova Scotia
NSW	New South Wales
NY	New York
NZ	New Zealand
OHIM	Office for Harmonisation in the Internal Market
OJ	The Official Journal of the European Community published by the Office for Official Publications of the European Community
Ont	Ontario
P	President
PC	Judicial Committee of the Privy Council
PEI	Prince Edward Island
Pat	Patents Court
q	question
QB	Queen's Bench Division
QBD	Queen's Bench Division of the High Court
Qld	Queensland
Que	Quebec
r	rule
RDC	Rural District Council
RPC	Restrictive Practices Court
RSC	Rules of the Supreme Court 1965 (as subsequently amended)
reg	regulation
Res	Resolution
revsd	reversed

Rly..	Railway
s..	section
SA..	South Africa
S Aust......................................	South Australia
SC..	Supreme Court
SI...	Statutory Instruments published by authority
SR & O.....................................	Statutory Rules and Orders published by authority
SR & O Rev 1904	Revised Edition comprising all Public and General Statutory Rules and Orders in force on 31 December 1903
SR & O Rev 1948	Revised Edition comprising all Public and General Statutory Rules and Orders and Statutory Instruments in force on 31 December 1948
SRNI	Statutory Rules of Northern Ireland
STI...	Simon's Tax Intelligence (1973–1995); Simon's Weekly Tax Intelligence (1996-current)
Sask	Saskatchewan
Sch...	Schedule
Sess..	Session
Sing	Singapore
TCC	Technology and Construction Court
TS..	Treaty Series
Tanz...	Tanzania
Tas...	Tasmania
UDC..	Urban District Council
UKHL.......................................	Official neutral citation for judgments of the House of Lords
UKPC	Official neutral citation for judgments of the Privy Council
UN	United Nations
V-C...	Vice-Chancellor
Vict..	Victoria
W Aust.....................................	Western Australia
Zimb	Zimbabwe

NOTE 1. A general list of the abbreviations of law reports and other sources used in this work can be found at the beginning of the Consolidated Table of Cases.

NOTE 2. Where references are made to other publications, the volume number precedes and the page number follows the name of the publication; eg the reference '12 Forms & Precedents (5th Edn) 44' refers to volume 12 of the Encyclopaedia of Forms and Precedents, page 44.

NOTE 3. An English statute is cited by short title or, where there is no short title, by regnal year and chapter number together with the name by which it is commonly known or a description of its subject matter and date. In the case of a foreign statute, the mode of citation generally follows the style of citation in use in the country concerned with the addition, where necessary, of the name of the country in parentheses.

NOTE 4. A statutory instrument is cited by short title, if any, followed by the year and number, or, if unnumbered, the date.

TABLE OF STATUTES

TABLE OF STATUTORY INSTRUMENTS

TABLE OF CIVIL PROCEDURE

Civil Procedure Rules 1998, SI 1998/3132 (CPR)

Practice Directions

TABLE OF EUROPEAN
UNION LEGISLATION

TABLE OF
NON-STATUTORY MATERIAL

TABLE OF CASES

PARA

PARA

PARA

PARA

Z

Decisions of the European Court of Justice are listed below numerically. These decisions
are also included in the preceding alphabetical list.

PARA

EMPLOYMENT

VOLUME 39

1. NATURE OF A CONTRACT OF EMPLOYMENT

(1) EMPLOYMENT UNDER CONTRACT

(i) In general

1. The importance of the contract of employment. Although much of modern employment law is contained in statutes and statutory instruments, the legal basis of employment remains the contract of employment between the employer and the employee[1]. The contract of employment is important in itself, in that it may give rise to a common law claim for its enforcement or for damages on account of its breach[2]. However, it is equally important in areas of statutory employment law because the expression 'employee' is defined[3] by reference to the contractual relationship at common law[4], although it is possible under the Employment Rights Act 1996 to contract out of certain of its provisions if specified circumstances apply[5], and an employee who agrees to take on the status of employee shareholder under the Employment Rights Act 1996 substitutes fundamental rights relating to unfair dismissal and redundancy with new rights of ownership[6].

1 Although historically employment law originated in what was termed the law of master and servant, the modern terminology adopted is that of 'employer' and 'employee'; and 'contract of employment' is used rather than the older phrase 'contract of service', except that the latter phrase is still used in social security and related legislation. An individual in business on his own account is known variously as an independent contractor or a self-employed person; and traditionally it has been said that such a person works under a 'contract for services' rather than a 'contract of employment' or a 'contract of service'.

2 See PARA 825 et seq. It has been held that '… a contract of service is but an example of contracts in general, so that the general law of contract will be applicable': *Laws v London Chronicle (Indicator Newspapers) Ltd* [1959] 2 All ER 285 at 287, [1959] 1 WLR 698 at 700, CA, per Lord Evershed MR. The contractual basis can, however, cause problems where the traditional rules of contract law do not produce solutions appropriate to the realities of employment (and, equally, where it is tempting to apply a principle to do justice in employment law that may affect the wider law of contract adversely if it is applied there), eg where an employee has suffered detriment due to an illegal contract (which remains unenforceable under employment law as in the law of contract: see PARA 18); and see *Bournemouth University Higher Education Corpn v Buckland* [2010] EWCA Civ 121, [2011] QB 323, [2010] 4 All ER 186 (there could not be in employment law the doctrine that a fundamental breach of a contractual term, if curable and if cured, takes away the innocent party's option of acceptance; to introduce that concept could only be on grounds that were capable of extension to other contracts) (cited in PARA 763 note 6). The relationship of express and implied terms in contracts of employment may also become problematic when viewed in the light of traditional approaches to contract law (see PARA 48 note 22) and it is arguable that implying terms into such contracts proceeds on a different basis from implying terms in traditional contract law anyway (see PARA 113 et seq). The approach of not deducting earnings during what should have been the notice period from a compensatory award for future loss of income (which is regarded as 'good Industrial Relations (IR) practice') provides a narrow exception to the normal rules on mitigation, however: see PARA 819 note 5. As to frustration see PARAS 728–729; and as to termination by mutual consent see PARAS 730–731.

3 See PARA 2.

4 See PARA 4. There is a note of caution to be sounded, however, in using the general law of contract to interpret the statute: see eg *GISDA Cyf v Barratt* [2010] UKSC 41, [2010] 4 All ER 851, [2010] ICR 1475, [2010] IRLR 1073; and PARA 764 note 6. Precedents in the law of tort also may need to be applied with care because, although the terminology used is similar, the person who is the employer for the purposes of vicarious liability in tort is not necessarily the same person as the employer for the purposes of employment law: see eg *Denham v Midland Employers' Mutual Assurance Ltd* [1955] 2 QB 437, [1955] 2 All ER 561, CA (loan of employee); *Morris v Breaveglen Ltd (t/a Anzac Construction Co)* [1993] ICR 766, [1993] IRLR 350, CA; and NEGLIGENCE vol 78 (2010) PARA 16; TORT vol 97 (2010) PARAS 506, 686 et seq.

5   See the Employment Rights Act 1996 s 203; and PARA 150.
6   See the Employment Rights Act 1996 s 205A; and PARA 154.

2.   Statutory meanings of 'employer'; 'employee'; 'employment'; and 'contract of employment'. 'Employer' means[1] the person[2] by whom the employee[3] is (or, where the employment has ceased, was) employed[4]; 'employee' means an individual who has entered into or works under (or, where the employment has ceased, worked under) a contract of employment[5]; 'employment', in relation to an employee, means[6] employment under a contract of employment and, in relation to a worker, means employment under his contract[7]; and 'contract of employment' means a contract of service or apprenticeship, whether express or implied, and, if it is express, whether it is oral or in writing[8].

Whether a person is or is not an employee is a question of fact[9] which, in proceedings under the Employment Rights Act 1996, is essentially a matter for the employment tribunal[10].

For the purposes of the Employment Rights Act 1996, it is immaterial whether the law which otherwise governs any person's employment[11] is the law of the United Kingdom[12] or of a part of the United Kingdom, or not[13].

1   Ie for the purpose of the Employment Rights Act 1996 (in relation to an employee or a worker: see PARA 69 et seq) and the Employment Tribunals Act 1996 (in relation to an employee only: see PARAS 152 et seq, 1399 et seq): see the Employment Rights Act 1996 s 230(4); and the Employment Tribunals Act 1996 s 42(1). The definition of 'employer' as worded in s 42(1) (ie with references to a worker omitted) is used also for the purposes of the Maternity and Parental Leave etc Regulations 1999, SI 1999/3312, reg 2(1) (see PARA 356 note 5); the Fixed-term Employees (Prevention of Less Favourable Treatment) Regulations 2002, SI 2002/2034, reg 1(2) (see PARA 86 note 4); the Paternity and Adoption Leave Regulations 2002, SI 2002/2788, reg 2(1) (see PARA 370 note 11); and the Flexible Working (Procedural Requirements) Regulations 2002, SI 2002/3207, reg 2(1) (see PARA 110 note 1). On the other hand, the definition of 'employer' given in the Employment Rights Act 1996 is used for the purposes of the Working Time Regulations 1998, SI 1998/1833, with references to an employee omitted: see reg 2(1); and PARA 269 note 5. As to the meaning of 'worker' see PARA 5.
2   In the case of an unincorporated association, this means the relevant management committee and its members as constituted from time to time: *Affleck v Newcastle MIND* [1999] ICR 852, [1999] IRLR 405, EAT (registered charity). It is permissible for an employee to bring a claim against an employer who is the management committee of an unincorporated association by using the name of the association: see *Asim v Nazir* [2010] ICR 1225, [2010] All ER (D) 113 (Aug), EAT (applying *Affleck v Newcastle MIND* (proceedings can be issued against a named committee member as respondent, representing all committee members)). As to the corporate or quasi-corporate status of employers' associations see PARA 1080.
3   Ie the employee or worker, in the case of the Employment Rights Act 1996 (see note 1): see s 230(4).
4   See the Employment Rights Act 1996 s 230(4); and the Employment Tribunals Act 1996 s 42(1). The Employment Rights Act 1996 s 230 has effect subject to s 43K (see PARA 69 notes 3, 5) and s 47B(3) (see PARA 619 note 1): see s 230(6) (added by the Public Interest Disclosure Act 1998 ss 15(1), 18(2)). The Employment Rights Act 1996 s 230 also has effect subject to s 75K(3), (5) (shared parental leave: see PARA 398 note 57): see s 230(7) (added by the Children and Families Act 2014 s 126(1), Sch 7 paras 29, 41).
    For the purposes of the Employment Rights Act 1996 Pt XIII (ss 191–209) (miscellaneous provisions), so far as relating to Pt IVA (ss 43A–43L) (protected disclosures: see PARAS 69, 70) or s 47B (see PARA 619), 'employer', 'employment' and 'employed' have the extended meaning given by s 43K: see s 230(6) (as so added). The wording of the definition of 'employer' given in s 230(4) is used also in relation to an employee or a worker for the purposes of the National Minimum Wage Act 1998 (see s 54(4); and PARA 170); the Part-time Workers (Prevention of Less Favourable Treatment) Regulations 2000, SI 2000/1551 (except where a provision of those regulations otherwise requires: see reg 1(2); and PARA 75 note 4); and the Agency Workers Regulations 2010, SI 2010/93 (see reg 2; and PARA 98 note 6). For the purposes of the National Minimum Wage Regulations 1999, SI 1999/584 (see PARA 172 et seq), 'employer' has the meaning given to it by the National Minimum Wage Act 1998 s 54(4) but, in relation to a

worker (as defined in s 54(3): see PARA 171), the definition is extended: see the National Minimum Wage Regulations 1999, SI 1999/584, reg 2(1); and PARA 170 note 4. 'Employer' is defined differently for the purposes of social security legislation: see the Social Security Contributions and Benefits Act 1992 s 163(1) (cited in PARA 571); s 171(1) (cited in PARA 414); s 171ZJ(1) (cited in PARA 414); and s 171ZS(1) (cited in PARA 502).

5 See the Employment Rights Act 1996 s 230(1); and the Employment Tribunals Act 1996 s 42(1). See *Melhuish v Redbridge Citizens Advice Bureau* [2005] IRLR 419, EAT. See also note 4. This wording of the definition of 'employee' is used also for the purposes of the National Minimum Wage Act 1998 (see s 54(1); and PARA 170); the Employment Act 2002 (see ss 40, 45(6); and PARAS 85 note 3, 700 note 4); the Maternity and Parental Leave etc Regulations 1999, SI 1999/3312 (see reg 2(1); and PARA 356 note 1); the Part-time Workers (Prevention of Less Favourable Treatment) Regulations 2000, SI 2000/1551 (except where a provision of the same regulations otherwise requires: see reg 1(2); and PARA 75 note 3); the Paternity and Adoption Leave Regulations 2002, SI 2002/2788 (see reg 2(1); and PARA 370 note 1); the Flexible Working (Procedural Requirements) Regulations 2002, SI 2002/3207 (see reg 2(1); and PARA 110 note 2); and the Agency Workers Regulations 2010, SI 2010/93 (see reg 2; and PARA 98 note 5). A modified and extended version of the wording used in the Employment Rights Act 1996 s 230(1) is used for the purposes of the Employers' Liability (Compulsory Insurance) Act 1969: see s 2(1) ('employee' means an individual who has entered into or works under a contract of service or apprenticeship with an employer whether by way of manual labour, clerical work or otherwise); and PARA 42.

'Employee' is specifically defined for the purposes of various other enactments: see the Health and Safety at Work etc Act 1974 Pt I (ss 1–54) (see s 53(1); and HEALTH AND SAFETY AT WORK vol 52 (2014) PARA 302); and the Transfer of Undertakings (Protection of Employment) Regulations 2006, SI 2006/246 (see reg 2(1); and PARA 137 note 8). It is also defined differently for the purposes of social security legislation: see the Social Security Contributions and Benefits Act 1992 s 163(1) (cited in PARA 562); s 171(1) (cited in PARA 406); s 171ZJ(2) (cited in PARA 448); and s 171ZS(2) (cited in PARA 494). See further PARA 5.

6 Ie in the Employment Rights Act 1996, except for the purposes of s 171 (see PARA 838): see s 230(5). As to the application of employment law in cases where the governing body of a school has the right to a delegated budget, and the Education Act 2002 provides for powers to be conferred and duties to be imposed on employers, for rights to be conferred on employees, and for relations between employers and employees otherwise to be regulated, when such bodies are acting in the exercise of their employment powers, see EDUCATION vol 35 (2011) PARA 355 et seq.

7 Employment Rights Act 1996 s 230(5). For the purposes of the Employment Tribunals Act 1996, 'employment' means employment under a contract of employment: see s 42(1). 'Employed' is to be construed accordingly: see the Employment Rights Act 1996 s 230(5); and the Employment Tribunals Act 1996 s 42(1). The wording of the definition of 'employment' given in the Employment Rights Act 1996 s 230(5) is used also for the purposes of the National Minimum Wage Act 1998 (see s 54(5); and PARA 170) and, in relation to a worker only, by the Working Time Regulations 1998, SI 1998/1833 (see reg 2(1); and PARA 269 note 5). A variation on the wording (which accommodates employment under a contract of service or apprenticeship or a contract for services or otherwise than under a contract) is used in both the Employment and Training Act 1973 (see s 13(1); and PARA 634 note 2) and the Industrial Training Act 1982 (see s 1(2); and PARA 658 note 2). See also PARA 5.

8 Employment Rights Act 1996 s 230(2); Employment Tribunals Act 1996 s 42(1). This wording of the definition of 'contract of employment' is used also for the purposes of the National Minimum Wage Act 1998 (see s 54(2); and PARA 170); the Employment Act 2002 (see s 45(6) (fixed-term work); and PARA 85 note 3); the Maternity and Parental Leave etc Regulations 1999, SI 1999/3312 (see reg 2(1); and PARA 356 note 1); the Part-time Workers (Prevention of Less Favourable Treatment) Regulations 2000, SI 2000/1551 (see reg 1(2); and PARA 75 note 2); the Paternity and Adoption Leave Regulations 2002, SI 2002/2788 (see reg 2(1); and PARA 370 note 1); the Flexible Working (Procedural Requirements) Regulations 2002, SI 2002/3207 (see reg 2(1); and PARA 110 note 2); and the Agency Workers Regulations 2010, SI 2010/93 (see reg 2; and PARA 97 note 5). A very similar definition (but using 'contract of employment' instead of 'contract of service') is used in the Health and Safety at Work etc Act 1974 s 53(1): see HEALTH AND SAFETY AT WORK vol 52 (2014) PARA 302. A different, wider, definition is used for the purposes of the Transfer of Undertakings (Protection of Employment) Regulations 2006, SI 2006/246: see reg 2(1) ('contract of employment' means any agreement between an employee and his employer determining the terms and conditions of his employment); and PARA 138 note 5. As to the meaning of 'contract of service' see PARA 1 note 1. In any Act, unless the contrary intention appears, 'writing' includes typing, printing, lithography, photography and

other modes of representing or reproducing words in a visible form; and expressions referring to writing are to be construed accordingly: see the Interpretation Act 1978 s 5, Sch 1.

9   As to the characteristics of the relationship of employer and employee see PARA 4. In a case where the status of a person's employment is in doubt, it is usual to ask the question whether that person is under a contract of employment or a contract for services, ie whether he is an employee or an independent contractor: see PARA 1 note 1. Usually that accurately reflects the possibilities, but they are not necessarily the only two categories. Exceptionally, another legal category could be relevant (see PARA 14 et seq) or, indeed, the person might fit into no particular category: see eg *Wiltshire Police Authority v Wynn* [1981] QB 95, [1980] ICR 649, CA (police cadet). See also *Wadi v Cornwall and Isles of Scilly Family Practitioner Committee* [1985] ICR 492, EAT (doctor and family practitioner committee); followed in *Ealing Hammersmith and Hounslow Family Health Services Authority v Shukla* [1993] ICR 710, EAT, and in *North Essex Health Authority v David-John* [2004] ICR 112, [2003] All ER (D) 84 (Aug), EAT. See further *Construction Industry Training Board v Labour Force Ltd* [1970] 3 All ER 220, DC; *Ironmonger v Movefield Ltd (t/a Deering Appointments)* [1988] IRLR 461, EAT (both cases where A agreed with B to work for C). In such a case, the correct approach is to consider whether that person is an employee within the meaning of the relevant statutory provision. As to the position of apprentices and youth trainees at common law see PARAS 112, 128–129, 636, 747–754. As to the statutory law on apprenticeships see EDUCATION vol 35 (2011) PARA 682 et seq. As to whether a majority shareholder in an employing company (whether or not also a director) can be an 'employee' see *Secretary of State for Trade and Industry v Bottrill* [1999] ICR 592, [1999] IRLR 326, CA; *Nesbitt v Secretary of State for Trade and Industry* [2007] IRLR 847, [2007] All ER (D) 23 (Sep); *Clarke v Clarke Construction Initiatives Ltd* [2008] ICR 635, [2008] IRLR 364, EAT (upheld on other grounds: [2008] EWCA Civ 1446, [2009] ICR 718, [2008] All ER (D) 191 (Dec)); and see PARA 8.

10 As to the employment tribunal as the tribunal of fact see *Carmichael v National Power plc* [1999] 4 All ER 897 at 902, [1999] 1 WLR 2042 at 2048, [2000] IRLR 43 at 45, HL, per Lord Hoffmann; *Franks v Reuters Ltd* [2003] EWCA Civ 417, [2003] ICR 1166, [2003] IRLR 423. As to employment tribunals see PARA 1399 et seq; as to the procedure on a complaint made to an employment tribunal see PARA 1453 et seq; and as to the restricted scope for an appeal against their decisions see PARA 1428.

11 In the case of most contracts of employment made after 1 April 1991, the question of which law governs the contract is answered by the rules of the European Parliament and Council Regulation (EC) 593/2008 (OJ L177, 4.7.2008, p 6) ('the Rome I Regulation'); and the Contracts (Applicable Law) Act 1990 s 2(4)(a), Sch 1 (setting out the English text of the Convention on the Law Applicable to Contractual Obligations opened for signature in Rome on 19 June 1980 (Rome, 19 June 1980; Cmnd 8489) ('the Rome Convention'): see CONFLICT OF LAWS vol 19 (2011) PARA 628.

12 In any Act, unless the contrary intention appears, 'United Kingdom' means Great Britain and Northern Ireland: see the Interpretation Act 1978 s 5, Sch 1. 'Great Britain' means England, Scotland and Wales: see the Union with Scotland Act 1706 preamble art I; and the Interpretation Act 1978 s 22(1), Sch 2 para 5(a). Neither the Channel Islands nor the Isle of Man are within the United Kingdom. 'England' means, subject to any alteration of the boundaries of local government areas, the areas consisting of the counties established by the Local Government Act 1972 s 1 (see LOCAL GOVERNMENT vol 69 (2009) PARAS 5, 22), and Greater London and the Isles of Scilly: see the Interpretation Act 1978 s 5, Sch 1. As to local government areas in England see LOCAL GOVERNMENT vol 69 (2009) PARA 22 et seq; and as to boundary changes see LOCAL GOVERNMENT vol 69 (2009) PARA 54 et seq. As to Greater London as an administrative area see LONDON GOVERNMENT vol 71 (2013) PARA 14. 'Wales' means the combined areas of the counties created by the Local Government Act 1972 s 20 (as originally enacted) (see LOCAL GOVERNMENT vol 69 (2009) PARAS 5, 37), but subject to any alteration made under s 73 (consequential alteration of boundary following alteration of watercourse: see LOCAL GOVERNMENT vol 69 (2009) PARA 90): see the Interpretation Act 1978 Sch 1 (definition substituted by the Local Government (Wales) Act 1994 s 1(3), Sch 2 para 9).

13 Employment Rights Act 1996 s 204(1).

3.   Statutory meaning of 'associated employer'.   Any two employers[1] are to be treated[2] as associated[3] if one is a company[4] of which the other (directly or indirectly) has control, or if both are companies of which a third person (directly or indirectly) has control; and 'associated employer' is to be construed accordingly[5].

For these purposes, 'control' means voting control, that is to say control by the majority of votes attaching to shares exercised in general meeting, not de facto control[6]. Control by a person may include control by a group of persons, together having the necessary voting power, provided that in practice they act as one[7].

1 As to the meaning of 'employer' see PARA 2. The concept of 'associated employer' exists to ensure that an employee is not unfairly prejudiced by the fact that his employing concern is divided into different companies each with its own corporate identity.

2 Ie for the purposes of the Employment Rights Act 1996 and the Employment Tribunals Act 1996: see the Employment Rights Act 1996 s 231; and the Employment Tribunals Act 1996 s 42(3).

3 See *Charnock v Barrie Muirhead Ltd* [1984] ICR 641, EAT; *Lucas v Henry Johnson (Packers and Shippers) Ltd* [1986] ICR 384, EAT.

4 'Company' means a limited company; but it does not apply to any other form of statutory body corporate: *Hasley v Fair Employment Agency* [1989] IRLR 106, NI CA. It does not include a local authority: *Merton London Borough v Gardiner* [1981] QB 269, [1981] ICR 186, CA. See also note 5. As to companies and other bodies corporate see COMPANIES vol 14 (2009) PARA 1 et seq.

5 See the Employment Rights Act 1996 s 231; and the Employment Tribunals Act 1996 s 42(3). The Employment Rights Act 1996 s 231 and the Employment Tribunals Act 1996 s 42(3) are exhaustive of the definition of 'associated employer': *Merton London Borough v Gardiner* [1981] QB 269, [1981] ICR 186, CA, applying *Southern Electricity Board v Collins* [1970] 1 QB 83, [1969] 2 All ER 1166, DC, and *Southwood Hostel Management Committee v Taylor* [1979] ICR 813, [1979] IRLR 397, EAT, and disapproving *Hillingdon Area Health Authority v Kauders* [1979] ICR 472, [1979] IRLR 197, EAT. A foreign company may, however, qualify as an associated employer if it does not differ in any material respects from a company incorporated under the Companies Acts (*Hancill v Marcon Engineering Ltd* [1990] ICR 103, [1990] IRLR 51, EAT), as may a partnership of companies (*Pinkney v Sandpiper Drilling Ltd* [1989] ICR 389, [1989] IRLR 425, EAT). As to the incorporation of a company under the Companies Acts see COMPANIES vol 14 (2009) PARA 24 et seq. A wider interpretation of 'company' is adopted for the purposes of the Equality Act 2010: see *Glasgow City Council v UNISON Claimants* [2014] CSIH 27, [2014] IRLR 532, 2014 SLT 716 (construing the statute by reference to the ordinary meaning of company, ie to mean essentially any body of persons with a common purpose, is consistent with the underlying purpose of the provision); and DISCRIMINATION vol 33 (2013) PARA 132.

6 *Secretary of State for Employment v Newbold* [1981] IRLR 305, EAT; *Umar v Pliastar Ltd* [1981] ICR 727, EAT; *Washington Arts Association Ltd v Forster* [1983] ICR 346, EAT; *South West Launderettes Ltd v Laidler* [1986] ICR 455, [1986] IRLR 305, CA. A 50% holding does not, however, constitute control: *Hair Colour Consultants Ltd v Mena* [1984] ICR 671, [1984] IRLR 386, EAT.

   Whereas voting control is the usual and normal test, there may, exceptionally, be other circumstances to be taken into account (*Payne v Secretary of State for Employment* [1989] IRLR 352 at 353, CA, obiter, per Balcombe LJ); but whether something less than a legal right to direct the voting of another, eg force of personality or economic reasons, might suffice to establish control remains undecided (*Payne v Secretary of State for Employment* at 355 per Staughton LJ).

7 *Zarb and Samuels v British and Brazilian Produce Co (Sales) Ltd* [1978] IRLR 78, EAT. If this view is correct, control must be by the same group in the case of each relevant company: *Poparm Ltd v Weekes* [1984] IRLR 388, EAT; *South West Launderettes Ltd v Laidler* [1986] ICR 455, [1986] IRLR 305, CA; *Strudwick v Iszatt Bros Ltd* [1988] ICR 796, [1988] IRLR 457, EAT; *Russell v Elmdon Freight Terminal Ltd* [1989] ICR 629, EAT. The concept of group control has, however, been doubted, though without being authoritatively disapproved (see *South West Launderettes Ltd v Laidler* at 459–460 and at 307, obiter, per Mustill LJ; *Strudwick v Iszatt Bros Ltd*); but cf *Harford v Swiftrim Ltd* [1987] ICR 439, [1987] IRLR 360, EAT; *Tice v Cartwright* [1999] ICR 769, EAT (where *Zarb and Samuels v British and Brazilian Produce Co (Sales) Ltd* was followed, on strong facts involving a very restricted shareholding in a family concern).

4. Test at common law as to whether a person is an employee. There is no single test for determining whether a person is an employee[1]. The test that used to be considered sufficient, that is to say the 'control' test[2], can no longer be considered sufficient, especially in the case of the employment of highly skilled individuals[3], and is now only one of the particular factors which may assist a court or tribunal in deciding the point[4]. More recently, the 'integration' or 'organisation' test had been suggested, proposing that the important question was whether the person was integrated into the enterprise or remained apart from, and independent of, it[5]. However, while both of these factors are still pertinent, the modern starting point for deciding whether a contract of service (now generally referred to as a 'contract of employment')[6] exists is to ascertain if:

(1)   the servant agrees that, in consideration of a wage or other remuneration, he will provide his own work and skill in the performance of some service for his master ('mutuality of obligation');

(2)   he agrees, expressly or impliedly, that in the performance of that service he will be subject to the other's control in a sufficient degree to make that other master ('control'); and

(3)   the other provisions of the contract are consistent with its being a contract of service[7].

The final classification of an individual now depends upon a balance of all relevant factors[8], fine though that balance sometimes might be[9], with 'mutuality of obligation' and 'control' being seen as the 'irreducible minimum' legal requirements for the existence of a contract of employment[10]. The factors taken into consideration may include: the method of payment; any obligation to work only for that employer[11]; stipulations as to hours; overtime, holidays etc; arrangements for payment of income tax and national insurance contributions[12]; how the contract may be terminated[13]; whether the individual may delegate work[14]; who provides tools and equipment[15]; and who, ultimately, bears the risk of loss and the chance of profit[16]. In some cases the nature of the work itself may be an important consideration[17].

The way in which the parties themselves treat the contract and the way in which they describe and operate it are not decisive[18]; and a court or tribunal must consider the categorisation of the person in question objectively[19]. Thus a person could have been described as self-employed during the currency of the engagement but, on its termination, claim to have been in fact an employee for the purpose of claiming unfair dismissal[20], although such a course of action could have unfortunate taxation implications[21].

In many employments, the contract will not be discernible just from one document, but will require consideration of several documents, oral exchanges (for example, at interview) and subsequent conduct[22]. In a case of what is often referred to as 'atypical employment', such as temporary or casual work, sporadic work or homeworking, it may be appropriate, when deciding on the employment status of an individual subject to such a regime, to consider whether there is sufficient mutuality of obligations to justify a finding that there was a contract of employment[23].

1   *Stevenson Jordan and Harrison Ltd v MacDonald and Evans* [1952] 1 TLR 101 at 111, CA, per Denning LJ.

2   Ie whether the employer could control not just what the employee did, but the way that he did it: see *Yewens v Noakes* (1880) 6 QBD 530, CA; *Simmons v Heath Laundry Co* [1910] 1 KB 543, CA; *Performing Right Society Ltd v Mitchell and Booker (Palais de Danse) Ltd* [1924] 1 KB 762; *Mersey Docks and Harbour Board v Coggins and Griffith (Liverpool) Ltd* [1947] AC 1, [1946] 2 All ER 345, HL. In circumstances which lack clarity, control is an important factor because it demonstrates the reality of a relationship: *Clifford v Union of Democratic Mineworkers* [1991] IRLR 518, CA (tribunal entitled to treat control as dominant factor in finding a national graded employee in reality to be employed by the area union). The limited

ambit of control exercised over sub-postmasters by the Post Office means that they do not constitute employees for the purposes of the Employment Rights Act 1996 s 230 (see PARA 2): *Wolstenholme v Post Office Ltd* [2003] ICR 546, sub nom *IRC v Post Office Ltd* [2003] IRLR 199, [2002] All ER (D) 282 (Dec), EAT. As to sub-postmasters and their classification under the National Minimum Wage Act 1998 see PARAS 171 note 9, 179 note 2.

A degree of control may be sufficient to establish an employment relationship between a hirer and an individual supplied by an employment agency: see PARA 11.

3   *Cassidy v Ministry of Health* [1951] 2 KB 343, [1951] 1 All ER 574, CA (surgeon); *Beloff v Pressdram Ltd* [1973] 1 All ER 241 (journalist).

4   See *Whittaker v Minister of Pensions and National Insurance* [1967] 1 QB 156, [1966] 3 All ER 531 (although the test of control is not as determinative as used to be thought the case, it is still of value in that the greater the degree of control exercisable by the employer, the more likely it is that the contract is one of service). Nevertheless, there may be an employment relationship even if there is little actual control; and a person can be under a high degree of control but still be an independent contractor because of other factors: *Ready Mixed Concrete (South East) Ltd v Minister of Pensions and National Insurance* [1968] 2 QB 497, [1968] 1 All ER 433; *Re CW and AL Hughes Ltd* [1966] 2 All ER 702, [1966] 1 WLR 1369; *Construction Industry Training Board v Labour Force Ltd* [1970] 3 All ER 220, DC; *Jones v Minton Construction Ltd* (1973) 15 KIR 309; and see *White v Troutbeck SA* [2013] EWCA Civ 1171, [2013] IRLR 949 (manager, caretaker and housekeeper of a substantial asset for absentee owners with day-to-day control of running farm and maintenance of buildings were employees for the purposes of the Employment Rights Act 1996, as owners retained a right of control to a sufficient degree: question was not by whom day-to-day control had been exercised but with whom and to what extent the ultimate right to control had resided); cf *Global Plant Ltd v Secretary of State for Social Services* [1972] 1 QB 139, sub nom *Global Plant Ltd v Secretary of State for Health and Social Security* [1971] 3 All ER 385; *BSM (1257) Ltd v Secretary of State for Social Services* [1978] ICR 894, EAT. The realities of the relationship between parties may require particular examination in the case of 'labour only' sub-contracting: *Re CW and AL Hughes Ltd*; *Jones v Minton Construction Ltd*; *Calder v H Kitson Vickers & Sons (Engineers) Ltd* [1988] ICR 232, CA (personal injury claimant viewed as self-employed even though the employer paid him 'wages' for ten weeks following accident); cf *Ferguson v John Dawson & Partners (Contractors) Ltd* [1976] 3 All ER 817, [1976] IRLR 346, CA (labour only sub-contractor held on the facts to have been an employee). See also *James v Redcats (Brands) Ltd* [2007] ICR 1006, [2007] IRLR 296, EAT (definition of 'worker' in the National Minimum Wage Act 1998 analysed); and PARA 171.

5   *Stevenson Jordan and Harrison Ltd v MacDonald and Evans* [1952] 1 TLR 101, CA; *Bank voor Handel en Scheepvaart NV v Slatford* [1953] 1 QB 248, [1952] 2 All ER 956, CA; *Whittaker v Minister of Pensions and National Insurance* [1967] 1 QB 156, [1966] 3 All ER 531 (trapeze artiste was 'employee' for purpose of claiming for industrial injury).

6   The terminology of 'contract of service' has been replaced by 'contract of employment' in the same way that 'master' and 'servant' have been replaced by 'employer' and 'employee': see PARA 1 note 1.

7   *Ready Mixed Concrete (South East) Ltd v Minister of Pensions and National Insurance* [1968] 2 QB 497 at 515, [1968] 1 All ER 433 at 439–440 per MacKenna J.
    Ready Mixed Concrete (South East) Ltd v Minister of Pensions and National Insurance has been applied in the context of tax cases eg in *Dragonfly Consultancy Ltd v Revenue and Customs Comrs* [2008] EWHC 2113 (Ch), [2008] STC 3030 (contractual statement of intention by the parties may be relevant, in a borderline case, to the issue of whether the notional contract involving certain individuals who provide their services through companies is a contract of employment for the purposes of taxation under the Income Tax (Earnings and Pensions) Act 2003, also applying *Express and Echo Publications Ltd v Tanton* [1999] ICR 693, [1999] IRLR 367, CA (see note 14)), and in *Matthews v Revenue and Customs Comrs* [2012] UKUT 229 (TCC), [2014] STC 297, [2013] All ER (D) 149 (Nov), UKUT (persons providing entertainment services on various cruises found to be engaged under contracts for services for the purposes of the Income Tax (Earnings and Pensions) Act 2003).

8   *Market Investigations Ltd v Minister of Social Security* [1969] 2 QB 173 at 184–185, [1968] 3 All ER 732 at 737–738 per Cooke J (factors which may be of importance include whether the man performing the services provides his own equipment, whether he hires his own helpers, what degree of financial risk he takes, what degree of responsibility for investment and management he has, and whether and how far he has an opportunity of profiting from sound management in the performance of his task); approved in *Lee Ting Sang v Chung Chi-Keung* [1990] 2 AC 374 at 382, [1990] ICR 409 at 412, PC. See further the text and notes 9–17. *Market Investigations Ltd v Minister of Social Security* and *Lee Ting Sang v Chung Chi-Keung*

were applied in *Dragonfly Consultancy Ltd v Revenue and Customs Comrs* [2008] EWHC 2113 (Ch), [2008] STC 3030 (taxation under the Income Tax (Earnings and Pensions) Act 2003: see note 7).

9 See *Market Investigations Ltd v Minister of Social Security* [1969] 2 QB 173, [1968] 3 All ER 732; *Ready Mixed Concrete (South East) Ltd v Minister of Pensions and National Insurance* [1968] 2 QB 497, [1968] 1 All ER 433; *Construction Industry Training Board v Labour Force Ltd* [1970] 3 All ER 220, DC; *Global Plant Ltd v Secretary of State for Social Services* [1972] 1 QB 139, sub nom *Global Plant Ltd v Secretary of State for Health and Social Security* [1971] 3 All ER 385. In such a case it may be largely a matter of impression: 'Was [the] contract a contract of service within the meaning which an ordinary person would give to the words?': *Cassidy v Ministry of Health* [1951] 2 KB 343 at 352, [1951] 1 All ER 574 at 579, CA, per Somervell LJ, citing *Simmons v Heath Laundry Co* [1910] 1 KB 543 at 553, CA, per Buckley LJ.

10 See *Johnson Underwood Ltd* v *Montgomery* [2001] EWCA Civ 318 at [18]–[22], [2001] ICR 819 at [18]–[22], [2001] IRLR 269 at [18]–[22] per Buckley J. In *Stephenson v Delphi Diesel Systems Ltd* [2003] ICR 471 at [11]–[14], EAT, Elias J (as he then was) held that where mutuality of obligation can establish that a contract of sorts exists (at least while the person is actually working), the only question then is whether there is sufficient control to give rise to a conclusion that the contractual relationship which does exist is one of a contract of service or not. However, in *Quashie v Stringfellows Restaurants Ltd* [2012] EWCA Civ 1735 at [14], [2013] IRLR 99 at [14], Elias LJ held that this particular element of his judgment was too sweeping as, even where the work-wage relationship is established, and there is substantial control, there may be other features of the relationship which will entitle a tribunal to conclude that there is no contract of employment in place even during an individual engagement. See also *Weight Watchers (UK) Ltd v Revenue and Customs Comrs* [2011] UKUT 433 (TCC), [2012] STC 265 (express and implied obligations agreed with leader of weight-loss meetings satisfied the mutuality of obligation condition sufficient to amount to contract of employment); and note 23.

11 In order to be an independent contractor (see PARA 1 note 1), it is not essential that the person works for more than one employer, although that would be important evidence. If the person does work for only one employer, questions of whether or not he is integrated into the enterprise may assume importance: see the text and note 5.

12 This is not determinative, especially as the tax authorities may decide to change the person's tax status later in the light of further evidence. Thus, a person's income tax and national insurance arrangements may not be regarded as decisive as to his employment status: *Davis v New England College of Arundel* [1977] ICR 6, EAT (lecturer had become an employed earner despite the fact that, at his own request, he had been treated by the college as self-employed for fiscal purposes); *Airfix Footwear Ltd v Cope* [1978] ICR 1210, [1978] IRLR 396, EAT (outworker held to be employee due to containing relationship which amounted to contract of employment); *Thames Television Ltd v Wallis* [1979] IRLR 136, EAT. As to the meanings of employment, employer, employee etc for the purposes of income tax legislation see INCOME TAXATION vol 58 (2014) PARA 732 et seq. Conversely, the fact that the person has been paying income tax as an employee on income from employment does not necessarily mean that he will be classified as an employee for the purposes of employment law: *O'Kelly v Trusthouse Forte plc* [1984] QB 90, [1983] ICR 728, CA; *Clark v Oxfordshire Health Authority* [1998] IRLR 125, CA; *Carmichael v National Power plc* [1999] 4 All ER 897, [2000] IRLR 43, HL. *Carmichael v National Power plc* was applied in *Action Contracts (East Midlands) Ltd v Ablitt* [2008] All ER (D) 456 (Jul), EAT; and see also *Lamarina v Bath Spa Experience (t/as Il Toco d'Italia)* [2008] All ER (D) 38 (Dec), EAT. See also *Quashie v Stringfellows Restaurants Ltd* [2012] EWCA Civ 1735, [2013] IRLR 99 (cited in note 16); and the cases cited in note 19, where the person is trying to establish a status for the purpose of claiming employment protection rights.

13 Theoretically an independent contractor works under a commercial contract which may be terminated in the ways envisaged by the contract, without there being a dismissal. As to the meaning of 'dismissal' see PARAS 762–763, 864.

14 A personal obligation to do the work in question was said to be a particularly important indicator of employment in *Express and Echo Publications Ltd v Tanton* [1999] ICR 693, [1999] IRLR 367, CA (express right to provide substitute inconsistent with a contract of service). However, a limited or occasional power of delegation is not automatically inconsistent with employee status: *Ready Mixed Concrete (South East) Ltd v Minister of Pensions and National Insurance* [1968] 2 QB 497 at 515, [1968] 1 All ER 433 at 440 per MacKenna J; *MacFarlane v Glasgow City Council* [2001] IRLR 7, EAT (employee status of gym instructors not affected by arranging for approved replacements to provide services in their absence);

cf *Staffordshire Sentinel Newspapers Ltd v Potter* [2004] IRLR 752, EAT (valid contractual term, providing that home delivery agent not required to perform work personally, was inconsistent with a contract of service).

Express and Echo Publications Ltd v Tanton was applied and *MacFarlane v Glasgow City Council* was distinguished in *Jozsa v Premier Groundworks Ltd* [2009] All ER (D) 22 (Apr), EAT (where a party had an unfettered right for any reason not personally to perform the contractual obligations under a contract, but could delegate them to someone else he could not be a 'worker' within the meaning of the Working Time Regulations 1998, SI 1998/1833 (see PARA 271), even though the person actually performing the contractual obligations had to meet certain conditions; the position would be different if the right not to perform the contractual obligation depended on some other event, such as where that party was 'unable' to perform his obligations).

15 As with all other factors, this is not determinative, and so there can be a 'labour only' independent contractor: see note 4. The question of who supplies tools and equipment could be important in industrial safety law if they are defective: see HEALTH AND SAFETY AT WORK vol 52 (2014) PARA 376 et seq.

16 This factor, looking at the economic realities, was first posited in *Montreal v Montreal Locomotive Works Ltd* [1947] 1 DLR 161, PC, and was later expressed in terms of whether the person in question was in business on his own account: *Market Investigations Ltd v Minister of Social Security* [1969] 2 QB 173, [1968] 3 All ER 732 (approved in *Lee Ting Sang v Chung Chi-Keung* [1990] 2 AC 374, [1990] ICR 409, PC). See also *Hitchcock v Post Office* [1980] ICR 100, EAT; *Warner Holidays Ltd v Secretary of State for Social Services* [1983] ICR 440; *Withers v Flackwell Heath Football Supporters' Club* [1981] IRLR 307, EAT ('are you your own boss?'). It would be an unusual case where a contract of service is found to exist when the worker takes the economic risk and is paid exclusively by third parties: see *Quashie v Stringfellows Restaurants Ltd* [2012] EWCA Civ 1735, [2013] IRLR 99 (lapdancer held to be self-employed rather than employed under a contract of employment, where she was responsible for various expenses (meaning that she might make no profit on any particular night), where also it was not part of her case that the whole thing was a sham and the fact that she herself had in the contract accepted that she was self-employed, that she had to deal with all matters of tax, and that there was no question of sickness or holiday pay). See also the factual analogy of *Cheng Yuen v Royal Hong Kong Golf Club* [1998] ICR 131, PC (self-employment found where golf caddy was licenced by the club to offer caddying services, had a discretion when to work and was remunerated by the golfers, not the club which merely administered the payments). As to employees who are also shareholders see PARAS 8–10.

17 Thus eg the exact position of a minister of religion in relation to employment law has been subject to argument: authority used to hold against a minister being presumed to have employment status: *President of the Methodist Conference v Parfitt* [1984] QB 368, [1984] ICR 176, [1984] IRLR 141, CA (the relationship between a church and a minister of religion is not apt, in the absence of clear indications of a contrary intention in the document, to be regulated by a contract of service); *Davies v Presbyterian Church of Wales* [1986] 1 All ER 705, [1986] ICR 280, [1986] IRLR 194, HL (it is possible for a man to be employed as a servant or as an independent contractor to carry out duties which are exclusively spiritual but in the present case the applicant cannot point to any contract between himself and the church); *Santokh Singh v Guru Nanak Gurdwara* [1990] ICR 309, CA (granthi at a Sikh temple was not employed under a contract of service); *Diocese of Southwark v Coker* [1998] ICR 140, CA (simple reason for the absence of a contract between the church and a minister of religion is the lack of an intention to create a contractual relationship); and see *Barthorpe v Exeter Diocesan Board of Finance* [1979] ICR 900, EAT (office holder not precluded from being an 'employee'). In *Percy v Board of National Mission of the Church of Scotland* [2005] UKHL 73, [2006] 2 AC 28, [2006] 4 All ER 1354, the House of Lords had to construe the word 'employment' for the purposes of a complaint made under the Sex Discrimination Act 1975 (repealed) by an associate minister in a Church of Scotland parish and, without overruling the employment cases, found that there was an intention to create a legally binding relationship so that the associate minister was employed by the Board of National Mission under a contract personally to execute work within the meaning of the Sex Discrimination Act 1975 (repealed). In *New Testament Church of God v Stewart* [2007] EWCA Civ 1004, [2008] ICR 282, [2008] IRLR 134, *Percy v Board of National Mission of the Church of Scotland* was held to have established that the fact-finding tribunal is no longer required to approach its consideration of the nature of the relationship between a minister and his church with the presumption that there was no intention to create legal relations; that an employment tribunal may find, on a careful and conscientious scrutiny of the evidence, that there is an intention to create legal relations between a church and one of its ministers; and that a spiritual motivation in working for a church does not necessarily preclude

an intention to create legal relations. However, this interpretation has been narrowed by the UK Supreme Court in *President of the Methodist Conference v Preston (formerly Moore)* [2013] UKSC 29, [2013] 2 AC 163, [2013] ICR 833, [2013] IRLR 646, so that, while there is no rule or presumption either way, neither office-holding status nor the spiritual nature of the work provided an answer in themselves, and a tribunal must apply the normal rules on employment to the terms of engagement of the particular church, to the rules and practices of the particular church, and to any special arrangements made with the particular minister, which, properly examined, might well prove to be inconsistent with contractual intention. The relevant documents in this case were the constitution and standing orders which provide the foundation of the minister's relationship with the Church and which had to be construed against their factual background; and the older line of authority is preserved but is similarly dependent upon the particular facts in play, hence: a Methodist minister is not an employee (*President of the Methodist Conference v Parfitt*) nor is a minister of the Church of Wales (*Davies v Presbyterian Church of Wales*); the employment status of a Church of Scotland minister (as opposed to his or her status in discrimination law) remains arguable (*Percy v Board of National Mission of the Church of Scotland*) and other churches are to be considered individually (see eg *New Testament Church of God v Stewart*). As from 1 January 2010, the position of Church of England clergy has been put onto a statutory footing: see the Ecclesiastical Offices (Terms of Service) Regulations 2009, SI 2009/2108; the Ecclesiastical Offices (Terms of Service) Directions 2010, SI 2010/1923; and ECCLESIASTICAL LAW vol 34 (2011) PARAS 407 et seq, 428.

18 It may be a factor for consideration, especially where other factors are evenly balanced: *Young and Woods Ltd v West* [1980] IRLR 201, CA, explaining *Massey v Crown Life Insurance Co* [1978] 2 All ER 576, [1978] ICR 590, CA, and *Ferguson v John Dawson & Partners (Contractors) Ltd* [1976] 3 All ER 817, [1976] IRLR 346, CA; *Calder v H Kitson Vickers & Sons (Engineers) Ltd* [1988] ICR 232, CA; *Carmichael v National Power plc* [1999] 4 All ER 897, [2000] IRLR 43, HL. *Carmichael v National Power plc* was applied in *Action Contracts (East Midlands) Ltd v Ablitt* [2008] All ER (D) 456 (Jul), EAT; and see also *Lamarina v Bath Spa Experience (t/as Il Toco d'Italia)* [2008] All ER (D) 38 (Dec), EAT. The test to be adopted should focus on the reality of the situation particularly where written documentation may not reflect the reality of the relationship: *Szilagyi v Protectacoat Firthglow Ltd* [2009] EWCA Civ 98, [2009] ICR 835, [2009] IRLR 365 (applying *Express and Echo Publications Ltd v Tanton* [1999] ICR 693, [1999] IRLR 367, CA (it is important that a tribunal should be alert to look at the reality of any obligations and to declare any that prove to be a sham); and *Kalwak v Consistent Group Ltd* [2007] IRLR 560 at [58], EAT, per Elias J (if the reality of the situation is that no one seriously expects that a worker will seek to provide a substitute, or refuse the work offered, the fact that the contract expressly provides for these unrealistic possibilities will not alter the true nature of the relationship) (decision revsd [2008] EWCA Civ 430, [2008] IRLR 505)). *Szilagyi v Protectacoat Firthglow Ltd* was adopted in *England v MPG Contracts Ltd* [2009] All ER (D) 92 (May), EAT, and approved in *Autoclenz Ltd v Belcher* [2011] UKSC 41, [2011] 4 All ER 745, [2011] IRLR 820 (in cases of contracts concerning work and services, court is not constrained by an apparently complete written contract to conclude that its terms represented the true agreement between the parties, and a tribunal is entitled to disregard the terms of the written documents in so far as they were inconsistent with that).

19 *Ferguson v John Dawson & Partners (Contractors) Ltd* [1976] 3 All ER 817, [1976] IRLR 346, CA; *Davis v New England College of Arundel* [1977] ICR 6, EAT; *Tyne and Clyde Warehouses Ltd v Hamerton* [1978] ICR 661, EAT; *BSM (1257) Ltd v Secretary of State for Social Services* [1978] ICR 894; *Young and Woods Ltd v West* [1980] IRLR 201, CA.

20 *Young and Woods Ltd v West* [1980] IRLR 201, CA. In *Massey v Crown Life Insurance Co* [1978] 2 All ER 576, [1978] ICR 590, CA, an employee deliberately negotiated with his employers to become self-employed and, when his engagement was later terminated, he was held not to have remained an employee for the purpose of claiming unfair dismissal.

21 The fact that the employee has been obtaining tax advantages by being self-employed may itself be a factor against allowing him to change that label when later dismissed: *Massey v Crown Life Insurance Co* [1978] 2 All ER 576, [1978] ICR 590, CA. See also the dissenting judgment of Lawton LJ in *Ferguson v John Dawson & Partners (Contractors) Ltd* [1976] 3 All ER 817 at 827, [1976] IRLR 346 at 350, CA. Even if such a change is permitted, the Inland Revenue (now Revenue and Customs) has a statutory duty to reclaim tax deductions which were granted to an individual as self-employed: *Young and Woods Ltd v West* [1980] IRLR 201 at 208, CA, per Ackner LJ (who stated that the applicant had probably won a 'hollow, indeed an expensive, victory').

22 *Carmichael v National Power plc* [1999] 4 All ER 897 at 902 et seq, [1999] 1 WLR 2042 at 2048 et seq, HL, per Lord Hoffmann. The question of whether the parties intended a document or documents to be the exclusive record of their agreement is a question of fact; so are the terms

of the contract where the intention of the parties, objectively ascertained, has to be gathered not only from documents but also from oral exchanges and conduct: *Carmichael v National Power plc* at 903 and 2049 per Lord Hoffmann. As to the employment tribunal as the tribunal of fact see PARA 2 notes 9, 10; and see generally PARA 1399 et seq.

23 *O'Kelly v Trusthouse Forte plc* [1984] QB 90, [1983] ICR 728, CA. See also *Nethermere (St Neots) Ltd v Gardiner* [1984] ICR 612 at 623, [1984] IRLR 240 at 245, CA, per Stephenson LJ ('irreducible minimum' of obligation required on each side to create a contract of service); approved in *Carmichael v National Power plc* [1999] 4 All ER 897 at 901, [1999] 1 WLR 2042 at 2047, [2000] IRLR 43 at 45, HL, per Lord Irvine of Lairg LC. *O'Kelly v Trusthouse Forte plc* and *Nethermere (St Neots) Ltd v Gardiner* were applied in *Haggerty v St Ives Plymouth Ltd* [2008] All ER (D) 317 (May), EAT. As to the application of this approach to temporary worker agreements made with employment agencies see further PARA 11. A homeworker can be an employee (*Airfix Footwear Ltd v Cope* [1978] ICR 1210, [1978] IRLR 396, EAT) but some casual workers may have difficulty satisfying a test of mutuality (*Mailway (Southern) Ltd v Willsher* [1978] ICR 511, [1978] IRLR 322, EAT; *Wickens v Champion Employment* [1984] ICR 365, EAT; *O'Kelly v Trusthouse Forte plc*), this being particularly the case in *Carmichael v National Power plc* [1999] 4 All ER 897, [1999] 1 WLR 2042, [2000] IRLR 43, HL (where a 'casual, as required' power station guide was held not to be under a contract of employment, failing primarily on lack of mutuality). Similarly, persons kept on some sort of 'pool' or 'bank' arrangement to be called on when necessary may have difficulty in establishing employed status: *Clark v Oxfordshire Health Authority* [1998] IRLR 125, CA. A casual worker may also have a difficulty, even if surmounting the initial obstacle of whether he is an employee at all, in showing that he has the necessary qualifying period of continuous employment for the statutory right in question; he may try to cure any gaps by either: (1) relying on the Employment Rights Act 1996 s 212(3)(b) on temporary cessation of work (see PARA 131); or (2) seeking to establish the existence of one overall 'umbrella' or 'global' contract unifying what would otherwise be separate and distinct contractual engagements: *Nethermere (St Neots) Ltd v Gardiner*; cf *Hellyer Bros Ltd v McLeod* [1987] 1 WLR 728, [1987] ICR 526, CA; *Carmichael v National Power plc*; *Stevedoring and Haulage Services Ltd v Fuller* [2001] EWCA Civ 651, [2001] IRLR 627, [2001] All ER (D) 106 (May) (terms cannot be implied so as to water down the effect of express terms which negative mutuality of obligation). See also *Royal National Lifeboat Institution v Bushaway* [2005] IRLR 674, EAT (initially temporary employee had necessary qualifying period of service despite written agreement between the parties to the contrary); *Wilson v Circular Distributors Ltd* [2006] IRLR 38, EAT (despite stipulation that worker would not be paid for periods when work not available, contract of employment existed as employer required to provide work where available); and *Prater v Cornwall County Council* [2006] EWCA Civ 102, [2006] 2 All ER 1013, [2006] ICR 731, [2006] IRLR 362 (individual agreements to provide tuition were contracts of employment as teacher obliged to see tuition through to completion). On the need (in atypical cases) to show an intent to create legal (ie employment contract) relations at all see *M & P Steelcraft Ltd v Ellis* [2008] ICR 578, sub nom *v Ellis v M & P Steelcraft Ltd* [2008] IRLR 355, EAT (arrangement was for a work placement for a shortly-to-be-released prisoner, not an employment contract). On mutuality of obligations (lack of which will only be a defence to an employer if it is lacking on both sides) see generally *Wilson v Circular Distributors Ltd.*

5. 'Worker' and the wider statutory definition of 'employee'. Some employment-related statutes achieve wider application by the use of either the term 'worker' or a deliberately wider definition of 'employment' and 'employee'[1].

The former approach has been used widely in the law relating to industrial relations and trade unions, where 'worker' is defined as an individual who works, or normally works or seeks to work:

(1) under a contract of employment; or

(2) under any other contract whereby he undertakes to do or perform personally any work or services for another party to the contract who is not a professional client of his; or

(3) in employment under or for the purposes of a government department,

otherwise than as a member of the naval, military or air forces of the Crown, in so far as such employment does not fall within head (1) or head (2) above[2].

For the purposes of the Employment Rights Act 1996, 'worker', except in the phrases 'shop worker'[3] and 'betting worker'[4], means an individual who has entered into or works under (or, where the employment has ceased, worked under):

(a)   a contract of employment[5]; or

(b)   any other contract, whether express or implied (and, if it is express, whether oral or in writing[6]), whereby the individual undertakes to do or perform personally any work or services for another party to the contract whose status is not, by virtue of the contract, that of a client or customer of any profession or business undertaking carried on by the individual;

and any reference to a worker's contract is to be construed accordingly[7]. The term 'worker' is used in the statutory provisions relating to deductions from wages[8], but is given an extended meaning in relation to protected disclosures[9] and in the statutory provisions governing the right to be accompanied at a disciplinary or grievance hearing[10]. The term 'worker' also appears in the National Minimum Wage Act 1998[11], the Working Time Regulations 1998[12], the Part-time Workers (Prevention of Less Favourable Treatment) Regulations 2000[13], and the Agency Workers Regulations 2010, SI 2010/93[14] (where in each case it is given a meaning that uses very similar or identical wording to that used in the Employment Rights Act 1996)[15].

The second approach, the use of the term 'employee' or 'employment' but with a deliberately wider definition has traditionally been seen in the legislation that prohibited various forms of discrimination (now embodied generally in the Equality Act 2010)[16]. It can also be seen in the Transfer of Undertakings (Protection of Employment) Regulations 2006[17].

Although containing some divergences which could be significant in an individual case, these extended definitions are essentially similar in their possible application to various forms of 'atypical' engagement which could fall outside the classic definition of an employee as a person under a contract of employment[18]. The case law on these definitions is relatively sparse, but the leading authority emphasises the importance of personal service as the dominant purpose of the contract[19], and other case law affirms that the definitions can include some self-employed persons[20].

A power was introduced by the Employment Relations Act 1999 whereby the Secretary of State[21] may by order extend any rights conferred on an individual against an employer, under or by virtue of specified legislation[22], to persons of a specified description[23].

1   See PARAS 2, 12 note 1; cf, for example, the Fixed-term Employees (Prevention of Less Favourable Treatment) Regulations 2002, SI 2002/2034 (which apply only to employees: see PARA 85 et seq).
2   See the Trade Union and Labour Relations (Consolidation) Act 1992 s 296(1); and PARA 892.
3   As to the meaning of 'shop worker' see PARA 321 note 1.
4   As to the meaning of 'betting worker' see PARA 321 note 2.
5   As to the meaning of 'contract of employment' see PARA 2.
6   As to the meaning of 'writing' see PARA 2 note 8.
7   See the Employment Rights Act 1996 s 230(3). See eg *Hospital Medical Group Ltd v Westwood* [2012] EWCA Civ 1005, [2013] ICR 415, [2012] IRLR 834 (general practitioner, who provided services to clinic providing cosmetic surgery procedures and non-surgical procedures, was a 'worker' under the 'any other contract' limb of the Employment Rights Act 1996 s 230(3) (see

head (b) in the text) because, even though he was in business on his own account, he was an integral part of HM government's undertaking when providing services in respect of hair restoration); *Bates van Winkelhof v Clyde & Co LLP* [2014] UKSC 32, [2014] ICR 730, [2014] IRLR 641 (the Limited Liability Partnerships Act 2000 s 4 (see PARTNERSHIP vol 79 (2014) PARA 238) did not mean that members of an LLP could only be 'workers' within the meaning of the Employment Rights Act 1996 s 230(3) if they would also have been 'workers' had the members of the LLP been partners in a traditional partnership). See also *Bullock v Norfolk County Council* [2011] All ER (D) 209 (Jan), EAT; and note 10. As to the Employment Rights Act 1996 and Crown employment see PARAS 6, 163.

8   Ie in the provisions of the Employment Rights Act 1996 Pt II (ss 13–27) (protection of wages: see PARA 254 et seq), originally enacted separately under the Wages Act 1986 (which used the term 'worker').

9   Ie in the provisions of the Employment Rights Act 1996 Pt IVA (ss 43A–43L) (protected disclosures: see PARAS 69, 70): see PARA 69 note 3.

10 See the Employment Relations Act 1999 s 13(1); and PARA 718. See eg *Bullock v Norfolk County Council* [2011] All ER (D) 209 (Jan), EAT (because authority established that the relationship between foster carer and local authority was not contractual, a carer did not work for the authority pursuant to a contract and accordingly was not a 'worker' within the meaning of the Employment Rights Act 1996 s 230(3) (see the text and notes 1–7), or a 'home worker' within the meaning of the Employment Relations Act 1999 s 13(3) so as to bring her within the scope of s 13(1)).

11 See the National Minimum Wage Act 1998 s 54(3); and PARA 171. In determining whether a person is a 'worker' for the purposes of s 54(3), a tribunal must be alive to the possibility that written documentation might include terms aimed at avoiding a particular statutory result ('sham' contractual terms), and must therefore focus on the actual legal obligations of the parties to ascertain what has been agreed, taking into account the parties' relative bargaining power: *Autoclenz Ltd v Belcher* [2011] UKSC 41, [2011] 4 All ER 745, [2011] IRLR 820 (documents had not reflected the true agreements between the parties which constituted a contract of employment; tribunal was entitled to disregard the terms of the written documents, in so far as they were inconsistent with that) (approving *Szilagyi v Protectacoat Firthglow Ltd* [2009] EWCA Civ 98, [2009] ICR 835, [2009] IRLR 365); and see PARA 4 note 18.

12 See the Working Time Regulations 1998, SI 1998/1833, reg 2(1); and PARA 271. See the guidance in *Cotswold Developments Construction Ltd v Williams* [2006] IRLR 181, EAT. See also *Express and Echo Publications Ltd v Tanton* [1999] ICR 693, [1999] IRLR 367, CA; *Jozsa v Premier Groundworks Ltd* [2009] All ER (D) 22 (Apr), EAT; and PARA 4 note 14.

13 See the Part-time Workers (Prevention of Less Favourable Treatment) Regulations 2000, SI 2000/1551, reg 1(2); and PARA 75 note 2.

14 See the Agency Workers Regulations 2010, SI 2010/93, reg 2; and PARA 98 note 7.

15 This definition is adopted also for the purposes of the Flexible Working (Procedural Requirements) Regulations 2002, SI 2002/3207, regs 14–16 (right of employee to be accompanied by a worker at the meeting following a request to allow for flexible working): see PARA 110 note 7.

16 'Employment' is defined as 'employment under a contract of service, a contract of apprenticeship, or a contract personally to execute any work or labour' and includes Crown employment and employment as a relevant member of the House of Commons staff, or of the House of Lords staff: see the Equality Act 2010 s 83(2); and DISCRIMINATION vol 33 (2013) PARA 110. As to the meaning of 'contract of service' see PARA 1 note 1. As to the position of apprentices and youth trainees at common law see PARAS 112, 128–129, 636, 747–754. As to the statutory law on apprenticeships see EDUCATION vol 35 (2011) PARA 682 et seq.

17 Ie the Transfer of Undertakings (Protection of Employment) Regulations 2006, SI 2006/246: see reg 2(1) ('employee' means any individual who works for another person whether under a contract of service or apprenticeship or otherwise but does not include anyone who provides services under a contract for services); and PARA 137 note 8.

18 See PARA 4.

19 *Gunning v Mirror Group Newspapers Ltd* [1986] 1 All ER 385, sub nom *Mirror Group Newspapers Ltd v Gunning* [1986] ICR 145, CA; followed and applied in *Sheehan v Post Office Counters Ltd* [1999] ICR 734, EAT.

20 *Writers' Guild of Great Britain v BBC* [1974] 1 All ER 574, [1974] ICR 234, NIRC. See also *Hugh-Jones v St John's College Cambridge* [1979] ICR 848, EAT; *Tanna v Post Office* [1981] ICR 374, EAT; *Quinnen v Hovells* [1984] ICR 525, [1984] IRLR 227, EAT. Legal services were held to be potentially covered by the equivalent provision in the Northern Ireland fair employment legislation: *Kelly v Northern Ireland Housing Executive, Loughran v Northern Ireland Housing Executive* [1999] 1 AC 428, [1998] ICR 828, HL. In *Byrne Bros*

(Formwork) Ltd v Baird [2002] ICR 667, [2002] IRLR 96, [2001] All ER (D) 321 (Nov), EAT, a case involving self-employed labour-only subcontractors, the purpose of the Working Time Regulations 1998, SI 1998/1833, was said to be 'to extend protection to workers who are, substantively and economically, in the same position'. This reasoning by the EAT was later criticised as being too policy-based in *Wright v Redrow Homes (Yorkshire) Ltd, Roberts v Redrow Homes (North West) Ltd* [2004] EWCA Civ 469, [2004] 3 All ER 98, sub nom *Redrow Homes (Yorkshire) Ltd v Wright, Roberts v Redrow Homes (North West) Ltd* [2004] ICR 1126, but the outcome of this latter case was similar, namely that self-employed brick-layers working personally for one employer were held to be 'workers' and so able to claim rights under the Working Time Regulations 1998, SI 1998/1833 (see also *Redrow Homes (Yorkshire) Ltd v Buckborough* [2009] IRLR 34, EAT).

21 In any enactment, 'Secretary of State' means one of Her Majesty's principal Secretaries of State: see the Interpretation Act 1978 s 5, Sch 1; and CONSTITUTIONAL AND ADMINISTRATIVE LAW vol 20 (2014) PARA 153. In general, ministerial functions relating to employment are divided between the Secretary of State for Business, Innovation and Skills (whose responsibilities include employment rights and relations) and the Secretary of State for Work and Pensions (whose responsibilities include welfare and pension policy). See also the Secretary of State for Business, Innovation and Skills Order 2009, SI 2009/2748.

In relation to Wales, the employment functions of the Secretary of State have not generally been transferred to the National Assembly for Wales. However, certain functions under the Employment and Training Act 1973, so far as they are exercisable in relation to Wales, have been transferred: see the National Assembly for Wales (Transfer of Functions) Order 1999, SI 1999/672, art 2, Sch 1; and PARA 634 note 1. The functions of the Secretary of State under the Disabled Persons (Employment) Act 1958 s 3, Schedule, so far as they are exercisable in relation to Wales, have also been transferred: see the National Assembly for Wales (Transfer of Functions) Order 1999, SI 1999/672, art 2, Sch 1; and PARA 611 note 2. The function under the Employers' Liability (Compulsory Insurance) Regulations 1998, SI 1998/2573, Sch 2 para 1 is exercisable by the Assembly concurrently with any Minister of the Crown by whom it is exercisable: see the National Assembly for Wales (Transfer of Functions) Order 2000, SI 2000/253, art 2(2), Sch 1; and see PARA 43 note 5. These transferred functions are now vested in the Welsh Ministers: see the Government of Wales Act 2006 s 162(1), Sch 11 para 30. 'Welsh Ministers' means the First Minister and the Welsh Ministers appointed under the Government of Wales Act 2006 s 48: see s 45(2). As to the First Minister and the Welsh Ministers see the Government of Wales Act 2006 ss 46–48; and CONSTITUTIONAL AND ADMINISTRATIVE LAW vol 20 (2014) PARAS 374, 375.

22 Ie the Trade Union and Labour Relations (Consolidation) Act 1992, the Employment Rights Act 1996, the Employment Act 2002, the Employment Relations Act 1999 and any instrument made under the European Communities Act 1972 s 2(2) (see CONSTITUTIONAL AND ADMINISTRATIVE LAW vol 20 (2014) PARA 156): see the Employment Relations Act 1999 s 23(1); and PARA 159.

23 See the Employment Relations Act 1999 s 23(1), (2); and PARA 159. At the date at which this volume states the law, no such order had been made.

6.   Crown employment. In the absence of special statutory provisions, all contracts of service under the Crown[1] are terminable without notice[2] on the part of the Crown, even if there is an express term to the contrary in the contract[3]. There is, however, nothing unconstitutional about the Crown entering into contracts of employment with civil servants, although the intention so to contract must be established[4]; and this may particularly be the case where the Crown is exercising a statutory power to engage staff, rather than a prerogative power[5].

Where a person holds any office or employment under the Crown on terms which do not constitute a contract of employment between that person and the Crown[6], those terms are nevertheless deemed to constitute such a contract for the purposes of[7]: (1) the law relating to the liability in tort of any person who commits an act which: (a) induces another person to break any contract, interferes with the performance of a contract or induces another person to interfere with its performance[8]; or (b) consists in a threat that a contract will be broken or its performance interfered with or that any person will be induced to break a contract or interfere with its performance[9]; and (2) the provisions of the Trade Union and Labour Relations (Consolidation) Act 1992 or any other Act which refer (whether in relation to contracts generally or only in relation to contracts of employment) to such an act[10].

1   As to Crown contracts for service see CONSTITUTIONAL AND ADMINISTRATIVE LAW vol 20 (2014) PARA 196; as to the application to Crown employment, to membership of House of Lords staff and to House of Commons staff of the Employment Rights Act 1996 and the Employment Tribunals Act 1996 see PARAS 163–165; as to the application of the Employment Rights Act 1996 and the Employment Tribunals Act 1996 to employment in police service see PARA 168; as to the application to Crown employment, membership of House of Lords staff and House of Commons staff of the statutory provisions governing the treatment of part-time workers see PARA 82; as to the application to Crown employment, membership of House of Lords staff and House of Commons staff of the statutory provisions governing the treatment of fixed-term employees see PARA 93; as to the application of the national minimum wage legislation to Crown employment, membership of House of Lords staff and House of Commons staff see PARAS 180–182; as to the application of the working hours legislation to Crown employment see PARA 274; as to the application of the working hours legislation to membership of House of Lords staff and House of Commons staff see PARAS 276–277; as to the application of statutory maternity pay to Crown employment see PARA 412; as to the application of statutory paternity pay to Crown employment see PARA 454; as to the application of statutory adoption pay to Crown employment see PARA 500; as to the application of statutory shared parental pay to Crown employment see PARA 541; and as to the application of statutory sick pay to Crown employment see PARA 569.

2   A Crown servant may thus not be able to bring a claim at common law for wrongful dismissal: *IRC v Hambrook* [1956] 2 QB 641 at 653, [1956] 1 All ER 807 at 811 per Lord Goddard CJ (affd on other grounds [1956] 2 QB 641 at 658, [1956] 3 All ER 338, CA); *Riordan v War Office* [1959] 3 All ER 552, [1959] 1 WLR 1046 (affd on another point [1960] 3 All ER 774n, [1961] 1 WLR 210, CA) (Army Council Regulations providing for a period of notice did not exclude Crown's right of summary dismissal). See also *A-G for Guyana v Nobrega* [1969] 3 All ER 1604, PC (no ruling on claim that the Crown could not unilaterally vary the terms of employment, the court finding that the employment under the original contract had actually been terminated and a new contract substituted for it). There may, however, be a statutory restriction on the power to dismiss: *Gould v Stuart* [1896] AC 575, PC. As to crown employment proceedings before employment tribunals with national security safeguards in place see PARA 1446 et seq.

      Formerly, in the event of a breach by the Crown of a contract entered into with the subject by a person having authority to contract on behalf of the Crown, a petition of right lay at the instance of a subject: see eg *Thomas v R* (1874) LR 10 QB 31; *Yeoman v R* [1904] 2 KB 429, CA; and CROWN PROCEEDINGS AND CROWN PRACTICE vol 12(1) (Reissue) PARA 111. Now, the subject is entitled to bring an action for breach of contract in such an event: see CONSTITUTIONAL AND ADMINISTRATIVE LAW vol 20 (2014) PARA 643. As to the principle that Crown servants are not in general personally liable on contracts see CONSTITUTIONAL AND ADMINISTRATIVE LAW vol 20 (2014) PARA 191; and as to the principle that civil proceedings against the Crown are now in general instituted and carried on in accordance with the ordinary rules of court, and for particular provisions relating to such proceedings, see CROWN PROCEEDINGS AND CROWN PRACTICE vol 12(1) (Reissue) PARAS 117, 118.

3   *Dunn v R* [1896] 1 QB 116, CA; *Denning v Secretary of State for India in Council* (1920) 37 TLR 138. In some cases, this has been explained on the basis that a Crown servant has no contract at all (see *Mulvenna v Admiralty* 1926 SC 842, Ct of Sess; *Lucas v Lucas and High Comr for India* [1943] P 68, [1943] 2 All ER 110), but this would mean that the individual had no legally enforceable rights even during the currency of his engagement as e g to recover arrears of pay, and so the balance of authority is in favour of there being a contract of employment of sorts, albeit terminable at will (see *Owners of SS Raphael v Brandy* [1911] AC 413, HL; *Sutton v A-G* (1923) 39 TLR 295, HL; *Reilly v R* [1934] AC 176, PC; *A-G for Guyana v Norbrega* [1969] 3 All ER 1604, PC; *Kodeeswaran v A-G of Ceylon* [1970] AC 1111, [1970] 2 WLR 456, PC (disapproving *Mulvenna v Admiralty* on the question of arrears of pay)).

4   *R v Civil Service Appeal Board, ex p Bruce* [1988] 3 All ER 686, [1988] ICR 649, DC; affd sub nom *R v Civil Service Appeal Board, ex p Bruce (A-G intervening)* [1989] 2 All ER 907, [1989] ICR 171, CA (civil servant held not to have been engaged under a contract of employment enforceable in the courts). Cf *R v Lord Chancellor's Department, ex p Nangle* [1991] ICR 743, [1991] IRLR 343, DC (objective construction of documents by which civil servant appointed

showed that contract of employment had been created). However, the Crown cannot deprive itself by contract of its prerogative power to dismiss civil servants: *R v Civil Service Appeal Board, ex p Bruce* at 698 and 665 per Roch J.

5 *McClaren v Home Office* [1990] ICR 824, [1990] IRLR 338, CA (prison officer had arguable case that he was employed under a contract of employment).

6 As to the meaning of 'contract of employment' in this context see PARA 893 note 3.

7 See the Trade Union and Labour Relations (Consolidation) Act 1992 s 245.

8 Trade Union and Labour Relations (Consolidation) Act 1992 s 245(a)(i). See further PARAS 1343, 1363. As to the tort of procuring breach of contract see TORT vol 97 (2010) PARA 614. Merely to prevent performance of a contract, or otherwise to interfere with its performance, is not so actionable, but may give rise to liability in the distinct tort of causing loss by unlawful means: see TORT vol 97 (2010) PARA 621.

9 Trade Union and Labour Relations (Consolidation) Act 1992 s 245(a)(ii). See further PARAS 1343, 1363.

10 Trade Union and Labour Relations (Consolidation) Act 1992 s 245(b). See further PARAS 1343, 1363.

7. Office-holders. The categorisation of an individual as an office-holder[1] tends to be of more significance in the law relating to income taxation than in employment law[2]. While it is true that in the case of certain major offices the individual's status as an office-holder may mean that he is not an employee[3], in most cases this will not be so and there will be nothing to prevent the ordinary definition of 'employee' from being satisfied[4]. Even if the office-holder does not qualify as an employee, there may still be aspects of employment law applicable to him, particularly in relation to the payment of wages, since the remuneration of a modern office-holder is likely to be construed as an ordinary salary for performing the duties of the office, not as the archaic form of an honorarium for filling the office[5].

There may, however, be one particular advantage to the status of office-holder in ordinary employment law, in that an office-holder wrongly deprived of his office may be able to challenge that dismissal as a breach of public law and seek administrative law remedies to quash it which are generally unavailable to ordinary employees[6].

1 In deciding whether an individual is an office-holder, the important matters to be taken into account are: (1) the nature of the payment made to the office-holder; (2) the mode and frequency of payment; (3) whether the individual has a right to payment; (4) the size of the payment; (5) whether the individual is exercising the functions of an independent office or is subject to the control and orders of others; (6) the extent and weight of the duties performed (the smaller they are, the less likely he is to be an employee); and (7) the description given to the payment, its treatment in the payer's accounts and for tax and national insurance purposes: *102 Social Club and Institute Ltd v Bickerton* [1977] ICR 911, EAT.

2 As to offices considered for the purposes of the Income Tax Acts see INCOME TAXATION vol 58 (2014) PARA 733 et seq.

3 As to the meaning of 'employee' see PARA 2. As to the position of individuals in the police service see PARA 168. The exact position of a minister of religion in relation to employment law has been subject to argument: see *Barthorpe v Exeter Diocesan Board of Finance* [1979] ICR 900, EAT (office holder not precluded from being an 'employee'); *President of the Methodist Conference v Preston (formerly Moore)* [2013] UKSC 29, [2013] 2 AC 163, [2013] ICR 833, [2013] IRLR 646 (while there is no rule or presumption either way, neither office-holding status nor the spiritual nature of the work provided an answer in themselves to the question); and PARA 4 note 17. As from 1 January 2010, the position of Church of England clergy has been put onto a statutory footing: see the Ecclesiastical Offices (Terms of Service) Regulations 2009, SI 2009/2108; the Ecclesiastical Offices (Terms of Service) Directions 2010, SI 2010/1923; and ECCLESIASTICAL LAW vol 34 (2011) PARAS 407 et seq, 428. However, the position of ministers in other churches is to be considered individually: see PARA 4 note 17.

4 *Johnson v Ryan* [2000] ICR 236, EAT (rent officer employed by local authority). A company director holding office under a service agreement may be both an office-holder and an employee of the company: see PARA 8.

5   *Miles v Wakefield Metropolitan District Council* [1987] AC 539, [1987] ICR 368, HL
    (superintendent registrar of births, deaths and marriages).
6   See PARA 827. See also, in particular, *Ridge v Baldwin* [1964] AC 40, [1963] 2 All ER 66, HL;
    Malloch v Aberdeen Corpn [1971] 2 All ER 1278, [1971] 1 WLR 1578, HL. However, the
    system whereby registration officers are unable to invoke directly the provisions of the
    Employment Rights Act 1996 (see the text and note 5) has been criticised (per curiam) as
    anachronistic and as perpetrating an injustice for which judicial review may provide an inapt
    remedy: *Lincolnshire County Council v Hopper* (2002) Times, 17 June, [2002] All ER (D) 401
    (May), EAT.

8.   **Company directors.** A company director is an office-holder who is not,
without more, an employee of the company[1]. A director who actually works for
the company, especially under a service agreement[2], may, however, also be an
employee of the company and so entitled to statutory rights such as the right not
to be unfairly dismissed or the right to a redundancy payment on termination of
his employment[3]. If the person works full-time as a managing director, there may
be a presumption of an employment relationship[4], but it is ultimately a question
of fact; and thus the fact that the director actually works for the company is not
in itself enough, and may be outweighed by other factors such as the absence of
any clear contract of employment, remuneration only by fees and treatment for
taxation and national insurance purposes[5]. Even where a director (or
ex-director) is claiming a statutory employment protection right, it remains a
question of fact whether he is or was an employee, with no rule of law against
such status, even where the director has or had considerable control over the
employing company[6].

1   *McMillan v Guest* [1942] AC 561, [1942] 1 All ER 606, HL. As to the status of directors see
    COMPANIES vol 14 (2009) PARA 478 et seq.
2   As to a company's obligation to keep at an appropriate place a copy of each director's written
    contract of service and a written memorandum setting out the terms of each director's contract
    of service which is not in writing see COMPANIES vol 14 (2009) PARA 525. The existence or
    non-existence of such a copy or memorandum may be evidence when deciding whether a
    director was also an employee, but it is not conclusive: *Parsons v Albert J Parsons & Sons Ltd*
    [1979] ICR 271, [1979] IRLR 117, CA; *Eaton v Robert Eaton Ltd* [1988] ICR 302, [1988]
    IRLR 83, EAT.
3   A director may be employed by his own ('one man') company: *Lee v Lee's Air Farming Ltd*
    [1961] AC 12, [1960] 3 All ER 420, PC. Moreover, a director will still be 'dismissed' as an
    employee in a case where he takes that decision himself qua director: *Morley v CT Morley Ltd*
    [1985] ICR 499, EAT.
4   *Folami v Nigerline (UK) Ltd* [1978] ICR 277, EAT.
5   *Parsons v Albert J Parsons & Sons Ltd* [1979] ICR 271, [1979] IRLR 117, CA; *Eaton v Robert
    Eaton Ltd* [1988] ICR 302, [1988] IRLR 83, EAT.
6   *Secretary of State for Trade and Industry v Bottrill* [1999] ICR 592, [1999] IRLR 326, CA
    (controlling shareholder can be an 'employee' for the purpose of claiming payments from
    Secretary of State on the company's insolvency), disapproving *Buchan v Secretary of State for
    Employment, Ivey v Secretary of State for Employment* [1997] IRLR 80, EAT; followed and
    applied in *Connolly v Sellars Arenascene Ltd* [2001] EWCA Civ 184, [2001] ICR 760, [2001]
    IRLR 222 (controlling shareholder with a stake in the future prosperity of the company not
    prevented from enjoying the status of employee for the purposes of unfair dismissal). See also
    PARA 2 note 9. As to whether a majority shareholder in the employing company (whether or not
    also a director) can also be an 'employee' see PARA 9.

9.   **Status of majority shareholder in employing company.** The question of
whether a majority shareholder in the employing company (whether or not also a
director) can also be an 'employee' has proved troublesome but settled authority
points to this being a question of fact, with evidence being required to resolve the
(relatively exceptional) issue of whether the putative contract is a genuine
contract or a sham, followed by the consideration, assuming a genuine contract,

of whether it amounts to a contract of employment[1]. The continuing receipt of monetary payment is not an absolute requirement, if a person was contractually entitled to it, and the fact that he did not take it (for instance, because he was a director and/or shareholder in a small company in financial difficulty) could not retrospectively diminish his right[2].

1 The only fixed point seemed to be that a majority shareholder was not automatically disqualified from employment status, but that it all remains a question of fact: *Secretary of State for Trade and Industry v Bottrill* [2000] 1 All ER 915, [1999] ICR 592, [1999] IRLR 326, CA. The uncertainty here was commented on unfavourably by Underhill J in *Nesbitt v Secretary of State for Trade and Industry* [2007] IRLR 847, EAT, who favoured a relatively straightforward view (at one extreme of the spectrum) that there should be employment status unless the employing company was a sham or 'mere simulacrum'. However, in *Clark v Clark Construction Initiatives Ltd* [2008] ICR 635 at [98], [2008] IRLR 364 at [98], EAT, Elias P revisited the whole area, in a case where the tribunal's view that there was no contract of employment during the period of majority shareholding (on the facts generally, not on the more restricted ground of 'sham or simulacrum') was upheld. The following guidance was supplied for tribunals to follow in such cases:

(1) the onus is on the party denying a contract; where an individual has paid an employee's tax and national insurance, prima facie he is entitled to an employee's rights;

(2) the mere fact of majority shareholding (or de facto control) does not in itself prevent a contract arising;

(3) similarly, entrepreneur status does not of itself prevent a contract arising;

(4) if the parties conduct themselves according to the contract (e g as to hours and holidays) that is a strong indicator towards employment;

(5) conversely, if their conduct is inconsistent with (or not governed by) the contract, that is a strong pointer against employment;

(6) the assertion that there is a genuine contract will be undermined if there is nothing in writing;

(7) the taking of loans from the company (or, conversely, the guaranteeing of its debts) is not intrinsically inconsistent with employment; and

(8) although majority shareholding and/or control will always be relevant and may be decisive, that fact alone should not justify a finding of no employment.

This guidance was approved on appeal (where the decision was affirmed on other grounds): [2008] EWCA Civ 1446, [2009] ICR 718, [2008] All ER (D) 191 (Dec). Subsequently, the Court of Appeal in *Neufeld v Secretary of State for Business, Enterprise and Regulatory Reform* [2009] EWCA Civ 280, [2009] 3 All ER 790, [2009] ICR 1183 responded to a request to clarify the approach to be adopted by employment tribunals in such cases, the issues in that case being as to whether a controlling shareholder and director of a trading company could become an employee of that company under a contract of employment and, if so, whether there were any guidelines to assist tribunals in deciding whether in any particular case such a shareholder-director has become an employee. The guidance set out in *Clark v Clark Construction Initiatives Ltd* at [98] per Elias P was approved in essence (see *Neufeld v Secretary of State for Business, Enterprise and Regulatory Reform* at [88]), subject to four qualifications:

(a) head (1) above should not be read as constituting a formal reversal of the burden of proof on to the party denying employment status; it may still be necessary for the putative employee to do more than produce documentation in order to satisfy the tribunal of that status (see *Neufeld v Secretary of State for Business, Enterprise and Regulatory Reform* at [88]);

(b) head (6) above might be too negative in its expression; it may be an important consideration but if the parties' conduct also shows a true contract of employment, 'we would not wish tribunals to seize too readily on the absence of a written agreement to justify the rejection of the claim' (see *Neufeld v Secretary of State for Business, Enterprise and Regulatory Reform* at [89]);

(c) heads (7) and (8) above had to be considered against the backdrop of a putative employee's shareholding in the company giving him control of the company (even total control) and how this affected the assessment of what has been done under the putative written or oral employment contract that is being asserted; however, control is not *ordinarily* of any special relevance in deciding whether or not he has a valid such contract, nor will the fact that he will have share capital invested in the company; or that he may have made loans to it; or that he has personally guaranteed its obligations; or that his personal investment in the company will stand to prosper in line with the company's prosperity; or that he has done any of the other things that the 'owner' of a business will commonly do on its behalf, all of which shows an 'owner' acting qua 'owner', which is inevitable in the sort of companies giving rise to the issue, and is *ordinarily* irrelevant to whether or not a valid contract of employment has been created; they do not show that the 'owner' cannot also be an employee (see *Neufeld v Secretary of State for Business, Enterprise and Regulatory Reform* at [86]–[87], [90]).

The following supplementary guidance was given:

(i)   a person, whose economic interest in a company and its business means that he is in practice properly to be regarded as their 'owner', can also be an employee of the company (see *Neufeld v Secretary of State for Business, Enterprise and Regulatory Reform* at [80]);

(ii)   whether or not such a shareholder-director is an employee of the company is a question of fact for the court or tribunal before which such issue arises (see *Neufeld v Secretary of State for Business, Enterprise and Regulatory Reform* at [81]); and: (A) the fact that the putative employee has control over the company and the board, and so was instrumental in the creation of the very contract that he is asserting, will obviously be a relevant matter in the court's consideration of whether the contract is or is not a sham (see *Neufeld v Secretary of State for Business, Enterprise and Regulatory Reform* at [82]); (B) it is a question of fact as to what conclusions are to be drawn from any investigation into how the parties have conducted themselves under the purported contract (which may show a variety of things and produce different outcomes) (see *Neufeld v Secretary of State for Business, Enterprise and Regulatory Reform* at [83]); (C) in a case in which no allegation of sham is raised, or in which the claimant proves that no question of sham arises, the question (or further question) for the court or tribunal will be whether the claimed contract amounts to a true contract of employment (see *Neufeld v Secretary of State for Business, Enterprise and Regulatory Reform* at [84]);

(iii)   in deciding whether a valid contract of employment was in existence, consideration will have to be given to the requisite conditions for the creation of such a contract and the court or tribunal will want to be satisfied that the contract meets them (see *Neufeld v Secretary of State for Business, Enterprise and Regulatory Reform* at [85]).

See also *Crawford v Department for Employment and Learning* [2014] NICA 26, [2014] IRLR 626, NICA, where guidance was given as to the matters that would fall to be considered on remittance to a tribunal in order to make adequate inquiry into the circumstances of the formation of contracts of employment between a brother and sister who were directors and shareholders of a company and the terms and conditions of any such contracts of employment and the conduct of the brother and sister in the performance of any duties under any claimed contracts of employment.

2   *Neufeld v Secretary of State for Business, Enterprise and Regulatory Reform* [2009] EWCA Civ 280, [2009] 3 All ER 790, [2009] ICR 1183; *Secretary of State for Business, Innovation and Skills v Knight* [2014] IRLR 605, EAT.

10. Employees participating in share option or profit sharing schemes.

10. Employees participating in share option or profit sharing schemes. Where an employee participates in a share option or profit sharing scheme[1], his status as an employee is not affected[2]. However, if the company is sold, including the employee's shares, he may be viewed primarily as a vendor rather than an employee, even if his holding is small, in any context where such a distinction is relevant[3].

1   Ie under the Income Tax (Earnings and Pensions) Act 2003 Pt 7 Ch 7 (ss 516–520) (approved SAYE option schemes: see INCOME TAXATION vol 58 (2014) PARA 903 et seq) and Pt 7 Ch 8 (ss 521–526) (approved company share option plan schemes: see INCOME TAXATION vol 58 (2014) PARA 886).

2   This is to be distinguished from the status of employee shareholder under the Employment Rights Act 1996 where an employee agrees to substitute fundamental rights relating to unfair dismissal and redundancy with new rights of ownership: see s 205A; and PARA 154.

3   *Systems Reliability Holdings plc v Smith* [1990] IRLR 377 (employee shareholder selling shares, with a restraint of trade clause in the sale agreement; the validity of that clause was to be judged according to the less stringent tests applied to vendor/purchaser restraints, rather than the more stringent tests applied to employer/employee restraints).

11. Employment agencies and agency workers. Statutory provisions regulate: (1) the carrying on and conduct of employment agencies and employment businesses[1]; and (2) the equal treatment of agency workers[2].

However, the fundamental legal position of the agency worker (that is, whether, and if so by whom, an individual dealing with an employment agency or an employment business is employed) is not addressed in the employment legislation[3], and this remains a question of common law[4].

1 See the Employment Agencies Act 1973; the Conduct of Employment Agencies and Employment Businesses Regulations 2003, SI 2003/3319; and TRADE AND INDUSTRY vol 97 (2010) PARA 881 et seq.
2 See the Agency Workers Regulations 2010, SI 2010/93 (amended by SI 2010/1901, SI 2011/1941, SI 2011/2345, SI 2012/2397; SI 2014/386), which give agency workers, from 1 October 2011, a right to equal treatment with directly recruited counterpart employees after 12 weeks in the job; and PARA 97 et seq. These regulations were intended to implement in part European Parliament and Council Directive (EC) 2008/104 of 19 November 2008 (OJ L327, 5.12.2008, p 9) on temporary agency work (see PARA 96), and affect neither the statutory rules on the conduct of agencies (see head (1) in the text) nor an agency worker's status at common law (see the text and notes 3–4).
3 Ie notwithstanding that the position of agency workers is recognised for the purposes of taxation, and in certain specific provisions of employment legislation such as the Employment Rights Act 1996 (see ss 57ZA–57ZS; PARA 337 et seq; ss 68A–68D, 69A, 70A; and PARAS 601–603, 605, 607); the Trade Union and Labour Relations (Consolidation) Act 1992 Sch A1 (see PARA 1103 et seq); the National Minimum Wage Act 1998 (see s 34; and PARA 178); the Working Time Regulations 1998, SI 1998/1833 (see reg 36; and PARA 273); the Information and Consultation of Employees Regulations 2004, SI 2004/3426 (see PARA 1289 et seq); the European Cooperative Society (Involvement of Employees) Regulations 2006, SI 2006/2059 (see reg 6A; and PARA 1338); and the European Public Limited-Liability Company (Employee Involvement) (Great Britain) Regulations 2009, SI 2009/2401 (see PARA 1317 et seq).
4 See PARA 95.

12. Workers supplied by gangmasters. The activities of persons who supply workers[1] to carry out certain kinds of agricultural and fisheries work ('gangmasters') are regulated by statute[2]. The work to which the legislation applies is agricultural work[3], the gathering of shellfish[4], and the processing or packaging of any produce derived from agricultural work or shellfish, fish or products derived therefrom[5]; the Secretary of State may also by regulations make provision excluding work of a prescribed description from being work to which the legislation applies[6], or including work of a specified nature[7], as being work to which it applies[8]. To fall within the legislation's ambit, the work in question must be carried out either in the United Kingdom, or on any portion of the shore or bed of the sea, or of an estuary or tidal river, adjacent to the United Kingdom, whether above or below (or partly above and partly below) the low water mark, or in UK coastal waters[9].

The legislation establishes a Gangmasters Licensing Authority to oversee a system of licensing for gangmasters[10], and makes it an offence to act as a gangmaster without a licence or to enter into arrangements with unlicensed gangmasters[11].

1 For these purposes, 'worker' means an individual who does work to which the Gangmasters (Licensing) Act 2004 applies (see the text and notes 3–9): see s 26(1). A person is not prevented from being a worker for these purposes by reason of the fact that he has no right to be, or to work, in the United Kingdom: see s 26(2). As to the meaning of 'United Kingdom' see PARA 2 note 12. See further AGRICULTURAL PRODUCTION AND MARKETING vol 1 (2008) PARA 1230.
2 See the Gangmasters (Licensing) Act 2004; and AGRICULTURAL PRODUCTION AND MARKETING vol 1 (2008) PARA 1252 et seq.
3 See the Gangmasters (Licensing) Act 2004 s 3(1)(a); and AGRICULTURAL PRODUCTION AND MARKETING vol 1 (2008) PARA 1230. For these purposes, 'agricultural work' means work in

agriculture (see s 3(2)); and 'agriculture' includes dairy-farming, the production for the purposes of any trade, business or other undertaking (whether carried on for profit or not) of consumable produce (ie produce grown for sale, consumption or other use after severance from the land on which it is grown), the use of land as grazing, meadow or pasture land, the use of land as an orchard or as osier land or woodland, and the use of land for market gardens or nursery grounds (see s 3(3)).

4   See the Gangmasters (Licensing) Act 2004 s 3(1)(b); and AGRICULTURAL PRODUCTION AND MARKETING vol 1 (2008) PARA 1230. For these purposes, 'shellfish' means crustaceans and molluscs of any kind, and includes any part of a shellfish and any (or any part of any) brood, ware, halfware or spat of shellfish, and any spawn of shellfish, and the shell, or any part of the shell, of a shellfish: see s 3(4).

5   See the Gangmasters (Licensing) Act 2004 s 3(1)(c); and AGRICULTURAL PRODUCTION AND MARKETING vol 1 (2008) PARA 1230.

6   See the Gangmasters (Licensing) Act 2004 s 3(5)(a); and AGRICULTURAL PRODUCTION AND MARKETING vol 1 (2008) PARA 1230. As to the Secretary of State see PARA 5 note 21.

7   Ie the gathering (by any manner) of wild creatures, or wild plants, of a prescribed description and the processing and packaging of anything so gathered; and the harvesting of fish from a fish farm: see the Gangmasters (Licensing) Act 2004 s 3(5)(b).

8   See the Gangmasters (Licensing) Act 2004 s 3(5)(b); and AGRICULTURAL PRODUCTION AND MARKETING vol 1 (2008) PARA 1230.

9   See the Gangmasters (Licensing) Act 2004 s 5(1); and AGRICULTURAL PRODUCTION AND MARKETING vol 1 (2008) PARA 1230. For these purposes, 'UK coastal waters' means waters adjacent to the United Kingdom to a distance of six miles (ie six international nautical miles of 1,852 metres each) measured from the baselines from which the breadth of the territorial sea is measured: see s 5(2).

10 See the Gangmasters (Licensing) Act 2004 s 1; and AGRICULTURAL PRODUCTION AND MARKETING vol 1 (2008) PARA 1262. The Gangmasters (Licensing Authority) Regulations 2005, SI 2005/448, make provision for the constitution, structure and other matters relating to the operation of the Gangmasters Licensing Authority: see AGRICULTURAL PRODUCTION AND MARKETING vol 1 (2008) PARA 1262 et seq.

11 See the Gangmasters (Licensing) Act 2004 ss 12–14; and AGRICULTURAL PRODUCTION AND MARKETING vol 1 (2008) PARAS 1253–1254.

13.   Agents, partners and bailees.   The alternative to being an employee is normally being an independent contractor, but this is not inevitably so[1]. Other possible legal categories may arise, including those of agent, partner or bailee[2].

An agent is a person who has authority to act on behalf of his principal in relation to third parties[3]. An employee may indeed have such authority, but it is not necessary to constitute him an employee for this purpose, and the fact that a person is referred to as an agent does not exclude him from being an employee[4]. Ultimately, the responsibility of the employer or principal for the acts of the employee or agent depends on the scope of the latter's authority; but the application of that test may produce different results depending on whether the test is applied to an employee or an agent[5].

A partner is not as such an employee[6]; and a contract for the remuneration of an employee or agent of a person engaged in a business by a share in the profits of the business does not of itself make the employee or agent a partner in the business or liable as such[7]. Where a salary is paid to a person by another in addition to a share of profit, it may be implied that the relationship between them is that of employer and employee rather than that of partners[8]. The term 'salaried partner' is apt to describe both an employee who is held out to third parties as being a partner and a person who is truly a partner under a partnership agreement but who is paid a fixed salary not dependent on profits[9]. A person who has formerly been a partner in a business may be re-employed on terms which are evidence of the relationship of employer and employee rather than that of partnership[10].

Where a person hands over to another a chattel to be used by him in the course of his trade at his own discretion and subject to no control by the owner, the relationship between the owner and the other person is likely to be that of bailor and bailee, rather than that of employer and employee[11].

1   See PARA 2 note 9.
2   Alternatively, the person may fit into no particular category: see PARA 2 note 9.
3   See AGENCY vol 1 (2008) PARA 1. As to contractual liabilities to third persons in employment law see PARAS 53–62.
4   *JC King Ltd v Valencia* (1966) 1 ITR 67; *Tyne and Clyde Warehouses Ltd v Hamerton* [1978] ICR 661, EAT.
5   *Heatons Transport (St Helens) Ltd v Transport and General Workers' Union* [1973] AC 15 at 99, [1972] ICR 308 at 392, HL.
6   *Palumbo v Stylianou* (1966) 1 ITR 407. See also *Cowell v Quilter Goodison & Co Ltd and QG Management Services Ltd* [1989] IRLR 392, CA (equity partner not covered by the Transfer of Undertakings (Protection of Employment) Regulations 1981, SI 1981/1794 (now the Transfer of Undertakings (Protection of Employment) Regulations 2006, SI 2006/246): see PARA 136 note 1); *Cobbetts LLP v Hodge* [2009] EWHC 786 (Ch), [2010] 1 BCLC 30, [2009] All ER (D) 156 (Apr) (partnership deed was powerful evidence that intention had been to distinguish between partners and employees, despite employee's title of 'employed partner'); and *Tiffin v Lester Aldridge LLP* [2012] EWCA Civ 35, [2012] 2 All ER 1113, [2012] ICR 647, [2012] IRLR 391 (an individual cannot be his or her own employer, so the existence of a genuine partnership per se rules out employment). The longstanding legal principle, held by the Court of Appeal in *Cowell v Quilter Goodison & Co Ltd and QG Management Services Ltd* and in *Tiffin v Lester Aldridge,* that a partner can never be an employee of the partnership, was raised as a subsidiary question before the UK Supreme Court in *Bates van Winkelhof v Clyde & Co LLP* [2014] UKSC 32, [2014] ICR 730, [2014] IRLR 641, but the issues in that case were dispensed with before the need arose to consider the question as part of the Court's decision.
7   See the Partnership Act 1890 s 2(3)(b); and PARTNERSHIP vol 79 (2014) PARA 17.
8   *Ross v Parkyns* (1875) LR 20 Eq 331 at 336 per Sir G Jessel MR.
9   *Stekel v Ellice* [1973] 1 All ER 465, [1973] 1 WLR 191. See also *Tiffin v Lester Aldridge LLP* [2012] EWCA Civ 35, [2012] 2 All ER 1113, [2012] ICR 647, [2012] IRLR 391 ('fixed share partner' in a LLP held to be a partner and not an employee), applying *Stekel v Ellice.* A salaried partner is not necessarily an employee: *Burgess v O'Brien* (1966) 1 ITR 164.
10 *Easdown v Cobb* [1940] 1 All ER 49, HL. As to continuity of employment through a change of partnership see PARA 135.
11 See BAILMENT AND PLEDGE vol 4 (2011) PARA 138.

(ii) Contracts of Employment

A. FORMATION AND FORM

14.   Form of contract of employment. In general, a contract of employment need not be in any particular form[1]. A contract of employment may thus be inferred from conduct which shows that such a contract was intended although never expressed, as where there has in fact been service of the kind usually performed by employees[2]. Accordingly, an employment tribunal should first examine all the relevant evidence, including what was said and done between the parties, to determine whether a contract of service may be implied, that is deduced, as a necessary inference from the conduct of the parties and the work done, before concluding that no contract of employment exists[3]. The inference of a contract of employment may be rebutted by evidence that some other relationship was intended[4], or that the relationship of the parties was on a charitable footing[5], or was a family relationship[6].

There are, however, certain statutory requirements to be complied with in respect of contracts of employment[7].

1   This is reflected in the statutory definition of 'contract of employment': see PARA 2. As to the written formalities required in the case of merchant seamen, however, see SHIPPING AND MARITIME LAW vol 93 (2008) PARA 450 et seq.

2   See *Browning v Great Central Mining Co of Devon Ltd* (1860) 5 H & N 856; *Churchward v R* (1865) LR 1 QB 173 at 195–196 per Cockburn CJ; *Thorn v London Corpn* (1875) LR 10 Exch 112 at 123, Ex Ch, per Brett J (on appeal (1876) 1 App Cas 120, HL); *Hamlyn & Co v Wood & Co* [1891] 2 QB 488, CA. Older cases were concerned with whether the hiring was a yearly hiring (see eg *R v Lyth Inhabitants* (1793) 5 Term Rep 327; *R v Pendleton Inhabitants* (1812) 15 East 449), a matter which is now outmoded: see PARA 723 note 5. As to whether a company director should be inferred to have been under a contract of employment from the fact that he has worked for the company see PARA 8. The status of a majority shareholder in an employing company (whether or not he is also a director) is solved by applying usual contractual principles to an investigation into how the parties have conducted themselves under any purported contract: see PARA 9.

3   *Franks v Reuters Ltd* [2003] EWCA Civ 417, [2003] ICR 1166, [2008] IRLR 423, applying *Carmichael v National Power plc* [1999] 4 All ER 897, [1999] 1 WLR 2042, [2000] IRLR 43, HL (cited in PARA 4). Few agency workers have been found to have implied contracts with the end user (see eg *Cairns v Visteon UK Ltd* [2007] ICR 616, [2007] IRLR 175, EAT; *Astbury v Gist Ltd* [2007] All ER (D) 480 (Mar), EAT) but there are occasional exceptions: see *Wood v National Grid Electricity Transmission plc* [2007] All ER (D) 358 (Oct), EAT; and see also PARA 11. As to the meaning of 'contract of service' see PARA 1 note 1.

4   *Fitzpatrick v Evans & Co* [1902] 1 KB 505, CA.

5   *R v Weyhill, Hants, Inhabitants* (1760) 1 Wm Bl 206; *R v Stokesley Inhabitants* (1796) 6 Term Rep 757.

6   *Gregory-Stoke Parish v Pitmister* (1726) 2 Sess Cas KB 132; *R v Sow Inhabitants* (1817) 1 B & Ald 178 at 181 per Bayley J; *Bradshaw v Hayward* (1842) Car & M 591.

7   See PARA 118 et seq.

15.   Capacity.   Any person of ordinary contractual capacity is competent to enter into a contract of employment either as employer or employee[1].

A contract of employment entered into by a minor will be binding if it is on the whole beneficial to him at the time when it is entered into[2]. It is generally considered a benefit for a minor to fit himself for, and employ himself in, work or business[3]; but the contract must not contain or omit stipulations, the inclusion or omission of which is so much to the detriment of the minor as to render it unfair that he should be bound by the contract[4]. If, however, the contract is generally for the minor's benefit, but contains covenants which are in any event invalid, the invalid covenants, if severable[5], may be disregarded and the rest of the contract enforced[6]. An arbitration clause is binding on a minor, provided that the contract as a whole is for his benefit[7]; and an employer may reserve a right to require a refund of an allowance if a trainee prematurely terminates the course of training, though the right must be exercised in good faith[8]. These rules may in any particular case be supplemented by, or take effect subject to, statutory provisions, in particular those relating to the employment of children[9].

Although an employer who is under a disability is not necessarily precluded from entering into a valid contract of employment[10], his liability for the employee's acts depends on the nature and extent of the disability to which he is subject. The employee of a minor may have an implied authority to pledge his employer's credit for necessaries[11], or on his behalf to enter into a contract, such as a contract for the purchase of land[12], belonging to the class of contracts which are binding on the minor, unless expressly repudiated on his coming of age[13]. The employee of a minor may also have an implied authority to protect his employer's property, and may therefore be entitled to expel a trespasser[14].

Where an employer is suffering from mental disorder he cannot, as a general rule, be made liable for the acts of persons to act on his behalf[15]. There may, however, be an implied authority to pledge his credit for the expenses necessary for the protection of his person or estate[16], although the implication of authority is rebutted by evidence that the person who is alleged to have pledged the credit had sufficient money in hand belonging to the estate of the person suffering from mental disorder[17]. Where the employer begins to suffer from mental disorder after the contract of employment has been entered into, the effect of his disorder is to revoke any authority which the employee may possess[18]. The employer remains liable, however, on all contracts made by the employee within the scope of his authority, provided they are made with persons to whom the employer, before his mental disorder, held out the employee as having authority to contract on his behalf, and provided those persons, at the time of making the contract, were not aware of the employer's mental disorder and consequent revocation of authority[19].

1   See CONTRACT vol 22 (2012) PARA 232. As to the capacity of a person suffering from mental disorder to enter into a contract see MENTAL HEALTH AND CAPACITY vol 75 (2013) PARA 614 et seq; and as to the power of one partner to bind a firm and as to the liability of partners to third persons see PARTNERSHIP vol 79 (2014) PARA 39 et seq.

2   *De Francesco v Barnum* (1890) 45 ChD 430; *Corn v Matthews* [1893] 1 QB 310, CA (a case concerning apprenticeship, but applied to minors generally in *Flower v London and North Western Rly Co* [1894] 2 QB 65, CA; *Clements v London and North Western Rly Co* [1894] 2 QB 482 at 495, CA, per AL Smith LJ); *Mackinlay v Bathurst* (1919) 36 TLR 31, CA; *Chaplin v Leslie Frewin (Publishers) Ltd* [1966] Ch 71 at 97, [1965] 3 All ER 764 at 774–775, CA, per Winn LJ. A reasonable restrictive covenant is enforceable against a minor after he comes of age (*Gadd v Thompson* [1911] 1 KB 304, DC) and possibly during his minority, provided that the contract as a whole is for his benefit (see *Gadd v Thompson* at 308 per Phillimore J; *Richards v Whitham* (1892) 66 LT 695, CA). As to covenants in restraint of trade between an employer and an employee see PARA 19. See also COMPETITION vol 18 (2009) PARA 418.

3   *Gylbert v Fletcher* (1629) Cro Car 179; *Cooper v Simmons* (1862) 7 H & N 707 at 721 per Wilde B; *De Francesco v Barnum* (1890) 45 ChD 430 at 439 per Fry LJ; *Clements v London and North Western Rly Co* [1894] 2 QB 482 at 491, CA, per Kay LJ, and at 495 per AL Smith LJ; *Mackinlay v Bathurst* (1919) 36 TLR 31, CA; *Denmark Productions Ltd v Boscobel Productions Ltd* [1969] 1 QB 699, [1968] 3 All ER 513, CA. A minor may enter into a valid contract of employment as an employer: see the text and notes 10–14.

4   *De Francesco v Barnum* (1890) 45 ChD 430 at 440, 442 per Fry LJ; *Corn v Matthews* [1893] 1 QB 310 at 316, CA, per AL Smith LJ; *Green v Thompson* [1899] 2 QB 1, DC. Thus it may be unfair eg:
    (1)   to provide for termination at will by the employer (*R v Lord* (1848) 12 QB 757 at 765 per Lord Denman CJ);
    (2)   to preclude the minor from suing for compensation for injury (*Flower v London and North Western Rly Co* [1894] 2 QB 65, CA; *Olsen v Corry and Gravesend Aviation Ltd* [1936] 3 All ER 241; *Murray v Schwachman Ltd* [1938] 1 KB 130, [1937] 2 All ER 68, CA; *Arabian v Tufnall and Taylor Ltd* [1944] KB 685, [1944] 2 All ER 317); or
    (3)   to include unusual or unnecessary restrictions (*Sir WC Leng & Co Ltd v Andrews* [1909] 1 Ch 763 at 769, CA, per Cozens-Hardy MR).
    Conditions normal in the usages of the particular employment may, however, be validly imposed on a minor where the contract as a whole is for his benefit: *Doyle v White City Stadium Ltd* [1935] 1 KB 110, CA (contract entered into by a boxer who was a minor and the British Boxing Board of Control, from whom the minor obtained a licence as a boxer, which contained a provision for forfeiture of the purse receivable by the boxer in case of disqualification held to be so closely connected with a contract of employment as to be binding on the minor, having regard to the fact that the contract as a whole was for his benefit); *Leslie v Fitzpatrick* (1877) 3 QBD 229; cf *Green v Thompson*; *Corn v Matthews*. *Doyle v White City Stadium Ltd* was distinguished in *Proform Sports Management Ltd v Proactive Sports Management Ltd* [2006] EWHC 2812 (Ch), [2007] 1 All ER 542 (agreement to act as executive agent and to carry out personal representation on behalf of professional football player who was a minor at the time when he entered into the agreement was at one remove from the class of contract that has been treated in the authorities as being subject to the exception to the general voidability of minors' contracts, applicable where such a contract is for the minor's benefit).

5   As to the doctrine of severance see CONTRACT vol 22 (2012) PARA 459.

6 *Bromley v Smith* [1909] 2 KB 235; *Gadd v Thompson* [1911] 1 KB 304, DC.
7 *Slade v Metrodent Ltd* [1953] 2 QB 112, [1953] 2 All ER 336 (apprenticeship deed providing for arbitration by the National Joint Council for the Craft of Dental Technicians might be beneficial to the infant).
8 *LCC v Mead* (1954) 52 LGR 533, 118 JP 514, CA (trainee teacher had obtained supplementary expenses grant for the academic year but left after one term for reasons which were deemed to be unsatisfactory).
9 See CHILDREN AND YOUNG PERSONS vol 10 (2012) PARA 705 et seq.
10 See *Chapple v Cooper* (1844) 13 M & W 252 at 258, per Alderson B; *Hands v Slaney* (1800) 8 Term Rep 578; and see CHILDREN AND YOUNG PERSONS vol 9 (2012) PARAS 18–19.
11 See note 10.
12 *Whittingham v Murdy* (1889) 60 LT 956.
13 As to such contracts, see *Duncan v Dixon* (1890) 44 ChD 211; *Carter v Silber* [1892] 2 Ch 278, CA (affd sub nom *Edwards v Carter* [1893] AC 360, HL); *Viditz v O'Hagan* [1900] 2 Ch 87, CA; and CHILDREN AND YOUNG PERSONS vol 9 (2012) PARA 12 et seq.
14 *Ewer v Jones* (1846) 9 QB 623; see AGENCY vol 1 (2008) PARA 5.
15 *Richardson v Du Bois* (1869) LR 5 QB 51; see generally MENTAL HEALTH AND CAPACITY vol 75 (2013) PARA 614.
16 *Williams v Wentworth* (1842) 5 Beav 325; c f *Re Wood's Estate, Davidson v Wood* (1863) 1 De GJ & Sm 465; *Read v Legard* (1851) 6 Exch 636; and see MENTAL HEALTH AND CAPACITY vol 75 (2013) PARA 727 et seq.
17 *Richardson v Du Bois* (1869) LR 5 QB 51.
18 *Drew v Nunn* (1879) 4 QBD 661, CA; *Richardson v Du Bois* (1869) LR 5 QB 51.
19 *Drew v Nunn* (1879) 4 QBD 661, CA; and see *Yonge v Toynbee* [1910] 1 KB 215, CA.

16. Consideration and certainty. In the absence of consideration, there can be no binding contract of employment unless it is by deed[1]. The adequacy of any particular consideration is not a matter into which a court will inquire[2].

In most contracts of employment, the employee's consideration is being ready and willing to serve[3]; and the employer's consideration is the provision of some form of remuneration, though this will not always take the form of a regular wage[4]. If an employee, during the course of a contract of employment, refuses or fails to supply the consideration for a particular period, especially by taking part in industrial action, that may justify the employer in refusing to pay some or all of the remuneration for that period[5]. Likewise, failure by the employer to supply his consideration may be a breach of contract sufficient to permit the employee to leave his employment and claim for statutory purposes to have been constructively dismissed[6].

To be legally binding, a contract must generally be sufficiently clear and certain[7]; but it is arguable that in the particular context of contracts of employment this requirement may have to be applied more liberally[8], for much the same reasons that implied terms have had to be found more easily[9], namely that historically this type of contract has often tended to be relatively informal with major areas not covered by express terms, or left to custom and practice[10].

1 *Lees v Whitcomb* (1828) 5 Bing 34 (written agreement to remain with an employer for two years for the purpose of learning the business held not to be binding because no consideration, as eg that the employer should teach, was disclosed); *Sykes v Dixon* (1839) 9 Ad & El 693 (contention that there might be implied in a contract, the operation of which was entirely on one side, a promise to pay for the services referred to in it was not upheld); *Hulse v Hulse* (1856) 17 CB 711 (future services). As to the doctrine of consideration see CONTRACT vol 22 (2012) PARA 308 et seq; and as to contracts by deed see DEEDS AND OTHER INSTRUMENTS vol 32 (2012) PARA 201 et seq.
2 *Hitchcock v Coker* (1837) 6 Ad & El 438, Ex Ch; *Pilkington v Scott* (1846) 15 M & W 657; *Middleton v Brown* (1878) 47 LJ Ch 411, CA; *Gaumont-British Picture Corpn Ltd v Alexander* [1936] 2 All ER 1686. See also COMPETITION vol 18 (2009) PARA 415; CONTRACT vol 22 (2012) PARA 317; c f SPECIFIC PERFORMANCE vol 95 (2013) PARA 368.
3 *Wallis v Warren* (1849) 4 Exch 361; *Warburton v Co-operative Wholesale Society Ltd* [1917] 1 KB 663, CA; *O'Grady v M Saper Ltd* [1940] 2 KB 469, [1940] 3 All ER 527, CA; *Henthorn*

and Taylor v Central Electricity Generating Board [1980] IRLR 361, CA; *Cresswell v Inland Revenue Board* [1984] 2 All ER 713, [1984] ICR 508. *Warburton v Co-operative Wholesale Society Ltd* was applied in *Kaur v British Library* [2008] All ER (D) 22 (Sep), EAT). This is significant in relation to the payment of wages during sickness or lay-off, since the basic obligation is to serve, not necessarily to work: see PARAS 27–28. It is for the employer to show that the contract permits the withholding of payment (eg through a clause specifically covering part payment or no payment during sickness): *Beveridge v KLM UK Ltd* [2000] IRLR 765, EAT.

4 See PARA 22. 'Mutuality of obligation' has been seen as one of the 'irreducible minimum' legal requirements for the existence of a contract of employment: see PARA 4.

5 *Miles v Wakefield Metropolitan District Council* [1987] AC 539, [1987] ICR 368, HL (registrar of births deaths and marriages declined to undertake marriages on a Saturday and employer lawfully deducted the pro rata amount of pay in respect of periods in which he declined to carry out part of his duties); *British Telecommunications plc v Ticehurst* [1992] ICR 383, sub nom *Ticehurst and Thompson v British Telecommunications plc* [1992] IRLR 219, CA; and see PARA 29.

6 See PARA 763.

7 See CONTRACT vol 22 (2012) PARA 273.

8 See eg *National Coal Board v Galley* [1958] 1 All ER 91, [1958] 1 WLR 16, CA (agreement by a deputy at a colliery to work such days or part days in each week as might reasonably be required by the management held to be enforceable), following *Foley v Classique Coaches Ltd* [1934] 2 KB 1, CA, and distinguishing *May and Butcher v R* [1934] 2 KB 17n, HL. If an agreement as to remuneration is too nebulous to enforce as a term, there may be implied, in an appropriate case, a contractual term to pay a reasonable sum for work done: *Way v Latilla* [1937] 3 All ER 759, HL; *Powell v Braun* [1954] 1 All ER 484, [1954] 1 WLR 401, CA; and see PARA 22.

9 See PARA 114.

10 See PARA 114. In such circumstances a strict interpretation of the requirement of certainty could lead to the unrealistic legal conclusion that there was no contract of employment when in practice there was clearly an employment relationship in existence. An employer has a statutory obligation to give an employee a written statement of the major terms and conditions of employment (see PARA 118 et seq); but, although this is clearly aimed at lessening the uncertainties inherent in many contracts of employment, it is not always observed properly or at all.

17. Applicability of the Unfair Contract Terms Act 1977. Whether the Unfair Contract Terms Act 1977[1] could apply to the terms of a contract of employment[2], and so subject them to a test of reasonableness, has caused uncertainty in the past. It was initially held (at first instance) that the Act could apply, but this involved straining the concept of a 'consumer' (to which the Act applies) to cover an employee[3]. Subsequently, however, the Court of Appeal disapproved that interpretation, held that 'consumer' has a natural meaning and further held that in normal circumstances that meaning does not include an employee[4]. Thus, the weight of authority is against the applicability of the Act here. Moreover, it must be stressed that, even if the Act did apply, it would only subject to the test of reasonableness a contract term excluding or restricting the employer's liability or purporting to entitle the employer to render a contractual performance substantially different from that reasonably expected of him, or to render no performance at all[5]. On that basis, an employee's claim, that a clause stating that he could be dismissed in the first two years of employment without implementation of the disciplinary procedure was subject to the Unfair Contract Terms Act 1977 and thus void for unreasonableness, failed because that clause did not purport to restrict or exclude an existing liability, but rather it set out the employee's entitlement and the limit of his rights in the first place[6]. Arguably, that would be so with most normal clauses in a contract of employment.

1 As to the Unfair Contract Terms Act 1977 generally see CONTRACT vol 22 (2012) PARA 408 et seq.

2   The question has been raised without being decided: see *Micklefield v SAC Technology Ltd* [1991] 1 All ER 275, [1990] IRLR 218; *Chapman v Aberdeen Construction Group plc* [1991] IRLR 505, Ct of Sess.

3   *Brigden v American Express Bank Ltd* [2000] IRLR 94. For these purposes, a party to a contract 'deals as consumer' in relation to another party if: (1) he neither makes the contract in the course of a business nor holds himself out as doing so; and (2) the other party does make the contract in the course of a business: see the Unfair Contract Terms Act 1977 s 12(1)(a), (b); and CONTRACT vol 22 (2012) PARA 420.

4   *Keen v Commerzbank AG* [2006] EWCA Civ 1536, [2007] ICR 623, sub nom *Commerzbank AG v Keen* [2007] IRLR 132.

5   See the Unfair Contract Terms Act 1977 s 3(2); and CONTRACT vol 22 (2012) PARA 411. Thus in spite of its name, the Unfair Contract Terms Act 1977 does not deal with unfair contract terms generally, but mostly with exclusion clauses in particular types of contract.

6   *Brigden v American Express Bank Ltd* [2000] IRLR 94. In *Keen v Commerzbank AG* [2006] EWCA Civ 1536, [2007] ICR 623, sub nom *Commerzbank AG v Keen* [2007] IRLR 132 (see note 4) a challenge under the Unfair Contract Terms Act 1977 to a clause stating that the employee had to be still in the employment at the date of declaration of a discretionary bonus in order to receive it failed.

B. TAINTED CONTRACTS

18.   Illegality. A contract of employment will not be enforced[1] if it is based on a consideration which is wholly illegal[2]; and the ordinary law of contract will apply[3]. A finding of illegality means, however, not only that no common law claim may be maintained on the contract, but also that the employee subject to the contract loses any statutory employment rights which rely on his having been an employee under a contract of employment, in particular the right to claim unfair dismissal[4].

A contract may generally be illegal because it is contrary to a statute or is an immoral contract[5]. A contract which is illegal in inception, that is to say in its purpose, is void regardless of the state of mind of the parties; but, where a contract is initially lawful but is later performed in an illegal manner, it is not necessarily void[6]. If both parties know of the illegality, it may be void; but, if one party did not know of the illegality, that party may still rely on the contract[7]. The tendency[8] has, however, been to treat cases of contracts tainted by tax evasion as cases of illegality in performance, so that an employee may still be able to avoid the doctrine and bring a statutory claim if it can be shown that he did not know of, or collude in, the tax evasion[9], or if his employer's conduct is so reprehensible in comparison with his own that public policy does not preclude his statutory claim[10].

Not every minor illegality is sufficient to render the whole contract unenforceable[11]; an employee's involvement in an act of dishonesty or fraud against his employer does not render the contract of employment illegal and thus unenforceable in the same way as an agreement between the employer and the employee for an illegal element in the contract[12]. If the illegality affects the contract only for a certain period during its currency, the contract may be unenforceable only for that period; but, if that period falls during a necessary qualifying period for the statutory right being claimed by the employee, his claim will still fail[13].

Although severance of the illegal element[14] in a contract may be possible in some cases, it is unlikely to be allowed in a case involving tax evasion[15].

1   'If during a case illegality emerges, it does not mean that the court or tribunal does not have jurisdiction to decide the issue in the case. It comes to no more than this, that, if a contract is an illegal one, it cannot be enforced at the suit of anyone who was knowingly a party to the illegality': *Wilkinson v Lugg* [1990] ICR 599 at 603, EAT, per Sir David Croom-Johnson.

2   *Davies v Makuna* (1885) 29 ChD 596, CA; *Kearney v Whitehaven Colliery Co* [1893] 1 QB
     700, CA; *Miller v Karlinksi* (1945) 62 TLR 85, CA; *Napier v National Business Agency Ltd*
     [1951] 2 All ER 264, CA. A characterisation of the relationship that is held to be erroneous,
     e g in relation to tax status, does not, in the absence of misrepresentation, necessarily prevent an
     employee subsequently claiming the advantages of being, or having been, an employee: *Enfield
     Technical Services Ltd v Payne, Grace v BF Components Ltd* [2008] EWCA Civ 393, [2008]
     IRLR 500 (employee must have both knowledge of the facts producing the illegality and an
     element of active participation). As to where it was possible to sever the illegal parts of a
     contract from the legal see for example *Helbawi v Blue Chip Trading Ltd* [2009] IRLR
     128, EAT (where employee had worked beyond the hours permitted by his foreign student visa,
     public policy would not be properly served by allowing him to recover for any of the work done
     in term when he was knowingly acting in breach of the licence conditions, but EAT was able to
     sever the lawful hours and allow the claim in relation to those, based on the important social
     goal of enforcing minimum standards).

3   See CONTRACT vol 22 (2012) PARA 452 et seq. These normal rules may not apply if the illegality
     relates to entirely extraneous payments, not themselves part of the contract of employment:
     Annandale Engineering v Samson [1994] IRLR 59, EAT. The defence of illegality does not give
     rise to a procedural bar so as to engage a claimant's rights under the Convention for the
     Protection of Human Rights and Fundamental Freedoms (Rome, 25 March 1957; TS 1 (1973);
     Cmnd 5179) art 6(1) and the Human Rights Act 1998 (see RIGHTS AND FREEDOMS vol 88A
     (2013) PARAS 243, 269 et seq): *Soteriou v Ultrachem Ltd* [2004] EWHC 983 (QB), [2004] IRLR
     870 (although a finding of illegality effectively stopped further litigation, the claimant was not
     denied a fair trial; rather at trial he had failed to prove an essential ingredient, namely an
     enforceable contract under the substantive law of contract).

4   *Tomlinson v Dick Evans 'U' Drive Ltd* [1978] ICR 639, [1978] IRLR 77, EAT. The argument
     that, whatever may be the position at common law, the doctrine of illegality should not as a
     matter of policy be applied in claims brought under employment protection legislation,
     especially for unfair dismissal, because of its harsh effects on employment rights, has been
     disapproved: *Coral Leisure Group Ltd v Barnett* [1981] ICR 503, [1981] IRLR 204, EAT;
     Newland v Simons & Willer (Hairdressers) Ltd [1981] ICR 521, [1981] IRLR 359, EAT;
     Hyland v JH Barker (North West) Ltd [1985] ICR 861, [1985] IRLR 403, EAT; and see *Zarkasi
     v Anindita* [2012] ICR 788, [2012] All ER (D) 202 (Jan), EAT (illegal contract was bar to unfair
     dismissal claim in circumstances where employee alleged she was victim of human trafficking,
     but tribunal route was not the only route by which a victim of trafficking could claim
     recompense). See also *Payne v Enfield Technical Services Ltd, Grace v BF Components Ltd*
     [2008] EWCA Civ 393, [2008] IRLR 500, [2008] All ER (D) 300 (Apr) (although a contract of
     employment might be unlawfully performed if there were misrepresentations, express or
     implied, as to the facts, there were limits to the circumstances which would deprive the
     employee of the right subsequently to claim the benefits of employment); the particular
     significance of this case was that a mere misunderstanding of the individual's status (with no
     misrepresentation to Her Majesty's Revenue and Customs) did *not* render the contract of
     employment illegal.
         Because the rights protected by statute on the grounds of discrimination are not founded
     upon the contract of employment and do not seek to enforce contractual obligations (although
     reference to the contract must be made to determine whether the person is 'employed' within the
     meaning of the statute), there is nothing in the statute, or as a matter of broad legislative policy,
     to disqualify a person, who is in fact employed, from protection by reason of illegality in the
     contract of employment if the claim is not founded upon, or seeking to enforce, contractual
     obligations: *Leighton v Michael* [1995] ICR 1091, [1996] IRLR 67, EAT (tribunal's jurisdiction
     to consider complaint under the Sex Discrimination Act 1975 of alleged sexual harassment and
     victimisation not affected by tainted contract of employment which involved a fraud on the
     Inland Revenue; contract for shop work was legal in its inception and transferred by operation
     of law to respondents who introduced the irregularity); approved in *Hall v Woolston Hall
     Leisure Ltd* [2000] 4 All ER 787, [2001] 1 WLR 225, CA (employee entitled to compensation
     for financial loss in respect of unlawful dismissal under the Sex Discrimination Act 1975 by
     reason of her pregnancy, notwithstanding that employers were not paying tax on part of her
     wages which tainted her contract of employment with illegality). However, this position may be
     modified where, in addition to knowledge of the facts which make the performance illegal, the
     employee actively participates in the illegal performance of a contract of employment (which is
     otherwise neither entered into for an illegal purpose nor prohibited by statute): *Hall v Woolston
     Hall Leisure Ltd* (employee's acquiescence in employers' illegal performance of the contract did
     not amount to actual participation (and she could in practice do nothing about it) and in any
     case was not causally linked with sex discrimination claim); applied in *Vakante v Addey &*

Stanhope School [2004] EWCA Civ 1065, [2004] 4 All ER 1056, [2005] ICR 231 (asylum seeker barred from claiming under the Race Relations Act 1976 on his dismissal because complaint was so inextricably bound up with the dishonest and criminal conduct by which he had achieved the whole employment relationship with the school (which was innocent of any illegality) that any compensation for discrimination would appear to condone that conduct). See also *Hounga v Allen* [2012] EWCA Civ 609, [2012] IRLR 685 (claim based on independent statutory tort under the Race Relations Act 1976 defeated where employment contract was illegal in its inception since both parties knew that employee arrived in UK on visitors' visa and was not entitled to work and allowance of claim would condone illegal conduct); revsd [2014] UKSC 47, [2014] 1 WLR 2889, [2014] ICR 847, [2014] IRLR 811 (tribunal's award compensated employee for injury to feelings consequent upon her dismissal, and did not permit evasion of a penalty prescribed by the criminal law or encourage those in the situation of the employee to enter into illegal contracts of employment). Where the issue is not dismissal, and where the actions complained of are not in any sense necessary, causative or inextricably linked with the employment itself, the approach of the Court of Appeal in *Vakante v Addey & Stanhope School* and in *Hounga v Allen* can be distinguished, and the illegality does not exclude a tort claim: *Wijesundera v Heathrow 3PL Logistics Ltd* [2014] ICR 523, EAT (there is nothing intrinsic about being an employee that leads to sexual harassment or freedom from it).

5   This was argued to be the case in *Coral Leisure Group Ltd v Barnett* [1981] ICR 503, [1981] IRLR 204, EAT, on the basis that during his employment the employee had hired prostitutes for the employer's clients. Most of the case law in the employment context has, however, involved contracts including or involving an element of unlawful tax evasion.

6   The burden of proof in cases where illegality is being alleged is on the party making the allegation to show that the contract had been entered into with the object of committing an illegal act, or had been performed with that objective: *Colen v Cebrian (UK) Ltd* [2003] EWCA Civ 1676, [2004] ICR 568, [2004] IRLR 210.

7   For these purposes, 'knowledge' means knowledge of the facts leading to the illegality, not knowledge that the act in question was illegal, ignorance of law being no defence; it refers to actual, subjective knowledge, not to what the employee ought to have known: *Davidson v Pillay* [1979] IRLR 275, EAT; *Corby v Morrison* [1980] ICR 564, [1980] IRLR 218, EAT; *Newland v Simons & Willer (Hairdressers) Ltd* [1981] ICR 521, [1981] IRLR 359, EAT. See also *Wheeler v Quality Deep Ltd (t/a Thai Royale Restaurant)* [2004] EWCA Civ 1085, [2005] ICR 265 (foreign national with limited knowledge of English and of tax and national insurance provisions not knowingly involved in fraudulent conduct); and see note 4.

8   See *Corby v Morrison* [1980] ICR 564, [1980] IRLR 218, EAT, where the primary ground for ruling out an unfair dismissal claim by an employee who had received an extra £5 per week without deduction of tax was that the contract was illegal in its inception and so void (applying the judgment of du Parcq LJ in *Miller v Karlinski* (1945) 62 TLR 85, CA); but the Employment Appeal Tribunal gave a second ground that, if it were only illegal in performance, the employee knew the facts and so the contract was, therefore, unenforceable. It was the second ground that was later emphasised in *Newland v Simons & Willer (Hairdressers) Ltd* [1981] ICR 521, [1981] IRLR 359, EAT.

9   *Tomlinson v Dick Evans 'U' Drive Ltd* [1978] ICR 639, [1978] IRLR 77, EAT; *Davidson v Pillay* [1979] IRLR 275, EAT; *Newland v Simons & Willer (Hairdressers) Ltd* [1981] ICR 521, [1981] IRLR 359, EAT. As to the position where the evasion is on the part of the employee only, without the employer's knowledge, see *McConnell v Bolik* [1979] IRLR 422, EAT. Where the employee does know the facts, there is a danger that an employer could make illegal payments and later rely on them to defeat a claim by the employee, thus profiting from his own misdeeds; this may be deterred by the tribunal's power in such a case to send the evidence that it has received to the Revenue and Customs: see *Corby v Morrison* [1980] ICR 564, [1980] IRLR 218, EAT; *Newland v Simons & Willer (Hairdressers) Ltd*. Cf *Hewcastle Catering Ltd v Ahmed and Elkamah* [1992] ICR 626, [1991] IRLR 473, CA; and see the text to note 10.

10   *Hewcastle Catering Ltd v Ahmed and Elkamah* [1992] ICR 626, [1991] IRLR 473, CA.

11   In the case of illegality through contravention of a statute, the test is whether the intention of the legislature was to affect contracts if necessary, not just to penalise the conduct in question in other ways: *St John Shipping Corpn v Joseph Rank Ltd* [1957] 1 QB 267 at 283, [1956] 3 All ER 683 at 687 per Devlin J (see CONTRACT vol 22 (2012) PARAS 452, 454, 457). This prevents eg a lorry driver's contract of employment from becoming unenforceable as soon as he exceeds a speed limit. It is clear, however, that breach of the taxation statutes is viewed as potentially leading to illegality and unenforceability: *Newland v Simons & Willer (Hairdressers) Ltd* [1981] ICR 521, [1981] IRLR 359, EAT; *Hyland v JH Barker (North West) Ltd* [1985] ICR 861, [1985] IRLR 403, EAT.

12 *Broaders v Kalkare Property Maintenance Ltd* [1990] IRLR 421, EAT. Likewise, the fact that
    the employee has committed some collateral act which is illegal or immoral, but which was not
    part of the contract itself or an integral part of performing it, will not debar the employee: *Coral
    Leisure Group Ltd v Barnett* [1981] ICR 503, [1981] IRLR 204, EAT.

13 *Hyland v JH Barker (North West) Ltd* [1985] ICR 861, [1985] IRLR 403, EAT (employee
    unable to claim unfair dismissal because of illegal payments during a four-week period falling
    within the two-year period prior to the date of dismissal (see PARA 758)).

14 As to the doctrine of severance see CONTRACT vol 22 (2012) PARA 459. See also note 2.

15 *Miller v Karlinski* (1945) 62 TLR 85, CA; *Napier v National Business Agency Ltd* [1951]
    2 All ER 264, CA; *Corby v Morrison* [1980] ICR 564, [1980] IRLR 218, EAT; *Hyland v JH
    Barker (North West) Ltd* [1985] ICR 861, [1985] IRLR 403, EAT.

19. Covenants in restraint of trade and 'garden leave' clauses. A covenant in
restraint of trade[1] between an employer and an employee is unenforceable unless
it is reasonable as between the parties and it is reasonable with reference to the
public interest[2].

However:

(1) a restraint clause in a contract of employment is enforceable only if it
     protects an interest of the employer that is considered by the law to be
     properly protectable; in the past this has essentially meant either trade
     secrets and other confidential information or trade connections,
     suppliers and customers[3] but more recently it has been accepted that an
     employer may have a legitimate interest in preserving workforce skills
     or keeping key staff, especially in a highly competitive business[4];

(2) the criteria for the validity of such a clause are stricter in the case of a
     contract of employment than in the case of a contract for the sale of a
     business, since the parties are less likely in the former case to be
     bargaining at arm's length and, further, it is particularly important in the
     case of an employee that the law is not used to stifle bona fide
     competition or to prevent the employee from using his own skills and
     knowledge, even if gained wholly or partly in the employer's service[5];

(3) it is likewise particularly important in the case of an employee that he
     can challenge a restraint even if it is contained in an agreement between
     other parties and not actually in his own contract of employment,
     especially where it is contained in an agreement of sorts between several
     employers but where it affects the livelihood of the employee[6];

(4) in a case of a restraint on an employee where the employer brings a
     claim to enforce the restraint but it is unlikely to be heard quickly, it
     may be appropriate for the court, when considering an interim
     injunction, to depart from the usual rule that only an arguable case
     needs to be shown by the claimant[7], and instead consider the strength of
     the parties' cases and the likelihood of success at the eventual trial[8];

(5) if the employee is wrongfully dismissed at common law, the employer
     cannot enforce the restraint clause[9] (but an employer who dismisses an
     employee unfairly may still take advantage of such a clause[10]).

An alternative to a formal covenant in restraint of trade in the case of a key
employee is the incorporation of a 'garden leave clause' into the contract by the
employer, whereby the employee is made subject to a lengthy notice requirement,
during which the employer continues to pay the employee his normal wage,
though not requiring him actually to work, in return for which the employee is
bound not to take employment elsewhere during that period[11].

However, if an employer, concerned about an employee leaving and
commencing work for a competitor, wishes to ensure that the employee is not

able to put himself in a position to misuse confidential information, the preferable course is to make him subject to an express restraint of trade clause, which is (if valid) a more certain and enforceable option than reliance on the residual implied duty of good faith as it applies after termination of employment, which by its nature is narrower, more vague and more difficult to enforce[12].

1 Contracts of employment, together with sales of businesses, form the two principal areas where potentially valid covenants in restraint of trade may be found: see COMPETITION vol 18 (2009) PARA 377 et seq. A clause restraining certain activities or imposing harsh conditions during employment may be subject to the doctrine of restraint of trade, as well as the more typical clause restraining post-termination activities: *A Schroeder Music Publishing Co Ltd v Macaulay* [1974] 3 All ER 616, [1974] 1 WLR 1308, HL; *Clifford Davis Management Ltd v WEA Records Ltd* [1975] 1 All ER 237, [1975] 1 WLR 61, CA.

2 *Nordenfelt v Maxim Nordenfelt Guns and Ammunition Co Ltd* [1894] AC 535, HL; *Mason v Provident Clothing and Supply Co Ltd* [1913] AC 724, HL; *Esso Petroleum Co Ltd v Harper's Garage (Stourport) Ltd* [1968] AC 269, [1967] 1 All ER 699, HL; *Watson v Prager* [1991] 3 All ER 487, [1991] ICR 603, EAT. See also *WRN Ltd v Ayris* [2008] EWHC 1080 (QB), [2008] IRLR 889, [2008] All ER (D) 276 (May) ('leaving contract' not valid and binding in law as there was insufficient relevant consideration). If a restrictive covenant is unreasonable at the date it is made, it cannot be saved simply because a subsequent change of circumstances means that it would have been reasonable at the time that it falls to be enforced: *Patsystems v Neilly* [2012] EWHC 2609 (QB), [2012] IRLR 979 (if the clause had been void when originally signed, then it was necessary for the first employer to show that a fresh agreement had been entered into).

3 *Herbert Morris Ltd v Saxelby* [1916] 1 AC 688, HL; *Faccenda Chicken Ltd v Fowler, Fowler v Faccenda Chicken Ltd* [1987] Ch 117, [1986] ICR 297, CA. See also *International Consulting Services (UK) Ltd v Hart* [2000] IRLR 227 (clause preventing former employee from dealing with companies with whom the employer had 'negotiated' was not too uncertain to be enforced; employer legitimately regarded the connection with customers resulting from negotiations as forming part of the goodwill of its business). In a modern business context, the term 'trade secrets' is not confined to secret formulae for the manufacture of products but can include highly confidential information of a non-technical or non-scientific nature, which may come within the ambit of information the employer is entitled to have protected, albeit for a limited period: *Lansing Linde Ltd v Kerr* [1991] 1 All ER 418 at 425–426, [1991] IRLR 80 at 84, CA, per Staughton LJ, and at 435 and 88 per Butler-Sloss LJ. See also *Townends Group Ltd v Cobb* [2004] EWHC 3432 (Ch), (2004) Times, 1 December, [2004] All ER (D) 421 (Nov) (clause restricting disclosure of customer information by former employee was unenforceable where it failed to define whether it applied to customers existing during employment or after); *Allan Janes LLP v Johal* [2006] EWHC 286 (Ch), [2006] ICR 742, [2006] IRLR 599 (clause preventing former employee from practising as solicitor within six miles of former employer was considered wider than necessary to protect latter's legitimate interests); and *Thomas v Farr plc* [2007] EWCA Civ 118, [2007] ICR 932, [2007] IRLR 419 (clause preventing director from competing with former employer within 12 months of termination of employment was reasonable; it was no argument against a restrictive covenant that it might be very difficult for either the employer or the employee to know exactly where the line might lie between information which remained confidential after the end of the employment and the information which did not). See also *Beckett Investment Management Group Ltd v Hall* [2007] EWCA Civ 613, [2007] ICR 1539, [2007] IRLR 793 (realistic interpretation of who was the protected 'company'); *Norbrook Laboratories (GB) Ltd v Adair* [2008] EWHC 978 (QB), [2008] IRLR 878 (restraint of trade by agreement); *CEF Holdings Ltd v Mundey* [2012] EWHC 1524 (QB), [2012] FSR 929, [2012] IRLR 912 (width of the non-competition clause was so great that it prevented ex-employees, who were in any case bound by a customer connection restriction clause, from having any interest in a competing company, such as even owning one share in a publicly quoted company); and *Threlfall v ECD Insight Ltd* [2012] EWHC 3543 (QB), [2013] IRLR 185 (ex-employee had not acted in breach of restrictive covenants in conducting event moderation at conferences after the termination of his employment, because he himself had developed it as part of the company's activities as a sideline to his work there and it stopped being part of the company's activities after he left).

As to the granting of 'barring-out relief' (ie the remedy of preventing an ex-employee from entering what the employer thinks is unacceptable further employment for a period of time) see *Bolkiah v KPMG (a firm)* [1999] 2 AC 222, [1999] 1 All ER 517, HL (professionals such as solicitors and accountants may be prevented from acting against former clients in connection with a matter in which they had previously acted for them, unless the court could be satisfied that there was no real risk of information confidential to a former client coming into the hands of anyone with an adverse interest); *Caterpillar Logistics Services (UK) Ltd v Huesca de Crean* [2012] EWCA Civ 156, [2012] 3 All ER 129, [2012] ICR 981, [2012] IRLR 410 (nothing to justify extension of 'barring-out relief' to the ordinary relationship of employer and employee, because only in the most exceptional circumstances could an employee be a fiduciary of the employer to the extent that is called for); and CONFIDENCE AND INFORMATIONAL PRIVACY vol 19 (2011) PARAS 36, 38.

4   *Alliance Paper Group plc v Prestwich* [1996] IRLR 25; *Dawnay, Day & Co Ltd v D'Alphen* [1998] ICR 1068, [1997] IRLR 442, CA. Thus a non-solicitation of staff clause may be valid, because a company does have a legitimate interest in maintaining a stable trained workforce, although it remains subject to the normal requirements of not being unreasonably wide: *TSC Europe (UK) Ltd v Massey* [1999] IRLR 22 (non-solicitation clause was held to be unenforceable where it purported to restrict the solicitation of any employee of the company, including those engaged after the termination of the employee's employment). See also *CEF Holdings Ltd v Mundey* [2012] EWHC 1524 (QB), [2012] FSR 929, [2012] IRLR 912 (ex-employees were subject to an unreasonable employee-recruitment restriction clause which would have precluded them from inducing, soliciting or endeavouring to entice away from their former company any of approximately 3,000 employees, only a very small percentage of whom would be known to them and about whose work they would know little and to whom no loyalty was due, and any injunction so granted would have had no legitimate interest to protect and would have been unenforceable anyway); and *Coppage v Safety Net Security Ltd* [2013] EWCA Civ 1176; [2013] IRLR 970 (post-termination restraint period as short as six months must be a powerful factor in assessing the overall reasonableness of the clause).

5   *Herbert Morris Ltd v Saxelby* [1916] 1 AC 688, HL; *Mason v Provident Clothing and Supply Co Ltd* [1913] AC 724, HL. It is unreasonable of the employer to ask employees to sign a new contract of employment incorporating a restrictive covenant limiting the scope in which they could, inter alia, compete with the employer should they cease to be employed by it, as an unreasonable fetter on their future trading activities and such a refusal could not amount to a potentially fair reason for dismissal (see PARA 762 et seq): *Forshaw v Archcraft Ltd* [2006] ICR 70, [2005] IRLR 600, EAT. See also *TFS Derivatives Ltd v Morgan* [2004] EWHC 3181 (QB), [2005] IRLR 246 (minor severance of overly-restrictive wording in covenant was enough to make it enforceable as doing no more than was necessary to protect legitimate business interests). In the context of computer knowledge and skills see *FSS Travel and Leisure Systems Ltd v Johnson* [1998] IRLR 382, CA. See also *Ward Evans Financial Services Ltd v Fox* [2001] EWCA Civ 1243, [2002] IRLR 120 (employees who formed a rival company breached a 'trust and confidence' agreement, even though the company was dormant during their employment, because their interest in the company impaired their ability to act at all times in the employers' best interests). When considering the interests of the contracting parties, the court may take into account the fact that employees had been paid extra for entering into an agreement to be bound by a restrictive covenant, although any restraint must still be justified according to the usual principles: *Turner v Commonwealth and British Minerals Ltd* [2000] IRLR 114, [1999] All ER (D) 1097, CA. An employee who is also a vendor (of shares in the employer's business) may be considered primarily the latter so that the less stringent tests appropriate to that category may be applicable: *Systems Reliability Holdings plc v Smith* [1990] IRLR 377; and see PARA 10 note 3.

6   *Eastham v Newcastle United Football Club* [1964] Ch 413, [1963] 3 All ER 139; *Pharmaceutical Society of Great Britain v Dickson* [1970] AC 403 at 433, [1968] 2 All ER 686 at 701, HL, per Lord Upjohn. Such an agreement between employers, not to employ anyone who had been in the other's employment in the previous five years, is exemplified in *Kores Manufacturing Co Ltd v Kolok Manufacturing Co Ltd* [1959] Ch 108, [1958] 2 All ER 65, CA; it was held to be unreasonable as between the parties, though it was later said in *Esso Petroleum Ltd v Harper's Garage (Stourport) Ltd* [1968] AC 269 at 300, [1967] 1 All ER 699 at 709, HL, per Lord Reid, and at 319 and 721 per Lord Hodson, to have been a case which should have been decided on the public interest limb and, moreover, it could be argued that mere labour stabilisation should not be acceptable as a protectable interest in any event.

7   *American Cyanamid Co v Ethicon Ltd* [1975] AC 396, [1975] 1 All ER 504, HL; and see CIVIL PROCEDURE vol 11 (2009) PARA 383 et seq.

8   *Lansing Linde Ltd v Kerr* [1991] 1 All ER 418, [1991] IRLR 80, CA, applying dicta of Balcombe LJ in *Lawrence David Ltd v Ashton* [1991] 1 All ER 385 at 395–396, [1989] ICR 123 at 135, CA.

9   *General Billposting Co Ltd v Atkinson* [1909] AC 118, HL; *Measures Bros Ltd v Measures* [1910] 2 Ch 248, CA; *Spafax Ltd v Harrison* [1980] IRLR 442, CA; *Rex Stewart Jeffries Parker*

Ginsberg Ltd v Parker [1988] IRLR 483, CA; *Briggs v Oates* [1991] 1 All ER 407, [1990] ICR 473. This rule cannot be circumvented by a clause purporting to apply on termination 'however caused': *Rock Refrigeration Ltd v Jones* [1997] ICR 938, [1996] IRLR 675, CA (where doubts were expressed as to the continued desirability of the rule but the court accepted that it was bound to apply *General Billposting Co Ltd v Atkinson*). As to wrongful dismissal see PARA 825.

10 *Lonmar Global Risks Ltd (formerly SBJ Global Risks Ltd) v West* [2010] EWHC 2878 (QB), [2011] IRLR 138 (it would be unfair on the employer, even as a matter of policy, to deprive it of the protection of an otherwise valid restraint clause where, for example, the employee was being dismissed for gross misconduct, including the obvious example of illegal solicitation, but the employer got the procedure wrong, thus leading to a dismissal which was unfair only procedurally). Unlike the common law action of wrongful dismissal (see the text and note 9), unfair dismissal operates through statute and does not destroy the contract so that any post-termination clauses would still apply: see the Employment Rights Act 1996 s 98; and PARA 765.

11 Such a clause may be enforceable, though ultimately the matter is one for the discretion of the court: *Provident Financial Group plc v Hayward* [1989] 3 All ER 298, [1989] ICR 160, CA; *William Hill Organisation Ltd v Tucker* [1999] ICR 291, [1998] IRLR 313, CA; *Symbian Ltd v Christensen* [2001] IRLR 77, CA (court's discretion not fettered by separate clause which allowed employee to engage in non-competing business after termination); and see PARA 734.

12 As to the duty of good faith during employment see PARA 67; and as to the (lesser) duty of continuing good faith after the termination of employment see PARA 71.

20. Unreasonable restrictions. Although the substance of a contract of employment is essentially a matter for agreement between the parties, so that in the case of certain peculiar employments[1] the contract may impose long, even life-long, obligations[2], or restrictions of an unusually personal nature[3], a contract of employment is invalid if it imposes conditions so harsh or one-sided, in the employer's favour[4], or so restrictive of personal freedom of action, as to amount to 'servile incidents'[5].

1 Eg contracts of great responsibility or sensitivity. See e g *A-G v Blake (Jonathan Cape Ltd, third party)* [2001] 1 AC 268, [2000] 4 All ER 385, HL, where, exceptionally, the court required a former member of the Secret Intelligence Service to account for the benefits he had received from the breach of an express contractual undertaking to the Crown not to divulge any confidential information during his period of service or after his employment had ceased. Members and former members of the security and intelligence services owe a life-long obligation of confidence to the Crown in relation to governmental secrets which is given statutory force by the Official Secrets Acts 1911 to 1989: see CRIMINAL LAW vol 26 (2010) PARA 427 et seq.

2 *Wallis v Day* (1837) 2 M & W 273; *Warner Bros Pictures Inc v Nelson* [1937] 1 KB 209, [1936] 3 All ER 160.

3 Cinema contracts in the past have contained personal restraints on the employee's diet, health, habits etc: see *Gaumont-British Picture Corpn Ltd v Alexander* [1936] 2 All ER 1686.

4 *Hepworth Manufacturing Co Ltd v Ryott* [1920] 1 Ch 1, CA (cinema company obtaining sole use of actor's name). A contract terminable only at the option of the employer may be bad: see *WH Milsted & Son Ltd v Hamp and Ross and Glendinning Ltd* (1927) 71 Sol Jo 845.

5 *Horwood v Millar's Timber and Trading Co Ltd* [1917] 1 KB 305, CA; *Denny's Trustee v Denny and Warr* [1919] 1 KB 583; c f *Davies v Davies* (1887) 36 ChD 359 at 393, CA, per Bowen LJ. A tie to pay back the cost of training is not necessarily illegal: *Strathclyde Regional Council v Neil* [1984] IRLR 11.

(iii) Employer's Obligations and Liabilities

A. EXERCISE OF DISCRETION TO SELECT EMPLOYEES

21. Limitation of exercise of employer's discretion to select employees. Traditionally, the law has not regulated the process of the selection of employees by an employer[1]. Such selection remains largely an area for managerial discretion[2]; and, even if employment is offered on the basis that it is subject to satisfactory references, that will probably be construed as meaning references satisfactory to the employer, not references that are objectively satisfactory[3].

Such managerial discretion must, however, be exercised subject to any statutory requirements, most obviously those under the Equality Act 2010, guaranteeing the equal treatment of actual and potential employees on the basis of 'protected characteristics'[4]. The Equality Act 2010 also restricts the circumstances in which potential employees can be asked questions about disability or health[5].

Employers must ensure compliance with the Employment Practices Data Protection Code (issued pursuant to the Data Protection Act 1998[6]) with regard to the processing of personal data in recruitment and selection, pre-employment vetting and employment records (as well as in connection with monitoring at work and workers' health)[7].

1   'An employer may ... refuse to employ [a workman] from the most mistaken, capricious, malicious or morally reprehensible motives that can be conceived, but the workman has no right of action against him': *Allen v Flood* [1898] AC 1 at 172, HL, per Lord Davey.
2   Once the person is taken into employment, however, the process of hiring could have an effect on the employee's terms and conditions (eg what he was told at an interview or saw in an advertisement), if such matters remain to be covered by implied or non-written express terms: see *Carmichael v National Power plc* [1999] 4 All ER 897 at 902 et seq, [1999] 1 WLR 2042 at 2048 et seq, [2000] IRLR 43 at 45 et seq, HL, per Lord Hoffmann; and PARA 113 et seq.
3   *Wishart v National Association of Citizens Advice Bureaux Ltd* [1990] ICR 794, [1990] IRLR 393, CA; and see PARA 724.
4   See the Equality Act 2010; and PARA 51. The Equality Act 2010 allows an employer, service provider or other organisation to take positive action so as to enable existing or potential employees or customers to overcome or minimise a disadvantage arising from a protected characteristic: see Pt 11 Ch 2 (ss 158–159); and DISCRIMINATION vol 33 (2013) PARA 286.
5   See the Equality Act 2010 s 60; and DISCRIMINATION vol 33 (2013) PARA 127.
6   As to the Data Protection Act 1998 generally see PARA 34; and CONFIDENCE AND INFORMATIONAL PRIVACY vol 19 (2011) PARA 95 et seq. As to the Information Commissioner's powers to prepare and disseminate codes of practice for guidance as to good practice see CONFIDENCE AND INFORMATIONAL PRIVACY vol 19 (2011) PARA 110.
7   See *Data Protection: the Employment Practices Code* (November 2011) and the *Supplementary Guidance* (June 2005) issued by the Information Commissioner's Office. As to guidance aimed specifically at securing compliance with the Data Protection Act 1998 when providing information about employees under the Transfer of Undertakings (Protection of Employment) Regulations 2006, SI 2006/246 (as amended by the Collective Redundancies and Transfer of Undertakings (Protection of Employment) (Amendment) Regulations 2014, SI 2014/16): see PARA 140 note 5. This guidance is available on the Information Commissioner's Office website, whose address, at the date at which this volume states the law, is to be found at: *http://ico. org.uk*. As to the Data Protection Act 1998 generally see PARA 34; and CONFIDENCE AND INFORMATIONAL PRIVACY vol 19 (2011) PARA 95 et seq. As to the Information Commissioner's powers to prepare and disseminate codes of practice for guidance as to good practice see CONFIDENCE AND INFORMATIONAL PRIVACY vol 19 (2011) PARA 110.

B.   REMUNERATION ETC

22.   Payment of remuneration. An employer's basic obligation under a contract of employment is normally the payment of remuneration, not the provision of work[1]. The rate of remuneration usually depends on the terms of the contract[2]; and the obligation to pay may be express[3] or implied[4]. Wages and salaries are deemed apportionable and accrue from day to day[5].

If a person is led by his employer to believe that he has been appointed to a position and he acts in that capacity, it is for the employer to show that his services were not to be remunerated[6]. Where it is agreed that it is to be left to the employer's discretion to determine whether or not remuneration is to be paid for any particular services, and he decides against making any payment, no remuneration is recoverable[7]. If, however, under a contract of employment the amount of an employee's remuneration is left to be fixed by agreement or to be decided by the employer, but it is nevertheless clear that some remuneration is intended to be paid, the employee is entitled, if the employer refuses to make any payment, to recover reasonable remuneration to pay him possibly on the basis of an implied contractual term[8]. In determining what is reasonable remuneration, the court may take into account any communications between the parties on the subject of remuneration as evidence of the value which each puts on the services in question[9].

If a person can prove the rendering of services under an unenforceable contract, the contract is admissible as evidence of the value of the services and he may recover on an implied contract to pay a reasonable sum[10].

Even where there is a definite requirement of remuneration, this does not necessarily mean that there must be a regular wage[11]. Thus there can be a valid contract of employment where the employee is to be rewarded only by fees or commission[12], or by the receipt of tips from customers[13], or by being given the chance to earn a salary[14].

1   As to the provision of work see PARA 30.
2   Ie subject to the national minimum wage legislation: see PARA 169 et seq. Under the Equality Act 2010, a term of a person's work that purports to prevent or restrict a person from disclosing or seeking to disclose information about the terms of his work, or seeking disclosure of information from a colleague about the terms of the colleague's work, is unenforceable against that person in so far as he makes or seeks a disclosure for the purpose of finding out whether or to what extent there is, in relation to the work in question, a connection between pay and having (or not having) a particular protected characteristic: see s 77(1), (2); and DISCRIMINATION vol 33 (2013) PARA 142.
3   As to the employer's obligation to give a written statement of an employee's terms and conditions of employment see PARA 119.
4   *Browning v Great Central Mining Co of Devon* (1860) 5 H & N 856.
5   See the Apportionment Act 1870 ss 2, 5 (all rents, annuities, dividends, and other periodical payments in the nature of income, whether reserved or made payable under an instrument in writing or otherwise, are to be considered as accruing from day to day, and are apportionable in respect of time accordingly; annuities including, for these purposes, salaries and pensions); and *Sim v Rotherham Metropolitan Borough Council* [1987] Ch 216, [1986] ICR 897. Under the Apportionment Act 1870, wages and salaries are deemed apportionable and accrue from day to day on a calendar days basis rather than a working days basis (*Thames Water Utilities v Reynolds* [1996] IRLR 186, EAT), although, if a worker claims unpaid amounts of holiday pay which have accrued under the Working Time Regulations 1998, SI 1998/1833 (see PARA 295), and have to be ascertained, calculation of the payment of holiday entitlement on the basis of day to day accrual has to be by reference to actual working days and not to calendar days (*Leisure Leagues UK Ltd v Maconnachie* [2002] IRLR 600, EAT). *Leisure Leagues UK Ltd v Maconnachie* was followed in *Yarrow v Edwards Chartered Accountants* [2007] All ER (D) 118 (Aug), EAT (in case of conflict, the most recent case of the EAT is followed in the interest of comity, and the approach found in the recent statutory employment provisions, ie the Working Time Regulations 1998, SI 1998/1833, is to be preferred to that found in the Victorian Apportionment Act). The matter may remain arguable, however, in the light of *Amey v Peter Symonds College* [2013] EWHC 2788 (QB), [2014] IRLR 206 (the Apportionment Act 1870 cannot be overridden simply because it achieves a poor fit with modern employment law; the reference to income accruing from 'day to day' in s 2 is to each calendar day, although in this case s 7 was applied in preference to s 2 due to countervailing contractual provisions which could not be reconciled with daily accrual).
    For the effect of the Apportionment Act 1870 ss 2, 5 on terminated contracts of employment see *Moriarty v Regent's Garage and Engineering Co Ltd* [1921] 1 KB 423 (revsd on another point [1921] 2 KB 766, CA); *Item Software (UK) Ltd v Fassihi* [2004] EWCA Civ 1244, [2005] ICR 450, [2004] IRLR 928 (revsg on this point [2002] EWHC 3116 (Ch), [2003] IRLR 769, [2003] 2 BCLC 1) (there is nothing in the Apportionment Act 1870 s 2 to exclude its application in the case of dismissal; the effect of s 2 is that, subject to any express agreement to the contrary

pursuant to s 7, the salary of an employee whose employment terminated during a pay period should be apportioned and paid in respect of the period actually worked, but with payment only becoming due and payable at the end of the relevant pay period).

6   *Davies v Davies* (1839) 9 C & P 87; *Higgins v Hopkins* (1848) 3 Exch 163 at 166 per Parke B; *Reeve v Reeve* (1858) 1 F & F 280; *Roberts v Smith* (1859) 4 H & N 315 at 321 per Martin B.

7   *Taylor v Brewer* (1813) 1 M & S 290 (employee did work under a committee resolution that any services to be rendered by him should 'be taken into consideration and such remuneration be made as should be deemed right'); *Roberts v Smith* (1859) 4 H & N 315 (employee agreed that, if a certain company were not formed, he would accept any remuneration the employers should think him deserving of and their means afforded); *Kofi Sunkersette Obu v A Strauss & Co Ltd* [1951] AC 243, PC (agent was to be paid a monthly sum for expenses and also a commission which he agreed to leave to his employers' discretion; the court could not determine the basis and rate of the commission since this would involve not only making a new agreement for the parties, but also varying the existing agreement by transferring to the court a discretion vested in the employers); *Re Richmond Gate Property Co Ltd* [1964] 3 All ER 936, [1965] 1 WLR 335.

8   *Way v Latilla* [1937] 3 All ER 759, HL (employee employed in obtaining mining concessions; no concluded contract between employee and employer as to share or interest which employee should receive, but contract of employment existed which indicated that work was not to be done gratuitously; employee entitled to reasonable remuneration). See also *Bryant v Flight* (1839) 5 M & W 114 (employee accepted a situation on the terms that the amount of the payment he was to receive he would leave entirely to the employer; a majority of the court concluded that a contract to pay something was to be inferred); *Craven-Ellis v Canons Ltd* [1936] 2 KB 403, [1936] 2 All ER 1066, CA; *Powell v Braun* [1954] 1 All ER 484, [1954] 1 WLR 401, CA (employer informed employee that he intended to pay her an annual bonus on profits, in addition to her salary, although he could not say at that moment what the amount would be; employee accepted the proposal; parties did not intend that payment of bonus should be in the employer's discretion, but that he should pay a reasonable sum); *Currencies Direct Ltd v Ellis* [2002] EWCA Civ 779, [2002] 2 BCLC 482 (sums received by a director in cash or in payments made on his behalf were properly to be regarded, up to the point at which he left the company, as remuneration for work done rather than as loans, despite the sums being shown in the company's accounts as emoluments and loans rather than remuneration because of the consequent tax and national insurance liability at a time when the company was not profitable). In *Powell v Braun*, the principle of quantum meruit was held to be no less applicable to additional remuneration than to basic remuneration; but c f *Kofi Sunkersette Obu v A Strauss & Co Ltd* [1951] AC 243 at 249, PC (where *Way v Latilla* was distinguished on the ground that the remuneration there in question was basic and not additional remuneration). *Way v Latilla* was distinguished also in *Benedetti v Sawiris* [2013] UKSC 50, [2013] 4 All ER 253, [2013] 3 WLR 351, and judged to be of no assistance, on the basis that the implied contract approach to restitutionary awards for unjust enrichment had since been decisively rejected in *Westdeutsche Landesbank Girozentrale v Islington London Borough Council* [1996] AC 669, [1996] 2 All ER 961, HL (see RESTITUTION vol 88 (2012) PARA 410 et seq). However, such cases as *Way v Latilla*, *Powell v Braun*, and *Currencies Direct Ltd v Ellis* were held to be consistent with the principle that there may in an appropriate case be an implied contractual term to pay a reasonable sum for work done in *Ajar-Tec Ltd v Stack* [2012] EWCA Civ 543 at [14], [2012] All ER (D) 136 (Apr) at [14] per Elias LJ.

See also *Loftus v Roberts* (1902) 18 TLR 532 at 534, CA, per Vaughan Williams LJ; *Broome v Speak* [1903] 1 Ch 586 at 599, CA, per Buckley J (where the decisions in *Taylor v Brewer* (1813) 1 M & S 290; *Roberts v Smith* (1859) 4 H & N 315; and *Bryant v Flight* were considered). The burden of establishing that a failure to pay a discretionary bonus payment amounts to a breach of contract is a very weighty one: *Keen v Commerzbank AG* [2006] EWCA Civ 1536, [2007] ICR 623 sub nom *Commerzbank AG v Keen* [2007] IRLR 132. See also PARAS 113 et seq, 142 et seq.

9   *Way v Latilla* [1937] 3 All ER 759 at 764, HL, per Lord Atkin, and at 766 per Lord Wright.

10 *Scarisbrick v Parkinson* (1869) 20 LT 175; c f *Bell Houses Ltd v City Wall Properties Ltd* [1966] 1 QB 207 at 226, [1965] 3 All ER 427 at 436 per Mocatta J; revsd on other grounds [1966] 2 QB 656, [1966] 2 All ER 674, CA.

11 As to the position of piece workers see PARA 30.

12 *Phillips v Curling* (1847) 10 LTOS 245; *Clayton Newbury Ltd v Findlay* [1953] 2 All ER 826n, [1953] 1 WLR 1194n; *Bronester Ltd v Priddle* [1961] 3 All ER 471, [1961] 1 WLR 1294, CA.

13 *Pauley v Kenaldo Ltd* [1953] 1 All ER 226, [1953] 1 WLR 187. Cf *Quashie v Stringfellows Restaurants Ltd* [2012] EWCA Civ 1735, [2013] IRLR 99 (it would be an unusual case where a contract of service is found to exist when the worker takes the economic risk and is paid

exclusively by third parties, eg where a lapdancer negotiated her own fees with clients, took the risk that on any particular night she might have been out of pocket, and received back from the employer only moneys received from clients after deductions); and see PARA 4.

14 *Gaumont-British Picture Corpn v Alexander* [1936] 2 All ER 1686.

23.   Performance of duty as condition precedent to remuneration. When the contract of employment is an entire contract[1], providing for payment on the completion of a definite period of service[2] or of a definite piece of work[3], it is a condition precedent to the recovery of any remuneration in respect of it that the service or duty is to be completely performed unless:

(1)   the employer has received substantial performance of the contract[4]; or

(2)   complete performance was prevented by the employer, in which case a claim for the value of the work actually performed may lie[5]; or

(3)   the employer so alters the contract as to entitle the employee to regard it as at an end, in which case the whole sum payable under the contract becomes due[6]; or

(4)   the contract has been frustrated[7], in which case the employee may recover either wages already earned under severable parts of the contract, or a just amount representing the work done up to the date of the frustration[8].

If, however, the contract, though in respect of work terminating at a particular time, is to be construed as providing that remuneration is to accrue due and become vested at stated periods, the remuneration constitutes a debt recoverable at the end of each such period of service[9].

1   Ie where all the promises on one side are to be performed before any of the promises of the other side. As to the distinction between entire and divisible contracts see CONTRACT vol 22 (2012) PARA 493.

2   *Countess of Plymouth v Throgmorton* (1688) 3 Mod Rep 153 (the contract being for service for a year, salary for three-quarters not recoverable); *Lilley v Elwin* (1848) 11 QB 742. Where a contract provided for a salary for a week, no portion became due until the end of the week: *Mapleson v Sears* (1911) 28 TLR 30, DC.

3   *Taylor v Laird* (1856) 1 H & N 266 (plaintiff accepted command of a vessel at 'fixed pay of £50 per month' and commission on the proceeds and, having abandoned the contract before completion, was held entitled to salary for as many months as he had served). *Quaere* whether, if necessary, reliance could be placed on the Apportionment Act 1870 ss 2, 5 (see PARA 22 note 5).

4   As to the doctrine of substantial performance see CONTRACT vol 22 (2012) PARA 495.

5   *Planché v Colburn* (1831) 8 Bing 14.

6   *O'Neil v Armstrong, Mitchell & Co* [1895] 2 QB 418, CA (seaman engaged to serve on a warship which had been built in England for the Japanese government and was to be taken to Japan; an outbreak of war between Japan and China during the voyage so altered the risks of the voyage as to entitle the seaman to leave the ship and claim the sum due for the whole voyage).

7   As to the application of the doctrine of frustration to contracts of employment see PARAS 728–729.

8   See the Law Reform (Frustrated Contracts) Act 1943 ss 1(3), 2(4); and CONTRACT vol 22 (2012) PARAS 486–487.

9   See *Cutter v Powell* (1795) 6 Term Rep 320; 2 Smith LC (13th Edn) 1 (a seaman having died during the voyage, no wages were held payable for the time actually served, the contract providing for payment 'provided he proceeded, continued and did his duty ... from Jamaica to the port of Liverpool'); *Sinclair v Bowles* (1829) 9 B & C 92; *Vigers v Cook* [1919] 2 KB 475, CA.

24.   Additional remuneration. Additional remuneration may be recovered only when it is the subject of a distinct agreement[1]. A promise to pay additional remuneration for services which are already within the scope of the employee's duty under his subsisting contract of employment[2] is void for lack of consideration[3]; but, since most contracts are now periodical, usually weekly or monthly, an agreement to pay additional remuneration will operate from the beginning of a period as a variation of the contract of employment.

A promise to pay additional remuneration is, however, founded on good consideration, and will be enforced, when the employee is no longer bound by the original contract:

(1)   where the employee undertakes increased responsibility or more work[4];

(2)   because the nature of the service has been entirely changed[5]; or

(3)   by reason of the risk having become greater than that within the contemplation of that contract[6].

1   *Bell v Drummond* (1791) Peake 45; *Carter v Hall* (1818) 2 Stark 361; *Farmer v LCC* [1943] 1 KB 522, [1943] 2 All ER 32, CA (wages for 'standing by'). As to the contractual term to be implied in an appropriate case for an employee to be paid a reasonable sum for work done, however, see PARA 22.

2   Eg a wage rise for performing the same work.

3   See the cases as to wages cited in CONTRACT vol 22 (2012) PARA 326.

4   *Powell v Braun* [1954] 1 All ER 484, [1954] 1 WLR 401, CA.

5   *Harris v Carter* (1854) 3 E & B 559 at 561 per Lord Campbell (where it was mentioned that an entire change of voyage would justify a new contract in place of the original articles).

6   *Hartley v Ponsonby* (1857) 7 E & B 872 (part of the crew deserted at a foreign port, and, as found by a jury, it was unreasonable and dangerous to proceed with the reduced crew; the captain promised extra pay to the remaining seamen if they would take the ship to the next port; the promise was held to be enforceable, as the members of the crew were not bound under their existing articles to proceed on a voyage which was dangerous to life).

25.   Mode of payment. The mode of payment of remuneration is usually governed by the contract of employment[1]. If, however, an employee is mistakenly overpaid, the employer has prima facie a right to recover the amount overpaid[2]; but, if the overpayment was through no fault of the employee who has changed his position, by spending some or all of it, without knowledge of having been overpaid[3], the right to recover may be defeated by estoppel[4] or by a defence of change of position in the law of restitution[5].

1   As to an employer's statutory obligations in respect of the payment of wages and the deductions he may make from them see PARA 254 et seq. A common law claim to recover wages due from the employer has been used to challenge an attempt by the employer to make unilateral changes to the employee's terms and conditions of employment, such as a unilateral reduction in hours or a laying-off where there is no contractual power to do so: see PARA 833. It may, however, be otherwise if it is impossible for the employees to continue to discharge their duties under the old contract: *MacPherson v Lambeth London Borough Council* [1988] IRLR 470. Although in form an individual claim for wages, such litigation may be intended to resolve a collective dispute over the terms or conditions in question, particularly where, in order to decide whether the wages are due, the court in fact has to decide which side is right in its interpretation of contractual rights and duties: see e g *Cresswell v Board of Inland Revenue* [1984] 2 All ER 713, [1984] ICR 508 (whether staff contractually obliged to operate new computers); *Sim v Rotherham Metropolitan Borough Council* [1987] Ch 216, [1986] ICR 897 (whether teachers contractually obliged to cover for absent colleagues).

    As to an employer's duty to continue providing non-financial benefits to an employee after retirement see *National Union of Mineworkers v Scargill* [2012] EWHC 3750 (Ch), [2013] All ER (D) 197 (Feb) (understanding had been that the payment of rent on a flat was a facility to enable the employee to do his job properly, and that he retained the right in due course to have a house bought for him by the union, but the national committee had never approved the contracts, so that, when the defendant retired, the contract that appeared to give him the right to have the union continue to pay the rent on the flat was not effective).

2   An employer may lawfully make a deduction from a worker's wages by way of reimbursement of any overpayment of wages: see the Employment Rights Act 1996 s 14(1)(a); and PARA 256 text head (1)(a).

3   If, however, the employee spends the amount with knowledge of the overpayment, that can be theft: see *A-G's Reference (No 1 of 1983)* [1985] QB 182, 79 Cr App Rep 288, CA; and CRIMINAL LAW vol 25 (2010) PARA 285.

4   *Avon County Council v Howlett* [1983] 1 All ER 1073, [1983] IRLR 171, CA (innocent spending of part of the money overpaid while the employee was off work sick held to defeat the employer's claim for return of any of the money).

5   *Lipkin Gorman (a firm) v Karpnale Ltd* [1991] 2 AC 548, [1992] 4 All ER 512, HL (where Lord Goff of Chievely suggested that cases such as *Avon County Council v Howlett* [1983] 1 All ER 1073, [1983] IRLR 171, CA (cited in note 4) should now be dealt with by way of a defence of change of position rather than under the law of estoppel, particularly as the former would allow pro tanto recovery in an appropriate case). There can be an anticipatory reliance on the defence where the recipient of the overpayment has changed his position in expectation of receiving a future benefit: see *Commerzbank AG v Price-Jones* [2003] EWCA Civ 1663, [2004] 1 P & CR D36, (2003) Times, 26 November (employer mistakenly paid two full bonuses instead of one bonus plus the difference between the two; although the employee would have sought employment elsewhere but for the expected second full bonus, his decision to stay fell outside the scope of the defence). As to the nature of the defence of change of position see RESTITUTION vol 88 (2012) PARA 567.

26. Minimum rates of pay. Although the fixing of wages has rarely been a concern of domestic law, there was formerly a system of statutory wages councils fixing minimum pay rates in certain industries. That system was, however, abolished as from 30 August 1993[1]. There has been no move towards the reinstatement of wages councils, the policy being instead the introduction of one comprehensive, statutory national minimum wage[2].

1   See the Trade Union Reform and Employment Rights Act 1993 s 35 (repealed), s 51, Sch 10; and the Trade Union Reform and Employment Rights Act 1993 (Commencement No 1 and Transitional Provisions) Order 1993, SI 1993/1908, art 2(1), Sch 1. The Agricultural Wages Board remained as a specific wage-fixing body (established under its own legislation) but was abolished, along with every agricultural wages committee for an area in England, by the Enterprise and Regulatory Reform Act 2013 s 72: see AGRICULTURAL PRODUCTION AND MARKETING vol 1 (2008) PARA 1231 et seq.

2   As to the National Minimum Wage Act 1998 see PARA 169 et seq.

27. Employee's temporary incapacity through illness. An employee who is unable to work because of illness[1] is likely to be eligible to receive statutory sick pay[2] from his employer. In addition, however, many contracts of employment contain terms relating to private sick pay, which may be payable in addition to statutory sick pay as long as the contract of employment subsists[3]. Whether any such private sick pay is payable, its amount, its duration, and its relationship with statutory sick pay or any other benefit[4] depend entirely on the terms of the individual employee's contract, since there is no rule of law that it either is or is not payable[5]. The relevant term may be expressed in the contract and this is common[6]; if not so expressed, a term may be implied. In the absence of an express term there is, however, no presumption that a term is to be implied[7]; it is rather a case of considering all the evidence in the particular case, including the normal method of remuneration[8], custom and practice[9] and any pronouncements by the employer[10]. Where a term is implied, it is likely to provide for deduction of state benefit, particularly statutory sick pay, and for the employer's liability to pay to be restricted to a reasonable period[11].

1   In an agreement to pay wages during illness, 'sickness' has been held to include incapacity, whether due to disease or accident (*Maloney v St Helens Industrial Co-operative Society Ltd* [1933] 1 KB 293, CA) and a period of convalescence (*Davies v Ebbw Vale UDC* (1911) 75 JP 533). See also *Manchester City Council v Thurston* [2002] IRLR 319 (term in contract excluding sick pay where absence is attributable to the employee's own misconduct did not entitle the employer to withhold sick pay for psychiatric illness resulting from disciplinary proceedings).

In an extreme case, the contract of employment may be frustrated by illness (see PARA 729), in which case nothing beyond the amounts required by statute and/or by the contract are payable. Even where the contract is not frustrated, the employer may dismiss an employee because of the illness; if this is done with proper notice, the dismissal will not be wrongful and again, in general, nothing further will be payable at common law, although an employee with the necessary two year's qualifying period of employment may challenge it as unfair: see PARA 775. It is also possible that the illness may constitute a disability, giving rise to arguments that the dismissal constituted unlawful discrimination contrary to the Equality Act 2010: see DISCRIMINATION vol 33 (2013) PARA 50 et seq.

2 Statutory sick pay is payable where an employee has a day of incapacity for work, subject to his fulfilling the statutory conditions: see PARA 558 et seq. As to the interaction between annual leave and absence due to illness see PARAS 291–292.

3 Contractual obligations may require the employer to take all reasonable steps on behalf of the employee, including the pursuit of legal proceedings, to procure benefits which have been provided for in this way: see *Marlow v East Thames Housing Group Ltd* [2002] IRLR 798 (employer who was contractually obliged to provide health benefits from an insurer should pursue the insurer in respect of an employee who had no other means of redress when her medical incapacity to work was incorrectly assessed). As to an employee's entitlement to remuneration following exhaustion of statutory and contractual entitlement to sick pay when ready, willing and able to return to work see *Beveridge v KLM UK Ltd* [2000] IRLR 765, EAT; and PARA 254.

4 Most contractual schemes work on a 'top up' basis, ie of supplementing state benefit (particularly statutory sick pay), to make up a certain level of wage stipulated in the contract. Such a scheme will normally also be found if a term is implied: see the text and note 11.

5 *Petrie v MacFisheries Ltd* [1940] 1 KB 258, [1939] 4 All ER 281, CA; *O'Grady v M Saper Ltd* [1940] 2 KB 469, [1940] 3 All ER 527, CA (explaining *Marrison v Bell* as reported in [1939] 2 KB 187, [1939] 1 All ER 745, CA). Such a rule could have been argued for logically on the basis that the employee's consideration is usually being ready and willing to serve, not actually working (see PARA 16) and that a distinction is drawn between voluntary and involuntary inability to work (*Cuckson v Stones* (1858) 1 E & E 248; applied in *Miles v Wakefield Metropolitan District Council* [1987] AC 539 at 568–569, [1987] ICR 368 at 399, HL, per Lord Oliver of Aylmerton). It is clear, however, that any uncertainty as to provision of sick pay is now to be dealt with by the implication of terms, not by any supposed rules of law: *Mears v Safecar Security Ltd* [1983] QB 54, [1982] ICR 626, CA.

6 Where such a term exists, the employer must incorporate it into an employee's written statement of terms and conditions of employment: see the Employment Rights Act 1996 s 1(4)(d)(ii) (terms and conditions relating to incapacity for work due to sickness or injury, including any provision for sick pay); *Mears v Safecar Security Ltd* [1983] QB 54, [1982] ICR 626, CA; *Howman & Son v Blyth* [1983] ICR 416, [1983] IRLR 139, EAT; and PARA 119.

7 *Mears v Safecar Security Ltd* [1983] QB 54, [1982] ICR 626, CA, disapproving dicta favouring such a presumption in *Orman v Saville Sportswear Ltd* [1960] 3 All ER 105, [1960] 1 WLR 1055.

8 *Browning v Crumlin Valley Collieries Ltd* [1926] 1 KB 522; *Hancock v BSA Tools Ltd* [1939] 4 All ER 538.

9 *O'Grady v M Saper Ltd* [1940] 2 KB 469, [1940] 3 All ER 527, CA.

10 *Petrie v MacFisheries Ltd* [1940] 1 KB 258, [1939] 4 All ER 281, CA.

11 *Howman & Son v Blyth* [1983] ICR 416, [1983] IRLR 139, EAT. On the deduction of other benefits older case law (see eg *Elliott v Liggens* [1902] 2 KB 84, DC; *Niblett v Midland Rly Co* (1907) 96 LT 462, DC; *Marrison v Bell* [1939] 2 KB 187, [1939] 1 All ER 745, CA) is probably no longer helpful.

28. Payment of wages during lay-off or short time. Whether an employer has a right to lay off an employee or shorten his hours, and, if so, on what terms, will often be governed, in a trade where it is particularly relevant, by a collective agreement or by express terms in the contracts of employment of the employees affected[1]. As in the case of the payment of wages during sickness[2], there are no general rules of law and the matter depends ultimately on the terms of the contract. If there is no express term, an employer may seek to establish an implied term permitting lay-off or short-time working[3]; and, in reaching its decision, a court may, in particular, look at custom and practice in the trade[4], at previous dealings[5] and at the nature of the work in question[6]. If, however, there is no term, express or implied, allowing the employer to lay off or shorten hours, then, as long as the employee remains ready and willing to work the normal hours[7], he may bring a claim for his normal wages[8], since there is no inherent power at common law for an employer to suspend an employee without pay[9].

1　Such an agreement may provide for some form of guaranteed minimum wage or number of hours per week: see eg *Powell Duffryn Wagon Co Ltd v House* [1974] ICR 123, NIRC. As to his right to continuity of employment see PARA 130 et seq; as to the right of an employee who is laid off, or put on certain forms of short-time working, to statutory guarantee payments see PARA 261 et seq; and as to his being able to leave and claim a redundancy payment see PARA 875 et seq.

2　See PARA 27.

3　*Browning v Crumlin Valley Collieries Ltd* [1926] 1 KB 522.

4　*Bird v British Celanese Ltd* [1945] KB 336, [1945] 1 All ER 488, CA; *Marshall v English Electric Co Ltd* [1945] 1 All ER 653, CA.

5　Mere acquiescence in a previous lay-off may not, however, be sufficient to establish an implied term or to raise an estoppel against the employee: *Waine v R Oliver (Plant Hire) Ltd* [1977] IRLR 434, EAT.

6　*Puttick v John Wright & Sons (Blackwall) Ltd* [1972] ICR 457, NIRC.

7　Ie thus providing what in most cases is the employee's consideration for the contract of employment: see PARA 16.

8　*Miller v Hamworthy Engineering Ltd* [1986] ICR 846, [1986] IRLR 461, CA; and see PARA 833. The employee could also leave and claim unfair dismissal, on the basis of having been constructively dismissed: see the cases cited in PARA 763.

9　*Devonald v Rosser & Sons* [1906] 2 KB 728, CA; *Hanley v Pease & Partners Ltd* [1915] 1 KB 698; *Marshall v English Electric Co Ltd* [1945] 1 All ER 653, CA; *Gorse v Durham County Council* [1971] 2 All ER 666, [1971] 1 WLR 775; *Bond v CAV Ltd, Neads v CAV Ltd* [1983] IRLR 360.

29.　Non-payment of wages for refusal to work.　Where an employee deliberately refuses to perform his contractual duties at all, whether or not through strike action, an employer is entitled, as a matter of contract, to rely on the principle of 'no work, no pay'[1].

More complicated is the case of a partial refusal to perform duties, either through a refusal to work certain hours or to perform a particular task, while remaining willing to work the remaining hours or perform the remaining tasks. In a case of breach of contract by the employee, the employer may sue the employee for damages[2], but in practice such a procedure could be cumbersome, especially in the case of widespread industrial action, and so the important question has been whether the employer in such circumstances may lawfully either refuse to pay wages at all or make pro rata deductions from wages[3].

An employer faced with partial performance by the employee may either:

(1)　make clear to the employee that he, the employer, is not willing to accept that performance at all and then pay no wages, even if the employee has in fact come to work and performed some of his duties[4]; or

(2)　allow the employee to tender the defective performance but make partial deductions from wages reasonably representing the services not performed[5].

If, however, the employer accepts the defective performance without objection, the employee may argue that the employer has in fact waived the breach of contract and so has lost the right to make deductions[6].

1　*Cresswell v Board of Inland Revenue* [1984] 2 All ER 713, [1984] ICR 508. This principle operates independently of any contractual right to suspend the employee, in that any procedures laid down in the contract as being necessary in order to impose a suspension do not apply:

Cresswell v Board of Inland Revenue, distinguishing *Gorse v Durham County Council* [1971] 2 All ER 666, [1971] 1 WLR 775. In a disputed case, the burden of proof is on the employee to show that he was in fact ready and willing to perform his contractual duties: *Henthorn and Taylor v Central Electricity Generating Board* [1980] IRLR 361, CA. See also *Luke v Stoke-on-Trent City Council* [2007] EWCA Civ 761, [2007] ICR 1678, [2007] IRLR 777 (employee not entitled to continued receipt of salary when refused to do that reasonably required by employer within scope of employment contract).

2   *National Coal Board v Galley* [1958] 1 All ER 91, [1958] 1 WLR 16, CA.

3   A deduction from wages on the basis of the employee's participation in a strike or other industrial action is not subject to the normal statutory requirements relating to the making of deductions: see the Employment Rights Act 1996 s 14(5); and PARA 256. That does not, however, resolve the primary question whether there is a common law right to make the deduction in the first place. Any power to deduct would be in relation to the period during which the part performance took place, since there is, in the absence of an express provision in the contract, no general power for the employer to retain, by way of forfeiture, wages already earned and due to the employee prior to the breach: *Parkin v South Hetton Coal Co* (1907) 24 TLR 193, CA; *Button v Thompson* (1869) LR 4 CP 330; *Warburton v Heyworth* (1880) 6 QBD 1, CA; *Boston Deep Sea Fishing and Ice Co v Ansell* (1888) 39 ChD 339, CA; *George v Davies* [1911] 2 KB 445, DC; *Healey v SA Française Rubastic* [1917] 1 KB 946.

4   *Wiluszynski v Tower Hamlets London Borough Council* [1989] ICR 493, [1989] IRLR 259, CA. The fact that the employee managed to attend work and do other things is irrelevant; and the employer is not required to pay for that (unwanted) service, a conclusion emphasised by the statement of Fox LJ in *Wiluszynski v Tower Hamlets London Borough Council* at 499 and 262 that the contractual doctrine of substantial performance (see CONTRACT vol 22 (2012) PARA 495) does not apply to cases such as these. This approach was strongly reaffirmed by the Court of Appeal in *British Telecommunications plc v Ticehurst* [1992] ICR 383, sub nom *Ticehurst and Thompson v British Telecommunications plc* [1992] IRLR 219, CA (employers faced with intermittent strike action permitted to issue an ultimatum that partial performance would not be accepted, and on that basis to refuse payment). See also *Bunn v Wilf Gilbert (Staffs) Ltd* [2008] All ER (D) 10 (Sep), EAT.

5   In *Sim v Rotherham Metropolitan Borough Council* [1987] Ch 216, [1986] ICR 897 (teachers refusing to cover for absent colleagues; small deduction from month's salary valid), Scott J put this on the basis of an equitable set-off by the employer (ie wages payable in full, but subject to a set-off of the damages that could have been claimed by the employer), having held that the Apportionment Act 1870 (see PARA 22 note 5) had limited applicability: see *Sim v Rotherham Metropolitan Borough Council* at 254–255 and 935–936 per Scott J. However, subsequently, in *Miles v Wakefield Metropolitan District Council* [1987] AC 539, [1987] ICR 368, HL (registrar refusing to work three hours, out of a normal working week of 37 hours; deduction of three-thirtysevenths of his salary valid), the House of Lords put it on the more fundamental basis of failure by the employee to provide consideration for the time not worked, so that nothing was payable in respect of that time in the first place. See also *Royle v Trafford Borough Council* [1984] IRLR 184 (five-thirtysixths of teacher's salary validly withheld when he refused to accept a further five children into his existing class of 31 children). The case of *Miles v Wakefield Metropolitan District Council*, however, concerned a readily quantifiable failure to work certain particular hours; and the position is more difficult in the case of a more general failure to perform fully (eg in a work-to-rule or go-slow or withdrawal of goodwill). To apply a straightforward 'failure of consideration' approach could lead to nothing at all being payable, even where the employer has not clearly adopted that option: see note 4. See also *Bunn v Wilf Gilbert (Staffs) Ltd* [2008] All ER (D) 10 (Sep), EAT; and *Burns v Santander UK plc* [2011] IRLR 639, EAT (employer acted lawfully in refusing to pay employee for six month period he was remanded in custody, and hence not available to work, since his detention had been an avoidable impediment to his work, and the period spent on remand was treated as part of the punishment on his conviction).

   Whether a claim for work actually performed could be made by the employee is undecided: see *Miles v Wakefield Metropolitan District Council*. It is arguable that the more general approach in *Sim v Rotherham Metropolitan Borough Council* is more appropriate to deal with such a case, allowing the set-off of a generally reasonable amount; *sed quaere* whether that approach is now open in the light of *Miles v Wakefield Metropolitan District Council*, even though *Sim v Rotherham Metropolitan Borough Council* was not actually disapproved.

The appropriate level of deductions to be made from an employee's wages, representing services not performed as a result of strike action, is dependent on whether the employee is able to sue for the wages withheld: *Cooper v Isle of Wight College* [2007] EWHC 2831 (QB), [2008] IRLR 124.

6   *Bond v CAV Ltd, Neads v CAV Ltd* [1983] IRLR 360.

C. PROVISION OF WORK

30. In general. The traditional view[1] is that the normal obligation on an employer under a contract of employment is to provide the employee with the agreed remuneration, not necessarily to provide him with work to do[2]. To this general rule there are exceptions where: (1) the employment is such that the work, and attendant publicity, are as important to the employee as the remuneration, as in the case of an actor or singer[3]; (2) it is necessary for the employee to be provided with work to do in order to earn the remuneration, as in the case of an employee remunerated by commission[4] or on a piece work basis[5]; or (3) the employee is engaged to fill a particular office, notably of a professional nature[6].

1   In *Langston v Amalgamated Union of Engineering Workers* [1974] 1 All ER 980 at 987, [1974] ICR 180 at 190, CA, per Lord Denning MR, it was held to be arguable that a contract of employment by implication gives to the employee not merely a right to be paid his agreed wage but also the right to have the opportunity of doing his work when it was there to be done. Although *Langston v Amalgamated Union of Engineering Workers* was applied in *NF Bosworth v Angus Jowett & Co Ltd* [1977] IRLR 374, the general concept of a right to work has, however, seen little significant development or application subsequently. It was revisited in *William Hill Organisation Ltd v Tucker* [1999] ICR 291, [1998] IRLR 313, CA, but only as an incidental point in a dispute over a 'garden leave clause' (ie an employer had no implied right to impose garden leave, and therefore to withhold work if this was available to be done).

2   *Turner v Sawdon & Co* [1901] 2 KB 653, CA (plaintiff's contention was that, being a salesman, if he were not given employment, he would be less efficient in his business; but the court refused to read the contract so as to 'convert the retainer at fixed wages into a contract to keep the servant in the service of his employer in such a manner as to enable the former to become *au fait* at his work': see at 657 per AL Smith MR); *Collier v Sunday Referee Publishing Co Ltd* [1940] 2 KB 647 at 650, [1940] 4 All ER 234 at 236 per Asquith J ('It is true that a contract of employment does not necessarily, or perhaps normally, oblige the master to provide the servant with work. Provided I pay my cook her wages regularly, she cannot complain if I choose to take any or all of my meals out'); *Williamson v Taylor* (1843) 5 QB 175; *Aspdin v Austin* (1844) 5 QB 671; *Dunn v Sayles* (1844) 5 QB 685; *Emmens v Elderton* (1853) 4 HL Cas 624; *Lagerwall v Wilkinson, Henderson and Clarke Ltd* (1899) 80 LT 55. This principle may be seen as lying behind the employer's ability normally: (1) to dismiss with wages in lieu of notice (see PARA 733); and (2) to suspend an employee with pay, eg while investigating a serious allegation against him (see PARA 699). As to the right to work generally and the power of an employer to impose 'garden leave' during a period of notice see *SG&R Valuation Service Co LLC v Boudrais* [2008] EWHC 1340 (QB), [2008] IRLR 770.

3   *Fechter v Montgomery* (1863) 33 Beav 22 (provincial actor engaged to appear in London theatre); *Bunning v Lyric Theatre Ltd* (1894) 71 LT 396; *Marbe v George Edwardes (Daly's Theatre) Ltd* [1928] 1 KB 269, CA. In a particular case, the obligation may be construed as not just to provide work, but to provide work of a certain kind or standard: *Herbert Clayton and Jack Waller Ltd v Oliver* [1930] AC 209, HL.

4   *Turner v Goldsmith* [1891] 1 QB 544, CA.

5   *R v Welch* (1853) 2 E & B 357; *Whittle v Frankland* (1862) 2 B & S 49; *Devonald v Rosser & Sons* [1906] 2 KB 728, CA (piece worker was employed on terms that he should not quit or be discharged except on 28 days' notice; employer unable to keep works open; worker entitled to damages for breach of implied agreement by employer to find work during interval between closing of works and expiration of notice subsequently given; it was unreasonable that he should be bound but unable to work or earn wages); *Bauman v Hulton Press Ltd* [1952] 2 All ER 1121; *Langston v Amalgamated Union of Engineering Workers (No 2)* [1974] ICR 510, [1974] IRLR 182, NIRC (premium payments for night shift and overtime).

6   *Collier v Sunday Referee Publishing Co Ltd* [1940] 2 KB 647, [1940] 4 All ER 234 (journalist
    appointed chief sub-editor of specific newspaper; newspaper sold). There could be further
    developments in this area, extending beyond office-holders to other employees who can be said
    to have an interest in their actual work or profession and who would suffer a disadvantage by
    being denied the opportunity to perform it (eg by not being able to keep up their skills in a
    rapidly developing field): *William Hill Organisation Ltd v Tucker* [1999] ICR 291, [1998] IRLR
    313, CA.

31.   Unlawful or dangerous orders.   It is an implied term of a contract of
employment that an employee is not to be required by his employer to do an
unlawful act[1]; and a dismissal for refusing to obey an order to do such an act is
likely to be unfair[2]. Similarly, an employer may not order the employee into
danger[3], though this is clearly a more vague rule than that against illegality; and
it seems that, in order to justify refusal to obey such an order, the danger must be
immediate and personal[4].

1   *Gregory v Ford* [1951] 1 All ER 121; *Strongman (1945) Ltd v Sincock* [1955] 2 QB 525 at 535,
    [1955] 3 All ER 90 at 93, CA, per Denning LJ; *Semtex Ltd v Gladstone* [1954] 2 All ER 206 at
    210, [1954] 1 WLR 945 at 951 per Finnemore J; *Lister v Romford Ice and Cold Storage Ltd*
    [1957] AC 555 at 570, [1957] 1 All ER 125 at 129, HL, per Viscount Simonds; *Buckoke v
    Greater London Council* [1971] 1 Ch 655, [1970] 2 All ER 193 (affd [1971] 1 Ch 662, [1971]
    2 All ER 254, CA).

2   *Morrish v Henlys (Folkestone) Ltd* [1973] 2 All ER 137, [1973] ICR 482, NIRC.

3   *Ottoman Bank v Chakarian* [1930] AC 277, PC.

4   *Bouzourou v Ottoman Bank* [1930] AC 271, PC; *Walmsley v Udec Refrigeration Ltd* [1972]
    IRLR 80.

D. DUTY OF CARE

32.   Implied duty of care for employee's health and safety.   A contract of
employment contains an implied term that the employer will take reasonable
care for the employee's health and safety[1]. The level of this duty is the same as
that of the employer's common law duty of care in the law of negligence; and so
an employee injured at work may theoretically have a cause of action in both
contract and tort[2]. Making unreasonable demands of the employee, especially as
to hours worked, could be a breach of this implied term[3]; but, if the subject
matter of the demands is expressly permitted by the contract itself, there is the
problem of the extent to which an implied term may be relied on to supplement
or restrict an express term[4].

The scope of the implied duty of care has been extended to cases where a third
party becomes responsible for the employee's safety[5], to rescuers of employees
endangered by their employers[6] and to a possible requirement to warn job
applicants of health risks inherent in the job but not a matter of common
knowledge[7]; but it does not extend to taking care of the safety of the employee's
belongings[8], nor to preventing economic loss to the employee[9]. Where, however,
a contract of employment contains a particular term conferring on the employee
a valuable right which is contingent on his taking steps to obtain that right, and
which he could not be expected to be aware of unless it is brought to his
attention, there is an implied obligation on the employer to take reasonable steps
to inform him of that right[10].

1   *Smith v Baker & Sons* [1891] AC 325, HL; *Wilsons and Clyde Coal Co Ltd v English* [1938]
    AC 57, [1937] 3 All ER 628, HL; *Latimer v AEC Ltd* [1953] AC 643, [1953] 2 All ER 449, HL;
    and see PARA 33.

2   *Matthews v Kuwait Bechtel Corpn* [1959] 2 QB 57, [1959] 2 All ER 345, CA; *Waters v Metropolitan Police Comr* [2000] 4 All ER 934, [2000] ICR 1064, [2000] IRLR 720, HL. As to the duty in tort see NEGLIGENCE vol 78 (2010) PARA 1 et seq; and see also HEALTH AND SAFETY AT WORK vol 52 (2014) PARA 376 et seq.

3   *Johnstone v Bloomsbury Health Authority* [1992] QB 333, [1991] 2 All ER 293, [1991] ICR 269, [1991] IRLR 118, CA (hospital doctor required by his contract to work 40 hours per week and to 'be available' for overtime of a further 48 hours per week on average, and sometimes actually working 100 hours per week; action for declaration that this broke the employer's duty not to injure the employee allowed to proceed). Failure to protect the employee from harassment which is known, or ought to have been known, to the employer may also constitute a breach of this duty: *Waters v Metropolitan Police Comr* [2000] ICR 1064, [2000] IRLR 720, HL. There is an implied term in the employee's contract that the employer will observe the statutory limit on weekly working hours in the Working Time Regulations 1998, SI 1998/1833 (see PARA 267 et seq): *Barber v RJB Mining (UK) Ltd* [1999] 2 CMLR 833, [1999] ICR 679.

4   In *Johnstone v Bloomsbury Health Authority* [1991] 2 All ER 293, [1991] ICR 269, CA, Stuart-Smith LJ at 299 and 277 considered that the express contractual power to require 88 hours per week had to be exercised in the light of the other contractual terms and, in particular, the duty to take care for the employee's safety; Browne-Wilkinson V-C at 305 and 284 considered that the employer's right to call for overtime was not an absolute right and that there was no reason why the discretion to call for overtime should not be exercised in conformity with the normal implied duty to take reasonable care not to injure the employee's health; and Leggatt LJ (dissenting) at 303 and 282 applied the traditional view that reliance on an express term cannot put the employer in breach of an implied term. As to stress suffered by employees under the normal exigencies of employment see PARA 33.

5   *McDermid v Nash Dredging and Reclamation Co Ltd* [1987] AC 906, [1987] ICR 917, HL (employee employed in dredging operations; employer in joint enterprise with third party; employee injured while working on third party's tug under control of third party's employee). The duty does not, however, extend to cases where the third party is in a foreign country at a considerable distance: *Cook* v *Square D Ltd* [1992] ICR 262, sub nom *Square D Ltd v Cook* [1992] IRLR 34, CA (employer who sent employee to work as computer consultant in Saudi Arabia not liable for injury to employee resulting from a fall on defective flooring at his work place there).

6   *Baker v TE Hopkins & Son Ltd* [1959] 3 All ER 225, [1959] 1 WLR 966, CA.

7   *White v Holbrook Precision Castings Ltd* [1985] IRLR 215, CA (employer has duty to warn employee to whom he is offering a particular job of the risks to health and safety that it involves where those risks are not common knowledge but are ones of which the employer knows or ought to know and against which he cannot guard by taking precautions and where, on information then available to him, knowledge of those risks would be likely to affect the decision of a sensible, level-headed prospective employee about accepting the offer); c f *Pape v Cumbria County Council* [1992] 3 All ER 211, [1991] IRLR 463 (duty on an employer to warn cleaners of the danger of handling chemical cleaning materials with unprotected hands and to instruct them as to the need to wear gloves at all times; danger of skin disease from sustained exposure to such materials well enough known to make it the duty of a reasonable employer to appreciate the risks it presents but not so well known as to make it obvious to the staff without any necessity for warning or instruction).

8   *Deyong v Shenburn* [1946] KB 227, [1946] 1 All ER 226, CA (actor's clothing stolen from theatre dressing room; no implied term in contract of service that his employer would take reasonable care of actor's clothing; no duty on employer to provide such a system of work as would not only protect employee from personal injury but also protect his clothing from theft); *Edwards v West Herts Group Hospital Management Committee* [1957] 1 All ER 541, [1957] 1 WLR 415, CA (house physician's clothing stolen from hostel at hospital; no duty owed by hospital management committee, as employer to employee, to take reasonable care of physician's effects; no term that the committee would take such care could be implied in the contract of employment).
    There is a statutory duty on the employer to provide suitable and sufficient accommodation for an employee's clothing not worn during working hours: see the Workplace (Health, Safety and Welfare) Regulations 1992, SI 1992/3004, reg 23; and HEALTH AND SAFETY AT WORK vol 52 (2014) PARA 441. In deciding what is suitable, risk of theft must be taken into account: *McCarthy v Daily Mirror Newspapers Ltd* [1949] 1 All ER 801, CA.

9   *Reid v Rush & Tompkins Group plc* [1989] 3 All ER 228, [1990] ICR 61, CA (no obligation on employer of employee working abroad to arrange, or advise the employee to arrange, personal accident insurance).

10 *Scally v Southern Health and Social Services Board (British Medical Association, third party)*
[1992] 1 AC 294, [1991] ICR 771, HL (contract of employment negotiated between employers
and an employees' representative body). This principle has been applied cautiously, so there is
no positive duty on an employer to make employees aware of their pension rights (or, indeed,
other terms and conditions of their employment): *University of Nottingham v Eyett* [1999] ICR
721, [1999] IRLR 87 (employer held not to be in breach when simply avoiding an employee's
query on pension entitlements, without positively pointing out that higher benefits could be
payable if the employee delayed retiring by a short period); *Outram v Academy Plastics* [2001]
ICR 367, [2000] IRLR 499, CA (employer who was a pension fund trustee held not to be in
breach by failing to advise a returning employee to rejoin the company pension scheme); *Hagen
v ICI Chemicals and Polymers Ltd* [2002] IRLR 31, [2002] PLR 1, [2002] Lloyd's Rep PN 288
(no general duty imposed on companies involved in a transfer of engineering operations to
ensure that the employees were made aware of the true position in regard to their pension
rights); *Crossley v Faithful & Gould Holdings* [2004] EWCA Civ 293, [2004] 4 All ER 447,
[2004] IRLR 377 (no duty imposed on employer to give his employee financial advice in relation
to benefits accruing from his employment). However, there is nothing to prevent the voluntary
assumption of responsibility principle (see NEGLIGENCE vol 78 (2010) PARA 14) applying to
statements made by the employer that he is under no obligation to make, or to an omission to
give advice, in circumstances where, if not handled carefully, the matter for which the employer
had voluntarily assumed responsibility could result in the employee suffering economic loss: see
Hagen v ICI Chemicals and Polymers Ltd; *Crossley v Faithful & Gould Holdings*; *Lennon v
Metropolitan Police Comr* [2004] EWCA Civ 130, [2004] 2 All ER 266, [2004] 1 WLR 2594.

33. Extent of duty of care at common law for employee's health and safety.
At common law[1], an employer is under a duty to take reasonable care for the
health and safety of his employees in all the circumstances of the case so as not to
expose them to an unnecessary risk[2]. For convenience, in applying the principle
in particular cases, the employer's obligation has long been recognised as
threefold in character, that is to say, to provide:

(1)   a competent staff of employees[3];
(2)   adequate material[4]; and
(3)   a proper system of work and effective supervision[5].

The duty may vary with the employee's particular circumstances which are
known, or ought reasonably to be known, to the employer[6]; and may encompass
a duty not to continue to employ an individual who is liable to develop some
illness if he carries out the job which he is employed to do[7].

An employer's duty to take reasonable care to carry on his operations so as
not to subject his employees to unnecessary risks is a single and continuing duty,
applicable in all circumstances[8]. The duty is personal to the employer; and, if he
entrusts its performance to some other person, he is vicariously liable for any
negligence on the part of the person so appointed in performing the duty[9]. It
should be noted that, in liability for damages, the common law may now be
supplemented by action under the Protection from Harassment Act 1997[10].

1   As to an employer's statutory obligations see PARA 34 et seq. As to negligence and breach of
statutory duty in the context of employment see HEALTH AND SAFETY AT WORK vol 52 (2014)
PARA 376 et seq.
2   *Wilsons and Clyde Coal Co Ltd v English* [1938] AC 57, [1937] 3 All ER 628, HL; *Latimer v
AEC Ltd* [1953] AC 643, [1953] 2 All ER 449, HL (employer held not negligent for failing to
close down premises when floors rendered slippery). The duty of care extends both to the
employee's physical health and to his mental health: see eg *Johnstone v Bloomsbury Health
Authority* [1992] QB 333, [1991] 2 All ER 293, CA (ill-health caused by working excessive
hours); *Walker v Northumberland County Council* [1995] 1 All ER 737, [1995] ICR 702, DC
(injury caused by work-induced stress); *Cross v Highlands and Islands Enterprise* [2001] IRLR
336, OH (duty to take reasonable care for employee's safety includes duty to ensure he is not
exposed to working conditions that might lead to him suffering foreseeable psychiatric harm);
Fraser v State Hospitals Board for Scotland 2001 SLT 1051, OH (no duty on employer to
protect against unpleasant emotions which do not give rise to injury); *Hone v Six Continents*

Retail Ltd [2005] EWCA Civ 922, [2006] IRLR 49 (duty in regard to excessive hours); and *Buck v Nottinghamshire Healthcare NHS Trust* [2006] EWCA Civ 1576, 93 BMLR 28 (psychiatric hospital owed duty to employees to take precautions against high-risk patients). See also *Simmons v British Steel plc* [2004] UKHL 20, [2004] ICR 585, where the principle in *Page v Smith* [1996] AC 155, [1995] 2 All ER 736, HL (see NEGLIGENCE vol 78 (2010) PARA 12) was applied in the case of an employee who suffered an injury at work which exacerbated a pre-existing medical condition and led to depressive illness. As to a recent case on an employer's potential liability for an employee's suicide see *Corr (Administratrix of Corr decd) v IBC Vehicles Ltd* [2008] UKHL 13, [2008] 1 AC 884, [2008] ICR 372 (the deceased had acted in a way he would not have done but for the injury which the defendant's breach of duty had caused him to suffer ... and his conduct ... could not be said to fall outside the scope of the duty which the defendant owed him).

3   There may thus be a common law obligation on an employer to remove a fellow employee with mischievous tendencies liable to cause danger: *Hudson v Ridge Manufacturing Co Ltd* [1957] 2 QB 348, [1957] 2 All ER 229. This could be an important factor if the employer in fact dismisses that person for a reason related to conduct and he brings a claim of unfair dismissal: see PARA 776 et seq.

4   Ie the duty to provide adequate plant and equipment. Where, after 25 October 1969 (ie after the commencement of the Employer's Liability (Defective Equipment) Act 1969: see s 2(2)):

   (1)   an employee suffers personal injury in the course of his employment in consequence of a defect in equipment provided by his employer for the purposes of the employer's business (s 1(1)(a)); and

   (2)   the defect is attributable wholly or partly to the fault of a third party (whether identified or not) (s 1(1)(b)),

   the injury is deemed to be also attributable to negligence on the part of the employer, whether or not he is otherwise liable in respect of the injury, but without prejudice to the law relating to contributory negligence and to any remedy by way of contribution or in contract or otherwise which is available to the employer in respect of the injury (see s 1(1)). As to contributory negligence see NEGLIGENCE vol 78 (2010) PARA 75 et seq. A broad approach has been taken to the meaning of 'equipment' for these purposes: *Coltman v Bibby Tankers Ltd, The Derbyshire* [1988] AC 276, [1988] ICR 67, HL (a whole ship qualified); *Knowles v Liverpool City Council* [1993] 4 All ER 321, [1994] ICR 243, HL (included material being worked on, ie paving stone supplied to employee). In so far as any agreement purports to exclude or limit any such liability of an employer, the agreement is void: Employer's Liability (Defective Equipment) Act 1969 s 1(2). See further HEALTH AND SAFETY AT WORK vol 52 (2014) PARA 377; TORT vol 97 (2010) PARA 675. The employer's duty to take reasonable care to provide adequate material also encompasses the need to maintain a reasonably safe place of work for his employees and reasonably safe access to it: see PARA 34; and HEALTH AND SAFETY AT WORK vol 52 (2014) PARA 420 et seq.

5   *Wilsons and Clyde Coal Co Ltd v English* [1938] AC 57 at 78, [1937] 3 All ER 628 at 640, HL, per Lord Wright. An employee who leaves because the system of work is unsafe may claim unfair dismissal on the grounds of breach of contract: see the cases cited in PARA 763 note 23.

6   *Paris v Stepney Borough Council* [1951] AC 367, [1951] 1 All ER 42, HL; *James v Hepworth and Grandage Ltd* [1968] 1 QB 94, [1967] 2 All ER 829, CA. The ordinary principles of employer's liability apply to claims for psychiatric (or physical) illness or injury arising from the stress of doing the work that an employee is required to do: *Hatton v Sutherland* [2002] EWCA Civ 76, [2002] 2 All ER 1, [2002] ICR 613, [2002] IRLR 263; affd on this point sub nom *Barber v Somerset County Council* [2004] UKHL 13 at [63]–[64], [2004] 2 All ER 385 at [63]–[64], [2004] 1 WLR 1089 at [63]–[64], [2004] IRLR 475 at [63]–[64] per Lord Walker of Gestingthorpe. The guidelines for determining employer liability for psychiatric illness caused by workplace stress given in *Hatton v Sutherland* at [17], [26]–[29], [31]–[36], [39], [42]–[43] per Hale LJ (see HEALTH AND SAFETY AT WORK vol 52 (2014) PARA 378) were approved in *Barber v Somerset County Council* at [63] and described as a valuable contribution to the development of the law. However, with regard to whether an employer is in breach of the duty of care owed to an employee in respect of psychiatric illness caused by work-related stress, the guidelines given in *Hatton v Sutherland* at [29] were described as useful practical guidance only, falling short of having anything like statutory force, and the dictum of Swanwick J in *Stokes v Guest, Keen and Nettlefold (Bolts and Nuts) Ltd* [1968] 1 WLR 1776 at 1783 ('... the overall test is still the conduct of the reasonable and prudent employer, taking positive thought for the safety of his workers in the light of what he knows or ought to know') was preferred as the best general statement of principle: *Barber v Somerset County Council* at [65]. Cf the general approval and application of Hale LJ's guidelines in *Hartman v South Essex Mental Health and Community Care NHS Trust* [2005] EWCA Civ 6, [2005] ICR 782, [2005] IRLR 293. As to

what puts an employer on notice that an employee's health is at risk of breaking down so that the employer should have acted to avert it see *Pratley v Surrey County Council* [2003] EWCA Civ 1067, [2004] ICR 159, [2003] IRLR 794 (what had been communicated, foreseen and foreseeable on both sides was the future risk if work overload continued; immediate collapse was unforeseeable); *Bonser v RJB Mining (UK) Ltd* [2003] EWCA Civ 1296, [2004] IRLR 164 (in order for an employee to recover damages, he must establish that sufficient indications have been given to the employer so that it was reasonably foreseeable not only that overwork would lead to stress but that the stress would lead to a breakdown in the employee's health). See also *Banks v Ablex Ltd* [2005] EWCA Civ 173, [2005] ICR 819, [2005] IRLR 357; *Vahidi v Fairstead House School Trust Ltd* [2005] EWCA Civ 765, [2005] ELR 607; *Hartman v South Essex Mental Health and Community Care NHS Trust* (foreseeability remains the key, and matters disclosed by the employee in confidence to the employer's counselling or occupational health service are not in that employer's direct knowledge, the mere fact that such a service exists not being evidence that the employer foresees stress-related injuries); *MacLennan v Hartford Europe Ltd* [2012] EWHC 346 (QB), [2012] All ER (D) 175 (Feb) (evidence did not support causative link between workplace stress and employee's chronic fatigue syndrome and or an immune deficiency syndrome she complained of, nor that employers were at fault in that they knew or ought to have known that, as a result of stress at work, there was a risk that the employee would suffer harm).

It is uncertain whether an employer who is on notice as to an employee's predisposition to illness arising from the normal exigencies of work is under a duty of care to provide the employee with assistance to enable him to perform his normal contractual duties: to this effect, see *Walker v Northumberland County Council* [1995] 1 All ER 737, [1995] ICR 702, DC (employer's failure to provide effective assistance contributed to employee's second breakdown); *Cross v Highlands and Islands Enterprise* [2001] IRLR 336, OH (employer had implemented new arrangements; duty not breached); *Young v Post Office* [2002] EWCA Civ 661, [2002] IRLR 660, [2002] All ER (D) 311 (Apr) (employer breached duty of care, despite creating a specific arrangement for employee, by failing to implement the arrangement properly). However, in *Barber v Somerset County Council* at [30]–[35], Lord Rodger of Earlsferry held that a duty of reasonable care imputed to the employer to provide such assistance would have implications for the parties' duties under the contract of employment (particularly with respect to sickness and termination provisions) and that these implications had not been examined in any depth in previous cases and were not analysed in the present case. See also *Dickins v 02 plc* [2008] EWCA Civ 1144, [2009] IRLR 58, [2008] All ER (D) 154 (Oct) (once an employee had told her manager that she was not coping with aspects of the job some responsibility for what became a psychiatric stress-related illness passed to the employer, as the employee's problems could only have been dealt with by management intervention).

7 See *Barber v Somerset County Council* [2004] UKHL 13 at [30], [2004] 2 All ER 385 at [30], [2004] 1 WLR 1089 at [30], [2004] IRLR 475 at [30] per Lord Rodger of Earlsferry. Where the risk is small, the employee may decide whether to run it, the employer being under no obligation (at common law) to offer alternative safe employment: *Withers v Perry Chain Co Ltd* [1961] 3 All ER 676 at 680, [1961] 1 WLR 1314 at 1320, CA, per Devlin LJ; followed in *Kossinski v Chrysler United Kingdom Ltd* (1973) 15 KIR 225, CA; *Henderson v Wakefield Shirt Co Ltd* [1997] PIQR P413, CA. In *Coxall v Goodyear Great Britain Ltd* [2002] EWCA Civ 1010 at [27]–[29], [2003] 1 WLR 536 at [27]–[29], [2003] ICR 152 at [27]–[29] per Simon Brown LJ, the principle in *Withers v Perry Chain Co Ltd* was held to be no less effective today, despite the growth in employers' responsibilities towards their workforce, because society's increasing respect for an employee's autonomy formed a countervailing consideration. However, Simon Brown LJ distinguished the line of authority derived from *Withers v Perry Chain Co Ltd* on the basis that the principal consideration must be the actual nature and extent of the known risk, so that where employers come to recognise that an employee should no longer continue in the work, they may be under a duty in law to dismiss the employee for his own good so as to protect him from physical danger: *Coxall v Goodyear Great Britain Ltd* at [29]; see also at [37] per Brooke LJ who felt that the employers' immediate duty was to discuss with the employee all the available options. See also *Dickins v 02 plc* [2008] EWCA Civ 1144, [2009] IRLR 58, [2008] All ER (D) 154 (Oct) (cited in note 6).

8 *Paris v Stepney Borough Council* [1951] AC 367 at 384, [1951] 1 All ER 42 at 50, HL, per Lord Oaksey; *Wilson v Tyneside Window Cleaning Co* [1958] 2 QB 110 at 124–125, [1958] 2 All ER 265 at 272, CA, per Parker LJ; *Morris v Breaveglen Ltd (t/a Anzac Construction Co)* [1993] ICR 766, [1993] IRLR 350, CA.

9 *Wilsons and Clyde Coal Co Ltd v English* [1938] AC 57, [1937] 3 All ER 628, HL; *Wilson v Tyneside Window Cleaning Co* [1958] 2 QB 110, [1958] 2 All ER 265, CA; and see TORT vol 97 (2010) PARA 680.

10 As to the Protection from Harassment Act 1997 see generally CRIMINAL LAW vol 25 (2010)
    PARAS 163–164. See also *Majrowski v Guy's and St Thomas's NHS Trust* [2006] UKHL 34,
    [2007] 1 AC 224, [2006] IRLR 695; *Sunderland City Council v Conn* [2007] EWCA Civ 1492,
    [2008] IRLR 324; and TORT vol 97 (2010) PARAS 426, 557.

34. General duties of employers under statute for health, safety and welfare of others. Under Part I of the Health and Safety at Work etc Act 1974[1], it is the duty of every employer[2] to ensure, so far as is reasonably practicable, the health, safety and welfare at work[3] of all his employees[4]. The matters to which that duty extends[5] include, in particular:

(1) the provision and maintenance of plant[6] and systems of work that are, so far as is reasonably practicable, safe and without risks to health;

(2) arrangements for ensuring, so far as is reasonably practicable, safety and absence of risks to health in connection with the use, handling, storage and transport of articles and substances[7];

(3) the provision of such information, instruction, training and supervision as is necessary to ensure, so far as is reasonably practicable, the health and safety at work of his employees;

(4) so far as is reasonably practicable as regards any place of work under the employer's control, the maintenance of it in a condition that is safe and without risks to health and the provision and maintenance of means of access to and egress from it that are safe and without such risks;

(5) the provision and maintenance of a working environment for his employees that is, so far as is reasonably practicable, safe, without risks to health, and adequate as regards facilities and arrangements for their welfare at work[8].

An employer is subject also to statutory obligations imposed by the Data Protection Act 1998 in relation to the processing of employees' personal data[9] and by the Regulation of Investigatory Powers Act 2000 in relation to the monitoring of employees' electronic communications[10].

1 Ie under the Health and Safety at Work etc Act 1974 Pt I (ss 1–54): see HEALTH AND SAFETY AT WORK vol 52 (2014) PARA 301 et seq.
2 The expression 'employer' is not defined for the purposes of the Health and Safety at Work etc Act 1974 Pt I; but nothing in that Part applies in relation to a person by reason only that he employs another, or is himself employed, as a domestic servant in a private household: see s 51; and HEALTH AND SAFETY AT WORK vol 52 (2014) PARA 302. As to the meaning of 'employer' and related expressions in relation to employment rights generally see PARA 2 et seq.
3 For these purposes:
   (1) 'work' means work as an employee or as a self-employed person (see the Health and Safety at Work etc Act 1974 s 52(1)(a); and HEALTH AND SAFETY AT WORK vol 52 (2014) PARA 302);
   (2) an employee is at work throughout the time when he is in the course of his employment, but not otherwise (see s 52(1)(b); and HEALTH AND SAFETY AT WORK vol 52 (2014) PARA 302);
   (3) a person holding the office of constable is at work throughout the time when he is on duty, but not otherwise (see s 52(1)(c); and HEALTH AND SAFETY AT WORK vol 52 (2014) PARA 302); and
   (4) a self-employed person is at work throughout such time as he devotes to work as a self-employed person (see s 52(1)(d); and HEALTH AND SAFETY AT WORK vol 52 (2014) PARA 302);
and the expressions 'work' and 'at work', in whatever context, are to be construed accordingly (see s 52(1); and HEALTH AND SAFETY AT WORK vol 52 (2014) PARA 302). Regulations may, however: (a) extend the meaning of 'work' and 'at work' for these purposes; and (b) in that connection provide for any of the relevant statutory provisions to have effect subject to such adaptations as may be specified in the regulations: see s 52(2); and HEALTH AND SAFETY AT

WORK vol 52 (2014) PARA 302. As to the meaning of 'relevant statutory provisions', and as to the regulations so made, see HEALTH AND SAFETY AT WORK vol 52 (2014) PARA 302.

For these purposes, 'employee' means an individual who works under a contract of employment, or is treated by s 51A (application of Pt I to police: see POLICE AND INVESTIGATORY POWERS vol 84 (2013) PARA 187) as being an employee; and related expressions are to be construed accordingly: see s 53(1); and HEALTH AND SAFETY AT WORK vol 52 (2014) PARA 302. 'Self-employed person' means an individual who works for gain or reward otherwise than under a contract of employment, whether or not he himself employs others; and 'contract of employment' means a contract of employment or apprenticeship (whether express or implied, and, if express, whether oral or in writing): see s 53(1); and HEALTH AND SAFETY AT WORK vol 52 (2014) PARA 302. As to the meanings of 'employee', 'contract of employment' and related expressions in relation to employment rights generally see PARA 2 et seq.

4   See the Health and Safety at Work etc Act 1974 s 2(1); and HEALTH AND SAFETY AT WORK vol 52 (2014) PARAS 303, 385. Nothing in Pt I (see HEALTH AND SAFETY AT WORK vol 52 (2014) PARA 302 et seq) is to be construed as conferring a right of action in any civil proceedings in respect of any failure to comply with any duty so imposed, however: see s 47; and HEALTH AND SAFETY AT WORK vol 52 (2014) PARA 380 et seq. Civil liability in this area is still governed by the common law and by those statutes whose breach does provide for civil liability: see TORT vol 97 (2010) PARA 491 et seq. See also *R v Swan Hunter Shipbuilders Ltd* [1982] 1 All ER 264, [1981] ICR 831, CA (duty to other person's employees); *West Bromwich Building Society Ltd v Townsend* [1983] ICR 257, [1983] IRLR 147 (erection of bandit screens; whether reasonably practicable).

5   Ie without prejudice to the generality of an employer's duty under the Health and Safety at Work etc Act 1974 s 2(1) (see the text and notes 1–4): see s 2(2); and HEALTH AND SAFETY AT WORK vol 52 (2014) PARA 385.

6   For these purposes, 'plant' includes any machinery, equipment or appliance: see the Health and Safety at Work etc Act 1974 s 53(1).

7   For these purposes, 'substance' means any natural or artificial substance (including micro-organisms), whether in solid or liquid form or in the form of a gas or vapour: see the Health and Safety at Work etc Act 1974 s 53(1) (amended by the Consumer Protection Act 1987 Sch 3 para 7).

8   See the Health and Safety at Work etc Act 1974 s 2(2); and HEALTH AND SAFETY AT WORK vol 52 (2014) PARA 385.

9   An employer's statutory obligations under the Data Protection Act 1998 are explained in *Data Protection: the Employment Practices Code* (November 2011) and *Supplementary Guidance* (June 2005) issued by the Information Commissioner's Office: see PARA 21 note 7. At common law see *Dalgleish v Lothian and Borders Police Board* [1991] IRLR 422, 1992 SLT 721, Ct of Sess; and PARA 67.

10 See the Telecommunications (Lawful Business Practice) (Interception of Communications) Regulations 2000, SI 2000/2699, made in exercise of the powers conferred by the Regulation of Investigatory Powers Act 2000 ss 4(2), 78(5); and POLICE AND INVESTIGATORY POWERS vol 84A (2013) PARA 659.

35. Statement of general policy.

It is the duty[1] of every employer to prepare, and as often as may be appropriate to revise, a written statement of his general policy with respect to the health and safety at work[2] of his employees[3] and the organisation and arrangements for the time being in force for carrying out that policy, and to bring the statement and any revision of it to the notice of all his employees[4].

1   The duty described in the text does not apply to an employer who carries on an undertaking in which for the time being he employs fewer than five employees: see the Employers' Health and Safety Policy Statements (Exception) Regulations 1975, SI 1975/1584, reg 2; and HEALTH AND SAFETY AT WORK vol 52 (2014) PARA 358.

2   As to the meaning of 'work' see HEALTH AND SAFETY AT WORK vol 52 (2014) PARA 302.

3   As to the meaning of 'employee' for these purposes see HEALTH AND SAFETY AT WORK vol 52 (2014) PARA 302.

4   See the Health and Safety at Work etc Act 1974 s 2(3); and HEALTH AND SAFETY AT WORK vol 52 (2014) PARA 358.

36. Safety representatives. Regulations made by the Secretary of State[1] may provide for the appointment in prescribed cases by recognised trade unions[2] of safety representatives from amongst the employees[3]; and those representatives must represent the employees in consultations[4] with the employers and have such other functions as may be prescribed[5].

It is the duty of every employer to consult[6] any such representatives with a view to the making and maintenance of arrangements which will enable him and his employees to co-operate effectively in promoting and developing measures to ensure the health and safety at work[7] of the employees and in checking the effectiveness of such measures[8].

Such representatives may also be significant on an informal and individual basis, in that one element of the employer's general duty of care is an obligation to act reasonably in dealing with matters of health and safety, and complaints relating thereto, which are drawn to his attention by employees[9]. If, therefore, the employee's complaint is ignored, and that breach by the employer is sufficiently serious on the facts to establish a fundamental breach of contract[10], the employee may leave his employment and claim to have been constructively dismissed[11].

1   As to the Secretary of State for these purposes see HEALTH AND SAFETY AT WORK vol 52 (2014) PARA 319 et seq.
2   Ie within the meaning of the Safety Representatives and Safety Committees Regulations 1977, SI 1977/500: see HEALTH AND SAFETY AT WORK vol 52 (2014) PARA 414.
3   As to the meaning of 'employee' and related expressions for these purposes see PARA 34 note 3. See also *Costain Building and Civil Engineering Ltd v Smith* [2000] ICR 215, EAT (appointment of a non-employee invalid).
4   Ie consultations under the Health and Safety at Work etc Act 1974 s 2(6): see the text and notes 6–8.
5   See the Health and Safety at Work etc Act 1974 s 2(4); and HEALTH AND SAFETY AT WORK vol 52 (2014) PARA 414.
6   As to the meaning of 'consult' see *Rollo v Minister of Town and Country Planning* [1948] 1 All ER 13, CA; *Agricultural, Horticultural and Forestry Industry Training Board v Aylesbury Mushrooms Ltd* [1972] 1 All ER 280, [1972] 1 WLR 190.
7   As to the meaning of 'work' see HEALTH AND SAFETY AT WORK vol 52 (2014) PARA 302.
8   See the Health and Safety at Work etc Act 1974 s 2(6); and HEALTH AND SAFETY AT WORK vol 52 (2014) PARAS 385, 414.
9   *British Aircraft Corpn Ltd v Austin* [1978] IRLR 332, EAT; *Keys v Shoefayre Ltd* [1978] IRLR 476; *Jagdeo v Smiths Industries Ltd* [1982] ICR 47, EAT. This may also be seen as an application of the term of trust and respect (see PARA 48), which may be broken by a refusal to take a complaint seriously, especially in the area of sexual harassment: *Bracebridge Engineering Ltd v Darby* [1990] IRLR 3, EAT. As to the implied term to treat grievances seriously see PARA 49.
10   *Graham Oxley Tool Steels Ltd v Firth* [1980] IRLR 135, EAT.
11   As to constructive dismissal see PARA 763.

37. Safety committees. In such cases as may be prescribed[1], it is the duty of every employer, if requested to do so by the safety representatives[2], to establish[3] a safety committee having the functions of keeping under review the measures taken to ensure the health and safety at work of his employees[4] and such other functions as may be prescribed[5].

1   See the Safety Representatives and Safety Committees Regulations 1977, SI 1977/500, reg 9(1); and HEALTH AND SAFETY AT WORK vol 52 (2014) PARA 414.
2   Ie the safety representatives mentioned in the Health and Safety at Work etc Act 1974 s 2(4): see PARA 36.
3   Ie in accordance with regulations made by the Secretary of State: see the Safety Representatives and Safety Committees Regulations 1977, SI 1977/500, reg 9(2); and HEALTH AND SAFETY AT WORK vol 52 (2014) PARA 414.

4   As to the meaning of 'employee' for these purposes see PARA 34 note 3.
5   See the Health and Safety at Work etc Act 1974 s 2(7); and HEALTH AND SAFETY AT WORK vol 52 (2014) PARA 385.

38. Consultation of employees. Notwithstanding the domestic statutory provisions requiring the appointment of safety representatives by recognised trade unions[1], the law of the European Union requires a level of consultation with all employees, whether members of a recognised trade union or not[2].

Accordingly, where there are employees who are not represented by safety representatives[3], the employer must consult those employees in good time on matters relating to their health and safety at work, and, in particular, with regard to:

(1)   the introduction of any measure at the workplace which may substantially affect the health and safety of those employees;

(2)   his arrangements for appointing or, as the case may be, nominating certain persons for statutory purposes[4];

(3)   any health and safety information he is required to provide to those employees;

(4)   the planning and organisation of any health and safety training he is required to provide to those employees; and

(5)   the health and safety consequences for those employees of the introduction, including the planning thereof, of new technologies into the workplace[5].

Such consultation must be with either the employees directly or with directly elected workforce representatives[6], who are entitled to be provided with training and facilities and to have paid time off for exercising their duties and receiving the training[7]. An employer is required to give to either the employees directly or the elected representatives, as appropriate, such information, within his knowledge, as is necessary to participate fully and effectively in the consultation[8].

1   See the Health and Safety at Work etc Act 1974 s 2(4); and HEALTH AND SAFETY AT WORK vol 52 (2014) PARA 414.

2   See Council Directive (EC) 89/391 of 12 June 1989 (OJ L183, 29.06.89, p 1) on the introduction of measures to encourage improvements in the safety and health of workers at work (known as the 'framework directive'), which contains general principles concerning the prevention of occupational risks, the protection of safety and health, the elimination of risk and accident factors, the informing, consultation, balanced participation in accordance with national laws and/or practices and training of workers and their representatives, as well as general guidelines for the implementation of those principles; and see HEALTH AND SAFETY AT WORK vol 52 (2014) PARA 311.

3   Ie under the Safety Representatives and Safety Committees Regulations 1977, SI 1977/500: see HEALTH AND SAFETY AT WORK vol 52 (2014) PARA 414.

4   Ie under the Regulatory Reform (Fire Safety) Order 2005, SI 2005/1541, art 13(3) (see HEALTH AND SAFETY AT WORK vol 53 (2014) PARA 627) or the Management of Health and Safety at Work Regulations 1999, SI 1999/3242, regs 7(1), 8(1)(b) (see HEALTH AND SAFETY AT WORK vol 52 (2014) PARAS 400, 401).

5   See the Health and Safety (Consultation with Employees) Regulations 1996, SI 1996/1513, reg 3; and HEALTH AND SAFETY AT WORK vol 52 (2014) PARA 415.

6   See the Health and Safety (Consultation with Employees) Regulations 1996, SI 1996/1513, reg 4; and HEALTH AND SAFETY AT WORK vol 52 (2014) PARA 415.

7   See the Health and Safety (Consultation with Employees) Regulations 1996, SI 1996/1513, reg 7; and HEALTH AND SAFETY AT WORK vol 52 (2014) PARA 415. Pay for time off is governed by reg 7(3), Sch 1, the right of complaint to an employment tribunal being set out in reg 7(3), Sch 2: see PARA 1210.

8　See the Health and Safety (Consultation with Employees) Regulations 1996, SI 1996/1513,
　　reg 5(1), (2); and HEALTH AND SAFETY AT WORK vol 52 (2014) PARA 415. As to the exceptions
　　to the obligation see reg 5(3); and HEALTH AND SAFETY AT WORK vol 52 (2014) PARA 415.

39. Implied duty to indemnify employee. An employer is under an implied
duty to indemnify or to reimburse the employee, as the case may be, against all
liabilities and losses and in respect of all expenses incurred by the employee
either in consequence of obedience to his orders, or incurred by him in the
execution of his authority, or in the reasonable performance of the duties of his
employment[1]. Notwithstanding the fact that an employee was acting in the
course of his employment, he may lose his right of indemnity or reimbursement
where the liabilities or expenses did not arise out of the nature of the transaction
which he was employed to carry out, but were solely attributable to his own
default or breach of duty, or where, by reason of his conduct, he has forfeited his
right to receive any remuneration for his services[2].

If the employer requires the employee to perform an act which, unknown to
the employee, is unlawful[3], the employee is entitled to be indemnified by the
employer against any damage suffered in consequence of its unlawful nature[4].
Even where the transaction is *prima facie* unlawful, he is entitled to his
indemnity if he was led to believe by the employer, and was justified in believing,
that in the circumstances of the case the transaction was one in which he might
lawfully engage[5].

Any person liable in respect of any damage suffered by another person may
recover contribution from any other person liable in respect of the same damage
(whether jointly with him or otherwise)[6].

1　*Adamson v Jarvis* (1827) 4 Bing 66; *Re Famatina Development Corpn Ltd* [1914] 2 Ch 271 at
　　282, CA, per Lord Cozens-Hardy MR; cf *Dugdale v Lovering* (1875) LR 10 CP 196; and see
　　AGENCY vol 1 (2008) PARA 111 et seq. No right to indemnity or reimbursement exists, however,
　　where the liabilities or expenses are incurred by the employee for his own purposes or where,
　　although incurred on the employer's behalf, they are not covered by the authority to be implied
　　from the course of the employee's employment, or from the employer's subsequent ratification:
　　see AGENCY vol 1 (2008) PARA 113.
2　*Lewis v Samuel* (1846) 8 QB 685. In such circumstances, if the employer is liable, he may have
　　a right to be indemnified by the employee: *Lister v Romford Ice and Cold Storage Co Ltd*
　　[1957] AC 555, [1957] 1 All ER 125, HL; *Morris v Ford Motor Co Ltd* [1973] QB 792, [1973]
　　2 All ER 1084, CA. See also PARA 65; and see AGENCY vol 1 (2008) PARA 113.
3　It is an implied term of the contract of employment that the employer will not order the
　　employee to do an unlawful act: see PARA 31. As to contracts to commit a legal wrong being
　　unenforceable at common law see CONTRACT vol 22 (2012) PARA 427 et seq.
4　*Gregory v Ford* [1951] 1 All ER 121 (employer required employee to drive vehicle not covered
　　by third party insurance; third party injured by employee's negligence; implied term in contract
　　of employment that employer would comply with statutory provisions as to motor vehicle
　　insurance; employee entitled to recover from employer damages and costs which he was liable to
　　pay to third party; employer not entitled to indemnity from employee). See also *Coulson v News
　　Group Newspapers Ltd* [2012] EWCA Civ 1547, [2013] IRLR 116 (agreement following
　　termination included clause guaranteeing indemnity for legal expenses properly incurred by
　　employee as a result of his employment; there was nothing in the criminal nature of the judicial
　　proceedings that did arise to have rendered it objectionable for such an indemnity to have been
　　applied).
　　　　If the act done by the employee is one which is not on the face of it unlawful, but one which
　　his employer appears to have the right to order him to do, the employee is not deprived of his
　　right of indemnity by reason of the act turning out to have been unlawful: *Adamson v Jarvis*
　　(1827) 4 Bing 66; *Dixon v Fawcus* (1861) 3 E & E 537; *Sheffield Corpn v Barclay* [1905] AC
　　392 at 397, HL, per Lord Halsbury LC (approving *Dugdale v Lovering* (1875) LR 10 CP 196).
　　See also CONTRACT vol 22 (2012) PARA 428; and TORT vol 97 (2010) PARA 683.
5　*Burrows v Rhodes* [1899] 1 QB 816, DC. See also CONTRACT vol 22 (2012) PARA 428. There is,
　　however, no right to indemnity in respect of a transaction involving a breach of the criminal law

if the party performing it knew or, if he had not been grossly negligent, would have known that it was illegal or if he knew the true circumstances which rendered it unlawful: see AGENCY vol 1 (2008) PARA 113; FINANCIAL SERVICES AND INSTITUTIONS vol 49 (2008) PARA 1269.

6 See the Civil Liability (Contribution) Act 1978 s 1; and DAMAGES vol 12(1) (Reissue) PARA 837 et seq; TORT vol 97 (2010) PARA 450 et seq.

E. DUTY TO INSURE

40. Insurance against liability for employees. Every employer carrying on any business[1] in Great Britain must[2] insure, and maintain insurance, under one or more approved policies[3] with an authorised insurer[4] or insurers against liability for bodily injury or disease sustained by his employees[5], and arising out of and in the course of their employment in Great Britain in that business (but, except in so far as regulations otherwise provide, not including injury or diseases suffered or contracted outside Great Britain)[6].

Regulations may provide that the amount for which an employer is so required to insure and maintain insurance is to be limited, either generally or in such cases or classes of case as may be prescribed by the regulations, and in such manner as may be so prescribed[7]. Accordingly, the amount for which an employer is so required to insure and maintain insurance in respect of relevant employees[8] under one or more policies of insurance must be, or must in aggregate be, not less than £5 million in respect of: (1) a claim relating to any one or more of those employees arising out of any one occurrence; and (2) any costs and expenses incurred in relation to any such claim[9].

An employer who on any day is not so insured when required to be so is guilty of an offence and liable on summary conviction to a fine[10]. Where such an offence committed by a corporation has been committed with the consent or connivance of, or facilitated by any neglect on the part of, any director, manager[11], secretary or other officer of the corporation, he, as well as the corporation, is deemed to be guilty of that offence and is liable to be proceeded against and punished accordingly[12].

1 For these purposes, 'business' includes a trade or profession, and includes any activity carried on by a body of persons, whether corporate or unincorporate: Employers' Liability (Compulsory Insurance) Act 1969 s 1(3)(c). Except as otherwise provided by regulations, an employer not having a place of business in Great Britain is deemed not to carry on business there: s 1(3)(d). As to the meaning of 'Great Britain' see PARA 2 note 12.

The Secretary of State may by statutory instrument make regulations for any purpose for which regulations are authorised to be made by the Employers' Liability (Compulsory Insurance) Act 1969; but any such statutory instrument is subject to annulment in pursuance of a resolution of either House of Parliament: s 6(1). Any such regulations may make different provision for different cases or classes of case, and may contain such incidental and supplementary provisions as appear to the Secretary of State to be necessary or expedient for the purposes of the regulations: s 6(2). As to regulations so made see notes 3, 7. As to the Secretary of State see PARA 5 note 21.

2 Ie except as otherwise provided by the Employers' Liability (Compulsory Insurance) Act 1969 (see also PARA 42 et seq): see s 1(1).

3 For these purposes, 'approved policy' means a policy of insurance not subject to any conditions or exceptions prohibited for those purposes by regulations: Employers' Liability (Compulsory Insurance) Act 1969 s 1(3)(a). In exercise of the power so conferred, the Secretary of State has made the Employers' Liability (Compulsory Insurance) Regulations 1998, SI 1998/2573, reg 2. Accordingly, as to the prohibited conditions see PARA 44.

4 For these purposes, 'authorised insurer' means:
   (1) a person who has permission under the Financial Services and Markets Act 2000 Pt 4A (ss 55A–55Z4) (permission to carry on regulated activities: see FINANCIAL SERVICES AND INSTITUTIONS vol 48 (2008) PARA 348 et seq) to effect and carry out contracts of insurance of a kind required by the Employers' Liability (Compulsory Insurance)

Act 1969 and regulations made thereunder (Employers' Liability (Compulsory Insurance) Act 1969 s 1(3)(b)(i) (s 1(3)(b) substituted, s 1(3A) added, by SI 2001/3649; Employers' Liability (Compulsory Insurance) Act 1969 s 1(3)(b)(i) amended by the Financial Services Act 2012 s 114(1), Sch 18 para 34)); or

(2) an EEA firm of the kind mentioned in the Financial Services and Markets Act 2000 ss 31(1)(b), 425(1)(a), Sch 3 para 5(d), which has permission under Sch 3 para 15 (permission granted to EEA firm to carry on regulated activities: see FINANCIAL SERVICES AND INSTITUTIONS vol 48 (2008) PARA 315) to effect and carry out contracts of insurance of a kind required by the Employers' Liability (Compulsory Insurance) Act 1969 and regulations made thereunder (Employers' Liability (Compulsory Insurance) Act 1969 s 1(3)(b)(ii) (s 1(3)(b) as so substituted)).

The Employers' Liability (Compulsory Insurance) Act 1969 s 1(3)(b) must be read with the Financial Services and Markets Act 2000 s 22, with any relevant order under s 22, and with Sch 2 (see FINANCIAL SERVICES AND INSTITUTIONS vol 48 (2008) PARAS 84–85): Employers' Liability (Compulsory Insurance) Act 1969 s 1(3A) (as so added). As to the meaning of 'United Kingdom' see PARA 2 note 12. As to the issue of certificates of insurance to employers by insurers see PARA 45.

5 As to the meaning of 'employee' for these purposes, and as to the employees to be covered, see PARA 42. Liability to maintain insurance under the Employers' Liability (Compulsory Insurance) Act 1969 is excluded by the Criminal Justice Act 2003 s 239(7), Sch 19 para 5(4) (employees of the Parole Board: see SENTENCING AND DISPOSITION OF OFFENDERS vol 92 (2010) PARA 772); the Data Protection Act 1998 s 6(7), Sch 5 Pt I para 4(6) (employees of the Information Commissioner: see CONFIDENCE AND INFORMATIONAL PRIVACY vol 19 (2011) PARA 109); the Immigration and Asylum Act 1999 s 83, Sch 5 Pt II para 17(4) (employees of the Immigration Services Commissioner: see IMMIGRATION AND ASYLUM vol 57 (2012) PARA 204); and the Police Reform Act 2002 s 9(6), Sch 2 para 7(2) (employees of the Independent Police Complaints Commission: see POLICE AND INVESTIGATORY POWERS vol 84 (2013) PARAS 288–290).

6 Employers' Liability (Compulsory Insurance) Act 1969 s 1(1).

7 Employers' Liability (Compulsory Insurance) Act 1969 s 1(2). In exercise of the power so conferred, the Secretary of State has made the Employers' Liability (Compulsory Insurance) Regulations 1998, SI 1998/2573, reg 3. Accordingly, as to the prescribed limit of the amount of compulsory insurance see the text and notes 8–9.

8 For these purposes, 'relevant employee' means an employee: (1) who is ordinarily resident in the United Kingdom; or (2) who, though not ordinarily resident in the United Kingdom, has been employed on or from an offshore installation or associated structure for a continuous period of not less than seven days; and (3) who, though not ordinarily resident in Great Britain, is present in Great Britain in the course of employment for a continuous period of not less than 14 days: see the Employers' Liability (Compulsory Insurance) Regulations 1998, SI 1998/2573, reg 1(2). See also the Employers' Liability (Compulsory Insurance) Act 1969 s 2(2); and PARA 42. As to ordinary residence see IMMIGRATION AND ASYLUM vol 57 (2012) PARA 140; CONFLICT OF LAWS vol 19 (2011) PARA 359.

For these purposes, 'offshore installation' has the same meaning as in the Offshore Installations and Pipe-line Works (Management and Administration) Regulations 1995, SI 1995/738 (see PARA 41 note 3); and, in relation to an offshore installation, 'associated structure' means a vessel, aircraft or hovercraft attendant on the installation or any floating structure used in connection with the installation: see the Employers' Liability (Compulsory Insurance) Regulations 1998, SI 1998/2573, reg 1(2). As to employers' liability insurance in respect of offshore installations see the Offshore Installations and Pipe-line Works (Management and Administration) Regulations 1995, SI 1995/738, reg 21; and PARA 41.

9 See the Employers' Liability (Compulsory Insurance) Regulations 1998, SI 1998/2573, reg 3(1). Where an employer is a company with one or more subsidiaries, the requirements of reg 3(1) are to be taken to apply to that company with any subsidiaries together, as if they were a single employer: reg 3(2). For these purposes, 'company' has the same meaning as in the Companies Act 1985 s 735 (repealed: see now the Companies Act 2006 ss 1, 1171; and COMPANIES vol 14 (2009) PARAS 1, 18, 24): see the Employers' Liability (Compulsory Insurance) Regulations 1998, SI 1998/2573, reg 1(2). 'Subsidiary' has the same meaning as in the Companies Act 1985 s 736 (repealed: see now the Companies Act 2006 s 1159; and COMPANIES vol 14 (2009) PARA 25): see the Employers' Liability (Compulsory Insurance) Regulations 1998, SI 1998/2573, reg 1(2). As to the effect of a company's insolvency on an employee's right to claim see the Third Parties (Rights against Insurers) Act 1930; and COMPANIES vol 15 (2009) PARA 1354.

10 The penalty is a fine not exceeding level 4 on the standard scale: see the Employers' Liability (Compulsory Insurance) Act 1969 s 5 (amended by the Criminal Justice Act 1982 s 46). As to the standard scale see SENTENCING AND DISPOSITION OF OFFENDERS vol 92 (2010) PARA 142.

11 Generally, 'manager' means a person who is connected with the management of the affairs of the company as a whole: see *Gibson v Barton* (1875) LR 10 QB 329; *Registrar of Restrictive Trading Agreements v WH Smith & Son Ltd* [1969] 3 All ER 1065, [1969] 1 WLR 1460, CA; *Tesco Supermarkets Ltd v Nattrass* [1971] 1 QB 133 at 142, [1970] 3 All ER 357 at 364, DC, per Fisher J (revsd without affecting this point [1972] AC 153, [1971] 2 All ER 127, HL); *R v Boal* [1992] QB 591, [1992] 3 All ER 177, CA; and COMPANIES vol 14 (2009) PARA 607.

12 Employers' Liability (Compulsory Insurance) Act 1969 s 5 (as amended: see note 10). The Employers' Liability (Compulsory Insurance) Act 1969 does not create civil liability on the part of the employer: *Richardson v Pitt-Stanley* [1995] QB 123, [1995] 1 All ER 460, CA.

41. Application to offshore installations. The Employers' Liability (Compulsory Insurance) Act 1969[1] applies to employers of relevant employees (as defined for the purpose)[2] employed for work on or from offshore installations[3], or on or from associated structures[4], in the course of activities undertaken on or in connection with such installations, subject to prescribed modifications and extensions[5], and subject to the following specific provision as to offences in respect of an offshore installation[6].

Accordingly, in respect of any offshore installation, it is the duty of the owner[7] of the installation to ensure that requirements imposed by or under the Employers' Liability (Compulsory Insurance) Act 1969 are complied with and, where, in respect of that installation[8]:

(1) any employer is on any day not insured in accordance with the Employers' Liability (Compulsory Insurance) Act 1969, the owner of the installation is guilty of an offence and liable on summary conviction to a fine[9]; or

(2) any person fails to comply with a requirement relating to certificates of insurance[10], the owner of the installation is guilty of an offence and liable on summary conviction to a fine[11].

In proceedings against the owner of an installation for such an offence, it is a defence for the accused to prove[12]:

(a) that he has used all due diligence to prevent the commission of the offence[13]; and

(b) that any relevant contravention was committed without his consent, connivance or wilful default[14].

No proceedings may, however, be instituted in England and Wales[15] for any such offence under the Employers' Liability (Compulsory Insurance) Act 1969 in respect of an offshore installation except by the Secretary of State[16] or by a person authorised in that behalf by the Secretary of State[17].

1 As to the Employers' Liability (Compulsory Insurance) Act 1969 see PARAS 40, 42, 43, 45.

2 For the purposes of the Offshore Installations and Pipe-line Works (Management and Administration) Regulations 1995, SI 1995/738, 'relevant employee' means an employee: (1) who is ordinarily resident in the United Kingdom; or (2) who is not ordinarily resident in the United Kingdom but who has been present in the United Kingdom and relevant waters in the course of employment there for a continuous period of not less than seven days: see reg 2(1). As to the meanings of 'United Kingdom' and 'Great Britain' see PARA 2 note 12. As to the meaning of 'relevant waters' for these purposes see HEALTH AND SAFETY AT WORK vol 53 (2014) PARA 687. As to ordinary residence see IMMIGRATION AND ASYLUM vol 57 (2012) PARA 140; CONFLICT OF LAWS vol 19 (2011) PARA 359. As to the meaning of 'relevant employee' for the purposes of the Employers' Liability (Compulsory Insurance) Regulations 1998, SI 1998/2573, see PARA 40 note 8.

3 For the purposes of the Offshore Installations and Pipe-line Works (Management and Administration) Regulations 1995, SI 1995/738, 'offshore installation' must be construed in accordance with reg 3 (see HEALTH AND SAFETY AT WORK vol 53 (2014) PARA 687): see reg 2(1). The Offshore Installations and Pipeline Works (Management and Administration) Regulations 1995, SI 1995/738, regs 6–21 (see also HEALTH AND SAFETY AT WORK vol 53 (2014) PARA 688 et seq) do not apply, however, in relation to an offshore installation which is in

transit to or from a location; and an offshore installation is not in transit to or from a location while it is being manoeuvred at the location: see reg 4(2); and HEALTH AND SAFETY AT WORK vol 53 (2014) PARA 687.

4   In relation to an offshore installation, 'associated structure' means a vessel, aircraft or hovercraft attendant on the installation or any floating structure used in connection with the installation: see the Offshore Installations and Pipe-line Works (Management and Administration) Regulations 1995, SI 1995/738, reg 2(1).

5   Offshore Installations and Pipe-line Works (Management and Administration) Regulations 1995, SI 1995/738, reg 21(1). The prescribed modifications mentioned in the text are as follows:

    (1)   In the Employers' Liability (Compulsory Insurance) Act 1969 s 1 (see PARA 40) as applied: (a) s 1(1) is modified to read: 'except as otherwise provided by the Employers' Liability (Compulsory Insurance) Act 1969, every employer must insure, and maintain insurance, under one or more approved policies with an authorised insurer or insurers against liability for bodily injury or disease sustained by those of his relevant employees who are employed by him for work on or from an offshore installation, or on or from an associated structure in the course of an activity undertaken on or in connection with an offshore installation, and arising out of and in the course of their employment for that work' (s 1(1) (modified by the Offshore Installations and Pipe-line Works (Management and Administration) Regulations 1995, SI 1995/738, reg 21(2)(a)); (b) the following is added to the Employers' Liability (Compulsory Insurance) Act 1969 s 1(3) (definitions): 'any expression to which a meaning is given by the Offshore Installations and Pipeline Works (Management and Administration) Regulations 1995, SI 1995/738, and to which a meaning is not given by the Employers' Liability (Compulsory Insurance) Act 1969, has the same meaning in the Act (s 1(3)(e) (added by the Offshore Installations and Pipe-line Works (Management and Administration) Regulations 1995, SI 1995/738, reg 21(2)(b)));

    (2)   the Employers' Liability (Compulsory Insurance) Act 1969 s 2(2)(b) (see PARA 42) has no effect (see the Offshore Installations and Pipe-line Works (Management and Administration) Regulations 1995, SI 1995/738, reg 21(3));

    (3)   the Employers' Liability (Compulsory Insurance) Act 1969 s 4(2)(a) (employer's duties during currency of insurance: see PARA 45) is modified to read: [the employer must] 'comply with any regulations requiring him to display copies of the certificate of insurance, or make arrangements to secure the maintenance of such copies on offshore installations or associated structures, for the information of his employees (s 4(2)(a) (modified by the Offshore Installations and Pipe-line Works (Management and Administration) Regulations 1995, SI 1995/738, reg 21(4)).

As to the meaning of 'approved policy' see PARA 40 note 3; as to the meaning of 'authorised insurer' see PARA 40 note 4; and as to the meaning of 'employee' see PARA 42.

6   See the Offshore Installations and Pipe-line Works (Management and Administration) Regulations 1995, SI 1995/738, reg 21(5); and the text and notes 7–17.

7   In relation to an offshore installation, references to the owner are references to the person who controls the operation of the installation: Employers' Liability (Compulsory Insurance) Act 1969 s 5A(6) (ss 5A, 5B added by SI 1995/738).

8   See the Employers' Liability (Compulsory Insurance) Act 1969 s 5A(1) (as added: see note 7).

9   Employers' Liability (Compulsory Insurance) Act 1969 s 5A(1)(a) (as added: see note 7). The penalty mentioned in the text is a fine not exceeding level 3 on the standard scale: see s 5A(1)(a) (as so added). As to the standard scale see SENTENCING AND DISPOSITION OF OFFENDERS vol 92 (2010) PARA 142.

    The Health and Safety at Work etc Act 1974 s 37 (offences by bodies corporate: see HEALTH AND SAFETY AT WORK vol 53 (2014) PARA 812) applies to an offence under the Employers' Liability (Compulsory Insurance) Act 1969 s 5A as if it were an offence under the Health and Safety at Work etc Act 1974: Employers' Liability (Compulsory Insurance) Act 1969 s 5A(3) (as so added). In proceedings for an offence under s 5A, an averment in any process of the fact that anything was done or situated within relevant waters is, until the contrary is proved, sufficient evidence of that fact: s 5A(4) (as so added). Proceedings for any offence under s 5A may be taken, and the offence may for all incidental purposes be treated as having been committed, in any place in Great Britain: s 5A(5) (as so added).

10   Ie fails to comply with a requirement imposed by or under the Employers' Liability (Compulsory Insurance) Act 1969 s 4 (see PARA 45): see the Employers' Liability (Compulsory Insurance) Act 1969 s 5A(1)(b) (as added: see note 7).

11 Employers' Liability (Compulsory Insurance) Act 1969 s 5A(1)(b) (as added: see note 7). The penalty mentioned in the text is a fine not exceeding level 2 on the standard scale: see s 5A(1)(b) (as so added). As to offences under s 5A see note 9.
12 See the Employers' Liability (Compulsory Insurance) Act 1969 s 5A(2) (as added: see note 7).
13 Employers' Liability (Compulsory Insurance) Act 1969 s 5A(2)(a) (as added: see note 7).
14 Employers' Liability (Compulsory Insurance) Act 1969 s 5A(2)(b) (as added: see note 7).
15 As to the meanings of 'England' and 'Wales' see PARA 2 note 12.
16 As to the Secretary of State see PARA 5 note 21.
17 Employers' Liability (Compulsory Insurance) Act 1969 s 5B (as added: see note 7).

42. Employees to be covered. For the purposes of the Employers' Liability (Compulsory Insurance) Act 1969[1], the term 'employee' means an individual who has entered into or works under a contract of service or apprenticeship[2] with an employer[3] whether by way of manual labour, clerical work or otherwise, whether such contract is expressed or implied, oral or in writing[4].

However, an employer is not so required[5] to insure[6]: (1) in respect of an employee of whom the employer is the husband, wife, civil partner, father, mother, grandfather, grandmother, stepfather, stepmother, son, daughter, grandson, granddaughter, stepson, stepdaughter, brother, sister, half-brother or half-sister[7]; or (2) except as otherwise provided by regulations, in respect of employees not ordinarily resident in Great Britain[8].

1 As to the Employers' Liability (Compulsory Insurance) Act 1969 see also PARAS 40, 43, 45.
2 As to the meaning of 'contract of service' see PARA 1 note 1. As to the position of apprentices and youth trainees at common law see PARAS 112, 128–129, 636, 747–754. As to the statutory law on apprenticeships see EDUCATION vol 35 (2011) PARA 682 et seq.
3 As to the meaning of 'employer' and related expressions in relation to employment rights generally see PARA 2 et seq. As to the employers exempted from insurance under the Employers' Liability (Compulsory Insurance) Act 1969 see PARA 43.
4 Employers' Liability (Compulsory Insurance) Act 1969 s 2(1). As to the meaning of 'writing' see PARA 2 note 8. As to the meaning of 'employee' and related expressions in relation to employment rights generally see PARA 2 et seq.
5 Ie is not required by the Employers' Liability (Compulsory Insurance) Act 1969 (see PARAS 40, 45): see s 2(2).
6 See the Employers' Liability (Compulsory Insurance) Act 1969 s 2(2).
7 Employers' Liability (Compulsory Insurance) Act 1969 s 2(2)(a) (amended by the Civil Partnerships Act 2004 s 261(1), Sch 27 para 33).
8 Employers' Liability (Compulsory Insurance) Act 1969 s 2(2)(b). As to the making of regulations see PARA 40 note 1. In exercise of the power conferred by s 2(2), the Secretary of State has made the Employers' Liability (Compulsory Insurance) Regulations 1998, SI 1998/2573, reg 1(2) (meaning of 'relevant employee': see PARA 40 note 8). As to the meaning of 'Great Britain' see PARA 2 note 12. As to ordinary residence see IMMIGRATION AND ASYLUM vol 57 (2012) PARA 140; CONFLICT OF LAWS vol 19 (2011) PARA 359. As to employers' liability insurance in respect of relevant employees employed for work on or from certain offshore installations see the Offshore Installations and Pipe-line Works (Management and Administration) Regulations 1995, SI 1995/738, reg 21; and PARA 41.

43. Employers exempted from insurance under the Employers' Liability (Compulsory Insurance) Act 1969. The Employers' Liability (Compulsory Insurance) Act 1969[1] does not require any insurance to be effected by[2]:

(1)   any such authority that is specified for this purpose in the Employers' Liability (Compulsory Insurance) Act 1969[3];

(2)   any body corporate established by or under any enactment for the carrying on of any industry or part of an industry, or of any undertaking, under national ownership or control[4]; or

(3)   in relation to any such cases as may be specified in the regulations, any employer exempted by regulations[5].

1   As to the Employers' Liability (Compulsory Insurance) Act 1969 see PARAS 40, 42, 45.
2   See the Employers' Liability (Compulsory Insurance) Act 1969 s 3(1).
3   Employers' Liability (Compulsory Insurance) Act 1969 s 3(1)(a). The text refers to any such authority that is mentioned in s 3(2) (amended by the Local Government Act 1972 s 272(1), Sch 30; the Local Government (Scotland) Act 1973 s 159; the Local Government Act 1985 ss 84, 102, Sch 14 para 46, Sch 17; the Education Reform Act 1988 s 237, Sch 13 Pt I; the Norfolk and Suffolk Broads Act 1988 s 21, Sch 6 para 7; the National Health Service and Community Care Act 1990 s 60, Sch 8 para 1; the Local Government (Wales) Act 1994 s 66(6), Sch 16 para 37; the Local Government etc (Scotland) Act 1994 s 180(1), Sch 13 para 83; the Environment Act 1995 s 120, Sch 10 para 9; the Police Act 1997 s 134(1), Sch 9 para 20; the Greater London Authority Act 1999 s 328, Sch 29 Pt I para 12; the Criminal Justice and Police Act 2001 Sch 6 Pt 3 para 57; the National Health Service Reform and Health Care Professions Act 2002 s 6(2), Sch 5 para 3(a), (b); the Health and Social Care (Community Health and Standards) Act 2003 s 34, Sch 4 paras 15, 16; the National Health Service (Consequential Provisions) Act 2006 s 2, Sch 1 paras 46, 47(a), (c); the Equality Act 2006 s 2, Sch 1 Pt 2 para 8; the Local Government and Public Involvement in Health Act 2007 s 209(2), Sch 13 Pt 2 para 28; the Local Democracy, Economic Development and Construction Act 2009 s 119, Sch 6 para 8; the Police Reform and Social Responsibility Act 2011 s 99, Sch 16 para 92; the Health and Social Care Act 2012 ss 55(2), 179(6), Sch 5 para 14(a), (b), Sch 14 para 44; and SI 2000/90; SI 2013/602): see the Employers' Liability (Compulsory Insurance) Act 1969 s 3(1)(a).
4   Employers' Liability (Compulsory Insurance) Act 1969 s 3(1)(b).
5   Employers' Liability (Compulsory Insurance) Act 1969 s 3(1)(c). As to the making of regulations see PARA 40 note 1. In exercise of the power conferred by s 3(1)(c), the Secretary of State has made the Employers' Liability (Compulsory Insurance) Regulations 1998, SI 1998/2573, reg 9, Sch 2 (amended by SI 1999/1820; SI 2000/253; SI 2003/1615; SI 2004/2882; SI 2009/801; SI 2010/677; SI 2011/686; SI 2012/725; SI 2012/765; SI 2013/1466). See also PARA 5 note 21.

44.   Prohibition of certain conditions in policies of insurance. For the purposes of the Employers' Liability (Compulsory Insurance) Act 1969[1], there is prohibited in any contract of insurance any condition which provides (in whatever terms) that no liability (either generally or in respect of a particular claim) is to arise under the policy, or that any such liability so arising is to cease, if[2]:

(1)   some specified thing is done or omitted to be done after the happening of the event giving rise to a claim under the policy[3];

(2)   the policy holder does not take reasonable care to protect his employees against the risk of bodily injury or disease in the course of their employment[4];

(3)   the policy holder fails to comply with the requirements of any enactment for the protection of employees against the risk of bodily injury or disease in the course of their employment[5]; or

(4)   the policy holder does not keep specified records or fails to provide the insurer with or make available to him information from such records[6].

Any condition in a policy of insurance which requires a relevant employee[7] to pay, or which requires an insured employer to pay the relevant employee, the first amount of any claim, or any aggregation of claims, is also prohibited for those purposes[8].

These provisions do not, however, prohibit for these purposes a condition in a policy of insurance which requires the employer to pay or contribute any sum to the insurer in respect of the satisfaction of any claim made under the contract of insurance by a relevant employee or any costs and expenses incurred in relation to any such claim[9].

1   Ie for the purposes of the Employers' Liability (Compulsory Insurance) Act 1969 s 1(3)(a): see PARA 40 note 3.
2   See the Employers' Liability (Compulsory Insurance) Regulations 1998, SI 1998/2573, reg 2(1).

3   Employers' Liability (Compulsory Insurance) Regulations 1998, SI 1998/2573, reg 2(1)(a).
4   Employers' Liability (Compulsory Insurance) Regulations 1998, SI 1998/2573, reg 2(1)(b).
5   Employers' Liability (Compulsory Insurance) Regulations 1998, SI 1998/2573, reg 2(1)(c).
6   Employers' Liability (Compulsory Insurance) Regulations 1998, SI 1998/2573, reg 2(1)(d).
7   As to the meaning of 'relevant employee' see PARA 40 note 8.
8   See the Employers' Liability (Compulsory Insurance) Regulations 1998, SI 1998/2573, reg 2(2).
     It is arguable in any case that a policy which contains this type of 'excess' clause would not meet
     in full the requirements of the Employers' Liability (Compulsory Insurance) Act 1969 s 1(1) (see
     PARA 40) as the employee would not be covered up to the level of the excess: see *Aitken v
     Independent Insurance Co Ltd* 2001 SLT 376, OH (considering the position under both the
     Employers' Liability (Compulsory Insurance) Regulations 1998, SI 1998/2573, and the
     predecessor regulations). Agreements containing excess clauses which allow the insurer to pay
     the employee's claim in full and then to claim reimbursement from the employer are allowed by
     the Employers' Liability (Compulsory Insurance) Regulations 1998, SI 1998/2573, reg 2(2): see
     Aitken v Independent Insurance Co Ltd.
9   See the Employers' Liability (Compulsory Insurance) Regulations 1998, SI 1998/2573, reg 2(3).

45.   Certificates of insurance.   Provision may be made by regulations[1] for
securing that certificates of insurance in such form and containing such
particulars as may be prescribed by the regulations are issued by insurers to
employers entering into contracts of insurance[2] and for the surrender in such
circumstances as may be so prescribed of certificates so issued[3]. Accordingly,
every authorised insurer who enters into a contract of insurance with an
employer[4] must issue the employer with a certificate of insurance in the
prescribed form[5] and containing the prescribed particulars[6]; and the certificate
must be issued by the insurer not later than 30 days after the date on which the
insurance commences or is renewed[7].

Where a certificate of insurance is required to be issued to an employer in
accordance with regulations so made, the employer must, subject to any
provision made by the regulations as to the surrender of the certificate, during
the currency of the insurance and such further period, if any, as may be provided
by regulations[8]:

(1)   comply with any regulations requiring him to display copies of the
       certificate of insurance for the information of his employees[9];

(2)   produce the certificate of insurance or a copy of it on demand to any
       inspector duly authorised by the Secretary of State[10] and produce or
       send the certificate or a copy of it to such other persons, at such place
       and in such circumstances as may be prescribed by regulations[11];

(3)   permit the policy of insurance or a copy of it to be inspected by such
       persons and in such circumstances as may be so prescribed[12].

A person who fails to comply with a requirement so imposed is liable on
summary conviction to a fine[13].

1   As to the making of regulations see PARA 40 note 1.
2   Ie in accordance with the requirements of the Employers' Liability (Compulsory Insurance)
     Act 1969 (see PARA 40): see s 4(1). As to employers exempted from insurance see PARA 43.
3   Employers' Liability (Compulsory Insurance) Act 1969 s 4(1). In exercise of the power conferred
     by s 4(1), (2), the Secretary of State has made the Employers' Liability (Compulsory Insurance)
     Regulations 1998, SI 1998/2573, regs 4–8, Sch 1 (see the text and notes 5–7).
4   Ie in accordance with the requirements of the Employers' Liability (Compulsory Insurance)
     Act 1969 (see PARA 40): see the Employers' Liability (Compulsory Insurance) Regulations 1998,
     SI 1998/2573, reg 4(1).
5   As to the prescribed form of certificate of employers' liability insurance see the Employers'
     Liability (Compulsory Insurance) Regulations 1998, SI 1998/2573, reg 4(1), Sch 1. In any case
     where it is intended that a contract of insurance for the purposes of the Employers' Liability
     (Compulsory Insurance) Act 1969 is to be effective, not only in Great Britain, but also:

(1) in Northern Ireland, the Isle of Man, the Island of Guernsey, the Island of Jersey or the Island of Alderney (Employers' Liability (Compulsory Insurance) Regulations 1998, SI 1998/2573, reg 4(6)(a));

(2) in any waters outside the United Kingdom to which the Employers' Liability (Compulsory Insurance) Act 1969 may have been applied by any enactment (Employers' Liability (Compulsory Insurance) Regulations 1998, SI 1998/2573, reg 4(6)(b)),

the prescribed form set out in Sch 1 may be modified by a reference to the relevant law which is applicable and a statement that the policy to which it relates satisfies the requirements of that law (see reg 4(6)). As to the meanings of 'United Kingdom' and 'Great Britain' see PARA 2 note 12.

6 Employers' Liability (Compulsory Insurance) Regulations 1998, SI 1998/2573, reg 4(1). As to the prescribed particulars see Sch 1. Where a contract of insurance for the purposes of the Employers' Liability (Compulsory Insurance) Act 1969 is entered into together with one or more other contracts of insurance which jointly provide insurance cover of no less than £5 million, the certificate must specify both the amount in excess of which insurance cover is provided by the policy and the maximum amount of that cover: see the Employers' Liability (Compulsory Insurance) Regulations 1998, SI 1998/2573, reg 4(3).

7 Employers' Liability (Compulsory Insurance) Regulations 1998, SI 1998/2573, reg 4(2).

8 See the Employers' Liability (Compulsory Insurance) Act 1969 s 4(2). See note 3.

9 Employers' Liability (Compulsory Insurance) Act 1969 s 4(2)(a). As to the meaning of 'employee', and as to the employees to be covered, see PARA 42. As to employers' liability insurance in respect of relevant employees employed for work on or from certain offshore installations see the Offshore Installations and Pipe-line Works (Management and Administration) Regulations 1995, SI 1995/738, reg 21; and PARA 41.

10 Ie authorised for the purposes of the Employers' Liability (Compulsory Insurance) Act 1969: see s 4(2)(b). As to the Secretary of State see PARA 5 note 21. As to the display of copies of certificates of insurance see PARA 46.

11 Employers' Liability (Compulsory Insurance) Act 1969 s 4(2)(b).

12 Employers' Liability (Compulsory Insurance) Act 1969 s 4(2)(c). As to production and inspection of certificates of insurance see PARA 47.

13 Employers' Liability (Compulsory Insurance) Act 1969 s 4(3) (amended by the Criminal Justice Act 1982 s 46). The penalty is a fine not exceeding level 3 on the standard scale: see the Employers' Liability (Compulsory Insurance) Act 1969 s 4(3) (as so amended). As to the standard scale see SENTENCING AND DISPOSITION OF OFFENDERS vol 92 (2010) PARA 142.

46. Display of copies of certificates of insurance. An employer who has been issued with a certificate of insurance[1] must display one or more copies of it at each place of business at which he employs any relevant employee[2] of the class or description to which the certificate relates[3]. This requirement is satisfied if the certificate is made available in electronic form and each relevant employee to whom it relates has reasonable access to it in that form[4].

Copies of a certificate which are required to be so displayed must be kept on display until the date of expiry or earlier termination of the approved policy mentioned in the certificate[5].

None of the above requirements[6] applies, however, where an employer employs a relevant employee on or from an offshore installation[7] or associated structure[8], but in such a case the employer must produce, at the request of that employee and within the period of ten days from such request, a copy of the certificate which relates to that employee[9].

1 Ie in accordance with the Employers' Liability (Compulsory Insurance) Regulations 1998, SI 1998/2573, reg 4 (see PARA 45): see reg 5(1) (reg 5(1), (2) substituted by SI 2008/1765).

2 As to the meaning of 'relevant employee' see PARA 40 note 8.

3 Employers' Liability (Compulsory Insurance) Regulations 1998, SI 1998/2573, reg 5(1) (as substituted: see note 1). As to the penalty for failure to comply with the requirements of the regulations see PARA 45.

4 Employers' Liability (Compulsory Insurance) Regulations 1998, SI 1998/2573, reg 5(2) (as substituted: see note 1).

5 Employers' Liability (Compulsory Insurance) Regulations 1998, SI 1998/2573, reg 5(3).

6   Ie the Employers' Liability (Compulsory Insurance) Regulations 1998, SI 1998/2573, reg 5(1)–(3) (see the text and notes 1–5): see reg 5(4).
7   As to the meaning of 'offshore installation' see PARA 40 note 8.
8   As to the meaning of 'associated structure' see PARA 40 note 8.
9   Employers' Liability (Compulsory Insurance) Regulations 1998, SI 1998/2573, reg 5(4). As to employers' liability insurance in respect of relevant employees employed for work on or from certain offshore installations see the Offshore Installations and Pipe-line Works (Management and Administration) Regulations 1995, SI 1995/738, reg 21; and PARA 41.

47.   Production and inspection of certificates of insurance. An employer who is required by a written notice issued by an inspector[1] to do so must produce or send to any person specified in the notice, at the address and within the time specified in the notice[2]:

(1)   either the original or a copy of every certificate of insurance issued[3] to him which relates to a period of insurance current at the date of issue of the notice[4];

(2)   either the original or a copy of every certificate issued[5] to him[6].

Where a certificate is required to be issued[7] to an employer, the employer must during the currency of the insurance permit the policy of insurance or a copy of it to be inspected by an inspector[8]:

(a)   at such reasonable time as the inspector may require[9];

(b)   at such place of business of the employer (which, in the case of an employer who is a company, may include its registered office[10]) as the inspector may require[11].

Any inspector must, if so required when visiting any premises[12], produce to an employer or his agent some duly authenticated document showing that he is authorised[13] by the Secretary of State[14].

1   For these purposes, 'inspector' means any inspector duly authorised by the Secretary of State under the Employers' Liability (Compulsory Insurance) Act 1969 s 4(2)(b) (see PARA 45): see the Employers' Liability (Compulsory Insurance) Regulations 1998, SI 1998/2573, reg 1(2). As to the Secretary of State see PARA 5 note 21.
2   See the Employers' Liability (Compulsory Insurance) Regulations 1998, SI 1998/2573, reg 6. As to the penalty for failure to comply with the requirements of the regulations see PARA 45.
3   Ie under the Employers' Liability (Compulsory Insurance) Regulations 1998, SI 1998/2573, reg 4 (see PARA 45): see reg 6(a).
4   Employers' Liability (Compulsory Insurance) Regulations 1998, SI 1998/2573, reg 6(a).
5   Ie under the Employers' Liability (Compulsory Insurance) Regulations 1998, SI 1998/2573, reg 4 (see PARA 45): see reg 6(b) (amended by SI 2008/1765).
6   Employers' Liability (Compulsory Insurance) Regulations 1998, SI 1998/2573, reg 6(b) (as amended: see note 5).
7   Ie in accordance with the Employers' Liability (Compulsory Insurance) Regulations 1998, SI 1998/2573, reg 4 (see PARA 45): see reg 7.
8   See the Employers' Liability (Compulsory Insurance) Regulations 1998, SI 1998/2573, reg 7.
9   Employers' Liability (Compulsory Insurance) Regulations 1998, SI 1998/2573, reg 7(a).
10 As to the meaning of 'company' for these purposes see PARA 40 note 9. As to a company's registered office see COMPANIES vol 14 (2009) PARA 129.
11 Employers' Liability (Compulsory Insurance) Regulations 1998, SI 1998/2573, reg 7(b).
12 Ie for the purposes of the Employers' Liability (Compulsory Insurance) Act 1969 (see PARA 45): see the Employers' Liability (Compulsory Insurance) Regulations 1998, SI 1998/2573, reg 8.
13 Ie under the Employers' Liability (Compulsory Insurance) Act 1969 s 4(2)(b) (see PARA 45): see the Employers' Liability (Compulsory Insurance) Regulations 1998, SI 1998/2573, reg 8.
14 Employers' Liability (Compulsory Insurance) Regulations 1998, SI 1998/2573, reg 8.

F. DUTY TO TREAT EMPLOYEE WITH RESPECT

48.   Implied term of trust and respect. In a contract of employment[1], there is an implied term that the employer will not, without reasonable and proper cause, conduct himself in a manner calculated[2] or likely to destroy or seriously damage the relationship of confidence and trust between employer and employee[3]. The term can, in appropriate circumstances, impose positive obligations on the employer[4].

The kinds of behaviour which may breach the term of trust and respect are in each case a question of fact for the tribunal[5], and entirely variable, but may include:

(1)   undermining the self-esteem and dignity of the employee[6];

(2)   abusive and false accusations[7];

(3)   failure to tell an employee of complaints made against him[8];

(4)   intolerable behaviour and bad language[9];

(5)   unwarranted docking of pay[10];

(6)   attaching unreasonable conditions to remuneration[11];

(7)   persistent attempts to vary conditions of employment[12];

(8)   capricious refusal to offer the same terms to a single employee as are offered to the rest of the workforce, whether by way of variation or by way of a new contract[13];

(9)   failure to notify an employee on maternity leave of a vacancy for which she believed she was suitable[14];

(10)   failure to give the employee necessary support[15];

(11)   failure to follow established procedures[16];

(12)   failure to take seriously a complaint of sexual harassment[17];

(13)   seducing the employee[18];

(14)   sudden withdrawal of an *ex gratia* loan by the employer[19];

(15)   persistent failure to make a reasonable adjustment in breach of discrimination legislation[20].

A series of actions by an employer or a series of incidents may cumulatively amount to a breach of the implied term of trust and confidence, even though each individual act or incident, perhaps trivial in itself, may not[21].

The implied term of trust and respect in the contract of employment has been held to have overriding effect, that is to say that, even where the employer has express power to act in a particular way under the terms of the contract, he must exercise that power in the light of his overall duty of trust and respect, with the result that, if he does not do so, the employee may be contractually entitled to leave his employment and claim constructive dismissal, in spite of the employer's claim that he was merely exercising his contractual rights[22].

An employee is entitled to rely on the implied term of trust and confidence as subsisting during a period of investigation of disciplinary charges against him[23].

The implied term has also been applied in the area of occupational pension schemes[24].

1   As to the formation and form of contracts of employment see PARA 14 et seq.

2   The behaviour of the employer complained of need not be deliberate (*Post Office v Roberts* [1980] IRLR 347, EAT); and it may be arguable that an employer is vicariously liable for a breach of the implied term (see *Moores v Bude-Stratton Town Council* [2001] ICR 271, [2000] IRLR 676, EAT (individual back-bench councillor verbally abused employee of council)).

3   *Woods v WM Car Services (Peterborough) Ltd* [1981] ICR 666, [1981] IRLR 347, EAT; affd [1982] ICR 693, [1982] IRLR 413, CA. The judgment of Browne-Wilkinson P in the Employment Appeal Tribunal in this case is regarded as the *locus classicus*. The term has, however, been variously described in the cases (trust and respect, confidence, co-operation, not rendering the contract impossible to perform), though a simple formulation as a term of reasonable behaviour by the employer has been rejected as too wide and uncertain: *Post Office v Roberts* [1980] IRLR 347, EAT; but cf *Brown v Merchant Ferries Ltd* [1998] IRLR 682, NI CA (where it was said that seriously unreasonable conduct may be evidence of breach of the

implied term). The existence of the term was approved in *Woods v WM Car Services (Peterborough) Ltd*; *Bliss v South East Thames Regional Health Authority* [1987] ICR 700, [1985] IRLR 308, CA (a rare common law application of it); *Lewis v Motorworld Garages Ltd* [1986] ICR 157, [1985] IRLR 465, CA. It was finally given the unqualified approval of the House of Lords in *Malik v Bank of Credit and Commerce International SA (in liquidation)*, *Mahmud v Bank of Credit and Commerce International SA (in liquidation)* [1998] AC 20, [1997] 3 All ER 1, HL. Employment tribunals have been advised to apply the tests stated in *Malik v Bank of Credit and Commerce International SA (in liquidation)*, *Mahmud v Bank of Credit and Commerce International SA (in liquidation)* and the cases cited therein using language which does not extend, or may appear to extend, the scope of the implied term of trust and confidence: *O'Brien v Transco plc (formerly BG plc)* [2002] EWCA Civ 379 at [24], [2002] ICR 721 at [24], [2002] IRLR 444 at [24] per Pill LJ (per curiam).

Where an employer's conduct is in breach of the implied term of trust and confidence, that will inevitably lead to a fundamental or repudiatory breach entitling an employee to claim constructive dismissal: *Morrow v Safeway Stores plc* [2002] IRLR 9, EAT. See also *Horkulak v Cantor Fitzgerald International* [2003] EWHC 1918 (QB), [2004] ICR 697, [2003] IRLR 756 (conduct of employers' chief executive included using foul and abusive language, not allowing the employee a chance to respond to criticism and setting standards of performance which the chief executive did not reasonably believe could be attained by the employee: see notes 5, 6); *Mayer v British Broadcasting Corpn* [2004] All ER (D) 34 (Nov), EAT (management had made mistakes in the presentation and timing of matters which they had been entitled to raise but, objectively speaking, these did not go to the root of the employment contract between the parties); *McBride v Falkirk Football and Athletic Club* [2012] IRLR 22, EAT (employer cannot pray in aid that behaviour complained of was part of the 'ethos' of the industry); *Lu v Nottingham University Hospitals NHS Trust* [2014] EWHC 690 (QB), 137 BMLR 172, [2014] All ER (D) 155 (Mar) (no breach of contract found in Trust's approach to draft programme providing for employee's resumption of surgical duties or in steps taken to inform the public and others of his resumption of work following his infection by antibiotic-resistant bacteria which caused problems in his performance of heart valve surgery). An employee can justify his refusal to perform his contract of employment on any grounds existing at the time of his leaving the employment and, once the degree of trust and confidence that the employee is entitled to have in the employer is destroyed or seriously damaged, the employee is entitled to leave: *Tullet Prebon plc v BGC Brokers LLP* [2010] EWHC 484 (QB), [2010] IRLR 648 (a person can have no trust and confidence in an employer who has recruited him in a manner which shows a cynical disregard for the law and for employees' duties) (affd [2011] EWCA Civ 131, [2011] IRLR 420 (obligations of trust and confidence can arise at a time of detailed contractual regulation between the parties, and a contract obliging a person to commence employment at a future date is a contract of employment for the purpose of the jurisdiction of the employment tribunal)). Arguments of repudiatory breach must not be constructed, however, as a means of avoiding notice periods and irksome covenants, especially where highly paid individuals and teams have already secured alternative employment with a competitor of their employer prior to resigning: *Tullet Prebon plc v BGC Brokers LLP* at [86] per Jack J. There had been a suggestion made in *Tullet Prebon plc v BGC Brokers LLP* at [83]–[85] per Jack J that an employee's misconduct may be relevant in the making of an objective judgement about whether the employer's conduct has sufficiently damaged the trust and confidence which the employee has in him (citing *RDF Media Group plc v Clements* [2007] EWHC 2892 (QB) at [140], [2008] IRLR 207 at [140] per Bernard Livesey QC (that where an employee is himself in repudiatory breach of a mutual obligation he is not entitled to accept any repudiation by his employer by reason of his own breaches)). However, the correct principle in English law has been stated by the EAT to be that, while a contract of employment subsists, the obligations which that contract imposes upon the parties continue to subsist; some of those obligations may in certain circumstances, be in suspense or not enforceable (for example, if an employee goes on strike, there is no obligation to pay him while he is on strike), but the obligation of trust and confidence which lies on each party to a contract of employment are not suspended or put in abeyance because one party has broken that obligation: *Atkinson v Community Gateway Association* [2014] All ER (D) 158 (Aug), EAT (citing *McNeill v Aberdeen City Council (No 2)* [2013] CSIH 102, [2014] IRLR 113, 2014 SLT 312, CSIH, with the proviso that neither the Scottish law doctrine of retention nor the Scottish approach to the principles of mutuality play any vital part in the conclusion thus reached).

As to the duty of good faith during employment see PARA 67; and as to the (lesser) duty of continuing good faith after the termination of employment see PARA 71. As to an employer's repudiatory breach of the employee's contract see *Bournemouth University Higher Education*

Corpn v Buckland [2010] EWCA Civ 121, [2011] QB 323, [2010] 4 All ER 186; *Assamoi v Spirit Pub Company (Services) Ltd (formerly known as Punch Pub Co Ltd)* [2012] All ER (D) 17 (Sep), EAT; and PARA 763.

4   *O'Brien v Transco plc (formerly BG plc)* [2002] EWCA Civ 379, [2002] ICR 721, [2002] IRLR 444.

5   *Woods v WM Car Services (Peterborough) Ltd* [1982] ICR 693, [1982] IRLR 413, CA. The test of whether there has been a breach of the implied term of trust and confidence is objective: *Malik v Bank of Credit and Commerce International SA (in liquidation), Mahmud v Bank of Credit and Commerce International SA (in liquidation)* [1998] AC 20 at 35, [1997] 3 All ER 1 at 5, HL, per Lord Nicholls of Birkenhead. In order to determine whether there has been a breach of the implied term, it has been suggested that two matters have to be determined: (1) whether, ignoring their cause, there have been acts which are likely on their face to seriously damage or destroy the relationship of trust and confidence between employer and employee; and (2) whether there is no reasonable and proper cause for those acts: *Hilton v Shiner Ltd (Builders Merchants)* [2001] IRLR 727, EAT (employer not in breach of the implied term of trust and confidence in removing cash handling and cashiering duties from an employee suspected on reasonable grounds of dishonesty). As to whether the test is for an employer not without reasonable and proper cause to conduct itself in a manner calculated *and* likely to destroy or seriously damage the relationship of confidence and trust between employer and employee see *Malik v Bank of Credit and Commerce International SA (in liquidation), Mahmud v Bank of Credit and Commerce International SA (in liquidation); Baldwin v Brighton and Hove City Council* [2007] ICR 680, [2007] IRLR 232, EAT (relevant test is satisfied if either of the requirements is met, ie if conduct is calculated *or* likely); *Leeds Dental Team Ltd v Rose* [2014] ICR 94, [2014] IRLR 8, EAT (test does not require a tribunal to make a factual finding as to what the actual intention of the employer was because If the employer acts in such a way, considered objectively, that his conduct is likely to destroy or seriously damage the relationship of trust and confidence, then he is taken to have the objective intention spoken of). As to an employee's remedies for breach of contract see PARA 826 et seq.

An employer, by paying substantial salaries, does not acquire a right to treat employees according to a different standard of conduct from that which might otherwise be required: *Horkulak v Cantor Fitzgerald International* [2003] EWHC 1918 (QB), [2004] ICR 697, [2003] IRLR 756 (revsd in part on the issue of quantum [2004] EWCA Civ 1287, [2005] ICR 402, [2004] IRLR 942).

6   *Hilton International Hotels (UK) Ltd v Protopapa* [1990] IRLR 316, EAT (unmerited reprimanding in humiliating circumstances); *Horkulak v Cantor Fitzgerald International* [2003] EWHC 1918 (QB), [2004] ICR 697, [2003] IRLR 756 (revsd in part on the issue of quantum [2004] EWCA Civ 1287, [2005] ICR 402, [2004] IRLR 942) (legitimate demands for high standards of performance must be balanced by a fair system of enforcement with criticisms properly raised and handled; the level of any rebuke must be proportionate to the alleged failing on the part of the employee).

7   *Robinson v Crompton Parkinson Ltd* [1978] ICR 401, [1978] IRLR 61, EAT; *Courtaulds Northern Textiles Ltd v Andrew* [1979] IRLR 84, EAT.

8   *TSB Bank plc v Harris* [2000] IRLR 157, EAT.

9   *Palmanor Ltd v Cedron* [1978] ICR 1008, [1978] IRLR 303, EAT; *Cantor Fitzgerald International v Bird* [2002] IRLR 867; *Horkulak v Cantor Fitzgerald International* [2003] EWHC 1918 (QB), [2004] ICR 697, [2003] IRLR 756 (revsd in part on the issue of quantum [2004] EWCA Civ 1287, [2005] ICR 402, [2004] IRLR 942) (frequent use of foul and abusive language, including use by the employee himself, did not sanitise its effect).

10   *Bristol Garage (Brighton) Ltd v Lowen* [1979] IRLR 86, EAT.

11   *Farrell Matthews & Weir v Hansen* [2005] ICR 509, [2005] IRLR 160, EAT (bonus to be paid in monthly instalments as long as employee did not give notice to terminate her employment). See also *Cantor Fitzgerald International v Bird* [2002] IRLR 867 (employers' representatives used aggressive and misleading tactics to persuade employees to accept new remuneration arrangements; erroneous implication that bonuses under existing contracts might be withheld if the employees did not agree to the new terms).

12   *Woods v WM Car Services (Peterborough) Ltd* [1981] ICR 666, [1981] IRLR 347, EAT; affd [1982] ICR 693, [1982] IRLR 413, CA.

13   *O'Brien v Transco plc (formerly BG plc)* [2002] EWCA Civ 379, [2002] ICR 721, [2002] IRLR 444 (single employee deprived of the opportunity to take advantage of new rights in erroneous belief that he was not a permanent employee).

14   *Paul v Visa International Service Association* [2004] IRLR 42, EAT (decision not affected by finding of fact that the applicant did not fulfil the criteria for the post).

15 *Wigan Borough Council v Davies* [1979] ICR 411, [1979] IRLR 127, EAT; *Associated Tyre Specialists (Eastern) Ltd v Waterhouse* [1977] ICR 218, [1976] IRLR 386, EAT.

16 *Post Office v Roberts* [1980] IRLR 347, EAT.

17 *Bracebridge Engineering Ltd v Darby* [1990] IRLR 3, EAT. Conversely, to suspend an employee too hastily, simply because an investigation was taking place, may contravene the term of trust and respect: see *Gogay v Hertfordshire County Council* [2000] IRLR 703, CA.

18 *Wood v Freeloader Ltd* [1977] IRLR 455.

19 *French v Barclays Bank plc* [1998] IRLR 646, CA.

20 *Meikle v Nottinghamshire County Council* [2004] EWCA Civ 859, [2004] 4 All ER 97, [2005] ICR 1, [2004] IRLR 703 (local authority in fundamental breach of contract as a result of its continuing failure to deal with disability discrimination against disabled teacher contrary to the Disability Discrimination Act 1996 (repealed)); *Greenhof v Barnsley Metropolitan Borough Council* [2006] IRLR 98, EAT (employee off sick with depression pressurised into taking a lesser job rather than having demands of existing job adjusted and claimed disability discrimination under the Disability Discrimination Act 1996 (repealed)). See also *Warner v Armfield Retail & Leisure Ltd* [2014] ICR 239, [2013] All ER (D) 260 (Oct), EAT (duty to make reasonable adjustments pursuant to the Equality Act 2010). As to the duty to make reasonable adjustments see DISCRIMINATION vol 33 (2013) PARA 84.

21 *Lewis v Motorworld Garages Ltd* [1986] ICR 157 at 167, [1985] IRLR 465 at 468, CA, per Neill LJ, and at 169 and 469 per Glidewell LJ (the 'last straw' principle). See also *Omilaju v Waltham Forest London Borough Council* [2004] EWCA Civ 1493, [2005] 1 All ER 75, [2005] ICR 481 (the conduct actually complained of does not need to be 'unreasonable' or 'blameworthy' in itself if it is a 'final straw', although the cause for complaint has to contribute something, however insignificant, to the breach of the implied term).

22 '... [T]here may well be conduct which is either calculated or likely to destroy or seriously damage the relationship of trust and confidence between employer and employee, which a literal interpretation of the written words of the contract might appear to justify, and it is in this sense that we consider that in the field of employment law it is proper to imply an overriding obligation [of trust and respect] which is independent of, and in addition to, the literal interpretation of the actions which are permitted to the employer under the terms of the contract': *United Bank Ltd v Akhtar* [1989] IRLR 507 at 512, EAT, per Knox J (failure by employer to give reasonable notice of a move under an express mobility clause entitled employee to leave his employment and claim constructive dismissal: see PARA 763). See also *Attrill v Dresdner Kleinwort Ltd, Anar v Dresdner Kleinwort Ltd* [2013] EWCA Civ 394, [2013] 3 All ER 607, [2013] IRLR 548 (variation of employment contract in relation to retention bonuses was effected in accordance with terms of employee handbook but adverse conditions clause undermined trust and confidence in light of bank's promises that bonus pool would be unaffected by efforts to reduce running costs). The judgment of Browne-Wilkinson V-C in *Imperial Group Pension Trust Ltd v Imperial Tobacco Ltd* [1991] ICR 524, [1991] IRLR 66 arguably shows signs of a similar approach. In the context of a contractual power to suspend an employee see also *McLory v Post Office* [1992] ICR 758, sub nom *McClory v Post Office* [1993] IRLR 159.

   If developed, this approach could have significant effects on employment law generally, and the law of constructive dismissal in particular; but it must be recognised that it is difficult to reconcile with traditional contract law on the relationship of express and implied terms. Not only does it pose problems of an express term being negated by an implied term, but it could be seen in simpler terms of being a requirement that an express term must always be exercised reasonably, an argument that has been rejected in other cases in other contexts: see *Express Lift Co Ltd v Bowles* [1977] ICR 474, [1977] IRLR 99, EAT; *Kenneth MacRae & Co Ltd v Dawson* [1984] IRLR 5, EAT; *Rank Xerox Ltd v Churchill* [1988] IRLR 280, EAT; *Courtaulds Northern Spinning Ltd v Sibson* [1988] ICR 451, [1988] IRLR 305, CA. See also *White v Reflecting Roadstuds Ltd* [1991] ICR 733, [1991] IRLR 331, EAT (argument based on implied requirement of reasonable exercise rejected, but implied term of trust and respect reaffirmed and held potentially applicable).

23 *King v University Court of the University of St Andrews* [2002] IRLR 252, OH. The term may inhibit an employer from pursuing disciplinary proceedings against an employee immediately before a public inquiry if there is a real risk that the proceedings will prevent the employee from participating properly in the inquiry: *R (on the application of Arthurworrey) v Haringey London Borough Council* [2001] EWHC 698 (Admin), [2002] ICR 279. The involvement of applicants and respondent as interested parties or witnesses before a public inquiry does not admit a public law dimension to this question: *R (on the application of Arthurworrey) v Haringey London Borough Council* (judicial review of the employer's decision to pursue disciplinary proceedings in these circumstances refused). An employee's right to fair treatment

can be derived from the implied term of trust and confidence in the employer-employee relationship, although fair treatment as a requirement is fact sensitive: *Yapp v Foreign and Commonwealth Office* [2013] EWHC 1098 (QB), [2013] IRLR 616, [2013] ICR D21 (employer had breached its obligation of fair treatment in failing to conduct some basic analysis of allegations of sexual misconduct before deciding to withdraw him).

24   *Imperial Group Pension Trust Ltd v Imperial Tobacco Ltd* [1991] ICR 524, [1991] IRLR 66 (employer's rights under a pension fund's rules must be exercised in accordance with the obligation of good faith towards the employees). See also *IBM United Kingdom Pensions Trust Ltd v IBM United Kingdom Holdings Ltd* [2012] EWHC 3540 (Ch), [2012] All ER (D) 118 (Dec); and PERSONAL AND OCCUPATIONAL PENSIONS vol 80 (2013) PARA 213.

G. DUTIES IN RELATION TO GRIEVANCES AND THE WORKING ENVIRONMENT

49.   Implied term to treat grievances seriously.   It is an implied term in a contract of employment[1] that an employer will deal properly and timeously with a grievance raised by the employee[2]; breach of this term could be the basis for constructive dismissal[3]. Employers are advised that fairness and transparency are promoted by developing and using proper procedures to help employers, employees and their representatives deal with disciplinary and grievance situations in the workplace[4], and an employee should have details regarding access to such a procedure included in the written particulars given to him on appointment[5].

If a grievance is raised relating to the performance of a duty by the employer and it is to lead to a grievance hearing[6], the employee has a statutory right, on a reasonable request, to be accompanied by a trade union official or a fellow worker[7].

1   As to the formation and form of contracts of employment see PARA 14 et seq.
2   *WA Goold (Pearmak) Ltd v McConnell* [1995] IRLR 516, EAT, which can be seen as putting on to a more generalised basis existing duties to take particular types of complaints seriously (see e g *British Aircraft Corpn Ltd v Austin* [1978] IRLR 332, EAT (complaints of health and safety breaches) (cited in PARA 36 note 9); *Bracebridge Engineering Ltd v Darby* [1990] IRLR 3, EAT (complaints of sexual harassment) (cited in PARA 48 note 17)).
3   As to constructive dismissal see PARA 763.
4   See the ACAS Code of Practice 1: Disciplinary and Grievance Procedures (2009) paras 1, 2; and PARA 702. Previously there was a statutory procedure that was a minimum requirement and could be supplemented by the employer's own regime so long as it was consistent with that requirement: see PARA 700.
5   See the Employment Rights Act 1996 s 3(1)(b), (c); and PARA 120.
6   As to the meaning of 'grievance hearing' see the Employment Relations Act 1999 s 13(5); and PARA 717 note 4.
7   See the Employment Relations Act 1999 s 10; and PARA 717.

50.   Implied term to provide a suitable working environment.   The implied term to take reasonable care for the employee's health and safety is well established and is considered elsewhere in this title[1]. This implied term is complemented by a wider obligation (which may be less dependent on the existence of a definable threat to health and safety) on an employer to provide and monitor for employees, as far as reasonably practicable, a working environment[2] which is reasonably suitable for the performance by them of their contractual duties[3].

1   See PARA 32 et seq.
2   The phrase 'working environment' is to be found in the general duties imposed on employers by the Health and Safety at Work etc Act 1974 s 2(2)(e) (see HEALTH AND SAFETY AT WORK vol 52 (2014) PARA 385) and in the Treaty on the Functioning of the European Union (Rome, 25 March 1957; TS 1 (1973); Cmnd 5179) ('TFEU') art 153 (which requires the European Union to support and complement the activities of member states in the field of (inter alia)

improvement of the working environment to protect workers' health and safety). The TFEU was formerly known as the Treaty Establishing the European Community (often abbreviated to TEC and also known as the 'EC Treaty' or the Treaty of Rome) and was renamed by the Treaty of Lisbon Amending the Treaty Establishing the European Union and the Treaty Establishing the European Community (Lisbon, 13 December 2007, ECS 13 (2007); Cm 7294) (often referred to as the 'Lisbon Treaty') which came into force on 1 December 2009: see CONSTITUTIONAL AND ADMINISTRATIVE LAW vol 20 (2014) PARA 25 et seq. The provisions of the TEC were renumbered by virtue of the Treaty of Amsterdam (see *Treaty Citation (No 2) (Note)* [1999] All ER (EC) 646, ECJ) and renumbered again by the Lisbon Treaty. Accordingly, art 153 TFEU was formerly known as art 137 TEC.

3 *Waltons & Morse v Dorrington* [1997] IRLR 488, EAT. In that case there was a failure to protect an employee from unwanted passive smoking (leading to a successful claim of constructive dismissal when she found conditions insufferable and left), but the implied term is cast in much more general terms and, in the absence of any further judicial authority, potentially open-ended.

H. EMPLOYER'S LIABILITIES

(A) Employer's Liability under the Equality Act 2010

51. Liability of employers under the Equality Act 2010. The Equality Act 2010 brings together previously-disparate elements of statutory law that dealt with discrimination[1] under a system that relies upon the key concepts of 'protected characteristics' (that is, age, disability, gender reassignment, marriage and civil partnership, race, religion or belief, sex and sexual orientation), and 'prohibited conduct' (that is, direct discrimination, discrimination arising from disability, indirect discrimination, harassment and victimisation)[2]. Although the scope of the Equality Act 2010 extends beyond work and employment, Part 5 of the Act deals specifically with those areas[3], and: (1) makes it unlawful to discriminate against, harass or victimise a person at work or in employment services[4]; and (2) contains provisions relating to equal pay between men and women, pregnancy and maternity pay, and making it unlawful for an employment contract to prevent an employee disclosing his or her pay (although regulations may require employers to publish information relating to the pay of employees for the purpose of showing whether, by reference to factors of such description as is prescribed, there are differences in the pay of male and female employees)[5].

1 Eg the Equal Pay Act 1970, the Sex Discrimination Act 1975, the Race Relations Act 1976, the Disability Discrimination Act 1995, the Employment Equality (Religion and Belief) Regulations 2003, SI 2003/1660, the Employment Equality (Sexual Orientation) Regulations 2003, SI 2003/1661, and the Employment Equality (Age) Regulations 2006, SI 2006/1031: see DISCRIMINATION vol 33 (2013) PARA 1 et seq.

2 See the Equality Act 2010 Pt 2 (ss 4–27, Sch 1); and DISCRIMINATION vol 33 (2013) PARAS 48–77. Part 8 (ss 108–112) prohibits other forms of conduct, including discriminating against or harassing an ex-employee or ex-pupil, instructing a third party to discriminate against another, or helping someone to discriminate against another: see DISCRIMINATION vol 33 (2013) PARAS 67, 74, 76, 77, 114, 227, 338. Part 14 (ss 191–197), Schs 22, 23 establishes exceptions to the prohibitions in the earlier parts of the 2010 Act in relation to a range of conduct: see DISCRIMINATION vol 33 (2013) PARAS 98, 307–321. Marriage of same sex couples is lawful in the law of England and Wales, and such marriages have the same effect as marriages of opposite sex couples: see the Marriage (Same Sex Couples) Act 2013 s 1(1), 11(1); and MATRIMONIAL AND CIVIL PARTNERSHIP LAW vol 72 (2009) PARA 1 et seq.

3 See the Equality Act 2010 Pt 5 (ss 39–83, Schs 6–9); and DISCRIMINATION vol 33 (2013) PARA 110 et seq. For the purposes of the Equality Act 2010, 'employment' is defined as 'employment under a contract of service, a contract of apprenticeship, or a contract personally to execute any work or labour' and includes Crown employment and employment as a relevant member of the House of Commons staff, or of the House of Lords staff: see s 83(2); and DISCRIMINATION vol 33 (2013) PARA 110.

4   See the Equality Act 2010 Pt 5 Ch 1 (ss 39–60, Sch 6); and DISCRIMINATION vol 33 (2013) PARA 110 et seq. As to an employer's vicarious liability under the 2010 Act see PARA 52. As to protected disclosures see also PARA 68.
5   See the Equality Act 2010 Pt 5 Ch 3 (ss 64–80, Sch 7); and DISCRIMINATION vol 33 (2013) PARA 130 et seq.

(B) Employer's Vicarious Liability for Employee's Actions

52.   Employer's vicarious liability for the acts of employees carried out in the course of employment.   The important issue of whether an employer can be made liable for an employee's acts that are carried out in the course of his employment is covered elsewhere in this work[1]. For the purposes of the Equality Act 2010, anything done by a person in the course of his employment is treated as also done by the employer[2].

1   See eg CRIMINAL LAW vol 25 (2010) PARA 58 et seq; NEGLIGENCE vol 78 (2010) PARA 16; SHIPPING AND MARITIME LAW vol 94 (2008) PARA 809; TORT vol 97 (2010) PARAS 506, 681, 693, 702, 712. See also PARA 53 et seq.
2   See the Equality Act 2010 Pt 8 (ss 108–112); and DISCRIMINATION vol 33 (2013) PARA 114.

(C) Employer's Liability to Third Persons made on Contracts

53.   Employer's liability on contract made by employee under express authority.   Where an employee, acting under his employer's express instructions[1], enters into a contract with a third person the employer is liable to the third person on the contract provided the employee, in making the contract, has strictly observed the tenor of his instructions[2]. If, therefore, without his employer's knowledge, the employee departs from his instructions[3] and makes a contract different from that which he was in fact authorised to make, the employer is not liable merely because of the existence of the original authority[4]. Thus, an employee who is authorised to buy goods on behalf of his employer must, in the absence of circumstances pointing to a contrary conclusion[5], buy them for cash[6]; he cannot, therefore, unless authorised to do so, render the employer liable to pay for them by buying them on credit[7]. Even the fact that the employer takes the benefit of his employee's contract does not necessarily impose any liability on the employer under it, since he may be unaware that the contract, the benefit of which he takes, differs in its terms from the contract which he authorised[8]. If, therefore, he has arranged that the employee is to pay for the goods himself[9], or if he has given the employee the money to pay for them[10], the employee's failure to pay for the goods in accordance with his instructions does not of itself render the employer liable, even though the goods are in fact used for the employer's purposes[11]. Where, however, the contract is capable of severance, the employer remains liable to the extent to which the contract, as actually made, is in accordance with his instructions, though his liability extends no further[12].

1   An act done under express instructions must be distinguished from an act done within the scope of the employee's general authority: see AGENCY vol 1 (2008) PARA 30.
2   *Metcalfe v Lumsden* (1844) 1 Car & Kir 309; *Helyear v Hawke* (1803) 5 Esp 72; cf *Hambro v Burnand* [1904] 2 KB 10, CA; *Gretton v Mees* (1878) 7 ChD 839. See generally AGENCY vol 1 (2008) PARA 121 et seq.
3   *Collen v Gardner* (1856) 21 Beav 540.
4   *Acey v Fernie* (1840) 7 M & W 151. An employer who employs an illiterate employee to enter into a contract which necessarily involves the signing of a written document will be bound by what the employee signs: see *Forenian v Great Western Rly Co* (1878) 38 LT 851.
5   *Maunder v Conyers* (1817) 2 Stark 281; *Summers v Solomon* (1857) 7 E & B 879.

6   *Wright v Glyn* [1902] 1 KB 745, CA; *Rusby v Scarlett* (1803) 5 Esp 76; *Stubbing v Heintz* (1791) Peake 47.

7   *Maunder v Conyers* (1817) 2 Stark 281; *Stubbing v Heintz* (1791) Peake 47; *Pearce v Rogers* (1800) 3 Esp 214. The same principle applies when the employee is authorised to sell goods on his employer's behalf (*Kaye v Brett* (1850) 5 Exch 269; *Curlewis v Birkbeck* (1863) 3 F & F 894; *Howard v Chapman* (1831) 4 C & P 508); or to receive payment (*Thorold v Smith* (1706) 11 Mod Rep 87; cf *Barrett v Deere* (1828) Mood & M 200; *Williams v Goodwin* (1826) 2 C & P 257). An employee who is authorised to receive payment by cheque may take a cheque payable to himself, provided that it is honoured: *Walker v Barker* (1900) 16 TLR 393; cf *Hogarth v Wherley* (1875) LR 10 CP 630. Tender of payment to an employee, although he has orders not to accept, has been held to be sufficient (*Moffat v Parsons* (1814) 5 Taunt 307); but where the employee at the time of tender disclaims authority to accept it has been held to be insufficient: *Bingham v Allport* (1833) 2 LJQB 86; see also *Finch v Boning* (1879) 4 CPD 143.

8   If, however, the employer takes the benefit of his employee's contract with knowledge of the facts, his conduct amounts to a ratification of the contract as made: *Bristowe v Whitmore* (1861) 9 HL Cas 391.

9   *Wright v Glyn* [1902] 1 KB 745, CA, commenting on *Precious v Abel* (1795) 1 Esp 350, and *Rimell v Sampayo* (1824) 1 C & P 254.

10 *Rusby v Scarlett* (1803) 5 Esp 76; *Miller v Hamilton* (1832) 5 C & P 433. It is otherwise, however, where the employer authorises the employee to buy on credit and the employee misappropriates the money which the employer afterwards gives him to pay with: *Rusby v Scarlett* (1803) 5 Esp 76.

11 *Stubbing v Heintz* (1791) Peake 47; *Maunder v Conyers* (1817) 2 Stark 281; *Pearce v Rogers* (1800) 3 Esp 214.

12 *Hunter v Countess Dowager of Berkeley* (1836) 7 C & P 413, where the defendant was also held entitled to set off a previous payment made under a contract which had been varied without her knowledge; cf *Marchioness of Bute v Mason, ex p Heard* (1849) 7 Moo PCC 1.

54.   Whether authority to bind employer can be implied. The employer is not, in principle, liable on contracts entered into by his employee without express authority, since the relation of employer and employee does not in itself confer on the employee an implied authority to bind his employer[1]. An authority to bind the employer may, however, be implied from the circumstances of the particular case, and the employer is then liable notwithstanding that the employee disobeyed his instructions[2].

Where the employer is aware that the employee is making a particular contract on his behalf and does not interfere, he is precluded from afterwards denying that the employee had no authority to make the contract in question, since he has by his conduct held out his employee to the person with whom the contract is made as having authority to make it[3].

1   *Hiscox v Greenwood* (1802) 4 Esp 174; *Maunder v Conyers* (1817) 2 Stark 281; *Waters v Brogden* (1827) 1 Y & J 457. The employer is not in any event liable if the third person looked exclusively to the employee: *Williamson v Barton* (1862) 7 H & N 899. As to acts within the apparent scope of the employee's authority, see PARAS 57–59.

2   See *Heatons Transport (St Helens) Ltd v Transport and General Workers' Union* [1973] AC 15 at 78, [1972] 3 All ER 101, HL. See also AGENCY vol 1 (2008) PARA 37. No authority to pledge the employer's credit is to be implied from the mere necessity of the case: see *Hawtayne v Bourne* (1841) 7 M & W 595, where money was borrowed for the purpose of preventing a distress; and AGENCY vol 1 (2008) PARA 37. As to the position where money borrowed has been applied for the employer's benefit, see *Bannatyne v MacIver* [1906] 1 KB 103, CA; and AGENCY vol 1 (2008) PARA 124.

3   See AGENCY vol 1 (2008) PARA 25. As to estoppel by conduct see ESTOPPEL vol 47 (2014) PARA 361 et seq.

55.   Employer's liability on unauthorised contract that is afterwards ratified. Where an unauthorised contract made by an employee is afterwards ratified by the employer with knowledge of its terms, he is liable on it[1]. He cannot, after ratification, rely either upon the defence that the employee had no authority to contract on his behalf[2], or on the defence that the employee departed from his instructions and made a contract differing from that which he was authorised to make[3].

If an employee, authorised to buy goods on the employer's behalf, buys them, in excess of his authority, on credit, the employer's retention of the goods in ignorance of the fact that his credit was pledged cannot be treated as a ratification[4], but where the employer has cause to suspect the employee's honesty and has refrained from making full inquiry he must be presumed to have ratified the employee's dishonest acts[5].

1   *Bristowe v Whitmore* (1861) 9 HL Cas 391. He may also enforce it: *Foster v Bates* (1843) 12 M & W 226. As to ratification generally, see AGENCY vol 1 (2008) PARA 57 et seq.
2   Cf *Bird v Brown* (1880) 4 Exch 786.
3   Cf *Bristowe v Whitmore* (1861) 9 HL Cas 391.
4   *Wright v Glyn* [1902] 1 KB 745, CA; *Rusby v Scarlett* (1803) 5 Esp 76; *Stubbing v Heintz* (1791) Peake 47; *Maunder v Conyers* (1817) 2 Stark 281; *Pearce v Rogers* (1800) 3 Esp 214.
5   *Morison v London County and Westminster Bank Ltd* [1914] 3 KB 356, CA.

56.   Employer's conduct amounting to representation that employee has authority to bind.   Where an employer from time to time allows his employee to make contracts of a particular class on his behalf without express authority, or ratifies them when made, without notifying the person with whom they were made of the fact that they were made without authority, the employer's conduct may amount to a representation to that person that the employee has authority to make contracts of that class on the employer's behalf[1].

1   *Hazard v Treadwell* (1722) 1 Stra 506; *Todd v Robinson* (1825) Ry & M 217; cf *Spooner v Browning* [1898] 1 QB 528, CA (where it was held on the facts that there had been no holding out by the employer); *Farquharson Bros & Co v G King & Co* [1902] AC 325, HL; and see AGENCY vol 1 (2008) PARA 25. As to estoppel by conduct see ESTOPPEL vol 47 (2014) PARA 361 et seq.

57.   Employer's liability on contract within apparent scope of employee's authority: general.   Where an employee, while acting in the ordinary course of his employment on his employer's behalf, makes a contract which falls within the apparent scope of his authority, the employer cannot escape liability on the ground that he did not authorise the making of the contract[1], nor even on the ground that he forbade his employer to make it[2]. All persons dealing with the employee are entitled to assume, unless they have notice to the contrary[3], that he possesses the authority which it is usual for an employee in his position to possess[4], and his employer, by placing him in that position, impliedly holds him out as having such authority[5]. Where it is sought on this ground to fix the employer with liability on his employee's contract it is necessary to take into consideration certain matters, namely the nature of the contract, the circumstances of the employee's employment, and the nature of the employer's business[6].

1   *Heatons Transport (St Helens) Ltd v Transport and General Workers' Union* [1973] AC 15 at 78, [1972] 3 All ER 101, HL; see also *Richardson v Cartwright* (1844) 1 Car & Kir 328; *Nickson v Brohan* (1712) 10 Mod Rep 109; *Smith v Hull Glass Co* (1852) 11 CB 897; *Smith v M'Guire* (1858) 3 H & N 554 at 562 (principal liable for contracts of general agent though agent exceeds instructions).
2   *Edmunds v Bushell and Jones* (1865) LR 1 QB 97 (principal employed agent to carry on business; business carried on in agent's name; agent forbidden by principal to accept bills of exchange; principal liable on bill accepted by agent); *Page v Great Northern Rly Co* (1868) IR 2 CL 228 (cattle booked by railway company's clerk before their delivery in company's yard, although clerk had express instructions not to book cattle before delivery; company liable for

delay in forwarding cattle despite irregularity of clerk in booking them); cf *Montaignac v Shitta* (1890) 15 App Cas 357, PC (where the authority was only to be exercised in certain circumstances); *Heatons Transport (St Helens) Ltd v Transport and General Workers' Union* [1973] AC 15 at 78, [1972] 3 All ER 101, HL; and see AGENCY vol 1 (2008) PARA 37.

3   *Jordan v Norton* (1838) 4 M & W 155; cf *International Sponge Importers Ltd v Andrew Watt & Sons* [1911] AC 279, HL.

4   *Watteau v Fenwick* [1893] 1 QB 346; *Richardson v Cartwright* (1844) 1 Car & Kir 328; *Smith v Hull Glass Co* (1852) 11 CB 897; *Howard v Sheward* (1866) LR 2 CP 148; cf *Barrett v Deere* (1828) Mood & M 200.

5   *Miller v Hamilton* (1832) 5 C & P 433; *Brooks v Hassall* (1883) 49 LT 569 (cf *Brady v Todd* (1861) 9 CBNS 592); *Real and Personal Advance Co v Phalempin* (1893) 9 TLR 569, CA.

6   See PARAS 58, 59.

58.   Employer's liability on contract within apparent scope of employee's authority: nature of contract and circumstances of employment. In order for a contract to fall within the apparent scope of an employee's authority[1], the contract must be one whose making is incidental to the duties which the employee is employed to perform[2]. The same tests are to be applied as for the purpose of determining the responsibility of a principal for the acts of his agent, although the tests might produce different results in the case of an employee[3].

The implied authority of an employee must, as a matter of course, vary according to the nature of his employment, and need not necessarily include an authority to contract at all. Employees are of different grades, and the authority to be implied in the case of one may be more extensive than in the case of another holding a more subordinate position[4]. The employee may be employed to perform a particular duty only, in which case he has no general authority to bind his employer by contract[5]. If the making of a particular class of contracts is incidental to the duty which he is employed to perform, any contract of that class will bind his employer on the ground that an authority to make it is to be implied from the nature of his employment[6]. Where, however, the contract belongs to a different class, the employer is not liable, since his employee is no longer acting in the course of his employment; and has therefore no implied authority to make it[7]. If, on the other hand, the employee is given a general authority to conduct his employer's business, his authority is wider in its scope, and the employer will be liable on all contracts made by the employee in the ordinary course of business[8].

1   As to the principle that an employer is liable on a contract within the apparent scope of his employee's authority see PARA 57.

2   *Richardson v Cartwright* (1844) 1 Car & Kir 328; *Graves v Masters (1883)* Cab & El 73; *Smith v Hull Glass Co* (1852) 11 CB 897; *Real and Personal Advance Co v Phalempin* (1893) 9 TLR 569, CA; cf *Sanderson v Bell* (1833) 2 Cr & M 304; *Lucas v Mason* (1875) LR 10 Exch 251.

3   *Heatons Transport (St Helens) Ltd v Transport and General Workers' Union* [1973] AC 15 at 78, [1972] 3 All ER 101, HL; and see AGENCY vol 1 (2008) PARA 37.

4   Contrast *Walker v Great Western Rly Co* (1867) LR 2 Exch 228, with *Cox v Midland Counties Rly Co* (1849) 3 Exch 268; and cf *Langan v Great Western Rly Co* (1873) 30 LT 173, Ex Ch; and see *Leckenby v Wolman* [1921] WN 100, where a salesman, employed at £3 per week plus 1 1/4 % commission on sales effected by him, was held not to be authorised to cancel sales made by him on behalf of his employer.

5   *Cox v Midland Counties Rly Co* (1849) 3 Exch 268; see also *Houghton v Pilkington* [1912] 3 KB 308, DC.

6   *Richardson v Cartwright* (1844) 1 Car & Kir 328. The fact that the employer has previously ratified similar contracts made by employees holding similar positions to that of the employee in question is evidence of the employee's authority: *Cox v Midland Counties Rly Co* (1849) 3 Exch 268; cf *Thorold v Smith* (1706) 11 Mod Rep 87.

7   *Hawtayne v Bourne* (1841) 7 M & W 595; *Linford v Provincial Horse and Cattle Insurance Co* (1864) 34 Beav 291; *Reynolds v Jex* (1865) 7 B & S 86; *A-G v Jackson* (1846) 5 Hare 355; *Re Southport and West Lancashire Banking Co* (1885) 1 TLR 204, CA; *Re Cunningham*

& Co Ltd, Simpson's Claim (1887) 36 ChD 532; cf *A-G v Briggs, A-G v Birmingham and Oxford Junction Rly Co* (1855) 1 Jur NS 1084.

8   *Fenn v Harnson* (1790) 3 Term Rep 757 at 760; *East India Co v Hensley* (1794) 1 Esp 111; *Walker v Great Western Rly Co* (1867) LR 2 Exch 228; *Smith v Hull Glass Co* (1852) 11 CB 897; *Myers v Willis* (1856) 18 CB 886, Ex Ch; *Summers v Solomon* (1857) 7 E & B 879; *Totterdell v Fareham Blue Brick and Tile Co Ltd* (1866) LR 1 CP 674; *Sandeman v Scurr* (1866) LR 2 QB 86; *Geake v Jackson* (1867) 36 LJCP 108; *Beer v London and Paris Hotel Co* (1875) LR 20 Eq 412; *Watteau v Fenwick* [1893] 1 QB 346 (cf *Daun v Simmins* (1879) 41 LT 783, CA, where the employee's authority was limited by usage).

59.   Employer's liability on contract within apparent scope of employee's authority: nature of employer's business.

In determining whether a contract falls within the apparent scope of the employee's authority[1], the employer's business must also be taken into consideration, since all employees employed to perform the same duty do not necessarily possess the same implied authority. Thus, an employee who is employed to sell goods on behalf of his employer has no implied authority to give a warranty if his employer is a private person[2], although if his employer is a dealer a warranty given by his employee will bind the employer, even though given contrary to his express instructions[3]. Where, however, the employer carries on a particular business, it is to be presumed that his employees possess the authority usually possessed by other employees in a similar position in the same kind of business[4].

1   As to the principle that an employer is liable on a contract within the apparent scope of his employee's authority see PARA 57.
2   *Brady v Todd* (1861) 9 CBNS 592; cf *Helyear v Hawke* (1803) 5 Esp 72, where the employee's authority extended to giving a warranty; see also *Miller v Lawton* (1864) 15 CBNS 834.
3   *Howard v Sheward* (1866) LR 2 CP 148. See also *Curtis v Chemical Cleaning and Dyeing Co* [1951] 1 KB 805, [1951] 1 All ER 631, CA.
4   See *Cox v Midland Counties Rly Co* (1849) 3 Exch 268; cf *Reynolds v Jex* (1865) 7 B & S 86.

60.   Employer's liability after notice of determination of authority.

Where an employee has been authorised to enter into contracts on his employer's behalf, the employer may be liable on contracts made by his employee with persons with whom he has been dealing on his employer's behalf, even after his employment has ended or the authority has been otherwise withdrawn[1]. The employer will continue to incur such liability until those persons have received notice[2] that the authority has been withdrawn[3]. It is immaterial whether the original authority was express[4], or whether it was to be implied from the employee's employment[5], or from the employer's conduct[6].

1   See AGENCY vol 1 (2008) PARA 192.
2   It may not be sufficient to give notice to an employee of a person with whom the employee has dealt on behalf of his employer: *Gratland v Freeman* (1800) 3 Esp 85. It may, however, be inferred from circumstances such as the lapse of time, or the failure to send in accounts to the employer, that such person is aware of the revocation of authority: *Stavely v Uzielli* (1860) 2 F & F 30.
3   *Aste v Montague* (1858) 1 F & F 264; cf *Anon v Harrison* (1699) 12 Mod Rep 346.
4   *Curlewis v Birkbeck* (1863) 3 F & F 894.
5   *Aste v Montague* (1858) 1 F & F 264.
6   *Stavely v Uzielli* (1860) 2 F & F 30; *Summers v Solomon* (1857) 7 E & B 879.

61.   Corporations.

Where the employer is a corporation aggregate[1], the identification of the employer with the acts of the employee is much closer than where the employer is an individual, since the corporation is incapable of doing any act itself but must necessarily avail itself of the services of others[2]. The liability of the corporation is nevertheless governed by the same general principles as in the case of an individual[3].

There is a common law rule that no employee can, even with express authority, bind a corporation to an act which is *ultra vires* the corporation[4]. Thus, where the employee of a corporation created by statute enters into a contract which is not expressly or impliedly authorised by its constitution, the corporation is not bound[5], even by a subsequent ratification[6]. This rule is, however, subject to the statutory exception in favour of a person dealing with a company in good faith, where the power of the directors to bind the company, or authorise others to do so, is deemed to be free of any limitation under the company's constitution[7].

1   As to the position of corporations generally see CORPORATIONS.
2   *Mersey Docks and Harbour Board Trustees v Gibbs* (1866) LR 1 HL 93 at 104, per Blackburn J.
3   See PARA 53 et seq.
4   *Montreal Assurance Co v M'Gillivray* (1859) 13 Moo PCC 87; and see further CORPORATIONS vol 24 (2010) PARA 478. As to the liability of a corporation for the torts of its employees see TORT vol 97 (2010) PARA 426.
5   *Directors of Shewsbury and Birmingham Rly Co v Directors of North-Western Rly Co* (1857) 6 HL Cas 113, approving *South Yorkshire Rly & River Dun Co v Great Northern Rly* (1853) 9 Exch 55 at 84, per Parke B; *Baroness Wenlock v River Dee Co* (1885) 10 App Cas 354, HL.
6   *Ashbury Railway Carriage and Iron Co v Riche* (1875) LR 7 HL 653; applied in *Baroness Wenlock v River Dee Co* (1885) 10 App Cas 354. HL.
7   See the Companies Act 2006 s 40; and COMPANIES vol 14 (2009) PARA 263.

62.   Liability of trustees and personal representatives for employees' acts.

Private trustees, personal representatives and other persons in a fiduciary position who are obliged, for the due performance of their duties, to engage employees, are liable personally for their employees' acts[1] done in the course of their employment and within the scope of their authority[2]. They are, however, entitled to be indemnified out of the trust estate, whether their liability is founded on contract[3] or on tort[4], provided the liability was incurred in the reasonable and proper management of the estate. Any third person who has succeeded in establishing the liability of a personal representative or trustee for any act done by his employee is subrogated to the right of indemnity of the representative or trustee, and may claim direct against the trust estate, whether he has recovered judgment against the personal representative or trustee in contract[5] or in tort[6].

1   As to statutory powers conferred on trustees and personal representatives to employ agents without being responsible for the default of the agents if employed in good faith see TRUSTS AND POWERS vol 98 (2013) PARA 439; and WILLS AND INTESTACY vol 103 (2010) PARA 1048.
2   As to the meanings of 'course of employment' and 'scope of authority' see TORT vol 97 (2010) PARAS 691–692. Cf *Brazier v Camp* (1894) 63 LJQB 257, CA.
3   *Farhall v Farhall* (1871) 7 Ch App 123. They may be entitled to be indemnified personally by the beneficiary if the trust estate is insufficient (*Matthews v Ruggles-Brise* [1911] 1 Ch 194, applying *Jervis v Wolferstan* (1874) LR 18 Eq 18 at 24, per Jessel MR; *Fraser v Murdoch* (1881) 6 App Cas 855 at 872, HL, per Lord Blackburn, and *Hardoon v Belilios* [1901] AC 118 at 123, PC); but this principle does not apply to a receiver and manager appointed by the court, who can look to the assets under the control of the court only (*Boehm v Goodall* [1911] 1 Ch 155). See RECEIVERS vol 88 (2012) PARA 194.
4   *Benett v Wyndham* (1862) 4 De GF & J 259.
5   *Dowse v Gorton* [1891] AC 190, HL; *Re Blundell, Blundell v Blundell* (1890) 44 ChD 1, CA; *Flower v Prechtel* (1934) 150 LT 491, CA; cf *Re Richardson, ex p Governors of St Thomas's Hospital* [1911] 2 KB 705, CA.
6   *Re Raybould, Raybould v Turner* [1900] 1 Ch 199; and see *Flower v Prechtel* (1934) 150 LT 491, CA.

(iv) Employee's Obligations

63.   Obedience to lawful orders.   An employee is under an obligation to carry out lawful orders from the employer, that is to say orders which are within the scope of the contract of employment[1]. There is, however, an implied obligation on the employer not to give the employee orders which are illegal or, in some cases, dangerous[2]; and an employee cannot lawfully be ordered to work beyond his contract (or to vary it, against his consent, in order to cover new duties) and insistence on such an order could found a claim of constructive dismissal[3].

Breach of the obligation to carry out a lawful order may mean that the employee may be lawfully dismissed at common law[4]; and such a dismissal will also *prima facie* be fair dismissal, as being for misconduct[5].

1   In deciding what is within the scope of the contract, assistance may be obtained from the job title given to the employee's work in the contract of employment or in the written statement of terms and conditions of employment: see PARA 118 et seq. As to the formation and form of contracts of employment see PARA 14 et seq.
2   See PARA 31.
3   As to constructive dismissal see PARA 763. Unfair pressure to change terms of employment could constitute a breach of the implied term of trust and respect: see PARA 48. In a case of a necessary business reorganisation, the employer may, however, argue that, although the order to alter the relevant contractual term was unlawful at common law, the reorganisation was so necessary that a dismissal for refusal to change, actual or constructive, was fair on the facts: see PARA 802. Thus the fact that the employee was in the right contractually will not necessarily mean that a dismissal is unfair: *Farrant v Woodroffe School* [1998] ICR 184, [1998] IRLR 176, EAT.
4   If the refusal to obey is serious enough to constitute gross misconduct, the employee may be dismissed summarily: see PARAS 743–746.
5   See PARAS 776–779. In order to be fair, however, the dismissal must also satisfy the general test in the Employment Rights Act 1996 s 98(4) (determination of question whether the dismissal is fair or unfair having regard to the reason shown by the employer: see PARA 765 et seq). If the employee's disobedience is not serious enough to warrant summary dismissal, it may warrant the giving of warnings under the employer's disciplinary procedure: see PARAS 707, 777.

64.   Extent of employee's requirement to adapt to new methods and techniques.   If an employer wishes to introduce new methods or techniques that are so different from what has happened previously that they would alter fundamentally the nature of the job that the employee is contracted to do, their introduction would constitute a variation of contract which, on ordinary principles, would require the consent of the employee[1].

An employee does not, however, have a vested right to preserve his working obligations completely unchanged as from the moment he first begins work, but is expected to adapt himself to new methods and techniques introduced in the course of his employment[2].

1   See PARAS 113, 121. If the employee refuses, and the employer dismisses him because of that refusal, the employer may try to establish that that dismissal was fair on the grounds of changing business needs or genuine reorganisation: see PARA 802.
2   *Cresswell v Board of Inland Revenue* [1984] 2 All ER 713, [1984] ICR 508 (civil servants required to change to computerised system which altered the methodology required to do the same job; although the content of some of the jobs might be affected considerably, it would not be altered so as to fall outside the original description of the employees' proper functions). 'Of course, in a proper case the employer must provide any necessary training or retraining ... It will, in all cases, be a question of pure fact as to whether the retraining involved the acquisition of such esoteric skills that it would not be reasonable to expect the employee to acquire them': *Cresswell v Board of Inland Revenue* at 721 and 519, obiter, per Walton J. This would be particularly important if, following the change, the employee were dismissed for incapability: see PARA 773.
    See also *Woods v WM Car Services (Peterborough) Ltd* [1982] ICR 693 at 702–703, [1982] IRLR 413 at 416, CA, per Watkins LJ ('The obdurate refusal of the appellant to accept

conditions very properly and sensibly being sought to be imposed upon her was unreasonable. Employers must not, in my opinion, be put in a position where, through the wrongful refusal of their employees to accept change, they are prevented from introducing improved business methods in furtherance of seeking success for their enterprise'); *Glitz v Watford Electric Co Ltd* [1979] IRLR 89 at 91, EAT, obiter, per Arnold J ('[It is] all the more necessary, where one is dealing with a small unit, where the job description tends to be wide precisely because to run a small unit one has to have flexibility, that it should be pointed out to employees, if it is not apparent that they understand this, either specifically or by means of some general hand-out or otherwise, that the ambit of the obligation in the contract of employment may very well be wider than the particular duties upon which the person is normally engaged'). Redundancy law has long been interpreted as not putting undue restraints on business innovation and change: see *Johnson v Nottinghamshire Combined Police Authority* [1974] 1 All ER 1082, [1974] ICR 170, CA; *Lesney Products & Co Ltd v Nolan* [1977] ICR 235, [1977] IRLR 77, CA; and PARA 870 note 9.

If the employee refuses to adapt where that is required of him and refuses to operate the new methods, the employer may lawfully refuse to pay some or all of his wages: see PARA 29.

65. Duty of care in the workplace. If an employee is engaged on the footing that he is skilled to perform certain duties, it is an implied term of the contract of employment that he will perform his duties with reasonable care[1]. If the employee commits a breach of this implied duty of care, and if the employer thereby suffers damage, the employer is entitled to recover damages from the employee, unless it is shown that the damage is too remote or that there is some other intervening factor which precludes recovery on general grounds[2]. If, as a result of the employee's breach of his implied duty of care, the employer becomes liable in damages to a third party, including the employee's fellow employee[3], injured by the employee's negligence, the employer is in general entitled to recover the amount of the damages from the employee in a claim for breach of contract[4]; but this right may not apply if:

(1)   at the time when the employee's alleged breach of his duty of care took place the employee was being employed on duties other than those in which he professed to be skilled at the time of his engagement[5]; or

(2)   he was required by his employer to perform an unlawful act[6]; or

(3)   the negligence of the employer or of some other and senior employee of the employer has contributed to the damage[7].

Even if there is no claim by the employer against the employee on a contractual basis because of the application of one of the above exceptions, the employer may, however, still seek, as an alternative, to recover the damages he has had to pay, in whole or in part, under the statutory provisions relating to contribution or indemnity between joint tortfeasors[8].

It is the statutory duty of every employee while at work[9]:

(a)   to take reasonable care for the health and safety of himself and others who may be affected by his acts or omissions at work[10]; and

(b)   as regards any duty or requirement imposed on his employer or any other person by or under any of the relevant statutory provisions[11], to co-operate with him so far as is necessary to enable that duty or requirement to be performed or complied with[12].

No person may intentionally or recklessly interfere with or misuse anything provided in the interest of health, safety or welfare in pursuance of any of the relevant statutory provisions[13].

1   *Lister v Romford Ice and Cold Storage Co Ltd* [1957] AC 555 at 572–573, [1957] 1 All ER 125 at 130, HL, per Viscount Simonds, citing *Harmer v Cornelius* (1858) 5 CBNS 236 at 246 per Willes J. The implied term extends only to those duties in which the employee professes, expressly or implicitly, to be skilled when he enters the contract of employment: *Harvey v RG O'Dell Ltd* [1958] 2 QB 78 at 105, [1958] 1 All ER 657 at 667 per McNair J.

2   *Lister v Romford Ice and Cold Storage Co Ltd* [1957] AC 555 at 573, [1957] 1 All ER 125 at 131, HL, per Viscount Simonds; and see eg *Lewson v Kirk* (1610) Cro Jac 265; *Hussy v Pacy* (1666) 1 Lev 188; *Stumore, Weston & Co v Breen* (1886) 12 App Cas 698, HL.

3   The doctrine of common employment which used to prevent an action against the employer in such circumstances (see *Priestley v Fowler* (1837) 3 M & W 1) was abolished by the Law Reform (Personal Injuries) Act 1948 s 1 (see NEGLIGENCE vol 78 (2010) PARA 74).

4   *Semtex Ltd v Gladstone* [1954] 2 All ER 206, [1954] 1 WLR 945; *Lister v Romford Ice and Cold Storage Co Ltd* [1957] AC 555, [1957] 1 All ER 125, HL (motor accident cases involving injury to the negligent employee's fellow workmen). In practice, such a claim is highly unusual, since the damages are usually paid by the employer's insurers (who are thereby subrogated into the employer's place) and insurers have a gentlemen's agreement *inter se* not to exercise these rights in most cases against negligent employees. In *Morris v Ford Motor Co Ltd* [1973] QB 792, [1973] 2 All ER 1084, CA, a party who was neither the employer nor an insurer sought to exercise a right of subrogation in order to recover damages from a negligent employee; the claim failed, but only because of the absence of an express subrogation clause, and the case does not limit the employer's theoretical rights under *Lister v Romford Ice and Cold Storage Co Ltd*.

5   *Harvey v RG O'Dell Ltd* [1958] 2 QB 78 at 105, [1958] 1 All ER 657 at 667 per McNair J (storekeeper acting as driver).

6   See *Gregory v Ford* [1951] 1 All ER 121 (employee required to drive vehicle not covered by a policy of third party insurance entitled to indemnity from employer). As to the employer's duty not to give illegal orders see PARA 31. Although it is an implied term of a driver's contract of employment that the employer will comply with the statutory obligations to insure, there is no implied term either that the employee is to be indemnified by his employers against claims in respect of negligent acts done in the course of his employment, or that he is entitled to the benefit of any contract of insurance effected by his employer: *Semtex Ltd v Gladstone* [1954] 2 All ER 206, [1954] 1 WLR 945; *Lister v Romford Ice and Cold Storage Co Ltd* [1957] AC 555, [1957] 1 All ER 125, HL.

7   *Jones v Manchester Corpn* [1952] 2 QB 852, [1952] 2 All ER 125, CA. This exception is based on the old common law rule that there was no contribution between joint tortfeasors in a case where each party bore some share of the responsibility (*Merryweather v Nixan* (1799) 8 Term Rep 186; *Adamson v Jarvis* (1827) 4 Bing 66; *Pearson v Skelton* (1836) 1 M & W 504).

8   See the Civil Liability (Contribution) Act 1978 s 1; and DAMAGES vol 12(1) (Reissue) PARA 837 et seq; TORT vol 97 (2010) PARA 450 et seq. Complete indemnities were awarded against employees on this ground in *Ryan v Fildes* [1938] 3 All ER 517; *Semtex Ltd v Gladstone* [1954] 2 All ER 206, [1954] 1 WLR 945; *Harvey v RG O'Dell Ltd* [1958] 2 QB 78, [1958] 1 All ER 657; *Lister v Romford Ice and Cold Storage Co Ltd* [1957] AC 555, [1957] 1 All ER 125, HL (all decided under the Law Reform (Married Women and Tortfeasors) Act 1935 s 6(1)(c) (repealed)).

9   See the Health and Safety at Work etc Act 1974 s 7; and HEALTH AND SAFETY AT WORK vol 52 (2014) PARA 410. As to the meanings of 'employee' and 'at work' for these purposes see PARA 34 note 3.

10 See the Health and Safety at Work etc Act 1974 s 7(a); and HEALTH AND SAFETY AT WORK vol 52 (2014) PARA 410.

11 As to the meaning of 'relevant statutory provisions' for these purposes see HEALTH AND SAFETY AT WORK vol 52 (2014) PARA 302.

12 See the Health and Safety at Work etc Act 1974 s 7(b); and HEALTH AND SAFETY AT WORK vol 52 (2014) PARA 410.

13 See the Health and Safety at Work etc Act 1974 s 8; and HEALTH AND SAFETY AT WORK vol 52 (2014) PARA 410.

66. Employee's duty not to disrupt the operation of the employer's business.

Although in general an employee may lawfully perform only those duties which are covered by his contract of employment and refuse to do more, difficult questions may arise if employees collectively decide, as part of industrial action, to perform duties in a way causing loss or disruption to their employer (as, for example, by way of a go-slow, work-to-rule or withdrawal of goodwill)[1]. This may be viewed as being in breach of an implied term. The employee's duty has been variously expressed, but at the least may be expressed as an obligation not to act in such a way as to disrupt the operation of the employer's business[2]. Where an employee has discretion in the way that he works, such disruption may also be viewed as breach of an implied term of fidelity, in that the discretion must be exercised to further the employer's interests, not so as to frustrate or hinder them (for example, as part of industrial action)[3].

Breach of such an implied term may entitle the employer to damages or may (more realistically) justify the employer in withholding pay until proper performance of the contract is resumed[4]. On a collective level, the question whether such conduct is in breach of contract is, in modern employment law, less likely to be of practical significance, since, in the case of an individual claim for unfair dismissal arising out of industrial action, the relevant statutory provisions[5] determining whether a former employee may bring proceedings in such a case cover both strike action and other industrial action; and it is well established that collective action can constitute the latter, whether or not it is technically in breach of contract[6].

1   As to the employee's right to take industrial action see PARA 1339 et seq.
2   *Secretary of State for Employment v Associated Society of Locomotive Engineers and Firemen (No 2)* [1972] 2 QB 455 at 491–492, [1972] 2 All ER 949 at 966–967, CA, per Lord Denning MR (in this case, an instruction to 'work to rule' was held to be a breach of an implied condition of employees' contracts because: (1) an employee must not wilfully obstruct his employer's business (at 491 and 967 per Lord Denning MR); (2) it involved breaches by employees of an implied term in the contract to serve the employer faithfully within the requirements of the contract (at 498 and 971–972 per Buckley LJ); (3) it involved breaches by employees of an implied term of the contract not to seek to obey lawful instructions so wholly unreasonably as to disrupt the efficient running of the system in which they were employed (at 508 and 980 per Roskill LJ)).
3   *British Telecommunications plc v Ticehurst* [1992] ICR 383, sub nom *Ticehurst and Thompson v British Telecommunications plc* [1992] IRLR 219, CA. As to the duty of good faith during employment see PARA 67; and as to the (lesser) duty of continuing good faith after the termination of employment see PARA 71.
4   See PARA 29. A deduction from wages on the basis of the employee's participation in a strike or other industrial action is not subject to the normal statutory requirements relating to the making of deductions: see the Employment Rights Act 1996 s 14(5); and PARA 256.
5   Ie the Trade Union and Labour Relations (Consolidation) Act 1992 ss 237, 238: see PARAS 1350–1351.
6   *Power Packing Casemakers Ltd v Faust* [1983] QB 471, [1983] 2 All ER 166, [1983] ICR 292, [1983] IRLR 117, CA; and see PARA 1351. As to legal action by an employer against a trade union at the collective level see PARA 1387 et seq.

67.   Duty of good faith during employment.   Although an employee does not, merely by reason of his role as an employee, assume fiduciary obligations to his employer, the employee is under an implied duty of good faith and fidelity during the currency of his employment[1], with the extent of that duty varying according to the nature of the contract[2]. The contract of employment is not a contract *uberrimae fidei*[3] but there may be a duty to disclose:

(1)   matters within the employee's knowledge which affect the confidential interests of the employer[4];

(2)   the employee's own misconduct which has been fraudulently concealed[5]; and

(3)   the misconduct of other employees, especially if the employee in question has responsibility for those others, even if that means the employee of necessity disclosing his own misconduct[6].

An employee must not make secret profits[7]; and, if he is found doing so, he may be made to account to the employer for them[8].

Although in general an employee's skills and spare time are his own, there may be cases where a court will restrain an employee from competing with his employer, or otherwise acting outside his employment, during the course of that employment if such activities can be shown to be harming the employer's business[9]. It will be a breach of the duty of good faith for an employee to canvass, during employment, his employer's customers to induce them to become his customers after the employment has terminated[10]. Improper competition by the employee may be a good ground for dismissal[11], however, as may solicitation of the employer's customers[12]; although merely planning during employment to leave to work for a competitor or to set up in competition, in the absence of improper conduct, will probably not be a fair reason for dismissal[13].

In the absence of an express term, there is a general implied term not to misuse confidential information belonging to the employer during the currency of the employment[14]. It is likely to be a breach of this implied duty if the employee during the employment, for use after the termination of the employment, makes or copies a list of the employer's customers or deliberately memorises such a list[15]. If an employee misuses confidential information during employment, that may be a good ground for dismissal[16]. However, as an exception to the general rule, there may be cases where the employee will not be in breach of the implied duty by disclosing confidential information because that disclosure is in the public interest and/or is permitted by statute[17].

In some cases[18], evidence of disclosure has been obtained by the employer by the use of a search order[19]; but such orders should be made only sparingly in this context[20]. The authorities indicate that the preferable course to take for an employer who is concerned about an employee leaving and commencing work for a competitor, and who wishes to ensure that the employee is not able to put himself in a position to misuse confidential information, is to make the employee subject to an express restraint of trade clause (which, if valid, is a more certain and enforceable option than reliance on the (lesser) duty of continuing good faith after the termination of employment, which by its nature is narrower, more vague and more difficult to enforce)[21]. Where, however, an employer can establish that future or further serious economic loss may be incurred by him on account of former staff members taking an unfair advantage of serious breaches of their contract of employment (or, if they are acting in concert with others, of any breach by any of those others), the employer may apply for an injunction on the basis of 'springboard relief'[22]. Nevertheless, direct liability can arise only if the defendant has knowledge of the true facts; the principles of strict liability and vicarious liability have no application to the implied duty of confidentiality[23].

1   An employee must not place himself in a position in which his acts or interests conflict with his duties as an employee: *Lacy v Osbaldiston* (1837) 8 C & P 80; *Pearce v Foster* (1886) 17 QBD 536, CA; *Boston Deep Sea Fishing and Ice Co v Ansell* (1888) 39 ChD 339, CA; *Eccles & Co v Louisville and Nashville Railroad Co* [1912] 1 KB 135, CA. As to the (lesser) duty of continuing good faith after the termination of employment see PARA 71.

     There may be an equivalent implied duty of confidentiality on the employer in relation to information about employees which is not in the public domain: see *Dalgleish v Lothian and Borders Police Board* [1991] IRLR 422, Ct of Sess (employers restrained from giving personal details of employees to local authority for purpose of community charge collection).

2   *Faccenda Chicken Ltd v Fowler, Fowler v Faccenda Chicken Ltd* [1987] Ch 117, [1986] ICR 297, CA. See also *Nottingham University v Fishel* [2000] ICR 1462, [2000] IRLR 471 (in determining whether a fiduciary relationship arises in the context of an employment relationship, it is necessary to identify with care the particular duties undertaken by the employee, and to ask whether in all the circumstances he has placed himself in a position where he must act solely in the interest of his employer); *Helmet Integrated Systems Ltd v Tunnard* [2006] EWCA Civ 1735, [2007] IRLR 126; *Ranson v Customer Systems plc* [2012] EWCA Civ 841, [2012] IRLR 769. Fiduciary obligations may lie more naturally and more heavily on directors of a company (and downwards to senior board level), requiring e g enhanced duties of disclosure: see note 3.

3   Ie so that an employee need not volunteer information about his own misdeeds: see *Bell v Lever Bros Ltd* [1932] AC 161, HL; *Nottingham University v Fishel* [2000] ICR 1462, [2000] IRLR 471 (by accepting work for embryologists and directing them abroad for his own financial gain, employee had breached his specific fiduciary duty to direct embryologists to work in the university's interests). If an employee commits fraud in order to obtain employment, that will usually be a fair ground for dismissal, however: *Birmingham City District Council v Beyer* [1978] 1 All ER 910, [1977] IRLR 211, EAT. As to the position in relation to spent convictions see PARA 779. As to criminal record certificates see the Police Act 1997 Pt V (ss 112–127); and SENTENCING AND DISPOSITION OF OFFENDERS vol 92 (2010) PARA 711 et seq.

The Companies Act 2006, in setting out general duties that are owed to the company, provides that a director of a company must act in the way he considers, in good faith, would be most likely to promote the success of the company for the benefit of its members as a whole: see the Companies Act 2006 s 172; and COMPANIES vol 14 (2009) PARA 544. This duty may require a director (as opposed to an employee) to disclose his own misconduct to his principal (or, more generally, information of relevance and concern to his principal) in order for the duty to be satisfied: *Item Software (UK) Ltd v Fassihi* [2004] EWCA Civ 1244, [2005] ICR 450, [2004] IRLR 928 (director obliged to disclose secret approach to client). As to a director's higher fiduciary duty see also *Cook v Deeks* [1916] 1 AC 554, PC; *Cranleigh Precision Engineering Ltd v Bryant* [1964] 3 All ER 289, [1965] 1 WLR 1293; *Industrial Development Consultants Ltd v Cooley* [1972] 2 All ER 162, [1972] 1 WLR 443; *Thomas Marshall (Exports) Ltd v Guinle* [1979] Ch 227, [1978] ICR 905. In relation to a director's duty to disclose his own misdeeds see *Regal (Hastings) Ltd v Gulliver* (1942) [1967] 2 AC 134n, [1942] 1 All ER 378, HL (employee who is a director of an employing company may have a fiduciary duty to disclose his own misdeeds in certain circumstances); *Horcal Ltd v Gatland* [1984] IRLR 288, CA; *Item Software (UK) Ltd v Fassihi*. A director with an interest in a contract with the company is in any case under a duty, again embodied in the Companies Act 2006, to disclose it to the board of directors, and non-disclosure may lead to a constructive trust to repay: see ss 182, 183, 185, 187 (formerly the Companies Act 1985 s 317); *Guinness plc v Saunders* [1988] 2 All ER 940, [1988] 1 WLR 863, CA (affd on other grounds [1990] 2 AC 663, [1990] 1 All ER 652, HL); and COMPANIES vol 14 (2009) PARA 560.

Although it is dangerous by analogy to introduce reasoning from cases about company directors to cases about employees generally (*Ranson v Customer Systems plc* [2012] EWCA Civ 841, [2012] IRLR 769), senior employees may have a positive obligation to disclose breaches of their fiduciary duty in the same way as company directors (see *Tesco Stores Ltd v Pook* [2003] EWHC 823 (Ch), [2004] IRLR 618). See also *QBE Management Services (UK) Ltd v Dymoke* [2012] EWHC 80 (QB), [2012] EWHC 116 (QB), [2012] IRLR 458 (there is a duty on directors and senior employees to disclose: (1) any action at all, if taken by others, that will lead to competitive activity; and (2) any action of their own, as soon as the irrevocable intention to compete is formed, unless they resign immediately).

4   *Cranleigh Precision Engineering Ltd v Bryant* [1964] 3 All ER 289, [1965] 1 WLR 1293. See also note 3. As to the position in relation to intellectual property rights arising in the course of employment see PARA 72.

5   *Sybron Corpn v Rochem Ltd* [1984] Ch 112, [1983] ICR 801, CA (employee had been party to fraudulent misconduct in conjunction with other employees subordinate to him). See also *IG Index plc v Colley* [2013] EWHC 478 (QB), [2013] All ER (D) 99 (Mar) (employee in breach of fiduciary duty by perpetrating fraud in spread betting transactions by acting in concert with clients); and see note 3.

6   *Sybron Corpn v Rochem Ltd* [1984] Ch 112, [1983] ICR 801, CA, applying *Swain v West (Butchers) Ltd* [1936] 3 All ER 261, CA. See also *Tesco Stores Ltd v Pook* [2003] EWHC 823 (Ch), [2004] IRLR 618 (absurd for senior employee to be under duty to disclose breaches by other employees but not his own); and see note 3.

7   *Boston Deep Sea Fishing and Ice Co v Ansell* (1888) 39 ChD 339, CA (employee was a managing director, but the principle holds good for ordinary employees); *Sinclair v Neighbour* [1967] 2 QB 279, [1966] 3 All ER 988, CA. See also *Cobbetts LLP v Hodge* [2009] EWHC 786 (Ch), [2010] 1 BCLC 30, [2009] All ER (D) 156 (Apr) ('employed partner' was held to have acquired shares in breach of his duty not to profit personally).

8   See *Reading v A-G* [1951] AC 507, [1951] 1 All ER 617, HL (soldier held accountable to Crown for money illegally received by him whilst ostensibly acting in military capacity); and RESTITUTION vol 88 (2012) PARA 555. Account of profits is a restitutionary remedy most often associated with the misuse of confidential information by a person who may be deprived of his profits for the benefit of the claimant: see CONFIDENCE AND INFORMATIONAL PRIVACY vol 19 (2011) PARA 89; and EQUITABLE JURISDICTION vol 47 (2014) PARA 235.

9   *Hivac Ltd v Park Royal Scientific Instruments Ltd* [1946] Ch 169, [1946] 1 All ER 350, CA; *Thomas Marshall (Exports) Ltd v Guinle* [1979] Ch 227, [1978] ICR 905. This implied duty not to compete does not, in the absence of a restraint of trade clause, apply after the termination of the employment: see PARA 71.

    As to whether an employer's business can be affected by comments made by an employee on a public forum about matters of public debate see *Smith v Trafford Housing Trust* [2012] EWHC 3221 (Ch), [2013] IRLR 86 (controversial but inoffensive postings about gay marriage in church made on Facebook wall at a weekend out of working hours by employee, a practising Christian and occasional lay preacher, did not bring and could not have brought the trust into disrepute).

10 *Wessex Dairies Ltd v Smith* [1935] 2 KB 80, CA; *Sanders v Parry* [1967] 2 All ER 803, [1967] 1 WLR 753. If, however, there is no such wrongdoing, an ex-employer cannot restrain competition by an ex-employee on these grounds: *JA Mont (UK) Ltd v Mills* [1993] IRLR 172, CA; *Wallace Bogan & Co v Cove* [1997] IRLR 453, CA. See also *Ranson v Customer Systems plc* [2012] EWCA Civ 841, [2012] IRLR 769 (in making preparations for the establishment of a competing business, which involved meeting with representatives of the employer's existing and potential clients before and during his notice period, employee had not breached any relevant fiduciary duty or contractual obligation of fidelity, duty of mutual trust and confidence, or duty to report; the main basis for determining whether such obligations arose was the contract of employment, which in this case did not include covenants restricting what employee could do after he had ceased to be employed by the employer, save for a prohibition from him taking employment with certain important customers).

11 *Gibson v National Union of Dyers, Bleachers and Textile Workers* (1972) 7 ITR 324; *Harris and Russell Ltd v Slingsby* [1973] 3 All ER 31, [1973] ICR 454, NIRC; *Golden Cross Hire Co Ltd v Lovell* [1979] IRLR 267, EAT; *Nova Plastics Ltd v Froggatt* [1982] IRLR 146, EAT.

12 *Hawkins v Prickett* [1976] IRLR 52.

13 *Harris and Russell Ltd v Slingsby* [1973] 3 All ER 31, [1973] ICR 454, NIRC; *Laughton v Bapp Industrial Supplies Ltd* [1986] ICR 634, [1986] IRLR 245, EAT. On the other hand (justifying dismissal) see *Marshall v Industrial Systems and Control Ltd* [1992] IRLR 294, EAT (managing director suborning employees and approaching customers before leaving); *Adamson v B & L Cleaning Services Ltd* [1995] IRLR 193, EAT (foreman putting in a tender in competition with employer before leaving to set up his own firm). See also *Ward Evans Financial Services Ltd v Fox* [2001] EWCA Civ 1243, [2002] IRLR 120, [2001] All ER (D) 415 (Jul) (clause in trust and confidence agreement prohibiting employees, during employment, from holding a material interest in a company which might impair their ability to act at all times in the employers' best interests, covered the formation, during employment, of a company which was dormant until after employment ended); *Helmet Integrated Systems Ltd v Tunnard* [2006] EWCA Civ 1735, [2007] IRLR 126 (employee entitled to prepare for future activities which he plans to undertake after leaving); *Foster Bryant Surveying Ltd v Bryant* [2007] EWCA Civ 200, [2007] IRLR 425, [2007] 2 BCLC 239 (no breach of fiduciary duty where director, who had been excluded from any role in company after his resignation, set up his own company during the notice period); and see *Thomson Ecology Ltd v APEM Ltd* [2013] EWHC 2875 (Ch), [2014] IRLR 184 (not consistent with employee's duty of fidelity to assist an actual or potential competitor to entice away staff, but his decision to notify other staff of his decision to join a competitor before he had told his employer was not necessarily a breach of the duty of fidelity because the context in which that information had been imparted to the other employee was likely to be determinative of the question whether or not a breach of duty had been involved).

    In *Cook v MSHK Ltd* [2009] EWCA Civ 624, [2009] IRLR 838, the employee went on sickness absence after he had arguably breached his duty of fidelity by agreeing to work for another company's dance music division which was in direct competition with his employer, but his employers were held to have affirmed the contract by their conduct in making it clear that they expected the employee to return to work and see out his contract to the bitter end before taking up his new employment.

14 *Bents Brewery Co Ltd v Luke Hogan* [1945] 2 All ER 570; *Faccenda Chicken Ltd v Fowler, Fowler v Faccenda Chicken Ltd* [1987] Ch 117, [1986] ICR 297, CA; *Robb v Green* [1895] 2 QB 315, CA; *Merryweather v Moore* [1892] 2 Ch 518; *Kirchner & Co v Gruban* [1909] 1 Ch 413; *Cranleigh Precision Engineering Ltd v Bryant* [1964] 3 All ER 289, [1965] 1 WLR 1293. This duty applies after the termination of employment, albeit in a modified form: see PARA 71. As to the implied or express duty of confidentiality owed by employees generally see CONFIDENCE AND INFORMATIONAL PRIVACY vol 19 (2011) PARA 23.

15 *Robb v Green* [1895] 2 QB 315, CA; *Faccenda Chicken Ltd v Fowler, Fowler v Faccenda Chicken Ltd* [1987] Ch 117, [1986] ICR 297, CA; *Roger Bullivant Ltd v Ellis* [1987] ICR 464, [1987] IRLR 491, CA.

16 *RS Components Ltd v Irwin* [1974] 1 All ER 41, [1973] ICR 535, NIRC; *Foot v Eastern Counties Timber Co Ltd* [1972] IRLR 83.

17 See PARA 68.

18 *Roger Bullivant Ltd v Ellis* [1987] ICR 464, [1987] IRLR 491, CA; *Johnson & Bloy (Holdings) Ltd and Johnson & Bloy Ltd v Wolstenholme Rink plc and Fallon* [1987] IRLR 499, CA; *Re a Company's Application* [1989] Ch 477, [1989] ICR 449.

19 As to search orders see CIVIL PROCEDURE vol 11 (2009) PARA 402 et seq.

20 *Lock International plc v Beswick* [1989] 3 All ER 373, [1989] IRLR 481.

21 See eg *Caterpillar Logistics Services (UK) Ltd v Huesca de Crean* [2012] EWCA Civ 156, [2012] 3 All ER 129, [2012] ICR 981, [2012] IRLR 410 ('barring out' relief (eg an injunction to prevent a leaver taking up new employment altogether, or requiring her not to undertake listed functions with the new employer) was not available for an alleged breach of the implied duty not to misuse confidential information, the employer being restricted to prior bargaining for an appropriate restrictive covenant, which is subject to definite restrictions relating to scope, timing and reasonableness). As to restraint of trade clauses see PARA 19; and COMPETITION vol 18 (2009) PARA 377 et seq. In the context of employers' confidences see also CONFIDENCE AND INFORMATIONAL PRIVACY vol 19 (2011) PARA 23. In some cases, a 'garden leave clause' may be a viable alternative: see PARAS 19, 734. As to the (lesser) duty of continuing good faith after the termination of employment see PARA 71.

22 As to the 'springboard' doctrine generally see CONFIDENCE AND INFORMATIONAL PRIVACY vol 19 (2011) PARA 63. In *UBS Wealth Management (UK) Ltd v Vestra Wealth LLP* [2008] EWHC 1974 (QB), [2008] IRLR 965, springboard relief was extended from restraining the misuse of confidential information acquired during the currency of former employment to protection afforded to a former employer against future and further losses caused eg by the poaching of staff. The legal requirements of a springboard injunction were considered further in *QBE Management Services (UK) Ltd v Dymoke* [2012] EWHC 80 (QB), [2012] EWHC 116 (QB), [2012] IRLR 458 (employees involved in numerous, repeated and continual breaches of their duties of fidelity and confidentiality, and other contractual duties, as part of a concerted and covert campaign with the illegitimate aim of acquiring part of their employer's people and business; attempts by senior employees to solicit more junior staff constituted particularly serious misconduct and the mere fact that activities were described by an employee as 'preparatory' to competition does not mean that they were legitimate).

23 *Vestergaard Frandsen A/S v Bestnet Europe Ltd* [2013] UKSC 31, [2013] 4 All ER 781, [2013] ICR 981, [2013] IRLR 654 (knowledge of true facts necessary for strict liability; secondary liability for participating in a 'common design' also requires full knowledge in the sense that each party must share in the design, although, once that is the case, an individual's participation can be variable in nature). Cf claims for breach of an existing obligation of confidence by disclosure or use of confidential information, where, if the obligation is equitable, even subconscious plagiarism may be sufficient for liability: see CONFIDENCE AND INFORMATIONAL PRIVACY vol 19 (2011) PARA 69.

68. Exceptions to the duty of confidentiality at common law; disclosure in the public interest and under statute. At common law, there has always been an ill-defined defence to an allegation of breach of the duty of confidentiality by an employee, where it can be said that disclosure of the information in question was in some sense in the public interest[1]. Originally, this was limited to the disclosure of criminal acts or a danger to the state[2], but later developments tended to expand the scope of the law beyond purely criminal acts or 'iniquity' by the employer[3]. It is recognised, however, that there is a difficult balance to be struck, with at least one pertinent warning that not everything that is interesting to the public may be disclosed in the public interest[4], and it may even be necessary to distinguish between different subject matters when deciding whether to make an order restraining disclosure[5].

Because of increasing concern about lack of protection for persons making *bona fide* disclosure (generally known as 'whistleblowers'), and the widespread use by employers of wide confidentiality or 'gagging' clauses, there is now special statutory protection for qualifying disclosures of information made by a worker[6] and protection from victimisation on such grounds[7], rendering any dismissal on such grounds automatically unfair[8]. The statutory regime under which a protected disclosure may be made does not, strictly speaking, govern the common law defence to an allegation of breach of the contractual duty of confidentiality[9]; rather, any provision in any agreement made between a worker and his employer is declared to be void in so far as it purports to preclude the worker from making a protected disclosure[10], and protection is afforded to the worker for any such disclosure that he or she may make so long as it falls within the provisions of the statutory disclosure regime[11]. Similar, but specific, provision is made in the Equality Act 2010 in relation to a 'relevant pay disclosure' (that is, a disclosure made for the purpose of enabling the person who makes it, or the person to whom it is made, to find out whether or to what extent there is, in relation to the work in question, a connection between pay and having, or not having, a particular protected characteristic)[12].

1   *Initial Services Ltd v Putterill* [1968] 1 QB 396, [1967] 3 All ER 145, CA; *Fraser v Evans* [1969] 1 QB 349, [1969] 1 All ER 8, CA; *Hubbard v Vosper* [1972] 2 QB 84, [1972] 1 All ER 1023, CA. See also *Tillery Valley Foods Ltd v Channel Four Television Corpn* [2004] EWHC 1075 (Ch), (2004) Times, 21 May (covert filming by journalist employed by food distributor; no requirement that owner of information be given right to reply). See further CONFIDENCE AND INFORMATIONAL PRIVACY vol 19 (2011) PARA 73.
2   *Weld-Blundell v Stephens* [1920] AC 956, HL.
3   *Lion Laboratories Ltd v Evans* [1985] QB 526, [1984] 2 All ER 417, CA, disapproving the narrower approach in *Beloff v Pressdram Ltd* [1973] 1 All ER 241.
4   *British Steel Corpn v Granada Television Ltd* [1981] AC 1096 at 1168, [1981] 1 All ER 417 at 455, HL, per Lord Wilberforce.
5   *Re a Company's Application* [1989] Ch 477, [1989] ICR 449 (order restraining certain disclosures, but not disclosure of irregularities to a regulatory body and the Inland Revenue).
6   See the Employment Rights Act 1996 Pt IVA (ss 43A–43L); and PARAS 69, 70. As to the meaning of 'worker' for these purposes see PARA 69 note 3; and as to the meaning of 'qualifying disclosure' see PARA 70.
7   See the Employment Rights Act 1996 s 47B; and PARA 619.
8   See the Employment Rights Act 1996 s 103A; and PARA 792. In such a case, there is no qualifying period of one year's employment (see s 108(2), (3)(ff); and PARA 758 note 9), and there is no statutory limit on the compensatory award (see s 124(1A); and PARA 823 note 6).
9   As to breach of an obligation of confidence generally see CONFIDENCE AND INFORMATIONAL PRIVACY vol 19 (2011) PARA 68 et seq; and as to defences particularly see CONFIDENCE AND INFORMATIONAL PRIVACY vol 19 (2011) PARA 73 et seq.
10 See the Employment Rights Act 1996 s 43J; and PARA 69.
11 As to the forms of making a protected disclosure see PARA 69; and as to the bases upon which a protected disclosure may be made see PARA 70.
12 See the Equality Act 2010 s 77; and DISCRIMINATION vol 33 (2013) PARA 142.

69.   Meaning of 'protected disclosure' made under statute. For the purposes of the statutory regime that protects certain disclosures of information under employment law[1], a 'protected disclosure' means a qualifying disclosure[2] which is made by a worker[3] in any of the following circumstances[4]:
  (1)   by the worker to his employer[5] (or, where the worker reasonably believes that the relevant failure[6] relates solely or mainly to the conduct of a person other than his employer, or to any other matter for which a person other than his employer has legal responsibility, to that other person)[7];
  (2)   in the course of obtaining legal advice[8];
  (3)   to a Minister of the Crown (where the worker's employer is an individual appointed under any enactment by a Minister of the Crown, or is a body any of whose members are so appointed)[9];

(4)   by a worker to a person prescribed by an order made by the Secretary of State for these purposes[10], where the worker reasonably believes that the relevant failure falls within any description of matters in respect of which that person is so prescribed, and reasonably believes that the information disclosed (and any allegation contained in it) are substantially true[11];

(5)   in other cases, if[12]:

   (a)   the worker reasonably believes that the information disclosed (and any allegation contained in it) are substantially true[13];

   (b)   he does not make the disclosure for purposes of personal gain[14];

   (c)   any of the prescribed conditions is met[15]; and

   (d)   in all the circumstances of the case, it is reasonable for him to make the disclosure[16];

(6)   if the relevant failure is of an exceptionally serious nature[17], and:

   (a)   the worker reasonably believes that the information disclosed (and any allegation contained in it) are substantially true[18];

   (b)   he does not make the disclosure for purposes of personal gain[19]; and

   (c)   in all the circumstances of the case, it is reasonable for him to make the disclosure[20].

Any provision in an agreement between a worker and his employer (whether a worker's contract or not)[21] is void in so far as it purports to preclude the worker from making a protected disclosure[22].

1   Ie for the purposes of the Employment Rights Act 1996 Pt IVA (ss 43A–43L) (see also PARA 70): see s 43A (ss 43A–43K, s 43L added by the Public Interest Disclosure Act 1998 s 1).

2   Ie as defined by the Employment Rights Act 1996 s 43B (see PARA 70): see s 43A (as added: see note 1). For the purposes of Pt IVA, 'qualifying disclosure' has the meaning given by s 43B: see s 43L(1) (as so added).

3   Ie made by a worker in accordance with any of the Employment Rights Act 1996 ss 43C–43H (see the text and notes 5–20): see s 43A (as added: see note 1). For the purposes of Pt IVA, 'worker' includes an individual who is not a worker as defined by s 230(3) (see PARA 5), but who:

   (1)   works or worked for a person in circumstances in which: (a) he is or was introduced or supplied to do that work by a third person; and (b) the terms on which he is or was engaged to do the work are or were in practice substantially determined not by him but by the person for whom he works or worked, by the third person or by both of them (s 43K(1)(a) (as so added));

   (2)   contracts or contracted with a person, for the purposes of that person's business, for the execution of work to be done in a place not under the control or management of that person and would not fall within s 230(3)(b) (see PARA 5) if the words '(whether personally or otherwise)' were substituted for 'personally' (s 43K(1)(b) (as so added));

   (3)   works or worked as a person performing services under a contract entered into by him with the National Health Service Commissioning Board under the National Health Service Act 2006 ss 83(2), 84, 92, 100, 107, 115(4), 117, 134, Sch 12 (see HEALTH SERVICES vol 54 (2008) PARA 241 et seq), or with a Local Health Board under the National Health Service (Wales) Act 2006 ss 41(2)(b), 42, 50, 57, 64, 92, Sch 7 (see HEALTH SERVICES vol 54 (2008) PARA 241 et seq) (Employment Rights Act 1996 s 43K(1)(ba) (s 43K as so added; s 43K(1)(ba) added by the Health and Social Care (Community Health and Standards) Act 2003 s 184, Sch 11 para 65(1), (2); and amended by the National Health Service (Consequential Provisions) Act 2006 s 2, Sch 1 paras 177, 178(a); the Health and Social Care Act 2012 s 55(2), Sch 5 paras 72, 73; the Enterprise and Regulatory Reform Act 2013 s 20(1), (2)));

   (4)   works or worked as a person providing services in accordance with arrangements made by the National Health Service Commissioning Board under the National Health Service Act 2006 s 126 or a Local Health Board under the National Health Service (Wales) Act 2006 s 71 or s 80 (see HEALTH SERVICES vol 54 (2008) PARAS 338, 339) (Employment Rights Act 1996 s 43K(1)(c) (s 43K as so added; s 43K(1)(c) amended by

the National Health Service Reform and Health Care Professions Act 2002 s 2(5), Sch 2 para 63; the National Health Service (Consequential Provisions) Act 2006 Sch 1 paras 177, 178(b); the Health and Social Care Act 2012 Sch 5 paras 72, 73; the Enterprise and Regulatory Reform Act 2013 s 20(1), (4); and SI 2007/961));

(5)   is or was provided with work experience provided pursuant to a training course or programme or with training for employment (or with both) otherwise than under a contract of employment or otherwise than by an educational establishment on a course run by that establishment (Employment Rights Act 1996 s 43K(1)(d) (as so added)),

and any reference to a worker's contract, to employment or to a worker being 'employed' is to be construed accordingly (see s 43K(1) (as so added)). 'Educational establishment' includes any university, college, school or other educational establishment: s 43K(3) (as so added). As to the meanings of 'employed', 'contract of employment', and related expressions in relation to employment rights generally, see PARA 2 et seq. In construing these provisions, it is relevant to have regard to the fact that s 43K was explicitly introduced for the purpose of providing protection to those who have made protected disclosures and it was appropriate to adopt a purposive construction, to provide protection rather than deny it, where one can properly do so: *Croke v Hydro Aluminium Worcester Ltd* [2007] ICR 1303, [2007] All ER (D) 71 (Apr), EAT (wording of 'the terms on which he is or was engaged to do the work' (see head (1)(b) above) does not imply a requirement for the existence of a contract; recruitment consultancy introduced individual to defendant as potential worker within meaning of the Employment Rights Act 1996 s 43K(1)(a) (see head (1)(a) above)); *Hinds v Keppel Seghers UK Ltd* [2014] IRLR 754, EAT (contractor engaged through intermediary company was 'sourced' as an individual meeting employer's specification and so was introduced as an individual for purposes of head (1)(a) above). The whole purpose of this statutory extension to the definition of 'worker' and 'employer' (see note 5) was to go beyond the normal contractual focus of those terms for statutory purposes in the employment field: see *Sharpe v Worcester Diocesan Board of Finance Ltd* [2014] ICR D9, EAT; *Hinds v Keppel Seghers UK Ltd* (tribunal was entitled to look at the various contracts relevant to the relationship and to see how these worked in practice).

The Secretary of State may by order make amendments to the Employment Rights Act 1996 s 43K as to what individuals count as 'workers' for the purposes of Pt IVA (despite not being within the definition in s 230(3)), but such an order may not make an amendment that has the effect of removing a category of individual unless the Secretary of State is satisfied that there are no longer any individuals in that category: see s 43K(4), (5) (s 43K as so added; s 43K(4), (5) added by the Enterprise and Regulatory Reform Act 2013 s 20(1), (7)). At the date at which this volume states the law, no such order had been made.

4   See the Employment Rights Act 1996 s 43A (as added: see note 1). In the Employment Rights Act 1996, except in so far as the context otherwise requires, 'protected disclosure' has the meaning given by s 43A: see s 235(1) (definition added by the Public Interest Disclosure Act 1998 ss 15(2), 18(2)).

5   For the purposes of the Employment Rights Act 1996 Pt IVA, 'employer' includes:

(1)   in relation to a worker falling within s 43K(1)(a) (see note 3), the person who substantially determines or determined the terms on which he is or was engaged (s 43K(2)(a) (as added: see note 1));

(2)   in relation to a worker falling within s 43K(1)(ba) (see note 3), the National Health Service Commissioning Board or the Local Health Board referred to therein (s 43K(2)(aa) (s 43K as so added; s 43K(2)(aa) added by the Health and Social Care (Community Health and Standards) Act 2003 Sch 11 para 65(1), (3); and amended by the Health and Social Care Act 2012 Sch 5 paras 72, 73));

(3)   in relation to a worker falling within the Employment Rights Act 1996 s 43K(1)(c) (see note 3), the authority or board referred to therein (s 43K(2)(b) (as so added)); and

(4)   in relation to a worker falling within 43K(1)(d) (see note 3), the person providing the work experience or training (s 43K(2)(d) (as so added)).

As to the meaning of 'employer' and related expressions in relation to employment rights generally see PARA 2 et seq. For the purposes of Pt IVA, s 47B (see PARA 619) (and s 48 (detriment (enforcement: complaint to employment tribunal): see PARA 625) and s 49 (detriment (enforcement: remedies): see PARA 626) so far as relating to s 47B), and s 103A (see PARA 792) (and the other provisions of Pt X (ss 94–134A) (unfair dismissal: see PARA 757 et seq) so far as relating to the right not to be unfairly dismissed in a case where the dismissal is unfair by virtue of s 103A), a person who holds (otherwise than under a contract of employment) the office of constable or an appointment as a police cadet is treated as an employee employed by the relevant officer under a contract of employment; and any reference to a worker being 'employed' and to his 'employer' is to be construed accordingly: see s 43KA(1) (s 43KA added by the Police Reform Act 2002 s 37(1)). As to the office of constable see POLICE AND

INVESTIGATORY POWERS vol 84 (2013) PARA 1 et seq; and as to police cadets see POLICE AND INVESTIGATORY POWERS vol 84 (2013) PARA 15 et seq. For this purpose, 'relevant officer' means:

  (a) in relation to a member of a police force or a special constable appointed for a police area, the chief officer of police (see POLICE AND INVESTIGATORY POWERS vol 84 (2013) PARA 112 et seq) (Employment Rights Act 1996 s 43KA(2)(a) (as so added));

  (b) in relation to a member of the police force seconded to the National Crime Agency to serve as a National Crime Agency officer, that Agency (s 43KA(2)(b) (s 43KA as so added; s 43KA(2)(b) substituted by the Serious Organised Crime and Police Act 2005 s 59, Sch 4 paras 84, 85; and amended by the Crime and Courts Act 2013 s 15(3), Sch 8 paras 49, 50));

  (c) in relation to any other person holding the office of constable or an appointment as police cadet, the person who has the direction and control of the body of constables or cadets in question (Employment Rights Act 1996 s 43KA(2)(d) (as so added)).

As to the National Crime Agency see POLICE AND INVESTIGATORY POWERS vol 84 (2013) PARA 424. The provisions of Pt IVA ought not to apply to a private conversation which is made in a confidential manner and does not involve the other party *qua* employer: *Douglas v Birmingham City Council* [2003] All ER (D) 329 (Jul), EAT (teacher spoke to fellow governor for advice regarding apparent lack of equal opportunities in the school).

 6 As to the meaning of 'relevant failure', in relation to a qualifying disclosure, see PARA 70 note 4.

 7 Employment Rights Act 1996 s 43C(1) (s 43C as added (see note 1); s 43C(1) amended by the Enterprise and Regulatory Reform Act 2013 s 18(1)(a)). A worker who, in accordance with a procedure whose use by him is authorised by his employer, makes a qualifying disclosure to a person other than his employer is to be treated as making the qualifying disclosure to his employer: Employment Rights Act 1996 s 43C(2) (as so added).

 8 Employment Rights Act 1996 s 43D (as added: see note 1). A disclosure of information in respect of which a claim to legal professional privilege could be maintained in legal proceedings is not a qualifying disclosure, however, if it is made by a person to whom the information had been disclosed in the course of obtaining legal advice: see s 43B(4); and PARA 70.

 9 See the Employment Rights Act 1996 s 43E (s 43E as added (see note 1); and amended by the Enterprise and Regulatory Reform Act 2013 s 18(1)(b)).

10 As to the making of orders under the Employment Rights Act 1996 generally see PARA 162. As to the Secretary of State see PARA 5 note 21.

11 See the Employment Rights Act 1996 s 43F(1) (s 43F as added (see note 1); s 43F(1) amended by the Enterprise and Regulatory Reform Act 2013 s 18(1)(c)). An order prescribing persons for the purposes of head (4) in the text may specify persons or descriptions of persons, and must specify the descriptions of matters in respect of which each person, or persons of each description, is or are prescribed: Employment Rights Act 1996 s 43F(2) (as so added). In exercise of the power so conferred, the Secretary of State has made the Public Interest Disclosure (Prescribed Persons) Order 1999, SI 1999/1549, which came into force on 2 July 1999: see art 1. Accordingly, in relation to a disclosure made after 1 October 2014, the persons and descriptions of persons and descriptions of matters prescribed for the purposes of the Employment Rights Act 1996 s 43F are those specified in the Public Interest Disclosure (Prescribed Persons) Order 2014, SI 2014/2418, art 3(1), (2) Schedule.

12 See the Employment Rights Act 1996 s 43G(1) (as added: see note 1). The provisions given in heads (5)(a) to (5)(d) in the text provide a collection of partially overlapping requirements, any one of which, if not fulfilled, will defeat a worker's right to maintain that his disclosure is 'protected': *Street v Derbyshire Unemployed Workers Centre* [2004] EWCA Civ 964, [2004] 4 All ER 839, [2005] ICR 97, [2004] IRLR 687. Where the motives for disclosure are mixed, the tribunal must look for the dominant purpose behind the making of the relevant disclosure: *Street v Derbyshire Unemployed Workers' Centre* (in considering good faith as distinct from reasonable belief, it is clearly open to a tribunal, satisfied as to the latter, to consider nevertheless whether the disclosure was made because of some ulterior motive which may or may not have made the disclosure unreasonable).

13 Employment Rights Act 1996 s 43G(1)(b) (s 43G as added (see note 1); s 43G(1)(b) amended by the Enterprise and Regulatory Reform Act 2013 s 18(2)).

14 Employment Rights Act 1996 s 43G(1)(c) (as added: see note 1). In determining for the purposes of Pt IVA whether a person makes a disclosure for purposes of personal gain, there is to be disregarded any reward payable by or under any enactment: s 43L(2) (as so added).

15 Employment Rights Act 1996 s 43G(1)(d) (as added: see note 1) The conditions prescribed as mentioned in the text are those set out in s 43G(2): see s 43G(1)(d) (as so added). Accordingly, the conditions so referred to are:

  (1) that, at the time he makes the disclosure, the worker reasonably believes that he will be

subjected to a detriment by his employer if he makes a disclosure to his employer or in accordance with s 43F (see head (4) in the text) (s 43G(2)(a) (as so added));

(2)   that, in a case where no person is prescribed for the purposes of s 43F in relation to the relevant failure, the worker reasonably believes that it is likely that evidence relating to the relevant failure will be concealed or destroyed if he makes a disclosure to his employer (s 43G(2)(b) (as so added)); or

(3)   that the worker has previously made a disclosure of substantially the same information either to his employer (s 43G(2)(c)(i) (as so added)); or in accordance with s 43F (s 43G(2)(c)(ii) (as so added)).

For these purposes, a subsequent disclosure may be regarded as a disclosure of substantially the same information as that disclosed by a previous disclosure as mentioned in head (3) above, even though the subsequent disclosure extends to information about action taken or not taken by any person as a result of the previous disclosure: s 43G(4) (as so added).

16   Employment Rights Act 1996 s 43G(1)(e) (as added: see note 1). In determining for the purposes of head (5)(d) in the text whether it is reasonable for the worker to make the disclosure, regard is to be had, in particular, to:

(1)   the identity of the person to whom the disclosure is made (s 43G(3)(a) (as so added));

(2)   the seriousness of the relevant failure (s 43G(3)(b) (as so added));

(3)   whether the relevant failure is continuing or is likely to occur in the future (s 43G(3)(c) (as so added));

(4)   whether the disclosure is made in breach of a duty of confidentiality owed by the employer to any other person (s 43G(3)(d) (as so added));

(5)   in a case falling within s 43G(2)(c)(i) (see note 15) or s 43G(2)(c)(ii) (see note 15), any action which the employer or the person to whom the previous disclosure in accordance with s 43F (see head (4) in the text) was made has taken or might reasonably be expected to have taken as a result of the previous disclosure (s 43G(3)(e) (as so added)); and

(6)   in a case falling within s 43G(2)(c)(i), whether, in making the disclosure to the employer, the worker complied with any procedure whose use by him was authorised by the employer (s 43G(3)(f) (as so added)).

As to breach of an obligation of confidence generally see CONFIDENCE AND INFORMATIONAL PRIVACY vol 19 (2011) PARA 68 et seq; and as to defences particularly see CONFIDENCE AND INFORMATIONAL PRIVACY vol 19 (2011) PARA 73 et seq.

17   See the Employment Rights Act 1996 s 43H(1)(d) (as added: see note 1).

18   Employment Rights Act 1996 s 43H(1)(b) (s 43H as added (see note 1); s 43H(1)(b) amended by the Enterprise and Regulatory Reform Act 2013 s 18(3)).

19   Employment Rights Act 1996 s 43H(1)(c) (as added: see note 1). See note 14.

20   Employment Rights Act 1996 s 43H(1)(e) (as added: see note 1). In determining for the purposes of head (6)(c) in the text whether it is reasonable for the worker to make the disclosure, regard is to be had, in particular, to the identity of the person to whom the disclosure is made: s 43H(2) (as so added).

21   Ie including an agreement to refrain from instituting or continuing any proceedings under the Employment Rights Act 1996 or any proceedings for breach of contract: see s 43J(2) (as added: see note 1).

22   See the Employment Rights Act 1996 s 43J(1), (2) (as added: see note 1).

70.   Meaning of 'qualifying disclosure' for purposes of protected disclosure made under statute.

For the purposes of the statutory regime that protects certain disclosures of information under employment law[1], a 'qualifying disclosure' means any disclosure of information[2] which, in the reasonable belief of the worker[3] making the disclosure, is made in the public interest and tends to show one or more of the following[4]:

(1)   that a criminal offence has been committed, is being committed, or is likely to be committed[5];

(2)   that a person has failed, is failing, or is likely to fail to comply with any legal obligation to which he is subject[6];

(3)   that a miscarriage of justice has occurred, is occurring, or is likely to occur[7];

(4)   that the health or safety of any individual has been, is being, or is likely to be endangered[8];

(5)   that the environment has been, is being, or is likely to be damaged[9]; or

(6)   that information tending to show any matter falling within heads (1) to (5) above has been, or is likely to be, deliberately concealed[10].

A disclosure of information is not a qualifying disclosure, however, if the person making it commits an offence by making it[11]; nor is a disclosure of information in respect of which a claim to legal professional privilege[12] could be maintained in legal proceedings a qualifying disclosure if it is made by a person to whom the information had been disclosed in the course of obtaining legal advice[13].

1   Ie for the purposes of the Employment Rights Act 1996 Pt IVA (ss 43A–43L) (see also PARA 69): see s 43B(1) (ss 43B, 43L added by the Public Interest Disclosure Act 1998 s 1).

2   For these purposes, any reference to the disclosure of information has effect, in relation to any case where the person receiving the information is already aware of it, as a reference to bringing the information to his attention: Employment Rights Act 1996 s 43L(3) (as added: see note 1). As to what constitutes 'disclosure' and 'information' for the purposes of s 43B(1) see *Cavendish Munro Professional Risks Management Ltd v Geduld* [2010] ICR 325, [2010] IRLR 38, EAT (an employee may be dissatisfied with the way he is being treated, and he or his solicitor may complain to the employer that if he is not going to be treated better, he will resign and claim constructive dismissal; however, if the employer then dismisses the employee, the dismissal does not follow from any disclosure of information for the purposes of the Employment Rights Act 1996 s 43B because it follows from a statement of the employee's position and even if such a letter conveyed 'information' for the purposes of the Act, it does not amount to a 'disclosure', and so it would not fall within the scope of s 43B); and *Shaw v Norbrook Laboratories (GB) Ltd* [2014] ICR 540, [2014] All ER (D) 139 (Mar), EAT (whilst two communications could, taken together, amount to a protected disclosure, whether they did so or not was a question of fact: where an employee had sent three emails to his employer expressing concerns about the danger posed to territory managers by driving in the snow to attend appointments, and sought guidance as well as enquired as to whether any company policy existed in relation to driving in snowy conditions, the tribunal had not erred in considering the three communications together in deciding whether the employee had made a disclosure which had amounted to a protected disclosure, notwithstanding that one email had been sent to a different individual in a different department from those sent prior to that).

3   As to the meaning of 'worker' for these purposes see PARA 69 note 3.

4   See the Employment Rights Act 1996 s 43B(1) (s 43B as added (see note 1); s 43B(1) amended by the Enterprise and Regulatory Reform Act 2013 s 17). For these purposes, it is immaterial whether the relevant failure occurred, occurs or would occur in the United Kingdom or elsewhere, and whether the law applying to it is that of the United Kingdom or of any other country or territory: Employment Rights Act 1996 s 43B(2) (as so added). As to the meaning of 'United Kingdom' see PARA 2 note 12. In relation to a qualifying disclosure, 'relevant failure' means the matter falling within s 43B(1)(a)–(f) (see heads (1)–(6) in the text): s 43B(5) (as so added). For the purposes of Pt IVA, the 'relevant failure', in relation to a qualifying disclosure, has the meaning given by s 43B(5): see s 43L(1) (as so added). The test to be applied when determining whether s 43B(1) applies in respect of a disclosure is whether the employee has a reasonable belief that a relevant failure has occurred: *Darnton v University of Surrey* [2003] ICR 615, [2003] IRLR 133, EAT. *Darnton v University of Surrey* was applied in *Muchesa v Central and Cecil Housing Care Support* [2008] All ER (D) 130 (Aug), EAT. See also *Evans v Bolton School* [2006] EWCA Civ 1653, [2007] ICR 641, sub nom *Bolton School v Evans* [2007] IRLR 140 (acts taken consequent to the disclosure are not part of it); and PARA 619 note 5. A reasonable belief may exist even if it later turns out to have been wrong: *Babula v Waltham Forest College* [2007] EWCA Civ 174, [2007] ICR 1026, [2007] IRLR 346 (overruling *Kraus v Penna plc* [2004] IRLR 260, [2003] All ER (D) 275 (Nov), EAT (see note 6) on this point). The requirement for a qualifying disclosure to be made in the public interest was added by the Enterprise and Regulatory Reform Act 2013 in order to reverse the decision in *Parkins v Sodexho Ltd* [2002] IRLR 109, EAT, to the extent that a legal obligation arising from a contract of employment was held to fall within the compass of 'any legal obligation to which he is subject' specified under head (2) in the text.

5   Employment Rights Act 1996 s 43B(1)(a) (as added: see note 1).

6   Employment Rights Act 1996 s 43B(1)(b) (as added: see note 1). As to the meaning of 'person' in head (2) in the text see *Hibbins v Hesters Way Neighbourhood Project* [2009] 1 All ER 949, [2009] ICR 319, EAT ('person' has a wide meaning and it was not to be limited to employers

but included all legal entities including a body of persons corporate or incorporate, the legislation being construed in light of its aim of encouraging whistle blowing).

The statutory test of 'likely to fail to comply' is not met by a belief that is limited to the possibility or the risk of a breach of a legal obligation: *Kraus v Penna plc* [2004] IRLR 260, [2003] All ER (D) 275 (Nov), EAT (employee informed a director of a company he was advising that proposed redundancies could breach employment legislation). A legal obligation which arises from a contract of employment may fall within the Employment Rights Act 1996 s 43B(1), but: (1) it must be shown that the breach of the employment contract was a breach of a legal obligation under that contact; (2) there must be a reasonable belief on the part of the employee that such a breach has, is or is likely to happen; and (3) there must be a disclosure of that which is alleged to be the reason for dismissal, that is to say, where there is a breach of contract, the reason for dismissal must be that the employee has complained that his employer has broken the contract of employment: *Parkins v Sodexho Ltd* [2002] IRLR 109, EAT (*quaere* whether this case is typical; the employee's complaint was framed in terms of a breach of health and safety constituting a breach of contract, thus evading limits placed on more direct routes of complaint regarding health and safety).

7   Employment Rights Act 1996 s 43B(1)(c) (as added: see note 1).
8   Employment Rights Act 1996 s 43B(1)(d) (as added: see note 1).
9   Employment Rights Act 1996 s 43B(1)(e) (as added: see note 1).
10 Employment Rights Act 1996 s 43B(1)(f) (as added: see note 1).
11 See the Employment Rights Act 1996 s 43B(3) (as added: see note 1). An example of such an offence as is mentioned in the text would be a contravention of the Official Secrets Acts 1911 to 1989: see CRIMINAL LAW vol 26 (2010) PARA 427 et seq.
12 As to legal professional privilege see CIVIL PROCEDURE vol 11 (2009) PARAS 558 et seq, 972; CRIMINAL PROCEDURE vol 28 (2010) PARA 506. See also LEGAL PROFESSIONS vol 65 (2008) PARAS 740–741; LEGAL PROFESSIONS vol 66 (2009) PARA 1146.
13 Employment Rights Act 1996 s 43B(4) (as added: see note 1).

71. Continuing duty of fidelity after termination of employment.

A former employee is entitled to make use of knowledge and skill acquired during the employment after its termination[1]; and he may set up in business in competition with his former employer, and use such knowledge and skill in the pursuit of that business[2]. If the employer wishes to prevent the employee from doing so, he may rely on an express restraint of trade clause[3]. However, even where such a clause is incorporated into the contract of employment, it will be valid only if reasonably necessary to protect the employer's trade secrets or customer connections; and such a clause will not be enforced if the employer's aim is merely to stifle *bona fide* competition by the former employee[4].

The implied duty not to misuse confidential information[5] survives the termination of employment, albeit in a restricted form[6]. The employer may be able to restrain misuse of such information by a former employee but only if the information is sufficiently confidential to amount to a trade secret[7], not if it is confidential only in the sense that unauthorised disclosure of it to a third party during employment would have been a breach of the duty of good faith[8].

1   *Printers and Finishers Ltd v Holloway* [1964] 3 All ER 731, [1965] 1 WLR 1; *United Sterling Corpn Ltd v Felton and Mannion* [1973] FSR 409, [1974] IRLR 314.The contract of employment is not a contract *uberrimae fidei* but an employee is under an implied duty of good faith and fidelity during the currency of his employment (a duty which is nevertheless stronger than the duty that applies after termination) with the extent of that duty varying according to the nature of the contract: see PARA 67.
2   *Attwood v Lamont* [1920] 3 KB 571, CA; *United Indigo Chemical Co Ltd v Robinson* (1931) 49 RPC 178; *Louis v Smellie* (1895) 73 LT 226 at 228, CA, per Lindley LJ; *Wallace Bogan & Co v Cove* [1997] IRLR 453, CA.
3   As to covenants in restraint of trade see PARA 19; and COMPETITION vol 18 (2009) PARA 377 et seq. See also e g *Caterpillar Logistics Services (UK) Ltd v Huesca de Crean* [2012] EWCA Civ 156, [2012] 3 All ER 129, [2012] ICR 981, [2012] IRLR 410; and note 8.
4   *Herbert Morris Ltd v Saxelby* [1916] 1 AC 688, HL; *Faccenda Chicken Ltd v Fowler, Fowler v Faccenda Chicken Ltd* [1987] Ch 117, [1986] ICR 297, CA.

5   See PARA 67.

6   See CONFIDENCE AND INFORMATIONAL PRIVACY vol 19 (2011) PARA 23. In the exceptional case
    of former employees of the intelligence and security services, the duty of confidentiality is a
    life-long duty, given statutory force by the Official Secrets Acts 1911 to 1989: see CRIMINAL LAW
    vol 26 (2010) PARA 427 et seq. A breach of that duty may also form the basis of a civil remedy:
    see *A-G v Blake (Jonathan Cape Ltd third party)* [2001] 1 AC 268, [2000] 4 All ER 385, HL
    (where, exceptionally, the court required the defendant to account for the benefits he had
    received from breach of an express contractual undertaking to the Crown not to divulge any
    confidential information during his period of service or after his employment had ceased);
    CONFIDENCE AND INFORMATIONAL PRIVACY vol 19 (2011) PARA 89; and EQUITABLE
    JURISDICTION vol 47 (2014) PARAS 14, 235.

7   See eg *PSM International plc v Whitehouse* [1992] IRLR 279, [1992] FSR 489, CA. As to
    matters to be considered when deciding what is a trade secret see *Faccenda Chicken Ltd v
    Fowler, Fowler v Faccenda Chicken Ltd* [1987] Ch 117 at 137–138, [1986] 1 All ER 617 at
    626–627, CA, per Neill LJ.

8   *Faccenda Chicken Ltd v Fowler, Fowler v Faccenda Chicken Ltd* [1987] Ch 117, [1986] ICR
    297, CA; *Johnson & Bloy (Holdings) Ltd and Johnson & Bloy Ltd v Wolstenholme Rink plc
    and Fallon* [1987] IRLR 499, CA; *Brooks v Olyslager OMS (UK) Ltd* [1998] IRLR 590, CA;
    cf *Roger Bullivant Ltd v Ellis* [1987] ICR 464, [1987] IRLR 491, CA. The employee may not
    take away from employment with him confidential documents (eg lists of customers) or copies
    of them, or commit such things to memory: see *Robb v Green* [1895] 2 QB 315, CA; *Sanders v
    Parry* [1967] 2 All ER 803, [1967] 1 WLR 753; *Roger Bullivant Ltd v Ellis*; and PARA 67.
    Although the existence of documents or copies may be important evidence for the employer,
    each case depends on its facts, and there is no rule that an employee is entitled to take away and
    use anything that is in his head when he leaves the employment: *Johnson & Bloy (Holdings) Ltd
    and Johnson & Bloy Ltd v Wolstendholme Rink plc and Fallon* above, disapproving dicta of
    Scott J in *Balston Ltd v Headline Fitters Ltd* [1987] FSR 330. See also *AT Poeton (Gloucester
    Plating) Ltd v Horton* [2000] ICR 1208, CA (information acquired by employee as part of
    general knowledge without any deliberate memorisation); *SBJ Stephenson Ltd v Mandy* [2000]
    IRLR 233 (the distinction between information learned with deliberate intent to misuse and that
    innocently carried in the employee's head is not determinative of protection afforded to
    information; the true distinction was drawn in *Herbert Morris Ltd v Saxelby* [1916] 1 AC
    688, HL, between 'objective' knowledge, which is the property of the employer, and 'subjective'
    knowledge, which is the employee's own property). See also *Crowson Fabrics Ltd v Rider*
    [2007] EWHC 2942 (Ch), [2008] IRLR 288 (much of information used improper but not
    confidential). As to the use of search orders in this context see PARA 67. Rather than relying on
    'barring out' relief (eg an injunction to prevent a leaver taking up new employment altogether
    from fear of the ex-employee breaching the implied duty not to misuse confidential information
    in a new employment) the courts tend to restrict employers to prior bargaining for an
    appropriate restrictive covenant to be included in the contract of employment, which the parties
    negotiate at arm's length: see eg *Caterpillar Logistics Services (UK) Ltd v Huesca de Crean*
    [2012] EWCA Civ 156, [2012] 3 All ER 129, [2012] ICR 981, [2012] IRLR 410; and the text
    and note 3.

72.   Intellectual property rights.   If an employee made an invention or
discovery in the course of his employment before 1 June 1978, he is normally, by
virtue of an implied term in his contract of employment, a trustee of that
invention or discovery for his employer and is obliged to communicate it to his
employer[1].

Notwithstanding anything in any rule of law, an invention made by an
employee after 31 May 1978 is to be taken, as between him and his employer, to
belong[2] to his employer if:

(1)   it was made in the course of the normal duties of the employee or in the
        course of duties falling outside his normal duties, but specifically
        assigned to him, and the circumstances in either case were such that an
        invention might reasonably be expected to result from the carrying out
        of his duties[3]; or

(2)   the invention was made in the course of the duties of the employee and,
        at the time of making the invention, because of the nature of his duties

and the particular responsibilities arising from the nature of his duties, he had a special obligation to further the interests of the employer's undertaking[4].

Any other invention made by an employee is to be taken, as between him and his employer, to belong[5] to the employee[6].

Where an invention so belongs, as between him and his employer, to an employee, nothing done:

(a)   by or on behalf of the employee or any person claiming under him for the purposes of pursuing an application for a patent; or

(b)   by any person for the purpose of performing or working the invention,

is to be taken to infringe the copyright or design right to which, as between him and his employer, his employer is entitled in any model or document relating to the invention[7].

Where a literary, dramatic, musical or artistic work or a film made on or after 1 July 1994 is made by an employee in the course of his employment, his employer is the first owner of any copyright in the work, subject to any agreement to the contrary[8].

Where, in the case of a design not created in pursuance of a commission, a design is created by an employee in the course of his employment, his employer is the first owner of any design right in the design[9].

Where a database is made by an employee in the course of his employment, his employer is to be regarded as the maker of the database, subject to any agreement to the contrary[10].

1   *Triplex Safety Glass Co v Scorah* [1938] Ch 211, [1937] 4 All ER 693; *British Celanese Ltd v Moncrieff* [1948] Ch 564, [1948] 2 All ER 44, CA; *Sterling Engineering Co Ltd v Patchett* [1955] AC 534, [1955] 1 All ER 369, HL; *British Syphon Co Ltd v Homewood* [1956] 2 All ER 897, [1956] 1 WLR 1190.

2   Ie for the purposes of the Patents Act 1977 and all other purposes (see PATENTS AND REGISTERED DESIGNS vol 79 (2014) PARA 301 et seq): see s 39(1)(a); and PATENTS AND REGISTERED DESIGNS vol 79 (2014) PARA 368.

3   See the Patents Act 1977 s 39(1)(a); and PATENTS AND REGISTERED DESIGNS vol 79 (2014) PARA 368. The duty of fidelity which an employee owes to his employer does not assist in the formulation of the actual duties which he was employed to do; and the wording 'an invention might reasonably be expected to result from the carrying out of his duties' must refer to an invention which achieves or contributes to achieving whatever was the aim or object to which the employee's efforts in carrying out his duties were directed: *Reiss Engineering Co Ltd v Harris* [1985] IRLR 232, EAT. Extra or different duties undertaken are not to be regarded only as duties 'specifically assigned' as it is possible for them to become 'normal' in the course of time under the Patents Act 1977 s 39(1): *LIFFE Administration and Management v Pinkava* [2007] EWCA Civ 217, [2007] 4 All ER 981, [2007] ICR 1489.

4   See the Patents Act 1977 s 39(1)(b); and PATENTS AND REGISTERED DESIGNS vol 79 (2014) PARA 368. As to the cases in which s 39 does not apply see PATENTS AND REGISTERED DESIGNS vol 79 (2014) PARA 368. As to compensation of employees for certain inventions see ss 40, 41; and PATENTS AND REGISTERED DESIGNS vol 79 (2014) PARAS 369–370. As to the enforceability of contracts relating to employees' inventions see s 42; and PATENTS AND REGISTERED DESIGNS vol 79 (2014) PARA 368.

5   Ie for the purposes of the Patents Act 1977 and all other purposes (see PATENTS AND REGISTERED DESIGNS vol 79 (2014) PARA 301 et seq): see s 39(2); and PATENTS AND REGISTERED DESIGNS vol 79 (2014) PARA 368.

6   See the Patents Act 1977 s 39(2); and PATENTS AND REGISTERED DESIGNS vol 79 (2014) PARA 368. As to the law protecting trade marks and trade names see TRADE MARKS AND TRADE NAMES vol 97A (2014) PARA 1 et seq.

7   See the Patents Act 1977 s 39(3); and PATENTS AND REGISTERED DESIGNS vol 79 (2014) PARA 368.

8   See the Copyright, Designs and Patents Act 1988 s 11(2); and COPYRIGHT vol 23 (2013) PARA 716. The Copyright, Designs and Patents Act 1988 s 11 does not apply to Crown copyright (see COPYRIGHT vol 23 (2013) PARA 738 et seq) or Parliamentary copyright (see COPYRIGHT vol 23

(2013) PARA 744 et seq) or to copyright which subsists by virtue of s 168 (copyright of certain international organisations: see COPYRIGHT vol 23 (2013) PARA 749): see s 11(3); and COPYRIGHT vol 23 (2013) PARA 716.

9 See the Copyright, Designs and Patents Act 1988 s 215(3); and COPYRIGHT vol 23 (2013) PARA 1065.

10 See the Copyright and Rights in Databases Regulations 1997, SI 1997/3032, reg 14(2); and INFORMATION TECHNOLOGY LAW vol 57 (2012) PARA 550.

(v) Part-time and Fixed-term Work

A. PART-TIME WORK

73. Framework Agreement on Part-time Work implemented by EU law. The purpose of the Framework Agreement on Part-time Work[1] is:

(1) to provide for the removal of discrimination against part-time workers and to improve the quality of part-time work[2];

(2) to facilitate the development of part-time work on a voluntary basis and to contribute to the flexible organisation of working time in a manner which takes into account the needs of employers and workers[3].

In respect of employment conditions, part-time workers must not be treated in a less favourable manner than comparable full-time workers[4] solely because they work part-time, unless different treatment is justified on objective grounds[5]; and, where appropriate, the principle of *pro rata temporis* applies[6].

In relation to opportunities for part-time work:

(a) member states, following consultations with the social partners in accordance with national law or practice, should identify and review obstacles of a legal or administrative nature which may limit the opportunities for part-time work and, where appropriate, eliminate them[7];

(b) the social partners, acting within their sphere of competence and through the procedures set out in collective agreements, should identify and review obstacles which may limit the opportunities for part-time work and, where appropriate, eliminate them[8];

(c) a worker's refusal to transfer from full-time to part-time work or *vice versa* should not in itself constitute a valid reason for termination of employment, without prejudice to termination in accordance with national law, collective agreements and practice, for other reasons such as may arise from the operational requirements of the establishment concerned[9];

(d) as far as possible, employers should give consideration to[10]:

(i) requests by workers to transfer from full-time to part-time work that becomes available in the establishment[11];

(ii) requests by workers to transfer from part-time to full-time work or to increase their working time should the opportunity arise[12];

(iii) the provision of timely information on the availability of part-time and full-time positions in the establishment in order to facilitate transfers from full-time to part-time or *vice versa*[13];

(iv) measures to facilitate access to part-time work at all levels of the enterprise, including skilled and managerial positions, and where appropriate, to facilitate access by part-time workers to vocational training to enhance career opportunities and occupational mobility[14];

(v)   the provision of appropriate information to existing bodies representing workers about part-time working in the enterprise[15].

1   Ie the Framework Agreement on Part-time Work concluded on 6 June 1997 between the general cross-industry organisations (the 'Framework Agreement'), which is annexed to, and is implemented by, Council Directive (EC) 97/81 of 15 December 1997 (OJ L14, 20.1.98, p 9) concerning the Framework Agreement on part-time work (the 'Part-time Work Directive'): see art 1. The general cross-industry organisations are: the Union of Industrial and Employers' Confederations of Europe (UNICE), the European Centre of Enterprises with Public Participation (CEEP) and the European Trade Union Confederation (ETUC): see art 1. The Part-time Work Directive was extended to the United Kingdom by Council Directive (EC) 98/23 of 7 April 1998 (OJ L131, 5.5.98, p 10) on the extension of Council Directive (EC) 97/81 to the United Kingdom of Great Britain and Northern Ireland. Member states and/or social partners may maintain or introduce more favourable provisions than those set out in the Framework Agreement: see Annex cl 6(1). The Framework Agreement is without prejudice to any more specific Community provisions and, in particular, Community provisions concerning equal treatment or opportunities for men and women: cl 6(4). Although the term 'social partners' is not defined for the purposes of the Part-time Work Directive, it is habitually used in EC Directives to indicate 'management and labour': see e g PARA 84 note 1 (the 'Fixed-term Work Directive'). As to legislation made for the purposes of implementing the Part-time Work Directive in the United Kingdom see PARA 74 et seq. As to the meaning of 'United Kingdom' see PARA 2 note 12.

2   Framework Agreement cl 1(a). The Agreement applies to part-time workers who have an employment contract or employment relationship as defined by the law, collective agreement or practice in force in each member state: cl 2(1). Member states, after consultation with the social partners in accordance with national law, collective agreements or practice, and/or the social partners at the appropriate level in conformity with national industrial relations practice may, for objective reasons, exclude wholly or partly from the terms of the Framework Agreement part-time workers who work on a casual basis; however, such exclusions should be reviewed periodically to establish if the objective reasons for making them remain valid: cl 2(2). For these purposes, the term 'part-time worker' refers to an employee whose normal hours of work, calculated on a weekly basis or on average over a period of employment of up to one year, are less than the normal hours of work of a comparable full-time worker: cl 3(1).

3   Framework Agreement cl 1(b).

4   The term 'comparable full-time worker' means a full-time worker in the same establishment having the same type of employment contract or relationship, who is engaged in the same or a similar work or occupation, due regard being given to other considerations which may include seniority and qualification or skills: Framework Agreement cl 3(2) para 1. Where there is no comparable full-time worker in the same establishment, the comparison must be made by reference to the applicable collective agreement or, where there is no applicable collective agreement, in accordance with national law, collective agreements or practice: cl 3(2) para 2.

5   Framework Agreement cl 4(1). The arrangements for the application of Annex cl 4 are defined by the member states and/or social partners, having regard to European legislation, national law, collective agreements and practice: cl 4(3).
      Where justified by objective reasons, member states, after consultation of the social partners in accordance with national law, collective agreements or practice and/or social partners may, where appropriate, make access to particular conditions of employment subject to a period of service, time worked or earnings qualification; qualifications relating to access by part-time workers to particular conditions of employment should be reviewed periodically having regard to the principle of non-discrimination as expressed in Annex cl 4(1): cl 4(4).

6   Framework Agreement cl 4(2). See Case C-285/02 *Elsner-Lakeberg v Land Nordrhein-Westfalen* [2004] 2 CMLR 874, [2005] IRLR 209, ECJ (national legislation which required that neither part-time nor full-time workers received any remuneration for additional hours worked when such work did not exceed three hours per calendar month was a breach of the *pro rata* principle). See also Case C-486/08 *Zentralbetriebsrat der Landeskrankenhauser Tirols v Land Tirol* [2010] ECR I-3527, [2010] IRLR 631, ECJ (the Part-time Workers Directive in particular precluded the reduction *pro rata* of unused leave entitlement where a worker changes from full-time to part-time working during the course of a leave year, without having taken all of her *pro rata* share of the year's leave allowance (referable to the period of full-time work before becoming part-time), but only if the worker concerned had not been able to take her full *pro rata* entitlement for the period of full-time work before becoming part-time); and Cases C-395/08 and C-396/08 *Istituto Nazionale Della Previdenza Sociale v Bruno; Istituto Nazionale Della Previdenza Sociale v Lotti* [2010] ECR I-5119, [2010] 3 CMLR 1225, [2010]

IRLR 890, ECJ (retirement pension not precluded from being calculated *pro rata temporis* in case of part-time employment but principle of *pro rata temporis* is not applicable for the purpose of determining the date required to acquire pension rights, since that depends solely on the worker's length of service, and that date should be calculated for a part-time worker as if he had held a full-time post, periods not worked being taken into account in their entirety). Case C-486/08 *Zentralbetriebsrat der Landeskrankenhauser Tirols v Land Tirol* was answered in part by reference to the general principles of EU social law, whose implementation by the competent national authorities is confined within the limits expressly laid down by the Working Time Directive: see PARA 267.

7   Framework Agreement cl 5(1)(a).
8   Framework Agreement cl 5(1)(b).
9   Framework Agreement cl 5(2). This provision seeks merely to exclude the refusal of a worker, as regards a conversion of a worker's part-time employment relationship to a full-time employment relationship, from being the only reason for the termination of his employment in the absence of other objective reasons; it does not require member states to adopt rules making such a conversion subject to his consent: Case C-221/13 *Mascellani v Ministero della Giustizia* [2014] All ER (D) 180 (Oct), CJEU.
10 See Framework Agreement cl 5(3).
11 Framework Agreement cl 5(3)(a).
12 Framework Agreement cl 5(3)(b).
13 Framework Agreement cl 5(3)(c).
14 Framework Agreement cl 5(3)(d).
15 Framework Agreement cl 5(3)(e).

74.   Secretary of State's power to make part-time workers regulations. The Secretary of State[1] must make regulations for the purpose of securing that persons in part-time employment are treated, for such purposes and to such extent as the regulations may specify, no less favourably than persons in full-time employment[2].

The regulations may:

(1)   specify classes of person who are to be taken to be, or not to be, in part-time employment[3];

(2)   specify classes of person who are to be taken to be, or not to be, in full-time employment[4];

(3)   specify circumstances in which persons in part-time employment are to be taken to be, or not to be, treated less favourably than persons in full-time employment[5];

(4)   make provision which has effect in relation to persons in part-time employment generally or provision which has effect only in relation to specified classes of persons in part-time employment[6].

The regulations also may:

(a)   confer jurisdiction, including exclusive jurisdiction, on employment tribunals[7] and on the Employment Appeal Tribunal[8];

(b)   create criminal offences[9] in relation to specified acts or omissions by an employer, by an organisation of employers, by an organisation of workers or by an organisation existing for the purposes of a profession or trade carried on by the organisation's members[10];

(c)   in specified cases or circumstances, extend liability for a criminal offence created under head (b) above to a person who aids the commission of the offence or to a person who is an agent, principal, employee, employer or officer of a person who commits the offence[11];

(d)   provide for specified obligations or offences not to apply in specified circumstances[12];

(e)   make provision about notices or information to be given, evidence to be produced and other procedures to be followed[13];

(f)   amend, apply with or without modifications, or make provision similar
        to any provision of the Employment Rights Act 1996[14] or the Trade
        Union and Labour Relations (Consolidation) Act 1992[15];
(g)   provide for the provisions of specified agreements to have effect in place
        of provisions of the regulations to such extent and in such circumstances
        as may be specified[16];
(h)   include supplemental, incidental, consequential and transitional
        provision, including provision amending an enactment[17];
(i)   make different provision for different cases or circumstances[18].

Without prejudice to the generality of the above, the regulations may make
any provision which appears to the Secretary of State to be necessary or
expedient:

(i)   for the purpose of implementing the Part-time Work Directive[19] in its
        application to terms and conditions of employment[20];
(ii)   for the purpose of dealing with any matter arising out of or related to
        the United Kingdom's obligations thereunder[21];
(iii)   for the purpose of any matter dealt with by the Framework Agreement[22]
        or for the purpose of applying the provisions of the Framework
        Agreement to any matter relating to part-time workers[23].

1   As to the Secretary of State see PARA 5 note 21.
2   Employment Relations Act 1999 s 19(1). Any power to make an order or regulations under the
    Employment Relations Act 1999 must be exercised by statutory instrument (see s 42(1)); but no
    such regulations are to be made under s 19 unless a draft has been laid before, and approved by
    resolution of, each House of Parliament (see s 42(2)). In exercise of the power so conferred, the
    Secretary of State has made the Part-time Workers (Prevention of Less Favourable Treatment)
    Regulations 2000, SI 2000/1551 (see PARA 75 et seq), which came into force on 1 July 2000 (see
    reg 1(1)), and the Part-time Workers (Prevention of Less Favourable Treatment)
    Regulations 2001, SI 2001/1107, which make minor amendments to the Employment Tribunals
    Act 1996 and to the Employment Rights Act 1996.
3   Employment Relations Act 1999 s 19(2)(a).
4   Employment Relations Act 1999 s 19(2)(b).
5   Employment Relations Act 1999 s 19(2)(c).
6   Employment Relations Act 1999 s 19(2)(d).
7   As to employment tribunals see PARA 1399 et seq; and as to the procedure on a complaint made
    to an employment tribunal see PARA 1453 et seq.
8   Employment Relations Act 1999 s 19(3)(a). As to the Employment Appeal Tribunal see PARAS
    1422 et seq, 1495 et seq.
9   Regulations under the Employment Relations Act 1999 s 19 which create an offence must
    provide for it to be triable summarily only and may not provide for it to be punishable by
    imprisonment or by a fine in excess of level 5 on the standard scale: see s 19(5). As to the
    standard scale see SENTENCING AND DISPOSITION OF OFFENDERS vol 92 (2010) PARA 142.
10 Employment Relations Act 1999 s 19(3)(b).
11 Employment Relations Act 1999 s 19(3)(c).
12 Employment Relations Act 1999 s 19(3)(d).
13 Employment Relations Act 1999 s 19(3)(e).
14 Ie including, in particular, the Employment Rights Act 1996 Pt V (ss 43M–49A) (protection
    from suffering detriment in employment: see PARA 612 et seq), Pt X (ss 94–134A) (unfair
    dismissal: see PARA 757 et seq) and Pt XIII (ss 191–209) (miscellaneous provisions): see the
    Employment Relations Act 1999 s 19(3)(f).
15 Employment Relations Act 1999 s 19(3)(f). As to the Trade Union and Labour Relations
    (Consolidation) Act 1992 see PARA 891 et seq.
16 Employment Relations Act 1999 s 19(3)(g).
17 Employment Relations Act 1999 s 19(3)(h).
18 Employment Relations Act 1999 s 19(3)(i).
19 Ie Council Directive (EC) 97/81 of 15 December 1997 (OJ L14, 20.1.98, p 9) concerning the
    Framework Agreement on part-time work (the 'Part-time Work Directive') (see PARA 73): see the
    Employment Relations Act 1999 s 19(4)(a).
20 Employment Relations Act 1999 s 19(4)(a).

21 Employment Relations Act 1999 s 19(4)(b).
22 As to the Framework Agreement see PARA 73.
23 Employment Relations Act 1999 s 19(4)(c).

75. Types of worker to be considered under part-time workers regulations.
The regulations that have been made for the purpose of implementing the
Part-time Work Directive[1] apply to workers[2], and not just to employees[3], and the
following distinctions between categories of 'worker' are further defined for
these purposes:

(1) a worker is a 'full-time worker' if he is paid wholly or in part by
     reference to the time he works and, having regard to the custom and
     practice of the employer[4] in relation to workers employed by the
     worker's employer under the same type of contract, is identifiable as a
     full-time worker[5];

(2) a worker is a 'part-time worker' if he is paid wholly or in part by
     reference to the time he works and, having regard to the custom and
     practice of the employer in relation to workers employed by the
     worker's employer under the same type of contract, is not identifiable as
     a full-time worker[6];

(3) a full-time worker is a 'comparable full-time worker' in relation to a
     part-time worker if, at the time when the treatment that is alleged to be
     less favourable to the part-time worker takes place[7]:

     (a) both workers are employed by the same employer under the same
          type of contract[8], and both workers are engaged in the same or
          broadly similar work having regard, where relevant, to whether
          they have a similar level of qualification, skills and experience[9];
          and

     (b) the full-time worker works or is based at the same establishment
          as the part-time worker or, where there is no full-time worker
          working or based at that establishment who satisfies the
          requirements of head (a) above, works or is based at a different
          establishment and satisfies those requirements[10].

For the purposes of heads (1) to (3) above, the following are regarded as being
employed under different types of contract[11]: (i) employees employed under a
contract that is not a contract of apprenticeship[12]; (ii) employees employed under
a contract of apprenticeship[13]; (iii) workers who are not employees[14]; (iv) any
other description of worker that it is reasonable for the employer to treat
differently from other workers on the ground that workers of that description
have a different type of contract[15].

1 As to Council Directive (EC) 97/81 of 15 December 1997 (OJ L14, 20.1.98, p 9) concerning the
   Framework Agreement on part-time work (the 'Part-time Work Directive') see PARA 73; and as
   to the Part-time Workers (Prevention of Less Favourable Treatment) Regulations 2000,
   SI 2000/1551, that were promulgated for the purpose of implementing that Directive, see also
   PARAS 74, 76 et seq.
2 For these purposes, 'worker' means an individual who has entered into or works under or
   (except where a provision of the Part-time Workers (Prevention of Less Favourable Treatment)
   Regulations 2000, SI 2000/1551, otherwise requires) where the employment has ceased, worked
   under:
   (1) a contract of employment (reg 1(2)(a)); or
   (2) any other contract, whether express or implied and (if it is express) whether oral or in
        writing, whereby the individual undertakes to do or perform personally any work or
        services for another party to the contract whose status is not, by virtue of the contract,
        that of a client or customer of any profession or business undertaking carried on by the
        individual (see reg 1(2)(b)).

'Contract of employment' means a contract of service or apprenticeship, whether express or implied and (if it is express) whether oral or in writing: see reg 1(2). As to the meaning of 'contract of service' in employment law generally see PARA 1 note 1; as to the meaning of 'contract of employment' and related expressions generally see PARA 2 et seq; as to the use of the term 'worker' generally see PARA 5. As to the position of apprentices and youth trainees at common law see PARAS 112, 128–129, 636, 747–754. As to the statutory law on apprenticeships see EDUCATION vol 35 (2011) PARA 682 et seq. As to the meaning of 'writing' see PARA 2 note 8.

3   For these purposes, 'employee' means an individual who has entered into or works under or, except where a provision of the Part-time Workers (Prevention of Less Favourable Treatment) Regulations 2000, SI 2000/1551, otherwise requires, where the employment has ceased, worked under a contract of employment: see reg 1(2). As to the meaning of 'employee' and related expressions in relation to employment rights generally see PARA 2 et seq.

4   For these purposes, 'employer', in relation to any employee or worker, means the person by whom the employee or worker is or, except where a provision of the Part-time Workers (Prevention of Less Favourable Treatment) Regulations 2000, SI 2000/1551, otherwise requires, where the employment has ceased, was employed: see reg 1(2). As to the meaning of 'employer' and related expressions in relation to employment rights generally see PARA 2 et seq.

5   Part-time Workers (Prevention of Less Favourable Treatment) Regulations 2000, SI 2000/1551, reg 2(1).

6   Part-time Workers (Prevention of Less Favourable Treatment) Regulations 2000, SI 2000/1551, reg 2(2).

7   See the Part-time Workers (Prevention of Less Favourable Treatment) Regulations 2000, SI 2000/1551, reg 2(4). The plain effect of the language of the Regulations is that a claimant cannot rely on a hypothetical comparator but can only rely on an actual comparator: *Carl v University of Sheffield* [2009] 3 CMLR 846, [2009] ICR 1286, [2009] IRLR 616, EAT.

8   Part-time Workers (Prevention of Less Favourable Treatment) Regulations 2000, SI 2000/1551, reg 2(4)(a)(i). Cf the definition of 'comparable full-time worker' given in the Framework Agreement on part-time work, which refers additionally to 'the same type of employment … relationship': see PARA 73 note 4.

9   Part-time Workers (Prevention of Less Favourable Treatment) Regulations 2000, SI 2000/1551, reg 2(4)(a)(ii). As to whether a fixed-term employee is or was employed on the same 'or broadly similar' work see *Matthews v Kent and Medway Towns Fire Authority* [2006] UKHL 8, [2006] 2 All ER 171, [2006] ICR 365, [2006] IRLR 367 (retained firefighters comparable with full-time firefighters) (revsng in part [2004] EWCA Civ 844, [2004] 3 All ER 620, [2005] ICR 84, [2004] IRLR 697 (full-time firefighters carried out measurable additional job functions and had fuller, wider jobs than retained firefighters)). The question of broad similarity posed by the Part-time Workers (Prevention of Less Favourable Treatment) Regulations 2000, SI 2000/1551, reg 2(4)(a), had to be approached in the context of regulations which were inviting a comparison between two types of worker whose work would almost inevitably be different to some extent and, in answering the question, particular weight must be given to the extent to which the work of the full-time and part-time workers was in fact the same and to the importance of that work to the enterprise as a whole; otherwise too much weight could be given to the differences in the work, which were the almost inevitable consequences of working less than full-time rather than working full-time: *Matthews v Kent and Medway Towns Fire Authority*.
    Under the Framework Agreement on Part-time Work (see PARA 73), it has been held that there was no proper comparison between a part-time worker and a full-time worker doing similar work where the part-time worker was engaged on a casual 'work on demand' basis: Case C-313/02 *Wippel v Peek and Cloppenburg GmbH & Co KG* [2004] ECR I-9483, [2005] IRLR 211, ECJ.

10 Part-time Workers (Prevention of Less Favourable Treatment) Regulations 2000, SI 2000/1551, reg 2(4)(b). See note 9.

11 See the Part-time Workers (Prevention of Less Favourable Treatment) Regulations 2000, SI 2000/1551, reg 2(3) (reg 2(3) substituted by SI 2002/2035). The different categories of working relationship listed in the Part-time Workers (Prevention of Less Favourable Treatment) Regulations 2000, SI 2000/1551, reg 2(3) (as originally enacted), within which part-time and full-time workers were to be regarded as comparable but between which they were not, were mutually exclusive: *Matthews v Kent and Medway Towns Fire Authority* [2006] UKHL 8, [2006] 2 All ER 171, [2006] ICR 365, [2006] IRLR 367.

12 Part-time Workers (Prevention of Less Favourable Treatment) Regulations 2000, SI 2000/1551, reg 2(3)(a) (as substituted: see note 11). See *Matthews v Kent and Medway Towns Fire Authority* [2006] UKHL 8, [2006] 2 All ER 171, [2006] ICR 365, [2006] IRLR 367 (retained and whole-time firefighters were employed under the same type of contract for these purposes).

13 Part-time Workers (Prevention of Less Favourable Treatment) Regulations 2000, SI 2000/1551, reg 2(3)(b) (as substituted: see note 11).

14 Part-time Workers (Prevention of Less Favourable Treatment) Regulations 2000, SI 2000/1551, reg 2(3)(c) (as substituted: see note 11).

15 Part-time Workers (Prevention of Less Favourable Treatment) Regulations 2000, SI 2000/1551, reg 2(3)(d) (as substituted: see note 11). Head (iv) in the text is to be construed as a residual category, put in as a catch-all by the parliamentary draftsmen in case something had been overlooked: see *Matthews v Kent and Medway Towns Fire Authority* [2006] UKHL 8, [2006] 2 All ER 171, [2006] ICR 365, [2006] IRLR 367.

76. Less favourable treatment of part-time workers under regulations. A part-time worker[1] has the right not to be treated by his employer[2] less favourably than the employer treats a comparable full-time worker[3]:

(1) as regards the terms of his contract; or

(2) by being subjected to any other detriment by any act, or deliberate failure to act, of his employer[4],

but the right so conferred applies only if the treatment is on the ground that the worker is a part-time worker, and only if the treatment is not justified on objective grounds[5].

In determining whether a part-time worker has been treated less favourably than a comparable full-time worker, the *pro rata* principle[6] is to be applied, unless it is inappropriate[7].

A part-time worker paid at a lower rate for overtime worked by him in a period than a comparable full-time worker is or would be paid for overtime worked by him in the same period is not, for that reason, to be regarded as treated less favourably than the comparable full-time worker where, or to the extent that, the total number of hours worked by the part-time worker in the period, including overtime, does not exceed the number of hours the comparable full-time worker is required to work in the period, disregarding absences from work and overtime[8].

If a worker who considers that his employer may have treated him in a manner which infringes the right not to be treated less favourably[9] requests in writing from his employer a written statement giving particulars of the reasons for the treatment, the worker is entitled to be provided with such a statement within 21 days of his request[10]. Such a statement in writing is admissible in evidence in any proceedings under the Part-time Workers (Prevention of Less Favourable Treatment) Regulations 2000[11]; and, if it appears to the tribunal in any such proceedings that the employer deliberately, and without reasonable excuse, omitted to provide a written statement, or that the written statement is evasive or equivocal, it may draw any inference which it considers it just and equitable to draw, including an inference that the employer has infringed the right in question[12].

The restrictions on contracting out that are imposed by the Employment Rights Act 1996[13] apply in relation to the Part-time Workers (Prevention of Less Favourable Treatment) Regulations 2000[14] as if those regulations were contained in the Employment Rights Act 1996[15].

1 As to the meaning of 'part-time worker' for these purposes see PARA 75.

2 As to the meaning of 'employer' for these purposes see PARA 75 note 4.

3 As to the meaning of 'comparable full-time worker' for these purposes see PARA 75.

4 See the Part-time Workers (Prevention of Less Favourable Treatment) Regulations 2000, SI 2000/1551, reg 5(1).

5 See the Part-time Workers (Prevention of Less Favourable Treatment) Regulations 2000, SI 2000/1551, reg 5(2). The defence of objective justification is specifically allowed by the Part-time Work Directive (ie Council Directive (EC) 97/81 of 15 December 1997 (OJ L14,

20.1.98, p 9) concerning the Framework Agreement on part-time work): see PARA 73. The part-time nature of an employee's status must be the effective and predominant cause of the less favourable treatment, although it need not be the only cause: *Sharma v Manchester City Council* [2008] ICR 623, [2008] IRLR 336, EAT (whereas domestic legislation must provide the protection contained in the Directive, it is not limited to such protection)/ *Sharma v Manchester City Council* was followed in *Carl v University of Sheffield* [2009] 3 CMLR 846, [2009] ICR 1286, [2009] IRLR 616, EAT; but c f *McMenemy v Capita Business Services Ltd* [2007] CSIH 25, [2007] IRLR 400 (less favourable treatment of part-time workers must, under the Directive, be for the reason that they work part-time and for that reason alone).

6   For these purposes, 'pro rata principle' means that, where a comparable full-time worker receives or is entitled to receive pay or any other benefit, a part-time worker is to receive or be entitled to receive not less than the proportion of that pay or other benefit that the number of his weekly hours bears to the number of weekly hours of the comparable full-time worker: see the Part-time Workers (Prevention of Less Favourable Treatment) Regulations 2000, SI 2000/1551, reg 1(2). 'Weekly hours' means the number of hours a worker is required to work under his contract of employment in a week in which he has no absences from work and does not work any overtime or, where the number of such hours varies according to a cycle, the average number of such hours: see reg 1(3). As to the meaning of 'contract of employment' for these purposes see PARA 75 note 2. The principle of *pro rata temporis* applies pursuant to the Framework Agreement cl 4: see PARA 73.

7   Part-time Workers (Prevention of Less Favourable Treatment) Regulations 2000, SI 2000/1551, reg 5(3).

8   Part-time Workers (Prevention of Less Favourable Treatment) Regulations 2000, SI 2000/1551, reg 5(4). See *James v Great North Eastern Railways* [2005] All ER (D) 15 (Mar), EAT (part-time employees' claims for more pay for contractual rostered hours worked not dependent on whether they worked overtime: statutory disregard in the Part-time Workers (Prevention of Less Favourable Treatment) Regulations 2000, SI 2000/1551, reg 5(4) inapplicable).

9   Ie infringes the right conferred on him by the Part-time Workers (Prevention of Less Favourable Treatment) Regulations 2000, SI 2000/1551, reg 5 (see the text and notes 1–8): see reg 6(1).

10 Part-time Workers (Prevention of Less Favourable Treatment) Regulations 2000, SI 2000/1551, reg 6(1). Regulation 6 does not apply, however, where the treatment in question consists of dismissal of an employee and the employee is entitled to a written statement of reason for his dismissal under the Employment Rights Act 1996 s 92 (see PARA 755): Part-time Workers (Prevention of Less Favourable Treatment) Regulations 2000, SI 2000/1551, reg 6(4). There is, however, no right to present a complaint to an employment tribunal for failure to provide such a statement. As to unfair dismissal for applying part-time workers regulations see PARA 78; and as to the right not to be subjected to any detriment for applying those regulations see PARA 79. As to the meaning of 'writing' see PARA 2 note 8.

11 See the Part-time Workers (Prevention of Less Favourable Treatment) Regulations 2000, SI 2000/1551, reg 6(2). See also note 10.

12 See the Part-time Workers (Prevention of Less Favourable Treatment) Regulations 2000, SI 2000/1551, reg 6(3). See also note 10.

13 Ie the Employment Rights Act 1996 s 203 (see PARA 150): see the Part-time Workers (Prevention of Less Favourable Treatment) Regulations 2000, SI 2000/1551, reg 9.

14 Ie in relation to the Part-time Workers (Prevention of Less Favourable Treatment) Regulations 2000, SI 2000/1551: see reg 9.

15 Part-time Workers (Prevention of Less Favourable Treatment) Regulations 2000, SI 2000/1551, reg 9.

77.   Treatment under part-time workers regulations of workers becoming part-time or returning part-time after absence.   Where a worker[1] who was identifiable as a full-time worker[2] continues, following a termination or variation of his contract, to work under a new or varied contract, whether of the same type or not, that requires him to work for a number of weekly hours[3] that is lower than the number he was required to work immediately before the termination or variation[4], the right not to be treated less favourably applies to him[5] as if he were a part-time worker[6] and as if there were a comparable full-time worker[7] employed under the terms that applied to him immediately before the variation or termination[8].

Where a worker:

(1)   was identifiable as a full-time worker[9] immediately before a period of absence (whether the absence followed a termination of the worker's contract or not)[10];

(2)   returns to work for the same employer[11] within a period of less than 12 months beginning with the day on which the period of absence started[12];

(3)   returns to the same job or to a job at the same level under a contract, whether it is a different contract or a varied contract and regardless of whether it is of the same type, under which he is required to work for a number of weekly hours that is lower than the number he was required to work immediately before the period of absence[13],

the right not to be treated less favourably applies to that worker[14] (the 'returning worker') as if he were a part-time worker and as if there were a comparable full-time worker employed under[15]: (a) the contract under which the returning worker was employed immediately before the period of absence[16]; or (b) where it is shown that, had the returning worker continued to work under the contract mentioned in head (a) above, a variation would have been made to its terms during the period of absence, that contract including that variation[17].

1   As to the meaning of 'worker' for these purposes see PARA 75 note 2.

2   Ie in accordance with the Part-time Workers (Prevention of Less Favourable Treatment) Regulations 2000, SI 2000/1551, reg 2(1) (see PARA 75): see reg 3(1).

3   As to the meaning of 'weekly hours' for these purposes see PARA 76 note 6.

4   See the Part-time Workers (Prevention of Less Favourable Treatment) Regulations 2000, SI 2000/1551, reg 3(1).

5   Ie notwithstanding the Part-time Workers (Prevention of Less Favourable Treatment) Regulations 2000, SI 2000/1551, reg 2(4) (see PARA 75), the right conferred by reg 5 (see PARA 76) applies to him: see reg 3(2). The fact that reg 3 applies to a worker does not affect any right he may have under the Part-time Workers (Prevention of Less Favourable Treatment) Regulations 2000, SI 2000/1551, by virtue of reg 2(4): reg 3(3).

6   As to the meaning of 'part-time worker' for these purposes see PARA 75.

7   As to the meaning of 'comparable full-time worker' for these purposes see PARA 75.

8   Part-time Workers (Prevention of Less Favourable Treatment) Regulations 2000, SI 2000/1551, reg 3(2).

9   Ie in accordance with the Part-time Workers (Prevention of Less Favourable Treatment) Regulations 2000, SI 2000/1551, reg 2(1) (see PARA 75): see reg 4(1)(a).

10   Part-time Workers (Prevention of Less Favourable Treatment) Regulations 2000, SI 2000/1551, reg 4(1)(a).

11   As to the meaning of 'employer' for these purposes see PARA 75 note 4.

12   Part-time Workers (Prevention of Less Favourable Treatment) Regulations 2000, SI 2000/1551, reg 4(1)(b).

13   Part-time Workers (Prevention of Less Favourable Treatment) Regulations 2000, SI 2000/1551, reg 4(1)(c).

14   Ie notwithstanding the Part-time Workers (Prevention of Less Favourable Treatment) Regulations 2000, SI 2000/1551, reg 2(4) (see PARA 75), the right conferred by reg 5 (see PARA 76) applies to him: see reg 4(2). The fact that reg 4 applies to a worker does not affect any right the worker may have under the Part-time Workers (Prevention of Less Favourable Treatment) Regulations 2000, SI 2000/1551, by virtue of reg 2(4): reg 4(3).

15   See the Part-time Workers (Prevention of Less Favourable Treatment) Regulations 2000, SI 2000/1551, reg 4(2).

16   Part-time Workers (Prevention of Less Favourable Treatment) Regulations 2000, SI 2000/1551, reg 4(2)(a).

17   Part-time Workers (Prevention of Less Favourable Treatment) Regulations 2000, SI 2000/1551, reg 4(2)(b).

78.   Employee's dismissal for applying part-time workers regulations to be regarded as unfair.   An employee[1] who is dismissed is to be regarded as unfairly dismissed for the purposes of the Employment Rights Act 1996[2] if the reason (or, if more than one, the principal reason) for the dismissal is a reason specified in heads (1) and (2) below[3], namely that:

(1)   the worker[4] has:

  (a)   brought proceedings against the employer[5] under the Part-time Workers (Prevention of Less Favourable Treatment) Regulations 2000[6];

  (b)   requested from his employer a written statement of reasons[7];

  (c)   given evidence or information in connection with such proceedings brought by any worker[8];

  (d)   otherwise done anything under the Part-time Workers (Prevention of Less Favourable Treatment) Regulations 2000 in relation to the employer or any other person[9];

  (e)   alleged that the employer had infringed the Part-time Workers (Prevention of Less Favourable Treatment) Regulations 2000[10]; or

  (f)   refused, or proposed to refuse, to forgo a right conferred on him by the Part-time Workers (Prevention of Less Favourable Treatment) Regulations 2000[11]; or

(2)   the employer believes or suspects that the worker has done or intends to do any of the things mentioned in head (1) above[12].

1   As to the meaning of 'employee' see PARA 75 note 3.
2   Ie for the purposes of the Employment Rights Act 1996 Pt X (ss 94–134A) (unfair dismissal: see PARA 757 et seq): see the Part-time Workers (Prevention of Less Favourable Treatment) Regulations 2000, SI 2000/1551, reg 7(1).
3   See the Part-time Workers (Prevention of Less Favourable Treatment) Regulations 2000, SI 2000/1551, reg 7(1). The text refers to a reason or principal reason specified in reg 7(3) (see heads (1) and (2) in the text): see reg 7(1). In an unfair dismissal complaint made under reg 7(1), neither the qualifying period nor the upper age applies: see the Employment Rights Act 1996 s 108(3)(i); and PARA 758 note 9. A redundancy selection for these reasons is also to be considered unfair: see s 105(7E); and PARA 781.
4   As to the meaning of 'worker' for these purposes see PARA 75 note 2.
5   As to the meaning of 'employer' for these purposes see PARA 75 note 4.
6   Part-time Workers (Prevention of Less Favourable Treatment) Regulations 2000, SI 2000/1551, reg 7(3)(a)(i). As to proceedings under the Part-time Workers (Prevention of Less Favourable Treatment) Regulations 2000, SI 2000/1551, see also PARAS 75 et seq, 79 et seq. As to the right to present a complaint to an employment tribunal see PARA 80.
7   Part-time Workers (Prevention of Less Favourable Treatment) Regulations 2000, SI 2000/1551, reg 7(3)(a)(ii). The text refers to a written statement of reasons requested under reg 6 (see PARA 76): see reg 7(3)(a)(ii).
8   Part-time Workers (Prevention of Less Favourable Treatment) Regulations 2000, SI 2000/1551, reg 7(3)(a)(iii).
9   Part-time Workers (Prevention of Less Favourable Treatment) Regulations 2000, SI 2000/1551, reg 7(3)(a)(iv).
10   Part-time Workers (Prevention of Less Favourable Treatment) Regulations 2000, SI 2000/1551, reg 7(3)(a)(v). Where the reason or principal reason for dismissal is that mentioned in reg 7(3)(a)(v), reg 7(1) (see the text and notes 1–3) does not apply if the allegation made by the worker is false and not made in good faith: see reg 7(4). See *Pipe v Hendrickson Europe Ltd* [2003] All ER (D) 280 (Apr), EAT (employer's insistence that an employee's retention was dependent on her agreeing to work full-time breached the Part-time Workers (Prevention of Less Favourable Treatment) Regulations 2000, SI 2000/1551).
11   Part-time Workers (Prevention of Less Favourable Treatment) Regulations 2000, SI 2000/1551, reg 7(3)(a)(vi).
12   Part-time Workers (Prevention of Less Favourable Treatment) Regulations 2000, SI 2000/1551, reg 7(3)(b). Where the reason or principal reason for dismissal is that mentioned in reg 7(3)(b),

so far as it relates to the ground mentioned in reg 7(3)(a)(v) (see head (1)(e) in the text), reg 7(1) (see the text and notes 1–3) does not apply if the allegation made by the worker is false and not made in good faith: see reg 7(4).

79. Worker's right not to be subjected to detriment for applying part-time workers regulations. A worker[1] has the right not to be subjected to any detriment by any act[2], or any deliberate failure to act, by his employer[3] done on a ground specified in heads (1) and (2) below[4], namely that:

(1) the worker has:

    (a) brought proceedings against the employer under the Part-time Workers (Prevention of Less Favourable Treatment) Regulations 2000[5];

    (b) requested from his employer a written statement of reasons[6];

    (c) given evidence or information in connection with such proceedings brought by any worker[7];

    (d) otherwise done anything under the Part-time Workers (Prevention of Less Favourable Treatment) Regulations 2000 in relation to the employer or any other person[8];

    (e) alleged that the employer had infringed the Part-time Workers (Prevention of Less Favourable Treatment) Regulations 2000[9]; or

    (f) refused, or proposed to refuse, to forgo a right conferred on him by the Part-time Workers (Prevention of Less Favourable Treatment) Regulations 2000[10]; or

(2) the employer believes or suspects that the worker has done or intends to do any of the things mentioned in head (1) above[11].

1 As to the meaning of 'worker' for these purposes see PARA 75 note 2.
2 The Part-time Workers (Prevention of Less Favourable Treatment) Regulations 2000, SI 2000/1551, reg 7(2) does not apply where the detriment in question amounts to the dismissal of an employee within the meaning of the Employment Rights Act 1996 Pt X (ss 94–134A) (unfair dismissal: see PARA 757 et seq): Part-time Workers (Prevention of Less Favourable Treatment) Regulations 2000, SI 2000/1551, reg 7(5). See, however, reg 7(1); and PARA 78. See also *Sharma v Manchester City Council* [2008] ICR 623, [2008] IRLR 336, EAT; and PARA 76 note 5.
3 As to the meaning of 'employer' for these purposes see PARA 75 note 4.
4 See the Part-time Workers (Prevention of Less Favourable Treatment) Regulations 2000, SI 2000/1551, reg 7(2). The text refers to a ground specified in reg 7(3) (see heads (1) and (2) in the text): see reg 7(2).
5 Part-time Workers (Prevention of Less Favourable Treatment) Regulations 2000, SI 2000/1551, reg 7(3)(a)(i). As to proceedings under the Part-time Workers (Prevention of Less Favourable Treatment) Regulations 2000, SI 2000/1551, see PARAS 75 et seq, 80 et seq. As to the right to present a complaint to an employment tribunal see PARA 80.
6 Part-time Workers (Prevention of Less Favourable Treatment) Regulations 2000, SI 2000/1551, reg 7(3)(a)(ii). The text refers to a written statement of reasons requested under reg 6 (see PARA 76): see reg 7(3)(a)(ii).
7 Part-time Workers (Prevention of Less Favourable Treatment) Regulations 2000, SI 2000/1551, reg 7(3)(a)(iii).
8 Part-time Workers (Prevention of Less Favourable Treatment) Regulations 2000, SI 2000/1551, reg 7(3)(a)(iv).
9 Part-time Workers (Prevention of Less Favourable Treatment) Regulations 2000, SI 2000/1551, reg 7(3)(a)(v). Where the ground for subjection to any act or deliberate failure to act is that mentioned in reg 7(3)(a)(v), reg 7(2) (see the text and notes 1–4) does not apply if the allegation made by the worker is false and not made in good faith: see reg 7(4).
10 Part-time Workers (Prevention of Less Favourable Treatment) Regulations 2000, SI 2000/1551, reg 7(3)(a)(vi).
11 Part-time Workers (Prevention of Less Favourable Treatment) Regulations 2000, SI 2000/1551, reg 7(3)(b). Where the ground for subjection to any act or deliberate failure to act is that mentioned in reg 7(3)(b), so far as it relates to the ground mentioned in reg 7(3)(a)(v) (see

head (1)(e) in the text), reg 7(2) (see the text and notes 1–4) does not apply if the allegation made by the worker is false and not made in good faith: see reg 7(4).

80.   Complaint to employment tribunal pursuant to part-time workers regulations. A worker[1] may[2] present a complaint to an employment tribunal[3] that his employer[4] has infringed his right as a part-time worker not to be treated less favourably than a comparable full-time worker[5] or not to be subjected to a detriment[6] for applying the part-time workers regulations[7].

An employment tribunal must not consider such a complaint, however, unless it is presented before the end of the period of three months[8] beginning with the date of the less favourable treatment or detriment[9] to which the complaint relates (or, where an act or failure to act is part of a series of similar acts or failures comprising the less favourable treatment or detriment, the last of them)[10]. In working out when the time limit set in this way[11] expires, the following period is not to be counted[12], namely the period that:

(1)   begins with the day after the day on which the worker concerned complies with the requirement to contact ACAS before instituting proceedings[13] in relation to the matter in respect of which the proceedings are brought ('the day after Day A')[14]; and

(2)   ends with the day on which the worker concerned receives (or, if earlier, is treated as receiving[15]) the certificate issued by the conciliation officer[16] to the effect either that he has concluded that a settlement is not possible within the prescribed period or that the prescribed period has expired without a settlement having been reached ('Day B')[17].

If the unextended time limit[18] would expire during the period beginning with Day A and ending one month after Day B, the time limit expires instead at the end of that period[19]. Nevertheless, a tribunal may consider any such complaint which is out of time if, in all the circumstances of the case, it considers that it is just and equitable to do so[20].

Where a worker presents such a complaint, it is for the employer to identify the ground for the less favourable treatment or detriment[21]. Where an employment tribunal finds that such a complaint presented to it is well founded, it must take such of the following steps as it considers just and equitable[22]: (a) making a declaration as to the rights of the complainant and the employer in relation to the matters to which the complaint relates[23]; (b) ordering the employer to pay compensation to the complainant[24]; (c) recommending[25] that the employer take, within a specified period, action appearing to the tribunal to be reasonable, in all the circumstances of the case, for the purpose of obviating or reducing the adverse effect on the complainant of any matter to which the complaint relates[26].

1   As to the meaning of 'worker' for these purposes see PARA 75 note 2.
2   Ie subject to the Part-time Workers (Prevention of Less Favourable Treatment) Regulations 2000, SI 2000/1551, reg 7(5) (see PARA 79 note 2): see reg 8(1).
3   As to employment tribunals see PARA 1399 et seq; and as to the procedure on a complaint made to an employment tribunal see PARA 1453 et seq. There is a requirement for early ACAS conciliation to be tried in order to promote a settlement before tribunal proceedings are instituted on a complaint under the Part-time Workers (Prevention of Less Favourable Treatment) Regulations 2000, SI 2000/1551, reg 8: see the Employment Tribunals Act 1996 s 18(1)(l); and PARA 152 note 1. As to the constitution and powers of ACAS see PARA 1213 et seq.
4   As to the meaning of 'employer' for these purposes see PARA 75 note 4.
5   Ie under the Part-time Workers (Prevention of Less Favourable Treatment) Regulations 2000, SI 2000/1551, reg 5 (see PARA 76): see reg 8(1). As to the meanings of 'comparable full-time worker' and 'part-time worker' for these purposes see PARA 75.

6 Ie under the Part-time Workers (Prevention of Less Favourable Treatment) Regulations 2000, SI 2000/1551, reg 7(2) (see PARA 79): see reg 8(1).

7 Part-time Workers (Prevention of Less Favourable Treatment) Regulations 2000, SI 2000/1551, reg 8(1).

8 Ie or six months, in a case to which the Part-time Workers (Prevention of Less Favourable Treatment) Regulations 2000, SI 2000/1551, reg 13 (members of the armed forces: see PARA 82) applies: see reg 8(2).

9 For the purposes of calculating the date of the less favourable treatment or detriment under the Part-time Workers (Prevention of Less Favourable Treatment) Regulations 2000, SI 2000/1551, reg 8(2):

    (1)   where a term in a contract is less favourable, that treatment is to be treated, subject to head (2) below, as taking place on each day of the period during which the term is less favourable (reg 8(4)(a));

    (2)   where an application relies on reg 3 (workers becoming part-time: see PARA 77) or reg 4 (workers returning as part-time after absence: see PARA 77), the less favourable treatment is treated as occurring on, and only on, in the case of reg 3, the first day on which the applicant worked under the new or varied contract and, in the case of reg 4, the day on which the applicant returned (reg 8(4)(b)); and

    (3)   a deliberate failure to act contrary to reg 5 (less favourable treatment of part-time workers: see PARA 76) or reg 7(2) (part-time workers subjected to detriment for applying regulations: see PARA 79) is to be treated as done when it was decided on (reg 8(4)(c)).

In the absence of evidence establishing the contrary, a person is to be taken for the purposes of head (3) above to decide not to act: (a) when he does an act inconsistent with doing the failed act (reg 8(5)(a)); or (b) if he has done no such inconsistent act, when the period expires within which he might reasonably have been expected to have done the failed act if it was to be done (reg 8(5)(b)).

10 Part-time Workers (Prevention of Less Favourable Treatment) Regulations 2000, SI 2000/1551, reg 8(2). Provision that is made for the extension of time limits in order to facilitate conciliation before the institution of proceedings (ie reg 8A: see the text and notes 11–19) applies for the purposes of reg 8(2): reg 8(2A) (regs 8(2A), 8A added by SI 2014/386). As to consideration of the circumstances in which the time for making a claim might be extended see *O'Brien v Department of Constitutional Affairs* [2008] EWCA Civ 1448, [2009] ICR 593, [2009] IRLR 294.

11 Ie set by the Part-time Workers (Prevention of Less Favourable Treatment) Regulations 2000, SI 2000/1551, reg 8(2) (see the text and notes 8–10): see reg 8A(2) (as added: see note 10).

12 See the Part-time Workers (Prevention of Less Favourable Treatment) Regulations 2000, SI 2000/1551, reg 8A(2) (as added: see note 10).

13 Ie the requirement in the Employment Tribunals Act 1996 s 18A(1) (see PARA 152): see the Part-time Workers (Prevention of Less Favourable Treatment) Regulations 2000, SI 2000/1551, reg 8A(1)(a) (as added: see note 10).

14 See the Part-time Workers (Prevention of Less Favourable Treatment) Regulations 2000, SI 2000/1551, reg 8A(1)(a), (2) (as added: see note 10).

15 Ie by virtue of regulations made under the Employment Tribunals Act 1996 s 18A(11) (see PARA 152): see the Part-time Workers (Prevention of Less Favourable Treatment) Regulations 2000, SI 2000/1551, reg 8A(1)(b) (as added: see note 10).

16 Ie the certificate issued under the Employment Tribunals Act 1996 s 18A(4) (see PARA 152): see the Part-time Workers (Prevention of Less Favourable Treatment) Regulations 2000, SI 2000/1551, reg 8A(1)(b) (as added: see note 10).

17 See the Part-time Workers (Prevention of Less Favourable Treatment) Regulations 2000, SI 2000/1551, reg 8A(1)(b), (2) (as added: see note 10).

18 Ie the time limit set by the Part-time Workers (Prevention of Less Favourable Treatment) Regulations 2000, SI 2000/1551, reg 8(2) (see the text and notes 8–10), if not extended by reg 8A(3): see reg 8A(3) (as added: see note 10).

19 See the Part-time Workers (Prevention of Less Favourable Treatment) Regulations 2000, SI 2000/1551, reg 8A(3) (as added: see note 10).

20 Part-time Workers (Prevention of Less Favourable Treatment) Regulations 2000, SI 2000/1551, reg 8(3). The power so conferred on the employment tribunal by reg 8(3) to extend the time limit set by reg 8(2) is exercisable in relation to any time limit as it is extended by reg 8A (see the text and notes 11–19): reg 8A(4) (as added: see note 10).

21 Part-time Workers (Prevention of Less Favourable Treatment) Regulations 2000, SI 2000/1551, reg 8(6).

22 See the Part-time Workers (Prevention of Less Favourable Treatment) Regulations 2000, SI 2000/1551, reg 8(7).

23 Part-time Workers (Prevention of Less Favourable Treatment) Regulations 2000, SI 2000/1551, reg 8(7)(a).

24 Part-time Workers (Prevention of Less Favourable Treatment) Regulations 2000, SI 2000/1551, reg 8(7)(b). Where a tribunal orders compensation to be paid under reg 8(7)(b), the amount of the compensation awarded must be such as the tribunal considers just and equitable in all the circumstances, having regard to (see reg 8(9) (amended by SI 2002/2035)):

   (1)   the infringement to which the complaint relates (Part-time Workers (Prevention of Less Favourable Treatment) Regulations 2000, SI 2000/1551, reg 8(9)(a)); and

   (2)   any loss which is attributable to the infringement having regard, in the case of an infringement of the right conferred by reg 5 (less favourable treatment of part-time workers: see PARA 76), to the *pro rata* principle except where it is inappropriate to do so (reg 8(9)(b)).

As to the meaning of '*pro rata* principle' see PARA 76 note 6. The loss is to be taken to include any expenses reasonably incurred by the complainant in consequence of the infringement, and loss of any benefit which he might reasonably be expected to have had but for the infringement: see reg 8(10). In ascertaining the loss, the tribunal must apply the same rule concerning the duty of a person to mitigate his loss as applies to damages recoverable under the common law of England and Wales: reg 8(12). As to the common law duty to mitigate loss see DAMAGES vol 12(1) (Reissue) PARA 1041 et seq. Compensation in respect of treating a worker in a manner which infringes the right conferred on him by reg 5 is not to include compensation for injury to feelings: reg 8(11). Where the tribunal finds that the act, or failure to act, to which the complaint relates was to any extent caused or contributed to by action of the complainant, it must reduce the amount of the compensation by such proportion as it considers just and equitable having regard to that finding: reg 8(13).

25 If the employer fails, without reasonable justification, to comply with such a recommendation made by an employment tribunal under the Part-time Workers (Prevention of Less Favourable Treatment) Regulations 2000, SI 2000/1551, reg 8(7)(c) (see head (c) in the text), the tribunal may, if it thinks it just and equitable to do so (see reg 8(14)): (1) increase the amount of compensation required to be paid to the complainant in respect of the complaint, where an order was made under reg 8(7)(b) (see head (b) in the text) (reg 8(14)(a)); or (2) make an order under reg 8(7)(b) (reg 8(14)(b)).

26 Part-time Workers (Prevention of Less Favourable Treatment) Regulations 2000, SI 2000/1551, reg 8(7)(c).

81.   Liability of employers and principals under part-time workers regulations. Anything done by a person in the course of his employment is to be treated for the purposes of the regulations that have been made for the purpose of implementing the Part-time Work Directive[1] as also done by his employer[2], whether or not it was done with the employer's knowledge or approval[3]; and anything done by a person as agent for the employer with the authority of the employer is to be treated for the purposes of those regulations as also done by the employer[4].

   In proceedings under those regulations against any person in respect of an act alleged to have been done by a worker[5] of his, it is a defence for that person to prove that he took such steps as were reasonably practicable to prevent the worker from doing that act, or doing, in the course of his employment, acts of that description[6].

1 As to Council Directive (EC) 97/81 of 15 December 1997 (OJ L14, 20.1.98, p 9) concerning the Framework Agreement on part-time work (the 'Part-time Work Directive') see PARA 73; and as to the Part-time Workers (Prevention of Less Favourable Treatment) Regulations 2000, SI 2000/1551, that were promulgated for the purpose of implementing that Directive, see also PARAS 74 et seq, 82 et seq.

2 As to the meaning of 'employer' for these purposes see PARA 75 note 4.

3 See the Part-time Workers (Prevention of Less Favourable Treatment) Regulations 2000, SI 2000/15551, reg 11(1). For the purposes of reg 11:

   (1)   the secondment of any constable to the National Crime Agency to serve as a member of its staff must be treated as employment by the National Crime Agency (and not as

being employment by any other person) (reg 16(1B)(a), (6) (reg 16(1B), (6) added by SI 2006/594; the Part-time Workers (Prevention of Less Favourable Treatment) Regulations 2000, SI 2000/15551, reg 16(1B)(a), (6) amended by virtue of the Crime and Courts Act 2013 s 15(3), Sch 8 para 190)); and

(2) anything done by a constable so seconded in the performance, or purported performance, of his functions must be treated as done in the course of that employment (Part-time Workers (Prevention of Less Favourable Treatment) Regulations 2000, SI 2000/15551, reg 16(1B)(b) (as so added)).

As to the secondment of police constables to the National Crime Agency generally see also PARA 82 note 14. As to the National Crime Agency see POLICE AND INVESTIGATORY POWERS vol 84 (2013) PARA 424.

4 See the Part-time Workers (Prevention of Less Favourable Treatment) Regulations 2000, SI 2000/15551, reg 11(2).

5 As to the meaning of 'worker' for these purposes see PARA 75 note 2.

6 See the Part-time Workers (Prevention of Less Favourable Treatment) Regulations 2000, SI 2000/1551, reg 11(3).

82. Special classes of person under part-time workers regulations. The regulations that have been made for the purpose of implementing the Part-time Work Directive[1]:

(1) have effect[2] in relation to Crown employment[3] and persons in Crown employment as they have effect in relation to other employment and other employees and workers[4];

(2) have effect in relation to employment as a relevant member of the House of Lords staff[5] as they have effect in relation to other employment[6];

(3) have effect in relation to employment as a relevant member of the House of Commons staff[7] as they have effect in relation to other employment[8];

(4) have effect[9] in relation to service as a member of the armed forces and to employment by an association established for the purposes of Part XI[10] of the Reserve Forces Act 1996[11],

However, the regulations do not apply to any individual in his capacity as the holder of a judicial office if he is remunerated on a daily fee-paid basis[12].

The holding, otherwise than under a contract of employment[13], of the office of constable or an appointment as a police cadet is to be treated as employment under a contract of employment by the relevant officer[14].

1 As to Council Directive (EC) 97/81 of 15 December 1997 (OJ L14, 20.1.98, p 9) concerning the Framework Agreement on part-time work (the 'Part-time Work Directive') see PARA 73; and as to the Part-time Workers (Prevention of Less Favourable Treatment) Regulations 2000, SI 2000/1551, that were promulgated for the purpose of implementing that Directive, see also PARA 74 et seq.

2 Ie subject to the Part-time Workers (Prevention of Less Favourable Treatment) Regulations 2000, SI 2000/1551, reg 13 (see head (4) in the text): see reg 12(1).

3 For these purposes, 'Crown employment' means employment under or for the purposes of a government department or any officer or body exercising on behalf of the Crown functions conferred by a statutory provision: see the Part-time Workers (Prevention of Less Favourable Treatment) Regulations 2000, SI 2000/1551, reg 12(2).

4 Part-time Workers (Prevention of Less Favourable Treatment) Regulations 2000, SI 2000/1551, reg 12(1). For the purposes of the application of the provisions of the Part-time Workers (Prevention of Less Favourable Treatment) Regulations 2000, SI 2000/1551, in relation to Crown employment in accordance with reg 12(1):

(1) references to an employee and references to a worker are to be construed as references to a person in Crown employment to whom the definition of employee (or, as the case may be, worker) is appropriate (reg 12(3)(a)); and

(2) references to a contract in relation to an employee and references to a contract in

relation to a worker are to be construed as references to the terms of employment of a person in Crown employment to whom the definition of employee (or, as the case may be, worker) is appropriate (reg 12(3)(b)).

As to the meaning of 'employee' see PARA 75 note 3; and as to the meaning of 'worker' for these purposes see PARA 75 note 2.

5   For these purposes, 'relevant member of the House of Lords staff' means any person who is employed under a contract with the Corporate Officer of the House of Lords by virtue of which he is a worker: see the Part-time Workers (Prevention of Less Favourable Treatment) Regulations 2000, SI 2000/1551, reg 14(2). As to the Corporate Officer of the House of Lords see PARLIAMENT vol 78 (2010) PARA 990 et seq.

6   Part-time Workers (Prevention of Less Favourable Treatment) Regulations 2000, SI 2000/1551, reg 14(1).

7   For these purposes, 'relevant member of the House of Commons staff' means any person:

    (1)   who was appointed by the House of Commons Commission (Part-time Workers (Prevention of Less Favourable Treatment) Regulations 2000, SI 2000/1551, reg 15(2)(a)); or

    (2)   who is a member of the Speaker's personal staff (reg 15(2)(b)).

As to the House of Commons Commission see PARLIAMENT vol 78 (2010) PARA 946; and as to the Speaker see PARLIAMENT vol 78 (2010) PARA 931 et seq.

8   Part-time Workers (Prevention of Less Favourable Treatment) Regulations 2000, SI 2000/1551, reg 15(1).

9   Ie subject to the Part-time Workers (Prevention of Less Favourable Treatment) Regulations 2000, SI 2000/1551, reg 13(2), (3) (see note 11) and apart from reg 7(1) (unfair dismissal for the purposes of the Employment Rights Act 1996: see PARA 78): see the Part-time Workers (Prevention of Less Favourable Treatment) Regulations 2000, SI 2000/1551, reg 13(1). See also *R (on the application of Manson) v Ministry of Defence* [2005] EWCA Civ 1678, [2006] ICR 355 (employment tribunal had jurisdiction to determine whether part-time worker's rights infringed compared to those of full-time worker).

10   Ie for the purposes of the Reserve Forces Act 1996 Pt XI (ss 110–119) (reserve associations: see ARMED FORCES vol 3 (2011) PARA 473): see the Part-time Workers (Prevention of Less Favourable Treatment) Regulations 2000, SI 2000/1551, reg 13(1).

11   Part-time Workers (Prevention of Less Favourable Treatment) Regulations 2000, SI 2000/1551, reg 13(1). The Part-time Workers (Prevention of Less Favourable Treatment) Regulations 2000, SI 2000/1551, do not have effect in relation to service as a member of the reserve forces in so far as that service consists in undertaking training obligations:

    (1)   under the Reserve Forces Act 1980 s 38, s 40 or s 41 (ss 38, 40, 41 prospectively repealed) (training of reserves: see ARMED FORCES vol 3 (2011) PARA 486) (Part-time Workers (Prevention of Less Favourable Treatment) Regulations 2000, SI 2000/1551, reg 13(2)(a));

    (2)   under the Reserve Forces Act 1996 s 22 (service of Marines in the Royal Fleet Reserve: see ARMED FORCES vol 3 (2011) PARA 487) (Part-time Workers (Prevention of Less Favourable Treatment) Regulations 2000, SI 2000/1551, reg 13(2)(b)); or

    (3)   pursuant to regulations made under the Reserve Forces Act 1996 s 4 (see ARMED FORCES vol 3 (2011) PARA 472), or consists in undertaking voluntary training or duties under s 27 (see ARMED FORCES vol 3 (2011) PARA 496) (Part-time Workers (Prevention of Less Favourable Treatment) Regulations 2000, SI 2000/1551, reg 13(2)(c)).

No complaint concerning the service of any person as a member of the armed forces may be presented to an employment tribunal under reg 8 (see PARA 80) unless:

    (a)   that person has made a complaint in respect of the same matter to an officer under the service redress procedures (reg 13(3)(a)); and

    (b)   that complaint has not been withdrawn (reg 13(3)(b)).

For the purposes of head (b) above, a person is treated as having withdrawn his complaint if, having made a complaint to an officer under the service redress procedures (see reg 13(4) (substituted by SI 2008/1696)):

    (i)   where the service redress procedures are those referred to in the Armed Forces Act 2006 s 334 (see ARMED FORCES vol 3 (2011) PARA 754), neither that officer nor a superior officer has decided to refer the complaint to the Defence Council, and the person who made the complaint fails to apply for such a reference to be made (Part-time Workers (Prevention of Less Favourable Treatment) Regulations 2000, SI 2000/1551, reg 13(4)(a) (as so substituted));

    (ii)   in any other case, the person who made the complaint fails to submit the complaint to the Defence Council under the service redress procedures (reg 13(4)(b) (as so substituted))).

As to the Defence Council see ARMED FORCES vol 3 (2011) PARA 302; CONSTITUTIONAL AND ADMINISTRATIVE LAW vol 20 (2014) PARA 562 et seq. Where a complaint of the kind referred to in reg 13(3) is presented to an employment tribunal, the service redress procedures may continue after the complaint is presented: reg 13(5). For these purposes, 'service redress procedures' means the procedures, excluding those which relate to the making of a report on a complaint to Her Majesty, referred to in the Army Act 1955 s 180 (repealed), the Air Force Act 1955 s 180 (repealed), the Naval Discipline Act 1957 s 130 (repealed) (see ARMED FORCES vol 3 (2011) PARA 303) or the Armed Forces Act 2006 (see ARMED FORCES vol 3 (2011) PARA 312 et seq): see the Part-time Workers (Prevention of Less Favourable Treatment) Regulations 2000, SI 2000/1551, reg 13(6) (amended by SI 2008/1696).

12 Part-time Workers (Prevention of Less Favourable Treatment) Regulations 2000, SI 2000/1551, reg 17. The exclusory effect of reg 17 had been upheld on the basis that there is no overarching EU law definition of 'worker', which leaves great discretion to member states in defining it: *Christie v Department for Constitutional Affairs* [2007] ICR 1553, [2007] All ER (D) 355 (Jul), EAT. However, when this interpretation was challenged in a case concerning a part-time fee-paid recorder, who had been denied a *pro rata* judicial pension on retirement (see *O'Brien v Ministry of Justice* [2010] UKSC 34, [2010] 4 All ER 62, [2010] IRLR 883 (a holder of judicial office is not employed under the necessary contract of employment, even in the wider definition of 'worker', and the Part-time Workers (Prevention of Less Favourable Treatment) Regulations 2000, SI 2000/1551, reg 17, makes it doubly clear that the part-time judiciary are not within the regulations), the UK Supreme Court made a reference to the Court of Justice of the European Union on the question as to whether there was a 'Community norm' which determined the concept of 'workers who have an employment contract or employment relationship' in the Framework Agreement on part-time work cl 2(1) (see PARA 73). The response made it clear that exclusion from the protection afforded by the Part-time Work Directive (and the Framework Agreement on part-time work which it adopted) may be permitted only if the relationship between judges and the Ministry of Justice is, by its nature, substantially different from an employment relationship between an employer and a worker: see Case C-393/10 *O'Brien v Ministry of Justice* [2012] All ER (EC) 757, [2012] 2 CMLR 728, [2012] ICR 955, [2012] IRLR 421, CJEU (it was for the national court to examine whether the pension-related inequality of treatment between full-time judges and part-time judges remunerated on a daily fee-paid basis may be justified by objective reasons). Subsequent to that reference, the UK Supreme Court held that a part-time recorder was in an employment relationship within the meaning of the Framework Agreement on part-time work cl 2(1), and therefore had to be treated as a 'worker' for the purposes of the Part-time Workers (Prevention of Less Favourable Treatment) Regulations 2000, SI 2000/1551: *Ministry of Justice (formerly Department for Constitutional Affairs) v O'Brien (Council of Immigration Judges intervening)* [2013] UKSC 6, [2013] 2 All ER 1, [2013] ICR 499, [2013] IRLR 315 (retired part-time recorder entitled to pension on terms equivalent to those applicable to circuit judge because the denial of a *pro rata* judicial pension to such workers, on the main ground of cost, could not under EU law constitute justification by itself). See further *O'Brien v Ministry of Justice* [2014] ICR 773, [2014] IRLR 440, EAT (employee's rights in respect of the level of his pension had begun with the date for the transposition of the Part-time Work Directive into domestic law, namely 7 April 2000; employee could not rely on the accrual of pension rights before that date, because he had enjoyed no such rights at that time, save in respect of any period needed for qualifying for access to a pension).

13 As to the meaning of 'contract of employment' for these purposes see PARA 75 note 2.

14 Part-time Workers (Prevention of Less Favourable Treatment) Regulations 2000, SI 2000/1551, reg 16(1). For these purposes, 'relevant officer' means (in relation to a member of a police force or a special constable or police cadet appointed for a police area) the chief officer of police and (in relation to any other person holding the office of constable or an appointment as a police cadet) the person who has the direction and control of the body of constables or cadets in question: see reg 16(2) (amended by SI 2006/594). For the purposes of the Part-time Workers (Prevention of Less Favourable Treatment) Regulations 2000, SI 2000/1551, the relevant officer, as so defined, must be treated as a corporation sole (reg 16(4) (added by SI 2005/2240)); and any constable who has been seconded to the National Crime Agency to serve as a member of its staff must be treated as employed by the National Crime Agency, in respect of actions taken by, or on behalf of, the National Crime Agency: reg 16(1A), (6) (reg 16(1A), (6) added by SI 2006/594; and amended by virtue of the Crime and Courts Act 2013 s 15(3), Sch 8 para 190). As to the secondment of police constables to the National Crime Agency for the purposes of the Part-time Workers (Prevention of Less Favourable Treatment) Regulations 2000, SI 2000/1551, reg 11 (liability of employers and principals) see PARA 81 note 3. As to the meaning of 'chief officer of police' see POLICE AND INVESTIGATORY POWERS vol 84 (2013) PARA 5; and as to the

meaning of 'police area' see POLICE AND INVESTIGATORY POWERS vol 84 (2013) PARA 52. As to the National Crime Agency see POLICE AND INVESTIGATORY POWERS vol 84 (2013) PARA 424.

83. Codes of practice relating to part-time workers. The Secretary of State[1] may issue codes of practice containing guidance for the purpose of[2]:

(1)   eliminating discrimination in the field of employment against part-time workers[3];

(2)   facilitating the development of opportunities for part-time work[4];

(3)   facilitating the flexible organisation of working time taking into account the needs of workers and employers[5];

(4)   any matter dealt with in the Framework Agreement annexed to the Part-time Work Directive[6].

The Secretary of State may revise a code and issue the whole or part of the revised code[7].

Before issuing or revising a code of practice in this way[8], however, the Secretary of State must consult such persons as he considers appropriate[9]; and he must, before issuing a code, publish a draft code, he must consider any representations made to him about the draft, and he must, if he thinks it appropriate, modify the draft in the light of any representations made to him[10].

A person's failure to observe a provision of a code does not make him liable to any proceedings[11].

A code is admissible in evidence in proceedings before an employment tribunal, and it must be taken into account by an employment tribunal in any case in which it appears to the tribunal to be relevant[12].

1   As to the Secretary of State see PARA 5 note 21.
2   See the Employment Relations Act 1999 s 20(1).
3   Employment Relations Act 1999 s 20(1)(a).
4   Employment Relations Act 1999 s 20(1)(b).
5   Employment Relations Act 1999 s 20(1)(c).
6   Employment Relations Act 1999 s 20(1)(d). As to Council Directive (EC) 97/81 of 15 December 1997 (OJ L14, 20.1.98, p 9) concerning the Framework Agreement on part-time work (the 'Part-time Work Directive') see PARA 73. At the date at which this volume states the law, no such code of practice had been issued.
7   Employment Relations Act 1999 s 20(2).
8   Ie before issuing or revising a code of practice under the Employment Relations Act 1999 s 20 (see the text and notes 1–7): see s 21(1).
9   Employment Relations Act 1999 s 21(1). For these purposes, and for the purposes of s 20(3), (4) (see the text and notes 11–12): (1) a reference to a code includes a reference to a revised code (s 21(5)(a)); (2) a reference to a draft code includes a reference to a draft revision (s 21(5)(b)); and (3) a reference to issuing a code includes a reference to issuing part of a revised code (s 21(5)(c)).
10   See the Employment Relations Act 1999 s 21(2). If, having followed the procedure under s 21(2), the Secretary of State decides to issue a code, he must lay a draft code before each House of Parliament (s 21(3)); and, if the draft code is approved by resolution of each House of Parliament, he must issue the code in the form of the draft (s 21(4)).
11   Employment Relations Act 1999 s 20(3).
12   Employment Relations Act 1999 s 20(4). As to employment tribunals see PARA 1399 et seq; and as to the procedure on a complaint made to an employment tribunal see PARA 1453 et seq.

B. FIXED-TERM WORK

84. Framework Agreement on Fixed-Term Work implemented by EU law. The purpose of the Framework Agreement on Fixed-Term Work[1] is:

(1)   to improve the quality of fixed-term work by ensuring the application of the principle of non-discrimination[2];

(2)   to establish a framework to prevent abuse arising from the use of successive fixed-term employment contracts or relationships[3].

In respect of employment conditions, fixed-term workers must not be treated in a less favourable manner than comparable permanent workers[4] solely because they have a fixed-term contract or relation, unless different treatment is justified on objective grounds[5]; and, where appropriate, the principle of *pro rata temporis* applies[6].

To prevent abuse arising from the use of successive fixed-term contracts or relationships, member states, after consultation with social partners in accordance with national law, collective agreements or practice, and/or the social partners, must, where there are no equivalent legal measures to prevent abuse, introduce, in a manner which takes account of the needs of specific sectors and/or categories of workers, one or more of the following measures[7]:

(a)   objective reasons justifying the renewal of such contracts or relationships[8];

(b)   the maximum total duration of successive fixed-term employment contracts or relationships[9];

(c)   the number of renewals of such contracts or relationships[10].

Employers must inform fixed-term workers about vacancies which become available in the undertaking or establishment to ensure that they have the same opportunity to secure permanent positions as other workers[11]; and, as far as possible, employers are to facilitate access by fixed-term workers to appropriate training opportunities to enhance their skills, career development and occupational mobility[12].

Fixed-term workers must be taken into account in calculating the threshold above which workers' representative bodies provided for in national and Community law may be constituted in the undertaking as required by national provisions[13]; and, as far as possible, employers should give consideration to the provision of appropriate information to existing workers' representative bodies about fixed-term work in the undertaking[14].

1   Ie the Framework Agreement on Fixed-term Work concluded on 18 March 1999 between the general cross-industry organisations (the 'Framework Agreement'), which is annexed to, and put into effect by, Council Directive (EC) 99/70 of 28 June 1999 (OJ L175, 10.7.99, p 43) concerning the framework agreement on fixed-term work concluded by ETUC, UNICE and CEEP (the 'Fixed-term Work Directive'): see art 1. The general cross-industry organisations are: the European Trade Union Confederation, the Union of Industrial and Employers' Confederations of Europe and the European Centre of Enterprises with Public Participation. Member states and/or the social partners (ie management and labour: see recital (2)) may maintain or introduce more favourable provisions for workers than those set out in the Framework Agreement: cl 8(1). The Framework Agreement is without prejudice to any more specific Community provisions and, in particular, Community provisions concerning equal treatment or opportunities for men and women: cl 8(2). As to legislation made for the purposes of implementing the Fixed-term Work Directive in the United Kingdom see the Fixed-term Employees (Prevention of Less Favourable Treatment) Regulations 2002, SI 2002/2034; and PARA 86 et seq (made under the Employment Act 2002 s 45: see PARA 85). As to the meaning of 'United Kingdom' see PARA 2 note 12.

2   Framework Agreement cl 1(a). The Framework Agreement applies to fixed-term workers who have an employment contract or employment relationship as defined in law, collective agreements or practice in each member state: cl 2(1). There is nothing in the Framework Agreement to suggest that it is limited to contracts for private sector workers: Case C–53/04 *Marrousu v Azienda Ospedaliera Ospedale San Martino di Genova e Cliniche Universitarie Convenzionate* [2006] ECR I-7213, [2006] All ER (D) 36 (Sep), ECJ. However, member states, after consultation with the social partners, and/or the social partners may provide that the Framework Agreement does not apply to:
    (1)   initial vocational training relationships and apprenticeship schemes (cl 2(2)(a));

(2)   employment contracts and relationships which have been concluded within the framework of a specific public or publicly-supported training, integration and vocational retraining scheme (cl 2(2)(b)).

For these purposes, the term 'fixed-term worker' means a person having an employment contract or relationship entered into directly between an employer and a worker where the end of the employment contract or relationship is determined by objective conditions such as reaching a specific date, completing a specific task, or the occurrence of a specific event: see cl 3(1). The Framework Agreement does not contain any provision that lays down the formal particulars that must be included in fixed-term employment contracts, however: Case C-362/13 *Fiamingo v Rete Ferroviaria Italiana SpA* [2014] All ER (D) 89 (Jul), CJEU (Framework Agreement applies to seafarers on board ferries making sea crossings between two ports situated in the same member state, who were employed as workers under fixed-term employment contracts that indicate only their duration (a 'maximum of 78 days') but not their termination date). The Fixed-term Work Directive and the Framework Agreement should be interpreted as not applying either to the fixed-term employment relationship between a temporary worker and a temporary employment business or to the employment relationship between such a worker and a user undertaking: Case C-290/12 *Rocca v Poste Italiane SpA* [2013] 3 CMLR 391, [2013] All ER (D) 111 (Apr), CJEU. See also *Duncombe v Secretary of State for Children, Schools and Families; Fletcher v Secretary of State for Children, Schools and Families* [2011] UKSC 14, [2011] 2 All ER 417, [2011] ICR 495, [2011] IRLR 498 (the purpose of the Fixed-term Work Directive was not to attack fixed-term contracts as such, but to ensure equal treatment for fixed-term workers by protecting them against discrimination and to prevent abuse arising from the use of successive fixed-term work agreements or contracts). As to jurisdiction see *Duncombe v Secretary of State for Children, Schools and Families (No 2)* [2011] UKSC 36, [2011] ICR 1312, [2011] IRLR 840; and PARA 757 note 4.

3   Framework Agreement cl 1(b). See Cases C-378–380/07 *Angelidaki v Organismos Nomarkhiaki Aftodiikisi Rethimnis; Giannoudi v Dimos Geropatamou* [2009] ECR I-3071, [2009] 3 CMLR 571, [2009] All ER (D) 86 (May), ECJ (the Framework Agreement did not preclude the application of a rule of national law which prohibited absolutely, in the public sector only, the conversion into a contract of indefinite duration of a succession of fixed-term employment contracts which, having been intended to cover fixed and permanent needs of the employer, had to be regarded as constituting an abuse).

4   The term 'comparable permanent worker' means a worker with an employment contract or relationship of indefinite duration, in the same establishment, engaged in the same or similar work/occupation, due regard being given to qualifications/skills: see Framework Agreement cl 3(2), para 1. Where there is no comparable permanent worker in the same establishment, the comparison must be made by reference to the applicable collective agreement or, where there is no applicable collective agreement, in accordance with national law, collective agreements or practice: cl 3(2), para 2.

5   Framework Agreement cl 4(1). The arrangements for the application of the Framework Agreement cl 4 are defined by the member states, after consultation with the social partners, and/or the social partners, having regard to European Union law, national law, collective agreements and practice: cl 4(3). Period-of-service qualifications relating to particular conditions of employment are the same for fixed-term workers as for permanent workers except where different length-of-service qualifications are justified on objective grounds: cl 4(4). See Joined Cases C-302/11–C-305/11 *Valenza v Autorita Garante della Concorrenza e del Mercato* [2013] 1 CMLR 1082, [2013] ICR 373, CJEU (provision under Italian law which allowed employee's wage for permanent post to be set without taking into account time spent previously doing the same work but on a fixed-term basis was held incompatible with the Framework Agreement cl 4(4) unless such discrimination could be objectively justified); and Case C-38/13 *Nierodzik v Samodzielny Publiczny Psychiatryczny Zaklad Opieki Zdrowotnej im. dr. Stanislawa Deresza w Choroszczy* [2014] 3 CMLR 262, [2014] ICR 600, [2014] All ER (D) 182 (Mar), CJEU (national rule which provided that a fixed notice period of two weeks might be applied for the termination of fixed-term contracts of more than six months, regardless of the length of service of the worker concerned, whereas the length of the notice period for contracts of indefinite duration was fixed in accordance with the length of service of the worker concerned, was precluded by the Framework Agreement cl 4(1) where those two categories of workers were in comparable situations).

As to a complaint based on the Framework Agreement cll 4, 5 and belated transposition of the Framework Agreement into Irish law and whether a national court is required to apply directly effective Community law in the absence of express jurisdiction see Case C-268/06 *Impact v Minister for Agriculture and Food* [2009] All ER (EC) 306, [2008] 2 CMLR 1265, ECJ.

6   Framework Agreement cl 4(2). See note 5.

7   See the Framework Agreement cl 5(1). Member states, after consultation with the social partners, and/or the social partners must, where appropriate, determine under what conditions fixed-term employment contracts or relationships are to be regarded as 'successive', or are to be deemed to be contracts or relationships of indefinite duration: cl 5(2).

8   Framework Agreement cl 5(1)(a). Head (a) in the text has to be interpreted as meaning that a temporary need for replacement staff, provided for by national legislation, might in principle constitute an objective reason, where the concept of 'objective reasons' must be understood for these purposes as referring to precise and concrete circumstances characterising a given activity: see Case C-586/10 *Kücük v Land Nordrhein-Westfalen* [2012] All ER (EC) 582, [2012] 2 CMLR 499, [2012] ICR 682, [2012] IRLR 697, CJEU (use of successive fixed-term employment contracts justified as cover for permanent employees temporarily away from work on parental or other such leave); and see Case C-212/04 *Adeneler v Ellinikos Organismos Galaktos (ELOG)* [2007] All ER (EC) 82, [2006] 3 CMLR 867, ECJ (a succession of fixed-term contracts which are intended to cover fixed and permanent needs of the employer constitutes an abuse, and the simple fact that national legislation requires the conclusion of fixed-term employment contracts cannot, by itself, constitute an objective reason for their renewal; the requirement is to show the presence of specific factors relating in particular to the activity in question and the conditions under which it is carried out). For the purposes of implementation, a member state can legitimately choose not to adopt the measure referred to in head (a) in the text and may prefer to adopt one or both of the measures referred to in head (b) or head (c) in the text instead, or it may even choose to maintain an existing equivalent legal measure, and it may do so provided that, whatever the measure thus chosen, the effective prevention of the misuse of fixed-term employment contracts or relationships is assured: Case C-362/13 *Fiamingo v Rete Ferroviaria Italiana SpA* [2014] All ER (D) 89 (Jul), CJEU (Framework Agreement cl 5 does not preclude, in principle, national legislation which provides for the conversion of fixed-term employment contracts into employment contracts of indefinite duration only in circumstances where the worker concerned has been employed continuously under such contracts by the same employer for a period longer than one year, the employment relationship being considered to be continuous where the fixed-term employment contracts are separated by time lapses of less than or equal to 60 days, but the referring court must satisfy itself that the conditions of application and the effective implementation of that legislation result in a measure that is adequate to prevent and punish the misuse of successive fixed-term employment contracts or relationships).

9   Framework Agreement cl 5(1)(b). The Framework Agreement cl 5 had to be interpreted as meaning that a member state which provided in its national legislation for conversion of fixed-term employment contracts into an employment contract of indefinite duration when the fixed-term contracts reached a certain duration was not obliged to require that the contract of indefinite duration reproduced in identical terms the principal clauses in the previous contracts; however, in order not to undermine the practical effect of, or the objectives pursued by, the Fixed-term Work Directive, the member state had to ensure that the conversion was not accompanied by material amendments to the clauses of the previous contracts in a way that was, overall, unfavourable to the person concerned when the subject-matter of that person's tasks and the nature of his functions remained unchanged: Case C-251/11 *Huet v Université de Bretagne Occidentale* [2012] 2 CMLR 755, [2012] ICR 694, [2012] IRLR 703, ECJ; and see Case C-180/04 *Vassallo v Azienda Ospedaliera Ospedale San Martino di Genova e Cliniche Universitarie Convenzionate* [2006] ECR I-7251, [2006] All ER (D) 45 (Sep), ECJ (legislation which prevents successive fixed-term contracts from being converted into indefinite contracts, where such conversion applies to contracts concluded with both public and private sector employers, is not contrary to the Framework Agreement if there are in place other measures which effectively prevent abuse of such contracts); Case C-109/09 *Deutsche Lufthansa AG v Kumpan* [2011] ECR I-1309, [2011] All ER (EC) 754, [2011] ICR 1278, ECJ (the concept in the national legislation of 'a close objective connection with a previous employment contract of indefinite duration concluded with the same employer' had to be applied to situations in which a fixed-term contract had not been immediately preceded by a contract of indefinite duration concluded with the same employer and an interval of several years separated those contracts, where, for that entire period, the initial employment relationship continued for the same activity, with the same employer, by means of an uninterrupted succession of fixed-term contracts). See also note 8.

10 Framework Agreement cl 5(1)(c). See also note 8.

11 Framework Agreement cl 6(1). Such information may be provided by way of a general announcement at a suitable place in the undertaking or establishment: see cl 6(1).

12 Framework Agreement cl 6(2).

13 Framework Agreement cl 7(1). The arrangements for the application of cl 7(1) are defined by
    member states, after consultation with the social partners, and/or the social partners in
    accordance with national law, collective agreements or practice and having regard to cl 4(1) (see
    the text and notes 4–5): cl 7(2).
14 Framework Agreement cl 7(3).

85.   Secretary of State's power to make fixed-term work regulations.   The
Secretary of State[1] must make regulations[2] for the purpose of securing that
employees[3] in fixed-term employment are treated, for such purposes and to such
extent as the regulations may specify, no less favourably than employees in
permanent employment, and for the purpose of preventing abuse arising from
the use of successive periods of fixed-term employment[4]. The regulations may:

(1)   specify classes of employee who are to be taken to be, or not to be, in
      fixed-term employment[5];

(2)   specify classes of employee who are to be taken to be, or not to be, in
      permanent employment[6];

(3)   specify circumstances in which employees in fixed-term employment are
      to be taken to be, or not to be, treated less favourably than employees in
      permanent employment[7];

(4)   specify circumstances in which periods of fixed-term employment are to
      be taken to be, or not to be, successive[8];

(5)   specify circumstances in which fixed-term employment is to have effect
      as permanent employment[9];

(6)   make provision which has effect in relation to employees in fixed-term
      employment generally or provision which has effect only in relation to
      specified classes of employee in fixed-term employment[10].

The regulations also may:

(a)   confer jurisdiction (including exclusive jurisdiction) on employment
      tribunals[11];

(b)   provide for specified obligations not to apply in specified
      circumstances[12];

(c)   make provision about notices or information to be given, evidence to be
      produced and other procedures to be followed[13];

(d)   amend, apply with or without modifications, or make provision similar
      to any provision of the Employment Rights Act 1996[14], the Trade Union
      and Labour Relations (Consolidation) Act 1992, or the Social Security
      Contributions and Benefits Act 1992[15];

(e)   provide for the provisions of specified agreements to have effect in place
      of provisions of the regulations to such extent and in such circumstances
      as may be specified[16].

Without prejudice to the generality of the provisions described above, the
regulations may make any provision in relation to employees which appears to
the Secretary of State to be necessary or expedient: (i) for the purpose of
implementing the Fixed-term Work Directive[17] in its application to terms and
conditions of employment[18]; (ii) for the purpose of dealing with any matter
arising out of or related to the United Kingdom's obligations under that
Directive[19]; (iii) for the purpose of any matter dealt with by the Framework
Agreement or for the purpose of applying the provisions of the Framework
Agreement to any matter relating to fixed-term workers[20].

1   As to the Secretary of State see PARA 5 note 21.
2   Any power of the Secretary of State to make orders or regulations under the Employment
    Act 2002 includes power:

(1)   to make different provision for different cases or circumstances (s 51(1)(a));

(2)   to make such incidental, supplementary, consequential or transitional provision as the Secretary of State thinks fit (s 51(1)(b)).

Any such power is exercisable by statutory instrument (s 51(2)); but no regulations may be made under s 45 unless a draft of the regulations has been laid before and approved by resolution of each House of Parliament (s 51(4) (amended by the Employment Act 2008 s 20, Schedule Pt 1)). Head (2) above, in its application to the Employment Act 2002 s 45, includes power to amend an enactment: s 45(5).

3   For these purposes, 'employee' means an individual who has entered into or works under (or, where the employment has ceased, worked under) a contract of employment, where 'contract of employment' means a contract of service or apprenticeship, whether express or implied, and (if it is express) whether oral or in writing: see the Employment Act 2002 s 45(6). As to the meaning of 'employee', 'contract of employment' and related expressions in relation to employment rights generally see PARA 2 et seq. As to the meaning of 'contract of service' see PARA 1 note 1. As to the position of apprentices and youth trainees at common law see PARAS 112, 128–129, 636, 747–754. As to the statutory law on apprenticeships see EDUCATION vol 35 (2011) PARA 682 et seq. As to the meaning of 'writing' see PARA 2 note 8.

4   See the Employment Act 2002 s 45(1). In exercise of this power, the Secretary of State has made the Fixed-term Employees (Prevention of Less Favourable Treatment) Regulations 2002, SI 2002/2034 (see PARA 86 et seq), which came into force on 1 October 2002: reg 1(1). The Fixed-term Employees (Prevention of Less Favourable Treatment) Regulations 2002, SI 2002/2034 (as so made under the Employment Act 2002 s 45) have been made for the purposes of implementing in the United Kingdom the Framework Agreement on Fixed-term Work concluded on 18 March 1999 between the general cross-industry organisations (the 'Framework Agreement'), which is annexed to, and put into effect by, Council Directive (EC) 99/70 of 28 June 1999 (OJ L175, 10.7.99, p 43) concerning the framework agreement on fixed-term work concluded by ETUC, UNICE and CEEP (the 'Fixed-term Work Directive'): see PARA 84. The Directive and the framework agreement are directed at discrimination against workers on fixed-term contracts in what is in reality an indefinite employment rather than the justifiable employment practice of employing people on single fixed-term contracts (which in itself does not offend against either the Directive or the Regulations): *Duncombe v Secretary of State for Children, Schools and Families, Fletcher v Secretary of State for Children, Schools and Families* [2011] UKSC 14, [2011] 2 All ER 417, [2011] ICR 495, [2011] IRLR 498. As to the meaning of 'United Kingdom' see PARA 2 note 12.

5   Employment Act 2002 s 45(2)(a).

6   Employment Act 2002 s 45(2)(b).

7   Employment Act 2002 s 45(2)(c).

8   Employment Act 2002 s 45(2)(d).

9   Employment Act 2002 s 45(2)(e).

10   Employment Act 2002 s 45(2)(f).

11   Employment Act 2002 s 45(3)(a). As to employment tribunals see PARA 1399 et seq; and as to the procedure on a complaint made to an employment tribunal see PARA 1453 et seq.

12   Employment Act 2002 s 45(3)(b).

13   Employment Act 2002 s 45(3)(c).

14   Ie including, in particular, the Employment Rights Act 1996 Pt V (ss 43M–49A) (protection from suffering detriment in employment: see PARA 612 et seq), Pt X (ss 94–134A) (unfair dismissal: see PARA 757 et seq) and Pt XIII (ss 191–209) (miscellaneous provisions): see the Employment Act 2002 s 45(3)(d).

15   Employment Act 2002 s 45(3)(d). As to the Trade Union and Labour Relations (Consolidation) Act 1992 see PARA 891 et seq.

16   Employment Act 2002 s 45(3)(e).

17   Ie Council Directive (EC) 99/70 of 28 June 1999 (OJ L175, 10.7.99, p 43) concerning the framework agreement on fixed-term work concluded by ETUC, UNICE and CEEP (the 'Fixed-term Work Directive') (see PARA 84): see the Employment Act 2002 s 45(4)(a).

18   Employment Act 2002 s 45(4)(a).

19   Employment Act 2002 s 45(4)(b).

20   Employment Act 2002 s 45(4)(c).

86.   Application of fixed-term work regulations.   For the purposes of the regulations that have been made for the purpose of implementing the Fixed-term Work Directive[1], an employee is a 'comparable permanent employee', in relation to a fixed-term employee[2], if, at the time when the treatment that is alleged to be less favourable to the fixed-term employee takes place[3]:

(1)   both employees are employed by the same employer[4], and engaged in the same or broadly similar work having regard, where relevant, to whether they have a similar level of qualification and skills[5]; and

(2)   the permanent employee[6] works or is based at the same establishment as the fixed-term employee or, where there is no comparable permanent employee working or based at that establishment who satisfies the requirements of head (1) above, works or is based at a different establishment and satisfies those requirements[7].

1   The Fixed-term Employees (Prevention of Less Favourable Treatment) Regulations 2002, SI 2002/2034, have been made under the Employment Act 2002 s 45 for the purposes of implementing in the United Kingdom the Framework Agreement on Fixed-term Work concluded on 18 March 1999 between the general cross-industry organisations (the 'Framework Agreement'), which is annexed to, and put into effect by, Council Directive (EC) 99/70 of 28 June 1999 (OJ L175, 10.7.99, p 43) concerning the framework agreement on fixed-term work concluded by ETUC, UNICE and CEEP (the 'Fixed-term Work Directive'): see PARA 84. As to the meaning of 'United Kingdom' see PARA 2 note 12.

2   For these purposes, 'fixed-term employee' means an employee who is employed under a fixed-term contract: see the Fixed-term Employees (Prevention of Less Favourable Treatment) Regulations 2002, SI 2002/2034, reg 1(2). 'Fixed-term contract' means a contract of employment that, under its provisions determining how it will terminate in the normal course, will terminate: (1) on the expiry of a specific term; (2) on the completion of a particular task; or (3) on the occurrence or non-occurrence of any other specific event other than the attainment by the employee of any normal and bona fide retiring age in the establishment for an employee holding the position held by him; and any reference to 'fixed-term' must be construed accordingly: see reg 1(2). As to the meanings of 'contract of employment' and 'employee' for these purposes see PARA 85 note 3. As to the termination of the contract of employment by expiry see PARA 725. By virtue of head (2) above, the effect of *Ryan v Shipboard Maintenance Ltd* [1980] ICR 88, [1980] IRLR 16, EAT, is reversed to the extent that an employee who has contracted to complete a specific task no longer has his contract terminated upon completion of the task without there being a dismissal. The ability of the parties to bring a contract to an end with notice at an earlier date does not make the contract anything other than one for a fixed term: see *Allen v National Australia Group Europe Ltd* [2004] IRLR 847, EAT (Sc) (provision for earlier notice did not negate the intention that the parties would see through the fixed term, unless and until some event which was not in the normal course occurred). A contract is not for a fixed term if it fixes merely the minimum duration: *Fuller-Shapcott v Chilton Electric Ltd* (1970) 5 ITR 186; *Weston v University College, Swansea* [1975] IRLR 102.

     As to the applicability of the principle in *Lawson v Serco Ltd, Botham v Ministry of Defence, Crofts v Veta Ltd* [2006] UKHL 3, [2006] 1 All ER 823 [2006] IRLR 289 about claims by employees overseas (see PARA 757 note 4) to the legislation protecting fixed-term workers see *Ashbourne v Department of Education and Skills, Collins v Department of Education and Skills* [2007] All ER (D) 390 (Nov), EAT.

3   See the Fixed-term Employees (Prevention of Less Favourable Treatment) Regulations 2002, SI 2002/2034, reg 2(1). For these purposes, an employee is not a comparable permanent employee if his employment has ceased: see reg 2(2).

4   Fixed-term Employees (Prevention of Less Favourable Treatment) Regulations 2002, SI 2002/2034, reg 2(1)(a)(i). For these purposes, 'employer', in relation to any employee, means the person by whom the employee is (or, where the employment has ceased, was) employed: see reg 1(2). As to the meaning of 'employer' and related expressions in relation to employment rights generally see PARA 2 et seq.

5   Fixed-term Employees (Prevention of Less Favourable Treatment) Regulations 2002, SI 2002/2034, reg 2(1)(a)(ii).

6   For these purposes, 'permanent employee' means an employee who is not employed under a fixed-term contract; and any reference to 'permanent employment' must be construed accordingly: see the Fixed-term Employees (Prevention of Less Favourable Treatment) Regulations 2002, SI 2002/2034, reg 1(2).

7   Fixed-term Employees (Prevention of Less Favourable Treatment) Regulations 2002, SI 2002/2034, reg 2(1)(b).

87. Less favourable treatment of fixed-term employees under regulations. A fixed-term employee[1] has the right not to be treated by his employer[2] less favourably than the employer treats a comparable permanent employee[3]:

(1) as regards the terms of his contract[4]; or

(2) by being subjected to any other detriment by any act, or deliberate failure to act, of his employer[5].

However, the right so conferred[6] applies only if the treatment is on the ground that the employee is a fixed-term employee[7], and the treatment is not justified on objective grounds[8].

In determining whether a fixed-term employee has been treated less favourably than a comparable permanent employee, the *pro rata* principle[9] is to be applied unless it is inappropriate[10].

If an employee who considers that his employer may have treated him in a manner which infringes the right not to be treated less favourably[11] requests in writing from his employer a written statement giving particulars of the reasons for the treatment, the employee is entitled to be provided with such a statement within 21 days of his request[12]. Such a written statement is admissible as evidence in any proceedings under the Fixed-term Employees (Prevention of Less Favourable Treatment) Regulations 2002[13]; and, if it appears to the tribunal in any such proceedings that the employer deliberately, and without reasonable excuse, omitted to provide a written statement, or that the written statement is evasive or equivocal, it may draw any inference which it considers it just and equitable to draw, including an inference that the employer has infringed the right in question[14].

The provisions of the Employment Rights Act 1996 that impose restrictions on contracting out[15] apply in relation to the Fixed-term Employees (Prevention of Less Favourable Treatment) Regulations 2002[16], as if those regulations were contained in the 1996 Act[17].

1 As to the meaning of 'fixed-term employee' see PARA 86 note 2.
2 As to the meaning of 'employer' for these purposes see PARA 86 note 4.
3 See the Fixed-term Employees (Prevention of Less Favourable Treatment) Regulations 2002, SI 2002/2034, reg 3(1). As to the meaning of 'comparable permanent employee' see PARA 86. The less favourable treatment applies to pay (if not pay determination) (see Case C–307/05 *Del Cerro Alonso v Osakidetza-Servicio Vasco de Salud* [2007] 3 CMLR 1492, [2007] IRLR 911, ECJ) and pensions (see Case C–268/06 *Impact v Minister for Agriculture and Food* [2009] All ER (EC) 306, [2008] IRLR 552, ECJ).
4 Fixed-term Employees (Prevention of Less Favourable Treatment) Regulations 2002, SI 2002/2034, reg 3(1)(a). As to the meaning of 'contract of employment' for these purposes see PARA 85 note 3. Once it was recognised that fixed-term contracts are not only lawful, but are recognised in the preamble to Council Directive (EC) 99/70 of 28 June 1999 (OJ L175, 10.7.99, p 43) concerning the framework agreement on fixed-term work concluded by ETUC, UNICE and CEEP (the 'Fixed-term Work Directive') (see PARA 84) as responding 'in certain circumstances, to the needs of both employers and workers' (see preamble, para 2), it follows that the termination of such a contract by the simple effluxion of time cannot, of itself, be said to fall within the Fixed-term Employees (Prevention of Less Favourable Treatment) Regulations 2002, SI 2002/2034, reg 3(1): *Webley v Department for Work and Pensions* [2004] EWCA Civ 1745, [2005] ICR 577, [2005] IRLR 288.
5 Fixed-term Employees (Prevention of Less Favourable Treatment) Regulations 2002, SI 2002/2034, reg 3(1)(b).
6 Subject to the Fixed-term Employees (Prevention of Less Favourable Treatment) Regulations 2002, SI 2002/2034, reg 3(3), (4) (see the text and notes 7–8), the right so conferred includes, in particular, the right of the fixed-term employee in question not to be treated less favourably than the employer treats a comparable permanent employee in relation to:

(1) any period of service qualification relating to any particular condition of service (reg 3(2)(a));

(2) the opportunity to receive training (reg 3(2)(b)); or

(3)   the opportunity to secure any permanent position in the establishment (reg 3(2)(c)).
In order to ensure that an employee is able to exercise the right conferred as described in
head (3) above, the employee has the right to be informed by his employer of available vacancies
in the establishment: reg 3(6). For this purpose, an employee is 'informed by his employer' only
if the vacancy is contained in an advertisement which the employee has a reasonable
opportunity of reading in the course of his employment or the employee is given reasonable
notification of the vacancy in some other way: reg 3(7).

7   Fixed-term Employees (Prevention of Less Favourable Treatment) Regulations 2002,
SI 2002/2034, reg 3(3)(a). The fact that an employer has applied discrimination to other
employee groups as well as to fixed-term employees is not relevant in answering the question as
to why the employer had decided to treat fixed-term employees differently: *Cure v Coutts
& Co plc* [2004] All ER (D) 393 (Oct), EAT (bonus payment made to specified employees,
excluding all non-permanent staff).

8   Fixed-term Employees (Prevention of Less Favourable Treatment) Regulations 2002,
SI 2002/2034, reg 3(3)(b). Regulation 3(3)(b) is subject to reg 4: reg 3(4). Accordingly, without
prejudice to the generality of reg 3(3)(b), where a fixed-term employee is treated by his employer
less favourably than the employer treats a comparable permanent employee as regards any term
of his contract, the treatment in question is regarded for the purposes of reg 3(3)(b) as justified
on objective grounds if the terms of the fixed-term employee's contract of employment, taken as
a whole, are at least as favourable as the terms of the comparable permanent employee's
contract of employment: see reg 4. See also Case C–307/05 *Del Cerro Alonso v
Osakidetza-Servicio Vasco de Salud* [2007] 3 CMLR 1492, [2007] IRLR 911, ECJ (unequal
treatment must be justified by the existence of precise and concrete factors, characterising the
employment conditions to which it relates, in the specific context in which it occurs and on the
basis of objective and transparent criteria in order to ensure that that unequal treatment in fact
responds to a genuine need, is appropriate for achieving the objective pursued and is necessary
for that purpose).
    The defence of objective justification is specifically allowed by the Framework Agreement on
Fixed-term Work concluded on 18 March 1999 between the general cross-industry
organisations (the 'Framework Agreement'), which is annexed to, and put into effect by, Council
Directive (EC) 99/70 of 28 June 1999 (OJ L175, 10.7.99, p 43) concerning the framework
agreement on fixed-term work concluded by ETUC, UNICE and CEEP (the 'Fixed-term Work
Directive'): see PARA 84.

9   '*Pro rata* principle' means that where a comparable permanent employee receives or is entitled
to pay or to any other benefit, a fixed-term employee is to receive or be entitled to such
proportion of that pay or other benefit as is reasonable in the circumstances having regard to the
length of his contract of employment and to the terms on which the pay or other benefit is
offered: see the Fixed-term Employees (Prevention of Less Favourable Treatment)
Regulations 2002, SI 2002/2034, reg 1(2).

10   Fixed-term Employees (Prevention of Less Favourable Treatment) Regulations 2002,
SI 2002/2034, reg 3(5).

11   Ie the right conferred on him by the Fixed-term Employees (Prevention of Less Favourable
Treatment) Regulations 2002, SI 2002/2034, reg 3 (see the text and notes 1–10): see reg 5(1).

12   Fixed-term Employees (Prevention of Less Favourable Treatment) Regulations 2002,
SI 2002/2034, reg 5(1). Regulation 5 does not apply where the treatment in question consists of
the dismissal of an employee and the employee is entitled to a written statement of reasons for
his dismissal under the Employment Rights Act 1996 s 92 (see PARA 755): Fixed-term Employees
(Prevention of Less Favourable Treatment) Regulations 2002, SI 2002/2034, reg 5(4). As to
unfair dismissal for applying fixed-term work regulations see PARA 89. As to the meaning of
'writing' see PARA 2 note 8.

13   Fixed-term Employees (Prevention of Less Favourable Treatment) Regulations 2002,
SI 2002/2034, reg 5(2). See note 12.

14   Fixed-term Employees (Prevention of Less Favourable Treatment) Regulations 2002,
SI 2002/2034, reg 5(3). See note 12.

15   Ie the Employment Rights Act 1996 s 203 (see PARA 150): see the Fixed-term Employees
(Prevention of Less Favourable Treatment) Regulations 2002, SI 2002/2034, reg 10.

16   Ie the Fixed-term Employees (Prevention of Less Favourable Treatment) Regulations 2002,
SI 2002/2034 (see also PARAS 86, 88 et seq): see reg 10.

17   Fixed-term Employees (Prevention of Less Favourable Treatment) Regulations 2002,
SI 2002/2034, reg 10.

88.   Treatment of successive fixed-term contracts under fixed-term work regulations.   Where:

(1) an employee[1] is employed under a contract purporting to be a fixed-term contract[2]; and

(2) the contract mentioned in head (1) above has previously been renewed[3] (or where the employee has previously been employed on a fixed-term contract before the start of the contract mentioned in head (1) above)[4],

then, with effect from the specified date[5], the provision of the contract mentioned in head (1) above that restricts the duration of the contract is of no effect, and the employee is a permanent employee[6], if:

(a) the employee has been continuously employed under the contract mentioned in head (1) above, or under that contract taken with a previous fixed-term contract, for a period of four years or more[7]; and

(b) the employment of the employee under a fixed-term contract was not justified on objective grounds[8]: (i) where the contract mentioned in head (1) above has been renewed, at the time when it was last renewed[9]; (ii) where that contract has not been renewed, at the time when it was entered into[10].

A collective agreement or a workforce agreement[11] may modify the application of these provisions in relation to any employee or specified description of employees[12].

If an employee who considers accordingly[13] that he is a permanent employee, requests in writing from his employer a written statement confirming that his contract is no longer fixed-term or that he is now a permanent employee, he is entitled to be provided, within 21 days of his request, with either such a statement or a statement giving reasons why his contract remains fixed-term[14]; and, if the reasons so stated include an assertion that there were objective grounds for the engagement of the employee under a fixed-term contract (or the renewal of such a contract), the statement must include a statement of those grounds[15].

Such a written statement is admissible as evidence in any proceedings before a court, an employment tribunal and the Commissioners for Revenue and Customs[16]; and, if it appears to the court or tribunal in any proceedings that the employer deliberately, and without reasonable excuse, omitted to provide a written statement, or that the written statement is evasive or equivocal, it may draw any inference which it considers it just and equitable to draw[17].

An employee who considers that[18] he is a permanent employee may present an application to an employment tribunal for a declaration to that effect[19].

1   As to the meaning of 'employee' for these purposes see PARA 85 note 3.
2   Fixed-term Employees (Prevention of Less Favourable Treatment) Regulations 2002, SI 2002/2034, reg 8(1)(a). As to the meaning of 'fixed-term contract' see PARA 86 note 2.
3   For these purposes, 'renewal' includes extension; and references to renewing a contract must be construed accordingly: see the Fixed-term Employees (Prevention of Less Favourable Treatment) Regulations 2002, SI 2002/2034, reg 1(2).
4   Fixed-term Employees (Prevention of Less Favourable Treatment) Regulations 2002, SI 2002/2034, reg 8(1)(b).
5   Ie with effect from the date specified in the Fixed-term Employees (Prevention of Less Favourable Treatment) Regulations 2002, SI 2002/2034, reg 8(3): see reg 8(2). The date referred to in reg 8(2) is whichever is the later of:
    (1) the date on which the contract mentioned in head (1) in the text was entered into or last renewed (reg 8(3)(a)); and
    (2) the date on which the employee acquired four years' continuous employment (reg 8(3)(b)).
    See also note 12. For the purposes of reg 8, the Employment Rights Act 1996 Pt XIV Ch I (ss 210–219) (see PARA 130 et seq) applies in determining whether an employee has been

continuously employed, and any period of continuous employment falling before 10 July 2002 is disregarded: Fixed-term Employees (Prevention of Less Favourable Treatment) Regulations 2002, SI 2002/2034, reg 8(4).

6   See the Fixed-term Employees (Prevention of Less Favourable Treatment) Regulations 2002, SI 2002/2034, reg 8(2). See also note 12. As to the meaning of 'permanent employee' see PARA 86 note 6.

7   Fixed-term Employees (Prevention of Less Favourable Treatment) Regulations 2002, SI 2002/2034, reg 8(2)(a). The United Kingdom could have chosen to implement the 'Fixed-term Work Directive' (see PARA 84) by setting a maximum number of renewals or successive fixed-term contracts, or by setting a maximum duration to the employment, but Parliament chose the alternative route of requiring objective justification after four years to provide a more flexible approach, capable of catering for the wide variety of circumstances in which a succession of fixed term contracts may be used: *Duncombe v Secretary of State for Children, Schools and Families, Fletcher v Secretary of State for Children, Schools and Families* [2011] UKSC 14, [2011] 2 All ER 417, [2011] ICR 495, [2011] IRLR 498.

8   It is the use of successive contracts to make up fixed-term employment that must be justified rather than any overarching limit on total employment achieved thereby: *Duncombe v Secretary of State for Children, Schools and Families; Fletcher v Secretary of State for Children, Schools and Families* [2011] UKSC 14, [2011] 2 All ER 417, [2011] ICR 495, [2011] IRLR 498 (it was objectively justified for the Secretary of State to employ teachers to work at European Schools on the basis of successive fixed-term contracts of 2, 3 then 4 years, because the board of governors had defined the terms of those secondments on the basis that teachers were employed to do a particular job which could only last for nine years). See also PARA 87.

9   Fixed-term Employees (Prevention of Less Favourable Treatment) Regulations 2002, SI 2002/2034, reg 8(2)(b)(i).

10 Fixed-term Employees (Prevention of Less Favourable Treatment) Regulations 2002, SI 2002/2034, reg 8(2)(b)(ii).

11 For these purposes, 'collective agreement' means a collective agreement within the meaning of the Trade Union and Labour Relations (Consolidation) Act 1992 s 178 (see PARA 1093), the trade union parties to which are independent trade unions within the meaning of s 5 (see PARA 904): see the Fixed-term Employees (Prevention of Less Favourable Treatment) Regulations 2002, SI 2002/2034, reg 1(2). 'Workforce agreement' means an agreement between an employer and his employees or their representatives in respect of which the following conditions are satisfied (see reg 1(2), Sch 1 para 1):

(1)   the agreement is in writing (Sch 1 para 1(a));

(2)   it has effect for a specified period not exceeding five years (Sch 1 para 1(b));

(3)   it applies either: (a) to all of the relevant members of the workforce (Sch 1 para 1(c)(i)); or (b) to all of the relevant members of the workforce who belong to a particular group (Sch 1 para 1(c)(ii));

(4)   the agreement is signed: (a) in the case of an agreement of the kind referred to in head (3)(a) above, by the representatives of the workforce and, in the case of an agreement of the kind referred to in head (3)(b) above by the representatives of the group to which the agreement applies, excluding (in either case) any representative not a relevant member of the workforce on the date on which the agreement was first made available for signature (Sch 1 para 1(d)(i)); or (b) if the employer employed 20 or fewer employees on the date referred to in head (4)(a) above, either by the appropriate representatives in accordance with that head or by the majority of the employees employed by him (Sch 1 para 1(d)(ii));

(5)   before the agreement was made available for signature, the employer provided all the employees to whom it was intended to apply on the date on which it came into effect with copies of the text of the agreement and such guidance as those employees might reasonably require in order to understand it fully (Sch 1 para 1(e)).

As to the meaning of 'employer' for these purposes see PARA 86 note 4. As to the meaning of 'writing' see PARA 2 note 8. For these purposes, 'relevant members of the workforce' are all of the employees employed by a particular employer, excluding any employee whose terms and conditions of employment are provided for, wholly or in part, in a collective agreement; 'a particular group' is a group of the relevant members of a workforce who undertake a particular function, work at a particular workplace or belong to a particular department or unit within their employer's business; 'representatives of the workforce' are employees duly elected to represent the relevant members of the workforce; and 'representatives of the group' are employees duly elected to represent the members of a particular group: see Sch 1 para 2. Representatives are 'duly elected' if the election at which they are elected satisfies the requirements of Sch 1 para 3 (see Sch 1 para 2), namely that:

- (i) the number of representatives to be elected is determined by the employer (Sch 1 para 3(a));
- (ii) the candidates for election as representatives of the workforce are relevant members of the workforce, and the candidates for election as representatives of a group are members of that group (Sch 1 para 3(b));
- (iii) no employee who is eligible to be a candidate is unreasonably excluded from standing for election (Sch 1 para 3(c));
- (iv) all the relevant members of the workforce are entitled to vote for representatives of the workforce, and all the members of a particular group are entitled to vote for representatives of the group (Sch 1 para 3(d));
- (v) the employees entitled to vote may vote for as many candidates as there are representatives to be elected (Sch 1 para 3(e));
- (vi) the election is conducted so as to secure that: (A) so far as is reasonably practicable, those voting do so in secret (Sch 1 para 3(f)(i)); and (B) the votes given at the election are fairly and accurately counted (Sch 1 para 3(f)(ii)).

12 Fixed-term Employees (Prevention of Less Favourable Treatment) Regulations 2002, SI 2002/2034, reg 8(5). Specifically, such an agreement may substitute for the provisions of reg 8(2) (see the text and notes 5–10) or reg 8(3) (see note 5), or for the provisions of both, one or more different provisions which, in order to prevent abuse arising from the use of successive fixed-term contracts, specify one or more of the following:

- (1) the maximum total period for which the employee or employees of that description may be continuously employed on a fixed-term contract or on successive fixed-term contracts (reg 8(5)(a));
- (2) the maximum number of successive fixed-term contracts and renewals of such contracts under which the employee or employees of that description may be employed (reg 8(5)(b)); or
- (3) objective grounds justifying the renewal of fixed-term contracts, or the engagement of the employee or employees of that description under successive fixed-term contracts (reg 8(5)(c)),

and those provisions have effect in relation to that employee or an employee of that description as if they were contained in reg 8(2), (3) (see reg 8(5)).

13 Ie by virtue of the Fixed-term Employees (Prevention of Less Favourable Treatment) Regulations 2002, SI 2002/2034, reg 8 (see the text and notes 1–12): see reg 9(1).

14 See the Fixed-term Employees (Prevention of Less Favourable Treatment) Regulations 2002, SI 2002/2034, reg 9(1).

15 Fixed-term Employees (Prevention of Less Favourable Treatment) Regulations 2002, SI 2002/2034, reg 9(2).

16 Fixed-term Employees (Prevention of Less Favourable Treatment) Regulations 2002, SI 2002/2034, reg 9(3). There is a requirement for early ACAS conciliation to be tried in order to promote a settlement before tribunal proceedings are instituted on a complaint under the Fixed-term Employees (Prevention of Less Favourable Treatment) Regulations 2002, SI 2002/2034, reg 9: see the Employment Tribunals Act 1996 s 18(1)(m); and PARA 152 note 1. As to the constitution and powers of ACAS see PARA 1213 et seq. As to employment tribunals see PARA 1399 et seq; and as to the procedure on a complaint made to an employment tribunal see PARA 1453 et seq. As to the Commissioners for Her Majesty's Revenue and Customs see INCOME TAXATION vol 58 (2014) PARAS 33–34.

17 See the Fixed-term Employees (Prevention of Less Favourable Treatment) Regulations 2002, SI 2002/2034, reg 9(4).

18 Ie by virtue of the Fixed-term Employees (Prevention of Less Favourable Treatment) Regulations 2002, SI 2002/2034, reg 8 (see the text and notes 1–12): see reg 9(5).

19 Fixed-term Employees (Prevention of Less Favourable Treatment) Regulations 2002, SI 2002/2034, reg 9(5). However, no application may be made under reg 9(5) unless: (1) the employee in question has previously requested a statement under reg 9(1) (see the text and notes 13–14) and the employer has either failed to provide a statement or given a statement of reasons why his contract remains fixed-term (reg 9(6)(a)); and (2) the employee is at the time the application is made employed by the employer (reg 9(6)(b)).

89. Employee's dismissal for applying fixed-term work regulations to be regarded as unfair. An employee[1] who is dismissed is regarded as unfairly dismissed for the purposes of the Employment Rights Act 1996[2] if the reason (or, if more than one, the principal reason) for the dismissal is[3]:

(1)   that the employee:

     (a)   has brought proceedings against the employer[4] under the Fixed-term Employees (Prevention of Less Favourable Treatment) Regulations 2002[5];

     (b)   has requested from his employer a written statement[6];

     (c)   has given evidence or information in connection with such proceedings brought by any employee[7];

     (d)   otherwise did anything under the Fixed-term Employees (Prevention of Less Favourable Treatment) Regulations 2002 in relation to the employer or any other person[8];

     (e)   has alleged that the employer has infringed the Fixed-term Employees (Prevention of Less Favourable Treatment) Regulations 2002[9];

     (f)   has refused or proposed to refuse to forgo a right conferred on him by the Fixed-term Employees (Prevention of Less Favourable Treatment) Regulations 2002[10];

     (g)   has declined to sign a workforce agreement[11]; or

     (h)   being either a representative of members of the workforce[12], or a candidate in an election in which any person elected will (on being elected) become such a representative, has performed (or proposed to perform) any functions or activities as such a representative or candidate[13]; or

(2)   that the employer believes or suspects that the employee has done or intends to do any of the things mentioned in head (1) above[14].

1   As to the meaning of 'employee' for these purposes see PARA 85 note 3.

2   Ie for the purposes of the Employment Rights Act 1996 Pt X (ss 94–134A) (unfair dismissal: see PARA 757 et seq): see the Fixed-term Employees (Prevention of Less Favourable Treatment) Regulations 2002, SI 2002/2034, reg 6(1).

3   See the Fixed-term Employees (Prevention of Less Favourable Treatment) Regulations 2002, SI 2002/2034, reg 6(1). The text refers to a reason specified in reg 6(3) (see heads (1), (2) in the text): see reg 6(1). A redundancy selection for a reason specified in reg 6(3) is also to be considered unfair: see the Employment Rights Act 1996 s 105(7F); and PARA 781.

     Where a dismissal is unfair under the Fixed-term Employees (Prevention of Less Favourable Treatment) Regulations 2002, SI 2002/2034, reg 6(1), the qualifying period for unfair dismissal does not apply: see the Employment Rights Act 1996 s 108(3)(j); and PARA 758 note 9. As to the right to make a complaint of unfair dismissal before an employment tribunal see PARA 804 et seq; and as to remedies see PARA 810 et seq.

4   As to the meaning of 'employer' for these purposes see PARA 86 note 4.

5   Fixed-term Employees (Prevention of Less Favourable Treatment) Regulations 2002, SI 2002/2034, reg 6(3)(a)(i). As to proceedings under the Fixed-term Employees (Prevention of Less Favourable Treatment) Regulations 2002, SI 2002/2034 see PARA 91.

6   Fixed-term Employees (Prevention of Less Favourable Treatment) Regulations 2002, SI 2002/2034, reg 6(3)(a)(ii). Head (1)(b) in the text applies to a request for a written statement made under reg 5 (see PARA 87) or reg 9 (see PARA 88): see reg 6(3)(a)(ii).

7   Fixed-term Employees (Prevention of Less Favourable Treatment) Regulations 2002, SI 2002/2034, reg 6(3)(a)(iii).

8   Fixed-term Employees (Prevention of Less Favourable Treatment) Regulations 2002, SI 2002/2034, reg 6(3)(a)(iv).

9   Fixed-term Employees (Prevention of Less Favourable Treatment) Regulations 2002, SI 2002/2034, reg 6(3)(a)(v).

10   Fixed-term Employees (Prevention of Less Favourable Treatment) Regulations 2002, SI 2002/2034, reg 6(3)(a)(vi).

11   Fixed-term Employees (Prevention of Less Favourable Treatment) Regulations 2002, SI 2002/2034, reg 6(3)(a)(vii). As to the meaning of 'workforce agreement' for these purposes see PARA 88 note 11.

12   Ie for the purposes of the Fixed-term Employees (Prevention of Less Favourable Treatment) Regulations 2002, SI 2002/2034, reg 1(2), Sch 1 (see PARA 88 note 11): see reg 6(3)(a)(viii).

13 See the Fixed-term Employees (Prevention of Less Favourable Treatment) Regulations 2002, SI 2002/2034, reg 6(3)(a)(viii).

14 Fixed-term Employees (Prevention of Less Favourable Treatment) Regulations 2002, SI 2002/2034, reg 6(3)(b). Where the reason or principal reason for dismissal is that mentioned in head (1)(e) in the text (or head (2) in the text so far as it relates thereto), reg 6(1) (see the text and notes 1–3) does not apply if the allegation made by the employee is false and not made in good faith: see reg 6(4).

90. Employee's right not to be subjected to detriment for applying fixed-term work regulations. An employee[1] has the right not to be subjected to any detriment by any act, or any deliberate failure to act, of his employer[2] done on one of the grounds specified in heads (1) and (2) below[3], namely:

(1) that the employee:

    (a) has brought proceedings against the employer under the Fixed-term Employees (Prevention of Less Favourable Treatment) Regulations 2002[4];

    (b) has requested from his employer a written statement[5];

    (c) has given evidence or information in connection with such proceedings brought by any employee[6];

    (d) otherwise did anything under the Fixed-term Employees (Prevention of Less Favourable Treatment) Regulations 2002 in relation to the employer or any other person[7];

    (e) has alleged that the employer has infringed the Fixed-term Employees (Prevention of Less Favourable Treatment) Regulations 2002[8];

    (f) has refused or proposed to refuse to forgo a right conferred on him by the Fixed-term Employees (Prevention of Less Favourable Treatment) Regulations 2002[9];

    (g) has declined to sign a workforce agreement[10]; or

    (h) being either a representative of members of the workforce[11], or a candidate in an election in which any person elected will (on being elected) become such a representative, has performed (or proposed to perform) any functions or activities as such a representative or candidate[12]; or

(2) that the employer believes or suspects that the employee has done or intends to do any of the things mentioned in head (1) above[13].

1 As to the meaning of 'employee' for these purposes see PARA 85 note 3.

2 As to the meaning of 'employer' for these purposes see PARA 86 note 4.

3 See the Fixed-term Employees (Prevention of Less Favourable Treatment) Regulations 2002, SI 2002/2034, reg 6(2). The text refers to a reason specified in reg 6(3) (see heads (1), (2) in the text): see reg 6(2). The provision made by reg 6(2) does not apply, however, where the detriment in question amounts to dismissal within the meaning of the Employment Rights Act 1996 Pt X (ss 94–134A) (unfair dismissal: see PARA 757 et seq): Fixed-term Employees (Prevention of Less Favourable Treatment) Regulations 2002, SI 2002/2034, reg 6(5).

4 Fixed-term Employees (Prevention of Less Favourable Treatment) Regulations 2002, SI 2002/2034, reg 6(3)(a)(i). As to proceedings under the Fixed-term Employees (Prevention of Less Favourable Treatment) Regulations 2002, SI 2002/2034 see PARA 91.

5 Fixed-term Employees (Prevention of Less Favourable Treatment) Regulations 2002, SI 2002/2034, reg 6(3)(a)(ii). Head (1)(b) in the text applies to a request for a written statement made under reg 5 (see PARA 87) or reg 9 (see PARA 88): see reg 6(3)(a)(ii).

6 Fixed-term Employees (Prevention of Less Favourable Treatment) Regulations 2002, SI 2002/2034, reg 6(3)(a)(iii).

7 Fixed-term Employees (Prevention of Less Favourable Treatment) Regulations 2002, SI 2002/2034, reg 6(3)(a)(iv).

8 Fixed-term Employees (Prevention of Less Favourable Treatment) Regulations 2002, SI 2002/2034, reg 6(3)(a)(v).

9 Fixed-term Employees (Prevention of Less Favourable Treatment) Regulations 2002, SI 2002/2034, reg 6(3)(a)(vi).

10 Fixed-term Employees (Prevention of Less Favourable Treatment) Regulations 2002, SI 2002/2034, reg 6(3)(a)(vii). As to the meaning of 'workforce agreement' for these purposes see PARA 88 note 11.

11 Ie for the purposes of the Fixed-term Employees (Prevention of Less Favourable Treatment) Regulations 2002, SI 2002/2034, reg 1(2), Sch 1 (see PARA 88 note 11): see reg 6(3)(a)(viii).

12 See the Fixed-term Employees (Prevention of Less Favourable Treatment) Regulations 2002, SI 2002/2034, reg 6(3)(a)(viii).

13 Fixed-term Employees (Prevention of Less Favourable Treatment) Regulations 2002, SI 2002/2034, reg 6(3)(b). Where the ground for subjection to any act or deliberate failure to act is that mentioned in head (1)(e) in the text (or head (2) in the text so far as it relates thereto), reg 6(2) (see the text and notes 1–3) does not apply if the allegation made by the employee is false and not made in good faith: see reg 6(4).

91. Complaint to employment tribunal pursuant to fixed-term work regulations. An employee[1] may present a complaint to an employment tribunal[2] that his employer[3] has infringed his right not to be treated less favourably as a fixed-term employee[4] or the right not to be subjected[5] to detriment[6].

An employment tribunal must not consider such a complaint, however, unless it is presented before the end of the period of three months beginning[7]:

(1) in the case of an alleged infringement of a right not to treated less favourably as a fixed-term employee[8], or the right not to be subjected to detriment[9], with the date of the less favourable treatment or detriment to which the complaint relates (or, where an act or failure to act is part of a series of similar acts or failures comprising the less favourable treatment or detriment, the last of them)[10];

(2) in the case of an alleged infringement of the right to be informed by his employer of available vacancies in the establishment[11], with the date (or, if more than one, the last date) on which other individuals, whether or not employees of the employer, were informed of the vacancy[12].

In working out when the time limit set in this way[13] expires, the following period is not to be counted[14], namely the period that:

(a) begins with the day after the day on which the worker concerned complies with the requirement to contact ACAS before instituting proceedings[15] in relation to the matter in respect of which the proceedings are brought ('the day after Day A')[16]; and

(b) ends with the day on which the worker concerned receives (or, if earlier, is treated as receiving[17]) the certificate issued by the conciliation officer[18] to the effect either that he has concluded that a settlement is not possible within the prescribed period or that the prescribed period has expired without a settlement having been reached ('Day B')[19].

If the unextended time limit[20] would expire during the period beginning with Day A and ending one month after Day B, the time limit expires instead at the end of that period[21]. Nevertheless, a tribunal may consider any such complaint which is out of time if, in all the circumstances of the case, it considers that it is just and equitable to do so[22].

Where an employee presents such a complaint, it is for the employer to identify the ground for the less favourable treatment or detriment[23].

Where an employment tribunal finds that such a complaint presented to it is well founded, it must take such of the following steps as it considers just and equitable[24]: (i) making a declaration as to the rights of the complainant and the employer in relation to the matters to which the complaint relates[25]; (ii) ordering the employer to pay compensation[26] to the complainant[27]; (iii) recommending[28] that the employer take, within a specified period, action appearing to the tribunal to be reasonable, in all the circumstances of the case, for the purpose of obviating or reducing the adverse effect on the complainant of any matter to which the complaint relates[29].

1   As to the meaning of 'employee' for these purposes see PARA 85 note 3.

2   As to employment tribunals see PARA 1399 et seq; and as to the procedure on a complaint made to an employment tribunal see PARA 1453 et seq. There is a requirement for early ACAS conciliation to be tried in order to promote a settlement before tribunal proceedings are instituted on a complaint under the Fixed-term Employees (Prevention of Less Favourable Treatment) Regulations 2002, SI 2002/2034, reg 7: see the Employment Tribunals Act 1996 s 18(1)(m); and PARA 152 note 1. As to the constitution and powers of ACAS see PARA 1213 et seq.

3   As to the meaning of 'employer' for these purposes see PARA 86 note 4.

4   Ie a right conferred on him by the Fixed-term Employees (Prevention of Less Favourable Treatment) Regulations 2002, SI 2002/2034, reg 3 (see PARA 87): see reg 7(1). As to the meaning of 'fixed-term employee' see PARA 86 note 2.

5   Ie under the Fixed-term Employees (Prevention of Less Favourable Treatment) Regulations 2002, SI 2002/2034, reg 6(2), subject to reg 6(5) (see PARA 90): see reg 7(1).

6   Fixed-term Employees (Prevention of Less Favourable Treatment) Regulations 2002, SI 2002/2034, reg 7(1).

7   See the Fixed-term Employees (Prevention of Less Favourable Treatment) Regulations 2002, SI 2002/2034, reg 7(2). Provision that is made for the extension of time limits in order to facilitate conciliation before the institution of proceedings (ie reg 7A: see the text and notes 13–21) applies for the purposes of reg 7(2): reg 7(2A) (regs 7(2A), 7A added by SI 2014/386). As to the right to present a complaint to an employment tribunal see PARA 80.

8   Ie a right conferred by the Fixed-term Employees (Prevention of Less Favourable Treatment) Regulations 2002, SI 2002/2034, reg 3(1) (see PARA 87): see reg 7(2)(a).

9   Ie a right conferred by the Fixed-term Employees (Prevention of Less Favourable Treatment) Regulations 2002, SI 2002/2034, reg 6(2) (see PARA 90): see reg 7(2)(a).

10   Fixed-term Employees (Prevention of Less Favourable Treatment) Regulations 2002, SI 2002/2034, reg 7(2)(a). For the purposes of calculating the date of the less favourable treatment or detriment under reg 7(2)(a):

   (1)   where a term in a contract is less favourable, that treatment is treated, subject to head (2) below, as taking place on each day of the period during which the term is less favourable (reg 7(4)(a)); and

   (2)   a deliberate failure to act contrary to reg 3 (see PARA 87) or reg 6(2) (see PARA 90) is treated as done when it was decided on (reg 7(4)(b)).

In the absence of evidence establishing the contrary, a person is taken for the purposes of head (2) above to decide not to act: (a) when he does an act inconsistent with doing the failed act (reg 7(5)(a)); or (b) if he has done no such inconsistent act, when the period expires within which he might reasonably have been expected to have done the failed act if it was to be done (reg 7(5)(b)).

11   Ie a right conferred by the Fixed-term Employees (Prevention of Less Favourable Treatment) Regulations 2002, SI 2002/2034, reg 3(6) (see PARA 87): see reg 7(2)(b).

12   Fixed-term Employees (Prevention of Less Favourable Treatment) Regulations 2002, SI 2002/2034, reg 7(2)(b).

13   Ie set by the Fixed-term Employees (Prevention of Less Favourable Treatment) Regulations 2002, SI 2002/2034, reg 7(2) (see the text and notes 7–12): see reg 7A(2) (as added: see note 7).

14   See the Fixed-term Employees (Prevention of Less Favourable Treatment) Regulations 2002, SI 2002/2034, reg 7A(2) (as added: see note 7).

15   Ie the requirement in the Employment Tribunals Act 1996 s 18A(1) (see PARA 152): see the Fixed-term Employees (Prevention of Less Favourable Treatment) Regulations 2002, SI 2002/2034, reg 7A(1)(a) (as added: see note 7).

16   See the Fixed-term Employees (Prevention of Less Favourable Treatment) Regulations 2002, SI 2002/2034, reg 7A(1)(a), (2) (as added: see note 7).

17   Ie by virtue of regulations made under the Employment Tribunals Act 1996 s 18A(11) (see PARA 152): see the Fixed-term Employees (Prevention of Less Favourable Treatment) Regulations 2002, SI 2002/2034, reg 7A(1)(b) (as added: see note 7).

18 Ie the certificate issued under the Employment Tribunals Act 1996 s 18A(4) (see PARA 152): see the Fixed-term Employees (Prevention of Less Favourable Treatment) Regulations 2002, SI 2002/2034, reg 7A(1)(b) (as added: see note 7).

19 See the Fixed-term Employees (Prevention of Less Favourable Treatment) Regulations 2002, SI 2002/2034, reg 7A(1)(b), (2) (as added: see note 7).

20 Ie the time limit set by the Fixed-term Employees (Prevention of Less Favourable Treatment) Regulations 2002, SI 2002/2034, reg 7(2) (see the text and notes 7–12), if not extended by reg 7A(3): see reg 7A(3) (as added: see note 7).

21 See the Fixed-term Employees (Prevention of Less Favourable Treatment) Regulations 2002, SI 2002/2034, reg 7A(3) (as added: see note 7).

22 Fixed-term Employees (Prevention of Less Favourable Treatment) Regulations 2002, SI 2002/2034, reg 7(3). The power so conferred on the employment tribunal by reg 7(3) to extend the time limit set by reg 7(2) (see the text and notes 7–12) is exercisable in relation to any time limit as it is extended by reg 7A (see the text and notes 13–21): reg 7A(4) (as added: see note 7).

23 Fixed-term Employees (Prevention of Less Favourable Treatment) Regulations 2002, SI 2002/2034, reg 7(6). The text refers to a complaint under reg 7 in relation to a right conferred by reg 3 (see PARA 87) or reg 6(2) (see PARA 90): see reg 7(6).

24 See the Fixed-term Employees (Prevention of Less Favourable Treatment) Regulations 2002, SI 2002/2034, reg 7(7).

25 Fixed-term Employees (Prevention of Less Favourable Treatment) Regulations 2002, SI 2002/2034, reg 7(7)(a).

26 Where a tribunal orders compensation to be paid under the Fixed-term Employees (Prevention of Less Favourable Treatment) Regulations 2002, SI 2002/2034, reg 7(7)(b) (see head (ii) in the text), the amount of the compensation awarded is such as the tribunal considers just and equitable in all the circumstances having regard to:
    (1)   the infringement to which the complaint relates (reg 7(8)(a)); and
    (2)   any loss which is attributable to the infringement (reg 7(8)(b)).
The loss is taken to include any expenses reasonably incurred by the complainant in consequence of the infringement, and loss of any benefit which he might reasonably be expected to have had but for the infringement: see reg 7(9). In ascertaining the loss, the tribunal must apply the same rule concerning the duty of a person to mitigate his loss as applies to damages recoverable under the common law of England and Wales: see reg 7(11). As to the common law duty to mitigate loss see DAMAGES vol 12(1) (Reissue) PARA 1041 et seq. Compensation in respect of treating an employee in a manner which infringes the right conferred on him by reg 3 (see PARA 87) does not include compensation for injury to feelings: reg 7(10). Where the tribunal finds that the act, or failure to act, to which the complaint relates was to any extent caused or contributed to by action of the complainant, it must reduce the amount of the compensation by such proportion as it considers just and equitable having regard to that finding: reg 7(12).

27 Fixed-term Employees (Prevention of Less Favourable Treatment) Regulations 2002, SI 2002/2034, reg 7(7)(b).

28 If the employer fails, without reasonable justification, to comply with a recommendation made by an employment tribunal under the Fixed-term Employees (Prevention of Less Favourable Treatment) Regulations 2002, SI 2002/2034, reg 7(7)(c) (see head (iii) in the text), the tribunal may, if it thinks it just and equitable to do so: (1) increase the amount of compensation required to be paid to the complainant in respect of the complaint, where an order was made under reg 7(7)(b) (see head (ii) in the text) (reg 7(13)(a)); or (2) make an order under reg 7(7)(b) (reg 7(13)(b)).

29 Fixed-term Employees (Prevention of Less Favourable Treatment) Regulations 2002, SI 2002/2034, reg 7(7)(c).

92.   Liability of employers and principals under fixed-term work regulations.
Anything done by a person in the course of his employment must be treated for the purposes of the regulations that have been made for the purpose of implementing the Fixed-term Work Directive[1] as also done by his employer[2], whether or not it was done with the employer's knowledge or approval[3]; and anything done by a person as agent for the employer with the authority of the employer must be treated for the purposes of those regulations as also done by the employer[4].

In proceedings under those regulations against any person in respect of an act alleged to have been done by an employee[5] of his, it is a defence for that person to prove that he took such steps as were reasonably practicable to prevent the employee from doing that act (or from doing, in the course of his employment, acts of that description)[6].

1   The Fixed-term Employees (Prevention of Less Favourable Treatment) Regulations 2002, SI 2002/2034, have been made under the Employment Act 2002 s 45 for the purposes of implementing in the United Kingdom the Framework Agreement on Fixed-term Work concluded on 18 March 1999 between the general cross-industry organisations (the 'Framework Agreement'), which is annexed to, and put into effect by, Council Directive (EC) 99/70 of 28 June 1999 (OJ L175, 10.7.99, p 43) concerning the framework agreement on fixed-term work concluded by ETUC, UNICE and CEEP (the 'Fixed-term Work Directive'): see PARA 84. As to the meaning of 'United Kingdom' see PARA 2 note 12.
2   As to the meaning of 'employer' for these purposes see PARA 86 note 4.
3   Fixed-term Employees (Prevention of Less Favourable Treatment) Regulations 2002, SI 2002/2034, reg 12(1). For the purposes of reg 12:
    (1)   the secondment of any constable or other person to the National Crime Agency to serve as a member of its staff must be treated as employment by the National Crime Agency (and not as being employment by any other person) (reg 17(1B)(a), (3) (reg 17(1B), (3) added by SI 2006/594; the Fixed-term Employees (Prevention of Less Favourable Treatment) Regulations 2002, SI 2002/2034, reg 17(1B), (3) amended by virtue of the Crime and Courts Act 2013 s 15(3), Sch 8 para 190)); and
    (2)   anything done by a person so seconded in the performance, or purported performance, of his functions must be treated as done in the course of that employment (Fixed-term Employees (Prevention of Less Favourable Treatment) Regulations 2002, SI 2002/2034, reg 17(1B)(b) (as so added)).
    As to the secondment of police constables to the National Crime Agency generally see also PARA 93 note 13. As to the National Crime Agency see POLICE AND INVESTIGATORY POWERS vol 84 (2013) PARA 424.
4   Fixed-term Employees (Prevention of Less Favourable Treatment) Regulations 2002, SI 2002/2034, reg 12(2).
5   As to the meaning of 'employee' for these purposes see PARA 85 note 3.
6   See the Fixed-term Employees (Prevention of Less Favourable Treatment) Regulations 2002, SI 2002/2034, reg 12(3).

93.   Special classes of person under fixed-term work regulations.   The regulations that have been made for the purpose of implementing the Fixed-term Work Directive[1]:

(1)   have effect[2] in relation to Crown employment[3] and persons in Crown employment as they have effect in relation to other employment and other employees and workers[4];

(2)   have effect in relation to employment as a relevant member of the House of Lords staff[5] as they have effect in relation to other employment[6];

(3)   have effect in relation to employment as a relevant member of the House of Commons staff[7] as they have effect in relation to other employment[8];

(4)   do not apply to service as a member of the naval, military or air forces of the Crown[9], but do apply to employment by an association established for the purposes of Part XI[10] of the Reserve Forces Act 1996[11],

The holding, otherwise than under a contract of employment[12], of the office of constable or an appointment as a police cadet is to be treated as employment under a contract of employment by the relevant officer[13].

1   The Fixed-term Employees (Prevention of Less Favourable Treatment) Regulations 2002, SI 2002/2034, have been made under the Employment Act 2002 s 45 for the purposes of

implementing in the United Kingdom the Framework Agreement on Fixed-term Work concluded on 18 March 1999 between the general cross-industry organisations (the 'Framework Agreement'), which is annexed to, and put into effect by, Council Directive (EC) 99/70 of 28 June 1999 (OJ L175, 10.7.99, p 43) concerning the framework agreement on fixed-term work concluded by ETUC, UNICE and CEEP (the 'Fixed-term Work Directive'): see PARA 84. As to the meaning of 'United Kingdom' see PARA 2 note 12.

2   Ie subject to the Fixed-term Employees (Prevention of Less Favourable Treatment) Regulations 2002, SI 2002/2034, reg 14 (see head (4) in the text): see reg 13(1).

3   For these purposes, a person is to be regarded as being in Crown employment only if: (1) he is in employment under or for the purposes of a government department or any officer or body exercising on behalf of the Crown functions conferred by a statutory provision (Fixed-term Employees (Prevention of Less Favourable Treatment) Regulations 2002, SI 2002/2034, reg 13(2)(a)); and (2) having regard to the terms and conditions under which he works, he would be an employee if he was not in Crown employment (reg 13(2)(b)). As to the meaning of 'employee' for these purposes see PARA 85 note 3.

4   Fixed-term Employees (Prevention of Less Favourable Treatment) Regulations 2002, SI 2002/2034, reg 13(1). For the purposes of the application of the provisions of the Fixed-term Employees (Prevention of Less Favourable Treatment) Regulations 2002, SI 2002/2034, in relation to Crown employment and persons in Crown employment in accordance with reg 13(1): (1) references to an employee must be construed as references to a person in Crown employment (reg 13(3)(a)); (2) references to a contract of employment must be construed, in relation to a person in Crown employment, as references to the terms and conditions mentioned in reg 13(2)(b) (see note 3) (reg 13(3)(b)); and (3) references to dismissal must be construed as references to the termination of Crown employment (reg 13(3)(c)).

5   For these purposes, 'relevant member of the House of Lords staff' means any person who is employed under a contract with the Corporate Officer of the House of Lords by virtue of which he is a worker: see the Fixed-term Employees (Prevention of Less Favourable Treatment) Regulations 2002, SI 2002/2034, reg 15(2). As to the Corporate Officer of the House of Lords see PARLIAMENT vol 78 (2010) PARA 990 et seq.

6   Fixed-term Employees (Prevention of Less Favourable Treatment) Regulations 2002, SI 2002/2034, reg 15(1).

7   For these purposes, 'relevant member of the House of Commons staff' means any person:

    (1)   who was appointed by the House of Commons Commission (Fixed-term Employees (Prevention of Less Favourable Treatment) Regulations 2002, SI 2002/2034, reg 16(2)(a)); or

    (2)   who is a member of the Speaker's personal staff (reg 16(2)(b)).

As to the House of Commons Commission see PARLIAMENT vol 78 (2010) PARA 946; and as to the Speaker see PARLIAMENT vol 78 (2010) PARA 931 et seq.

8   Fixed-term Employees (Prevention of Less Favourable Treatment) Regulations 2002, SI 2002/2034, reg 16(1).

9   Fixed-term Employees (Prevention of Less Favourable Treatment) Regulations 2002, SI 2002/2034, reg 14(1)(a).

10   Ie for the purposes of the Reserve Forces Act 1996 Pt XI (ss 110–119) (reserve associations: see ARMED FORCES vol 3 (2011) PARA 473): see the Fixed-term Employees (Prevention of Less Favourable Treatment) Regulations 2002, SI 2002/2034, reg 14(1)(b).

11   Fixed-term Employees (Prevention of Less Favourable Treatment) Regulations 2002, SI 2002/2034, reg 14(1)(b).

12   As to the meaning of 'contract of employment' for these purposes see PARA 85 note 3.

13   Fixed-term Employees (Prevention of Less Favourable Treatment) Regulations 2002, SI 2002/2034, reg 17(1). For these purposes, 'relevant officer' means (in relation to a member of a police force or a special constable or police cadet appointed for a police area) the chief officer of police and (in relation to any other person holding the office of constable or an appointment as a police cadet) the person who has the direction and control of the body of constables or cadets in question: see reg 17(2) (amended by SI 2006/594). For the purposes of the Fixed-term Employees (Prevention of Less Favourable Treatment) Regulations 2002, SI 2002/2034, any constable or other person who has been seconded to the National Crime Agency to serve as a member of its staff must be treated as employed by the National Crime Agency, in respect of actions taken by, or on behalf of, the National Crime Agency: reg 17(1A), (3) (reg 17(1A), (3) added by SI 2006/594; and amended by virtue of the Crime and Courts Act 2013 s 15(3), Sch 8 para 190). As to the secondment of police constables to the National Crime Agency for the purposes of the Fixed-term Employees (Prevention of Less Favourable Treatment) Regulations 2002, SI 2002/2034, reg 12 (liability of employers and principals) see PARA 92 note 3. As to the meaning of 'chief officer of police' see POLICE AND INVESTIGATORY POWERS

vol 84 (2013) PARA 5; and as to the meaning of 'police area' see POLICE AND INVESTIGATORY POWERS vol 84 (2013) PARA 52. As to the National Crime Agency see POLICE AND INVESTIGATORY POWERS vol 84 (2013) PARA 424.

94. Excluded classes of person under fixed-term work regulations. The regulations that have been made for the purpose of implementing the Fixed-term Work Directive[1] do not have effect:

(1) in relation to a fixed-term employee[2] who is employed on a scheme, designed to provide him with training or work experience for the purpose of assisting him to seek or obtain work, which is either provided to him under arrangements made by the government, or funded in whole or part by an institution of the European Union[3];

(2) in relation to a fixed-term employee whose employment consists in attending a period of work experience not exceeding one year that he is required to attend as part of a higher education course[4];

(3) in relation to employment under a fixed-term contract where the employee is an agency worker[5];

(4) in relation to employment under a fixed-term contract where the contract is a contract of apprenticeship or an apprenticeship agreement[6].

1 The Fixed-term Employees (Prevention of Less Favourable Treatment) Regulations 2002, SI 2002/2034, have been made under the Employment Act 2002 s 45 for the purposes of implementing in the United Kingdom the Framework Agreement on Fixed-term Work concluded on 18 March 1999 between the general cross-industry organisations (the 'Framework Agreement'), which is annexed to, and put into effect by, Council Directive (EC) 99/70 of 28 June 1999 (OJ L175, 10.7.99, p 43) concerning the framework agreement on fixed-term work concluded by ETUC, UNICE and CEEP (the 'Fixed-term Work Directive'): see PARA 84. As to the meaning of 'United Kingdom' see PARA 2 note 12.

2 As to the meaning of 'employee' for these purposes see PARA 85 note 3; and as to the meaning of 'fixed-term employee' see PARA 86 note 2.

3 Fixed-term Employees (Prevention of Less Favourable Treatment) Regulations 2002, SI 2002/2034, reg 18(1) (amended by SI 2011/1043). See *Hudson v Department for Work and Pensions* [2012] EWCA Civ 1416, [2013] 1 All ER 1370, [2013] ICR 329, [2013] IRLR 32 (period during which employee employed under fixed-term contract pursuant to government scheme not taken into account when determining whether employed for requisite period despite employment under further fixed-term contract when scheme ended).

4 Fixed-term Employees (Prevention of Less Favourable Treatment) Regulations 2002, SI 2002/2034, reg 18(2). For these purposes, 'higher education course' means, in England and Wales, a course of a description referred to in the Education Reform Act 1988 s 120, s 235(1), Sch 6 (see EDUCATION vol 35 (2011) PARA 23): see the Fixed-term Employees (Prevention of Less Favourable Treatment) Regulations 2002, SI 2002/2034, reg 18(3). As to the meanings of 'England' and 'Wales' see PARA 2 note 12.

5 Fixed-term Employees (Prevention of Less Favourable Treatment) Regulations 2002, SI 2002/2034, reg 19(1) (substituted by SI 2008/2776). There is an exception in respect of the Fixed-term Employees (Prevention of Less Favourable Treatment) Regulations 2002, SI 2002/2034, Sch 2 Pt 1 para 1: see reg 19(1) (as so substituted). For these purposes, 'agency worker' means any person who is supplied by an employment business to do work for another person under a contract or other arrangements made between the employment business and the other person (see reg 19(2)); and 'employment business' means the business, whether or not carried on with a view to profit and whether or not carried on in conjunction with any other business, of supplying persons in the employment of the person carrying on the business, to act for, and under the control of, other persons in any capacity (see reg 19(3)). As to special regulations made for the purposes of guaranteeing equal treatment of agency workers see PARA 95 et seq.

6 Fixed-term Employees (Prevention of Less Favourable Treatment) Regulations 2002, SI 2002/2034, reg 20 (amended by SI 2012/3112). Head (4) in the text refers to an apprenticeship agreement within the meaning of the Apprenticeships, Skills, Children and Learning Act 2009 s 32 (see EDUCATION vol 35 (2011) PARA 683): see the Fixed-term Employees

(Prevention of Less Favourable Treatment) Regulations 2002, SI 2002/2034, reg 20 (as so amended). As to the position of apprentices and youth trainees at common law see PARAS 112, 128–129, 636, 747–754.

(vi) Agency Workers

A. RIGHTS AT COMMON LAW

95.   Employment rights of agency workers at common law. The fundamental legal position of the agency worker (that is, whether, and if so by whom, an individual dealing with an employment agency or an employment business is employed) is not addressed either in the employment legislation, or in the statutory provisions which regulate the carrying on and conduct of employment agencies and employment businesses[1]. It, therefore, remains a matter to be determined on ordinary principles whether that individual is employed by the employment agency[2], the employment business or the hirer[3], or is self-employed[4], or whether he is subject to an arrangement which is neither employment nor self-employment[5]. Equally, it is possible for the individual to be under two contracts of employment, namely a general engagement with the agency (through being 'on the books') and a specific engagement with the hirers, if the facts show such an arrangement[6]. The court should also consider the possibility of an implied contract of employment arising between an individual and a client of the agency to which the individual has been posted over a long period of time although recent case law seems to be against this[7].

1   See PARA 11.
2   See *Stephenson v Delphi Diesel Systems Ltd* [2003] ICR 471, EAT (control by hirer over individual explained by contract between individual and agency).
3   In determining whether an individual who has hired himself out through the machinery of an agency to a third party is an employee of that third party, the employment tribunal must first ascertain whether there was a contract of any kind between the individual and the third party: *Hewlett Packard Ltd v O'Murphy* [2002] IRLR 4, EAT (individual contractor who provided his services through an employment agency to a third party, with whom there is no direct contractual relationship, is not the employee of that third party, there being no contractual nexus).
4   *Warner Holidays Ltd v Secretary of State for Social Services* [1983] ICR 440; *Wickens v Champion Employment* [1984] ICR 365, EAT. In such a case, the treatment for tax purposes of the individual is likely to be of little relevance as a factor, since special provisions apply to the taxation of workers supplied by agencies, irrespective of the precise employment status of the individual: see the Income Tax (Earnings and Pensions) Act 2003 Pt 2 Ch 7 (ss 44–47) (agency workers); and INCOME TAXATION vol 58 (2014) PARAS 742–743. See also *Costain Building and Civil Engineering Ltd v Smith* [2000] ICR 215, EAT (individual chose to operate on a self-employed agent basis; possible motives for doing so irrelevant).
5   *Construction Industry Training Board v Labour Force Ltd* [1970] 3 All ER 220 at 225, DC, obiter, per Cooke J ('where A contracts with B to render services exclusively to C, the contract is not a contract for services, but a contract sui generis, a different type of contract from either of the familiar two'); *Ironmonger v Movefield Ltd (t/a Deering Appointments)* [1988] IRLR 461, EAT.
6   *McMeechan v Secretary of State for Employment* [1997] ICR 549, [1997] IRLR 353, CA. See also *Motorola Ltd v Davidson* [2001] IRLR 4, EAT (despite contract between employment agency and individual, hirer exercised sufficient degree of practical control over individual to establish employment relationship for purposes of unfair dismissal). It is in reality more likely that individual contracts in respect of specific assignments or tasks will exist with the employment agency where there is no master agreement containing detailed terms in being, as in *McMeechan v Secretary of State for Employment*, than where there is, since the terms of the latter may well cover what is to happen on each assignment: *Bunce v Postworth Ltd (t/a Skyblue)* [2005] EWCA Civ 490, [2005] IRLR 557, [2005] All ER (D) 38 (May) (very detailed provisions in written agreement governed relationship between the applicant and the employment agency in respect of each assignment).

7   *Franks v Reuters Ltd* [2003] EWCA Civ 417, [2003] ICR 1166, [2003] IRLR 423 (employment
tribunal should determine as a fact whether, on a consideration of all the relevant evidence, there
was an implied contract of service between the relevant parties); *Dacas v Brook Street Bureau
(UK) Ltd* [2004] EWCA Civ 217, [2004] ICR 1437, [2004] IRLR 358 (even where the
individual is not an employee of the agency, a contract of service between the hirer and the
individual may be deduced as a necessary inference from the conduct of parties and the work
done). As to the meaning of 'contract of service' see PARA 1 note 1. See also *Montgomery v
Johnson Underwood Ltd* [2001] EWCA Civ 318, [2001] ICR 819, [2001] IRLR 269 (agency
did not retain sufficient control for there to be a contract of employment between it and an
individual who was assigned to same client over long period of time). *Dacas v Brook Street
Bureau (UK) Ltd* was applied in *Cable & Wireless plc v Muscat* [2006] EWCA Civ 220, [2006]
ICR 975, [2006] IRLR 354. However, there was an immediate reaction against this approach; it
was held e g that where a person is employed by the agency, there can be no implied contract of
employment with a second employer: *Cairns v Visteon UK Ltd* [2007] ICR 616, [2007] IRLR
175, EAT. This more cautious approach was upheld in *James v London Borough of Greenwich*
[2008] EWCA Civ 35, [2008] ICR 545, [2008] IRLR 302 (agency worker supplied to same
end-user for several years; unnecessary to imply contract of employment) which as at the date
this volume states the law is the dominant case in the area and represents a strong line against
finding a direct employment relationship between a long-serving agency worker and the
client/end-user, seemingly going against (at least the spirit of) Court of Appeal cases like *Dacas v
Brook Street Bureau (UK) Ltd* and *Cable & Wireless plc v Muscat* (with the latter now being
viewed as an unusual decision reliant on its particular facts). Its 'necessity' test means that there
will rarely be a contract of employment with the client/end-user. *James v London Borough of
Greenwich* was applied in *Beck v London Borough of Camden* [2008] All ER (D) 09
(Sep), EAT; and in *Sridhar v East Living Ltd* [2008] All ER (D) 290 (Nov), EAT. In *Cave v
Portsmouth City Council* [2008] All ER (D) 313 (May), EAT, *James v London Borough of
Greenwich* was followed in holding that there needed to be two distinct stages in the analysis of
whether there was a contract between an agency worker and an end-user: (1) whether there was
a contract in existence at all; and (2) whether, if there was, the contract was a contract of
employment or some other contract. Since *Cable & Wireless plc v Muscat*, courts and tribunals
have become more vigilant in exposing sham arrangements: however the Court of Appeal would
not carry this to extremes where the evidence was not sufficient: see *Kalwak v Consistent
Group Ltd* [2008] EWCA Civ 430, [2008] IRLR 505. See also PARA 14 note 3.

B. EQUAL TREATMENT OF AGENCY WORKERS

96.   EU requirements on temporary agency work. The purpose of the
European Parliament and Council Directive of 19 November 2008 on temporary
agency work[1] is:

(1)   to ensure the protection of temporary agency workers[2]; and

(2)   to improve the quality of temporary agency work,

by ensuring that the principle of equal treatment[3] is applied to temporary agency
workers, and by recognising temporary-work agencies as employers, while
taking into account the need to establish a suitable framework for the use of
temporary agency work with a view to contributing effectively to the creation of
jobs and to the development of flexible forms of working[4]. Prohibitions or
restrictions on the use of temporary agency work may be justified only on
grounds of general interest relating in particular to the protection of temporary
agency workers, the requirements of health and safety at work or the need to
ensure that the labour market functions properly and abuses are prevented[5].

Temporary agency workers must be:

(a)   informed of any vacant posts in the user undertaking to give them the
      same opportunity as other workers in that undertaking to find
      permanent employment[6]; and

(b)   given access to the amenities or collective facilities in the user
      undertaking (in particular, any canteen, child-care facilities and

transport services) under the same conditions as workers employed directly by the undertaking, unless the difference in treatment is justified by objective reasons[7].

Temporary-work agencies may not charge workers any fees in exchange for arranging for them to be recruited by a user undertaking, or for concluding a contract of employment or an employment relationship with a user undertaking after carrying out an assignment in that undertaking[8].

Member states must:

(i)   take suitable measures or promote dialogue between the social partners, in accordance with their national traditions and practices, in order to improve temporary agency workers' access to training and to child-care facilities in the temporary-work agencies, even in the periods between their assignments, in order to enhance their career development and employability, and in order to improve temporary agency workers' access to training for user undertakings' workers[9]; and

(ii)   take any action required to ensure that any clauses prohibiting or having the effect of preventing the conclusion of a contract of employment or an employment relationship between the user undertaking and the temporary agency worker after his assignment are null and void or may be declared null and void[10]; and

(iii)   provide for appropriate measures in the event of non-compliance with the Temporary Agency Work Directive by temporary-work agencies or user undertakings[11]; and they must lay down rules on effective, proportionate and dissuasive penalties applicable in the event of infringements of national provisions implementing the Directive and take all necessary measures to ensure that they are applied[12].

Temporary agency workers must count, under conditions established by the member states, for the purposes of calculating the threshold above which bodies representing workers provided for under EU and national law and collective agreements are to be formed at the temporary-work agency[13]; and member states may provide that, under conditions that they define, temporary agency workers count for the purposes of calculating the threshold above which bodies representing workers provided for by EU and national law and collective agreements are to be formed in the user undertaking, in the same way as if they were workers employed directly for the same period of time by the user undertaking[14]. Without prejudice to national and EU provisions on information and consultation which are more stringent and/or more specific[15], the user undertaking must provide suitable information on the use of temporary agency workers when providing information on the employment situation in that undertaking to bodies representing workers set up in accordance with national and EU legislation[16].

1   Ie European Parliament and Council Directive (EC) 2008/104 of 19 November 2008 (OJ L327, 05.12.2008, p 9) on temporary agency work (the 'Temporary Agency Work Directive').

2   For these purposes, 'temporary agency worker' means a worker with a contract of employment or an employment relationship with a temporary-work agency with a view to being assigned to a user undertaking to work temporarily under its supervision and direction, where 'worker' means any person who, in the member state concerned, is protected as a worker under national employment law; 'temporary-work agency' means any natural or legal person who, in compliance with national law, concludes contracts of employment or employment relationships with temporary agency workers in order to assign them to user undertakings to work there temporarily under their supervision and direction; and 'user undertaking' means any natural or legal person for whom and under the supervision and direction of whom a temporary agency worker works temporarily: see the Temporary Agency Work Directive art 3(1)(a)–(d). The

Directive is without prejudice to national law as regards the definition of pay, contract of employment, employment relationship or worker; but member states may not exclude from its scope workers, contracts of employment or employment relationships solely because they relate to part-time workers, fixed-term contract workers or persons with a contract of employment or employment relationship with a temporary-work agency: see art 3(2).

The Temporary Agency Work Directive applies to workers with a contract of employment or employment relationship with a temporary-work agency who are assigned to user undertakings to work temporarily under their supervision and direction (art 1(1)); and it applies to public and private undertakings which are temporary-work agencies or user undertakings engaged in economic activities whether or not they are operating for gain (art 1(2)). Member states may, after consulting the social partners, provide that the Directive does not apply, however, to employment contracts or relationships concluded under a specific public or publicly supported vocational training, integration or retraining programme: art 1(3).

3   Ie as set out in the Temporary Agency Work Directive art 5: see art 2. Accordingly, the basic working and employment conditions of temporary agency workers must be, for the duration of their assignment at a user undertaking, at least those that would apply if they had been recruited directly by that undertaking to occupy the same job: art 5(1) para 1. For these purposes, 'basic working and employment conditions' means working and employment conditions laid down by legislation, regulations, administrative provisions, collective agreements and/or other binding general provisions in force in the user undertaking relating to pay and to the duration of working time, overtime, breaks, rest periods, night work, holidays and public holidays: art 3(1)(f). 'Assignment' means the period during which the temporary agency worker is placed at the user undertaking to work temporarily under its supervision and direction: art 3(1)(e).

For the purposes of the application of art 5(1) para 1, the rules in force in the user undertaking on protection of pregnant women and nursing mothers and protection of children and young people; and on equal treatment for men and women and any action to combat any discrimination based on sex, race or ethnic origin, religion, beliefs, disabilities, age or sexual orientation, must be complied with as established by legislation, regulations, administrative provisions, collective agreements and/or any other general provisions: art 5(1) para 2. Member states may, after consulting the social partners: (1) as regards pay, provide that an exemption be made to the principle established in art 5(1) where temporary agency workers who have a permanent contract of employment with a temporary-work agency continue to be paid in the time between assignments (art 5(2)); and (2) give them, at the appropriate level and subject to the conditions laid down by the member states, the option of upholding or concluding collective agreements which, while respecting the overall protection of temporary agency workers, may establish arrangements concerning the working and employment conditions of temporary agency workers which may differ from those referred to in art 5(1) (art 5(3)). Provided that an adequate level of protection is provided for temporary agency workers, member states in which there is either no system in law for declaring collective agreements universally applicable or no such system in law or practice for extending their provisions to all similar undertakings in a certain sector or geographical area, may, after consulting the social partners at national level and on the basis of an agreement concluded by them, establish arrangements concerning the basic working and employment conditions which derogate from the principle established in art 5(1): see art 5(4) para 1. Such arrangements may include a qualifying period for equal treatment: see art 5(4) para 1. The arrangements referred to must be in conformity with EU legislation and sufficiently precise and accessible to allow the sectors and firms concerned to identify and comply with their obligations: see art 5(4) para 2. In particular, member states must specify, in application of art 3(2) (see note 2), whether occupational social security schemes, including pension, sick pay or financial participation schemes are included in the basic working and employment conditions referred to in in art 5(1): see art 5(4) para 2. Such arrangements must also be without prejudice to agreements at national, regional, local or sectoral level that are no less favourable to workers: see art 5(4) para 2. Member states must take appropriate measures, in accordance with national law and/or practice, with a view to preventing misuse in the application of art 5 and, in particular, to preventing successive assignments designed to circumvent the provisions of the Temporary Agency Work Directive; and they must inform the Commission about such measures: see art 5(5).

4   Temporary Agency Work Directive art 2.

5   Temporary Agency Work Directive art 4(1). As to the treatment of agency workers for the purposes of implementing cross-border mergers legislation see COMPANIES vol 15 (2009) PARA 1451; and as to health and safety protection afforded to agency workers (especially new or expectant mothers who are agency workers) see HEALTH AND SAFETY AT WORK vol 52 (2014) PARA 392 et seq.

Provision was made for member states, after consulting the social partners in accordance with national legislation, collective agreements and practices, to review, by 5 December 2011, any restrictions or prohibitions on the use of temporary agency work in order to verify whether they are justified on the grounds mentioned in art 4(1): see art 4(2), (3), (5). The provision made by art 4(1)–(3) was without prejudice to national requirements with regard to registration, licensing, certification, financial guarantees or monitoring of temporary-work agencies: art 4(4). The Temporary Agency Work Directive also was without prejudice to the member states' right to apply or introduce legislative, regulatory or administrative provisions more favourable to workers or to promote or permit collective agreements concluded between the social partners more favourable to workers (art 9(1)); but implementation under no circumstances constituted sufficient grounds for justifying a reduction in the general level of protection of workers in the fields covered by the Directive (see art 9(2)). This was without prejudice to the rights of member states and/or management and labour to lay down, in the light of changing circumstances, different legislative, regulatory or contractual arrangements to those prevailing at the time of the adoption of the Directive, provided always that the minimum requirements laid down in the Directive are respected: see art 9(2). As to implementation and review see further arts 11, 12. For the purposes of implementing the 'Temporary Agency Work Directive' in England and Wales, the Agency Workers Regulations 2010, SI 2010/93, which came into force on 1 October 2011, have been made in exercise of the powers conferred on the Secretary of State by the European Communities Act 1972 s 2(2) (see CONSTITUTIONAL AND ADMINISTRATIVE LAW vol 20 (2014) PARA 156): see PARA 97 et seq.

6   Temporary Agency Work Directive art 6(1). Such information may be provided by a general announcement in a suitable place in the undertaking for which, and under whose supervision, temporary agency workers are engaged: see art 6(1).

7   Temporary Agency Work Directive art 6(4). This provision is without prejudice to art 5(1) (principle of equal treatment: see note 3): see art 6(4).

8   Temporary Agency Work Directive art 6(3).

9   See Temporary Agency Work Directive art 6(5).

10 Temporary Agency Work Directive art 6(2). This provision is without prejudice to provisions under which temporary agencies receive a reasonable level of recompense for services rendered to user undertakings for the assignment, recruitment and training of temporary agency workers: see art 6(2).

11 Temporary Agency Work Directive art 10(1). In particular, member states must ensure that adequate administrative or judicial procedures are available to enable the obligations deriving from the Directive to be enforced: see art 10(1).

12 See Temporary Agency Work Directive art 10(2). In particular, member states must ensure that workers and/or their representatives have adequate means of enforcing the obligations under the Directive: see art 10(2).

13 Temporary Agency Work Directive art 7(1). See note 14.

14 Temporary Agency Work Directive art 7(2). Those member states which avail themselves of the option provided for in art 7(2) are not obliged to implement the provisions of art 7(1) (see the text and note 13): art 7(3).

15 Ie, in particular, European Parliament and Council Directive (EC) 2002/14 of 11 March 2002 (OJ L80, 23.2.2002, p 29) establishing a general framework for informing and consulting employees in the European Union (see PARA 1288 note 13; and see also COMPANIES vol 14 (2009) PARA 23): see the Temporary Agency Work Directive art 8.

16 Temporary Agency Work Directive art 8.

97.   Meanings of 'agency worker' and 'temporary work agency' for purposes of agency worker regulations.   For the purposes of regulations that have been made for the purpose of implementing the Temporary Agency Work Directive[1], 'agency worker' means an individual who[2]:

(1)   is supplied by a temporary work agency to work temporarily for and under the supervision and direction of a hirer[3]; and

(2)   has a contract with the temporary work agency[4] which is either a contract of employment with the agency[5], or any other contract with the agency to perform work or services personally[6].

However, an individual is not an agency worker if:

(a)   the contract the individual has with the temporary work agency has the effect that the status of the agency is that of a client or customer of a profession or business undertaking carried on by the individual[7]; or

(b)   there is a contract, by virtue of which the individual is available to work for the hirer, having the effect that the status of the hirer is that of a client or customer of a profession or business undertaking carried on by the individual[8].

An individual is not prevented from being an agency worker because[9]:

(i)   the temporary work agency supplies the individual through one or more intermediaries[10];

(ii)   one or more intermediaries supply that individual[11];

(iii)   the individual is supplied pursuant to any contract or other arrangement between the temporary work agency, one or more intermediaries and the hirer[12];

(iv)   the temporary work agency pays for the services of the individual through one or more intermediaries[13]; or

(v)   the individual is employed by or otherwise has a contract with one or more intermediaries[14].

For these purposes, 'temporary work agency' means a person engaged in the economic activity, public or private, whether or not operating for profit, and whether or not carrying on such activity in conjunction with others, of: (A) supplying individuals to work temporarily for and under the supervision and direction of hirers[15]; or (B) paying for, or receiving or forwarding payment for, the services of individuals who are supplied to work temporarily for and under the supervision and direction of hirers[16].

1   Ie the Agency Workers Regulations 2010, SI 2010/93, which were made in exercise of the powers conferred on the Secretary of State by the European Communities Act 1972 s 2(2) (see CONSTITUTIONAL AND ADMINISTRATIVE LAW vol 20 (2014) PARA 156) for the purposes of implementing European Parliament and Council Directive (EC) 2008/104 of 19 November 2008 (OJ L327, 05.12.2008, p 9) on temporary agency work (the 'Temporary Agency Work Directive') (see PARA 96). The Agency Workers Regulations 2010, SI 2010/93, came into force on 1 October 2011: see reg 1(1).

2   See the Agency Workers Regulations 2010, SI 2010/93, reg 3(1).

3   Agency Workers Regulations 2010, SI 2010/93, reg 3(1)(a). For these purposes, 'hirer' means a person engaged in economic activity, public or private, whether or not operating for profit, to whom individuals are supplied, to work temporarily for and under the supervision and direction of that person: see reg 2. For the purposes of head (1) in the text, an individual is to be treated as having been supplied by a temporary work agency to work temporarily for and under the supervision and direction of a hirer if:
   (1)   the temporary work agency initiates or is involved as an intermediary in the making of the arrangements that lead to the individual being supplied to work temporarily for and under the supervision and direction of the hirer (reg 3(3)(a)); and
   (2)   the individual is supplied by an intermediary, or one of a number of intermediaries, to work temporarily for and under the supervision and direction of the hirer (reg 3(3)(b)).
   An individual treated by virtue of reg 3(3) as having been supplied by a temporary work agency, must be treated, for the purposes of reg 3(1)(b) (see head (2) in the text), as having a contract with the temporary work agency: reg 3(4).

4   See note 3.

5   Agency Workers Regulations 2010, SI 2010/93, reg 3(1)(b)(i). For these purposes, 'contract of employment' means a contract of service or of apprenticeship, whether express or implied, and (if it is express) whether oral or in writing: see reg 2.

6   Agency Workers Regulations 2010, SI 2010/93, reg 3(1)(b)(ii) (substituted by SI 2011/1941).

7   Agency Workers Regulations 2010, SI 2010/93, reg 3(2)(a).

8   Agency Workers Regulations 2010, SI 2010/93, reg 3(2)(b).

9   See the Agency Workers Regulations 2010, SI 2010/93, reg 3(5). The provision made by reg 3(5) (see heads (i) to (v) in the text) does not prejudice the generality of reg 3(1)–(4) (see the text and notes 1–8): reg 3(6).

10   Agency Workers Regulations 2010, SI 2010/93, reg 3(5)(a).

11 Agency Workers Regulations 2010, SI 2010/93, reg 3(5)(b).
12 Agency Workers Regulations 2010, SI 2010/93, reg 3(5)(c).
13 Agency Workers Regulations 2010, SI 2010/93, reg 3(5)(d).
14 Agency Workers Regulations 2010, SI 2010/93, reg 3(5)(e).
15 Agency Workers Regulations 2010, SI 2010/93, reg 4(1)(a).
16 Agency Workers Regulations 2010, SI 2010/93, reg 4(1)(b). Notwithstanding reg 4(1)(b), a person is not a temporary work agency if the person is engaged in the economic activity of paying for, or receiving or forwarding payments for, the services of individuals regardless of whether the individuals are supplied to work for hirers: reg 4(2).

98. Temporary agency worker's entitlement to basic working and employment conditions. An agency worker[1] is entitled to the same basic working and employment conditions as he would be entitled to for doing the same job had he been recruited by the hirer[2]:

(1) other than by using the services of a temporary work agency[3]; and
(2) at the time the qualifying period commenced[4].

For these purposes, the basic working and employment conditions are:

(a) where the agency worker would have been recruited as an employee[5], the relevant terms and conditions that are ordinarily included in the contracts of employees of the hirer[6];
(b) where the agency worker would have been recruited as a worker[7], the relevant terms and conditions that are ordinarily included in the contracts of workers of the hirer[8],

whether by collective agreement or otherwise, including any variations in those relevant terms and conditions made at any time after the qualifying period commenced[9].

This requirement[10] is deemed to have been complied with where[11]: (i) an agency worker is working under the same relevant terms and conditions as an employee who is a comparable employee[12]; and (ii) the relevant terms and conditions of that comparable employee are terms and conditions ordinarily included in the contracts of employees, who are comparable employees of the hirer, whether by collective agreement or otherwise[13].

An agency worker who considers that the hirer or a temporary work agency may have treated that agency worker in a manner which infringes a right to basic working and employment conditions[14] may make a written request to the temporary work agency for a written statement containing information relating to the treatment in question[15]; and a temporary work agency that receives such a request from an agency worker must, within 28 days of receiving it, provide the agency worker with a written statement setting out[16]:

(A) relevant information relating to the basic working and employment conditions of the workers of the hirer[17];
(B) the factors the temporary work agency considered when determining the basic working and employment conditions which applied to the agency worker at the time when the breach[18] is alleged to have taken place[19]; and
(C) where the temporary work agency seeks to rely on deemed compliance[20], relevant information which explains the basis on which it is considered that an individual is a comparable employee[21], and which describes the relevant terms and conditions, which apply to that employee[22].

If an agency worker has made such a request and has not been provided with such a statement within 30 days of making that request, the agency worker may make a written request to the hirer for a written statement containing information relating to the relevant basic working and employment conditions of the workers of the hirer[23]; and a hirer that receives such a request[24] must, within 28 days of receiving it, provide the agency worker with such a statement[25].

Information provided in this way[26], whether in the form of a written statement or otherwise, is admissible as evidence in any proceedings under the Agency Workers Regulations 2010[27]; and, if it appears to the tribunal in any proceedings under those regulations either that a temporary work agency or the hirer (as the case may be) deliberately, and without reasonable excuse, failed to provide information, whether in the form of a written statement or otherwise[28], or that any written statement supplied is evasive or equivocal[29], it may draw any inference which it considers it just and equitable to draw, including an inference that that temporary work agency or hirer (as the case may be) has infringed the right in question[30].

The restrictions on contracting out that are imposed by the Employment Rights Act 1996[31] apply in relation to the Agency Workers Regulations 2010[32] as if those regulations were contained in the Employment Rights Act 1996[33].

1   As to the meaning of 'agency worker' for these purposes see PARA 97.
2   See the Agency Workers Regulations 2010, SI 2010/93, reg 5(1). The provision made by reg 5 does not apply unless an agency worker has completed the qualifying period (as to which see reg 7; and PARA 99): see reg 5(1). As to the meaning of 'hirer' for these purposes see PARA 97 note 3.
3   Agency Workers Regulations 2010, SI 2010/93, reg 5(1)(a). As to the meaning of 'temporary work agency' for these purposes see PARA 97.
4   Agency Workers Regulations 2010, SI 2010/93, reg 5(1)(b). As to the qualifying period see note 2.
5   For these purposes, 'employee' means an individual who has entered into or works under or, where the employment has ceased, worked under a contract of employment: see the Agency Workers Regulations 2010, SI 2010/93, reg 2. In relation to an employee, 'employment' means employment under a contract of employment; and 'employed' must be construed accordingly: see reg 2. As to the meaning of 'contract of employment' for these purposes see PARA 97 note 5.
6   Agency Workers Regulations 2010, SI 2010/93, reg 5(2)(a). For these purposes, 'relevant terms and conditions' means terms and conditions relating to:
    (1)   pay (reg 6(1)(a));
    (2)   the duration of working time (reg 6(1)(b));
    (3)   night work (reg 6(1)(c));
    (4)   rest periods (reg 6(1)(d));
    (5)   rest breaks (reg 6(1)(e)); and
    (6)   annual leave (reg 6(1)(f)).
    For the purposes of head (1) above, 'pay' means any sums payable to a worker of the hirer in connection with the worker's employment, including any fee, bonus, commission, holiday pay or other emolument referable to the employment, whether payable under contract or otherwise, but excluding any payments or rewards within the following heads (reg 6(2)):
    (a)   any payment by way of occupational sick pay (reg 6(3)(a));
    (b)   any payment by way of a pension, allowance or gratuity in connection with the worker's retirement or as compensation for loss of office (reg 6(3)(b));
    (c)   any payment in respect of maternity, paternity or adoption leave (reg 6(3)(c));
    (d)   any payment referable to the worker's redundancy (reg 6(3)(d));
    (e)   any payment or reward made pursuant to a financial participation scheme (reg 6(3)(e));
    (f)   any bonus, incentive payment or reward which is not directly attributable to the amount or quality of the work done by a worker, and which is given to a worker for a reason other than the amount or quality of work done such as to encourage the worker's loyalty or to reward the worker's long-term service (reg 6(3)(f));
    (g)   any payment for time off under the Employment Rights Act 1996 Pt VI (ss 50–63C) (time off work: see PARA 325 et seq) or the Trade Union and Labour Relations (Consolidation) Act 1992 s 169 (payment for time off for carrying out trade union activities: see PARA 1065) (Agency Workers Regulations 2010, SI 2010/93, reg 6(3)(g));
    (h)   a guarantee payment under the Employment Rights Act 1996 s 28 (see PARA 261) (Agency Workers Regulations 2010, SI 2010/93, reg 6(3)(h));

(i)   any payment by way of an advance under an agreement for a loan or by way of an advance of pay, but without prejudice to the application of the Employment Rights Act 1996 s 13 to any deduction made from the worker's wages in respect of any such advance (see PARA 255) (Agency Workers Regulations 2010, SI 2010/93, reg 6(3)(i));

(j)   any payment in respect of expenses incurred by the worker in carrying out the employment (reg 6(3)(j)); and

(k)   any payment to the worker otherwise than in that person's capacity as a worker (reg 6(3)(k)).

Any monetary value attaching to any payment or benefit in kind furnished to a worker by the hirer is not to be treated as pay of the worker, however, except any voucher or stamp which is of fixed value expressed in monetary terms, and is capable of being exchanged (whether on its own or together with other vouchers, stamps or documents, and whether immediately or only after a time) for money, goods or services (or for any combination of two or more of those things): see reg 6(4). For these purposes, 'financial participation scheme' means any scheme that offers workers of the hirer either a distribution of shares or options, or a share of profits in cash or in shares; 'night work' means work during night time; and 'night time', in relation to an individual, means a period whose duration is not less than seven hours (and which includes the period between midnight and 5 am) which is determined for the purposes of the Agency Workers Regulations 2010, SI 2010/93, by a working time agreement (or, in default of such a determination, the period between 11 pm and 6 am); 'rest period', in relation to an individual, means a period which is not working time, other than a rest break or leave to which that individual is entitled either under the Working Time Regulations 1998, SI 1998/1833 (see PARA 267 et seq) or under the contract between that individual and the employer of that individual; 'working time', in relation to an individual, means any period during which that individual is working, at the disposal of the employer of that individual and carrying out the activity or duties of that individual, any period during which that individual is receiving relevant training, and any additional period which is to be treated as working time for the purposes of the Working Time Regulations 1998, SI 1998/1833, under a working time agreement; 'relevant training' means work experience provided pursuant to a training course or programme, training for employment, or both (other than work experience or training the immediate provider of which is an educational institution or a person whose main business is the provision of training, and which is provided on a course run by that institution or person); and 'working time agreement', in relation to an individual, means a workforce agreement (within the meaning of the Working Time Regulations 1998, SI 1998/1833, reg 2(1): see PARA 272), which applies to the individual any provision of a collective agreement which forms part of a contract between that individual and the employer of that individual, or any other agreement in writing which is legally enforceable as between the individual and the employer of that individual: see the Agency Workers Regulations 2010, SI 2010/93, reg 6(5). In relation to an employee or worker, 'employer' means the person by whom the employee or worker is (or where the employment has ceased, was) employed: see reg 2.

7   For these purposes, 'worker' means an individual who is not an agency worker but who has entered into or works under (or where the employment has ceased, worked under) either a contract of employment, or any other contract, whether express or implied and (if it is express) whether oral or in writing, whereby the individual undertakes to do or perform personally any work or services for another party to the contract whose status is not by virtue of the contract that of a client or customer of any profession or business undertaking carried on by the individual (and any reference to a worker's contract must be construed accordingly): see the Agency Workers Regulations 2010, SI 2010/93, reg 2. In relation to a worker, 'employment' means employment under that worker's contract; and 'employed' must be construed accordingly: see reg 2.

8   Agency Workers Regulations 2010, SI 2010/93, reg 5(2)(b). As to the meaning of 'relevant terms and conditions' for these purposes see note 6.

9   See the Agency Workers Regulations 2010, SI 2010/93, reg 5(2). The provision made by reg 5 has no effect in relation to an agency worker who has a permanent contract of employment with a temporary work agency which provides for pay between assignments: see regs 5(6), 10; and 100.

10   Ie the Agency Workers Regulations 2010, SI 2010/93, reg 5(1) (see the text and notes 1–4): see reg 5(3).

11   See the Agency Workers Regulations 2010, SI 2010/93, reg 5(3).

12   Agency Workers Regulations 2010, SI 2010/93, reg 5(3)(a). For these purposes, an employee is a comparable employee in relation to an agency worker if at the time when the breach of reg 5(1) (see the text and notes 1–4) is alleged to take place:

(1)   both that employee and the agency worker are: (a) working for and under the

supervision and direction of the hirer (reg 5(4)(a)(i)); and (b) engaged in the same or broadly similar work having regard, where relevant, to whether they have a similar level of qualification and skills (reg 5(4)(a)(ii)); and

(2) the employee works or is based at the same establishment as the agency worker or, where there is no comparable employee working or based at that establishment who satisfies the requirements of head (1) above, works or is based at a different establishment and satisfies those requirements (reg 5(4)(b)).

An employee is not a comparable employee, however, if that employee's employment has ceased: reg 5(5).

13 Agency Workers Regulations 2010, SI 2010/93, reg 5(3)(b).
14 Ie a right conferred by the Agency Workers Regulations 2010, SI 2010/93, reg 5 (see the text and notes 1–13): see reg 16(1).
15 Agency Workers Regulations 2010, SI 2010/93, reg 16(1). The provision made by reg 16(1) applies only to an agency worker who at the time that worker makes such a request is entitled to the right conferred by reg 5 (see the text and notes 1–13): see reg 16(7).
16 See the Agency Workers Regulations 2010, SI 2010/93, reg 16(2).
17 Agency Workers Regulations 2010, SI 2010/93, reg 16(2)(a).
18 Ie the breach of the Agency Workers Regulations 2010, SI 2010/93, reg 5 (see the text and notes 1–13): see reg 16(2)(b).
19 Agency Workers Regulations 2010, SI 2010/93, reg 16(2)(b).
20 Ie seeks to rely on the Agency Workers Regulations 2010, SI 2010/93, reg 5(3) (see the text and notes 10–13): see reg 16(2)(c).
21 Agency Workers Regulations 2010, SI 2010/93, reg 16(2)(c)(i).
22 Agency Workers Regulations 2010, SI 2010/93, reg 16(2)(c)(ii).
23 Agency Workers Regulations 2010, SI 2010/93, reg 16(3). The provision made by reg 16(3) applies only to an agency worker who at the time that worker makes such a request is entitled to the right conferred by reg 5 (see the text and notes 1–13): see reg 16(7).
24 Ie a request made in accordance with the Agency Workers Regulations 2010, SI 2010/93, reg 16(3) (see the text and note 23): see reg 16(4).
25 Agency Workers Regulations 2010, SI 2010/93, reg 16(4).
26 Ie provided under the Agency Workers Regulations 2010, SI 2010/93, reg 16 (see the text and notes 14–25): see reg 16(8).
27 Agency Workers Regulations 2010, SI 2010/93, reg 16(8). As to proceedings under the Agency Workers Regulations 2010, SI 2010/93, see PARA 105.
28 Agency Workers Regulations 2010, SI 2010/93, reg 16(9)(a).
29 Agency Workers Regulations 2010, SI 2010/93, reg 16(9)(b).
30 See the Agency Workers Regulations 2010, SI 2010/93, reg 16(9). As to employment tribunals see PARA 1399 et seq; and as to the procedure on a complaint made to an employment tribunal see PARA 1453 et seq.
31 Ie the Employment Rights Act 1996 s 203 (see PARA 150): see the Agency Workers Regulations 2010, SI 2010/93, reg 15.
32 Ie in relation to the Agency Workers Regulations 2010, SI 2010/93: see reg 15.
33 Agency Workers Regulations 2010, SI 2010/93, reg 15.

99. Qualifying period for temporary agency worker's entitlement to basic working and employment conditions. The entitlement of an agency worker[1] to basic working and employment conditions[2] does not apply unless the agency worker has completed the qualifying period[3]; and to complete the qualifying period the agency worker must work in the same role with the same hirer for 12 continuous calendar weeks, during one or more assignments[4]. For these purposes[5], the agency worker works in 'the same role' unless[6]:

(1) the agency worker has started a new role with the same hirer, whether supplied by the same or by a different temporary work agency[7];

(2) the work or duties that make up the whole or the main part of that new role are substantively different from the work or duties that made up the whole or the main part of the previous role[8]; and

(3) the temporary work agency has informed the agency worker in writing of the type of work the agency worker will be required to do in the new role[9].

Where an agency worker has completed the qualifying period with a particular hirer, the entitlement to basic working and employment conditions[10] applies and continues to apply to that agency worker in relation to that particular hirer unless that agency worker is no longer working in the same role[11] with that hirer[12], or unless there is a break between assignments, or during an assignment, which disrupts that agency worker's continuity of employment with that hirer[13].

When an agency worker has: (a) completed two or more assignments with a hirer ('H')[14]; (b) completed at least one assignment with H and one or more earlier assignments with hirers connected to H[15]; or (c) worked in more than two roles during an assignment with H, and on at least two occasions has worked in a role that was not the 'same role' as the previous role[16], and where:

(i)   the most likely explanation for the structure of the assignment, or assignments, mentioned in heads (a) to (c) above is that H (or the temporary work agency supplying the agency worker to H, or, where applicable, H and one or more hirers connected to H) intended to prevent the agency worker from being entitled to, or from continuing to be entitled to, basic working and employment conditions[17]; and

(ii)   the agency worker would be entitled to, or would continue to be entitled to, basic working and employment conditions[18] in relation to H, but for that structure[19],

then:

(A)   an agency worker is to be treated[20] as having completed the qualifying period from the time at which the agency worker would have completed the qualifying period but for the structure of the assignment or assignments mentioned in heads (a) to (c) above[21]; and

(B)   an agency worker who has completed the qualifying period and who is no longer entitled to basic working and employment conditions[22], but who would be so entitled but for the structure of the assignment or assignments mentioned in heads (a) to (c) above, is to be treated[23] as continuing to be entitled to those rights from the time at which the agency worker completed that period[24].

For these purposes, hirers are connected to a hirer if one hirer (directly or indirectly) has control of the other hirer or a third person (directly or indirectly) has control of both hirers[25].

1   As to the meaning of 'agency worker' for these purposes see PARA 97.
2   Ie the rights conferred by the Agency Workers Regulations 2010, SI 2010/93, reg 5 (see PARA 98): see reg 7(1). As to the meaning of 'basic working and employment conditions' for these purposes see PARA 98.
3   Agency Workers Regulations 2010, SI 2010/93, reg 7(1).
4   Agency Workers Regulations 2010, SI 2010/93, reg 7(2). For these purposes, 'assignment' means a period of time during which an agency worker is supplied by one or more temporary work agencies to a hirer to work temporarily for and under the supervision and direction of the hirer: see reg 2. Time spent by an agency worker working during an assignment before 1 October 2011 does not count for the purposes of reg 7, however: reg 7(12). As to the meaning of 'temporary work agency' for these purposes see PARA 97; and as to the meaning of 'hirer' for these purposes see PARA 97 note 3.
     For the purposes of reg 7 and reg 10 (see PARA 100), any week during the whole or part of which an agency worker works during an assignment is counted as a calendar week (reg 7(4)); and, for the purposes of regs 7–9 (see also the text and notes 5–25), when calculating whether any weeks completed with a particular hirer are continuous, where:
    (1)   the agency worker has started working during an assignment, and there is a break, either between assignments or during an assignment, when the agency worker is not working (reg 7(5)(a));

(2)   reg 7(8) applies to that break (reg 7(5)(b)); and

(3)   the agency worker returns to work in the same role with the same hirer (reg 7(5)(c)),

any continuous weeks during which the agency worker worked for that hirer before the break must be carried forward and treated as continuous with any weeks during which the agency worker works for that hirer after the break (see reg 7(5)). The provision made by reg 7(8) applies where there is a break between assignments, or during an assignment, when the agency worker is not working (see reg 7(8)), and the break is:

(a)   for any reason and the break is not more than six calendar weeks (reg 7(8)(a));

(b)   wholly due to the fact that the agency worker is incapable of working in consequence of sickness or injury, and the requirements of reg 7(9) are satisfied (reg 7(8)(b));

(c)   related to pregnancy, childbirth or maternity and is at a time in a protected period (reg 7(8)(c));

(d)   wholly for the purpose of taking time off or leave, whether statutory or contractual, to which the agency worker is otherwise entitled which is: (i) ordinary, compulsory or additional maternity leave (reg 7(8)(d)(i)); (ii) ordinary or additional adoption leave (reg 7(8)(d)(ii)); (iii) paternity leave (reg 7(8)(d)(iii)); (iv) time off or other leave not listed in head (i), head (ii) or head (iii) above (reg 7(8)(d)(iv)); or (v) for more than one of the reasons listed in heads (i)–(iv) above (reg 7(8)(d)(v));

(e)   wholly due to the fact that the agency worker is required to attend at any place in pursuance of being summoned for service as a juror under the Juries Act 1974 (see JURIES vol 61 (2010) PARA 801 et seq) or under the Coroners Act 1988 (see now the Coroners and Justice Act 2009; and CORONERS vol 24 (2010) PARA 41), and the break is 28 calendar weeks or less (reg 7(8)(e));

(f)   wholly due to a temporary cessation in the hirer's requirement for any worker to be present at the establishment and work in a particular role, for a pre-determined period of time according to the established custom and practices of the hirer (reg 7(8)(f)); or

(g)   wholly due to a strike, lock-out or other industrial action at the hirer's establishment (reg 7(8)(g)); or

(h)   wholly due to more than one of the reasons listed in heads (b), (c), (d), (e), (f) or (g) above (reg 7(8)(h)).

Head (b) above applies only where the break is 28 calendar weeks or less, where head (c) above does not apply, and where, if required to do so by the temporary work agency, the agency worker has provided such written medical evidence as may reasonably be required: see reg 7(9). For the purposes of head (c) above, a protected period begins at the start of the pregnancy, and the protected period associated with any particular pregnancy ends at the end of the 26 weeks beginning with childbirth or, if earlier, when the agency worker returns to work (see reg 7(10)), where 'childbirth' means the birth of a living child or the birth of a child whether living or dead after 24 weeks of pregnancy (see reg 7(11)). As to the meaning of working in the 'same role' see reg 7(3); and the text and notes 5–9.

For the purposes of reg 7 and reg 8 (see the text and notes 10–13), when calculating the number of weeks during which the agency worker has worked, where the agency worker has (see reg 7(6)):

(A)   started working in a role during an assignment (reg 7(6)(a)); and

(B)   is unable to continue working for a reason described in head (c) or in head (d)(i), (d)(ii) or (d)(iii) above (reg 7(6)(b)),

for the period that is covered by one or more such reasons, that agency worker is deemed to be working in that role with the hirer, for the original intended duration, or likely duration of the assignment, whichever is the longer (see reg 7(6)). Where an assignment ends on grounds which are maternity grounds within the meaning of the Employment Rights Act 1996 s 68A (ending the supply of an agency worker on maternity grounds: see PARA 601), and where the agency worker is deemed to be working in that role in accordance with reg 7(6), the fact that an agency worker is actually working in another role, whether for the same or a different hirer during the period mentioned in reg 7(6) or any part of that period, does not affect the operation of reg 7(6): see reg 7(7).

5   Ie for the purposes of the Agency Workers Regulations 2010, SI 2010/93, regs 7–9 (see also the text and notes 6–25): see reg 7(3).

6   See the Agency Workers Regulations 2010, SI 2010/93, reg 7(3).

7   Agency Workers Regulations 2010, SI 2010/93, reg 7(3)(a).

8   Agency Workers Regulations 2010, SI 2010/93, reg 7(3)(b).

9   Agency Workers Regulations 2010, SI 2010/93, reg 7(3)(c).

10   Ie the rights conferred by the Agency Workers Regulations 2010, SI 2010/93, reg 5 (see PARA 98): see reg 8.

11 Ie within the meaning of the Agency Workers Regulations 2010, SI 2010/93, reg 7(3) (see the text and notes 5–9): see reg 8(a).
12 Agency Workers Regulations 2010, SI 2010/93, reg 8(a).
13 Agency Workers Regulations 2010, SI 2010/93, reg 8(b). The text refers to a break between assignments, or during an assignment, when the agency worker is not working, to which reg 7(8) does not apply (see note 4): see reg 8(b).
14 Agency Workers Regulations 2010, SI 2010/93, reg 9(3)(a).
15 Agency Workers Regulations 2010, SI 2010/93, reg 9(3)(b). As to when hirers are connected to a hirer see the text and note 25.
16 Agency Workers Regulations 2010, SI 2010/93, reg 9(3)(c). The text refers to working in the 'same role' within the meaning of reg 7(3) (see the text and notes 5–9): see reg 9(3)(c).
17 Agency Workers Regulations 2010, SI 2010/93, reg 9(4)(a). The text refers to the right to basic working and employment conditions conferred by reg 5 (see PARA 98): see reg 9(4)(a).
   The following matters in particular are to be taken into account in determining whether the structure of the assignment or assignments mentioned in reg 9(3) (see the text and notes 14–16) shows that the most likely explanation for it is that mentioned in reg 9(4)(a), namely:
   (1) the length of the assignments (reg 9(5)(a));
   (2) the number of assignments with H (and, where applicable, hirers connected to H) (reg 9(5)(b));
   (3) the number of times the agency worker has worked in a new role with H (and, where applicable, hirers connected to H) and that new role is not the 'same role' within the meaning of reg 7(3) (see the text and notes 5–9) (reg 9(5)(c));
   (4) the number of times the agency worker has returned to work in the same role within the meaning of reg 7(3) with H (and, where applicable, hirers connected to H) (reg 9(5)(d));
   (5) the period of any break between assignments with H (and, where applicable, hirers connected to H) (reg 9(5)(e)).
18 Ie the rights conferred by the Agency Workers Regulations 2010, SI 2010/93, reg 5 (see PARA 98): see reg 9(4)(b).
19 Agency Workers Regulations 2010, SI 2010/93, reg 9(4)(b).
20 Ie notwithstanding the Agency Workers Regulations 2010, SI 2010/93, reg 7(1), (2) (see the text and notes 1–4) and reg 8 (see the text and notes 10–13): see reg 9(1).
21 See the Agency Workers Regulations 2010, SI 2010/93, reg 9(1).
22 Ie is no longer entitled to the rights conferred by the Agency Workers Regulations 2010, SI 2010/93, reg 5 (see PARA 98): see reg 9(2).
23 Ie notwithstanding the Agency Workers Regulations 2010, SI 2010/93, reg 7(1), (2) (see the text and notes 1–4) and reg 8 (see the text and notes 10–13): see reg 9(2).
24 See the Agency Workers Regulations 2010, SI 2010/93, reg 9(2).
25 Agency Workers Regulations 2010, SI 2010/93, reg 9(6).

100.   Treatment of permanent contracts of employment with a temporary work agency providing for pay between assignments.

To the extent to which it relates to pay[1], the entitlement of an agency worker[2] to basic working and employment conditions[3] does not have effect in relation to an agency worker who has a permanent contract of employment[4] with a temporary work agency[5] if:

(1)   the contract of employment was entered into before the beginning of the first assignment[6] under that contract and includes terms and conditions in writing relating to[7]: (a) the minimum scale or rate of remuneration or the method of calculating remuneration[8]; (b) the location or locations where the agency worker may be expected to work[9]; (c) the expected hours of work during any assignment[10]; (d) the maximum number of hours of work that the agency worker may be required to work each week during any assignment[11]; (e) the minimum hours of work per week that may be offered to the agency worker during any assignment provided that it is a minimum of at least one hour[12]; and (f) the nature of the work that the agency worker may expect to be offered including any relevant requirements relating to qualifications or experience[13];

(2)   the contract of employment contains a statement that the effect of

entering into it is that the employee does not, during the currency of the contract, have any entitlement to basic working and employment conditions[14] insofar as they relate to pay[15];

(3)   during any period under the contract after the end of the first assignment under that contract in which the agency worker is not working temporarily for and under the supervision and direction of a hirer[16], but is available to do so[17]: (a) the temporary work agency takes reasonable steps to seek suitable work for the agency worker[18]; (b) if suitable work is available, the temporary work agency offers the agency worker to be proposed to a hirer who is offering such work[19]; and (c) the temporary work agency pays the agency worker a minimum amount of remuneration in respect of that period ('the minimum amount')[20]; and

(4)   the temporary work agency does not terminate the contract of employment until it has complied with its obligations in head (3) above for an aggregate of not less than four calendar weeks during the contract[21].

The minimum amount to be paid to the agency worker during a pay reference period falling within a period to which head (3) above applies must not be less than 50% of the pay paid to the agency worker in the relevant pay reference period[22].

1   As to the meaning of 'pay' for these purposes see PARA 98 note 6.
2   As to the meaning of 'agency worker' for these purposes see PARA 97.
3   Ie the rights conferred by the Agency Workers Regulations 2010, SI 2010/93, reg 5 (see PARA 98): see reg 10(1). As to the meaning of 'basic working and employment conditions' for these purposes see PARA 98.
4   As to the meaning of 'contract of employment' for these purposes see PARA 97 note 5.
5   See the Agency Workers Regulations 2010, SI 2010/93, reg 10(1). As to the meaning of 'temporary work agency' for these purposes see PARA 97.
6   As to the meaning of 'assignment' for these purposes see PARA 99 note 4.
7   See the Agency Workers Regulations 2010, SI 2010/93, reg 10(1)(a).
8   Agency Workers Regulations 2010, SI 2010/93, reg 10(1)(a)(i).
9   Agency Workers Regulations 2010, SI 2010/93, reg 10(1)(a)(ii).
10 Agency Workers Regulations 2010, SI 2010/93, reg 10(1)(a)(iii).
11 Agency Workers Regulations 2010, SI 2010/93, reg 10(1)(a)(iv). For the purposes of reg 10, any week during the whole or part of which an agency worker works during an assignment is counted as a calendar week: see reg 7(4).
12 Agency Workers Regulations 2010, SI 2010/93, reg 10(1)(a)(v).
13 Agency Workers Regulations 2010, SI 2010/93, reg 10(1)(a)(vi).
14 Ie entitlement to the rights conferred by the Agency Workers Regulations 2010, SI 2010/93, reg 5 (see PARA 98): see reg 10(1)(b).
15 Agency Workers Regulations 2010, SI 2010/93, reg 10(1)(b).
16 As to the meaning of 'hirer' for these purposes see PARA 97 note 3.
17 See the Agency Workers Regulations 2010, SI 2010/93, reg 10(1)(c) (amended by SI 2011/1941).
18 Agency Workers Regulations 2010, SI 2010/93, reg 10(1)(c)(i). For work to be suitable for the purposes of head (3) in the text, the nature of the work, and the terms and conditions applicable to the agency worker whilst performing the work, must not differ from the nature of the work and the terms and conditions included in the contract of employment under head (1) in the text: reg 10(2).
19 Agency Workers Regulations 2010, SI 2010/93, reg 10(1)(c)(ii).
20 Agency Workers Regulations 2010, SI 2010/93, reg 10(1)(c)(iii). As to the minimum amount see the text and note 22.
21 Agency Workers Regulations 2010, SI 2010/93, reg 10(1)(d).
22 Agency Workers Regulations 2010, SI 2010/93, reg 11(1). For these purposes, 'pay reference period' is a month (or, in the case of a worker who is paid wages by reference to a period shorter than a month, that period) (see reg 11(5)); and the relevant pay reference period is the pay reference period in which the agency worker received the highest level of pay which fell:

(1) within the 12 weeks immediately preceding the end of the previous assignment (where the assignment lasted for longer than 12 weeks) (reg 11(2)(a)); or (2) during the assignment (where the assignment lasted for 12 or fewer weeks) (reg 11(2)(b)). For the purposes of calculating the minimum amount as set out in the text, only payments in respect of basic pay whether by way of annual salary, payments for actual time worked or by reference to output or otherwise are to be taken into account: reg 11(4). The minimum amount must be not less than the amount that the agency worker would have been entitled to for the hours worked in the relevant pay reference period if the provisions of the National Minimum Wage Regulations 1999, SI 1999/584, applied: Agency Workers Regulations 2010, SI 2010/93, reg 11(3) (substituted by SI 2010/1901; amended by SI 2012/2397). As to the rate, and the method of calculation, of the national minimum wage see PARA 199 et seq.

101.   Temporary agency worker's rights of access to permanent employment opportunities and collective facilities etc.   An agency worker[1] has during an assignment[2]:

  (1)   the right to be treated no less favourably than a comparable worker[3] in relation to the collective facilities and amenities provided by the hirer[4]; and

  (2)   the right to be informed by the hirer of any relevant vacant posts with the hirer[5], to give that agency worker the same opportunity as a comparable worker[6] to find permanent employment with the hirer[7].

The right conferred by head (1) above applies, however, only if the treatment is not justified on objective grounds[8].

An agency worker who considers that the hirer may have treated that agency worker in a manner which infringes a right conferred under head (1) or head (2) above, may make a written request to the hirer for a written statement containing information relating to the treatment in question[9]. A hirer that receives such a request from an agency worker must, within 28 days of receiving it, provide the agency worker with a written statement setting out[10]:

  (a)   all relevant information relating to the rights of a comparable worker in relation to the rights mentioned in head (1) above or, as the case may be, in head (2) above[11], and

  (b)   the particulars of the reasons for the treatment of the agency worker in respect of the right conferred by head (1) above or, as the case may be, by head (2) above[12].

Information provided in this way[13], whether in the form of a written statement or otherwise, is admissible as evidence in any proceedings under the Agency Workers Regulations 2010[14]; and, if it appears to the tribunal in any proceedings under those regulations either that a temporary work agency or the hirer (as the case may be) deliberately, and without reasonable excuse, failed to provide information, whether in the form of a written statement or otherwise[15], or that any written statement supplied is evasive or equivocal[16], it may draw any inference which it considers it just and equitable to draw, including an inference that that temporary work agency or hirer (as the case may be) has infringed the right in question[17].

1   As to the meaning of 'agency worker' for these purposes see PARA 97.
2   As to the meaning of 'assignment' for these purposes see PARA 99 note 4.
3   For these purposes, an individual is a comparable worker in relation to an agency worker if at the time when the breach of the Agency Workers Regulations 2010, SI 2010/93, reg 12(1) (see head (1) in the text) is alleged to take place:
      (1)   both that individual and the agency worker are: (a) working for and under the supervision and direction of the hirer (reg 12(4)(a)(i)); and (b) engaged in the same or broadly similar work having regard, where relevant, to whether they have a similar level of qualification and skills (reg 12(4)(a)(ii));

(2) that individual works or is based at the same establishment as the agency worker (or, where there is no comparable worker working or based at that establishment who satisfies the requirements of head (1) above, works or is based at a different establishment and satisfies those requirements) (reg 12(4)(b)); and

(3) that individual is an employee of the hirer (or, where there is no employee satisfying the requirements of heads (1) and (2) above, is a worker of the hirer and satisfies those requirements) (reg 12(4)(c)).

As to the meaning of 'hirer' for these purposes see PARA 97 note 3. As to the meaning of 'employee' for these purposes see PARA 98 note 5.

4 Agency Workers Regulations 2010, SI 2010/93, reg 12(1). For these purposes, 'collective facilities and amenities' includes, in particular, canteen or other similar facilities, child care facilities, and transport services: see reg 12(3).

5 For these purposes, the hirer may inform the agency worker by a general announcement in a suitable place in the hirer's establishment: Agency Workers Regulations 2010, SI 2010/93, reg 13(4).

6 For these purposes, an individual is a comparable worker in relation to an agency worker if at the time when the breach of the Agency Workers Regulations 2010, SI 2010/93, reg 13(1) (see head (2) in the text) is alleged to take place:

(1) both that individual and the agency worker are: (a) working for and under the supervision and direction of the hirer (reg 13(2)(a)(i)); and (b) engaged in the same or broadly similar work having regard, where relevant, to whether they have a similar level of qualification and skills (reg 13(2)(a)(ii));

(2) that individual works or is based at the same establishment as the agency worker (reg 13(2)(b)); and

(3) that individual is an employee of the hirer (or, where there is no employee satisfying the requirements of heads (1) and (2) above, is a worker of the hirer and satisfies those requirements) (reg 13(2)(c)).

For these purposes, an individual is not a comparable worker, however, if that individual's employment with the hirer has ceased: reg 13(3).

7 Agency Workers Regulations 2010, SI 2010/93, reg 13(1).

8 Agency Workers Regulations 2010, SI 2010/93, reg 12(2).

9 Agency Workers Regulations 2010, SI 2010/93, reg 16(5).

10 See the Agency Workers Regulations 2010, SI 2010/93, reg 16(6).

11 Agency Workers Regulations 2010, SI 2010/93, reg 16(6)(a).

12 Agency Workers Regulations 2010, SI 2010/93, reg 16(6)(b).

13 Ie provided under the Agency Workers Regulations 2010, SI 2010/93, reg 16 (see the text and notes 9–12): see reg 16(8).

14 Agency Workers Regulations 2010, SI 2010/93, reg 16(8). As to proceedings under the Agency Workers Regulations 2010, SI 2010/93, see PARA 105.

15 Agency Workers Regulations 2010, SI 2010/93, reg 16(9)(a).

16 Agency Workers Regulations 2010, SI 2010/93, reg 16(9)(b).

17 See the Agency Workers Regulations 2010, SI 2010/93, reg 16(9). As to employment tribunals see PARA 1399 et seq; and as to the procedure on a complaint made to an employment tribunal see PARA 1453 et seq.

102. Liabilities of temporary work agency and hirer under agency worker regulations. A temporary work agency[1] is liable[2] for any breach of the right conferred on an agency worker[3] to basic working and employment conditions[4], to the extent that it is responsible for that breach[5]; and the hirer[6] is liable also for any such breach[7], to the extent that it is responsible for that breach[8]. A temporary work agency is not so liable[9], however, where it is established that the temporary work agency[10]:

(1) obtained, or has taken reasonable steps to obtain, relevant information from the hirer[11]:

(a) about the basic working and employment conditions in force in the hirer[12];

(b) if needed to assess compliance with the agency worker's right to basic working and employment conditions[13], about the relevant terms and conditions under which an employee[14] of the hirer is working[15], where: (i) that employee is considered to be a comparable employee[16] in relation to that agency worker[17]; and (ii) those terms and conditions are ordinarily included in the contract of such a comparable employee[18]; and

(c)   which explains the basis on which it is considered that the employee referred to in head (b)(i) above is a comparable employee[19];

(2)   where it has received such information, has acted reasonably in determining what the agency worker's basic working and employment conditions should be at the end of the qualifying period[20] and during the period after that until[21] the agency worker ceases to be entitled to basic working and employment conditions[22]; and

(3)   ensured that, where it has responsibility for applying those basic working and employment conditions to the agency worker, that agency worker has been treated in accordance with the determination described in head (2) above[23],

and, to the extent that the temporary work agency is not so liable, the hirer is liable[24]. Where more than one temporary work agency is a party to the proceedings, when deciding whether or not each temporary work agency is responsible in full or in part, the employment tribunal[25] must have regard to the extent to which each agency was responsible for the determination, or application, of any of the agency worker's basic working and employment conditions[26].

The hirer alone is liable for any breach of an agency worker's right during an assignment[27] to be treated no less favourably than a comparable worker in relation to the collective facilities and amenities[28] provided by the hirer, and for any breach of an agency worker's right during an assignment[29] to be informed by the hirer of any relevant vacant posts with the hirer[30].

In relation to the protections conferred on an employee who applies the agency worker regulations, so that his dismissal may be regarded as unfair[31], and any detriment to which he may be subjected is prohibited[32]: (A) a temporary work agency is liable for any act, or any deliberate failure to act, of that temporary work agency[33]; and (B) the hirer is liable for any act, or any deliberate failure to act, of the hirer[34].

1   As to the meaning of 'temporary work agency' for these purposes see PARA 97.
2   Ie subject to the Agency Workers Regulations 2010, SI 2010/93, reg 14(3) (see the text and notes 9–24): see reg 14(1) (reg 14(1), (2) amended, reg 14(3)(a) substituted, by SI 2011/1941).
3   As to the meaning of 'agency worker' for these purposes see PARA 97.
4   Ie any breach of the Agency Workers Regulations 2010, SI 2010/93, reg 5 (see PARA 98): see reg 14(1) (as amended: see note 2). As to the meaning of 'basic working and employment conditions' for these purposes see PARA 98.
5   Agency Workers Regulations 2010, SI 2010/93, reg 14(1) (as amended: see note 2).
6   As to the meaning of 'hirer' for these purposes see PARA 97 note 3.
7   Ie any breach of the Agency Workers Regulations 2010, SI 2010/93, reg 5 (see PARA 98): see reg 14(2) (as amended: see note 2).
8   Agency Workers Regulations 2010, SI 2010/93, reg 14(2) (as amended: see note 2).
9   Ie is not liable for a breach of the Agency Workers Regulations 2010, SI 2010/93, reg 5 (see PARA 98): see reg 14(3).
10 See the Agency Workers Regulations 2010, SI 2010/93, reg 14(3).
11 Agency Workers Regulations 2010, SI 2010/93, reg 14(3)(a) (as substituted: see note 2).
12 Agency Workers Regulations 2010, SI 2010/93, reg 14(3)(a)(i) (as substituted: see note 2).
13 Ie compliance with the Agency Workers Regulations 2010, SI 2010/93, reg 5 (see PARA 98): see reg 14(3)(a)(ii) (as substituted: see note 2).
14 As to the meaning of 'employee' for these purposes see PARA 98 note 5.

15 Agency Workers Regulations 2010, SI 2010/93, reg 14(3)(a)(ii) (as substituted: see note 2).
16 Ie for the purposes of the Agency Workers Regulations 2010, SI 2010/93, reg 5(4) (see PARA 98 note 12): see reg 14(3)(a)(ii)(aa) (as substituted: see note 2).
17 Agency Workers Regulations 2010, SI 2010/93, reg 14(3)(a)(ii)(aa) (as substituted: see note 2). As to the meaning of 'a comparable employee' in relation to an agency worker for these purposes see PARA 98 note 12.
18 Agency Workers Regulations 2010, SI 2010/93, reg 14(3)(a)(ii)(bb) (as substituted: see note 2).
19 Agency Workers Regulations 2010, SI 2010/93, reg 14(3)(a)(iii) (as substituted: see note 2).
20 As to the qualifying period for these purposes see PARA 99.
21 Ie in accordance with the Agency Workers Regulations 2010, SI 2010/93, reg 8 (see PARA 99): see reg 14(3)(b).
22 Agency Workers Regulations 2010, SI 2010/93, reg 14(3)(b). The text refers to the rights to basic working and employment conditions conferred by reg 5 (see PARA 98): see reg 14(3)(b).
23 Agency Workers Regulations 2010, SI 2010/93, reg 14(3)(c).
24 See the Agency Workers Regulations 2010, SI 2010/93, reg 14(3).
25 As to employment tribunals see PARA 1399 et seq; and as to the procedure on a complaint made to an employment tribunal see PARA 1453 et seq.
26 Agency Workers Regulations 2010, SI 2010/93, reg 14(5).
27 Ie any breach of the Agency Workers Regulations 2010, SI 2010/93, reg 12 (see PARA 101): see reg 14(6). As to the meaning of 'assignment' for these purposes see PARA 99 note 4.
28 As to the meaning of 'collective facilities and amenities' see PARA 101 note 4.
29 Ie any breach of the Agency Workers Regulations 2010, SI 2010/93, reg 13 (see PARA 101): see reg 14(6).
30 Agency Workers Regulations 2010, SI 2010/93, reg 14(6).
31 Ie in relation to the right conferred by the Agency Workers Regulations 2010, SI 2010/93, reg 17 (see PARA 103): see reg 14(7).
32 Ie in relation to the right conferred by the Agency Workers Regulations 2010, SI 2010/93, reg 17 (see PARA 104): see reg 14(7).
33 Agency Workers Regulations 2010, SI 2010/93, reg 14(7)(a).
34 Agency Workers Regulations 2010, SI 2010/93, reg 14(7)(b).

103. Employee's dismissal for applying agency worker regulations to be regarded as unfair. An agency worker[1] who is an employee[2], and is dismissed, is regarded as unfairly dismissed for the purposes of the Employment Rights Act 1996[3] if the reason (or, if more than one, the principal reason) for the dismissal is[4]:

(1) that the agency worker:
   (a) brought proceedings under the Agency Workers Regulations 2010[5];
   (b) gave evidence or information in connection with such proceedings brought by any agency worker[6];
   (c) made a request to either the temporary work agency[7] or the hirer[8] for a written statement[9];
   (d) otherwise did anything under the Agency Workers Regulations 2010 in relation to a temporary work agency, or hirer, or any other person[10];
   (e) alleged that a temporary work agency, or hirer, has breached the Agency Workers Regulations 2010[11];
   (f) refused (or proposed to refuse) to forgo a right conferred by the Agency Workers Regulations 2010[12]; or
(2) that the temporary work agency, or hirer, believes or suspects that the agency worker has done or intends to do any of the things mentioned in head (1) above[13].

1 As to the meaning of 'agency worker' for these purposes see PARA 97.
2 As to the meaning of 'employee' for these purposes see PARA 98 note 5.
3 Ie for the purposes of the Employment Rights Act 1996 Pt X (ss 94–134A) (unfair dismissal: see PARA 757 et seq): see the Agency Workers Regulations 2010, SI 2010/93, reg 17(1).

4   See the Agency Workers Regulations 2010, SI 2010/93, reg 17(1). The text refers to a reason
     specified in reg 17(3) (see heads (1), (2) in the text): see reg 17(1). A redundancy selection for a
     reason specified in reg 17(3) is also to be considered unfair: see the Employment Rights
     Act 1996 s 105(7N); and PARA 781.
         Where a dismissal is unfair under the Agency Workers Regulations 2010, SI 2010/93,
     reg 17(1), the qualifying period for unfair dismissal does not apply: see the Employment Rights
     Act 1996 s 108(3)(r); and PARA 758 note 9. As to the right to make a complaint of unfair
     dismissal before an employment tribunal see PARA 804 et seq; and as to remedies see PARA 810
     et seq.
5   Agency Workers Regulations 2010, SI 2010/93, reg 17(3)(a)(i). As to proceedings under the
     Agency Workers Regulations 2010, SI 2010/93, see PARA 105.
6   Agency Workers Regulations 2010, SI 2010/93, reg 17(3)(a)(ii).
7   As to the meaning of 'temporary work agency' for these purposes see PARA 97.
8   As to the meaning of 'hirer' for these purposes see PARA 97 note 3.
9   Agency Workers Regulations 2010, SI 2010/93, reg 17(3)(a)(iii). Head (1)(c) in the text applies
     to a request for a written statement made under reg 16 (see PARAS 98, 101): see reg 17(3)(a)(iii).
10   Agency Workers Regulations 2010, SI 2010/93, reg 17(3)(a)(iv).
11   Agency Workers Regulations 2010, SI 2010/93, reg 17(3)(a)(v).
12   Agency Workers Regulations 2010, SI 2010/93, reg 17(3)(a)(vi).
13   Agency Workers Regulations 2010, SI 2010/93, reg 17(3)(b). Where the reason or principal
     reason for dismissal is that mentioned in head (1)(e) in the text (or head (2) in the text so far as
     it relates thereto), reg 17(1) (see the text and notes 1–4) does not apply if the allegation made by
     the agency worker is false and not made in good faith: see reg 17(4).

**104. Agency worker's right not to be subjected to detriment for applying
agency worker regulations.** An agency worker[1] has the right not to be subjected
to any detriment by, or as a result of, any act, or any deliberate failure to act, of
a temporary work agency[2], or the hirer[3], done on one of the grounds specified in
heads (1) and (2) below[4], namely:

(1)   that the agency worker:
       (a)   brought   proceedings   under   the   Agency   Workers
              Regulations 2010[5];
       (b)   gave evidence or information in connection with such proceedings
              brought by any agency worker[6];
       (c)   made a request to either the temporary work agency or the hirer
              for a written statement[7];
       (d)   otherwise   did   anything   under   the   Agency   Workers
              Regulations 2010 in relation to a temporary work agency, or
              hirer, or any other person[8];
       (e)   alleged that a temporary work agency, or hirer, has breached the
              Agency Workers Regulations 2010[9];
       (f)   refused (or proposed to refuse) to forgo a right conferred by the
              Agency Workers Regulations 2010[10]; or
(2)   that the temporary work agency, or hirer, believes or suspects that the
       agency worker has done or intends to do any of the things mentioned in
       head (1) above[11].

1   As to the meaning of 'agency worker' for these purposes see PARA 97.
2   As to the meaning of 'temporary work agency' for these purposes see PARA 97.
3   As to the meaning of 'hirer' for these purposes see PARA 97 note 3.
4   See the Agency Workers Regulations 2010, SI 2010/93, reg 17(2). The text refers to a reason
     specified in reg 17(3) (see heads (1), (2) in the text): see reg 17(2). The provision made by
     reg 17(2) does not apply, however, where the detriment in question amounts to dismissal within
     the meaning of the Employment Rights Act 1996 Pt X (ss 94–134A) (unfair dismissal: see PARA
     757 et seq): Agency Workers Regulations 2010, SI 2010/93, reg 17(5).
5   Agency Workers Regulations 2010, SI 2010/93, reg 17(3)(a)(i). As to proceedings under the
     Agency Workers Regulations 2010, SI 2010/93, see PARA 105.
6   Agency Workers Regulations 2010, SI 2010/93, reg 17(3)(a)(ii).

7   Agency Workers Regulations 2010, SI 2010/93, reg 17(3)(a)(iii). Head (1)(c) in the text applies
    to a request for a written statement made under reg 16 (see PARAS 98, 101): see reg 17(3)(a)(iii).
8   Agency Workers Regulations 2010, SI 2010/93, reg 17(3)(a)(iv).
9   Agency Workers Regulations 2010, SI 2010/93, reg 17(3)(a)(v).
10 Agency Workers Regulations 2010, SI 2010/93, reg 17(3)(a)(vi).
11 Agency Workers Regulations 2010, SI 2010/93, reg 17(3)(b). Where the ground for subjection
    to any act or deliberate failure to act is that mentioned in head (1)(e) in the text (or head (2) in
    the text so far as it relates thereto), reg 17(2) (see the text and notes 1–4) does not apply if the
    allegation made by the employee is false and not made in good faith: see reg 17(4).

**105.   Complaint to employment tribunal pursuant to agency worker
regulations.**   An agency worker[1] may present a complaint to an employment
tribunal[2] that a temporary work agency[3], or the hirer[4], has infringed any of the
following rights[5], namely:
(1)   his right to basic working and employment conditions[6];
(2)   his right, during an assignment[7], to be treated no less favourably than a
       comparable worker in relation to the collective facilities and amenities
       provided by the hirer[8];
(3)   his right, during an assignment, to be informed by the hirer of any
       relevant vacant posts with the hirer[9]; or
(4)   his right not to be subjected to detriment for applying the Agency
       Workers Regulations 2010[10].
An agency worker may also present a complaint to an employment tribunal
that a temporary work agency has breached[11]:
(a)   a term of a permanent contract of employment[12] with a temporary work
       agency that provides for pay between assignments[13]; or
(b)   a duty arising from such a contract[14].
An employment tribunal must not consider any such complaint, however,
unless it is presented before the end of the period of three months beginning[15]:
(i)   in the case of an alleged infringement under heads (1), (2) or (4) above,
       or a breach of a term of the contract under head (a) above, or a breach
       of a duty under head (b) above, with the date of the infringement,
       detriment or breach to which the complaint relates (or, where an act or
       failure to act is part of a series of similar acts or failures comprising the
       infringement, detriment or breach, the last of them)[16];
(ii)   in the case of an alleged infringement of the right under head (3) above,
       with the date (or, if more than one, the last date) on which other
       individuals, whether or not employed by the hirer, were informed of the
       vacancy[17].
In working out when the time limit set in this way[18] expires, the following period
is not to be counted[19], namely the period that:
(A)   begins with the day after the day on which the worker concerned
       complies with the requirement to contact ACAS before instituting
       proceedings[20] in relation to the matter in respect of which the
       proceedings are brought ('the day after Day A')[21]; and
(B)   ends with the day on which the worker concerned receives (or, if earlier,
       is treated as receiving[22]) the certificate issued by the conciliation
       officer[23] to the effect either that he has concluded that a settlement is
       not possible within the prescribed period or that the prescribed period
       has expired without a settlement having been reached ('Day B')[24].
If the unextended time limit[25] would expire during the period beginning with
Day A and ending one month after Day B, the time limit expires instead at the

end of that period[26]. Nevertheless, a tribunal may consider any such complaint which is out of time if, in all the circumstances of the case, it considers that it is just and equitable to do so[27].

Where an employment tribunal finds that such a complaint presented to it is well founded, it must take such of the following steps as it considers just and equitable[28]: (aa) making a declaration as to the rights of the complainant in relation to the matters to which the complaint relates[29]; (bb) ordering the respondent[30] to pay compensation[31] to the complainant[32]; (cc) recommending[33] that the respondent take, within a specified period, action appearing to the tribunal to be reasonable, in all the circumstances of the case, for the purpose of obviating or reducing the adverse effect on the complainant of any matter to which the complaint relates[34].

1   As to the meaning of 'agency worker' for these purposes see PARA 97.
2   As to employment tribunals see PARA 1399 et seq; and as to the procedure on a complaint made to an employment tribunal see PARA 1453 et seq. There is a requirement for early ACAS conciliation to be tried in order to promote a settlement before tribunal proceedings are instituted on a complaint under the Agency Workers Regulations 2010, SI 2010/93, reg 18: see the Employment Tribunals Act 1996 s 18(1)(z); and PARA 152 note 1. As to the constitution and powers of ACAS see PARA 1213 et seq.
3   As to the meaning of 'temporary work agency' for these purposes see PARA 97.
4   As to the meaning of 'hirer' for these purposes see PARA 97 note 3.
5   See the Agency Workers Regulations 2010, SI 2010/93, reg 18(2).
6   Ie a right conferred by the Agency Workers Regulations 2010, SI 2010/93, reg 5 (see PARA 98): see reg 18(2). As to the meaning of 'basic working and employment conditions' for these purposes see PARA 98.
7   As to the meaning of 'assignment' for these purposes see PARA 99 note 4.
8   Ie a right conferred by the Agency Workers Regulations 2010, SI 2010/93, reg 12 (see PARA 101): see reg 18(2). As to the meaning of 'collective facilities and amenities' see PARA 101 note 4.
9   Ie a right conferred by the Agency Workers Regulations 2010, SI 2010/93, reg 13 (see PARA 101): see reg 18(2).
10 Ie a right conferred by the Agency Workers Regulations 2010, SI 2010/93, reg 17(2), subject to reg 17(5) (see PARA 104 note 4): see reg 18(2).
11 See the Agency Workers Regulations 2010, SI 2010/93, reg 18(3).
12 As to the meaning of 'contract of employment' for these purposes see PARA 97 note 5.
13 Ie has breached a term of the contract of employment described in the Agency Workers Regulations 2010, SI 2010/93, reg 10(1)(a) (see PARA 100): see reg 18(3).
14 Ie has breached a duty under the Agency Workers Regulations 2010, SI 2010/93, reg 10(1)(b), (c), or (d) (see PARA 100): see reg 18(3).
15 See the Agency Workers Regulations 2010, SI 2010/93, reg 18(4). Provision that is made for the extension of time limits in order to facilitate conciliation before the institution of proceedings (ie reg 18A: see the text and notes 18–26) applies for the purposes of reg 18(4): reg 18(4A) (regs 18(4A), 18A added by SI 2014/386).
16 Agency Workers Regulations 2010, SI 2010/93, reg 18(4)(a). For the purposes of calculating the date of the infringement, detriment or breach under reg 18(4)(a):
    (1)   where a term in a contract infringes a right conferred by reg 5 (see PARA 98), reg 12 (see PARA 101), or reg 17(2) (see PARA 104), or breaches reg 10(1) (see PARA 100), that infringement or breach is treated, subject to head (2) below, as taking place on each day of the period during which the term infringes that right or breaches that duty (reg 18(6)(a)); and
    (2)   a deliberate failure to act that is contrary to reg 5, reg 12, reg 17(2), or reg 10(1), is treated as done when it was decided on (reg 18(6)(b)).
    In the absence of evidence establishing the contrary, a person is taken for the purposes of head (2) above to decide not to act: (a) when he does an act inconsistent with doing the failed act (reg 18(7)(a)); or (b) if he has done no such inconsistent act, when the period expires within which he might reasonably have been expected to have done the failed act if it was to be done (reg 18(7)(b)).
17 Agency Workers Regulations 2010, SI 2010/93, reg 18(4)(b).
18 Ie set by the Agency Workers Regulations 2010, SI 2010/93, reg 18(4) (see the text and notes 15–17): see reg 18A(2) (as added: see note 15).

19 See the Agency Workers Regulations 2010, SI 2010/93, reg 18A(2) (as added: see note 15).

20 Ie the requirement in the Employment Tribunals Act 1996 s 18A(1) (see PARA 152): see the Agency Workers Regulations 2010, SI 2010/93, reg 18A(1)(a) (as added: see note 15).

21 See the Agency Workers Regulations 2010, SI 2010/93, reg 18A(1)(a), (2) (as added: see note 15).

22 Ie by virtue of regulations made under the Employment Tribunals Act 1996 s 18A(11) (see PARA 152): see the Agency Workers Regulations 2010, SI 2010/93, reg 18A(1)(b) (as added: see note 15).

23 Ie the certificate issued under the Employment Tribunals Act 1996 s 18A(4) (see PARA 152): see the Agency Workers Regulations 2010, SI 2010/93, reg 18A(1)(b) (as added: see note 15).

24 See the Agency Workers Regulations 2010, SI 2010/93, reg 18A(1)(b), (2) (as added: see note 15).

25 Ie the time limit set by the Agency Workers Regulations 2010, SI 2010/93, reg 18(4) (see the text and notes 15–17), if not extended by reg 18A(3): see reg 18A(3) (as added: see note 15).

26 See the Agency Workers Regulations 2010, SI 2010/93, reg 18A(3) (as added: see note 15).

27 Agency Workers Regulations 2010, SI 2010/93, reg 18(5). The power so conferred on the employment tribunal by reg 18(5) to extend the time limit set by reg 18(4) (see the text and notes 15–17) is exercisable in relation to any time limit as it is extended by reg 18A (see the text and notes 18–26): reg 18A(4) (as added: see note 15).

28 See the Agency Workers Regulations 2010, SI 2010/93, reg 18(8).

29 Agency Workers Regulations 2010, SI 2010/93, reg 18(8)(a).

30 For these purposes, 'respondent' includes the hirer and any temporary work agency: see the Agency Workers Regulations 2010, SI 2010/93, reg 18(1).

31 Where a tribunal orders compensation to be paid under the Agency Workers Regulations 2010, SI 2010/93, reg 18(8)(b) (see head (bb) in the text), and there is more than one respondent, the amount of compensation payable by each or any respondent is to be such as may be found by the tribunal to be just and equitable having regard to the extent of each respondent's responsibility for the infringement to which the complaint relates: reg 18(9).

Where a tribunal orders compensation to be paid under reg 18(8)(b), the amount of the compensation awarded is such as the tribunal considers just and equitable in all the circumstances having regard to (see reg 18(10)):

(1)   the infringement or breach to which the complaint relates (reg 18(10)(a)); and

(2)   any loss which is attributable to the infringement (reg 18(10)(b)).

The loss is taken to include any expenses reasonably incurred by the complainant in consequence of the infringement or breach, and loss of any benefit which the complainant might reasonably be expected to have had but for the infringement or breach: see reg 18(11). In ascertaining the loss, the tribunal must apply the same rule concerning the duty of a person to mitigate his loss as applies to damages recoverable under the common law of England and Wales: see reg 18(16). As to the common law duty to mitigate loss see DAMAGES vol 12(1) (Reissue) PARA 1041 et seq. Compensation in respect of treating an agency worker in a manner which infringes the right conferred on him by reg 5 (see PARA 98), reg 12 (see PARA 101), or reg 13 (see PARA 101), or which breaches reg 10(1)(b), (c), or (d) (see PARA 100), or which breaches a term of the contract described in reg 10(1)(a) (see PARA 100), does not include compensation for injury to feelings: reg 18(15). Where the tribunal finds that the act, or failure to act, to which the complaint relates was to any extent caused or contributed to by action of the complainant, it must reduce the amount of the compensation by such proportion as it considers just and equitable having regard to that finding: reg 18(17).

The provision made by reg 18(10) is subject to reg 18(12), (13): see reg 18(10). Accordingly, except where the tribunal considers that in all the circumstances of the case, taking into account the conduct of the claimant and respondent, two weeks' pay is not a just and equitable amount of compensation (and the amount is reduced as the tribunal considers appropriate) (see reg 18(13)), where a tribunal orders compensation under reg 18(8)(b), any compensation which relates to an infringement or breach of the rights conferred by reg 5 or reg 10 (see PARA 100), or conferred by reg 17(2) (see PARA 104) to the extent that the infringement or breach relates to reg 5 or reg 10, must not be less than two weeks' pay, calculated in accordance with reg 19 (see reg 18(12)). For these purposes, a week's pay is the higher of:

(a)   the average weekly pay received by the agency worker, in relation to the assignment to which the claim relates, in the relevant period (reg 19(1)(a)(i)); and

(b)   the average weekly pay the agency worker should have been receiving by virtue of reg 5, in relation to the assignment to which the claim relates, in the relevant period (reg 19(1)(a)(ii)).

However, only payments in respect of basic pay whether by way of annual salary, payments for actual time worked, or by reference to output or otherwise, must be taken into account for these purposes: see reg 19(1)(b). The 'relevant period' is:

(i) where the assignment has ended on or before the date the complaint was presented to the tribunal under reg 18(2) (see the text and notes 1–5), the four week period (or, in a case where the assignment was shorter than four weeks, that period) ending with the last day of the assignment to which the claim relates (reg 19(2)(a)); or

(ii) where the assignment has not so ended, the four week period (or in the case where that assignment was shorter than four weeks, that period) ending with the date of the complaint (reg 19(2)(b)).

Where a tribunal finds that reg 9(4) applies (ie where the structure of assignments is found to have been designed to deprive the worker of rights conferred on him: see PARA 99), and where it orders compensation under reg 18(8)(b), the tribunal may make an additional award of compensation under reg 18(8)(b), which may not be more than £5,000 (and, where there is more than one respondent, the proportion of any additional compensation awarded that is payable by each of them must be such as the tribunal considers just and equitable having regard to the extent to which it considers each to have been responsible for the fact that reg 9(4)(a) applies): reg 18(14). In relation to an infringement or breach for which a tribunal orders a respondent to pay compensation under reg 18(8)(b), the tribunal may order the respondent also to pay a penalty under the Employment Tribunals Act 1996 s 12A (financial penalty payable to Secretary of State for aggravated breach of worker's rights: see PARA 1477), but only if the tribunal decides not to exercise the power under the Agency Workers Regulations 2010, SI 2010/93, reg 18(14) to make an additional award of compensation against the respondent: reg 18(14A) (added by the Enterprise and Regulatory Reform Act 2013 s 16(2), Sch 3 para 6).

32 Agency Workers Regulations 2010, SI 2010/93, reg 18(8)(b).

33 If a temporary work agency, or the hirer, fails, without reasonable justification, to comply with a recommendation made by an employment tribunal under the Agency Workers Regulations 2010, SI 2010/93, reg 18(8)(c) (see head (cc) in the text), the tribunal may, if it thinks it just and equitable to do so: (1) increase the amount of compensation required to be paid to the complainant in respect of the complaint, where an order was made under reg 18(8)(b) (see head (bb) in the text) (reg 18(18)(a)); or (2) make an order under reg 18(8)(b) (reg 18(18)(b)).

34 Agency Workers Regulations 2010, SI 2010/93, reg 18(8)(c).

106. Liability of employers and principals under agency worker regulations.

Anything done by a person in the course of his employment must be treated for the purposes of regulations that have been made for the purpose of implementing the Temporary Agency Work Directive[1] as also done by his employer[2], whether or not it was done with the employer's knowledge or approval[3]; and anything done by a person as agent for the employer with the authority of the employer must be treated for the purposes of those regulations as also done by the employer[4].

In proceedings under those regulations against any person in respect of an act alleged to have been done by an employee[5] of his, it is a defence for that person to prove that he or she took such steps as were reasonably practicable to prevent the employee from doing that act (or from doing, in the course of his employment, acts of that description)[6].

1 Ie the Agency Workers Regulations 2010, SI 2010/93, which were made in exercise of the powers conferred on the Secretary of State by the European Communities Act 1972 s 2(2) (see CONSTITUTIONAL AND ADMINISTRATIVE LAW vol 20 (2014) PARA 156) for the purposes of implementing European Parliament and Council Directive (EC) 2008/104 of 19 November 2008 (OJ L327, 05.12.2008, p 9) on temporary agency work (the 'Temporary Agency Work Directive') (see PARA 96).

2 As to the meaning of 'employer' for these purposes see PARA 98 note 6.

3 Agency Workers Regulations 2010, SI 2010/93, reg 20(1). For the purposes of reg 20:

(1) the secondment of any constable or other person to the National Crime Agency to serve as a member of its staff must be treated as employment by the National Crime Agency (and not as being employment by any other person) (reg 24(3)(a), (5) (reg 24(3)(a), (5) amended by virtue of the Crime and Courts Act 2013 s 15(3), Sch 8 para 190)); and

(2) anything done by a person so seconded in the performance, or purported performance, of his functions must be treated as done in the course of that employment (Agency Workers Regulations 2010, SI 2010/93, reg 24(3)(b)).

As to the National Crime Agency see POLICE AND INVESTIGATORY POWERS vol 84 (2013) PARA 424.

4 Agency Workers Regulations 2010, SI 2010/93, reg 20(2).
5 As to the meaning of 'employee' for these purposes see PARA 98 note 5.
6 See the Agency Workers Regulations 2010, SI 2010/93, reg 20(3).

107. Special classes of person under agency worker regulations. The regulations that have been made for the purpose of implementing the Temporary Agency Work Directive[1]:

(1) have effect in relation to Crown employment[2], service as a member of the armed forces of the Crown, persons in Crown employment, and persons in service as a member of the armed forces of the Crown, as they have effect in relation to other employment and other employees[3];

(2) have effect in relation to employment as a relevant member of the House of Lords staff[4] as they have effect in relation to other employment[5];

(3) have effect in relation to employment as a relevant member of the House of Commons staff[6] as they have effect in relation to other employment[7].

The holding, otherwise than under a contract of employment[8], of the office of constable or an appointment as a police cadet is to be treated as employment under a contract of employment by the relevant officer[9].

1 Ie the Agency Workers Regulations 2010, SI 2010/93, which were made in exercise of the powers conferred on the Secretary of State by the European Communities Act 1972 s 2(2) (see CONSTITUTIONAL AND ADMINISTRATIVE LAW vol 20 (2014) PARA 156) for the purposes of implementing European Parliament and Council Directive (EC) 2008/104 of 19 November 2008 (OJ L327, 05.12.2008, p 9) on temporary agency work (the 'Temporary Agency Work Directive') (see PARA 96).

2 For these purposes, 'Crown employment' means employment under or for the purposes of a government department or any officer or body exercising on behalf of the Crown functions conferred by a statutory provision: Agency Workers Regulations 2010, SI 2010/93, reg 21(2). Crown employment includes employment by an association established for the purposes of the Reserve Forces Act 1996 Pt XI (ss 110–119) (reserve associations: see ARMED FORCES vol 3 (2011) PARA 473) (see the Agency Workers Regulations 2010, SI 2010/93, reg 21(4)(b)), but it does not include service as a member of the armed forces of the Crown (see reg 21(4)(a)).

3 Agency Workers Regulations 2010, SI 2010/93, reg 21(1). As to the meaning of 'employee' and 'employment' for these purposes see PARA 98 note 5.
   For the purposes of the application of the provisions of the Agency Workers Regulations 2010, SI 2010/93, in relation to Crown employment, and service as a member of the armed forces of the Crown, in accordance with reg 21(1): (1) references to an employee must be construed as references to a person in Crown employment or in service as a member of the armed forces of the Crown to whom the definition of 'employee' is appropriate (reg 21(3)(a)); (2) references to a contract in relation to an employee must be construed as references to the terms of employment of a person in Crown employment or in service as a member of the armed forces of the Crown to whom the definition of 'employee' is appropriate (reg 21(3)(b)).

4 For these purposes, 'relevant member of the House of Lords staff' means any person who is employed under a contract with the Corporate Officer of the House of Lords by virtue of which he is a worker: see the Agency Workers Regulations 2010, SI 2010/93, reg 22(2). As to the Corporate Officer of the House of Lords see PARLIAMENT vol 78 (2010) PARA 990 et seq.

5 Agency Workers Regulations 2010, SI 2010/93, reg 22(1).

6 For these purposes, 'relevant member of the House of Commons staff' means any person:
   (1) who was appointed by the House of Commons Commission (Agency Workers Regulations 2010, SI 2010/93, reg 23(2)(a)); or
   (2) who is a member of the Speaker's personal staff (reg 23(2)(b)).

As to the House of Commons Commission see PARLIAMENT vol 78 (2010) PARA 946; and as to the Speaker see PARLIAMENT vol 78 (2010) PARA 931 et seq.

7 Agency Workers Regulations 2010, SI 2010/93, reg 23(1).

8 As to the meaning of 'contract of employment' for these purposes see PARA 97 note 5.

9 Agency Workers Regulations 2010, SI 2010/93, reg 24(1). For these purposes, 'relevant officer' means (in relation to a member of a police force or a special constable or police cadet appointed for a police area) the chief officer of police, and (in relation to any other person holding the office of constable or an appointment as a police cadet) the person who has the direction and control of the body of constables or cadets in question: see reg 24(4). For these purposes, any constable or other person who has been seconded to the National Crime Agency to serve as a member of its staff must be treated as employed by the National Crime Agency, in respect of actions taken by, or on behalf of, the National Crime Agency: reg 24(2), (5) (reg 24(2), (5) amended by virtue of the Crime and Courts Act 2013 s 15(3), Sch 8 para 190). As to the secondment of police constables to the National Crime Agency for the purposes of the Agency Workers Regulations 2010, SI 2010/93, reg 20 (liability of employers and principals) see PARA 106 note 3. As to the meaning of 'chief officer of police' see POLICE AND INVESTIGATORY POWERS vol 84 (2013) PARA 5; and as to the meaning of 'police area' see POLICE AND INVESTIGATORY POWERS vol 84 (2013) PARA 52. As to the National Crime Agency see POLICE AND INVESTIGATORY POWERS vol 84 (2013) PARA 424.

(vii) Flexible Working

108. Statutory right to request contract variation. Under the Employment Rights Act 1996, a qualifying employee[1] may apply to his employer[2] for a change in his terms and conditions of employment[3] if the change relates to[4]:

(1) the hours he is required to work[5];

(2) the times when he is required to work[6];

(3) where, as between his home and a place of business of his employer, he is required to work[7]; or

(4) such other aspect of his terms and conditions of employment as the Secretary of State may specify by regulations[8].

Such an application must:

(a) state that it is such an application[9];

(b) specify the change applied for and the date on which it is proposed the change should become effective[10];

(c) explain what effect, if any, the employee thinks making the change applied for would have on his employer and how, in his opinion, any such effect might be dealt with[11].

The Secretary of State has power to make regulations providing for the form of such applications, and when such an application is to be taken as made[12].

Accordingly, an employee who has been continuously employed for a period of at least 26 weeks is entitled to make a flexible working application[13]. Such an application must:

(i) be in writing[14];

(ii) state whether the employee has previously made any such application to the employer (and, if so, when)[15]; and

(iii) be dated[16].

Any such application is taken as made on the day the application is received[17].

1 For these purposes, an employee is a qualifying employee if he satisfies such conditions as to duration of employment as the Secretary of State may specify by regulations, and if he is not an agency worker (other than an agency worker who is returning to work from a period of parental leave under regulations under the Employment Rights Act 1996 s 76 (see PARA 390)): see s 80F(8)(a) (s 80F added by the Employment Act 2002 s 47(1), (2); the Employment Rights Act 1996 s 80F(8)(a) amended by SI 2013/283). An employee is an agency worker if he is supplied by a person (the 'agent') to do work for another (the 'principal') under a contract or other arrangement made between the agent and the principal: see the Employment Rights

Act 1996 s 80F(8)(b) (as so added). As to the meaning of 'employee' and related expressions in relation to employment rights generally see PARA 2 et seq. As to agency workers see PARAS 11, 95 et seq. As to the Secretary of State see PARA 5 note 21. As to the making of regulations under the Employment Rights Act 1996 generally see PARA 162. In exercise of the powers conferred by s 80F(1)(b), (5), (8)(a), the Secretary of State has made the Flexible Working Regulations 2014, SI 2014/1398, which came into force on 30 June 2014, and apply to a flexible working application made on or after that date: see regs 1(1), 2(1). For these purposes, 'flexible working application' means an application made under the Employment Rights Act 1996 s 80F (statutory right to request contract variation): see the Flexible Working Regulations 2014, SI 2014/1398, reg 1(2). As to the regulations so made see further the text and notes 13–17.

The Flexible Working (Eligibility, Complaints and Remedies) Regulations 2002, SI 2002/3236, are revoked but continue to apply to a flexible working application made before 30 June 2014: see the Flexible Working Regulations 2014, SI 2014/1398, reg 2(2).

2   As to the meaning of 'employer' and related expressions in relation to employment rights generally see PARA 2 et seq.

3   See the Employment Rights Act 1996 s 80F(1) (as added: see note 1).

4   See the Employment Rights Act 1996 s 80F(1)(a) (as added: see note 1).

5   Employment Rights Act 1996 s 80F(1)(a)(i) (as added: see note 1).

6   Employment Rights Act 1996 s 80F(1)(a)(ii) (as added: see note 1).

7   Employment Rights Act 1996 s 80F(1)(a)(iii) (as added: see note 1).

8   Employment Rights Act 1996 s 80F(1)(a)(iv) (s 80F as added (see note 1); s 80F(1)(a)(iv) amended by the Children and Families Act 2014 s 131(1), (2)(a), (b)). Regulations under the Employment Rights Act 1996 s 80F may make different provision for different cases: s 80F(9) (s 80F as so added; s 80F(9) added by the Work and Families Act 2006 s 12(1), (5)).

The Secretary of State must from time to time carry out a review of the Children and Families Act 2014 ss 131–133 (see also PARAS 109, 111), and set out the conclusions of the review in a report, which he must publish: see s 134(1). The report must in particular set out the objectives intended to be achieved by the amendments of the Employment Rights Act 1996 made by the Children and Families Act 2014 ss 131–133, assess the extent to which those objectives are achieved, and assess whether those objectives remain appropriate and, if so, the extent to which they could be achieved in a way that imposes less regulation: see s 134(2). The first report to be published under s 134 must be published before the end of the period of seven years beginning with the day on which ss 131–133 come into force (s 134(3)); and such reports are afterwards to be published at intervals not exceeding seven years (s 134(4)).

9   Employment Rights Act 1996 s 80F(2)(a) (as added: see note 1).

10 Employment Rights Act 1996 s 80F(2)(b) (as added: see note 1).

11 Employment Rights Act 1996 s 80F(2)(c) (s 80F as added (see note 1); s 80F(2)(c) amended by the Children and Families Act 2014 s 131(1), (2)(c)). See note 8.

12 See the Employment Rights Act 1996 s 80F(5) (as added: see note 1). As to the regulations so made see note 1.

13 Flexible Working Regulations 2014, SI 2014/1398, reg 3.

14 Flexible Working Regulations 2014, SI 2014/1398, reg 4(a).

15 Flexible Working Regulations 2014, SI 2014/1398, reg 4(b).

16 Flexible Working Regulations 2014, SI 2014/1398, reg 4(c).

17 Flexible Working Regulations 2014, SI 2014/1398, reg 5(1). Any such application is received, unless the contrary is proved: (1) where the employer has agreed that the application can be sent by electronic transmission, and has specified an electronic address to which the application can be sent, and the electronic form to be used by the employee, and where the application is sent by electronic transmission, on the day of transmission (reg 5(2)(a), (3)); (2) if sent by post, on the day on which it would have been delivered in the ordinary course of post (reg 5(2)(b)); and (3) if it is delivered personally, on the day of delivery (reg 5(2)(c)).

109. Employer's duties in relation to application for a contract variation. An employer[1] to whom a qualifying employee[2] has made an application for a change in his terms and conditions of employment[3], must:

(1)   deal with the application in a reasonable manner[4];

(2)   notify the employee of the decision on the application within the decision period[5]; and

(3)   only refuse such an application because he considers that one or more of the following grounds applies[6]:

    (a)   the burden of additional costs[7];

    (b)   detrimental effect on ability to meet customer demand[8];

    (c)   inability to re-organise work among existing staff[9];

    (d)   inability to recruit additional staff[10];

    (e)   detrimental impact on quality[11];

    (f)   detrimental impact on performance[12];

    (g)   insufficiency of work during the periods the employee proposes to work[13];

    (h)   planned structural changes[14]; and

    (i)   such other grounds as the Secretary of State may specify by regulations[15].

Such an application is to be treated as having been withdrawn by the employee if[16]:

    (i)   the employee without good reason has failed to attend both the first meeting arranged by the employer to discuss the application and the next meeting arranged for that purpose[17]; or

    (ii)   where the employer allows the employee to appeal a decision to reject an application or to make a further appeal, the employee without good reason has failed to attend both the first meeting arranged by the employer to discuss the appeal and the next meeting arranged for that purpose[18],

and if the employer has notified the employee that the employer has decided to treat that conduct of the employee as a withdrawal of the application[19].

1   As to the meaning of 'employer' and related expressions in relation to employment rights generally see PARA 2 et seq.

2   As to the meaning of 'qualifying employee' for these purposes see PARA 108 note 1. As to the meaning of 'employee' and related expressions in relation to employment rights generally see PARA 2 et seq.

3   Ie an application under the Employment Rights Act 1996 s 80F (see PARA 108): see s 80G(1) (ss 80F, 80G added by the Employment Act 2002 s 47(1), (2)). If an employee has made an application under the Employment Rights Act 1996 s 80F, he may not make a further application to the same employer before the end of the period of 12 months beginning with the date on which the previous application was made: s 80F(4) (as so added).

4   Employment Rights Act 1996 s 80G(1)(a) (s 80G as added (see note 3); s 80G(1)(a) substituted, s 80G(1)(aa) added, by the Children and Families Act 2014 s 132(1), (2)). As to the amendments made by s 132 see PARA 108 note 8.
     The ACAS (Flexible Working) Arbitration Scheme (Great Britain) Order 2004, SI 2004/2333, sets out a revised scheme, prepared by the Advisory, Conciliation and Arbitration Service ('ACAS') pursuant to the Trade Union and Labour Relations (Consolidation) Act 1992 s 212A, providing for arbitration in the case of disputes involving proceedings, or claims which could be the subject of proceedings, before an employment tribunal arising out of a contravention or alleged contravention of the Employment Rights Act 1996 ss 80G(1), 80H(1)(b) (flexible working: see also PARA 111): see PARA 824.

5   Employment Rights Act 1996 s 80G(1)(aa) (s 80G as added (see note 3); s 80G(1)(aa) as added (see note 4)). If an employer allows an employee to appeal a decision to reject an application, the reference in s 80G(1)(aa) to the decision on the application is a reference to the decision on the appeal, or (if more than one appeal is allowed) to the decision on the final appeal: see s 80G(1A) (s 80G(1A)–(1D) added by the Children and Families Act 2014 s 132(1), (3)). For the purposes of the Employment Rights Act 1996 s 80G(1)(aa), the decision period applicable to an employee's application under s 80F (see PARA 108) is the period of three months beginning with the date on which the application is made, or such longer period as may be agreed by the employer and the employee: see s 80G(1B) (as so added). An agreement to extend the decision period in a particular case may be made either before it ends (s 80G(1C)(a) (as so added)), or with retrospective effect, before the end of a period of three months beginning with the day after that on which the decision period that is being extended came to an end (s 80G(1C)(b) (as so added)).

6 See the Employment Rights Act 1996 s 80G(1)(b) (as added: see note 3). See *Commotion Ltd v Rutty* [2006] ICR 290, sub nom *Rutty v Commotion Ltd* [2006] IRLR 171, EAT (employer had not made out a reason for refusal of request for flexible working).

7 Employment Rights Act 1996 s 80G(1)(b)(i) (as added: see note 3).

8 Employment Rights Act 1996 s 80G(1)(b)(ii) (as added: see note 3).

9 Employment Rights Act 1996 s 80G(1)(b)(iii) (as added: see note 3).

10 Employment Rights Act 1996 s 80G(1)(b)(iv) (as added: see note 3).

11 Employment Rights Act 1996 s 80G(1)(b)(v) (as added: see note 3).

12 Employment Rights Act 1996 s 80G(1)(b)(vi) (as added: see note 3).

13 Employment Rights Act 1996 s 80G(1)(b)(vii) (as added: see note 3).

14 Employment Rights Act 1996 s 80G(1)(b)(viii) (as added: see note 3).

15 Employment Rights Act 1996 s 80G(1)(b)(ix) (as added: see note 3). As to the Secretary of State see PARA 5 note 21. As to the making of regulations under the Employment Rights Act 1996 generally see PARA 162. At the date at which this volume states the law, no such regulations had been made. However, the Flexible Working (Eligibility, Complaints and Remedies) Regulations 2002, SI 2002/3236, made in exercise of the powers conferred by the Employment Rights Act 1996 s 80G(1)(b), are revoked but continue to apply to any such application made before 30 June 2014: see the Flexible Working Regulations 2014, SI 2014/1398, reg 2.

16 See the Employment Rights Act 1996 s 80G(1D) (s 80G as added (see note 3); s 80G(1D) as added (see note 5)).

17 Employment Rights Act 1996 s 80G(1D)(a) (s 80G as added (see note 3); s 80G(1D) as added (see note 5)).

18 Employment Rights Act 1996 s 80G(1D)(b) (s 80G as added (see note 3); s 80G(1D) as added (see note 5)).

19 See the Employment Rights Act 1996 s 80G(1D) (s 80G as added (see note 3); s 80G(1D) as added (see note 5)).

110. Right of employee to be accompanied at meeting discussing application for a contract variation. Where a meeting is held by an employer[1] either to discuss an application for a contract variation with an employee[2] or to discuss an employee's appeal[3] against the employer's decision to refuse such an application[4], and where the employee reasonably requests to be accompanied at the meeting[5], the employer must permit the employee to be accompanied at the meeting by a single companion who:

(1)   is chosen by the employee[6], and is a worker employed by the same employer as the employee[7];

(2)   is to be permitted to address the meeting (but not to answer questions on behalf of the employee)[8]; and

(3)   is to be permitted to confer with the employee during the meeting[9].

If an employee has such a right to be accompanied at a meeting, but his chosen companion will not be available at the time proposed for the meeting by the employer, and the employee proposes an alternative time (which must be convenient for employer, employee and companion, and must fall before the end of the period of seven days beginning with the first day after the day proposed by the employer[10]), the employer must postpone the meeting to the time proposed by the employee[11].

A person has the right not to be subjected to any detriment by any act, or any deliberate failure to act, by his employer done on the ground that he exercised or sought to exercise the right to be accompanied at a meeting[12] or accompanied or sought to accompany an employee pursuant to such a request[13].

A person who is dismissed must be regarded for the purposes of Part X of the Employment Rights Act 1996[14] as unfairly dismissed if the reason or, if more than one, the principal reason for the dismissal is either that he exercised or sought to exercise the right to be accompanied at a meeting[15], or that he accompanied or sought to accompany an employee pursuant to such a request[16].

1   For these purposes, 'employer' means the person by whom an employee is (or, where the employment has ceased, was) employed: see the Flexible Working (Procedural Requirements) Regulations 2002, SI 2002/3207, reg 2(1).

2   Ie an application made under relevant provisions (see PARA 108): see the Flexible Working (Procedural Requirements) Regulations 2002, SI 2002/3207, reg 14(1)(a). For these purposes, 'employee' means an individual who has entered into or works under (or, where the employment has ceased, worked under) a contract of employment; and 'contract of employment' means a contract of service or apprenticeship, whether express or implied, and (if it is express) whether oral or in writing: see reg 2(1). 'Application' means an application under the Employment Rights Act 1996 s 80F (statutory right to request a contract variation: see PARA 108); and 'contract variation' means a change in the terms and conditions of a contract of employment of a kind specified in s 80F(1)(a) (see PARA 108): see the Flexible Working (Procedural Requirements) Regulations 2002, SI 2002/3207, reg 2(1).

3   See PARA 109.

4   See the Flexible Working (Procedural Requirements) Regulations 2002, SI 2002/3207, reg 14(1)(a).

5   See the Flexible Working (Procedural Requirements) Regulations 2002, SI 2002/3207, reg 14(1)(b).

6   Flexible Working (Procedural Requirements) Regulations 2002, SI 2002/3207, reg 14(2)(a). The companion chosen by the employee must be within reg 14(3) (see the text and note 7): see reg 14(2)(a).

7   Flexible Working (Procedural Requirements) Regulations 2002, SI 2002/3207, reg 14(3). For these purposes, 'worker' means an individual who has entered into or works under, or, where the employment has ceased, worked under: (1) a contract of employment; or (2) any other contract, whether express or implied and (if it is express) whether oral or in writing, whereby the individual undertakes to do or perform personally any work or services for another party to the contract whose status is not by virtue of the contract that of a client or customer of any profession or business undertaking carried on by the individual: see reg 2(1). An employer must permit a worker to take time off during working hours for the purpose of accompanying an employee in accordance with a request under reg 14(1)(b) (see the text and note 5): reg 14(6). The Trade Union and Labour Relations (Consolidation) Act 1992 ss 168(3), (4), 169, 171–173 (time off and payment for carrying out trade union duties: see PARAS 1065, 1068) apply in relation to the Flexible Working (Procedural Requirements) Regulations 2002, SI 2002/3207, reg 14(6) as they apply in relation to the Trade Union and Labour Relations (Consolidation) Act 1992 s 168(1) (see PARA 1065): Flexible Working (Procedural Requirements) Regulations 2002, SI 2002/3207, reg 14(7).

8   Flexible Working (Procedural Requirements) Regulations 2002, SI 2002/3207, reg 14(2)(b).

9   Flexible Working (Procedural Requirements) Regulations 2002, SI 2002/3207, reg 14(2)(c).

10   See the Flexible Working (Procedural Requirements) Regulations 2002, SI 2002/3207, reg 14(5).

11   See the Flexible Working (Procedural Requirements) Regulations 2002, SI 2002/3207, reg 14(4).

12   Ie under the Flexible Working (Procedural Requirements) Regulations 2002, SI 2002/3207, reg 14(2) (see the text and notes 6–9) or reg 14(4) (see the text and notes 10–11): see reg 16(1).

13   Flexible Working (Procedural Requirements) Regulations 2002, SI 2002/3207, reg 16(1). The Employment Rights Act 1996 s 48 (detriment (enforcement: complaint to employment tribunal): see PARA 625) applies in relation to contraventions of the Flexible Working (Procedural Requirements) Regulations 2002, SI 2002/3207, reg 16(1) as it applies in relation to contraventions of the Employment Rights Act 1996 that are specified in s 48: Flexible Working (Procedural Requirements) Regulations 2002, SI 2002/3207, reg 16(2).

14   Ie the Employment Rights Act 1996 Pt X (ss 94–134A) (unfair dismissal: see PARA 757 et seq): see the Flexible Working (Procedural Requirements) Regulations 2002, SI 2002/3207, reg 16(3). In the application of the Employment Rights Act 1996 Pt X Ch II (ss 111–132) (remedies for unfair dismissal: see PARA 804 et seq) in relation to the Flexible Working (Procedural Requirements) Regulations 2002, SI 2002/3207, reg 16(3), a reference to an employee must be taken as a reference to a worker: reg 16(6).

15   Ie he exercised or sought to exercise his right under the Flexible Working (Procedural Requirements) Regulations 2002, SI 2002/3207, reg 14(2) (see the text and notes 6–9) or reg 14(4) (see the text and notes 10–11): see reg 16(3).

16   See the Flexible Working (Procedural Requirements) Regulations 2002, SI 2002/3207, reg 16(3). The Employment Rights Act 1996 s 108 (qualifying period of employment: see PARA) does not apply in relation to the Flexible Working (Procedural Requirements) Regulations 2002, SI 2002/3207, reg 16(3): see reg 16(4). However, the Employment Rights Act 1996 ss 128–132 (interim relief: see PARAS 805–808) do apply in relation to dismissal for the reason specified in the Flexible Working (Procedural Requirements) Regulations 2002, SI 2002/3207, reg 16(3), as

those provisions of the Employment Rights Act 1996 apply in relation to dismissal for a reason specified in s 128(1)(b) (see PARA 805): Flexible Working (Procedural Requirements) Regulations 2002, SI 2002/3207, reg 16(5).

111.   Complaints to employment tribunal in relation to application for a contract variation. An employee[1] who makes an application for a change in his terms and conditions of employment[2] may present a complaint to an employment tribunal[3]:

(1)   that his employer[4] has failed to comply with his statutory duties in relation to such an application[5];

(2)   that a decision by his employer to reject the application was based on incorrect facts[6]; or

(3)   that the employer's notification of withdrawal[7] was given in circumstances that did not satisfy one of the statutory requirements[8].

In the case of an application which has not been disposed of by agreement or withdrawn, no such complaint may be made under head (1) or head (2) above[9], however, until either[10]:

(a)   the employer notifies the employee of the employer's decision on the application[11]; or

(b)   if the decision period applicable to the application[12] comes to an end without the employer notifying the employee of the employer's decision on the application, the end of the decision period[13].

A complaint may be made under head (3) above as soon as the notification complained of[14] is given to the employee[15].

An employment tribunal must not consider any such complaint under any of heads (1) to (3) above unless it is presented either:

(i)   before the end of the period of three months beginning with the relevant date[16]; or

(ii)   within such further period as the tribunal considers reasonable in a case where it is satisfied that it was not reasonably practicable for the complaint to be presented before the end of that period of three months[17].

Where an employment tribunal finds any such complaint well-founded, it must make a declaration to that effect[18], and it may: (A) make an order for reconsideration of the application[19]; and (B) make an award of compensation to be paid by the employer to the employee[20]. The amount of compensation must be such amount, not exceeding the permitted maximum[21], as the tribunal considers just and equitable in all the circumstances[22].

1   As to the meaning of 'employee' see PARA 110 note 2.

2   Ie who makes an application under the Employment Rights Act 1996 s 80F (see PARA 108): see s 80H(1) (ss 80H, 80I added by the Employment Act 2002 s 47(1), (2)).

3   See the Employment Rights Act 1996 s 80H(1) (as added: see note 2). No complaint to a tribunal may be made under s 80H(1)(a) (see head (1) in the text) or s 80H(1)(b) (see head (2) in the text), however, in respect of an application which has been disposed of by agreement or withdrawn: s 80H(2) (s 80H as so added; s 80H(2) amended by the Children and Families Act 2014 s 133(1), (3)). As to the amendments made by s 133 see PARA 108 note 8. As to disposal of an application see PARA 109. As to employment tribunals see PARA 1399 et seq; and as to the procedure on a complaint made to an employment tribunal see PARA 1453 et seq.

The ACAS (Flexible Working) Arbitration Scheme (Great Britain) Order 2004, SI 2004/2333, sets out a revised scheme, prepared by the Advisory, Conciliation and Arbitration Service ('ACAS') pursuant to the Trade Union and Labour Relations (Consolidation) Act 1992 s 212A, providing for arbitration in the case of disputes involving proceedings, or claims which could be the subject of proceedings, before an employment tribunal arising out of a contravention or alleged contravention of the Employment Rights Act 1996 s 80G(1), s 80H(1)(b): see PARA 824.

4   As to the meaning of 'employer' and related expressions in relation to employment rights generally see PARA 2 et seq.

5   Employment Rights Act 1996 s 80H(1)(a) (as added: see note 2). The text refers to the employer's failure to comply with s 80G(1) (see PARA 109): see s 80H(1)(a) (as so added).

6   Employment Rights Act 1996 s 80H(1)(b) (as added: see note 2). Although the reference to 'incorrect facts' means that a tribunal cannot adjudicate the reasonableness of the employer's refusal, it may still be necessary to look at what would have been the effects of granting the application: *Commotion Ltd v Rutty* [2006] ICR 290, sub nom *Rutty v Commotion Ltd* [2006] IRLR 171.

7   Ie notification under the Employment Rights Act 1996 80G(1D) (see PARA 109): see s 80H(1)(c) (s 80H as added (see note 2); s 80H(1)(c) added by the Children and Families Act 2014 s 133(1), (2)).

8   Employment Rights Act 1996 s 80H(1)(c) (as added: see note 7). The text refers to one of the requirements in s 80G(1D)(a) (see PARA 109) and s 80G(1D)(b) (see PARA 109): see s 80H(1)(c) (as so added).

9   Ie no complaint under the Employment Rights Act 1996 s 80H(1)(a) (see head (1) in the text) or s 80H(1)(b) (see head (2) in the text) may be made: see s 80H(3) (s 80H as added (see note 2); s 80H(3) substituted, s 80H(3A), (3B) added, by the Children and Families Act 2014 s 133(1), (4)).

10   See the Employment Rights Act 1996 s 80H(3) (s 80H as added (see note 2); s 80H(3) as substituted (see note 9)).

11   Employment Rights Act 1996 s 80H(3)(a) (s 80H as added (see note 2); s 80H(3) as substituted (see note 9)). If an employer allows an employee to appeal a decision to reject an application, a reference in s 80H to the decision on the application is a reference to the decision on the appeal (or, if more than one appeal is allowed, the decision on the final appeal): s 80H(3A) (s 80H as added (see note 2); s 80H(3A) as added (see note 9)).

12   Ie under the Employment Rights Act 1996 80G(1B) (see PARA 109 note 5): see s 80H(3)(b) (s 80H as added (see note 2); s 80H(3) as substituted (see note 9)).

13   Employment Rights Act 1996 s 80H(3)(b) (s 80H as added (see note 2); s 80H(3) as substituted (see note 9)). If an agreement to extend the decision period is made as described in s 80G(1C)(b) (see PARA 109 note 5), s 80H(3)(b) is to be treated as not allowing a complaint until the end of the extended period: s 80H(3B) (s 80H as so added; s 80H(3B) as added (see note 9)).

14   Ie notification under the Employment Rights Act 1996 s 80G(1D) (see PARA 109): see s 80H(3C) (s 80H as added (see note 2); s 80H(3C) added by the Children and Families Act 2014 s 133(1), (5)).

15   Employment Rights Act 1996 s 80H(3C) (as added: see note 15).

16   Employment Rights Act 1996 s 80H(5)(a) (as added: see note 2). For these purposes, the reference to the relevant date is a reference to the first date on which the employee may make a complaint under s 80H(1)(a) (see head (1) in the text), s 80H(1)(b) (see head (2) in the text), or s 80H(1)(c) (see head (3) in the text), as the case may be: s 80H(6) (s 80H as so added; s 80H(6) amended by the Children and Families Act 2014 s 133(1), (6)). Also for these purposes, the provisions of the Employment Rights Act 1996 s 207A(3) (extended time limit where mediation required in certain cross-border disputes: see PARA 1454) and s 207B (extension of time limits to facilitate conciliation before institution of proceedings: see PARA 1455) apply: s 80H(7) (added by SI 2011/1133; and amended by the Enterprise and Regulatory Reform Act 2013 s 8, Sch 2 paras 15, 32).

17   Employment Rights Act 1996 s 80H(5)(b) (as added: see note 2).

18   Employment Rights Act 1996 s 80I(1) (as added: see note 2).

19   Employment Rights Act 1996 s 80I(1)(a) (as added: see note 2). Where an employment tribunal makes an order under s 80I(1)(a), the provision made by s 80G (see PARA 109) applies as if the application had been made on the date of the order: s 80I(4) (s 80I as so added; s 80I(4) amended by the Children and Families Act 2014 s 132(1), (5)(d)).

20   Employment Rights Act 1996 s 80I(1)(b) (as added: see note 2).

21   For these purposes, the permitted maximum is such number of weeks' pay as the Secretary of State may specify by regulations: Employment Rights Act 1996 s 80I(3) (as added: see note 2). Accordingly, for the purposes of s 80I, the maximum amount of compensation is 8 weeks' pay of the employee who presented the complaint under s 80H (complaints to employment tribunals): Flexible Working Regulations 2014, SI 2014/1398, reg 6. As to the Secretary of State see PARA 5 note 21. As to the making of regulations under the Employment Rights Act 1996 generally see PARA 162.

22   Employment Rights Act 1996 s 80I(2) (as added: see note 2).

(viii) Contracts of Apprenticeship

112. Apprentices; trainees. At common law, a contract of apprenticeship is something more than, and distinct from, a contract of employment[1]. It envisages a purpose of learning a trade or calling, the apprentice undertaking to serve the master for that purpose and the master undertaking to teach the apprentice[2]; there are certain requirements as to form[3] and special provisions relating to enforcement and termination[4].

The separate existence of a contract of apprenticeship is, however, of lesser practical significance in modern employment law because: (1) the expression 'employee' means an individual who has entered into or works under (or, where the employment has ceased, worked under) a contract of employment, where 'contract of employment' includes a contract of apprenticeship (whether express or implied, and (if it is express) whether oral or in writing)[5]; and (2) in modern employment conditions, traditional apprenticeships are rare[6].

Nevertheless, the old common law on apprenticeship still exists and may be applicable where still relevant[7].

1   As to the meaning of 'contract of employment' and related expressions in relation to employment rights generally see PARA 2 et seq.
2   *R v Laindon Inhabitants* (1799) 8 Term Rep 379; *St Pancras Parish v Clapham Parish* (1860) 2 E & E 742. If, however, teaching by the master was only an incidental object, the contract remains one of employment: *R v Crediton Inhabitants* (1831) 2 B & Ad 493. The word 'apprenticeship' does not have to be used: *R v Laindon Inhabitants*. A solicitor's articled clerk could be an apprentice for the purposes of the poor law (*St Pancras Parish v Clapham Parish*; *R v Edingale Inhabitants* (1830) 10 B & C 739; *R v Wooldale Inhabitants* (1844) 6 QB 549); but a pupil barrister is not under a contract of apprenticeship for the purposes of the national minimum wage legislation (see PARA 169 et seq) (*Edmonds v Lawson* [2000] QB 501, [2000] ICR 567, CA). Payment of a premium is strong but not conclusive evidence of a contract of apprenticeship: *R v St Margaret's, King's Lynn, Inhabitants* (1826) 6 B & C 97 at 99 per Bayley J; *R v Rainham Inhabitants* (1801) 1 East 531; cf *James v Krauth* (1910) 26 TLR 240, DC.

    A government-sponsored apprenticeship can give rise to a contract of apprenticeship at common law, even though it is a tripartite relationship (with the academic component being provided by a third party): see *Flett v Matheson* [2006] EWCA Civ 53, [2006] ICR 673, [2006] IRLR 277. As to the position of apprentices and youth trainees at common law see also PARAS 128–129, 636, 747–754. As to the statutory law on apprenticeships see EDUCATION vol 35 (2011) PARA 682 et seq.
3   See PARA 128.
4   See PARAS 747–754.
5   See the Employment Rights Act 1996 s 230(1), (2); and PARA 2.
6   Although modern apprenticeships leading to certification have been established under statute (see note 2), traditional apprenticeships have in practice often been replaced by various training schemes (see note 7; and PARA 636).
7   *Wallace v CA Roofing Services Ltd* [1996] IRLR 435 (no power of early termination of apprenticeship contract for redundancy), followed and applied in *Whitely v Marton Electrical Ltd* [2003] ICR 495, [2003] IRLR 197, EAT (individual engaged under a modern 'apprenticeship pact', following the standard-form agreement promoted by national training organisations).

(2) TERMS OF EMPLOYMENT

(i) Express Terms

113. Express terms of employment. Express coverage of terms and conditions in a contract of employment is clearly advantageous: parties may not rely on the use of implied terms[1] to cure gaps in contracts on all occasions[2]; and, where there is an express term, the general law is that it cannot be overridden, or indeed materially altered[3], by reliance on an implied term[4].

It is not clear, however, to what extent an express term giving an employer a particular right or power[5] may have added to it an implied qualification that, in exercising that right or power, the employer must behave reasonably[6]. On the one hand, applying a traditional contractual approach, it has been held that, for instance, if a mobility term is clear, it may be exercised as it stands, without the addition of a requirement of reasonable exercise[7]; likewise, it has been held that an express lay-off clause is not to be read as being subject to an implied limitation that the lay-off will last only for a reasonable period[8]. On the other hand, it has been held that a mobility clause may be construed as subject to an implied requirement that the employer will give the employee reasonable notice before moving him[9], that a general power to suspend an employee is subject to a requirement of exercise on reasonable grounds (and only for such period as those grounds continue)[10], and that the exercise of an employer's rights under a disciplinary procedure is subject to requirements of reasonableness and proportionality[11]. The contractual rights of the employer may be subject generally to the implied term of trust and respect[12], so that any unreasonable exercise of those contractual rights puts the employer in breach of contract, entitling the employee to leave his employment and claim constructive dismissal[13]. An employer's unreasonable exercise of a discretion under the contract may be challenged, even though the express term appears to be in unlimited terms in giving that discretion (for example, over the amount of an annual bonus or the exercise of share options); and such a challenge would be founded on breach of contract, either on the basis of a breach of the implied contractual term of trust and respect[14], or because an employer is in breach of contract if he exercises a discretion in a manner which no reasonable employer would have done[15].

A contract of employment does not need to be in writing, although there is a statutory obligation to give a written statement of the principal terms and conditions[16]; and, even where the contract of employment is in writing, it may still be possible, unless the contract is expressed to be exhaustive[17], to discern other expressly agreed terms, for example, from the dealings of the parties[18] or from other documents such as a letter of appointment[19].

1   As to implied terms see PARA 114. As to terms and obligations that may be considered to be imposed, rather than genuinely implied, see PARA 115.

2   *Stubbes v Trower, Still & Keeling* [1987] IRLR 321, CA.

3   Any variation of contractual terms must be by bilateral agreement and must be accepted either expressly or impliedly: *Burdett-Coutts v Hertfordshire County Council* [1984] IRLR 91 (changes to conditions of service had effect of repudiating the contracts; employees entitled to stand on the original contract and claim recovery); *Rigby v Ferodo Ltd* [1988] ICR 29, [1987] IRLR 516, HL (no implied acceptance of the employers' repudiation or of the new terms where employees continued working under protest); *Security and Facilities Division v Hayes* [2001] IRLR 81, CA. An employer's repudiation allows an employee to terminate the contract of employment without notice: see PARA 763.

4   *Nelson v BBC* [1977] ICR 649 at 656, [1977] IRLR 148 at 151, CA, per Roskill LJ.

5   Eg to order the employee to move job location.

6   This question is particularly important in the context of constructive dismissal: see PARA 763. See also the text and note 15.

7   *Rank Xerox Ltd v Churchill* [1988] IRLR 280, EAT; *Courtaulds Northern Spinning Ltd v Sibson* [1988] ICR 451, [1988] IRLR 305, CA (implied mobility/location term, the term implied being to work anywhere within reasonable daily reach of home; the court refused to imply any further requirement of reasonable exercise of the clause by the employer or use of it only for genuine operational reasons); *White v Reflecting Roadstuds Ltd* [1991] ICR 733, [1991] IRLR

331, EAT (no general requirement of reasonableness). See also *Qantas Cabin Crew (UK) Ltd v Lopez* [2013] IRLR 4, EAT (true terms of the contract could not depend on the subjective interpretation of the employees, who had in mind the tax consequences of the expatriation arrangements they were making); *Verma v Barts and the London NHS Trust* [2013] UKSC 20, [2013] ICR 727, [2013] IRLR 567 (applying ordinary principles of construction, condition designed to confer important rights on employees, ie entitlement to payment protection when moving to training post, was clearly not well drafted, and required reconsideration).

8   *Kenneth MacRae & Co Ltd v Dawson* [1984] IRLR 5, EAT, disapproving *A Dakri & Co Ltd v Tiffen* [1981] ICR 256, [1981] IRLR 57, EAT, on this point; but cf *McLory v Post Office* [1992] ICR 758, sub nom *McClory v Post Office* [1993] IRLR 159 (where support was expressed in principle for *A Dakri & Co Ltd v Tiffen*, with the decision in *Kenneth MacRae & Co Ltd v Dawson* being thought explicable on the wide express power to lay off).

9   *Prestwick Circuits Ltd v McAndrew* [1990] IRLR 191, Ct of Sess (implied mobility clause); *United Bank Ltd v Akhtar* [1989] IRLR 507, EAT, considered in *White v Reflecting Roadstuds Ltd* [1991] ICR 733, [1991] IRLR 331, EAT.

10   *McLory v Post Office* [1992] ICR 758, sub nom *McClory v Post Office* [1993] IRLR 159.

11   *BBC v Beckett* [1983] IRLR 43, EAT; *Cawley v South Wales Electricity Board* [1985] IRLR 89, EAT.

12   As to the implied term of trust and respect see PARA 48.

13   This was the second ground of decision in *United Bank Ltd v Akhtar* [1989] IRLR 507 at 512, EAT, per Knox J ('... in the field of employment law it is proper to imply an overriding obligation [of confidence and trust] which is independent of, and in addition to, the literal interpretation of the actions which are permitted to the employer under the terms of the contract').

14   See *Clark v BET plc* [1997] IRLR 348; and as to remedies in such an action see PARA 828 et seq.

15   *Clark v Nomura International plc* [2000] IRLR 766 (exercise of discretion stigmatised as perverse or irrational; test of perversity or irrationality simpler to apply than a test of capriciousness, which entailed aspects of arbitrariness or whimsicality); *Mallone v BPB Industries plc* [2002] EWCA Civ 126, [2002] ICR 1045, [2002] IRLR 452, [2002] All ER (D) 242 (Feb). For a synthesis of these two approaches see *Horkulak v Cantor Fitzgerald International* [2003] [2004] EWCA Civ 1287, [2005] ICR 402, [2004] IRLR 942 (revsg in part EWHC 1918 (QB), [2004] ICR 697, [2003] IRLR 756).

16   See PARA 118 et seq.

17   See eg *White v Bristol Rugby Ltd* [2002] IRLR 204 (employee sought to 'opt out' of his contract before joining the club in exercise of a right he felt was represented to him by the club's chief executive; however, the contract could not be interpreted as containing a separate oral term because it was expressly worded to exclude claims based on collateral warranties or oral terms outside the written document). If, however, there are significant ambiguities in the case it may be possible to look beyond an 'entire agreement' clause: *Bushaway v Royal National Lifeboat Institution* [2005] IRLR 674, EAT.

18   Eg at interview, when accepting an offer of employment. Cf *Judge v Crown Leisure Ltd* [2005] EWCA Civ 571, [2005] IRLR 823 (casual conversation at Christmas party in regard to employee's future not sufficient).

19   *Tayside Regional Council v McIntosh* [1982] IRLR 272, EAT. This need (ie in many cases to look to several sources for the whole of the contract) was strongly affirmed in *Carmichael v National Power plc* [1999] 4 All ER 897 at 902 et seq, [1999] 1 WLR 2042 at 2048 et seq, HL, per Lord Hoffmann. However, where an employee's entitlement to long-term disability payments is governed by the express provisions laid down in his contract of employment, an employer cannot rely on the terms of the insurance policy which is taken out in order to meet obligations under a scheme that is designed to provide an income during lengthy periods of absence due to prolonged sickness or injury: *Jowitt v Pioneer Technology (UK) Ltd* [2003] EWCA Civ 411, [2003] ICR 1120, [2003] IRLR 356. See also *Geys v Société Générale, London Branch* [2012] UKSC 63, [2013] 1 AC 523, [2013] 1 All ER 1061, [2013] IRLR 122, [2013] ICR 117 (there was no conflict between a contractual term allowing termination on three months' notice and an employee handbook provision allowing for immediate termination with payment in lieu of notice); and as to the incorporation of terms see PARA 116.

(ii)   Implied Terms

114.   Implication of terms of employment.   Given that the employment relationship is explained legally in contractual terms[1], the ordinary law of contract is applicable[2]. Classically, a term may be implied into a contract either on the 'officious bystander' test[3] or the 'business efficacy' test[4]; both of these tests are essentially subjective, looking for implied agreement by the parties, with the emphasis against the implication of a term merely because it appears reasonable to the court. These tests may well be applied in cases concerning contracts of employment[5], but arguably a generally wider approach is justified in this context, not only because the implied term will be more frequently used as a device to impose a particular legal solution or requirement on to contracts of employment as such[6], but also because historically contracts of employment have left more to be filled in by implied terms than most other types of contract[7]. Moreover, the need to fill such gaps may be more urgent, either to fulfil statutory obligations[8], or simply in order to make legal sense of an employment relationship that clearly exists in practice[9]. Arguably, therefore, orthodox contract law on the implication of terms may need to be stretched in the context of employment, in particular by placing more emphasis on what would be reasonable terms[10], and by allowing the court to look at the parties' behaviour during the employment but subsequent to the entering of the contract of employment[11].

A term may be implied from custom and practice, provided that it is certain, general and reasonable; this will particularly be the case where either the employee took the employment subject to the custom or practice, or that custom or practice grew up during the employment and the employee impliedly accepted it (as, for example, by taking benefits under it)[12]. An implied term, even one based on custom and practice, cannot, however, negate or alter a clear express term[13], although there may be scope for the use of implication in order to interpret an express term[14].

1 See PARA 1.

2 *Laws v London Chronicle (Indicator Newspapers) Ltd* [1959] 2 All ER 285 at 287, [1959] 1 WLR 698 at 700, CA, per Lord Evershed MR. As to contractual terms and their interpretation in the law of contract see CONTRACT vol 22 (2012) PARA 352 et seq. As to the caution that also must attend any interaction between ordinary contract law and employment law, however, see PARA 1 notes 2, 4.

3 See *Shirlaw v Southern Foundries (1926) Ltd* [1939] 2 KB 206 at 227, [1939] 2 All ER 113 at 124, CA, per MacKinnon LJ; and CONTRACT vol 22 (2012) PARA 369.

4 See *The Moorcock* (1889) 14 PD 64, CA; *Reigate v Union Manufacturing Co (Ramsbottom) Ltd and Elton Cop Dyeing Co Ltd* [1918] 1 KB 592, CA; and CONTRACT vol 22 (2012) PARAS 370, 371.

5 *Lake v Essex County Council* [1979] ICR 577, [1979] IRLR 241, CA; *Deeley v British Rail Engineering* [1980] IRLR 147, CA; *Stubbes v Trower, Still & Keeling* [1987] IRLR 321, CA; *Ali v Christian Salvesen Food Services Ltd* [1997] ICR 25, [1997] IRLR 17, CA; *Glendale Managed Services v Graham* [2003] EWCA Civ 773, [2003] IRLR 465 (term implied that notice was required from the employer before he could decline to pay a nationally agreed pay increase).

6 See PARA 115.

7 Before the Contracts of Employment Act 1963, there was no requirement for a contract of employment to be in writing, and most contracts were informal, but the Employment Rights Act 1996 ss 1–7B now require fundamental terms of employment particulars to be recorded in a written statement (see PARAS 119–123). However, this document does not constitute a contract of employment itself (*System Floors UK Ltd v Daniel* [1982] ICR 54, [1981] IRLR 475, EAT (statement is neither the contract nor conclusive evidence of the terms of the contract); approved in *Robertson v British Gas Corpn, Jackson v British Gas Corpn* [1983] ICR 351, [1983] IRLR 302, CA); and its terms should not be construed as if they were agreed terms in a written commercial contract (*Glendale Managed Services v Graham* [2003] EWCA Civ 773, [2003] IRLR 465). See also *Bull v Nottinghamshire and City of Nottingham Fire and Rescue Authority, Lincolnshire County Council v Fire Brigades Union* [2007] EWCA Civ 240, [2007] ICR 1631, [2007] All ER (D) 372 (Feb) (no implication in firefighters' employment contract that firefighters obliged to co-respond to calls for ambulance crews). Written agreements or

statements are, therefore, now more common, but are certainly not exhaustive, thus leaving scope for implication of other terms into particular contracts.

8 Eg to comply with the Employment Rights Act 1996 s 1 under which, on a complaint under s 11, an employment tribunal may have to find and record in writing a term or condition required to be in a written statement (see PARA 115 note 1); *Mears v Safecar Security Ltd* [1983] QB 54, [1982] ICR 626, CA; *Eagland v British Telecommunications plc* [1993] ICR 644, [1992] IRLR 323, CA. It is not possible to imply a contractual term to cover every aspect of statutory protection or statutory obligations: *Doherty v British Midland Airways Ltd* [2006] IRLR 90, [2005] All ER (D) 12 (Apr), EAT.

9 Although the contractual doctrine of certainty has not been applied strictly in employment law (*Powell v Braun* [1954] 1 All ER 484, [1954] 1 WLR 401, CA; *National Coal Board v Galley* [1958] 1 All ER 91, [1958] 1 WLR 16, CA), it may still be necessary, in order to decide a common law or (increasingly) a statutory claim, to rule on contractual rights and obligations, which may mean filling a gap in the contract with an implied term. This has been seen particularly in the context of mobility clauses; the existence or otherwise of such a clause, or its terms, may decide a redundancy or unfair dismissal case (see PARA 870), and thus, if the contract in question is silent on the matter, it is essential to imply a term one way or another, even if the parties themselves had never put their minds to it: *Jones v Associated Tunnelling Co Ltd* [1981] IRLR 477, EAT; *Courtaulds Northern Spinning Ltd v Sibson* [1988] ICR 451, [1988] IRLR 305, CA. See also *Geys v Société Générale, London Branch* [2012] UKSC 63, [2013] 1 AC 523, [2013] 1 All ER 1061, [2013] IRLR 122, [2013] ICR 117 (a term should be implied as a necessary incident of the employment relationship that the parties would notify each other in 'clear and unambiguous terms' when a right to terminate the contract was exercised, and that the party exercising the right would specify how and when the right was intended to operate).

In the same way that a term in a contract of employment can be varied by implication, even the identity of the employer can be altered by implied agreement constituted by conduct: see *Khatri v London Central Mosque Trust Ltd* [2012] All ER (D) 357 (Jul) (employment as nursery manager had transferred to the second employer, the employee having been hired as a teacher at the first employer mosque's weekend school).

10 *Lister v Romford Ice and Cold Storage Co Ltd* [1957] AC 555, [1957] 1 All ER 125, HL; *Shell UK Ltd v Lostock Garage Ltd* [1977] 1 All ER 481 at 487, [1976] 1 WLR 1187 at 1196, CA, per Lord Denning MR; *Pepper and Hope v Daish* [1980] IRLR 13, EAT; *Mears v Safecar Security Ltd* [1983] QB 54, [1982] ICR 626, CA; *Howman & Son v Blyth* [1983] ICR 416, [1983] IRLR 139, EAT; *Courtaulds Northern Spinning Ltd v Sibson* [1988] ICR 451, [1988] IRLR 305, CA.

11 *Courtaulds Northern Spinning Ltd v Sibson* [1988] ICR 451, [1988] IRLR 305, CA; *Mears v Safecar Security Ltd* [1983] QB 54, [1982] ICR 626, CA; *Carmichael v National Power plc* [1999] 4 All ER 897 at 902 et seq, [2000] IRLR 43 at 1232 et seq, HL, per Lord Hoffmann. See also *Consistent Group Ltd v Kalwak* [2008] EWCA Civ 430, [2008] IRLR 505 (not enough details given for conclusion that obligations clause was a sham); *McBride v Falkirk Football and Athletic Club* [2012] IRLR 22, EAT (rejection of implied term that football manager would eventually be replaced by another employee yet to be appointed at the time of contracting).

12 *George v Davies* [1911] 2 KB 445, DC; *Meek v Port of London Authority* [1918] 2 Ch 96, CA; *Sagar v H Ridehalgh & Son Ltd* [1931] 1 Ch 310, CA; *Marshall v English Electric Ltd* [1945] 1 All ER 653, CA; *Spencer Jones v Timmens Freeman* [1974] IRLR 325; *Samways v Swan Hunter Shipbuilders Ltd* [1975] IRLR 190. See also *FW Farnsworth Ltd v Lacy* [2012] EWHC 2830 (Ch), [2013] IRLR 198 (by applying for private medical insurance in a form not previously available to him, and which had its source ultimately in benefits available under a new contract, redefining his relationship with his employer, the employee accepted legal incidents of the new definition of his relationship).

The question of whether a practice, followed without exception for a period of time, may lead to the inference that a contractual term to that effect has been agreed between the parties, can be solved by a tribunal's enquiry, whose essential object is to ascertain what the parties must have or must be taken to have understood from each other's conduct and words, applying ordinary contractual principles: *Garratt v Mirror Group Newspapers Ltd* [2011] EWCA Civ 425, [2011] ICR 880, [2011] IRLR 591 (practice of requiring a compromise agreement before payment of an enhanced redundancy payment was very well established with the workforce; from the standpoint of the reasonable, notorious and certain test, in this context, 'notoriety' is no more than widespread knowledge and understanding, and 'certainty' relates to the established nature of the arrangement). Applying this principle, the focus must be what the employer actually has communicated to the employees (and what the employer may have personally understood or intended is irrelevant except to the extent that the employees are, or should reasonably have been, aware of it): *Park Cakes Ltd v Shumba* [2013] EWCA Civ 974,

[2013] IRLR 800 (if, by his conduct in making available a particular benefit to employees over a period, the employer had evinced to the relevant employees an intention that they should enjoy that benefit as of right, the benefit formed part of the remuneration which was offered to the employee for his work (or, perhaps more accurately in most cases, his willingness to work), and the employee worked on that basis) (followed in *McAlinden v CSC Computer Sciences Ltd* [2013] EWCA Civ 1435, [2013] All ER (D) 138 (Nov) (if the employer's communications had conveyed the impression to the employees that annual pay increases in line at least with the increase in the retail price index (RPI), subject to satisfactory performance, had been a contractual right, the fact that it might have been acting on a mistaken belief was irrelevant); and applied in *Peregrine v Peacock Stores* [2014] All ER (D) 22 (Apr), EAT (based on employer's consistent past practice of making redundancy payments based on statutory terms, but without a cap on either years of service or the amount of a weekly wage, a contractual term to that effect could be inferred from the conduct of the parties, and that term would continue to apply unless there was some reason why it should not, particularly, whether it was varied by agreement, whether actual or itself to be inferred)).

13 See *Stevedoring and Haulage Services Ltd v Fuller* [2001] EWCA Civ 651, [2001] IRLR 627 (terms upon which casual work was offered and accepted expressly negatived mutuality of obligation); *Luke v Stoke-on-Trent City Council* [2007] EWCA Civ 761, [2007] ICR 1678, [2007] IRLR 777 (employment contract contained express term governing employee's claim for salary arrears so that implied term unnecessary). See also *Thorne v House Of Commons Commission* [2014] EWHC 93 (QB), [2014] IRLR 260, [2014] All ER (D) 105 (Mar) (suggested implied term of custom and practice, namely that annual progression payments would be made to staff, subject to satisfactory performance and reaching the maximum of their pay scale, is inconsistent with the express terms set out in the letters of appointment, read together with the staff handbook and the collectively negotiated pay agreement from 2008–2010 which was limited in time).

14 See eg *Dunlop Tyres Ltd v Blows* [2001] EWCA Civ 1032, [2001] IRLR 629 (where the terms of a contract of employment are truly ambiguous, it is open to the court to look at the practice adopted by the parties as being evidence of their intentions and to attach considerable importance to it as indicating the proper interpretation of the contractual terms). The borderline may, however, be a difficult one to draw: *McColl v Norman Insurance Co Ltd* (1969) 4 ITR 285.

(iii) Imposed Terms

115. Imposed terms of employment. A particular term may be imposed on a contract of employment by statute[1]. In addition, however, a court may find an 'implied term'[2] in a particular contract, not because of any supposed implied intent of the parties, or even because of the particular circumstances of the case, but because such a term is to be included either in contracts of employment generally or in contracts of employment of that type[3]. Such terms and the obligations they contain may be considered to be imposed, rather than genuinely implied[4].

1 Thus, under the Equality Act 2010, if the terms of a person's work do not (by whatever means) include a sex equality clause, they are to be treated as including one: see s 66; and DISCRIMINATION vol 33 (2013) PARA 133. Also, the Pensions Act 2008 creates duties on employers to enrol eligible jobholders into automatic enrolment schemes and to contribute to those arrangements, although a jobholder has the right to opt in to such a scheme or to opt out of it: see PERSONAL AND OCCUPATIONAL PENSIONS vol 80 (2013) PARA 737 et seq. As to personal and occupational pension provision generally see PERSONAL AND OCCUPATIONAL PENSIONS vol 80 (2013) PARA 201 et seq. For discussion of the pension schemes relating to particular public service occupations, reference should be made to the appropriate title in this work: eg in relation to teachers' superannuation see EDUCATION vol 36 (2011) PARA 1004 et seq; and in relation to parliamentary pensions see PARLIAMENT vol 78 (2010) PARA 926 et seq. As to other pensions for members of the armed forces see generally ARMED FORCES vol 3 (2011) PARA 707 et seq. As to state pensions see WELFARE BENEFITS AND STATE PENSIONS vol 104 (2014) PARA 487 et seq.

Where an employer does not give an employee a statement as required by the Employment Rights Act 1996 s 1 (statement of initial employment particulars: see PARAS 119–120), s 4 (statement of changes in required particulars: see PARA 121) or s 8 (written itemised pay statement: see PARA 124), either because he gives him no statement or because the statement he gives does not comply with what is required, the employee may require a reference to be made to an employment tribunal to determine what particulars ought to have been included or referred to in a statement so as to comply with the requirements of the section concerned: see s 11; and PARAS 125–126.

The Central Arbitration Committee may make an award imposing a particular substantive term on contracts of employment as a means of enforcing an order for disclosure of bargaining information: see the Trade Union and Labour Relations (Consolidation) Act 1992 s 185; and PARA 1182.

2   As to implied terms see PARA 114.

3   'The phrase 'implied term' can be used to denote a term inherent in the nature of the contract which the law will imply in every case unless the parties agree to vary or exclude it': *Sterling Engineering Co Ltd v Patchett* [1955] AC 534 at 547, [1955] 1 All ER 369 at 376, HL, per Lord Reid. ' ... in the world in which we live today, it is a necessary condition of the relationship of master and man': *Lister v Romford Ice and Cold Storage Co Ltd* [1957] AC 555 at 576, [1957] 1 All ER 125 at 132, HL, per Viscount Simonds. See also *Scally v Southern Health and Social Service Board (British Medical Association, third party)* [1992] 1 AC 294, sub nom *Scally v Southern Health and Social Services Board* [1991] ICR 771, HL; *Malik v Bank of Credit and Commerce International SA (in liquidation), Mahmud v Bank of Credit and Commerce International SA (in liquidation)* [1998] AC 20, [1997] 3 All ER 1, HL (where at 45 and 15 Lord Steyn referred to standardised terms implied by law operating as 'default rules' of the contract of employment).

4   As to terms so imposed (the employee's duty of fidelity and the employer's duty of mutual respect being good examples) see PARA 14 et seq. In addition, such imposed terms have been used more specifically in relation to strike notices (*Morgan v Fry* [1968] 2 QB 710, [1968] 3 All ER 452, CA; but cf *Simmons v Hoover Ltd* [1977] ICR 61, [1976] IRLR 266, EAT); exclusion of subrogation (*Morris v Ford Motor Co Ltd* [1973] QB 792, [1973] 2 All ER 1084, CA); provision of work (*Langston v Amalgamated Union of Engineering Workers* [1974] 1 All ER 980, [1974] ICR 180, CA); disruption of an employer's business (*Secretary of State for Employment v Associated Society of Locomotive Engineers and Firemen (No 2)* [1972] 2 QB 455, [1972] ICR 19, CA); sick pay (*Howman & Son v Blyth* [1983] ICR 416, [1983] IRLR 139, EAT); pension entitlement (*Mihlenstedt v Barclays Bank International Ltd and Barclays Bank plc* [1989] IRLR 522, CA); provision of information by the employer (*Scally v Southern Health and Social Services Board (British Medical Association, third party)* [1992] 1 AC 294, sub nom *Scally v Southern Health and Social Service Board* [1991] ICR 771, HL); and observing the requirements of the Working Time Regulations 1998, SI 1998/1833 (see PARA 267 et seq) (*Barber v RJB Mining (UK) Ltd* [1999] 2 CMLR 833, [1999] ICR 679). For an example of this contractual usage in a different area of law (ie landlord and tenant) see *Liverpool City Council v Irwin* [1977] AC 239, [1976] 2 All ER 39, HL; and LANDLORD AND TENANT vol 62 (2012) PARAS 132, 169, 554.

(iv) Incorporated Terms

116.   Incorporation of terms of employment. As well as being implied[1], terms of a contract of employment may be incorporated from some other source. Historically, the principal source of such terms has been a collective bargain[2], but more recently documents such as works manuals, company handbooks or company policy statements have become potential sources of terms and conditions of employment.

A collective agreement[3] is not legally binding, unless in writing and stating expressly that the parties intend it to be a legally enforceable contract[4]; it is thus not generally enforceable by the parties or by an employee subject to it[5]. However, one or more provisions of a particular collective agreement may be apt for incorporation into an individual contract of employment of an employee covered by it, in which case the provision in question gains contractual legal effect[6]; but the basis of that legal effect is the contract, so that it is only the employee who may sue on it, not the trade union[7], and, if a dispute arises as to the meaning of the term, it is to be interpreted according to the normal canons of interpretation in the law of contract, even though it originated in a non-legalistic collective agreement[8].

A provision of a collective agreement may be expressly incorporated into the contract of employment[9]; if the employer adopts the procedure of giving a written statement of terms and conditions of employment[10] rather than a formal written contract, the statement must give particulars of any collective agreements which directly affect the terms and conditions of employment[11]. If not expressly incorporated, a provision of a collective agreement may be incorporated impliedly[12], particularly if there is a record of acceptance of such provisions[13], or a custom or practice to apply the agreement's provisions on the point in question[14]. Whether a particular provision is impliedly incorporated depends on the facts of the case; incorporation must be considered in the light of individual provisions, so that the fact that one provision is incorporated does not necessarily mean that a different provision of the same agreement will be[15]. A provision will be incorporated only if its subject matter is appropriate for inclusion in an individual contract[16]; and the fact that the employer belongs to an employers' association that bargains collectively with a trade union does not mean that the resulting collective agreement will necessarily be incorporated into the contracts of employment of that employer's employees[17].

In one area, statute has intervened; any terms of a collective agreement which prohibit or restrict the right of workers[18] to engage in a strike or other industrial action, or have the effect of prohibiting or restricting that right, do not form part of any contract between any worker and the person for whom he works unless the collective agreement:

(1)   is in writing;

(2)   contains a provision expressly stating that those terms are to be or may be incorporated in such a contract;

(3)   is reasonably accessible at his place of work to the worker to whom it applies and is available for him to consult during working hours; and

(4)   is one where each trade union which is a party to the agreement is an independent trade union[19],

and unless the contract with the worker expressly or impliedly incorporates those terms in the contract[20].

Particular candidates for appropriate express incorporation are the company handbook or other form of in-house manual[21], which may well contain matters such as grievance and disciplinary procedures[22]. Such a handbook or manual may, however, contain both provisions intended to have contractual effect and 'works rules' which are not meant to be contractual but merely instructions to employees as to how to carry out parts of the employment, the control of which remains within managerial prerogative; the latter are not appropriate for incorporation into contracts of employment[23]. Policy statements by the employer will generally remain non-contractual[24] unless introduced in such a way as to show an intent that they should form part of the employees' individual contracts[25].

1   As to implied terms see PARA 114; and as to terms and obligations that may be considered to be imposed, rather than genuinely implied, see PARA 115.

2   See, however, *Ackinclose v Gateshead Metropolitan Borough Council* [2005] IRLR 79, EAT (where contracts of employment made reference to a predecessor negotiating body, and only made reference to that body's national agreement as the relevant collective bargain, no successor body or successor agreement could be held to be part of the contracts of employment without any further reference or incorporation).

3   For these purposes, 'collective agreement' means any agreement or arrangement made by or on behalf of one or more trade unions and one or more employers or employers' associations and relating to one or more of the matters mentioned in the Trade Union and Labour Relations (Consolidation) Act 1992 s 178(2): see s 178(1); and PARA 1093.

4   See the Trade Union and Labour Relations (Consolidation) Act 1992 s 179(1); and PARA 1175. As to the meaning of 'writing' see PARA 2 note 8. A mere statement that the parties agree to be bound by the agreement is not enough to displace the presumption in s 179: *National Coal Board v National Union of Mineworkers* [1986] ICR 736, [1986] IRLR 439.

5   The employee is not a party to the agreement, even if it were legally enforceable; and a trade union is not generally considered to act as the agent of its members: *Holland v London Society of Compositors* (1924) 40 TLR 440; *Burton Group Ltd v Smith* [1977] IRLR 351, EAT (agency of union representatives must be supported in the particular case by the creation of some specific agency); *Harris v Richard Lawson Autologistics Ltd* [2002] EWCA Civ 442, [2002] ICR 765, [2002] IRLR 476, [2002] All ER (D) 214 (Mar) (shop steward had apparent or ostensible authority to negotiate agreement on behalf of union members); c f *Edwards v Skyways Ltd* [1964] 1 All ER 494, [1964] 1 WLR 349.

6   *Hullard v William Sanders & Son* [1945] KB 78, [1944] 2 All ER 568, CA; *Donelan v Kerrby Constructions Ltd* [1983] ICR 237, [1983] IRLR 191; *Robertson v British Gas Corpn, Jackson v British Gas Corpn* [1983] ICR 351, [1983] IRLR 302, CA; *Marley v Forward Trust Group Ltd* [1986] ICR 891, [1986] IRLR 369, CA; cf *Malone v British Airways plc* [2010] EWCA Civ 1225, [2011] ICR 125, [2011] IRLR 32 (disputed term of collective agreement regarding complements was not intended as an enforceable undertaking towards cabin crew employees collectively but, rather, as binding in honour only and so not 'apt' to be incorporated).

    Where a term is incorporated, or otherwise incorporated by reference, there may be an implied obligation on the employer to take reasonable steps to bring such a term to the employee's attention: *Scally v Southern Health and Social Services Board (British Medical Association, third party)* [1992] 1 AC 294, sub nom *Scally v Southern Health and Social Services Board* [1991] ICR 771, HL.

7   See e g the joining of individual named miners as parties to the action in *National Coal Board v National Union of Mineworkers* [1986] ICR 736, [1986] IRLR 439 in order to argue that the national procedure in question was enforceable as a term of their individual contracts; this argument failed. Cf, however, *Dalgleish v Lothian and Borders Police Board* [1991] IRLR 422, Ct of Sess (collective agreement on access to employees' personal files arguably not yet incorporated into individual contracts of employment; *prima facie* case that it was binding to the extent that each individual employee could found on it to prevent disclosure of confidential information without his express knowledge and consent).

8   *Hooper v British Railways Board* [1988] IRLR 517, CA. See e g *Agnew v North Lanarkshire Council* [2010] All ER (D) 157 (Oct), EAT (it might not be possible to reach a view on the aptness for incorporation of the terms of a collective agreement without first determining what exactly the clause meant). See also *Kershaw v Mirror Colour Print (Oldham) Ltd* [2004] All ER (D) 336 (Oct), EAT (terms of employment governed by collective agreement could not have intended the normal operation of the shift system to create overtime; implied term found by tribunal did not pass the 'officious bystander' test or the 'business efficacy' test (as to which see CONTRACT vol 22 (2012) PARAS 369–371)). As to contractual terms and their interpretation in the law of contract generally see CONTRACT vol 22 (2012) PARA 352 et seq.

9   *National Coal Board v Galley* [1958] 1 All ER 91, [1958] 1 WLR 16, CA; *Keir and Williams v Hereford and Worcester County Council* [1985] IRLR 505, CA. Some care is needed to make it clear which collective agreement is being referred to in the contract (see *Gascol Conversions Ltd v Mercer* [1974] ICR 420, [1974] IRLR 155, CA), as there may be several contenders (*Bond v CAV Ltd, Neads v CAV Ltd* [1983] IRLR 360).

10 See the Employment Rights Act 1996 s 1; and PARAS 119–120.

11 See the Employment Rights Act 1996 s 1(4)(j); and PARA 119.

12 See *Young v Canadian Northern Rly Co* [1931] AC 83, PC (where on the facts no contractual obligation to observe the provisions of the collective agreement was found); *MacLea v Essex Line Ltd* (1933) 45 Ll L Rep 254 (implied incorporation of national agreement allowed employee to claim payment in lieu of leave despite his signing of a settlement at the end of the voyage).

13 *Tocher v General Motors Scotland Ltd* [1981] IRLR 55, EAT. See also *Glendale Managed Services v Graham* [2003] EWCA Civ 773, [2003] IRLR 465 (where a contract provides in effect that nationally agreed pay increases will normally be paid, a term was implied that notice was required from the employer before he could decline to pay those increases).

14 *Howman & Son v Blyth* [1983] ICR 416, [1983] IRLR 139. In order to establish a custom and practice, clear evidence is required and there should be a scrutiny commensurate with the particular circumstances but the burden of proof on custom and practice is upon the balance of probabilities rather than a 'strict' level of proof, which suggests a different and higher standard: *Henry v London General Transport Services Ltd* [2002] EWCA Civ 488, [2002] ICR 910, [2002] IRLR 472 (tradition of collective negotiation between employers and recognised trade unions sufficient to establish a custom and practice that fundamental changes such as those set out in a framework agreement were incorporated into individual contracts by virtue of the collective bargaining).

15 *Jewell v Neptune Concrete Ltd* [1975] IRLR 147; and see *Cadoux v Central Regional Council* [1986] IRLR 131, Ct of Sess.

16 While this does not mean that only substantive provisions such as those covering pay and hours will be capable of incorporation, a court may take the view that collective provisions of the agreement are meant to be applicable only to the relations of employer and trade union and so not appropriate for incorporation into individual contracts: see *Young v Canadian Northern Rly Co* [1931] AC 83, PC (seniority provisions); *Gallagher v Post Office* [1970] 3 All ER 712 (recognition) (but c f *City and Hackney Health Authority v National Union of Public Employees* [1985] IRLR 252, CA); *National Coal Board v National Union of Mineworkers* [1986] ICR 736, [1986] IRLR 439 (disputes procedures); *Alexander v Standard Telephones and Cables Ltd (No 2), Wall v Standard Telephones and Cables Ltd (No 2)* [1991] IRLR 286 (redundancy procedures) (but c f *Anderson v Pringle of Scotland Ltd* [1998] IRLR 64, Ct of Sess); *Kaur v MG Rover Group Ltd* [2004] EWCA Civ 1507, [2005] ICR 625, [2005] IRLR 40 (principles in document intended to be a commitment by management and trade unions to communicate effectively on business issues; principles characterised as overwhelmingly aspirational and not to be regarded as amending contracts of employment). See also *Tadd v Eastwood and Daily Telegraph Ltd* [1983] IRLR 320; *British Leyland UK Ltd v McQuilken* [1978] IRLR 245, EAT (policy planning). Not only may a provision of a collective agreement concerning pay be considered apt for incorporation into an individual contract of employment, but also the decision as to whether any such matters are contractual or not can be determined upon by a tribunal and the tribunal may also imply meaning to the terms of a contract where those terms are ambiguous: see *Anderson v London Fire and Emergency Planning Authority* [2013] EWCA Civ 321, [2013] IRLR 459 (construction of collective agreement adopted by the EAT was wholly improbable: properly construed, choice of two options for amount of increase depended on which amount turned out to be the greater, not on the employer's unfettered right to choose which of the options to implement); and PARA 255.

17 *Hamilton v Futura Floors Ltd* [1990] IRLR 478, Ct of Sess. There is a parallel rule in the law relating to recognition: see *National Union of Gold, Silver and Allied Trades v Albury Bros Ltd* [1979] ICR 84, [1978] IRLR 504, CA; and PARA 1094.

18 As to the meaning of 'worker' see PARA 5; and see also PARA 892.

19 As to the meaning of 'independent trade union' for these purposes see the Trade Union and Labour Relations (Consolidation) Act 1992 s 5; and PARA 904.

20 See the Trade Union and Labour Relations (Consolidation) Act 1992 s 180(1), (2); and PARA 1177. The provisions of s 180(1), (2) have effect notwithstanding any provision to the contrary in any agreement including a collective agreement or a contract with any worker: see s 180(3); and PARA 1177. Section 180 was enacted to reverse the decision in *Rookes v Barnard* [1964] AC 1129, [1964] 1 All ER 367, HL (no-strike clause incorporated into individual contracts and formed a basis for the tort of intimidation). See also *Camden Exhibition and Display Ltd v Lynott* [1966] 1 QB 555, [1965] 3 All ER 28, CA. As to no-strike clauses in collective agreements generally see further PARA 1177.

21 The modern practice of consolidating guidance in handbooks etc supersedes cruder devices such as the posting of notices (see *Petrie v MacFisheries Ltd* [1940] 1 KB 258, [1939] 4 All ER 281, CA); and the use of company handbooks is encouraged by the Advisory, Conciliation and Arbitration Service (ACAS) (see *ACAS Advisory Handbook: the A to Z of Work* (September 2008)). The leading case of incorporation of terms from company handbooks is *Keeley v Fosroc International Ltd* [2006] EWCA Civ 1277, [2006] IRLR 961. See also *Bateman v Asda Stores Ltd* [2010] IRLR 370, EAT (incorporation of term in company handbook permitting unilateral variation of policies); *Attrill v Dresdner Kleinwort Ltd, Anar v Dresdner Kleinwort Ltd* [2013] EWCA Civ 394, [2013] 3 All ER 607, [2013] IRLR 548 (variation of employment contract in relation to retention bonuses was effected in accordance with terms of employee handbook but adverse conditions clause undermined trust and confidence in light of bank's promises that bonus pool would be unaffected by efforts to reduce running costs). Provision for redundancy has become a widely accepted feature of an employee's remuneration package and tribunals should scrutinise with care arguments by employers that payments which

were intended to be part of an employee's remuneration package, once promised and communicated, were merely matters of policy and discretion: *Allen v TRW Systems Ltd* [2013] IRLR 699, [2013] ICR D13, EAT (enhanced redundancy terms contained in employee handbook source of contractual obligation); and see *Albion Automotive Ltd v Walker* [2002] EWCA Civ 946, [2002] All ER (D) 170 (Jun) (relevant factors deployed in proper approach to cases concerning enhanced redundancy benefits). See also *Geys v Société Générale, London Branch* [2012] UKSC 63, [2013] 1 AC 523, [2013] 1 All ER 1061, [2013] IRLR 122, [2013] ICR 117 (there was no conflict between a contractual term allowing termination on three months' notice and an employee handbook provision allowing for immediate termination with payment in lieu of notice). As to ACAS see PARA 1213 et seq.

22 See eg *Deadman v Bristol City Council* [2007] EWCA Civ 822, [2007] IRLR 888 (considered a contractual term that employer would follow its published procedure when conducting an investigation, unless and until withdrawn by agreement); *Hussain v Surrey and Sussex Healthcare NHS Trust* [2011] EWHC 1670 (QB), [2011] All ER (D) 91 (Jul), [2012] Med LR 163 (Secretary of State for Health's national guidance and procedure contained in Maintaining High Professional Standards in the Modern NHS (MHPS) was implemented locally in the Trust's Disciplinary Procedure, which was incorporated into individual contracts, but it was still necessary to consider separately whether each of the particular provisions was apt for incorporation); *Fynes v St George's Hospital NHS Trust* [2014] EWHC 756 (QB), 138 BMLR 170, [2014] All ER (D) 210 (Mar) (MHPS was implemented locally in the Medical and Dental Staff Conduct and Capability Policy which had been incorporated into the contract of employment but the MHPS (or any part of it) had not been incorporated into the contract of employment such that its terms could be directly relied on by the employee).

23 *Secretary of State for Employment v Associated Society of Locomotive Engineers and Firemen (No 2)* [1972] 2 QB 455, [1972] 2 All ER 949, CA; *Dal v Orr* [1980] IRLR 413, EAT (provision in an employees' handbook impliedly incorporated into contracts); *Dryden v Greater Glasgow Health Board* [1992] IRLR 469, EAT (introduction of a no smoking policy was within the managerial prerogative). The leading case is now *Keeley v Fosroc Industrial Ltd* [2006] EWCA Civ 1277, [2006] IRLR 961 where an enhanced redundancy package which was intended by the employer to be discretionary but was referred to in the company handbook (under the heading 'Employee benefits and rights') as an entitlement was held to be contractually binding. Where a staff handbook has been recast into an internet site, it is unlikely that that change will alone be construed as altering or negating existing contractual rights: *Harlow v Artemis International Corpn Ltd* [2008] EWHC 1126 (QB), [2008] IRLR 629.

24 *Grant v South-West Trains Ltd* [1998] IRLR 188 (equal opportunities policy referring to discrimination on grounds of sexual orientation held not to be contractual); *Wandsworth London Borough Council v D'Silva* [1998] IRLR 193, CA (council's code of practice on staff sickness was not intended to be contractual, but rather meant as guidance on good practice for managers).

25 *Secretary of State for Scotland v Taylor* [1997] IRLR 608, EAT (equal opportunities policy held to be contractual, having been introduced by the employer as a substantive change of terms and conditions); affd on other grounds sub nom *Taylor v Secretary of State for Scotland* [2000] ICR 595, [2000] IRLR 502, HL.

117.   Incorporated terms of employment survive the demise of the instrument itself.   Where a provision of a collective agreement[1] or other source is incorporated into an individual contract of employment, that provision then gains independent contractual effect as a term of that contract, which may be relied on by the individual employee[2]. If the employer subsequently withdraws from the collective agreement and refuses to abide by it any longer[3], that does not mean that a contractual term incorporated from the agreement lapses or is automatically varied; as it has independent contractual effect, that term stands and the employee may seek to enforce it unless and until it is varied in some contractually acceptable way, usually requiring the employee's assent. If, therefore, the employer wishes to be rid of a collective agreement and its effects, he must both withdraw from the agreement and lawfully vary the terms in the contracts of employment incorporated from that agreement[4].

1   As to the meaning of 'collective agreement' for these purposes see PARA 116 note 3.

2   See PARA 116. The collective agreement itself is not legally binding, however, and the employer
    may not be held to it legally by the trade union: see PARA 116.
3   Withdrawing from the collective agreement could be part of a move to derecognise the union;
    unless recognition was gained by use of the statutory recognition procedure, a union has no
    legal right to continued recognition: see PARA 1094.
4   *Morris v CH Bailey Ltd* [1969] 2 Lloyd's Rep 215, CA; *Burroughs Machines Ltd v Timmoney*
    [1977] IRLR 404, Ct of Sess; *Gibbons v Associated British Ports* [1985] IRLR 376; *Cadoux v
    Central Regional Council* [1986] IRLR 131, Ct of Sess; *National Coal Board v National Union
    of Mineworkers* [1986] ICR 736, [1986] IRLR 439; and see *Whent v T Cartledge Ltd* [1997]
    IRLR 153, EAT (where a clause incorporating a particular collective agreement survived a
    transfer of the business to a new employer). This may work to the opposite effect, in that, where
    an employee's contract expressly incorporates terms from a collective agreement and is subject
    to negotiated changes in that agreement, the employee may not refuse unilaterally to accept any
    particular negotiated change: *Tocher v General Motors Scotland Ltd* [1981] IRLR 55, EAT.

(v) Employment Particulars

A. WRITTEN PARTICULARS OF EMPLOYMENT

**118.   General obligations regarding basic terms and conditions of
employment.** At common law, there is no need for any particular form or
formality in order for a contract of employment to exist, and it certainly does not
need to be in writing[1]. An employer is, however, under a statutory obligation[2] to
give to an employee, not later than two months after the beginning of the
employee's employment, a written statement setting out certain basic terms and
conditions of employment[3]. Such a statement is not itself a written contract of
employment and so is not conclusive of the true terms and conditions, but in
practice it will be strong evidence of what those terms and conditions are[4]. A
court or tribunal should not, however, always assume that acquiescence in, or
lack of objection to, a written statement by an employee signifies consent to its
contents[5], particularly where the employer has issued a new statement
purporting to vary the terms and conditions[6]. Merely acknowledging receipt of a
written statement by signing it does not turn the statement into a written
contract[7]; but a bilateral agreement in writing that the stated terms are correct
may have the effect of turning the statement into a contract, with
correspondingly less scope at a later date for arguing that the statement was
inaccurate[8].

1   See PARA 14.
2   Ie by virtue of the Employment Rights Act 1996 s 1(1): see PARA 119.
3   See the Employment Rights Act 1996 s 1; and PARA 119. Although certain of the required
    particulars must be included in a single document (see PARA 119), the statutory strictures are
    more as to content than as to form (see PARA 122).
4   *System Floors (UK) Ltd v Daniel* [1982] ICR 54, [1981] IRLR 475, EAT; approved in
    Robertson v British Gas Corpn, Jackson v British Gas Corpn [1983] ICR 351, [1983] IRLR
    302, CA. See also *Camden Exhibition and Display Ltd v Lynott* [1966] 1 QB 555, [1965]
    3 All ER 28, CA; *Parkes Classic Confectionery v Ashcroft* (1973) 8 ITR 43.
5   *System Floors (UK) Ltd v Daniel* [1982] ICR 54, [1981] IRLR 475, EAT.
6   *Jones v Associated Tunnelling Co Ltd* [1981] IRLR 477 at 481, EAT, obiter, per
    Browne-Wilkinson P. Any variation of contractual terms must be by bilateral agreement: see
    PARA 113.
7   *System Floors (UK) Ltd v Daniel* [1982] ICR 54, [1981] IRLR 475, EAT.
8   *Gascol Conversions Ltd v Mercer* [1974] ICR 420, [1974] IRLR 155, CA (distinguished in
    Hawker Siddeley Power Engineering Ltd v Rump [1979] IRLR 425, EAT); *Robertson v British
    Gas Corpn, Jackson v British Gas Corpn* [1983] ICR 351, [1983] IRLR 302, CA.

119. Statutory requirement for written statement of initial particulars of employment. Where an employee[1] begins employment[2] with an employer[3], the employer must give to the employee a written statement of particulars of employment[4]. The statement must contain particulars of:

(1) the names of the employer and employee[5];

(2) the date when the employment began[6]; and

(3) the date on which the employee's period of continuous employment began, taking into account any employment with a previous employer which counts towards that period[7].

The statement must also contain particulars[8], as at a specified date not more than seven days before the statement (or the instalment containing them) is given[9], of:

(a) the scale or rate of remuneration or the method of calculating remuneration[10];

(b) the intervals at which remuneration is paid (that is, weekly, monthly or other specified intervals)[11];

(c) any terms and conditions relating to hours of work, including any terms and conditions relating to normal working hours[12];

(d) any terms and conditions relating to any of the following:

    (i) entitlement to holidays, including public holidays, and holiday pay (the particulars given being sufficient to enable the employee's entitlement, including any entitlement to accrued holiday pay on the termination of employment, to be precisely calculated)[13];

    (ii) incapacity for work due to sickness or injury, including any provision for sick pay[14]; and

    (iii) pensions and pension schemes[15];

(e) the length of notice which the employee is obliged to give, and entitled to receive, to determine his contract of employment[16];

(f) the title of the job[17] which the employee is employed to do or a brief description of the work for which he is employed[18];

(g) where the employment is not intended to be permanent, the period for which it is expected to continue (or, if it is for a fixed term, the date when it is to end)[19];

(h) either the place of work or, where the employee is required or permitted to work at various places, an indication of that and of the address of the employer[20];

(i) any collective agreements[21] which directly affect the terms and conditions of the employment including, where the employer is not a party, the persons by whom they were made[22]; and

(j) where the employee is required to work outside the United Kingdom for a period of more than one month[23]:

    (i) the period for which he is to work outside the United Kingdom[24];

    (ii) the currency in which remuneration is to be paid while he is working outside the United Kingdom[25];

    (iii) any additional remuneration payable to him, and any benefits to be provided to or in respect of him, by reason of his being required to work outside the United Kingdom[26]; and

    (iv) any terms and conditions relating to his return to the United Kingdom[27].

The required statement of particulars may refer the employee to the provisions of some other document which is reasonably accessible to him[28] for particulars of any of the matters specified under either head (d)(ii) or head (d)(iii) above[29]; and for particulars of either of the matters specified in head (e) above, it may refer the employee to the law, or to the provisions of any collective agreement directly affecting the terms and conditions of employment which is reasonably accessible to him[30].

The particulars required by heads (1)–(3), (a)–(c), (d)(i), (f) and (h) above[31] must be included in a single document[32].

The Secretary of State[33] may by order provide that the statutory provisions which require a written statement of initial particulars of employment to be given to the employee[34] are to have effect as if particulars of such further matters as may be specified in the order were included in the particulars required to be included in such a statement[35].

1   As to the meaning of 'employee' see PARA 2.
2   As to the meaning of 'employment' see PARA 2.
3   As to the meaning of 'employer' see PARA 2.
4   Employment Rights Act 1996 s 1(1). Subject to s 2(4) (see the text and notes 31–32), the statement may be given in instalments and (whether or not given in instalments) must be given not later than two months after the beginning of the employment: s 1(2). A statement must be given to a person under s 1 even if his employment ends before the end of the period within which the statement is required to be given: s 2(6). As to the meaning of 'written' see PARA 2 note 8. As to the cases in which such a statement need not be given see PARA 123. As to particulars of disciplinary procedures etc which must be included in the statement see PARA 120; and as to the use of alternative documents to give particulars see PARA 122.
     The written statement of particulars does not normally constitute the contract of employment itself: *System Floors (UK) Ltd v Daniel* [1982] ICR 54, [1981] IRLR 475, EAT (statement is neither the contract nor conclusive evidence of the terms of the contract), approved in *Robertson v British Gas Corpn, Jackson v British Gas Corpn* [1983] ICR 351, [1983] IRLR 302, CA. See also *Glendale Managed Services v Graham* [2003] EWCA Civ 773, [2003] IRLR 465 (terms in the particulars of employment were evidence of the agreement between the employer and employee and not to be construed as if they were agreed terms in a written commercial contract). The statement required by the Employment Rights Act 1996 s 1(1), amongst other things, serves to implement Council Directive (EC) 91/533 (OJ L288, 18.10.91, p 32) on an employer's obligation to inform employees of the conditions applicable to the contract or employment relationship. As to the scope and effect of this Directive see Case C-350/99 *Lange v Georg Schünemann GmbH* [2001] [2001] All ER (EC) 481, ECR I-1061, [2001] IRLR 244, ECJ.
5   Employment Rights Act 1996 s 1(3)(a).
6   Employment Rights Act 1996 s 1(3)(b). The fact that s 1 is directed by s 5(1) (see PARA 123 note 6) to apply to an employee as if his employment began on his ceasing to come within the exceptions referred to in s 5(1) does not affect the obligation under s 1(3)(b) to specify the date on which his employment actually began: see s 5(2); and PARA 123 note 6. See also note 23.
7   Employment Rights Act 1996 s 1(3)(c). As to the date when an employee's period of continuous employment begins see s 211(1); and PARA 130. An agreement by the parties to count previous employment, with the same or a different employer, may have contractual effect; but, for statutory purposes, continuity of employment is computed according to the statutory rules (see PARA 130 et seq) which may not be superseded by any agreement of the parties, whether by estoppel or otherwise: *Secretary of State for Employment v Globe Elastic Thread Co Ltd* [1979] ICR 706, [1979] IRLR 327, HL (overruling *Evenden v Guildford City Association Football Club Ltd* [1975] ICR 367, [1975] IRLR 213, CA).
8   If, in the case of a statement under the Employment Rights Act 1996 s 1, there are no particulars to be entered under any of the heads of s 1(4)(d) (see head (d) in the text) or s 1(4)(k) (see head (j) in the text) or under any of the other provisions of s 1(3) (see heads (1) to (3) in the text) or s 1(4) (see heads (a) to (j) in the text), that fact must be stated: s 2(1). There is a distinction between 'mandatory terms' which are required to be present in the statement and 'non-mandatory terms' which are required to be in the statement only if agreement on them has actually been reached: see *Eagland v British Telecommunications plc* [1990] ICR 248, [1990] IRLR 328, EAT. For an example of a non-mandatory term see *Morley v Heritage plc* [1993] IRLR 400, CA (holiday pay accrued on termination).

9 See the Employment Rights Act 1996 s 1(4). As to the instalments that may contain the required particulars see note 4.

10 Employment Rights Act 1996 s 1(4)(a). As to the statutory right to an itemised pay statement see PARA 124.

11 Employment Rights Act 1996 s 1(4)(b).

12 Employment Rights Act 1996 s 1(4)(c). As to the computation of normal working hours see PARA 142. Council Directive (EC) 91/533 (OJ L288, 18.10.91, p 32) (see note 4) places employers under an obligation to notify employees only in relation to normal working hours and not in relation to the working of overtime: Case C-350/99 *Lange v Georg Schünemann GmbH* [2001] All ER (EC) 481, [2001] ECR I-1061, [2001] IRLR 244, ECJ.

13 Employment Rights Act 1996 s 1(4)(d)(i). The provision made by s 1(4)(d)(i) requires only that the parties are able to calculate the holiday pay that would be received, not that it could be predicted: *Walker v Co-operative Insurance Society* [2003] EWCA Civ 632, [2003] All ER (D) 219 (Apr).

14 Employment Rights Act 1996 s 1(4)(d)(ii). As to an employee's eligibility to receive pay during temporary incapacity through illness see PARA 27; and as to statutory sick pay see PARA 558 et seq.

15 Employment Rights Act 1996 s 1(4)(d)(iii). The provision made by s 1(4)(d)(iii) does not, however, apply to an employee of a body or authority if: (1) the employee's pension rights depend on the terms of a pension scheme established under any provision contained in, or having effect under, any Act (s 1(5)(a)); and (2) any such provision requires the body or authority to give to a new employee information concerning the employee's pension rights or the determination of questions affecting those rights (s 1(5)(b)).

16 Employment Rights Act 1996 s 1(4)(e). As to the meaning of 'contract of employment' see PARA 2. As to dismissal by notice see PARA 733; and as to minimum periods of notice see PARAS 735–736.

17 Except in so far as the context otherwise requires, 'job', in relation to an employee, means the nature of the work which he is employed to do in accordance with his contract and the capacity and place in which he is so employed: see the Employment Rights Act 1996 s 235(1).

18 Employment Rights Act 1996 s 1(4)(f).

19 Employment Rights Act 1996 s 1(4)(g).

20 Employment Rights Act 1996 s 1(4)(h).

21 For these purposes, except in so far as the context otherwise requires, 'collective agreement' has the meaning given by the Trade Union and Labour Relations (Consolidation) Act 1992 s 178(1), (2) (see PARA 116 note 3): see the Employment Rights Act 1996 s 235(1).

22 Employment Rights Act 1996 s 1(4)(j).

23 See the Employment Rights Act 1996 s 1(4)(k). Where, before the end of the period of two months after the beginning of an employee's employment, the employee is to begin to work outside the United Kingdom for a period of more than one month, the statement under s 1 must be given to him not later than the time when he leaves the United Kingdom in order to begin so to work: s 2(5). As to the meaning of 'United Kingdom' see PARA 2 note 12.

24 Employment Rights Act 1996 s 1(4)(k)(i).

25 Employment Rights Act 1996 s 1(4)(k)(ii).

26 Employment Rights Act 1996 s 1(4)(k)(iii).

27 Employment Rights Act 1996 s 1(4)(k)(iv).

28 For the purposes of the Employment Rights Act 1996 ss 2–4 (see also PARAS 120–121), references to a document or collective agreement which is reasonably accessible to an employee are references to a document or collective agreement which: (a) the employee has reasonable opportunities of reading in the course of his employment (s 6(a)); or which is made reasonably accessible to him in some other way (s 6(b)).

29 See the Employment Rights Act 1996 s 2(2).

30 See the Employment Rights Act 1996 s 2(3).

31 Ie the particulars required by the Employment Rights Act 1996 s 1(3), (4)(a)–(c), (d)(i), (f), (h) (see heads (1)–(3), (a)–(c), (d)(i), (f), (h) in the text): see s 2(4).

32 Employment Rights Act 1996 s 2(4).

33 As to the Secretary of State see PARA 5 note 21.

34 Ie the Employment Rights Act 1996 s 1 (see the text and notes 1–27): see s 7.

35 Employment Rights Act 1996 s 7. For this purpose, the order may include such provisions amending s 1 (see the text and notes 1–27) as appear to the Secretary of State to be expedient: see s 7. As to the making of orders under the Employment Rights Act 1996 generally see PARA 162. At the date at which this volume states the law, no such order had been made.

120. Particulars of disciplinary procedures etc. A written statement of initial particulars of employment, required by statute[1], must include a note[2]:

(1) specifying any disciplinary rules applicable to the employee or referring the employee to the provisions of a document which specifies such rules and which is reasonably accessible to the employee[3];

(2) specifying any procedure applicable to the taking of disciplinary decisions relating to the employee, or to a decision to dismiss the employee, or referring the employee to the provisions of a document which is reasonably accessible to the employee and which specifies such a procedure[4];

(3) specifying, by description or otherwise[5]:
    (a) a person to whom the employee can apply if he is dissatisfied with any disciplinary decision relating to him, or any decision to dismiss him[6]; and
    (b) a person to whom the employee can apply for the purpose of seeking redress of any grievance relating to his employment[7],
    and the manner in which any such application should be made[8]; and

(4) where there are further steps consequent on any such application, explaining those steps or referring to the provisions of a document which is reasonably accessible to the employee and which explains them[9]; and

(5) stating whether a contracting-out certificate[10] is in force for the employment in respect of which the statement is given[11].

The provisions of heads (1) to (4) above do not apply to rules, disciplinary decisions, decisions to dismiss, grievances or procedures relating to health or safety at work, however[12].

1 Ie the statement required to be given to an employee under the Employment Rights Act 1996 s 1 (see PARA 119): see s 3(1). As to the meanings of 'employee' and 'employment' see PARA 2; and as to the meaning of 'written' see PARA 2 note 8. As to excluded classes of employment see PARA 123.

2 See the Employment Rights Act 1996 s 3(1).

3 Employment Rights Act 1996 s 3(1)(a). As to the meaning of references to a document being reasonably accessible see PARA 119 note 28.

4 Employment Rights Act 1996 s 3(1)(aa) (added by the Employment Act 2002 s 35(1), (2)). As to dismissal procedures generally see PARA 698 et seq; and as to dismissal on notice generally see PARA 733 et seq.

5 See the Employment Rights Act 1996 s 3(1)(b).

6 Employment Rights Act 1996 s 3(1)(b)(i) (amended by the Employment Act 2002 s 35(1), (3)).

7 Employment Rights Act 1996 s 3(1)(b)(ii).

8 See the Employment Rights Act 1996 s 3(1)(b). As to grievance procedures generally see PARA 698 et seq.

9 Employment Rights Act 1996 s 3(1)(c).

10 As to the issue of contracting-out certificates by the Occupational Pensions Board see the Pension Schemes Act 1993 Pt III Ch I (ss 7–39); and PERSONAL AND OCCUPATIONAL PENSIONS vol 80 (2013) PARA 395 et seq.

11 Employment Rights Act 1996 s 3(5).

12 Employment Rights Act 1996 s 3(2) (amended by the Employment Act 2002 s 35(1), (4)). As to health and safety at work generally see HEALTH AND SAFETY AT WORK vol 52 (2014) PARA 301 et seq.

121. Written particulars where there are changes in the terms of employment. If, after the material date[1], there is a change in any of the matters particulars of which are required[2] to be included or referred to in the written statement of initial particulars of employment[3], the employer[4] must, at the earliest opportunity and in any event not more than one month after the change in question, give to the employee a written statement containing particulars of the change[5].

Where, after an employer has given to an employee a statement of initial employment particulars[6], either:

(1) the name of the employer (whether an individual or a body corporate or partnership) is changed without any change in the identity of the employer[7]; or

(2) the identity of the employer is changed in circumstances in which the continuity of the employee's period of employment is not broken[8],

and where the change does not involve any change in the matters (other than the names of the parties) whose particulars are required[9] to be included or referred to in that statement[10], the person who is the employer immediately after the change is not required to give to the employee such a statement[11]. A statement[12] which informs an employee of a change such as is referred to in head (2) above must, however, specify the date on which the employee's period of continuous employment began[13].

1 For these purposes:
   (1) in relation to a matter particulars of which are included or referred to in a statement given under the Employment Rights Act 1996 s 1 (see PARAS 119–120) otherwise than in instalments, the material date is the date to which the statement relates (s 4(2)(a));
   (2) in relation to a matter particulars of which: (a) are included or referred to in an instalment of a statement given under s 1 (s 4(2)(b)(i)); or (b) are required by s 2(4) (see PARA 119) to be included in a single document but are not included in an instalment of a statement given under s 1 which does include other particulars to which that provision applies (s 4(2)(b)(ii)), the material date is the date to which the instalment relates (s 4(2)(b));
   (3) in relation to any other matter, the material date is the date by which a statement under s 1 is required to be given (s 4(2)(c)).
  As to the delivery of particulars in instalments see PARA 119 note 4.
2 Ie required by the Employment Rights Act 1996 ss 1–3 (see PARAS 119–120): see s 4(1).
3 Ie under the Employment Rights Act 1996 s 1 (see PARAS 119–120): see s 4(1). As to the meanings of 'employee' and 'employment' see PARA 2; and as to the meaning of 'written' see PARA 2 note 8. As to excluded classes of employment see PARA 123.
4 As to the meaning of 'employer' see PARA 2.
5 See the Employment Rights Act 1996 s 4(1), (3)(a). Where, however, the change results from the employee being required to work outside the United Kingdom for a period of more than one month, the statement must be given not later than the time when he leaves the United Kingdom in order to begin so to work, if that is earlier: s 4(3)(b). As to the meaning of 'United Kingdom' see PARA 2 note 12.
  A statement under s 4(1) may:
   (1) refer the employee to the provisions of some other document which is reasonably accessible to the employee for a change in any of the matters specified in s 1(4)(d)(ii), (iii) (see PARA 119) and s 3(1)(a), (c) (see PARA 120) (s 4(4));
   (2) refer the employee for a change in either of the matters specified in s 1(4)(e) (see PARA 119) to the law or to the provisions of any collective agreement directly affecting the terms and conditions of the employment which is reasonably accessible to the employee (s 4(5)).
  As to the meaning of 'collective agreement' see PARA 119 note 21; and as to the meaning of references to a document being reasonably accessible see PARA 119 note 28.
  The provision made by s 4 does not, however, give the employer a right of unilateral variation of the contract of employment; the aim of s 4 is to ensure proper notification of changes which have been agreed in some contractually valid way. It is true that employers sometimes seek to vary contracts by issuing amendments under s 4(1), or indeed reissuing the whole written statement, including the altered terms, putting the onus on the employees to object or be considered as having accepted the variation by acquiescence, but in such a case a court or tribunal should be wary of finding implied acceptance too readily, particularly where the change is to a term not having an immediate impact, such as a sick pay term: *Jones v*

Associated Tunnelling Co Ltd [1981] IRLR 477 at 481, EAT, obiter, per Browne-Wilkinson P; *Robertson v British Gas Corpn, Jackson v British Gas Corpn* [1983] ICR 351, [1983] IRLR 302, CA. An employee's place of work could in certain cases be of such importance as to amount to a fundamental term, the breach of which would constitute a repudiatory breach: *Norris v Great Dawley Parish Council* [2008] All ER (D) 278 (Nov), EAT. As to the variation of terms in a contract of employment see PARA 113 note 3.

6   Ie under the Employment Rights Act 1996 s 1 (see PARAS 119–120): see s 4(6). The reference in s 4(6) to an employer having given a statement under s 1 (see PARAS 119–120) is treated as including his having given a document by virtue of which his duty to give such a statement is treated as met: s 7A(7) (s 7A added by the Employment Act 2002 s 37). As to the use of alternative documents to give particulars see further PARA 122.

7   Employment Rights Act 1996 s 4(6)(a).

8   Employment Rights Act 1996 s 4(6)(b). As to continuity of employment see PARA 130 et seq.

9   Ie by the Employment Rights Act 1996 ss 1–3 (see PARAS 119–120): see s 4(7).

10 See the Employment Rights Act 1996 s 4(7).

11 See the Employment Rights Act 1996 s 4(6). The change is, however, to be treated as a change falling within s 4(1) (see the text and notes 1–5): see s 4(6).

12 Ie under the Employment Rights Act 1996 s 4(1) (see the text and notes 1–5): see s 4(8).

13 Employment Rights Act 1996 s 4(8).

122.   Use of alternative documents to give particulars.   Where:

(1)   an employer[1] gives an employee[2] a document in writing[3] in the form of a contract of employment[4] or letter of engagement[5];

(2)   the document contains information which, were the document in the form of a statement of initial particulars of employment[6], would meet the employer's obligation[7] in relation to the names of the employer and employee[8], the date when the employment began[9], the date on which the employee's period of continuous employment began[10], the scale or rate of remuneration or the method of calculating remuneration[11], the intervals at which remuneration is paid[12], any terms and conditions relating to hours of work[13] or to entitlement to holidays[14], the job title or description[15] and details relating to[16] the place or places of work[17]; and

(3)   the document is given after the beginning of the employment and before the end of the period for giving a statement of initial particulars of employment[18],

the employer's duty to give a written statement of particulars[19] in relation to any matter is treated as met if the document given to the employee contains information which, were the document in the form of a statement of particulars, would meet the employer's obligation in relation to that matter[20]. The employer's duty in relation to particulars of disciplinary procedures and pensions[21] is also treated as met if such a document given to the employee contains information which, were the document in the form of a statement of initial particulars and the information included in the form of a note, would meet the employer's obligation in that regard[22].

1   As to the meaning of 'employer' see PARA 2.

2   As to the meaning of 'employee' see PARA 2.

3   As to the meaning of 'writing' see PARA 2 note 8.

4   As to the meaning of 'contract of employment' see PARA 2.

5   Employment Rights Act 1996 s 7A(1)(a) (ss 7A, 7B added by the Employment Act 2002 s 37). For these purposes, a document to which the Employment Rights Act 1996 s 7A(1)(a) applies is treated, in relation to information in respect of any of the matters mentioned in s 1(4) (see PARA 119), as specifying the date on which the document is given to the employee as the date as at which the information applies: see s 7A(4) (as so added). A document in the form of a contract of employment or letter of engagement given by an employer to an employee before the

beginning of the employee's employment with the employer is treated for the purposes of s 7A as having been given when the employment begins: s 7B (as so added).

6   Ie a statement under the Employment Rights Act 1996 s 1 (see PARA 119): see s 7A(1)(b) (as added: see note 5).

7   Ie his obligation under the Employment Rights Act 1996 s 1 (see PARA 119): see s 7A(1)(b) (as added: see note 5).

8   Ie his obligation in relation to matters mentioned in the Employment Rights Act 1996 s 1(3)(a) (see PARA 119): see s 7A(1)(b) (as added: see note 5).

9   Ie his obligation in relation to matters mentioned in the Employment Rights Act 1996 s 1(3)(b) (see PARA 119): see s 7A(1)(b) (as added: see note 5).

10 Ie his obligation in relation to matters mentioned in the Employment Rights Act 1996 s 1(3)(c), taking into account any employment with a previous employer which counts towards that period (see PARA 119): see s 7A(1)(b) (as added: see note 5).

11 Ie his obligation in relation to matters mentioned in the Employment Rights Act 1996 s 1(4)(a) (see PARA 119): see s 7A(1)(b) (as added: see note 5).

12 Ie his obligation in relation to matters mentioned in the Employment Rights Act 1996 s 1(4)(b) (see PARA 119): see s 7A(1)(b) (as added: see note 5).

13 Ie his obligation in relation to matters mentioned in the Employment Rights Act 1996 s 1(4)(c), including any terms and conditions relating to normal working hours (see PARA 119): see s 7A(1)(b) (as added: see note 5).

14 Ie his obligation in relation to matters mentioned in the Employment Rights Act 1996 s 1(4)(d)(i), including public holidays and holiday pay (see PARA 119): see s 7A(1)(b) (as added: see note 5).

15 Ie his obligation in relation to matters mentioned in the Employment Rights Act 1996 s 1(4)(f) (see PARA 119): see s 7A(1)(b) (as added: see note 5).

16 Ie his obligation in relation to matters mentioned in the Employment Rights Act 1996 s 1(4)(h) (see PARA 119): see s 7A(1)(b) (as added: see note 5).

17 Employment Rights Act 1996 s 7A(1)(b) (as added: see note 5).

18 Employment Rights Act 1996 s 7A(1)(c) (as added: see note 5). As to the period for giving a statement of particulars of employment under s 1 see PARA 119.

19 Ie his obligation under the Employment Rights Act 1996 s 1 (see PARA 119): see s 7A(2) (as added: see note 5).

20 Employment Rights Act 1996 s 7A(2) (as added: see note 5). Where s 7A(2) applies in relation to any matter, the date on which the document by virtue of which s 7A(2) applies is given to the employee is the material date in relation to that matter for the purposes of s 4(1) (see PARA 121): s 7A(5) (as so added).

21 Ie his duty under the Employment Rights Act 1996 s 3 (see PARA 120): see s 7A(3) (as added: see note 5).

22 See the Employment Rights Act 1996 s 7A(3) (as added: see note 5). Where s 7A(3) applies, the date on which the document by virtue of which s 7A(3) applies is given to the employee is the material date for the purposes of s 4(1) (see PARA 121) in relation to the matters of which particulars are required to be given under s 3 (see PARA 120): s 7A(6) (as so added).

123.   Exclusion from rights to statements.   The provisions that require a written statement of initial particulars of an employee's terms of employment[1] do not apply to: (1) an employee if his employment[2] continues for less than one month[3]; (2) a person employed[4] as a seaman in a ship registered in the United Kingdom[5] under a crew agreement, the provisions and form of which are of a kind approved by the Secretary of State[6].

1   Ie the Employment Rights Act 1996 ss 1–7 (see PARAS 119–121): see ss 198, 199(1). As to the meaning of 'employee' see PARA 2.

2   As to the meaning of 'employment' see PARA 2.

3   See the Employment Rights Act 1996 s 198.

4   As to the meaning of 'employed' see PARA 2.

5   As to the registration of ships in the United Kingdom see the Merchant Shipping Act 1995 Pt II (ss 8–23); and SHIPPING AND MARITIME LAW vol 93 (2008) PARA 245 et seq. As to the meaning of 'United Kingdom' see PARA 2 note 12.

6   See the Employment Rights Act 1996 s 199(1). As to the Secretary of State see PARA 5 note 21. See further PARA 167. As to crew agreements see SHIPPING AND MARITIME LAW vol 93 (2008) PARA 450.

The provisions of ss 1–4 (see PARAS 119–121) apply to an employee who at any time comes or ceases to come within the exceptions from ss 1–4 provided by s 199 (see PARA 167), and under s 209 (see PARA 158), as if his employment with his employer terminated or began at that time: s 5(1) (amended by the Employment Relations Act 1999 s 32(3)). The fact that the Employment Rights Act 1996 s 1 (see PARA 119) is directed by s 5(1) to apply to an employee as if his employment began on his ceasing to come within the exceptions referred to in s 5(1) does not affect the obligation under s 1(3)(b) (see PARA 119) to specify the date on which his employment actually began: s 5(2). As to the meaning of 'employer' see PARA 2.

B. ITEMISED PAY STATEMENTS

124. Right to itemised pay statement. An employee[1] has the right to be given by his employer[2], at or before the time at which any payment of wages or salary is made to him, a written itemised pay statement[3], containing particulars of:

(1)   the gross amount of the wages or salary[4];

(2)   the amounts of any variable, and[5] any fixed, deductions from that gross amount and the purposes for which they are made[6];

(3)   the net amount of wages or salary payable[7]; and

(4)   where different parts of the net amount are paid in different ways, the amount and method of payment of each part-payment[8].

A pay statement given in this way need not contain separate particulars of a fixed deduction if it contains instead an aggregate amount of fixed deductions (including that deduction)[9], and if the employer has given to the employee, at or before the time at which the pay statement is given, a standing statement of fixed deductions[10], in writing[11], which contains, in relation to each deduction comprised in the aggregate amount of deductions, particulars of:

(a)   the amount of the deduction[12];

(b)   the intervals at which the deduction is to be made[13]; and

(c)   the purpose for which it is made[14],

and which is effective[15] at the date on which the pay statement is given[16]. An employer who has given to an employee a standing statement of fixed deductions in this way must, within the period of 12 months beginning with the date on which the first standing statement was given[17], and at intervals of not more than 12 months afterwards[18], reissue it in a consolidated form incorporating any amendments that have been duly notified[19].

1   As to the meaning of 'employee' see PARA 2; and as to excluded classes of employment see PARAS 166–168.

2   As to the meaning of 'employer' see PARA 2.

3   Employment Rights Act 1996 s 8(1). The right under s 8 is an inherent right, not conditional on the employee's having asked for the statement: *Coales v John Wood & Co* [1986] ICR 71, [1986] IRLR 129, EAT. As to the meaning of 'written' see PARA 2 note 8.

    The Secretary of State may by order vary the provisions of s 8 and s 9 as to the particulars which must be included in a pay statement or a standing statement of fixed deductions by adding items to, or removing items from, the particulars listed therein or by amending any such particulars: s 10(a). As to the Secretary of State see PARA 5 note 21. As to the making of orders under the Employment Rights Act 1996 generally see PARA 162. At the date at which this volume states the law, no such order had been made.

4   Employment Rights Act 1996 s 8(2)(a). The statement does not have to include sums payable to the employee from sources other than the employer: *Cofone v Spaghetti House Ltd* [1980] ICR 155, EAT (tips). See also note 6.

5   Ie subject to the Employment Rights Act 1996 s 9 (see the text and notes 9–19): see s 8(2)(b).

6   Employment Rights Act 1996 s 8(2)(b). It is not sufficient, with regard to variable deductions, just to have one general item 'miscellaneous deductions': *Milsom v Leicestershire County Council* [1978] IRLR 433. Where a payment by way of salary or wages for a period is reduced by the recovery of an overpayment in a previous period, that reduction is a 'deduction' for the purposes of the Employment Rights Act 1996 s 8, and both the deduction and its purpose

should be identified on the itemised pay statement relating to the payment: *Ridge v Her Majesty's Land Registry* [2014] All ER (D) 169 (Sep), EAT. As to when a deduction may be made see the Employment Rights Act 1996 Pt II (ss 13–27) (protection of wages); and PARA 254 et seq. As to the overlap between remedies under Pt II and these provisions see PARA 126 note 12.

7 Employment Rights Act 1996 s 8(2)(c). See also note 6.
8 Employment Rights Act 1996 s 8(2)(d). See also note 6.
9 Employment Rights Act 1996 s 9(1)(a). See also note 6.
10 Employment Rights Act 1996 s 9(1)(b). See also note 6.
11 Employment Rights Act 1996 s 9(2)(a). See also note 6.
12 Employment Rights Act 1996 s 9(2)(b)(i). See also note 6.
13 Employment Rights Act 1996 s 9(2)(b)(ii). See also note 6.
14 Employment Rights Act 1996 s 9(2)(b)(iii). See also note 6.
15 For these purposes, a standing statement of fixed deductions becomes effective on the date on which it is given to the employee, and it ceases to be effective at the end of the period of 12 months beginning with that date, or, where it is reissued in accordance with the Employment Rights Act 1996 s 9(4) (see the text and notes 17–19), with the end of the period of 12 months beginning with the date on which it was last reissued: s 9(5). The Secretary of State may by order vary the provisions of s 9(4) and s 9(5) so as to shorten or extend the periods of 12 months therein referred to, or those periods as varied from time to time under s 10: s 10(b). At the date at which this volume states the law, no such order had been made.
16 Employment Rights Act 1996 s 9(2)(c). A standing statement of fixed deductions may be amended (whether by addition of a new deduction, by a change in the particulars, or by cancellation of an existing deduction) by notice in writing, containing particulars of the amendment, given by the employer to the employee: see s 9(3). See also note 6.
17 Employment Rights Act 1996 s 9(4)(a). See note 15.
18 Employment Rights Act 1996 s 9(4)(b). See note 15.
19 Employment Rights Act 1996 s 9(4). The text refers to any amendments notified in accordance with s 9(3) (see note 16): see s 9(4). See also note 6. As to the application of Pt I (ss 1–12) (employment particulars: see PARA 119 et seq), so far as it relates to itemised pay statements, where an employee or employer dies see PARA 1456. As to the application of these provisions to Crown employment, House of Lords staff and House of Commons staff see PARAS 163–165.

C. ENFORCEMENT OF STATUTORY RIGHTS

125. Reference to employment tribunal. Where an employer does not give an employee[1] either a written statement of initial particulars of employment[2], or itemised pay statements[3], as required by statute[4], the employee may require a reference to be made to an employment tribunal[5] to determine what particulars ought to have been included or referred to in a statement so as to comply with those requirements[6].

Where:

(1)   a statement purporting to be a written statement of initial particulars of employment, or a statement of changes in those terms[7]; or

(2)   a pay statement, or a standing statement of fixed deductions, purporting to comply with the statutory requirements[8],

has been given to an employee[9], and where a question arises as to the particulars which ought[10] to have been included or referred to in the statement[11], either the employer or the employee may require that question to be referred to, and determined by, an employment tribunal[12].

An employment tribunal must not consider any such reference, however, in a case where the employment[13] to which the reference relates has ceased, unless an application requiring the reference to be made was made[14] either: (a) before the end of the period of three months beginning with the date on which the employment ceased[15]; or (b) within such further period as the tribunal considers reasonable in a case where it is satisfied that it was not reasonably practicable for the application to be made before the end of that period of three months[16].

1   As to the meanings of 'employee' and 'employer' see PARA 2.
2   Ie as required by the Employment Rights Act 1996 s 1 (statement of initial employment
    particulars: see PARAS 119–120) or s 4 (statement of changes: see PARA 121): see s 11(1)
    (s 11(1), (2), (4) amended by the Employment Rights (Dispute Resolution) Act 1998 s 1(2)(a)).
    As to the meaning of 'written' see PARA 2 note 8.
3   Ie as required by the Employment Rights Act 1996 s 8 (itemised pay statement: see PARA 124):
    see s 11(1) (as amended: see note 2).
4   Ie either because the employer gives the employee no statement at all or because the statement he
    gives does not comply with what is required by statute: see the Employment Rights Act 1996
    s 11(1) (as amended: see note 2).
5   As to employment tribunals see PARA 1399 et seq; and as to the procedure on an application to
    a tribunal see PARA 1453 et seq.
6   Employment Rights Act 1996 s 11(1) (as amended: see note 2). The remedy of an employee for
    infringement of any of the rights conferred on him by s 8 (itemised pay statement: see PARA 124)
    is by way of a reference to an employment tribunal and not otherwise: see s 205(1); and PARA
    1406.
7   Ie purporting to be a statement under the Employment Rights Act 1996 s 1 (statement of initial
    employment particulars: see PARAS 119–120) or s 4 (statement of changes: see PARA 121): see
    s 11(2)(a).
8   Ie purporting to comply with the requirements of the Employment Rights Act 1996 s 8 or s 9
    (see PARA 124): see s 11(2)(a).
9   Employment Rights Act 1996 s 11(2)(a).
10 Ie so as to comply with the requirements of the Employment Rights Act 1996 Pt I (ss 1–12)
    (employment particulars: see PARA 119 et seq): see s 11(2) (as amended: see note 2).
11 Employment Rights Act 1996 s 11(2)(b). For these purposes, a question as to the particulars
    which ought to have been included: (1) in the note required by s 3 (see PARA 120) to be included
    in the statement under s 1 (see PARA 119) does not include any question whether the
    employment is, has been or will be contracted-out employment for the purposes of the Pension
    Schemes Act 1993 Pt III (ss 7–68) (see **PERSONAL AND OCCUPATIONAL PENSIONS** vol 80 (2013)
    PARA 395 et seq) (Employment Rights Act 1996 s 11(3)(a)): (2) in a pay statement or standing
    statement of fixed deductions does not include a question solely as to the accuracy of an amount
    stated in any such particulars (s 11(3)(b)).
12 Employment Rights Act 1996 s 11(2) (as amended: see note 2). As to the determination of such
    a reference by the employment tribunal see PARA 126.
13 As to the meaning of 'employment' see PARA 2. As to excluded classes of employment see PARAS
    166–168.
14 Employment Rights Act 1996 s 11(4) (as amended: see note 2). As to time limits generally see
    PARA 1453; and as to the similar time limit on unfair dismissal claims see PARA 804. As to the
    determination of references by the tribunal see PARA 126.
15 Employment Rights Act 1996 s 11(4)(a). For the purposes of head (a) in the text: (1) the
    provisions of the s 207A(3) (extended time limit where mediation required in certain
    cross-border disputes: see PARA 1454) (s 11(5) (added by SI 2011/1133)); and (2) where the
    reference concerns compliance with the Employment Rights Act 1996 s 8 (itemised pay
    statement: see PARA 124), the provisions of s 207B (extension of time limits to facilitate
    conciliation before institution of proceedings: see PARA 1455) (s 11(6) (added by the Enterprise
    and Regulatory Reform Act 2013 s 8, Sch 2 paras 15, 16; amended by SI 2014/431)), both
    apply.
16 Employment Rights Act 1996 s 11(4)(b).

126.   Determination of reference by employment tribunal. Where, on a
reference[1] involving the failure of an employer to give to an employee the
required statements relating to the terms of his employment[2], an employment
tribunal[3] determines particulars as being those which ought to have been
included or referred to in a written statement of initial particulars[4], the employer
is deemed to have given to the employee a statement in which those particulars
were included, or referred to, as specified in the decision of the tribunal[5].

On determining a reference where a statement has been given purporting to be
a written statement of initial particulars of employment, or a statement of
changes in those terms, or where a pay statement, or a standing statement of
fixed deductions, has been given purporting to comply with the statutory

requirements[6], an employment tribunal may confirm the particulars as included or referred to in the statement given by the employer, it may amend those particulars, or it may substitute other particulars for them, as the tribunal may determine to be appropriate; and the statement is deemed to have been given by the employer to the employee in accordance with the decision of the tribunal[7].

Where, on any such reference[8], an employment tribunal finds that an employer has failed to give an employee any pay statement[9], or finds that a pay statement or standing statement of fixed deductions does not, in relation to a deduction, contain the particulars required[10] to be included in that statement, the tribunal must make a declaration to that effect[11]. Where, in such a case, the tribunal further finds that any unnotified deductions[12] have been made from the employee's pay during the period of 13 weeks[13] immediately preceding the date of the application for the reference (whether or not the deductions were made in breach of the contract of employment[14]), the tribunal may order the employer to pay the employee a sum not exceeding the aggregate of the unnotified deductions so made[15].

1 Ie a reference under the Employment Rights Act 1996 s 11(1) (see PARA 125): see s 12(1) (s 12(1)–(3) amended by the Employment Rights (Dispute Resolution) Act 1998 s 1(2)(a)).

2 Ie as required by the Employment Rights Act 1996 s 1 (statement of initial employment particulars: see PARAS 119–120), s 4 (statement of changes: see PARA 121), or s 8 (itemised pay statement: see PARA 124): see s 12(1) (as amended: see note 1). As to the meanings of 'employee', 'employer', and 'employment', see PARA 2. As to excluded classes of employment see PARAS 166–168.

3 As to employment tribunals see PARA 1399 et seq; and as to the procedure on a complaint made to an employment tribunal see PARA 1453 et seq.

4 Ie in a statement given under the Employment Rights Act 1996 s 1 (statement of initial employment particulars: see PARAS 119–120) or s 4 (statement of changes: see PARA 121): see s 12(1) (as amended: see note 1). As to the meaning of 'written' see PARA 2 note 8.

5 Employment Rights Act 1996 s 12(1) (as amended: see note 1). The tribunal's function is restricted to declaring what term should be included in the written statement, with any question of interpretation or enforcement of such a term remaining a matter for the ordinary courts: *Cuthbertson v AML Distributors* [1975] IRLR 228; *Construction Industry Training Board v Leighton* [1978] 2 All ER 723, sub nom *Leighton v Construction Industry Training Board* [1978] ICR 577, EAT; *Mears v Safecar Security Ltd* [1983] QB 54, [1982] ICR 626, CA. This distinction has not always been an easy one to draw: see *Owens v Multilux Ltd* [1974] IRLR 113, NIRC.

   In determining what particulars ought to be included, the tribunal should look primarily to see whether anything was agreed between the parties; if not, the tribunal should look at all the circumstances, including the subsequent conduct of the parties, to find the term that must have been agreed: *Mears v Safecar Security Ltd*. In that case, it was suggested at 80–81 and 653 per Stephenson LJ that, in the unlikely event of there being no reliable evidence, the tribunal may have to 'invent' such a term, in order to discharge its duty under what is now the Employment Rights Act 1996 s 11 (see PARA 125). This was subsequently said to be an overstatement in *Eagland v British Telecommunications plc* [1993] ICR 644, [1992] IRLR 323, CA (cited in PARA 119 note 8). See also *Perkins v Southern Cross Healthcare Co Ltd* [2010] EWCA Civ 1442, [2011] ICR 285, [2011] IRLR 247 (although it might be regrettable that an employment tribunal lacks jurisdiction to construe written statements of particulars of employment made pursuant to the Employment Rights Act 1996, that was the consequence of ss 11, 12, coupled with the unwillingness of successive governments to broaden the contractual jurisdiction of employment tribunals).

6 Ie a reference under the Employment Rights Act 1996 s 11(2) (regarding a statement purporting to be a statement under s 1 (statement of initial employment particulars: see PARAS 119–120) or s 4 (statement of changes: see PARA 121), or a statement purporting to comply with the requirements of s 8 or s 9 (see PARA 124): see PARA 125): see s 12(2) (as amended: see note 1).

7 See the Employment Rights Act 1996 s 12(2) (as amended: see note 1). See note 5. At one time it was queried whether, on this rather tortuous drafting, there was a power to amend an inaccurate statement (*Construction Industry Training Board v Leighton* [1978] 2 All ER 723, sub nom *Leighton v Construction Industry Training Board* [1978] ICR 577, EAT; *Brown v*

Stuart Scott & Co [1981] ICR 166, EAT); but it was held by the Court of Appeal in *Mears v Safecar Security Ltd* [1983] QB 54, [1982] ICR 626, CA, that such a gap does not exist, the power to amend an inaccurate statement being contained in a combination of what are now the Employment Rights Act 1996 s 11(2) (see PARA 125) and s 12(2).

8   Ie on a reference under the Employment Rights Act 1996 s 11 (see PARA 125): see s 12(3) (as amended: see note 1).

9   Ie in accordance with the Employment Rights Act 1996 s 8 (see PARA 124): see s 12(3) (as amended: see note 1).

10 Ie by the Employment Rights Act 1996 s 8 or s 9 (see PARA 124): see s 12(3) (as amended: see note 1).

11 See the Employment Rights Act 1996 s 12(3) (as amended: see note 1). See note 5.

12 For these purposes, a deduction is an 'unnotified deduction' if it is made without the employer giving the employee, in any pay statement or standing statement of fixed deductions, the particulars of that deduction required by the Employment Rights Act 1996 s 8 or s 9 (see PARA 124): see s 12(5). The tribunal may thus disallow, and order payment of, an unnotified deduction, even though the employer was otherwise entitled to make it: *Milsom v Leicestershire County Council* [1978] IRLR 433; *Scott v Creager* [1979] ICR 403, [1979] IRLR 162, EAT.

The powers under the Employment Rights Act 1996 s 12(3) (see the text and notes 8–11), s 12(4) (see also the text to notes 13–15) are not affected by the provisions of Pt II (ss 13–27) (protection of wages: see PARA 254 et seq); but the aggregate of any amounts ordered to be paid under s 12(4) and s 24 (see PARA 260) in respect of any particular deduction may not exceed the amount of that deduction: see s 26; and PARA 259.

13 For these purposes, 'week' means, in relation to an employee whose remuneration is calculated weekly by a week ending with a day other than Saturday, a week ending with that other day, and, in relation to any other employee, a week ending with Saturday: see the Employment Rights Act 1996 s 235(1) (definition amended by the Employment Act 2002 s 53, Sch 7 paras 24, 48(1), (3)). This definition does not apply for the purposes of the Employment Rights Act 1996 s 80A (regulations in relation to paternity leave upon birth: see PARA 368) or s 80B (regulations in relation to paternity leave upon adoption: see PARA 369), s 86 (minimum period of notice: see PARA 736) or Pt XIV Ch I (ss 210–219) (continuous employment: see PARA 130 et seq): see s 235(1) (definition of 'week' as so amended).

14 As to the meaning of 'contract of employment' see PARA 2.

15 Employment Rights Act 1996 s 12(4). See note 12.

127. Sanctions for failure to comply with statutory employment protections.

If, in the case of proceedings before an employment tribunal[1] relating to a claim by an employee[2] under specified jurisdictions[3]:

  (1)   the employment tribunal finds in favour of the employee, but makes no award to him in respect of the claim to which the proceedings relate[4]; and

  (2)   when the proceedings were begun the employer was in breach of his duty to give a written statement of initial employment particulars[5], or of particulars of change[6], to the employee[7],

the tribunal must[8] make an award of the minimum amount[9] to be paid by the employer to the employee and may, if it considers it just and equitable in all the circumstances, award the higher amount[10] instead[11].

If, in the case of such proceedings:

  (a)   the employment tribunal makes an award to the employee in respect of the claim to which the proceedings relate[12]; and

  (b)   when the proceedings were begun, the employer was in breach of his duty to give a written statement of initial employment particulars[13], or of particulars of change[14], to the employee[15],

the tribunal must[16] increase the award by the minimum amount[17] and may, if it considers it just and equitable in all the circumstances, increase the award by the higher amount[18] instead[19].

1   As to employment tribunals see PARA 1399 et seq; and as to the procedure on a complaint made to an employment tribunal see PARA 1453 et seq.

2   As to the meaning of 'employee' see PARA 2.

3   See the Employment Act 2002 s 38(1), (2). The jurisdictions referred to in the text are any listed in s 38(1), Sch 5 (amended by the Tax Credits Act 2002 s 60, Sch 6; the Employment Relations Act 2004 s 57(1), Sch 1 para 43; the Equality Act 2010 s 211, Sch 26 Pt 1 para 49(1)–(3), Sch 27 Pt 1 (Sch 26 amended, Sch 27 Pt 1 substituted, by SI 2010/2279); SI 2003/1660; SI 2006/1031; SI 2006/2059; SI 2007/30; SI 2007/2974; and SI 2008/1660): see the Employment Act 2002 s 38(1). The Secretary of State may by order: (1) amend Sch 5 for the purpose of adding a jurisdiction to or removing a jurisdiction from the list in Sch 5 (s 38(8)(a)); (2) make provision, in relation to a jurisdiction listed in Sch 5, for s 38 not to apply to proceedings relating to claims of a description specified in the order (s 38(8)(b)); (3) make provision for s 38 to apply, with or without modifications, as if any individual of a description specified in the order who would not otherwise be an employee for the purposes of s 38 were an employee for those purposes, and as if a person of a description specified in the order were, in the case of any such individual, the individual's employer for those purposes (s 38(8)(c)). As to the Secretary of State see PARA 5 note 21. As to the making of orders under the Employment Act 2002 see PARA 85 note 2. In exercise of the powers conferred on him by s 38(8) (*inter alia*), the Secretary of State has made the Employment Act 2002 (Amendment of Schedules 3, 4 and 5) Order 2007, SI 2007/30, accordingly. As to the relationship of the Employment Act 2002 s 38 with the Trade Union and Labour Relations (Consolidation) Act 1992 s 207A see PARA 1234.

4   Employment Act 2002 s 38(2)(a).

5   Ie his duty to the employee under the Employment Rights Act 1996 s 1(1) (see PARA 119): see the Employment Act 2002 s 38(2)(b).

6   Ie his duty to the employee under the Employment Rights Act 1996 s 4(1) (see PARA 121): see the Employment Act 2002 s 38(2)(b).

7   Employment Act 2002 s 38(2)(b).

8   Ie subject to the Employment Act 2002 s 38(5): see s 38(2). Accordingly, the duty under s 38(2) does not apply if there are exceptional circumstances which would make an award or increase unjust or inequitable: see s 38(5).

9   For these purposes, references to the minimum amount are references to an amount equal to two weeks' pay: see the Employment Act 2002 s 38(4)(a). The amount of a week's pay of an employee must: (1) be calculated for these purposes in accordance with the Employment Rights Act 1996 Pt XIV Ch II (ss 220–229) (calculation of a week's pay: see PARA 143 et seq) (Employment Act 2002 s 38(6)(a)); and (2) not exceed the amount for the time being specified in the Employment Rights Act 1996 s 227 (maximum amount of week's pay) (see PARA 147) (Employment Act 2002 s 38(6)(b)). For the purposes of the Employment Rights Act 1996 Pt XIV Ch II as so applied, the calculation date is taken to be: (a) if the employee was employed by the employer on the date the proceedings were begun, that date (Employment Act 2002 s 38(7)(a)); and (b) if he was not, the effective date of termination as defined by the Employment Rights Act 1996 s 97 (see PARA 764) (Employment Act 2002 s 38(7)(b)).

10 For these purposes, references to the higher amount are references to an amount equal to four weeks' pay: see the Employment Act 2002 s 38(4)(b). As to a week's pay see note 9.

11 Employment Act 2002 s 38(2).

12 Employment Act 2002 s 38(3)(a).

13 Ie his duty to the employee under the Employment Rights Act 1996 s 1(1) (see PARA 119): see the Employment Act 2002 s 38(3)(b).

14 Ie his duty to the employee under the Employment Rights Act 1996 s 4(1) (see PARA 121): see the Employment Act 2002 s 38(3)(b).

15 Employment Act 2002 s 38(3)(b).

16 Ie subject to the Employment Act 2002 s 38(5): see s 38(3). Accordingly, the duty under s 38(3) does not apply if there are exceptional circumstances which would make an award or increase unjust or inequitable: see s 38(5).

17 For these purposes, references to the minimum amount are references to an amount equal to two weeks' pay: see the Employment Act 2002 s 38(4)(a).

18 For these purposes, references to the higher amount are references to an amount equal to four weeks' pay: see the Employment Act 2002 s 38(4)(b). As to a week's pay see note 9.

19 See the Employment Act 2002 s 38(3).

(vi) Apprenticeship Agreements

128. Form of apprenticeship agreements and parties. At common law, under an apprenticeship agreement, a person is bound to another for the purpose of learning a trade or calling, the apprentice undertaking for an agreed period[1] to serve his master for the purpose of being taught, and the master undertaking to teach the apprentice and either to maintain the apprentice or pay his wages[2].

Technical words are not necessary to effect an apprenticeship agreement[3]. However, an apprenticeship agreement is unenforceable if it is not in writing[4]. Because of its particular characteristics, apprenticeship does not come within the law of master and servant (or employer and employee), and an apprenticeship agreement is not, therefore, a contract of service[5].

An apprentice cannot be bound without his own consent[6]; and consent without execution of the agreement is insufficient[7]. The agreement must be executed by the apprentice himself for no-one else has the right to bind him[8]. In the case of a minor his parent or guardian, although not necessarily parties to the agreement[9], usually execute it too in order to covenant for the apprentice's due performance of the agreement since, in the absence of a local custom[10], an apprentice who is a minor cannot be sued on his own covenant[11]. An apprenticeship agreement is binding on a minor only if it is on the whole beneficial to him[12].

It is not essential that the master should execute an apprenticeship agreement[13]; but, where a master had in fact executed one part of an apprenticeship agreement, a recital in that part of the agreement that the apprentice had bound himself apprentice to the master was evidence against the master that the apprentice had executed the other part of the agreement[14]. A corporation may take an apprentice[15].

1　An apprenticeship agreement is not terminable at will as a contract of employment is at common law: *Wallace v CA Roofing Services Ltd* [1996] IRLR 435. See also *Whitely v Marton Electrical Ltd* [2003] ICR 495, [2003] IRLR 197, EAT (a 'modern apprenticeship pact' under which the employer agrees to employ the apprentice 'for the duration of the training plan' is not terminable on notice). As to covenants in apprenticeship agreements see PARA 129. As to the position of apprentices and youth trainees at common law see also PARAS 112, 636, 747–754. As to the statutory law on apprenticeships see EDUCATION vol 35 (2011) PARA 682 et seq.

2　*R v Laindon Inhabitants* (1799) 8 Term Rep 379; *R v Crediton Inhabitants* (1831) 2 B & Ad 493; *Horan v Hayhoe* [1904] 1 KB 288, DC. See also PARA 112. As to the special requirements which apply in the case of contracts for trainee solicitors see LEGAL PROFESSIONS vol 65 (2008) PARA 651 et seq. As to the application of the National Minimum Wage Act 1998 to workers participating in a traineeship in England see PARA 195.

3　*R v Rainham Inhabitants* (1801) 1 East 531. It is not essential that the word 'apprentice' should be used: *R v Laindon Inhabitants* (1799) 8 Term Rep 379. In the City of London, apprenticeship agreements should, in observance of custom, be enrolled: *Code v Holmes* (1623) Palm 361. In a field of employment in which traditional apprenticeships are still to be found, the word 'apprenticeship' will ordinarily carry with it the legal connotations of such an agreement. While it is possible to create a contract which is otherwise one of apprenticeship but is subject to a provision for termination on the ground of redundancy, it would require clear words to produce that result once the contract has been characterised within an industrial context as one of apprenticeship. Merely to remark in the course of concluding an agreement for an apprenticeship that it can be terminated during its currency on the ground of redundancy would not be sufficient: *Wallace v CA Roofing Services Ltd* [1996] IRLR 435. See also *Whitely v Marton Electrical Ltd* [2003] ICR 495, [2003] IRLR 197, EAT (uncertainty as to when a modern 'apprenticeship pact' would in fact end did not connote any conceptual uncertainty so as to make the pact unenforceable).

4　See *Kirkby v Taylor* [1910] 1 KB 529, DC; *McDonald v John Twiname Ltd* [1953] 2 QB 304, [1953] 2 All ER 589, CA. In *Wallace v CA Roofing Services Ltd* [1996] IRLR 435, there was held to be no written apprenticeship agreement but the plaintiff's written statement of terms and conditions stated that his job title was 'apprentice sheet metalworker' and also included a provision that 'at the end of your apprenticeship your employment will terminate unless there is a suitable vacancy that we can offer you at the time'.

5　*Horan v Hayhoe* [1904] 1 KB 288, DC. The terminology of 'master' and 'servant' has been replaced by that of 'employer' and 'employee' in the same way that 'contract of service' has been replaced by 'contract of employment' (see PARA 1 note 1). As to the meanings of 'contract of employment', 'employee', 'employer', and 'employment', in relation to employment rights generally, see PARA 2.

6   *R v Arnesby Inhabitants* (1820) 3 B & Ald 584.

7   *R v Ripon Inhabitants* (1808) 9 East 295.

8   *R v Margram Inhabitants* (1793) 5 Term Rep 153; *R v Cromford Inhabitants* (1806) 8 East 25; *R v Arnesby Inhabitants* (1820) 3 B & Ald 584; *R v Chillesford Inhabitants, R v Winslow Inhabitants* (1825) 4 B & C 94; *St Nicholas, Rochester, Churchwardens and Overseers v St Botolph-without-Bishopsgate Churchwardens and Overseers* (1862) 12 CBNS 645. If the apprentice is illiterate, someone else may sign for him: *R v Longnor Inhabitants* (1833) 4 B & Ad 647.

9   *R v Arundel Inhabitants* (1816) 5 M & S 257.

10 By the custom of the City of London, an apprentice who is a minor above the age of 14 can bind himself by the covenants in his apprenticeship agreement: *Stanton's Case* (1583) Moore KB 135; *Horn v Chandler* (1670) 1 Mod Rep 271.

11 *Walker v Nicholson* (1599) Cro Eliz 652; *Whittingham v Hill* (1618) Cro Jac 494; *Gylbert v Fletcher* (1629) Cro Car 179; *Lylly's Case* (1702) 7 Mod Rep 15; *Branch v Ewington* (1780) 2 Doug KB 518; *De Francesco v Barnum* (1889) 43 ChD 165 at 171. An exception to the rule is the case of a covenant which takes effect only after the expiration of the term of the apprenticeship: *Gadd v Thompson* [1911] 1 KB 304, DC.

12 As to the general principles for construing contracts with minors see PARA 15. Although seven years was mentioned in *R v Saltren* (1784) Cald Mag Cas 444 as the minimum age at which an apprentice could be bound, there appears to be no common law rule about this. As to the statutory restrictions on the employment of children see CHILDREN AND YOUNG PERSONS vol 10 (2012) PARA 705 et seq.

13 *R v St Peter's-on-the-Hill* (1741) 2 Bott (6th Edn) 394; *R v Fleet* (1777) 2 Bott (6th Edn) 396; *McDonald v John Twiname Ltd* [1953] 2 QB 304, [1953] 2 All ER 589, CA; and see DEEDS AND OTHER INSTRUMENTS vol 32 (2012) PARA 262.

14 *Burleigh v Stibbs* (1793) 5 Term Rep 465.

15 See CORPORATIONS vol 24 (2010) PARA 471.

129. Covenants in apprenticeship agreements. At common law, covenants entered into by the master, and also those entered into on behalf of or, where there is a special custom, by the minor, are mutual and independent, entitling each party to his remedy for a breach of them[1]. The covenants by the parent are not released by the minor electing not to be bound by the apprenticeship agreement[2]; but they may be released by a change in the circumstances of the master[3]. A parent who enters into a covenant on behalf of a minor apprentice is liable for a breach of the covenant committed after the apprentice has attained full age[4]. The master is not released by misconduct on the part of the apprentice if it is only slight[5]; but he is released if it is of a gross character and causes him actual injury or renders it impossible for him to fulfil his part of the agreement[6]. The master is liable in damages if he changes his place of business or otherwise alters the circumstances to the detriment of the apprentice[7].

1   *Winstone v Linn* (1823) 1 B & C 460 at 467 per Bayley J; *Waterman v Fryer* [1922] 1 KB 499 at 503 per Horridge J. As to the form of apprenticeship agreements, and parties to them, see PARA 128. As to the position of apprentices and youth trainees at common law see also PARAS 112, 636, 747–754. As to the statutory law on apprenticeships see EDUCATION vol 35 (2011) PARA 682 et seq.

2   *Cuming v Hill* (1819) 3 B & Ald 59. The minor may so elect on attaining full age (*Ex p Davis* (1794) 5 Term Rep 715; *Wray v West* (1866) 15 LT 180) but does not do so merely by absenting himself from the service (*Gray v Cookson* (1812) 16 East 13).

3   *Ellen v Topp* (1851) 6 Exch 424. Where an apprentice is bound to two masters, it is a question of construction of the apprenticeship agreement whether he remains bound to one after they have dissolved the partnership: *Lloyd v Blackburn* (1842) 9 M & W 363; *Popham v Jones* (1853) 13 CB 225; *Brook v Dawson* (1869) 20 LT 611; *Couchman v Sillar* (1870) 18 WR 757; *Eaton v Western* (1882) 9 QBD 636, CA.

4   *Cuming v Hill* (1819) 3 B & Ald 59.

5   *Winstone v Linn* (1823) 1 B & C 460; *Wise v Wilson* (1845) 1 Car & Kir 662 at 669; *Phillips v Clift* (1859) 4 H & N 168.

6   *Hughes v Humphreys* (1827) 6 B & C 680; *Wise v Wilson* (1845) 1 Car & Kir 662; *Cox v Mathews* (1861) 2 F & F 397; *Raymond v Minton* (1866) LR 1 Exch 244; *Westwick v Theodor* (1875) LR 10 QB 224; *Learoyd v Brook* [1891] 1 QB 431; *Waterman v Fryer* [1922] 1 KB 499.

7   *Eaton v Western* (1882) 9 QBD 636, CA, overruling *Royce v Charlton* (1881) 8 QBD 1.

(3) CONTINUITY OF EMPLOYMENT

(i) Computation of Period of Continuous Employment; in general

130. Computation of period of continuous employment. Unless the contrary is shown, a person's employment[1] during any period is presumed to have been continuous[2]; and any week[3] during the whole or part of which an employee's[4] relations with his employer[5] is governed by a contract of employment[6] counts in computing the employee's period of employment[7], but a week which does not count in computing the length of a period of continuous employment[8] breaks[9] continuity of employment[10].

In computing an employee's period of continuous employment for the purposes of any provision of the Employment Rights Act 1996[11], any question:

  (1)   whether the employee's employment is of a kind counting towards a period of continuous employment[12]; or

  (2)   whether periods (consecutive or otherwise) are to be treated as forming a single period of continuous employment[13],

must be determined week by week[14]. However, where it is necessary to compute the length of an employee's period of employment it must be computed in months and years of 12 months in accordance with the following provisions[15], namely:

  (a)   an employee's period of continuous employment for the purposes of any provision of the Employment Rights Act 1996 begins, subject to head (b) below, with the day on which the employee starts work, and it ends with the day by reference to which the length of the employee's period of continuous employment is to be ascertained for the purposes of the statutory provision in question[16]; and

  (b)   if an employee's period of continuous employment includes one or more periods which[17], while not counting in computing the length of the period, do not break continuity of employment, the beginning of the period is treated as postponed by the number of days falling within that intervening period[18], or by the aggregate number of days falling within those periods, calculated in accordance with the statutory provision in question[19].

The provisions of the Employment Rights Act 1996 that govern computation of a period of continuous employment[20]: (i) apply[21] to a period of employment even where during that period the employee was engaged in work wholly or mainly outside Great Britain[22]; and (ii) apply even where the employee was excluded by or under the Employment Rights Act 1996 from any right conferred thereby[23].

1   As to the meaning of 'employment' see PARA 2.

2   Employment Rights Act 1996 s 210(5). The burden is, therefore, on the employer to show that continuity was not present or was broken: *Nicoll v Nocorrode Ltd* [1981] ICR 348, [1981] IRLR 163, EAT. If, however, the employer can establish a break, there is no continuity even if the employer has deliberately arranged the break: *Booth v United States of America* [1999] IRLR 16, EAT. The presumption does not, however, apply in the case of a transfer of business

under the Employment Rights Act 1996 s 218(2) (see PARA 135): *Secretary of State for Employment v Cohen* [1987] ICR 570, [1987] IRLR 169, EAT. Continuity of employment is significant in the context of statutory rights, e g unfair dismissal, where, except in a case where the Employment Rights Act 1996 s 108(3) (see PARA 758 note 9) applies, an employee must have been employed continuously for a period of not less than two year before he may claim unfair dismissal: see s 108(1); and PARA 758.

3   For the purposes of the Employment Rights Act 1996 Pt XIV Ch I (ss 210–219) (continuous employment: see also PARAS 131 et seq, 861 et seq), 'week' means a week ending with Saturday: see s 235(1). Cf PARA 126 note 13.

4   As to the meaning of 'employee' see PARA 2.

5   As to the meaning of 'employer' see PARA 2.

6   As to the meaning of 'contract of employment' see PARA 2.

7   See the Employment Rights Act 1996 s 212(1). This statutory rule is to be applied as it stands and not subject to any glosses: *Carrington v Harwich Dock Co Ltd* [1998] ICR 1112, [1998] IRLR 567, EAT; *Sweeney v J & S Henderson (Concessions) Ltd* [1999] IRLR 306, EAT (disapproving *Roach v CSB (Moulds) Ltd* [1991] ICR 349, [1991] IRLR 200, EAT).

8   Ie under the Employment Rights Act 1996 ss 211–219 (see also PARA 131 et seq): see s 210(4).

9   Ie except so far as otherwise provided in the Employment Rights Act 1996 ss 215–217 (see PARAS 132, 134, 863): see s 210(4).

10 See the Employment Rights Act 1996 s 210(4). Continuity of employment is an entirely statutory concept, not to be supplemented or detracted from by the parties' own intentions or understandings, or by arguments on Parliamentary intent: *Morris v Walsh Western UK Ltd* [1997] IRLR 562, EAT; *Collison v BBC* [1998] ICR 669, [1998] IRLR 238, EAT. The corollary of the principle in the Employment Rights Act 1996 s 210(4) is that, where an employee's employment does consist of consecutive counting weeks, his employment is continuous even if events have happened which would otherwise have broken continuity, e g one job ending and another beginning the next week: *Loggie v Alexander Hall & Son (Builders) Ltd* (1969) 4 ITR 390; *Wood v York City Council* [1978] ICR 840, [1978] IRLR 228, CA; *Jennings v Salford Community Service Agency* [1981] ICR 399, [1981] IRLR 76, EAT; *Tipper v Roofdec Ltd* [1989] IRLR 419, EAT. See also note 2.

11 See the Employment Rights Act 1996 s 210(3). References in any provision of the Employment Rights Act 1996 to a period of continuous employment are, unless provision is expressly made to the contrary, references to a period computed in accordance with the provisions of Pt XIV Ch I (continuous employment: see also PARAS 131 et seq, 861 et seq) (s 210(1)); and, in any such provision which refers to a period of continuous employment expressed in months or years, a 'month' means a calendar month, and a 'year' means a year of 12 calendar months (s 210(2)). As to the rules on continuity of employment for the purposes of statutory maternity pay see PARA 415 et seq. See also note 2.

12 Employment Rights Act 1996 s 210(3)(a). See also note 2.

13 Employment Rights Act 1996 s 210(3)(b). See also note 2.

14 See the Employment Rights Act 1996 s 210(3). See also note 2.

15 See the Employment Rights Act 1996 s 210(3). The text refers to computation in accordance with s 211 (see heads (a), (b) in the text): see s 210(3). See also note 2.

16 See the Employment Rights Act 1996 s 211(1) (amended by SI 2006/1031). The period starts on commencement of the contract of employment, not necessarily when the employee actually starts performing work under it (which could be later): *General of the Salvation Army v Dewsbury* [1984] ICR 498, [1984] IRLR 222, EAT. See also note 2.

17 Ie by virtue of any provision of the Employment Rights Act 1996 s 215, s 216 or s 217 (see PARAS 132, 134, 863): see s 211(3).

18 The number of days falling within such an intervening period is: (1) in the case of a period to which the Employment Rights Act 1996 s 215 applies, seven days for each week within s 215(3) (see s 215(3); and PARA 863); (2) in the case of a period to which s 216 applies, the number of days between the last working day before the strike or lockout and the day on which work was resumed (see s 216(2), (3); and PARA 134); (3) in the case of a period to which s 217 applies, the number of days between the employee's last day of employment with the employer (or, if there was more than one such period, the last of them) and the first day of the period of employment beginning in the six-month period mentioned in s 217(1) (see s 217(2); and PARA 132 note 6).

19 Employment Rights Act 1996 s 211(3). See also note 2.

20 Ie the Employment Rights Act 1996 Pt XIV Ch I (continuous employment: see also PARAS 131 et seq, 861 et seq): see s 215(1).

21 Ie subject to the Employment Rights Act 1996 s 215(2)–(6) (see PARA 863): see s 215(1)(a).

22 Employment Rights Act 1996 s 215(1)(a). See also note 2. As to the meaning of 'Great Britain'
    see PARA 2 note 12.
23 Employment Rights Act 1996 s 215(1)(b). See also note 2.

**131.   Weeks counting in computing the period in cases of incapacity or
absence.**   Any week[1] during the whole or part of which an employee[2] is:

(1)   incapable of work in consequence of sickness or injury[3]; or
(2)   absent from work[4] on account of a temporary cessation of work[5]; or
(3)   absent from work[6] in circumstances such that, by arrangement or
        custom, he is regarded as continuing in the employment[7] of his
        employer[8] for any purpose[9],

counts in computing the employee's period of employment[10]. However, not more
than 26 weeks count under head (1) above between any periods falling within
the general statutory provision[11] for computing a period of continuous
employment[12].

1   As to the meaning of 'week' for these purposes see PARA 130 note 3. This means a week not
    falling under the general rule in the Employment Rights Act 1996 s 212(1): see PARA 130.
2   As to the meaning of 'employee' see PARA 2.
3   Employment Rights Act 1996 s 212(3)(a). The absence must be connected with sickness or
    injury: *Kolatsis v Rockware Glass Ltd* [1974] 3 All ER 555, [1974] ICR 580, NIRC; *Scarlett v
    Godfrey Abbott Group Ltd* [1978] ICR 1106, [1978] IRLR 456, EAT; *Pearson v Kent County
    Council* [1993] IRLR 165, CA. The requirement is only that the employee is unfit for *that* work,
    and so the Employment Rights Act 1996 s 212(3)(a) can apply if the employee has taken lighter
    work during the gap: *Donnelly v Kelvin International Services* [1992] IRLR 496, EAT. Weeks
    counting under the Employment Rights Act 1996 s 212(3)(a) may count against a transferee
    employer if the business is transferred during the absence: *Green v Wavertree Heating and
    Plumbing Co Ltd* [1978] ICR 928, EAT.
4   'Absent from work' merely means away from work: *Fitzgerald v Hall, Russell & Co Ltd* [1970]
    AC 984, [1969] 3 All ER 1140, HL; *Ford v Warwickshire County Council* [1983] 2 AC 71,
    [1983] 1 All ER 753, [1983] ICR 273, HL. A definite intention of the parties to end the
    employment, eg a dismissal or resignation meant to be final, but followed shortly in fact by a
    re-engagement of the employee, may mean that head (2) in the text does not apply: *Clark v
    Blairs Ltd* (1966) 1 ITR 545; *Todd v Sun Ventilating Co Ltd* [1975] IRLR 4; *McAree v GKN
    Sankey Ltd* [1976] IRLR 58, DC. However, where, as usual, that is not the case, the fact that the
    employee takes a job temporarily, eg during a period when laid off, will not prevent him from
    being absent from work on account of a temporary cessation of work: *Thompson v Bristol
    Channel Ship Repairers and Engineers Ltd* (1970) 5 ITR 85, CA; *Bentley Engineering Co Ltd v
    Crown, Bentley Engineering Co Ltd v Miller* [1976] ICR 225, [1976] IRLR 146, DC.
5   Employment Rights Act 1996 s 212(3)(b) (s 212(3)(b), (c) amended by the Employment
    Relations Act 1999 ss 9, 44, Sch 4 Pt III paras 1, 5, 38(1), (3), Sch 9). See also note 3.
        For the Employment Rights Act 1996 s 212(3)(b) to apply, there must be a temporary
    cessation of work, in the sense that the quantum of work has ceased to be available, at least as
    respects the employee in question; and it is not sufficient merely that the employee is temporarily
    absent from work: *Fitzgerald v Hall, Russell & Co Ltd* [1970] AC 984, [1969] 3 All ER
    1140, HL; *Byrne v Birmingham City District Council* [1987] ICR 519, [1987] IRLR 191, CA;
    Letheby & Christopher Ltd v Bond [1988] ICR 480, EAT; and see *Welton v Deluxe Retail Ltd
    (t/a Madhouse) (in administration)* [2013] ICR 428, [2013] IRLR 166, EAT (the first question in
    any case where there is an interval to be bridged is whether in fact there was a sufficient break
    between contracts; a contract of employment can arise before any contractual duty to work
    arises, eg between the ending of employment with an employer at one business which had closed
    down and starting work with the same employer at another); *quaere* whether *Bentley
    Engineering Co Ltd v Crown, Bentley Engineering Co Ltd v Miller* [1976] ICR 225, [1976]
    IRLR 146, DC, is wrong on this point. Normally the Employment Rights Act 1996 s 212(3)(b)
    will, therefore, cover events in the nature of a lay-off due to some involuntary suspension of the
    employer's normal operations: see eg *Hunter v Smiths Dock Co Ltd* [1968] 2 All ER 81, [1968]
    1 WLR 1865; *Fitzgerald v Hall, Russell & Co Ltd*; *Newsham v Dunlop Textiles Ltd (No 2)*
    (1969) 4 ITR 268, DC; *McCartney v Sir Robert McAlpine & Sons Ltd* (1967) 2 ITR 399. If the
    work is not available, the Employment Rights Act 1996 s 212(3)(b) is potentially applicable,
    without the tribunal investigating the reason for the lack of work: *University of Aston in*

Birmingham v Malik [1984] ICR 492, EAT. If, however, the work is available but the employer chooses not to give it to a particular employee, the Employment Rights Act 1996 s 212(3)(b) will not apply: *Booth v United States of America* [1999] IRLR 16, EAT. Whether the cessation of work was 'temporary' is to be looked at after the event, with the benefit of hindsight; 'temporary' merely means 'transient' and is to be considered in all the circumstances: *Fitzgerald v Hall, Russell & Co Ltd*; *Ford v Warwickshire County Council* [1983] 2 AC 71, [1983] 1 All ER 753, [1983] ICR 273, HL; *Flack v Kodak Ltd* [1986] 2 All ER 1003, [1986] ICR 775, CA; and see *Hussain v Acorn Independent College Ltd* [2011] IRLR 463, EAT (if the first contract of employment ended because of a temporary cessation of work (in this case, caused effectively by the college's summer vacation), and the claimant is employed again, then the case falls under the Employment Rights Act 1996 s 212(3)(b)).

The Employment Rights Act 1996 s 212(3)(b) can apply even where the temporary cessations of work are:

(1)   foreseeable, predictable or even regular (*Ford v Warwickshire County Council* (overruling *Rashid v ILEA* [1977] ICR 157, EAT; and probably impliedly overruling *Ryan v Shipboard Maintenance Ltd* [1980] ICR 88, [1980] IRLR 16, EAT)); or

(2)   highly irregular, over a considerable period (*Flack v Kodak Ltd*).

Where a tribunal is considering a case of regular gaps, it may be appropriate to determine whether the gaps are temporary by adopting a mathematical approach (suggested by Lord Diplock in *Ford v Warwickshire County Council*, ie by contrasting the length of a gap with the length of the periods of employment on either side of it; and see *Berwick Salmon Fisheries Co Ltd v Rutherford* [1991] IRLR 203, EAT); but when considering a case of irregular gaps, such a mathematical approach can produce illogical results and so it may be appropriate to adopt a 'broad brush' approach of putting the gaps into the whole employment history (as done by the Court of Appeal in *Flack v Kodak Ltd*): *Sillars v Charrington Fuels Ltd* [1989] ICR 475, [1989] IRLR 152, CA (mathematical approach appropriate on the facts).

See also *Prater v Cornwall County Council* [2006] EWCA Civ 102, [2006] 2 All ER 1013, [2006] ICR 731, [2006] IRLR 362 (a succession of individual contracts for work in providing tuition within each of which there was mutuality of obligation relating to the work provided and performed under that contract could be contracts of employment with the necessary continuity despite the fact that there was no continuing or further obligation on the one party to offer more work or on the other party to accept the work).

6   See note 4.

7   As to the meaning of 'employment' see PARA 2.

8   As to the meaning of 'employer' see PARA 2.

9   Employment Rights Act 1996 s 212(3)(c) (as amended: see note 5). It has been held that head (3) in the text applies only where there is no subsisting contract (see note 10); but, if the contract subsists (eg in a lent servant case such as *Wishart v National Coal Board* [1974] ICR 460, NIRC; cf *Southern Electricity Board v Collins* [1970] 1 QB 83, [1969] 2 All ER 1166), the employee may be able to claim continuity under the general rules, especially under the Employment Rights Act 1996 s 212(1) (see PARA 130): *Puttick v John Wright & Sons (Blackwall) Ltd* [1972] ICR 457, NIRC. See also note 3.

For the Employment Rights Act 1996 s 212(3)(c) to apply, there must be some 'arrangement or custom' by which both the employer and the employee regard the employee as continuing in employment in that week: *Moore v James Clarkson & Co Ltd* (1970) 5 ITR 298; *Taylor v Triumph Motors, British Leyland UK Ltd and Secretary of State for Employment* [1975] IRLR 369; *Curr v Marks & Spencer plc* [2002] EWCA Civ 1852, [2003] ICR 443, [2003] IRLR 74, [2002] All ER (D) 205 (Dec) ('arrangement' not found where employee extended maternity leave under a scheme which required her resignation and re-employment and she returned to work on temporary fixed-term contracts; 'for any purpose' may include eg for pension purposes). Such an arrangement or custom may be shown if the contract has ended but the employee's name has been put on some form of 'holding list': *O'Reilly v Hotpoint Ltd* (1969) 5 ITR 68, DC; *Normanton v Southalls (Birmingham) Ltd* [1975] IRLR 74. If, however, no such arrangement or custom can be shown, and the employee is not in some way regarded as carrying on in employment, the Employment Rights Act 1996 s 212(3)(c) will not apply: *Rhodes v Pontins Ltd* (1971) 6 ITR 88; *Duff v Evan Thomas Radcliffe & Co Ltd* [1979] ICR 720, EAT; *Brown v Southall & Knight* [1980] ICR 617, [1980] IRLR 130, EAT. An arrangement or custom may be particularly difficult to show where the employee was engaged on a series of single, separate contracts not constituting one overall 'global' contract: *Letheby & Christopher Ltd v Bond* [1988] ICR 480, EAT; *Booth v United States of America* [1999] IRLR 16, EAT. In *Murphy v A Birrell & Sons Ltd* [1978] IRLR 458, EAT, it was held that an ex post facto arrangement (where the employee leaves, apparently permanently, but then returns and is assured by the employer that his continuity will be treated as unbroken) is not sufficient; but cf *Taylor v*

Triumph Motors, British Leyland UK Ltd and Secretary of State for Employment; Ingram v Foxon [1984] ICR 685, [1985] IRLR 5, EAT. In *Morris v Walsh Western UK Ltd* [1997] IRLR 562, EAT, *Murphy v A Birrell & Sons Ltd* was followed in preference to *Ingram v Foxon*; but in *London Probation Board v Kirkpatrick* [2005] ICR 965, [2005] IRLR 443, sub nom *Kirkpatrick v London Probation Board* [2005] All ER (D) 148 (Feb), EAT ('arrangement' found where the employee was dismissed following a disciplinary hearing notwithstanding his successful internal appeal against the decision to dismiss), *Ingram v Foxon* was followed in preference to *Murphy v A Birrell & Sons Ltd*.

10 See the Employment Rights Act 1996 s 212(3). There is no express requirement for s 212(3) to govern the situation where no contract of employment subsists at all, but that requirement used to be contained in the cross-heading appearing over the predecessor to s 212, ie the Employment Protection (Consolidation) Act 1978 s 151, Sch 13 para 9 (repealed) ('*Periods in which there is no contract of employment*'). It was, therefore, accepted as a requirement in the leading case of *Ford v Warwickshire County Council* [1983] 2 AC 71, [1983] 1 All ER 753, [1983] ICR 273, HL (decided under the Employment Protection (Consolidation) Act 1978 Sch 13 para 9 (repealed)). In the light of this, certain earlier cases which had effectively ignored it had to be considered doubtful: see, in particular, *Jones v William Smith (Poplar) Ltd* (1969) 4 ITR 317; *Lloyds Bank Ltd v Secretary of State for Employment* [1979] 2 All ER 573, [1979] ICR 258, EAT; *Corton House Ltd v Skipper* [1981] ICR 307, [1981] IRLR 78, EAT. Now that there is no such cross-heading in the legislation, it could be argued that there is no such requirement, but conversely: (1) the Employment Rights Act 1996 was only a consolidating Act; and (2) s 212(3) is expressed to apply to a week not falling within s 212(1) (which applies where there is a subsisting contract: see PARA 130). As to the status of marginal notes see STATUTES AND LEGISLATIVE PROCESS vol 96 (2012) PARA 682.

11 Ie the Employment Rights Act 1996 s 212(1) (see PARA 130): see s 212(4) (amended by the Employment Relations Act 1999 Sch 4 Pt III paras 1, 5, 38(1), (4), Sch 9).

12 Employment Rights Act 1996 s 212(4) (as amended: see note 11).

(ii) Special Cases

132. Reinstatement after military service. If a person, entitled to apply to his former employer[1] under the Reserve Forces (Safeguard of Employment) Act 1985[2], enters his employer's employment[3] not later than the end of the six-month period after which the former employer's obligation under that Act may lawfully cease[4], his period of service in the armed forces of the Crown[5] does not break his continuity of employment[6].

1 As to the meaning of 'employer' see PARA 2.
2 Where a member of the reserve forces in permanent service under the Reserve Forces Act 1996 applies to his former employer to be taken into his employment, the former employer is obliged to employ the applicant, at the first opportunity, in the occupation which he previously held and on terms and conditions not less favourable than those which he previously enjoyed, or if this is not practicable, then in the most favourable occupation and on the most favourable terms and conditions as is reasonable and practicable: see the Reserve Forces (Safeguard of Employment) Act 1985 s 1; and ARMED FORCES vol 3 (2011) PARA 370.
3 As to the meaning of 'employment' see PARA 2.
4 Ie the period mentioned in the Reserve Forces (Safeguard of Employment) Act 1985 s 1(4)(b) (in no case is the former employer under any obligation under s 1 to take the applicant into his employment after six months have elapsed from the end of the applicant's whole-time service: see ARMED FORCES vol 3 (2011) PARA 370): see the Employment Rights Act 1996 s 217(1).
5 Ie in the circumstances specified in the Reserve Forces (Safeguard of Employment) Act 1985 s 1(1) (ie a person's 'whole-time service': see ARMED FORCES vol 3 (2011) PARA 370): see the Employment Rights Act 1996 s 217(1).
6 Employment Rights Act 1996 s 217(1). In the case of such a person, the number of days which, for the purposes of s 211(3) (see PARA 130), fall within the intervening period is the number of days between the last day of his previous period of employment with the employer (or, if there was more than one such period, the last of them) and the first day of the period of employment beginning in the six-month period: s 217(2).

133. Reinstatement or re-engagement of dismissed employee. Regulations made by the Secretary of State under the Employment Rights Act 1996[1] may make provision[2]:

(1) for preserving the continuity of a person's period of employment[3] for the purposes of those provisions of the Employment Rights Act 1996 that govern the computation of a period of continuous employment[4] (or for the purposes of those provisions as applied by or under any other enactment specified in the regulations)[5]; or

(2) for modifying or excluding the operation of the special provision made by the Employment Rights Act 1996 for redundancy payments[6] (subject to the recovery of any such payment[7] that may be made in accordance with that provision)[8],

in cases where a dismissed employee[9] is reinstated, re-engaged or otherwise re-employed by his employer or by a successor[10] or associated employer[11] of that employer in any circumstances prescribed by the regulations[12].

If, in consequence of any applicable action[13], a dismissed employee is reinstated or re-employed by his employer or by a successor or associated employer of the employer[14]: (a) the continuity of that employee's period of employment is preserved[15]; and (b) the period beginning with the date on which the dismissal takes effect and ending with the date of reinstatement or re-engagement counts in the computation of the employee's period of continuous employment[16].

1 As to the Secretary of State see PARA 5 note 21. As to the making of orders and regulations under the Employment Rights Act 1996 generally see PARA 162. As to the regulations so made see the text and notes 13–16.

2 See the Employment Rights Act 1996 s 219(1) (amended by the Employment Rights (Dispute Resolution) Act 1998 s 15, Sch 1 para 25(1), (2), Sch 2).

3 As to the meaning of 'employment' see PARA 2.

4 Ie for the purposes of the Employment Rights Act 1996 Pt XIV Ch I (ss 210–219) (continuous employment: see also PARAS 130 et seq, 134 et seq, 861 et seq): see the Employment Rights Act 1996 s 219(1)(a).

5 Employment Rights Act 1996 s 219(1)(a).

6 Ie the operation of the Employment Rights Act 1996 s 214 (see PARA 862): see s 219(1)(b).

7 Ie any such payment as is mentioned in the Employment Rights Act 1996 s 214 (see PARA 862): see s 219(1)(b).

8 Employment Rights Act 1996 s 219(1)(b).

9 As to the meaning of 'employee' see PARA 2.

10 For these purposes, except in so far as the context otherwise requires, 'successor', in relation to the employer of an employee, means a person who, in consequence of a change occurring (whether by virtue of a sale or other disposition or by operation of law) in the ownership of the undertaking, or of the part of the undertaking, for the purposes of which the employee was employed, has become the owner of the undertaking or part: see the Employment Rights Act 1996 s 235(1); and the Employment Tribunals Act 1996 s 42(1). However, that definition of 'successor' has effect (subject to the necessary modifications) in relation to a case where:

(1) the person by whom an undertaking or part of an undertaking is owned immediately before a change is one of the persons by whom (whether as partners, trustees or otherwise) it is owned immediately after the change (Employment Rights Act 1996 s 235(2)(a); Employment Tribunals Act 1996 s 42(2)(a)); or

(2) the persons by whom an undertaking or part of an undertaking is owned immediately before a change (whether as partners, trustees or otherwise) include the persons by whom, or include one or more of the persons by whom, it is owned immediately after the change, as it has effect where the previous owner and the new owner are wholly different persons (Employment Rights Act 1996 s 235(2)(b); Employment Tribunals Act 1996 s 42(2)(b)).

As to the meaning of 'employer' see PARA 2.

11 As to the meaning of 'associated employer' see PARA 3.

12 Employment Rights Act 1996 s 219(1) (as amended: see note 2). In exercise of the powers conferred on him by s 219, the Secretary of State has made the Employment Protection (Continuity of Employment) Regulations 1996, SI 1996/3147: see the text and notes 13–16. Those regulations apply also to exclude the operation of the Employment Rights Act 1996 s 214 where a redundancy payment (or an equivalent payment paid in respect of a relevant dismissal) is repaid: see PARA 862.

13 Ie any action to which the Employment Protection (Continuity of Employment) Regulations 1996, SI 1996/3147, apply: see reg 3(2). The Employment Protection (Continuity of Employment) Regulations 1996, SI 1996/3147, apply to any action taken in relation to the dismissal of an employee which consists of (see reg 2):

    (1)   his making a claim in accordance with a dismissal procedures agreement designated by an order under the Employment Rights Act 1996 s 110 (see PARAS 759, 760) (Employment Protection (Continuity of Employment) Regulations 1996, SI 1996/3147, reg 2(a));

    (2)   the presentation by him of a relevant complaint of dismissal (reg 2(b));

    (3)   any action taken by a conciliation officer under any of the Employment Tribunals Act 1996 ss 18A–18C (requirement to contact ACAS before instituting proceedings: see PARAS 152, 153) (Employment Protection (Continuity of Employment) Regulations 1996, SI 1996/3147, reg 2(c) (amended by the Employment Rights (Dispute Resolution) Act 1998 s 1(2)(c); SI 2001/1188; SI 2014/386));

    (4)   the making of a relevant settlement agreement (see PARA 151) (Employment Protection (Continuity of Employment) Regulations 1996, SI 1996/3147, reg 2(d) (amended by SI 2001/1188; SI 2004/752; SI 2013/1956));

    (5)   the making of an agreement to submit a dispute to arbitration in accordance with a scheme having effect by virtue of an order under the Trade Union and Labour Relations (Consolidation) Act 1992 s 212A (see PARA 824) (Employment Protection (Continuity of Employment) Regulations 1996, SI 1996/3147, reg 2(e) (added by SI 2001/1188; and amended by SI 2004/752));

    (6)   a decision taken arising out of the use of a statutory dispute resolution procedure contained in the Employment Act 2002 s 29, Sch 2 (repealed) in a case where, in accordance with the Employment Act 2002 (Dispute Resolution) Regulations 2004, SI 2004/752 (revoked), such a procedure applies (Employment Protection (Continuity of Employment) Regulations 1996, SI 1996/3147, reg 2(f) (added by SI 2004/752; and amended by SI 2006/1031)); or

    (7)   a decision arising out of the statutory duty to consider procedure contained in the Employment Equality (Age) Regulations 2006, SI 2006/1031, Sch 6 (revoked) (Employment Protection (Continuity of Employment) Regulations 1996, SI 1996/3147, reg 2(g) (added by SI 2006/1031)).

As to head (6) above now see PARA 698 et seq; and as to head (7) above see now the Equality Act 2010; and PARA 51.

14 See the Employment Protection (Continuity of Employment) Regulations 1996, SI 1996/3147, reg 3(2). The provision made by reg 3 has effect to preserve the continuity of a person's period of employment for the purposes of the Employment Rights Act 1996 Pt XIV Ch I (continuous employment: see also PARAS 130 et seq, 134, 135, 861 et seq), and for the purposes of Pt XIV Ch I as applied by the Trade Union and Labour Relations (Consolidation) Act 1992 s 282(2) for the purposes of s 282 (employment under a fixed term contract: see PARA 1194): see the Employment Protection (Continuity of Employment) Regulations 1996, SI 1996/3147, reg 3(1).

15 Employment Protection (Continuity of Employment) Regulations 1996, SI 1996/3147, reg 3(2)(a).

16 Employment Protection (Continuity of Employment) Regulations 1996, SI 1996/3147, reg 3(2)(b).

(iii) Industrial Disputes

134. Continuity in cases of strike or lockout. A week[1] does not count under the provisions of the Employment Rights Act 1996 that are used to compute the period of employment[2] if during the week, or any part of the week, the employee[3] takes part in a strike[4].

The continuity of an employee's period of employment is not, however, broken by: (1) a week which does not count[5], if during the week, or any part of the week, the employee takes part in a strike[6]; (2) a week if, during the week, or any part of the week, the employee is absent from work because of a lockout[7] by the employer[8].

1   As to the meaning of 'week' for these purposes see PARA 130 note 3.
2   Ie under the Employment Rights Act 1996 s 212 (see PARA 131): see s 216(1). As to the meaning of 'employment' see PARA 2.
3   As to the meaning of 'employee' see PARA 2.
4   Employment Rights Act 1996 s 216(1). For these purposes, 'strike' means:
     (1)   the cessation of work by a body of employed persons acting in combination (s 235(5)(a)); or
     (2)   a concerted refusal or a refusal under a common understanding of any number of employed persons to continue to work for an employer in consequence of a dispute (s 235(5)(b)),
  done as a means of compelling their employer or any employed person or body of employed persons, or to aid other employees in compelling their employer or any employed person or body of employed persons, to accept or not to accept terms or conditions of or affecting employment (see s 235(5)). As to the meaning of 'employer' see PARA 2.
5   Ie under the Employment Rights Act 1996 Pt XIV Ch I (ss 210–219) (continuous employment: see also PARAS 130 et seq, 135, 861 et seq), whether or not by virtue only of s 216(1) (see the text and notes 1–4): see s 216(2).
6   See the Employment Rights Act 1996 s 216(2). The number of days which, for the purposes of s 211(3) (see PARA 130), fall within the intervening period is the number of days between the last working day before the strike and the day on which work was resumed: see s 216(2). The provisions of s 216(1), (2) thus effect a compromise that the weeks on strike do not break continuity, but equally they do not count for continuity purposes. The preservation of continuity applies whether or not the employer dismisses during the strike: *Hanson v Fashion Industries (Hartlepool) Ltd* [1981] ICR 35, [1980] IRLR 393, EAT; *Bloomfield v Springfield Hosiery Finishing Co Ltd* [1972] 1 All ER 609, [1972] ICR 91, NIRC. If the strike ends but is followed by a period when the employee is laid off, until the business resumes, that latter period may be covered by the Employment Rights Act 1996 s 212(3)(b) (see PARA 131) as a temporary cessation of work: *Clarke Chapman-John Thompson Ltd v Walters* [1972] 1 All ER 614, [1972] ICR 83, NIRC.
7   For these purposes, 'lockout' means:
     (1)   the closing of a place of employment (Employment Rights Act 1996 s 235(4)(a));
     (2)   the suspension of work (s 235(4)(b)); or
     (3)   the refusal by an employer to continue to employ any number of persons employed by him in consequence of a dispute (s 235(4)(c)),
  done with a view to compelling persons employed by the employer, or to aid another employer in compelling persons employed by him, to accept terms or conditions of or affecting employment (see s 235(4)).
8   See the Employment Rights Act 1996 s 216(3). The number of days which, for the purposes of s 211(3) (see PARA 130), fall within the intervening period is the number of days between the last working day before the lockout and the day on which work was resumed: see s 216(3). Although s 216(3) preserves continuity, in the case of a lockout there is no equivalent of s 216(1) (see the text and notes 1–4) which expressly states that a week on strike is not to count. Thus the question whether a week locked out is to count towards a period of employment depends on the general continuity provisions. A lockout does not automatically terminate a contract of employment: *E and J Davis Transport Ltd v Chattaway* [1972] ICR 267, NIRC. If, therefore, the contract does not terminate, the relevant week or weeks will count on ordinary principles under the Employment Rights Act 1996 s 212(1) (see PARA 130); but, if the contract is actually terminated by the employer, the provisions of s 211(3) (see PARA 130) will apply, this being a case where a week does not count but does not break continuity. See also note 6.

(iv)   Change of Employer

135. Change of employer. Subject to the exceptions set out under heads (1) to (7) below, the provisions of the Employment Rights Act 1996 that govern the computation of a period of continuous employment[1] relate only to employment[2] by the one employer[3], but:

     (1)   if a trade or business[4], or an undertaking[5], is transferred from one

person to another, the period of employment of an employee[6] in the trade or business or undertaking at the time of the transfer[7] counts as a period of employment with the transferee, and the transfer does not break the continuity of the period of employment[8];

(2)   if, by or under an Act of Parliament[9], a contract of employment[10] between any body corporate and an employee is modified, and some other body corporate is substituted as the employer, the employee's period of employment at the time when the modification takes effect counts as a period of employment with the second body corporate, and the change of employer does not break the continuity of the period of employment[11];

(3)   if, on the death of an employer, the employee is taken into the employment of the personal representatives or trustees of the deceased, the employee's period of employment at the time of the death counts as a period of employment with the employer's personal representatives or trustees, and the death does not break the continuity of the period of employment[12];

(4)   if there is a change in the partners, personal representatives or trustees who employ any person, the employee's period of employment at the time of the change counts as a period of employment with the partners, personal representatives or trustees after the change, and the change does not break the continuity of the period of employment[13];

(5)   if an employee of an employer is taken into the employment of another employer who, at the time when the employee enters the second employer's employment, is an associated employer[14] of the first employer, the employee's period of employment at that time counts as a period of employment with the second employer, and the change of employer does not break the continuity of the period of employment[15];

(6)   if an employee of the governing body of a school maintained by a local authority[16] is taken into the employment of the authority, or if an employee of a local authority is taken into the employment of the governing body of a school maintained by the authority, his period of employment at the time of the change of employer counts as a period of employment with the second employer, and the change does not break the continuity of the period of employment[17];

(7)   if a person employed in relevant employment by a health service employer[18] is taken into relevant employment by another such employer, his period of employment at the time of the change of employment counts as a period of employment with the second employer, and the change does not break the continuity of the period of employment[19].

1   Ie the Employment Rights Act 1996 Pt XIV Ch I (ss 210–219) (continuous employment: see also PARAS 130 et seq, 861 et seq): see s 218(1).
2   As to the meaning of 'employment' see PARA 2.
3   Employment Rights Act 1996 s 218(1); and see *Lee v Barry High Ltd* [1970] 3 All ER 1040, [1970] 1 WLR 1549, CA; *Harold Fielding Ltd v Mansi* [1974] 1 All ER 1035, [1974] ICR 347, NIRC (see note 13). The employment need not be under a single contract: *Re Mack Trucks (Britain) Ltd* [1967] 1 All ER 977, [1967] 1 WLR 780. As to the meaning of 'employer' see PARA 2.
4   For these purposes, except in so far as the context otherwise requires, 'business' includes a trade or profession and includes any activity carried on by a body of persons (whether corporate or unincorporated): see the Employment Rights Act 1996 s 235(1). 'Activity' in this context includes the whole of the operations carried out, whether or not they amount to a business,

trade or profession in the ordinary sense, and so can include the operations of a charity, school, college or statutory undertaking: *Dallow Industrial Properties Ltd v Else* [1967] 2 QB 449, [1967] 2 All ER 30; *Robinson v Bournemouth County Borough Council* (1970) 5 ITR 100.

5   Ie whether or not it is an undertaking established by or under an Act of Parliament: see the Employment Rights Act 1996 s 218(2). As to the construction of references to undertakings in relation to Crown employment see PARA 163.

6   As to the meaning of 'employee' see PARA 2.

7   The meaning of 'at the time of the transfer' has been unclear: see the different interpretations given (obiter) by Stephenson LJ, Goff LJ and Eveleigh LJ in *Teesside Times Ltd v Drury* [1980] ICR 338, [1980] IRLR 72, CA. In *Macer v Abafast Ltd* [1990] ICR 234, [1990] IRLR 137, EAT, the tribunal adopted the opinion of Eveleigh LJ in *Teesside Times Ltd v Drury* and held that 'at the time of the transfer' qualifies 'period of employment', not 'employee'; thus there is no formal requirement that the employee be still in the transferor's employment at the moment of transfer in order for these provisions to operate; a gap is not fatal to continuity and employers cannot evade the application of the Employment Rights Act 1996 s 218(2) by the device of dismissing shortly prior to the transfer (provided that any gap is related to the machinery of the transfer: *Gibson v Motortune Ltd* [1990] ICR 740, EAT). However, a similar result was reached in *Clark & Tokeley Ltd (t/a Spellbrook) v Oakes* [1998] 4 All ER 353, [1999] ICR 276, CA, by reliance on the opinion of Stephenson LJ in *Teesside Times Ltd v Drury* to the effect that a transfer will often take place over a period of time, and it is open to a tribunal to find as a fact that the dismissal took place during that period of time. In effect, this produces the same result as was produced under the Transfer of Undertakings (Protection of Employment) Regulations 1981, SI 1981/1794 (see now the Transfer of Undertakings (Protection of Employment) Regulations 2006, SI 2006/246), by the decision in *Litster v Forth Dry Dock and Engineering Co Ltd (in receivership)* [1990] 1 AC 546, [1989] ICR 341, HL, but by different reasoning (see PARA 139 note 4). See also *Castro v D36 Ltd* [2004] All ER (D) 287 (Jul), sub nom *Castro v Design 36 Ltd* (2004) Times, 28 July, EAT, where it was held that the Transfer of Undertakings (Protection of Employment) Regulations 1981, SI 1981/1794 (see now the Transfer of Undertakings (Protection of Employment) Regulations 2006, SI 2006/246; and PARA 136 et seq), Council Directive (EC) 77/187 (OJ L161, 5.3.77, p 26) (see now Council Directive (EC) 2001/23 (OJ L82, 22.3.2001, p 16) (see PARA 136)) and the Employment Rights Act 1996 s 218(2) were part of a single scheme for the protection of employees' rights, to be interpreted consistently, and with an identical interpretation of the word 'transfer'. See also Case C-108/10 *Scattolon v Ministero dell'Istruzione, dell'Universita e della Ricerca* [2011] ECR I-7491, [2012] 1 CMLR 432, [2012] ICR 740, [2011] IRLR 1020, ECJ (transfer of staff from local authority to lists of state employees constituted transfer of undertaking for purposes of Business Transfers Directive, whose objective consists in preventing workers subject to a transfer from being placed in a less favourable position solely as a result of the transfer).

8   See the Employment Rights Act 1996 s 218(2). The presumption of continuity in s 210(5) (see PARA 130) does not apply to a transfer of business under s 218(2): *Secretary of State for Employment v Cohen* [1987] ICR 570, [1987] IRLR 169, EAT.

The Employment Rights Act 1996 s 218(2) may apply to the transfer of a business or part of a business: *GD Ault (Isle of Wight) Ltd v Gregory* (1967) 2 ITR 301, DC; *McLeod v John Rostron & Sons Ltd* (1972) 7 ITR 144, NIRC; *Newlin Oil Co Ltd v Trafford* [1974] IRLR 205, NIRC (no transfer on the facts); *Green v Wavertree Heating and Plumbing Co Ltd* [1978] ICR 928, EAT; *Rastill v Automatic Refreshment Services Ltd* [1978] ICR 289, EAT. In either case, however, the central point is that there must be the transfer of a going concern; a mere sale or other transfer of an asset or assets is not sufficient (a point of particular significance and potential difficulty where only part of a business is involved): *Melon v Hector Powe Ltd* [1981] 1 All ER 313, [1981] ICR 43, HL; *Kenmir Ltd v Frizzell* [1968] 1 All ER 414, [1968] 1 WLR 329; *Lloyd v Brassey* [1969] 2 QB 98, [1969] 1 All ER 382, CA; *Crompton v Truly Fair (International) Ltd* [1975] ICR 359, [1975] IRLR 250; *Gibson v Motortune Ltd* [1990] ICR 740, EAT. In deciding this point, matters such as the sale of goodwill and the transfer of customers will be important as evidence, but not decisive: *Luckey v Hockley* (1966) 2 ITR 38; *Kenmir Ltd v Frizzell*; *HA Rencoule (Joiners and Shopfitters) Ltd v Hunt* (1967) 2 ITR 475; *Chapman v Wilkinson* (1967) 3 ITR 39, DC; *Ward v Haines Watts* [1983] ICR 231, sub nom *Atkin v Ward and Haines Watts* [1983] IRLR 285, EAT; *Jeetle v Elster* [1985] ICR 389, [1985] IRLR 227, EAT. The concern need not necessarily be a going concern at the time of transfer: see *Teesside Times Ltd v Drury* [1980] ICR 338, [1980] IRLR 72, CA (transfer of insolvent business); and *Oakland v Wellswood (Yorkshire) Ltd* [2009] EWCA Civ 1094, [2010] ICR 902, [2010] IRLR 82 (Employment Rights Act 1996 s 218(2) applied where there was a transfer of the assets and employees of a business which had gone into administration). There may be exceptional cases where on the facts the asset in question is the business, so that transfer of that asset will be transfer of the business: *Lloyd v Brassey* (farming land); *Young v Daniel Thwaites & Co Ltd* [1977] ICR 877, EAT (tenancy of public house); c f *Bumstead v John L Cars Ltd* (1967) 2 ITR 137; *Port Talbot Engineering Co Ltd v Passmore* [1975] ICR 234, [1975] IRLR 156. The proper test is whether 'B' has become the proprietor of the trade, business or undertaking in succession to 'A'; there must, therefore, be a change internally in the ownership of the business: *Woodhouse v Peter Brotherhood Ltd* [1972] 2 QB 520, [1972] 3 All ER 91, CA; *Kenmir Ltd v Frizzell; Lloyd v Brassey; Melon v Hector Powe Ltd*. If this is not the case, the Employment Rights Act 1996 s 218(2) does not apply even if to the employee or some other objective observer there is the outward appearance of a transfer and a continuation of the work: *Umar v Pliastar Ltd* [1981] ICR 727, EAT; *SI (Systems and Instrumentation) Ltd v Grist* [1983] ICR 788, sub nom *SI (Systems and Instruments) Ltd v Grist and Riley* [1983] IRLR 391, EAT. A tribunal should not, however, apply an over-strict standard of proof, given that an employee may have little detailed knowledge of the financial dealings, and may be able to infer the existence of a transfer from the employee's knowledge of what outwardly happened, in the absence of more detailed evidence: *Secretary of State for Employment v Cohen* at 577 and 172 per Scott J. Once the substance of a transfer has taken place, the Employment Rights Act 1996 s 218(2) may apply even if certain final steps remain to be taken: *Dabell v Vale Industrial Services (Nottingham) Ltd* [1988] IRLR 439, CA.

The Transfer of Undertakings (Protection of Employment) Regulations 1981, SI 1981/1794 (see now the Transfer of Undertakings (Protection of Employment) Regulations 2006, SI 2006/246; and PARA 136 et seq) were not integrated into the existing statutory framework but simply added to it and their relationship with the Employment Rights Act 1996 s 218(2) is, therefore, unclear. It has been suggested that the Transfer of Undertakings (Protection of Employment) Regulations 1981, SI 1981/1794 (now the Transfer of Undertakings (Protection of Employment) Regulations 2006, SI 2006/246) are aimed at qualifying and regulating the contractual position of the employee, so that questions of continuity of employment for statutory purposes remain governed by the statute only: *Macer v Abafast Ltd* [1990] ICR 234 at 244, [1990] IRLR 137 at 141 per Wood P; and see *Keabeech Ltd v Mulcahy* [1985] ICR 791, EAT. On the other hand, it has also been suggested that the Transfer of Undertakings (Protection of Employment) Regulations 1981, SI 1981/1794 (see now the Transfer of Undertakings (Protection of Employment) Regulations 2006, SI 2006/246), Council Directive (EC) 77/187 (OJ L161, 5.3.77, p 26) (see now Council Directive (EC) 2001/23 (OJ L82, 22.3.2001, p 16)) and the Employment Rights Act 1996 s 218(2) form a single scheme for the protection of employees' rights, to be interpreted consistently: see *Castro v D36 Ltd* [2004] All ER (D) 287 (Jul), sub nom *Castro v Design 36 Ltd* (2004) Times, 28 July, EAT. There was little guidance in Council Directive (EC) 77/187 (OJ L161, 5.3.77, p 26) (see now Council Directive (EC) 2001/23 (OJ L82, 22.3.2001, p 16) (see PARA 136 note 3)) which merely states (in art 3(1) in both directives) that 'the transferor's rights and obligations arising from a contract of employment or from an employment relationship existing on the date of a transfer ... shall, by reason of such transfer, be transferred to the transferee'. It could certainly be said that continuity of employment is a right of the employee, but neither Council Directive (EC) 77/187 (OJ L161, 5.3.77, p 26) (see now Council Directive (EC) 2001/23 (OJ L82, 22.3.2001, p 16)) nor the Transfer of Undertakings (Protection of Employment) Regulations 1981, SI 1981/1794, reg 5(2) (see now the Transfer of Undertakings (Protection of Employment) Regulations 2006, SI 2006/246, reg 4) (see PARA 139) is drafted from the employee's point of view, referring instead to the transferor's rights and liabilities; technically, therefore, the question is whether continuity of employment is a liability of the employer, not whether it is a right of the employee. In practical terms it makes little difference what interpretation is adopted since continuity of employment will be preserved in either event; the only potential difficulty would be in a case where there was a transfer of an undertaking under the Transfer of Undertakings (Protection of Employment) Regulations 1981, SI 1981/1794 (see now the Transfer of Undertakings (Protection of Employment) Regulations 2006, SI 2006/246) which did not qualify as a transfer of business under the Employment Rights Act 1996.

9　Ie whether public or local and whether passed before or after the Employment Rights Act 1996: see s 218(3).

10　As to the meaning of 'contract of employment' see PARA 2.

11　See the Employment Rights Act 1996 s 218(3). For head (2) in the text to apply, the employee must have been transferred from one body to the other as part of the statutory scheme: *Gale v Northern General Hospital NHS Trust* [1994] IRLR 292, CA.

12　See the Employment Rights Act 1996 s 218(4). For the purposes of s 218(4), an employee who is also his deceased employer's personal representative can make a contract of employment with himself: *Rowley, Holmes & Co v Barber* [1977] 1 All ER 801, [1977] ICR 387, EAT.

For the purposes of the application of the Employment Rights Act 1996 Pt XI (ss 135–181) (redundancy payments: see PARA 836 et seq), in accordance with s 161(2) (see PARA 856), to an employee who was employed as a domestic servant in a private household, any reference in s 218(4) or s 218(5) (see head (4) in the text) to a personal representative includes a reference to any person to whom, otherwise than in pursuance of a sale or other disposition for valuable consideration, the management of the household has passed in consequence of the death of the employer: see s 174(6). As to the meaning of 'personal representative' for these purposes see PARA 1456 note 5.

13 See the Employment Rights Act 1996 s 218(5). See also note 12. The circumstances covered by s 218(5) include those where a partnership of two is continued by a sole principal who had previously been one of the partners: *Stevens v Bower* [2004] EWCA Civ 496, [2004] ICR 1582, [2004] IRLR 957 (approving on this point *Jeetle v Elster* [1985] ICR 389, [1985] IRLR 227, EAT, and overruling *Harold Fielding Ltd v Mansi* [1974] 1 All ER 1035, [1974] ICR 347, NIRC). *Quaere* whether the Employment Rights Act 1996 s 218(5) applies where employment by an individual is followed by employment by a partnership including that individual: see *Wynne v Hair Control* [1978] ICR 870, EAT (following *Harold Fielding Ltd v Mansi*), the reasoning in which was doubted in *Allen & Son v Coventry* [1980] ICR 9, [1979] IRLR 399, EAT, and in *Jeetle v Elster*.

14 As to the meaning of 'associated employer' see PARA 3.

15 See the Employment Rights Act 1996 s 218(6). Continuity is preserved even if the employee enters the employment of the associated employer after a gap, provided that the gap is covered by some other provision of Pt XIV Ch I (continuous employment: see also PARAS 130 et seq, 861 et seq), and even if the associated employer had not previously been employing persons: *Binns v Versil Ltd* [1975] IRLR 273; *Bentley Engineering Co Ltd v Crown, Bentley Engineering Co Ltd v Miller* [1976] ICR 225, [1976] IRLR 146, DC; *Charnock v Barrie Muirhead Ltd* [1984] ICR 641, EAT; *Lucas v Henry Johnson (Packers and Shippers) Ltd* [1986] ICR 384, EAT. Parliament's purpose was to provide continuity of employment for employees where there was a change of employer and to avoid the effect of manipulation of the employment relationship, depriving employees of their rights by setting up by the same owners of a new business, shorn of continuity of service: *Da Silva Junior v Composite Mouldings & Design Ltd* [2009] ICR 416, [2008] All ER (D) 157 (Aug), EAT.

16 For these purposes, 'local authority' has the meaning given by Education Act 1996 s 579(1) (see EDUCATION vol 35 (2011) PARA 24): Employment Rights Act 1996 s 218(11) (added by SI 2010/1158).

17 See the Employment Rights Act 1996 s 218(7) (amended by the Education Act 2002 s 215(1), Sch 21 para 32; and SI 2010/1158).

18 For these purposes, employment is relevant employment if it is employment of a description:
   (1)   in which persons are engaged while undergoing professional training which involves their being employed successively by a number of different health service employers (Employment Rights Act 1996 s 218(9)(a)); and
   (2)   which is specified in an order made by the Secretary of State (s 218(9)(b)).
As to the Secretary of State see PARA 5 note 21. As to the making of orders and regulations under the Employment Rights Act 1996 generally see PARA 162. At the date at which this volume states the law, no such order had been made under the powers conferred by s 218, but, by virtue of s 241, Sch 2 para 2(1) (see PARA 162), the Employment Protection (Continuity of Employment of National Health Service Employees) (Modification) Order 1996, SI 1996/1023 (see PARA 326 note 13) has effect as if so made. As to the health service employers that are specified for the purposes of the Employment Rights Act 1996 s 218(8), (9) (see head (7) in the text) see s 218(10) (amended by the Health and Social Care (Community Health and Standards) Act 2003 ss 34, 190(2), 196, Sch 4 paras 99, 101, Sch 13 para 8, Sch 14 Pts 4, 7; the Health Protection Agency Act 2004 s 11(1), Sch 3 para 13; the National Health Service (Consequential Provisions) Act 2006 s 2, Sch 1 paras 177, 180; the Health and Social Care Act 2012 ss 55(2), 56(4), 179(6), 249(1), 277, Sch 5 para 75, Sch 7 para 9, Sch 14 Pt 2 paras 68, 70, Sch 17 para 6(1), (3), Sch 19 para 6(1), (3); and SI 2000/90; SI 2007/961).

19 See the Employment Rights Act 1996 s 218(8).

(v) Transfers of Undertakings

A. EU OBLIGATIONS

136.   Implementation of the Acquired Rights Directive. The Transfer of Undertakings (Protection of Employment) Regulations 2006[1] have been made[2] in order to give effect in the United Kingdom to EC Council Directive 2001/23 of 12 March 2001 on the approximation of the laws of the member states relating to the safeguarding of employees' rights in the event of transfers of undertakings, businesses or parts of undertakings or businesses ('the Acquired Rights Directive')[3].

1   Ie the Transfer of Undertakings (Protection of Employment) Regulations 2006, SI 2006/246 (which came into force on 6 April 2006: see reg 1(2)), replacing and revoking the Transfer of Undertakings (Protection of Employment) Regulations 1981, SI 1981/1794 (see the Transfer of Undertakings (Protection of Employment) Regulations 2006, SI 2006/246, regs 20(1), 21): see PARA 137 et seq. The Transfer of Undertakings (Protection of Employment) Regulations 1981, SI 1981/1794, continue to apply to any transfer of an undertaking (or part of an undertaking) that took place before 6 April 2006. See also note 3.

     The Department for Business, Innovation and Skills has published guidance in order to help employers, employees and their representatives understand the Regulations and to help parties comply with their legal requirements: see *Employment Rights on the Transfer of an Undertaking: A Guide to the 2006 TUPE Regulations (as amended by the Collective Redundancies and Transfer of Undertakings (Protection of Employment) (Amendment) Regulations 2014) for Employees, Employers and Representatives* (Jan 2014). This guidance is available on the website of the Department for Business, Innovation and Skills, whose address, at the date at which this volume states the law, is to be found at: *http://www.bis.gov.uk*. The Advisory, Conciliation and Arbitration Service (ACAS) has also published guidance on how to conduct a TUPE transfer primarily from an employment relations perspective: see *Handling TUPE Transfers: the Acas Guide* (June 2014), which is available on ACAS's website, whose address, at the date at which this volume states the law, is to be found at: *http://www.acas.org.uk*. As to the constitution and powers of ACAS see PARA 1213 et seq.

2   Ie made by the Secretary of State in exercise of the powers conferred upon him by the European Communities Act 1972 s 2(2) (see CONSTITUTIONAL AND ADMINISTRATIVE LAW vol 20 (2014) PARA 156), and the Employment Relations Act 1999 s 38: see the Transfer of Undertakings (Protection of Employment) Regulations 2006, SI 2006/246, Preamble. Where regulations under the European Communities Act 1972 s 2(2) make provision for the purpose of implementing, or for a purpose concerning, an EU obligation of the United Kingdom which relates to the treatment of employees on the transfer of an undertaking or business or part of an undertaking or business, the Secretary of State may by regulations make the same or similar provision in relation to the treatment of employees in circumstances other than those to which the EU obligation applies (including circumstances in which there is no transfer, or no transfer to which the EU obligation applies): Employment Relations Act 1999 s 38(1), (2) (amended by virtue of SI 2011/1043). The power to make such regulations is exercisable by statutory instrument (Employment Relations Act 1999 s 42(1)); and such regulations are subject to annulment in pursuance of a resolution of either House of Parliament (s 38(3)). In exercise of the powers conferred upon him by s 38, the Secretary of State has made (ie in addition to the Transfer of Undertakings (Protection of Employment) Regulations 2006, SI 2006/246: see note 1):

     (1)   the Transfer of Undertakings (Protection of Employment) (Rent Officer Service) Regulations 1999, SI 1999/2511 (see LOCAL GOVERNMENT vol 69 (2009) PARA 453);

     (2)   the Transfer of Undertakings (Protection of Employment) (Transfer to OFCOM) Regulations 2003, SI 2003/2715;

     (3)   the Transfer of Undertakings (Protection of Employment) (RCUK Shared Services Centre Limited) Regulations 2012, SI 2012/2413;

     (4)   the Transfer of Undertakings (Protection of Employment) (Transfers of Public Health Staff) Regulations 2013, SI 2013/278 (see HEALTH SERVICES); and

     (5)   the Transfer of Undertakings (Protection of Employment) (Transfers of Staff to the Department for Work and Pensions) Regulations 2014, SI 2014/1139.

As to the meaning of 'United Kingdom' see PARA 2 note 12. As to the Secretary of State see PARA 5 note 21. To the extent that the Transfer of Undertakings (Protection of Employment) Regulations 2006, SI 2006/246, relate to 'service provision change' (ie outsourcing, re-tendering of out-sourced services and in-sourcing: see reg 3(1)(b); and PARA 137), they are made under the Employment Relations Act 1999 s 38 (because the Acquired Rights Directive contains no specific reference to outsourcing, re-tendering or in-sourcing).

     The Energy Act 2004 provides for the Transfer of Undertakings (Protection of Employment) Regulations 2006, SI 2006/246, to apply to a transfer of an undertaking or business (or part of an undertaking or business) either in accordance with a nuclear transfer scheme, or in accordance with a modification agreement (see ENERGY AND CLIMATE CHANGE vol 44 (2011)

PARA 834), as if (in so far as that would not otherwise be the case) the references in those regulations to the transferor were references to the person in whom that undertaking or business or that part of an undertaking or business was vested immediately before the coming into force of the transfer: Energy Act 2004 s 38(8), Sch 5 para 10(1) (Sch 5 para 10(1), (2)–(4) amended, Sch 5 para 10(1A) added, by SI 2006/246). The Transfer of Undertakings (Protection of Employment) Regulations 2006, SI 2006/246, apply also to a service provision change either in accordance with a nuclear transfer scheme, or in accordance with a modification agreement, as if (in so far as that would not otherwise be the case) the references in those Regulations to the transferor were references to the person by whom the activities affected by the service provision change were carried out immediately before the coming into force of the service provision change: Energy Act 2004 Sch 5 para 10(1A) (as so added). It is the duty of the Secretary of State, before making such a nuclear transfer scheme, or approving such a modification agreement, to give such notice of his proposals to such persons as he considers appropriate for enabling the provisions of the Transfer of Undertakings (Protection of Employment) Regulations 2006, SI 2006/246, applicable to a transfer or service provision change in accordance with the scheme or agreement to be complied with by the transferor: Energy Act 2004 Sch 5 para 10(2) (as so amended). For this purpose, the 'transferor', in relation to a transfer or service provision change, means the person who is the transferor or service provision change in relation to that transfer for the purposes of the Transfer of Undertakings (Protection of Employment) Regulations 2006, SI 2006/246: see the Energy Act 2004 Sch 5 para 10(3) (as so amended). References to a service provision change are references to a service provision change falling within the Transfer of Undertakings (Protection of Employment) Regulations 2006, SI 2006/246, reg 3(1)(b): see the Energy Act 2004 Sch 5 para 10(4) (as so amended).

The Transfer of Undertakings (Protection of Employment) Regulations 2006, SI 2006/246, have been applied further to transfers of staff (if they do not otherwise apply to such transfers) made by means of transfer orders under the Greater London Authority Act 1999 s 408 (see LONDON GOVERNMENT vol 71 (2013) PARA 13) or transfer schemes under s 409 (see LONDON GOVERNMENT vol 71 (2013) PARA 13): see the Transfer of Undertakings (Protection of Employment) (Greater London Authority) Order 2000, SI 2000/686; and LONDON GOVERNMENT vol 71 (2013) PARA 12.

3   Ie Council Directive (EC) 2001/23 of 12 March 2001 (OJ L82, 22.03.2001, p 16) on the approximation of the laws of the member states relating to the safeguarding of employees' rights in the event of transfers of undertakings, businesses or parts of undertakings or businesses ('the Acquired Rights Directive'). The Directive of 12 March 2001 replaced Council Directive (EEC) 77/187 of 14 February 1977 (OJ L61, 05.03.77, p 26) on the approximation of the laws of the Member States relating to the safeguarding of employees' rights in the event of transfers of undertakings, businesses or parts of undertakings or businesses (which had been substantially amended and it was thought necessary to codify it in the interests of clarity and rationality: see Council Directive (EC) 2001/23 of 12 March 2001 (OJ L82, 22.03.2001, p 16) recital (1)). The decisions of domestic courts in cases brought under the Transfer of Undertakings (Protection of Employment) Regulations 1981, SI 1981/1794 (revoked: see note 1), and the jurisprudence of the European Court of Justice (ECJ) (now the Court of Justice of the European Union (CJEU)), in cases brought under reference from United Kingdom courts and from the courts of other members states in relation to Council Directive (EEC) 77/187 of 14 February 1977 (OJ L61, 05.03.77, p 26) have aided the application and interpretation of those provisions and have been reflected in the drafting of both the Transfer of Undertakings (Protection of Employment) Regulations 2006, SI 2006/246 (see note 1) and Council Directive (EC) 2001/23 of 12 March 2001 (OJ L82, 22.03.2001, p 16), and may continue to have relevance (although the novel statutory concept of 'service provision change' in the Transfer of Undertakings (Protection of Employment) Regulations 2006, SI 2006/246, may have rendered some of the previous case-law, e g on 'contracting-out' cases, redundant: see PARA 137).

The Acquired Rights Directive has not been held to have direct effect, but United Kingdom courts are under a duty to give the regulations, where necessary, a purposive construction in order to comply with the Directive: *Litster v Forth Dry Dock and Engineering Co Ltd (in receivership)* [1990] 1 AC 546, [1989] ICR 341, HL (considering the Transfer of Undertakings (Protection of Employment) Regulations 1981, SI 1981/1794 (revoked), in the light of Council Directive (EEC) 77/187 of 14 February 1977 (OJ L61, 05.03.77, p 26) (revoked): see also PARA 139 note 4). As to the presumption favouring purposive construction of legislation generally see STATUTES AND LEGISLATIVE PROCESS vol 96 (2012) PARA 1177.

The subject-matter of the Acquired Rights Directive was previously governed only by the common law, which had hardly developed in England in this respect. At common law, a contract of service cannot be novated by substituting a new employer without the express or implied consent of the employee, so that, where such consent is absent, any transfer of a business from one party to another automatically terminates the contract of employment and gives rise to a dismissal: *Nokes v Doncaster Amalgamated Collieries Ltd* [1940] AC 1014, [1940] 3 All ER 549, HL (employee's right to choose for himself whom he would serve constituted the main difference between a servant and a serf). *Nokes v Doncaster Amalgamated Collieries Ltd* remains the position at common law (i e where a transfer has taken place outside the application of the Transfer of Undertakings (Protection of Employment) Regulations 2006, SI 2006/246): see *Gabriel v Peninsula Business Services* [2012] All ER (D) 199 (Jun), EAT (there had been no question of the employee giving her express assent to a transfer of her employment in view of the company's abject failure to advise her of the change of employer). The decision in *Bolwell v Redcliffe Homes Ltd and O'Connor* [1999] IRLR 485, CA (circumstances fell far short of what would be necessary to imply a workman's consent to a proposed transfer of his employment of which he knows nothing) is consistent with *Nokes v Doncaster Amalgamated Collieries Ltd*, although that case was not put in argument (see *Bolwell v Redcliffe Homes Ltd and O'Connor* at [13] per Simon Brown LJ).

B. RELEVANT TRANSFERS UNDER THE TRANSFER OF UNDERTAKINGS REGULATIONS

137. Relevant transfers to which the Transfer of Undertakings (Protection of Employment) Regulations 2006 apply. The Transfer of Undertakings (Protection of Employment) Regulations 2006[1] apply to[2]:

(1)   a transfer of an undertaking[3], business, or part of an undertaking or business[4], situated immediately before the transfer in the United Kingdom[5] to another person where there is a transfer of an economic entity[6] which retains its identity[7]; and

(2)   a service provision change[8].

Such a transfer or a service provision change is known for these purposes as a 'relevant transfer'; and 'transferor' and 'transferee' are to be construed accordingly[9].

Subject to heads (1) and (2) above[10], the Transfer of Undertakings (Protection of Employment) Regulations 2006 apply to[11]:

(a)   public and private undertakings engaged in economic activities whether or not they are operating for gain[12];

(b)   a transfer or service provision change howsoever effected[13], notwithstanding: (i) that the transfer of an undertaking, business (or part of an undertaking or business) is governed or effected by the law of a country or territory outside the United Kingdom, or that the service provision change is governed or effected by the law of a country or territory outside Great Britain[14]; (ii) that the employment of persons employed in the undertaking, business or part transferred (or, in the case of a service provision change, persons employed in the organised grouping of employees) is governed by any such law[15];

(c)   a transfer of an undertaking, business (or part of an undertaking or business), which may also be a service provision change, where persons employed in the undertaking, business or part transferred ordinarily work outside the United Kingdom[16].

An administrative reorganisation of public administrative authorities or the transfer of administrative functions between public administrative authorities is not a relevant transfer for these purposes, however[17].

A relevant transfer:

(A)   may be effected by a series of two or more transactions[18]; and

(B)   may take place whether or not any property is transferred to the transferee from the transferor[19].

The Employment Rights Act 1996 restrictions on contracting out[20] apply in relation to the Transfer of Undertakings (Protection of Employment)

Regulations 2006[21] as if they were contained in the 1996 Act, except that those restrictions do not apply in so far as the 2006 Regulations provide for an agreement (whether a contract of employment or not) to exclude or limit the operation of those Regulations[22].

1 Ie the Transfer of Undertakings (Protection of Employment) Regulations 2006, SI 2006/246, made by the Secretary of State in exercise of the powers conferred upon him by the European Communities Act 1972 s 2(2) (see CONSTITUTIONAL AND ADMINISTRATIVE LAW vol 20 (2014) PARA 156), and the Employment Relations Act 1999 s 38, in order to give effect in the United Kingdom to Council Directive (EC) 2001/23 of 12 March 2001 (OJ L82, 22.03.2001, p 16) on the approximation of the laws of the member states relating to the safeguarding of employees' rights in the event of transfers of undertakings, businesses or parts of undertakings or businesses ('the Acquired Rights Directive'), and for associated purposes: see PARA 136.

2 See the Transfer of Undertakings (Protection of Employment) Regulations 2006, SI 2006/246, reg 3(1).

3 The definition of 'undertaking' used for the purposes of the Transfer of Undertakings (Protection of Employment) Regulations 1981, SI 1981/1794, included any trade or business (and so was presumed not to include any undertaking or part of an undertaking that was not in the nature of a commercial venture): see reg 2(1) (as originally enacted). However, Council Directive (EC) 77/187 (OJ L161, 5.3.77, p 26) (revoked: see PARA 136 note 3) did not contain such a limitation (see Case C–29/91 *Dr Sophie Redmond Stichting v Bartol* [1992] ECR I-3189, [1992] IRLR 366, ECJ, in which it was held that there was a 'legal transfer' when a public body switched its subsidy from a foundation providing assistance to drug addicts to another legal person with comparable aims and objects) and the limitation itself was eventually held to have been contrary to European Community law (Case C–382/92 *EC Commission v United Kingdom* [1994] ECR I-2435, [1994] ICR 664, ECJ). In the meantime, the definition of 'undertaking' in the Transfer of Undertakings (Protection of Employment) Regulations 1981, SI 1981/1794, reg 2(1) had already been amended to exclude that limitation (but see *Alderson v Secretary of State for Trade and Industry* [2003] EWCA Civ 1767, [2004] 1 All ER 1148, [2004] ICR 512, where the wording of the unamended provision was held to have been 'elastic' enough for it to be read in a manner which accorded with the Acquired Rights Directive). The issues of what constitutes an undertaking and what constitutes a relevant transfer tend to become intertwined: see further note 4.

4 Certainly in the context of predecessor regulations (ie the Transfer of Undertakings (Protection of Employment) Regulations 1981, SI 1981/1794 (revoked: see PARA 136 note 1)) there was a distinction between a transfer of part of a business (covered by the statutory provisions) and the mere sale or other transfer of an asset or assets of the business (not covered): see *Robert Seligman Corpn v Baker* [1983] ICR 770, EAT; *Premier Motors (Medway) Ltd v Total Oil Great Britain Ltd* [1984] 1 WLR 377, [1984] ICR 58, EAT; Case 24/85 *Spijkers v Gebr Benedik Abattoir CV* [1986] ECR 1119, [1986] 2 CMLR 296, ECJ; *Fairhurst Ward Abbotts Ltd v Botes Building Ltd* [2004] EWCA Civ 83, [2004] ICR 919, [2004] IRLR 304 (undertaking fractured following a transfer); *NUMAST v P & O Scottish Ferries Ltd* [2005] ICR 1270, [2005] All ER (D) 27 (Apr), EAT. This is now perhaps reinforced in the Transfer of Undertakings (Protection of Employment) Regulations 2006, SI 2006/246, with the wording of reg 3(1)(a) (see head (1) in the text); and see Case C-466/07 *Klarenberg v Ferrotron Technologies GmbH* [2009] ECR I-803, [2009] ICR 1263, [2009] IRLR 301, ECJ (Acquired Rights Directive may apply where the part of the undertaking or business transferred does not retain its organisational autonomy, provided that: (1) the functional link between the various elements of production transferred is preserved; and (2) that functional link enables the transferee to use those elements to pursue an identical or analogous economic activity).

As to the transfer of shares, as distinct from a transfer of business, see *Brookes v Borough Care Services* [1998] ICR 1198, [1998] IRLR 636, EAT (no relevant transfer of business occurred when company shares were acquired by legal person which assumed management of the care homes in which employees worked, notwithstanding that this form of transaction was adopted with the purpose of avoiding the consequences of the acquired rights provisions as set out in *Wilson v St Helens Borough Council* [1996] ICR 711, [1996] IRLR 320, EAT (cited in PARA 139 note 10)); cf *Millam v Print Factory (London) 1991 Ltd* [2007] EWCA Civ 322, [2007] ICR 1331, [2007] IRLR 526 (question is whether as a matter of fact the business in which the claimant is employed has been transferred from one company to another; formulation of the issue in terms of piercing the corporate veil led the EAT to misdirect itself) (applied in *Smith v Jackson Lloyd Ltd* [2014] All ER (D) 157 (Apr), EAT (relevant transfer found following

100% acquisition of the first employer's shares by a subsidiary of the second employer which wholly subsumed the activities and practical identity of the first employer)).

5   As to the meaning of 'United Kingdom' see PARA 2 note 12. The location of an undertaking for these purposes must be the operational base of the employer rather than its physical location at any particular time: *Addison v Denholm Ship Management (UK) Ltd* [1997] ICR 770, [1997] IRLR 389, EAT (per curiam). The extension of employment protection legislation to the continental shelf (see PARA 156) does not apply for these purposes: *Addison v Denholm Ship Management (UK) Ltd* (case under the Employment Protection (Offshore) Employment Order 1976, SI 1976/766, and the Transfer of Undertakings (Protection of Employment) Regulations 1981, SI 1981/1794). As to the application (with modifications) of the Transfer of Undertakings (Protection of Employment) Regulations 2006, SI 2006/246, to Northern Ireland see regs 1(3), 2(3), Sch 1 (Sch 1 amended by SR 2006/177; SI 2009/592; SI 2014/386); and the Service Provision Change (Protection of Employment) Regulations (Northern Ireland) 2006, SR 2006/177. The acquired rights provisions have the potential to apply to a transfer from the UK to a non-EU entity in the event that on the transfer the undertaking did not remain in the jurisdiction: *GMB v Holis Metal Industries Ltd* [2008] ICR 464, [2008] IRLR 187, EAT (a purposive approach requires that those employees should be protected even if the transfer is to be across borders, although enforcement may present a problem).

    Where, in consequence (whether directly or indirectly) of the transfer of an undertaking, business or part of an undertaking or business which was situated immediately before the transfer in the United Kingdom, a ship (within the meaning of the Merchant Shipping Act 1995: see SHIPPING AND MARITIME LAW vol 93 (2008) PARA 229) registered in the United Kingdom ceases to be so registered, the Transfer of Undertakings (Protection of Employment) Regulations 2006, SI 2006/246, do not affect the right conferred by the Merchant Shipping Act 1995 s 29 (right of seamen to be discharged when ship ceases to be registered in the United Kingdom: see SHIPPING AND MARITIME LAW vol 93 (2008) PARA 463) on a seaman employed in the ship: Transfer of Undertakings (Protection of Employment) Regulations 2006, SI 2006/246, reg 3(7).

6   For this purpose, 'economic entity' means an organised grouping of resources which has the objective of pursuing an economic activity, whether or not that activity is central or ancillary: Transfer of Undertakings (Protection of Employment) Regulations 2006, SI 2006/246, reg 3(2). See Case C-458/05 *Jouini v Princess Personal Service GmbH* [2007] ECR I-7301, [2008] ICR 128, [2007] IRLR 1005, ECJ (concept of economic entity refers to an organised group of persons and assets enabling the exercise of an economic activity which pursues a specific objective); and Case C-108/10 *Scattolon v Ministero dell'Istruzione, dell'Università e della Ricerca* [2011] ECR I-7491, [2012] 1 CMLR 432, [2012] ICR 740, [2011] IRLR 1020, ECJ (any grouping of persons and assets enabling the exercise of an economic activity pursuing a specific objective and which is sufficiently structured and independent will constitute an economic entity).

7   Transfer of Undertakings (Protection of Employment) Regulations 2006, SI 2006/246, reg 3(1)(a).

    In determining whether there has been the transfer of an economic entity, the court must apply a multi-factorial test and adopt a common sense approach in order to adjudge whether there was a stable economic entity which retained its identity after what was said to be a transfer falling within head (1) in the text: *Cheesman v R Brewer Contracts Ltd* [2001] IRLR 144, EAT (distilling principles derived from the decisions in Cases C-127/96, C-229/96 and C-74/97 *Vidal (Francisco Hernandez) SA v Gomez Perez* [1998] ECR I-8179, [1999] IRLR 132, ECJ; Case C-173/96 *Sanchez Hidalgo v Asociacion de Servicios Aser and Sociedad Cooperativa Minerva* [1998] ECR I-8237, [2002] ICR 73, [1999] IRLR 136, ECJ; C-234/98 *Allen v Amalgamated Construction Co Ltd* [1999] ECR I-8643, [2000] All ER (EC) 97, [2000] IRLR 119, ECJ; and *ECM (Vehicle Delivery Service) v Cox* [1999] 4 All ER 669, [1999] ICR 1162, [1999] IRLR 559, CA); approved in *McCarrick v Hunter* [2012] EWCA Civ 1399, [2013] ICR 235, [2013] IRLR 26. All facts are required to be taken into account and each is to be no more than a single factor with none to be considered in isolation: *Cheesman v R Brewer Contracts Ltd*.

    The test for determining whether a business is being transferred has generated much debate, especially in the context of the earlier implementing regulations (ie the Transfer of Undertakings (Protection of Employment) Regulations 1981, SI 1981/1794 (revoked), replaced by the Transfer of Undertakings (Protection of Employment) Regulations 2006, SI 2006/246: see PARA 136 note 1), and the predecessor version of 'the Acquired Rights Directive' (ie Council Directive (EEC) 77/187 of 14 February 1977 (OJ L61, 05.03.77, p 26) (revoked), replaced by Council Directive (EC) 2001/23 of 12 March 2001 (OJ L82, 22.03.2001, p 16): see PARA 136 note 3). The provisions of the Acquired Rights Directive have been construed as applying not just where there has been a change in the ownership of the undertaking, but also to cases where there has been some other form of change of employer, eg the transfer of a lease, on the basis that what really matters is the continuation of the economic entity, albeit under the operation of some new natural or legal person: Case 24/85 *Spijkers v Gebr Benedik Abattoir CV* [1986] ECR 1119, [1986] 2 CMLR 296, ECJ; Case 324/86 *Foreningen af Arbejdsledere i Danmark v Daddy's Dance Hall A/S* [1988] ECR 739, [1988] IRLR 315, ECJ; Case 287/86 *Landsorganisationen i Danmark v Ny Mølle Kro* [1989] ICR 330, [1989] IRLR 37, ECJ; Case 101/87 *P Bork International A/S (in liquidation) v Foreningen af Arbejdsledere i Danmark* [1990] 3 CMLR 701, [1989] IRLR 41, ECJ; Joined Cases 144/87, 145/87 *Berg and Busschers v Besselsen* [1988] ECR 2559, [1990] ICR 396, ECJ; Case C-172/99 *Oy Liikenne Ab v Liskojärvi* [2001] All ER (EC) 544, [2002] ICR 155, [2001] IRLR 171, ECJ (no direct contractual link between two undertakings successively awarded operation of public transport service by a legal person governed by public law); and see Case C-458/05 *Jouini v Princess Personal Service GmbH* [2007] ECR I-7301, [2008] ICR 128, [2007] IRLR 1005, ECJ (cited in note 6); Case C-242/09 *Albron Catering BV v FNV Bondgenoten* [2010] ECR I-10309, [2011] All ER (EC) 625, [2011] 1 CMLR 1267, [2011] ICR 373, [2011] IRLR 76, ECJ (transfer of an undertaking found where persons employed by one company in a group are permanently assigned to another company in the group and the activities of the latter company are transferred to a third party); and Case C-108/10 *Scattolon v Ministero dell'Istruzione, dell'Università e della Ricerca* [2011] ECR I-7491, [2012] 1 CMLR 432, [2012] ICR 740, [2011] IRLR 1020, ECJ (cited in note 6). There is a general requirement for the transfer of some recognisable business: *Banking Insurance and Finance Union v Barclays Bank plc* [1987] ICR 495, EAT (staff continued to do the same work as they did when employed by subsidiaries). A change in employment status of employees is not sufficient, eg when changing from direct employment to agency employment (*Wynnwith Engineering Co Ltd v Bennett* [2002] IRLR 170, EAT) or where some employees are dedicated to servicing one contract which is then transferred (*Davies v Eton Air Ltd* [2004] All ER (D) 355 (Oct), EAT). The transfer purely of a contract between two enterprises may not come within the Acquired Rights Directive, even if employees move with it (Case C-48/94 *Ledernes Hovedorganisation (acting on behalf of Rygaard) v Dansk Arbejdsgiverforening (acting on behalf of Strø Mølle Akustik A/S)* [1995] ECR I-2745, [1996] ICR 333, ECJ), but it is likely that such a situation will be exceptional, with other factors usually pointing to an economic entity retaining its identity and being transferred; and Case C-48/94 *Ledernes Hovedorganisation (acting for Rygaard) v Dansk Arbejdsgiverforening (acting for Strø Mølle Akustik A/S)* has been restrictively distinguished by both the Employment Appeal Tribunal (*BSG Property Services v Tuck* [1996] IRLR 134, EAT; *Argyll Training Ltd v Sinclair* [2000] IRLR 630, EAT) and the European Court of Justice (Case C-234/98 *Allen v Amalgamated Construction Co Ltd*). See also note 4.

As to the transfer of an economic activity from a legal person governed by private law to one governed by public law see the text and note 17.

It is possible for the undertaking to retain its identity where there is a time gap between the date of the transfer and the transferee taking up the business (ie it may be enough if the transferee resumes the activity, rather than immediately continuing it): see *Wood v Caledon Social Club Ltd* [2010] All ER (D) 79 (Sep), EAT (there was a transfer for the purposes of the Transfer of Undertakings (Protection of Employment) Regulations 2006, SI 2006/246, reg 3(1)(a) of a members' club which at the time was closed having had its liquor licence revoked but by the transfer date, the second respondent had intended to obtain a fresh premises licence certificate and to re-open the bar area itself, operating precisely as it had done under the employer).

8 Transfer of Undertakings (Protection of Employment) Regulations 2006, SI 2006/246, reg 3(1)(b). For these purposes, a 'service provision change' is a situation in which:

(1) activities cease to be carried out by a person (a 'client') on his own behalf and are carried out instead by another person on the client's behalf (a 'contractor') (reg 3(1)(b)(i));

(2) activities cease to be carried out by a contractor on a client's behalf (whether or not those activities had previously been carried out by the client on his own behalf) and are carried out instead by another person (a 'subsequent contractor') on the client's behalf (reg 3(1)(b)(ii)); or

(3) activities cease to be carried out by a contractor or a subsequent contractor on a client's behalf (whether or not those activities had previously been carried out by the client on his own behalf) and are carried out instead by the client on his own behalf (reg 3(1)(b)(iii)),

and in which the following conditions are satisfied (see reg 3(1)(b)), namely that:

(a) immediately before the service provision change: (i) there is an organised grouping of employees situated in Great Britain which has as its principal purpose the carrying out of the activities concerned on behalf of the client (reg 3(3)(a)(i)); (ii) the client intends that the activities will, following the service provision change, be carried out by the transferee other than in connection with a single specific event or task of short-term duration (reg 3(3)(a)(ii)); and

(b)   the activities concerned do not consist wholly or mainly of the supply of goods for the client's use (reg 3(3)(b)).

For these purposes, references to 'organised grouping of employees' includes a single employee; and references to a contractor in reg 3 include a sub-contractor: see reg 2(1) (and see Case C-392/92 *Schmidt v Spar-und Leihkasse Der Früheren ämter Bordesholm Kiel and Cronshagen* [1995] ICR 237, [1994] IRLR 302, ECJ). As to the meaning of 'Great Britain' see PARA 2 note 12. For these purposes, 'employee' means any individual who works for another person, whether under a contract of service or apprenticeship or otherwise, but does not include anyone who provides services under a contract for services; and references to a person's employer must be construed accordingly: see the Transfer of Undertakings (Protection of Employment) Regulations 2006, SI 2006/246, reg 2(1). As to the meanings of 'employee', 'employer' and related expressions in relation to employment rights generally see PARA 2 et seq. As to the meaning of 'contract of service' see PARA 1 note 1. As to the position of apprentices and youth trainees at common law see PARAS 112, 128–129, 636, 747–754. As to the statutory law on apprenticeships see EDUCATION vol 35 (2011) PARA 682 et seq. Despite this wide definition of 'employee' there must be an employment relationship of sorts: *Cowell v Quilter Goodison Co Ltd and QG Management Services Ltd* [1989] IRLR 392, CA (partnership as a concept is quite different from an employment relationship). Moreover, the test remains contract-based, and the definition cannot be applied to what is arguably an employment relationship if that is not reflected in the contractual arrangements: *Clifton Middle School Governing Body v Askew* [2000] ICR 286, sub nom *Askew v Governing Body of Clifton Middle School* [1999] IRLR 708, CA (no relevant transfer between schools, when the employment contract remained with the local authority; in spite of the phrase 'or otherwise' in the definition of employee, it is not possible to separate an employment relationship from the employment contract). The applicable definition of 'contract of employment' is equally wide: see PARA 138 note 5.

References in the Transfer of Undertakings (Protection of Employment) Regulations 2006, SI 2006/246, reg 3(1)(b) (see heads (1) to (3) above) to activities being carried out instead by another person (including the client) are to activities which are fundamentally the same as the activities carried out by the person who has ceased to carry them out: reg 3(2A) (added by SI 2014/16). This appears to codify the approach to the Transfer of Undertakings (Protection of Employment) Regulations 2006, SI 2006/246, reg 3(1)(b) that has been seen in case law since 2006, when the wholly new statutory concept of a transfer of undertakings by service provision change was intended to remove or at least alleviate the uncertainties and difficulties created, in a variety of familiar commercial settings, by the need under the Transfer of Undertakings (Protection of Employment) Regulations 1981, SI 1981/1794 (revoked: see PARA 136 note 1) to establish a transfer of a stable economic identity which retained its identity in the hands of the alleged transferee, particularly in the case of labour-intensive operations, by including within the definition of a transfer of undertaking the situations falling within the Transfer of Undertakings (Protection of Employment) Regulations 2006, SI 2006/246, reg 3(1)(b) in which the conditions set out in reg 3(3) were satisfied (see heads (a), (b) above): *Metropolitan Resources Ltd v Churchill Dulwich Ltd (in liquidation)* [2009] ICR 1380 at [26], [2009] IRLR 700 at [26], EAT, per Burke QC J. The three situations falling within the Transfer of Undertakings (Protection of Employment) Regulations 2006, SI 2006/246, reg 3(1)(b) can be described as:

(A)   outsourcing (see reg 3(1)(b)(i));

(B)   change in the provision of activities or services carried out on behalf of a client between one contractor and another (see reg 3(1)(b)(ii));

(C)   in-sourcing (see reg 3(1)(b)(iii)):

see *Metropolitan Resources Ltd v Churchill Dulwich Ltd (in liquidation)* at [26]. Since 'service provision change' is not defined in terms of economic entity or of other concepts which have developed under the Transfer of Undertakings (Protection of Employment) Regulations 1981, SI 1981/1794, or by jurisprudence arising under the Acquired Rights Directive prior to April 2006 (when the Transfer of Undertakings (Protection of Employment) Regulations 2006, SI 2006/246, took effect), the application of the 'service provision change' provisions to an individual case is essentially one of fact and there is no need for a judicially prescribed multi-factorial approach (ie such as that required for the purposes of head (1) in the text, as described in note 7) : see *Metropolitan Resources Ltd v Churchill Dulwich Ltd (in liquidation)* at [27]–[29]. In a case falling within the Transfer of Undertakings (Protection of Employment) Regulations 2006, SI 2006/246, reg 3(1)(b) (see head (2) in the text), there is no call for a formal list of factors which the tribunal has to consider before it could make a decision as to whether there was a relevant transfer: *Metropolitan Resources Ltd v Churchill Dulwich Ltd (in liquidation)*; cf *Enterprise Management Services Ltd v Connect-up Ltd* [2012] IRLR 190 at [8], EAT, per Peter Clark J (guidelines for identifying under head (2) above relevant 'activities' carried out by the original contractor, and whether the activities carried on by the subsequent contractor after the relevant date are fundamentally or essentially the same as those carried on by the original contractor, being essentially a question of fact and degree). For there to be a service provision change within the meaning of the Transfer of Undertakings (Protection of Employment) Regulations 2006, SI 2006/246, reg 3(1)(b), the activities carried out by different contractors before and after the transfer must be carried out for the same client, so there is no service provision change where both the client and the contractor change: *McCarrick v Hunter* [2012] EWCA Civ 1399, [2013] ICR 235, [2013] IRLR 26 (no basis for seeking to apply a purposive construction to 'the client' for these purposes as no underlying EU provision requires it: this is a purely domestic provision); *SNR Denton UK LLP v Kirwan* [2013] ICR 101, [2012] IRLR 966, EAT (solicitors retained by administrator were not themselves acting on behalf of the company when they acted in the administration merely because the administrator could act as agent, and in exercise of its functions as administrator did so act).

There is no organised grouping of employees within the meaning of the Transfer of Undertakings (Protection of Employment) Regulations 2006, SI 2006/246, reg 3(3)(a)(i) (see head (a)(i) above) where a group of employees work in practice, but without any deliberate planning or intent, mostly on tasks which benefit a particular client: *Eddie Stobart Ltd v Moreman* [2012] ICR 919, [2012] IRLR 356, EAT (if the putative 'grouping' did not reflect any existing organisational unit, there could be real practical difficulties in identifying which employees belonged to it).

There is no special definition of 'intends' in the Transfer of Undertakings (Protection of Employment) Regulations 2006, SI 2006/246, reg 3(3)(a)(ii) (see head (a)(ii) above), and it should be given its ordinary meaning: *Robert Sage Ltd (t/a Prestige Nursing Care Ltd) v O'Connell* [2014] IRLR 428, [2014] All ER (D) 309 (Mar), EAT (a hope and wish that, following a service provision change, activities would be carried out by a transferee in connection with a task of short term duration was not an intention that they would be so carried out). Whether or not a client intends that certain activities will be carried out in connection with a task of short term duration must be a matter of fact and degree and very much for assessment by the tribunal of first instance in the context of their findings in fact about the whole circumstances of the change of service provision: *SNR Denton UK LLP v Kirwan* at [44] per Langstaff J; *Liddells Coaches v Cook* [2013] ICR 547 at [32] per Lady Smith. As to whether, as a matter of construction, 'a single specific event or task of short-term duration' in the Transfer of Undertakings (Protection of Employment) Regulations 2006, SI 2006/246, reg 3(3)(a)(ii) uses the phrase 'of short-term duration' to qualify both 'a single specific event' and the word 'task' see *SNR Denton UK LLP v Kirwan* at [41], obiter, per Langstaff J ('of short-term duration' applies to both 'task' and 'single specific event'); and *Liddells Coaches v Cook* at [28]–[30], EAT, per Lady Smith ('of short-term duration' governs 'task' only because 'event', of itself, connotes short duration and to refer to a single specific event of short term duration would be tautologous). The interpretation of Langstaff J was preferred in *Swanbridge Hire & Sales Ltd v Butler* (2013) UKEAT/0056/13/BA, which was applied in *Ndeze v Horizon Security Services Ltd* [2014] All ER (D) 72 (Aug), EAT.

As to the principles and approach to be taken in the context of a service provision change when there has been a transfer of one transferor's activities to more than one transferee (ie plural use of the word 'transferee': cf head (a)(ii) above) see *Kimberley Group Housing Ltd v Hambley, Angel Services (UK) Ltd v Hambley* [2008] ICR 1030, [2008] IRLR 682, EAT (transferee who took the greater part of the transferor's activities took all the employees of the transferor), applying *Duncan Web Offset (Maidstone) Ltd v Cooper* [1995] IRLR 633, EAT (where the whole of their employer's only business was transferred, all employees were assigned to the business of his employer, notwithstanding that some duties were performed for other entities within the group). There may be some circumstances in which a service which is being provided by one contractor to a client is in the event so fragmented that nothing which one can properly determine as being a service provision change has taken place: *Kimberley Group Housing Ltd v Hambley, Angel Services (UK) Ltd v Hambley*, applied in *Ankers v Clearsprings Management Ltd* [2009] All ER (D) 261 (Feb), EAT (service users looked after by employer whose contract was not renewed were randomly allocated to incoming contractors, so no particular transferee cold be identified as having taken over the activity).

The application of the Transfer of Undertakings (Protection of Employment) Regulations 2006, SI 2006/246, reg 3(3)(b) (see head (b) above) to individual cases is also essentially one of fact: *Pannu v Geo W King Ltd (in liquidation)* [2012] IRLR 193, EAT (where a motor company switched suppliers of axles from company A to company B, the fact that the employees of company A were providing a service to their employer did not prevent their activities being the supply of goods, and a relevant transfer was precluded by failure to meet condition for a service provision change in the Transfer of Undertakings (Protection of Employment) Regulations 2006, SI 2006/246, reg 3(3)(b)).

9   See the Transfer of Undertakings (Protection of Employment) Regulations 2006, SI 2006/246, reg 2(1). Note that the two categories of 'relevant transfer' given under head (1) and head (2) in the text are not mutually exclusive, but that the 'service provision change' provisions are made under the Employment Relations Act 1999 s 38 (because the Acquired Rights Directive contains no specific reference to outsourcing, re-tendering or in-sourcing: see PARA 136 note 2). In the case of a service provision change falling within the Transfer of Undertakings (Protection of Employment) Regulations 2006, SI 2006/246, reg 3(1)(b) (see head (2) in the text), the 'transferor' means the person who carried out the activities prior to the service provision change; and the 'transferee' means the person who carries out the activities as a result of the service provision change: see reg 2(1).

10 Ie the Transfer of Undertakings (Protection of Employment) Regulations 2006, SI 2006/246, reg 3(1) (see the text and notes 1–8): see reg 3(4).

11 See the Transfer of Undertakings (Protection of Employment) Regulations 2006, SI 2006/246, reg 3(4).

12 Transfer of Undertakings (Protection of Employment) Regulations 2006, SI 2006/246, reg 3(4)(a).

13 See the Transfer of Undertakings (Protection of Employment) Regulations 2006, SI 2006/246, reg 3(4)(b).

14 Transfer of Undertakings (Protection of Employment) Regulations 2006, SI 2006/246, reg 3(4)(b)(i).

15 Transfer of Undertakings (Protection of Employment) Regulations 2006, SI 2006/246, reg 3(4)(b)(ii).

16 Transfer of Undertakings (Protection of Employment) Regulations 2006, SI 2006/246, reg 3(4)(c).

17 Transfer of Undertakings (Protection of Employment) Regulations 2006, SI 2006/246, reg 3(5). This provision reflects Case C–298/94 *Henke v Gemeinde* [1996] ECR I-4989, [1997] ICR 746, ECJ (reorganisation of structures of the public administration or the transfer of administrative functions between public administrative authorities are excluded from the Acquired Rights Directive), a decision which itself is now reflected in Council Directive (EC) 2001/23 of 12 March 2001 (OJ L82, 22.3.2001, p 16) art 1(1)(c). This exception has been narrowly construed, however: Case C-175/99 *Mayeur v Association Promotion de L'Information Messine (APIM)* [2000] ECR I-7755, [2002] ICR 1316, ECJ (transfer of an economic activity from a legal person governed by private law to a legal person governed by public law is not excluded from the scope of the Acquired Rights Directive solely on the ground that the person to whom the activity is transferred is a public law body); Case C-343/98 *Collino v Telecom Italia SpA* [2001] All ER (EC) 405, [2002] ICR 38, [2000] IRLR 788, ECJ (transfer of an entity operating telecommunications services and managed by a public body within the State administration to a private law company falls within the scope of the Acquired Rights Directive). See also Case E-3/01 *Viggósdóttir v Íslandspóstur HF* [2002] 2 CMLR 18, [2002] IRLR 425, EFTA Ct (conversion of a State entity into a limited liability company owned by the State may constitute a transfer within the meaning of the Acquired Rights Directive (as annexed to the European Economic Agreement and deemed to be part of that Agreement), notwithstanding that there was no transfer of proprietary rights). As to the application of the Transfer of Undertakings (Protection of Employment) Regulations 2006, SI 2006/246, reg 3(5) specifically see *Employment Rights on the Transfer of an Undertaking: A Guide to the 2006 TUPE Regulations for Employees, Employers and Representatives* (Jan 2014) pp 7–8. As to this guidance see PARA 136 note 1.

In principle, the Directive does not preclude, in the event of a transfer of an undertaking from a legal person governed by private law to the state, the latter (as new employer) from reducing the amount of the remuneration of the employees concerned for the purpose of complying with the national rules in force for public employees: Case C-425/02 *Delahaye v Ministre de la Fonction Publique de la Réforme Administrative* [2005] All ER (EC) 575 sub nom *Boor (née Delahaye) v Ministre de la Fonction Publique et de la Réforme Administrative* [2005] IRLR 61, ECJ (following a transfer of training services from the private sector to the civil service, the applicant was placed on the appropriate civil service scales, resulting in a 37% reduction in monthly salary). See also *Wain v Guernsey Ship Management Ltd* [2007] EWCA Civ 294, [2007] ICR 1350, [2007] All ER (D) 35 (Apr) (although the claimants could be said to belong to a group which could be identified because all members had short term contracts and fulfilled a specific role in the business but they all did different work on different vessels, and it was thus considered that the group was not an economic entity).

18 Transfer of Undertakings (Protection of Employment) Regulations 2006, SI 2006/246, reg 3(6)(a). Even before the current version of this provision came into force, it had been held that there could be a four-stage transfer, particularly in a case of the re-tendering of a contract: *Dines v Initial Healthcare Services Ltd* [1995] ICR 11, [1994] IRLR 336, CA. However, for the provision to apply, the transfer must be 'effected' by the transactions in question so that, if necessary, the causal link must still be shown: *Longden v Ferrari Ltd* [1994] ICR 443, [1994] IRLR 157, EAT (transfer in fact effected by the final sale, not by a previous series of transactions which were too remote to come within the regulation).

Where a transfer of an undertaking does occur over an extended period of time, an employee who has continued to be employed by the relevant business is entitled to rights accrued throughout the transfer; and in such a case the establishment of the period of time during which the transfer takes place is a task for the tribunal of fact: *Celtec Ltd v Astley* [2002] EWCA Civ 1035, [2002] ICR 1289, [2002] IRLR 629, [2002] All ER (D) 287 (Jul). For reference to the European Court of Justice as to whether there is a particular point in time at which the transfer of the undertaking is deemed to have been completed, see Case C-478/03 *Celtec Ltd v Astley* [2005] ICR 1409, [2005] IRLR 647, ECJ. Following that ruling, the House of Lords has confirmed the Court of Appeal's decision: see *Astley v Celtec Ltd* [2006] UKHL 29, [2006] 4 All ER 27, [2006] 1 WLR 2420. *Astley v Celtec Ltd* was applied in *Communication Workers Union v Royal Mail Group Ltd* [2009] IRLR 108, [2009] All ER (D) 07 (Jan), EAT. See also *Metropolitan Resources Ltd v Churchill Dulwich Ltd (in liquidation)* [2009] ICR 1380 at [38], [2009] IRLR 700 at [38], EAT, per Burke QC J (*Astley v Celtec Ltd* requires the tribunal to find one date on which any type of relevant transfer occurred on the facts before them but does not require that all the steps which constitute such a transfer must take place on the same day).

19 Transfer of Undertakings (Protection of Employment) Regulations 2006, SI 2006/246, reg 3(6)(b).

20 Ie the Employment Rights Act 1996 s 203 (see PARA 150): see the Transfer of Undertakings (Protection of Employment) Regulations 2006, SI 2006/246, reg 18.

21 Ie in relation to the Transfer of Undertakings (Protection of Employment) Regulations 2006, SI 2006/246: see reg 18.

22 Transfer of Undertakings (Protection of Employment) Regulations 2006, SI 2006/246, reg 18. Compromise agreements which do not arise by reason of the transfer were held not to offend against the earlier version of this provision (ie the Transfer of Undertakings (Protection of Employment) Regulations 1981, SI 1981/1794, reg 12): *Solectron Scotland Ltd v Roper* [2004] IRLR 4, EAT (employer was not purporting to vary the contract, which had come to an end, but merely to compromise a dispute as to its value).

138. Transfers where transferor is subject to relevant insolvency proceedings.
If, at the time of a relevant transfer[1], the transferor[2] is subject to relevant insolvency proceedings[3]:

(1) the relevant statutory scheme under the Employment Rights Act 1996 that applies where an employer has become insolvent[4] applies in the case of a relevant employee[5], irrespective of the fact that the qualifying requirement that the employee's employment has been terminated is not met, and for those purposes the date of the transfer must be treated as the date of the termination and the transferor must be treated as the employer[6]; and

(2) the provisions that govern the effect of a relevant transfer on contracts of employment[7] do not operate to transfer liability for the sums payable to the relevant employee under the relevant statutory schemes[8].

However, neither the provisions mentioned in head (2) above nor the provisions that govern dismissal of an employee because of a relevant transfer[9] apply where the transferor is the subject of bankruptcy proceedings or any analogous insolvency proceedings which have been instituted with a view to the liquidation of the assets of the transferor, and which are under the supervision of an insolvency practitioner[10].

If, at the time of a relevant transfer, the transferor is subject to relevant insolvency proceedings[11], the provisions of the Transfer of Undertakings (Protection of Employment) Regulations 2006[12], do not prevent the transferor or transferee (or an insolvency practitioner), and appropriate representatives of assigned employees[13], agreeing to permitted variations[14]. An individual may be an appropriate representative both for this purpose[15], and for the purposes of informing and consulting employees affected by a relevant transfer[16], provided that where the representative is not a trade union representative he is either elected by or has authority from assigned employees[17], and affected employees, as the case may be[18]. Where assigned employees are represented by non-trade union representatives[19]:

(a)   the agreement recording a permitted variation must be in writing and signed by each of the representatives who have made it (or, where that is not reasonably practicable, by a duly authorised agent of that representative)[20]; and

(b)   the employer must, before the agreement is made available for signature, provide all employees to whom it is intended to apply on the date on which it is to come into effect with copies of the text of the agreement and such guidance as those employees might reasonably require in order to understand it fully[21].

A permitted variation must take effect as a term or condition of the assigned employee's contract of employment in place, where relevant, of any term or condition which it varies[22].

1   As to the meaning of 'relevant transfer' see PARA 137.

2   As to the meaning of 'transferor' see PARA 137.

3   See the Transfer of Undertakings (Protection of Employment) Regulations 2006, SI 2006/246, reg 8(1). In the circumstances described in the text, reg 8(2)–(6) (see heads (1), (2) in the text) applies: see reg 8(1). The scheme set out by reg 8 envisages the operation of two different sub-schemes: (1) a scheme that arises under reg 8(3)–(6) (see heads (1), (2) in the text) and which applies where there are relevant insolvency proceedings but no bankruptcy proceedings or analogous insolvency proceedings instituted with a view to the liquidation of the assets of the transferor; (2) the other scheme, which falls within reg 8(7) (see the text and notes 9–10): *Secretary of State for Trade and Industry v Slater* [2008] ICR 54 at [13]–[19], [2007] IRLR 928 at [13]–[19], EAT, per Elias J.

    For these purposes 'relevant insolvency proceedings' means insolvency proceedings which have been opened in relation to the transferor not with a view to the liquidation of the assets of the transferor and which are under the supervision of an insolvency practitioner: see the Transfer of Undertakings (Protection of Employment) Regulations 2006, SI 2006/246, reg 8(6). 'Insolvency practitioner' has the meaning given to the expression by the Insolvency Act 1986 Pt XIII (ss 388–398) (insolvency practitioners and their qualification: see BANKRUPTCY AND INDIVIDUAL INSOLVENCY vol 5 (2013) PARA 35 et seq): see the Transfer of Undertakings (Protection of Employment) Regulations 2006, SI 2006/246, reg 2(1). The transferor cannot be subject to relevant insolvency proceedings before the appointment of an insolvency practitioner because the concept of when the proceedings begin has to be the same under the Transfer of Undertakings (Protection of Employment) Regulations 2006, SI 2006/246, as it is in the legislation defining the relevant statutory proceedings (see note 4): *Secretary of State for Trade and Industry v Slater* (liquidation occurred as a consequence of the creditors' voluntary liquidation which commenced as a result of the resolution of either the members' or the creditors' meeting, but in any event did not occur until after the transfer). The guidance published by the Department for Business, Innovation and Skills (see PARA 136 note 1) takes the view that '[the Transfer of Undertakings (Protection of Employment) Regulations 2006, SI 2006/246, regs 8 and 9] do not attempt to list all [the] different types of [relevant insolvency proceedings] individually. It is the Department's view that 'relevant insolvency proceedings' mean any collective insolvency proceedings in which the whole or part of the business or undertaking is transferred to another entity as a going concern. That is to say, it covers an insolvency proceeding in which all creditors of a debtor may participate, and in relation to which the insolvency office-holder owes a duty to all creditors. The Department considers that 'relevant insolvency proceedings' does not cover winding-up by either creditors or members where there is no such transfer': see *Employment Rights on the Transfer of an Undertaking: A Guide to the 2006 TUPE Regulations* (Jan 2014) p 27. See also note 10.

4 Ie the relevant statutory scheme specified in the Transfer of Undertakings (Protection of Employment) Regulations 2006, SI 2006/246, reg 8(4)(b): see reg 8(3). For the purposes of reg 8, the 'relevant statutory schemes' are:

    (1)   the Employment Rights Act 1996 Pt XI Ch VI (ss 166–170) (redundancy payments etc made by Secretary of State: see PARAS 884, 885, 887) (Transfer of Undertakings (Protection of Employment) Regulations 2006, SI 2006/246, reg 8(4)(a));

    (2)   the Employment Rights Act 1996 Pt XII (ss 182–190) (insolvency of employers: see PARAS 628–631) (Transfer of Undertakings (Protection of Employment) Regulations 2006, SI 2006/246, reg 8(4)(b)).

As to the meaning of 'employer' and related expressions in relation to employment rights generally see PARA 2 et seq.

5 For these purposes 'relevant employee' means an employee of the transferor:

    (1)   whose contract of employment transfers to the transferee by virtue of the operation of the Transfer of Undertakings (Protection of Employment) Regulations 2006, SI 2006/246 (see reg 8(2)(a)); or

    (2)   whose employment with the transferor is terminated before the time of the relevant transfer in the circumstances described in reg 7(1) (dismissal of an employee because of a relevant transfer: see PARA 803) (see reg 8(2)(b)).

As to the meaning of 'transferee' see PARA 137. As to the meaning of 'employee' for these purposes see PARA 137 note 8. 'Contract of employment' means any agreement between an employee and his employer determining the terms and conditions of his employment: reg 2(1). As to the meanings of 'contract of employment' and 'employee', and related expressions in relation to employment rights generally, see PARA 2 et seq. It is, however, the overall relationship which is preserved and transferred, not necessarily one specific contract of employment: *DJM International Ltd v Nicholas* [1996] ICR 214, [1996] IRLR 76, EAT. A continuation order made under the Trade Union and Labour Relations (Consolidation) Act 1992 s 164 (see PARA 1060), which deems certain contractual provisions to continue pending settlement of a complaint, does not revive the contract and so the transferee does not become liable under such an order for the purposes of the Transfer of Undertakings (Protection of Employment) Regulations 1981, SI 1981/1794 (see now the Transfer of Undertakings (Protection of Employment) Regulations 2006, SI 2006/246; and PARA 136 note 1): *Dowling v ME Ilic Haulage* [2004] ICR 1176, EAT.

6 Transfer of Undertakings (Protection of Employment) Regulations 2006, SI 2006/246, reg 8(3). The date of transfer is not treated as the date of termination in relation to a dismissal which occurs after the date of the transfer, however: *Pressure Coolers Ltd v Molloy* [2011] IRLR 630, EAT.

7 Ie the Transfer of Undertakings (Protection of Employment) Regulations 2006, SI 2006/246, reg 4 (see PARA 139): see reg 8(5).

8 Transfer of Undertakings (Protection of Employment) Regulations 2006, SI 2006/246, reg 8(5). As to the meaning of 'relevant statutory schemes' see note 4.

9 Ie neither the Transfer of Undertakings (Protection of Employment) Regulations 2006, SI 2006/246, reg 4 (see PARA 139) nor reg 7 (dismissal of an employee because of a relevant transfer: see PARA 803): see reg 8(7).

10 Transfer of Undertakings (Protection of Employment) Regulations 2006, SI 2006/246, reg 8(7). Administration proceedings instituted in England pursuant to the Insolvency Act 1986 s 8, Sch B1 (see COMPANY AND PARTNERSHIP INSOLVENCY vol 16 (2011) PARA 158 et seq) are not capable of constituting 'bankruptcy proceedings or any analogous insolvency proceedings which have been instituted with a view to the liquidation of the assets of the transferor' within the meaning of the Transfer of Undertakings (Protection of Employment) Regulations 2006, SI 2006/246, reg 8(7): *OTG Ltd v Barke* [2011] ICR 781, [2011] IRLR 272, EAT (formally, it cannot be said at the moment of the institution of any administration proceedings that their object is to liquidate the assets); approved in *Key2Law (Surrey) LLP v De'Antiquis (Secretary of State for Business, Innovation and Skills intervening)* [2011] EWCA Civ 1567, [2012] ICR 881, [2012] IRLR 212 (the Acquired Rights Directive art 5(1) (see PARA 136 note 3), which is transposed almost verbatim into the Transfer of Undertakings (Protection of Employment) Regulations 2006, SI 2006/246, reg 8(7), was concerned with the purpose of 'analogous insolvency proceedings which have been instituted ...'. and that meant a consideration of the purpose of administration order when actually made rather than a consideration of what the applicants for the order hoped to achieve by it if it were to be made; given the alternatives open to the administrator upon the making of an administration order, it had not been possible

rationally to conclude that such an appointment had been made 'with a view' to the liquidation of the transferor's assets). *Oakland v Wellswood (Yorkshire) Ltd* [2009] All ER (D) 12 (Jan), EAT (whether the Transfer of Undertakings (Protection of Employment) Regulations 2006, SI 2006/246, reg 8(7) applies is a question of fact, not simply a question of categorising the type of insolvency) was not followed in *OTG Ltd v Barke* (a fact-based approach inevitably increases the likelihood of disputes as to who is liable for the transferor's obligations, and a 'bright-line' rule has clear advantages), and on appeal *Oakland v Wellswood (Yorkshire) Ltd* was decided on a different basis: see [2009] EWCA Civ 1094, [2010] IRLR 82 (employment tribunal had jurisdiction without any need to rely upon the provisions of the Transfer of Undertakings (Protection of Employment) Regulations 2006, SI 2006/246, and, in those circumstances, it was not necessary to determine whether, pursuant to reg 8(7), the administration excluded the application of reg 4). As to ECJ case law that is reflected in the wording of the Acquired Rights Directive art 5(1) see Case 135/83 *Abels v Administrative Board of the Bedrijfsvereniging voor de Metaalindustrie en de Electrotechnische Industrie* [1985] ECR 469, [1987] 2 CMLR 406, ECJ; Case C-362/89 *d'Urso v Ercole Marelli Elettromeccanica Generale SpA* [1991] ECR I-4105, [1993] 3 CMLR 513, [1992] IRLR 136, ECJ; Case C-472/93 *Spano v Fiat Geotech SpA and Fiat Hitachi Excavators SpA* [1995] ECR 1–4321, ECJ; Case C-319/94 *Jules Dethier Équipement v Dassy and Sovam SPRL (in liquidation)* [1998] ECR I-1061, [1998] All ER (EC) 346, [1998] 2 CMLR 611, ECJ; Case C-399/96 *Europièces SA (in liquidation) v Wilfried Sanders and Automotive Industries Holding Company SA* [1998] ECR I-6965, [1999] All ER (EC) 831, [2001] 1 CMLR 667, ECJ. See also note 3.

11 For the purposes of the Transfer of Undertakings (Protection of Employment) Regulations 2006, SI 2006/246, reg 9, 'relevant insolvency proceedings' has the meaning given to the expression by reg 8(6) (see note 3): see reg 9(7).

12 Ie the Transfer of Undertakings (Protection of Employment) Regulations 2006, SI 2006/246: see reg 9(1).

13 For these purposes 'appropriate representatives' are:
    (1) if the employees are of a description in respect of which an independent trade union is recognised by their employer, representatives of the trade union (Transfer of Undertakings (Protection of Employment) Regulations 2006, SI 2006/246, reg 9(2)(a)); or
    (2) in any other case, whichever of the following employee representatives the employer chooses: (a) employee representatives appointed or elected by the assigned employees (whether they make the appointment or election alone or with others) otherwise than for the purposes of reg 9, who (having regard to the purposes for, and the method by which they were appointed or elected) have authority from those employees to agree permitted variations to contracts of employment on their behalf (reg 9(2)(b)(i)); (b) employee representatives elected by assigned employees (whether they make the appointment or election alone or with others) for these particular purposes, in an election satisfying requirements identical to those contained in reg 14 (except those in reg 14(1)(d)) (see PARA 1196 text head (iv)) (reg 9(2)(b)(ii)).
    For the purposes of reg 9, 'permitted variation' is a variation to the contract of employment of an assigned employee where:
    (i) the sole or principal reason for the variation is the transfer, and not a reason referred to in reg 4(5)(a) (ie an economic, technical or organisational reason entailing changes in the workforce: see PARA 139) (reg 9(7)(a) (substituted by SI 2014/16)); and
    (ii) it is designed to safeguard employment opportunities by ensuring the survival of the undertaking, business or part of the undertaking or business that is the subject of the relevant transfer (Transfer of Undertakings (Protection of Employment) Regulations 2006, SI 2006/246, reg 9(7)(b)).
    For the purposes of reg 9, 'assigned employees' means those employees assigned to the organised grouping of resources or employees that is the subject of a relevant transfer: see reg 9(7). Generally, 'assigned' means assigned other than on a temporary basis: see reg 2(1); and see Case 186/83 *Botzen v Rotterdamsche Droogdok Maatschappij BV* [1985] ECR 519, [1986] 2 CMLR 50, ECJ (where only part of business was transferred, the Acquired Rights Directive (see PARA 136 note 3) applied only to employees that could be said to have been transferred or assigned to that part, excluding those not transferred but who carried out administrative duties in relation to the transferred department) (applied in *Michael Peters Ltd v Michael Peters Group plc* [1995] IRLR 190, EAT; *Duncan Web Offset (Maidstone) Ltd v Cooper* [1995] IRLR 633, EAT; *Buchanan-Smith v Schleicher & Co International Ltd* [1996] ICR 613, [1996] IRLR 547, EAT).
    For the purposes of the Transfer of Undertakings (Protection of Employment) Regulations 2006, SI 2006/246, the representative of a trade union recognised by an employer is an official or other person authorised to carry on collective bargaining with that employer by

that trade union: reg 2(2). 'Recognised' has the meaning given to the expression by the Trade Union and Labour Relations (Consolidation) Act 1992 s 178(3) (see PARA 1094); and 'collective agreement', 'collective bargaining' and 'trade union' have the same meanings respectively as in the Trade Union and Labour Relations (Consolidation) Act 1992: see the Transfer of Undertakings (Protection of Employment) Regulations 2006, SI 2006/246, reg 2(1). Accordingly, as to the meaning of 'trade union' see the Trade Union and Labour Relations (Consolidation) Act 1992 s 1; and PARA 891. As to the meanings of 'collective agreement' and 'collective bargaining' see s 178(1); and PARA 1093. As to the modifications that are made to s 168 (time off work for trade union duties and industrial relations training: see PARA 1020) for these purposes see the Transfer of Undertakings (Protection of Employment) Regulations 2006, SI 2006/246, reg 9(4); and see PARA 1020. As to the effect of a relevant transfer on trade union recognition see reg 6; and PARA 1095.

14 Transfer of Undertakings (Protection of Employment) Regulations 2006, SI 2006/246, reg 9(1).

15 Ie the purposes of the Transfer of Undertakings (Protection of Employment) Regulations 2006, SI 2006/246, reg 9: see reg 9(3).

16 Ie the purposes of the Transfer of Undertakings (Protection of Employment) Regulations 2006, SI 2006/246, reg 13 (see PARA 1196): see reg 9(3).

17 Ie within the meaning of the Transfer of Undertakings (Protection of Employment) Regulations 2006, SI 2006/246, reg 9 (see note 13): see reg 9(3).

18 Transfer of Undertakings (Protection of Employment) Regulations 2006, SI 2006/246, reg 9(3). The reference to 'affected employees' is to employees who are so described in reg 13(1) (see PARA 1196): see reg 9(3).

19 See the Transfer of Undertakings (Protection of Employment) Regulations 2006, SI 2006/246, reg 9(5).

20 Transfer of Undertakings (Protection of Employment) Regulations 2006, SI 2006/246, reg 9(5)(a).

21 Transfer of Undertakings (Protection of Employment) Regulations 2006, SI 2006/246, reg 9(5)(b).

22 Transfer of Undertakings (Protection of Employment) Regulations 2006, SI 2006/246, reg 9(6).

C. EFFECT ON CONTRACTS OF EMPLOYMENT

139. Effect of relevant transfer on contracts of employment. A relevant transfer[1] does not operate so as to terminate the contract of employment[2] of any person employed by the transferor[3] and assigned to the organised grouping of resources or employees that is subject to the relevant transfer[4] (which would otherwise be terminated by the transfer) but any such contract will have effect after the transfer as if originally made between the person so employed and the transferee[5]. Without prejudice to this provision[6], on the completion of a relevant transfer[7]:

(1) all the transferor's rights, powers, duties and liabilities under or in connection with any such contract[8] are to be transferred[9] to the transferee[10]; and

(2) any act or omission before the transfer is completed, of or in relation to the transferor in respect of that contract or a person assigned to that organised grouping of resources or employees, is to be deemed to have been an act or omission of or in relation to the transferee[11].

The provision so made[12] does not transfer or otherwise affect the liability of any person to be prosecuted for, convicted of and sentenced for any offence[13], and it is subject to other provisions that preserve liabilities for civil penalties imposed for a failure to inform or consult affected employees[14], and those provisions which govern relevant insolvency proceedings that have been opened in relation to a transferor[15]. Subject to contract variations that are permitted in prescribed circumstances where such insolvency proceedings have been opened[16], any purported variation of a contract of employment that is, or will be, otherwise transferred[17], is void if the sole or principal reason for the variation is the transfer[18]. This restriction does not prevent a variation of the contract of employment, however, if[19]:

(a)   the sole or principal reason for the variation is an economic, technical, or organisational reason entailing changes in the workforce[20], provided that the employer and employee agree that variation[21]; or

(b)   the terms of that contract permit the employer to make such a variation[22].

Nor does that restriction[23] apply in respect of a variation of the contract of employment in so far as it varies a term or condition incorporated from a collective agreement[24], provided that[25]:

(i)   the variation of the contract takes effect on a date more than one year after the date of the transfer[26]; and

(ii)   following that variation, the rights and obligations in the employee's contract, when considered together, are no less favourable to the employee than those which applied immediately before the variation[27].

Neither such exception to the restriction on purported contract variations[28] affects any rule of law as to whether a contract of employment is effectively varied[29].

Where a contract of employment, which is transferred by the effect of a relevant transfer[30], incorporates provisions of collective agreements as may be agreed from time to time, any rights, powers, duties and liabilities are not transferred under heads (1) and (2) above[31] in relation to any provision of a collective agreement if the following conditions are met[32], namely:

(A)   the provision of the collective agreement is agreed after the date of the transfer[33]; and

(B)   the transferee is not a participant in the collective bargaining for that provision[34].

The contract of employment has effect[35] after the transfer as if it does not incorporate provisions of a collective agreement which meet the conditions set out in heads (A) and (B) above[36].

Any such transfer of an employee's contract of employment[37] may not be effected to an employee who informs the transferor or the transferee that he objects to becoming employed by the transferee[38].

1   As to the meaning of 'relevant transfer' see PARA 137.

2   As to the meaning of 'contract of employment' see PARA 138 note 5.

3   As to the meaning of 'transferor' see PARA 137.

4   Any reference in the Transfer of Undertakings (Protection of Employment) Regulations 2006, SI 2006/246, reg 4(1) to a person employed by the transferor and assigned to the organised grouping of resources or employees that is subject to a relevant transfer, is a reference to a person so employed immediately before the transfer, or who would have been so employed if he had not been dismissed in the circumstances described in reg 7(1) (dismissal of an employee because of a relevant transfer: see PARA 803) (including, where the transfer is effected by a series of two or more transactions, a person so employed and assigned or who would have been so employed and assigned immediately before any of those transactions): reg 4(3). As to the meaning of 'employee' and as to references to 'organised grouping of employees' for these purposes see PARA 137 note 8. As to the meaning of 'assigned' see PARA 138 note 13.

     When applying the Transfer of Undertakings (Protection of Employment) Regulations 2006, SI 2006/246, reg 4(3) to the issue of whether an employee who was not at work immediately before a transfer was assigned to the part transferred, the issue is a question of fact to be determined having regard to all the circumstances and by reference to where the employee would have been required to work immediately before the transfer: *Robert Sage Ltd (t/a Prestige Nursing Care Ltd) v O'Connell* [2014] IRLR 428, [2014] All ER (D) 309 (Mar), EAT (the fact that the employee was not permitted to return to work immediately before the service provision change means that she was not assigned to the grouping of employees subject to the relevant transfer). In the context of the predecessor provision (ie the Transfer of Undertakings (Protection of Employment) Regulations 1981, SI 1981/1794, reg 5(3)), 'immediately before' was held to mean that the employee is still in the transferor's employment at the moment of the transfer: *Secretary of State for Employment v Spence* [1987] QB 179, [1986] ICR 651, CA (applying *Premier Motors (Medway) Ltd v Total Oil Great Britain Ltd* [1984] 1 WLR 377, [1984] ICR 58, EAT; Case 19/83 *Wendelboe v LJ Music ApS (in liquidation)* [1985] ECR 457, [1986] 1 CMLR 476, ECJ; disapproving *Alphafield v Barratt* [1984] 3 All ER 795, sub nom *Apex Leisure Hire v Barratt* [1984] ICR 452, EAT; *Secretary of State for Employment v Anchor Hotel (Kippford) Ltd* [1985] ICR 724, [1985] IRLR 452, EAT; *Fenton v Stablegold Ltd* [1986] ICR 236, [1986] IRLR 64, EAT; *Bullard v Marchant* [1986] 3 CMLR 641, [1986] ICR 389, EAT). The decision in *Secretary of State for Employment v Spence* also impliedly overruled *Kestongate Ltd v Miller* [1986] ICR 672, EAT (in which it was held that a 'transfer' could cover a period of time, eg between contract and completion): *Wheeler v Patel* [1987] ICR 631, [1987] IRLR 211, EAT. The holding in *Secretary of State for Employment v Spence* that 'immediately before' meant 'at the moment of transfer' led to the possibility of the avoidance of the regulations by the device of an artificially created gap; but this was prevented by the subsequent decision in *Litster v Forth Dry Dock and Engineering Co Ltd (in receivership)* [1990] 1 AC 546, [1989] ICR 341, HL (applying Case 101/87 *P Bork International A/S (in liquidation) v Foreningen af Arbejdsledere i Danmark* [1990] 3 CMLR 701, [1989] IRLR 41, ECJ, on the equivalent provision of the Acquired Rights Directive), which required the words 'immediately before the transfer' in the Transfer of Undertakings (Protection of Employment) Regulations 1981, SI 1981/1794, reg 5(3) to be read as if 'or would have been so employed if he had not been unfairly dismissed ...' were implied. The current wording of the Transfer of Undertakings (Protection of Employment) Regulations 2006, SI 2006/246, reg 4(3) reflects the decision in *Litster v Forth Dry Dock and Engineering Co Ltd (in receivership)*. See also *Brook Lane Finance Co Ltd v Bradley* [1988] ICR 423, [1988] IRLR 283, EAT (date of transfer was the date when the transfer was completed rather than the date on which the transferees were let into possession and control of the business by a deed of assignment); *Macer v Abafast Ltd* [1990] ICR 234, [1990] IRLR 137, EAT (*Brook Lane Finance Co Ltd v Bradley* not followed); *Clark & Tokeley Ltd (t/a Spellbrook) v Oakes* [1998] 4 All ER 353, [1999] ICR 276, CA; *G4S Justice Services (UK) Ltd v Anstey* [2006] IRLR 588, EAT (employment was transferred, notwithstanding that employees' appeal against dismissal on grounds of misconduct had not been heard by the transferors by the time of the transfer).

5   Transfer of Undertakings (Protection of Employment) Regulations 2006, SI 2006/246, reg 4(1). This provision does not apply where the right of objection under reg 4(7) is exercised (see the text and notes 37–38; and PARA 141): see reg 4(1). As to the meaning of 'transferee' see PARA 137.

The Transfer of Undertakings (Protection of Employment) Regulations 1981, SI 1981/1794, reg 5(1) (ie the predecessor provision to the Transfer of Undertakings (Protection of Employment) Regulations 2006, SI 2006/246, reg 4(1)) effectively provides for the automatic continuation between different parties of the contract of employment, on certain conditions being satisfied, but irrespective of the wishes or consent of the parties: *Premier Motors (Medway) Ltd v Total Oil Great Britain Ltd* [1984] 1 WLR 377, [1984] ICR 58, EAT; Joined Cases 144/87, 145/87 *Berg and Busschers v Besselsen* [1988] ECR 2559, [1990] ICR 396, [1989] IRLR 447, ECJ. See also *Preston v Wolverhampton Healthcare Trust* [2006] UKHL 13, [2006] ICR 606, sub nom *Powerhouse Retail Ltd v Burroughs* [2006] IRLR 381. At common law, the employee has a right to choose for himself whom he would serve so that the transfer of a business would automatically terminate contracts of employment giving rise to a dismissal: see *Nokes v Doncaster Amalgamated Collieries Ltd* [1940] AC 1014, [1940] 3 All ER 549, HL; and PARA 136 note 3.

6   Ie without prejudice to the Transfer of Undertakings (Protection of Employment) Regulations 2006, SI 2006/246, reg 4(1) (see the text and notes 1–5): see reg 4(2).

7   See the Transfer of Undertakings (Protection of Employment) Regulations 2006, SI 2006/246, reg 4(2). The two elements of reg 4(2), ie reg 4(2)(a) (see head (1) in the text) and reg 4(2)(b) (see head (2) in the text), are to be construed separately: see *Lindley v Perry's Motor Sales Ltd* [2008] All ER (D) 32 (Jun), EAT.

8   It was suggested under the predecessor provisions (ie under the Transfer of Undertakings (Protection of Employment) Regulations 1981, SI 1981/1794 (revoked: see PARA 136 note 1)) that, for these purposes, a distinction must be drawn between a liability which arises under the Regulations, which does not transfer, and a general liability, arising under a contract of employment and applying in relation to all employees, which does: see *Transport and General Workers' Union v James McKinnon Jnr (Haulage) Ltd* [2001] ICR 1281, [2001] IRLR

597, EAT. Cf *Kerry Foods Ltd v Creber* [2000] IRLR 10, EAT (liability for a failure to inform and consult was 'under or in connection with the contract of employment' and so transfers); and see *Alamo Group (Europe) Ltd v Tucker* [2003] ICR 829, [2003] IRLR 266, EAT, which preferred the decision in *Kerry Foods Ltd v Creber* to that in *Transport and General Workers' Union v James McKinnon Jnr (Haulage) Ltd*.

Recent authority seems to prefer a more purposive approach, taking the aim of the acquired rights provisions as being to prevent the employee from being prejudiced as a result of the transfer, whilst at the same time not conferring additional rights on the employee or improving the situation of the employee: *Jackson v Computershare Investor Services plc* [2007] EWCA Civ 1065, [2008] ICR 341, [2008] IRLR 70 (transferred employee has no entitlement to enhanced redundancy payments that were applicable only to the transferee's staff, and to which the transferred employee never had any freestanding entitlement) (applied in *Small v Boots Co plc* [2009] IRLR 328, [2009] All ER (D) 200 (Jan), EAT). See also Case E-3/01 *Viggósdóttir v Íslandspóstur HF* [2002] 2 CMLR 18, [2002] IRLR 425, EFTA Ct (transfer within the meaning of the Acquired Rights Directive as annexed to the European Economic Agreement and deemed to be part of that Agreement); and Case C-108/10 *Scattolon v Ministero dell'Istruzione, dell'Università e della Ricerca* [2011] ECR I-7491, [2012] 1 CMLR 432, [2012] ICR 740, [2011] IRLR 1020, ECJ. Perhaps a more than ordinary flexibility of approach is required as the price of the conclusion that every sort of right, even an expectation which is subject to the exercise of a discretionary power, is to be transferred pursuant to the acquired rights provisions: *Procter & Gamble Co v Svenska Cellulosa Aktiebolaget SCA* [2012] EWHC 1257 (Ch), [2012] IRLR 733. What is important throughout is not the label but the substance of the right, power, duty and liability concerned because, to satisfy the objectives, it is necessary in each case to unpack the economic components, with a view to providing for substantial identity (or failing which substantive equivalence) of economic benefit after the transfer as before: *Procter & Gamble Co v Svenska Cellulosa Aktiebolaget SCA* (phrase 'rights and obligations' in the Acquired Rights Directive art 3 is to be liberally interpreted without regard to domestic distinctions between a discretionary entitlement and a legally enforceable right; relevant right to be considered for early retirement benefits had been a liability which had transferred under the Regulations). As to the Acquired Rights Directive see PARA 136 note 3.

9   Ie by virtue of the Transfer of Undertakings (Protection of Employment) Regulations 2006, SI 2006/246, reg 4: see reg 4(2)(a). See eg *Rossiter v Pendragon plc, Crosby-Clarke v Air Foyle Ltd* [2002] EWCA Civ 745, [2002] ICR 1063, [2002] IRLR 483 (transferor's contractual right to alter terms of employment passed to transferee); *Dowling v ME Ilic Haulage* [2004] ICR 1176, EAT (liability under a continuation of employment order pursuant to the Trade Union and Labour Relations (Consolidation) Act 1992 s 164 (see PARA 1060), without a voluntary order being made under s 163, did not transfer); *British Telecommunications plc v Royal Mail Group Ltd* [2010] EWHC 8 (QB), [2010] All ER (D) 10 (Jan) (liabilities towards employees passed in accordance with the British Telecommunications Act 1981 s 10(2) (see TELECOMMUNICATIONS vol 97 (2010) PARA 57)).

10   Transfer of Undertakings (Protection of Employment) Regulations 2006, SI 2006/246, reg 4(2)(a). Where, by virtue of the Employers' Liability (Compulsory Insurance) Act 1969 s 3(1)(a) (exemption for specified authorities: see PARA 43) or s 3(1)(b) (exemption for body corporates under national ownership or control: see PARA 43), the transferor is not required by the 1969 Act to effect any insurance, or where, by virtue of s 3(1)(c) (exemption for such cases as may be specified in regulations: see PARA 43), the transferor is exempted from the requirement of the 1969 Act to effect insurance, the transferor and the transferee are to be jointly and severally liable, on completion of a relevant transfer, in respect of any liability referred to in s 1(1) (general duty to insure: see PARA 40), in so far as such liability relates to the employee's employment with the transferor: see the Transfer of Undertakings (Protection of Employment) Regulations 2006, SI 2006/246, reg 17(1), (2). See also note 7.

The Acquired Rights Directive (see PARA 136 note 3) has been construed as transferring to the transferee all debts arising out of the employment contract or relationship unless they come under the exceptions set out in art 3(3) (for the purposes of implementation in the United Kingdom the Transfer of Undertakings (Protection of Employment) Regulations 1981, SI 1981/1794, reg 7 was made: see now the Transfer of Undertakings (Protection of Employment) Regulations 2006, SI 2006/246, reg 10 (occupational pension schemes); and PARA 141): Case 135/83 *Abels v Administrative Board of the Bedrijfsvereniging voor de Metaalindustrie en de Electrotechnische Industrie* [1985] ECR 469, [1987] 2 CMLR 406, ECJ. However, the exceptions are to be construed narrowly: see Case C-164/00 *Beckmann v Dynamco Whicheloe MacFarlane Ltd* [2002] All ER (EC) 865, [2003] ICR 50, ECJ (employer's obligations under a scheme providing for benefits upon dismissal by reason of redundancy are transferred); Case C-4/01 *Martin v South Bank University* [2003] ECR I–12859, [2004]

1 CMLR 472, [2004] IRLR 74, ECJ (redundancy provision under a collective agreement entitled an employee to early retirement benefit). See also Case C-343/98 *Collino v Telecom Italia SpA* [2001] All ER (EC) 405, [2002] ICR 38, [2000] IRLR 788, ECJ (in calculating the employee's financial rights, the transferee must take into account the entire length of service, in so far as the obligation to do so derives from the employment relationship between employee and transferor). As to whether occupational pension schemes are supplementary schemes within the Acquired Rights Directive art 3 see *Walden Engineering Co Ltd v Warrener* [1993] ICR 967, [1993] IRLR 420, EAT.

Cases in domestic law have shown the width of the formulation in the Transfer of Undertakings (Protection of Employment) Regulations 1981, SI 1981/1794, reg 5(1) (but see now the slightly reworded Transfer of Undertakings (Protection of Employment) Regulations 2006, SI 2006/246, reg 4(1) (see the text and notes 1–5)), transferring to the transferee not just the ordinary incidents of the contract of employment and contractual or statutory liabilities (eg for unfair dismissal or a redundancy payment) but also:

(1)   liability under a protective award for failure to consult on collective redundancies (see the Trade Union and Labour Relations (Consolidation) Act 1992 ss 188, 189; and PARA 1189) (*Kerry Foods Ltd v Creber* [2000] IRLR 10, EAT; *Alamo Group (Europe) Ltd v Tucker* [2003] ICR 829, [2003] IRLR 266, EAT (both disapproving *Angus Jowett & Co Ltd v National Union of Tailors and Garment Workers* [1985] ICR 646, [1985] IRLR 326, EAT));

(2)   liability under statute for alleged discrimination (*DJM International Ltd v Nicholas* [1996] ICR 214, [1996] IRLR 76, EAT; cf *Gutridge v Sodexo Ltd* [2009] EWCA Civ 729, [2009] ICR 1486, [2009] IRLR 721 (employee's rights against transferor were limited in time so claim had to be made within six months of the termination of her employment with the transferor));

(3)   the benefit of a restraint of trade clause (*Morris Angel & Son Ltd v Hollande* [1993] 3 All ER 569, [1993] ICR 71, CA);

(4)   liability in tort for an industrial accident (*Bernadone v Pall Mall Services Group Ltd (Independent Insurance Ltd, third party)* [2000] 3 All ER 544, [2000] IRLR 487, CA);

(5)   the benefit of a collective agreement incorporated into the employees' contracts of employment (but see the text and notes 23–36);

(6)   the benefit of a profit-sharing scheme operated by the transferor on its performance (*Unicorn Consultancy Services Ltd v Westbrook* [2000] IRLR 80, EAT (profit-related pay); *Mitie Management Services Ltd v French* [2002] ICR 1395, [2002] IRLR 512, EAT (right to participate in profit-sharing scheme of 'substantial equivalence')).

As to head (1) above, see now the Transfer of Undertakings (Protection of Employment) Regulations 2006, SI 2006/246, reg 15(9); and PARA 1200.

Liabilities (and occasionally rights) such as these transfer wholly to the transferee because the United Kingdom chose to implement the Acquired Rights Directive so as not to leave any concurrent liability on the transferor: *Allan v Stirling District Council* [1995] ICR 1082, sub nom *Stirling District Council v Allan* [1995] IRLR 301, Ct of Sess. In *Kerry Foods Ltd v Creber*, the Employment Appeal Tribunal stated that, exceptionally, liability for a dismissal by the transferor for an 'economic, technical or organisational reason' within the Transfer of Undertakings (Protection of Employment) Regulations 1981, SI 1981/1794, reg 8 (see now the Transfer of Undertakings (Protection of Employment) Regulations 2006, SI 2006/246, reg 7) (see PARA 803) which was held in substance to have been unfair remained personal to the transferor and would not transfer to the transferee.

Once the Transfer of Undertakings (Protection of Employment) Regulations 1981, SI 1981/1794, reg 5 (but see now the Transfer of Undertakings (Protection of Employment) Regulations 2006, SI 2006/246, reg 4) has operated to transfer contractual rights and liabilities, an orthodox approach based on domestic contract law would allow the parties (transferee and transferred employees) to reach an agreement to alter the existing terms and conditions for good consideration, just as the transferor might have done had there been no transfer; and initially that appeared to be the position under the Acquired Rights Directive: Case 324/86 *Foreningen af Arbejdsledere i Danmark v Daddy's Dance Hall A/S* [1988] ECR 739, [1988] IRLR 315, ECJ. However, in the light of certain dicta in that case, the Employment Appeal Tribunal held that the intent of the Acquired Rights Directive is that a transferee employer may not lawfully change the existing terms and conditions, if the change is transfer-related, and that any attempt to do so (even for good consideration, and with the agreement of the transferred employees) is void: *Wilson v St Helens Borough Council* [1996] ICR 711, [1996] IRLR 320, EAT. When this case was heard by the House of Lords, sub nom *British Fuels Ltd v Baxendale, Wilson v St Helens*

Borough Council [1998] 4 All ER 609, [1998] ICR 1141, HL, that invalidity was assumed and argument centred on when a change might be effective. The House of Lords held that this would be so in two cases:

(a) where a post-transfer change can be shown not to be transfer-related, but for some other independent reason; and

(b) where the employees are dismissed and then re-engaged on the new terms (which operates as a valid change, there being in domestic law no concept of a dismissal being a nullity, but which exposes the employer to a claim for unfair dismissal, with compensation potentially reflecting any worsening in the terms of employment: *Cornwall County Care Ltd v Brightman* [1998] ICR 529, [1998] IRLR 228, EAT).

On this basis, the addition of restraint clauses to transferred employees' contracts on a transfer has been held to be invalid (and so the clauses were held to be unenforceable), even where good consideration was given by the transferee employer: *Crédit Suisse First Boston (Europe) Ltd v Padiachy* [1999] ICR 569, [1998] IRLR 504; *Crédit Suisse First Boston (Europe) Ltd v Lister* [1999] ICR 794, [1998] IRLR 700, CA. See now also *Power v Regent Security Services Ltd* [2007] EWCA Civ 1188, [2008] 2 All ER 977, [2008] ICR 442 (safeguarding of an employee's acquired rights on the transfer of an undertaking meant that a transferred employee, who wished to take the benefit of an original retiring age of 60 agreed with the transferor, was entitled to do so as against the transferee: if the retiring age was then varied by agreement with the transferee, the employee had to be treated as obtaining an additional right not as waiving an acquired right) in which *Crédit Suisse First Boston (Europe) Ltd v Lister* and Case 324/86 *Foreningen af Arbejdsledere i Danmark v Daddy's Dance Hall A/S* were distinguished. The approach taken in head (a) above has been supported (without reference to *British Fuels Ltd v Baxendale, Wilson v St Helens Borough Council*) in Case C-343/98 *Collino v Telecom Italia SpA* (under the Acquired Rights Directive, a transferee may alter the terms of the employment relationship, where national law allowed, in situations other than the transfer of an undertaking); and see Case C-108/10 *Scattolon v Ministero dell'Istruzione, dell'Università e della Ricerca* [2011] ECR I-7491, [2012] 1 CMLR 432, [2012] ICR 740, [2011] IRLR 1020, ECJ (on transfer of local authority workers to the state, employee was put on a salary scale that did not reflect her full service within the local authority but as her pay was in a collective agreement it was unlawful for a transferee to apply terms and conditions under the new state collective agreement).

An order for interim relief made under the Trade Union and Labour Relations (Consolidation) Act 1992 ss 163, 164 (see PARA 1060; and note 9) does not operate primarily through the contract and so does not transfer to the transferee: *Dowling v ME Ilic Haulage* [2004] ICR 1176, EAT. Also, the transfer, under the Transfer of Undertakings (Protection of Employment) Regulations 2006, SI 2006/246, reg 4, of rights and obligations under or in connection with an occupational pension scheme is subject to reg 10: see PARA 141.

The Transfer of Undertakings (Protection of Employment) Regulations 2006, SI 2006/246, provide for the transferor to notify the transferee of any relevant employee liability information, including any collective agreement which has effect after the transfer: see regs 11, 12; and PARA 140.

11 Transfer of Undertakings (Protection of Employment) Regulations 2006, SI 2006/246, reg 4(2)(b). See note 7.

12 Ie the provision made by the Transfer of Undertakings (Protection of Employment) Regulations 2006, SI 2006/246, reg 4(2) (see the text and notes 6–11): see reg 4(2).

13 See the Transfer of Undertakings (Protection of Employment) Regulations 2006, SI 2006/246, reg 4(6). The provision made by reg 4(2) (see the text and notes 6–11) is subject to reg 4(6): see reg 4(2).

14 Ie the provision made by the Transfer of Undertakings (Protection of Employment) Regulations 2006, SI 2006/246, reg 4(2) (see the text and notes 6–11) is subject to reg 15(9) (see PARA 1200): see reg 4(2). As to the meaning of 'affected employees' see PARA 1196 note 8.

15 Ie the provision made by the Transfer of Undertakings (Protection of Employment) Regulations 2006, SI 2006/246, reg 4(2) (see the text and notes 6–11) is subject to reg 8 (see PARA 138): see reg 4(2). As to the meaning of 'relevant insolvency proceedings' for these purposes see PARA 138 note 3.

16 Ie subject to the Transfer of Undertakings (Protection of Employment) Regulations 2006, SI 2006/246, reg 9 (see PARA 138): see reg 4(4) (reg 4(4), (5) substituted, regs 4(5A)–(5C), 4A added, by SI 2014/16). As to the meaning of 'permitted variation' for these purposes see PARA 138 note 13.

17 Ie that is, or will be, transferred by the Transfer of Undertakings (Protection of Employment) Regulations 2006, SI 2006/246, reg 4(1) (see the text and notes 1–5): see reg 4(4) (as substituted: see note 16).

18 Transfer of Undertakings (Protection of Employment) Regulations 2006, SI 2006/246, reg 4(4) (as substituted: see note 16).

19 See the Transfer of Undertakings (Protection of Employment) Regulations 2006, SI 2006/246, reg 4(5) (as substituted: see note 16).

20 For these purposes, the expression 'changes in the workforce' includes a change to the place where employees are employed by the employer to carry on the business of the employer or to carry out work of a particular kind for the employer (and the reference to such a place has the same meaning as in the Employment Rights Act 1996 s 139: see PARA 870): Transfer of Undertakings (Protection of Employment) Regulations 2006, SI 2006/246, reg 4(5A) (as added: see note 16). *Berriman v Delabole Slate Ltd* [1984] ICR 636, [1984] IRLR 394, EAT (affd [1985] ICR 546, [1985] IRLR 305, CA) held that 'changes in the workforce' should entail changes in the actual numbers employed or in any event in the jobs which the employees do (ie redundancies or redeployment); and see *Manchester College v Hazel* [2014] EWCA Civ 72, [2014] IRLR 392 (principal reason for dismissal was refusal to accept changed terms, which did not constitute a 'change in the workforce', and dismissal had been automatically unfair) (cited also in PARA 803 note 7); cf *Nationwide Building Society v Benn* [2010] IRLR 922, EAT (it was enough that a section of employees were affected, here the group of, transferring employees).

21 Transfer of Undertakings (Protection of Employment) Regulations 2006, SI 2006/246, reg 4(5)(a) (as substituted: see note 16).

22 Transfer of Undertakings (Protection of Employment) Regulations 2006, SI 2006/246, reg 4(5)(b) (as substituted: see note 16).

23 Ie the Transfer of Undertakings (Protection of Employment) Regulations 2006, SI 2006/246, reg 4(4) (see the text and notes 16–18): see reg 4(5B) (as added: see note 16).

24 Where, at the time of a relevant transfer, there exists a collective agreement made by or on behalf of the transferor with a trade union recognised by the transferor in respect of any employee whose contract of employment is preserved by the Transfer of Undertakings (Protection of Employment) Regulations 2006, SI 2006/246, reg 4(1) (see the text and notes 1–5) (see reg 5), then:

(1) without prejudice to the Trade Union and Labour Relations (Consolidation) Act 1992 ss 179, 180 (collective agreements presumed to be unenforceable in specified circumstances: see PARAS 1175–1177), that agreement, in its application in relation to the employee, must, after the transfer, have effect as if made by or on behalf of the transferee with that trade union, and accordingly anything done under or in connection with it, in its application in relation to the employee, by or in relation to the transferor before the transfer, is, after the transfer, deemed to have been done by or in relation to the transferee (Transfer of Undertakings (Protection of Employment) Regulations 2006, SI 2006/246, reg 5(a)); and

(2) any order made in respect of that agreement, in its application in relation to the employee, must, after the transfer, have effect as if the transferee were a party to the agreement (reg 5(b)).

As to the meanings of 'collective agreement', 'recognised', and 'trade union' for these purposes see PARA 138 note 13. See generally Case C-4/01 *Martin v South Bank University* [2003] ECR I–12859, [2004] 1 CMLR 472, [2004] IRLR 74, ECJ (redundancy provision under a collective agreement); Case C-499/04 *Werhof v Freeway Traffic Systems GmbH & Co KG* [2005] ECR I-2397, [2006] IRLR 400, ECJ (see note 32); Case C-396/07 *Juuri v Fazer Amica Oy* [2008] ECR I-8883, [2009] 1 CMLR 902, [2008] All ER (D) 302 (Nov), ECJ (Directive cannot impose on the transferee the obligation to observe the original working conditions after the agreed date of expiry of the collective agreement since, after that date, the agreement is no longer in force); Case C-108/10 *Scattolon v Ministero dell'Istruzione, dell'Università e della Ricerca* [2011] ECR I-7491, [2012] 1 CMLR 432, [2012] ICR 740, [2011] IRLR 1020, ECJ (unlawful for transferee to apply terms and conditions under new collective agreement); Case C-328/13 *Österreichischer Gewerkschaftsbund v Wirtschaftskammer Österreich*, [2014] All ER (D) 110 (Sep), CJEU (terms and conditions laid down in a collective agreement, which continue to produce their effects as regards the employment relationship which was governed by them before the agreement was terminated, constitute 'terms and conditions agreed in any collective agreement' so long as that employment relationship is not subject to a new collective agreement or a new individual agreement is not concluded with the employees concerned). The protection afforded under heads (1) and (2) above does not apply in any case to so much of a collective agreement as relates to an occupational pension scheme within the meaning of the Pension Schemes Act 1993 (see PERSONAL AND OCCUPATIONAL PENSIONS vol 80 (2013) PARA 208 et seq), in so far as the scheme provides benefits for old age, invalidity or survivors, and does not apply to any rights, powers, duties or liabilities subsisting by virtue of any such agreement and relating to such a scheme or otherwise arising in connection with that person's employment and relating to such a scheme: see the Transfer of Undertakings (Protection of Employment) Regulations 2006, SI 2006/246, reg 10; and PARA 141.

The Acquired Rights Directive (see PARA 136 note 3) is aimed at ensuring that a transferee safeguards the working conditions agreed under a collective agreement only in respect of employees already employed by the undertaking at the time of transfer and that this excludes those who were recruited after that date: Case C-287/86 *Landsorganisationen i Danmark v Ny Mølle Kro* [1987] ECR 5465, [1989] ICR 330, [1989] IRLR 37, ECJ (transferee not placed under an obligation to observe terms of the collective agreement in respect of any workers who are not employees on the undertaking at the time it was transferred); and see *Ralton v Havering College of Further and Higher Education* [2001] 3 CMLR 1452, [2001] IRLR 738, EAT (transferee not bound to incorporate the terms of a collective agreement into a new contract of employment unrelated to the transfer). At common law, a provision of a collective agreement may be expressly incorporated into the contract of employment: see PARA 116. As to whether transferees are bound by clauses in employment contracts allowing for collective agreements to determine pay and conditions, in circumstances where the transferee is not a party to the collective bargaining machinery, see the Transfer of Undertakings (Protection of Employment) Regulations 2006, SI 2006/246, reg 4A; and the text and notes 30–36.

25　See the Transfer of Undertakings (Protection of Employment) Regulations 2006, SI 2006/246, reg 4(5B) (as added: see note 16).

26　Transfer of Undertakings (Protection of Employment) Regulations 2006, SI 2006/246, reg 4(5B)(a) (as added: see note 16).

27　Transfer of Undertakings (Protection of Employment) Regulations 2006, SI 2006/246, reg 4(5B)(b) (as added: see note 16).

28　Ie neither the Transfer of Undertakings (Protection of Employment) Regulations 2006, SI 2006/246, reg 4(5) (see the text and notes 19–22) nor reg 4(5B) (see the text and notes 23–27): see reg 4(5C) (as added: see note 16).

29　Transfer of Undertakings (Protection of Employment) Regulations 2006, SI 2006/246, reg 4(5C) (as added: see note 16).

30　Ie which is transferred by the Transfer of Undertakings (Protection of Employment) Regulations 2006, SI 2006/246, reg 4(1) (see the text and notes 1–5): see reg 4A(1) (as added: see note 16).

31　Ie are not transferred by the Transfer of Undertakings (Protection of Employment) Regulations 2006, SI 2006/246, reg 4(2) (see the text and notes 6–11): see reg 4A(1) (as added: see note 16).

32　See the Transfer of Undertakings (Protection of Employment) Regulations 2006, SI 2006/246, reg 4A(1) (as added: see note 16). The provision made by reg 4A codifies the 'static' approach to collective agreements that was adopted in Case C-426/11 *Alemo-Herron v Parkwood Leisure Ltd* [2014] All ER (EC) 400, [2014] 1 CMLR 585, [2013] ICR 1116, [2013] IRLR 744, CJEU (Acquired Rights Directive precludes member states from adopting a 'dynamic' interpretation of collective bargaining clauses that would allow them to transfer and continue to bind the new employer, even where the transferee does not have the possibility of participating in the negotiation process of such collective agreements concluded after the date of the transfer, as the Directive cannot be interpreted as entitling member states to take measures which, while being more favourable to employees, are liable to adversely affect the very essence of the transferee's freedom to conduct a business). As to the 'static' interpretation of collective agreement clauses see also Case C-499/04 *Werhof v Freeway Traffic Systems GmbH & Co KG* [2005] ECR I-2397, [2006] IRLR 400, ECJ (Acquired Rights Directive had not intended a transferee to be bound by a collective agreement other than the one in force at the time of the transfer); cf *Whent v T Cartlidge Ltd* [1997] IRLR 153, EAT (transferee employers still bound by collective agreement, so far as incorporated in individual contracts of employment and until the bargaining arrangements were validly varied, notwithstanding their withdrawal from the collective agreement).

33　Transfer of Undertakings (Protection of Employment) Regulations 2006, SI 2006/246, reg 4A(1)(a) (as added: see note 16).

34　Transfer of Undertakings (Protection of Employment) Regulations 2006, SI 2006/246, reg 4A(1)(b) (as added: see note 16).

35　Ie for the purposes of the Transfer of Undertakings (Protection of Employment) Regulations 2006, SI 2006/246, reg 4(1) (see the text and notes 1–5): see reg 4A(2) (as added: see note 16).

36　See the Transfer of Undertakings (Protection of Employment) Regulations 2006, SI 2006/246, reg 4A(2) (as added: see note 16).

37 Ie the Transfer of Undertakings (Protection of Employment) Regulations 2006, SI 2006/246, reg 4(1), (2) (see the text and notes 1–11): see reg 4(7).
38 See the Transfer of Undertakings (Protection of Employment) Regulations 2006, SI 2006/246, reg 4(7), (8); and PARA 141. As to other effects of relevant transfer on employee's rights under the contract see also PARA 141.

140. Notification of employee liability information, and remedy for failure to do so. The transferor[1] must notify to the transferee[2] the employee liability information[3] of any person employed by him who is assigned to the organised grouping of resources or employees[4] that is the subject of a relevant transfer[5]. The notification:

(1)   must be made either in writing[6], or by making it available to the transferee in a readily accessible form[7];

(2)   must be given not less than 28 days before the relevant transfer (or, if special circumstances make this not reasonably practicable, as soon as reasonably practicable thereafter)[8]; and

(3)   may be given in more than one instalment or indirectly, through a third party[9].

On or after a relevant transfer, the transferee may present a complaint to an employment tribunal[10] that the transferor has failed to comply with any of the employee liability information provisions[11]. An employment tribunal must not consider such a complaint, however, unless it is presented[12]:

(a)   before the end of the period of three months beginning with the date of the relevant transfer[13]; or

(b)   within such further period as the tribunal considers reasonable in a case where it is satisfied that it was not reasonably practicable for the complaint to be presented before the end of that period of three months[14].

In working out when the time limit set in this way expires, the following period is not to be counted[15], namely the period that:

(i)   begins with the day after the day on which the worker concerned complies with the requirement to contact ACAS before instituting proceedings[16] in relation to the matter in respect of which the proceedings are brought ('the day after Day A')[17]; and

(ii)   ends with the day on which the worker concerned receives (or, if earlier, is treated as receiving[18]) the certificate issued by the conciliation officer[19] to the effect either that he has concluded that a settlement is not possible within the prescribed period or that the prescribed period has expired without a settlement having been reached ('Day B')[20].

If the unextended time limit[21] would expire during the period beginning with Day A and ending one month after Day B, the time limit expires instead at the end of that period[22].

Where an employment tribunal finds such a complaint well founded, the tribunal must make a declaration to that effect, and it may make an award of compensation to be paid by the transferor to the transferee[23]. The amount of the compensation is to be such as the tribunal considers just and equitable in all the circumstances[24], having particular regard to[25]:

(A)   any loss sustained by the transferee which is attributable to the matters complained of[26]; and

(B)   the terms of any contract between the transferor and the transferee relating to the transfer under which the transferor may be liable to pay any sum to the transferee in respect of a failure to notify the transferee of employee liability information[27].

In ascertaining the loss referred to in head (A) above, the tribunal must apply the same rule concerning the duty of a person to mitigate his loss as applies to any damages recoverable under the common law of England and Wales[28].

1   As to the meaning of 'transferor' see PARA 137.
2   As to the meaning of 'transferee' see PARA 137.
3   For these purposes, 'employee liability information' means:
    (1)   the identity and age of the employee (Transfer of Undertakings (Protection of Employment) Regulations 2006, SI 2006/246, reg 11(2)(a));
    (2)   those particulars of employment that an employer is obliged to give to an employee pursuant to the Employment Rights Act 1996 s 1 (see PARA 119) (Transfer of Undertakings (Protection of Employment) Regulations 2006, SI 2006/246, reg 11(2)(b));
    (3)   information of any: (a) disciplinary procedure taken against an employee (reg 11(2)(c)(i)); or (b) grievance procedure taken by an employee (reg 11(2)(c)(ii)), within the previous two years, in circumstances where a Code of Practice issued under the Trade Union and Labour Relations (Consolidation) Act 1992 Pt IV (ss 178–218) (industrial relations: see PARAS 1223, 1231), which relates exclusively or primarily to the resolution of disputes, applies (Transfer of Undertakings (Protection of Employment) Regulations 2006, SI 2006/246, reg 11(2)(c) (amended by SI 2009/592));
    (4)   information of any court or tribunal case, claim or action: (a) brought by an employee against the transferor, within the previous two years (Transfer of Undertakings (Protection of Employment) Regulations 2006, SI 2006/246, reg 11(2)(d)(i)); or (b) that the transferor has reasonable grounds to believe that an employee may bring against the transferee, arising out of the employee's employment with the transferor (reg 11(2)(d)(ii)); and
    (5)   information of any collective agreement which will have effect after the transfer, in its application in relation to the employee, pursuant to reg 5(a) (see PARA 139 note 24) (reg 11(2)(e)).
    Employee liability information must contain information as at a specified date not more than 14 days before the date on which the information is notified to the transferee (reg 11(3)); and, following notification of the employee liability information in accordance with reg 11, the transferor must notify the transferee in writing of any change in that information (see reg 11(5)). As to the meaning of 'employee' see PARA 137 note 8. As to the meaning of 'collective agreement' for these purposes see PARA 138 note 13.
4   As to the meaning of 'assigned' for these purposes see PARA 138 note 13; and as to references to 'organised grouping of employees' see PARA 137 note 8.
5   Transfer of Undertakings (Protection of Employment) Regulations 2006, SI 2006/246, reg 11(1). The duty to provide employee liability information in reg 11(1) includes a duty to provide employee liability information of any person who would have been employed by the transferor and assigned to the organised grouping of resources or employees that is the subject of a relevant transfer immediately before the transfer if he had not been dismissed in the circumstances described in reg 7(1) (see PARA 803), including, where the transfer is effected by a series of two or more transactions, a person so employed and assigned or who would have been so employed and assigned immediately before any of those transactions: reg 11(4). As to the meaning of 'relevant transfer' see PARA 137.
    The Information Commissioner's Office has issued guidance explaining what organisations need to do in order to comply with the Data Protection Act 1998 when providing information about their employees under the Transfer of Undertakings (Protection of Employment) Regulations 2006, SI 2006/246 (as amended by the Collective Redundancies and Transfer of Undertakings (Protection of Employment) (Amendment) Regulations 2014, SI 2014/16): see *Disclosure of employee information under TUPE* (June 2014). This guidance is available on the Information Commissioner's Office website, whose address, at the date at which this volume states the law, is to be found at: *http://ico.org.uk*. As to the Data Protection Act 1998 generally see PARA 34; and CONFIDENCE AND INFORMATIONAL PRIVACY vol 19 (2011) PARA 95 et seq. As to the Information Commissioner's powers to prepare and disseminate codes of practice for guidance as to good practice see CONFIDENCE AND INFORMATIONAL PRIVACY vol 19 (2011) PARA 110.
6   Transfer of Undertakings (Protection of Employment) Regulations 2006, SI 2006/246, reg 11(1)(a). As to the meaning of 'writing' see PARA 2 note 8.
7   Transfer of Undertakings (Protection of Employment) Regulations 2006, SI 2006/246, reg 11(1)(b).

8   Transfer of Undertakings (Protection of Employment) Regulations 2006, SI 2006/246, reg 11(6) (amended by SI 2014/16).

9   See the Transfer of Undertakings (Protection of Employment) Regulations 2006, SI 2006/246, reg 11(7).

10 As to employment tribunals see PARA 1399 et seq; and as to the procedure on a complaint made to an employment tribunal see PARA 1453 et seq.

11 Transfer of Undertakings (Protection of Employment) Regulations 2006, SI 2006/246, reg 12(1). The reference in the text a failure to comply with any provision of reg 11 (see the text and notes 1–9): see reg 12(1). The Employment Tribunals Act 1996 ss 18A–18C (requirement to contact ACAS before instituting proceedings: see PARAS 152, 153) apply to the right conferred by the Transfer of Undertakings (Protection of Employment) Regulations 2006, SI 2006/246, reg 12, and to proceedings under reg 12, as they apply to the rights conferred by the Employment Tribunals Act 1996, and to the employment tribunal proceedings mentioned in that Act: Transfer of Undertakings (Protection of Employment) Regulations 2006, SI 2006/246, reg 12(7) (amended by SI 2014/386).

12 See the Transfer of Undertakings (Protection of Employment) Regulations 2006, SI 2006/246, reg 12(2). Provision that is made for the extension of time limits in order to facilitate conciliation before the institution of proceedings (ie reg 16A: see the text and notes 14–22) applies for the purposes of reg 12(2): reg 12(2A) (regs 12(2A), 16A added by SI 2014/853). See note 14.

13 Transfer of Undertakings (Protection of Employment) Regulations 2006, SI 2006/246, reg 12(2)(a).

14 Transfer of Undertakings (Protection of Employment) Regulations 2006, SI 2006/246, reg 12(2)(b). Where an employment tribunal has power under the Transfer of Undertakings (Protection of Employment) Regulations 2006, SI 2006/246, to extend the time limit set by any provision in those Regulations which also provides for reg 16A to apply for the purpose ('a relevant provision'), the power is exercisable in relation to that time limit as it is extended by reg 16A (see also the text and notes 15–22): see reg 16A(1), (5) (as added: see note 12). Accordingly, reg 12(2) is a 'relevant provision', for whose purposes reg 12(2A) has provided for reg 16A to apply: see note 12.

15 See the Transfer of Undertakings (Protection of Employment) Regulations 2006, SI 2006/246, reg 16A(3) (as added: see note 12). The text refers to working out when the time limit set by a relevant provision of the Transfer of Undertakings (Protection of Employment) Regulations 2006, SI 2006/246 (ie, in this case, reg 12(2): see note 14), expires: see reg 16A(3) (as added: see note 12).

16 Ie the requirement in the Employment Tribunals Act 1996 s 18A(1) (see PARA 152): see the Transfer of Undertakings (Protection of Employment) Regulations 2006, SI 2006/246, reg 16A(2)(a) (as added: see note 12).

17 See the Transfer of Undertakings (Protection of Employment) Regulations 2006, SI 2006/246, reg 16A(2)(a), (3) (as added: see note 12).

18 Ie by virtue of regulations made under the Employment Tribunals Act 1996 s 18A(11) (see PARA 152): see the Transfer of Undertakings (Protection of Employment) Regulations 2006, SI 2006/246, reg 16A(2)(b) (as added: see note 12).

19 Ie the certificate issued under the Employment Tribunals Act 1996 s 18A(4) (see PARA 152): see the Transfer of Undertakings (Protection of Employment) Regulations 2006, SI 2006/246, reg 16A(2)(b) (as added: see note 12).

20 See the Transfer of Undertakings (Protection of Employment) Regulations 2006, SI 2006/246, reg 16A(2)(b), (3) (as added: see note 12).

21 Ie the time limit set by a relevant provision of the Transfer of Undertakings (Protection of Employment) Regulations 2006, SI 2006/246 (ie, in this case, reg 12(2): see note 14), if not extended by reg 16A(4): see reg 16A(4) (as added: see note 12).

22 See the Transfer of Undertakings (Protection of Employment) Regulations 2006, SI 2006/246, reg 16A(4) (as added: see note 12).

23 See the Transfer of Undertakings (Protection of Employment) Regulations 2006, SI 2006/246, reg 12(3).

24 Ie subject to the Transfer of Undertakings (Protection of Employment) Regulations 2006, SI 2006/246, reg 12(5): see reg 12(4). Accordingly, subject to reg 12(6) (see the text and note 28), the amount of compensation awarded under reg 12(3) must not be less than £500 per employee in respect of whom the transferor has failed to comply with a provision of reg 11 (see the text and notes 1–9), unless the tribunal considers it just and equitable, in all the circumstances, to award a lesser sum: reg 12(5).

25 See the Transfer of Undertakings (Protection of Employment) Regulations 2006, SI 2006/246, reg 12(4).

26 Transfer of Undertakings (Protection of Employment) Regulations 2006, SI 2006/246, reg 12(4)(a).
27 Transfer of Undertakings (Protection of Employment) Regulations 2006, SI 2006/246, reg 12(4)(b).
28 Transfer of Undertakings (Protection of Employment) Regulations 2006, SI 2006/246, reg 12(6). As to the common law duty to mitigate loss see DAMAGES vol 12(1) (Reissue) PARA 1041 et seq.

141. Employees' rights under contract before and after relevant transfer. The normal rules that govern business transfers[1] do not operate to transfer the contract of employment[2] (and the rights, powers, duties and liabilities under or in connection with such a contract) of an employee[3] who informs either the transferor[4] or the transferee[5] that he objects to becoming employed by the transferee[6]. Where an employee so objects, the relevant transfer[7] operates so as to terminate his contract of employment with the transferor (but he must not be treated, for any purpose, as having been dismissed by the transferor)[8].

Subject to contract variations that are permitted[9] in prescribed circumstances where relevant insolvency proceedings[10] have been opened in relation to a transferor[11], where a relevant transfer involves or would involve a substantial change in working conditions to the material detriment of a person whose contract of employment is or would be so transferred[12], such an employee may treat the contract of employment as having been terminated (and the employee must be treated for any purpose as having been dismissed by the employer)[13].

However, the general provisions that govern the transfer of a contract of employment[14], and the rules that govern consequential termination of the contract[15], are without prejudice to any right of an employee arising apart from the Transfer of Undertakings (Protection of Employment) Regulations 2006[16] to terminate his contract of employment without notice in acceptance of a repudiatory breach of contract by his employer[17].

The normal rules that govern the deemed transfer of a contract of employment[18] and terms of a collective agreement[19] under a relevant business transfer do not apply to[20]:

(1) so much of a contract of employment or collective agreement as relates to an occupational pension scheme[21]; or

(2) any rights, powers, duties or liabilities under or in connection with any such contract or subsisting by virtue of any such agreement and relating to such a scheme or otherwise arising in connection with that person's employment and relating to such a scheme[22].

An employee whose contract of employment is deemed to be transferred as a result of a relevant transfer[23] is not entitled to bring a claim against the transferor for[24]:

(a) breach of contract[25]; or

(b) constructive unfair dismissal under the Employment Rights Act 1996[26], arising out of a loss or reduction in his rights under an occupational pension scheme in consequence of the transfer (save in so far as the alleged breach of contract or dismissal, as the case may be, occurred prior to 6 April 2006)[27].

An employer has a duty to inform and consult employees' representatives regarding a transfer and the implications of such a transfer for the affected employees[28].

1 Ie the provision made by the Transfer of Undertakings (Protection of Employment) Regulations 2006, SI 2006/246, reg 4(1), (2) (see PARA 139): see reg 4(7).
2 As to the meaning of 'contract of employment' see PARA 138 note 5.
3 As to the meaning of 'employee' see PARA 137 note 8.
4 As to the meaning of 'transferor' see PARA 137.

5   As to the meaning of 'transferee' see PARA 137.

6   Transfer of Undertakings (Protection of Employment) Regulations 2006, SI 2006/246, reg 4(7). This corresponds to an earlier version of the provision (ie the Transfer of Undertakings (Protection of Employment) Regulations 1981, SI 1981/1794, reg 5(4A)) which was added in response to a European Court of Justice decision to the effect that the Acquired Rights Directive (see PARA 136 note 3) impliedly preserves the employee's right not to be obliged to work for a new employer: Joined Cases C-132/91, C-138/91 and C-139/91 *Katsikas v Konstantinidis* [1992] ECR I-6577, [1993] 1 CMLR 845, [1993] IRLR 179, ECJ (fate of the contract of employment or of the employment relationship is for the member state to determine since the Directive does not oblige the contract or the employment relationship to be continued with the transferor where an employee freely decides not to continue in employment with the transferee) (applied in Joined Cases C-171/94, 172/94 *Merckx and Neuhuys v Ford Motors Co Belgium SA* [1996] ECR I-1253, [1997] ICR 352, [1996] IRLR 467, ECJ). At common law in England, the employee has a right to choose for himself whom he would serve so that the transfer of a business would automatically terminate contracts of employment giving rise to a dismissal: see *Nokes v Doncaster Amalgamated Collieries Ltd* [1940] AC 1014, [1940] 3 All ER 549, HL; and PARA 136 note 3.

Whether an employee has objected to becoming employed by a transferee depends on the facts and circumstances of each case: *Capita Health Solutions Ltd v McLean* [2008] IRLR 595, EAT. There is no particular procedure prescribed for making such an objection, and it may, therefore, be inferred from words or conduct: *Hay v George Hanson (Building Contractors) Ltd* [1996] IRLR 427, EAT (but cf *Senior Heat Treatment Ltd v Bell* [1997] IRLR 614, EAT (expression of a preference for an offered redundancy package was not enough in itself to constitute an objection); *Hamilton v Stonehouse Coaches Ltd* [2013] All ER (D) 116 (Sep), EAT(Sc) (it is not necessary that the employee seek a transfer; rather it is necessary that she objects to a transfer if that be her position)). Where the employee does not know the identity of the transferee before the date of the transfer, a purposive construction of the Transfer of Undertakings (Protection of Employment) Regulations 2006, SI 2006/246, reg 4(7) would be adopted, to avoid an undermining of the regulations' protective intent, with the result that an objection can be made after a transfer: *New ISG Ltd v Vernon* [2007] EWHC 2665 (Ch), [2008] ICR 319, [2008] IRLR 115 (letters of resignation were construed as objections within the Transfer of Undertakings (Protection of Employment) Regulations 2006, SI 2006/246, reg 4(7) in circumstances where the employee did not know the identity of the transferee before the date of transfer).

7   As to the meaning of 'relevant transfer' see PARA 137.

8   Transfer of Undertakings (Protection of Employment) Regulations 2006, SI 2006/246, reg 4(8). This provision is subject to reg 4(9), (11) (see the text and notes 9–17): see reg 4(8).

9   As to the meaning of 'permitted variation' for these purposes see PARA 138 note 13.

10 As to the meaning of 'relevant insolvency proceedings' for these purposes see PARA 138 note 3.

11 Ie subject to the Transfer of Undertakings (Protection of Employment) Regulations 2006, SI 2006/246, reg 9 (see PARA 138): see reg 4(9).

12 Ie whose contract of employment is or would be transferred under the Transfer of Undertakings (Protection of Employment) Regulations 2006, SI 2006/246, reg 4(1) (see PARA 139): see reg 4(9).

In determining whether a 'substantial change' is to the 'material detriment' of the employee, the test to be applied is whether the treatment is of such a kind that a reasonable worker could or would take the subjective view that in all the circumstances it was to his or her detriment, with the corollary that a tribunal must consider objectively the effect of what has taken place upon someone in that person's position: *Tapere v South London and Maudsley NHS Trust* [2009] ICR 1563, [2009] IRLR 972, EAT; *Abellio London Ltd (formerly Travel London Ltd) v Musse, Centrewest London Buses Ltd v Musse* [2012] IRLR 360, EAT. 'Working conditions' is a phrase that is wider than 'contractual conditions', and is capable of relating to both contractual and physical conditions, including matters such as the place of work: *Abellio London Ltd (formerly Travel London Ltd) v Musse, Centrewest London Buses Ltd v Musse* (tribunal justified in concluding that the move of depots had been a substantial change in working conditions to the material detriment of the bus drivers). The question of whether there has been a 'substantial change' is a question of fact: *Abellio London Ltd (formerly Travel London Ltd) v Musse, Centrewest London Buses Ltd v Musse*.

13 Transfer of Undertakings (Protection of Employment) Regulations 2006, SI 2006/246, reg 4(9). No damages are payable by an employer as a result of a dismissal falling within reg 4(9) in respect of any failure by the employer to pay wages to an employee in respect of a notice period which the employee has failed to work: reg 4(10).

The predecessor provision to reg 4(9) (ie the Transfer of Undertakings (Protection of Employment) Regulations 1981, SI 1981/1794, reg 5(5): see PARA 136 note 1) was worded differently but was to be construed in the same way as the Employment Rights Act 1996 s 95(1)(c) (see PARA 762): see *Rossiter v Pendragon plc, Crosby-Clarke v Air Foyle Ltd* [2002] EWCA Civ 745, [2002] ICR 1063, [2002] IRLR 483. The Transfer of Undertakings (Protection of Employment) Regulations 1981, SI 1981/1794, reg 5(5), was also held not to apply to mere fears of detrimental change (*Sita (GB) Ltd v Burton* [1998] ICR 17, [1997] IRLR 501, EAT); but it did apply if changes were actually being threatened (*University of Oxford v Humphreys and Associated Examining Board* [2000] 1 All ER 996, [2000] IRLR 183, CA).

14 Ie in particular, the Transfer of Undertakings (Protection of Employment) Regulations 2006, SI 2006/246, reg 4(1) (see PARA 139), and reg 4(7) (see the text and notes 1–6): see reg 4(11).

15 Ie in particular, the Transfer of Undertakings (Protection of Employment) Regulations 2006, SI 2006/246, reg 4(8), (9) (see the text and notes 7–13): see reg 4(11).

16 Ie apart from the Transfer of Undertakings (Protection of Employment) Regulations 2006, SI 2006/246: see reg 4(11).

17 Transfer of Undertakings (Protection of Employment) Regulations 2006, SI 2006/246, reg 4(11). As to a situation where the effect of working for the transferee was to transfer the contract see *Capita Health Solutions Ltd v McLean* [2008] IRLR 595, EAT (employee objected to transfer and gave notice of termination of her employment but she worked six weeks of her notice period on secondment to transferee to assist in transition, and so lost her right to object). It cannot be right, however, that an employee is automatically assigned on a temporary basis, thereby losing the protection of the acquired rights provisions, simply as a result of handing in notice prior to the transfer: *Marcroft v Heartland (Midlands) Limited* [2011] EWCA Civ 438, [2011] IRLR 599 (employee transferred to transferee during time he was working out his notice with the transferor).

18 Ie the Transfer of Undertakings (Protection of Employment) Regulations 2006, SI 2006/246, reg 4 (see PARA 139): see reg 10(1).

19 Ie the Transfer of Undertakings (Protection of Employment) Regulations 2006, SI 2006/246, reg 5 (see PARA 139 note 24): see reg 10(1). As to the meaning of 'collective agreement' for these purposes see PARA 138 note 13.

20 See the Transfer of Undertakings (Protection of Employment) Regulations 2006, SI 2006/246, reg 10(1).

21 Transfer of Undertakings (Protection of Employment) Regulations 2006, SI 2006/246, reg 10(1)(a). Head (1) in the text applies to an occupational pension scheme within the meaning of the Pension Schemes Act 1993 (see PERSONAL AND OCCUPATIONAL PENSIONS vol 80 (2013) PARA 201 et seq): see the Transfer of Undertakings (Protection of Employment) Regulations 2006, SI 2006/246, reg 10(1)(a). For the purposes of reg 10(1) and reg 10(3) (see the text and notes 23–27), any provisions of an occupational pension scheme which do not relate to benefits for old age, invalidity or survivors are not to be treated as being part of the scheme: reg 10(2).

The effect of the predecessor provision to reg 10 (ie the Transfer of Undertakings (Protection of Employment) Regulations 1981, SI 1981/1794, reg 7) was to shear the specified pension rights provided by the transferor from the continuing contract of employment (which is deemed otherwise always to have been with the transferee): see *Preston v Wolverhampton Healthcare Trust* [2006] UKHL 13, [2006] 3 All ER 193, [2007] 2 CMLR 980, [2006] ICR 606, [2006] IRLR 381, sub nom *Powerhouse Retail Ltd v Burroughs* [2006] IRLR 381 (claim based on deficiency in the terms of the contract which existed between the transferor and the employee before the transfer took place, in so far as its terms have not been transferred, was subject to limitation). The pensions exception given in the Transfer of Undertakings (Protection of Employment) Regulations 1981, SI 1981/1794, reg 7 was held to have correctly implemented the Acquired Rights Directive, and there was no additional requirement of providing equivalent pension rights: *Adams v Lancashire County Council* [1997] ICR 834, [1997] IRLR 436, CA; Case E-2/95 *Eidesund v Stavanger Catering A/S* [1996] IRLR 684, EFTA Ct. An element of pension protection is provided separately, however, under the Pensions Act 2004 ss 257, 258, and the Transfer of Employment (Pension Protection) Regulations 2005, SI 2005/649: see PERSONAL AND OCCUPATIONAL PENSIONS vol 80 (2013) PARA 612.

22 Transfer of Undertakings (Protection of Employment) Regulations 2006, SI 2006/246, reg 10(1)(b). See note 21.

23 Ie whose contract of employment is transferred in the circumstances described in the Transfer of Undertakings (Protection of Employment) Regulations 2006, SI 2006/246, reg 4(1) (see PARA 139): see reg 10(3). See note 21.

24 See the Transfer of Undertakings (Protection of Employment) Regulations 2006, SI 2006/246, reg 10(3). See note 21.

25 Transfer of Undertakings (Protection of Employment) Regulations 2006, SI 2006/246, reg 10(3)(a). See note 21.
26 Transfer of Undertakings (Protection of Employment) Regulations 2006, SI 2006/246, reg 10(3)(b). Head (b) in the text refers to constructive unfair dismissal under the Employment Rights Act 1996 s 95(1)(c) (see PARA 762): see the Transfer of Undertakings (Protection of Employment) Regulations 2006, SI 2006/246, reg 10(3)(b). See note 21.
27 See the Transfer of Undertakings (Protection of Employment) Regulations 2006, SI 2006/246, reg 10(3). The date of 6 April 2006 refers to the date on which the Transfer of Undertakings (Protection of Employment) Regulations 2006, SI 2006/246, took effect (see reg 1(2); and PARA 136 note 1): see reg 10(3). See note 21.
28 See the Transfer of Undertakings (Protection of Employment) Regulations 2006, SI 2006/246, regs 13–16; European Parliament and Council Directive (EC) 2002/14 (OJ L80, 23.3.2002, p 29), which establishes a general framework for informing and consulting employees in the European Community (for the purposes of its implementation in the United Kingdom the Information and Consultation of Employees Regulations 2004, SI 2004/3426, were made, which, inter alia, provide that an employer can consult under the Transfer of Undertakings (Protection of Employment) Regulations 2006, SI 2006/246, rather than under the Information and Consultation of Employees Regulations 2004, SI 2004/3426 (see reg 20(5))); and PARAS 1095, 1196 et seq. As to the Information and Consultation of Employees Regulations 2004, SI 2004/3426, see PARA 1289 et seq.
    As well as this statutory duty, an employer has a duty in tort as well as an implied contractual duty to take reasonable care in making statements to its employees where: (1) an employer proposes that the employees transfer their employment; (2) the transfer would impact on the employees' future economic interests; (3) an employer needs the employees' support for the proposed transfer; (4) an employer has access to certain information unavailable to the employees; and (5) an employer knows that the information would carry considerable weight with the employees: *Hagen v ICI Chemicals and Polymers Ltd* [2002] IRLR 31. Nevertheless, these duties do not alter the scope of an employer's implied duty of care, which does not extend to any general duty to prevent economic loss to the employee: see PARA 32.

(4) CALCULATION OF NORMAL WORKING HOURS AND A WEEK'S PAY

(i) Normal Working Hours

142. Normal working hours. Where an employee[1] is entitled to overtime pay when employed for more than a fixed number of hours in a week[2] or other period, there are[3] normal working hours in his case[4]; and the normal working hours in such a case are the fixed number of hours[5]. Where, however, in such a case:

(1) the contract of employment[6] fixes the number, or the minimum number, of hours of employment in the relevant week or other period (whether or not it also provides for the reduction of that number or minimum in certain circumstances)[7]; and

(2) that number or minimum number of hours exceeds the number of hours without overtime[8],

the normal working hours are that number or minimum number of hours (and not the number of hours without overtime)[9].

1 As to the meaning of 'employee' see PARA 2.
2 As to the meaning of 'week' for these purposes see PARA 126 note 13.
3 Ie for the purposes of the Employment Rights Act 1996: see s 234(1).
4 Employment Rights Act 1996 s 234(1).
    Where the contract expressly states the normal working hours, that will usually be conclusive, and it will not avail the employee that he in fact works longer hours than those expressed, unless he can prove an actual variation of contract to increase the hours as originally stated: *Lynch v Dartmouth Auto Castings Ltd* (1969) 4 ITR 273, DC; *Truelove v Matthew Hall Mechanical Services Ltd* (1968) 3 ITR 65; *Armstrong Whitworth Rolls Ltd v Mustard* [1971]

1 All ER 598, DC; *Friend v PMA Holdings Ltd* [1976] ICR 330, EAT; *ITT Components (Europe) Group v Kolah* [1977] ICR 740, [1977] IRLR 53, EAT; *Barrett v National Coal Board* [1978] ICR 1101, EAT. Where there is a contractual term covering normal working hours, it should be included in the written statement of terms and conditions of employment: see the Employment Rights Act 1996 s 1(4)(c); and PARA 119. As to the calculation of a week's pay where there are no normal working hours see PARA 145.

5   Employment Rights Act 1996 s 234(2). This provision is subject to s 234(3) (which provides the exception that overtime can count in certain circumstances: see the text and notes 6–9): see s 234(2).
    The provision set out in the text, however, enacts the basic rule that voluntary overtime is not to count towards normal working hours, a rule also found in Pt XIV Ch II (ss 220–229) (calculation of a week's pay: see PARA 143 et seq). Thus, a term providing for the payment of overtime rates 'after X hours per week' means that X hours are to be the normal working hours, even if there is no express term to that effect: *Fox v C Wright (Farmers) Ltd* [1978] ICR 98, EAT; *Pearson v William Jones Ltd* [1967] 2 All ER 1062, [1967] 1 WLR 1140, DC; *Minister of Labour v Country Bake Ltd* (1968) 3 ITR 379, DC. 'Fixed number of hours' means actual fixed hours, not a notional number of hours, even if it is a genuine pre-estimate: *Sanderson v Exel Management Services Ltd* [2006] 4 All ER 107, [2006] ICR 1337, EAT. See also note 9.

6   As to the meaning of 'contract of employment' see PARA 2.
7   Employment Rights Act 1996 s 234(3)(a).
8   Employment Rights Act 1996 s 234(3)(b).
9   See the Employment Rights Act 1996 s 234(3). This provision provides the exception that overtime can count, but only if, and to the extent that, it is obligatory on both sides (i e where a contract of employment requires an employer to provide overtime and requires an employee to work it): *Tarmac Roadstone Holdings Ltd v Peacock* [1973] 2 All ER 485, [1973] ICR 273, CA; *Gascol Conversions Ltd v Mercer* [1974] ICR 420, [1974] IRLR 155, CA; *Lotus Cars Ltd v Sutcliffe and Stratton* [1982] IRLR 381, CA; *Bamsey v Albon Engineering and Manufacturing plc* [2004] EWCA Civ 359, [2004] ICR 1083, [2004] IRLR 457 (discussing the Employment Rights Act 1996 s 234 in the context of the Working Time Regulations 1998, SI 1998/1833, reg 16: see PARA 295 note 3). 'Overtime', however, is not a defined term in employment legislation nor is it a term of art at common law. Its meaning and its financial implications will depend on the way the parties have defined it contractually or, in the absence of an express agreement, on the particular circumstances leading to a claim that overtime has been worked and should be remunerated: *Driver v Air India Ltd* [2011] EWCA Civ 830, [2011] EWCA Civ 986, [2011] IRLR 992 (in the circumstances, the contract had given the employee, even in the absence of any guidelines from the employer, a contractual right to be paid for overtime where overtime was required). See also *Czarnecki v Choice Textiles Ltd* [2013] All ER (D) 77 (Sep), EAT (effect of the employee's contract was that if it was shown that an employee had worked beyond the 52 hours averaged across the working year, he was entitled to be paid the ordinary rate for the job for those additional hours and any enhanced rate to be paid for those hours was subject to the discretion of the employer).

(ii) A Week's Pay

143.   Calculation of week's pay of employee for the purposes of the Employment Rights Act 1996. The Employment Rights Act 1996 provides for the amount of a week's pay of an employee[1] to be calculated[2] in the following cases[3]:

(1)   where there are normal working hours[4] for the employee when employed under the contract of employment[5] in force on the calculation date[6];

(2)   where there are no normal working hours for the employee when employed under the contract of employment in force on the calculation date[7];

(3)   where the employee has not been employed for a sufficient period to enable a calculation to be made under either head (1) or head (2) above[8].

1   As to the meaning of 'employee' see PARA 2.
2   Ie for the purposes of the Employment Rights Act 1996: see s 220.

3 See the Employment Rights Act 1996 s 220. The text refers to calculation made in accordance with Pt XIV Ch II (ss 220–229) (calculation of a week's pay: see also PARAS 144–148): see s 220.
4 As to normal working hours see PARA 142.
5 As to the meaning of 'contract of employment' see PARA 2.
6 See the Employment Rights Act 1996 ss 221–223; and PARA 144. The provision made by s 221 is subject to s 227 (maximum amount of week's pay: see PARA 147) and s 228 (see head (3) in the text): see s 221(5); and PARA 144 note 4. As to the calculation date see ss 225, 226; and PARA 146.
7 See the Employment Rights Act 1996 s 224; and PARA 145. The provision made by s 222 is subject to s 227 (maximum amount of week's pay: see PARA 147) and s 228 (see head (3) in the text): see s 224(4); and PARA 145.
8 See the Employment Rights Act 1996 s 228; and PARA 148.

144. Employments for which there are normal working hours. Where there are normal working hours[1] for the employee[2] when employed under the contract of employment[3] in force on the calculation date[4], the amount of a week's pay of an employee is calculated[5] as follows[6]:

(1)   if the employee's remuneration[7] for employment in normal working hours (whether by the hour or week[8] or other period) does not vary with the amount of work[9] done in the period, the amount of a week's pay is, subject to head (3) below, the amount which is payable by the employer[10] under the contract of employment in force on the calculation date if the employee works throughout his normal working hours in a week[11];

(2)   if the employee's remuneration for employment in normal working hours (whether by the hour or week or other period) does vary with the amount of work done in the period, then, subject to head (3) below, the amount of a week's pay is the amount of remuneration for the number of normal working hours in a week calculated at the average hourly rate of remuneration payable by the employer to the employee in respect of the period of 12 weeks ending[12]: (a) where the calculation date is the last day of a week, with that week[13]; and (b) otherwise, with the last complete week before the calculation date[14];

(3)   if there are normal working hours for an employee when employed under the contract of employment in force on the calculation date, and he is required under that contract to work during those hours on days of the week, or at times of the day, which differ from week to week or over a longer period so that the remuneration payable for, or apportionable to, any week varies according to the incidence of those days or times[15], then the amount of a week's pay is the amount of remuneration for the average number of weekly normal working hours[16] at the average hourly rate of remuneration[17].

In arriving at the average hourly rate of remuneration for the purposes of heads (1) to (3) above, only the hours when the employee was working, and only the remuneration payable for (or apportionable to) those hours of work are to be brought in[18]; and, if for any of the 12 weeks mentioned in heads (1) to (3) above, no such remuneration was payable for (or apportionable to) those hours by the employer to the employee, account must be taken of remuneration in earlier weeks so as to bring up to 12 the number of weeks of which account is taken[19]. Where, in arriving at the hourly rate of remuneration, account has to be taken of remuneration payable for (or apportionable to) work done in hours other than normal working hours, and where the amount of that remuneration was greater than it would have been if the work had been done in normal working hours, account must be taken of that remuneration as if the work had been done in such hours and the amount of that remuneration had been reduced accordingly[20].

1   As to normal working hours see PARA 142.
2   As to the meaning of 'employee' see PARA 2.
3   As to the meaning of 'contract of employment' see PARA 2.

4   See the Employment Rights Act 1996 s 221(1). The provision made by s 221 is subject to s 227 (maximum amount of week's pay: see PARA 147) and s 228 (employee not employed for sufficient period to enable usual calculation to be made: see PARA 148): s 221(5). The provisions of ss 222–223 (see also the text and notes 15–20) also apply where s 221 applies: see s 221(1). As to the calculation date see PARA 146.

5   Ie in accordance with the Employment Rights Act 1996 Pt XIV Ch II (ss 220–229) (calculation of a week's pay: see also PARAS 143, 145–148): see s 220; and PARA 143.

6   See the Employment Rights Act 1996 s 220; and PARA 143.

7   Notwithstanding the Employment Rights Act 1996 ss 222–223 (see the text and notes 15–20), there is no statutory definition of 'remuneration' for these purposes. Case law has, however, established the following major propositions for these purposes:
   (1)   a week's pay generally means the employee's gross weekly pay, not his net weekly pay (*Secretary of State for Employment v John Woodrow & Sons (Builders) Ltd* [1983] ICR 582, [1983] IRLR 11, EAT, disapproving dicta to the contrary in *Secretary of State for Employment v Jobling* [1980] ICR 380, EAT);
   (2)   the relevant rate of pay is that in force at the calculation date, and so a backdated pay rise may not normally be included (*Valentine v Great Lever Spinning Co* (1966) 1 ITR 71; c f *Dawson v Effingham Steel Works Ltd* (1967) 2 ITR 286; *Leyland Vehicles Ltd v Reston* [1981] ICR 403, [1981] IRLR 19, EAT (distinguishing *Carrod v Pullman Spring Filled Co Ltd* (1967) 2 ITR 650 and *Tsoukka v Potomac Restaurants Ltd* (1968) 3 ITR 259));
   (3)   where a week's pay is less than the statutory minimum, the starting point should be not less than the national minimum wage (see PARA 169 et seq), less notional tax and national insurance (*Paggetti v Cobb* [2002] IRLR 861, [2002] All ER (D) 394 (Mar), EAT (notwithstanding the fact that free accommodation was provided to the employee under the terms of his employment), applying *Cooner v PS Doal & Sons* [1988] ICR 495, [1988] IRLR 338, EAT (wages order, now mostly obsolete: see PARA 26));
   (4)   the employee's real rate of pay must be taken, even if expressed unusually, and this may include bonuses and commissions to which the employee is entitled (*Adams v John Wright & Sons (Blackwall) Ltd* [1972] ICR 463, NIRC; *Mole Mining Ltd v Jenkins* [1972] ICR 282, NIRC; *Amalgamated Asphalte Companies Ltd v Dockrill* (1972) 7 ITR 198, NIRC; *Ogden v Ardphalt Asphalt Ltd* [1977] 1 All ER 267, [1977] ICR 604, EAT; *Weevsmay Ltd v Kings* [1977] ICR 244, EAT; *A & B Marcusfield Ltd v Melhuish* [1977] IRLR 484, EAT; *Donelan v Kerrby Constructions Ltd* [1983] ICR 237, [1983] IRLR 191, EAT);
   (5)   an annual bonus may be treated as accruing on a weekly basis, either generally or under the Employment Rights Act 1996 s 229(2) (see PARA 148) (*J & S Bickley Ltd v Washer* [1977] ICR 425, EAT);
   (6)   holiday pay will not normally be included (*Secretary of State for Employment v Haynes* [1980] ICR 371, [1980] IRLR 270, EAT);
   (7)   expenses may be included if they are a profit in the employee's hands (*S & U Stores Ltd v Wilkes* [1974] 3 All ER 401, [1974] ICR 645, NIRC (*quaere* whether the tribunal should involve itself with any illegality through tax evasion in such a case: see *S & U Stores Ltd v Lee* [1969] 2 All ER 417, [1969] 1 WLR 626, DC; *Cole v Fred Stacey Ltd* [1974] IRLR 73; *Jennings v Westwood Engineering Ltd* [1975] IRLR 245; and as to illegality generally see PARA 18));
   (8)   payments in kind are not normally included (*S & U Stores Ltd v Wilkes* at 405 and 649; *Skillen v Eastwoods Froy Ltd* (1966) 2 ITR 112; *British Transport Hotels Ltd v Minister of Labour* (1966) 2 ITR 165, EAT; *Lyford v Turquand (liquidator of GA Sprott Ltd)* (1966) 1 ITR 554; *AM Carmichael Ltd (in liquidation) v Laing* (1972) 7 ITR 1);
   (9)   any payment by someone other than the employer is not normally included, unless there is some special contractual provision (*S & U Stores Ltd v Wilkes* at 405 and 649; *Palmanor Ltd v Cedron* [1978] ICR 1008, [1978] IRLR 303, EAT (waiter cannot

include tips); cf *Tsoukka v Potomac Restaurants Ltd*; *Donelan v Kerrby Constructions Ltd* (site bonus included in remuneration); *Nerva v RL & G Ltd* [1997] ICR 11, [1996] IRLR 461, CA).

As to customers' tips being part of remuneration see Application 42295/98 *Nerva v United Kingdom* [2002] IRLR 815, 13 BHRC 246, [2002] All ER (D) 137 (Sep), ECtHR (employees should come to a contractual arrangement with their employer as to how the tips at issue were to be dealt with).

8 As to the meaning of 'week' for these purposes see PARA 126 note 13.

9 For these purposes, references to remuneration varying with the amount of work done include references to remuneration which may include any commission or similar payment which varies in amount: Employment Rights Act 1996 s 221(4); and see *Keywest Club Ltd (t/a Veeraswamys Restaurant) v Choudhury* [1988] IRLR 51, EAT. What the Employment Rights Act 1996 s 221(4) achieves is to make clear that, where remuneration does in fact vary with the amount of work done, commission, bonuses and similar payments are included in the calculation of an employee's week's pay; s 221(4) does not control whether a contract is placed in s 221(2) (see the text and notes 10–11) or in s 221(3) (see the text and notes 12–14): *Evans v Malley Organisation Ltd (t/a First Business Support)* [2002] EWCA Civ 1834, [2003] ICR 432, [2003] IRLR 156 (commission paid to an employee in respect of performance, and not the amount of work undertaken, not included when calculating the average hourly rate of remuneration).

10 As to the meaning of 'employer' see PARA 2.

11 Employment Rights Act 1996 s 221(2). See also notes 4, 7. Payments should be calculated on the basis of the weeks actually worked and not on the basis of a notional 52-week calculation which takes into account weeks employees were not required to work and for which they were not paid to work: *Gilbert v Barnsley Metropolitan Borough Council* [2002] All ER (D) 45 (Apr), EAT.

12 Employment Rights Act 1996 s 221(3). See also notes 4, 7.

13 Employment Rights Act 1996 s 221(3)(a).

14 Employment Rights Act 1996 s 221(3)(b).

15 See the Employment Rights Act 1996 s 222(1). The provision made by s 222 is subject to s 227 (maximum amount of week's pay: see PARA 147) and s 228 (employee not employed for sufficient period to enable usual calculation to be made: see PARA 148): s 222(5).

16 For these purposes, the average number of weekly hours must be calculated by dividing by 12 the total number of the employee's normal working hours during the relevant period of 12 weeks (see the Employment Rights Act 1996 s 222(3)(a)), where the 'relevant period of 12 weeks' means (where the calculation date is the last day of a week) the period of 12 weeks ending with that week, and, otherwise, the period of 12 weeks ending with the last complete week before the calculation date (see s 222(4)).

17 See the Employment Rights Act 1996 s 222(2). For these purposes, the average hourly rate of remuneration is the average hourly rate of remuneration payable by the employer to the employee in respect of the relevant period of 12 weeks: see s 222(3)(b). See also note 15.

18 See the Employment Rights Act 1996 s 223(1). See also *Gilbert v Barnsley Metropolitan Borough Council* [2002] All ER (D) 45 (Apr), EAT (cited in note 11).

19 See the Employment Rights Act 1996 s 223(2).

20 See the Employment Rights Act 1996 s 223(3). The provision made by s 223(3) also applies to a case within s 234(3) (see PARA 142) in the event of normal working hours falling within the number of hours without overtime: see s 223(3). This means that hours worked as overtime are to be taken into account but with the element of overtime premium 'stripped out' of the pay, even if that has the effect of artificially decreasing the average hourly rate of remuneration: *British Coal Corpn v Cheesbrough* [1990] 2 AC 256, [1990] ICR 317, HL.

145. Employments for which there are no normal working hours. Where there are no normal working hours[1] for an employee[2] when employed under the contract of employment[3] in force on the calculation date[4], the amount of a week's pay[5] for such an employee is calculated[6] as follows[7]: (1) the amount of a week's pay is the amount of the employee's average weekly remuneration[8] in the period of 12 weeks ending[9]: (a) where the calculation date is the last day of a week, with that week[10]; and (b) otherwise, with the last complete week before the calculation date[11]; and (2) in arriving at the average weekly rate of remuneration, no account is to be taken of a week in which no remuneration was payable by the employer[12] to the employee, and remuneration in earlier weeks must be brought in so as to bring up to 12 the number of weeks of which account is taken[13].

1   As to normal working hours see PARA 142.
2   As to the meaning of 'employee' see PARA 2.
3   As to the meaning of 'contract of employment' see PARA 2.
4   See the Employment Rights Act 1996 s 224(1). As to the calculation date see PARA 146. As to the general requirement to follow s 224 see *Alderson v Wings Aeromedical Services Ltd* [2009] All ER (D) 11 (Jan), EAT.
5   As to the meaning of 'week' see PARA 126 note 13.
6   Ie in accordance with the Employment Rights Act 1996 Pt XIV Ch II (ss 220–229) (calculation of a week's pay: see also PARAS 143, 144, 146–148): see s 220; and PARA 143.
7   See the Employment Rights Act 1996 s 220; and PARA 143.
8   As to the meaning of 'remuneration' for these purposes see PARA 144 note 7.
9   See the Employment Rights Act 1996 s 224(2). The provision made by s 224 is subject to s 227 (maximum amount of week's pay: see PARA 147) and s 228 (employee not employed for sufficient period to enable usual calculation to be made: see PARA 148): s 224(4).
10 Employment Rights Act 1996 s 224(2)(a).
11 Employment Rights Act 1996 s 224(2)(b).
12 As to the meaning of 'employer' see PARA 2.
13 See the Employment Rights Act 1996 s 224(3). See note 9. This provision applies when nothing is legally payable in the particular week, regardless of the reason: *Secretary of State for Employment v Crane* [1988] IRLR 238, EAT.

146.   The calculation date.   For the purposes of calculating the amount of a week's pay[1] in accordance with the Employment Rights Act 1996[2], the 'calculation date' is:

(1)   where the calculation is of the amount of a guarantee payment[3], the day in respect of which the guarantee payment is payable (or, where the employee's[4] contract has been varied, or a new contract entered into, in connection with a period of short-time working, the last day on which the original contract was in force)[5];

(2)   where the calculation is of the amount of remuneration for time off to look for work or make arrangements for training[6], the day on which the employer's[7] notice was given[8];

(3)   where the calculation is of the amount of remuneration for time off for ante-natal care[9], the day of the appointment[10];

(4)   where the calculation is of the amount of remuneration for time off for employee representatives[11], the day on which the time off was taken or on which it is alleged the time off should have been permitted[12];

(5)   where the calculation is of the amount of remuneration for time off for study or training[13], the day on which the time off was taken (or on which it is alleged the time off should have been permitted) in Wales, or the day on which the application was made in England (as the case may be)[14];

(6)   where the calculation is of the amount of remuneration payable on suspension on medical or maternity grounds[15]: (a) in the case of an employee suspended on medical grounds, the day before that on which the suspension begins[16]; or (b) in the case of an employee suspended on maternity grounds, where the day before that on which the suspension begins falls during a period of ordinary or additional maternity[17] leave, the day before the beginning of that period, and otherwise the day before that on which the suspension began[18];

(7)   where the calculation is for the purposes of providing compensation for

a complaint brought under the flexible working provisions[19], the day on which the application to request a contract variation was made[20];

(8) where the calculation is of the amount of remuneration payable during periods of notice[21], the day immediately preceding the first day of notice[22] that is required[23];

(9) where the calculation is for certain purposes of compensation relating to unfair dismissal[24], the date on which the employer's notice was given (if the dismissal was with notice) and otherwise the effective date of termination[25];

(10) where the calculation is for the purposes[26] of a basic award of compensation for unfair dismissal[27]: (a) if a date is to be treated[28] as the effective date of termination[29] which is later than the effective date of termination[30], the effective date of termination as so defined[31]; and (b) otherwise, the date on which notice would have been given had the statutory conditions been fulfilled[32], whether those conditions were in fact fulfilled or not[33];

(11) where the calculation is for the purposes of the statutory provisions relating to short-time working[34], the day immediately preceding the first of the four or, as the case may be, the four or six specified[35] weeks[36];

(12) where the calculation is for the purposes of the statutory provisions relating to redundancy payments[37]: (a) where a date is to be treated[38] as the relevant date for the purposes of certain statutory provisions which is later than the relevant date[39], the relevant date as so defined[40]; or (b) otherwise, the date on which notice would have been given had the statutory conditions been fulfilled[41], whether those conditions were in fact fulfilled or not[42].

1 As to the meaning of 'week' see PARA 126 note 13.
2 Ie in accordance with the Employment Rights Act 1996 Pt XIV Ch II (ss 220–229) (calculation of a week's pay: see also PARAS 143, 144, 145, 147, 148): see s 220; and PARA 143.
3 Ie for the purposes of the Employment Rights Act 1996 s 30 (calculation of guarantee payment: see PARA 263): see s 225(1).
4 As to the meaning of 'employee' see PARA 2.
5 See the Employment Rights Act 1996 s 225(1).
6 Ie for the purposes of the Employment Rights Act 1996 s 53 (remuneration for time off to look for work or make arrangements for training: see PARA 326) or s 54 (complaint to employment tribunal: see PARA 327): see s 225(2).
7 As to the meaning of 'employer' see PARA 2.
8 Employment Rights Act 1996 s 225(2).
9 Ie for the purposes of the Employment Rights Act 1996 s 56 (remuneration for time off for ante-natal care: see PARA 333): see s 225(3).
10 Employment Rights Act 1996 s 225(3). Where the calculation is for the purposes of:
　　(1) s 57ZF (complaint to employment tribunal regarding right to time off to accompany to ante-natal appointment: see PARA 336), the calculation date is the day of the appointment (s 225(3A) (added by the Children and Families Act 2014 s 127(2)(c))); and
　　(2) the Employment Rights Act 1996 s 57ZK (right to remuneration for time off to attend adoption appointments: see PARA 341) or s 57ZM (complaint to employment tribunal regarding right to time off to attend or accompany to adoption appointment: see PARA 343), the calculation date is the day of the appointment (s 225(3B) (added by the Children and Families Act 2014 s 128(2)(d))).
11 Ie for the purposes of the Employment Rights Act 1996 s 62 (remuneration for time off for employee representatives: see PARA 1209): see s 225(4).
12 Employment Rights Act 1996 s 225(4).
13 Ie for the purposes of the Employment Rights Act 1996 s 63B (remuneration for time off for study or training for young person in Wales or Scotland: see PARA 331), or s 63J (remuneration for time off for study or training: see PARA 330): see s 225(4A) (added by the Teaching and

Higher Education Act 1998 s 44(1), Sch 3 paras 10, 14), the Employment Rights Act 1996 s 225(4B) (added by the Apprenticeships, Skills, Children and Learning Act 2009 s 40(5), Sch 1 paras 1, 8).

14 Employment Rights Act 1996 ss 225(4A), (4B) (as added: see note 13). Head (5) in the text refers to the day on which the time off was taken (or on which it is alleged the time off should have been permitted) where s 63B applies (see PARA 331), or the day on which the application under s 63D was made where s 63J applies (see PARA 330): see ss 225(4A), (4B) (as so added).

15 Ie for the purposes of the Employment Rights Act 1996 s 69 (see PARA 604): see s 225(5).

16 Employment Rights Act 1996 s 225(5)(a).

17 As to ordinary and additional maternity leave see PARAS 356–362.

18 Employment Rights Act 1996 s 225(5)(b) (amended by the Employment Relations Act 1999 s 9, Sch 4 Pt III paras 5, 39).

19 Ie for the purposes of the Employment Rights Act 1996 s 80I (see PARA 111): see s 225(6) (added by the Employment Act 2002 s 53, Sch 7 paras 24, 45).

20 Employment Rights Act 1996 s 225(6) (as added: see note 19). Head (7) in the text refers to the day on which the application under s 80F for a contract variation was made (see PARAS 108–111): see s 225(6) (as so added)

21 Ie for the purposes of the Employment Rights Act 1996 s 88 (see PARA 738) or s 89 (see PARA 739): see s 226(1).

22 Ie the period of notice required by Employment Rights Act 1996 s 86(1) or (2) (see PARA 736): see s 226(1).

23 Employment Rights Act 1996 s 226(1).

24 Ie for the purposes of the Employment Rights Act 1996 s 93 (written statement of reasons for dismissal) (see PARA 756) or s 117 (compensation for failure to reinstate or re-engage) (see PARA 813) or s 125 (repealed): see s 226(2).

25 See the Employment Rights Act 1996 s 226(2).

26 Ie for the purposes of the Employment Rights Act 1996 s 112 (remedy on complaint of unfair dismissal) (see PARA 810), s 119 (basic award of compensation for unfair dismissal) (see PARA 815), s 120 and s 121 (minimum amounts of basic award of compensation for unfair dismissal) (see PARA 816) or s 124 (maximum amounts for award: see PARA 823): see s 226(3) (amended by the Employment Act 2002 Sch 7 paras 24, 46; and SI 2013/1949).

27 See the Employment Rights Act 1996 s 226(3) (as amended: see note 26).

28 Ie by virtue of the Employment Rights Act 1996 s 97(2) or (4) (see PARA 764): see s 226(3)(b).

29 Ie for the purposes of the Employment Rights Act 1996 s 108(1) (see PARA 758), s 119(1) (see PARA 815) or s 227(3) (repealed): see s 226(3)(b).

30 Ie as defined by the Employment Rights Act 1996 s 97(1) (see PARA 764): see s 226(3)(b).

31 Employment Rights Act 1996 s 226(3)(b).

32 For these purposes, and for the purposes of the Employment Rights Act 1996 s 226(5)(c) (see the text and notes 41–42), the date referred to is the date on which notice would have been given: (1) had the contract been terminable by notice. and it had been terminated by the employer giving such notice as is required by s 86 (see PARAS 735–736) to terminate that contract (s 226(6)(a)); and (2) had the notice expired on the effective date of termination, or on the relevant date (s 226(6)(b)).

33 See the Employment Rights Act 1996 s 226(3)(c), (6).

34 Ie the Employment Rights Act 1996 s 147(2) (see PARA 875): see s 226(4).

35 Ie referred to in the Employment Rights Act 1996 s 148(2) (see PARA 876): see s 226(4).

36 Employment Rights Act 1996 s 226(4).

37 See the Employment Rights Act 1996 s 226(5). Head (12) in the text refers to a calculation for the purposes of s 162 (see PARA 881): see s 226(5).

38 Ie by virtue of the Employment Rights Act 1996 s 145(5) (see PARA 871): see s 226(5)(b).

39 Ie as defined by the Employment Rights Act 1996 s 145(1)–(4) (see PARA 871): see s 226(5)(b).

40 Employment Rights Act 1996 s 226(5)(b).

41 See note 32.

42 See the Employment Rights Act 1996 s 226(5)(c), (6).

147. Maximum amount of week's pay for certain purposes. Notwithstanding the general provision made for calculating the amount of a week's pay[1] in accordance with the Employment Rights Act 1996[2], the amount of a week's pay for the purpose of calculating:

(1) an award of compensation[3] for a complaint brought under the provisions that allow time off for study or training[4];

(2)   an award of compensation[5] for a complaint brought under the flexible working provisions[6];

(3)   a basic award of compensation[7] for unfair dismissal[8];

(4)   an additional award of compensation[9] for unfair dismissal[10];

(5)   an award of compensation[11] for unfair dismissal on grounds of procedural fairness[12];

(6)   a redundancy payment[13],

must not exceed £464[14].

1   As to the meaning of 'week' see PARA 126 note 13.
2   Ie in accordance with the Employment Rights Act 1996 Pt XIV Ch II (ss 220–229) (calculation of a week's pay: see also PARAS 143 et seq, 148): see s 220; and PARA 143.
3   Ie under the Employment Rights Act 1996 s 63J(1)(b) (see PARA 330): see s 227(1)(zza) (added by the Apprenticeships, Skills, Children and Learning Act 2009 s 40(5), Sch 1 paras 1, 9). At the date at which this volume states the law, the amendment made by Sch 1 has come into force for all purposes except in relation to small employers and their employees (see the Apprenticeships, Skills, Children and Learning Act 2009 (Commencement No 2 and Transitional and Saving Provisions) Order 2010, SI 2010/303, art 4, Sch 3) and will come into force for all remaining purposes on a day to be appointed under the Apprenticeships, Skills, Children and Learning Act 2009 s 269(4). However, at the date at which this volume states the law, no such day had been appointed.
4   Employment Rights Act 1996 s 227(1)(zza) (as added: see note 3).
5   Ie under the Employment Rights Act 1996 s 80I(1)(b) (see PARA 111): see s 227(1)(za) (added by the Employment Act 2002 s 53, Sch 7 paras 24, 47(1), (2)).
6   Employment Rights Act 1996 s 227(1)(za) (as added: see note 5).
7   Ie within the meaning of the Employment Rights Act 1996 s 119 (see PARA 815): see s 227(1)(a).
8   Employment Rights Act 1996 s 227(1)(a).
9   Ie within the meaning of the Employment Rights Act 1996 s 117(3)(b) (see PARA 813): see s 227(1)(b).
10 Employment Rights Act 1996 s 227(1)(b).
11 Ie under the Employment Rights Act 1996 s 112(5) (see PARA 810): see s 227(1)(ba) (substituted by the Employment Act 2002 Sch 7 paras 24, 47(1), (3)).
12 Employment Rights Act 1996 s 227(1)(ba) (as substituted: see note 11).
13 Employment Rights Act 1996 s 227(1)(c). As to redundancy payments see PARA 835 et seq.
14 See the Employment Rights Act 1996 s 227(1) (amended by SI 2014/382). As to the Secretary of State's duty to increase or decrease the amount in the Employment Rights Act 1996 s 227(1) in line with the retail prices index see the Employment Relations Act 1999 s 34(1)(e), (2), (3)(c); and PARA 160. The Work and Families Act 2006 s 14 also applies to the sum specified in the Employment Rights Act 1996 s 227(1), however: see the Work and Families Act 2006 s 14(1)(b). Accordingly, the Secretary of State may, on one occasion only, by order substitute for the sum specified in the Employment Rights Act 1996 s 227(1) such higher sum as may be specified in the order: Work and Families Act 2006 s 14(2). An order under s 14 must be made by statutory instrument, it may include transitional provision, and it may exclude (on a single occasion specified in the order under s 14) any duty to make an order under the Employment Relations Act 1999 s 34 (indexation of certain amounts etc: see PARA 160), so far as relating to the sum specified in the Employment Rights Act 1996 s 227(1): see the Work and Families Act 2006 s 14(3). Subject to any provision so made, s 14 does not affect the operation of the Employment Relations Act 1999 s 34 in relation to the sum specified in the Employment Rights Act 1996 s 227(1) as so substituted: see the Work and Families Act 2006 s 14(4). No statutory instrument containing an order under s 14 may be made unless a draft of the instrument has been laid before, and approved by a resolution of, each House of Parliament: s 14(5). At the date at which this volume states the law, no such order had been made under s 14. As to the Secretary of State see PARA 5 note 21.

148.   Special cases. In any case in which an employee[1] has not been employed[2] for a sufficient period to enable a calculation of the amount of a week's pay[3] to be made otherwise in accordance with the Employment Rights Act 1996[4], the amount of a week's pay is an amount which fairly represents a week's pay[5]. In determining that amount, the employment tribunal[6]:

(1)   must apply, as nearly as may be, such of those general provisions[7] as it considers appropriate[8]; and

(2)   may have regard to such of the following considerations as it thinks fit[9], that is to say:

(a)   any remuneration[10] received by the employee in respect of the employment in question[11];

(b)   the amount offered to the employee as remuneration in respect of the employment in question[12];

(c)   the remuneration received by other persons engaged in relevant comparable employment with the same employer[13];

(d)   the remuneration received by other persons engaged in relevant comparable employment with other employers[14].

In arriving at an average hourly rate of remuneration, or at an average weekly remuneration[15], account is to be taken of work for a former employer within the period for which the average is to be taken if a period of employment with the former employer counts[16] as part of the employee's continuous period of employment[17]. Where account is to be taken for these purposes[18] of remuneration or other payments for a period which does not coincide with the periods for which the remuneration or other payments are calculated, the remuneration or other payments must be apportioned in such manner as may be just[19].

The Secretary of State[20] may by regulations[21] provide that in prescribed cases the amount of a week's pay is to be calculated in such manner as may be so prescribed[22].

1   As to the meaning of 'employee' see PARA 2.
2   As to the meaning of 'employed' see PARA 2.
3   As to the meaning of 'week' see PARA 126 note 13.
4   Ie to be made under the Employment Rights Act 1996 ss 220–227 (calculation of a week's pay: see also PARA 143 et seq): see s 228(1).
5   See the Employment Rights Act 1996 s 228(1).
6   See the Employment Rights Act 1996 s 228(2) (amended by the Employment Rights (Dispute Resolution) Act 1998 s 1(2)(a)).
7   Ie such of the Employment Rights Act 1996 ss 220–227 (calculation of a week's pay: see also PARA 143 et seq): see s 228(2)(a).
8   Employment Rights Act 1996 s 228(2)(a).
9   See the Employment Rights Act 1996 s 228(2)(b). Head (2) in the text refers to such of the considerations specified in s 228(3) (see heads (a)–(d) in the text) as the employment tribunal thinks fit: see s 228(2)(b).
10   As to the meaning of 'remuneration' for these purposes see PARA 144 note 7.
11   Employment Rights Act 1996 s 228(3)(a). As to the meaning of 'employment' see PARA 2.
12   Employment Rights Act 1996 s 228(3)(b).
13   Employment Rights Act 1996 s 228(3)(c). As to the meaning of 'employer' see PARA 2.
14   Employment Rights Act 1996 s 228(3)(d).
15   Ie under the Employment Rights Act 1996 Pt XIV Ch II (ss 220–229) (calculation of a week's pay: see also PARA 143 et seq): see s 229(1).
16   Ie by virtue of the Employment Rights Act 1996 Pt XIV Ch I (ss 210–219) (continuous employment: see PARAS 130 et seq, 861 et seq): see s 229(1).
17   See the Employment Rights Act 1996 s 229(1).
18   Ie under the Employment Rights Act 1996 Pt XIV Ch II (calculation of a week's pay: see also PARA 143 et seq): see s 229(2).
19   Employment Rights Act 1996 s 229(2).
20   As to the Secretary of State see PARA 5 note 21.
21   As to making of regulations under the Employment Rights Act 1996 generally see PARA 162.
22   Employment Rights Act 1996 s 228(4). At the date at which this volume states the law, no such regulations had been made.

2. RIGHTS ARISING IN THE COURSE OF EMPLOYMENT

(1) IN GENERAL

(i) Introductory

149. In general. Although employment protection rights[1] are statutory in origin and nature, their background remains tied to the concept of the contract of employment, which, therefore, continues to underlie this area of law, for three reasons:

(1) with the exception of some statutory provisions which adopt a wider definition[2], an 'employee' is defined, for most statutory purposes, as an individual who has entered into or works under, or, where the employment has ceased, worked under, a contract of employment[3];

(2) if, for any reason, there is a legal defect in the contractual basis of employment, that defect may prejudice not just the employee's rights under contract, but also his rights under statute (because most statutory rights are given to employees as described under head (1) above)[4];

(3) the statutory protections have been said to provide a 'floor of rights', in the sense that they establish a legal minimum[5].

Any discussion of the idea of a 'floor of rights' must be tempered, however, by the fact that: (a) it is possible under the Employment Rights Act 1996 to contract out of certain of its provisions if specified circumstances apply because it is open to the parties to negotiate or contract for better rights from the employee's point of view (which then normally take effect as terms of individual contracts of employment)[6]; and (b) an employee who agrees to take on the status of employee shareholder under the Employment Rights Act 1996 forgoes certain fundamental rights (primarily those relating to unfair dismissal and redundancy) in return for new rights of ownership and tax advantages[7].

1 Ie those rights that are discussed at PARA 150 et seq.
2 See PARA 5.
3 See the Employment Rights Act 1996 s 230(1); and PARA 2. The question as to what constitutes a contract of employment (and, therefore, as to who is an employee) remains to be decided under common law, however: see PARAS 2–4.
4 Examples of such legal defects might be where the contract of employment is illegal (see PARA 18), or where it is frustrated (see PARAS 728–729).
5 Examples of such rights might be where lay-off pay is negotiated at a higher rate than the statutory guarantee payment (see PARA 261), or where a contract contains more generous terms on maternity leave than those in the statutory right (see PARA 367). Collective agreements may also provide for enhanced protection, or for enhanced rights, and the terms of such agreements may be incorporated into individual contracts of employment, either expressly or impliedly: see PARA 116.
6 See the Employment Rights Act 1996 s 203; and PARA 150.
7 See the Employment Rights Act 1996 s 205A; and PARA 154. Employment rights underwritten by EU law remain unaffected: see PARA 154.

(ii) Restrictions on Contracting Out

A. STATUTORY RESTRICTIONS

150. Restrictions on contracting out of statutory protections. Any provision in an agreement (whether a contract of employment[1] or not) is void in so far as it purports[2]:

(1) to exclude or limit the operation of any provision of the Employment Rights Act 1996[3]; or

(2) to preclude any person from bringing any proceedings under the Employment Rights Act 1996 before an employment tribunal[4].

The restriction set out in heads (1) and (2) above does not, however, apply to:

(a) any provision in a collective agreement[5] excluding rights to guarantee payments[6] if an exemption order[7] is for the time being in force in respect of it[8];

(b) any provision in a dismissal procedures agreement[9] excluding rights under the Employment Rights Act 1996 provisions[10] relating to unfair dismissal if that provision is not to have effect unless an exclusion order is for the time being in force[11] in respect of it[12];

(c) any provision in an agreement if a redundancy payments exemption order[13] is for the time being in force in respect of it[14];

(d) any agreement to refrain from instituting or continuing proceedings before an employment tribunal[15] where a conciliation officer has taken action under the Employment Tribunals Act 1996[16];

(e) any agreement to refrain from instituting or continuing any proceedings falling within the jurisdiction of the Employment Tribunals Act 1996 where conciliation is available[17], being proceedings under the Employment Rights Act 1996[18], or are proceedings arising out of the Part-time Workers (Prevention of Less Favourable Treatment) Regulations 2000[19], or arising out of the Fixed-term Employees (Prevention of Less Favourable Treatment) Regulations 2002[20], if the conditions regulating settlement agreements under the Employment Rights Act 1996[21] are satisfied in relation to the agreement[22].

Furthermore, any provision in an agreement (whether a contract of employment[23] or not) is also void in so far as it purports[24]:

(i) to exclude or limit the operation of any provision of the Trade Union and Labour Relations (Consolidation) Act 1992[25]; or

(ii) to preclude a person from bringing proceedings before an employment tribunal, or the Central Arbitration Committee, under any provision of the Trade Union and Labour Relations (Consolidation) Act 1992[26].

The restriction set out in heads (i) and (ii) above does not, however, apply to:

(A) an agreement to refrain from instituting or continuing proceedings before an employment tribunal[27] where a conciliation officer has taken action under the Employment Tribunals Act 1996[28];

(B) an agreement to refrain from instituting or continuing specified proceedings under the Trade Union and Labour Relations (Consolidation) Act 1992[29] before an employment tribunal if the conditions regulating settlement agreements under the Trade Union and Labour Relations (Consolidation) Act 1992[30] are satisfied in relation to the agreement[31];

(C) a collective agreement or individual agreement effecting an improvement of terms and conditions[32], to the extent that it varies or supersedes an award made by the Central Arbitration Committee[33]; or

(D) any provision in a collective agreement excluding rights under the procedure that is provided by the Trade Union and Labour Relations (Consolidation) Act 1992 for handling redundancies[34], if there is an exclusion order[35] in force in respect of it[36].

1   As to the meaning of 'contract of employment' see PARA 2.

2   See the Employment Rights Act 1996 s 203(1). The word 'purports' is not designed only to
     catch provisions which expressly claim to limit the operation of a provision of the Employment
     Rights Act 1996 (see head (1) in the text); it is there to take account of the fact that s 203(1)
     makes such provisions void: *Fitzgerald v University of Kent at Canterbury* [2004] EWCA Civ
     143, [2004] ICR 737, [2004] IRLR 300 (consensual arrangement to antedate termination of
     employment caught by the restriction in the Employment Rights Act 1996 s 203(1)). The
     agreement must be valid in the first place: see note 17.
          The provision made by the Employment Rights Act 1996 s 203 is not exhaustive, however;
     and thus it may be possible for an applicant wishing to avoid an agreement also to attack the
     validity of that agreement on common law grounds: *Hennessy v Craigmyle & Co Ltd* [1986]
     ICR 461, [1986] IRLR 300, CA (principle that economic duress is capable of rendering a
     contract voidable is applicable to employment law, although the circumstances in which it is
     likely to be successfully alleged will arise only most exceptionally in such cases).

3   Employment Rights Act 1996 s 203(1)(a). There must be an existing legal effect of the
     contractual arrangements out of which the offending provision purports to contract: see *M & P
     Steelcraft Ltd v Ellis* [2008] ICR 578, [2008] IRLR 355, EAT (no existing employment
     relationship found). Any provision in an agreement which is void under head (1) in the text is
     otherwise valid: *Sutherland v Network Appliance Ltd* [2001] IRLR 12, EAT. One of the most
     significant applications of the Employment Rights Act 1996 s 203 was to an agreement that
     employment would terminate automatically (ie without the need for a dismissal) on the
     happening of a particular event in *Igbo v Johnson, Matthey Chemicals Ltd* [1986] ICR 505,
     [1986] IRLR 215, CA (failure to return from leave); but this case was distinguished, and the
     Employment Rights Act 1996 s 203 was not applied, where there was a genuine agreement to
     take early retirement (*Scott v Coalite Fuels and Chemicals Ltd* [1988] ICR 355, [1988] IRLR
     131, EAT) and in the case of an agreement to resign, reached without undue pressure and on
     agreed terms (*Logan Salton v Durham County Council* [1989] IRLR 99, EAT). As to
     termination by mutual consent generally see PARAS 730–731.
          The Employment Rights Act 1996 s 203 is also applied directly for the purposes of:
     (1)   the Part-time Workers (Prevention of Less Favourable Treatment) Regulations 2000,
            SI 2000/1551 (see reg 9; and PARA 76);
     (2)   the   Fixed-term   Employees   (Prevention   of   Less   Favourable   Treatment)
            Regulations 2002, SI 2002/2034 (see reg 10; and PARA 87);
     (3)   the Transfer of Undertakings (Protection of Employment) Regulations 2006,
            SI 2006/246 (see reg 18; and PARA 137);
     (4)   the Agency Workers Regulations 2010, SI 2010/93 (see reg 15; and PARA 98),
     as if each of heads (1) to (4) above was contained in the Employment Rights Act 1996 s 203. A
     form of words that is very similar to that found in s 203 is found also (without invoking that
     provision directly) in:
     (a)   the Trade Union and Labour Relations (Consolidation) Act 1992 (see s 288; and heads
            (i)–(ii), (A)–(D) in the text);
     (b)   the National Minimum Wage Act 1998 (see s 49; and PARA 173);
     (c)   the Social Security Contributions and Benefits Act 1992 Pt 12ZA (ss 171ZA–171ZK)
            (ordinary and additional statutory paternity pay), Pt 12ZB (ss 171ZL–171ZT)
            (statutory adoption pay), Pt 12ZC (ss 171ZU–171ZZ5) (statutory shared parental pay:
            see ss 171ZF, 171ZO, 171ZZ; and PARAS 443, 488, 534);
     (d)   the Working Time Regulations 1998, SI 1998/1833 (see reg 35; and PARA); and
     (e)   the Transnational Information and Consultation of Employees Regulations 1999,
            SI 1999/3323 (see regs 40, 41; and PARA 1238).
          A term of a contract is unenforceable also by a person in whose favour it would operate in so
     far as it purports to exclude or limit a provision of or made under the Equality Act 2010 (see
     s 144; and DISCRIMINATION vol 33 (2013) PARA 6).

4   Employment Rights Act 1996 s 203(1)(b) (amended by the Employment Rights (Dispute
     Resolution) Act 1998 s 1(2)(a)). As to employment tribunals see PARA 1399 et seq; and as to the
     procedure on a complaint made to an employment tribunal see PARA 1453 et seq.
          The Employment Rights Act 1996 s 203 is principally of significance in unfair dismissal
     claims, with the effect that, unless an agreement to settle such a claim has been reached after an
     ACAS conciliation officer (see note 16) has taken action or by way of agreement (see heads (d),
     (e) in the text), that agreement is not binding on the parties (*Courage Take Home Trade Ltd v
     Keys* [1986] ICR 874, [1986] IRLR 427, EAT); but it has also been applied in several areas
     other than settling unfair dismissal claims, eg rendering void:
     (1)   an agreement not to pursue a claim in return for ex gratia payment (*Council of
            Engineering Institutions v Maddison* [1977] ICR 30, [1976] IRLR 389, EAT);

(2)   an agreement not to continue with a complaint (*Naqvi v Stephens Jewellers Ltd* [1978] ICR 631, EAT);

(3)   a provision in a staff code that limited the effect of statutory maternity rights (*ILEA v Nash* [1979] ICR 229, [1979] IRLR 29, EAT);

(4)   a clause in a contract of employment that was made on re-engagement after a strike negativing the normal rules on continuity of employment (*Hanson v Fashion Industries (Hartlepool) Ltd* [1981] ICR 35, [1980] IRLR 393, EAT);

(5)   an agreement reducing the number of hours worked to a figure below that necessary to qualify for statutory rights (*Secretary of State for Employment v Deary* [1984] ICR 413, [1984] IRLR 180, EAT);

(6)   a 'bumping' arrangement in redundancy law allowing for compulsory redeployment (*Tocher v General Motors Scotland Ltd* [1981] IRLR 55, EAT).

If an employment tribunal has made a consent order allowing a complaint to be withdrawn following a voluntary agreement between the parties, that will bind the applicant, in the absence of fraud or misrepresentation, and no further proceedings may be instituted: *Times Newspapers Ltd v Fitt* [1981] ICR 637, EAT. Where a tribunal has made a finding on liability, the parties can validly agree on compensation without falling foul of the Employment Rights Act 1996 s 203: *Carter v Reiner Moritz Associates Ltd* [1997] ICR 881, EAT; and see *Mayo-Deman v University of Greenwich* [2005] IRLR 845, EAT (claim for discrimination on grounds of sex and race dismissed on the basis that parties had agreed on compensation in full and final settlement of the proceedings and all her claims, notwithstanding that the settlement was not a [settlement] agreement complying with the terms of the discrimination legislation then in force). If, however, there is no withdrawal or abandonment of the claim, further proceedings may be brought: *Milestone School of English Ltd v Leakey* [1982] IRLR 3, EAT. Settlement agreements were formerly known as compromise agreements (ie before 29 July 2013: see the Enterprise and Regulatory Reform Act 2013 s 23 (renaming of 'compromise agreements', 'compromise contracts' and 'compromises'); and the Enterprise and Regulatory Reform Act 2013 (Commencement No 2) Order 2013, SI 2013/1648, art 2(c)).

5   As to the meaning of 'collective agreement' see PARA 119 note 21.

6   Ie under the Employment Rights Act 1996 s 28 (see PARA 261): see s 203(2)(a).

7   Ie under the Employment Rights Act 1996 s 35 (see PARA 266): see s 203(2)(a).

8   Employment Rights Act 1996 s 203(2)(a).

9   For these purposes, except in so far as the context otherwise requires, 'dismissal procedures agreement' means an agreement in writing with respect to procedures relating to dismissal made by or on behalf of one or more independent trade unions and one or more employers or employers' associations: see the Employment Rights Act 1996 s 235(1). 'Independent trade union' means, except in so far as the context otherwise requires, a trade union which: (1) is not under the domination or control of an employer or a group of employers or of one or more employers' associations; and (2) is not liable to interference by an employer or any such group or association, arising out of the provision of financial or material support or by any other means whatsoever, tending towards such control: see s 235(1). 'Employers' association', except in so far as the context otherwise requires, has the same meaning as in the Trade Union and Labour Relations (Consolidation) Act 1992 (see PARA 1079); and 'trade union' has the meaning given by s 1 (see PARA 891): see the Employment Rights Act 1996 s 235(1); and the Employment Tribunals Act 1996 s 42(1). As to the meaning of 'employer' see PARA 2; and as to the meaning of 'associated employer' see PARA 3. As to the meaning of 'writing' see PARA 2 note 8.

10 Ie under the Employment Rights Act 1996 s 94 (see PARA 757): see s 203(2)(b).

11 Ie an order under the Employment Rights Act 1996 s 110 (see PARAS 759–760): see s 203(2)(b).

12 Employment Rights Act 1996 s 203(2)(b).

13 Ie an order under the Employment Rights Act 1996 s 157 (see PARA 857): see s 203(2)(c).

14 Employment Rights Act 1996 s 203(2)(c).

15 An agreement under which the parties agree to submit a dispute to arbitration:

(1)   is to be regarded for the purposes of the Employment Rights Act 1996 s 203(2)(e) and s 203(2)(f) (see head (e) in the text) as being an agreement to refrain from instituting or continuing proceedings, if: (a) the dispute is covered by a scheme having effect by virtue of an order under the Trade Union and Labour Relations (Consolidation) Act 1992 s 212A (see PARA 824) (Employment Rights Act 1996 s 203(5)(a)(i) (s 203(5) added by the Employment Rights (Dispute Resolution) Act 1998 s 8(5))); and (b) the agreement is to submit it to arbitration in accordance with the scheme (Employment Rights Act 1996 s 203(5)(a)(ii) (as so added)); but

(2)   is to be regarded as neither being nor including such an agreement in any other case (s 203(5)(b) (as so added)).

16 Employment Rights Act 1996 s 203(2)(e) (amended by the Employment Rights (Dispute Resolution) Act 1998 s 1(2)(c); and the Enterprise and Regulatory Reform Act 2013 s 7(2), Sch 1 para 10). The text refers to action taken by a conciliation officer under any of the Employment Tribunals Act 1996 ss 18A–18C (requirement to contact ACAS before instituting proceedings: see PARAS 152, 153): see the Employment Rights Act 1996 s 203(2)(e) (as so amended). For these purposes, except in so far as the context otherwise requires, 'conciliation officer' means an officer designated by the Advisory, Conciliation and Arbitration Service (ACAS) under the Trade Union and Labour Relations (Consolidation) Act 1992 s 211 (see PARA 1214): see the Employment Rights Act 1996 s 235(1). 'Taking action' is not further defined, and so must be given its ordinary meaning, so as to cover any action taken by an ACAS officer in pursuance of his statutory duty (which goes no further than that he is to endeavour to promote a settlement of the proceedings in relation to the claim): *Allma Construction Ltd v Bonner* [2011] IRLR 204, EAT (jurisdiction of tribunal ousted as ACAS officer had taken action by communicating claimant's acceptance of offer); and see *Freeman v Sovereign Chicken Ltd* [1991] ICR 853, [1991] IRLR 408, EAT (cited in PARA 809 note 6). As to the constitution and powers of ACAS see PARA 1213 et seq.

17 Ie proceedings within the Employment Tribunals Act 1996 s 18(1)(b), (l), (m) (cases where conciliation available: see notes 18–20): see the Employment Rights Act 1996 s 203(2)(f) (amended by the Employment Rights (Dispute Resolution) Act 1998 s 15, Sch 2; the Enterprise and Regulatory Reform Act 2013 s 23(1)(b); and SI 2001/1107). See note 15. The word 'agreement' in the Employment Rights Act 1996 s 203(2) must mean a valid agreement and the employment tribunal has to ensure that any purported [settlement] agreement is valid: *Horizon Recruitment Ltd v Vincent* [2010] ICR 491, sub nom *Industrious Ltd v Horizon Recruitment Ltd (in liquidation) and Vincent* [2010] IRLR 204, EAT ([settlement] agreement in this case was voidable on ground of misrepresentation).

18 Ie proceedings within the Employment Tribunals Act 1996 s 18(1)(b) (see PARA 152 note 1), Employment Rights Act 1996: see s 203(2)(f)(i) (s 203(2)(f)(i), (ii) added by SI 2001/1107; and amended by SI 2014/431).

19 Ie proceedings within the Employment Tribunals Act 1996 s 18(1)(l) (see PARA 152 note 1), arising out of the Part-time Workers (Prevention of Less Favourable Treatment) Regulations 2000, SI 2000/1551 (see PARA 75 et seq): see the Employment Rights Act 1996 s 203(2)(f)(ii) (as added and amended: see note 18).

20 Ie proceedings within the Employment Tribunals Act 1996 s 18(1)(m) (see PARA 152 note 1), arising out of the Fixed-term Employees (Prevention of Less Favourable Treatment) Regulations 2002, SI 2002/2034 (see PARA 86 et seq): see the Employment Rights Act 1996 s 203(2)(f)(iii) (added by SI 2002/2034; and amended by SI 2014/431).

21 As to the conditions regulating the validity of settlement agreements under the Employment Rights Act 1996 see s 203(3), (3A), (3B), (4); and PARA 151.

22 Employment Rights Act 1996 s 203(2)(f) (as amended: see note 17).

23 As to the meaning of 'contract of employment' for these purposes see PARA 892.

24 See the Trade Union and Labour Relations (Consolidation) Act 1992 s 288(1). Sere also note 2.

25 Trade Union and Labour Relations (Consolidation) Act 1992 s 288(1)(a).

26 Trade Union and Labour Relations (Consolidation) Act 1992 s 288(1)(b) (amended by the Trade Union Reform and Employment Rights Act 1993 Sch 10; the Employment Rights (Dispute Resolution) Act 1998 s 1(2)(a); and the Employment Relations Act 2004 s 57, Sch 1 para 19, Sch 2). As to the Central Arbitration Committee see PARA 1226 et seq.

27 An agreement under which the parties agree to submit a dispute to arbitration:
  (1) is to be regarded for the purposes of the Trade Union and Labour Relations (Consolidation) Act 1992 s 288(2) and s 288(2A) (see head (B) in the text) as being an agreement to refrain from instituting or continuing proceedings, if: (a) the dispute is covered by a scheme having effect by virtue of an order under s 212A (see PARA 824) (s 288(6)(a)(i) (s 288(6) added by the Employment Rights (Dispute Resolution) Act 1998 s 8(3))); and (b) the agreement is to submit it to arbitration in accordance with the scheme (Trade Union and Labour Relations (Consolidation) Act 1992 s 288(6)(a)(ii) (as so added)); but
  (2) is to be regarded as neither being nor including such an agreement in any other case (s 288(6)(b) (as so added)).

28 Trade Union and Labour Relations (Consolidation) Act 1992 s 288(2) (amended by the Employment Tribunals Act 1996 Sch 1 para 8(a); the Employment Rights (Dispute Resolution) Act 1998 s 1(2)(c); and the Enterprise and Regulatory Reform Act 2013 Sch 1 para 1). The text refers to action taken by a conciliation officer under any of the Employment Tribunals Act 1996

ss 18A–18C (requirement to contact ACAS before instituting proceedings: see PARAS 152, 153): see the Trade Union and Labour Relations (Consolidation) Act 1992 s 288(2) (as so amended). See note 16.

29 Ie any proceedings, other than excepted proceedings, specified in the Employment Tribunals Act 1996 s 18(1)(a) (see PARA 152 note 1): see the Trade Union and Labour Relations (Consolidation) Act 1992 s 288(2A) (s 288(2A), (2C) added by the Trade Union Reform and Employment Rights Act 1993 s 39(2), Sch 6 para 4; the Trade Union and Labour Relations (Consolidation) Act 1992 s 288(2A) amended by the Employment Tribunals Act 1996 Sch 1 para 8(b); the Employment Rights (Dispute Resolution) Act 1998 s 1(2)(a); and the Enterprise and Regulatory Reform Act 2013 s 23(1)(a)); Interpretation Act 1978 s 17(2). The proceedings excepted from the Trade Union and Labour Relations (Consolidation) Act 1992 s 288(2A) are proceedings on a complaint of non-compliance with s 188 (see PARAS 1185–1188): s 288(2C) (as so added). See note 27.

30 As to the conditions regulating the validity of settlement agreements under the Trade Union and Labour Relations (Consolidation) Act 1992 see s 288(2B), (4), (4A)–(4C), (5); and PARA 151.

31 Trade Union and Labour Relations (Consolidation) Act 1992 s 288(2A) (as added and amended: see note 29).

32 Ie such an agreement as is referred to in the Trade Union and Labour Relations (Consolidation) Act 1992 s 185(5)(b) or s 185(5)(c) (see PARA 1182): see s 288(3)(a).

33 Trade Union and Labour Relations (Consolidation) Act 1992 s 288(3)(a). The text refers to an award that is varied or superseded under s 185 (see PARA 1182): see s 288(3)(a).

34 Ie rights under the Trade Union and Labour Relations (Consolidation) Act 1992 Pt IV Ch II (ss 188–198B) (see PARA 1185 et seq): see s 288(3)(b).

35 Ie an order under the Trade Union and Labour Relations (Consolidation) Act 1992 s 198 (see PARA 1195): see s 288(3)(b).

36 Trade Union and Labour Relations (Consolidation) Act 1992 s 288(3)(b).

151. Conditions that regulate settlement agreements under employment protection legislation. Given that, as a matter of policy, the Advisory, Conciliation and Arbitration Service (ACAS)[1] will indorse a settlement under the Employment Rights Act 1996 and the Employment Tribunals Act 1996[2] only if it has been involved in its negotiation and that any simple settlement between the parties is void[3], it was perceived that there was a need for a half-way house, allowing the parties to settle without ACAS conciliation, but ensuring that the employee (or ex-employee) had some statutory protection, at least to the extent of understanding his rights and what he was agreeing to forgo. To meet this need, the Trade Union Reform and Employment Rights Act 1993[4] introduced the compromise agreement (now known as a 'settlement agreement'[5]) which, like an ACAS-conciliated settlement, constitutes an exception to the statutory restrictions on contracting out[6], and so is binding[7]. The relevant provisions are now contained in the Employment Rights Act 1996[8] and, in identical form, in other relevant employment protection and related legislation[9].

The conditions regulating settlement agreements[10] under the Employment Rights Act 1996 are that[11]:

(1) the agreement must be in writing[12];

(2) the agreement must relate to the particular proceedings[13];

(3) the employee or worker[14] must have received advice from a relevant independent adviser[15] as to the terms and effect of the proposed agreement (and, in particular, its effect on his ability to pursue his rights before an employment tribunal)[16];

(4) there must be in force, when the adviser gives the advice, a contract of insurance, or an indemnity provided for members of a profession or professional body, covering the risk of a claim by the employee or worker in respect of loss arising in consequence of the advice[17];

(5) the agreement must identify the adviser[18]; and

(6)	the agreement must state that the conditions regulating settlement agreements under the Employment Rights Act 1996 are satisfied[19].

The conditions regulating settlement agreements[20] under the Trade Union and Labour Relations (Consolidation) Act 1992 are that[21]:

(a)	the agreement must be in writing[22];

(b)	the agreement must relate to the particular proceedings[23];

(c)	the complainant must have received advice from a relevant independent adviser[24] as to the terms and effect of the proposed agreement (and, in particular, its effect on his ability to pursue his rights before an employment tribunal)[25];

(d)	there must be in force, when the adviser gives the advice, a contract of insurance or an indemnity provided for members of a profession or professional body covering the risk of a claim by the complainant in respect of loss arising in consequence of the advice[26];

(e)	the agreement must identify the adviser[27]; and

(f)	the agreement must state that the conditions regulating settlement agreements under the Trade Union and Labour Relations (Consolidation) Act 1992 are satisfied[28].

The requirements that the agreement must relate to the particular proceedings (see heads (2), (b) above) and that the agreement must state that it satisfies the relevant statutory conditions (see heads (6), (f) above) mean that a settlement agreement cannot be used on a simple 'all claims' basis, and that, if it fails to mention a particular statutory provision under which a claim or possible claim is meant to be settled[29], it will be ineffective to that extent, and a claim under that statutory provision could still be brought[30].

1	As to the constitution and powers of ACAS see PARA 1213 et seq.
2	Ie under the Employment Rights Act 1996 s 203(2)(e) (see PARA 150) and the Employment Tribunals Act 1996 ss 18A–18C (requirement to contact ACAS before instituting proceedings: see PARAS 152, 153).
3	See the Employment Rights Act 1996 s 203(1); and PARA 150. As to the equivalent provisions in other relevant legislation see PARA 150 note 3.
4	Ie the Trade Union Reform and Employment Rights Act 1993 s 39(2), Sch 6 para 3 (repealed).
5	'Compromise agreements' were renamed 'settlement agreements' with effect from 29 July 2013: see the Enterprise and Regulatory Reform Act 2013 s 23 (renaming of 'compromise agreements', 'compromise contracts' and 'compromises'); and the Enterprise and Regulatory Reform Act 2013 (Commencement No 2) Order 2013, SI 2013/1648, art 2(c).
6	Ie in the Employment Rights Act 1996 s 203(1) and the equivalent provisions.
7	See the Employment Rights Act 1996 s 203(2)(e); and PARA 150.
8	Ie the Employment Rights Act 1996 s 203(3), (3A), (3B), (4) (see heads (1)–(6) in the text).
9	See eg the National Minimum Wage Act 1998 s 49(3)–(10) (see PARA 173); and the Working Time Regulations 1998, SI 1998/1833, reg 35(2)–(7) (see PARA 282). As to the Trade Union and Labour Relations (Consolidation) Act 1992 s 288(2B), (4), (4A)–(4C), (5) see PARA 150; and the text and notes 20–28.
10	Ie for the purposes of the Employment Rights Act 1996 s 203(2)(f) (see PARA 150): see s 203(3) (amended by Enterprise and Regulatory Reform Act 2013 s 23(1)(b)).
11	See the Employment Rights Act 1996 s 203(3) (as amended: see note 10).
12	Employment Rights Act 1996 s 203(3)(a). As to the meaning of 'writing' see PARA 2 note 8.
13	Employment Rights Act 1996 s 203(3)(b) (amended by the Employment Rights (Dispute Resolution) Act 1998 s 15, Sch 1 para 24(1), (2)). The wording of the condition set out in head (2) in the text must be construed as requiring the particular proceedings to which the agreement relates to be clearly identified, either by a generic description or by reference to the provision of the statute giving rise to the claim: *University of East London v Hinton* [2005] EWCA Civ 532, [2005] ICR 1260, [2005] IRLR 552. Good practice dictates that if actual proceedings are settled, the particulars of the proceedings and of the particular allegations made in them should be inserted in the [settlement] agreement in the form of a brief factual and legal description; and if the [settlement] is of a particular claim raised which is not yet the subject of proceedings, it is

good practice for the particulars of the nature of the allegations and of the statute under which they are made or the common law basis of the alleged claim to be inserted in the [settlement] agreement in the form of a brief factual and legal description: *University of East London v Hinton*.

14 As to the meaning of 'employee' see PARA 2; and as to the meaning of 'worker' see PARA 5.

15 For these purposes, a person is a relevant independent adviser (see the Employment Rights Act 1996 s 203(3A) (s 203(3A), (3B) added, s 203(4) substituted, by the Employment Rights (Dispute Resolution) Act 1998 Sch 1 para 24(1), (3))):

   (1)   if he is a qualified lawyer (Employment Rights Act 1996 s 203(3A)(a) (as so added));
   (2)   if he is an officer, official, employee or member of an independent trade union who has been certified in writing by the trade union as competent to give advice and as authorised to do so on behalf of the trade union (s 203(3A)(b) (as so added));
   (3)   if he works at an advice centre, whether as an employee or a volunteer, and has been certified in writing by the centre as competent to give advice and as authorised to do so on behalf of the centre (s 203(3A)(c) (as so added)); or
   (4)   if he is a person of a description specified in an order made by the Secretary of State (s 203(3A)(d) (as so added)).

For the purposes of head (1) above, 'qualified lawyer' means, as respects England and Wales, a person who, for the purposes of the Legal Services Act 2007, is an authorised person in relation to an activity which constitutes the exercise of a right of audience or the conduct of litigation (within the meaning of that Act: see LEGAL PROFESSIONS vol 65 (2008) PARAS 497–498): Employment Rights Act 1996 s 203(4)(a) (s 203(4) as so substituted; s 203(4)(a) amended by the Legal Services Act 2007 s 208(1), Sch 21 para 120). As to the meaning of 'independent trade union' see PARA 150 note 9. A person is not, however, a relevant independent adviser for the purposes of head (3) in the text, in relation to the employee or worker:

   (a)   if he is, is employed by or is acting in the matter for the employer or an associated employer (Employment Rights Act 1996 s 203(3B)(a) (as so added));
   (b)   in the case of a person within heads (2) or (3) above, if the trade union or advice centre is the employer or an associated employer (s 203(3B)(b) (as so added));
   (c)   in the case of a person within head (3) above, if the employee or worker makes a payment for the advice received from him (s 203(3B)(c) (as so added)); or
   (d)   in the case of a person of a description specified in an order under head (4) above, if any condition specified in the order in relation to the giving of advice by persons of that description is not satisfied (s 203(3B)(d) (as so added)).

As to the meaning of 'employer' see PARA 2; and as to the meaning of 'associated employer' see PARA 3. As to orders, rules and regulations made under the Employment Rights Act 1996 see PARA 162. As to the Secretary of State see PARA 5 note 21. As to the order that has been made under the powers conferred by head (4) above see the Settlement Agreements (Description of Person) Order 2004, SI 2004/754 (amended by SI 2004/2515; SI 2009/3348; SI 2013/1956).

16 Employment Rights Act 1996 s 203(3)(c) (amended by the Employment Rights (Dispute Resolution) Act 1998 ss 1(2)(a), 9(1), (2)(e)). As to employment tribunals see PARA 1399 et seq; and as to the procedure on a complaint made to an employment tribunal see PARA 1453 et seq.

17 Employment Rights Act 1996 s 203(3)(d) (amended by the Employment Rights (Dispute Resolution) Act 1998 s 10(1), (2)(e)).

18 Employment Rights Act 1996 s 203(3)(e).

19 Employment Rights Act 1996 s 203(3)(f) (amended by Enterprise and Regulatory Reform Act 2013 s 23(1)(b)).

20 Ie for the purposes of the Trade Union and Labour Relations (Consolidation) Act 1992 s 288(2A) (see PARA 150): see s 288(2B) (added by the Trade Union Reform and Employment Rights Act 1993 s 39(2), Sch 6 para 4; and amended by the Enterprise and Regulatory Reform Act 2013 s 23(1)(a)).

21 See the Trade Union and Labour Relations (Consolidation) Act 1992 s 288(2B) (as added and amended: see note 20).

22 Trade Union and Labour Relations (Consolidation) Act 1992 s 288(2B)(a) (as added: see note 20).

23 Trade Union and Labour Relations (Consolidation) Act 1992 s 288(2B)(b) (s 288(2B) as added (see note 20); s 288(2B)(b) amended by the Employment Rights (Dispute Resolution) Act 1998 Sch 1 para 9(1), (2)).

24 For these purposes, a person is a relevant independent adviser (see the Trade Union and Labour Relations (Consolidation) Act 1992 s 288(4) (s 288(4), (5) added by the Trade Union Reform and Employment Rights Act 1993 s 39(2), Sch 6 para 4(b); and substituted by the Employment Rights (Dispute Resolution) Act 1998 Sch 1 para 9(1), (3))):

(1) if he is a qualified lawyer (Trade Union and Labour Relations (Consolidation) Act 1992 s 288(4)(a) (as so added and substituted));

(2) if he is an officer, official, employee or member of an independent trade union who has been certified in writing by the trade union as competent to give advice and as authorised to do so on behalf of the trade union (s 288(4)(b) (as so added and substituted));

(3) if he works at an advice centre, whether as an employee or a volunteer, and has been certified in writing by the centre as competent to give advice and as authorised to do so on behalf of the centre (s 288(4)(c) (as so added and substituted)); or

(4) if he is a person of a description specified in an order made by the Secretary of State (s 288(4)(d) (as so added and substituted)).

For the purposes of head (1) above, 'qualified lawyer' means, as respects England and Wales, a person who, for the purposes of the Legal Services Act 2007, is an authorised person in relation to an activity which constitutes the exercise of a right of audience or the conduct of litigation (within the meaning of that Act: see LEGAL PROFESSIONS vol 65 (2008) PARAS 497–498): Trade Union and Labour Relations (Consolidation) Act 1992 s 288(4B)(a) (s 288(4A)–(4C) added by the Employment Rights (Dispute Resolution) Act 1998 Sch 1 para 9(1), (3); the Trade Union and Labour Relations (Consolidation) Act 1992 s 288(4B)(a) amended by the Legal Services Act 2007 Sch 21 paras 104, 107)). A person is not, however, a relevant independent adviser for the purposes of head (c) in the text in relation to the complainant:

(a) if he is, is employed by or is acting in the matter for the other party or a person who is connected with the other party (Trade Union and Labour Relations (Consolidation) Act 1992 s 288(4A)(a) (as so added));

(b) in the case of a person within heads (2) or (3) above, if the trade union or advice centre is the other party or a person who is connected with the other party (s 288(4A)(b) (as so added));

(c) in the case of a person within head (3) above, if the complainant makes a payment for the advice received from him (s 288(4A)(c) (as so added)); or

(d) in the case of a person of a description specified in an order under head (4) above, if any condition specified in the order in relation to the giving of advice by persons of that description is not satisfied (s 288(4A)(d) (as so added)).

Any two persons are to be treated as connected for the purposes of heads (a)–(d) above if one is a company of which the other, directly or indirectly, has control, or if both are companies of which a third person, directly or indirectly, has control: see s 288(5) (as so added and substituted). Any order under head (4) above must be made by statutory instrument, subject to annulment in pursuance of a resolution of either House of Parliament: s 288(4C) (as so added). As to the order that has been made under the powers conferred by head (4) above see the Settlement Agreements (Description of Person) Order 2004, SI 2004/754 (amended by SI 2004/2515; SI 2009/3348; SI 2013/1956).

25 Trade Union and Labour Relations (Consolidation) Act 1992 s 288(2B)(c) (s 288(2B) as added (see note 20); s 288(2B)(c) amended by the Employment Rights (Dispute Resolution) Act 1998 ss 1(2)(a), 9(1), (2)(c)).

26 Trade Union and Labour Relations (Consolidation) Act 1992 s 288(2B)(d) (s 288(2B) as added (see note 20); s 288(2B)(d) amended by the Employment Rights (Dispute Resolution) Act 1998 s 10(1), (2)(c)).

27 Trade Union and Labour Relations (Consolidation) Act 1992 s 288(2B)(e) (s 288(2B) as added: see note 20).

28 Trade Union and Labour Relations (Consolidation) Act 1992 s 288(2B)(f) (s 288(2B) as added (see note 20); s 288(2B)(f) amended by the Enterprise and Regulatory Reform Act 2013 s 23(1)(a)).

29 Although a party to a [settlement] agreement may intend a general release for good consideration of rights unknown to both parties, the court, in the absence of clear language, will be slow to infer that a party had agreed to such terms: *Bank of Credit and Commerce International SA (in liquidation) v Ali* [2001] UKHL 8, [2002] 1 AC 251, [2001] 1 All ER 961.

30 *Lunt v Merseyside TEC Ltd* [1999] ICR 17, [1999] IRLR 458, EAT. See also note 13.

B. EMPLOYMENT TRIBUNAL PROCEEDINGS

152. Requirement for early conciliation to promote a settlement before tribunal proceedings are instituted. Before a person ('the prospective claimant') presents an application to institute relevant proceedings[1] relating to any matter[2], the prospective claimant must provide to ACAS[3] prescribed information (in the prescribed manner)[4] about that matter[5] (although a person may institute relevant proceedings without complying with this requirement in prescribed cases)[6]. On receiving the prescribed information in the prescribed manner, ACAS must send a copy of it to a conciliation officer[7]; and the conciliation officer must, during the prescribed period, endeavour to promote a settlement[8] between the persons who would be parties to the proceedings[9]. If:

(1) during the prescribed period the conciliation officer concludes that a settlement is not possible[10]; or

(2) the prescribed period expires without a settlement having been reached[11],

the conciliation officer must issue a certificate to that effect, in the prescribed manner, to the prospective claimant[12]. A person who is subject to satisfy the requirement for early conciliation to promote a settlement before instituting tribunal proceedings[13] may not present an application to institute relevant proceedings without such a certificate[14].

The conciliation officer may continue to endeavour to promote a settlement after the expiry of the prescribed period[15].

A conciliation officer also must endeavour to promote a settlement[16] between the persons who would be parties to the proceedings, in circumstances where[17]:

(a) a person contacts ACAS requesting the services of a conciliation officer in relation to a matter that (if not settled) is likely to give rise to relevant proceedings against that person[18], and where ACAS has not received the prescribed information[19] from the prospective claimant[20]; or

(b) a person contacts ACAS requesting the services of a conciliation officer in relation to a matter that (if not settled) is likely to give rise to relevant proceedings by that person[21], and the requirement for early conciliation[22] would apply to that person but for an exemption[23].

If at any time: (i) the conciliation officer concludes that a settlement is not possible[24]; or (ii) a conciliation officer comes under the duty[25] to promote a settlement between the persons who would be parties to the proceedings[26], the duty mentioned in head (ii) above ceases to apply at that time[27].

Provision is made for the recovery of any sums that are payable under settlements reached in this way[28].

In proceeding to promote a settlement before tribunal proceedings are instituted[29], a conciliation officer must, where appropriate, have regard to the desirability of encouraging the use of other procedures available for the settlement of grievances[30].

The statutory restrictions on contracting out[31] of certain provisions of the employment protection legislation do not render void any agreement to refrain from instituting or continuing any proceedings before an employment tribunal where a conciliation officer has taken action in accordance with the provisions described above[32].

1   For the purposes of the Employment Tribunals Act 1996 ss 18, 18A–18C (see also PARA 153), 'relevant proceedings' means employment tribunal proceedings under the following provisions (see s 18(1) (amended by the Enterprise and Regulatory Reform Act 2013 s 7(2), Sch 1 paras 2, 5(1), (3)), ie under:

    (1)   the Trade Union and Labour Relations (Consolidation) Act 1992 s 66 (see PARA 1031), s 68A (see PARA 1035), s 70C (see PARA 1173), s 87 (see PARA 990), s 137 (see PARA 1042), s 138 (see PARA 1043), s 145A (see PARA 1051), s 145B (see PARA 1052), s 146 (see PARA 1048), ss 168, 168A, 169 (see PARA 1065), s 170 (see PARA 1066), s 174 (see PARA 1026), s 189 (see PARA 1189) and s 192 (see PARA 1190), or under Sch A1

para 156 (see PARA 1169) (Employment Tribunals Act 1996 s 18(1)(a) (s 18(1)(a)–(y) substituted, s 18(1)(z)–(z2) added, by SI 2014/431);

(2) the Employment Rights Act 1996 s 11 (see PARA 125), s 23 (see PARA 259), s 34 (see PARA 265), s 63I (see PARA 330), ss 70, 70A (see PARAS 606, 607), s 80(1) (see PARA 397), s 80H (see PARA 111), s 93 (see PARA 756), s 111 (see PARA 804), s 163 (see PARA 886), or s 177(see PARA 888), and Pt V (ss 43M–49A) (protection from suffering detriment in employment: see PARA 612 et seq), Pt VI (ss 50–63C) (time off work: see PARA 326 et seq) (Employment Tribunals Act 1996 s 18(1)(b) (as so substituted));

(3) the National Minimum Wage Act 1998 s 11 (see PARA 228), s 19D(1)(a) (see PARA 246) and s 24 (see PARA 249) (Employment Tribunals Act 1996 s 18(1)(c) (as so substituted));

(4) the Pensions Act 2008 s 56 (see PERSONAL AND OCCUPATIONAL PENSIONS vol 80 (2013) PARA 764) (Employment Tribunals Act 1996 s 18(1)(d) (as so substituted));

(5) the Equality Act 2010 s 120 (see DISCRIMINATION vol 33 (2013) PARA 344) or s 127 (see DISCRIMINATION vol 33 (2013) PARA 347) (Employment Tribunals Act 1996 s 18(1)(e) (as so substituted));

(6) the Safety Representatives and Safety Committees Regulations 1977, SI 1977/500, reg 11 (see PARA 1074) (Employment Tribunals Act 1996 s 18(1)(f) (as so substituted));

(7) the Employment Tribunals Extension of Jurisdiction (England and Wales) Order 1994, SI 1994/1623, art 6 (see PARA 1408) (Employment Tribunals Act 1996 s 18(1)(g) (as so substituted));

(8) the Health and Safety (Consultation with Employees) Regulations 1996, SI 1996/1513, Sch 2 para 2 (see PARA 1210) (Employment Tribunals Act 1996 s 18(1)(i) (as so substituted));

(9) the Working Time Regulations 1998, SI 1988/1833, reg 30 (see PARA 319) (Employment Tribunals Act 1996 s 18(1)(j) (as so substituted));

(10) the Transnational Information and Consultation of Employees Regulations 1999, SI 1999/3323, reg 27 (see PARA 1276) or reg 32 (see PARA 1278) (Employment Tribunals Act 1996 s 18(1)(k) (as so substituted));

(11) the Part-time Workers (Prevention of Less Favourable Treatment) Regulations 2000, SI 2000/1551, reg 8 (see PARA 80) (Employment Tribunals Act 1996 s 18(1)(l) (as so substituted));

(12) the Fixed-term Employees (Prevention of Less Favourable Treatment) Regulations 2002, SI 2002/2034, reg 7 (see PARA 91) or reg 9 (see PARA 88) (Employment Tribunals Act 1996 s 18(1)(m) (as so substituted));

(13) the Merchant Shipping (Hours of Work) Regulations 2002, SI 2002/2125, reg 22 (see SHIPPING AND MARITIME LAW vol 93 (2008) PARA 499) (Employment Tribunals Act 1996 s 18(1)(n) (as so substituted));

(14) the Flexible Working (Procedural Requirements) Regulations 2002, SI 2002/3207, reg 15 (see now the Employment Rights Act 1996 s 80H; and PARA 111) (Employment Tribunals Act 1996 s 18(1)(o) (as so substituted));

(15) the Merchant Shipping (Working Time: Inland Waterways) Regulations 2003, SI 2003/3049, reg 18 (see SHIPPING AND MARITIME LAW vol 94 (2008) PARA 625) (Employment Tribunals Act 1996 s 18(1)(p) (as so substituted));

(16) the Civil Aviation (Working Time) Regulations 2004, SI 2004/756, reg 18 (see AIR LAW vol 2 (2008) PARA 476) (Employment Tribunals Act 1996 s 18(1)(q) (as so substituted));

(17) the Fishing Vessels (Working Time: Sea-fishermen) Regulations 2004, SI 2004/1713, reg 19 (see SHIPPING AND MARITIME LAW vol 94 (2008) PARA 626) (Employment Tribunals Act 1996 s 18(1)(r) (as so substituted));

(18) the Information and Consultation of Employees Regulations 2004, SI 2004/3426, reg 29 (see PARA 1311) or reg 33 (see PARA 1313) (Employment Tribunals Act 1996 s 18(1)(s) (as so substituted));

(19) the Occupational and Personal Pension Schemes (Consultation by Employers and Miscellaneous Amendment) Regulations 2006, SI 2006/349, Schedule paras 4, 8 (see PERSONAL AND OCCUPATIONAL PENSIONS vol 80 (2013) PARA 486) (Employment Tribunals Act 1996 s 18(1)(t) (as so substituted));

(20) the European Cooperative Society (Involvement of Employees) Regulations 2006, SI 2006/2059, regs 30, 34 (see PARA 1338) (Employment Tribunals Act 1996 s 18(1)(u) (as so substituted));

(21) the Companies (Cross-Border Mergers) Regulations 2007, SI 2007/2974, regs 45, 51 (see COMPANIES vol 15 (2009) PARA 1451) (Employment Tribunals Act 1996 s 18(1)(v) (as so substituted)); or

(22) the Cross-border Railways Services (Working Time) Regulations 2008, SI 2008/1660,

reg 17 (see RAILWAYS AND TRAMWAYS vol 86 (2013) PARAS 33, 328) (Employment Tribunals Act 1996 s 18(1)(w) (as so substituted));

(23) the Ecclesiastical Offices (Terms of Service) Regulations 2009, SI 2009/2108, reg 9 (see ECCLESIASTICAL LAW vol 34 (2011) PARA 434) (Employment Tribunals Act 1996 s 18(1)(x) (as so substituted));

(24) the European Public Limited-Liability Company (Employee Involvement) (Great Britain) Regulations 2009, SI 2009/2401, reg 28 (see PARA 1332), reg 32 (see PARA 1334) (Employment Tribunals Act 1996 s 18(1)(y) (as so substituted));

(25) the Agency Workers Regulations 2010, SI 2010/93, reg 18 (see PARA 105) (Employment Tribunals Act 1996 s 18(1)(z) (as so added));

(26) the Employee Study and Training (Procedural Requirements) Regulations 2010, SI 2010/155, reg 17 (see PARA 330) (Employment Tribunals Act 1996 s 18(1)(z1) (as so added));

(27) the Employment Relations Act 1999 (Blacklists) Regulations 2010, SI 2010/493, regs 5, 6 or 9 (see PARAS 1038, 1040) (Employment Tribunals Act 1996 s 18(1)(z2) (as so added)).

The Secretary of State and the Lord Chancellor, acting jointly, may by order amend the definition of 'relevant proceedings' in s 18(1) by adding to or removing from the list particular types of employment tribunal proceedings: s 18(8) (amended by the Tribunals, Courts and Enforcement Act 2007 Sch 8 paras 35, 38; and the Enterprise and Regulatory Reform Act 2013 s 9(1), (2)). An order under the Employment Tribunals Act 1996 s 18(8) that:

(a) adds employment tribunal proceedings to the list in s 18(1) may amend an enactment so as to extend the time limit for instituting those proceedings in such a way as appears necessary or expedient in order to facilitate the conciliation process provided for by s 18A (see the text and notes 2–15) (s 18(9) (s 18(9), (10) added by the Enterprise and Regulatory Reform Act 2013 s 9(1), (3))); and

(b) removes employment tribunal proceedings from the list in the Employment Tribunals Act 1996 s 18(1) may repeal or revoke any provision of an enactment that, for the purpose mentioned in s 18(9), extends the time limit for instituting those proceedings, and may make further amendments which are consequential on that repeal or revocation (see s 18(10) (as so added)).

In exercise of the powers conferred by s 18(8), the Secretary of State has made the Employment Tribunals Act 1996 (Application of Conciliation Provisions) Order 2014, SI 2014/431 (cited at head (1) above). As to the making of orders under the Employment Tribunals Act 1996 generally see PARA 162. As to the Secretary of State see PARA 5 note 21. As to the Lord Chancellor see CONSTITUTIONAL AND ADMINISTRATIVE LAW vol 20 (2014) PARAS 255–261. As to employment tribunals see PARA 1399 et seq; and as to the procedure on a complaint made to an employment tribunal see PARA 1453 et seq.

2   The Employment Tribunals Act 1996 ss 18A, 18B apply in the case of matters which could be the subject of relevant proceedings: see s 18(1A) (added by the Enterprise and Regulatory Reform Act 2013 Sch 1 paras 2, 5(1), (7)). The Employment Tribunals Act 1996 s 18C applies in the case of relevant proceedings themselves: see s 18(1A) (as so added); and PARA 153.

3   Ie the Advisory, Conciliation and Arbitration Service (ACAS): see the Employment Tribunals Act 1996 s 42(1) (definition added by the Enterprise and Regulatory Reform Act 2013 Sch 1 paras 2, 9(a)). As to the constitution and powers of ACAS see PARA 1213 et seq.

4   For the purposes of the Employment Tribunals Act 1996 s 18A(1)–(7) (see also the text and notes 1–3, 5–12, 15), 'prescribed' means prescribed in employment tribunal procedure regulations: s 18A(10) (ss 18A, 18B added by the Enterprise and Regulatory Reform Act 2013 s 7(1)). 'Employment tribunal procedure regulations' is to be construed in accordance with the Employment Tribunals Act 1996 s 7 (see PARA 1410): see s 42(1) (definition amended by the Employment Rights (Dispute Resolution) Act 1998 s 1(2)(a)). The Secretary of State may by employment tribunal procedure regulations make such further provision as appears to the Secretary of State to be necessary or expedient with respect to the conciliation process provided for by the Employment Tribunals Act 1996 s 18A(1)–(8) (see also the text and notes 1–3, 5–15): see s 18A(11) (as so added). Employment tribunal procedure regulations may (in particular) make provision:

(1) authorising the Secretary of State to prescribe, or prescribe requirements in relation to, any form which is required by such regulations to be used for the purpose of providing information to ACAS under s 18A(1) (see also the text and notes 1–3, 5) or issuing a certificate under s 18(4) (see the text and notes 10–12) (see s 18A(12)(a) (as so added));

(2) requiring ACAS to give a person any necessary assistance to comply with the requirement in s 18A(1) (see s 18A(12)(b) (as so added));

(3)   for the extension of the period prescribed for the purposes of s 18A(3) (see the text and notes 8–9) (see s 18A(12)(c) (as so added));

(4)   treating the requirement in s 18A(1) as complied with, for the purposes of any provision extending the time limit for instituting relevant proceedings, by a person who is relieved of that requirement by virtue of s 18A(7)(a) (see s 18A(12)(d) (as so added)).

It is submitted that the reference in head (4) above refers to cases where the requirement is complied with by another person instituting relevant proceedings relating to the same matter (see note 6), although doubt arises because s 18A(7) is not further sub-divided. In exercise of the powers conferred by s 18A(7), (11), (12) and s 41(4), the Secretary of State has made the Employment Tribunals (Early Conciliation: Exemptions and Rules of Procedure) Regulations 2014, SI 2014/254. Accordingly, to satisfy the requirement for early conciliation, a prospective claimant must either:

(a)   present a completed early conciliation form to ACAS in accordance with reg 5, Schedule r 2 (Schedule r 1(a)); or

(b)   telephone ACAS in accordance with Schedule r 3 (Schedule r 1(b)).

For these purposes, 'requirement for early conciliation' means the requirement set out in the Employment Tribunals Act 1996 s 18A(1) (see also the text and notes 1–3, 5); and 'early conciliation form' means a form prescribed by the Secretary of State in accordance with the Employment Tribunals (Constitution and Rules of Procedure) Regulations 2013, SI 2013/1237, reg 4(1)(a): see the Employment Tribunals (Early Conciliation: Exemptions and Rules of Procedure) Regulations 2014, SI 2014/254, reg 2. The Secretary of State may prescribe one or more forms to be used by all prospective claimants for the purpose of complying with the early conciliation requirement (reg 4(1)(a)); and he must publish any forms so prescribed under reg 4(1)(a) in a manner which the Secretary of State considers appropriate to bring them to the attention of prospective claimants and their advisers (reg 4(2)). 'ACAS' means the Advisory, Conciliation and Arbitration Service referred to in the Trade Union and Labour Relations (Consolidation) Act 1992 s 247 (see PARA 1213); 'prospective claimant' means a person who is considering presenting a claim form to an employment tribunal in relation to relevant proceedings; 'claim form' means the form prescribed by the Secretary of State in accordance with the Employment Tribunals (Constitution and Rules of Procedure) Regulations 2013, SI 2013/1237, reg 12(1)(a) (see PARA 1461); 'employment tribunal' means an employment tribunal established in accordance with reg 4 (see PARA 1399); and 'relevant proceedings' are those proceedings listed in the Employment Tribunals Act 1996 s 18(1) (see note 1): see the Employment Tribunals (Early Conciliation: Exemptions and Rules of Procedure) Regulations 2014, SI 2014/254, reg 2.

An early conciliation form which is presented to ACAS must be either submitted using the online form on the ACAS website (Schedule r 2(1)(a)), or sent by post to the ACAS address set out on the early conciliation form (Schedule r 2(1)(b)). An early conciliation form must contain the prospective claimant's name and address, and the prospective respondent's name and address: see Schedule r 2(2). ACAS may reject a form that does not contain the information specified in Schedule r 2(2) or may contact the prospective claimant to obtain any missing information: Schedule r 2(3). If ACAS rejects a form under Schedule r 2(3), it must return the form to the prospective claimant: Schedule r 2(4). 'Respondent' means the person against whom proceedings are brought in the employment tribunal; and 'prospective respondent' means the person who would be the respondent on the claim form which the prospective claimant is considering presenting to an employment tribunal: see reg 2. The address of the ACAS website, at the date at which this volume states the law, is to be found at: *http://www.acas.org.uk*.

A prospective claimant telephoning ACAS for early conciliation must call the telephone number set out on the early conciliation form and tell ACAS the prospective claimant's name and address, and the prospective respondent's name and address: Schedule r 3(1). ACAS must insert the information so provided on to an early conciliation form: Schedule r 3(2).

If there is more than one prospective respondent, the prospective claimant must present a separate early conciliation form under Schedule r 2 in respect of each respondent or, in the case of a telephone call made under Schedule r 3, must name each prospective respondent: Schedule r 4 (substituted by SI 2014/847). The amendment made by SI 2014/847 was needed to make it clear that the restriction allowing the details of only one prospective respondent to appear on an early conciliation form does not alter the scope of the early conciliation requirement in the Employment Tribunals Act 1996 s 18A(1).

5   Employment Tribunals Act 1996 s 18A(1) (as added: see note 4). This provision is subject to s 18A(7) (see the text and note 6): see s 18A(1) (as so added).

6   See the Employment Tribunals Act 1996 s 18A(7) (as added: see note 4). The prescribed cases referred to in the text may include (in particular) cases where the requirement is complied with by another person instituting relevant proceedings relating to the same matter, cases where

proceedings that are not relevant proceedings are instituted by means of the same form as proceedings that are, or cases where the Employment Tribunals Act 1996 s 18B applies (see the text and notes 16–27) because ACAS has been contacted by a person against whom relevant proceedings are being instituted: see s 18A(7) (as so added). Accordingly, a person ('A') may institute relevant proceedings without complying with the requirement for early conciliation (see the Employment Tribunals (Early Conciliation: Exemptions and Rules of Procedure) Regulations 2014, SI 2014/254, reg 3(1)), where:

(1) another person ('B') has complied with that requirement in relation to the same dispute and A wishes to institute proceedings on the same claim form as B (reg 3(1)(a));

(2) A institutes those relevant proceedings on the same claim form as proceedings which are not relevant proceedings (reg 3(1)(b));

(3) A is able to show that the respondent has contacted ACAS in relation to a dispute, ACAS has not received information from A under the Employment Tribunals Act 1996 s 18A(1) (see the text and notes 1–5) in relation to that dispute, and the proceedings on the claim form relate to that dispute (Employment Tribunals (Early Conciliation: Exemptions and Rules of Procedure) Regulations 2014, SI 2014/254, reg 3(1)(c));

(4) the proceedings are proceedings under the Employment Rights Act 1996 Pt X (ss 94–134A) (unfair dismissal: see PARA 757 et seq) and the application to institute those proceedings is accompanied by an application under s 128 (interim relief pending determination of claim: see PARA 805) or the Trade Union and Labour Relations (Consolidation) Act 1992 s 161 (application for interim relief where dismissal is by reason of trade union membership etc: see PARA 1058) (Employment Tribunals (Early Conciliation: Exemptions and Rules of Procedure) Regulations 2014, SI 2014/254, reg 3(1)(d)); or

(5) A is instituting proceedings against the Security Service, the Secret Intelligence Service or the Government Communications Headquarters (reg 3(1)(e)).

Where A benefits from the exemption in head (1) above, the requirement for early conciliation must be treated as complied with for the purposes of any provision extending the time limit for instituting relevant proceedings in relation to that matter: reg 3(2). As to the Security Service, the Secret Intelligence Service, and the Government Communications Headquarters, see CONSTITUTIONAL AND ADMINISTRATIVE LAW vol 20 (2014) PARAS 243–245.

7 Employment Tribunals Act 1996 s 18A(2) (as added: see note 4). Anything communicated to a conciliation officer in connection with the performance of his functions under any of ss 18, 18A–18C (see also PARA 153) is not admissible in evidence in any proceedings before an employment tribunal, except with the consent of the person who communicated it to that officer: s 18(7) (amended by the Employment Rights (Dispute Resolution) Act 1998 s 1(2)(a); and the Enterprise and Regulatory Reform Act 2013 Sch 1 paras 2, 5(1), (9)). The Employment Tribunals Act 1996 s 18(7) does not, however, render inadmissible evidence which exists in an admissible form apart from evidence based on communication to the conciliation officer: *M & W Grazebrook Ltd v Wallens* [1973] 2 All ER 868, [1973] ICR 256, NIRC. As to the meaning of 'conciliation officer' see PARA 150 note 16.

Employment tribunal procedure regulations must include, in relation to employment tribunal proceedings, in the case of which any enactment makes provision for conciliation, provisions requiring a copy of the application by which the proceedings are instituted, and a copy of any notice relating to it which is lodged by or on behalf of the person against whom the proceedings are brought, to be sent to a conciliation officer, and provisions securing that the applicant and the person against whom the proceedings are brought are notified that the services of a conciliation officer are available to them: see the Employment Tribunals Act 1996 s 19(1); and PARA 1420. Accordingly, where employment tribunal proceedings concern an enactment which provides for conciliation, the Employment Tribunal must send a copy of the claim form and the response to an ACAS conciliation officer; and inform the parties that the services of an ACAS conciliation officer are available to them: see the Employment Tribunals (Constitution and Rules of Procedure) Regulations 2013, SI 2013/1237, Sch 1 r 93; and PARA 1468. Where an application instituting relevant proceedings has been presented to an employment tribunal, and a copy of it has been sent to a conciliation officer, the conciliation officer must endeavour to promote a settlement: see the Employment Tribunals Act 1996 s 18C; and PARA 153. A Tribunal must in any case wherever practicable and appropriate encourage the use by the parties of the services of ACAS, judicial or other mediation, or other means of resolving their disputes by agreement: see the Employment Tribunals (Constitution and Rules of Procedure) Regulations 2013, SI 2013/1237, Sch 1 r 3; and PARA 1466.

8 For the purposes of the Employment Tribunals Act 1996 s 18A(3)–(5) (see also the text and notes 9–12, 15), 'settlement' means a settlement that avoids proceedings being instituted: see s 18A(6) (as added: see note 4). Where a conciliation officer acts under s 18A in a case where the

prospective claimant has ceased to be employed by the employer, and the proposed proceedings are proceedings under the Employment Rights Act 1996 s 111 (remedy for unfair dismissal: see PARA 804), the conciliation officer may in particular:

    (1)   seek to promote the reinstatement or re-engagement of the prospective claimant by the employer, or by a successor of the employer or by an associated employer, on terms appearing to the conciliation officer to be equitable (Employment Tribunals Act 1996 s 18A(9)(a) (as so added)); or

    (2)   where the prospective claimant does not wish to be reinstated or re-engaged, or where reinstatement or re-engagement is not practicable, seek to promote agreement between them as to a sum by way of compensation to be paid by the employer to the prospective claimant (Employment Tribunals Act 1996 s 18A(9)(b) (as so added)).

As to the meaning of 'employer' see PARA 2; and as to the meaning of 'associated employer' see PARA 3.

9   Employment Tribunals Act 1996 s 18A(3) (as added: see note 4). For up to one calendar month starting on the date:

    (1)   of receipt by ACAS of the early conciliation form presented in accordance with the Employment Tribunals (Early Conciliation: Exemptions and Rules of Procedure) Regulations 2014, SI 2014/254, Schedule r 2 (see note 4) (Schedule r 6(1)(a)); or

    (2)   the prospective claimant telephoned ACAS in accordance with Schedule r 3 (see note 4) (Schedule r 6(1)(b)),

the conciliation officer must endeavour to promote a settlement between the prospective claimant and the prospective respondent (see Schedule r 6(1)). The period for early conciliation may be extended by a conciliation officer, provided that the prospective claimant and prospective respondent consent to the extension and the conciliation officer considers that there is a reasonable prospect of achieving a settlement before the expiry of the extended period: Schedule r 6(2). Such an extension of the period for early conciliation may only occur once, however, and may be for up to a maximum of 14 days: Schedule r 6(3). For these purposes, 'conciliation officer' means an officer designated by the Advisory, Conciliation and Arbitration Service (ACAS) under the Trade Union and Labour Relations (Consolidation) Act 1992 s 211 (see PARA 1214): see the Employment Tribunals (Early Conciliation: Exemptions and Rules of Procedure) Regulations 2014, SI 2014/254, reg 2.

ACAS must make reasonable attempts to contact the prospective claimant: Schedule r 5(1). If the prospective claimant consents to ACAS contacting the prospective respondent, ACAS must make reasonable attempts to contact the prospective respondent: Schedule r 5(2). If ACAS is unable to make contact with the prospective claimant or prospective respondent it must conclude that settlement is not possible: Schedule r 5(3).

10   Employment Tribunals Act 1996 s 18A(4)(a) (as added: see note 4). See note 8.

11   Employment Tribunals Act 1996 s 18A(4)(b) (as added: see note 4). See note 8.

12   Employment Tribunals Act 1996 s 18A(4) (as added: see note 4). Accordingly, if:

    (1)   at any point during the period for early conciliation (or during any extension of that period) the conciliation officer concludes that a settlement of a dispute (or part of it) is not possible (Employment Tribunals (Early Conciliation: Exemptions and Rules of Procedure) Regulations 2014, SI 2014/254, Schedule r 7(1)); or

    (2)   the period for early conciliation (including any extension of that period) expires without a settlement having been reached (Schedule r 7(2)),

ACAS must issue an early conciliation certificate (see Schedule r 7(1), (2)). 'Early conciliation certificate' means a form prescribed by the Secretary of State in accordance with reg 4(1)(b): see reg 2. The Secretary of State may prescribe a certificate to be issued by ACAS if Schedule r 6 applies: reg 4(1)(b). An early conciliation certificate must contain:

    (a)   the name and address of the prospective claimant (Schedule r 8(a));

    (b)   the name and address of the prospective respondent (Schedule r 8(b));

    (c)   the date of receipt by ACAS of the early conciliation form presented in accordance with Schedule r 2 (see note 4), or the date that the prospective claimant telephoned ACAS in accordance with Schedule r 3 (see note 4) (Schedule r 8(c));

    (d)   the unique reference number given by ACAS to the early conciliation certificate (Schedule r 8(d)); and

    (e)   the date of issue of the certificate (which will be the date that the certificate is sent by ACAS) and a statement indicating the method by which the certificate is to be sent (Schedule r 8(e)).

Where ACAS issues an early conciliation certificate, it must send a copy to the prospective claimant and, if ACAS has had contact with the prospective respondent during the period for early conciliation, to the prospective respondent: Schedule r 9(1). If the prospective claimant or prospective respondent has provided an email address to ACAS, ACAS must send the early conciliation certificate by email and in any other case must send the early conciliation certificate by post: Schedule r 9(2). An early conciliation certificate will be deemed received (if sent by email) on the day it is sent, or (if sent by post) on the day on which it would be delivered in the ordinary course of the post: see Schedule r 9(3).

13 Ie a person who is subject to the requirement in the Employment Tribunals Act 1996 s 18A(1) (see the text and notes 1–5): see s 18A(8) (as added: see note 4).

14 Employment Tribunals Act 1996 s 18A(8) (as added: see note 4).

15 Employment Tribunals Act 1996 s 18A(5) (as added: see note 4). See note 8.

16 For the purposes of the Employment Tribunals Act 1996 s 18B(3), (4) (see the text and notes 17, 24–27), 'settlement' means a settlement that avoids proceedings being instituted: see s 18B(5) (as added: see note 4). Where a conciliation officer acts under s 18B in a case where the prospective claimant has ceased to be employed by the employer and the proposed proceedings are proceedings under the Employment Rights Act 1996 s 111 (remedy for unfair dismissal: see PARA 804), the conciliation officer may in particular:

    (1)   seek to promote the reinstatement or re-engagement of the prospective claimant by the employer, or by a successor of the employer or by an associated employer, on terms appearing to the conciliation officer to be equitable (Employment Tribunals Act 1996 s 18A(9)(a) (as so added) (s 18A(9) applied by s 18B(6) (as so added))); or

    (2)   where the prospective claimant does not wish to be reinstated or re-engaged, or where reinstatement or re-engagement is not practicable, seek to promote agreement between them as to a sum by way of compensation to be paid by the employer to the prospective claimant (Employment Tribunals Act 1996 s 18A(9)(b) (as so added and applied)).

17 See the Employment Tribunals Act 1996 s 18B(3) (as added: see note 4).

18 Employment Tribunals Act 1996 s 18B(1)(a) (as added: see note 4).

19 Ie under the Employment Tribunals Act 1996 s 18A(1) (see the text and notes 1–5): see s 18B(1)(b) (as added: see note 4).

20 Employment Tribunals Act 1996 s 18B(1)(b) (as added: see note 4).

21 Employment Tribunals Act 1996 s 18B(2)(a) (as added: see note 4).

22 Ie the requirement in the Employment Tribunals Act 1996 s 18A(1) (see the text and notes 1–5): see s 18B(2)(b) (as added: see note 4).

23 Employment Tribunals Act 1996 s 18B(2)(b) (as added: see note 4). Head (b) in the text refers to a situation where the requirement in s 18A(1) (see the text and notes 1–5) would apply but for s 18A(7) (see the text and note 6): see s 18B(2)(b) (as so added).

24 Employment Tribunals Act 1996 s 18B(4)(a) (as added: see note 4). See note 16.

25 Ie the duty in the Employment Tribunals Act 1996 s 18A(3) (see the text and note 17): see s 18B(4)(b) (as added: see note 4).

26 Employment Tribunals Act 1996 s 18B(4)(b) (as added: see note 4). See note 16.

27 See the Employment Tribunals Act 1996 s 18B(4) (as added: see note 4).

28 See the Employment Tribunals Act 1996 s 19A; and PARA 1420.

29 Ie in proceeding under any of the Employment Tribunals Act 1996 ss 18, 18A–18C (see also PARA 153): see s 18(6) (amended by the Enterprise and Regulatory Reform Act 2013 Sch 1 paras 2, 5(1), (9)).

30 Employment Tribunals Act 1996 s 18(6) (as amended: see note 29).

31 Ie the Employment Rights Act 1996 s 203 and equivalent provisions: see PARA 150.

32 See the Employment Rights Act 1996 s 203(2)(e); and PARA 150. As to the meaning of 'taking action' for these purposes see *Allma Construction Ltd v Bonner* [2011] IRLR 204, EAT (cited in PARA 150 note 16).

153. Conciliation to promote a settlement after institution of proceedings.
Where an application instituting relevant proceedings[1] has been presented to an employment tribunal[2], and a copy of it has been sent to a conciliation officer[3], the conciliation officer must endeavour to promote a settlement[4]:

    (1)   if requested to do so by the person by whom and the person against whom the proceedings are brought[5]; or

    (2)   if, in the absence of any such request, the conciliation officer considers that the officer could act accordingly[6] with a reasonable prospect of success[7].

Provision is made for the recovery of any sums that are payable under settlements reached in this way[8].

In proceeding to promote a settlement after tribunal proceedings are instituted[9], a conciliation officer must, where appropriate, have regard to the desirability of encouraging the use of other procedures available for the settlement of grievances[10].

The statutory restrictions on contracting out[11] of certain provisions of the employment protection legislation do not render void any agreement to refrain from instituting or continuing any proceedings before an employment tribunal where a conciliation officer has taken action in accordance with the provisions described above[12].

1   As to the meaning of 'relevant proceedings' for the purposes of the Employment Tribunals Act 1996 ss 18, 18A–18C (see also PARA 152) see PARA 152 note 1.

2   As to employment tribunals see PARA 1399 et seq; and as to the procedure on a complaint made to an employment tribunal see PARA 1453 et seq.

3   Anything communicated to a conciliation officer in connection with the performance of his functions under any of the Employment Tribunals Act 1996 ss 18, 18A–18C (see also PARA 152) is not admissible in evidence in any proceedings before an employment tribunal, except with the consent of the person who communicated it to that officer: s 18(7) (amended by the Employment Rights (Dispute Resolution) Act 1998 s 1(2)(a); and the Enterprise and Regulatory Reform Act 2013 s 7(2), Sch 1 paras 2, 5(1), (9)). The Employment Tribunals Act 1996 s 18(7) does not, however, render inadmissible evidence which exists in an admissible form apart from evidence based on communication to the conciliation officer: *M & W Grazebrook Ltd v Wallens* [1973] 2 All ER 868, [1973] ICR 256, NIRC. As to the meaning of 'conciliation officer' see PARA 150 note 16.

4   See the Employment Tribunals Act 1996 s 18C(1) (s 18C added by the Enterprise and Regulatory Reform Act 2013 s 7(2), Sch 1 paras 2, 6). The Employment Tribunals Act 1996 s 18C applies in the case of relevant proceedings (whereas ss 18A, 18B (see PARA 152) apply in the case of matters which could be the subject of relevant proceedings): see s 18(1A) (added by the Enterprise and Regulatory Reform Act 2013 Sch 1 paras 2, 5(1), (7)). The resulting settlement is usually recorded on a form COT 3, such settlements often being referred to as 'COT 3 settlements' rather than settlement agreements (see PARA 151). Although a 'COT3 settlement' will be binding pursuant to the Employment Rights Act 1996 s 203(2)(e) (see PARA 150), there is a general equitable power for a court or tribunal to allow a claim to proceed in spite of such a settlement where it would be unconscionable not to do so: *Bank of Credit and Commerce International SA (in liquidation) v Ali* [2000] 3 All ER 51, [2000] IRLR 398, CA; affd [2001] UKHL 8, [2002] 1 AC 251, [2001] 1 All ER 961. An oral agreement is also enforceable: *Gilbert v Kembridge Fibres Ltd* [1984] ICR 188, [1984] IRLR 52, EAT.

For these purposes, 'settlement' means a settlement that brings proceedings to an end without their being determined by an employment tribunal: see the Employment Tribunals Act 1996 s 18C(3) (as so added). Where a person who has presented a complaint to an employment tribunal under the Employment Rights Act 1996 s 111 (remedy for unfair dismissal: see PARA 804) has ceased to be employed by the employer against whom the complaint was made, the conciliation officer may in particular:

(1)   seek to promote the reinstatement or re-engagement of the complainant by the employer, or by a successor of the employer or by an associated employer, on terms appearing to the conciliation officer to be equitable (Employment Tribunals Act 1996 s 18C(2)(a) (as so added)); or

(2)   where the prospective claimant does not wish to be reinstated or re-engaged, or where reinstatement or re-engagement is not practicable, and the parties desire the conciliation officer to act, seek to promote agreement between them as to a sum by way of compensation to be paid by the employer to the claimant (Employment Tribunals Act 1996 s 18C(2)(b) (as so added)).

As to the meaning of 'employer' see PARA 2; and as to the meaning of 'associated employer' see PARA 3.

5   Employment Tribunals Act 1996 s 18C(1)(a) (as added: see note 4).

6   Ie act under the Employment Tribunals Act 1996 s 18C: see s 18C(1)(b) (as added: see note 4).

7   Employment Tribunals Act 1996 s 18C(1)(b) (as added: see note 4).

8   See the Employment Tribunals Act 1996 s 19A; and PARA 1420.

9   Ie in proceeding under any of the Employment Tribunals Act 1996 ss 18, 18A–18C (see also PARA 152): see s 18(6) (amended by the Enterprise and Regulatory Reform Act 2013 Sch 1 paras 2, 5(1), (9)).

10 Employment Tribunals Act 1996 s 18(6) (as amended: see note 9).
11 Ie the Employment Rights Act 1996 s 203 and equivalent provisions: see PARA 150.
12 See the Employment Rights Act 1996 s 203(2)(e); and PARA 150. As to the meaning of 'taking action' for these purposes see *Allma Construction Ltd v Bonner* [2011] IRLR 204, EAT (cited in PARA 150 note 16).

(iii) Status of Employee Shareholder

154. Employment status of employee shareholder. An individual who is or becomes an employee of a company[1] is an 'employee shareholder' if[2]:

(1) the company and the individual agree that the individual is to be an employee shareholder[3];

(2) in consideration of that agreement, the company issues or allots to the individual fully paid up shares in the company[4], or procures the issue or allotment to the individual of fully paid up shares in its parent undertaking[5], which have a value, on the day of issue or allotment, of no less than £2,000[6];

(3) the company gives the individual a written statement of the particulars of the status of employee shareholder and of the rights which attach to the shares referred to in head (2) above ('the employee shares')[7]; and

(4) the individual gives no consideration other than by entering into the agreement[8].

An employee who is an employee shareholder does not have the following rights under the Employment Rights Act 1996[9]:

(a) the right to make an application to undertake study or training[10];

(b) the right to make an application for flexible working[11];

(c) the right not to be unfairly dismissed[12]; or

(d) the right to a redundancy payment[13].

Certain other statutory rights, pertaining to maternity, additional paternity or adoption leave, are modified, in the case of an employee who is an employee shareholder, to require extended periods of notice to an employer if such an employee intends to return early from such leave[14].

Agreement between a company and an individual that the individual is to become an employee shareholder is of no effect unless, before the agreement is made[15]:

(i) the individual, having been given the statement referred to in head (3) above, receives advice from a relevant independent adviser[16] as to the terms and effect of the proposed agreement[17]; and

(ii) seven days have passed since the day on which the individual receives the advice[18].

Any reasonable costs incurred by the individual in obtaining the advice (whether or not the individual becomes an employee shareholder) which would otherwise[19] have to be met by the individual are instead to be met by the company[20].

An employee has a right not to suffer a detriment or dismissal as a result of refusing to accept an offer by his employer to become an employee shareholder[21].

1 For these purposes, 'company' means: (1) either a company within the meaning of the Companies Act 2006 (see COMPANIES vol 14 (2009) PARA 24), or an overseas company within the meaning of that Act (see COMPANIES vol 15 (2009) PARA 1824), which has a share capital; or (2) a European Public Limited-Liability Company (or Societas Europaea) within the meaning of Council Regulation (EC) 2157/2001 of 8 October 2001 (OJ L294, 10.11.2001, p 1) on the Statute for a European Company (see COMPANIES vol 15 (2009) PARA 1633 et seq): see the

Employment Rights Act 1996 s 205A(13) (s 205A added by the Growth and Infrastructure Act 2013 s 31(1)). As to the meaning of references in the Companies Acts to a 'company having a share capital' see COMPANIES vol 15 (2009) PARA 1042. As to the meaning of 'employee' generally see PARA 2.

2	See the Employment Rights Act 1996 s 205A(1) (as added: see note 1).

Employee shareholder status is a creature of statute and the Department for Business, Innovation and Skills has published guidance in recognition of the fact that the process for offering or accepting a job on an employee shareholder basis is different to jobs offered on other employment contracts: see *Guidance: Employee shareholders* (February 2014) ('BIS guidance on Employee shareholders'), which is available via the website of the Department for Business, Innovation and Skills, whose address, at the date at which this volume states the law, is to be found at: *http://www.bis.gov.uk.*

3	Employment Rights Act 1996 s 205A(1)(a) (as added: see note 1).

4	As to the meaning of references to 'issued' and 'allotted' shares see COMPANIES vol 15 (2009) PARA 1045; and as to the meaning of 'fully paid up shares' in a company see COMPANIES vol 15 (2009) PARA 1048. The requirement that any such shares be fully paid up means that in the majority of cases the shares will have to be paid out of distributable reserves: see *BIS guidance on Employee shareholders (Action for companies if considering offering an employee shareholder job).* As to distributions of profits and assets to company members generally see COMPANIES vol 15 (2009) PARA 1389 et seq.

5	For these purposes, 'parent undertaking' has the same meaning as in the Companies Act 2006 (see COMPANIES vol 14 (2009) PARA 26): see the Employment Rights Act 1996 s 205A(13) (as added: see note 1).

6	Employment Rights Act 1996 s 205A(1)(b) (as added: see note 1). References to the value of shares in a company are references to their market value within the meaning of the Taxation of Chargeable Gains Act 1992 (see ss 272, 273; and CAPITAL GAINS TAXATION vol 6 (2011) PARA 647): see the Employment Rights Act 1996 s 205A(14) (as so added). An employee who is not satisfied with the value of the shares may request his own valuation (although this option will incur a cost) or refuse to become an employee shareholder at any time prior to signing the contract: see *BIS guidance on Employee shareholders.* If an employee shareholder sells his shares, his employment status does not change (because a change of employment status would require a change of employment contract to alter the employment status): see *BIS guidance on Employee shareholders.* As to the treatment for tax purposes of shares acquired by employee shareholders see the Income Tax (Earnings and Pensions) Act 2003 ss 226A–226D; and INCOME TAXATION vol 58 (2014) PARA 791.

The Secretary of State may by order amend the Employment Rights Act 1996 s 205A(1) so as to increase the sum for the time being specified there (s 205A(11) (as so added)); and by regulations he may provide that any agreement for a company to buy back from an individual the shares referred to in head (2) in the text in the event that the individual ceases to be an employee shareholder or ceases to be an employee must be on terms which meet the specified requirements (s 205A(12) (as so added)). As to the making of orders and regulations under the Employment Rights Act 1996 generally see PARA 162. As to the Secretary of State see PARA 5 note 21. At the date at which this volume states the law, no such order or regulation had been made.

7	Employment Rights Act 1996 s 205A(1)(c) (as added: see note 1). The statement referred to in s 205A(1)(c) must:
   (1)	state that, as an employee shareholder, the individual would not have the rights specified in s 205A(2) (see heads (a) to (d) in the text) (s 205A(5)(a) (as so added));
   (2)	specify the notice periods that would apply in the individual's case as a result of s 205A(3), (4) (see the text and note 14) (s 205A(5)(b) (as so added));
   (3)	state whether any voting rights attach to the employee shares (s 205A(5)(c) (as so added));
   (4)	state whether the employee shares carry any rights to dividends (s 205A(5)(d) (as so added));
   (5)	state whether the employee shares would, if the company were wound up, confer any rights to participate in the distribution of any surplus assets (s 205A(5)(e) (as so added));
   (6)	if the company has more than one class of shares and any of the rights referred to in heads (3) to (5) above attach to the employee shares, explain how those rights differ from the equivalent rights that attach to the shares in the largest class (or next largest class if the class which includes the employee shares is the largest) (s 205A(5)(f) (as so added));

(7)   state whether the employee shares are redeemable and, if they are, at whose option (s 205A(5)(g) (as so added));
(8)   state whether there are any restrictions on the transferability of the employee shares and, if there are, what those restrictions are (s 205A(5)(h) (as so added));
(9)   state whether any of the requirements of the Companies Act 2006 s 561 (existing shareholders' right of pre-emption: see COMPANIES vol 15 (2009) PARA 1098) and s 562 (communication of pre-emption offers to shareholders: see COMPANIES vol 15 (2009) PARA 1104) are excluded in the case of the employee shares (Employment Rights Act 1996 s 205A(5)(i) (as so added)); and
(10)   state whether the employee shares are subject to drag-along rights or tag-along rights and, if they are, explain the effect of the shares being so subject (s 205A(5)(j) (as so added)).

For these purposes, 'drag-along rights', in relation to shares in a company, means the right of the holders of a majority of the shares, where they are selling their shares, to require the holders of the minority to sell theirs; and 'tag-along rights', in relation to shares in a company, means the right of the holders of a minority of the shares to sell their shares, where the holders of the majority are selling theirs, on the same terms as those on which the holders of the majority are doing so: see s 205A(13) (as so added). As to the meaning of 'dividend' see COMPANIES vol 15 (2009) PARA 1408; and as to the meaning of 'redeemable shares' see COMPANIES vol 15 (2009) PARA 1052. As to the voting rights of company members see COMPANIES vol 14 (2009) PARA 652 et seq; as to the transferability of shares generally see COMPANIES vol 15 (2009) PARA 1055; as to classes of share capital see COMPANIES vol 15 (2009) PARA 1057 et seq; and as to winding up a company generally see COMPANY AND PARTNERSHIP INSOLVENCY vol 16 (2011) PARA 399 et seq.

8   Employment Rights Act 1996 s 205A(1)(d) (as added: see note 1).
9   See the Employment Rights Act 1996 s 205A(2) (as added: see note 1).
10   Employment Rights Act 1996 s 205A(2)(a) (as added: see note 1). Head (a) in the text refers to the right under s 63D (statutory right to make request in relation to study or training: see PARA 328): see s 205A(2)(a) (as so added).
11   Employment Rights Act 1996 s 205A(2)(b) (as added: see note 1). Head (b) in the text refers to the right under s 80F (right to request contract variation in relation to flexible working: see PARA 108): see s 205A(2)(b) (as so added).The reference in head (b) in the text to making an application under s 80F does not, however, include a reference to making an application within the period of 14 days beginning with the day on which the employee shareholder returns to work from a period of parental leave under regulations made under s 76 (see PARA 390): s 205A(8) (as so added).
12   Employment Rights Act 1996 s 205A(2)(c) (as added: see note 1). Head (c) in the text refers to the right under s 94 (right not to be unfairly dismissed: see PARA 757): see s 205A(2)(c) (as so added).The reference in head (c) in the text to unfair dismissal does not include a reference to (see s 205A(9) (as so added)):
      (1)   a dismissal which is required to be regarded as unfair for the purposes of Pt X (ss 94–134A) (unfair dismissal: see PARA 757 et seq) by a provision (whenever made) contained in or made under the Employment Rights Act 1996 or any other Act (s 205A(9)(a) (as so added));
      (2)   a dismissal which amounts to a contravention of the Equality Act 2010 (Employment Rights Act 1996 s 205A(9)(b) (as so added)).
      As to contraventions of the Equality Act 2010 generally see DISCRIMINATION vol 33 (2013) PARA 65 et seq. Nor does the reference in head (c) in the text to the right not to be unfairly dismissed include a reference to that right in a case where the Employment Rights Act 1996 s 108(2) (qualifying period applicable to suspension from work on medical grounds: see PARA 758) applies: s 205A(10) (as so added).
13   Employment Rights Act 1996 s 205A(2)(d) (as added: see note 1). Head (d) in the text refers to the right under s 135 (right to redundancy payment: see PARA 836): see s 205A(2)(d) (as so added).
14   See the Employment Rights Act 1996 s 205A(3), (4) (as added: see note 1). Accordingly 16 weeks' notice is required to be given by an employee who is an employee shareholder, in the following cases:
      (1)   the Maternity and Parental Leave etc Regulations 1999, SI 1999/3312, reg 11 (notices to be given by the employee entitled to maternity leave: see PARA 365) (ie in place of 8 weeks' notice) (see the Employment Rights Act 1996 s 205A(3)(a) (as so added));
      (2)   the Paternity and Adoption Leave Regulations 2002, SI 2002/2788, reg 25 (notification of employee's intention to return during additional adoption leave period: see PARA 384) (ie in place of 8 weeks' notice) (see the Employment Rights Act 1996 s 205A(3)(b) (as so added));

(3)   the Additional Paternity Leave Regulations 2010, SI 2010/1055, reg 30 (requirement for employee to notify employer of intention to return to work during additional paternity leave period) (lapsed) (see the Employment Rights Act 1996 s 205A(4) (as so added)).

15   See the Employment Rights Act 1996 s 205A(6) (as added: see note 1).
16   For these purposes, 'relevant independent adviser' has the meaning that it has for the purposes of the Employment Rights Act 1996 s 203(3)(c) (see PARA 151 note 15): see s 205A(13) (as added: see note 1).
17   Employment Rights Act 1996 s 205A(6)(a) (as added: see note 1).
18   Employment Rights Act 1996 s 205A(6)(b) (as added: see note 1).
19   Ie but for the Employment Rights Act 1996 s 205A(7): see s 205A(7) (as added: see note 1).
20   See the Employment Rights Act 1996 s 205A(7) (as added: see note 1).
21   See the Employment Rights Act 1996 s 47G (cited in PARA 624), s 104G (cited in PARA 800).

(iv) Powers to amend Scope of Legislation

155. Power to extend provisions of the Employment Rights Act 1996 (and equivalent Northern Ireland legislation). Her Majesty may by Order in Council provide that[1]:

(1)   the provisions of the Employment Rights Act 1996[2]; and
(2)   any Northern Ireland legislation[3] making provision for purposes corresponding to any of the purposes of the Employment Rights Act 1996[4],

apply, to such extent and for such purposes as may be specified in the Order in Council (with or without modification) to or in relation to a person in offshore employment[5].

Such an Order in Council may:

(a)   make different provision for different cases[6];
(b)   provide that all or any of the provisions referred to under heads (1) and (2) above (as applied by such an Order in Council) are to apply: (i) to individuals (whether or not they are British subjects)[7]; and (ii) to bodies corporate (whether or not they are incorporated under the law of a part of the United Kingdom)[8], and are to apply even where the application may affect their activities outside the United Kingdom[9];
(c)   make provision for conferring jurisdiction[10] on any court or class of court specified in the Order in Council, or on employment tribunals[11], in respect of offences, causes of action or other matters arising in connection with offshore employment[12];
(d)   without prejudice to the generality of heads (1) and (2) or head (a) above, provide that the provisions referred to under heads (1) and (2) above (as applied by such an Order in Council) are to apply in relation to any person in employment in any part[13] of the territorial waters of the United Kingdom, or in any part of the United Kingdom sector of the continental shelf[14];
(e)   exclude from the operation of the Territorial Waters Jurisdiction Act 1878[15] proceedings for offences under the provisions referred to under heads (1) and (2) above in connection with offshore employment[16];
(f)   provide that such proceedings are not to be brought without such consent as may be required by the Order in Council[17];
(g)   without prejudice to the generality of the power under heads (1) and (2) above, modify or exclude the operation of specified statutory provisions[18] or of any corresponding provision in any Northern Ireland legislation[19].

The Employment Relations (Offshore Employment) Order 2000[20] has been made in exercise of these powers, and the Employment Protection (Offshore Employment) Order 1976[21] has effect as if so made.

1   See the Employment Rights Act 1996 s 201(2). A statutory instrument made under any power conferred by the Employment Rights Act 1996 to make an Order in Council (unless the empowering provision is excepted) is subject to annulment in pursuance of a resolution of either House of Parliament: see s 236; and PARA 162.

2   Employment Rights Act 1996 s 201(2)(a).

3   As to the meaning, in any Act, unless the contrary intention appears, of 'Northern Ireland legislation' see the Interpretation Act 1978 ss 5, 24(5), Sch 1; and STATUTES AND LEGISLATIVE PROCESS vol 96 (2012) PARA 1213.

4   Employment Rights Act 1996 s 201(2)(b).

5   See the Employment Rights Act 1996 s 201(2). For these purposes, 'offshore employment' means employment for the purposes of activities:
   (1)   in the territorial waters of the United Kingdom (s 201(1)(a));
   (2)   connected with the exploration of the sea bed or subsoil or the exploitation of their natural resources in the United Kingdom sector of the continental shelf (s 201(1)(b)); or
   (3)   connected with the exploration or exploitation, in a foreign sector of the continental shelf, of a cross-boundary petroleum field (s 201(1)(c)).
   'United Kingdom sector of the continental shelf' means any area designated by order under the Continental Shelf Act 1964 s 1(7) (see ENERGY AND CLIMATE CHANGE vol 44 (2011) PARA 1046); 'cross-boundary petroleum field' means a petroleum field that extends across the boundary between an area designated by order under s 1(7) and a foreign sector of the continental shelf; 'foreign sector of the continental shelf' means an area outside the territorial waters of any state, within which rights with respect to the sea bed and subsoil and their natural resources are exercisable by a state other than the United Kingdom; and 'petroleum field' means a geological structure identified as an oil or gas field by the Order in Council concerned: see the Employment Rights Act 1996 s 201(5). As to the meaning of 'employment' see PARA 2. As to the meaning of 'United Kingdom' see PARA 2 note 12. As to the territorial sea (or waters) of the United Kingdom see the Territorial Sea Act 1987 s 1; and INTERNATIONAL RELATIONS LAW vol 61 (2010) PARA 123 et seq; WATER AND WATERWAYS vol 100 (2009) PARA 31.
   As from a day to be appointed under the Petroleum Act 1998 s 52(2)–(4), all definitions contained in the Employment Rights Act 1996 s 201(5) are repealed by the Petroleum Act 1998 ss 50, 51(1), Sch 4 para 40(1), (3), Sch 5 Pt I; and the definition of 'offshore employment' contained in the Employment Rights Act 1996 s 201(1) is substituted so that it means employment for the purposes of: (a) any activities in the territorial sea adjacent to the United Kingdom; or (b) any such activities as are mentioned in the Petroleum Act 1998 s 11(2) in waters within s 11(8)(b), (c) (see ENERGY AND CLIMATE CHANGE vol 44 (2011) PARA 1080) (see the Employment Rights Act 1996 s 201(1) (prospectively substituted by the Petroleum Act 1998 Sch 4 para 40(1), (2))). However, at the date at which this volume states the law, no such day had been so appointed in relation to either the amendment or the repeal.

6   Employment Rights Act 1996 s 201(3)(a).

7   Employment Rights Act 1996 s 201(3)(b)(i). Although the legislation refers to 'British subject', the status of British subject ceased to be a common status enjoyed in addition to citizenship as from 1 January 1983 and became a miscellaneous, residual and disappearing category: see BRITISH NATIONALITY vol 4 (2011) PARA 407.

8   Employment Rights Act 1996 s 201(3)(b)(ii).

9   See the Employment Rights Act 1996 s 201(3)(b).

10   Any jurisdiction conferred on any court or tribunal under the Employment Rights Act 1996 s 201 is without prejudice to jurisdiction exercisable apart from s 201 by that or any other court or tribunal: s 201(4).

11   Where an Order in Council under the Employment Rights Act 1996 s 201 confers jurisdiction on an employment tribunal, the jurisdiction conferred includes power to make an order under the Employment Tribunals Act 1996 s 12A (financial penalty payable to Secretary of State for aggravated breach of worker's rights: see PARA 1477), and s 12A applies accordingly: Employment Rights Act 1996 s 201(3A) (added by the Enterprise and Regulatory Reform Act 2013 s 16(2), Sch 3 para 5). As to employment tribunals see PARA 1399 et seq; and as to the procedure on a complaint made to an employment tribunal see PARA 1453 et seq.

12   Employment Rights Act 1996 s 201(3)(c) (amended by the Employment Rights (Dispute Resolution) Act 1998 s 1(2)(b)).

13 Ie in a part of the areas specified in the Employment Rights Act 1996 s 201(1)(a), (b) (see note 5): see s 201(3)(d).

14 Employment Rights Act 1996 s 201(3)(d).

15 Ie the operation of the Territorial Waters Jurisdiction Act 1878 s 3 (consents required for prosecutions: see CRIMINAL PROCEDURE vol 27 (2010) PARA 12): see the Employment Rights Act 1996 s 201(3)(e).

16 Employment Rights Act 1996 s 201(3)(e).

17 Employment Rights Act 1996 s 201(3)(f).

18 Ie the Employment Rights Act 1996 s 199 (mariners: see PARA 167) and s 215(2)–(6) (continuity of employment; employment abroad: see PARA 863): see s 201(3)(g) (amended by the Employment Relations Act 1999 s 44, Sch 9).

19 Employment Rights Act 1996 s 201(3)(g) (as amended: see note 18).

20 Ie the Employment Relations (Offshore Employment) Order 2000, SI 2000/1828: see PARA 156.

21 Ie the Employment Protection (Offshore Employment) Order 1976, SI 1976/766, by virtue of the Employment Rights Act 1996 s 241, Sch 2 para 2(1): see PARA 156.

156. Extension of employment protection legislation to offshore areas. Much of the employment protection legislation[1] applies[2] to or in relation to persons in employment[3] for the purposes of any of the following activities[4], that is to say:

(1) any activities (other than activities connected with a ship[5] which is in the course of navigation or is a survey ship or is engaged in dredging[6] or fishing) in the territorial waters[7];

(2) any activities connected with the exploration of the sea bed or subsoil or the exploitation of their natural resources in any designated area (other than an area or part of an area in which the law of Northern Ireland applies) being activities carried out on or from an offshore installation[8] in any such designated area[9];

(3) any activities in the foreign sector of the continental shelf connected with the exploration or exploitation of the Frigg Gas Field[10].

These provisions apply to individuals whether or not they are British subjects[11], and to bodies corporate whether or not they are incorporated under the law of any part of the United Kingdom, notwithstanding that such application may affect their activities outside the United Kingdom[12].

Trade Union and Labour Relations (Consolidation) Act 1992 provisions relating to the recognition of trade unions for collective bargaining purposes[13], the exclusion of protection for certain acts in contemplation or furtherance of a trade dispute[14], and the requirement of a ballot etc before industrial action[15], and Employment Rights Act 1996 provisions relating to unfair dismissal for reasons connected with union recognition[16], apply to and in relation to employment for the purposes of activities[17]:

(a) in the territorial waters of the United Kingdom (other than an area or part of an area to which the law of Northern Ireland applies)[18];

(b) connected with the exploration of the sea bed or its subsoil, or the exploitation of their natural resources, in the United Kingdom sector of the continental shelf (other than an area to which the law of Northern Ireland applies)[19]; or

(c) in the foreign sector of the continental shelf connected with the exploration or exploitation of the Frigg Gas Field, where the employer is a company registered under the Companies Acts, is an oversea company[20] which has an established place of business within Great Britain from which it directs the activities in question, or is any other person who has a place of business within Great Britain from which he directs the activities in question[21], but those provisions do not apply to or in relation to: (i) any employment wholly or mainly for the purposes of any activities connected with the Ekofisk Field[22]; (ii) employment in connection with a ship which is in the course of navigation or a ship which is engaged in dredging[23] or fishing[24].

Employment tribunals[25] have: (A) such jurisdiction in respect of matters arising[26] from acts or omissions taking place in the English area as they would have if those acts or omissions had taken place in England or Wales[27]; and (B) jurisdiction in respect of matters arising in connection with employment wholly or mainly for the purposes of any activities connected with the Frigg Gas Field[28].

1   References in the Employment Protection (Offshore Employment) Order 1976, SI 1976/766, to enactments are references to those enactments as amended or extended by or under any other enactment: art 1(5).
        Offences under the applied provisions (ie offences connected with employment to which the Employment Protection (Offshore Employment) Order 1976, SI 1976/766, applies) are excluded from the operation of the Territorial Waters Jurisdiction Act 1878 s 3 (consents required for prosecution: see CRIMINAL PROCEDURE vol 27 (2010) PARA 12); but proceedings for any such offence, including cases where s 3 would otherwise apply, may not be brought in England and Wales except by or with the consent of the Secretary of State: see the Employment Protection (Offshore Employment) Order 1976, SI 1976/766, art 5. For these purposes, 'applied provisions' means the provisions applied by art 3, Schedule as they are so applied: see art 1(2). As to the meanings of 'England' and 'Wales' see PARA 2 note 12. As to the Secretary of State see PARA 5 note 21.
2   Ie to the extent and for the purposes, and subject to the modifications, specified in the Employment Protection (Offshore Employment) Order 1976, SI 1976/766, Schedule: see art 3 (amended by SI 1981/208; SI 1984/1149). Accordingly, for these purposes:
    (1)   all the provisions of the Industrial Training Act 1982 apply for such purposes as are relevant to or in relation to persons in employment to which the Employment Protection (Offshore Employment) Order 1976, SI 1976/766, applies; and such application is subject to the modification that, in respect of employment to which the Employment Protection (Offshore Employment) Order 1976, SI 1976/766, applies, the references in the Industrial Training Act 1982 s 10 (training for employment overseas: see PARA 668) to Great Britain are to be treated as including the territorial waters, the waters in any designated area (other than an area or part of an area in which the law of Northern Ireland applies) and the waters in the foreign sector of the continental shelf (Employment Protection (Offshore Employment) Order 1976, SI 1976/766, art 3(a), Schedule paras 1, 2 (art 3(a)–(f), Schedule Pts I–VII (paras 1–12) substituted by SI 1981/208); Employment Rights Act 1996 s 241, Sch 2 para 2(1));
    (2)   the provisions of the Trade Union and Labour Relations (Consolidation) Act 1992 apply for such purposes as are relevant to or in relation to persons in employment to which the Employment Protection (Offshore Employment) Order 1976, SI 1976/766, applies; and such application is subject to the modification that the Trade Union and Labour Relations (Consolidation) Act 1992 s 285 (employment outside Great Britain: see PARA 1071) has effect in respect of employment to which the Employment Protection (Offshore Employment) Order 1976, SI 1976/766, applies as if: (a) the reference in the Trade Union and Labour Relations (Consolidation) Act 1992 s 285(1) to Great Britain included the territorial waters, the waters in any designated area, other than an area or part of an area in which the law of Northern Ireland applies, and the waters in the foreign sector of the continental shelf; and (b) s 285(2) were omitted (Employment Protection (Offshore Employment) Order 1976, SI 1976/766, art 3(b), (c), Schedule paras 3–5 (as so substituted); Employment Rights Act 1996 Sch 2 para 2(1));
    (3)   the provisions of the Employment Rights Act 1996 except s 50 (right to time off work for public duties: see PARA 350) apply for such purposes as are relevant to or in relation to persons in employment to which the Employment Protection (Offshore Employment) Order 1976, SI 1976/766, applies; but such application is subject to the modification that: (a) the reference in the Employment Rights Act 1996 s 215(2) (computing a period of employment where employee was engaged in work wholly or mainly outside Great Britain: see PARA 863) to Great Britain is to be treated as including the territorial waters, the waters in any designated area, other than an area or part of an area in which the law of Northern Ireland applies, and the waters in the foreign sector of the

continental shelf; (b) the provisions of Pt XI (ss 135–181) (redundancy payments: see PARA 835 et seq) do not apply so as to affect the exclusion of any merchant seaman from Pt XI by the Redundancy Payments (Merchant Seamen Exclusion) Order 1973, SI 1973/1281 (revoked), or the disregarding of any period of employment pursuant to art 4 (revoked) (Employment Protection (Offshore Employment) Order 1976, SI 1976/766, art 3(d), Schedule paras 6–8 (as so substituted); Employment Rights Act 1996 Sch 2 para 2(1)).

For these purposes, 'designated area' means any area designated by order under the Continental Shelf Act 1964 s 1(7) (see ENERGY AND CLIMATE CHANGE vol 44 (2011) PARA 1040); and the 'territorial waters' means the territorial waters of the United Kingdom other than the territorial waters adjacent to Northern Ireland: see the Employment Protection (Offshore Employment) Order 1976, SI 1976/766, art 1(2). 'Foreign sector of the continental shelf' has the same meaning as in the Employment Rights Act 1996 s 201 (see PARA 155 note 5): see the Employment Protection (Offshore Employment) Order 1976, SI 1976/766, art 1(2) (definition added by SI 1981/208); and the Employment Rights Act 1996 Sch 2 para 2(1). References to an area or part of an area in which the law of Northern Ireland applies are references to the Northern Irish Area: see the Employment Protection (Offshore Employment) Order 1976, SI 1976/766, art 1(4). For these purposes, 'Northern Irish Area' means such of the offshore area adjacent to Northern Ireland which lies to the west of the Northern Irish border together with the internal waters of Northern Ireland, in so far as they are tidal or constitute parts of the sea: Civil Jurisdiction (Offshore Activities) Order 1987, SI 1987/2197, art 1(2); applied by the Employment Protection (Offshore Employment) Order 1976, SI 1976/766, art 1(4). As to the meanings of 'Great Britain' and 'United Kingdom' see PARA 2 note 12. As to the territorial sea (or waters) of the United Kingdom see the Territorial Sea Act 1987 s 1; and INTERNATIONAL RELATIONS LAW vol 61 (2010) PARA 123 et seq; WATER AND WATERWAYS vol 100 (2009) PARA 31.

3   Where, however, apart from the Employment Protection (Offshore Employment) Order 1976, SI 1976/766, any provision of any Act mentioned in art 3 (see note 2) to any extent applies to or in relation to a person's employment, then that employment is not as respects that Act to be regarded as an employment to which the Employment Protection (Offshore Employment) Order 1976, SI 1976/766, applies; and accordingly nothing therein affects the application of those Acts in cases to which they apply apart from the Employment Protection (Offshore Employment) Order 1976, SI 1976/766: art 2(1A) (added by SI 1977/588). As to the application of national minimum wage legislation to offshore employment see the National Minimum Wage (Offshore Employment) Order 1999, SI 1999/1128; and PARA 184.

4   See the Employment Protection (Offshore Employment) Order 1976, SI 1976/766, art 2(1) (art 2(1) amended by SI 1977/588). The Employment Protection (Offshore Employment) Order 1976, SI 1976/766, art 2(1) is subject to art 2(1A) (see note 3) and art 2(2): see art 2(1) (as so amended). Accordingly, the Employment Protection (Offshore Employment) Order 1976, SI 1976/766, does not apply to any employment wholly or mainly for the purpose of any activities connected with the Ekofisk Field: art 2(2) (amended by SI 1981/208).

In its application to any employment wholly or mainly for the purpose of any activities connected with the Frigg Gas Field (whether or not that employment wholly or mainly takes place in the foreign sector of the continental shelf) the Employment Protection (Offshore Employment) Order 1976, SI 1976/766, is subject to the modification that the employment to which it applies is employment within art 2 and in respect of which the employer is:

(1)   a company registered under the Companies Acts (Employment Protection (Offshore Employment) (Amendment) Order 1981, SI 1981/208, art 3(a)(i); Employment Rights Act 1996 Sch 2 para 2(1));

(2)   an oversea company which has established a place of business within Great Britain from which it directs the offshore operations in question (Employment Protection (Offshore Employment) (Amendment) Order 1981, SI 1981/208, art 3(a)(ii); or

(3)   any other person who has a place of business within Great Britain from which he directs the offshore operations in question (art 3(a)(iii)).

For these purposes, 'Frigg Gas Field' means the naturally occurring gas-bearing sand formations of the lower Eocene age located in the vicinity of the intersection of the line of latitude 59° 53' North and of the dividing line between the sectors of the Continental Shelf of the United Kingdom and the Kingdom of Norway and includes all other gas-bearing strata from which gas at the start of production is capable of flowing into the above-mentioned gas-bearing sand formations; and 'oversea company' has the same meaning as in the Companies Act 2006 s 1044 (see COMPANIES vol 15 (2009) PARA 1824): Employment Protection (Offshore Employment) (Amendment) Order 1981, SI 1981/208, art 1(2); Employment Rights Act 1996 Sch 2 para 2(1).

5   For these purposes, 'ship' includes vessel: see the Employment Protection (Offshore Employment) Order 1976, SI 1976/766, art 1(2).

6   For these purposes, 'dredging' does not include the excavation of the sea bed or its subsoil in the course of pipe laying: see the Employment Protection (Offshore Employment) Order 1976, SI 1976/766, art 1(2).

7   Employment Protection (Offshore Employment) Order 1976, SI 1976/766, art 2(1)(a).

8   For these purposes, an offshore installation is any structure, whether fixed or otherwise, which is for use offshore for purposes connected with the exploration of the sea bed or its subsoil or the exploitation of their natural resources: Employment Protection (Offshore Employment) Order 1976, SI 1976/766, art 1(3)(a). A structure may, however, be treated as being for use for the purposes described in art 1(3)(a) notwithstanding that it is not in operation or that it is undergoing construction, modification, maintenance, repair, demolition or any similar works: art 1(3)(b). 'Structure' includes ship (whether registered in the United Kingdom or elsewhere) (see art 1(2)); and a structure which is a ship (whether registered in the United Kingdom or elsewhere) is not to be treated, notwithstanding that it is for use as described in art 1(3)(a), as an offshore installation if it is:
    (1)   in the course of navigation or engaged in dredging, other than navigation or dredging which is wholly or mainly attributable to activities for the purposes described in art 1(3)(a) in which it is for the time being actually engaged (art 1(3)(c)(i));
    (2)   a survey ship (art 1(3)(c)(ii)).
    The purposes described in art 1(3)(a) do not include fishing: art 1(3)(d). As to the registration of ships in the United Kingdom see the Merchant Shipping Act 1995 Pt II (ss 8–23); and SHIPPING AND MARITIME LAW vol 93 (2008) PARA 245 et seq.

9   Employment Protection (Offshore Employment) Order 1976, SI 1976/766, art 2(1)(b).

10 Employment Protection (Offshore Employment) Order 1976, SI 1976/766, art 2(1)(c) (added by SI 1981/208).

11 Although the legislation refers to 'British subjects', the status of British subject ceased to be a common status enjoyed in addition to citizenship as from 1 January 1983 and became a miscellaneous, residual and disappearing category: see BRITISH NATIONALITY vol 4 (2011) PARA 407.

12 Employment Protection (Offshore Employment) Order 1976, SI 1976/766, art 4.

13 Ie the Trade Union and Labour Relations (Consolidation) Act 1992 ss 70A–70C, Sch A1 (see PARA 1097 et seq): see the Employment Relations (Offshore Employment) Order 2000, SI 2000/1828, art 2(5)(a).

14 Ie the Trade Union and Labour Relations (Consolidation) Act 1992 ss 222–224 (see PARAS 1365–1367): see the Employment Relations (Offshore Employment) Order 2000, SI 2000/1828, art 2(5)(b).

15 Ie the Trade Union and Labour Relations (Consolidation) Act 1992 ss 226–235 (and s 246 (definitions) as it applies to ss 226–235) (see PARA 1370 et seq) : see the Employment Relations (Offshore Employment) Order 2000, SI 2000/1828, art 2(5)(c).

16 Ie the Employment Rights Act 1996 Pt X (ss 94–134A) (unfair dismissal: see PARA 757 et seq) for the purposes of the Trade Union and Labour Relations (Consolidation) Act 1992 s 70A, Sch A1 paras 161–165 (see PARA 1171), to the extent that the Employment Rights Act 1996 provisions would not otherwise apply: see the Employment Relations (Offshore Employment) Order 2000, SI 2000/1828, art 2(6).

17 See the Employment Relations (Offshore Employment) Order 2000, SI 2000/1828, arts 2(1), (5)(a)–(c), (6).

18 Employment Relations (Offshore Employment) Order 2000, SI 2000/1828, art 2(1)(a). For these purposes, references to the United Kingdom sector of the continental shelf to which the law of Northern Ireland applies are references to the Northern Irish Area: see art 1(2). For these purposes, 'Northern Irish Area' means such of the offshore area adjacent to Northern Ireland which lies to the west of the Northern Irish border together with the internal waters of Northern Ireland, in so far as they are tidal or constitute parts of the sea: Civil Jurisdiction (Offshore Activities) Order 1987, SI 1987/2197, art 1(2); applied by the Employment Relations (Offshore Employment) Order 2000, SI 2000/1828, art 1(2).

19 Employment Relations (Offshore Employment) Order 2000, SI 2000/1828, art 2(1)(b).

20 For these purposes, 'oversea company' has the same meaning as in the Companies Act 2006 s 1044 (see COMPANIES vol 15 (2009) PARA 1824): Employment Relations (Offshore Employment) Order 2000, SI 2000/1828, art 1(2); Employment Rights Act 1996 Sch 2 para 2(1).

21 Employment Relations (Offshore Employment) Order 2000, SI 2000/1828, art 2(1)(c).

22 Employment Relations (Offshore Employment) Order 2000, SI 2000/1828, art 2(2).

23 For these purposes, 'dredging' does not include the excavation of the sea bed or its subsoil in the course of pipe laying: Employment Relations (Offshore Employment) Order 2000, SI 2000/1828, art 2(4).

24 Employment Relations (Offshore Employment) Order 2000, SI 2000/1828, art 2(3).

25 Ie the employment tribunals established in pursuance of the Employment Tribunals (Constitution and Rules of Procedure) Regulations 2013, SI 2013/1237: see the Employment Protection (Offshore Employment) Order 1976, SI 1976/766, art 1(2) (definition amended by the Employment Rights (Dispute Resolution) Act 1998 s 1(2)(b)). As to employment tribunals see PARA 1399 et seq; and as to the procedure on a complaint made to an employment tribunal see PARA 1453 et seq.

26 Ie in connection with employment to which the Employment Protection (Offshore Employment) Order 1976, SI 1976/766, and the Employment Relations (Offshore Employment) Order 2000, SI 2000/1828, apply.

27 Employment Protection (Offshore Employment) Order 1976, SI 1976/766, art 6(1) (amended by the Employment Rights (Dispute Resolution) Act 1998 s 1(2)(b)); Employment Relations (Offshore Employment) Order 2000, SI 2000/1828, art 3(1); Employment Rights Act 1996 Sch 2 para 2(1). For these purposes, 'English area' means such of the offshore area adjacent to England and Wales which lies to the south of the Scottish border and east of the Northern Irish border together with the internal waters of England and Wales, in so far as they are tidal or constitute parts of the sea: Civil Jurisdiction (Offshore Activities) Order 1987, SI 1987/2197, art 1(2) (applied by the Employment Protection (Offshore Employment) Order 1976, SI 1976/766, art 1(4)); Employment Relations (Offshore Employment) Order 2000, SI 2000/1828, art 1(2); Employment Rights Act 1996 Sch 2 para 2(1).

28 Employment Protection (Offshore Employment) Order 1976, SI 1976/766, art 6(3) (added by SI 1981/208; and amended by the Employment Rights (Dispute Resolution) Act 1998 s 1(2)(b)); Employment Relations (Offshore Employment) Order 2000, SI 2000/1828, art 3(3).

157. Reciprocal arrangements for co-ordinating the Employment Rights Act 1996 with equivalent provisions of Northern Ireland legislation. If provision is made by Northern Ireland legislation[1] for purposes corresponding to any of the purposes of the Employment Rights Act 1996 (other than an excepted provision)[2], the Secretary of State[3] may, with the consent of the Treasury[4], make reciprocal arrangements with the appropriate Northern Ireland authority[5] for co-ordinating the relevant provisions of the Employment Rights Act 1996 with the corresponding provisions of the Northern Ireland legislation, so as to secure that they operate, to such extent as may be provided by the arrangements, as a single system[6].

The Secretary of State may make regulations for giving effect to any such arrangements[7]. Any such regulations may make different provision for different cases[8]; and they may provide that the relevant provisions of the Employment Rights Act 1996 have effect in relation to persons affected by the arrangements subject to such modifications and adaptations as may be specified in the regulations[9], including provision: (1) for securing that acts, omissions and events having any effect for the purposes of the Northern Ireland legislation have a corresponding effect for the purposes of the Employment Rights Act 1996 (but not so as to confer a right to double payment in respect of the same act, omission or event)[10]; and (2) for determining, in cases where rights accrue both under the Employment Rights Act 1996 and under the Northern Ireland legislation, which of those rights is available to the person concerned[11].

1 As to the meaning, in any Act, unless the contrary intention appears, of 'Northern Ireland legislation' see the Interpretation Act 1978 ss 5, 24(5), Sch 1; and STATUTES AND LEGISLATIVE PROCESS vol 96 (2012) PARA 1213.

2 Ie for the purposes of the Employment Rights Act 1996, except ss 1–7 (statements of employment particulars: see PARAS 119–123), Pt II (ss 13–27) (protection of wages: see PARA 254 et seq), Pt IV (ss 36–43) (Sunday working for shop and betting workers: see PARA 321 et seq), s 45 (detriment (Sunday working for shop and betting workers): see PARA 615), s 46 (detriment (trustees of occupational pension schemes): see PARA 617), s 58 (right to time off for trustees of occupational pension schemes: see PARA 352), s 59 (right to payment for time off under s 58: see PARA 352), s 60 (complaint relating to time off work: see PARA 353), s 86 (termination (minimum notice): see PARAS 735–736), s 87 (termination (rights of employee in

notice period): see PARAS 737, 738 note 4), s 88 (termination (employments with normal working hours): see PARA 738), s 89 (termination (employments without normal working hours): see PARA 739), s 90 (termination (benefits): see PARA 740), s 91 (termination (supplementary): see PARAS 736–737, 741), s 101 (unfair dismissal (shop and betting workers who refuse Sunday work): see PARA 787) and s 102 (unfair dismissal (trustees of occupational pension schemes): see PARA 790): see s 238(2).

3   As to the Secretary of State see PARA 5 note 21.
4   As to the Treasury see CONSTITUTIONAL AND ADMINISTRATIVE LAW vol 20 (2014) PARAS 262–265.
5   For these purposes, 'appropriate Northern Ireland authority' means such authority as may be specified in that behalf in the Northern Ireland legislation: Employment Rights Act 1996 s 238(6).
6   Employment Rights Act 1996 s 238(1).
7   Employment Rights Act 1996 s 238(3). As to the making of regulations under the Employment Rights Act 1996 generally see PARA 162. At the date at which this volume states the law, no such regulations had been made but, by virtue of s 241, Sch 2 para 2(1) (see PARA 162), the Redundancy Payments Northern Ireland Reciprocal Arrangements Regulations 1965, SI 1965/2027, have effect as if so made.
8   Employment Rights Act 1996 s 238(4).
9   See the Employment Rights Act 1996 s 238(5).
10 Employment Rights Act 1996 s 238(5)(a).
11 Employment Rights Act 1996 s 238(5)(b).

158.   General power under the Employment Rights Act 1996 to amend employment protection legislation.   The Secretary of State may by order[1]:

(1)   provide that any provision of the Employment Rights Act 1996 (unless it is excepted[2]), which is specified in the order is not to apply to persons or to employments[3] of such classes as may be prescribed in the order[4];

(2)   provide that any provision of the Employment Rights Act 1996 (unless it is excepted[5]) is to apply to persons or employments of such classes as may be prescribed in the order subject to such exceptions and modifications as may be so prescribed[6]; or

(3)   vary, or exclude the operation of, any of the provisions that are applied for this purpose[7].

The power to make such orders is without prejudice to any other power of the Secretary of State to amend, vary or repeal any provision of the Employment Rights Act 1996, or to extend or restrict its operation in relation to any person or employment[8].

1   See the Employment Rights Act 1996 s 209(1). Any power conferred by any provision of the Employment Rights Act 1996 to make any order (other than an Order in Council) is exercisable by statutory instrument: see s 236; and PARA 162. No order may be made under s 209, however, unless a draft of the order has been laid before Parliament and approved by a resolution of each House of Parliament (see s 236(3); and PARA 162), although s 236(3) does not apply to an order under s 209(1)(b) (see head (2) in the text) which specifies only provisions contained in Pt XI (ss 135–181) (redundancy payments: see PARA 835 et seq) (s 236(4)). As to the Secretary of State see PARA 5 note 21.
2   Ie any provision of the Employment Rights Act 1996 other than any to which s 209(1)(a) does not apply: see s 209(1)(a). Accordingly, s 209(1)(a) does not apply to:
    (1)   Pt II (ss 13–27) (protection of wages: see PARA 254 et seq) and Pt IV (ss 36–43) (Sunday working for shop and betting workers: see PARA 321 et seq) (s 209(2)(a));
    (2)   in Pt V (ss 43M–49A) (protection from suffering detriment in employment: see PARA 612 et seq), s 45 (Sunday working for shop and betting workers: see PARA 615), s 46 (trustees of occupational pension schemes: see PARA 617), and s 48 (detriment (enforcement: complaint to employment tribunal): see PARA 625) and s 49 (detriment (enforcement: remedies): see PARA 626) (so far as ss 48, 49 relate to ss 45, 46) (s 209(2)(b));
    (3)   in Pt VI (ss 50–63C) (time off work: see PARA 326 et seq), s 58 (right to time off for

trustees of occupational pension schemes: see PARA 352), s 59 (right to payment for time off under s 58: see PARA 352), s 60 (complaint relating to time off work: see PARA 353) (s 209(2)(c));

(4) in Pt IX (ss 86–93) (termination of employment: see PARA 735 et seq), s 87(3) (period of notice: see PARA 738 note 4), s 88 (employments with normal working hours: see PARA 738), s 89 (employments without normal working hours: see PARA 739), s 90 (benefits: see PARA 740), s 91(1)–(4), (6) (termination (supplementary): see PARAS 736, 741–742), s 92(6)–(8) (right to written statement of reasons for dismissal: see PARA 755 note 11) (s 209(2)(d));

(5) in Pt X (ss 94–134A) (unfair dismissal: see PARA 757 et seq), s 95 (circumstances of dismissal: see PARA 762), s 97(1)–(5) (effective date of termination: see PARA 764), s 98(1)–(4), (6) (fairness: see PARA 765 et seq), s 100 (health and safety cases: see PARA 786), s 101 (shop and betting workers who refuse Sunday work: see PARA 787), s 101A (working time cases: see PARA 788), s 102 (trustees of occupational pension schemes: see PARA 790), s 103 (employee representatives: see PARA 791), s 105 (redundancy: see PARA 781), s 107 (influence of industrial action: see PARA 771), s 110 (exclusion agreement: see PARAS 759–760), s 111 (remedy of complaint: see PARA 804), s 120(2) (repealed), s 124(1), (2), (5) (s 124(2) repealed) (limit of compensatory award: see PARA 823), s 125(7) (s 125 repealed), s 134 (effect of death of party: see PARA 757) (s 209(2)(e) (amended by SI 1998/1833));

(6) in the Employment Rights Act 1996 Pt XI (redundancy payments: see PARA 835 et seq), s 143 (notice of extension on account of strike action: see PARA 868), s 144 (supplementary: see PARA 868), s 160(2), (3) (exclusion in respect of employment in any capacity under the government of an overseas territory: see PARA 854 note 6), s 166 (application for payments by Secretary of State: see PARA 884), s 167 (making of payments by Secretary of State: see PARA 884), s 168 (amount of payments by Secretary of State: see PARA 884), s 169 (information regarding applications for payments: see PARA 885), s 170 (complaint regarding payments: see PARA 887), s 171 (exclusion where employment not under contract: see PARA 838), s 172 (exclusion where termination was by statute: see PARA 869), s 173 (exclusion where employees paid by third party: see PARA 836), s 177 (complaint under s 171: see PARA 888), s 178 (former statutory schemes: see PARA 883), s 179 (notices: see PARA 837), s 180 (offences: see PARAS 882, 885) (s 209(2)(f));

(7) Pt XIV Ch 1 (ss 210–219) (continuous employment: see PARAS 130 et seq, 861 et seq) (s 209(2)(h)); and

(8) in Pt XV (ss 236–245) (general and supplementary), s 236(3) (procedure for Orders in Council: see PARA 162) (so far as relating to ss 120(2), 124(2), s 125(7) (all repealed)) (s 209(2)(j)).

3   As to the meaning of 'employment' see PARA 2.
4   Employment Rights Act 1996 s 209(1)(a).
5   Head (2) in the text does not apply to any of the provisions to which the Employment Rights Act 1996 s 209(1)(a) (see head (1) in the text) does not apply (see note 2), nor to ss 1–7 (statements of employment particulars: see PARAS 119–123) or the provisions of ss 86–91 (termination of employment: see PARA 735 et seq) not specified in s 209(2) (see note 2): see s 209(3).
6   Employment Rights Act 1996 s 209(1)(b). The provision which may be made by virtue of head (2) in the text in relation to s 94 (see PARA 757) does not include provision for application subject to exceptions and modifications; but this does not prejudice s 209(1)(a) (see head (1) in the text): s 209(4). See also note 1.
    In exercise of the power conferred by head (2) in the text, the Secretary of State has made the Redundancy Payment (Continuity of Employment in Local Government etc) (Modification) Order 1999, SI 1999/2277 (amended by SI 2000/1042; SI 2001/866; SI 2002/532; SI 2004/1682; SI 2004/3168; SI 2005/2929; SI 2005/3226; SI 2007/3224; SI 2008/912; SI 2008/2250; SI 2008/2831; SI 2009/462; SI 2009/801; SI 2010/903; SI 2010/1172; SI 2010/1836; SI 2011/2581; SI 2012/641; SI 2012/666; SI 2012/2733; SI 2013/1465; SI 2013/1784) (see PARA 839 et seq). By virtue of the Employment Rights Act 1996 s 241, Sch 2 para 2(1) (see PARA 162), the following orders have effect as if made under ss 209(1)(b), 236(5): Redundancy Payments (National Health Service) (Modification) Order 1993, SI 1993/3167 (amended by SI 2000/694; SI 2002/2469; SI 2004/696; SI 2005/1622; SI 2005/2078;SI 2013/235) (see PARA 851 et seq); and the Employment Protection (Continuity of Employment of National Health Service Employees) (Modification) Order 1996, SI 1996/1023 (amended by SI 2000/694; SI 2002/2469; SI 2004/696; SI 2005/1622; SI 2011/2581; SI 2013/235) (see PARA 326 note 13).

7   Employment Rights Act 1996 s 209(1)(c). Head (3) in the text refers to provisions to which s 209(1)(c) applies: see s 209(1)(c). Accordingly, s 209(1)(c) applies to s 29(2) (repealed), s 65(2) (repealed), s 86(5) (repealed), s 92(3) (right to written statement of reasons for dismissal: see PARA 755), s 108(1) (disapplication of 94 to dismissal of employee unless he has been continuously employed for a period of not less than two years ending with the effective date of termination: see PARA 758), s 159 (redundancy (exclusion of public offices etc): see PARA 854), s 160(1) (redundancy (exclusion in respect of employment in any capacity under the government of an overseas territory): see PARA 854) and s 199(1), (2), (4), (5) (exclusion of mariners from certain protections: see PARA 167): s 209(5) (amended by the Employment Relations Act 1999 Sch 9; and SI 2006/1031).

       In exercise of the power conferred by head (3) in the text, the Secretary of State has made the Unfair Dismissal and Statement of Reasons for Dismissal (Variation of Qualifying Period) Order 2012, SI 2012/989 (amending) (see PARAS 755, 758).

8   Employment Rights Act 1996 s 209(8).

159. Power under the Employment Relations Act 1999 to confer rights on individuals. The Secretary of State[1] may by order[2] make provision which has the effect of conferring certain statutory rights[3] on individuals[4] who are of a specified description[5]. Such an order may: (1) provide that individuals are to be treated as parties to workers' contracts or contracts of employment[6]; (2) make provision as to who are to be regarded as the employers of individuals[7]; (3) make provision which has the effect of modifying the operation of any right as conferred on individuals by the order[8]; (4) include such consequential, incidental or supplementary provisions as the Secretary of State thinks fit[9].

1   As to the Secretary of State see PARA 5 note 21.
2   Such an order may make provision in such way as the Secretary of State thinks fit: Employment Relations Act 1999 s 23(5) (amended by the Employment Act 2002 s 41; and the Employment Relations Act 2004 ss 39(1), (2), 57(2), Sch 2). The ways in which an order under the Employment Relations Act 1999 s 23 may make provision include, in particular, amending any enactment, and excluding or applying (whether with or without amendment) any enactment: see s 23(5A) (s 23(5A), (5B) added by the Employment Relations Act 2004 s 39(1), (3)). For this purpose, 'enactment' includes an enactment comprised in subordinate legislation made under an Act: Employment Relations Act 1999 s 23(5B) (as so added). Any power to make an order under the Employment Relations Act 1999 must be made by statutory instrument (s 42(1)); but no such order may be made under s 23 unless a draft has been laid before, and approved by resolution of, each House of Parliament (s 42(2)). At the date at which this volume states the law, no such order had been made. The Employment Relations Act 1999 s 23 supersedes the Employment Rights Act 1996 s 209(7), which is repealed (see the Employment Relations Act 1999 ss 23(6), 44, Sch 9); and any order made or having effect as if made under that provision, and having effect immediately before 25 October 1999, has effect as if made under s 23 (see s 23(7)).
3   The Employment Relations Act 1999 s 23 applies to any right conferred on an individual against an employer, however defined, under or by virtue of the Trade Union and Labour Relations (Consolidation) Act 1992, the Employment Rights Act 1996, the Employment Act 2002, the Employment Relations Act 1999, or any instrument made under the European Communities Act 1972 s 2(2) (see CONSTITUTIONAL AND ADMINISTRATIVE LAW vol 20 (2014) PARA 156): see the Employment Relations Act 1999 s 23(1) (amended by the Employment Act 2002 s 53, Sch 7 para 54).
4   For these purposes, the reference to individuals includes a reference to individuals expressly excluded from exercising the right: see the Employment Relations Act 1999 s 23(3).
5   Employment Relations Act 1999 s 23(2).
6   Employment Relations Act 1999 s 23(4)(a).
7   Employment Relations Act 1999 s 23(4)(b).
8   Employment Relations Act 1999 s 23(4)(c).
9   Employment Relations Act 1999 s 23(4)(d).

160. Review of monetary limits. If, in relation to the following sums, that is to say:

    (1)   the limit on the amount[1] of a guarantee payment[2];

(2)   the minimum amount payable[3] as the basic award for unfair dismissal[4];

(3)   the limit of compensatory award[5] for unfair dismissal[6];

(4)   the maximum amount payable[7] on the insolvency of an employer[8];

(5)   the maximum amount[9] of a week's pay for calculating certain maximum amounts[10];

(6)   the amount of the award made[11] for unlawful inducements in relation to collective bargaining or to trade union membership or activities[12];

(7)   remedies[13] for breach of the right to membership of a trade union[14],

the retail prices index[15] for September of a year is higher or lower than the index for the previous September, the Secretary of State must make an order[16] in relation to each sum mentioned in heads (1) to (7) above, increasing each sum (if the new index is higher) or decreasing each sum (if the new index is lower), by the same percentage as the amount of the increase or decrease of the index, with effect from the following 6 April[17].

1   Ie the sum specified in the Employment Rights Act 1996 s 31(1) (see PARA 264): see the Employment Relations Act 1999 s 34(1)(a).
2   Employment Relations Act 1999 s 34(1)(a).
3   Ie the sum specified in the Employment Rights Act 1996 s 120(1) (see PARA 816) or in the Trade Union and Labour Relations (Consolidation) Act 1992 s 156(1) (see PARA 1057): see the Employment Relations Act 1999 s 34(1)(b), (f) (s 34(1)(ea) added, s 34(1)(f) substituted, by the Employment Relations Act 2004 s 57(1), Sch 1 para 42(1), (2)).
4   Employment Relations Act 1999 s 34(1)(b), (f) (s 34(1)(f) as substituted: see note 3).
5   Ie the sum specified in the Employment Rights Act 1996 s 124(1) (see PARA 823): see the Employment Relations Act 1999 s 34(1)(c). A reference in s 34 to a sum specified in the Employment Rights Act 1996 s 124(1) does not include anything specified by virtue of the Enterprise and Regulatory Reform Act 2013 s 15(2)(b)(ii) (specified number multiplied by a week's pay of the individual concerned: see PARA 823 note 6): Employment Relations Act 1999 s 34(4A) (s 34(4A), (4B) added by the Enterprise and Regulatory Reform Act 2013 s 15(10)). See note 17.
6   Employment Relations Act 1999 s 34(1)(c).
7   Ie the sum specified in the Employment Rights Act 1996 s 186(1)(a), (b) (see PARA 628): see the Employment Relations Act 1999 s 34(1)(d).
8   Employment Relations Act 1999 s 34(1)(d).
9   Ie the sum specified in the Employment Rights Act 1996 s 227(1) (see PARA 147): see the Employment Relations Act 1999 s 34(1)(e).
10 Employment Relations Act 1999 s 34(1)(e).
11 Ie the sum specified in the Trade Union and Labour Relations (Consolidation) Act 1992 s 145E(3) (see PARA 1055): see the Employment Relations Act 1999 s 34(1)(ea) (as added: see note 3).
12 Employment Relations Act 1999 s 34(1)(ea) (as added: see note 3).
13 Ie the sum specified in the Trade Union and Labour Relations (Consolidation) Act 1992 s 176(6A) (see PARA 1028 note 10): see the Employment Relations Act 1999 s 34(1)(g) (amended by the Employment Relations Act 2004 s 57(1), Sch 1 para 42(1), (3)).
14 Employment Relations Act 1999 s 34(1)(g) (as amended: see note 13).
15 For these purposes, 'retail prices index' means: (1) the general index of retail prices (for all items) published by the Statistics Board; or (2) where that index is not published for a month, any substituted index or figures published by the Board: see the Employment Relations Act 1999 s 34(5) (amended by the Statistics and Registration Service Act 2007 s 60(1), Sch 3 para 11). As to the Statistics Board see REGISTRATION CONCERNING THE INDIVIDUAL vol 88 (2012) PARA 353.
16 Such an order must be made by statutory instrument, must be laid before Parliament after being made, and may include transitional provision: see the Employment Relations Act 1999 s 34(6). In exercise of the power so conferred the Secretary of State has made the Employment Rights (Revision of Limits) Order 2014, SI 2014/382 (see PARAS 147 note 14, 264 note 4, 628 note 22, 816 note 5, 823 note 6, 1028 note 10, 1055 note 3, 1057 note 3), which came into force on 6 April 2014 (see art 1(1)). As to the Secretary of State see PARA 5 note 21.
17 Employment Relations Act 1999 s 34(2) (amended by the Enterprise and Regulatory Reform Act 2013 s 22(1), (2)). In making the calculation so required, the Secretary of State must round the result to the nearest whole pound, taking 50 pence as nearest to the next whole pound

above: Employment Relations Act 1999 s 34(3) (amended by the Enterprise and Regulatory Reform Act 2013 s 22(1), (3)). As regards a sum specified in the Employment Rights Act 1996 s 124(1) (see head (3) in the text), the duty under the Employment Relations Act 1999 s 34(2) to make an order with effect from 6 April in a particular year does not arise where an order varying such a sum with effect from a day within 12 months before that date has been made under the Enterprise and Regulatory Reform Act 2013 s 15(1) (see PARA 823 note 6): Employment Relations Act 1999 s 34(4B) (as added: see note 5).

161. Recoupment of benefits. The Secretary of State[1] may by regulations make, with respect to specified employment-related payments which are the subject of proceedings before employment tribunals[2], provision for any or all of the following purposes[3]:

(1) enabling the Secretary of State to recover from an employer, by way of total or partial recoupment of universal credit[4], jobseeker's allowance[5] or income support[6] (or income-related employment and support allowance)[7], a sum not exceeding the amount of the prescribed element of the monetary award[8] (or, in the case of a protective award, the amount of the remuneration)[9];

(2) requiring or authorising an employment tribunal to order payment of such a sum, by way of total or partial recoupment of universal credit, jobseeker's allowance, income support or income-related employment and support allowance, to the Secretary of State instead of to an employee[10]; and

(3) requiring an employment tribunal to order the payment to an employee of only the excess of the prescribed element of the monetary award over the amount of any universal credit, jobseeker's allowance, income support or income-related employment and support allowance shown to the tribunal to have been paid to the employee and enabling the Secretary of State to recover from the employer, by way of total or partial recoupment of the benefit, a sum not exceeding that amount[11].

Such regulations may:

(a) be framed so as to apply to all such payments or to one or more classes of those payments[12], and be framed so as to apply to all or any of the benefits mentioned in heads (1) to (3) above[13];

(b) confer powers and impose duties on employment tribunals or other persons[14];

(c) impose on an employer to whom a monetary award or protective award relates a duty to furnish particulars connected with the award, and a duty to suspend payments in pursuance of the award during any period prescribed by the regulations[15];

(d) provide for an employer who pays a sum to the Secretary of State in pursuance of the provisions described above to be relieved from any liability to pay the sum to another person[16];

(e) provide for the determination by the Secretary of State of any issue arising as to the total or partial recoupment, in pursuance of the regulations, of universal credit, a jobseeker's allowance, unemployment benefit, income support or income-related employment and support allowance[17];

(f) confer on an employee a right of appeal to the First-tier Tribunal[18] against any decision of the Secretary of State on any such issue[19];

(g) provide for the proof in proceedings before employment tribunals, whether by certificate or in any other manner, of any amount of universal credit, jobseeker's allowance, income support or income-related employment and support allowance paid to an employee[20];

(h) make different provision for different cases[21].

Where, in pursuance of any such regulations, a sum has been recovered by or paid to the Secretary of State by way of total or partial recoupment of universal credit, jobseeker's allowance, income support or income-related employment and support allowance, no sum is recoverable under the Social Security Administration Act 1992[22], and no abatement, payment or reduction is to be made by reference to the universal credit, jobseeker's allowance, income support or income-related employment and support allowance recouped[23].

Any amount found to have been duly recovered by or paid to the Secretary of State in pursuance of such regulations by way of total or partial recoupment of jobseeker's allowance must be paid into the National Insurance Fund[24].

1 As to the Secretary of State see PARA 5 note 21.

2 The Employment Tribunals Act 1996 s 16 applies to payments which are the subject of proceedings before employment tribunals (see s 16(1) (amended by the Employment Rights (Dispute Resolution) Act 1996 s 1(2)(b))), and which are:

(1) payments of wages or compensation for loss of wages (Employment Tribunals Act 1996 s 16(1)(a));

(2) payments by employers to employees under the Trade Union and Labour Relations (Consolidation) Act 1992 ss 146–151 (detriment on grounds related to trade union membership or activities: see PARA 1048 et seq), ss 168–173 (time off for carrying out trade union duties and for union learning representatives: see PARA 1065 et seq) or s 192 (protective award: see PARA 1190) (Employment Tribunals Act 1996 s 16(1)(b));

(3) payments by employers to employees under the Employment Rights Act 1996 Pt III (ss 28–35) (guarantee payments: see PARA 261 et seq), Pt V (ss 43M–49A) (protection from suffering detriment in employment: see PARA 612 et seq), Pt VI (ss 50–63C) (time off work: see PARA 326 et seq), Pt VII (ss 64–70A) (suspension from work: see PARA 596 et seq), s 93 (termination (complaint related to right to written statement of reasons for dismissal): see PARA 756) or Pt X (ss 94–134A) (unfair dismissal: see PARA 757 et seq) (Employment Tribunals Act 1996 s 16(1)(c) (s 16(1)(c) amended, s 16(1)(e) added, by SI 2010/493));

(4) payments by employers to employees of a nature similar to, or for a purpose corresponding to the purpose of, payments within heads (1), (2) above (Employment Tribunals Act 1996 s 16(1)(d));

(5) payments by employers to employees under the Employment Relations Act 1999 (Blacklists) Regulations 2010, SI 2010/493, regs 5, 6 or 9 (see PARAS 1038, 1040) (Employment Tribunals Act 1996 s 16(1)(e) (as so added)),

and payments of remuneration under a protective award under the Trade Union and Labour Relations (Consolidation) Act 1992 s 189 (see PARA 1189) (see the Employment Tribunals Act 1996 s 16(1) (as so amended). As to the meanings of 'employer' and 'employee' see PARA 2. As to employment tribunals see PARA 1399 et seq; and as to the procedure on a complaint made to an employment tribunal see PARA 1453 et seq.

3 Employment Tribunals Act 1996 s 16(2). The Secretary of State and the Lord Chancellor, acting jointly, may by order: (1) provide that ss 16, 17, if specified in the order, are not to apply to persons, or to employments, of such classes as may be prescribed in the order; or (2) provide that ss 16, 17 are to apply to persons or employments of such classes as may be prescribed in the order subject to such exceptions and modifications as may be so prescribed: see s 40(1), (2) (s 40(1) amended by the Tribunals, Courts and Enforcement Act 2007 Sch 8 paras 35, 38). No such order may be made unless a draft of the order has been laid before Parliament and approved by resolution of each House of Parliament: s 41(2). As to the making of orders under the Employment Rights Act 1996 generally see PARA 162. At the date at which this volume states the law, no such order had been made. As to the Lord Chancellor see CONSTITUTIONAL AND ADMINISTRATIVE LAW vol 20 (2014) PARAS 255–261.

4 As to universal credit see WELFARE BENEFITS AND STATE PENSIONS vol 104 (2014) PARA 124 et seq.

5 As to jobseeker's allowance see WELFARE BENEFITS AND STATE PENSIONS vol 104 (2014) PARA 419 et seq.

6   As to income support see WELFARE BENEFITS AND STATE PENSIONS vol 104 (2014) PARA 292 et seq. See note 10.

7   In the Employment Tribunals Act 1996 ss 16, 17, 'income-related employment and support allowance' means an income-related allowance (which has been partly abolished and, as from a day to be appointed, will be abolished fully) currently payable under the Welfare Reform Act 2007 Pt 1 (ss 1–29) (see WELFARE BENEFITS AND STATE PENSIONS vol 104 (2014) PARAS 252–261): see the Employment Tribunals Act 1996 s 17(5) (added by the Welfare Reform Act 2007 s 28(1), Sch 3 para 15(1), (4)).

8   For these purposes, 'monetary award' means the amount which is awarded, or ordered to be paid, to the employee by the tribunal or would be so awarded or ordered apart from any provision of regulations under Employment Tribunals Act 1996 s 16; and 'prescribed element', in relation to any monetary award, means so much of that award as is attributable to such matters as may be prescribed by regulations under the Employment Tribunals Act 1996 s 16: see s 17(3).

9   Employment Tribunals Act 1996 s 16(3)(a) (amended by the Welfare Reform Act 2007 Sch 3 para 15(1), (2)(a); and SI 2013/630). See also note 3. In exercise of the power so conferred the Secretary of State has made the Employment Protection (Recoupment of Benefits) Regulations 1996, SI 1996/2349: see PARAS 1190, 1478.
     As from a day to be appointed under the Welfare Reform Act 2009 ss 9, 61(3), (4), the Employment Tribunals Act 1996 s 16(3)(a) is further amended so that the reference to income support is repealed: see s 16(3)(a) (prospectively further amended by the Welfare Reform Act 2009 ss 9(3)(b), 58(1), Sch 7 Pt 1). However, at the date at which this volume states the law, no such day had been appointed.

10   Employment Tribunals Act 1996 s 16(3)(b) (amended by the Employment Rights (Dispute Resolution) Act 1998 s 1(2)(a); the Welfare Reform Act 2007 Sch 3 para 15(1), (2)(b); and SI 2013/630). See also note 3.
     As from a day to be appointed under the Welfare Reform Act 2009 ss 9, 61(3), (4), the Employment Tribunals Act 1996 s 16(3)(b) is further amended so that the reference to income support is repealed: see s 16(3)(b) (prospectively further amended by the Welfare Reform Act 2009 Sch 7 Pt 1). However, at the date at which this volume states the law, no such day had been appointed.

11   Employment Tribunals Act 1996 s 16(3)(c) (amended by the Employment Rights (Dispute Resolution) Act 1998 s 1(2)(a); the Welfare Reform Act 2007 Sch 3 para 15(1), (2)(a); and SI 2013/630). See also note 3.
     As from a day to be appointed under the Welfare Reform Act 2009 ss 9, 61(3), (4), the Employment Tribunals Act 1996 s 16(3)(c) is further amended so that the reference to income support is repealed: see s 16(3)(c) (prospectively further amended by the Welfare Reform Act 2009 Sch 7 Pt 1). However, at the date at which this volume states the law, no such day had been appointed.

12   Employment Tribunals Act 1996 s 16(4)(a). See also note 3.

13   Employment Tribunals Act 1996 s 16(4)(b) (substituted by the Welfare Reform Act 2007 Sch 3 para 15(1), (2)(c)). See also note 3.

14   Employment Tribunals Act 1996 s 16(5)(a) (amended by the Employment Rights (Dispute Resolution) Act 1998 s 1(2)(b); and the Social Security Act 1998 s 86(1), (2), Sch 7 para 147(a), Sch 8). See also note 3.

15   Employment Tribunals Act 1996 s 16(5)(b). See also note 3.

16   Employment Tribunals Act 1996 s 16(5)(c). See also note 3.

17   Employment Tribunals Act 1996 s 16(5)(cc) (added by the Social Security Act 1998 Sch 7 para 147(b); and amended by the Welfare Reform Act 2007 Sch 3 para 15(1), (2)(a); and SI 2013/630). See also note 3.

18   As to the First-tier Tribunal see COURTS AND TRIBUNALS vol 24 (2010) PARAS 876–882.

19   Employment Tribunals Act 1996 s 16(5)(d) (substituted by the Social Security Act 1998 Sch 7 para 147(b); and amended by SI 2008/2833). See also note 3.

20   Employment Tribunals Act 1996 s 16(5)(e) (amended by the Employment Rights (Dispute Resolution) Act 1998 s 1(2)(b); the Welfare Reform Act 2007 Sch 3 para 15(1), (2)(a); and SI 2013/630). See also note 3.
     As from a day to be appointed under the Welfare Reform Act 2009 ss 9, 61(3), (4), the Employment Tribunals Act 1996 s 16(5)(e) is further amended so that the reference to income support is repealed: see s 16(5)(e) (prospectively further amended by the Welfare Reform Act 2009 Sch 7 Pt 1). However, at the date at which this volume states the law, no such day had been appointed.

21   Employment Tribunals Act 1996 s 16(6). See also note 3.

22 Ie under the Social Security Administration Act 1992 Pt III (ss 71–80) or Pt V (ss 105–108) (see WELFARE BENEFITS AND STATE PENSIONS vol 104 (2014) PARA 527 et seq): see the Employment Tribunals Act 1996 s 17(1) (amended by the Welfare Reform Act 2007 Sch 3 para 15(1), (3); and SI 2013/630).

23 Employment Tribunals Act 1996 s 17(1) (as amended: see note 22). See also note 3.

As from a day to be appointed under the Welfare Reform Act 2009 ss 9, 61(3), (4), the Employment Tribunals Act 1996 s 17(1) is further amended so that the reference to income support is repealed: see s 17(1) (prospectively further amended by the Welfare Reform Act 2009 Sch 7 Pt 1). However, at the date at which this volume states the law, no such day had been appointed.

24 Employment Tribunals Act 1996 s 17(2). See also note 3. As to the National Insurance Fund see WELFARE BENEFITS AND STATE PENSIONS vol 104 (2014) PARA 15.

162. Orders, rules and regulations made under the Employment Rights Act 1996 or under the Employment Tribunals Act 1996. Any power conferred by any provision of the Employment Rights Act 1996 to make any order (other than an Order in Council) or to make regulations is exercisable by statutory instrument[1]. A statutory instrument made under any power conferred by that Act to make an Order in Council or other order or regulations is, with certain exceptions[2], subject to annulment in pursuance of a resolution of either House of Parliament[3].

Any power conferred by the Employment Tribunals Act 1996 on a Minister of the Crown to make an order, and any power conferred by that Act to make regulations or rules, is exercisable by statutory instrument[4].

Anything done or having effect as done (including the making of subordinate legislation) under or for the purposes of any provision repealed or revoked by the Employment Rights Act 1996 or, as the case may be, the Employment Tribunals Act 1996 has effect as if done under or for the purposes of any corresponding provision of the Employment Rights Act 1996 or, as the case may be, the Employment Tribunals Act 1996[5].

1 Employment Rights Act 1996 s 236(1). Any power so conferred which is exercisable by statutory instrument includes power to make such incidental, supplementary or transitional provisions as appear to the authority exercising the power to be necessary or expedient: s 236(5).

2 Ie except for:
    (1)   an Order in Council or other order or regulations to which s 236(3) applies (s 236(2)(a) (amended by the Employment Relations Act 1999 s 9, Sch 4 Pt III paras 5, 42(1), (2)));
    (2)   an order made under the Employment Rights Act 1996 s 35 (see PARA 266) or s 241, Sch 2 Pt II paras 16–18 (transitory provisions) (s 236(2)(b)); or
    (3)   an order made in accordance with s 208 (repealed) (s 236(2)(c)).
    As from a day to be appointed under the Employment Relations Act 1999 s 45(1), head (3) above is repealed by s 44, Sch 9. At the date at which this volume states the law, no such day had been appointed.
    No recommendation is to be made to Her Majesty to make an Order in Council under the Employment Rights Act 1996 s 192(3) (see PARA 163 note 5), and no order or regulations is or are to be made under s 43K(4) (see PARA 69 note 3), s 47C (see PARA 620), s 63D (see PARA 328), s 63F(7) (see PARA 328), s 71 (see PARA 355), s 72 (see PARA 355), s 73 (see PARA 355), s 75A (see PARA 377), s 75B (see PARA 377), s 76 (see PARA 390), s 80A (see PARA 368), s 80AA (repealed), s 80B (see PARA 369), s 80BB (repealed), s 80G (see PARA 109), s 99 (see PARA 784), s 120(2) (repealed), s 124(2) (repealed), s 125(7) (repealed) or s 205A(11), (12) (see PARA 154 note 6), or s 209 (see PARA 158), unless a draft of the Order in Council, order or regulations has been laid before Parliament and approved by a resolution of each House of Parliament: see s 236(3) (amended by the Employment Relations Act 1999 ss 9, 44, Sch 4 Pt III paras 5, 42, Sch 9; the Employment Act 2002 s 53, Sch 7 paras 24, 49; the Work and Families Act 2006 s 11(1), Sch 1 para 44; the Apprenticeships, Skills, Children and Learning Act 2009 s 40(5), Sch 1 paras 1, 11; the Enterprise and Regulatory Reform Act 2013 s 20(8); and the Growth and Infrastructure Act 2013 s 31(6)). The Employment Rights Act 1996 s 236(3) does not apply to an order under s 209(1)(b): see s 236(4); and PARA 158 note 1.

3   See the Employment Rights Act 1996 s 236(2).
4   Employment Tribunals Act 1996 s 41(1). Any power conferred by the Employment Tribunals
    Act 1996 which is exercisable by statutory instrument includes power to make such incidental,
    supplementary or transitional provision as appears to the minister exercising the power to be
    necessary or expedient: s 41(4). No recommendation is to be made to Her Majesty to make an
    Order in Council under s 38(4) (see PARA 163), and no order is to be made under s 3 (see PARA
    1407), s 4(4), (6D) (see PARAS 1403, 1404), s 12A(12) (see PARA 1477), s 28(5) (see PARA 1426),
    or s 40 (see PARAS 161 note 3, 1407 note 5), unless a draft of the Order in Council or order has
    been laid before Parliament and approved by a resolution of each House of Parliament: s 41(2)
    (amended by the Enterprise and Regulatory Reform Act 2013 ss 11(12), 12(1), (4), 16(2), Sch 3
    paras 2, 4(1)). A statutory instrument containing an order made by a Minister of the Crown
    under any other provision of the Employment Tribunals Act 1996, except s 44, Sch 2 Pt II
    paras 7–10 (transitory provisions), or containing regulations or rules made under the
    Employment Tribunals Act 1996, is subject to annulment in pursuance of a resolution of either
    House of Parliament: see s 41(3).
5   Employment Rights Act 1996 Sch 2 para 2(1); Employment Tribunals Act 1996 Sch 2 para 2.
    The Employment Rights Act 1996 Sch 2 para 2(1) does not apply to the making of any
    subordinate legislation, however, to the extent that it is reproduced in the Employment Rights
    Act 1996: Sch 2 para 2(2).
        The substitution of the Employment Rights Act 1996 or, as the case may be, the Employment
    Tribunals Act 1996 for the provisions repealed or revoked by the Employment Rights Act 1996
    or, as the case may be, the Employment Tribunals Act 1996 does not affect the continuity of the
    law: Employment Rights Act 1996 Sch 2 para 1; Employment Tribunals Act 1996 Sch 2 para 1.
        Any reference, express or implied, in the Employment Rights Act 1996 or, as the case may
    be, the Employment Tribunals Act 1996 or any other enactment, or in any instrument or
    document, to a provision of the Employment Rights Act 1996 or, as the case may be, the
    Employment Tribunals Act 1996 is, so far as the context permits, to be read as, according to the
    context, being or including in relation to times, circumstances and purposes before the
    commencement of the Employment Rights Act 1996 or, as the case may be, the Employment
    Tribunals Act 1996 a reference to the corresponding provision repealed or revoked by the
    Employment Rights Act 1996 or, as the case may be, the Employment Tribunals Act 1996:
    Employment Rights Act 1996 Sch 2 para 3; Employment Tribunals Act 1996 Sch 2 para 3.
        Any reference, express or implied, in any enactment, or in any instrument or document, to a
    provision repealed or revoked by the Employment Rights Act 1996 or, as the case may be, the
    Employment Tribunals Act 1996 is, so far as the context permits, to be read as, according to the
    context, being or including in relation to times, circumstances and purposes after the
    commencement of the Employment Rights Act 1996 or, as the case may be, the Employment
    Tribunals Act 1996 a reference to the corresponding provision of the Employment Rights
    Act 1996 or, as the case may be, the Employment Tribunals Act 1996: Employment Rights
    Act 1996 Sch 2 para 4(1); Employment Tribunals Act 1996 Sch 2 para 4(1). In particular, where
    a power conferred by an Act is expressed to be exercisable in relation to enactments contained in
    Acts passed before or in the same session as the Act conferring the power, the power is also
    exercisable in relation to provisions of the Employment Rights Act 1996 or, as the case may be,
    the Employment Tribunals Act 1996 which reproduce such enactments: Employment Rights
    Act 1996 Sch 2 para 4(2); Employment Tribunals Act 1996 Sch 2 para 4(2).
        The Employment Rights Act 1996 Sch 2 paras 1–4 or, as the case may be, the Employment
    Tribunals Act 1996 Sch 2 paras 1–4 have effect in place of the Interpretation Act 1978 s 17(2)
    (see STATUTES AND LEGISLATIVE PROCESS vol 96 (2012) PARA 702), but are without prejudice to
    any other provision of the Interpretation Act 1978: Employment Rights Act 1996 Sch 2 para 5;
    Employment Tribunals Act 1996 Sch 2 para 5.

(2) CROWN EMPLOYMENT; PARLIAMENTARY STAFF

163.   Application of employment protection legislation to Crown employment.   Certain provisions of the Employment Rights Act 1996 have effect[1] in relation to Crown employment[2] and to persons in Crown employment[3] as they have effect in relation to other employment and to other employees or workers[4]. At the date at which this volume states the law, those provisions do not have such effect in relation to service as a member of the naval, military or air forces of the Crown[5]; but they do have such effect in relation to employment by any reserve association[6].

For the purposes of the application of the provisions of the Employment Rights Act 1996[7] in relation to Crown employment[8]:

(1)   references to an employee or a worker are to be construed as references to a person in Crown employment[9];

(2)   references to a contract of employment[10], or a worker's contract, are to be construed as references to the terms of employment of a person in Crown employment[11];

(3)   references to dismissal, or to the termination of a worker's contract, are to be construed as references to the termination of Crown employment[12];

(4)   references to redundancy[13] are to be construed as references to the existence of such circumstances as are treated[14] as equivalent to redundancy in relation to Crown employment[15];

(5)   the reference to an employer's undertaking in the provisions governing unfair dismissal for jury service[16] must be construed as a reference to the national interest[17]; and

(6)   any other reference to an undertaking is to be construed (in relation to a Minister of the Crown) as a reference to his functions or, as the context may require, to the department of which he is in charge, and (in relation to a government department, officer or body) is to be construed as a reference to the functions of the department, officer or body or, as the context may require, to the department, officer or body[18].

The Employment Tribunals Act 1996 has effect in relation to Crown employment[19] and persons in Crown employment as it has effect in relation to other employment and other employees[20]. At the date at which this volume states the law, this application does not have such effect in relation to service as a member of the naval, military or air forces of the Crown[21]; but it does have such effect in relation to employment by any reserve association[22]. For the purposes of such application of the Employment Tribunals Act 1996 in relation to Crown employment: (i) references to an employee are to be construed as references to a person in Crown employment[23]; and (ii) references to a contract of employment are to be construed as references to the terms of employment of a person in Crown employment[24].

1   The provisions of the Employment Rights Act 1996 to which s 191 applies are:
    (1)   Pt I (ss 1–12) (employment particulars: see PARA 119 et seq), Pt II (ss 13–27) (protection of wages: see PARA 254 et seq) and Pt III (ss 28–35) (guarantee payments: see PARA 261 et seq) (s 191(2)(a));
    (2)   Pt IVA (ss 43A–43L) (protected disclosures: see PARAS 69, 70) (s 191(2)(aa) (added by the Public Interest Disclosure Act 1998 s 10));
    (3)   the Employment Rights Act 1996 Pt V (ss 43M–49A) (protection from suffering detriment in employment: see PARA 612 et seq), except s 45 (Sunday working for shop and betting workers: see PARA 615) (s 191(2)(b));
    (4)   Pt VI (ss 50–63C) (time off work: see PARA 326 et seq), Pt VII (ss 64–70A) (suspension from work: see PARA 596 et seq), Pt VIII (ss 71–80E) (family leave: see PARA 355 et seq), Pt VIIIA (ss 80F–80I) (flexible working: see PARAS 108–111) (s 191(2)(c) (substituted by the Employment Act 2002 s 53, Sch 7 paras 24, 41));
    (5)   in the Employment Rights Act 1996 Pt IX (ss 86–93) (termination of employment: see PARA 735 et seq), s 92 (right to written statement of reasons for dismissal: see PARA 755) and s 93 (complaint: see PARA 756) (s 191(2)(d));
    (6)   Pt X (ss 94–134A) (unfair dismissal: see PARA 757 et seq), except s 101 (shop and betting workers who refuse Sunday work: see PARA 787) (s 191(2)(e));
    (7)   Pt XIII (miscellaneous) (ss 191–209) (see also PARA 164 et seq), Pt XIV (ss 210–235) (interpretation: see PARAS 130 et seq, 861 et seq) and Pt XV (ss 236–245) (general and supplementary) (s 191(2)(f)).

The provision made by s 191(1) is subject to s 192 (armed forces: see the text and notes 5–6) and s 193 (national security: the Secret and Intelligence Services): see s 191(1). Accordingly, the provision made by Pt IVA and s 47B (protected disclosures: see PARA 619) does not apply in relation to employment for the purposes of the Security Service, the Secret Intelligence Service, or the Government Communications Headquarters: see s 193 (substituted by the Employment Relations Act 1999 s 41, Sch 8 para 1). As to the Security Service, the Secret Intelligence Service, and the Government Communications Headquarters, see CONSTITUTIONAL AND ADMINISTRATIVE LAW vol 20 (2014) PARAS 243–245.

2   For the purposes of the Employment Rights Act 1996, 'Crown employment' means employment under or for the purposes of a government department or any officer or body exercising on behalf of the Crown functions conferred by a statutory provision: see s 191(3). Except where the context otherwise requires, 'statutory provision' means a provision, whether of a general or a special nature, contained in, or in any document made or issued under any Act, whether of a general or special nature: see s 235(1).

3   Where the terms of employment of a person in Crown employment restrict his right to take part in:
(1)   certain political activities (Employment Rights Act 1996 s 191(5)(a)); or
(2)   activities which may conflict with his official functions (s 191(5)(b)),
nothing in s 50 (right to time off for public duties: see PARA 350) requires him to be allowed time off work for public duties connected with any such activities (see s 191(5)). As to persons in Crown employment generally see PARA 6.

4   Employment Rights Act 1996 s 191(1). As to the meanings of 'employee' and 'employment' see PARA 6. As to the meaning of 'worker' see PARA 6.

5   Employment Rights Act 1996 s 192(1)(a) (s 192 substituted by s 241, Sch 2 para 16(1)).
The substitution of s 192 by Sch 2 para 16(1) was to have effect until the relevant commencement date if the Trade Union Reform and Employment Rights Act 1993 s 31 did not come into force before the commencement of the Employment Rights Act 1996: see Sch 2 para 16(1). For these purposes, the reference to the relevant commencement date is a reference:
(1)   if an order was made before the commencement of the Employment Rights Act 1996 appointing a day after that commencement as the day on which the Trade Union Reform and Employment Rights Act 1993 s 31 was to come into force, to that day as so appointed (Employment Rights Act 1996 Sch 2 para 16(2)(a)); and
(2)   otherwise, to such day as the Secretary of State may appoint (Sch 2 para 16(2)(b)).
The Trade Union Reform and Employment Rights Act 1993 s 31 was not brought into force prior to the passing of the Employment Rights Act 1996, and in fact has been repealed (with effect from 22 August 1996: see s 243; Sch 3 Pt I). Thus s 192 has effect as substituted by Sch 2 para 16(1) until the Secretary of State provides otherwise, as from a day to be appointed. As from such a day, the provisions of s 191 apply to:
(a)   service as a member of the naval, military or air forces of the Crown (but subject to s 192(2)–(8)) (see s 192(1)(a) (not yet in force)); and
(b)   employment by an association established for the purposes of the Reserve Forces Act 1996 Pt XI (ss 110–119) (reserve associations: see ARMED FORCES vol 3 (2011) PARA 473) (see the Employment Rights Act 1996 s 192(1)(b) (not yet in force).
The provisions of the Employment Rights Act 1996 which have effect by virtue of s 191 in relation to service as a member of the naval, military or air forces of the Crown are:
(i)   Pt I (employment particulars: see PARA 119 et seq) (s 192(2)(a) (not yet in force));
(ii)   in Pt V (ss 43M–49A) (protection from suffering detriment in employment: see PARA 612 et seq), s 43M (jury service: see PARA 613), s 45A (working time cases: see PARA 616), s 47C (leave for family or domestic reasons: see PARA 620), s 47D (tax credits: see PARA 621) (and s 48 (detriment (enforcement): complaint to employment tribunal): see PARA 625) and s 49 (detriment (enforcement): remedies): see PARA 626), so far as relating to ss 43M, 45A, 47C, 47D) (s 192(2)(aa) (added by SI 1998/1833; and amended by the Tax Credits Act 2002 s 27, Sch 1 para 1(1), (5); and the Employment Relations Act 2004 s 57(1), Sch 1 para 35(a)) (not yet in force));
(iii)   in the Employment Rights Act 1996 Pt VI (ss 50–63C) (time off work: see PARA 326 et seq), s 55 (see PARA 333), s 56 (see PARA 333), s 57 (see PARA 334), s 57A (see PARA 347), s 57B (see PARA 348) (s 192(2)(b) (amended by the Employment Relations Act 1999 s 9, Sch 4 Pt III paras 5, 31(a), (b)) (not yet in force));
(iv)   the Employment Rights Act 1996 Pt VII (ss 64–70A) (suspension from work: see PARA 596 et seq), and Pt VIII (ss 71–80E) (family leave: see PARA 355 et seq) (s 192(2)(c) (not yet in force));

(v)   in Pt IX (ss 86–93) (termination of employment: see PARA 735 et seq), s 92 (right to written statement of reasons for dismissal: see PARA 755) and s 93 (complaint: see PARA 756) (s 192(2)(d) (not yet in force));

(vi)   Pt X (ss 94–134A) (unfair dismissal: see PARA 757 et seq), apart from s 98B(2), (3) (see PARA 785), ss 100–103 (see PARAS 786–788, 790–791), s 104C (see PARA 796), s 108(5) (qualifying period of employment: see PARA 758), and s 134 (see PARA 757) (s 192(2)(e) (amended by the Employment Act 2002 s 53, Sch 7 paras 24, 42; the Employment Relations Act 2004 Sch 1 para 35(b); and the Defence Reform Act 2014 s 48(1), (3)) (not yet in force));

(vii)   the Employment Rights Act 1996 Pt XIII (miscellaneous) (ss 191–209) (see also PARA 164 et seq), Pt XIV (ss 210–235) (interpretation: see PARAS 130 et seq, 861 et seq) and Pt XV (ss 236–245) (general and supplementary) (s 192(2)(f) (not yet in force)).

Her Majesty may by Order in Council amend s 192(2) by making additions to, or omissions from, the provisions for the time being therein specified; and may make any provision for the time being so specified apply to service as a member of the naval, military or air forces of the Crown subject to such exceptions and modifications as may be specified in the Order in Council; but no provision contained in Pt II (ss 13–27) (protection of wages: see PARA 254 et seq) may be added to the provisions for the time being specified in s 192(2): see s 192(3) (not yet in force). Modifications made by an Order in Council under s 192(3) may include provision precluding the making of a complaint or reference to any employment tribunal unless the person aggrieved has made a service complaint, and unless the Defence Council has made a determination with respect to the service complaint: see s 192(4) (amended by the Armed Forces Act 1996 s 26(1), (2); the Employment Rights (Dispute Resolution) Act 1998 s 1(2)(a); and the Armed Forces Act 2006 s 378(1), Sch 16 para 136(a)) (not yet in force). No provision, however, is to be made by virtue of the Employment Rights Act 1996 s 192(4) which has the effect of substituting a period longer than six months for any period specified as the normal period for a complaint or reference: s 192(7) (not yet in force). For these purposes, 'normal period for a complaint or reference', in relation to any matter within the jurisdiction of an employment tribunal, means the period specified in the relevant enactment as the period within which the complaint or reference must be made, disregarding any provision permitting an extension of that period at the discretion of the tribunal: see s 192(8) (amended by the Employment Rights (Dispute Resolution) Act 1998 s 1(2)(a)). Where modifications made by an Order in Council under the Employment Rights Act 1996 s 192(3) include provision such as is mentioned in s 192(4), the Order in Council must also include provision (see s 192(5) (substituted by the Armed Forces Act 1996 s 26(1), (3)) (not yet in force)):

(A)   enabling a complaint or reference to be made to an employment tribunal in such circumstances as may be specified in the Order in Council, notwithstanding that provision such as is mentioned in the Employment Rights Act 1996 s 192(4) would otherwise preclude the making of the complaint or reference (s 192(5)(a) (s 192(5) as so substituted; s 192(5)(a) amended by the Employment Rights (Dispute Resolution) Act 1998 s 1(2)(a)) (not yet in force)); and

(B)   where a complaint or reference is made to an employment tribunal by virtue of a provision such as is mentioned in head (A) above, enabling the service complaint procedures to continue after the complaint or reference is made (Employment Rights Act 1996 s 192(5)(b) (s 192(5) as so substituted; s 192(5)(b) amended by the Employment Rights (Dispute Resolution) Act 1998 s 1(2)(a); and the Armed Forces Act 2006 Sch 16 para 136(b)) (not yet in force)).

For the purposes of the Employment Rights Act 1996 s 192(4), (5), 'service complaint' means a complaint under the Armed Forces Act 2006 s 334 (see ARMED FORCES vol 3 (2011) PARA 754); and 'service complaint procedures' means the procedures prescribed by regulations under s 334: see the Employment Rights Act 1996 s 192(6A) (s 192(6) repealed, s 192(6A) added, by the Armed Forces Act 2006 Sch 16 para 136(c)) (not yet in force). As to the making of Orders in Council under the Employment Rights Act 1996 generally see PARA 162. As to employment tribunals see PARA 1399 et seq; and as to the procedure on a complaint made to an employment tribunal see PARA 1453 et seq. As to the Defence Council see ARMED FORCES vol 3 (2011) PARA 302.

The failure to bring into force the Employment Rights Act 1996 s 192 does not constitute an infringement of the right to a fair trial under the Convention for the Protection of Human Rights and Fundamental Freedoms (Rome, 25 March 1957; TS 1 (1973); Cmnd 5179), art 6(1) and the Human Rights Act 1998 (see RIGHTS AND FREEDOMS vol 88A (2013) PARAS 243, 269 et seq): *McQuade, Petitioner* 2004 SLT 182, OH (a person dismissed from the armed forces does not have a civil right capable of protection because members of armed forces have no substantive right not to be unfairly dismissed under domestic law).

6 Employment Rights Act 1996 s 192(1)(b) (as substituted: see note 5). The text refers to an association established for the purposes of the Reserve Forces Act 1996 Pt XI (ss 110–119) (reserve associations: see ARMED FORCES vol 3 (2011) PARA 473): see the Employment Rights Act 1996 s 192(1)(b) (as so substituted).

7 Ie in accordance with the Employment Rights Act 1996 s 191(1) (see the text and notes 1–4): see s 191(4).

8 See the Employment Rights Act 1996 s 191(4).

9 Employment Rights Act 1996 s 191(4)(a).

10 As to the meaning of 'contract of employment' see PARA 2.

11 Employment Rights Act 1996 s 191(4)(b).

12 Employment Rights Act 1996 s 191(4)(c).

13 As to the meaning of 'redundancy' see PARA 870.

14 Ie in accordance with any arrangements falling within the Employment Rights Act 1996 s 177(3) (payments equivalent to redundancy payment by way of compensation for loss of employment: see PARA 888) for the time being in force: see s 191(4)(d) (amended by the Employment Relations Act 2004 Sch 1 para 34(1), (2), Sch 2).

15 Employment Rights Act 1996 s 191(4)(d) (as amended : see note 14). The provisions made by s 159 (exclusion from right to redundancy payment in respect of employment in a public office: see PARA 854) and s 160 (exclusion from right to redundancy payment in respect of employment in any capacity under the government of an overseas territory: see PARA 854) are without prejudice to any exemption or immunity of the Crown: s 191(6).

16 Ie the Employment Rights Act 1996 s 98B(2)(a) (see PARA 785): see s 191(4)(da) (added by the Employment Relations Act 2004 Sch 1 para 34(1), (2)).

17 Employment Rights Act 1996 s 191(4)(da) (as added: see note 16).

18 See the Employment Rights Act 1996 s 191(4)(e) (amended by the Employment Relations Act 2004 Sch 1 para 34(1), (3)).

19 For the purposes of the Employment Tribunals Act 1996, 'Crown employment' means employment under or for the purposes of a government department or any officer or body exercising on behalf of the Crown functions conferred by a statutory provision: see s 38(2). For these purposes, 'statutory provision' means a provision, whether of a general or a special nature, contained in, or in any document made or issued under any Act, whether of a general or special nature: see s 42(1).

20 Employment Tribunals Act 1996 s 38(1).

21 Employment Tribunals Act 1996 s 38(4)(a) (s 38(4) substituted by s 44, Sch 2 para 9(1)).
    The substitution of s 38(4) by Sch 2 para 9(1) was to have effect until the relevant commencement date if the Trade Union Reform and Employment Rights Act 1993 s 31 did not come into force before the commencement of the Employment Tribunals Act 1996: see Sch 2 para 9(1). For these purposes, the reference to the relevant commencement date is a reference:

    (1)   if an order was made before the commencement of the Employment Tribunals Act 1996 appointing a day after that commencement as the day on which the Trade Union Reform and Employment Rights Act 1993 s 31 was to come into force, to that day as so appointed (Employment Tribunals Act 1996 Sch 2 para 9(2)(a)); and

    (2)   otherwise, to such day as the Secretary of State may appoint (Sch 2 para 9(2)(b)).

    The Trade Union Reform and Employment Rights Act 1993 s 31 was not brought into force prior to the passing of the Employment Tribunals Act 1996, and in fact has been repealed (with effect from 22 August 1996: see the Employment Rights Act 1996 s 243; Sch 3 Pt I). Thus the Employment Tribunals Act 1996, s 38(4) has effect as substituted by Sch 2 para 9(1) until the Secretary of State provides otherwise, as from a day to be appointed. As from such a day, the provisions of s 38(1) apply to:

    (a)   service as a member of the naval, military or air forces of the Crown (s 38(4)(a) (not yet in force)); and

    (b)   employment by an association established for the purposes of the Reserve Forces Act 1996 Pt XI (ss 110–119) (reserve associations: see ARMED FORCES vol 3 (2011) PARA 473) (Employment Tribunals Act 1996 s 38(4)(b) (not yet in force));

but Her Majesty may by Order in Council make any provision of the Employment Tribunals Act 1996 apply to service as a member of the naval, military or air forces of the Crown subject to such exceptions and modifications as may be specified in the Order in Council (see s 38(4) (not yet in force)). No recommendation is to be made to Her Majesty to make an Order in Council under s 38(4), however, unless a draft of the Order in Council or order has been laid before Parliament and approved by a resolution of each House of Parliament: see s 41(2); and PARA 162. At the date at which this volume states the law, no such Order in Council had been made.

22 Employment Tribunals Act 1996 s 38(4)(b) (as substituted: see note 21). The text refers to an association established for the purposes of the Reserve Forces Act 1996 Pt XI (ss 110–119) (reserve associations: see ARMED FORCES vol 3 (2011) PARA 473): see the Employment Tribunals Act 1996 s 38(4)(b) (as so substituted).
23 See the Employment Tribunals Act 1996 s 38(3)(a).
24 See the Employment Tribunals Act 1996 s 38(3)(b).

164. Application of employment protection legislation to House of Lords staff. Certain provisions of the Employment Rights Act 1996 have effect[1] in relation to employment[2] as a relevant member of House of Lords staff[3] as they have effect in relation to other employment[4]. For the purposes of the application of such provisions[5], in relation to a relevant member of the House of Lords staff, references to an undertaking are to be construed as references to the House of Lords[6], except that, for the purposes of the application of the provisions governing unfair dismissal for jury service[7], the reference to an employer's undertaking must be construed in relation to a relevant member of the House of Lords staff as a reference to the national interest or, if the case so requires, the interests of the House of Lords[8]. Nothing in any rule of law or the law or practice of Parliament prevents a relevant member of the House of Lords staff from bringing before the High Court or the County Court[9]: (1) a claim arising out of, or relating to, a contract of employment or any other contract connected with employment[10]; or (2) a claim in tort arising in connection with employment[11].

The Employment Tribunals Act 1996 has effect in relation to employment as a relevant member of the House of Lords staff[12] as it has effect in relation to other employment[13]. Nothing in any rule of law or the law or practice of Parliament prevents a relevant member of the House of Lords staff from bringing before an employment tribunal proceedings of any description which could be brought before such a tribunal by a person who is not a relevant member of the House of Lords staff[14].

1 The provisions of the Employment Rights Act 1996 to which s 194 applies are:
  (1) Pt I (ss 1–12) (employment particulars: see PARA 119 et seq) (s 194(2)(a));
  (2) Pt III (ss 28–35) (guarantee payments: see PARA 261 et seq) (s 194(2)(b));
  (3) in Pt V (ss 43M–49A) (protection from suffering detriment in employment: see PARA 612 et seq), s 43M (jury service: see PARA 613), s 44 (health and safety cases: see PARA 614), s 45A (working time cases: see PARA 616), s 47 (employee representatives: see PARA 1208), s 47C (leave for family or domestic reasons: see PARA 620), s 47D (tax credits: see PARA 621), s 47E (flexible working: see PARA 622) (and s 48 (detriment (enforcement: complaint to employment tribunal): see PARA 625) and s 49 (detriment (enforcement: remedies): see PARA 626), so far as relating to ss 43M, 44, 45A, 47, 47C, 47D, 47E) (s 194(2)(c) (amended by the Employment Relations Act 1999 s 9, Sch 4 Pt III paras 5, 32; the Employment Act 2002 s 53, Sch 7 paras 24, 43(a); the Employment Relations Act 2004 ss 41(7), 57(1), Sch 1 para 36(1), (2); and SI 1998/1833));
  (4) the Employment Rights Act 1996 Pt VI (ss 50–63C) (time off work: see PARA 326 et seq), apart from ss 58–60 (occupational pension scheme trustees: see PARAS 352–353) (s 194(2)(d));
  (5) Pt VIA (ss 63D–63K) (study and training: see PARA 328), Pt VII (ss 64–70A) (suspension from work: see PARA 596 et seq), Pt VIII (ss 71–80E) (family leave: see PARA 355 et seq), and Pt VIIIA (ss 80F–80I) (flexible working: see PARAS 108–111) (s 194(2)(e) (substituted by the Employment Act 2002 Sch 7 paras 24, 43(b); and amended by the Apprenticeships, Skills, Children and Learning Act 2009 s 40(1), (5), Sch 1 paras 1, 5));
  (6) in the Employment Rights Act 1996 Pt IX (ss 86–93) (termination of employment: see PARA 735 et seq), s 92 (right to written statement of reasons for dismissal: see PARA 755) and s 93 (complaint: see PARA 756) (s 194(2)(f));
  (7) Pt X (ss 94–134A) (unfair dismissal: see PARA 757 et seq), apart from s 101 (shop and

betting workers who refuse Sunday work: see PARA 787) and s 102 (occupational pension scheme trustees: see PARA 790) (s 194(2)(g));

(8)   Pt XIII (miscellaneous) (ss 191–209) (see also PARAS 163, 165 et seq), Pt XIV (ss 210–235) (interpretation: see PARAS 130 et seq, 861 et seq) and Pt XV (ss 236–245) (general and supplementary) (s 194(2)(h)).

As from a day to be appointed under the Education and Skills Act 2008 s 173(4), a reference to the Employment Rights Act 1996 s 47AA (participation in education or training: see PARA 618) is added to head (3) above: see s 194(2)(c) (as so amended; prospectively further amended by the Education and Skills Act 2008 s 39(1), (5)). At the date at which this volume states the law, no such day had been appointed.

2   As to the meaning of 'employment' see PARA 2.

3   For these purposes, 'relevant member of the House of Lords staff' means any person who is employed under a contract of employment with the Corporate Officer of the House of Lords: see the Employment Rights Act 1996 s 194(6). As to the Corporate Officer of the House of Lords see PARLIAMENT vol 78 (2010) PARA 990 et seq. As to the meaning of 'contract of employment' see PARA 2.

4   Employment Rights Act 1996 s 194(1). Where the terms of employment of a relevant member of the House of Lords staff restrict his right to take part in:
(1)   certain political activities (s 194(5)(a)); or
(2)   activities which may conflict with his official functions (s 194(5)(b)),
nothing in s 50 (right to time off for public duties: see PARA 350) requires him to be allowed time off work for public duties connected with any such activities (see s 194(5)).
      For the purposes of the application of the provisions of the Employment Rights Act 1996 to which s 194 applies, or the application of a claim within s 194(4) (see the text and note 9), in relation to a person continuously employed in or for the purposes of the House of Lords up to the time when he became so employed under a contract of employment with the Corporate Officer of the House of Lords, his employment is not to be treated as having been terminated by reason only of a change in his employer before or at that time: see s 194(7). As to the meaning of 'employer' see PARA 2.

5   Ie the application of the other provisions of the Employment Rights Act 1996 to which s 194 applies: see s 194(3) (s 194(2A) added, s 194(3) amended, by the Employment Relations Act 2004 Sch 1 para 36(1), (3), (4)).

6   See the Employment Rights Act 1996 s 194(3) (as amended: see note 5).

7   Ie the Employment Rights Act 1996 s 98B(2)(a) (see PARA 785): see s 194(2A) (as added: see note 5).

8   See the Employment Rights Act 1996 s 194(2A) (as added: see note 5).

9   See the Employment Rights Act 1996 s 194(4) (amended by the Crime and Courts Act 2013 s 17(5), Sch 9 Pt 3 para 52(1)(b), (2)).

10   Employment Rights Act 1996 s 194(4)(a).

11   Employment Rights Act 1996 s 194(4)(b).

12   For the purposes of the Employment Tribunals Act 1996, 'relevant member of the House of Lords staff' means any person who is employed under a contract of employment with the Corporate Officer of the House of Lords: see s 39(4).

13   See the Employment Tribunals Act 1996 s 39(1).

14   See the Employment Tribunals Act 1996 s 39(2) (amended by the Employment Rights (Dispute Resolution) Act 1998 s 1(2)(a)). As to employment tribunals see PARA 1399 et seq; and as to the procedure on a complaint made to an employment tribunal see PARA 1453 et seq.

165.   Application of employment protection legislation to House of Commons staff.   Certain provisions of the Employment Rights Act 1996 have effect[1] in relation to employment[2] as a relevant member of the House of Commons staff[3] as they have effect in relation to other employment[4]; and, accordingly, for the purposes of the application of those provisions in relation to a relevant member of the House of Commons staff[5]:

(1)   references to an employee[6] are to be construed as references to a relevant member of the House of Commons staff[7];

(2)   references to a contract of employment[8] are to be construed as including a reference to the terms of employment of a relevant member of the House of Commons staff[9];

(3) references to dismissal are to be construed as including a reference to the termination of the employment of a relevant member of the House of Commons staff[10];

(4) references to an undertaking[11] are to be construed as a reference to the House of Commons[12].

For the purposes of the application of the provisions relating to unfair dismissal for jury service[13], the reference to an employer's undertaking must be construed in relation to a relevant member of the House of Commons staff as a reference to the national interest or, if the case so requires, the interests of the House of Commons[14].

Nothing in any rule of law or the law or practice of Parliament prevents a relevant member of the House of Commons staff from bringing before the High Court or the County Court[15]:

(a) a claim arising out of, or relating to, a contract of employment or any other contract connected with employment[16]; or

(b) a claim in tort arising in connection with employment[17].

Where any proceedings are so brought against the House of Commons Commission, against the Speaker[18] or against any designated person[19], the person against whom the proceedings are brought may apply to the court or employment tribunal concerned to have some other person against whom the proceedings could at the time of the application be properly brought substituted for him as a party to those proceedings[20].

The Employment Tribunals Act 1996 has effect in relation to employment as a relevant member of the House of Commons staff[21] as it has effect in relation to other employment[22]. For the purposes of the application of the Employment Tribunals Act 1996 in relation to a relevant member of the House of Commons staff: (i) references to an employee are to be construed as references to a relevant member of the House of Commons staff[23]; and (ii) references to a contract of employment are to be construed as including references to the terms of employment of a relevant member of the House of Commons staff[24]. Nothing in any rule of law or the law or practice of Parliament prevents a relevant member of the House of Commons staff from bringing before an employment tribunal proceedings of any description which could be brought before such a tribunal by a person who is not a relevant member of the House of Commons staff[25].

1 The provisions of the Employment Rights Act 1996 to which s 195 applies are:
  (1) Pt I (ss 1–12) (employment particulars: see PARA 119 et seq) (s 195(2)(a));
  (2) Pt III (ss 28–35) (guarantee payments: see PARA 261 et seq) (s 195(2)(b));
  (3) in Pt V (ss 43M–49A) (protection from suffering detriment in employment: see PARA 612 et seq), s 43M (jury service: see PARA 613), s 44 (health and safety cases: see PARA 614), s 45A (working time cases: see PARA 616), s 47 (employee representatives: see PARA 1208), s 47C (leave for family or domestic reasons: see PARA 620), s 47D (tax credits: see PARA 621), s 47E (flexible working: see PARA 622) (and s 48 (detriment (enforcement: complaint to employment tribunal): see PARA 625) and s 49 (detriment (enforcement: remedies): see PARA 626), so far as relating to ss 43M, 44, 45A, 47, 47C, 47D, 47E) (s 195(2)(c) (amended by the Employment Relations Act 1999 s 9, Sch 4 Pt III paras 5, 33; the Employment Act 2002 s 53, Sch 7 paras 24, 43(a); the Employment Relations Act 2004 ss 41(7), 57(1), Sch 1 para 37(1), (2); and SI 1998/1833));
  (4) the Employment Rights Act 1996 Pt VI (ss 50–63C) (time off work: see PARA 326 et seq), apart from ss 58–60 (occupational pension scheme trustees: see PARAS 352–353) (s 195(2)(d));
  (5) Pt VIA (ss 63D–63K) (study and training: see PARA 328), Pt VII (ss 64–70A) (suspension from work: see PARA 596 et seq), Pt VIII (ss 71–80E) (family leave: see PARA 355 et seq), and Pt VIIIA (ss 80F–80I) (flexible working: see PARAS 108–111)

(s 195(2)(e) (substituted by the Employment Act 2002 Sch 7 paras 24, 43(b); and amended by the Apprenticeships, Skills, Children and Learning Act 2009 s 40(1), (5), Sch 1 paras 1, 6));

(6)   in the Employment Rights Act 1996 Pt IX (ss 86–93) (termination of employment: see PARA 735 et seq), s 92 (right to written statement of reasons for dismissal: see PARA 755) and s 93 (complaint: see PARA 756) (s 195(2)(f));

(7)   Pt X (ss 94–134A) (unfair dismissal: see PARA 757 et seq), apart from s 101 (shop and betting workers who refuse Sunday work: see PARA 787) and s 102 (occupational pension scheme trustees: see PARA 790) (s 195(2)(g));

(8)   Pt XIII (miscellaneous) (ss 191–209) (see also PARAS 163, 164, 166 et seq), Pt XIV (ss 210–235) (interpretation: see PARAS 130–135, 861–863) and Pt XV (ss 236–245) (general and supplementary) (s 195(2)(h)).

As from a day to be appointed under the Education and Skills Act 2008 s 173(4), a reference to the Employment Rights Act 1996 s 47AA (participation in education or training: see PARA 618) is added to head (3) above: see s 195(2)(c) (as so amended; prospectively further amended by the Education and Skills Act 2008 s 39(1), (6)). At the date at which this volume states the law, no such day had been appointed.

2   As to the meaning of 'employment' see PARA 2.

3   For these purposes, 'relevant member of the House of Commons staff' means any person:

(1)   who was appointed by the House of Commons Commission (the 'Commission') or is employed in the refreshment department (Employment Rights Act 1996 s 195(5)(a)); and

(2)   who is a member of the Speaker's personal staff (s 195(5)(b)).

The House of Commons Commission is a statutory body established by the House of Commons (Administration) Act 1978 and is responsible for the administration and services of the House of Commons, employing staff who are not civil servants but whose complimenting, grading and pay are kept broadly in line with those in the Home Civil Service: see PARLIAMENT vol 78 (2010) PARA 946. As to whether House of Commons staff have a contractual right to annual pay increases until they reach the top of the pay scale for their respective pay bands, in circumstances where the Cabinet Office had advised that, in the Civil Service, progression payments would be payable to staff where there was a contractual entitlement to them (but not otherwise), see *Thorne v House Of Commons Commission* [2014] EWHC 93 (QB), [2014] IRLR 260 (words used in the letters of appointment, staff handbook and collectively negotiated pay agreements, meant that House of Commons staff had not had a contractual right to annual pay increases).

If the House of Commons resolves at any time that any provision of the Employment Rights Act 1996 s 195(5)–(8) (see also notes 18–20) should be amended in its application to any member of the staff of that House, Her Majesty may by Order in Council amend that provision accordingly: s 195(12). As to the making of Orders in Council under the Employment Rights Act 1996 generally see PARA 162. At the date at which this volume states the law, no such Order in Council had been made.

4   Employment Rights Act 1996 s 195(1).

5   See the Employment Rights Act 1996 s 195(3).

6   As to the meaning of 'employee' see PARA 2.

7   Employment Rights Act 1996 s 195(3)(a).

8   As to the meaning of 'contract of employment' see PARA 2.

9   Employment Rights Act 1996 s 195(3)(b).

10   Employment Rights Act 1996 s 195(3)(c).

11   Ie other than in the Employment Rights Act 1996 s 98B (unfair dismissal for jury service: see PARA 785): see s 195(3)(d) (s 195(2A) added, s 195(3)(d) amended, by the Employment Relations Act 2004 Sch 1 para 37(1), (3), (4)).

12   Employment Rights Act 1996 s 195(3)(d) (as amended: see note 11).

13   Ie for the purposes of the application of the Employment Rights Act 1996 s 98B(2)(a) (unfair dismissal for jury service: see PARA 785): see s 195(2A) (as added: see note 11).

14   Employment Rights Act 1996 s 195(2A) (as added: see note 11).

15   See the Employment Rights Act 1996 s 195(4) (amended by the Crime and Courts Act 2013 s 17(5), Sch 9 Pt 3 para 52(1)(b), (2)).

16   Employment Rights Act 1996 s 195(4)(a).

17   Employment Rights Act 1996 s 195(4)(b).

18   Subject to the Employment Rights Act 1996 s 195(7), for the purposes of:

(1)   the provisions of the Employment Rights Act 1996 to which s 195 applies (see note 1) (s 195(6)(a));

(2)   Pt XI (ss 135–181) (redundancy payments: see PARA 835 et seq), where applicable to relevant members of the House of Commons (s 195(6)(b)); and

(3)   a claim within s 195(4) (see heads (a), (b) in the text) (s 195(6)(c)),
the House of Commons Commission is the employer of staff appointed by the Commission and
the Speaker is the employer of his personal staff and of any person employed in the refreshment
department and not appointed by the Commission (see s 195(6)). Where the House of
Commons Commission or the Speaker designates a person to be treated for all or any of the
purposes mentioned in s 195(6) as the employer of any description of staff (other than the
Speaker's personal staff) the person so designated is to be treated for those purposes as their
employer: s 195(7).

For the purposes mentioned in s 195(6), a person's employment in or for the purposes of the
House of Commons is not (provided that he continues to be employed in such employment) to
be treated as terminated by reason only of a change in his employer, and (provided that he so
continues) his first appointment to such employment is deemed after the change to have been
made by his employer for the time being: see s 195(9). In accordance with s 195(9):

(a)   an employee is to be treated for the purposes mentioned in s 195(6) as being
continuously employed by his employer for the time being from the commencement of
his employment until its termination (s 195(10)(a)); and

(b)   anything done by or in relation to his employer for the time being in respect of his
employment before the change is to be so treated as having been done by or in relation
to the person who is his employer for the time being after the change (s 195(10)(b)).

For these purposes, 'employer for the time being', in relation to a person who has ceased to be
employed in or for the purposes of the House of Commons, means the person who was his
employer immediately before he ceased to be so employed, except that, where some other person
would have been his employer for the time being if he had not ceased to be so employed, it
means that other person: see s 195(11).

19 Ie any person designated under the Employment Rights Act 1996 s 195(7) (see note 18): see
s 195(8) (amended by the Employment Rights (Dispute Resolution) Act 1998 s 1(2)(a)).

20 Employment Rights Act 1996 s 195(8) (as amended: see note 19).

21 For the purposes of the Employment Tribunals Act 1996, 'relevant member of the House of
Commons staff' has the same meaning as in the Employment Rights Act 1996 s 195 (see note 3):
see the Employment Tribunals Act 1996 s 39(5). Subject to an Order in Council under the
Employment Rights Act 1996 s 195(12) (see note 3): (1) the provisions of s 195(6), (7) (see note
18) have effect for determining who is the employer of a relevant member of the House of
Commons staff for the purposes of the Employment Tribunals Act 1996 (see s 39(5)(a)); and (2)
the Employment Rights Act 1996 s 195(8) (see the text and notes 19–20) applies in relation to
proceedings brought by virtue of the Employment Tribunals Act 1996 s 39 (see s 39(5)(b)).

22 See the Employment Tribunals Act 1996 s 39(1).

23 Employment Tribunals Act 1996 s 39(3)(a).

24 Employment Tribunals Act 1996 s 39(3)(b).

25 See the Employment Tribunals Act 1996 s 39(2) (amended by the Employment Rights (Dispute
Resolution) Act 1998 s 1(2)(a)).

(3) EXCLUDED CLASSES OF EMPLOYMENT

166.   Employment outside Great Britain. The Employment Rights Act 1996,
as originally enacted, did not give jurisdiction to many of its provisions where
the employee's contract of employment required him ordinarily to work outside
Great Britain, nor did the 1996 Act apply its provisions relating to employment
particulars or termination of employment in relation to employment during any
period when the employee was engaged in work wholly or mainly outside Great
Britain unless: (1) the employee ordinarily worked in Great Britain and the work
outside Great Britain was for the same employer; or (2) the law which governed
his contract of employment was the law of England and Wales or the law of
Scotland[1]. That exclusion, however, was repealed by the Employment Relations
Act 1999[2], partly in reaction to perceived unfairness to those seconded to work
in Great Britain but remaining based abroad[3], and partly in order to comply with
the relevant European Directive[4]. The absence of the statutory test previously
found in the Employment Rights Act 1996 does not prevent an employee who
sometimes works outside the United Kingdom from claiming unfair dismissal,

however, but, for the tribunal to exercise jurisdiction, he must establish the necessary link with the United Kingdom (for instance, where his absences from the United Kingdom are short, or by demonstrating that he falls within one of the recognised categories of worker: (a) peripatetic workers based in Great Britain; (b) certain expatriate workers posted abroad by a British employer for the purpose of a business carried on in Great Britain; or (c) certain workers operating in what is in effect an extra-territorial British 'enclave' in a foreign country)[5].

1   See the Employment Rights Act 1996 s 196(1)–(7) (repealed by the Employment Relations Act 1999 ss 32(3), 44, Sch 9). As to the meanings of 'contract of employment', 'employee', 'employer' and 'employment' see PARA 2. As to the meanings of 'England' and 'Wales' and 'Great Britain' see PARA 2 note 12. As to the governing law in contract generally see CONFLICT OF LAWS vol 19 (2011) PARA 628 et seq.

2   See note 1. When the repeal was enacted, it was thought that the question of application of statutory rights under the Employment Rights Act 1996 could be left to the normal rules of private international law. The advice given by the Department of Trade and Industry (now the Department for Business, Enterprise and Regulatory Reform) was that the matter would be covered by the Convention on Jurisdiction and Enforcement of Judgments in Civil and Commercial Matters (Brussels, 27 September 1968; EC 46 (1976); Cmnd 7395) (the 'Brussels Convention') (see CONFLICT OF LAWS vol 19 (2011) PARA 366) and the Convention on the Law applicable to Contractual Obligations (Rome, 19 June 1980; Cmnd 8489) (the 'Rome Convention') (see CONFLICT OF LAWS vol 19 (2011) PARA 628 et seq) but those Conventions deal primarily with contracts (including employment contracts), whereas statutory employment rights, such as unfair dismissal, operate on a separate legislative basis and are arguably not governed by conflict rules relating to contracts. See eg *Lawson v Serco Ltd* [2004] EWCA Civ 12 at [19], [2004] 2 All ER 200 at [19], [2004] ICR 204 at [19] per Pill LJ (on the question whether it is only to an employment in Great Britain that the right to claim for unfair dismissal attaches, the Rome Convention is not material) but see note 5 where overall the case was reversed on further appeal. Moreover, there is authority that there is no contractual right to be implied that an employee will not be unfairly dismissed: *Focsa Services (UK) Ltd v Birkett* [1996] IRLR 325, EAT.

    If these rules do not deal with the matter, the position is that the Employment Rights Act 1996 now has no jurisdiction provision. If it is true that the conflict of laws rules do not apply, and there is now no jurisdiction provision in the Employment Rights Act 1996, then arguably it becomes a matter of statutory interpretation as to the jurisdictional application of the Employment Rights Act 1996 (see STATUTES AND LEGISLATIVE PROCESS vol 96 (2012) PARA 1078 et seq). The application of the rule in *Pepper (Inspector of Taxes) v Hart* [1993] AC 593, [1993] ICR 291, HL (see STATUTES AND LEGISLATIVE PROCESS vol 96 (2012) PARA 1122), permitting Parliamentary debates to be considered, is of limited assistance since the repeal effected by the Employment Relations Act 1999 s 32(3) was incorporated into the Employment Relations Act 1999 only at a late stage in reaction to a more limited amendment originally proposed (in order to deal with the point in *Carver (née Mascarenhas) v Saudi Arabian Airlines* [1999] 3 All ER 61, [1999] ICR 991, CA): see 602 HL Official Report (5th series) cols 384–385. Lord Simon of Highbury, introducing the repeal, merely said that, for domestic employment protection laws to apply in the future, 'there must be some proper connection with the United Kingdom first, and in such cases it is right that United Kingdom law should apply': see 603 HL Official Report (5th series) cols 1089–1090. Cf the discrimination legislation that preceded the Equality Act 2010, which was subject to a more limited reform, retaining the jurisdiction provisions in modified form; the Equality Act 2010 now makes no specific provision, in relation to its provisions that concern discrimination at work, for territorial application but leaves it to tribunals to determine whether the law applies, depending eg on the connection between the employment relationship and Great Britain: see the Equality Act 2010 Explanatory Notes paras 14, 15; and DISCRIMINATION vol 33 (2013) PARA 7.

3   Ie as demonstrated by the decision in *Carver (née Mascarenhas) v Saudi Arabian Airlines* [1999] 3 All ER 61, [1999] ICR 991, CA (contract of employment provided for employee to be based at any location to which the airline operates in or out of the Saudi Kingdom and for her to be transferred from one location to another).

4   Ie Council Directive (EC) 96/71 of 16 December 1996 (OJ L18, 21.1.97, p 1) concerning the posting of workers in the framework of the provision of services, with which the Employment Rights Act 1996 s 196 (repealed) was inconsistent.

Statutory rights based on EU directives have to be given wide territorial jurisdiction in order to enhance those rights: *Bleuse v MBT Transport Ltd* [2008] ICR 488, [2008] IRLR 264, EAT; and see *Ministry of Defence v Wallis* [2011] EWCA Civ 231, [2011] ICR 617, [2011] All ER (D) 97 (Mar) (principle of direct effect did not allow a domestic statute to be framed, eg in terms of territorial restrictions, so as to defeat a claim to a directly effective right; to suggest that the rights of employees, eg wives of British service personnel posted to NATO organisations abroad, had to be enforced elsewhere infringed the fundamental principle of EU law that there should be an effective remedy for a breach of any EU right, and it was not an effective remedy to require that remedy to be pursued in Belgium). See also Case C-346/06 *Ruffert v Land Niedersachsen* [2008] All ER (EC) 902, [2008] IRLR 467, ECJ (payment of non-domestic workers in accordance with terms of collective agreement).

5   See *Lawson v Serco Ltd, Botham v Ministry of Defence, Crofts v Veta Ltd* [2006] UKHL 3, [2006] 1 All ER 823, [2006] IRLR 289; and PARA 757 note 4.

167.   Mariners.   The statutory provisions relating to:

(1)   written statements of terms and conditions of employment[1];

(2)   deductions from wages[2]; and

(3)   rights to minimum notice and rights during notice[3],

do not apply to a person employed as a seaman in a ship registered in the United Kingdom[4] under a crew agreement[5] the provisions and form of which are of a kind approved by the Secretary of State[6].

Certain provisions of the employment protection legislation[7] do not apply to employment[8] as master, or as a member of the crew, of a fishing vessel where the employee[9] is remunerated only by a share in the profits or gross earnings of the vessel[10]; nor do certain provisions[11] of the employment protection legislation apply to employment as a merchant seaman[12]. Other provisions[13] are, however, applied to employment on board a registered ship[14] if, and only if:

(a)   the ship's entry in the register specifies a port in Great Britain[15] as the port to which the vessel is to be treated as belonging[16];

(b)   under his contract of employment[17] the person employed does not work wholly outside Great Britain[18]; and

(c)   the person employed is ordinarily resident in Great Britain[19].

1   Ie the Employment Rights Act 1996 ss 1–7 (see PARA 119 et seq): see s 199(1).
2   Ie the Employment Rights Act 1996 Pt II (ss 13–27) (protection of wages: see PARA 254 et seq): see s 199(1).
3   Ie the Employment Rights Act 1996 ss 86–91 (see PARA 735 et seq): see s 199(1).
4   See note 14. As to the meaning of 'United Kingdom' see PARA 2 note 12.
5   As to crew agreements see SHIPPING AND MARITIME LAW vol 93 (2008) PARA 450 et seq.
6   Employment Rights Act 1996 s 199(1). As to the Secretary of State see PARA 5 note 21.
7   Ie the Employment Rights Act 1996 ss 8–10 (right to itemised pay statement: see PARA 124), Pt III (ss 28–35) (guarantee payments: see PARA 261 et seq), s 44 (health and safety cases: see PARA 614), s 45 (detriment (Sunday working for shop and betting workers): see PARA 615), s 47 (employee representative: see PARA 1208), s 47C (leave for family or domestic reasons: see PARA 620), s 47E (flexible working: see PARA 622), s 47F (study and training: see PARA 623), ss 50–57B (time off work: see PARA 326 et seq), ss 61–63 (employee representatives: see PARA 1209), Pt VIA (ss 63D–63K) (study and training: see PARA 328), Pt VII (ss 64–70A) (suspension from work: see PARA 596 et seq), Pt VIII (ss 71–80E) (family leave: see PARA 355 et seq), and Pt VIIIA (ss 80F–80I) (flexible working: see PARAS 108–111), s 92 (right to written statement of reasons for dismissal: see PARA 755), s 93 (complaint: see PARA 756), Pt X (ss 94–134A) (unfair dismissal: see PARA 757 et seq), Pt XI (ss 135–181) (redundancy payments: see PARA 835 et seq), and Pt XII (ss 182–190) (insolvency of employers: see PARAS 628–631): see s 199(2) (amended by the Employment Relations Act 1999 ss 9, 44, Sch 4 Pt III paras 5, 34(a), (b), Sch 9; the Employment Act 2002 s 53, Sch 7 paras 24, 44(1), (2)(a), (b); the Employment Relations Act 2004 s 41(8); and the Apprenticeships, Skills, Children and Learning Act 2009 s 40(1), (5), Sch 1 paras 1, 7(a), (b)).
8   As to the meaning of 'employment' see PARA 2.
9   As to the meaning of 'employee' see PARA 2.

10 Employment Rights Act 1996 s 199(2) (as amended: see note 7). On the true construction of s 199(2), the singular cannot be read as including the plural in the words 'the vessel'; and, therefore, the application of s 199(2) is restricted to those members of a crew who are remunerated only by a share in the profits or gross earnings of the vessel on which they were employed: *Goodeve v Gilsons (a firm)* [1985] ICR 401, CA.

11 Ie the Employment Rights Act 1996 ss 8–10 (right to itemised pay statement: see PARA 124), ss 50–54 (time off work: see PARAS 326, 327, 350, 351) and Pt XII (ss 182–190) (insolvency of employers: see PARAS 628–631): see s 199(4).

12 Employment Rights Act 1996 s 199(4). For these purposes, 'employment as a merchant seaman':
    (1) does not include employment in the fishing industry or employment on board a ship otherwise than by the owner, manager or charterer of that ship except employment as a radio officer (s 199(5)(a)); but
    (2) subject to that, includes employment: (a) as a master or a member of the crew of any ship (s 199(5)(b)(i)); (b) as a trainee undergoing training for the sea service (s 199(5)(b)(ii)); and (c) in or about a ship in port by the owner, manager or charterer of the ship to do work of the kind ordinarily done by a merchant seaman on a ship while it is in port (s 199(5)(b)(iii)).

13 Ie the provisions mentioned in the Employment Rights Act 1996 s 199(8): see s 199(7) (s 199(7), (8) added by the Employment Relations Act 1999 s 32(4)). Accordingly, the provisions are:
    (1) the Employment Rights Act 1996 ss 8–10 (right to itemised pay statement: see PARA 124) (s 199(8)(a) (as so added));
    (2) Pt II (protection of wages: see PARA 254 et seq), Pt III (guarantee payments: see PARA 261 et seq), and Pt V (ss 43M–49A) (protection from suffering detriment in employment: see PARA 612 et seq) (s 199(8)(b) (as so added));
    (3) Pt VI (ss 50–63C) (time off work: see PARA 326 et seq), apart from ss 58–60 (occupational pension scheme trustees: see PARAS 352–353) (s 199(8)(c) (as so added));
    (4) Pt VIA (ss 63D–63K) (study and training: see PARA 328), Pt VII (ss 64–70A) (suspension from work: see PARA 596 et seq), Pt VIII (ss 71–80E) (family leave: see PARA 355 et seq), and Pt VIIIA (ss 80F–80I) (flexible working: see PARAS 108–111) (s 199(8)(d) (s 199(8) as so added; s 199(8)(d) substituted by the Employment Act 2002 Sch 7 paras 24, 44(1), (3); and amended by the Apprenticeships, Skills, Children and Learning Act 2009 Sch 1 paras 1, 7(c)));
    (5) the Employment Rights Act 1996 s 92 (right to written statement of reasons for dismissal: see PARA 755) and s 93 (complaint: see PARA 756) (s 199(8)(e) (as so added)); and
    (6) Pt X (ss 94–134A) (unfair dismissal: see PARA 757 et seq) (s 199(8)(f) (as so added)).

14 Ie a ship registered in the register maintained under the Merchant Shipping Act 1995 s 8: see SHIPPING AND MARITIME LAW vol 93 (2008) PARA 254. It would not be the natural reading of the Employment Rights Act 1996 s 199(7) to say that it was intended to deal exhaustively with the position of all persons employed on ships, and it would not be inconsistent with the principle of comity if the jurisdiction of the English courts were to extend to regulating the social affairs of those who work on board vessels with a foreign flag: *Diggins v Condor Marine Crewing Services Ltd* [2009] EWCA Civ 1133, [2010] ICR 213, [2010] IRLR 119, EAT (the issue would be what link with the United Kingdom ought to be established in order to justify a tribunal in Great Britain exercising unfair dismissal jurisdiction; tribunal had jurisdiction to hear claim of a peripatetic employee whose base was Great Britain at the time he was dismissed, he had no connection with Guernsey where company was based and even less with Bahamas where ship was registered). See also *Lawson v Serco Ltd, Botham v Ministry of Defence, Crofts v Veta Ltd* [2006] UKHL 3, [2006] 1 All ER 823, [2006] IRLR 289; and PARAS 166, 757.

15 As to the meaning of 'Great Britain' see PARA 2 note 12.

16 Employment Rights Act 1996 s 199(7)(a) (as added: see note 13).
    The predecessor of the Employment Rights Act 1996 s 199(7), ie the Employment Protection (Consolidation) Act 1978 s 141(5) (repealed), was held not to apply where a seaman was employed under a contract which required him to work on non-British, as well as British, ships: *Royle v Globtik Management Ltd* [1977] ICR 552, EAT.

17 As to the meaning of 'contract of employment' see PARA 2.

18 Employment Rights Act 1996 s 199(7)(b) (as added: see note 13). See *Wood v Cunard Line Ltd* [1991] ICR 13, [1990] IRLR 281, CA (person working on a British ship which never entered United Kingdom waters held to be working wholly outside Great Britain, even though himself

British, paid in sterling (with tax and national insurance contributions deducted) and travelling back to the United Kingdom for holidays). As to the meaning of 'British ship' see SHIPPING AND MARITIME LAW vol 93 (2008) PARA 230.

19 Employment Rights Act 1996 s 199(7)(c) (as added: see note 13). As to ordinary residence see IMMIGRATION AND ASYLUM vol 57 (2012) PARA 140; CONFLICT OF LAWS vol 19 (2011) PARA 359.

168. Police officers. Certain provisions of the employment protection legislation[1] do not apply to employment[2] under a contract of employment[3] in police service[4], or to persons engaged in such employment[5].

1 Ie the Employment Rights Act 1996 ss 8–10 (right to itemised pay statement: see PARA 124), Pt III (ss 28–35) (guarantee payments: see PARA 261 et seq), s 43M (jury service: see PARA 613), s 45 (detriment (Sunday working for shop and betting workers): see PARA 615), s 45A (working time cases: see PARA 616), s 47 (employee representatives: see PARA 1208), s 47C (leave for family or domestic reasons: see PARA 620), ss 50–57B (time off work: see PARA 326 et seq), ss 61–63 (time off work (employee representatives): see PARA 1209), Pt VII (ss 64–70A) (suspension from work: see PARA 596 et seq), Pt VIII (ss 71–80E) (family leave: see PARA 355 et seq), s 92 (right to written statement of reasons for dismissal: see PARA 755) and s 93 (complaint: see PARA 756), and Pt X (ss 94–134A) (unfair dismissal: see PARA 757 et seq) (except s 100 (health and safety cases: see PARA 786), s 103A (protected disclosure: see PARA 792) and s 134A (police: see PARA 786) and the other provisions of Pt X so far as relating to the right not to be unfairly dismissed in a case where the dismissal is unfair by virtue of s 100 or s 103A): see s 200(1) (amended by the Police (Health and Safety) Act 1997 s 6(2); the Public Interest Disclosure Act 1998 ss 13(a), (b), 18(2); the Employment Relations Act 1999 ss 9, 44, Sch 4 Pt III paras 5, 35(a)–(d), Sch 9; the Police Reform Act 2002 ss 37(2), 107(2), Sch 8; the Employment Relations Act 2004 s 57(1), Sch 1 para 38; and SI 1998/1833).

2 As to the meaning of 'employment' see PARA 2.

3 As to the meaning of 'contract of employment' see PARA 2.

4 For these purposes, 'police service' means:
   (1) service as a member of a constabulary maintained by virtue of an enactment (Employment Rights Act 1996 s 200(2)(a)); or
   (2) subject to the Criminal Justice and Public Order Act 1994 s 126 (prison staff not to be regarded as in police service: see PRISONS AND PRISONERS vol 85 (2012) PARA 423), service in any other capacity by virtue of which a person has the powers or privileges of a constable (Employment Rights Act 1996 s 200(2)(b)).
   The transport police who make up the British Transport Police Force are a constabulary maintained by virtue of an enactment as defined by head (1) above and are thus employed under a contract of employment in police service and so cannot claim unfair dismissal: *Spence v British Railways Board* [2001] ICR 232, [2000] All ER (D) 1956, EAT. See also *Redbridge London Borough Council v Dhinsa* [2014] EWCA Civ 178, [2014] ICR 834, sub nom *McKinnon v London Borough of Redbridge* [2014] All ER (D) 10 (Mar) (Redbridge Parks Police Service was a constabulary analogous to other constabularies (apart from the police) and constituted a 'constabulary maintained by virtue of an enactment' within head (1) above, which operated to deny the claimant sergeant any remedy for unfair dismissal).

5 Employment Rights Act 1996 s 200(1) (as amended: see note 1). A police cadet does not come within this exclusion, but is not an employee and thus cannot claim unfair dismissal in any event: *Wiltshire Police Authority v Wynn* [1981] QB 95, [1980] ICR 649, CA. The statutory exclusion used to apply to prison officers, even if the officer was dismissed for misconduct at a time when he was not exercising those powers or privileges: see *Home Office v Robinson and the Prison Officers' Association* [1982] ICR 31, [1981] IRLR 524, EAT. This was an important factor in permitting a disciplined prison officer to seek judicial review: *R v Secretary of State for the Home Department, ex p Benwell* [1984] ICR 723, [1985] IRLR 6; cf *McClaren v Home Office* [1990] ICR 824, [1990] IRLR 338, CA; and see PARA 827.

(4) ENTITLEMENT TO THE NATIONAL MINIMUM WAGE

(i) Introduction

169. Basic scope of the National Minimum Wage Act 1998. Workers who qualify for the national minimum wage[1] must be remunerated by their employers at a rate which is not less than the national minimum wage[2]. Certain categories of workers are, however, excluded from the right to be paid at such a rate[3].

Workers have a right not to be subjected to any detriment for taking, or proposing to take, any action to enforce or otherwise secure the benefit of their statutory right to be paid at a rate which is not less than the national minimum wage[4], that right being enforceable by application to an employment tribunal[5]; and the dismissal of a worker on account of any such action constitutes unfair dismissal[6].

There must be paid out of money provided by Parliament: (1) any expenditure incurred under the National Minimum Wage Act 1998 by a Minister of the Crown or government department[7] or by a body performing functions on behalf of the Crown[8]; and (2) any increase attributable to the provisions of the National Minimum Wage Act 1998 in the sums payable out of such money under any other Act[9].

1   As to persons who qualify for the national minimum wage see PARA 177 et seq. As to the meaning of 'worker' for these purposes see PARA 171.
2   See the National Minimum Wage Act 1998 s 1(1); and PARA 176. As to the meaning of 'employer' for these purposes see PARA 170 note 4.
       As to the rate, and the method of calculation, of the national minimum wage see PARA 199 et seq. As to offences under the National Minimum Wage Act 1998 see PARA 251 et seq.
3   See PARA 186 et seq.
4   See the National Minimum Wage Act 1998 s 23; and PARA 249.
5   See the National Minimum Wage Act 1998 s 24; and PARA 249.
6   See the Employment Rights Act 1996 s 104A; and PARA 794.
7   For the purposes of head (1) in the text, 'government department' does not include a Northern Ireland department: see the National Minimum Wages Act 1998 s 55(1).
8   National Minimum Wages Act 1998 s 52(a).
9   National Minimum Wages Act 1998 s 52(b).

170.   Meaning of 'employee' etc for the purposes of national minimum wage provisions.   For the purposes of the National Minimum Wage Act 1998, 'employee' means an individual who has entered into or works[1] under (or, where the employment has ceased, worked under) a contract of employment[2]. In relation to an employee or a worker[3], 'employer' means the person by whom the employee or worker is (or, where the employment has ceased, was) employed[4]. Where: (1) the immediate employer of a worker is himself in the employment of some other person[5]; and (2) the worker is employed on the premises of that other person[6], that other person is deemed, for the purposes of the National Minimum Wage Act 1998, to be the employer of the worker jointly with the immediate employer[7].

For the purposes of the National Minimum Wage Act 1998, 'employment' means: (a) in relation to an employee, employment under a contract of employment[8]; and (b) in relation to a worker, employment under his contract[9]; and 'employed' is to be construed accordingly[10].

1   As to the meaning of 'work' for these purposes see PARA 172.
2   National Minimum Wage Act 1998 s 54(1). For these purposes, 'contract of employment' means a contract of service or apprenticeship, whether express or implied, and, if it is express, whether oral or in writing: s 54(2). As to the meaning of 'contract of service' see PARA 1 note 1; and as to the meaning of 'writing' see PARA 2 note 8. As to the meanings of 'employee', 'contract of employment' and related expressions in relation to employment rights generally see PARA 2 et seq. As to the position of apprentices and youth trainees at common law see PARAS 112, 128–129, 636, 747–754. As to the statutory law on apprenticeships see EDUCATION vol 35 (2011) PARA 682 et seq. A contract of pupillage is not one of apprenticeship for the purposes of the National Minimum Wage Act 1998: *Edmonds v Lawson* [2000] QB 501, [2000] ICR 567, CA.

3   As to the meaning of 'worker' for these purposes see PARA 171.
4   National Minimum Wage Act 1998 s 54(4). Under s 54(4) the notion of 'person' and, therefore,
    'employer' includes a partnership: see 591 HL Official Report (5th series) col 80.
        For the purposes of the National Minimum Wage Regulations 1999, SI 1999/584, 'employer'
    has the meaning given to it by the National Minimum Wage Act 1998 s 54(4): see the National
    Minimum Wage Regulations 1999, SI 1999/584, reg 2(1). However, in relation to a 'worker'
    (ie as defined in the National Minimum Wage Act 1998 s 54(3): see PARA 171), 'employer'
    includes, in addition, except in the National Minimum Wage Regulations 1999, SI 1999/584,
    reg 12(6) (see PARA 194): (1) an agent or principal in relation to whom, by virtue of the National
    Minimum Wage Act 1998 s 34(2) (see PARA 178), the provisions of the National Minimum
    Wage Act 1998 have effect as if there were a worker's contract between him and an agency
    worker for the doing of work by the agency worker; and (2) an employer of a home worker who
    is a worker by virtue of s 35 (see PARA 179): see the National Minimum Wage Regulations 1999,
    SI 1999/584, reg 2(1). As to the meaning of 'employer' and related expressions in relation to
    employment rights generally see PARA 2 et seq. As to the fundamental legal position of the
    agency worker at common law see PARAS 11, 95; and as to special regulations made for the
    purposes of guaranteeing equal treatment of agency workers see PARA 96 et seq.
5   National Minimum Wage Act 1998 s 48(a).
6   National Minimum Wage Act 1998 s 48(b).
7   See the National Minimum Wage Act 1998 s 48.
8   National Minimum Wage Act 1998 s 54(5)(a).
9   National Minimum Wage Act 1998 s 54(5)(b).
10 See the National Minimum Wage Act 1998 s 54(5). As to the meaning of 'employment',
    'employed' and related expressions in relation to employment rights generally see PARA 2 et seq.

171.   Meaning of 'worker' for the purposes of national minimum wage provisions.   For the purposes of the National Minimum Wage Act 1998, 'worker' (except in the phrases 'agency worker'[1] and 'home worker'[2]) means an individual who has entered into or works[3] under (or, where the employment[4] has ceased, worked under)[5]:

(1)   a contract of employment[6]; or

(2)   any other contract, whether express or implied and, if it is express, whether oral or in writing[7], whereby the individual undertakes to do or perform personally any work or services for another party to the contract whose status is not by virtue of the contract that of a client or customer of any profession or business undertaking carried on by the individual[8];

and any reference to a worker's contract is to be construed accordingly[9].

1   As to the meaning of 'agency worker' see PARA 178.
2   As to the meaning of 'home worker' (which applies a modified definition of the term 'worker'
    given in the National Minimum Wage Act 1998 s 54(3)) see PARA 179.
3   As to the meaning of 'work' for these purposes see PARA 172.
4   As to the meaning of 'employment' for these purposes see PARA 170.
5   See the National Minimum Wage Act 1998 s 54(3).
6   National Minimum Wage Act 1998 s 54(3)(a). As to the meaning of 'contract of employment'
    for these purposes see PARA 170 note 2.
7   As to the meaning of 'writing' see PARA 2 note 8.
8   National Minimum Wage Act 1998 s 54(3)(b).
9   See the National Minimum Wage Act 1998 s 54(3). The following are not workers within the
    meaning of the National Minimum Wage Act 1998: (1) a pupil barrister (*Edmonds v Lawson*
    [2000] QB 501, [2000] ICR 567, CA (payment of the national minimum wage is not required
    during pupillage)); (2) a sub-postmaster (*Wolstenholme v Post Office Ltd* [2003] ICR 546, sub
    nom *IRC v Post Office Ltd* [2003] IRLR 199, EAT). As to guidance on the matters to be
    considered in determining 'worker' status see *James v Redcats (Brands) Ltd* [2007] ICR 1006,
    [2007] IRLR 296, EAT (which related to a self-employed parcel courier). As to special categories
    of worker who do qualify under the national minimum wage provisions see PARA 177 et seq;
    and as to categories of worker who do not so qualify see PARA 186 et seq.
        For the purposes of the National Minimum Wage Regulations 1999, SI 1999/584, 'worker'
    has the same meaning as in the National Minimum Wage Act 1998 s 54(3): see the National

Minimum Wage Regulations 1999, SI 1999/584, reg 2(1). However, except in reg 12(5) (see PARA 194) and reg 12(6) (see PARA 194), 'worker' includes in addition: (a) an agency worker in relation to whom, by virtue of the National Minimum Wage Act 1998 s 34(2) (see PARA 178), the provisions of the National Minimum Wage Act 1998 have effect as if there were a worker's contract for the doing of his work between him and an agent or principal; and (b) a home worker who is a worker by virtue of s 35 (see PARA 179): see the National Minimum Wage Regulations 1999, SI 1999/584, reg 2(1) (definition of 'worker' amended by SI 2010/1901). See also the definition of 'worker' used for purpose of the Working Time Regulations 1998, SI 1998/1833, reg 2(1) (cited in PARA 271), around which important case law has developed. As to use of the term 'worker' in employment law generally see PARA 5.

172.   Meaning of 'work' for the purposes of national minimum wage provisions. For the purposes of the National Minimum Wage Act 1998, any reference to doing work includes a reference to performing services; and 'work' and other related expressions are to be construed accordingly[1].

For the purposes of the National Minimum Wage Regulations 1999[2], 'work' does not include work (of whatever description) relating to the employer's[3] family household done by a worker where the conditions in head (1) or head (2) below are satisfied[4]:

(1)   the conditions to be satisfied under this head are:
    (a)   that the worker[5] resides in the family home of the employer for whom he works[6];
    (b)   that the worker is not a member of that family, but is treated as such, in particular as regards to the provision of accommodation and meals and the sharing of tasks and leisure activities[7];
    (c)   that the worker is neither liable to any deduction, nor to make any payment to the employer, or any other person, in respect of the provision of the living accommodation or meals[8]; and
    (d)   that, had the work been done by a member of the employer's family, it would not be treated as being performed under a worker's contract or as being work because the conditions in head (2) below would be satisfied[9];

(2)   the conditions to be satisfied under this head are:
    (a)   that the worker is a member of the employer's family[10];
    (b)   that the worker resides in the family home of the employer[11];
    (c)   that the worker shares in the tasks and activities of the family[12],
and that the work is done in that context[13].

For the purposes of the National Minimum Wage Regulations 1999, 'work' does not include work (of whatever description) relating to an employer's family business, done by a worker who satisfies the following conditions[14]:

(i)   that the worker is a member of the employer's family[15];
(ii)   that the worker resides in the family home of the employer[16];
(iii)   that the worker participates in the running of the family business[17],
and that the work is done in that context[18].

1   See the National Minimum Wage Act 1998 s 55(3).
2   Ie for the purposes of the National Minimum Wage Regulations 1999, SI 1999/584 (see also PARAS 170 note 4, 171 note 9, 193 et seq).
3   As to the meaning of 'employer' for these purposes see PARA 170 note 4.
4   See the National Minimum Wage Regulations 1999, SI 1999/584, reg 2(2). For the purposes of reg 2(2), the worker's place within the family must be considered holistically, with due consideration given to the fact that all families are different in terms of their approaches to performing household tasks and taking meals: *Nambalat v Taher, Udin v Chamsi-Pasha* [2012] EWCA Civ 1249, [2013] ICR 1024, [2012] IRLR 1004 (foreign nationals employed as live-in domestic help not performing qualifying work).

5 As to the meaning of 'worker' for these purposes see PARA 171.
6 National Minimum Wage Regulations 1999, SI 1999/584, reg 2(2)(a)(i).
7 National Minimum Wage Regulations 1999, SI 1999/584, reg 2(2)(a)(ii).
8 National Minimum Wage Regulations 1999, SI 1999/584, reg 2(2)(a)(iii).
9 National Minimum Wage Regulations 1999, SI 1999/584, reg 2(2)(a)(iv).
10 National Minimum Wage Regulations 1999, SI 1999/584, reg 2(2)(b)(i).
11 National Minimum Wage Regulations 1999, SI 1999/584, reg 2(2)(b)(ii).
12 National Minimum Wage Regulations 1999, SI 1999/584, reg 2(2)(b)(iii).
13 See the National Minimum Wage Regulations 1999, SI 1999/584, reg 2(2)(b).
14 See the National Minimum Wage Regulations 1999, SI 1999/584, reg 2(3).
15 National Minimum Wage Regulations 1999, SI 1999/584, reg 2(4)(i).
16 National Minimum Wage Regulations 1999, SI 1999/584, reg 2(4)(ii).
17 National Minimum Wage Regulations 1999, SI 1999/584, reg 2(4)(iii).
18 See the National Minimum Wage Regulations 1999, SI 1999/584, reg 2(4).

173. Restrictions on contracting out of the National Minimum Wage Act 1998. Any provision in any agreement, whether a worker's contract[1] or not, is void in so far as it purports[2]:

(1) to exclude or limit the operation of any provision of the National Minimum Wage Act 1998[3]; or

(2) to preclude a person from bringing proceedings under the National Minimum Wage Act 1998 before an employment tribunal[4].

The restriction set out in heads (1) and (2) above does not, however, apply to:

(a) any agreement to refrain from instituting or continuing proceedings where a conciliation officer has taken action[5] under the Employment Tribunals Act 1996[6];

(b) any agreement to refrain from instituting or continuing before an employment tribunal any proceedings arising under the National Minimum Wage Act 1998 that fall within the jurisdiction of the Employment Tribunals Act 1996[7] where conciliation is available[8], if the conditions regulating settlement agreements under the National Minimum Wage Act 1998 are satisfied in relation to the agreement[9].

For the purposes of head (b) above, the conditions regulating settlement agreements under the National Minimum Wage Act 1998 are that[10]:

(i) the agreement is in writing[11];

(ii) the agreement relates to the particular proceedings[12];

(iii) the employee[13] or worker[14] has received advice from a relevant independent adviser[15] as to the terms and effect of the proposed agreement and, in particular, its effect on his ability to pursue his rights before an employment tribunal[16];

(iv) there is in force, when the adviser gives the advice, a contract of insurance, or an indemnity provided for members of a profession or a professional body, covering the risk of a claim by the employee or worker in respect of loss arising in consequence of the advice[17];

(v) the agreement identifies the adviser[18]; and

(vi) the agreement states that the conditions regulating settlement agreements under the National Minimum Wage Act 1998 are satisfied[19].

1 As to the meaning of references to a worker's contract see PARA 171.
2 See the National Minimum Wage Act 1998 s 49(1).
3 National Minimum Wage Act 1998 s 49(1)(a).
4 National Minimum Wage Act 1998 s 49(1)(b). Any reference in the National Minimum Wage Act 1998 to an employment tribunal must, in relation to Northern Ireland, be construed as a

reference to an industrial tribunal: see s 55(6). As to proceedings brought under the National Minimum Wage Act 1998 before an employment tribunal see PARAS 228, 242 et seq.

5　Ie under any of the Employment Tribunals Act 1996 ss 18A–18C (requirement to contact ACAS before instituting proceedings: see PARAS 152, 153): see the National Minimum Wage Act 1998 s 49(2)(a) (amended by the Enterprise and Regulatory Reform Act 2013 s 7(2), Sch 1 para 11). As to conciliation officers see PARA 1214. As to 'taking action' under equivalent provisions of the Employment Rights Act 1996 see PARA 150 note 16.

6　See the National Minimum Wage Act 1998 s 49(2)(a) (as amended: see note 5).

7　Ie any proceedings within the Employment Tribunals Act 1996 s 18(1)(c) (arising out of the National Minimum Wage Act 1998 s 11 (see PARA 228), s 19D(1)(a) (see PARA 246) or s 24 (see PARA 249): see PARA 152 note 1): see the National Minimum Wage Act 1998 s 49(3)(a) (amended by SI 2014/431).

8　See the National Minimum Wage Act 1998 s 49(3)(a) (as amended: see note 7).

9　See the National Minimum Wage Act 1998 s 49(3) (s 49(3), (4), (4)(f) amended by the Enterprise and Regulatory Reform Act 2013 s 23(3)(a)). Settlement agreements were formerly known as compromise agreements (ie before 29 July 2013: see the Enterprise and Regulatory Reform Act 2013 s 23 (renaming of 'compromise agreements', 'compromise contracts' and 'compromises'); and the Enterprise and Regulatory Reform Act 2013 (Commencement No 2) Order 2013, SI 2013/1648, art 2(c)). In the application of the National Minimum Wage Act 1998 s 49 in relation to Northern Ireland, however, the terminology of 'compromise agreements' is retained and other modifications have effect: see s 49(8A), (9)–(11) (s 49(8A) added by the Enterprise and Regulatory Reform Act 2013 s 23(3)(b)).

10　See the National Minimum Wage Act 1998 s 49(4) (as amended: see note 9).

11　National Minimum Wage Act 1998 s 49(4)(a). As to the meaning of 'writing' see PARA 2 note 8.

12　National Minimum Wage Act 1998 s 49(4)(b).

13　As to the meaning of 'employee' for these purposes see PARA 170.

14　As to the meaning of 'worker' for these purposes see PARA 171.

15　For these purposes, a person is a relevant independent adviser (see the National Minimum Wage Act 1998 s 49(5)):

(1)　if he is a qualified lawyer (s 49(5)(a));

(2)　if he is an officer, official, employee or member of an independent trade union who has been certified in writing by the trade union as competent to give advice and as authorised to do so on behalf of the trade union (s 49(5)(b));

(3)　if he works at an advice centre, whether as an employee or a volunteer, and has been certified in writing by the centre as competent to give advice and as authorised to do so on behalf of the centre (s 49(5)(c)); or

(4)　if he is a person of a description specified in an order made by the Secretary of State (s 49(5)(d)).

For the purposes of head (1) above, 'qualified lawyer' means, as respects England and Wales, a person who, for the purposes of the Legal Services Act 2007, is an authorised person in relation to an activity which constitutes the exercise of a right of audience or the conduct of litigation (within the meaning of that Act: see LEGAL PROFESSIONS vol 65 (2008) PARAS 497–498): see the National Minimum Wage Act 1998 s 49(7)(a) (substituted by the Legal Services Act 2007 s 208(1), Sch 21 paras 124, 126). A person is not, however, a relevant independent adviser for the purposes of head (iii) in the text, in relation to the employee or worker:

(a)　if he is, is employed by or is acting in the matter for the employer or an associated employer (National Minimum Wage Act 1998 s 49(6)(a));

(b)　in the case of a person within heads (2) or (3) above, if the trade union or advice centre is the employer or an associated employer (s 49(6)(b));

(c)　in the case of a person within head (3) above, if the employee or worker makes a payment for the advice received from him (s 49(6)(c)); or

(d)　in the case of a person of a description specified in an order under head (4) above, if any condition specified in the order in relation to the giving of advice by persons of that description is not satisfied (s 49(6)(d)).

As to the meaning of 'employer' for these purposes see PARA 170 note 4. Any two employers are to be treated as associated if one is a company of which the other (directly or indirectly) has control, or if both are companies of which a third person (directly or indirectly) has control; and 'associated employer' is to be construed accordingly: see s 49(8). As to the making of regulations under the National Minimum Wage Act 1998 see PARA 175. As to the Secretary of State see PARA 5 note 21. As to the order that has been made under the powers conferred by head (4) above see the Settlement Agreements (Description of Person) Order 2004, SI 2004/754 (amended by SI 2004/2515; SI 2009/3348; SI 2013/1956).

16　National Minimum Wage Act 1998 s 49(4)(c).

17 National Minimum Wage Act 1998 s 49(4)(d).
18 National Minimum Wage Act 1998 s 49(4)(e).
19 National Minimum Wage Act 1998 s 49(4)(f) (as amended: see note 9).

174. Publication of information about provisions relating to the national minimum wage. The Secretary of State[1] must arrange for information about the National Minimum Wage Act 1998, and regulations under it[2], to be published by such means as appear to the Secretary of State to be most appropriate for drawing the provisions of that Act, and those regulations, to the attention of persons affected by them[3]. The information required to be so published includes, in particular, information about:

(1) the hourly rate for the time being prescribed under the National Minimum Wage Act 1998[4];

(2) the method or methods to be used for determining under the National Minimum Wage Act 1998[5] the hourly rate at which a person is to be regarded for the purposes of that Act as remunerated by his employer[6] in respect of his work[7] in any pay reference period[8];

(3) the methods of enforcing rights under the National Minimum Wage Act 1998[9]; and

(4) the persons who are excluded from the National Minimum Wage Act 1998 or subject to modifications[10], and the provision that is made in relation to them by regulations[11].

1 As to the Secretary of State see PARA 5 note 21.
2 For the purposes of the National Minimum Wage Act 1998, unless the context otherwise requires, 'prescribe' means prescribe by regulations: see s 55(1). As to the making of regulations under the National Minimum Wage Act 1998 see PARA 175.
3 National Minimum Wage Act 1998 s 50(1).
4 National Minimum Wage Act 1998 s 50(2)(a). Head (1) in the text refers to the hourly rate for the time being prescribed under s 1 (see PARA 176): see s 50(2)(a). See note 2.
5 Ie under the National Minimum Wage Act 1998 s 2 (see PARA 200): see s 50(2)(b).
6 As to the meaning of 'employer' for these purposes see PARA 170.
7 As to the meaning of 'work' for these purposes see PARA 172.
8 National Minimum Wage Act 1998 s 50(2)(b). As to the meaning of 'pay reference period' see PARA 202. Any reference to a person being remunerated for a pay reference period is a reference to the person being remunerated by his employer in respect of his work in that pay reference period: s 55(2).
9 National Minimum Wage Act 1998 s 50(2)(c). As to enforcement and remedies for underpayment see PARA 242 et seq.
10 Ie persons to whom the National Minimum Wage Act 1998 s 3 applies (see PARA 186): see s 50(2)(d).
11 National Minimum Wage Act 1998 s 50(2)(d). Head (4) in the text refers to the provision made by regulations under s 3 (see PARA 186): see s 50(2)(d).

175. Regulations and orders under the National Minimum Wage Act 1998. Except to the extent that the National Minimum Wage Act 1998 makes provision to the contrary, any power conferred by the Act to make an Order in Council, regulations or an order includes power[1]:

(1) to make different provision for different cases or for different descriptions of person[2]; and

(2) to make incidental, consequential, supplemental or transitional provision and savings[3].

No recommendation is to be made to Her Majesty to make an Order in Council under any provision of the National Minimum Wage Act 1998 unless a draft of the Order in Council has been laid before Parliament and approved by a resolution of each House of Parliament[4].

Any power of a Minister of the Crown to make regulations or an order under the National Minimum Wage Act 1998 is exercisable by statutory instrument[5].

A statutory instrument containing (whether alone or with other provisions) regulations under the National Minimum Wage Act 1998 may not be made unless a draft of the instrument has been laid before, and approved by a resolution of, each House of Parliament[6].

1   See the National Minimum Wage Act 1998 s 51(1).
2   National Minimum Wage Act 1998 s 51(1)(a). Section 51(1)(a) does not have effect in relation to regulations under s 1(3) (see PARA 199) or an order under s 49 (see PARA 173): s 51(2). As to the regulations that have been made see the National Minimum Wage Regulations 1999, SI 1999/584. See also note 3.
3   National Minimum Wage Act 1998 s 51(1)(b). See note 2. See also eg the National Minimum Wage Act 1998 (Commencement No 1 and Transitional Provisions) Order 1998, SI 1998/2574, the National Minimum Wage Act 1998 (Commencement No 2 and Transitional Provisions) Order 1999, SI 1999/685, and the National Minimum Wage (Offshore Employment) Order 1999, SI 1999/1128.
4   National Minimum Wage Act 1998 s 51(3).
5   National Minimum Wage Act 1998 s 51(4). A statutory instrument which:
    (1)   contains, whether alone or with other provisions, any regulations under s 47(2) or (4) (s 47 repealed in relation to England and repealed, as from a day to be appointed, in relation to Wales: see AGRICULTURAL PRODUCTION AND MARKETING vol 1 (2008) PARA 1228 et seq) or an order under s 49 (see PARA 173) (s 51(7)(a) (s 51(6), (7)(a) amended by the Employment Act 2008 ss 9(3), 20, Schedule Pt 2)); and
    (2)   is not subject to any requirement that a draft of the instrument be laid before, and approved by a resolution of, each House of Parliament (National Minimum Wage Act 1998 s 51(7)(b)),
   is subject to annulment in pursuance of a resolution of either House of Parliament (see s 51(7)).
6   National Minimum Wage Act 1998 s 51(5). Section 51(5) does not have effect in relation to a statutory instrument if the only regulations under the National Minimum Wage Act 1998 which the instrument contains are regulations under s 47(2) or (4) (s 47 repealed in relation to England and repealed, as from a day to be appointed, in relation to Wales: see AGRICULTURAL PRODUCTION AND MARKETING vol 1 (2008) PARA 1228 et seq): s 51(6) (as amended: see note 5).

(ii) Right to be Paid the National Minimum Wage

176. Workers to be paid at least the national minimum wage. A person who qualifies for the national minimum wage must be remunerated by his employer[1] in respect of his work[2] in any pay reference period[3] at a rate which is not less than the national minimum wage[4].

A person qualifies for the national minimum wage if he is an individual who[5]:
(1)   is a worker[6];
(2)   is working, or ordinarily works, in the United Kingdom[7] under his contract[8]; and
(3)   has ceased to be of compulsory school age[9].

1   As to the meaning of 'employer' for these purposes see PARA 170.
2   As to the meaning of 'work' for these purposes see PARA 172.
3   As to the meanings of 'pay reference period', and of references to a person being remunerated for a pay reference period, see PARA 174 note 8.
4   National Minimum Wage Act 1998 s 1(1). The provision made by s 1(1)–(4) (see also the text and notes 5–9; and PARAS 199, 202) is subject to ss 2–56 (see also PARAS 169 et seq, 177 et seq): s 1(5).
   As to the rate, and the method of calculation, of the national minimum wage see PARA 199 et seq; and as to the restriction on contracting out see PARA 173. As to offences under the National Minimum Wage Act 1998 see PARA 251 et seq.
5   See the National Minimum Wage Act 1998 s 1(2). For the purposes of the National Minimum Wage Act 1998, unless the context otherwise requires, 'person who qualifies for the national minimum wage' is to be construed in accordance with s 1(2); and related expressions are to be

construed accordingly: see s 55(1). As to persons who are excluded from qualifying for the national minimum wage see PARAS 186–198; and as to persons who qualify for the national minimum wage at a different rate to that prescribed see PARA 199.

6   National Minimum Wage Act 1998 s 1(2)(a). As to the meaning of 'worker' for these purposes see PARA 171.
7   As to the meaning of 'United Kingdom' see PARA 2 note 12.
8   National Minimum Wage Act 1998 s 1(2)(b). As to the meaning of references to a worker's contract see PARA 171. For the purposes of applying the National Minimum Wage Act 1998 to offshore employment, s 1(2)(b) is modified: see PARA 184 note 17.
9   National Minimum Wage Act 1998 s 1(2)(c). As to the compulsory school age and its upper limit see the Education Act 1996 s 8; and EDUCATION vol 35 (2011) PARA 18. As to persons ceasing to be of compulsory school age, in relation to Northern Ireland, see the National Minimum Wage Act 1998 s 55(5).

(iii) Special Categories of Worker qualifying for the National Minimum Wage

177. In general. Although the National Minimum Wage Act 1998 sets out general criteria by which a person qualifies for the national minimum wage[1], special provision is made in relation to the following categories of worker[2]:

(1)   agency workers[3];
(2)   home workers[4];
(3)   persons in Crown employment[5];
(4)   relevant members of the House of Lords staff[6];
(5)   relevant members of the House of Commons staff[7];
(6)   mariners[8];
(7)   persons in offshore employment[9]; and
(8)   individuals who are not otherwise classified as 'workers' for the purposes of the legislation[10].

1   See the National Minimum Wage Act 1998 s 1(2); and PARA 176.
    As to the rate, and the method of calculation, of the national minimum wage see PARA 199 et seq. As to offences under the National Minimum Wage Act 1998 see PARA 251 et seq.
2   As to the meaning of 'worker' for these purposes see PARA 171. As to use of the term 'worker' in employment law generally see PARA 5.
3   See PARA 178.
4   See PARA 179.
5   See PARA 180.
6   See PARA 181.
7   See PARA 182.
8   See PARA 183.
9   See PARA 184.
10 See PARA 185.

178. Treatment of agency workers who are not otherwise 'workers'. In any case where an individual (the 'agency worker')[1]:

(1)   is supplied by a person (the 'agent') to do work for another (the 'principal') under a contract or other arrangements made between the agent and the principal[2]; but
(2)   is not, as respects that work[3], a worker[4], because of the absence of a worker's contract[5] between the individual and the agent or the principal[6]; and
(3)   is not a party to a contract under which he undertakes to do the work for another party to the contract whose status is, by virtue of the contract, that of a client or customer of any profession or business undertaking carried on by the individual[7],

then the provisions of the National Minimum Wage Act 1998 have effect as if there were a worker's contract for the doing of the work by the agency worker, made between the agency worker[8] and: (a) whichever of the agent and the principal is responsible for paying the agency worker in respect of the work[9]; or (b) if neither the agent nor the principal is so responsible, whichever of them pays the agency worker in respect of the work[10].

1   See the National Minimum Wage Act 1998 s 34(1). As to the fundamental legal position of the agency worker at common law see PARAS 11, 95; and as to special regulations made for the purposes of guaranteeing equal treatment of agency workers see PARA 96 et seq.
2   National Minimum Wage Act 1998 s 34(1)(a). At common law, a degree of control may be sufficient to establish an employment relationship between a hirer and an individual supplied by an employment agency: see PARA 95.
3   As to the meaning of 'work' for these purposes see PARA 172.
4   As to the meaning of 'worker' for these purposes see PARA 171.
5   As to the meaning of references to a worker's contract see PARA 171.
6   National Minimum Wage Act 1998 s 34(1)(b).
7   National Minimum Wage Act 1998 s 34(1)(c).
8   See the National Minimum Wage Act 1998 s 34(2).
9   National Minimum Wage Act 1998 s 34(2)(a).
10 National Minimum Wage Act 1998 s 34(2)(b).

179.   Treatment of home workers who are not 'workers' (as defined).   For the purposes of the National Minimum Wage Act 1998, 'home worker' means an individual who contracts with a person, for the purposes of that person's business, for the execution of work[1] to be done in a place not under the control or management of that person[2]. For the purposes of determining whether a home worker is or is not a 'worker'[3], the latter term is defined as an individual who has entered into or works under (or, where the employment[4] has ceased, worked under)[5]:

(1)   a contract of employment[6]; or
(2)   any other contract, whether express or implied and, if it is express, whether oral or in writing[7], whereby the individual undertakes to do or perform (whether personally or otherwise) any work or services for another party to the contract whose status is not by virtue of the contract that of a client or customer of any profession or business undertaking carried on by the individual[8].

1   As to the meaning of 'work' for these purposes see PARA 172.
2   National Minimum Wage Act 1998 s 35(2). Sub-postmasters are not 'home workers' as defined in s 35 because the Post Office has material control over the place of work: *Wolstenholme v Post Office Ltd* [2003] ICR 546, sub nom *IRC v Post Office Ltd* [2003] IRLR 199, EAT. See also *James v Redcats (Brands) Ltd* [2007] ICR 1006, [2007] IRLR 296, EAT in regard to a self-employed parcel courier (ie a homeworker not working from home).
3   As to the meaning of 'worker' generally see PARA 171.
4   As to the meaning of 'employment' for these purposes see PARA 170.
5   See the National Minimum Wage Act 1998 s 54(3) (modified by s 35(1)). For these purposes, the definition of 'worker' given in s 54(3) (see PARA 171) is modified so that s 54(3)(b) (see head (2) in the text) has effect as if for the word 'personally' there were substituted '(whether personally or otherwise)': see s 35(1).
6   National Minimum Wage Act 1998 s 54(3)(a) (s 54(3) as modified: see note 5). As to the meaning of 'contract of employment' for these purposes see PARA 170 note 2.
7   As to the meaning of 'writing' see PARA 2 note 8.
8   National Minimum Wage Act 1998 s 54(3)(b) (s 54(3) as modified: see note 5).

180.   Effect of the National Minimum Wage Act 1998 in relation to Crown employment.   The provisions of the National Minimum Wage Act 1998 have effect[1] in relation to Crown employment[2] and persons in Crown employment as they have effect in relation to other employment and other workers[3].

For the purposes of the application of the provisions of the National Minimum Wage Act 1998 in relation to Crown employment[4]:

(1) references to an employee[5], or a worker, are to be construed as references to a person in Crown employment[6];

(2) references to a contract of employment[7], or a worker's contract[8], are to be construed as references to the terms of employment of a person in Crown employment[9]; and

(3) references to dismissal, or to the termination of a worker's contract, are to be construed as references to the termination of Crown employment[10].

1 Ie subject to the National Minimum Wage Act 1998 s 37 (armed forces: see PARA 192): see s 36(1).

2 For these purposes, subject to the National Minimum Wage Act 1998 s 37 (armed forces: see PARA 192), 'Crown employment' means employment under or for the purposes of a government department or any officer or body exercising on behalf of the Crown functions conferred by statutory provision: see s 36(2). As to the meaning of 'employment' for these purposes see PARA 170.

3 National Minimum Wage Act 1998 s 36(1). As to the meaning of 'worker' for these purposes see PARA 171.
 Notwithstanding anything in the National Minimum Wage Act 1998 s 37(1) (see PARA 192), s 36 applies to employment by an association established for the purposes of the Reserve Forces Act 1996 Pt XI (ss 110–119) (see ARMED FORCES vol 3 (2011) PARA 473): see the National Minimum Wage Act 1998 s 37(2).

4 Ie in accordance with the National Minimum Wage Act 1998 s 36(1) (see the text and notes 1–3): see s 36(3).

5 As to the meaning of 'employee' for these purposes see PARA 170.

6 National Minimum Wage Act 1998 s 36(3)(a).

7 As to the meaning of 'contract of employment' for these purposes see PARA 170 note 2.

8 As to the meaning of references to a worker's contract see PARA 171.

9 National Minimum Wage Act 1998 s 36(3)(b).

10 National Minimum Wage Act 1998 s 36(3)(c).

181. Treatment of House of Lords staff under the National Minimum Wage Act 1998. The provisions of the National Minimum Wage Act 1998[1] have effect in relation to employment[2] as a relevant member of the House of Lords staff[3] as they have effect in relation to other employment[4].

Nothing in any rule of law or the law or practice of Parliament prevents a relevant member of the House of Lords staff from bringing before the High Court or the County Court any claim under the National Minimum Wage Act 1998[5].

1 Ie apart from the National Minimum Wage Act 1998 ss 19A–19H (financial penalty for underpayment: see PARAS 244–248): see s 38(1); and the Interpretation Act 1978 s 17(2).

2 As to the meaning of 'employment' for these purposes see PARA 170.

3 For these purposes, 'relevant member of the House of Lords staff' means any person who is employed under a worker's contract with the Corporate Officer of the House of Lords: see the National Minimum Wage Act 1998 s 38(3). As to the meaning of 'employed' for these purposes see PARA 170; and as to the meaning of references to a worker's contract see PARA 171. As to the Corporate Officer of the House of Lords see PARLIAMENT vol 78 (2010) PARA 990 et seq.

4 National Minimum Wage Act 1998 s 38(1); Interpretation Act 1978 s 17(2).

5 National Minimum Wage Act 1998 s 38(2) (amended by the Crime and Courts Act 2013 s 17(5), Sch 9 Pt 3 para 52(1)(b), (2)).

182. Treatment of House of Commons staff under the National Minimum Wage Act 1998. The provisions of the National Minimum Wage Act 1998[1] have effect in relation to employment[2] as a relevant member of the House of Commons staff[3] as they have effect in relation to other employment[4].

Nothing in any rule of law or the law or practice of Parliament prevents a relevant member of the House of Commons staff from bringing before the High Court or the County Court any claim under the National Minimum Wage Act 1998[5].

1   Ie apart from the National Minimum Wage Act 1998 ss 19A–19H (financial penalty for underpayment: see PARAS 244–248): see s 39(1); and the Interpretation Act 1978 s 17(2).
2   As to the meaning of 'employment' for these purposes see PARA 170.
3   For these purposes, 'relevant member of the House of Commons staff' means any person:
    (1)   who was appointed by the House of Commons Commission (National Minimum Wage Act 1998 s 39(3)(a)); or
    (2)   who is a member of the Speaker's personal staff (s 39(3)(b)).
    As to the House of Commons Commission see PARLIAMENT vol 78 (2010) PARA 946. As to the Speaker of the House of Commons see PARLIAMENT vol 78 (2010) PARA 931 et seq.
4   National Minimum Wage Act 1998 s 39(1); Interpretation Act 1978 s 17(2).
5   National Minimum Wage Act 1998 s 39(2) (amended by the Crime and Courts Act 2013 s 17(5), Sch 9 Pt 3 para 52(1)(b), (2)).

183.   Treatment of mariners under the National Minimum Wage Act 1998. For the purposes of the National Minimum Wage Act 1998, an individual employed[1] to work on board a ship registered in the United Kingdom[2] is to be treated as an individual who under his contract ordinarily works[3] in the United Kingdom[4], unless:
    (1)   the employment[5] is wholly outside the United Kingdom[6]; or
    (2)   the person is not ordinarily resident in the United Kingdom[7].
Related expressions are to be construed accordingly[8].

1   As to the meaning of 'employed' for these purposes see PARA 170.
2   Ie under the Merchant Shipping Act 1995 Pt II (ss 8–23) (registration: see SHIPPING AND MARITIME LAW vol 93 (2008) PARA 245 et seq): see the National Minimum Wage Act 1998 s 40. As to the meaning of 'United Kingdom' see PARA 2 note 12.
3   As to the meaning of 'work' for these purposes see PARA 172.
4   See the National Minimum Wage Act 1998 s 40.
5   As to the meaning of 'employment' for these purposes see PARA 170.
6   National Minimum Wage Act 1998 s 40(a).
7   National Minimum Wage Act 1998 s 40(b). As to ordinary residence see CONFLICT OF LAWS vol 19 (2011) PARA 359; IMMIGRATION AND ASYLUM vol 57 (2012) PARA 140.
8   See the National Minimum Wage Act 1998 s 40.

184.   Application of the National Minimum Wage Act 1998 to offshore employment. Her Majesty may by Order in Council provide that the provisions of the National Minimum Wage Act 1998 apply, to such extent and for such purposes as may be specified in the Order (with or without modification), to or in relation to a person in offshore employment[1]. For these purposes, 'offshore employment' means employment for the purposes of activities:
    (1)   in the territorial waters of the United Kingdom[2]; or
    (2)   connected with the exploration of the sea bed or subsoil, or the exploitation of their natural resources, in the United Kingdom sector of the continental shelf[3]; or
    (3)   connected with the exploration or exploitation, in a foreign sector of the continental shelf[4], of a cross-boundary petroleum field[5].
Such an Order in Council:
    (a)   may provide that all or any of the provisions of the National Minimum Wage Act 1998, as applied by such an Order in Council, apply[6]:
        (i)   to individuals, whether or not they are British subjects[7]; and
        (ii)   to bodies corporate, whether or not they are incorporated under the law of a part of the United Kingdom[8],

and apply even where the application may affect their activities outside the United Kingdom[9];

(b)   may make provision for conferring jurisdiction on any court or class of court specified in the Order in Council, or on employment tribunals, in respect of offences, causes of action or other matters arising in connection with offshore employment[10];

(c)   may[11] provide that the provisions of the National Minimum Wage Act 1998, as applied by the Order in Council, apply in relation to any person in employment in a part of the areas specified in heads (1) and (2) above[12];

(d)   may exclude from the operation of the provisions in the Territorial Waters Jurisdiction Act 1878 requiring consents for prosecutions[13] proceedings for offences under the National Minimum Wage Act 1998 in connection with offshore employment[14];

(e)   may provide that such proceedings are not to be brought without such consent as may be required by the Order in Council[15];

(f)   may[16] modify or exclude the operation of provisions of the National Minimum Wage Act 1998[17] relating to mariners and individuals who ordinarily works in the United Kingdom under their contract[18].

Any jurisdiction conferred on a court or tribunal under these provisions is without prejudice to jurisdiction exercisable apart from those provisions by that or any other court or tribunal[19].

1   National Minimum Wage Act 1998 s 42(2).
        As to the Order that has been made see the National Minimum Wage (Offshore Employment) Order 1999, SI 1999/1128, which came into force on 1 May 1999 (see art 1(1)). Nothing in the National Minimum Wage (Offshore Employment) Order 1999, SI 1999/1128, applies to work done before 1 May 1999: art 5(1). The National Minimum Wage Regulations 1999, SI 1999/584 (see PARAS 170 note 4, 171 note 9, 172, 193 et seq), apply to employment to which the National Minimum Wage (Offshore Employment) Order 1999, SI 1999/1128, relates as if the National Minimum Wage Regulations 1999, SI 1999/584, had come into force on 1 May 1999: National Minimum Wage (Offshore Employment) Order 1999, SI 1999/1128, art 5(2). The National Minimum Wage (Offshore Employment) Order 1999, SI 1999/1128, has no application to employment in connection with a ship which is in the course of navigation or a ship which is engaged in dredging or fishing: art 2(2). For these purposes, 'dredging' does not include the excavation of the sea bed or its subsoil in the course of pipe-laying: art 2(3).

2   National Minimum Wage Act 1998 s 42(1)(a). As to the meaning of 'United Kingdom' see PARA 2 note 12. As to the territorial sea (or waters) of the United Kingdom see the Territorial Sea Act 1987 s 1; and INTERNATIONAL RELATIONS LAW vol 61 (2010) PARA 123 et seq; WATER AND WATERWAYS vol 100 (2009) PARA 31.

3   National Minimum Wage Act 1998 s 42(1)(b). For these purposes, 'United Kingdom sector of the continental shelf' means the area designated under the Continental Shelf Act 1964 s 1(7) (see ENERGY AND CLIMATE CHANGE vol 44 (2011) PARA 1040): see the National Minimum Wage Act 1998 s 42(5).

4   For these purposes, 'foreign sector of the continental shelf' means an area outside the territorial waters of any state, within which rights with respect to the sea bed and subsoil and their natural resources are exercisable by a state other than the United Kingdom: see the National Minimum Wage Act 1998 s 42(5).

5   National Minimum Wage Act 1998 s 42(1)(c). For these purposes, 'cross-boundary petroleum field' means a petroleum field that extends across the boundary between the United Kingdom sector of the continental shelf and a foreign sector of the continental shelf; and 'petroleum field' means a geological structure identified as an oil or gas field by the Order in Council concerned: see s 42(5).

6   See the National Minimum Wage Act 1998 s 42(3)(a).

7   National Minimum Wage Act 1998 s 42(3)(a)(i). Although the legislation refers to 'British subjects', the status of British subject ceased to be a common status enjoyed in addition to

citizenship as from 1 January 1983 and became a miscellaneous, residual and disappearing category: see BRITISH NATIONALITY vol 4 (2011) PARA 407.

8   National Minimum Wage Act 1998 s 42(3)(a)(ii).

9   National Minimum Wage Act 1998 s 42(3)(a). Accordingly the National Minimum Wage (Offshore Employment) Order 1999, SI 1999/1128, applies to individuals whether or not they are British subjects, and to bodies corporate whether or not they are incorporated under the law of the United Kingdom, and applies even when the application may affect their activities outside the United Kingdom: art 2(4). As to use of the term 'British subjects' see note 7.

10 National Minimum Wage Act 1998 s 42(3)(b). Accordingly, in England and Wales, the employment tribunals have jurisdiction to determine complaints or appeals arising, in connection with employment to which the National Minimum Wage (Offshore Employment) Order 1999, SI 1999/1128, applies (see note 1), from acts or omissions taking place in the English area, as they have if those acts or omissions had taken place in England and Wales: art 3(2). For these purposes, 'English area' has the same meaning as in the Civil Jurisdiction (Offshore Activities) Order 1987, SI 1987/2197 (see PARA 156 note 27): see the National Minimum Wage (Offshore Employment) Order 1999, SI 1999/1128, art 3(1). As to employment tribunals see PARA 1399 et seq; and as to the procedure on a complaint made to an employment tribunal see PARA 1453 et seq. As to the meanings of 'England' and 'Wales' see PARA 2 note 12.

11 Ie without prejudice to the National Minimum Wage Act 1998 s 42(2) (see the text and note 1): see s 42(3)(c).

12 National Minimum Wage Act 1998 s 42(3)(c).

13 Ie the Territorial Waters Jurisdiction Act 1878 s 3 (consents required for prosecutions: see CRIMINAL PROCEDURE vol 27 (2010) PARA 12): see the National Minimum Wage Act 1998 s 42(3)(d).

14 National Minimum Wage Act 1998 s 42(3)(d). As to offences under the National Minimum Wage Act 1998 see PARA 251 et seq.

15 National Minimum Wage Act 1998 s 42(3)(e). Accordingly, proceedings for any offence connected with employment to which the National Minimum Wage (Offshore Employment) Order 1999, SI 1999/1128, applies (see note 1) may not be brought in England and Wales except by, or with the consent of, the Secretary of State: art 4. As to the Secretary of State see PARA 5 note 21.

16 Ie without prejudice to the National Minimum Wage Act 1998 s 42(2) (see the text and note 1): see s 42(3)(f).

17 Ie the National Minimum Wage Act 1998 s 1(2)(b) (workers qualifying ordinarily for the national minimum wage: see PARA 176) and s 40 (mariners: see PARA 183): see s 42(3)(f). Accordingly, the provisions of the National Minimum Wage Act 1998 apply to offshore employment as if the reference in s 1(2)(b) to an individual who is working, or ordinarily works in the United Kingdom included a reference to an individual who is working, or ordinarily works in the territorial waters of the United Kingdom or in the United Kingdom sector of the continental shelf: see the National Minimum Wage (Offshore Employment) Order 1999, SI 1999/1128, art 2(1).

18 National Minimum Wage Act 1998 s 42(3)(f).

19 National Minimum Wage Act 1998 s 42(4).

185.   Power to make provision for individuals who are not otherwise 'workers' for the purposes of the National Minimum Wage Act 1998.   The Secretary of State[1] may by regulations[2] make provision for the National Minimum Wage Act 1998 to apply, with or without modifications, as if:

(1)   any individual of a prescribed[3] description who would not otherwise be a worker for the purposes of the National Minimum Wage Act 1998 were a worker for those purposes[4];

(2)   there were in the case of any such individual a worker's contract[5] of a prescribed description under which the individual works[6]; and

(3)   a person of a prescribed description were the employer[7] under that contract[8].

1   As to the Secretary of State see PARA 5 note 21.

2   As to the making of regulations under the National Minimum Wage Act 1998 see PARA 175.

3   For these purposes, unless the context otherwise requires, 'prescribe' means prescribe by regulations: see the National Minimum Wage Act 1998 s 55(1). At the date at which this volume states the law, no such regulations had been made under s 41.

4   National Minimum Wage Act 1998 s 41(a). As to the meaning of 'worker' for these purposes see PARA 171.
5   As to the meaning of references to a worker's contract see PARA 171.
6   National Minimum Wage Act 1998 s 41(b). As to the meaning of 'work' for these purposes see PARA 172.
7   As to the meaning of 'employer' for these purposes see PARA 170.
8   National Minimum Wage Act 1998 s 41(c).

(iv) Workers not qualifying for the National Minimum Wage

186.   In general.   The following workers do not qualify for the national minimum wage under the National Minimum Wage Act 1998[1]:

(1)   share fishermen[2];
(2)   voluntary workers[3];
(3)   resident workers in religious and other communities[4];
(4)   prisoners[5];
(5)   members of the armed forces[6]; and
(6)   persons detained in removal centres under the Immigration and Asylum Act 1999, in respect of work done in pursuance of removal centre rules[7].

In addition, the Secretary of State[8] may by regulations make provision in relation to any of the following persons[9], that is say:

(a)   persons who have not attained the age of 26[10];
(b)   persons who have attained the age of 26[11] who are:
   (i)   within the first six months after the commencement of their employment[12] with an employer[13] by whom they have not previously been employed[14];
   (ii)   participating in a scheme under which shelter is provided in return for work[15];
   (iii) participating in a scheme designed to provide training, work experience or temporary work[16];
   (iv)   participating in a scheme to assist in the seeking or obtaining of work[17];
   (v)   undertaking a course of higher education requiring attendance for a period of work experience[18]; or
   (vi)   undertaking a course of further education requiring attendance for a period of work experience[19],

either preventing them from being persons who qualify for the national minimum wage[20], or prescribing an hourly rate for the national minimum wage other than the single hourly rate for the time being otherwise[21] prescribed[22]. No provision is to be so made which treats persons differently in relation to: (A) different areas[23]; (B) different sectors of employment[24]; (C) undertakings of different sizes[25]; or (D) different occupations[26].

1   As to the general criteria by which a person qualifies for the national minimum wage see PARA 176. As to the rate of the national minimum wage see PARA 199.
2   As to share fishermen see PARA 187.
3   As to voluntary workers see PARA 188.
4   As to resident workers in religious and other communities see PARA 189.
5   As to prisoners see PARA 190.
6   As to members of the armed forces see PARA 192.
7   The Immigration and Asylum Act 1999 s 153A (see IMMIGRATION AND ASYLUM vol 57 (2012) PARA 192) disqualifies certain persons for the national minimum wage: National Minimum Wage Act 1998 s 45B (added by the Immigration, Asylum and Nationality Act 2006 s 59(2)).
8   As to the Secretary of State see PARA 5 note 21.

9   See the National Minimum Wage Act 1998 s 3(2). If any description of persons who have attained the age of 26 is added by regulations under s 4 (see note 11) to the descriptions of person to whom s 3 applies, no provision is to be made under s 3(2) which treats persons of that description differently in relation to different ages over 26: s 3(4). As to the making of regulations under the National Minimum Wage Act 1998 see PARA 175. As to the regulations so made under s 3 see PARAS 193–198, 199.

10 National Minimum Wage Act 1998 s 3(1). A person attains a particular age expressed in years at the commencement of the relevant anniversary of the date of his birth: see the Family Law Reform Act 1969 s 9; and CHILDREN AND YOUNG PERSONS vol 9 (2012) PARA 2.

11 See the National Minimum Wage Act 1998 s 3(1A) (added by SI 1999/583).
    The Secretary of State may by regulations amend the National Minimum Wage Act 1998 s 3 by adding descriptions of persons who have attained the age of 26 to the descriptions of person to whom s 3 applies: s 4(1). No amendment is to be so made which treats persons differently in relation to:
    (1) different areas (s 4(2)(a));
    (2) different sectors of employment (s 4(2)(b));
    (3) undertakings of different sizes (s 4(2)(c));
    (4) different ages over 26 (s 4(2)(d)); or
    (5) different occupations (s 4(2)(e)).
    As to the regulations so made see the National Minimum Wage Act 1998 (Amendment) Regulations 1999, SI 1999/583; and the National Minimum Wage Act 1998 (Amendment) Regulations 2007, SI 2007/2042.

12 As to the meaning of 'employment' for these purposes see PARA 170.

13 As to the meaning of 'employer' for these purposes see PARA 170.

14 National Minimum Wage Act 1998 s 3(1A)(a) (as added: see note 11). As to the meaning of 'employed' for these purposes see PARA 170.

15 National Minimum Wage Act 1998 s 3(1A)(b) (as added: see note 11).

16 National Minimum Wage Act 1998 s 3(1A)(c) (as added: see note 11).

17 National Minimum Wage Act 1998 s 3(1A)(d) (s 3(1A) as added (see note 11); s 3(1A)(d), (e) amended, s 3(1A)(f) added, by SI 2007/2042).

18 National Minimum Wage Act 1998 s 3(1A)(e) (as added and amended: see note 17).

19 National Minimum Wage Act 1998 s 3(1A)(f) (s 3(1A) as added (see note 11); s 3(1A)(f) as added (see note 17)).

20 National Minimum Wage Act 1998 s 3(2)(a). As to the meaning of 'person who qualifies for the national minimum wage' see PARA 176 note 5. As to persons so prevented by regulations from qualifying for the national minimum wage see PARA 186 et seq.

21 Ie under the National Minimum Wage Act 1998 s 1(3) (see PARA 199): see s 3(2)(b).

22 National Minimum Wage Act 1998 s 3(2)(b). For these purposes, unless the context otherwise requires, 'prescribe' means prescribe by regulations: see s 55(1).

23 National Minimum Wage Act 1998 s 3(3)(a).

24 National Minimum Wage Act 1998 s 3(3)(b).

25 National Minimum Wage Act 1998 s 3(3)(c).

26 National Minimum Wage Act 1998 s 3(3)(d).

187. Share fishermen. A person:

(1) employed[1] as master, or as a member of the crew, of a fishing vessel[2]; and

(2) remunerated, in respect of that employment[3], only by a share in the profits or gross earnings of the vessel[4],

does not qualify for the national minimum wage in respect of that employment[5].

1   As to the meaning of 'employed' for these purposes see PARA 170.

2   National Minimum Wage Act 1998 s 43(a).

3   As to the meaning of 'employment' for these purposes see PARA 170.

4   National Minimum Wage Act 1998 s 43(b).

5   See the National Minimum Wage Act 1998 s 43. As to the meaning of 'person who qualifies for the national minimum wage' see PARA 176 note 5. As to the rate of the national minimum wage see PARA 199.

188. Voluntary workers. A worker[1] employed[2] by a charity[3], a voluntary organisation[4], an associated fund-raising body[5], or a statutory body[6], does not qualify for the national minimum wage[7] in respect of that employment[8] if he receives[9], and under the terms of his employment[10] is entitled to[11]:

(1)   no monetary payments of any description, or no monetary payments except in respect of expenses actually incurred in the performance of his duties, or expenses reasonably estimated as likely to be or to have been so incurred[12]; and

(2)   no benefits in kind of any description, or no benefits in kind other than the provision of some or all of his subsistence[13] or of such accommodation as is reasonable in the circumstances of the employment[14].

A person who would satisfy these conditions but for receiving monetary payments made solely for the purpose of providing him with means of subsistence is to be taken to satisfy those conditions, however, if[15]: (a) he is employed to do the work in question as a result of arrangements made between a charity acting in pursuance of its charitable purposes and the body for which the work is done[16]; and (b) the work is done for a charity, a voluntary organisation, an associated fund-raising body or a statutory body[17].

1   As to the meaning of 'worker' for these purposes see PARA 171.
2   As to the meaning of 'employed' for these purposes see PARA 170.
3   For these purposes, 'charity' means a body of persons, or the trustees of a trust, established for charitable purposes only: see the National Minimum Wage Act 1998 s 44(4). The exclusions made by s 44 do not apply to volunteering in non-charitable commercial enterprises: see 308 HC Official Report (6th Series) cols 24–25. As to charitable purposes see CHARITIES vol 8 (2010) PARA 1 et seq.
      A volunteer who assists a charitable organisation with no obligation to do so is not a worker for the purposes of the National Minimum Wage Act 1998: *Best v St Austell China Clay Museum Ltd* [2004] All ER (D) 106 (Aug), EAT.
4   For these purposes, 'voluntary organisation' means a body of persons, or the trustees of a trust, which is established only for charitable purposes (whether or not those purposes are charitable within the meaning of any rule of law), benevolent purposes or philanthropic purposes, but which is not a charity: see the National Minimum Wage Act 1998 s 44(4).
5   For these purposes, 'associated fund-raising body' means a body of persons the profits of which are applied wholly for the purposes of a charity or voluntary organisation: see the National Minimum Wage Act 1998 s 44(4).
6   For these purposes, 'statutory body' means a body established by or under an enactment (including an enactment comprised in Northern Ireland legislation) and includes the Children's Panel: see the National Minimum Wage Act 1998 s 44(4) (definition amended by SI 2013/1465). As to the meaning of 'Northern Ireland legislation' see PARA 155 note 3. As to the Children's Panel see the Children's Hearings (Scotland) Act 2011 s 4.
7   As to the meaning of 'person who qualifies for the national minimum wage' see PARA 176 note 5. As to the rate of the national minimum wage see PARA 199.
8   As to the meaning of 'employment' for these purposes see PARA 170.
9   For these purposes, 'receive', in relation to a monetary payment or a benefit in kind, means receive in respect of, or otherwise in connection with, the employment in question, whether or not under the terms of the employment: see the National Minimum Wage Act 1998 s 44(4).
10 Ie apart from the National Minimum Wage Act 1998: see s 44(1).
11 See the National Minimum Wage Act 1998 s 44(1).
12 See the National Minimum Wage Act 1998 s 44(1)(a). For the purposes of head (1) in the text, expenses which are (see s 44(1A) (added by the Employment Act 2008 s 14)):
      (1)   incurred in order to enable the worker to perform his duties (National Minimum Wage Act 1998 s 44(1A)(a) (as so added));
      (2)   reasonably so incurred (s 44(1A)(b) (as so added)); and
      (3)   not accommodation expenses (s 44(1A)(c) (as so added)),
      are to be regarded as actually incurred in the performance of his duties (see s 44(1A) (as so added)).
13 For these purposes, 'subsistence' means such subsistence as is reasonable in the circumstances of the employment in question, and does not include accommodation: see the National Minimum Wage Act 1998 s 44(4). See also note 12.

14 National Minimum Wage Act 1998 s 44(1)(b). See also note 12. For the purposes of head (2) in the text:

    (1)   any training (other than that which a person necessarily acquires in the course of doing his work) is to be taken to be a benefit in kind (s 44(3)(a)); but

    (2)   there is to be left out of account any training provided for the sole or main purpose of improving the worker's ability to perform the work which he has agreed to do (s 44(3)(b)).

As to the meaning of 'work' for these purposes see PARA 172.

15 See the National Minimum Wage Act 1998 s 44(2).

16 National Minimum Wage Act 1998 s 44(2)(a).

17 National Minimum Wage Act 1998 s 44(2)(b).

189.   Resident workers in religious and other communities.   A residential member of a community[1]:

    (1)   which is a charity[2] or is established by a charity[3];

    (2)   one of whose purposes is to practise or advance a belief of a religious or similar nature[4]; and

    (3)   all or some of whose members live together for that purpose[5],

other than a community which[6]:

    (a)   is an independent school[7] or an alternative provision Academy that is not an independent school[8]; or

    (b)   provides a course of further or higher education[9],

does not qualify for the national minimum wage[10] in respect of employment[11] by the community[12].

1   Ie a community to which the National Minimum Wage Act 1998 s 44A applies (see s 44A(2), (3); and the text and notes 2–9): see s 44A(1) (s 44A added by the Employment Relations Act 1999 s 22). For these purposes, the residential members of a community are those who live together as mentioned in the National Minimum Wage Act 1998 s 44A(2)(c) (see head (3) in the text): see s 44A(4) (as so added).

2   For these purposes, 'charity' has the same meaning as in the National Minimum Wage Act 1998 s 44 (see PARA 188 note 3): s 44A(5)(a) (as added: see note 1).

3   National Minimum Wage Act 1998 s 44A(2)(a) (as added: see note 1).

4   National Minimum Wage Act 1998 s 44A(2)(b) (as added: see note 1).

5   National Minimum Wage Act 1998 s 44A(2)(c) (as added: see note 1).

6   See the National Minimum Wage Act 1998 s 44A(3) (as added: see note 1).

7   For these purposes, 'independent school' has the same meaning as in the Education Act 1996 s 463 (see EDUCATION vol 35 (2011) PARA 440): National Minimum Wage Act 1998 s 44A(5)(b) (as added: see note 1).

8   National Minimum Wage Act 1998 s 44A(3)(a) (s 44A as added (see note 1); s 44A(3)(a) amended by SI 2012/976). As to alternative provision Academies see the Academies Act 2010 ss 1C, 1D; and EDUCATION vol 35 (2011) PARA 510.

9   National Minimum Wage Act 1998 s 44A(3)(b) (as added: see note 1). For these purposes, 'course of further or higher education' means a course of a description referred to in the Education Reform Act 1988 s 120(1), Sch 6 (see EDUCATION vol 35 (2011) PARA 23) or the Further and Higher Education Act 1992 s 3(1), Sch 2 (repealed): National Minimum Wage Act 1998 s 44A(6)(a) (as so added).

10   As to the meaning of 'person who qualifies for the national minimum wage' see PARA 176 note 5. As to the rate of the national minimum wage see PARA 199.

11   As to the meaning of 'employment' for these purposes see PARA 170.

12   See the National Minimum Wage Act 1998 s 44A(1) (as added: see note 1).

190.   Prisoners.   A prisoner[1] does not qualify for the national minimum wage[2] in respect of any work[3] which he does in pursuance of prison rules[4].

1   For these purposes, 'prisoner' means a person detained in, or on temporary release from, a prison; and 'prison' includes any other institution to which prison rules apply: see the National Minimum Wage Act 1998 s 45(2). 'Prison rules' means rules made under the Prison Act 1952 s 47 (see PRISONS AND PRISONERS vol 85 (2012) PARA 404): see the National Minimum Wage Act 1998 s 45(2).

As from a day to be appointed under the Legal Aid, Sentencing and Punishment of Offenders Act 2012 s 151(1), the definition of 'prison rules' given in the National Minimum Wage Act 1998 s 45(2) is amended to include rules made also under the Prison Act 1952 s 47A (not yet in force) (rules about employment in prisons etc: see PRISONS AND PRISONERS vol 85 (2012) PARA 405): see the National Minimum Wage Act 1998 s 45(2) (definition of 'prison rules' prospectively amended by the Legal Aid, Sentencing and Punishment of Offenders Act 2012 s 129(9)). However, at the date at which this volume states the law, no such day had been appointed.

2   As to the meaning of 'person who qualifies for the national minimum wage' see PARA 176 note 5. As to the rate of the national minimum wage see PARA 199.
3   As to the meaning of 'work' for these purposes see PARA 172.
4   National Minimum Wage Act 1998 s 45(1).

191. Persons discharging fines by unpaid work. A person does not qualify for the national minimum wage[1] in respect of any work[2] that he does in pursuance of a work order under the Courts Act 2003[3].

1   As to the meaning of 'person who qualifies for the national minimum wage' see PARA 176 note 5. As to the rate of the national minimum wage see PARA 199.
2   As to the meaning of 'work' for these purposes see PARA 172.
3   National Minimum Wage Act 1998 s 45A (added by the Courts Act 2003 s 109(1), Sch 8 para 382). The text refers to a work order under the Courts Act 2003 s 97(2), Sch 6 (see MAGISTRATES vol 71 (2013) PARA 665 et seq): see the National Minimum Wage Act 1998 s 45A (as so added).

192. Armed forces. A person serving as a member of the naval, military or air forces of the Crown does not qualify for the national minimum wage[1] in respect of that service[2]. Members of the Cadet Forces who assist the activities of those forces otherwise than in the course of Crown employment are also excluded in respect of anything done in so assisting those activities[3].

1   As to the meaning of 'person who qualifies for the national minimum wage' see PARA 176 note 5. As to the rate, and the method of calculation, of the national minimum wage see PARA 199 et seq. As to offences under the National Minimum Wage Act 1998 see PARA 251 et seq.
2   National Minimum Wage Act 1998 s 37(1).
3   A person (not being a person to whom the National Minimum Wage Act 1998 s 37(1) applies: see the text and notes 1–2) who:
     (1)   is a member of any of the forces specified in s 37A(2) (see s 37A(1)(a) (s 37A added by the Employment Act 2008 s 13)); and
     (2)   assists the activities of those forces otherwise than in the course of Crown employment (National Minimum Wage Act 1998 s 37A(1)(b) (as so added),
   does not qualify for the national minimum wage in respect of anything done by him in so assisting those activities (see s 37A(1) (as so added)). The forces referred to in head (1) above are: (a) the Combined Cadet Force (s 37A(2)(a) (as so added)); (b) the Sea Cadet Corps (s 37A(2)(b) (as so added)); (c) the Army Cadet Force (s 37A(2)(c) (as so added)); (d) the Air Training Corps (s 37A(2)(d) (as so added)). As to the organisation and administration of the Army Cadet Force, the Air Training Corps, the Combined Cadet Force and the Sea Cadet Corps see ARMED FORCES vol 3 (2011) PARA 473.
   Notwithstanding anything in the National Minimum Wage Act 1998 s 37(1), s 36 (Crown employment: see PARA 180) applies to employment by an association established for the purposes of the Reserve Forces Act 1996 Pt XI (ss 110–119) (see ARMED FORCES vol 3 (2011) PARA 473): see the National Minimum Wage Act 1998 s 37(2); and PARA 180 note 3. As to Crown employment generally see PARA 6.

193. Workers participating in a government work-based learning programme. A worker[1] who is participating in a scheme provided to that worker[2]:
     (1)   in England[3], under the government arrangements[4] known, at 1 October 2010, as Programme Led Apprenticeships[5]; or

(2)   in Wales, under the government arrangements known, at 1 October 2010, as Skill Build (or known, at 1 August 2011, as Traineeships or Steps to Employment)[6],

does not qualify for the national minimum wage[7] in respect of work done for the employer[8] as part of the scheme[9].

1   As to the meaning of 'worker' for these purposes see PARA 171 note 9.
2   See the National Minimum Wage Regulations 1999, SI 1999/584, reg 12(4A) (added by SI 2004/1930; and substituted by SI 2010/1901).
3   As to the meaning of 'England' see PARA 2 note 12.
4   For these purposes, 'government arrangements' means, in England and Wales, arrangements made by the Secretary of State under the Employment and Training Act 1973 s 2 (see PARA 634), or under the Jobseekers Act 1995 s 17B (see WELFARE BENEFITS AND STATE PENSIONS vol 104 (2014) PARA 442): see the National Minimum Wage Regulations 1999, SI 1999/584, reg 2(1) (definition amended by SI 2008/1894; SI 2011/2345). As to the meaning of 'Wales' see PARA 2 note 12. As to the Secretary of State see PARA 5 note 21.
5   National Minimum Wage Regulations 1999, SI 1999/584, reg 12(4A)(a) (as added and substituted: see note 2).
6   National Minimum Wage Regulations 1999, SI 1999/584, reg 12(4A)(d) (reg 12(4A) as added and substituted (see note 2); reg 12(4A)(d) amended by SI 2011/2345).
7   As to the meaning of 'person who qualifies for the national minimum wage' see PARA 176 note 5. As to the power to make regulations preventing a person from qualifying for the national minimum wage see the National Minimum Wage Act 1998 s 3; and PARA 186. As to the rate of the national minimum wage see PARA 199.
8   As to the meaning of 'employer' for these purposes see PARA 170.
9   See the National Minimum Wage Regulations 1999, SI 1999/584, reg 12(4A) (as added and substituted: see note 2).

194. Workers participating in training, work experience or temporary work scheme provided under government arrangements. A worker[1] who is participating in a scheme, designed to provide training, work experience or temporary work, or to assist in seeking or obtaining work[2], which is:

(1)   a scheme provided under government arrangements that are not already specified[3] for the purposes of disqualifying him for the national minimum wage[4]; or

(2)   a scheme, not being one provided under government arrangements, funded in whole or part under the European Social Fund[5],

does not qualify for the national minimum wage[6] in respect of work done for the employer[7] as part of that scheme, except to the extent it is otherwise[8] provided[9]. This restriction does not apply, however:

(a)   to a person who: (i) is a worker within the meaning of the National Minimum Wage Act 1998[10]; (ii) is participating in a scheme falling within head (1) above[11]; (iii) is employed by the employer for whom he works under the scheme[12]; and (iv) is remunerated by the employer in respect of that employment[13], or is entitled to remuneration from the employer under his contract with the employer[14], or is participating in a trial period of work with a prospective employer under government arrangements for a period in excess of six weeks[15];

(b)   to an employee who is participating in a scheme falling within head (2) above if he is employed by the employer for whom he works under the scheme, unless the employee is engaged, for a period not exceeding six weeks, in a trial period of work with a prospective employer under government arrangements[16].

1   As to the extended meaning of 'worker' that is applied for the purposes of the National Minimum Wage Regulations 1999, SI 1999/584, reg 12(5), (6) (see also the text and notes 2–15) see PARA 171 note 9.

2 See the National Minimum Wage Regulations 1999, SI 1999/584, reg 12(5) (reg 12(5) substituted, reg 12(5A) added, by SI 2010/1901).

3 Ie arrangements that are not specified in either the National Minimum Wage Regulations 1999, SI 1999/584, reg 12(4A) (see PARA 193) or reg 12(5A): see reg 12(5)(a) (as substituted: see note 2). For the purposes of reg 12(5), the government arrangements specified by reg 12(5A) are:

    (1)   in England, government arrangements known, at 1st October 2010, as Apprenticeships or Advanced Apprenticeships (or known as Intermediate Level Apprenticeships or Advanced Level Apprenticeships) (reg 12(5A)(a) (reg 12(5A) as added (see note 2); reg 12(5A)(a) amended by SI 2012/2397); and

    (2)   in Wales, government arrangements known, at 1st October 2010, as Foundation Modern Apprenticeships, Modern Apprenticeships, Foundation Apprenticeships or Apprenticeships (National Minimum Wage Regulations 1999, SI 1999/584, reg 12(5A)(d) (as so added)).

As to the meanings of 'England' and 'Wales' see PARA 2 note 12. As to the meaning of 'government arrangements' see PARA 193 note 4.

4 National Minimum Wage Regulations 1999, SI 1999/584, reg 12(5)(a) (as substituted: see note 2).

5 National Minimum Wage Regulations 1999, SI 1999/584, reg 12(5)(b) (as substituted: see note 2).

6 As to the meaning of 'person who qualifies for the national minimum wage' see PARA 176 note 5. As to the power to make regulations preventing a person from qualifying for the national minimum wage see the National Minimum Wage Act 1998 s 3; and PARA 186. As to the rate of the national minimum wage see PARA 199.

7 As to the meaning of 'employer' for these purposes see PARA 170.

8 Ie by the National Minimum Wage Regulations 1999, SI 1999/584, reg 12(6), (7) (see the text and notes 9–16): see reg 12(5) (as substituted: see note 2).

9 See the National Minimum Wage Regulations 1999, SI 1999/584, reg 12(5) (as substituted: see note 2).

10 National Minimum Wage Regulations 1999, SI 1999/584, reg 12(6)(a) (reg 12(6) substituted, reg 12(6A), (6B) added, by SI 2008/1894). Head (a)(i) in the text applies to a worker within the meaning of the National Minimum Wage Act 1998 s 54(3) (see PARA 171): see the National Minimum Wage Regulations 1999, SI 1999/584, reg 12(6)(a) (as so substituted).

11 National Minimum Wage Regulations 1999, SI 1999/584, reg 12(6)(b) (as substituted: see note 10).

12 National Minimum Wage Regulations 1999, SI 1999/584, reg 12(6)(c) (as substituted: see note 10). As to the meaning of 'employed' for these purposes see PARA 170.

13 National Minimum Wage Regulations 1999, SI 1999/584, reg 12(6)(d)(i) (as substituted: see note 10). For these purposes (and for the purposes of reg 12(6)(d)(ii) (see the text and note 14)), remuneration does not include a payment by an employer to a person in respect of expenses:

    (1)   actually incurred in the performance of that person's duties (reg 12(6A)(a) (as added: see note 10)); or

    (2)   reasonably estimated as likely to be or to have been so incurred (reg 12(6A)(b) (as so added)).

For these purposes, expenses which are incurred in order to enable the person to perform his duties and are reasonably so incurred, are to be regarded as actually incurred in the performance of his duties: see reg 12(6B) (as so added).

14 National Minimum Wage Regulations 1999, SI 1999/584, reg 12(6)(d)(ii) (as substituted: see note 10). As to 'remuneration' for these purposes see note 13.

15 National Minimum Wage Regulations 1999, SI 1999/584, reg 12(6)(d)(iii) (as substituted: see note 10).

16 National Minimum Wage Regulations 1999, SI 1999/584, reg 12(7) (amended by SI 2001/1108; SI 2008/1894; and SI 2010/1901).

195. Workers participating in a traineeship in England. A worker[1] does not qualify for the national minimum wage[2] for work done as part of that worker's participation in a traineeship in England[3], consisting of a skills programme which meets the following conditions[4]:

    (1)   the programme includes a work experience placement and work preparation training[5];

    (2)   the programme lasts no more than six months[6];

(3) the programme is funded in whole or in part by the Secretary of State under the Education Act 2002[7] or by the Chief Executive of Skills Funding[8]; and

(4) the programme is open only to persons aged on the first day of the traineeship[9]: (a) at least 16 years but under the age of 25 years[10]; or (b) at least 16 years but under the age of 26 years in the case of persons subject to learning difficulty assessment within the meaning of the Education Act 1996[11].

1 As to the meaning of 'worker' for these purposes see PARA 171 note 9.
2 As to the meaning of 'person who qualifies for the national minimum wage' see PARA 176 note 5. As to the power to make regulations preventing a person from qualifying for the national minimum wage see the National Minimum Wage Act 1998 s 3; and PARA 186. As to the rate of the national minimum wage see PARA 199.
3 See the National Minimum Wage Regulations 1999, SI 1999/584, reg 12(7A) (reg 12(7A), (7B) added by SI 2014/546). The text refers to participation in a traineeship in England to which the National Minimum Wage Regulations 1999, SI 1999/584, reg 12(7B) (see heads (1) to (4) in the text) applies: see reg 12(7A) (as so added).
4 See the National Minimum Wage Regulations 1999, SI 1999/584, reg 12(7B) (as added: see note 3).
5 National Minimum Wage Regulations 1999, SI 1999/584, reg 12(7B)(a) (as added: see note 3).
6 National Minimum Wage Regulations 1999, SI 1999/584, reg 12(7B)(b) (as added: see note 3).
7 Ie under the Education Act 2002 s 14 (financial assistance for purposes related to education or children etc: see EDUCATION vol 35 (2011) PARA 77): see the National Minimum Wage Regulations 1999, SI 1999/584, reg 12(7B)(c) (as added: see note 3). As to the Secretary of State see PARA 5 note 21.
8 National Minimum Wage Regulations 1999, SI 1999/584, reg 12(7B)(c) (as added: see note 3). As to the Chief Executive of Skills Funding see EDUCATION vol 36 (2011) PARA 1279 et seq.
9 See the National Minimum Wage Regulations 1999, SI 1999/584, reg 12(7B)(d) (as added: see note 3). A person attains a particular age expressed in years at the commencement of the relevant anniversary of the date of his birth: see the Family Law Reform Act 1969 s 9; and CHILDREN AND YOUNG PERSONS vol 9 (2012) PARA 2.
10 National Minimum Wage Regulations 1999, SI 1999/584, reg 12(7B)(d)(i) (as added: see note 3).
11 National Minimum Wage Regulations 1999, SI 1999/584, reg 12(7B)(d)(ii) (as added: see note 3). The text refers to persons subject to learning difficulty assessment within the meaning of the Education Act 1996 s 13(4), (5) (see EDUCATION vol 35 (2011) PARA 26): see the National Minimum Wage Regulations 1999, SI 1999/584, reg 12(7B)(d)(ii) (as so added).

196. Workers attending courses involving work experience. A worker[1] who is undertaking either:

(1) a higher education course[2]; or

(2) a further education course[3], and

who, before the course ends, is required, as part of that course, to attend a period of work experience not exceeding one year, does not qualify for the national minimum wage[4] in respect of work done for his employer[5] as part of that course[6].

1 As to the meaning of 'worker' for these purposes see PARA 171 note 9.
2 For these purposes, 'higher education course' means, in England and Wales, a course of a description referred to in the Education Reform Act 1988 s 120(1), Sch 6 (see EDUCATION vol 35 (2011) PARA 23): see the National Minimum Wage Regulations 1999, SI 1999/584, reg 2(1) (definition added by SI 2011/2347). To define a higher education course for these purposes so as to relate only to courses undertaken within the United Kingdom does not disproportionately exclude EU and foreign students who were not taking such courses from having as favourable an opportunity of gaining work experience: *Daler-Rowney Ltd v Revenue and Customs Comrs* [2014] All ER (D) 308 (Jul), FAT (tribunal entitled to decide that the

definition was (indirectly) discriminatory, but justified as a proportionate means of preventing abuse of the national minimum wage system, which was a legitimate aim). As to the meanings of 'England' and 'Wales' see PARA 2 note 12.

3   For these purposes, 'further education course' means:

   (1)   in England, a course of education that is suitable to the requirements of persons who are over compulsory school age, and that: (a) is funded by the Secretary of State under the Education Act 2002 s 14 (financial assistance for purposes related to education or children etc: see EDUCATION vol 35 (2011) PARA 77); (b) is funded by the Chief Executive of Skills Funding; (c) is funded by a local authority; (d) leads to a qualification to which the Apprenticeships, Skills, Children and Learning Act 2009 Pt 7 (ss 127–174) (see EDUCATION vol 36 (2011) PARA 1147 et seq) applies which is awarded or authenticated by a body which is recognised by the Office of Qualifications and Examinations Regulation under s 132 (see EDUCATION vol 36 (2011) PARA 1152) in respect of the qualification; or (e) leads to a qualification that is approved pursuant to the Learning and Skills Act 2000 s 98 (see EDUCATION vol 36 (2011) PARA 1137), except that it does not include a higher education course (see the National Minimum Wage Regulations 1999, SI 1999/584, reg 2(1) (definition added by SI 2011/2347; and amended in relation to England by SI 2012/956));

   (2)   in Wales, a course of education that is suitable to the requirements of persons who are over compulsory school age, and that: (a) is funded by the Welsh Ministers; (b) is funded by a local authority; (c) leads to a qualification that is accredited by the Welsh Ministers pursuant to the Education Act 1997 s 30 (see EDUCATION vol 36 (2011) PARA 1050); or (d) leads to a qualification that is approved pursuant to the Learning and Skills Act 2000 s 99 (see EDUCATION vol 36 (2011) PARA 1139), except that it does not include a higher education course (see the National Minimum Wage Regulations 1999, SI 1999/584, reg 2(1) (definition as so added)).

   For these purposes,' compulsory school age' has the meaning given to it by the Education Act 1996 s 8 (see EDUCATION vol 35 (2011) PARA 18): see the National Minimum Wage Regulations 1999, SI 1999/584, reg 2(1) (definition added by SI 2011/2347). As to the Chief Executive of Skills Funding see EDUCATION vol 36 (2011) PARA 1279 et seq.

4   As to the meaning of 'person who qualifies for the national minimum wage' see PARA 176 note 5. As to the power to make regulations preventing a person from qualifying for the national minimum wage see the National Minimum Wage Act 1998 s 3; and PARA 186. As to the rate of the national minimum wage see PARA 199.

5   As to the meaning of 'employer' for these purposes see PARA 170.

6   National Minimum Wage Regulations 1999, SI 1999/584, reg 12(8) (substituted by SI 2000/1989; National Minimum Wage Regulations 1999, SI 1999/584, reg 12(8) amended, reg 12(9A) added, by SI 2007/2318); National Minimum Wage Regulations 1999, SI 1999/584, reg 12(9A) (as so added).

197.   Homeless workers provided with shelter and other benefits. A worker[1] does not qualify for the national minimum wage[2] in respect of work performed for his employer[3] under a scheme in which he is participating, and under which he is provided with shelter and other benefits[4] in return for performing work[5], if:

   (1)   the worker himself satisfies the necessary condition[6], that is to say that, immediately before his entry into the scheme[7]:

      (a)   he was either homeless or residing in a hostel for homeless persons[8]; and

      (b)   he was in receipt of, or entitled to, universal credit[9], income support[10], income-based jobseeker's allowance[11] or income-related employment and support allowance[12], or he was not entitled to receive any of those benefits only because he was not habitually resident in the United Kingdom[13]; and

   (2)   the scheme satisfies the prescribed conditions[14], that is to say that[15]:

      (a)   the arrangements under which the scheme operates prevent the person operating the scheme or any other person from making a profit out of the provision of the scheme, other than one which may only be applied in running the scheme or other schemes satisfying the necessary requirements[16] or, where the person operating the scheme is a charity, for a purpose (being a purpose of the charity) relating to the alleviation of poverty[17];

(b)   every person participating in the scheme satisfies the condition set out under head (1) above (or would satisfy it if he were a worker)[18];

(c)   the accommodation available under the scheme is provided by the person operating the scheme or under arrangements made between that person and another person[19]; and

(d)   the work done under the scheme is both provided by, and performed for, the person operating the scheme[20].

1   As to the meaning of 'worker' for these purposes see PARA 171 note 9.
2   As to the meaning of 'person who qualifies for the national minimum wage' see PARA 176 note 5. As to the power to make regulations preventing a person from qualifying for the national minimum wage see the National Minimum Wage Act 1998 s 3; and PARA 186. As to the rate of the national minimum wage see PARA 199.
3   As to the meaning of 'employer' for these purposes see PARA 170.
4   Ie which may include money benefits: see the National Minimum Wage Regulations 1999, SI 1999/584, reg 12(10).
5   See the National Minimum Wage Regulations 1999, SI 1999/584, reg 12(10).
6   Ie if the worker satisfies the condition set out in the National Minimum Wage Regulations 1999, SI 1999/584, reg 12(11) (see head (1) in the text): see reg 12(10).
7   See the National Minimum Wage Regulations 1999, SI 1999/584, reg 12(11).
8   National Minimum Wage Regulations 1999, SI 1999/584, reg 12(11)(a).
9   Ie under the Welfare Reform Act 2012 Pt 1 (ss 1–43) (see WELFARE BENEFITS AND STATE PENSIONS vol 104 (2014) PARA 124 et seq): see the National Minimum Wage Regulations 1999, SI 1999/584, reg 12(11)(b)(i) (amended by SI 2008/1879; SI 2013/630).
10 As to income support see WELFARE BENEFITS AND STATE PENSIONS vol 104 (2014) PARA 292 et seq.
11 As to income-based jobseeker's allowance (which has been partly abolished and, as from a day to be appointed, will be abolished fully) see WELFARE BENEFITS AND STATE PENSIONS vol 104 (2014) PARA 262 et seq.
12 National Minimum Wage Regulations 1999, SI 1999/584, reg 12(11)(b)(i) (as amended: see note 9). The text refers to income-related employment and support allowance (which has been partly abolished and, as from a day to be appointed, will be abolished fully) payable under the Welfare Reform Act 2007 Pt 1 (ss 1–29) (see WELFARE BENEFITS AND STATE PENSIONS vol 104 (2014) PARAS 252–261): see the National Minimum Wage Regulations 1999, SI 1999/584, reg 12(11)(b)(i) (as so amended).
12 National Minimum Wage Regulations 1999, SI 1999/584, reg 12(11)(b)(ii) (amended by SI 2013/630). As to the meaning of 'United Kingdom' see PARA 2 note 12. As to habitual residence see CONFLICT OF LAWS vol 19 (2011) PARA 360 et seq.
14 Ie if the scheme satisfies the conditions set out in the National Minimum Wage Regulations 1999, SI 1999/584, reg 12(12) (see head (2) in the text): see reg 12(10).
15 See the National Minimum Wage Regulations 1999, SI 1999/584, reg 12(12).
16 Ie the requirements of the National Minimum Wage Regulations 1999, SI 1999/584, reg 12(12) (see heads (2)(a)–(2)(d) in the text): see reg 12(12)(a).
17 National Minimum Wage Regulations 1999, SI 1999/584, reg 12(12)(a).
18 National Minimum Wage Regulations 1999, SI 1999/584, reg 12(12)(b).
19 National Minimum Wage Regulations 1999, SI 1999/584, reg 12(12)(c).
20 National Minimum Wage Regulations 1999, SI 1999/584, reg 12(12)(d).

198.   Workers participating in certain EU programmes.   A worker[1] who was participating in a specified European Union programme for education, training, and youth[2] did not qualify for the national minimum wage[3] in respect of work done for his employer[4] as part of that programme[5].

1   As to the meaning of 'worker' for these purposes see PARA 171 note 9.
2   The programmes currently so specified by the National Minimum Wage Regulations 1999, SI 1999/584, reg 12, are:

(1)   the second phase of the European Community 'Leonardo da Vinci' established pursuant to Council Decision (EC) 99/382 of 26 April 1999 (OJ L146, 11.6.99, p 33) establishing the second phase of the Community vocational training action programme 'Leonardo da Vinci' (see the National Minimum Wage Regulations 1999, SI 1999/584, reg 12(13) (added by SI 2005/2019));

(2)   the European Community Leonardo da Vinci programme established pursuant to European Parliament and Council Decision (EC) 1720/2006 of 15 November 2006 (OJ L327, 24.11.2006, p 45) establishing an action programme in the field of lifelong learning (see the National Minimum Wage Regulations 1999, SI 1999/584, reg 12(14) (added by SI 2007/2318));

(3)   the European Community Youth in Action Programme established pursuant to European Parliament and Council Decision (EC) 1719/2006 of 15 November 2006 (OJ L327, 24.11.2006, p 30) establishing the Youth Action programme for the period 2007 to 2013 (see the National Minimum Wage Regulations 1999, SI 1999/584, reg 12(15) (added by SI 2007/2318)); and

(4)   the European Community Erasmus or Comenius programmes, both also established pursuant to European Parliament and Council Decision (EC) 1720/2006 of 15 November 2006 (OJ L327, 24.11.2006, p 45) (see the National Minimum Wage Regulations 1999, SI 1999/584, reg 12(16) (added by SI 2009/1902)).

However, the programme established under head (1) above was intended to implemented over the period from 1 January 2000 to 31 December 2006 (see Council Decision (EC) 99/382 of 26 April 1999 (OJ L146, 11.6.99, p 33) art 1(2)); and the programmes established under heads (2)–(4) above have lapsed following the repeal of European Parliament and Council Decision (EC) 1719/2006 of 15 November 2006 (OJ L327, 24.11.2006, p 30) and European Parliament and Council Decision (EC) 1720/2006 of 15 November 2006 (OJ L327, 24.11.2006, p 45) by European Parliament and Council Regulation (EU) 1288/2013 of 11 December 2013 (OJ L347, 20.12.2013, p 50) establishing 'Erasmus+' (the Union programme for education, training, youth and sport).

3   As to the meaning of 'person who qualifies for the national minimum wage' see PARA 176 note 5. As to the power to make regulations preventing a person from qualifying for the national minimum wage see the National Minimum Wage Act 1998 s 3; and PARA 186. As to the rate of the national minimum wage see PARA 199.

4   As to the meaning of 'employer' for these purposes see PARA 170.

5   See the National Minimum Wage Regulations 1999, SI 1999/584, reg 12(13)–(16) (as added: see note 2).

(v) Rate of the National Minimum Wage

199. Single hourly rate of the national minimum wage and persons qualifying for different hourly rates. The national minimum wage must be such single hourly rate as the Secretary of State[1] may from time to time prescribe[2].

The rate is subject to frequent change but. at the date at which this volume states the law, the single hourly rate of the national minimum wage is £6.50[3], except that[4]:

(1)   subject to head (3) below, the hourly rate of the national minimum wage is £5.13 for a worker who has attained the age of 18 but not the age of 21[5]; and

(2)   subject to head (3) below, the hourly rate of the national minimum wage is £3.79 for a worker who has not attained the age of 18[6];

(3)   the hourly rate of the national minimum wage is £2.73 for a worker[7] who: (a) is employed under a contract of apprenticeship[8], or is to be treated[9] as employed under a contract of apprenticeship[10]; and (b) is within the first 12 months after the commencement of that employment[11], or has not attained the age of 19[12].

1   As to the Secretary of State see PARA 5 note 21.

2   National Minimum Wage Act 1998 s 1(3). The provision made by s 1(1)–(4) (see also PARAS 176, 202) is subject to ss 2–56 (see also PARAS 169 et seq, 200 et seq): s 1(5).

For the purposes of the National Minimum Wage Act 1998, unless the context otherwise requires, 'prescribe' means prescribe by regulations: see s 55(1). As to the making of regulations under the National Minimum Wage Act 1998 see PARA 175. As to the regulations so made under s 1(3) see the National Minimum Wage Regulations 1999, SI 1999/584; and the text and notes 3–12. As to regulations made for the purposes of determining the hourly rate in any pay reference period see PARA 200 et seq.

3   National Minimum Wage Regulations 1999, SI 1999/584, reg 11 (amended by SI 2014/2485).

See *Hughes v Graham (t/a Graylyns Residential Home)* [2008] All ER (D) 137 (Oct), EAT (employee entitled to the benefit of the National Minimum Wage Regulations 1999, SI 1999/584 (entitling her to the minimum wage for the hours worked), and the Working Time Regulations 1998, SI 1998/1833, in circumstances where she had actually worked eight hours a week and was required to be on call for 77, giving her a working week of 85 hours).

4   As to the power to prescribe an hourly rate for the national minimum wage other than the single hourly rate for the time being otherwise prescribed see the National Minimum Wage Act 1998 s 3; and PARA 186.

5   National Minimum Wage Regulations 1999, SI 1999/584, reg 13(1) (reg 13 substituted by SI 2010/1901; the National Minimum Wage Regulations 1999, SI 1999/584 reg 13(1)–(3) amended by SI 2014/2485). As to the meaning of 'worker' for these purposes see PARA 171 note 9. A person attains a particular age expressed in years at the commencement of the relevant anniversary of the date of his birth: see the Family Law Reform Act 1969 s 9; and CHILDREN AND YOUNG PERSONS vol 9 (2012) PARA 2.

The National Minimum Wage Regulations 1999, SI 1999/584, reg 13(1)–(3) (see also heads (2), (3) in the text) do not apply in relation to a worker who, by virtue of reg 12 (see PARAS 193–197), does not qualify for the national minimum wage: reg 13(4) (as so substituted).

6   National Minimum Wage Regulations 1999, SI 1999/584, reg 13(2) (reg 13 as substituted (see note 5); reg 13(2) as amended (see note 5)). See note 5.

7   See the National Minimum Wage Regulations 1999, SI 1999/584, reg 13(3) (reg 13 as substituted (see note 5); reg 13(3) as amended (see note 5)).

8   For the purposes of the National Minimum Wage Regulations 1999, SI 1999/584, the expression 'a worker who is employed under a contract of apprenticeship' includes a worker who is working under an apprenticeship agreement (within the meaning of the Apprenticeships, Skills, Children and Learning Act 2009 s 32: see EDUCATION vol 35 (2011) PARA 683): National Minimum Wage Regulations 1999, SI 1999/584, reg 13A (added by SI 2012/3112). As to the position of apprentices and youth trainees at common law see PARAS 112, 128–129, 636, 747–754. As to the statutory law on apprenticeships see EDUCATION vol 35 (2011) PARA 682 et seq. See also PARA 170.

9   Ie in accordance with the National Minimum Wage Regulations 1999, SI 1999/584, reg 13(6): see reg 13(3)(a) (as substituted: see note 5). Accordingly, a person is to be treated for the purposes of head (3)(a) in the text as a worker who is employed under a contract of apprenticeship, if, and only if, that person is:

    (1)   a worker within the meaning given by the National Minimum Wage Act 1998 s 54(3) (see PARA 171) (National Minimum Wage Regulations 1999, SI 1999/584, reg 13(6)(a) (as so substituted)); and

    (2)   engaged: (a) in England, under the government arrangements known, at 1 October 2010, as Apprenticeships or Advanced Apprenticeships, or known as Intermediate Level Apprenticeships or Advanced Level Apprenticeships, or under a Trailblazer Apprenticeship (reg 13(6)(b)(i) (reg 13 as so substituted; reg 13(6)(b)(i) amended by SI 2012/2397; and SI 2014/2832)); or (b) in Wales, under the government arrangements known, at 1 October 2010, as Foundation Modern Apprenticeships, Modern Apprenticeships, Foundation Apprenticeships or Apprenticeships (National Minimum Wage Regulations 1999, SI 1999/584, reg 13(6)(b)(iv) (as so substituted)).

For the purposes of head (2)(a) above, a 'Trailblazer Apprenticeship' is an agreement between an employer and a worker which provides for the worker to perform work for that employer and for the employer, or another person, to provide training in order to assist the worker to achieve the apprenticeship standard in the work done under the agreement, where 'apprenticeship standard' means the standard published by the Secretary of State in connection with the government arrangements known as Trailblazer Apprenticeships, which applies as respects the work done under the agreement: see reg 13(7), (8) (added by SI 2014/2832). As to the meanings of 'England' and 'Wales' see PARA 2 note 12.

10   National Minimum Wage Regulations 1999, SI 1999/584, reg 13(3)(a) (as substituted: see note 5).

11   For the purposes of head (3)(b) in the text, a person does not commence employment with an employer where that person has previously been employed by another employer and continuity

of employment is preserved between the two employments by or under any enactment: National Minimum Wage Regulations 1999, SI 1999/584, reg 13(5) (as substituted: see note 5).

12 National Minimum Wage Regulations 1999, SI 1999/584, reg 13(3)(b) (as substituted: see note 5).

200. Secretary of State's power to make regulations for determining the hourly rate in any pay reference period. The Secretary of State[1] may by regulations[2] make provision for determining what is the hourly rate at which a person is to be regarded for the purposes of the National Minimum Wage Act 1998 as remunerated by his employer[3] in respect of his work[4] in any pay reference period[5].

The regulations may make provision for determining the hourly rate in cases where[6]:

(1) the remuneration, to the extent that it is at a periodic rate, is at a single rate[7];

(2) the remuneration is, in whole or in part, at different rates applicable at different times or in different circumstances[8];

(3) the remuneration is, in whole or in part, otherwise than at a periodic rate or rates[9];

(4) the remuneration consists, in whole or in part, of benefits in kind[10].

The regulations may make provision with respect to[11]:

(a) circumstances in which, times at which, or the time for which, a person is to be treated as, or as not, working, and the extent to which a person is to be so treated[12];

(b) the treatment of periods of paid or unpaid absence from, or lack of, work and of remuneration in respect of such periods[13].

The provision that may be made by virtue of head (a) above includes provision for or in connection with[14]:

(i) treating a person as, or as not, working for a maximum or minimum time, or for a proportion of the time, in any period[15];

(ii) determining any matter to which head (a) above relates by reference to the terms of an agreement[16].

The regulations may also make provision with respect to[17]:

(A) what is to be treated as, or as not, forming part of a person's remuneration, and the extent to which it is to be so treated[18];

(B) the valuation of benefits in kind[19];

(C) the treatment of deductions from earnings[20];

(D) the treatment of any charges or expenses which a person is required to bear[21];

(E) the attribution to a period, or the apportionment between two or more periods, of the whole or any part of any remuneration or work, whether or not the remuneration is received or the work is done within the period or periods in question[22];

(F) the aggregation of the whole or any part of the remuneration for different periods[23];

(G) the time at which remuneration is to be treated as received or accruing[24].

No such provision is to be made however which treats the same circumstances differently in relation to different areas[25], different sectors of employment[26], undertakings of different sizes[27], persons of different ages[28], or persons of different occupations[29].

1 As to the Secretary of State see PARA 5 note 21.

2   As to the making of regulations under the National Minimum Wage Act 1998 see PARA 175. See also note 5.

3   As to the meaning of 'employer' for these purposes see PARA 170.

4   As to the meaning of 'work' for these purposes see PARA 172.

5   National Minimum Wage Act 1998 s 2(1). As to the meaning of references to a person being remunerated for a pay reference period see PARA 174 note 8; and as to the meaning of 'pay reference period' see PARA 202. As to the referral of certain matters to the Low Pay Commission before the making of the first regulations see PARA 234; and as to the regulations that have been made under s 2 see the National Minimum Wage Regulations 1999, SI 1999/584; and PARAS 170 et seq, 201 et seq. Failure to remunerate a worker who qualifies for the national minimum wage at the appropriate hourly rate is an offence: see PARA 251.

6   See the National Minimum Wage Act 1998 s 2(2). Section 2(2)–(6) (see also the text and notes 7–24) is without prejudice to s 2(1) (see the text and notes 1–5): see s 2(7).

7   National Minimum Wage Act 1998 s 2(2)(a). See note 6.

8   National Minimum Wage Act 1998 s 2(2)(b). See note 6.

9   National Minimum Wage Act 1998 s 2(2)(c). See note 6.

10   National Minimum Wage Act 1998 s 2(2)(d). See note 6.

11   See the National Minimum Wage Act 1998 s 2(3). See note 6.

12   National Minimum Wage Act 1998 s 2(3)(a). See note 6.

13   National Minimum Wage Act 1998 s 2(3)(b). See note 6.

14   See the National Minimum Wage Act 1998 s 2(4). See note 6.

15   National Minimum Wage Act 1998 s 2(4)(a). See note 6.

16   National Minimum Wage Act 1998 s 2(4)(b). See note 6.

17   See the National Minimum Wage Act 1998 s 2(5). See note 6.

18   National Minimum Wage Act 1998 s 2(5)(a). See note 6.

19   National Minimum Wage Act 1998 s 2(5)(b). See note 6.

20   National Minimum Wage Act 1998 s 2(5)(c). See note 6.

21   National Minimum Wage Act 1998 s 2(5)(d). See note 6.

22   National Minimum Wage Act 1998 s 2(6)(a). See note 6.

23   National Minimum Wage Act 1998 s 2(6)(b). See note 6.

24   National Minimum Wage Act 1998 s 2(6)(c). See note 6.

25   National Minimum Wage Act 1998 s 2(8)(a).

26   National Minimum Wage Act 1998 s 2(8)(b). As to the meaning of 'employment' for these purposes see PARA 170.

27   National Minimum Wage Act 1998 s 2(8)(c).

28   National Minimum Wage Act 1998 s 2(8)(d).

29   National Minimum Wage Act 1998 s 2(8)(e).

201. Method of determining the hourly rate in a pay reference period paid to a worker who qualifies for the national minimum wage. The hourly rate paid to a worker[1] in a pay reference period[2] is determined by dividing[3]:

(1)   the total calculated by subtracting from the total of remuneration[4] in the pay reference period[5], the total of reductions[6]; by

(2)   the total number of hours of time work[7], salaried hours work[8], output work[9], and unmeasured work[10], worked by the worker in the pay reference period[11].

1   As to the meaning of 'worker' for these purposes see PARA 171.

2   The hourly rate at which a worker is entitled to be remunerated in respect of his work in any pay reference period is the rate, prescribed by regulations, that is in force on the first day of that period: National Minimum Wage Regulations 1999, SI 1999/584, reg 14A (added by SI 2002/1999). As to the meaning of 'pay reference period' see PARA 202.

3   See the National Minimum Wage Regulations 1999, SI 1999/584, reg 14(1). The hourly rate mentioned in the text is determined by dividing the total calculated in accordance with reg 14(2) (see head (1) in the text) by the number of hours specified in reg 14(3) (see head (2) in the text): see reg 14(1).

4   For these purposes, the 'total of remuneration' means the total of money payments determined in accordance with the National Minimum Wage Regulations 1999, SI 1999/584, reg 30 (see PARA 220): see reg 2(1).

5   Ie the payments to the worker that are taken into account as determined under the National Minimum Wage Regulations 1999, SI 1999/584, reg 30 (see PARA 220): see reg 14(2).

6 See the National Minimum Wage Regulations 1999, SI 1999/584, reg 14(2). Head (1) in the text refers to the total of reductions determined under regs 31–37 (see PARA 221 et seq): see reg 14(2). For the purposes of the National Minimum Wage Regulations 1999, SI 1999/584, generally, the 'total of reductions' means the total of reductions determined in accordance with regs 31–37: see reg 2(1).

7 As to the meaning of 'time work' see PARA 203.

8 As to the meaning of 'salaried hours work' see PARA 204.

9 As to the meaning of 'output work' see PARA 205.

10 As to the meaning of 'unmeasured work' see PARA 206.

11 See the National Minimum Wage Regulations 1999, SI 1999/584, reg 14(3) (amended by SI 2000/1989). Head (2) in the text refers to the hours worked in a pay reference period ascertained in accordance with the National Minimum Wage Regulations 1999, SI 1999/584, regs 20–29A (see PARA 213 et seq): see reg 14(3) (as so amended).

202. Meaning of 'pay reference period' under national minimum wage provisions. For the purposes of the National Minimum Wage Act 1998, a 'pay reference period' is such period as the Secretary of State[1] may prescribe for the purpose[2].

The pay reference period so prescribed is a month (or, in the case of a worker[3] who is paid wages by reference to a period shorter than a month, that period)[4].

1 As to the Secretary of State see PARA 5 note 21.

2 National Minimum Wage Act 1998 s 1(4). The provision made by s 1(1)–(4) (see also PARAS 176, 199) is subject to ss 2–56 (see also PARAS 169 et seq, 207 et seq): s 1(5).

For the purposes of the National Minimum Wage Act 1998, unless the context otherwise requires, 'prescribe' means prescribe by regulations: see s 55(1). As to the making of regulations under the National Minimum Wage Act 1998 see PARA 175. As to the regulations so made under s 1(4) see the National Minimum Wage Regulations 1999, SI 1999/584; the text and notes 3–4; and PARA 203 et seq.

3 As to the meaning of 'worker' for these purposes see PARA 171.

4 National Minimum Wage Regulations 1999, SI 1999/584, reg 10(1). For the purposes of the National Minimum Wage Regulations 1999, SI 1999/584, 'pay reference period' has the meaning assigned to it by reg 10: see reg 2(1).

When a worker's contract terminates, reg 14 (method of determining the national minimum wage has been paid to a worker: see PARA 201) and regs 30–37 (remuneration counting towards the national minimum wage: see PARA 220 et seq) must be applied in relation to payments made in the period of a month beginning with the day immediately following the last day on which the worker worked under the contract as if such payments had been made in the worker's final pay reference period: reg 10(2).

203. Meaning of 'time work' under national minimum wage regulations. 'Time work' means[1]:

(1) work[2] that is paid for under a worker's contract by reference to the time for which a worker[3] works and is not salaried hours work[4];

(2) work that is paid for under a worker's contract by reference to a measure of the output of the worker per hour or other period of time during the whole of which the worker is required to work, and is not salaried hours work[5]; and

(3) work that would fall within head (2) above but for the fact that the worker is paid by reference to the length of the period of time alone when his output does not exceed a particular level[6].

1 Ie for the purposes of the National Minimum Wage Regulations 1999, SI 1999/584 (see also PARAS 170 et seq, 204 et seq): see reg 3.

Where work is time work within the meaning of reg 3, the question of whether the scope of time work is extended by reg 15 (see PARA 208) does not arise: *Scottbridge Construction Ltd v Wright* [2003] IRLR 21, IH (employee's work was his attendance as a night watchman, even though he was permitted to sleep, because he could be required at any time to perform duties such as answering the telephone). *Scottbridge Construction Ltd v Wright* was applied in *Rossiter v Burrow Down Support Services Ltd* [2008] ICR 1172, [2008] All ER (D) 49 (Oct), EAT.

2   As to the meaning of 'work' for these purposes see PARA 172.
3   As to the meaning of 'worker' for these purposes see PARA 171.
4   National Minimum Wage Regulations 1999, SI 1999/584, reg 3(a). As to the meaning of 'salaried hours work' see PARA 204.
5   National Minimum Wage Regulations 1999, SI 1999/584, reg 3(b).
6   National Minimum Wage Regulations 1999, SI 1999/584, reg 3(c).

204.   Meaning of 'salaried hours work' under national minimum wage regulations. 'Salaried hours work' means[1]:
   (1)   work that is done under a contract to do salaried hours work[2]; and
   (2)   is work in respect of which the worker[3] is entitled to no payment in addition to his annual salary (or to no payment in addition to his annual salary other than a performance bonus)[4].
A contract to do salaried hours work is a contract under which a worker:
   (a)   is entitled to be paid for an ascertainable basic number of hours in a year (the 'basic hours')[5]; and
   (b)   is entitled, in respect of hours that consist of or include the basic hours, to be paid an annual salary (either by equal weekly or monthly instalments of wages, or by monthly instalments of wages that vary but have the result that the worker is entitled to be paid an equal amount in each quarter), regardless of the number of hours in respect of which the worker is entitled to the annual salary that are actually worked by him, if any, in any particular week or month[6]; and
   (c)   has, in respect of those hours, no entitlement to any payment other than his annual salary or no such entitlement other than an entitlement to a performance bonus[7].
A contract that satisfies the conditions in heads (a) to (c) above does so:
   (i)   whether or not all the basic hours are working hours[8];
   (ii)   whether or not the worker can be required under his contract to work, or does in fact work, any hours in addition to the total of hours in respect of which he is entitled to his annual salary, and regardless of any payments made in respect of those additional hours[9].
Circumstances having the result that in practice a worker may not be or is not paid by equal instalments of wages, or by an equal amount in each quarter, for hours in respect of which he is entitled under his contract only to his annual salary, do not prevent the contract from being a contract for salaried hours work[10], for example:
   (A)   where a worker may be awarded a performance bonus[11];
   (B)   where the amount of a worker's annual salary may be varied[12];
   (C)   where the worker is entitled[13] to the national minimum wage[14] in respect of hours in addition to his basic hours when, under his contract, there is no entitlement to any payment in addition to his annual salary for those additional hours (or to no payment in addition other than a performance bonus)[15]; and
   (D)   where the worker's employment may start or terminate during a week or month with the result that the worker is paid a proportionate amount of his annual salary for the week or month in question[16].
The fact that, by reason of an absence from work for hours in respect of which his annual salary is normally payable, a worker is entitled under his contract, in

respect of those hours, to be paid less than he would be but for the absence or to no payment does not prevent the worker's contract from being a contract for salaried hours work[17].

1 Ie for the purposes of the National Minimum Wage Regulations 1999, SI 1999/584 (see also PARAS 170 et seq, 205 et seq): see reg 4.
2 National Minimum Wage Regulations 1999, SI 1999/584, reg 4(1)(a). As to the meaning of 'work' for these purposes see PARA 172.
3 As to the meaning of 'worker' for these purposes see PARA 171.
4 See the National Minimum Wage Regulations 1999, SI 1999/584, reg 4(1)(b), (6). Head (2) in the text refers to work that falls within reg 4(6): see reg 4(1)(b). For these purposes, 'performance bonus' means a performance bonus or other merit payment attributable to the quality or amount of work done in the course of more than one pay reference period, and not, therefore, payable directly in respect of work done in specific hours: see reg 2(1). See also note 13. As to the meaning of 'pay reference period' see PARA 202.
5 National Minimum Wage Regulations 1999, SI 1999/584, reg 4(2)(a).
6 See the National Minimum Wage Regulations 1999, SI 1999/584, reg 4(2)(b).
7 National Minimum Wage Regulations 1999, SI 1999/584, reg 4(2)(c).
8 National Minimum Wage Regulations 1999, SI 1999/584, reg 4(3)(a).
9 National Minimum Wage Regulations 1999, SI 1999/584, reg 4(3)(b).
10 See the National Minimum Wage Regulations 1999, SI 1999/584, reg 4(4).
11 National Minimum Wage Regulations 1999, SI 1999/584, reg 4(4)(a).
12 National Minimum Wage Regulations 1999, SI 1999/584, reg 4(4)(b).
13 Ie by virtue of the National Minimum Wage Regulations 1999, SI 1999/584, reg 22 (see PARA 215) or reg 23 (see PARA 216): see reg 4(4)(c). References in reg 22 to work or hours of work in respect of which a worker is entitled to no payment other than his annual salary refer also to work or hours of work in respect of which the only payment to which the worker is entitled other than his annual salary is payment of a performance bonus: reg 4(7).
14 As to entitlement to the national minimum wage see PARA 176; and as to the rate of the national minimum wage see PARA 199.
15 National Minimum Wage Regulations 1999, SI 1999/584, reg 4(4)(c).
16 National Minimum Wage Regulations 1999, SI 1999/584, reg 4(4)(d).
17 National Minimum Wage Regulations 1999, SI 1999/584, reg 4(5).

205. Meaning of 'output work' under national minimum wage regulations.
'Output work' means[1] work that is paid for under a worker's contract that is not time work[2] and would[3] be paid for under that contract wholly by reference to the number of pieces made or processed by the worker[4], or wholly by reference to some other measure of output such as the number or value of sales made or transactions completed by the worker or as a result of his work[5].

1 Ie for the purposes of the National Minimum Wage Regulations 1999, SI 1999/584 (see also PARAS 170 et seq, 206 et seq): see reg 5.
2 As to the meaning of 'work' for these purposes see PARA 172; and as to the meaning of 'time work' see PARA 203.
3 Ie but for the effect of the National Minimum Wage Act 1998 and the National Minimum Wage Regulations 1999, SI 1999/584, or anything done pursuant to the National Minimum Wage Regulations 1999, SI 1999/584: see reg 5.
4 As to the meaning of 'worker' for these purposes see PARA 171.
5 National Minimum Wage Regulations 1999, SI 1999/584, reg 5.

206. Meaning of 'unmeasured work' under national minimum wage regulations. 'Unmeasured work' means[1] any other work that is not time work[2], salaried hours work[3] or output work[4] including, in particular, work in respect of which there are no specified hours, and the worker[5] is required to work when needed or when work is available[6].

1 Ie for the purposes of the National Minimum Wage Regulations 1999, SI 1999/584 (see also PARAS 170 et seq): see reg 6.

2 As to the meaning of 'work' for these purposes see PARA 172; and as to the meaning of 'time work' see PARA 203.
3 As to the meaning of 'salaried hours work' see PARA 204.
4 As to the meaning of 'output work' see PARA 205.
5 As to the meaning of 'worker' for these purposes see PARA 171.
6 National Minimum Wage Regulations 1999, SI 1999/584, reg 6. See *Walton v Independent Living Organisation* [2003] EWCA Civ 199, [2003] ICR 688, [2003] IRLR 469 (a carer carried out unmeasured work where she was employed to look after a disabled client in the client's own home which required her being on the premises 24 hours a day, three days a week, though not all the time performing services for the client).

207.   Employer to provide worker with national minimum wage statement.

Regulations under the National Minimum Wage Act 1998[1] may make provision for the purpose of conferring on a worker[2] the right to be given by his employer[3], at or before the time at which any payment of remuneration is made to the worker, a written statement[4]. The regulations may make provision with respect to the contents of any such statement and may, in particular, require it to contain[5]:

(1)   prescribed[6] information relating to the National Minimum Wage Act 1998 or any regulations under it[7]; or

(2)   prescribed information for the purpose of assisting the worker to determine whether he has been remunerated at a rate at least equal to the national minimum wage[8] during the period to which the payment of remuneration relates[9].

Any statement required to be so given to a worker by his employer may, if the worker is an employee[10], be included in the written itemised pay statement required to be given to him[11] by his employer[12].

1 As to the making of regulations under the National Minimum Wage Act 1998 see PARA 175.
2 As to the meaning of 'worker' for these purposes see PARA 171.
3 As to the meaning of 'employer' for these purposes see PARA 170.
4 National Minimum Wage Act 1998 s 12(1). At the date at which this volume states the law, no such regulations had been made.
5 See the National Minimum Wage Act 1998 s 12(2).
6 For the purposes of the National Minimum Wage Act 1998, unless the context otherwise requires, 'prescribe' means prescribe by regulations: see s 55(1). See notes 1, 4.
7 National Minimum Wage Act 1998 s 12(2)(a).
8 As to the rate of the national minimum wage see PARA 199.
9 National Minimum Wage Act 1998 s 12(2)(b). The regulations may also make provision for the purpose of applying the Employment Rights Act 1996 s 11 (reference to employment tribunal where employer does not give employee statements required by statute: see PARA 125) and s 12 (determination by employment tribunal of particulars which ought to have been included in statements: see PARA 126), in relation to a worker and any such statement as is mentioned in the National Minimum Wage Act 1998 s 12(1), as the Employment Rights Act 1996 ss 11, 12 apply in relation to an employee and a statement required to be given to him by his employer under s 8 (right to itemised pay statement see PARA 124): see the National Minimum Wage Act 1998 s 12(4).
10 As to the meaning of 'employee' for these purposes see PARA 170.
11 Ie under the Employment Rights Act 1996 s 8 (see PARA 124): see the National Minimum Wage Act 1998 s 12(3).
12 National Minimum Wage Act 1998 s 12(3).

(vi) Determining Working Time for the Purposes of the National Minimum Wage

208.   Extension of scope of time work.

For the purposes of the National Minimum Wage Act 1998, 'time work'[1] includes time when a worker[2] is available at or near a place of work for the purpose of doing time work and is required to be available for such work[3], except where:

(1)   the worker's home is at or near the place of work[4]; and

(2)   the time is time the worker is entitled to spend at home[5].

In relation to a worker who by arrangement sleeps at or near a place of work and is provided with suitable facilities for sleeping, time during the hours he is permitted to use those facilities for the purpose of sleeping is, however, only to be treated as being time work when the worker is awake for the purpose of working[6].

Time when a worker is travelling for the purpose of duties carried out by him in the course of time work is treated as being time work[7], except where:

(a)   the travelling is incidental to the duties carried out in the course of time work[8], the time work is not assignment work[9] and the time is time when the worker would not otherwise be working[10]; or

(b)   the travelling is between the worker's home, or an address where he is temporarily residing other than for the purposes of performing work, and his place of work or a place where an assignment is carried out[11].

Where a worker's hours of work vary either as to their length or in respect of the time at which they are performed and, as a result, it is uncertain in relation to particular time when the worker is travelling whether he would otherwise be working, that time is to be treated, for the purposes of head (a) above, as time when he would otherwise be working[12].

Time work does not include[13] time when a worker is absent from work[14]; and a worker engaged in taking industrial action in the course of time work is to be treated as being absent from work for the time during which he is so engaged[15]. Where a worker is entitled to a rest break in the course of time work, the period of the break is to be treated as time when the worker is absent from work; but a worker is not to be treated as being entitled to any rest breaks during time which is otherwise[16] required to be treated as time work[17].

1   As to the usual meaning of 'time work' see PARA 203.

2   As to the meaning of 'worker' for these purposes see PARA 171.

3   See the National Minimum Wage Regulations 1999, SI 1999/584, reg 15(1) (reg 15(1)–(3) substituted, reg 15(1A) added, by SI 2000/1989). The provision made by the National Minimum Wage Regulations 1999, SI 1999/584, reg 15(1) is subject to reg 15(1A) (see the text and note 6): see reg 15(1) (as so substituted). See also *British Nursing Association v Inland Revenue (National Minimum Wage Compliance Team)* [2002] EWCA Civ 494, [2003] ICR 19, [2002] IRLR 480 (employees operating the employers' emergency telephone booking service from home during night-time hours were 'working' throughout their shifts for the purposes of the National Minimum Wage Regulations 1999, SI 1999/584, reg 15(1) (as originally enacted), even though they were not actually answering telephone calls for the whole of that time and could spend part of their shift doing other activities, such as reading or watching television).

4   National Minimum Wage Regulations 1999, SI 1999/584, reg 15(1)(a) (as substituted: see note 3).

5   National Minimum Wage Regulations 1999, SI 1999/584, reg 15(1)(b) (as substituted: see note 3).

6   National Minimum Wage Regulations 1999, SI 1999/584, reg 15(1A) (as added : see note 3). The provision set out in the text (ie reg 15(1A)) is not a self-standing provision intended to qualify the definition of 'time work' in reg 3 (see PARA 203) but had to be seen rather as qualifying the effect of reg 15(1) (see the text and notes 1–5); it has no impact on periods of actual work: *Rossiter v Burrow Down Support Services Ltd* [2008] ICR 1172, [2008] All ER (D) 49 (Oct), EAT ('night sleeper' employed to ensure the security of the work premises, a care home for people with learning difficulties, was at work for the whole of his shift because even during the time when he was permitted to be asleep, he was still required to deal with anything untoward that might arise). *Rossiter v Burrow Down Support Services Ltd* was applied in

Whittlestone v BJP Home Support Ltd [2014] ICR 275, [2014] IRLR 176, EAT (care assistant entitled to have the time she spent doing sleepovers included in the overall calculation of the national minimum wage).

For the purposes of the national minimum wage, the case law shows a clear dichotomy between: (1) those cases where an employee is working merely by being present at the employer's premises (eg a nightwatchman) whether or not provided with sleeping accommodation (where sleeping time will count as working time); and (2) those case where the employee is provided with sleeping accommodation and is simply on-call: *South Manchester Abbeyfield Society Ltd v Hopkins* [2011] ICR 254, [2011] IRLR 300, EAT. In cases under head (2) above, the employee may be able to rely on the National Minimum Wage Regulations 1999, SI 1999/584, to assert that all the hours on-call are working hours, but he can only bring into account such hours as he is awake for the purpose of working (because of the effect of regs 15(1A), 16(1A) (see also PARA 209)): *South Manchester Abbeyfield Society Ltd v Hopkins*. See also *Wray v JW Lees & Co (Brewers) Ltd* [2012] ICR 43, [2011] All ER (D) 124 (Sep), EAT; and PARA 209 note 7. As to distinguishing between 'at-work' cases, where the employee is paid simply to be there 'just in case', and 'on-call' cases where he is required to be there on call and is not deemed to be working the whole time see also *Esparon (t/a Middle West Residential Care Home) v Slavikovska* [2014] IRLR 598, EAT (an important consideration must be why the employer requires the employee to be on the premises: if he requires the employee to be on the premises pursuant to a statutory requirement to have a suitable person on the premises 'just in case', that would be a powerful indicator that the employee is being paid simply to be there and is thus deemed to be working regardless of whether work is actually carried out).

7   See the National Minimum Wage Regulations 1999, SI 1999/584, reg 15(2) (as substituted: see note 3). For the purposes of the National Minimum Wage Regulations 1999, SI 1999/584, reg 15(2), reg 16(2), (5)(b) (see PARA 209), reg 17(1) (see PARA 210), reg 18(1) (see PARA 211) and reg 19(1)(b) (see PARA 212), a worker is to be treated as travelling if:
    (1)   he is in the course of a journey by a mode of transport or is making a journey on foot (reg 7(a));
    (2)   he is waiting at a place of departure to begin his journey by a mode of transport (reg 7(b));
    (3)   where his journey is broken, he is waiting at a place of departure for his journey to recommence either by the same or another mode of transport, except for any time during such a period he spends in taking a rest break (reg 7(c)); or
    (4)   he is waiting at the end of a journey (in the case of reg 15(2), reg 16(2), reg 17(1) or reg 18(1)) for the purpose of carrying out his duties or (in the case of regs 16(5)(b), 19(1)(b)) to receive training, except for any time before he is due to carry out his duties or receive training which he spends in taking a rest break (reg 7(d)).

8   For the purposes of head (a) in the text, travelling is incidental to the duties carried out by a worker unless duties involved in his work are necessarily carried out in the course of the travelling (as in the case of a worker driving a bus, or serving in a bar on a train) or whose main duty is to transport items from one place to another: National Minimum Wage Regulations 1999, SI 1999/584, reg 15(3)(a) (as substituted: see note 3).

9   For the purposes of head (a) in the text, time work is assignment work if it consists of assignments of work to be carried out at different places between which the worker is obliged to travel that are not places occupied by the worker's employer: National Minimum Wage Regulations 1999, SI 1999/584, reg 15(3)(b) (as substituted: see note 3). As to the meaning of 'employer' for these purposes see PARA 170.

10 National Minimum Wage Regulations 1999, SI 1999/584, reg 15(2)(a) (as substituted: see note 3).

11 National Minimum Wage Regulations 1999, SI 1999/584, reg 15(2)(b) (as substituted: see note 3).

12 National Minimum Wage Regulations 1999, SI 1999/584, reg 15(4).

13 Ie except as mentioned in the National Minimum Wage Regulations 1999, SI 1999/584, reg 15(2) (see the text and notes 7–11) and reg 19 (see PARA 212): see reg 15(5).

14 National Minimum Wage Regulations 1999, SI 1999/584, reg 15(5).

15 National Minimum Wage Regulations 1999, SI 1999/584, reg 15(6).

16 Ie by the National Minimum Wage Regulations 1999, SI 1999/584, reg 15(2) (see the text and notes 7–11): see reg 15(7).

17 National Minimum Wage Regulations 1999, SI 1999/584, reg 15(7).

209.   Extension of scope of salaried hours work.   For the purposes of the National Minimum Wage Act 1998, time when a worker[1] is available at or near

a place of work for the purpose of doing salaried hours work[2], and is required to be available for such work, is to be treated[3] as being working hours[4], except where:

(1) the worker is at or near the place of work[5]; and

(2) the time is time the worker is entitled to spend at home[6].

In relation to a worker who by arrangement sleeps at or near a place of work and is provided with suitable facilities for sleeping, time during the hours he is permitted to use those facilities for the purpose of sleeping is, however, only to be treated as being salaried hours work when the worker is awake for the purpose of working[7].

Time when a worker is travelling for the purpose of duties carried out by him in the course of salaried hours work[8] is to be treated[9] as being working hours[10], except where:

(a) the travelling is incidental to the duties[11] carried out in the course of salaried hours work, the salaried hours work is not assignment work[12] and the time is time when the worker would not otherwise be working[13]; or

(b) the travel is between the worker's home, or an address where he is temporarily residing other than for the purposes of performing work, and his place of work or a place where an assignment is carried out[14].

Where a worker's hours of work vary either as to their length or in respect of the time at which they are performed and, as a result, it is uncertain in relation to particular time when the worker is travelling whether he would otherwise be working, that time is to be treated, for the purposes of head (a) above, as time when he would otherwise be working[15].

Time when a worker is:

(i) attending at a place other than his normal place of work, when he would otherwise be working, for the purpose of receiving training wholly or mainly in connection with salaried hours work that has been approved by his employer[16];

(ii) travelling, when he would otherwise be working, between a place of work and a place where he is receiving such training[17]; or

(iii) receiving such training at his normal place of work[18],

is to be treated[19] as working hours[20].

1 As to the meaning of 'worker' for these purposes see PARA 171.
2 As to the meaning of 'salaried hours work' see PARA 204.
3 Ie for the purpose of, and to the extent mentioned in, the National Minimum Wage Regulations 1999, SI 1999/584, reg 22(3)(d) (see PARA 215) and reg 22(4)(b) (see PARA 215): see reg 16(1) (reg 16(1)–(3) substituted, reg 16(1A) added, by SI 2000/1989).
4 See the National Minimum Wage Regulations 1999, SI 1999/584, reg 16(1) (as substituted: see note 3). The provision made by reg 16(1) is subject to reg 16(1A) (see the text and note 7): see reg 16(1) (as so substituted).
5 National Minimum Wage Regulations 1999, SI 1999/584, reg 16(1)(a) (as substituted: see note 3). See note 4.
6 National Minimum Wage Regulations 1999, SI 1999/584, reg 16(1)(b) (as substituted: see note 3). See note 4.
7 National Minimum Wage Regulations 1999, SI 1999/584, reg 16(1A) (as added : see note 3). See *Wray v JW Lees & Co (Brewers) Ltd* [2012] ICR 43, [2011] All ER (D) 124 (Sep), EAT (requirement that pub manager reside and sleep at premises as a 'minimum security measure', with sleeping facilities provided, not sufficient to count her sleeping time as working hours for the purposes of the National Minimum Wage Regulations 1999, SI 1999/584, reg 16(1), (1A); only time spent awake dealing with an actual emergency could be counted).
8 As to when a worker is to be treated as travelling for these purposes see PARA 208 note 7.

9   Ie for the purpose of, and to the extent mentioned in, the National Minimum Wage Regulations 1999, SI 1999/584, reg 22(3)(d) (see PARA 215) and reg 22(4)(b) (see PARA 215): see reg 16(2) (as substituted: see note 3).

10   See the National Minimum Wage Regulations 1999, SI 1999/584, reg 16(2) (as substituted: see note 3).

11   For the purposes of head (a) in the text, travelling is incidental to the duties carried out by a worker unless duties involved in his work are necessarily carried out in the course of the travelling (as in the case of a worker driving a bus, or serving in a bar on a train) or whose main duty is to transport items from one place to another: National Minimum Wage Regulations 1999, SI 1999/584, reg 16(3)(a) (as substituted: see note 3).

12   For the purposes of head (a) in the text, salaried hours work is assignment work if it consists of assignments of work to be carried out at different places between which the worker is obliged to travel that are not places occupied by the worker's employer: National Minimum Wage Regulations 1999, SI 1999/584, reg 16(3)(b) (as substituted: see note 3). As to the meaning of 'employer' for these purposes see PARA 170.

13   National Minimum Wage Regulations 1999, SI 1999/584, reg 16(2)(a) (as substituted: see note 3).

14   National Minimum Wage Regulations 1999, SI 1999/584, reg 16(2)(b) (as substituted: see note 3).

15   National Minimum Wage Regulations 1999, SI 1999/584, reg 16(4).

16   National Minimum Wage Regulations 1999, SI 1999/584, reg 16(5)(a).

17   National Minimum Wage Regulations 1999, SI 1999/584, reg 16(5)(b). As to when a worker is to be treated as travelling for these purposes see PARA 208 note 7.

18   National Minimum Wage Regulations 1999, SI 1999/584, reg 16(5)(c).

19   Ie for the purpose of, and to the extent mentioned in, the National Minimum Wage Regulations 1999, SI 1999/584, reg 22(3)(d) (see PARA 215) and reg 22(4)(b) (see PARA 215): see reg 16(5).

20   See the National Minimum Wage Regulations 1999, SI 1999/584, reg 16(5).

210. Extension of scope of output work. Time spent by a worker[1] in travelling for the purposes of doing output work[2] is to be treated as time spent doing output work, except for time spent travelling between his home (or a place where he is temporarily residing)[3], and:

(1)   premises from which he works[4]; or

(2)   except in the case of a worker whose work consists in producing tangible items at his home, premises to which he reports[5].

A worker is not to be treated as doing output work[6] during time when he is engaged in taking industrial action nor as having worked[7] during such time[8].

1   As to the meaning of 'worker' for these purposes see PARA 171.
2   As to the meaning of 'output work' see PARA 205. As to when a worker is to be treated as travelling for these purposes see PARA 208 note 7.
3   See the National Minimum Wage Regulations 1999, SI 1999/584, reg 17(1).
4   National Minimum Wage Regulations 1999, SI 1999/584, reg 17(1)(a).
5   National Minimum Wage Regulations 1999, SI 1999/584, reg 17(1)(b).
6   Ie for the purposes of the National Minimum Wage Regulations 1999, SI 1999/584, reg 24 (see PARA 217): see reg 17(2).
7   Ie for the purposes of the National Minimum Wage Regulations 1999, SI 1999/584, reg 26 (see PARA 217): see reg 17(2).
8   National Minimum Wage Regulations 1999, SI 1999/584, reg 17(2).

211. Extension of scope of unmeasured work. Time when a worker[1] is travelling for the purpose of unmeasured work[2] is to be treated as being unmeasured work[3].

A worker is not to be treated, however, as carrying out his contractual duties to do unmeasured work[4] during time when he is engaged in taking industrial action, nor as being available to carry out those duties[5] during such time[6].

1   As to the meaning of 'worker' for these purposes see PARA 171.

2   As to the meaning of 'unmeasured work' see PARA 206. As to when a worker is to be treated as travelling for these purposes see PARA 208 note 7.
3   National Minimum Wage Regulations 1999, SI 1999/584, reg 18(1).
4   Ie for the purposes of the National Minimum Wage Regulations 1999, SI 1999/584, reg 27 (see PARA 218): see reg 18(2).
5   Ie for the purposes of the National Minimum Wage Regulations 1999, SI 1999/584, reg 29 (see PARA 218): see reg 18(2).
6   National Minimum Wage Regulations 1999, SI 1999/584, reg 18(2).

212. Time spent on training to be treated as time work. Time when a worker is[1]:

   (1) attending at a place other than his normal place of work (when he would otherwise be working) for the purpose of receiving training that has been approved by his employer[2];

   (2) travelling (when he would otherwise be working) between a place of work and a place where he is receiving such training[3]; or

   (3) receiving such training at his normal place of work[4],

is to be treated as time work[5]. This provision does not apply, however, in relation to training wholly or mainly in connection with salaried hours work[6].

Where a worker's hours of work vary either as to their length or in respect of the time at which they are performed and, as a result, it is uncertain in relation to particular time when the worker is attending at a place or travelling, whether he would otherwise be working, that time is to be treated for the purposes of head (1) above, or, as the case may be, head (2) above, as time when he would otherwise be working[7].

1   See the National Minimum Wage Regulations 1999, SI 1999/584, reg 19(1). As to the meaning of 'worker' for these purposes see PARA 171.
2   National Minimum Wage Regulations 1999, SI 1999/584, reg 19(1)(a). See the text and note 6. As to the meaning of 'employer' for these purposes see PARA 170.
3   National Minimum Wage Regulations 1999, SI 1999/584, reg 19(1)(b). See the text and note 6. As to when a worker is to be treated as travelling for these purposes see PARA 208 note 7.
4   National Minimum Wage Regulations 1999, SI 1999/584, reg 19(1)(c).See the text and note 6.
5   See the National Minimum Wage Regulations 1999, SI 1999/584, reg 19(1).
6   National Minimum Wage Regulations 1999, SI 1999/584, reg 19(3). As to the meaning of 'salaried hours work' see PARA 204.
7   National Minimum Wage Regulations 1999, SI 1999/584, reg 19(2).

(vii) Hours Worked in a Pay Reference Period

213. Determining the hours of time work. The time work[1] worked by a worker[2] in a pay reference period[3] is the total number of hours of time work done by him in the pay reference period[4].

1   As to the meaning of 'time work' see PARA 203.
2   As to the meaning of 'worker' for these purposes see PARA 171.
3   As to the meaning of 'pay reference period' see PARA 202.
4   National Minimum Wage Regulations 1999, SI 1999/584, reg 20.

214. Determining the hours of salaried hours work. The salaried hours work[1] worked by a worker[2] in a pay reference period[3] is determined[4] by dividing the basic hours by[5]:

   (1) where the pay reference period is a week, 52[6];

   (2) where the pay reference period is a month, 12[7]; and

   (3) where the pay reference period is any other period, by the figure obtained by dividing 365 by the number of days in the pay reference period (including non-working days)[8].

Where in a pay reference period:

(a)   a worker is absent from work for a number of hours in respect of which his annual salary is payable[9]; and

(b)   is, for that reason, entitled to be paid less and is paid less than the normal proportion of his annual salary in respect of the pay reference period[10],

the salaried hours work worked by the worker in the pay reference period is the number of hours determined under heads (1) to (3) above in relation to the pay reference period reduced by the number of hours referred to in head (a) above[11].

Hours in a pay reference period during which a worker is engaged in taking industrial action and in respect of which his annual salary is or, but for his engagement in the action, would be payable, are to be regarded as satisfying the requirements in heads (a) and (b) above, whether or not the worker's entitlement to the normal proportion of his annual salary is affected by his engagement in the action, and whether or not he is paid any amount in respect of those hours[12].

1   As to the meaning of 'salaried hours work' see PARA 204.
2   As to the meaning of 'worker' for these purposes see PARA 171.
3   As to the meaning of 'pay reference period' see PARA 202.
4   Ie except as mentioned in the National Minimum Wage Regulations 1999, SI 1999/584, reg 21(3) (see the text and note 11), reg 22 (see PARA 215) and reg 23 (see PARA 216): see reg 21(2).
5   See the National Minimum Wage Regulations 1999, SI 1999/584, reg 21(2). For these purposes, 'basic hours' means the basic number of hours in a year in respect of which a worker is entitled under his contract to his annual salary as ascertained in accordance with his contract on the first day of the pay reference period in question: see reg 21(1). As to determining the hours of salaried hours work where the basic hours have been exceeded see reg 22; and PARA 215.
6   National Minimum Wage Regulations 1999, SI 1999/584, reg 21(2)(a).
7   National Minimum Wage Regulations 1999, SI 1999/584, reg 21(2)(b).
8   National Minimum Wage Regulations 1999, SI 1999/584, reg 21(2)(c).
9   National Minimum Wage Regulations 1999, SI 1999/584, reg 21(3)(a).
10 National Minimum Wage Regulations 1999, SI 1999/584, reg 21(3)(b).
11 See the National Minimum Wage Regulations 1999, SI 1999/584, reg 21(3).
12 National Minimum Wage Regulations 1999, SI 1999/584, reg 21(4).

215.   Determining the hours of salaried hours work where the basic hours have been exceeded.   Where in any calculation year[1] the total of the hours of salaried hours work[2] exceeds the basic hours[3], the following provisions apply[4] for the purpose of determining the salaried hours work worked by a worker[5] in the pay reference period[6] during which the basic hours are exceeded and in the subsequent pay reference periods, if any, in the calculation year[7].

Accordingly, in determining for this purpose whether the basic hours have been exceeded by a worker in any calculation year (and, if so, when they were exceeded), the following hours in that year are to be taken into account[8]:

(1)   the number of the worker's working hours that fell within the basic hours[9];

(2)   the number of hours for which the worker has been absent from work that fell within the basic hours[10];

(3)   any hours worked by the worker outside the basic hours in respect of which the worker had no entitlement under his contract to any payment other than his annual salary[11];

(4)   time required to be treated as working hours[12], to the extent that such time consisted of hours in respect of which the worker had no entitlement under his contract to his annual salary or to any other payment[13],

but excluding the number of hours, if any, during which the worker was engaged in taking industrial action[14].

In that part of the pay reference period during which the basic hours are exceeded which is referred to in head (ii) below and in each subsequent pay reference period, if any, in the calculation year, a worker is to be treated as working for the sum of the following[15]:

(a) the number of hours in the pay reference period that would have fallen to be taken into account under head (1) above if the basic hours had not been exceeded, but excluding any time during those hours in which the worker was engaged in taking industrial action[16]; and

(b) time required to be treated as working hours[17], to the extent that such time consists of hours in respect of which the worker is not entitled under his contract to his annual salary or to any other payment[18],

and the number of hours so determined is referred to[19] as the 'actual working hours'[20].

The salaried hours work worked by a worker in the pay reference period during which the basic hours are exceeded is the sum of the following[21]:

(i) in relation to the part of the pay reference period before the day on which the basic hours are exceeded, the number of hours that result from applying the basic calculation of salaried hours work[22] to the part as if it were a pay reference period containing the number of days in the part[23]; and

(ii) in relation to the part of the pay reference period beginning with the day on which the basic hours are exceeded, the sum of[24]: (A) the number of hours that result from applying the basic calculation of salaried hours work[25] to the part as if it were a pay reference period containing the number of days in the part (but ignoring any reduction required[26] otherwise)[27]; and (B) the actual working hours in that part[28].

The salaried hours work worked by a worker in each subsequent pay reference period until the end of the calculation year is the sum of: (aa) the number of hours that result from applying the basic calculation of salaried hours work[29] in relation to the pay reference period (but ignoring any reduction required[30] otherwise)[31]; and (bb) the actual working hours in the pay reference period[32].

1   For the purposes of the National Minimum Wage Regulations 1999, SI 1999/584, reg 22 and reg 23 (see also PARA 216), 'calculation year' means: (1) in the case of a worker employed by an employer on 1 April 1999 (ie the date on which the National Minimum Wage Regulations 1999, SI 1999/584, came into force: see reg 1), for so long as he continues in that employment, the year beginning on that day, and each subsequent year beginning on the anniversary of that day; (2) in the case of a worker whose annual salary is payable monthly and who becomes employed by an employer after that date, for so long as he continues in the same employment: (a) where the worker becomes employed on the first day of a month, the year beginning with the first day of that month and each subsequent year beginning on the anniversary of that day; (b) where the worker becomes employed on any other day of a month, the period beginning with that day and ending with the day before the first anniversary of the first day of the next month, and each year beginning on that anniversary or on a subsequent anniversary of the first day of that month; (3) in the case of a worker whose annual salary is payable weekly and who becomes employed by an employer after that date, for so long as he continues in the same employment, the year beginning with the first day of his employment and each subsequent year beginning on the anniversary of that day: see reg 22(2).

2   Ie the total of the hours referred to in the National Minimum Wage Regulations 1999, SI 1999/584, reg 22(3) (see the text and notes 8–14): see reg 22(1). As to the meaning of 'salaried hours work' see PARA 204.

3   For the purposes of the National Minimum Wage Regulations 1999, SI 1999/584, reg 22 and reg 23 (see also PARA 216), 'basic hours' means: (1) in a calculation year when the basic number

of hours in respect of which the worker is entitled under his contract to his annual salary is not varied, that basic number; (2) in a calculation year when that basic number of hours is varied: (a) where the basic hours are determined in respect of the calculation year before the only or first variation takes effect, the basic number of hours ignoring the effect of the variation; (b) where the basic hours are determined after a variation has taken effect, the sum of the following numbers of hours: (i) for the period beginning with the day on which the variation in question takes effect until the end of the year, the proportion of the basic number of hours in respect of which the worker would be entitled to his annual salary, in accordance with that variation, in a year of 365 days, which the number of days in the period bears to 365; (ii) for the period starting with the beginning of the year and ending with the day before the day on which the only or first variation took effect, the proportion of the basic number of hours in respect of which the worker would be entitled to his annual salary, before the variation, in a year of 365 days, which the number of days in the period bears to 365; and (iii) where there has been more than one variation, for each period beginning with the day on which a particular variation took effect and ending on the last day before the next variation took effect, the proportion of the basic number of hours in respect of which the worker would be entitled to his annual salary, in accordance with the earlier variation, in a year of 365 days, which the number of days in the period bears to 365: see reg 22(2). However, in applying reg 21 (see PARA 214) for the purposes of reg 22(5)(a) (see head (i) in the text), reg 22(5)(b)(i) (see head (ii)(A) in the text), reg 22(6)(a) (see the text and notes 29–31), the definition of 'basic hours' in reg 21(1) (see PARA 214 note 5) is to be used: see reg 22(2) (amended by SI 2000/1989).

4 Ie the National Minimum Wage Regulations 1999, SI 1999/584, reg 22 applies instead of reg 21 (see PARA 214): see reg 22(1).

5 As to the meaning of 'worker' for these purposes see PARA 171.

6 As to the meaning of 'pay reference period' see PARA 202.

7 National Minimum Wage Regulations 1999, SI 1999/584, reg 22(1).

8 See the National Minimum Wage Regulations 1999, SI 1999/584, reg 22(3).

9 National Minimum Wage Regulations 1999, SI 1999/584, reg 22(3)(a).

10 National Minimum Wage Regulations 1999, SI 1999/584, reg 22(3)(b).

11 National Minimum Wage Regulations 1999, SI 1999/584, reg 22(3)(c). References in reg 22 to work or hours of work in respect of which a worker is entitled to no payment other than his annual salary refer also to work or hours of work in respect of which the only payment to which the worker is entitled other than his annual salary is payment of a performance bonus: see reg 4(7); and PARA 204 note 13.

12 Ie by the National Minimum Wage Regulations 1999, SI 1999/584, reg 16 (see PARA 209): see reg 22(3).

13 National Minimum Wage Regulations 1999, SI 1999/584, reg 22(3)(d).

14 See the National Minimum Wage Regulations 1999, SI 1999/584, reg 22(3).

15 See the National Minimum Wage Regulations 1999, SI 1999/584, reg 22(4).

16 National Minimum Wage Regulations 1999, SI 1999/584, reg 22(4)(a).

17 Ie by the National Minimum Wage Regulations 1999, SI 1999/584, reg 16 (see PARA 209): see reg 22(4)(b).

18 National Minimum Wage Regulations 1999, SI 1999/584, reg 22(4)(b).

19 Ie in the National Minimum Wage Regulations 1999, SI 1999/584, reg 22(5), (6) (see the text and notes 21–32) and reg 23(3) (see PARA 216): see reg 22(4).

20 See the National Minimum Wage Regulations 1999, SI 1999/584, reg 22(4).

21 See the National Minimum Wage Regulations 1999, SI 1999/584, reg 22(5).

22 Ie the number of hours that result from applying the National Minimum Wage Regulations 1999, SI 1999/584, reg 21 (see PARA 214): see reg 22(5)(a).

23 National Minimum Wage Regulations 1999, SI 1999/584, reg 22(5)(a).

24 See the National Minimum Wage Regulations 1999, SI 1999/584, reg 22(5)(b).

25 Ie the number of hours that result from applying the National Minimum Wage Regulations 1999, SI 1999/584, reg 21(2) (see PARA 214): see reg 22(5)(b)(i).

26 Ie by the National Minimum Wage Regulations 1999, SI 1999/584, reg 21(3) (see PARA 214): see reg 22(5)(b)(i).

27 National Minimum Wage Regulations 1999, SI 1999/584, reg 22(5)(b)(i).

28 National Minimum Wage Regulations 1999, SI 1999/584, reg 22(5)(b)(ii).

29 Ie the number of hours that result from applying the National Minimum Wage Regulations 1999, SI 1999/584, reg 21(2) (see PARA 214): see reg 22(6)(a).

30 Ie by the National Minimum Wage Regulations 1999, SI 1999/584, reg 21(3) (see PARA 214): see reg 22(6)(a).

31 National Minimum Wage Regulations 1999, SI 1999/584, reg 22(6)(a).

32 National Minimum Wage Regulations 1999, SI 1999/584, reg 22(6)(b).

216. Determining the hours of salaried work in certain cases where the employment terminates. In relation to the final pay reference period[1] of a worker[2] whose employment terminates in the course of a calculation year[3], and in cases where the employment of a worker is treated[4] as being terminated[5], then:

(1) where the basic hours[6] have not been exceeded at the end of the final pay reference period but, at the end of that pay reference period, the total of the hours to be taken into account[7] since the beginning of the calculation year (the 'A' hours) exceeds the total of the number of hours[8] in relation to all of the pay reference periods (including the final pay reference period) since the beginning of the calculation year (the 'B' hours), the salaried hours work worked by the worker in that pay reference period is to be regarded as including (in addition to the number of hours determined[9] in relation to the pay reference period) the number of hours by which the 'A' hours exceed the 'B' hours[10];

(2) where the basic hours have been exceeded at any time during the calculation year before the end of the final pay reference period, the salaried hours work worked by the worker in that pay reference period is to be regarded as including (in addition to the number of hours determined in relation to the pay reference period[11]) the number of hours that result from applying the basic calculation of salaried hours work[12] in relation to the period beginning with the day immediately following the last day of the worker's final pay reference period and ending at the end of the calculation year (the 'subsequent period')[13], as if: (a) the whole of the subsequent period were a single pay reference period (containing the number of days in it)[14]; and (b) the worker had continued to be employed under his contract to do salaried hours work for the whole of the subsequent period and had not been absent from work during it for any hours in respect of which a reduction is[15] required[16].

1 As to the meaning of 'pay reference period' see PARA 202.
2 As to the meaning of 'worker' for these purposes see PARA 171.
3 As to the meaning of 'calculation year' see PARA 215 note 1.
4 Ie by virtue of the National Minimum Wage Regulations 1999, SI 1999/584, reg 23(4): see reg 23(1). Where a worker's contract is varied so that any salaried hours work required to be done under the contract becomes work that is not salaried hours work, reg 23 applies as if:
  (1) the employment of the worker had been terminated (reg 23(4)(a)); and
  (2) the last day of the worker's final pay reference period had fallen on the day before the day on which the variation took effect (reg 23(4)(b)).
  As to the meaning of 'salaried hours work' see PARA 204.
5 See the National Minimum Wage Regulations 1999, SI 1999/584, reg 23(1).
6 As to the meaning of 'basic hours' see PARA 215 note 3.
7 Ie under the National Minimum Wage Regulations 1999, SI 1999/584, reg 22(3) (see PARA 215): see reg 23(2).
8 Ie determined in accordance with the National Minimum Wage Regulations 1999, SI 1999/584, reg 21 (see PARA 214): see reg 23(2).
9 See note 8.
10 National Minimum Wage Regulations 1999, SI 1999/584, reg 23(2).
11 Ie determined in accordance with the National Minimum Wage Regulations 1999, SI 1999/584, reg 22(5) or, as the case may be, reg 22(6) (see PARA 215): see reg 23(3).
12 Ie the number of hours that result from applying the National Minimum Wage Regulations 1999, SI 1999/584, reg 21(2) (see PARA 214): see reg 23(3).
13 See the National Minimum Wage Regulations 1999, SI 1999/584, reg 23(3).
14 National Minimum Wage Regulations 1999, SI 1999/584, reg 23(3)(a).

15 Ie under the National Minimum Wage Regulations 1999, SI 1999/584, reg 21(3) (see PARA 214): see reg 23(3)(b).
16 National Minimum Wage Regulations 1999, SI 1999/584, reg 23(3)(b).

217. Determining the hours of output work; 'fair estimate' agreements for output work. The output work[1] of a worker[2] in a pay reference period[3] relating to a type of piece produced, or a type of task performed, is the number of hours spent by the worker during the pay reference period in producing that type of piece, or performing that type of task, except where the output work relating to that type of piece or task is rated output work[4]. Output work is 'rated output work' if[5]:

(1) it satisfies the conditions that[6]: (a) the output work relating to the type of piece in question (the 'subject piece') or the type of task in question (the 'subject task') is work in respect of which the worker's contract does not set any normal, minimum or maximum working hours[7]; (b) the employer[8] does not in practice determine or control the hours worked by the worker in relation to the subject piece or the subject task[9]; and (c) the employer has determined the mean hourly output rate[10] for the subject piece or the subject task[11]; and

(2) it is work in respect of which the employer has given the worker a notice that satisfies the following requirements[12], namely that: (a) it has been given in writing[13] to the worker at any time before the beginning of the pay reference period (whether or not the notice was given before the beginning of, and had effect in relation to, any earlier pay reference periods)[14]; and (b) it contains statements conveying[15]: (i) that it is being given to inform the worker that, for the purpose of securing compliance with the national minimum wage legislation, he is to be treated, in respect of his production of the subject piece or his performance of the subject task (as appropriate) during the pay reference period, as working for a certain period of time[16]; (ii) that, for the purpose of determining the period of time the worker will be treated as working, the employer has conducted a test or, where applicable, made an estimate of the average speed at which workers employed by the employer produce the subject piece or perform the subject task (as appropriate)[17]; (iii) what the mean hourly output rate for the subject piece or the subject task is[18]; (iv) the rate to be paid to the worker for the production of a single subject piece or the performance of a single subject task (as appropriate)[19]; and (v) the telephone number of the national minimum wage helpline, which is identified as being the national minimum wage helpline number[20].

Where output work is rated output work consisting of the production of subject pieces, the number of hours of output work spent by the worker in producing subject pieces during the pay reference period is to be treated as being 120 per cent of the number of hours that a worker producing the subject pieces at the mean hourly output rate would have taken to produce the number of subject pieces produced by the worker in the pay reference period[21].

Where output work is rated output work consisting of the performance of subject tasks, the number of hours of output work spent by the worker in performing subject tasks during the pay reference period is to be treated as being 120 per cent of the number of hours that a worker performing at the mean hourly output rate would have taken to perform the number of subject tasks performed by the worker in the pay reference period[22].

To determine the mean hourly rate for a subject piece or a subject task, an employer must[23]:

(A)   conduct a satisfactory test[24] of the speed at which every worker in one of the groups[25] produces the subject piece or performs the subject task, and then divide the total number of subject pieces or subject tasks (or the fraction of a subject piece or subject task) that all the workers in the group tested have produced or performed per hour during the period of the test by the number of workers in the group tested[26]; or

(B)   make a satisfactory estimate[27] of the average speed, in terms of pieces or tasks per hour, at which the workers producing the subject piece or performing the subject task are likely to produce that piece or perform that task[28].

Where a satisfactory test has been conducted, or a satisfactory estimate has been made, subsequent changes in the number or identity of the workers of the employer who produce the subject piece or perform the subject task do not require the employer to conduct a further satisfactory test or make a further satisfactory estimate unless the employer has reason to believe that the changes materially affect the mean hourly output rate[29].

1   As to the meaning of 'output work' see PARA 205.
2   As to the meaning of 'worker' for these purposes see PARA 171.
3   As to the meaning of 'pay reference period' see PARA 202.
4   National Minimum Wage Regulations 1999, SI 1999/584, reg 24(1) (regs 24–26 substituted, reg 26A added, reg 26(1), (2) amended, by SI 2004/1161). The substitutions and addition made by the National Minimum Wage Regulations 1999 (Amendment) Regulations 2004, SI 2004/1161, reg 2, did not apply in relation to any pay reference period beginning before 1 October 2004 (see reg 4(1)); and the amendments made by reg 3 did not apply in relation to any pay reference period beginning before 6 April 2005 (see reg 4(3)). See also note 24.
5   See the National Minimum Wage Regulations 1999, SI 1999/584, reg 24(2) (as substituted: see note 4).
6   See the National Minimum Wage Regulations 1999, SI 1999/584, reg 24(2)(a) (as substituted: see note 4). Head (1) in the text refers to output work that satisfies the conditions in reg 25(1) (see heads (1)(a)–(1)(c) in the text): see reg 24(2)(a) (as so substituted).
7   National Minimum Wage Regulations 1999, SI 1999/584, reg 25(1)(a) (as substituted: see note 4).
8   As to the meaning of 'employer' for these purposes see PARA 170.
9   National Minimum Wage Regulations 1999, SI 1999/584, reg 25(1)(b) (as substituted: see note 4).
10 For the purposes of the National Minimum Wage Regulations 1999, SI 1999/584, reg 25, reg 26 (see the text and notes 21–22) and reg 26A (see the text and notes 23–29), 'mean hourly output rate' means the average number, including any fraction, of:
   (1)   subject pieces, or fraction of a subject piece, produced in an hour by workers of the employer producing the subject piece (reg 26(3)(a) (as substituted: see note 4)); or
   (2)   subject tasks, or fraction of a subject task, performed in an hour by workers of the employer performing the subject task (reg 26(3)(b) (as so substituted)),
  as determined in accordance with reg 26A (see reg 26(3) (as so substituted)).
11 National Minimum Wage Regulations 1999, SI 1999/584, reg 25(1)(c) (as substituted: see note 4).
12 See the National Minimum Wage Regulations 1999, SI 1999/584, reg 24(2)(b) (as substituted: see note 4). Head (2) in the text refers to a notice that satisfies the requirements of reg 25(2) (see heads (2)(a)–(2)(b) in the text): see reg 24(2)(b) (as so substituted). As to the employer's duty to keep a copy of the notice referred to in reg 24(2)(b) see PARA 226.
13 As to the meaning of 'writing' see PARA 2 note 8.
14 National Minimum Wage Regulations 1999, SI 1999/584, reg 25(2)(a) (as substituted: see note 4).
15 See the National Minimum Wage Regulations 1999, SI 1999/584, reg 25(2)(b) (as substituted: see note 4).
16 National Minimum Wage Regulations 1999, SI 1999/584, reg 25(2)(b)(i) (as substituted: see note 4).

17 National Minimum Wage Regulations 1999, SI 1999/584, reg 25(2)(b)(ii) (as substituted: see note 4).

18 National Minimum Wage Regulations 1999, SI 1999/584, reg 25(2)(b)(iii) (as substituted: see note 4). As to the employer's duty to keep a copy of such data as is necessary to show how he has determined the rate referred to in reg 25(2)(b)(iii) see PARA 226.

19 National Minimum Wage Regulations 1999, SI 1999/584, reg 25(2)(b)(iv) (as substituted: see note 4). As to the employer's duty to keep a copy of such data as is necessary to show how he has determined the rate referred to in reg 25(2)(b)(iv) see PARA 226.

20 National Minimum Wage Regulations 1999, SI 1999/584, reg 25(2)(b)(v) (as substituted: see note 4).

21 National Minimum Wage Regulations 1999, SI 1999/584, reg 26(1) (as substituted and amended: see note 4).

22 National Minimum Wage Regulations 1999, SI 1999/584, reg 26(2) (as substituted and amended: see note 4).

23 National Minimum Wage Regulations 1999, SI 1999/584, reg 26A(1) (as added: see note 4).

24 Ie in accordance with the National Minimum Wage Regulations 1999, SI 1999/584, reg 26A(2): see reg 26A(1)(a) (as added: see note 4). Accordingly, for this purpose, a test is satisfactory only if all the workers in the group are tested in working circumstances similar to those in which the worker is or will be producing the subject piece or performing the subject task: see reg 26A(2) (as so added). The permitted groups for the purposes of the test mentioned in head (A) in the text are:
> (1) all of the workers of the employer who produce the subject piece or perform the subject task (reg 26A(2)(a) (as so added)); or
> (2) a sample of those workers of the employer which, in respect of the speed at which the workers in the sample work, is representative of all those workers (reg 26A(2)(b) (as so added)).

In relation to a pay reference period beginning on or after 1 October 2004, it is irrelevant whether a satisfactory test was conducted before or after 1 October 2004 (ie the date on which regs 24–26 and reg 26A came into force): see the National Minimum Wage Regulations 1999 (Amendment) Regulations 2004, SI 2004/1161, reg 4(2).

25 Ie one of the groups specified in the National Minimum Wage Regulations 1999, SI 1999/584, reg 26A(2) (see note 24): see reg 26A(1)(a) (as added: see note 4).

26 National Minimum Wage Regulations 1999, SI 1999/584, reg 26A(1)(a) (as added: see note 4).

27 Ie in accordance with the National Minimum Wage Regulations 1999, SI 1999/584, reg 26A(3): see reg 26A(1)(b) (as added: see note 4). Accordingly, for the purposes of head (B) in the text, and subject to reg 26A(4) (see the text and note 29), an estimate is satisfactory if the employer:
> (1) has tested the average speed, in terms of pieces or tasks per hour, at which a sample of workers of the employer working in similar working circumstances to the worker produce a piece or perform a task that is reasonably similar to the subject piece or subject task and, in making the estimate, has fairly adjusted that average speed to take account of the increased or decreased time involved in production of the subject piece or performance of the subject task (reg 26A(3)(a) (as so added)); or
> (2) has tested the average speed, in terms of pieces or tasks per hour, at which a sample of workers of the employer working in different working circumstances from the worker produce the subject piece or perform the subject task and, in making the estimate, has fairly adjusted that average speed to take account of the increased or decreased time involved in producing the subject piece or performing the subject task in the same working circumstances as the worker (reg 26A(3)(b) (as so added)).

A sample of workers tested in this way must be, so far as is reasonably practicable, representative, in respect of the speed at which they work, of the speed at which the workers who produce the subject piece or perform the subject task work: see reg 26A(3) (as so added); and see also note 24.

28 National Minimum Wage Regulations 1999, SI 1999/584, reg 26A(1)(b) (as added: see note 4).

29 National Minimum Wage Regulations 1999, SI 1999/584, reg 26A(4) (as added: see note 4).

218. Determining the hours of unmeasured work. The unmeasured work[1] worked by a worker[2] in a pay reference period[3] is the total of the number of hours spent by him during the pay reference period in carrying out the contractual duties required of him under his contract to do such work, unless the following condition is satisfied[4], that is to say that there is an agreement[5] in writing[6] between the worker and his employer[7], made at any time before the beginning of the pay reference period, determining the average daily number of hours the worker is likely to spend in carrying out the duties required of him under his contract to do unmeasured work on days when he is available to carry out those duties for the full amount of time contemplated by the contract[8]. That condition is not satisfied, however, if the employer cannot show that the average daily number of hours determined is a realistic average[9]. Where that condition is satisfied, the hours of unmeasured work worked by a worker in the pay reference period is to be treated as being the ascertained hours[10].

1 As to the meaning of 'unmeasured work' see PARA 206.
2 As to the meaning of 'worker' for these purposes see PARA 171.
3 As to the meaning of 'pay reference period' see PARA 202.
4 See the National Minimum Wage Regulations 1999, SI 1999/584, reg 27. The text refers to the condition in reg 28(1) (see the text and notes 5–8) being satisfied: see reg 27.
5 For these purposes, unless otherwise agreed, such an agreement has effect solely for the purpose of determining the amount of unmeasured work the worker is to be treated as having worked for the purpose of the National Minimum Wage Regulations 1999, SI 1999/584, and does not vary the worker's contract: see reg 28(3).
6 As to the meaning of 'writing' see PARA 2 note 8.
7 As to the meaning of 'employer' for these purposes see PARA 170.
8 National Minimum Wage Regulations 1999, SI 1999/584, reg 28(1). A work day assessment, agreed between an employer and an employee, of how many hours a live-in carer actually spends actively caring for a patient constitutes an agreement for the purposes of reg 28(1), and may be used to calculate the amount of unmeasured work carried out by an employee: *Walton v Independent Living Organisation Ltd* [2003] EWCA Civ 199, [2003] ICR 688, [2003] IRLR 469. As to the employer's duty to keep a copy of the agreement referred to in the National Minimum Wage Regulations 1999, SI 1999/584, reg 28(1), see PARA 226.
9 National Minimum Wage Regulations 1999, SI 1999/584, reg 28(2).
10 National Minimum Wage Regulations 1999, SI 1999/584, reg 29(2). For these purposes, the term 'ascertained hours' means the number of hours of unmeasured work that would have been worked by the worker in a pay reference period if he had worked: (1) on each day worked by him in the pay reference period on which he was available to carry out his duties for at least the full amount of time contemplated by the contract, for the average daily number of hours specified in the agreement referred to in reg 28(1) (see the text and notes 5–8) (reg 29(1)(a)); and (2) on each day worked by him in the pay reference period on which he was available to carry out his duties for only part of that amount of time, for the proportion of that average number of hours which the part bears to the full amount of time contemplated by the contract (reg 29(1)(b)).

219. Payment for work due only on submission of record. Where, at the time of the making of a determination whether the national minimum wage has been paid[1], any work[2] done by a worker[3] in the pay reference period[4] in question is work in respect of which[5]:

    (1)   the worker is not entitled to payment until a record of the work has been submitted to the employer[6]; and

    (2)   no such record has been so submitted[7],

the number of hours attributable to that work must be excluded from the total number of hours to be taken into account[8] in making that determination[9].

1 Ie a determination under the National Minimum Wage Regulations 1999, SI 1999/584, reg 14 (see PARA 201): see reg 29A (added by SI 2000/1989).
2 As to the meaning of 'work' for these purposes see PARA 172.
3 As to the meaning of 'worker' for these purposes see PARA 171.
4 As to the meaning of 'pay reference period' see PARA 202.
5 See the National Minimum Wage Regulations 1999, SI 1999/584, reg 29A (as added: see note 1).
6 National Minimum Wage Regulations 1999, SI 1999/584, reg 29A(a) (as added: see note 1). As to the meaning of 'employer' for these purposes see PARA 170.
7 National Minimum Wage Regulations 1999, SI 1999/584, reg 29A(b) (as added: see note 1).

8   Ie under the National Minimum Wage Regulations 1999, SI 1999/584, reg 14(3) (see PARA 201):
     see reg 29A (as added: see note 1).
9   See the National Minimum Wage Regulations 1999, SI 1999/584, reg 29A (as added: see
     note 1).

(viii) Remuneration counting towards the National Minimum Wage

220.   Payments to the worker to be taken into account.   The total of
remuneration in a pay reference period is calculated by adding together[1]:
(1)   all money payments paid by the employer[2] to the worker in the pay
       reference period[3];
(2)   any money payments paid by the employer to the worker in the
       following pay reference period in respect of the pay reference period
       (whether in respect of work or not)[4];
(3)   any money payment paid by the employer to the worker later than the
       end of the following pay reference period in respect of work done in the
       pay reference period[5], being work in respect of which:
       (a)   the worker is under an obligation to complete a record of the
              amount of work done[6];
       (b)   the worker is not entitled to payment until the completed record
              has been submitted by him to the employer[7]; and
       (c)   the worker has failed to submit a record before the fourth
              working day before the end of that following pay reference
              period[8],
       provided that the payment is paid in either the pay reference period in
       which the record is submitted to the employer or the pay reference
       period after that[9];
(4)   where the employer has provided the worker with living
       accommodation during the pay reference period, but in respect of that
       provision is neither entitled to make any deduction from the wages of
       the worker nor to receive any payment from him, the amount[10]
       permitted to be taken into account[11].

1   See the National Minimum Wage Regulations 1999, SI 1999/584, reg 30. As to the meaning of
     'pay reference period' see PARA 202.
2   References in the National Minimum Wage Regulations 1999, SI 1999/584, to payments paid
     by the employer to the worker are references to payments paid by the employer to the worker in
     his capacity as a worker before any deductions are made (see reg 8), excluding:
     (1)   any payment by way of an advance under an agreement for a loan or by way of an
            advance of wages (reg 8(a));
     (2)   any payment by way of a pension, by way of an allowance or gratuity in connection
            with the worker's retirement or as compensation for loss of office (reg 8(b));
     (3)   any payment of an award made by a court or tribunal or to settle proceedings which
            have been or might be brought before a court or tribunal, other than the payment of an
            amount due under the worker's contract (reg 8(c));
     (4)   any payment referable to the worker's redundancy (reg 8(d));
     (5)   any payment by way of an award under a suggestions scheme (reg 8(e)).
     Note that the definition of 'allowance' that applies elsewhere in the regulations does not apply
     to head (2) above: see reg 2(1); and PARA 221 note 17. The following are not, however, to be
     treated as payments by the employer to the worker:
     (a)   any benefit in kind provided to the worker, whether or not a monetary value is attached
            to the benefit, other than living accommodation (reg 9(a));
     (b)   any voucher, stamp or similar document capable of being exchanged for money, goods
            or services, or for any combination of those things, provided by the employer to the
            worker (reg 9(b)).
     As to the meaning of 'employer' for these purposes see PARA 170; and as to the meaning of
     'worker' see PARA 171.

3   National Minimum Wage Regulations 1999, SI 1999/584, reg 30(a). As to whether tips can be counted as payments paid by the employer to the worker for the purposes of reg 30(a) see *Revenue and Customs Comrs v Annabel's (Berkeley Square)* [2009] EWCA Civ 361, [2009] 4 All ER 55, [2009] ICR 1123; and PARA 221 note 19.

4   National Minimum Wage Regulations 1999, SI 1999/584, reg 30(b).

5   See the National Minimum Wage Regulations 1999, SI 1999/584, reg 30(c).

6   National Minimum Wage Regulations 1999, SI 1999/584, reg 30(c)(i).

7   National Minimum Wage Regulations 1999, SI 1999/584, reg 30(c)(ii).

8   National Minimum Wage Regulations 1999, SI 1999/584, reg 30(c)(iii).

9   See the National Minimum Wage Regulations 1999, SI 1999/584, reg 30(c).

10 Ie the amount determined in accordance with the National Minimum Wage Regulations 1999, SI 1999/584, reg 36 (see PARA 224): see reg 30(d).

11 National Minimum Wage Regulations 1999, SI 1999/584, reg 30(d). For an example of the application of these principles in the case of head (4) in the text see *Paggetti v Cobb* [2002] IRLR 861, [2002] All ER (D) 394 (Mar), EAT (calculation of a week's pay under the Employment Rights Act 1996 ss 221–229 (see PARAS 144–148) for the purposes of compensation in an unfair dismissal case).

221.   Reductions from payments to be taken into account. The total of reductions[1] required to be subtracted from the total of remuneration[2] is calculated by adding together[3]:

(1)   any money payments paid by the employer[4] to the worker in the pay reference period[5] that are required[6] to be included in the total of remuneration for an earlier pay reference period[7];

(2)   in the case of: (a) work[8] other than salaried hours work[9], any money payments paid by the employer to the worker in respect of periods when the worker was absent from work or engaged in taking industrial action[10]; (b) salaried hours work, any money payment paid by the employer to the worker attributable to the hours, if any, by which the number of hours[11] is required to be reduced[12] where the worker is entitled[13] to less than the normal proportion of annual salary because of his absence from work[14];

(3)   any money payments paid by the employer to the worker in respect of: (a) time work worked by him in the pay reference period involving particular duties that is paid for at a higher rate per hour than the lowest rate per hour payable to the worker in respect of time work worked by him involving those duties during the pay reference period, to the extent that the total of those payments exceeds the total of the money payments that would have been payable in respect of the work if that lowest rate per hour had been applicable to the work[15]; (b) particular output work worked by him in the pay reference period that is paid for at a higher rate than the normal rate applicable to that work by reason of the work being done at a particular time or in particular circumstances, to the extent that the total of those payments exceeds the total of the money payments that would have been payable in respect of the work if the normal rate had been applicable to the work[16];

(4)   any money payment paid by the employer to the worker by way of an allowance[17] other than an allowance attributable to the performance of the worker in carrying out his work[18];

(5)   any money payment paid by the employer to the worker representing amounts paid by customers by way of a service charge, tip, gratuity or cover charge[19];

(6)   any money payment paid by the employer to the worker to meet a payment by the worker that is a payment by the worker on account of

expenditure in connection with his employment to persons other than his employer[20] but for the worker's payment being met or designed to be met by the employer[21];

(7)   any deduction that is required to be subtracted[22];

(8)   any payment made by or due from the worker in the pay reference period that is required to be subtracted[23];

(9)   the amount of any deduction the employer is entitled to make, or payment he is entitled to receive from the worker, in respect of the provision of living accommodation by him to the worker in the pay reference period (as adjusted, where applicable[24]) to the extent that it exceeds the amount otherwise permitted to be taken into account[25] where living accommodation is provided[26];

(10)   any money payments paid by the employer to the worker in the pay reference period in respect of travelling expenses that are allowed as deductions from earnings under the Income Tax (Earnings and Pensions) Act 2003[27].

Any payment made to, or deduction by, a local housing authority[28] or a registered social landlord[29] in respect of the provision of living accommodation must be exempted from the operation of head (9) above, except where the living accommodation is provided to the worker in connection with his employment with the local housing authority or registered social landlord[30]; and any payment made to, or deduction by, a Higher Education Institution[31], Further Education Institution[32], or a 16 to 19 Academy[33], in respect of the provision of living accommodation must be exempted from the operation of head (9) above, except where the living accommodation is provided to the worker who is enrolled on a full-time higher education course, or a full-time further education course at that Higher Education or Further Education Institution, or on a full-time course provided by a 16 to 19 Academy[34].

To the extent that any payment or deduction is required to be subtracted from the total of remuneration by virtue of more than one of heads (1) to (10) above, it is to be subtracted only once[35].

1   As to the meaning of 'total of reductions' see PARA 201 note 6.
2   As to the meaning of 'total of remuneration' see PARA 201 note 4.
3   See the National Minimum Wage Regulations 1999, SI 1999/584, reg 31(1).
4   As to the meaning of references to payments paid by the employer to the worker see PARA 220 note 2. As to the meaning of 'employer' for these purposes see PARA 170; and as to the meaning of 'worker' for these purposes see PARA 171.
5   As to the meaning of 'pay reference period' see PARA 202.
6   Ie by virtue of the National Minimum Wage Regulations 1999, SI 1999/584, reg 30(b) or reg 30(c) (see PARA 220): see reg 31(1)(a).
7   National Minimum Wage Regulations 1999, SI 1999/584, reg 31(1)(a).
8   As to the meaning of 'work' for these purposes see PARA 172.
9   As to the meaning of 'salaried hours work' see PARA 204.
10   National Minimum Wage Regulations 1999, SI 1999/584, reg 31(1)(b)(i).
11   Ie determined under the National Minimum Wage Regulations 1999, SI 1999/584, reg 21(2) (see PARA 214): see reg 31(1)(b)(ii).
12   Ie whether under the direct application of the National Minimum Wage Regulations 1999, SI 1999/584, reg 21(2) (see PARA 214) or reg 21(3) (see PARA 214) or the application of those provisions required by reg 22(5)(a) (see PARA 215): see reg 31(1)(b)(ii).
13   Ie under the National Minimum Wage Regulations 1999, SI 1999/584, reg 21(3) (see PARA 214): see reg 31(1)(b)(ii).
14   National Minimum Wage Regulations 1999, SI 1999/584, reg 31(1)(b)(ii).
15   National Minimum Wage Regulations 1999, SI 1999/584, reg 31(1)(c)(i).
16   National Minimum Wage Regulations 1999, SI 1999/584, reg 31(1)(c)(ii).

17 For these purposes, 'allowance', other than in the National Minimum Wage Regulations 1999, SI 1999/584, reg 8(b) (see PARA 220 note 2), means any payment paid by the employer to a worker attributable to a particular aspect of his working arrangements or to his working or personal circumstances that is not consolidated into his standard pay (but does not include an allowance designed to refund a worker in respect of expenses incurred by him in connection with his employment): reg 2(1). See *Laird v AK Stoddart* [2001] IRLR 591, [2001] All ER (D) 261 (Jan), EAT (attendance allowances must be left out of account other than for productivity purposes in determining whether a worker is being remunerated at a rate not less than the national minimum wage). Cf the position under the Employment Rights Act 1996 s 27 for the purposes of calculating wages in terms of s 13: see PARAS 254–255.

18 National Minimum Wage Regulations 1999, SI 1999/584, reg 31(1)(d). See *Smith v Oxfordshire Learning Disability NHS Trust* [2009] ICR 1395, [2009] All ER (D) 170 (Aug), EAT (flat rate payment for sleep-in work made to part-time lifestyle support worker at a residential care home for adults with learning disabilities not an allowance within the meaning of the National Minimum Wage Regulations 1999, SI 1999/584, reg 31(1)(d), but a payment for performing a duty as per the employee's contract of employment; flat-rate payment was inherently different from the unsocial hours 'enhancements' to which the employee had separately been entitled for the hours immediately before and after a sleep-in, or the special payments that he would receive if he had a disturbed night, each of which was made on top of the basic remuneration for the work in question, and both of which were good examples of genuine 'allowances' within the meaning of the National Minimum Wage Regulations 1999, SI 1999/584).

19 National Minimum Wage Regulations 1999, SI 1999/584, reg 31(1)(e) (amended by SI 2009/1902). The amendment made to the National Minimum Wage Regulations 1999, SI 1999/584, reg 31(1)(e) (ie by deleting the words 'not paid through the payroll', so as to ensure, with effect from 1 October 2009, that no service charge, tip, gratuity or cover charge may be counted by the employer towards their National Minimum Wage obligation) gives legislative effect to the decision in *Revenue and Customs Comrs v Annabel's (Berkeley Square)* [2009] EWCA Civ 361, [2009] 4 All ER 55, [2009] ICR 1123 (tips can be counted as payments paid by the employer to the worker, for the purposes of the National Minimum Wage Regulations 1999, SI 1999/584, reg 30(a) (see PARA 220 note 3), if paid though the employer (eg when given by credit card or cheque) but not if paid in cash or if paid through a 'tronc' operated independently of the employer). Cash tips that are passed direct from a customer and not through the employer are unaffected, so they do not count as payments made for the purposes of the employer's National Minimum Wage obligation.

20 Ie a payment that would fall within the National Minimum Wage Regulations 1999, SI 1999/584, reg 34(1)(b) (see PARA 223): see reg 31(1)(f).

21 National Minimum Wage Regulations 1999, SI 1999/584, reg 31(1)(f).

22 National Minimum Wage Regulations 1999, SI 1999/584, reg 31(1)(g). Head (7) in the text refers to any deduction falling within reg 32 (see PARA 222): see reg 31(1)(g).

23 National Minimum Wage Regulations 1999, SI 1999/584, reg 31(1)(h). Head (8) in the text refers to any payment falling within reg 34 (see PARA 223): see reg 31(1)(h).

24 Ie as adjusted, where applicable, in accordance with the National Minimum Wage Regulations 1999, SI 1999/584, reg 37 (see PARA 225): see reg 31(1)(i).

25 Ie under the National Minimum Wage Regulations 1999, SI 1999/584, reg 36 (see PARA 224): see reg 31(1)(i).

26 National Minimum Wage Regulations 1999, SI 1999/584, reg 31(1)(i).

27 National Minimum Wage Regulations 1999, SI 1999/584, reg 31(1)(j) (added by SI 2010/3001). Head (10) in the text refers to travelling expenses that are allowed as deductions from earnings under the Income Tax (Earnings and Pensions) Act 2003 s 338 (see INCOME TAXATION vol 58 (2014) PARA 853): see the National Minimum Wage Regulations 1999, SI 1999/584, reg 31(1)(j) (as so added). An application for judicial review of the amendment proposed by the National Minimum Wage (Amendment) (No 2) Regulations 2010, SI 2010/3001, was rebutted by the Secretary of State's 'reasoned and convincing' analysis that the amendment either brought very substantial benefits to, or removed discrimination as between, low paid workers, without the certainty that they would suffer detriment by reason of the payment of significantly reduced wages: see *R (on the application of Cordant Group plc) v Secretary of State for Business, Innovation and Skills* [2010] EWHC 3442 (Admin), [2011] All ER (D) 04 (Jan).

28 For these purposes, 'local housing authority' means, in England and Wales, a local housing authority as defined in the Housing Act 1985 Pt 1 (ss 1–7) (see HOUSING vol 56 (2011) PARA 9) (and must in addition include county councils): see the National Minimum Wage Regulations 1999, SI 1999/584, reg 31(4) (reg 31(3)–(5) added by SI 2007/2318). As to the meanings of 'England' and 'Wales' see PARA 2 note 12.

29 For these purposes, 'registered social landlord' means, in England and Wales, either a private registered provider of social housing (and must in addition include subsidiaries or associates as defined in the Housing and Regeneration Act 2008 Pt 2 (ss 59–278A) (regulation of social housing: see HOUSING vol 56 (2011) PARA 30 et seq)), or a social landlord registered under the Housing Act 1996 Pt 1 (ss A1–64) (social rented sector regulated by the Welsh Ministers: see HOUSING vol 56 (2011) PARAS 11, 124) (and must in addition include subsidiaries or associates as defined in that Act): see the National Minimum Wage Regulations 1999, SI 1999/584, reg 31(5) (as added (see note 28); and amended by SI 2010/671).

30 National Minimum Wage Regulations 1999, SI 1999/584, reg 31(3) (as added: see note 28). Where the provision of accommodation was dependent on the pre-condition of a compulsory charge for heating and light, it must be taken into account in calculating the permitted accommodation deduction: *Leisure Employment Services Ltd v Revenue and Customs Comrs* [2007] EWCA Civ 92, [2007] ICR 1056, [2007] IRLR 450.

31 For these purposes, 'Higher Education Institution' refers to an institution within the higher education sector as defined by the Further and Higher Education Act 1992 s 91(5) (see EDUCATION vol 36 (2011) PARA 809): see the National Minimum Wage Regulations 1999, SI 1999/584 reg 2(1) (definition added by SI 2011/2347).

32 For these purposes, 'Further Education Institution' refers to an institution within the further education sector as defined by the Further and Higher Education Act 1992 s 91(3) (see EDUCATION vol 36 (2011) PARA 729): see the National Minimum Wage Regulations 1999, SI 1999/584 reg 2(1) (definition added by SI 2011/2347).

33 As to 16 to 19 Academies see EDUCATION vol 35 (2011) PARA 510.

34 National Minimum Wage Regulations 1999, SI 1999/584, reg 31(6) (added by SI 2011/2347; and amended in relation to England by SI 2012/979).

35 National Minimum Wage Regulations 1999, SI 1999/584, reg 31(2).

222. Deductions to be subtracted from the total of remuneration. The deductions required to be subtracted[1] from the total of remuneration are[2]:

    (1)   any deduction in respect of the worker's[3] expenditure in connection with his employment[4];

    (2)   any deduction made by the employer[5] for his own use and benefit (and accordingly not attributable to any amount paid or payable by the employer to any other person on behalf of the worker), except[6]:

        (a)   any deduction in respect of conduct of the worker, or any other event, in respect of which he, whether together with any other workers or not, is contractually liable[7];

        (b)   any deduction on account of an advance under an agreement for a loan or an advance of wages[8];

        (c)   any deduction made to recover an accidental overpayment of wages made to the worker[9];

        (d)   any deduction in respect of the purchase by the worker of any shares, other securities or share option, or of any share in a partnership[10]; or

        (e)   any deduction in respect of the provision of living accommodation which is exempted[11].

To the extent that any deduction is required to be subtracted by virtue of both heads (1) and (2) above, it is to be subtracted only once[12].

1   Ie under the National Minimum Wage Regulations 1999, SI 1999/584, reg 31(1)(g) (see PARA 221): see reg 32(1).

2   See the National Minimum Wage Regulations 1999, SI 1999/584, reg 32(1). As to the meaning of 'total of remuneration' see PARA 201 note 4.

3   As to the meaning of 'worker' for these purposes see PARA 171.

4   National Minimum Wage Regulations 1999, SI 1999/584, reg 32(1)(a).

5   As to the meaning of 'employer' for these purposes see PARA 170. Deductions made by an employer providing accommodation to pay for gas and electricity that result in an employee being paid less than the minimum wage are unlawful: *Leisure Employment Services Ltd v Revenue and Customs Comrs* [2007] EWCA Civ 92, [2007] ICR 1056, [2007] IRLR 450.

6   See the National Minimum Wage Regulations 1999, SI 1999/584, reg 32(1)(b). Head (2) in the text refers to the exception specified in reg 33 (see heads (a)–(e) in the text): see reg 32(1)(b).
7   National Minimum Wage Regulations 1999, SI 1999/584 reg 33(a).
8   National Minimum Wage Regulations 1999, SI 1999/584 reg 33(b).
9   National Minimum Wage Regulations 1999, SI 1999/584 reg 33(c).
10 National Minimum Wage Regulations 1999, SI 1999/584, reg 33(d) (reg 33(d) amended, reg 33(e) added, by SI 2007/2318).
11 National Minimum Wage Regulations 1999, SI 1999/584 reg 33(e) (as added (see note 10); and amended by SI 2012/2397). Head (e) in the text refers to deductions exempted from the National Minimum Wage Regulations 1999, SI 1999/584 reg 31(1)(i) by reg 31(3) or reg 31(6) (see PARA 221): see reg 33(e) (as so added and amended).
12 National Minimum Wage Regulations 1999, SI 1999/584, reg 32(2).

223.   Payments made by, or due from, a worker to be subtracted from the total of remuneration.   The payments made by, or due from, the worker[1] required to be subtracted[2] from the total of remuneration are[3]:

(1)   any payment due from the worker to the employer[4] in the pay reference period[5] on account of the worker's expenditure in connection with his employment[6];

(2)   any payment paid in the pay reference period on account of the worker's expenditure in connection with his employment to the extent that the expenditure consists of a payment to a person other than the employer and is not met, or designed to be met, by a payment paid to him by the employer[7];

(3)   any other payment due from the worker to the employer in the pay reference period that the employer retains or is entitled to retain for his own use and benefit except for a payment required to be left out of account[8], that is to say:

   (a)   any payment in respect of conduct of the worker, or any other event, in respect of which he, whether together with any other workers or not, is contractually liable[9];

   (b)   any payment on account of an advance under an agreement for a loan or an advance of wages[10];

   (c)   any payment made to refund the employer in respect of an accidental overpayment of wages made by the employer to the worker[11];

   (d)   any payment in respect of the purchase by the worker of any shares, other securities or share option, or of any share in a partnership[12];

   (e)   any payment in respect of the purchase by the worker of any goods or services from the employer, unless the purchase is made in order to comply with a requirement in the worker's contract or any other requirement imposed on him by the employer in connection with his employment[13]; or

   (f)   any deduction in respect of the provision of living accommodation which is exempted[14].

To the extent that any payment is required to be subtracted by virtue of more than one of heads (1) to (3) above, it is to be subtracted only once[15].

1   As to the meaning of 'worker' for these purposes see PARA 171.
2   Ie under the National Minimum Wage Regulations 1999, SI 1999/584, reg 31(1)(h) (see PARA 221): see reg 34(1).
3   See the National Minimum Wage Regulations 1999, SI 1999/584, reg 34(1). As to the meaning of 'total of remuneration' see PARA 201 note 4.
4   As to the meaning of 'employer' for these purposes see PARA 170.

5   As to the meaning of 'pay reference period' see PARA 202.
6   National Minimum Wage Regulations 1999, SI 1999/584, reg 34(1)(a).
7   National Minimum Wage Regulations 1999, SI 1999/584, reg 34(1)(b).
8   See the National Minimum Wage Regulations 1999, SI 1999/584, reg 34(1)(c). Head (3) in the
    text refers to a payment required to be left out of account by reg 35 (see heads (a)–(f) in the
    text): see reg 34(1)(c).
9   National Minimum Wage Regulations 1999, SI 1999/584 reg 35(a).
10 National Minimum Wage Regulations 1999, SI 1999/584 reg 35(b).
11 National Minimum Wage Regulations 1999, SI 1999/584 reg 35(c).
12 National Minimum Wage Regulations 1999, SI 1999/584 reg 35(d).
13 National Minimum Wage Regulations 1999, SI 1999/584, reg 35(e) (reg 35(e) amended,
    reg 35(f) added, by SI 2007/2318).
14 National Minimum Wage Regulations 1999, SI 1999/584 reg 35(f) (as added (see note 13); and
    amended by SI 2012/2397). Head (f) in the text refers to deductions exempted from reg 31(1)(i)
    by reg 31(3) or reg 31(6) (see PARA 221): see reg 33(f) (as so added and amended).
15 National Minimum Wage Regulations 1999, SI 1999/584, reg 34(2).

**224.   Amount to be taken into account where living accommodation is
provided.**   The amount to be taken into account where living accommodation is
provided[1] is the amount resulting from multiplying the number of days in the
pay reference period[2] for which accommodation was provided[3] by a specified
sum[4].

1   Ie the amount referred to in the National Minimum Wage Regulations 1999, SI 1999/584,
    reg 30(d) (see PARA 220) and reg 31(1)(i) (see PARA 221): see reg 36(1) (substituted by
    SI 2003/1923; and amended by SI 2014/2485).
2   Any amounts required to be determined for the purpose of the National Minimum Wage
    Regulations 1999, SI 1999/584, reg 30(d) (see PARA 220) or reg 31(1)(i) (see PARA 221) in
    respect of any pay reference period is to be determined in accordance with the regulations as
    they are in force on the first day of the pay reference period: reg 36A (added by SI 2003/1923).
    As to the meaning of 'pay reference period' see PARA 202.
3   For these purposes, living accommodation is provided for a day only if it is provided for the
    whole of a day from midnight to midnight: National Minimum Wage Regulations 1999,
    SI 1999/584, reg 36(2).
4   See the National Minimum Wage Regulations 1999, SI 1999/584, reg 36(1) (as substituted and
    amended: see note 1). At the date at which this volume states the law, the specified sum is £5.08:
    see reg 36(1) (as so substituted and amended). See e g *Paggetti v Cobb* [2002] IRLR 861, [2002]
    All ER (D) 394 (Mar), EAT (calculation of a week's pay under the Employment Rights Act 1996
    ss 221–229 (see PARAS 144–148) for the purposes of compensation in an unfair dismissal case).

225.   Adjusted deductions and payments in respect of living accommodation.
Where an employer[1] is entitled to make deductions or receive payments in
respect of the provision of living accommodation to a worker[2], and where, in a
pay reference period[3]:

(1)   a worker is absent from work for a day or more when, but for his
      absence, he would be expected to perform time work (for example,
      because he is sick or taking a holiday)[4];

(2)   during that period of absence he is paid, for the hours of time work for
      which he is absent, an amount not less than the amount to which he
      would have been entitled[5], but for his absence[6];

(3)   the hours of time work worked by the worker in the pay reference
      period are, by reason of his absence, less than they would be in a pay
      reference period containing the same number of working days in which
      the worker worked for the normal number of working hours (and for
      no additional hours)[7]; and

(4)   the amount of the deduction the employer is entitled to make or
      payment he is entitled to receive in respect of the provision of living

accommodation to the worker during the pay reference period does not increase by reason of the worker's absence from work[8],
the amount of the deduction the employer is entitled to make or payment he is entitled to receive in respect of the provision of living accommodation is to be adjusted[9] by multiplying that amount by the number of hours of time work actually worked by the worker in the pay reference period[10] and dividing the figure so obtained by the total number of hours of time work the worker would have worked in the pay reference period (including the hours of time work actually worked), but for his absence[11].

1 As to the meaning of 'employer' for these purposes see PARA 170.
2 As to the meaning of 'worker' for these purposes see PARA 171.
3 See the National Minimum Wage Regulations 1999, SI 1999/584, reg 37(1). As to the meaning of 'pay reference period' see PARA 202.
4 National Minimum Wage Regulations 1999, SI 1999/584, reg 37(1)(a). As to the meaning of 'time work' see PARA 203.
5 Ie under the National Minimum Wage Regulations 1999, SI 1999/584: see reg 37(1)(b).
6 National Minimum Wage Regulations 1999, SI 1999/584, reg 37(1)(b).
7 National Minimum Wage Regulations 1999, SI 1999/584, reg 37(1)(c).
8 National Minimum Wage Regulations 1999, SI 1999/584, reg 37(1)(d).
9 Ie for the purposes of the National Minimum Wage Regulations 1999, SI 1999/584, reg 31(1)(i) (see PARA 221): see reg 37(2).
10 Ie as determined Ie in accordance with the National Minimum Wage Regulations 1999, SI 1999/584, reg 20 (see PARA 213): see reg 37(2).
11 See the National Minimum Wage Regulations 1999, SI 1999/584, reg 37(2).

(ix) Access to Records and Information required to be kept for the purposes of the National Minimum Wage Act 1998

226. Duty of employers to keep records. For the purposes of the National Minimum Wage Act 1998, the Secretary of State[1] may by regulations[2] make provision requiring employers[3]:

(1) to keep, in such form and manner as may be prescribed, such records as may be prescribed[4]; and

(2) to preserve those records for such period as may be prescribed[5].

Accordingly, the employer of a worker[6] who qualifies for the national minimum wage[7] must keep in respect of that worker records sufficient to establish that he is remunerating the worker at a rate at least equal to the national minimum wage[8]. The records required to be so kept must be in a form which enables the information kept about a worker in respect of a pay reference period[9] to be produced in a single document[10].

The employer of a worker who qualifies for the national minimum wage who has entered into any agreement with the worker in respect of unmeasured work[11] must keep a copy of that agreement[12]; and the employer of a worker who qualifies for the national minimum wage, who has given the worker a notice in respect of output work[13], must keep a copy of that notice and a copy of such data as is necessary to show how he has determined the rates[14] for the subject piece or task or for the production of a single subject piece or task[15].

The records required to be kept: (a) must be kept by the employer for a period of three years beginning with the day on which the pay reference period immediately following that to which they relate ends[16]; and (b) may be kept by means of a computer[17].

1 As to the Secretary of State see PARA 5 note 21.

2   As to the making of regulations under the National Minimum Wage Act 1998 see PARA 175. See further note 4.
3   See the National Minimum Wage Act 1998 s 9. As to the meaning of 'employer' for these purposes see PARA 170.
4   National Minimum Wage Act 1998 s 9(a). For these purposes, unless the context otherwise requires, 'prescribe' means prescribe by regulations: see s 55(1). In exercise of the power so conferred, the Secretary of State has made the National Minimum Wage Regulations 1999, SI 1999/584, reg 38: see the text and notes 6–17.
5   National Minimum Wage Act 1998 s 9(b). See further note 4. As to the worker's right of access to such records see PARA 227; as to the power of officers appointed by the Secretary of State to require the production etc of such records see PARA 238; as to offences in connection with records see PARA 251; and as to offences by bodies corporate see PARA 252.
6   As to the meaning of 'worker' for these purposes see PARA 171.
7   As to the meaning of 'person who qualifies for the national minimum wage' see PARA 176 note 5. As to the rate of the national minimum wage see PARA 199.
8   National Minimum Wage Regulations 1999, SI 1999/584, reg 38(1).
    The provision made by the National Minimum Wage Regulations 1999, SI 1999/584, reg 38(4)–(6) (reg 38(4) amended by SI 2004/1930), in relation to a minimum rate of wages fixed under the Agricultural Wages Act 1948 s 3(1)(a) (see AGRICULTURAL PRODUCTION AND MARKETING vol 1 (2008) PARA 1231), is revoked, and most of the 1948 Act repealed, as from a date to be appointed under the Enterprise and Regulatory Reform Act 2013 s 103(3), by s 72(4), Sch 20 para 2. That day has been appointed as 1 October 2013 in relation to England (see the Enterprise and Regulatory Reform Act 2013 (Commencement No 1, Transitional Provisions and Savings) Order 2013, SI 2013/1455, art 3(b), Sch 2 para 6 (art 3(b) amended by SI 2013/2271)), but such a day has not been appointed, at the date at which this volume states the law, in relation to Wales. As to the meanings of 'England' and 'Wales' see PARA 2 note 12.
9   As to the meaning of 'pay reference period' see PARA 202.
10 National Minimum Wage Regulations 1999, SI 1999/584, reg 38(2).
11 Ie an agreement under the National Minimum Wage Regulations 1999, SI 1999/584, reg 28(1) (see PARA 218): see reg 38(3) (amended by SI 2010/1901).
12 National Minimum Wage Regulations 1999, SI 1999/584, reg 38(3) (as amended: see note 11).
13 Ie a notice in accordance with the National Minimum Wage Regulations 1999, SI 1999/584, reg 24(2)(b) (see PARA 217): see reg 38(3A) (added by SI 2004/1930).
14 Ie the rates referred to in the National Minimum Wage Regulations 1999, SI 1999/584, reg 25(2)(b)(iii), (iv) (see PARA 217): see reg 38(3A) (as added: see note 13).
15 National Minimum Wage Regulations 1999, SI 1999/584, reg 38(3A) (as added: see note 13).
16 See the National Minimum Wage Regulations 1999, SI 1999/584, reg 38(7).
17 See the National Minimum Wage Regulations 1999, SI 1999/584, reg 38(8).

227.   Worker's right of access to records.   A worker may[1] require his employer[2] to produce any relevant records[3], and the worker may inspect and examine those records and copy any part of them[4]. Such rights of access are, however, exercisable:

(1)   only if the worker believes on reasonable grounds that he is or may be being, or has or may have been, remunerated for any pay reference period by his employer at a rate which is less than the national minimum wage[5];

(2)   only for the purpose of establishing whether or not the worker is being, or has been, remunerated for any pay reference period by his employer at a rate which is less than the national minimum wage[6];

(3)   either: (a) by the worker alone[7]; or (b) by the worker accompanied by such other person as the worker may think fit[8];

(4)   only if the worker gives notice[9] (a 'production notice') to his employer requesting the production of any relevant records relating to such period as may be described in the notice[10].

If the worker intends to exercise the right conferred by head (3)(b) above, the production notice must contain a statement of that intention[11]. Where a production notice is given, the employer must give the worker reasonable notice of the place and time at which the relevant records will be produced[12].

The place at which the relevant records are produced must be:

(i)   the worker's place of work[13]; or

(ii)   any other place at which it is reasonable, in all the circumstances, for the worker to attend to inspect the relevant records[14]; or

(iii)   such other place as may be agreed between the worker and the employer[15];

and the relevant records must be produced: (A) before the end of the period of 14 days following the date of receipt of the production notice[16]; or (B) at such later time as may be agreed during that period between the worker and the employer[17].

1   Ie in accordance with the National Minimum Wage Act 1998 s 10(2)–(10) (see the text and notes 5–17): see s 10(1). As to the meaning of 'worker' for these purposes see PARA 171.
2   As to the meaning of 'employer' for these purposes see PARA 170.
3   National Minimum Wage Act 1998 s 10(1)(a). For these purposes, 'records' means records which the worker's employer is required to keep and, at the time of receipt of the production notice (see head (4) in the text), preserve in accordance with s 9 (see PARA 226); and 'relevant records' means such parts of, or such extracts from, any records as are relevant to establishing whether or not the worker has, for any pay reference period to which the records relate, been remunerated by the employer at a rate which is at least equal to the national minimum wage: see s 10(10). As to the meaning of references to a person being remunerated for a pay reference period see PARA 174 note 8; and as to the meaning of 'pay reference period' see PARA 202. As to the rate of the national minimum wage see PARA 199.
4   National Minimum Wage Act 1998 s 10(1)(b). As to the consequences of a failure to allow access to records see PARA 228.
5   National Minimum Wage Act 1998 s 10(2).
6   National Minimum Wage Act 1998 s 10(3).
7   National Minimum Wage Act 1998 s 10(4)(a).
8   National Minimum Wage Act 1998 s 10(4)(b).
9   For these purposes, unless the context otherwise requires, 'notice' means notice in writing: see the National Minimum Wage Act 1998 s 55(1). As to the meaning of 'writing' see PARA 2 note 8.
10 National Minimum Wage Act 1998 s 10(5).
11 National Minimum Wage Act 1998 s 10(6).
12 National Minimum Wage Act 1998 s 10(7).
13 National Minimum Wage Act 1998 s 10(8)(a).
14 National Minimum Wage Act 1998 s 10(8)(b).
15 National Minimum Wage Act 1998 s 10(8)(c).
16 National Minimum Wage Act 1998 s 10(9)(a).
17 National Minimum Wage Act 1998 s 10(9)(b).

228.   Failure of employer to allow access to records.   A complaint may be presented to an employment tribunal[1] by a worker[2] on the ground that the employer[3]:

(1)   failed to produce at the proper time or place[4] some or all of the relevant records[5]; or

(2)   failed to allow the worker to exercise some or all of his rights of access[6] to records[7].

An employment tribunal must not consider such a complaint unless it is presented to the tribunal before the expiry of the period of three months following the end of the period of 14 days after the date of receipt of the production notice[8] or, in a case where a later day was duly agreed[9], that later day[10]. In working out when the time limit set in this way[11] expires, the following period is not to be counted[12], namely the period that:

(a)   begins with the day after the day on which the worker concerned complies with the requirement to contact ACAS before instituting proceedings[13] in relation to the matter in respect of which the proceedings are brought ('the day after Day A')[14]; and

(b)   ends with the day on which the worker concerned receives (or, if earlier, is treated as receiving[15]) the certificate issued by the conciliation officer[16] to the effect either that he has concluded that a settlement is not possible within the prescribed period or that the prescribed period has expired without a settlement having been reached ('Day B')[17].

If the unextended time limit[18] would expire during the period beginning with Day A and ending one month after Day B, the time limit expires instead at the end of that period[19]. Where, however, the employment tribunal is satisfied that it was not reasonably practicable for such a complaint to be presented before the expiry of such a period of three months, the tribunal may consider the complaint if it is presented within such further period as the tribunal considers reasonable[20].

Where an employment tribunal finds such a complaint well-founded, the tribunal must make a declaration to that effect[21], and must make an award that the employer pay to the worker a sum equal to 80 times the hourly amount of the national minimum wage[21] (as in force when the award is made)[22].

1   As to employment tribunals see PARA 1399 et seq; and as to the procedure on a complaint made to an employment tribunal see PARA 1453 et seq. There is a requirement for early ACAS conciliation to be tried in order to promote a settlement before tribunal proceedings are instituted on a complaint under the National Minimum Wage Act 1998 s 11, however: see the Employment Tribunals Act 1996 s 18(1)(c); and PARA 152 note 1. As to the constitution and powers of ACAS see PARA 1213 et seq.
2   As to the meaning of 'worker' for these purposes see PARA 171.
3   See the National Minimum Wage Act 1998 s 11(1). As to the meaning of 'employer' for these purposes see PARA 170.
4   Ie in accordance with the National Minimum Wage Act 1998 s 10(8) (place at which relevant records must be produced: see PARA 227) or s 10(9) (time when relevant records must be produced: see PARA 227): see s 11(1)(a).
5   National Minimum Wage Act 1998 s 11(1)(a). For these purposes, 'records' and 'relevant records' have the same meanings as they have in s 10 (see PARA 227 note 3): see s 11(5).
6   Ie the rights conferred by the National Minimum Wage Act 1998 s 10(1)(b) (inspection, examination and copying: see PARA 227) or s 10(4)(b) (right to be accompanied: see PARA 227): see s 11(1)(b).
7   National Minimum Wage Act 1998 s 11(1)(b).
8   Ie the end of the period of 14 days mentioned in the National Minimum Wage Act 1998 s 10(9)(a) (see PARA 227): see s 11(3).
9   Ie under the National Minimum Wage Act 1998 s 10(9)(b) (see PARA 227): see s 11(3).
10 See the National Minimum Wage Act 1998 s 11(3). Provision that is made for the extension of time limits in order to facilitate conciliation before the institution of proceedings (ie s 11A: see the text and notes 11–19) applies for the purposes of s 11(3): s 11(4A) (ss 11(4A), 11A added by the Enterprise and Regulatory Reform Act 2013, s 8, Sch 2, paras 36–38). As to the right to present a complaint to an employment tribunal see PARA 80.
11 Ie set by the National Minimum Wage Act 1998 s 11(3) (see the text and notes 8–10): see s 11A(2) (as added: see note 10).
12 See the National Minimum Wage Act 1998 s 11A(2) (as added: see note 10).
13 Ie the requirement in the Employment Tribunals Act 1996 s 18A(1) (see PARA 152): see the National Minimum Wage Act 1998 s 11A(1)(a) (as added: see note 10).
14 See the National Minimum Wage Act 1998 s 11A(1)(a), (2) (as added: see note 10).
15 Ie by virtue of regulations made under the Employment Tribunals Act 1996 s 18A(11) (see PARA 152): see the National Minimum Wage Act 1998 s 11A(1)(b) (as added: see note 10).
16 Ie the certificate issued under the Employment Tribunals Act 1996 s 18A(4) (see PARA 152): see the National Minimum Wage Act 1998 s 11A(1)(b) (as added: see note 10).
17 See the National Minimum Wage Act 1998 s 11A(1)(b), (2) (as added: see note 10).
18 Ie the time limit set by the National Minimum Wage Act 1998 s 11(3) (see the text and notes 8–10), if not extended by s 11A(3): see s 11A(3) (as added: see note 10).

19 See the National Minimum Wage Act 1998 s 11A(3) (as added: see note 10).
20 National Minimum Wage Act 1998 s 11(4). The power so conferred on the employment
    tribunal by s 11(4) to extend the time limit set by s 11(3) is exercisable in relation to any time
    limit as it is extended by s 11A (see the text and notes 11–19): s 11A(4) (as added: see note 10).
21 National Minimum Wage Act 1998 s 11(2)(a).
22 As to the amount of the national minimum wage see PARA 199.
23 National Minimum Wage Act 1998 s 11(2)(b).

(x) The Low Pay Commission

229. Appointment of the Low Pay Commission. The National Minimum
Wage Act 1998 enabled the Secretary of State[1] to appoint a body, known as the
'Low Pay Commission', to discharge the functions conferred or imposed on the
Commission under that Act[2].

1 As to the Secretary of State see PARA 5 note 21.
2 National Minimum Wage Act 1998 s 8(9). As to the exercise of the Secretary of State's power
   under s 8(9) see also s 8(11). As to membership etc of the Low Pay Commission see PARA 230 et
   seq.

230. Membership of the Low Pay Commission. The Low Pay Commission[1]
(the 'Commission') consists of a chairman and eight other members appointed by
the Secretary of State[2]. In appointing members, the Secretary of State must have
regard to the desirability of securing that there is such a balance as the Secretary
of State considers appropriate between[3]:
  (1) members with knowledge or experience of, or interest in, trade unions
       or matters relating to workers generally[4];
  (2) members with knowledge or experience of, or interest in, employers'
       associations or matters relating to employers generally[5]; and
  (3) members with other relevant knowledge or experience[6].
Members hold and must vacate office in accordance with their terms of
appointment, subject to the following provisions[7]:
  (a) a member may resign his membership by giving notice[8] to the Secretary
       of State[9]; and
  (b) the Secretary of State may by notice to the member concerned remove
       from office a member who: (i) has become bankrupt, has had a debt
       relief order made in respect of him[10], has made an arrangement with his
       creditors, has had his estate sequestrated, has granted a trust deed for
       his creditors, or has made a composition contract with his creditors[11];
       or (ii) has been absent from two or more consecutive meetings of the
       Commission otherwise than for a reason approved by it[12]; or (iii) is, in
       the opinion of the Secretary of State, unable or unfit to perform his
       duties as member[13].

1 Ie the Low Pay Commission appointed under the National Minimum Wage Act 1998 s 8(9) (see
   PARA 229): see s 8(10), Sch 1 para 1(1).
2 National Minimum Wage Act 1998 Sch 1 para 1(1). As to the Secretary of State see PARA 5 note
   21. Members of the Low Pay Commission are disqualified for membership of the House of
   Commons: see the House of Commons Disqualification Act 1975 s 1(1)(f), Sch 1 Pt II; and
   PARLIAMENT vol 78 (2010) PARA 908.
3 See the National Minimum Wage Act 1998 Sch 1 para 1(2).
4 National Minimum Wage Act 1998 Sch 1 para 1(2)(a). As to the meaning of 'worker' for these
   purposes see PARA 171.
5 National Minimum Wage Act 1998 Sch 1 para 1(2)(b). As to the meaning of 'employer' for
   these purposes see PARA 170.
6 National Minimum Wage Act 1998 Sch 1 para 1(2)(c).
7 See the National Minimum Wage Act 1998 Sch 1 para 1(3).

8   As to the meaning of 'notice' for these purposes see PARA 227 note 9.
9   National Minimum Wage Act 1998 Sch 1 para 1(4). A person who ceases to be a member is eligible for re-appointment: Sch 1 para 1(5).
10 Ie under the Insolvency Act 1986 Pt VIIA (ss 251A–251X) (debt relief orders: see BANKRUPTCY AND INDIVIDUAL INSOLVENCY vol 5 (2013) PARA 91 et seq): see the National Minimum Wage Act 1998 Sch 1 para 1(6)(a) (amended by SI 2012/2404).
11 National Minimum Wage Act 1998 Sch 1 para 1(6)(a) (as amended: see note 10).
12 National Minimum Wage Act 1998 Sch 1 para 1(6)(b).
13 National Minimum Wage Act 1998 Sch 1 para 1(6)(c).

231.   Financial provisions. The Secretary of State[1] may pay the members of the Low Pay Commission[2] such remuneration, and such allowances in respect of travel or other expenses properly incurred by them, or in respect of loss of remuneration sustained by them, in the performance of their duties, as the Secretary of State may determine[3].

The Secretary of State may determine to pay in respect of a person's office as member of the Commission[4]:

(1)   such pension, allowance or gratuity to or in respect of that person on his retirement or death[5]; or

(2)   such contributions or other payment towards the provision of such a pension, allowance or gratuity[6],

as the Secretary of State may determine[7].

Where a person ceases to be a member of the Commission (otherwise than on the expiry of his term of office), and where it appears to the Secretary of State that there are special circumstances which make it right for him to receive compensation, the Secretary of State may determine to make a payment to him by way of compensation of such amount as the Secretary of State may determine[8].

1   As to the Secretary of State see PARA 5 note 21.
2   Ie the Low Pay Commission appointed under the National Minimum Wage Act 1998 s 8(9) (see s 8(10), Sch 1 para 1(1); and PARA 230).
3   National Minimum Wage Act 1998 Sch 1 para 2(1).
4   See the National Minimum Wage Act 1998 Sch 1 para 2(2).
5   National Minimum Wage Act 1998 Sch 1 para 2(2)(a).
6   National Minimum Wage Act 1998 Sch 1 para 2(2)(b).
7   See the National Minimum Wage Act 1998 Sch 1 para 2(2).
8   National Minimum Wage Act 1998 Sch 1 para 2(3).

232.   Staff, facilities and money. The Secretary of State[1] must provide the Low Pay Commission[2] with:

(1)   such staff[3];

(2)   such accommodation, equipment and other facilities[4]; and

(3)   such sums[5],

as the Secretary of State may reasonably determine are required by the Commission for carrying out its duties in preparing any report on matters referred to it under the National Minimum Wage Act 1998[6].

1   As to the Secretary of State see PARA 5 note 21.
2   Ie the Low Pay Commission appointed under the National Minimum Wage Act 1998 s 8(9) (see s 8(10), Sch 1 para 1(1); and PARA 230).
3   National Minimum Wage Act 1998 Sch 1 para 3(a).
4   National Minimum Wage Act 1998 Sch 1 para 3(b).
5   National Minimum Wage Act 1998 Sch 1 para 3(c).
6   See the National Minimum Wage Act 1998 Sch 1 para 3.

233. Proceedings. The quorum of the Low Pay Commission[1], and the arrangements relating to its meetings, are such as the Commission may determine[2].

The validity of proceedings of the Commission is not affected by[3]: (1) any vacancy among the members, whether occurring by reason of death, resignation or otherwise[4]; (2) the appointment of a member at any time to fill such a vacancy[5]; or (3) any defect in the appointment of a member[6].

1   Ie the Low Pay Commission appointed under the National Minimum Wage Act 1998 s 8(9) (see s 8(10), Sch 1 para 1(1); and PARA 230).
2   National Minimum Wage Act 1998 Sch 1 para 4(1).
3   See the National Minimum Wage Act 1998 Sch 1 para 4(2).
4   National Minimum Wage Act 1998 Sch 1 para 4(2)(a). As to membership of the Commission see PARA 230.
5   National Minimum Wage Act 1998 Sch 1 para 4(2)(b).
6   National Minimum Wage Act 1998 Sch 1 para 4(2)(c).

234. Initial referral of matters to the Low Pay Commission. Before making the first regulations[1] relating to the national minimum wage's single hourly rate[2], pay reference periods[3], or the method used for determining the hourly rate of remuneration[4], the Secretary of State[5] had a duty to refer the following matters to the Low Pay Commission for its consideration[6]:

(1)   what single hourly rate should be prescribed[7] as the national minimum wage[8];

(2)   what period or periods should be prescribed[9] as pay reference periods[10];

(3)   what method or methods should be used for determining[11] the hourly rate at which a person is to be regarded as remunerated for the purposes of the National Minimum Wage Act 1998[12];

(4)   whether any, and if so what, provision should be made[13] to exclude, or modify the provisions relating to, certain classes of person[14]; and

(5)   whether any, and if so what, descriptions of person should be added to the descriptions of person to whom head (4) above applies[15] and what provision should be made[16] in relation to persons of those descriptions[17].

Where matters were so referred to the Commission, it had a duty to consider those matters, then make a report to the Prime Minister and the Secretary of State which had to contain the Commission's recommendations about each of those matters[18]. If, following that report, the Secretary of State decided[19]:

(a)   not to make any regulations implementing the Commission's recommendations[20]; or

(b)   to make regulations implementing only some of the Commission's recommendations[21]; or

(c)   to prescribe[22] a single hourly rate which was different from the rate recommended by the Commission[23]; or

(d)   to make regulations which in some other respect differed from the recommendations of the Commission[24]; or

(e)   to make regulations which did not relate to a recommendation of the Commission[25],

the Secretary of State had a duty to lay a report before each House of Parliament containing a statement of the reasons for the decision[26].

1   As to the making of regulations under the National Minimum Wage Act 1998 see PARA 175. As to the regulations that have been so made see the National Minimum Wage Regulations 1999, SI 1999/584; and PARA 170 et seq.

2   Ie the first regulations under the National Minimum Wage Act 1998 s 1(3) (see PARA 199): see s 5(1). See note 1.
3   Ie the first regulations under the National Minimum Wage Act 1998 s 1(4) (see PARA 202): see s 5(1). See note 1.
4   Ie the first regulations under the National Minimum Wage Act 1998 s 2 (see PARA 200): see s 5(1). See note 1.
5   As to the Secretary of State see PARA 5 note 21.
6   See the National Minimum Wage Act 1998 s 5(1). Matters relating to the National Minimum Wage Act 1998 may be referred by the Secretary of State to the Commission at any time: see s 6; and PARA 235. As to the Low Pay Commission see also PARAS 229 et seq, 235, 236.
7   Ie under the National Minimum Wage Act 1998 s 1(3) (see PARA 199): see s 5(2)(a). For these purposes, unless the context otherwise requires, 'prescribe' means prescribe by regulations: s 55(1). See note 1.
8   National Minimum Wage Act 1998 s 5(2)(a).
9   Ie under the National Minimum Wage Act 1998 s 1(4) (see PARA 202): see s 5(2)(b). See note 1.
10   National Minimum Wage Act 1998 s 5(2)(b).
11   Ie under the National Minimum Wage Act 1998 s 2 (see PARA 200): see s 5(2)(c). See note 1.
12   National Minimum Wage Act 1998 s 5(2)(c).
13   Ie under the National Minimum Wage Act 1998 s 3 (see PARA 186): see s 5(2)(d). See note 1.
14   National Minimum Wage Act 1998 s 5(2)(d).
15   Ie the descriptions of person to whom the National Minimum Wage Act 1998 s 3 applies (see PARA 186): see s 5(2)(e). See note 1.
16   Ie under the National Minimum Wage Act 1998 s 3 (see PARA 186): see s 5(2)(e). See note 1.
17   National Minimum Wage Act 1998 s 5(2)(e).
18   National Minimum Wage Act 1998 s 5(3). If the Commission failed to make its report under s 5(3) within the time allowed for doing so under s 7 (see PARA 236), any power of the Secretary of State to make regulations under the National Minimum Wage Act 1998 was exercisable as if s 5(1) (see the text and notes 1–6) had not been enacted: s 5(5).
19   See the National Minimum Wage Act 1998 s 5(4).
20   National Minimum Wage Act 1998 s 5(4)(a).
21   National Minimum Wage Act 1998 s 5(4)(b).
22   Ie under the National Minimum Wage Act 1998 s 1(3) (see PARA 199): see s 5(4)(c).
23   National Minimum Wage Act 1998 s 5(4)(c).
24   National Minimum Wage Act 1998 s 5(4)(d).
25   National Minimum Wage Act 1998 s 5(4)(e).
26   See the National Minimum Wage Act 1998 s 5(4).

235. Referral of matters to the Low Pay Commission at any time. The Secretary of State[1] may at any time refer to the Low Pay Commission[2] such matters relating to the National Minimum Wage Act 1998 as he thinks fit[3]. Where matters are referred in this way to the Commission, it must, after considering those matters, make a report to the Prime Minister and the Secretary of State which must contain the Commission's recommendations about each of those matters[4].

If, on such a referral:

(1)   the Secretary of State seeks the opinion of the Commission on a matter[5] which was to be referred to the Commission before making the first regulations[6];

(2)   the Commission's report[7] contains recommendations in relation to that matter[8]; and

(3)   implementation of any of those recommendations involves the exercise of any of the statutory powers[9] to make regulations[10],

the Secretary of State's duty to lay a report before each House of Parliament[11] applies in relation to the report, so far as relating to the recommendations falling within head (3) above, as it applies in relation to a report[12] relating to the first regulations[13]; and if, on such a referral:

(a)   the Secretary of State seeks the opinion of the Commission on any matter[14] which was to be referred to the Commission before making the first regulations[15]; but

(b)   the Commission fails to make its report[16] within the time allowed[17],

the Secretary of State may make regulations[18] as if the opinion of the Commission had not been sought in relation to that matter[19].

1   As to the Secretary of State see PARA 5 note 21.
2   As to the Low Pay Commission see PARA 229 et seq.
3   National Minimum Wage Act 1998 s 6(1).
4   National Minimum Wage Act 1998 s 6(2).
5   Ie a matter falling within the National Minimum Wage Act 1998 s 5(2) (see PARA 234): see s 6(3)(a).
6   National Minimum Wage Act 1998 s 6(3)(a).
7   Ie under the National Minimum Wage Act 1998 s 6(2) (see the text and note 4): see s 6(3)(b).
8   National Minimum Wage Act 1998 s 6(3)(b).
9   Ie under the National Minimum Wage Act 1998 s 1 (see PARAS 176, 199, 202), s 2 (see PARA 200), s 3 (see PARA 186) or s 4 (see PARA 186 note 11): see s 6(3)(c).
10 National Minimum Wage Act 1998 s 6(3)(c).
11 Ie the duty imposed by the National Minimum Wage Act 1998 s 5(4) (see PARA 234): see s 6(3).
12 Ie under the National Minimum Wage Act 1998 s 5(3) (see PARA 234): see s 6(3).
13 See the National Minimum Wage Act 1998 s 6(3).
14 Ie a matter falling within the National Minimum Wage Act 1998 s 5(2) (see PARA 234): see s 6(4)(a).
15 National Minimum Wage Act 1998 s 6(4)(a).
16 Ie under the National Minimum Wage Act 1998 s 6(2) (see the text and note 4): see s 6(4)(b).
17 National Minimum Wage Act 1998 s 6(4)(b). The text refers to the time allowed under s 7 (see PARA 236): see s 6(4)(b).
18 Ie under the National Minimum Wage Act 1998 s 1 (see PARAS 176, 199, 202), s 2 (see PARA 200), s 3 (see PARA 186) or s 4 (see PARA 186 note 11): see s 6(4).
19 See the National Minimum Wage Act 1998 s 6(4).

236.   Procedure on referrals to, and reports of, the Low Pay Commission.
Where matters are referred[1] to the Low Pay Commission[2], the Secretary of State[3] may by notice[4] require the Commission to make its report[5] within such time as may be specified in the notice[6], although the time allowed to the Commission for making its report may from time to time be extended by further notice given to it by the Secretary of State[7].

Before arriving at the recommendations[8] to be included in its report, the Commission must consult[9]:

(1)   such organisations representative of employers as it thinks fit[10];
(2)   such organisations representative of workers as it thinks fit[11]; and
(3)   if it thinks fit, any other body or person[12].

In considering what recommendations to include in its report, the Commission must[13]:

(a)   have regard to the effect of the National Minimum Wage Act 1998 on the economy of the United Kingdom[14] as a whole, and on competitiveness[15]; and

(b)   take into account any additional factors which the Secretary of State specifies in referring the matters to it[16].

The report of the Commission must[17]:

(i)   identify the members of the Commission making the report[18];
(ii)   explain the procedures adopted in respect of consultation, the taking of evidence, and the receiving of representations[19];
(iii)   set out the reasons for its recommendations[20]; and
(iv)   if the Secretary of State has specified any additional factor to be taken

into account under head (b) above, state that it has taken that factor into account in making its recommendations[21].

The Secretary of State must lay a copy of any report of the Commission before each House of Parliament[22], and he must arrange for the report to be published[23].

1   Ie under the National Minimum Wage Act 1998 s 5 (see PARA 234) or s 6 (see PARA 235): see s 7(1).
2   See the National Minimum Wage Act 1998 s 7(1). As to the Low Pay Commission see PARA 229 et seq.
3   As to the Secretary of State see PARA 5 note 21.
4   As to the meaning of 'notice' for these purposes see PARA 227 note 9.
5   For these purposes, 'report' means the report which the Low Pay Commission is required to make under the National Minimum Wage Act 1998 s 5(3) (see PARA 234) or s 6(2) (see PARA 235), as the case may be, on the matters referred to it as mentioned in s 7(1): see s 7(8).
6   See the National Minimum Wage Act 1998 s 7(2).
7   See the National Minimum Wage Act 1998 s 7(3).
8   For these purposes, 'recommendations' means the recommendations required to be contained in a report under the National Minimum Wage Act 1998 s 5(3) (see PARA 234) or s 6(2) (see PARA 235), as the case may be: see s 7(8).
9   See the National Minimum Wage Act 1998 s 7(4).
10 National Minimum Wage Act 1998 s 7(4)(a). As to the meaning of 'employer' for these purposes see PARA 170.
11 National Minimum Wage Act 1998 s 7(4)(b). As to the meaning of 'worker' for these purposes see PARA 171.
12 National Minimum Wage Act 1998 s 7(4)(c).
13 See the National Minimum Wage Act 1998 s 7(5).
14 As to the meaning of 'United Kingdom' see PARA 2 note 12.
15 National Minimum Wage Act 1998 s 7(5)(a).
16 National Minimum Wage Act 1998 s 7(5)(b).
17 See the National Minimum Wage Act 1998 s 7(6).
18 National Minimum Wage Act 1998 s 7(6)(a).
19 National Minimum Wage Act 1998 s 7(6)(b).
20 National Minimum Wage Act 1998 s 7(6)(c).
21 National Minimum Wage Act 1998 s 7(6)(d).
22 National Minimum Wage Act 1998 s 7(7)(a).
23 National Minimum Wage Act 1998 s 7(7)(b).

(xi)   Officers appointed for the purposes of the National Minimum Wage Act 1998

237.   Appointment of officers.   The Secretary of State[1]:
(1)   may appoint officers to act for the purposes of the National Minimum Wage Act 1998[2]; and
(2)   may, instead of or in addition to appointing any officers in this way[3], arrange with any Minister of the Crown or government department, or any body performing functions on behalf of the Crown, that officers of that minister, department or body are to act for those purposes[4].

When acting for the purposes of the National Minimum Wage Act 1998, an officer must, if so required, produce some duly authenticated document showing his authority so to act[5].

If it appears to an officer that any person with whom he is dealing while acting for the purposes of the National Minimum Wage Act 1998 does not know that he is an officer so acting, the officer must identify himself as such to that person[6].

1   See the National Minimum Wage Act 1998 s 13(1). As to the Secretary of State see PARA 5 note 21.

2   National Minimum Wage Act 1998 s 13(1)(a). As to the powers of such officers see PARA 238;
     as to the powers of such officers to issue notices of underpayment see PARA 243; as to the
     powers of such officers to sue on behalf of workers for non-compliance with notices of
     underpayment see PARA 246; as to the powers of such officers to serve notices see PARA 248; and
     as to the penalty for obstructing such officers see PARA 251.
3   Ie under the National Minimum Wage Act 1998 s 13: see s 13(1)(b).
4   National Minimum Wage Act 1998 s 13(1)(b).
5   National Minimum Wage Act 1998 s 13(2).
6   National Minimum Wage Act 1998 s 13(3).

238.   Powers of officers. An officer acting for the purposes of the National
Minimum Wage Act 1998[1] has power for the performance of his duties[2]:

(1)   to require the production by a relevant person[3] of any records required
       to be kept and preserved[4] and to inspect and examine those records and
       to copy them[5];

(2)   to require a relevant person to furnish to him (either alone or in the
       presence of any other person, as the officer thinks fit) an explanation of
       any such records[6];

(3)   to require a relevant person to furnish to him (either alone or in the
       presence of any other person, as the officer thinks fit) any additional
       information known to the relevant person which might reasonably be
       needed in order to establish whether the National Minimum Wage
       Act 1998, or any notice of underpayment[7], is being or has been
       complied with[8];

(4)   at all reasonable times to enter any relevant premises[9] in order to
       exercise any power conferred on the officer by heads (1) to (3) above[10].

The powers so conferred include power, on reasonable written notice, to require
a relevant person[11]:

(a)   to produce any such records as are mentioned in head (1) above to an
       officer at such time and place as may be specified in the notice[12]; or

(b)   to attend before an officer at such time and place as may be specified in
       the notice to furnish any such explanation or additional information as
       is mentioned in head (2) or head (3) above[13].

No person may be required under head (2) or head (3) above to answer any
question or furnish any information which might incriminate the person (or, if
married or a civil partner, the person's spouse or civil partner)[14].

1   As to the appointment of officers see PARA 237.
2   See the National Minimum Wage Act 1998 s 14(1).
3   For these purposes, 'relevant person' means any person whom an officer acting for the purposes
     of the National Minimum Wage Act 1998 has reasonable cause to believe to be:
     (1)   the employer of a worker (s 14(4)(a));
     (2)   a person who for the purposes of s 34 (agency workers: see PARA 178) is the agent or
            the principal (s 14(4)(b));
     (3)   a person who supplies work to an individual who qualifies for the national minimum
            wage (s 14(4)(c));
     (4)   a worker, servant or agent of a person falling within head (1), head (2) or head (3)
            above (s 14(4)(d)); or
     (5)   a person who qualifies for the national minimum wage (s 14(4)(e)).
     As to the meaning of 'employer' for these purposes see PARA 170; as to the meaning of 'worker'
     for these purposes see PARA 171; and as to the meaning of 'person who qualifies for the national
     minimum wage' see PARA 176 note 5.
4   Ie in accordance with regulations under the National Minimum Wage Act 1998 s 9 (see PARA
     226): see s 14(1)(a) (s 14(1)(a) amended, s 14(3A) added, by the Employment Act 2008
     ss 10(1)–(3), 20, Schedule Pt 3).
5   National Minimum Wage Act 1998 s 14(1)(a) (as amended: see note 4). The power of an officer
     to copy records under head (1) in the text includes a power to remove such records from the

place where they are produced to him in order to copy them; but such records must be returned as soon as reasonably practicable to the relevant person by whom they are produced: s 14(3A) (as added: see note 4).

6   National Minimum Wage Act 1998 s 14(1)(b).
7   Ie under the National Minimum Wage Act 1998 s 19 (see PARA 243): see s 14(1)(c). As to the meaning of 'notice of underpayment' see PARA 243.
8   National Minimum Wage Act 1998 s 14(1)(c).
9   For these purposes, 'relevant premises' means any premises which an officer acting for the purposes of the National Minimum Wage Act 1998 has reasonable cause to believe to be:
      (1)   premises at which an employer carries on business (s 14(5)(a));
      (2)   premises which an employer uses in connection with his business (including any place used, in connection with that business, for giving out work to home workers, within the meaning of s 35 (see PARA 179)) (s 14(4)(b)); or
      (3)   premises of a person who for the purposes of s 34 (agency workers: see PARA 178) is the agent or the principal (s 14(4)(c)).
10   National Minimum Wage Act 1998 s 14(1)(d). As to offences see PARA 251; and as to offences by bodies corporate see PARA 252.
11   See the National Minimum Wage Act 1998 s 14(3).
12   National Minimum Wage Act 1998 s 14(3)(a).
13   National Minimum Wage Act 1998 s 14(3)(b).
14   National Minimum Wage Act 1998 s 14(2) (amended by the Civil Partnership Act 2004 s 261(1), Sch 27 para 155).
      Marriage of same sex couples is lawful in the law of England and Wales, and such marriages have the same effect as marriages of opposite sex couples: see the Marriage (Same Sex Couples) Act 2013 s 1(1), 11(1); and MATRIMONIAL AND CIVIL PARTNERSHIP LAW vol 72 (2009) PARA 1 et seq.

(xii) Information obtained or supplied for the purposes of the National Minimum Wage Act 1998

239.   Information obtained by officers.   Any information obtained by an officer acting[1] for the purposes of the National Minimum Wage Act 1998[2]:

(1)   vests in the Secretary of State[3];
(2)   may be used for any purpose relating to the National Minimum Wage Act 1998 either by the Secretary of State or by any relevant authority[4] whose officer obtained the information[5];
(3)   may be supplied by, or with the authorisation of, the Secretary of State to any relevant authority for any purpose relating to the National Minimum Wage Act 1998[6]; and
(4)   may be used by the recipient for any purpose relating to the National Minimum Wage Act 1998[7],

but information supplied under heads (3) and (4) above: (a) must not be supplied by the recipient to any other person or body unless it is supplied for the purposes of any civil or criminal proceedings relating to the National Minimum Wage Act 1998[8]; and (b) must not be supplied in those circumstances without the authorisation of the Secretary of State[9].

Information so obtained by an officer acting for the purposes of the National Minimum Wage Act 1998[10]: (i) may be supplied by, or with the authorisation of, the Secretary of State to an officer acting for the purposes of the Employment Agencies Act 1973 for any purpose relating to that Act[11]; and (ii) may be used by an officer acting for the purposes of that Act for any purpose relating to that Act[12].

These provisions do not limit the circumstances in which information may otherwise be supplied or used[13]; nor do they prevent the disclosure of information[14] by enforcement officers[15].

1 Ie whether by virtue of the National Minimum Wage Act 1998 s 13(1)(a) (see PARA 237) or s 13(1)(b) (see PARA 237): see s 15(1).

2 See the National Minimum Wage Act 1998 s 15(1). As to the appointment of officers see PARA 237.

3 See the National Minimum Wage Act 1998 s 15(2). Head (1) in the text applies to information to which s 15 applies (see the text and notes 1–2): see s 15(2). As to the Secretary of State see PARA 5 note 21. Head (1) in the text does not affect the title or rights of:
   (1) any person whose property the information was immediately before it was obtained as mentioned in s 15(1) (see the text and notes 1–2) (s 15(7)(a)); or
   (2) any person claiming title or rights through or under such a person otherwise than by virtue of any power conferred by or under the National Minimum Wage Act 1998 (s 15(7)(b)).

4 For these purposes, 'relevant authority' means any Minister of the Crown who, or government department or other body which, is party to arrangements made with the Secretary of State which are in force under the National Minimum Wage Act 1998 s 13(1)(b) (see PARA 237): see s 15(8).

5 See the National Minimum Wage Act 1998 s 15(3). Head (2) in the text applies to information to which s 15 applies (see the text and notes 1–2): see s 15(3). As to the disclosure of information obtained by enforcement officers see PARA 240; and as to the supply of information obtained by revenue officials see PARA 241.

6 See the National Minimum Wage Act 1998 s 15(4)(a). Head (3) in the text applies to information to which s 15 applies (see the text and notes 1–2): see s 15(4).

7 See the National Minimum Wage Act 1998 s 15(4)(b). Head (4) in the text applies to information to which s 15 applies (see the text and notes 1–2): see s 15(4).

8 National Minimum Wage Act 1998 s 15(5)(a). For the purposes of the National Minimum Wage Act 1998, unless the context otherwise requires, 'civil proceedings' means proceedings before an employment tribunal or civil proceedings before any other court: see s 55(1). As to employment tribunals see PARA 1399 et seq; and as to the procedure on a complaint made to an employment tribunal see PARA 1453 et seq.

9 National Minimum Wage Act 1998 s 15(5)(b).

10 See the National Minimum Wage Act 1998 s 15(5A) (added by the Employment Act 2008 s 18(1)). The National Minimum Wage Act 1998 s 15(5A) applies to information to which s 15 applies (see the text and notes 1–2): see s 15(5A) (as so added).

11 National Minimum Wage Act 1998 s 15(5A)(a) (as added: see note 10). As to the Employment Agencies Act 1973 see TRADE AND INDUSTRY vol 97 (2010) PARA 881 et seq. See also PARA 11.

12 National Minimum Wage Act 1998 s 15(5A)(b) (as added: see note 10).

13 National Minimum Wage Act 1998 s 15(6)(a) (s 15(6) substituted by the Finance Act 2000 s 148(4)). The text refers to circumstances in which information may be supplied or used apart from the National Minimum Wage Act 1998 s 15: see s 15(6)(a) (as so substituted). In particular, s 15 is subject to the Finance Act 2000 s 148 (use of minimum wage information: see INCOME TAXATION vol 59 (2014) PARA 2325): National Minimum Wage Act 1998 s 15(6)(b) (as so substituted).

14 Ie in accordance with the National Minimum Wage Act 1998 s 16A (see PARA 240): see s 15(6A) (added by the Employment Relations Act 2004 s 57(1), Sch 1 para 40).

15 National Minimum Wage Act 1998 s 15(6A) (as added: see note 14).

240. Disclosure of information by enforcement officers. Where information has been obtained by an enforcement officer acting[1] for the purposes of the National Minimum Wage Act 1998[2], then, in order to enable or assist him to act for those purposes[3]: (1) so far as that information relates to an identifiable worker or agency worker[4], he may disclose all or any of the information to the worker or, as the case may be, agency worker concerned[5]; and (2) so far as that information relates to an identifiable employer[6] or person who is the agent or the principal[7], he may disclose all or any of the information to the employer, the agent or, as the case may be, the principal concerned[8].

1 Ie whether by virtue of the National Minimum Wage Act 1998 s 13(1)(a) (see PARA 237) or s 13(1)(b) (see PARA 237): see s 16A(5) (s 16A added by the Employment Relations Act 2004 s 44).

   The provision made by the National Minimum Wage Act 1998 s 16A(5) refers also to enforcement officers acting for the purposes of the Agricultural Wages Act 1948 (see

AGRICULTURAL PRODUCTION AND MARKETING vol 1 (2008) PARA 1241) but the National Minimum Wage Act 1998 s 16A(5) is amended, as from a date to be appointed under the Enterprise and Regulatory Reform Act 2013 s 103(3), by s 72(4), Sch 20 para 2, so as to remove those references, and indeed to repeal most of the 1948 Act itself. That day has been appointed as 1 October 2013 in relation to England (see the Enterprise and Regulatory Reform Act 2013 (Commencement No 1, Transitional Provisions and Savings) Order 2013, SI 2013/1455, art 3(b), Sch 2 para 5 (art 3(b) amended by SI 2013/2271)), but such a day has not been appointed, at the date at which this volume states the law, in relation to Wales. As to the meanings of 'England' and 'Wales' see PARA 2 note 12.

2   See the National Minimum Wage Act 1998 s 16A(1), (3) (as added: see note 1). As to the appointment of officers see PARA 237.
3   See the National Minimum Wage Act 1998 s 16A(2), (4) (as added: see note 1).
4   See the National Minimum Wage Act 1998 s 16A(1) (as added: see note 1). For these purposes, 'agency worker' is to be construed in accordance with s 34 (see PARA 178): see s 16A(5) (as so added). As to the meaning of 'worker' for these purposes see PARA 171.
5   See the National Minimum Wage Act 1998 s 16A(2) (as added: see note 1).
6   As to the meaning of 'employer' for these purposes see PARA 170.
7   See the National Minimum Wage Act 1998 s 16A(3) (as added: see note 1). The text refers to a person who is the agent or the principal for the purposes of s 34 (see PARA 178): see s 16A(3) (as so added).
8   See the National Minimum Wage Act 1998 s 16A(4) (as added: see note 1).

241.   Supply of information obtained by revenue officials.   Information obtained by a revenue official[1] in the course of carrying out a function of the Commissioners for Revenue and Customs[2] may be[3]: (1) supplied by the Commissioners to the Secretary of State[4] for any purpose relating to the National Minimum Wage Act 1998[5]; (2) supplied by the Secretary of State with the authority of the Commissioners to any person appointed by him[6] to act for the purposes of the National Minimum Wage Act 1998[7].

1   For these purposes, 'revenue official' means an officer of the Commissioners for Revenue and Customs appointed under the Commissioners for Revenue and Customs Act 2005 s 1 (see CONSTITUTIONAL AND ADMINISTRATIVE LAW vol 20 (2014) PARA 479): Employment Relations Act 1999 s 39(2); Interpretation Act 1978 s 17(2).
2   As to the Commissioners for Her Majesty's Revenue and Customs see INCOME TAXATION vol 58 (2014) PARAS 33–34.
3   See the Employment Relations Act 1999 s 39(1). In addition to heads (1) and (2) in the text, provision is made under s 39(1)(c), and under the National Minimum Wage Act 1998 s 16, in relation to information supplied by the Secretary of State with the authority of the Commissioners to an officer acting for the purposes of the Agricultural Wages Act 1948 s 15A (see AGRICULTURAL PRODUCTION AND MARKETING vol 1 (2008) PARA 1242). However, the latter provision is repealed, along with most of the 1948 Act itself, as from a date to be appointed under the Enterprise and Regulatory Reform Act 2013 s 103(3), by s 72(4), Sch 20 para 2. That day has been appointed as 1 October 2013 in relation to England (see the Enterprise and Regulatory Reform Act 2013 (Commencement No 1, Transitional Provisions and Savings) Order 2013, SI 2013/1455, art 3(b), Sch 2 para 6 (art 3(b) amended by SI 2013/2271)), but such a day has not been appointed, at the date at which this volume states the law, in relation to Wales. As to the meanings of 'England' and 'Wales' see PARA 2 note 12.
4   As to the Secretary of State see PARA 5 note 21.
5   Employment Relations Act 1999 s 39(1)(a).
6   Ie any person acting under the National Minimum Wage Act 1998 s 13(1)(b) (see PARA 237): see s 39(1)(b).
7   Employment Relations Act 1999 s 39(1)(b).

(xiii) Enforcement and Underpayment

242.   Worker entitled to additional remuneration.   If a worker who qualifies for the national minimum wage[1] is remunerated for any pay reference period[2] by his employer[3] at a rate which is less than the national minimum wage[4], the worker must at any time (the 'time of determination') be taken to be entitled under his contract[5] to be paid, as additional remuneration in respect of that period, whichever is the higher of the amount described in head (1) below and the amount described in head (2) below[6], being:

(1)   the difference between[7]: (a) the relevant remuneration received by the worker for the pay reference period[8]; and (b) the relevant remuneration which the worker would have received for that period had he been remunerated by the employer at a rate equal to the national minimum wage[9]; and

(2)   the amount determined by a statutory formula which modifies the amount described in head (1) above[10].

1   As to the meaning of 'worker' for these purposes see PARA 171; and as to the meaning of 'person who qualifies for the national minimum wage' see PARA 176 note 5.

2   As to the meaning of references to a person being remunerated for a pay reference period see PARA 174 note 8; and as to the meaning of 'pay reference period' see PARA 202.

3   As to the meaning of 'employer' for these purposes see PARA 170.

4   As to the rate of the national minimum wage see PARA 199.

5   As to the meaning of references to a worker's contract see PARA 171.

6   See the National Minimum Wage Act 1998 s 17(1) (s 17(1), (2) amended, s 17(4)–(6) added, by the Employment Act 2008 s 8(1)–(5)). The National Minimum Wage Act 1998 s 17(1) ceases to apply to a worker in relation to any pay reference period when he is at any time paid the additional remuneration for that period to which he is at that time entitled under s 17(1): s 17(5) (as so added). Where any additional remuneration is paid to the worker under s 17 in relation to the pay reference period but s 17(1) has not ceased to apply in relation to him, the amounts described in s 17(2) (see head (1) in the text) and in s 17(4) (see head (2) in the text) must be regarded as reduced by the amount of that remuneration: s 17(6) (as so added).
    If the persons who are the worker and the employer for the purposes of s 17 would not, apart from s 18, fall to be regarded as the worker and the employer for the purposes of the Employment Rights Act 1996 Pt II (ss 13–27) (protection of wages: see PARA 254 et seq), they are to be so regarded for the purposes of the application of Pt II in relation to the entitlement conferred by the National Minimum Wage Act 1998 s 17: see s 18(1). In the application, by virtue of s 18(1), of the Employment Rights Act 1996 Pt II in a case where there is or was, for the purposes of Pt II, no worker's contract between the persons who are the worker and the employer for the purposes of the National Minimum Wage Act 1998 s 17, it is to be assumed that there is or, as the case may be, was such a contract: s 18(2). For the purpose of enabling the amount described as additional remuneration in s 17(1) to be recovered in civil proceedings on a claim in contract in a case where in fact there is or was no worker's contract between the persons who are the worker and the employer for the purposes of s 17, it is to be assumed for the purpose of any civil proceedings, so far as relating to that amount, that there is or, as the case may be, was such a contract: s 18(3). As to the meaning of 'civil proceedings' for these purposes see PARA 239 note 8.

7   See the National Minimum Wage Act 1998 s 17(2) (as amended: see note 6).

8   National Minimum Wage Act 1998 s 17(2)(a). For these purposes, 'relevant remuneration' means remuneration which falls to be brought into account for the purposes of regulations under s 2 (see PARA 200): see s 17(3).

9   National Minimum Wage Act 1998 s 17(2)(b).

10   See the National Minimum Wage Act 1998 s 17(4) (as added: see note 6). Head (2) in the text refers to an amount that is determined by the formula:

$$\frac{A}{R1} \times R2$$

where A is the amount described in s 17(2) (see head (1) in the text); R1 is the rate of national minimum wage which was payable in respect of the worker during the pay reference period; and R2 is the rate of national minimum wage which would have been payable in respect of the worker during that period had the rate payable in respect of him during that period been determined by reference to regulations under s 1 (see PARAS 199, 202) and s 3 (see PARA 186) in force at the time of determination: see s 17(4) (as so added).

243.   Notices of underpayment: arrears.   Where an officer acting for the purposes of the National Minimum Wage Act 1998[1] is of the opinion that, on any day (the 'relevant day'), a sum was due[2] for any one or more pay reference periods[3] ending before the relevant day to a worker[4] who at any time qualified for the national minimum wage[5], the officer may[6] serve a notice (a 'notice of underpayment')[7] requiring the employer[8] to pay to the worker, within the 28-day period[9], the sum due to the worker[10] for any one or more of those pay reference periods in which he was so underpaid[11]. A notice of underpayment must specify, for each worker to whom it relates[12]:

(1)   the relevant day in relation to that worker[13];

(2)   the pay reference period or periods in respect of which the employer is required to pay a sum to the worker[14] in respect of the underpayment[15];

(3)   the amounts of additional remuneration[16] in relation to the worker in respect of each such period[17];

(4)   the sum due[18] to the worker for each such period[19].

Where a notice of underpayment relates to more than one worker, the notice may identify the workers either by name or by description[20].

1   As to the appointment of officers see PARA 237.
2   Ie under the National Minimum Wage Act 1998 s 17 (see PARA 242): see s 19(1) (s 19 substituted by the Employment Act 2008 s 9(1)).
3   The reference in the National Minimum Wage Act 1998 s 19(1) to a pay reference period includes (subject to s 19(7)) a pay reference period ending before the coming into force of s 19: s 19(6) (as substituted: see note 2). A notice of underpayment may not relate to a pay reference period ending more than six years before the date of service of the notice: s 19(7) (as so substituted). As to the meaning of 'pay reference period' generally see PARA 202.
4   As to the meaning of 'worker' for these purposes see PARA 171.
5   See the National Minimum Wage Act 1998 s 19(1) (as substituted: see note 2). As to the meaning of 'person who qualifies for the national minimum wage' see PARA 176 note 5.
6   Ie subject to the National Minimum Wage Act 1998 s 19: see s 19(2) (as substituted: see note 2).
7   In the National Minimum Wage Act 1998, 'notice of underpayment' means a notice under s 19: see s 19(3) (as substituted: see note 2). As to the meaning of 'notice' for these purposes see PARA 227 note 9.
8   As to the meaning of 'employer' for these purposes see PARA 170.
9   In the National Minimum Wage Act 1998 ss 19–19C (see also PARAS 244–245), '28-day period' means the period of 28 days beginning with the date of service of the notice of underpayment: s 19(8) (as substituted: see note 2).
10   Ie under the National Minimum Wage Act 1998 s 17 (see PARA 242): see s 19(2) (as substituted: see note 2).
11   National Minimum Wage Act 1998 s 19(2) (as substituted: see note 2). The pay reference periods mentioned in the text are those referred to in s 19(1) (see the text and notes 1–5): see s 19(2) (as so substituted).
12   See the National Minimum Wage Act 1998 s 19(4) (as substituted: see note 2).
13   National Minimum Wage Act 1998 s 19(4)(a) (as substituted: see note 2).
14   Ie as specified in the National Minimum Wage Act 1998 s 19(2) (see the text and notes 6–11): see s 19(4)(b) (as substituted: see note 2).
15   National Minimum Wage Act 1998 s 19(4)(b) (as substituted: see note 2).
16   Ie the amounts described in the National Minimum Wage Act 1998 s 17(2) (see PARA 242) or in s 17(4) (see PARA 242): see s 19(4)(c), (d) (as substituted: see note 2).
17   National Minimum Wage Act 1998 s 19(4)(c), (d) (as substituted: see note 2).
18   Ie under the National Minimum Wage Act 1998 s 17 (see PARA 242): see s 19(4)(e) (as substituted: see note 2).
19   National Minimum Wage Act 1998 s 19(4)(e) (as substituted: see note 2).
20   National Minimum Wage Act 1998 s 19(5) (as substituted: see note 2).

244.   Notices of underpayment: financial penalty.   A notice of underpayment[1] must[2] require the employer[3] to pay a financial penalty specified in the notice to the Secretary of State[4] within the 28-day period[5].

The Secretary of State may by directions specify circumstances in which a notice of underpayment is not to impose a requirement to pay a financial penalty[6]. Such directions may be amended or revoked by further such directions[7].

The amount of any financial penalty is[8] to be 100 per cent of the total of amounts specified for all workers to whom the notice relates in respect of specified pay reference periods[9]. A notice of underpayment must, in addition to specifying the amount of any financial penalty, state how that amount was calculated[10].

In a case where a notice of underpayment imposes a requirement to pay a financial penalty, if the employer on whom the notice is served, within the period of 14 days beginning with the day on which the notice was served[11]:

(1)   pays the amount required[12]; and
(2)   pays at least half the financial penalty[13],

he is regarded as having paid the financial penalty[14].

A financial penalty paid to the Secretary of State in this way[15] must be paid by the Secretary of State into the Consolidated Fund[16].

In any case where it appears to the officer serving a notice of underpayment which imposes a requirement to pay a financial penalty that:

(a)   relevant proceedings have been instituted[17]; or
(b)   relevant proceedings may be instituted[18],

the notice of underpayment may contain provision suspending the requirement to pay the financial penalty payable under the notice until a notice terminating the suspension is served on the employer[19].

An officer acting for the purposes of the National Minimum Wage Act 1998[20] may serve on the employer a notice terminating the suspension (a 'penalty activation notice') if it appears to the officer:

(i)   in a case referred to in head (a) above, that relevant proceedings have concluded without the employer having been convicted of a criminal offence for refusal or wilful neglect to pay the proper rate[21]; or
(ii)   in a case referred to in head (b) above that relevant proceedings will not be instituted, or that relevant proceedings have been concluded without the employer having been convicted of a criminal offence mentioned in head (i) above[22].

Where a penalty activation notice is served, the requirement to pay the financial penalty has effect as if the notice of underpayment had been served on the day on which the penalty activation notice was served[23].

An officer acting for the purposes of the National Minimum Wage Act 1998 must serve on the employer a notice withdrawing the requirement to pay the financial penalty if it appears to the officer that, pursuant to relevant proceedings, the employer has been convicted of a criminal offence mentioned in head (i) above[24].

1   As to the meaning of 'notice of underpayment' see PARA 243 note 7.
2   Ie subject to the National Minimum Wage Act 1998 s 19A: see s 19A(1) (ss 19A, 19B added by the Employment Act 2008 s 9(1)).
3   As to the meaning of 'employer' for these purposes see PARA 170.
4   As to the Secretary of State see PARA 5 note 21.
5   National Minimum Wage Act 1998 s 19A(1) (as added: see note 2). As to the meaning of '28-day period' for these purposes see PARA 243 note 9.
6   National Minimum Wage Act 1998 s 19A(2) (as added: see note 2).
7   National Minimum Wage Act 1998 s 19A(3) (as added: see note 2).
8   Ie subject to the National Minimum Wage Act 1998 s 19A(5)–(8) (see note 9): see s 19A(4) (s 19A as added (see note 2); s 19A(4), (7) amended by SI 2014/547).

9   National Minimum Wage Act 1998 s 19A(4) (as added and amended: see note 8). As to the meaning of 'worker' for these purposes see PARA 171. The reference is to amounts referred to in s 19A(5): see s 19A(4) (as so added and amended). Accordingly, those amounts are the amounts specified under s 19(4)(c) (see PARA 243) for all workers to whom the notice relates in respect of pay reference periods specified under s 19(4)(b) (see PARA 243) which commence after 6 April 2009 (ie after the coming into force of s 19A: see the Employment Act 2008 (Commencement No 2, Transitional Provisions and Savings) Order 2009, SI 2009/603, art 2): National Minimum Wage Act 1998 s 19A(5) (as so added). If a financial penalty as calculated under s 19A(4) would be less than £100, or more than £20,000, the financial penalty specified in the notice must be that amount: see s 19A(6), (7) (s 19A as so added and s 19A(7) as amended).

     The Secretary of State may by regulations:
     (1)   amend s 19A(4) so as to substitute a different percentage for the percentage at any time specified there (s 19A(8)(a) (as so added));
     (2)   amend s 19A(6) or s 19A(7) so as to substitute a different amount for the amount at any time specified there (s 19A(8)(b) (as so added)).
As to the making of regulations under the National Minimum Wage Act 1998 see PARA 175. As to regulations so made under s 19A(8) see the National Minimum Wage (Variation of Financial Penalty) Regulations 2014, SI 2014/547 (amending the National Minimum Wage Act 1998 s 19A(4), (7)).

10   National Minimum Wage Act 1998 s 19A(9) (as added: see note 2).

11   See the National Minimum Wage Act 1998 s 19A(10) (as added: see note 2).

12   National Minimum Wage Act 1998 s 19A(10)(a) (as added: see note 2). Head (1) in the text refers to the amount required under s 19(2) (see PARA 243): see s 19A(10) (as so added).

13   National Minimum Wage Act 1998 s 19A(10)(b) (as added: see note 2).

14   See the National Minimum Wage Act 1998 s 19A(10) (as added: see note 2).

15   Ie pursuant to the National Minimum Wage Act 1998 s 19A: see s 19A(11) (as added: see note 2).

16   National Minimum Wage Act 1998 s 19A(11) (as added: see note 2). As to the Consolidated Fund see CONSTITUTIONAL AND ADMINISTRATIVE LAW vol 20 (2014) PARA 480 et seq; PARLIAMENT vol 78 (2010) PARAS 1028–1031.

17   National Minimum Wage Act 1998 s 19B(1)(a) (as added: see note 2). For these purposes, 'relevant proceedings' means proceedings against the employer for an offence under s 31(1) (see PARA 251) in relation to a failure to remunerate any worker to whom the notice relates for any pay reference period specified under s 19(4)(b) (see PARA 243) in relation to that worker: see s 19B(2) (as so added).

18   National Minimum Wage Act 1998 s 19B(1)(b) (as added: see note 2).

19   See the National Minimum Wage Act 1998 s 19B(3) (as added: see note 2).

20   As to the appointment of officers see PARA 237.

21   National Minimum Wage Act 1998 s 19B(4)(a) (as added: see note 2). Head (i) in the text refers to an offence under s 31(1) (see PARA 251): see s 19B(4)(a) (as so added).

22   See the National Minimum Wage Act 1998 s 19B(4)(b) (as added: see note 2). See note 21.

23   National Minimum Wage Act 1998 s 19B(5) (as added: see note 2).

24   National Minimum Wage Act 1998 s 19B(6) (as added: see note 2). See note 21.

245. Notices of underpayment: appeals. A person on whom a notice of underpayment[1] is served may[2] appeal against any one or more of the following[3]:
     (1)   the decision to serve the notice[4];
     (2)   any requirement imposed by the notice to pay a sum to a worker[5];
     (3)   any requirement imposed by the notice to pay a financial penalty[6].
Such an appeal[7] lies to an employment tribunal[8]. It must be made before the end of the 28-day period[9]; and:
     (a)   if made under head (1) above, it must be made on the ground that no sum was due[10] to any worker to whom the notice relates on the day specified[11] in relation to him in respect of any pay reference period[12] specified[13] in relation to him[14];
     (b)   if made under head (2) above in relation to a worker, it must be made on either or both of the following grounds[15]: (i) that, on the day specified[16] in relation to the worker, no sum was due to the worker[17] in

respect of any pay reference period specified[18] in relation to him[19]; (ii) that the amount specified in the notice as the sum due to the worker is incorrect[20].

(c)   if made under head (3) above, it must be made on either or both of the following grounds[21]: (i) that the notice was served in circumstances specified by the Secretary of State[22] in a direction[23]; or (ii) that the amount of the financial penalty specified in the notice of underpayment has been incorrectly calculated (whether because the notice is incorrect in some of the particulars which affect that calculation or for some other reason)[24].

Where the employment tribunal allows an appeal under head (1) above, it must rescind the notice[25]; but, where the employment tribunal allows an appeal under either head (2) or head (3) above[26]: (A) the employment tribunal must rectify the notice[27]; and (B) the notice of underpayment has effect as rectified from the date of the employment tribunal's determination[28].

1   As to the meaning of 'notice of underpayment' see PARA 243 note 7.
2   Ie in accordance with the National Minimum Wage Act 1998 s 19C: see s 19C(1) (s 19C added by the Employment Act 2008 s 9(1)).
3   See the National Minimum Wage Act 1998 s 19C(1) (as added: see note 2).
4   National Minimum Wage Act 1998 s 19C(1)(a) (as added: see note 2).
5   National Minimum Wage Act 1998 s 19C(1)(b) (as added: see note 2). As to the meaning of 'worker' for these purposes see PARA 171.
6   National Minimum Wage Act 1998 s 19C(1)(c) (as added: see note 2). As to the financial penalty see PARA 244.
7   Ie an appeal under the National Minimum Wage Act 1998 s 19C: see s 19C(2) (as added: see note 2).
8   National Minimum Wage Act 1998 s 19C(2) (as added: see note 2). As to employment tribunals and the procedure before them see PARA 1399 et seq; and as to the procedure on a complaint made to an employment tribunal see PARA 1453 et seq.
9   National Minimum Wage Act 1998 s 19C(3) (as added: see note 2). As to the meaning of '28–day period' see PARA 243 note 9.
10 Ie under the National Minimum Wage Act 1998 s 17 (see PARA 242): see s 19C(4) (as added: see note 2).
11 Ie under the National Minimum Wage Act 1998 s 19(4)(a) (see PARA 243): see s 19C(4) (as added: see note 2).
12 As to the meaning of 'pay reference period' see PARA 202.
13 Ie under the National Minimum Wage Act 1998 s 19(4)(b) (see PARA 243): see s 19C(4) (as added: see note 2).
14 National Minimum Wage Act 1998 s 19C(4) (as added: see note 2).
15 See the National Minimum Wage Act 1998 s 19C(5) (as added: see note 2).
16 Ie under the National Minimum Wage Act 1998 s 19(4)(a) (see PARA 243): see s 19C(5)(a) (as added: see note 2).
17 Ie under the National Minimum Wage Act 1998 s 17 (see PARA 242): see s 19C(5)(a) (as added: see note 2).
18 Ie under the National Minimum Wage Act 1998 s 19(4)(b) (see PARA 243): see s 19C(5)(a) (as added: see note 2).
19 National Minimum Wage Act 1998 s 19C(5)(a) (as added: see note 2).
20 National Minimum Wage Act 1998 s 19C(5)(b) (as added: see note 2).
21 See the National Minimum Wage Act 1998 s 19C(6) (as added: see note 2).
22 Ie in circumstances specified in a direction under the National Minimum Wage Act 1998 s 19A(2) (Secretary of State may by directions specify circumstances in which a notice of underpayment is not to impose a requirement to pay a financial penalty: see PARA 244): see s 19C(6)(a) (as added: see note 2). As to the Secretary of State see PARA 5 note 21.
23 National Minimum Wage Act 1998 s 19C(6)(a) (as added: see note 2).
24 National Minimum Wage Act 1998 s 19C(6)(b) (as added: see note 2).
25 National Minimum Wage Act 1998 s 19C(7) (as added: see note 2).
26 See the National Minimum Wage Act 1998 s 19C(8) (as added: see note 2). The text refers to a case where s 19C(7) does not apply (see the text and note 25): see s 19C(8) (as so added).

27 National Minimum Wage Act 1998 s 19C(8)(a) (as added: see note 2).

28 National Minimum Wage Act 1998 s 19C(8)(b) (as added: see note 2).

246.   Non-compliance with notice of underpayment: recovery of arrears. If a requirement to pay a sum to a worker[1] contained in a notice of underpayment[2] is not complied with in whole or in part, an officer acting for the purposes of the National Minimum Wage Act 1998[3] may, on behalf of any worker to whom the requirement relates[4]:

(1)   present a complaint to an employment tribunal[5] in respect of any sums due[6] to the worker[7]; or

(2)   commence other civil proceedings[8] for the recovery, on a claim in contract, of any sums due[9] to the worker[10].

The powers so conferred[11] for the recovery of sums due from an employer to a worker are not in derogation of any right which the worker may have to recover such sums by civil proceedings[12].

A financial penalty[13], payable under a notice of underpayment in England and Wales[14], is recoverable, if the County Court so orders, under the County Courts Act 1984[15] or otherwise as if it were payable under an order of that court[16].

1   As to the meaning of 'worker' for these purposes see PARA 171.

2   As to the meaning of 'notice of underpayment' see PARA 243 note 7.

3   As to the appointment of officers see PARA 237.

4   See the National Minimum Wage Act 1998 s 19D(1) (ss 19D, 19E added by the Employment Act 2008 s 9(1)).

5   Ie under the Employment Rights Act 1996 s 23(1)(a) (deductions from worker's wages in contravention of s 13: see PARA 259): see the National Minimum Wage Act 1998 s 19D(1)(a) (as added: see note 4). As to employment tribunals see PARA 1399 et seq; and as to the procedure on a complaint made to an employment tribunal see PARA 1453 et seq.

6   Ie by virtue of the National Minimum Wage Act 1998 s 17 (see PARA 242): see s 19D(1)(a) (as added: see note 4).

7   National Minimum Wage Act 1998 s 19D(1)(a) (as added: see note 4).

8   As to the meaning of 'civil proceedings' for these purposes see PARA 239 note 8.

9   Ie by virtue of the National Minimum Wage Act 1998 s 17 (see PARA 242): see s 19D(1)(b) (as added: see note 4).

10 National Minimum Wage Act 1998 s 19D(1)(b) (as added: see note 4).

11 Ie the powers conferred by the National Minimum Wage Act 1998 s 19D(1) (see the text and notes 1–10): see s 19D(2) (as added: see note 4).

12 National Minimum Wage Act 1998 s 19D(2) (as added: see note 4).

13 As to the financial penalty see PARA 244.

14 As to the meanings of 'England' and 'Wales' see PARA 2 note 12.

15 Ie under the County Courts Act 1984 s 85 (sum of money payable under a judgment or order of the County Court: see CIVIL PROCEDURE vol 12 (2009) PARA 1283): see the National Minimum Wage Act 1998 s 19E(a) (s 19E as added (see note 4); s 19E(a) amended by the Crime and Courts Act 2013 s 17(5), Sch 9 Pt 3 para 52(1)(b), (2)).

16 National Minimum Wage Act 1998 s 19E(a) (as added and amended: see note 15).

247.   Withdrawal of notice of underpayment. Where a notice of underpayment[1] has been served (and not already withdrawn or rescinded), and where it appears to an officer acting for the purposes of the National Minimum Wage Act 1998[2] that the notice incorrectly includes or omits any requirement or is incorrect in any particular, the officer may withdraw it by serving notice of the withdrawal on the employer[3].

Where a notice of underpayment is withdrawn and no replacement notice of underpayment is[4] served[5]:

(1)   any sum paid by or recovered from the employer by way of financial

penalty[6] payable under the notice must be repaid to him with interest at the appropriate rate[7] running from the date when the sum was paid or recovered[8];

(2)   any appeal against the notice must be dismissed[9];

(3)   after the withdrawal no complaint may be presented or other civil proceedings commenced[10] in reliance on any non-compliance with the notice before it was withdrawn[11];

(4)   any complaint or proceedings so commenced before the withdrawal may be proceeded with despite the withdrawal[12].

In a case where heads (1) to (4) above[13] apply, the notice of withdrawal must indicate the effect[4] (but a failure to do so does not make the withdrawal ineffective)[15].

1   As to the meaning of 'notice of underpayment' see PARA 243 note 7.
2   As to the appointment of officers see PARA 237.
3   National Minimum Wage Act 1998 s 19F(1) (s 19F added by the Employment Act 2008 s 9(1)). As to the meaning of 'employer' for these purposes see PARA 170.
4   Ie in accordance with the National Minimum Wage Act 1998 s 19G (see PARA 248): see s 19F(2) (as added: see note 3).
5   See the National Minimum Wage Act 1998 s 19F(2) (as added: see note 3).
6   As to the financial penalty see PARA 244.
7   For these purposes, 'appropriate rate' means the rate that, on the date the sum was paid or recovered, was specified in the Judgments Act 1838 s 17 (judgment debts to carry interest: see CIVIL PROCEDURE vol 12 (2009) PARA 1149): National Minimum Wage Act 1998 s 19F(4) (as added: see note 3).
8   National Minimum Wage Act 1998 s 19F(2)(a) (as added: see note 3).
9   National Minimum Wage Act 1998 s 19F(2)(b) (as added: see note 3).
10   Ie by virtue of the National Minimum Wage Act 1998 s 19D (see PARA 246): see s 19F(2)(c) (as added: see note 3). As to the meaning of 'civil proceedings' for these purposes see PARA 239 note 8.
11   National Minimum Wage Act 1998 s 19F(2)(c) (as added: see note 3).
12   National Minimum Wage Act 1998 s 19F(2)(d) (as added: see note 3).
13   Ie where the National Minimum Wage Act 1998 s 19F(2) applies (see the text and notes 4–12): see s 19F(3) (as added: see note 3).
14   Ie the effect of the National Minimum Wage Act 1998 s 19F(2) (see the text and notes 4–12): see s 19F(3) (as added: see note 3).
15   National Minimum Wage Act 1998 s 19F(3) (as added: see note 3).

248. Replacement notice of underpayment and its effect. Where an officer acting for the purposes of the National Minimum Wage Act 1998[1] serves a notice of withdrawal[2], and where he is of the opinion that a sum was due in respect of underpayment[3] to any worker[4] specified in the notice which is being withdrawn (the 'original notice'), he may at the same time serve another notice[5] (the 'replacement notice')[6].

The replacement notice may not relate to any worker to whom the original notice did not relate[7]; and if the replacement notice contravenes this requirement[8], that fact is an additional ground of appeal[9]. The replacement notice may relate to a pay reference period ending after the date of service of the original notice[10].

The replacement notice must:

(1)   indicate the differences between it and the original notice that it is reasonable for the officer to consider are material[11]; and

(2)   indicate its effect[12].

Failure to comply with heads (1) and (2) above[13] does not, however, make the replacement notice ineffective[14].

Where a replacement notice is withdrawn[15], no further replacement notice may be served[16] pursuant to the withdrawal[17].

Nothing in the provisions providing for replacement notices[18] affects any power that arises apart from the provisions to serve a notice of underpayment in relation to any worker[19].

Where a notice of underpayment is withdrawn[20], and where a replacement notice is[21] served[22], then, if an appeal has been made[23] against the original notice, and if the appeal has not been withdrawn or finally determined before the time when that notice is withdrawn[24]:

(a)   that appeal (the 'earlier appeal') has effect after that time as if it were against the replacement notice[25]; and

(b)   the employer[26] may exercise his right of appeal[27] against the replacement notice only if he withdraws the earlier appeal[28].

After the withdrawal no complaint may be presented or other civil proceedings commenced[29] in reliance on any non-compliance with the notice before it was withdrawn[30]. Any complaint or proceedings so commenced before the withdrawal may be proceeded with despite the withdrawal, however[31].

If a sum was paid by or recovered from the employer by way of financial penalty[32] under the original notice[33]: (i) an amount equal to that sum (or, if more than one, the total of those sums) is treated as having been paid in respect of the replacement notice[34]; and (ii) any amount by which that sum (or total) exceeds the amount payable under the replacement notice must be repaid to the employer with interest at the appropriate rate[35] running from the date when the sum (or, if more than one, the first of them) was paid or recovered[36].

1   As to the appointment of officers see PARA 237.
2   Ie under the National Minimum Wage Act 1998 s 19F (see PARA 247): see s 19G(1) (ss 19G, 19H added by the Employment Act 2008 s 9(1)).
3   Ie is of the opinion referred to in the National Minimum Wage Act 1998 s 19(1) (see PARA 243): see s 19G(1) (as added: see note 2).
4   As to the meaning of 'worker' for these purposes see PARA 171.
5   Ie under the National Minimum Wage Act 1998 s 19 (see PARA 243): see s 19G(1) (as added: see note 2).
6   National Minimum Wage Act 1998 s 19G(1) (as added: see note 2). In relation to the replacement notice, s 19(7) (see PARA 243) applies as if the reference to six years before the date of service of the notice were a reference to six years before the date of service of the original notice: see s 19G(5) (as so added).
7   National Minimum Wage Act 1998 s 19G(2) (as added: see note 2).
8   Ie the National Minimum Wage Act 1998 s 19G(2) (see the text and note 7): see s 19G(3) (as added: see note 2).
9   National Minimum Wage Act 1998 s 19G(3) (as added: see note 2). This text refers to an additional ground of appeal for the purposes of s 19C (see PARA 245): see s 19G(3) (as so added).
10   National Minimum Wage Act 1998 s 19G(4) (as added: see note 2).
11   National Minimum Wage Act 1998 s 19G(6)(a) (as added: see note 2).
12   National Minimum Wage Act 1998 s 19G(6)(b) (as added: see note 2). Head (2) in the text requires the notice specifically to indicate the effect of s 19H (see the text and notes 20–36): see s 19G(6)(b) (as so added).
13   Ie the National Minimum Wage Act 1998 s 19G(6) (see the text and notes 11–12): see s 19G(7) (as so added).
14   National Minimum Wage Act 1998 s 19G(7) (as added: see note 2).
15   Ie under the National Minimum Wage Act 1998 s 19F (see PARA 247): see s 19G(8) (as added: see note 2).
16   Ie under the National Minimum Wage Act 1998 s 19G(1) (see the text and notes 1–6): see s 19G(8) (as added: see note 2).
17   National Minimum Wage Act 1998 s 19G(8) (as added: see note 2).
18   Ie the National Minimum Wage Act 1998 s 19G (see the text and notes 1–17): see s 19G(9) (as added: see note 2).

19 National Minimum Wage Act 1998 s 19G(9) (as added: see note 2).
20 Ie under the National Minimum Wage Act 1998 s 19F (see PARA 247): see s 19H(1) (as added: see note 2).
21 Ie in accordance with the National Minimum Wage Act 1998 s 19G (see the text and notes 1–19): see s 19H(1) (as added: see note 2).
22 See the National Minimum Wage Act 1998 s 19H(1) (as added: see note 2).
23 Ie under the National Minimum Wage Act 1998 s 19C (see PARA 245): see s 19H(2) (as added: see note 2).
24 See the National Minimum Wage Act 1998 s 19H(2) (as added: see note 2).
25 National Minimum Wage Act 1998 s 19H(2)(a) (as added: see note 2).
26 As to the meaning of 'employer' for these purposes see PARA 170.
27 Ie under the National Minimum Wage Act 1998 s 19C (see PARA 245): see s 19H(2)(b) (as added: see note 2).
28 National Minimum Wage Act 1998 s 19H(2)(b) (as added: see note 2).
29 Ie by virtue of the National Minimum Wage Act 1998 s 19D (see PARA 246): see s 19H(3) (as added: see note 2). As to the meaning of 'civil proceedings' for these purposes see PARA 239 note 8.
30 See the National Minimum Wage Act 1998 s 19H(3) (as added: see note 2).
31 See the National Minimum Wage Act 1998 s 19H(3) (as added: see note 2).
32 As to the financial penalty see PARA 244.
33 See the National Minimum Wage Act 1998 s 19H(4) (as added: see note 2).
34 National Minimum Wage Act 1998 s 19H(4)(a) (as added: see note 2).
35 For these purposes, 'appropriate rate' means the rate that, on the date mentioned in that provision, was specified in the Judgments Act 1838 s 17 (judgment debts to carry interest: see CIVIL PROCEDURE vol 12 (2009) PARA 1149): National Minimum Wage Act 1998 s 19H(5) (as added: see note 2).
36 National Minimum Wage Act 1998 s 19H(4)(b) (as added: see note 2).

(xiv) Right Not to Suffer Detriment

249. Right not to suffer detriment. A worker[1] has the right not to be subjected to any detriment[2] by any act, or any deliberate failure to act, by his employer[3], done on the ground that[4]:

(1) any action was taken, or was proposed to be taken, by or on behalf of the worker with a view to enforcing, or otherwise securing the benefit of[5]: (a) any right of the worker conferred by, or by virtue of, any provision of the National Minimum Wage Act 1998, for which the remedy for its infringement is by way of a complaint to an employment tribunal[6]; or (b) any right of the worker to additional remuneration[7];

(2) the employer was prosecuted for an offence[8] as a result of action taken by or on behalf of the worker for the purpose of enforcing, or otherwise securing the benefit of, a right of the worker specified in head (1)(a) or head (1)(b) above[9]; or

(3) the worker qualifies, or will or might qualify, for the national minimum wage[10] or for a particular rate of national minimum wage[11].

It is immaterial for the purposes of head (1) or head (2) above whether or not the worker has the right, or whether or not the right has been infringed; but the claim to the right and, if applicable, the claim that it has been infringed must[12] be made in good faith[13].

A worker may present a complaint to an employment tribunal that he has been subjected to a detriment falling within any of heads (1) to (3) above[14]. Where the detriment to which the worker is subjected is the termination of his worker's contract[15] (but where that contract is not a contract of employment)[16], any compensation awarded[17] must not exceed the following limit[18], being: (i) the sum which would be the basic award for unfair dismissal, calculated in accordance with the Employment Rights Act 1996[19], if the worker had been an employee and the contract terminated had been a contract of employment[20]; and (ii) the sum for the time being specified in the Employment Rights Act 1996[21] which is the limit for a compensatory award[22].

1   As to the meaning of 'worker' for these purposes see PARA 171.
2   The National Minimum Wage Act 1998 s 23 does not apply, however, where the detriment in question amounts to dismissal within the meaning of the Employment Rights Act 1996 Pt X (ss 94–134A) (unfair dismissal: see PARA 757 et seq): see the National Minimum Wage Act 1998 s 23(4) (substituted by the Employment Relations Act 1999 s 18(1), (4)). As to unfair dismissal and the national minimum wage see PARA 794.
3   As to the meaning of 'employer' for these purposes see PARA 170.
4   See the National Minimum Wage Act 1998 s 23(1).
5   National Minimum Wage Act 1998 s 23(1)(a). Head (1) in the text refers to enforcing, or otherwise securing the benefit of, a right to which s 23 applies (see s 23(3); and heads (1)(a), (1)(b) in the text): see s 23(1)(a).
6   National Minimum Wage Act 1998 s 23(3)(a). As to employment tribunals see PARA 1399 et seq; and as to the procedure on a complaint made to an employment tribunal see PARA 1453 et seq.
7   National Minimum Wage Act 1998 s 23(3)(b). Head (1)(b) in the text refers to any right conferred by s 17 (see PARA 242): see s 23(3)(b).
8   Ie under the National Minimum Wage Act 1998 s 31 (see PARA 251): see s 23(1)(b).
9   National Minimum Wage Act 1998 s 23(1)(b).
10 As to the meaning of 'person who qualifies for the national minimum wage' see PARA 176 note 5.
11 National Minimum Wage Act 1998 s 23(1)(c). As to the rate of the national minimum wage see PARA 199.
12 Ie for the National Minimum Wage Act 1998 s 23(1) to apply (see the text and notes 1–11): see s 23(2).
13 See the National Minimum Wage Act 1998 s 23(2).
14 National Minimum Wage Act 1998 s 24(1). The text refers to a detriment in contravention of s 23 (see the text and notes 1–13): see s 24(1). Subject to s 24(3)–(5) (see the text and notes 15–22), the provisions of the Employment Rights Act 1996 s 48(2)–(4A) (detriment (enforcement: complaint to employment tribunal): see PARA 625) and s 49 (detriment (enforcement: remedies): see PARA 626) apply in relation to a complaint under the National Minimum Wage Act 1998 s 24 as they apply in relation to a complaint under the Employment Rights Act 1996 s 48, but taking references in those provisions to the employer as references to the employer within the meaning of the National Minimum Wage Act 1998 s 23(1) (see the text and notes 1–11): see s 24(2) (amended by the Enterprise and Regulatory Reform Act 2013 s 8, Sch 2 paras 36, 39).
    The Employment Act 2002 also applies to proceedings before an employment tribunal relating to a claim by an employee under the National Minimum Wage Act 1998 s 24: see the Employment Act 2002 s 38, Sch 5 (failure to give statement of employment particulars etc); and PARA 127. There is a requirement also for early ACAS conciliation to be tried in order to promote a settlement before tribunal proceedings are instituted on a complaint under the National Minimum Wage Act 1998 s 24: see the Employment Tribunals Act 1996 s 18(1)(c); and PARA 152 note 1. As to the constitution and powers of ACAS see PARA 1213 et seq.
15 National Minimum Wage Act 1998 s 24(3)(a). Where the worker has been working under arrangements which do not fall to be regarded as a worker's contract for the purposes of the Employment Rights Act 1996, he is to be treated for the purposes of the National Minimum Wage Act 1998 s 24(3), (4) (see also the text and notes 16–22) as if any arrangements under which he has been working constituted a worker's contract falling within the Employment Rights Act 1996 s 230(3)(b) (see PARA 5): National Minimum Wage Act 1998 s 24(5). See note 14. As to the meaning of references to a worker's contract see PARA 171.
16 National Minimum Wage Act 1998 s 24(3)(b). See note 14. As to the meaning of 'contract of employment' see PARA 2.
17 Ie under the Employment Rights Act 1996 s 49 (see PARA 626): see s 24(3).
18 See the National Minimum Wage Act 1998 s 24(3). The limit referred to in the text is the limit specified in s 24(4) (see heads (i), (ii) in the text): see s 24(3),
19 Ie calculated in accordance with the Employment Rights Act 1996 s 119 (see PARA 815): see the National Minimum Wage Act 1998 s 24(4)(a).
20 National Minimum Wage Act 1998 s 24(4)(a). See note 14.

21 Ie the sum for the time being specified in the Employment Rights Act 1996 s 124(1) (see PARA 823): see the National Minimum Wage Act 1998 s 24(4)(b).
22 National Minimum Wage Act 1998 s 24(4)(b). The text refers to the limit for a compensatory award to a person calculated in accordance with the Employment Rights Act 1996 s 123 (see PARA 818): see the National Minimum Wage Act 1998 s 24(4)(b).

(xv) Burden of Proof

250. Reversal of burden of proof. Where in any civil proceedings[1] any question arises as to whether an individual qualifies or qualified at any time for the national minimum wage[2], it is to be presumed that the individual qualifies or, as the case may be, qualified at that time for the national minimum wage unless the contrary is established[3].

Where a complaint:

(1)   is made to an employment tribunal[4] in respect of unauthorised deductions from wages[5]; and

(2)   relates in whole or in part to the deduction of additional remuneration[6],

it is to be presumed for the purposes of the complaint, so far as relating to the deduction of that amount, that the worker[7] in question was remunerated at a rate less than the national minimum wage unless the contrary is established[8].

Where in any civil proceedings a person seeks to recover on a claim in contract additional remuneration[9], it is to be presumed for the purposes of the proceedings, so far as relating to that amount, that the worker in question was remunerated at a rate less than the national minimum wage unless the contrary is established[10].

1   As to the meaning of 'civil proceedings' see PARA 239 note 8.
2   As to the meaning of 'person who qualifies for the national minimum wage' see PARA 176 note 5. As to the rate of the national minimum wage see PARA 199.
3   National Minimum Wage Act 1998 s 28(1).
4   Ie under the Employment Rights Act 1996 s 23(1)(a) (see PARA 259): see the National Minimum Wage Act 1998 s 28(2)(a). As to employment tribunals see PARA 1399 et seq; and as to the procedure on a complaint made to an employment tribunal see PARA 1453 et seq.
5   National Minimum Wage Act 1998 s 28(2)(a).
6   National Minimum Wage Act 1998 s 28(2)(b). Head (2) in the text refers to the amount described as additional remuneration in s 17(1) (see PARA 242): see s 28(2)(b).
7   As to the meaning of 'worker' for these purposes see PARA 171.
8   See the National Minimum Wage Act 1998 s 28(2).
9   Ie the amount described as additional remuneration in the National Minimum Wage Act 1998 s 17(1) (see PARA 242): see s 28(3).
10   National Minimum Wage Act 1998 s 28(3).

(xvi) Offences

251. Offences. If the employer[1] of a worker who qualifies for the national minimum wage[2] refuses or wilfully neglects to remunerate the worker for any pay reference period[3] at a rate which is at least equal to the national minimum wage[4], that employer is guilty of an offence[5] and liable to a penalty[6].

If a person who is required to keep or preserve any record[7] fails to do so, that person is guilty of an offence[8] and liable to a penalty[9].

In any proceedings for either such offence[10], it is a defence for the person charged to prove that he exercised all due diligence and took all reasonable precautions to secure that the provisions of the National Minimum Wage Act 1998, and of any relevant regulations made under it, were complied with by himself and by any person under his control[11].

If a person makes, or knowingly causes or allows to be made, in a record required to be kept[12] any entry which he knows to be false in a material particular, that person is guilty of an offence[13] and liable to a penalty[14].

If a person, for purposes connected with the provisions of the National Minimum Wage Act 1998, produces or furnishes, or knowingly causes or allows to be produced or furnished, any record or information which he knows to be false in a material particular, that person is guilty of an offence[15] and liable to a penalty[16].

If a person:

(1)   intentionally delays or obstructs an officer acting for the purposes of the National Minimum Wage Act 1998 in the exercise of any power conferred by that Act[17]; or

(2)   refuses or neglects to answer any question, furnish any information or produce any document when required to do so[18],

that person is guilty of an offence[19] and liable to a penalty[20].

1   As to the meaning of 'employer' for these purposes see PARA 170.
2   As to the meaning of 'worker' for these purposes see PARA 171; and as to the meaning of 'person who qualifies for the national minimum wage' see PARA 176 note 5.
3   As to the meaning of 'pay reference period' see PARA 202.
4   As to the rate of the national minimum wage see PARA 199.
5   National Minimum Wage Act 1998 s 31(1).
6   See the National Minimum Wage Act 1998 s 31(9) (amended by the Employment Act 2008 s 11(1)). The penalty (on conviction on indictment) is a fine or (on summary conviction) a fine not exceeding the statutory maximum: see the National Minimum Wage Act 1998 s 31(9) (as so amended). As to the statutory maximum see SENTENCING AND DISPOSITION OF OFFENDERS vol 92 (2010) PARA 140. As to proceedings for offences see PARA 253.
       Where the commission by any person of an offence under the National Minimum Wage Act 1998 s 31(1) (see the text and notes 1–5) or s 31(2) (see the text and notes 7–8) is due to the act or default of some other person, that other person is also guilty of the offence: s 31(6). A person may be charged with and convicted of an offence by virtue of s 31(6) whether or not proceedings are taken against any other person: s 31(7). As to offences by bodies corporate see PARA 252.
7   Ie in accordance with regulations under the National Minimum Wage Act 1998 s 9 (see PARA 226): see s 31(2).
8   National Minimum Wage Act 1998 s 31(2). See also note 6.
9   See the National Minimum Wage Act 1998 s 31(9) (as amended: see note 6). As to the penalty see note 6.
10   Ie an offence under the National Minimum Wage Act 1998 s 31(1) or (2) (see the text and notes 1–8): see s 31(8).
11   National Minimum Wage Act 1998 s 31(8).
12   Ie in accordance with regulations under the National Minimum Wage Act 1998 s 9 (see PARA 226): see s 31(3).
13   National Minimum Wage Act 1998 s 31(3).
14   See the National Minimum Wage Act 1998 s 31(9) (as amended: see note 6). As to the penalty see note 6.
15   National Minimum Wage Act 1998 s 31(4).
16   See the National Minimum Wage Act 1998 s 31(9) (as amended: see note 6). As to the penalty see note 6.
17   National Minimum Wage Act 1998 s 31(5)(a).
18   National Minimum Wage Act 1998 s 31(5)(b). Head (2) in the text refers to information or documents required to be furnished or produced under s 14(1) (see PARA 238): see s 31(5)(b).
19   See the National Minimum Wage Act 1998 s 31(5).
20   See the National Minimum Wage Act 1998 s 31(9) (as amended: see note 6). As to the penalty see note 6.

252.   Offences by bodies corporate etc.   If any offence under the National Minimum Wage Act 1998[1], committed by a body corporate, is proved[2]:

(1) to have been committed with the consent or connivance of an officer of the body[3]; or

(2) to be attributable to any neglect on the part of such an officer[4],

the officer, as well as the body corporate, is guilty of the offence and liable to be proceeded against and punished accordingly[5].

1 See the National Minimum Wage Act 1998 s 32(1). As to offences under the National Minimum Wage Act 1998 see PARA 251; and as to proceedings for offences see PARA 253.
2 See the National Minimum Wage Act 1998 s 32(2).
3 National Minimum Wage Act 1998 s 32(2)(a). For these purposes, 'officer', in relation to a body corporate, means a director, manager, secretary or other similar officer of the body, or a person purporting to act in any such capacity: see s 32(3). As to the meaning of 'manager' at common law see PARA 40 note 11.
4 National Minimum Wage Act 1998 s 32(2)(b).
5 See the National Minimum Wage Act 1998 s 32(2). If the affairs of a body corporate are managed by its members, s 32(2) applies in relation to the acts and defaults of a member in connection with his functions of management as if he were a director of the body corporate: s 32(4).

253. Proceedings for offences. The persons who may conduct proceedings for an offence under the National Minimum Wage Act 1998 in England and Wales[1], before a magistrates' court[2], include any person authorised for the purpose by the Secretary of State[3].

1 As to offences under the National Minimum Wage Act 1998 see PARA 251; and as to offences by bodies corporate see PARA 252. As to the meanings of 'England' and 'Wales' see PARA 2 note 12.
  Provision was made under the National Minimum Wage Act 1998 s 46 to avoid conflict with proceedings for offences under the Agricultural Wages Act 1948 (see AGRICULTURAL PRODUCTION AND MARKETING vol 1 (2008) PARA 1240). However, the National Minimum Wage Act 1998 s 46 is repealed, along with most of the 1948 Act itself, as from a date to be appointed under the Enterprise and Regulatory Reform Act 2013 s 103(3), by s 72(4), Sch 20 para 2. That day has been appointed as 1 October 2013 in relation to England (see the Enterprise and Regulatory Reform Act 2013 (Commencement No 1, Transitional Provisions and Savings) Order 2013, SI 2013/1455, art 3(b), Sch 2 para 6 (art 3(b) amended by SI 2013/2271)), but such a day has not been appointed, at the date at which this volume states the law, in relation to Wales.
2 As to proceedings for offences tried in magistrates' courts see generally CRIMINAL PROCEDURE vol 27 (2010) PARA 220 et seq.
3 National Minimum Wage Act 1998 s 33(1A) (added by the Legal Services Act 2007 s 208(1), Sch 21 paras 124, 125). As to the Secretary of State see PARA 5 note 21.

(5) DEDUCTIONS FROM WAGES

(i) Protection of Workers in relation to Payment of Wages

254. Meaning of 'wages'. For the purposes of the statutory provisions relating to the protection of workers[1] in respect of the payment of wages[2], 'wages', in relation to a worker, means any sums payable to the worker in connection with his employment[3], including:

(1) any fee, bonus[4], commission, holiday pay or other emolument referable to his employment, whether payable under his contract or otherwise[5];
(2) statutory sick pay[6];
(3) statutory maternity pay[7];
(4) statutory paternity pay[8];
(5) statutory shared parental pay[9];
(6) statutory adoption pay[10];
(7) a guarantee payment[11];

(8)   any payment for time off[12];

(9)   remuneration on suspension on medical or maternity grounds[13];

(10)   remuneration on ending the supply of an agency worker on maternity grounds[14];

(11)   any sum payable in pursuance of an order for reinstatement or re-engagement[15];

(12)   any sum payable in pursuance of an order for the continuance of a contract of employment[16]; and

(13)   remuneration under a protective award[17],

but excluding any payment[18]:

(a)   by way of an advance under an agreement for a loan or by way of an advance of wages[19];

(b)   in respect of expenses incurred by the worker in carrying out his employment[20];

(c)   by way of a pension, allowance or gratuity in connection with the worker's retirement or as compensation for loss of office[21];

(d)   referable to the worker's redundancy[22];

(e)   to the worker otherwise than in his capacity as a worker[23].

For these purposes, any monetary value attaching to any payment or benefit in kind furnished to a worker by his employer is not to be treated as wages of the worker[24], except in the case of any voucher, stamp or similar document which is: (i) of a fixed value expressed in monetary terms[25]; and (ii) capable of being exchanged (whether on its own or together with other vouchers, stamps or documents, and whether immediately or only after a time) for money, goods or services, or for any combination of two or more of those things[26].

1   As to the meaning of 'worker' see PARA 5.
2   Ie in the Employment Rights Act 1996 Pt II (ss 13–27) (protection of wages: see also PARA 255 et seq): see s 27(1).
3   See the Employment Rights Act 1996 s 27(1). As to the meaning of 'employment' see PARA 2. Where the employer gives the employee proper notice of termination but then tells him not to work the notice out, the amount payable during the notice period is 'wages' for this purpose, but it is otherwise if either the contract has a payment in lieu of notice (PILON) clause or the employer summarily dismisses tendering payment in lieu, in which cases the amount is no longer payable in connection with the employment, and so (if unpaid) cannot be claimed in proceedings under the Employment Rights Act 1996 Pt II: *Delaney v Staples (t/a De Montfort Recruitment)* [1992] 1 AC 687, [1992] ICR 483, HL. It is open to the contracting parties to agree that a PILON clause should be calculated without the preconception that it necessarily seeks to give the employee what he would have earned as an employee had he remained in employment during the notice period, and, as a matter of contractual construction, this can deprive an employee of his entitlement to be paid a bonus as part of the PILON: *Locke v Candy and Candy Ltd* [2010] EWCA Civ 1350, [2011] ICR 769, [2011] IRLR 163 (reading the contract as a whole, the employee had to be employed by the company in order to receive the bonus and, provided the employer made the right payment in lieu of notice, the employment came to an end on the immediate date of termination).
4   Where any payment in the nature of a non-contractual bonus is, for any reason, made to a worker by his employer, the amount of the payment is, for the purposes of the Employment Rights Act 1996 Pt II, to be treated as wages of the worker, and treated as payable to him as such on the day on which the payment is made: see s 27(3). As to the meaning of 'employer' see PARA 2. However, this provision is not exhaustive and so an unpaid bonus may also fall within the general provisions of s 27(1): *Farrell Matthews & Weir v Hansen* [2005] ICR 509, [2005] IRLR 160, EAT. In the case of a bonus which once declared involved a quantifiable sum which the employee was legally entitled to receive and which could be enforced under the Employment Rights Act 1996 for non-payment, the form of the payment was irrelevant and in any event it fell within the definition of 'bonus' in s 27: *Mouradian v Tradition Securities and Futures SA* [2009] EWCA Civ 60, [2009] All ER (D) 100 (Feb).

5 Employment Rights Act 1996 s 27(1)(a). As to the meaning of 'contract of employment' see PARA 2. Commission outstanding to a self-employed worker has been held to constitute wages for this purpose: *Robertson v Blackstone Franks Investment Management Ltd* [1998] IRLR 376, CA.

The reference to 'or otherwise' permits the Employment Rights Act 1996 Pt II to be used to recover non-payment of an amount such as a discretionary bonus in the reasonable contemplation of the parties as being payable: *Kent Management Services Ltd v Butterfield* [1992] ICR 272, [1992] IRLR 394, EAT. This might be the case particularly where the employer has stated that the bonus will be paid: *Farrell Matthews & Weir v Hansen* [2005] ICR 509, [2005] IRLR 160, EAT. As to the possible right to sue for a discretionary bonus at common law see *Clark v Nomura International plc* [2000] IRLR 766; and PARA 113. There must, however, be some legal right of sorts to the payment, even if not contractual: *New Century Cleaning Co Ltd v Church* [2000] IRLR 27, CA (no entitlement to a payment for a job that had not yet been fixed by the parties). See also *Revenue and Customs Comrs v Stringer* [2009] UKHL 31, [2009] 4 All ER 1205, [2009] ICR 985 (payment due for a period of statutory annual leave under the Working Time Regulations 1998, SI 1998/1833, could be categorised as 'wages' for the purpose of the Employment Rights Act 1996 s 27, giving the employee a choice of remedy either under the Working Time Regulations 1998, SI 1998/1833, or under the Employment Rights Act 1996 Pt II); and see PARA 293.

6 Employment Rights Act 1996 s 27(1)(b). Head (2) in the text refers to sums payable under the Social Security Contributions and Benefits Act 1992 Pt XI (ss 151–163) (see PARA 558 et seq): see the Employment Rights Act 1996 s 27(1)(b). As to an employee's entitlement to remuneration at common law following exhaustion of statutory and contractual entitlement to sick pay when ready and willing to work see *Beveridge v KLM UK Ltd* [2000] IRLR 765, EAT.

7 Employment Rights Act 1996 s 27(1)(c). Head (3) in the text refers to sums payable under the Social Security Contributions and Benefits Act 1992 Pt XII (ss 164–171) (see PARA 401 et seq): see the Employment Rights Act 1996 s 27(1)(c).

8 Employment Rights Act 1996 s 27(1)(ca) (s 27(1)(ca), (cb) added by the Employment Act 2002 s 53, Sch 7 paras 24, 25; the Employment Rights Act 1996 s 27(1)(ca) amended by the Work and Families Act 2006 s 11(1), Sch 1 para 29; and the Children and Families Act 2014 s 126, Sch 7 paras 29, 30(a)). Head (4) in the text refers to sums payable under the Social Security Contributions and Benefits Act 1992 Pt XIIZA (ss 171ZA–171ZK) (see PARA 443 et seq): see the Employment Rights Act 1996 s 27(1)(ca) (as so added and amended).

9 Employment Rights Act 1996 s 27(1)(cc) (added by the Children and Families Act 2014 Sch 7 paras 29, 30(b)). Head (5) in the text refers to statutory shared parental pay under the Social Security Contributions and Benefits Act 1992 Pt 12ZC (ss 171ZU–171ZZ5) (see PARA 534): see the Employment Rights Act 1996 s 27(1)(cc) (as so added).

10 Employment Rights Act 1996 s 27(1)(cb) (as added: see note 8). Head (6) in the text refers to sums payable under the Social Security Contributions and Benefits Act 1992 Pt XIIZB (ss 171ZL–171ZT) (see PARA 488 et seq): see the Employment Rights Act 1996 s 27(1)(cb) (as so added).

11 Employment Rights Act 1996 s 27(1)(d). Head (7) in the text refers to sums payable under s 28 (see PARA 261): see s 27(1)(d).

12 Employment Rights Act 1996 s 27(1)(e). Head (8) in the text refers to sums payable under Pt VI (ss 50–63C) (see PARA 326 et seq) or the Trade Union and Labour Relations (Consolidation) Act 1992 s 169 (payment for time off for carrying out trade union activities: see PARA 1065): see the Employment Rights Act 1996 s 27(1)(e).

13 Employment Rights Act 1996 s 27(1)(f). Head (9) in the text refers to sums payable under s 64 (medical grounds: see PARA 596) or s 68 (maternity grounds: see PARA 598): see s 27(1)(f).

14 Employment Rights Act 1996 s 27(1)(fa) (added by SI 2010/93). Head (10) in the text refers to sums payable under s 68C (see PARA 601): see s 27(1)(fa) (as so added).

15 Employment Rights Act 1996 s 27(1)(g). Head (11) in the text refers to sums payable under s 113 (see PARA 811): see s 27(1)(g).

16 Employment Rights Act 1996 s 27(1)(h). Head (12) in the text refers to sums payable under s 130 (see PARA 807) or the Trade Union and Labour Relations (Consolidation) Act 1992 s 164 (see PARA 1060): see the Employment Rights Act 1996 s 27(1)(h).

17 Employment Rights Act 1996 s 27(1)(i). Head (13) in the text refers to sums payable under the Trade Union and Labour Relations (Consolidation) Act 1992 s 189 (see PARA 1189): see the Employment Rights Act 1996 s 27(1)(i).

18 See the Employment Rights Act 1996 s 27(1). The text refers to the exclusion of any payments within s 27(2) (see heads (a)–(e) in the text): see s 27(1).

19 Employment Rights Act 1996 s 27(2)(a). Head (a) in the text is without prejudice to the application of s 13 (see PARA 255) to any deduction made from the worker's wages in respect of any such advance: see s 27(2)(a).

20 Employment Rights Act 1996 s 27(2)(b). The exclusion given in head (b) in the text applies widely, both to true expenses and to those which in reality contain an element of remuneration: *Southwark London Borough v O'Brien* [1996] IRLR 420, EAT.

21 Employment Rights Act 1996 s 27(2)(c).

22 Employment Rights Act 1996 s 27(2)(d). As to the meaning of 'redundancy' see PARA 870.

23 Employment Rights Act 1996 s 27(2)(e).

24 See the Employment Rights Act 1996 s 27(5).

25 Employment Rights Act 1996 s 27(5)(a).

26 Employment Rights Act 1996 s 27(5)(b).

255. General restrictions on deductions made, or payments received by, employers. An employer[1] must not make a deduction from wages[2] of a worker[3] employed[4] by him unless[5]:

(1)   the deduction is required or authorised to be made by virtue of a statutory provision[6] or a relevant provision of the worker's contract[7]; or

(2)   the worker has previously[8] signified in writing his agreement or consent to the making of the deduction[9].

Nor may an employer receive any payment[10] from a worker employed by him unless[11]:

(a)   the payment is required or authorised to be made by virtue of a statutory provision or a relevant provision of the worker's contract[12]; or

(b)   the worker has previously signified in writing his agreement or consent to the making of the payment[13].

Where the total amount of wages paid on any occasion by an employer to a worker employed by him is less than the total amount of the wages properly payable by him to the worker on that occasion[14] (after deductions), then the amount of the deficiency is to be treated for these purposes (except in so far as the deficiency is attributable to an error of computation[15]) as a deduction made by the employer from the worker's wages on that occasion[16].

These provisions[17] do not affect any other statutory provision by virtue of which a sum payable to a worker by his employer but not constituting wages[18] is not to be subject to a deduction at the instance of the employer[19].

1   As to the meaning of 'employer' see PARA 2.

2   As to deductions which are excluded from these provisions see PARA 256. As to the meaning of 'wages' see PARA 254.

     An attendance allowance can be taken into account for the purposes of calculating wages in terms of the Employment Rights Act 1996 s 13: *Laird v AK Stoddart Ltd* [2001] IRLR 591, EAT. Cf the position regarding attendance allowances under the National Minimum Wage Regulations 1999, SI 1999/584: see PARA 221 note 17.

3   As to the meaning of 'worker' see PARA 5; and as to the exclusion of mariners see PARA 167.

4   As to the meaning of 'employed' see PARA 2.

5   See the Employment Rights Act 1996 s 13(1). Failure by an employer to pay any or all of an employee's wages on time amounts to an unlawful deduction from wages under s 13(1): *Elizabeth Claire Care Management Ltd v Francis* [2005] IRLR 858, [2005] All ER (D) 244 (Jun), EAT (term 'deduction from wages' has a wide meaning and applies as much to an employee who had been paid all but £1 of her wages as to one who was not paid any of her wages). Any failure to pay holiday pay under the Working Time Regulations 1998, SI 1998/1833, can also constitute an unauthorised deduction from wages contrary to the Employment Rights Act 1996 s 13: see *Revenue and Customs Comrs v Stringer* [2009] UKHL 31, [2009] 4 All ER 1205, [2009] ICR 985; and PARA 291 note 3.

6   Accordingly, an employer has no power unilaterally to:

     (1)   vary a worker's contract upon the abolition of the Truck Acts (ie the Truck Acts 1831–1944 (repealed)), so as to withdraw a wage supplement paid in respect of the loss of the right to cash pay by absorbing it into an overall increase, unless one of the

conditions set out in head (1) in the text is met (*McCree v Tower Hamlets London Borough Council* [1992] ICR 99, [1992] IRLR 56, EAT) (decided under the Wages Act 1986 s 1(1) (repealed));

(2) reduce an employee's contractual rate of pay in order to discharge the employer's liability under the Working Time Regulations 1998, SI 1998/1833 (see PARA 268 et seq) (*Davies v MJ Wyatt (Decorators) Ltd* [2000] IRLR 759, EAT (wages reduced to fund holiday scheme));

(3) introduce new arrangements to meet his obligations under the National Minimum Wage Regulations 1999, SI 1999/584 (see PARA 200 et seq) (*Laird v AK Stoddart Ltd* [2001] IRLR 591, EAT (employer removed part of attendance allowance to supplement the rate of pay up to the appropriate level; level of take-home pay not affected)).

As to claims under the Employment Rights Act 1996 s 13 which are founded on the holiday pay arrangements guaranteed under the Working Time Regulations 1998, SI 1998/1833, see further PARA 293.

7 Employment Rights Act 1996 s 13(1)(a). For these purposes, 'relevant provision', in relation to a worker's contract, means a provision of the contract comprised:

(1) in one or more written terms of the contract of which the employer has given the worker a copy on any occasion prior to the employer making the deduction in question (Employment Rights Act 1996 s 13(2)(a)); or

(2) in one or more terms of the contract, whether express or implied and, if express, whether oral or in writing, the existence and effect, or combined effect, of which in relation to the worker the employer has notified to the worker in writing on such an occasion (s 13(2)(b)).

As to the meaning of references to a worker's contract see PARA 5. As to the meaning of 'writing' see PARA 2 note 8.

For these purposes, a relevant provision of a worker's contract having effect by virtue of a variation of the contract does not, however, operate to authorise the making of a deduction on account of any conduct of the worker, or any other event occurring, before the variation took effect (s 13(5)); and an agreement or consent signified by a worker does not operate to authorise the making of a deduction on account of any conduct of the worker, or any other event occurring, before the agreement or consent was signified (s 13(6)). This means that, where there has been a variation of contract to permit deductions, for the variation to be effective for these purposes it must have been: (a) agreed before the date of the conduct on account of which the deduction was made; and (b) notified in writing to the employee before the date of the deduction: *York City and District Travel Ltd v Smith* [1990] ICR 344, [1990] IRLR 213, EAT. The change must be notified in writing to the worker individually (not just by a factory notice): *Kerr v Sweater Shop (Scotland) Ltd, Sweater Shop (Scotland) Ltd v Park* [1996] IRLR 424, EAT.

8 The reference to 'previously' means that the signed agreement for the deduction must pre-date not just the deduction, but the event giving rise to the deduction, so that an ad hoc agreement after the event but before the deduction will not qualify: *Discount Tobacco and Confectionery Ltd v Williamson* [1993] ICR 371, [1993] IRLR 327, EAT.

9 Employment Rights Act 1996 s 13(1)(b). See *International Packaging Corpn (UK) Ltd v Balfour* [2003] IRLR 11, [2002] All ER (D) 146 (Nov), EAT (Sc) (reduction in employee's pay following the unilateral introduction of short-time working by the employers amounted to an unauthorised deduction from wages in terms of the Employment Rights Act 1996 s 13(1)); cf *Hussman Manufacturing Ltd v Weir* [1998] IRLR 288, 599 IRLB 5, EAT (reduction in employee's pay resulting from an alteration in shift patterns, which the employers were contractually entitled to make, did not amount to an unauthorised deduction). See also *Briggs v Nottingham University Hospitals NHS Trust* [2010] EWCA Civ 264, [2010] IRLR 504, [2010] All ER (D) 152 (Mar) (NHS workers unsuccessfully argued that refusal to classify their positions as qualifying for 'recruitment and retention premium' constituted unlawful deduction from wages); *Deakin v Kuehne & Nagel Drinks Logistics Ltd* [2012] EWCA Civ 22, [2012] IRLR 513 (no unauthorised deduction where employer deducted sum for planned break periods not actually taken because agreement meant that the worker was obliged to take the planned break); *Hay v Gilgrove Ltd* [2013] EWCA Civ 412, [2013] ICR 1139, [2013] All ER (D) 220 (Apr) (collective agreement not incorporated into contracts of employment of new employees who were not registered market porters but employer's construction of 'registered market porters' as including all porters was correct); *Anderson v London Fire and Emergency Planning Authority* [2013] EWCA Civ 321, [2013] IRLR 459 (amount of increase depended on which amount specified by the formula in the agreement turned out to be the greater, not on the employer's unfettered right to choose which of the options to implement); *Glasson v Bexley London Borough Council* [2014] All ER (D) 134 (Apr), EAT (after restructuring, assimilation, and job evaluation undertaken in respect of employee's new role, the conditions giving rise to the

exercise of employer's discretion to make payments under an honorarium scheme, by reason of the additional duties within the employee's area of responsibility being undertaken by the employee, had ceased). See also *Verma v Barts and the London NHS Trust* [2013] UKSC 20, [2013] ICR 727, [2013] IRLR 567; and PARA 113 note 7.

10   For the purposes of the Employment Rights Act 1996 Pt II (ss 13–27) (protection of wages: see also PARAS 254, 256 et seq), any reference to an employer receiving a payment from a worker employed by him is a reference to his receiving such a payment in his capacity as the worker's employer: see s 15(5).

11   See the Employment Rights Act 1996 s 15(1).

12   Employment Rights Act 1996 s 15(1)(a). For these purposes, 'relevant provision', in relation to a worker's contract, means a provision of the contract comprised:

    (1)   in one or more written terms of the contract of which the employer has given the worker a copy on any occasion prior to the employer receiving the payment in question (s 15(2)(a)); or

    (2)   in one or more terms of the contract, whether express or implied and, if express, whether oral or in writing, the existence and effect, or combined effect, of which in relation to the worker the employer has notified to the worker in writing on such an occasion (s 15(2)(b)).

A relevant provision of a worker's contract having effect by virtue of a variation of the contract does not operate to authorise the receipt of a payment on account of any conduct of the worker, or any other event occurring, before the variation took effect (s 15(3)); and an agreement or consent signified by a worker does not operate to authorise the receipt of a payment on account of any conduct of the worker, or any other event occurring, before the agreement or consent was signified (s 15(4)).

13   Employment Rights Act 1996 s 15(1)(b).

14   The words 'properly payable' in the Employment Rights Act 1996 s 13(3) referred to a legal, but not necessarily a contractual, entitlement on the part of the employee to the payment, and consideration of whether there was a sum legally payable in accordance with s 13(3) was an exercise which had to be completed before s 13(1), (2) (see the text and notes 1–9) could apply; it was only if the answer was in the affirmative that there had to be a consideration as to whether there was a deduction from that sum so as to invoke s 13(1), (2): *Hellewell v Axa Services Ltd* [2011] ICR D29, [2011] All ER (D) 89 (Aug), EAT (bonus payments were not payable pursuant to a legal obligation, and so were not 'properly payable' for these purposes).

15   The Employment Rights Act 1996 s 13(3) does not apply in so far as the deficiency is attributable to an error of any description on the part of the employer affecting the computation by him of the gross amount of the wages properly payable by him to the worker on that occasion: see s 13(4). 'Gross amount', in relation to any wages payable to a worker, means the total amount of those wages before deductions of whatever nature: see s 27(4). A deliberate refusal to pay in the belief that there is no obligation to do so is not an error of computation: *Yemm v British Steel plc* [1994] IRLR 117, EAT.

16   Employment Rights Act 1996 s 13(3). The application of s 13(3) caused initially a sharp disagreement within the Employment Appeal Tribunal as to what was meant by a 'deduction', especially in a case where the worker complained that the employer had refused to pay an amount, which the worker said was due under the contract, at all (eg a refusal to pay accrued holiday pay or bonus). The wider view was that s 13(3) had to apply as it stood, so that any such shortfall constituted a deemed deduction, and so might be recoverable by a claim before a tribunal; the narrower view was that, in spite of s 13(3), a simple refusal to pay by an employer was not a 'deduction' at all, but rather a breach of contract, and so was not within the tribunal's jurisdiction, and had to be pursued at common law before an ordinary court. This disagreement was resolved by the Court of Appeal in favour of the wider approach and applying the literal meaning of s 13(3) that any shortfall in the amount of wages properly payable is to be treated as a deduction: *Delaney v Staples (t/a De Montfort Recruitment)* [1991] 2 QB 47, [1991] ICR 331, CA (affd on other grounds [1992] 1 AC 687, [1992] ICR 483, HL), approving on this point *Greg May (Carpet Fitters and Contractors) Ltd v Dring* [1990] ICR 188, [1990] IRLR 19, EAT, and *Kournavous v JR Masterton & Sons (Demolition) Ltd* [1990] ICR 387, [1990] IRLR 119, EAT, and disapproving *Barlow v Whittle (t/a Micro Management)* [1990] ICR 270, [1990] IRLR 79, EAT, and *Alsop v Star Vehicle Contracts Ltd* [1990] ICR 378, [1990] IRLR 83, EAT. See also *Small v Boots Co plc* [2009] IRLR 328, [2009] All ER (D) 200 (Jan), EAT. Thus tribunal proceedings under these provisions can be used by a worker to challenge a unilateral change of terms by the employer, where that results in a lesser amount being payable: *McCree v Tower Hamlets London Borough Council* [1992] ICR 99, [1992] IRLR 56, EAT; *Bruce v Wiggins Teape (Stationery) Ltd* [1994] IRLR 536, EAT; *Morgan v West Glamorgan County Council* [1995] IRLR 68, EAT; *Saavedra v Aceground Ltd (t/a Terrazza Est)* [1995]

IRLR 198, EAT; *Farrell Matthews & Weir v Hansen* [2005] ICR 509, [2005] IRLR 160, EAT (once employee had a legal entitlement to bonus, it became a wage properly payable under the Employment Rights Act 1996 s 13(3) in accordance with terms properly notified until those terms were altered and notice of the alteration was given); *Mouradian v Tradition Securities and Futures SA* [2009] EWCA Civ 60, [2009] All ER (D) 100 (Feb) (in a claim for unlawful deduction of wages if the relevant deductible costs had been overstated any additional fixed sum was held to have been unlawfully deducted from the employee's wages).

For a claim to be successful an employee has to establish what was properly due as wages under the Employment Rights Act 1996 s 13(3) before it is possible to discern whether or not there has been a deduction and whether or not that deduction was authorised by the contract: *Fisher v London Underground Ltd* [2004] All ER (D) 126 (Nov), EAT (contractual documents separated contractual salary from the anti-social hours allowance so 5% increase on promotion applied to the basic salary only, giving a lower figure; no unlawful deduction).

Even where there is a term in the contract permitting a deduction, a worker may still argue that the deduction actually made is contrary to these provisions by being excessive in amount, in the light of the contract term: *Fairfield Ltd v Skinner* [1992] ICR 836, [1993] IRLR 4, EAT.

The fact that a deduction extinguishes the amount payable altogether does not prevent its being a deduction: *Alsop v Star Vehicle Contracts Ltd* above; *New Centurion Trust v Welch* [1990] ICR 383, [1990] IRLR 123, EAT. An arrangement whereby an employee forfeits an amount of money owed to him if he fails to give the notice required by the contract comes within the Employment Rights Act 1996 s 13(1) and its requirements of notification (*Pename Ltd v Paterson* [1989] ICR 12, [1989] IRLR 195, EAT; *Chiltern House Ltd v Chambers* [1990] IRLR 88 at 90, EAT, per Wood P (obiter)); but cf the different position if the employer refuses to pay an amount due in lieu of notice (see PARA 254 note 3).

See also *Campbell & Smith Construction Group Ltd v Greenwood* [2001] IRLR 588, EAT (refusal to give employee an extra day's holiday where a working day, normally given by employer as holiday, was declared a public holiday, was not unlawful deduction); *Bates v Chubb Security Personnel Lt*d [2004] All ER (D) 121 (Sep), EAT (continuing deduction from wages occurred where employer had chosen not to adhere to the Transfer of Undertakings (Protection of Employment) Regulations 1981, SI 1981/1794 (now the Transfer of Undertakings (Protection of Employment) Regulations 2006, SI 2006/246) (see PARAS 137–141, 803) so that an employee could claim overtime for those weeks when the hours worked were in excess of the previously-agreed number of hours per week); *Adcock v Coors Brewers Ltd* [2007] EWCA Civ 19, [2007] ICR 983, sub nom *Coors Brewers Ltd v Adcock* [2007] IRLR 440 (discontinuance of profit share scheme did not constitute unauthorised deduction). *Adcock v Coors Brewers Ltd* was applied in *Lucy v British Airways plc* [2009] All ER (D) 58 (Jan), EAT.

17 Ie the Employment Rights Act 1996 s 13: see s 13(7).
18 Ie within the meaning of the Employment Rights Act 1996 Pt II (see PARA 254): see s 13(7).
19 Employment Rights Act 1996 s 13(7). The provisions of Pt II operate in addition to those of ss 8–11 on itemised pay statements and standing statements of fixed deductions (see PARAS 124–125). As to the overlapping remedies see PARA 259 note 17.

256. Exceptions to the rules on deductions made, or payments received by, employers. The general statutory restrictions on deductions made[1], or payments received[2], by employers[3] do not apply:

(1) to a deduction from a worker's[4] wages[5] made by his employer, or to a payment received from a worker by his employer[6], where the purpose of the deduction or, as the case may be, payment is the reimbursement of the employer in respect of: (a) an overpayment of wages; or (b) an overpayment in respect of expenses incurred by the worker in carrying out his employment[7], made, for any reason, by the employer to the worker[8];

(2) to a deduction from a worker's wages made by his employer, or to a payment received from a worker by his employer, in consequence of any disciplinary proceedings if those proceedings were held by virtue of a statutory provision[9];

(3) to a deduction from a worker's wages made by his employer in pursuance of a requirement imposed on the employer by a statutory provision to deduct and pay over to a public authority amounts

determined by that authority as being due to it from the worker, if the deduction is made in accordance with the relevant determination of that authority[10];

(4) to a deduction from a worker's wages made by his employer in pursuance of any arrangements which have been established: (a) in accordance with a relevant provision of his contract[11] to the inclusion of which in the contract the worker has signified his agreement or consent in writing[12]; or (b) otherwise with the prior agreement or consent of the worker signified in writing, and under which the employer is to deduct and pay over to a third person amounts notified to the employer by that person as being due to him from the worker, if the deduction is made in accordance with the relevant notification by that person[13];

(5) to a deduction from a worker's wages made by his employer, or to a payment received from a worker by his employer, where the worker has taken part in a strike or other industrial action and the deduction is made, or the payment has been required, by the employer on account of the worker's having taken part in that strike or other action[14]; or

(6) to a deduction from a worker's wages made by his employer with his prior agreement or consent signified in writing, or a payment received from a worker by his employer, where the purpose of the deduction or, as the case may be, payment is the satisfaction, whether wholly or in part, of an order of a court or tribunal requiring the payment of any amount by the worker to the employer[15].

1   Ie in the Employment Rights Act 1996 s 13 (see PARA 255): see s 14(1).
2   Ie in the Employment Rights Act 1996 s 15 (see PARA 255): see s 16(1).
3   As to the meaning of 'employer' see PARA 2.
4   As to the meaning of 'worker' see PARA 5.
5   As to the meaning of 'wages' see PARA 254.
6   As to the meaning of references to an employer receiving a payment from a worker employed by him see PARA 255 note 10.
7   As to the meaning of 'employment' see PARA 2.
8   See the Employment Rights Act 1996 ss 14(1), 16(1). The wording of the statutory exception is to be applied as it stands, ie to any such deduction whether lawfully made under the contract or not (because the tribunal's jurisdiction does not extend to deciding the lawfulness of the deduction and any breach of contract can be remedied by proceedings in the civil courts): *Sunderland Polytechnic v Evans* [1993] ICR 392, [1993] IRLR 196, EAT (disapproving obiter *Home Office v Ayres* [1992] ICR 175, [1992] IRLR 59, EAT, on this point); and see *SIP Industrial Products Ltd v Swinn* [1994] ICR 473, [1994] IRLR 323, EAT (overpayment in respect of expenses dishonestly obtained by employee altering receipts for diesel fuel properly characterised as a common law dispute which should be resolved in the civil courts). Making findings of fact as to the existence of the jurisdictional question, ie whether or not the Employment Rights Act 1996 s 14 is engaged, does not involve any consideration of the lawfulness of the deduction: *Gill v Ford Motor Co Ltd, Wong v BAE Systems Operations Ltd* [2004] IRLR 840, EAT.

     See also *Southwark London Borough v O'Brien* [1996] IRLR 420, EAT (where there is an element in the payment which is not reimbursement of expenses, it is not possible to perform the kind of apportionment that would be necessary to distinguish between wages and expenses and, therefore, a finding has to be made that the deduction is wholly in respect of wages, or wholly in respect of expenses (decided under the Wages Act 1986 s 7 (repealed))).

9   See the Employment Rights Act 1996 ss 14(2), 16(2); and see *Chiltern House Ltd v Chambers* [1990] IRLR 88 at 90, EAT, per Wood P (obiter) (the Employment Rights Act 1996 s 14(2) applies not to private sector employers but only to those in the public sector such as the police and fire service where disciplinary procedures are established under statute).

10   Employment Rights Act 1996 s 14(3). 'Determination' in s 14(3) is to be interpreted in a wide, non-technical way and includes all decisions by which a direction is given to an employer by a public authority in accordance with statute to make a deduction from an employee's wages: *Patel v Marquette Partners (UK) Ltd* [2009] ICR 569, [2009] IRLR 425, EAT (in the area of

income tax, it does not require HMRC to have made a formal 'determination' (under tax law) before a deduction for tax is permitted, and an employer who makes a deduction following a communication from HMRC to make deductions according to the employee's notice of coding will be making it in a way which is authorised by reason of the Employment Rights Act 1996 s 14(3)).

11 As to the meaning of references to a worker's contract see PARA 5.
12 As to the meaning of 'writing' see PARA 2 note 8.
13 Employment Rights Act 1996 s 14(4).
14 See the Employment Rights Act 1996 ss 14(5), 16(3). There are no statutory definitions of 'strike' and 'other industrial action' for these purposes; but as to their meaning in the Trade Union and Labour Relations (Consolidation) Act 1992 s 238 (dismissal in connection with a lockout, strike or other industrial action) see PARA 1351. As with the Employment Rights Act 1996 s 14(1) (see the text and notes 1–8), s 14(5) is to be applied as it stands, without consideration of the overall legality or otherwise of the deduction: *Sunderland Polytechnic v Evans* [1993] ICR 392, [1993] IRLR 196, EAT. See also *Gill v Ford Motor Co Ltd, Wong v BAE Systems Operations Ltd* [2004] IRLR 840, EAT; *Norris v London Fire and Emergency Planning Authority* [2013] ICR 819, [2013] IRLR 428, EAT (firefighter's individual refusal to 'act up' as a watch manager after official industrial dispute had been resolved did not constitute participation in industrial action); and note 8.
15 See the Employment Rights Act 1996 ss 14(6), 16(4).

(ii) Special Protection for Workers in Retail Employment

257. Deductions from wages of workers in retail employment on account of cash shortages etc. Where the employer[1] of a worker[2] in retail employment[3] makes[4], on account of one or more cash shortages[5] or stock deficiencies[6], a deduction[7] or deductions from any wages[8] payable to the worker on a pay day[9], the amount or aggregate amount of the deduction or deductions must not exceed one-tenth of the gross amount[10] of the wages payable to the worker on that day[11]. Where the employer makes such a deduction, he is not to be treated as making the deduction in compliance with the statutory restriction[12] unless (in addition to those requirements being satisfied with respect to the deduction)[13]:

(1) the deduction is made[14]; or
(2) in the case of a deduction which is one of a series of deductions relating to the shortage or deficiency, the first deduction in the series was made[15],

not later than the end of the relevant period[16] (being the end of the period of 12 months beginning with the date when the employer established the existence of the shortage or deficiency or, if earlier, the date when he ought reasonably to have done so)[17]. Where:

(a) by virtue of an agreement between a worker in retail employment and his employer, the amount of the worker's wages or any part of them is or may be determined by reference to the incidence of cash shortages or stock deficiencies[18]; and
(b) the gross amount of the wages payable to the worker on any pay day is, on account of any such shortages or deficiencies, less than the gross amount of the wages that would have been payable to him on that day if there had been no such shortages or deficiencies[19],

then:

(i) the amount representing the difference between the two amounts referred to in head (b) above (the 'relevant amount') is to be treated[20] as a deduction from the wages payable to the worker on that day made by the employer on account of the cash shortages or stock deficiencies in question[21]; and

(ii)   the second of the amounts referred to in head (b) above is to be treated[22] as the gross amount of the wages payable to him on that day[23],

and the statutory restriction on unauthorised deductions[24] has effect in relation to the relevant amount accordingly[25].

Where, in any legal proceedings, the court finds that the employer of a worker in retail employment is entitled[26] to recover an amount from the worker in respect of a cash shortage or stock deficiency, the court must, in ordering the payment by the worker to the employer of that amount, make such provision as appears to the court to be necessary to ensure that it is paid by the worker at a rate not exceeding that at which it could be duly recovered from him by the employer[27].

1   As to the meaning of 'employer' see PARA 2.
2   As to the meaning of 'worker' see PARA 5.
3   For the purposes of the Employment Rights Act 1996 ss 18–27 (see also PARA 258 et seq), in relation to a worker, 'retail employment' means employment involving (whether on a regular basis or not):
     (1)   the carrying out by the worker of retail transactions directly with members of the public or with fellow workers or other individuals in their personal capacities (s 17(2)(a)); or
     (2)   the collection by the worker of amounts payable in connection with retail transactions carried out by other persons directly with members of the public or with fellow workers or other individuals in their personal capacities (s 17(2)(b));
     and, for these purposes, references to a 'retail transaction' are references to the sale or supply of goods or the supply of services (including financial services) (see s 17(3)). As to the meaning of 'employment' see PARA 2.
4   Ie in accordance with the Employment Rights Act 1996 s 13 (see PARA 255): see s 18(1).
5   For these purposes, 'cash shortage' means a deficit arising in relation to amounts received in connection with retail transactions: see the Employment Rights Act 1996 s 17(1).
6   For these purposes, 'stock deficiency' means a stock deficiency arising in the course of retail transactions: see the Employment Rights Act 1996 s 17(1).
7   For the purposes of the Employment Rights Act 1996 ss 18–27 (see also PARA 258 et seq), references to a deduction made from wages of a worker in retail employment on account of a cash shortage or stock deficiency include references to a deduction so made on account of:
     (1)   any dishonesty or other conduct on the part of the worker which resulted in any such shortage or deficiency (s 17(4)(a)); or
     (2)   any other event in respect of which he, whether together with any other workers or not, has any contractual liability and which so resulted (s 17(4)(b)),
     whether or not the amount of the deduction is designed to reflect the exact amount of the shortage or deficiency (see s 17(4)); and references to the recovery from a worker of an amount in respect of a cash shortage or stock deficiency include references to the recovery from him of an amount in respect of any such conduct that is mentioned in head (1) or head (2) above (see s 17(5)).
8   As to the meaning of 'wages' see PARA 254.
9   For the purposes of the Employment Rights Act 1996 ss 18–27 (see also PARA 258 et seq), in relation to a worker, 'pay day' means a day on which wages are payable to the worker: see the Employment Rights Act 1996 s 17(6).
10   As to the meaning of 'gross amount' see PARA 255 note 15.
11   Employment Rights Act 1996 s 18(1). The provision made by s 18(1) does not, however, operate to restrict the amount of any deductions which may, in accordance with s 13(1) (see PARA 255), be made by the employer of a worker in retail employment from the worker's final instalment of wages: s 22(2). For these purposes, 'final instalment of wages', in relation to a worker, means:
     (1)   the amount of wages payable to the worker which consists of or includes an amount payable by way of contractual remuneration in respect of the last of the periods for which he is employed under his contract prior to its termination for any reason (but excluding any wages referable to any earlier such period) (s 22(1)(a)); or
     (2)   where an amount in lieu of notice is paid to the worker later than the amount referred to in head (1) above, the amount so paid (s 22(1)(b)),
     in each case whether the amount in question is paid before or after the termination of the worker's contract (see s 22(1)).
12   Ie in accordance with the Employment Rights Act 1996 s 13 (see PARA 255): see s 18(2).
13   See the Employment Rights Act 1996 s 18(2).

14 Employment Rights Act 1996 s 18(2)(a).

15 Employment Rights Act 1996 s 18(2)(b).

16 See the Employment Rights Act 1996 s 18(2).

17 See the Employment Rights Act 1996 s 18(3).

18 Employment Rights Act 1996 s 19(1)(a).

19 Employment Rights Act 1996 s 19(1)(b).

20 Ie for the purposes of the Employment Rights Act 1996 Pt II (ss 13–27) (protection of wages: see also PARAS 254 et seq, 258 et seq): see s 19(2).

21 Employment Rights Act 1996 s 19(2).

22 Ie for the purposes of the Employment Rights Act 1996 Pt II (protection of wages: see also PARAS 254 et seq, 258 et seq), except s 19(1): see s 19(3).

23 Employment Rights Act 1996 s 19(3).

24 Ie the Employment Rights Act 1996 s 13 (see PARA 255) and, if the requirements of s 13 and s 18(2) (see the text and notes 12–13) are satisfied, s 18(1) (see the text and notes 1–11): see s 19(4).

25 Employment Rights Act 1996 s 19(4).

26 Ie in accordance with the Employment Rights Act 1996 s 15 (see PARA 255) as it applies apart from s 20(1) (see PARA 258): see s 21(3).

27 Employment Rights Act 1996 s 21(3). The text refers to payment that could be recovered by the employer in accordance with s 21: see s 21(3). The provision made by s 21(3) does not, however, apply to any amount which is to be paid by a worker on or after the day on which his final instalment of wages is paid: s 22(4).

258. Payments by workers in retail employment on account of cash shortages etc. Where the employer[1] of a worker[2] in retail employment[3] receives[4] from the worker a payment[5] on account of a cash shortage or stock deficiency, the employer is not to be treated as receiving the payment in compliance with the statutory restriction[6] unless, in addition to those requirements being satisfied with respect to the payment, he has previously[7]:

(1) notified the worker in writing[8] of the worker's total liability to him in respect of that shortage or deficiency[9]; and

(2) required the worker to make the payment by means of a demand for payment made as follows[10]: (a) a demand for payment made by the employer of a worker in retail employment in respect of a cash shortage or stock deficiency must be made in writing[11], and must be made on one of the worker's pay days[12]; (b) a demand for payment in respect of a particular cash shortage or stock deficiency (or, in the case of a series of such demands, the first such demand) must not be made[13]: (i) earlier than the first pay day of the worker following the date when he is notified of his total liability in respect of the shortage or deficiency in pursuance of head (1) above[14] or, where he is so notified on a pay day, earlier than that day[15]; or (ii) later than the end of the period of 12 months beginning with the date when the employer established the existence of the shortage or deficiency (or, if earlier, the date when he ought reasonably to have done so)[16].

Where the employer of a worker in retail employment makes on any pay day one or more demands for payment in this way[17], the amount or aggregate amount required to be paid by the worker in pursuance of the demand or demands must not exceed[18]:

(A) one-tenth of the gross amount[19] of the wages payable to the worker on that day[20]; or

(B) where one or more deductions on account of one or more cash shortages or stock deficiencies[21] is or are made by the employer from those wages, such amount as represents the balance of that one-tenth after subtracting the amount or aggregate amount of the deduction or deductions[22].

Legal proceedings by the employer of a worker in retail employment for the recovery from the worker of an amount in respect of a cash shortage or stock deficiency[23] may not be instituted by the employer after the end of the period referred to in head (B) above, unless he has within that period duly made a demand for payment in respect of that amount[24].

1 As to the meaning of 'employer' see PARA 2.

2 As to the meaning of 'worker' see PARA 5.

3 As to the meaning of 'retail employment' see PARA 257 note 3.

4 As to the meaning of references to an employer receiving a payment from a worker employed by him see PARA 255 note 10; and as to the meaning of references to a payment received from a worker in retail employment on account of a cash shortage or stock deficiency see PARA 257 note 7. As to the meaning of 'cash shortage' see PARA 257 note 5; and as to the meaning of 'stock deficiency' see PARA 257 note 6.

5 Nothing in the Employment Rights Act 1996 s 20 or in s 21 (see also the text and notes 17–22) applies to any payment falling within s 20(1) which is made on or after the day on which any such worker's final instalment of wages is paid, but, even if the requirements of s 15 (see PARA 255) would otherwise be satisfied with respect to it, his employer is not to be treated as receiving any such payment in accordance with s 15 if the payment was first required to be made after the end of the period referred to in s 20(3)(b) (see head (b)(ii) in the text): s 22(3). As to the meaning of 'final instalment of wages' see PARA 257 note 11.

6 Ie in accordance with the Employment Rights Act 1996 s 15 (see PARA 255): see s 20(1).

7 See the Employment Rights Act 1996 s 20(1).

8 As to the meaning of 'writing' see PARA 2 note 8.

9 Employment Rights Act 1996 s 20(1)(a).

10 Employment Rights Act 1996 s 20(1)(b). Head (2) in the text refers to a demand for payment made in accordance with s 20(2)–(5) (see the text and notes 11–16, 23–24): see s 20(1)(b).

11 Employment Rights Act 1996 s 20(2)(a).

12 Employment Rights Act 1996 s 20(2)(b). For these purposes, a demand for payment is to be treated as made by the employer on one of the worker's pay days if it is given to the worker, or posted to or left at his last known address:
    (1)   on that pay day (s 20(4)(a); or
    (2)   in the case of a pay day which is not a working day of the employer's business, on the first such working day following that pay day (s 20(4)(b)).
As to the meaning of 'pay day' see PARA 257 note 9.

13 See the Employment Rights Act 1996 s 20(3).

14 Ie in pursuance of the Employment Rights Act 1996 s 20(1)(a) (see head (1) in the text): see s 20(3)(a).

15 Employment Rights Act 1996 s 20(3)(a).

16 Employment Rights Act 1996 s 20(3)(b).

17 Ie in accordance with the Employment Rights Act 1996 s 20 (see the text and notes 1–16): see s 21(1). Once an amount has been required to be paid by means of a demand for payment made in accordance with s 20 on any pay day, that amount is not to be taken into account under s 21(1) as it applies to any subsequent pay day, even if the employer is obliged to make further requests for it to be paid: s 21(2).

18 See the Employment Rights Act 1996 s 21(1).

19 As to the meaning of 'gross amount' see PARA 255 note 15.

20 Employment Rights Act 1996 s 21(1)(a).

21 Ie falling within the Employment Rights Act 1996 s 18(1) (see PARA 257): see s 21(1)(b).

22 Employment Rights Act 1996 s 21(1)(b).

23 As to the meaning of references to the recovery from a worker of an amount in respect of a cash shortage or stock deficiency see PARA 257 note 7.

24 Employment Rights Act 1996 s 20(5). The text refers to payment in respect of the amount made in accordance with s 20: see s 20(5).

(iii) Remedies

259. Complaint to employment tribunal. A worker[1] may present a complaint to an employment tribunal[2] that his employer[3]:

(1)   has made a deduction from his wages[4] in contravention of the statutory restrictions[5];

(2)   has received from him a payment[6] in contravention of the restrictions[7];

(3)   has recovered from his wages on account of any cash shortages or stock deficiencies[8] an amount or aggregate amount exceeding the limit applying to the deduction or deductions so made[9]; or

(4)   has received from him, in pursuance of one or more demands for payment made on a particular pay day[10], a payment or payments of an amount or aggregate amount exceeding the limit applying to the demand or demands so made[11].

An employment tribunal must not consider such a complaint, however, unless it is presented before the end of the period of three months beginning with[12]:

(a)   in the case of a complaint relating to a deduction by the employer, the date of payment of the wages from which the deduction was made[13]; or

(b)   in the case of a complaint relating to a payment received by the employer, the date when the payment was received[14].

Where the employment tribunal is satisfied that it was not reasonably practicable for such a complaint to be presented before the end of the relevant period of three months, the tribunal may consider the complaint if it is presented within such further period as the tribunal considers reasonable[15].

The provision made for such a complaint does not affect the jurisdiction of an employment tribunal to consider a reference made pursuant to an alleged failure by an employer to provide the required particulars of employment (including an itemised pay statement)[16] in relation to any deduction from the wages of a worker[17].

1   As to the meaning of 'worker' see PARA 5.

2   See the Employment Rights Act 1996 s 23(1) (ss 23(1), (2), (4), 26 amended by the Employment Rights (Dispute Resolution) Act 1998 s 1(2)(a)). As to employment tribunals see PARA 1399 et seq; and as to the procedure on a complaint made to an employment tribunal see PARA 1453 et seq. As to the relief available from an employment tribunal on a complaint under the Employment Rights Act 1996 s 23 see PARA 260. The Employment Act 2002 also applies to proceedings before an employment tribunal relating to a claim by an employee under the Employment Rights Act 1996 s 23: see the Employment Act 2002 s 38, Sch 5 (employer in breach of duty to give written statement of initial employment particulars or of particulars of change); and PARA 127. There is a requirement also for early ACAS conciliation to be tried in order to promote a settlement before tribunal proceedings are instituted on a complaint under the Employment Rights Act 1996 s 23: see the Employment Tribunals Act 1996 s 18(1)(b); and PARA 152 note 1. As to the constitution and powers of ACAS see PARA 1213 et seq.

3   As to the meaning of 'employer' see PARA 2.

4   As to the meaning of 'wages' see PARA 254.

5   Employment Rights Act 1996 s 23(1)(a). Head (1) in the text refers to a deduction made in contravention of s 13 (see PARA 255) including a deduction made in contravention of s 13 as it applies by virtue of s 18(2) (see PARA 257): see s 23(1)(a). However, no complaint may be presented under s 23 in respect of any deduction made in contravention of the Trade Union and Labour Relations (Consolidation) Act 1992 s 86 (deduction of political fund contribution where certificate of exemption or objection has been given: see PARA 989): Employment Rights Act 1996 s 23(5) (added by the Employment Rights (Dispute Resolution) Act 1998 Sch 1 para 18). An officer acting for the purposes of the National Minimum Wage Act 1998 may present a complaint under head (1) in the text where a notice of underpayment served under that Act has not been complied with: see PARA 246.

6   As to the meaning of references to an employer receiving a payment from a worker employed by him see PARA 255 note 10; and as to the meaning of references to a payment received from a worker in retail employment on account of a cash shortage or stock deficiency see PARA 257 note 7.

7   Employment Rights Act 1996 s 23(1)(b). Head (2) in the text refers to a deduction made in contravention of s 15 (see PARA 255) including a payment received in contravention of s 15 as it applies by virtue of s 20(1) (see PARA 258): see s 23(1)(b).

8   Ie by means of one or more deductions falling within the Employment Rights Act 1996 s 18(1) (see PARA 257): see s 23(1)(c). As to the meaning of references to the recovery of an amount see PARA 257 note 7.

9   Employment Rights Act 1996 s 23(1)(c). Head (3) in the text refers to the limit applying to the deduction or deductions under s 18(1) (see PARA 257): see s 23(1)(c).

10 Ie in accordance with the Employment Rights Act 1996 s 20 (see PARA 258): see s 23(1)(d). As to the meaning of 'pay day' see PARA 257 note 9.

11 Employment Rights Act 1996 s 23(1)(d). Head (4) in the text refers to the limit applying to the demand or demands under s 21(1) (see PARA 258): see s 23(1)(d).

12 See the Employment Rights Act 1996 s 23(2) (as amended: see note 2). The provision made by s 23(2) is subject to s 23(4) (see the text and note 15): see s 23(2) (as so amended). For the purposes of s 23(2), s 207A(3) (extension because mediation in certain European cross-border disputes starts before the time limit expires: see PARA 1454) and s 207B (extension of time limits to facilitate conciliation before institution of proceedings: see PARA 1455) apply: s 23(3A) (added by SI 2011/1133; and amended by the Enterprise and Regulatory Reform Act 2013 s 8, Sch 2 paras 15, 17). As to time limits generally see PARA 1453.

13 Employment Rights Act 1996 s 23(2)(a). Where a complaint is brought under s 23 in respect of a series of deductions, the references in s 23(2) to the deduction are references to the last deduction in the series: see s 23(3)(a). Where a complaint relates to non-payment of remuneration, the three-month period flows from when it was due to be paid under the contract: *Group 4 Nightspeed Ltd v Gilbert* [1997] IRLR 398, EAT. The three-month period relates to the presentation of the complaint; it does not mean that a tribunal may only award three months' back deductions: *Reid v Camphill Engravers* [1990] ICR 435, [1990] IRLR 268, EAT. As to the correct approach to applying the Employment Rights Act 1996 s 23 see further *Taylorplan Services Ltd v Jackson* [1996] IRLR 184, EAT.

14 Employment Rights Act 1996 s 23(2)(b). Where a complaint is brought under s 23 in respect of a series of payments, or a number of payments falling within s 23(1)(d) (see head (4) in the text) and made in pursuance of demands for payments subject to the same limit under s 21(1) (see PARA 258) but received by the employer on different dates, the references in s 23(2) to the payment are references to the last payment in the series, or to the last of the payments so received: see s 23(3)(a), (b).

15 Employment Rights Act 1996 s 23(4) (as amended: see note 2).

16 Ie a reference under the Employment Rights Act 1996 s 11 (see PARA 125): see s 26 (as amended: see note 2).

17 See the Employment Rights Act 1996 s 26 (as amended: see note 2). The aggregate of any amounts ordered by an employment tribunal to be paid under s 12(4) (see PARA 126) and under s 24 (see PARA 260), whether on the same or different occasions, in respect of a particular deduction may not, however, exceed the amount of the deduction: see s 26 (as so amended).

    The existence of the statutory remedies does not remove the right of a party to a contract of employment to bring common law proceedings in the courts for any moneys due under the contract where liability to pay those moneys is denied by the other party: *Rickard v PB Glass Supplies Ltd* [1990] ICR 150, CA.

260.   Relief available from employment tribunal.

Where an employment tribunal[1] finds that a worker's complaint relating to unauthorised deductions by, or payments to, an employer[2] is well-founded, it must make a declaration to that effect[3]; and it must:

(1)   in the case of a complaint relating to unauthorised deductions by an employer[4], order the employer to pay to the worker the amount of any deduction unduly made[5]; and

(2)   in the case of a complaint relating to unauthorised payments to an employer[6], order the employer to repay to the worker the amount of any payment unduly received[7]; and

(3)　in the case of a complaint relating to unauthorised deductions from wages of workers in retail employment[8], order the employer to pay any amount recovered from him in excess of the limit so allowed[9];

(4)　in the case of a complaint relating to unauthorised payments by workers in retail employment[10], order the employer to repay to the worker any amount received from him in excess of the limit so allowed[11].

Where, in the case of any complaint under head (1) or head (2) above, a tribunal finds that, although neither of the statutory conditions[12] was satisfied with respect to the whole amount of a deduction or payment, one of those conditions was satisfied with respect to any lesser amount, the amount of the deduction or payment is to be treated[13] as reduced by the amount with respect to which that condition was satisfied[14].

An employer may not be ordered under any of heads (1) to (4) above to pay or repay to a worker any amount in respect of a deduction or payment or in respect of any combination of deductions or payments, in so far as it appears to the tribunal that he has already paid or repaid any such amount to the worker[15].

Where a tribunal has ordered an employer under any of heads (1) to (4) above to pay or repay to a worker any amount in respect of a particular deduction or payment that was the subject of a complaint[16], the amount which the employer is entitled to recover, by whatever means, in respect of the matter in relation to which the deduction or payment was originally made or received is to be treated as reduced by that amount[17]. Where a tribunal has ordered[18] an employer to pay or repay to a worker in retail employment any amount in respect of any combination of deductions or payments falling within head (3) or head (4) above, the aggregate amount which the employer is entitled to recover, by whatever means, in respect of the cash shortages[19] or stock deficiencies[20] in respect of which the deductions or payments were originally made or required to be made is to be treated as reduced by that amount[21].

1　As to employment tribunals see PARA 1399 et seq; and as to the procedure on a complaint made to an employment tribunal see PARA 1453 et seq.

2　Ie a complaint under the Employment Rights Act 1996 s 23 (see PARA 259): see s 24(1) (s 24(1) renumbered, s 24(2) added, by the Employment Act 2008 s 7(1)). As to the meaning of 'employer' see PARA 2. As to the meaning of 'worker' see PARA 5. As to the meaning of references to an employer receiving a payment from a worker employed by him see PARA 255 note 10; and as to the meaning of references to a payment received from a worker in retail employment on account of a cash shortage or stock deficiency see PARA 257 note 7.

3　See the Employment Rights Act 1996 s 24(1) (as renumbered: see note 2). Where a tribunal makes a declaration under s 24(1), it may order the employer to pay to the worker (in addition to any amount ordered to be paid under a 24(1)) such amount as the tribunal considers appropriate in all the circumstances to compensate the worker for any financial loss sustained by him which is attributable to the matter complained of: s 24(2) (as added: see note 2).

4　Ie a complaint under the Employment Rights Act 1996 s 23(1)(a) (see PARA 259): see s 24(1)(a) (s 24(1) as renumbered: see note 2).

5　Employment Rights Act 1996 s 24(1)(a) (s 24(1) as renumbered: see note 2). Head (1) in the text refers to any deduction made in contravention of s 13 (see PARA 255): see s 24(1)(a) (as so renumbered).

6　Ie a complaint under the Employment Rights Act 1996 s 23(1)(b) (see PARA 259): see s 24(1)(b) (s 24(1) as renumbered: see note 2).

7　Employment Rights Act 1996 s 24(1)(b) (s 24(1) as renumbered: see note 2). Head (2) in the text refers to any payment made in contravention of s 15 (see PARA 255): see s 24(1)(b) (as so renumbered).

8　Ie a complaint under the Employment Rights Act 1996 s 23(1)(c) (see PARA 259): see s 24(1)(c) (s 24(1) as renumbered: see note 2). As to the meaning of 'retail employment' see PARA 257 note 3.

9　Employment Rights Act 1996 s 24(1)(c) (s 24(1) as renumbered: see note 2). Head (3) in the text refers to any amount recovered from the worker in excess of the limit mentioned in s 23(1)(c) (see PARA 259): see s 24(1)(c) (as so renumbered). As to the meaning of references to the recovery of an amount from a worker see PARA 257 note 7.

10 Ie a complaint under the Employment Rights Act 1996 s 23(1)(d) (see PARA 259): see s 24(1)(d) (s 24(1) as renumbered: see note 2).

11 Employment Rights Act 1996 s 24(1)(d) (s 24(1) as renumbered: see note 2). Head (4) in the text refers to any amount received from the worker in excess of the limit mentioned in s 23(1)(d) (see PARA 259): see s 24(1)(d) (as so renumbered).

12 Ie the conditions set out in the Employment Rights Act 1996 s 13(1)(a), (b) (see PARA 255) or in s 15(1)(a), (b) (see PARA 255), as the case may be: see s 25(1), (2).

13 Ie for the purposes of the Employment Rights Act 1996 s 24(1)(a) (see head (1) in the text) or s 24(1)(b) (see head (2) in the text), as the case may be: see s 25(1), (2).

14 See the Employment Rights 1996 s 25(1), (2).

15 Employment Rights 1996 s 25(3). Section 25(3) is to be applied broadly, covering an amount paid before the deduction, not just an amount repaid afterwards: *Robertson v Blackstone Franks Investment Management Ltd* [1998] IRLR 376, CA (advance of commission set off against subsequent non-payment of commission).

16 Ie a particular deduction or payment falling within the Employment Rights Act 1996 s 23(1)(a)–(d) (see PARA 259): see s 25(4).

17 Employment Rights Act 1996 s 25(4). The effect of s 25(4) (and s 25(5) in relation to payments: see the text and notes 18–21) is that, if an employer makes an illegal deduction (or receives an illegal payment) and the tribunal orders repayment of that amount, the employer loses all right to it and may not seek to recover it by a common law claim: *Potter v Hunt Contracts Ltd* [1992] ICR 337, [1992] IRLR 108, EAT.

18 Ie under the Employment Rights Act 1996 s 24: see s 25(5).

19 As to the meaning of 'cash shortage' see PARA 257 note 5.

20 As to the meaning of 'stock deficiency' see PARA 257 note 6.

21 Employment Rights Act 1996 s 25(5). As to the overlapping remedy under s 12(4) and the overall limit applying to amounts which the tribunal may order to be paid see PARA 126. As to procedure on a complaint to an employment tribunal see PARA 1453 et seq.

(6) GUARANTEE PAYMENTS

261. Right to a guarantee payment. Where, throughout a day[1], during any part of which an employee would normally be required to work in accordance with his contract of employment[2], he is not provided with work by his employer[3] by reason of[4]:

(1)   a diminution in the requirements of the employer's business[5] for work of the kind which the employee is employed to do[6]; or

(2)   any other occurrence[7] affecting the normal working of the employer's business in relation to work of the kind which the employee is employed to do[8],

he is entitled to be paid by his employer an amount in respect of that day[9]. For the purposes of the Employment Rights Act 1996, a payment to which an employee is so entitled is referred to as a 'guarantee payment'[10].

A right to a guarantee payment does not, however, affect any right of an employee in relation to remuneration under his contract of employment ('contractual remuneration')[11]. Any contractual remuneration paid to an employee in respect of a workless day[12] goes towards discharging any liability of the employer to pay a guarantee payment in respect of that day; and, conversely, any guarantee payment paid in respect of a day goes towards discharging any liability of the employer to pay contractual remuneration in respect of that day[13].

1   For the purposes of the Employment Rights Act 1996 Pt III (ss 28–35) (guarantee payments: see also PARAS 262–266), 'day' means the period of 24 hours from midnight to midnight (s 28(4)); and, where a period of employment begun on any day extends, or would normally extend, over midnight into the following day, then:

(1)　if the employment before midnight is, or would normally be, of longer duration than that after midnight, the period of employment is to be treated as falling wholly on the first day (s 28(5)(a)); and

(2)　in any other case, the period of employment is to be treated as falling wholly on the second day (s 28(5)(b)).

As to the meaning of 'employment' see PARA 2. The Secretary of State may by order provide that, in relation to any description of employees, the provisions of s 28(4), (5), s 30 (see PARA 263), s 31(3)–(5) (as originally enacted or as varied under s 31(7)) (see PARA 264) and s 32 (see the text and notes 11–13) and, so far as they apply for the purposes of those provisions, Pt XIV Ch II (ss 220–229) (calculation of a week's pay: see PARA 143 et seq) and s 234 (normal working hours: see PARA 142) are to have effect subject to such modifications and adaptations as may be prescribed by the order: s 33. As to the meaning of 'employee' see PARA 2. As to the Secretary of State see PARA 5 note 21. As to the making of orders under the Employment Rights Act 1996 generally see PARA 162. At the date at which this volume states the law, no such order had been made under s 33.

2　As to the meaning of 'contract of employment' see PARA 2. If there is no contract of employment (eg in the case of a self-employed casual worker), there is no entitlement to a guarantee payment: *Mailway (Southern) Ltd v Willsher* [1978] ICR 511, [1978] IRLR 322, EAT; distinguished in *Miller v Harry Thornton (Lollies) Ltd* [1978] IRLR 430.

3　As to the meaning of 'employer' see PARA 2. For the purposes of the Employment Rights Act 1996 Pt III (guarantee payments: see also PARAS 262–266), a day falling within s 35(1) is referred to as a 'workless day'; and 'workless period' has a corresponding meaning: see s 28(3). A workless day will not include a holiday, a day of sickness or lack of voluntary overtime: *York and Reynolds v Colledge Hosiery Co Ltd* [1978] IRLR 53. The contrast which the Employment Rights Act 1996 s 28 imports is between the state of affairs as it actually is (ie where, *ex hypothesi*, the employee is not being required to work) and the state of affairs as it would be but for the (abnormal) non-provision of work for him to do: *Abercrombie v Aga Rangemaster Ltd* [2013] EWCA Civ 1148, [2014] 1 All ER 1101, [2014] ICR 209, [2013] IRLR 953 (agreement to five-day working had always been intended as a temporary arrangement but it had remained the norm and, in so far as work was not provided on Fridays, they were workless days within the meaning of the Employment Rights Act 1996 Pt III in respect of which employees were entitled to guarantee payments).

4　See the Employment Rights Act 1996 s 28(1).

5　As to the meaning of 'business' see PARA 135 note 4.

6　Employment Rights Act 1996 s 28(1)(a). As to the meaning of 'employed' see PARA 2.

7　'Occurrence' does not include a voluntary closure by the employer: *North v Pavleigh Ltd, Skeet v Carr Mills Clothing Co Ltd* [1977] IRLR 461.

8　Employment Rights Act 1996 s 28(1)(b).

9　See the Employment Rights Act 1996 s 28(1).

10　See the Employment Rights Act 1996 s 28(2). Accordingly, except in so far as the context otherwise requires, 'guarantee payment' has the meaning given by s 28: see s 235(1). No guarantee payment is payable, however, to an employee in whose case there are no normal working hours on the day in question: see s 30(1); and PARA 263. If an employee's contract of employment has been lawfully varied to reduce the number of days per week worked, he cannot claim a guarantee payment for the missing days: *Clemens v Peter Richards Ltd (t/a John Bryan)* [1977] IRLR 332; *Daley v Strathclyde Regional Council* [1977] IRLR 414. See, however, the Employment Rights Act 1996 s 31(6); and PARA 264. As to employees excluded from the right to a guarantee payment see PARAS 166–168, 262.

Any amount owed by an employer to an employee in respect of a guarantee payment is treated as arrears of remuneration or pay for the purposes of counting as a preferential debt (see PARA 627), or as an amount which may be claimed from the Secretary of State in the event of the employer's insolvency (see PARA 628). As to the National Insurance Fund see WELFARE BENEFITS AND STATE PENSIONS vol 104 (2014) PARA 15.

11　Employment Rights Act 1996 s 32(1). See also note 1.

12　For these purposes, contractual remuneration is to be treated as paid in respect of a workless day:

(1)　where it is expressed to be calculated or payable by reference to that day or any part of that day, to the extent that it is so expressed (Employment Rights Act 1996 s 32(3)(a)); and

(2)　in any other case, to the extent that it represents guaranteed remuneration, rather than remuneration for work actually done, and is referable to that day when apportioned rateably between that day and any other workless period falling within the period in respect of which the remuneration is paid (s 32(3))(b)).

See also note 1.
13 Employment Rights Act 1996 s 32(2). See also note 1. Thus where the employee has received contractual payments up to the specified number of days in the three-month period under s 31 (see PARA 264), there is no statutory entitlement to any further payment: *Cartwright v G Clancey Ltd* [1983] ICR 552, [1983] IRLR 355, EAT.

262. General exclusions from right to guarantee payment. An employee[1] is not entitled to a guarantee payment[2]:

(1)   unless he has been continuously employed[3] for a period of not less than one month ending with the day[4] before that in respect of which the guarantee payment is claimed[5];

(2)   in respect of a workless day[6]: (a) if the failure to provide him with work for that day occurs in consequence of a strike, lockout or other industrial action[7] involving any employee of his employer[8] or of an associated employer[9]; or (b) if his employer has offered to provide alternative work for that day which is suitable in all the circumstances (whether or not it is work which the employee is under his contract employed to perform)[10], and if the employee has unreasonably refused that offer[11]; or

(3)   if he does not comply with reasonable requirements imposed by his employer with a view to ensuring that his services are available[12].

1   As to the meaning of 'employee' see PARA 2.
2   As to the meaning of 'guarantee payment' see PARA 261.
3   As to the meaning of 'employed' see PARA 2. As to continuity of employment see PARAS 130 et seq, 861 et seq.
4   As to the meaning of 'day' for these purposes see PARA 261 note 1.
5   See the Employment Rights Act 1996 s 29(1).
6   As to the meaning of 'workless day' for these purposes see PARA 261 note 3.
7   In the Employment Protection (Consolidation) Act 1978 s 13(3) (as originally enacted) the wording was 'in consequence of a trade dispute'; but the Employment Act 1982 materially narrowed the definition of 'trade dispute' for the purposes of the law on industrial disputes (see PARA 1360). It is apprehended that the phrase 'strike, lockout or other industrial action', which is wider than 'trade dispute', will be construed in the like manner as in the Trade Union and Labour Relations (Consolidation) Act 1992 s 238 (dismissal in connection with a lockout, strike or other industrial action: see PARA 1351) where it is similarly undefined.
8   As to the meaning of 'employer' see PARA 2.
9   See the Employment Rights Act 1996 s 29(3). As to the meaning of 'associated employer' see PARA 3. The industrial action must affect the employer's own employees, or those of an associated employer, but this could come about through sympathy action with outside action, e g by not crossing picket lines when required by the employer to do so: *Garvey v J and J Maybank (Oldham) Ltd* [1979] IRLR 408. The industrial action need not be the sole cause of the lay-off, provided that it is the immediate cause: *Thomson v Priest (Lindley) Ltd* [1978] IRLR 99.
10 Employment Rights Act 1996 s 29(4)(a). A wide variety of work may be suitable if it is only temporary, particularly if the rearrangement is to meet an emergency: *Purdy v Willowbrook International Ltd* [1977] IRLR 388.
11 Employment Rights Act 1996 s 29(4)(b).
12 See the Employment Rights Act 1996 s 29(5); and see *Meadows v Faithful Overalls Ltd* [1977] IRLR 330.

263. Calculation of guarantee payment. The amount of a guarantee payment[1] payable to an employee[2] in respect of any day[3] is[4] the sum produced by multiplying the number of normal working hours[5] on that day by the guaranteed hourly rate[6].

The guaranteed hourly rate, in relation to an employee, is the amount of one week's pay[7] divided by the number of normal working hours in a week for that employee when employed under the contract of employment[8] in force on the day in respect of which the guarantee payment is payable[9]. However, where the number of normal working hours differs from week to week or over a longer period, the amount of one week's pay is divided instead by[10]:

(1) the average number of normal working hours calculated by dividing by 12 the total number of the employee's normal working hours during the period of 12 weeks ending with the last complete week before the day in respect of which the guarantee payment is payable[11]; or

(2) where the employee has not been employed for a sufficient period to enable the calculation to be made under head (1) above, a number which fairly represents the number of normal working hours in a week having regard to such of the following considerations as are appropriate in the circumstances[12], that is to say: (a) the average number of normal working hours in a week which the employee could expect in accordance with the terms of his contract[13]; and (b) the average number of normal working hours of other employees engaged in relevant comparable employment with the same employer[14].

1   As to the meaning of 'guarantee payment' see PARA 261.
2   As to the meaning of 'employee' see PARA 2.
3   As to the meaning of 'day' for these purposes see PARA 261 note 1.
4   Ie subject to the limits set by the Employment Rights Act 1996 s 31 (see PARA 264): see s 30(1).
5   As to the computation of normal working hours see PARA 142.
6   See the Employment Rights Act 1996 s 30(1). No guarantee payment is payable, accordingly, to an employee in whose case there are no normal working hours on the day in question: see s 30(1). As to the power to vary the provisions of s 30 see PARA 261 note 1.
7   As to the computation of a week's pay see PARA 143; and as to the calculation date for these purposes see the Employment Rights Act 1996 s 225(1); and PARA 146. As to the meaning of 'week' see PARA 126 note 13.
8   As to the meanings of 'contract of employment' and 'employed' see PARA 2.
9   Employment Rights Act 1996 s 30(2). If in any case an employee's contract has been varied, or if a new contract has been entered into, in connection with a period of short-time working, the provisions of s 30(2), (3) (see also the text and notes 10–12) have effect as if for the reference to the day in respect of which the guarantee payment is payable there were substituted a reference to the last day on which the original contract was in force: s 30(5).
10 See the Employment Rights Act 1996 s 30(3).
11 See the Employment Rights Act 1996 s 30(3)(a). See also note 9.
12 See the Employment Rights Act 1996 s 30(3)(b).
13 Employment Rights Act 1996 s 30(4)(a).
14 Employment Rights Act 1996 s 30(4)(b). As to the meanings of 'employer' and employment' see PARA 2.

264. Limits on amount of and entitlement to guarantee payment. The amount of a guarantee payment[1] payable to an employee[2] in respect of any day[3] is not to exceed the specified limit[4].

An employee is not entitled to guarantee payments in respect of more than the specified number of days in any period of three months[5]; and, for these purposes, the specified number of days is:

(1) the number of days, not exceeding five, on which the employee normally works in a week[6] under the contract of employment[7] in force on the day in respect of which the guarantee payment is claimed[8]; but

(2) where that number of days varies from week to week or over a longer period: (a) the average number of such days, not exceeding five, calculated by dividing by 12 the total number of such days during the period of 12 weeks ending with the last complete week before the day in respect of which the guarantee payment is claimed, and rounding up the resulting figure to the next whole number[9]; or (b) where the employee

has not been employed[10] for a sufficient period to enable the calculation
to be made under head (a) above, a number which fairly represents the
number of the employee's normal working days in a week, not
exceeding five, having regard to such of the following considerations as
are appropriate in the circumstances[11], that is to say: (i) the average
number of normal working days in a week which the employee could
expect in accordance with the terms of his contract[12]; and (ii) the
average number of such days of other employees engaged in relevant
comparable employment with the same employer[13].

1   As to the meaning of 'guarantee payment' see PARA 261.
2   As to the meaning of 'employee' see PARA 2.
3   As to the meaning of 'day' for these purposes see PARA 261 note 1.
4   Employment Rights Act 1996 s 31(1) (amended by SI 2014/382). At the date at which this
    volume states the law, the limit is £25.00: see the Employment Rights Act 1996 s 31(1) (as so
    amended). As to the Secretary of State's duty to increase or decrease the amount in s 31(1) in
    line with the retail prices index see the Employment Relations Act 1999 s 34(1)(a), (2), (3); and
    PARA 160.
5   Employment Rights Act 1996 s 31(2). As to the position where contractual remuneration has
    been paid see PARA 261. The Secretary of State may by order vary the length of the period
    specified in s 31(2) or a limit specified in s 31(3) or (4) (see the text and notes 6–11): s 31(7)
    (substituted by the Employment Relations Act 1999 s 35). As to the making of orders under the
    Employment Rights Act 1996 generally see PARA 162. At the date at which this volume states
    the law, no such order had been made under s 31.
6   As to the meaning of 'week' see PARA 126 note 13.
7   As to the meaning of 'contract of employment' see PARA 2.
8   Employment Rights Act 1996 s 31(3). If in any case an employee's contract has been varied, or
    if a new contract has been entered into, in connection with a period of short-time working,
    s 31(3) and s 31(4) (see the text and notes 9–11) have effect as if for the references to the day in
    respect of which the guarantee payment is claimed there were substituted references to the last
    day on which the original contract was in force: s 31(6). As to the Secretary of State's power to
    vary the provisions of s 31(3) and of s 31(4), (5) (see the text and notes 9–13), as originally
    enacted or as varied under s 31(7) (see note 5), see PARA 261 note 1.
9   Employment Rights Act 1996 s 31(4)(a). See also notes 5, 8.
10 As to the meaning of 'employed' see PARA 2.
11 Employment Rights Act 1996 s 31(4)(b). See also notes 5, 8.
12 Employment Rights Act 1996 s 31(5)(a). See also notes 5, 8.
13 Employment Rights Act 1996 s 31(5)(b). See also notes 5, 8. As to the meanings of
    'employment' and 'employer' see PARA 2.

265. Complaint to employment tribunal relating to guarantee payments. An
employee[1] may present a complaint to an employment tribunal[2] that his
employer[3] has failed to pay the whole or any part of a guarantee payment[4] to
which the employee is entitled[5].

An employment tribunal must not consider a complaint relating to a
guarantee payment in respect of any day[6], however, unless the complaint is
presented to it[7]:

(1)   before the end of the period of three months beginning with that day[8];
       or

(2)   within such further period as it considers reasonable in a case where it is
       satisfied that it was not reasonably practicable for the complaint to be
       presented before the end of that period of three months[9].

Where an employment tribunal finds such a complaint well-founded, the
tribunal must order the employer to pay to the employee the amount of
guarantee payment which it finds is due to him[10].

1   As to the meaning of 'employee' see PARA 2.

2   As to employment tribunals see PARA 1399 et seq; and as to the procedure on a complaint made to an employment tribunal see PARA 1453 et seq.
3   As to the meaning of 'employer' see PARA 2.
4   As to the meaning of 'guarantee payment' see PARA 261.
5   Employment Rights Act 1996 s 34(1) (s 34(1), (2), (3) amended by the Employment Rights (Dispute Resolution) Act 1998 s 1(2)(a)). The remedy of an employee for infringement of the right to a guarantee payment is by way of complaint to an employment tribunal and not otherwise: see the Employment Rights Act 1996 s 205(1); and PARA 1406. There is a requirement also for early ACAS conciliation to be tried in order to promote a settlement before tribunal proceedings are instituted on a complaint under the Employment Rights Act 1996 s 34: see the Employment Tribunals Act 1996 s 18(1)(b); and PARA 152 note 1. As to the constitution and powers of ACAS see PARA 1213 et seq.
6   As to the meaning of 'day' for these purposes see PARA 261 note 1.
7   See the Employment Rights Act 1996 s 34(2) (as amended: see note 5).
8   Employment Rights Act 1996 s 34(2)(a). For the purposes of s 34(2)(a), s 207A(3) (extension because mediation in certain European cross-border disputes starts before the time limit expires: see PARA 1454) and s 207B (extension of time limits to facilitate conciliation before institution of proceedings: see PARA 1455) apply: s 34(2A) (added by SI 2011/1133; and amended by the Enterprise and Regulatory Reform Act 2013 s 8, Sch 2 paras 15, 18). As to time limits generally see PARA 1453.
9   Employment Rights Act 1996 s 34(2)(b). See *Abercrombie v Aga Rangemaster Ltd* [2013] EWCA Civ 1148, [2014] 1 All ER 1101, [2014] ICR 209, [2013] IRLR 953 (claimants permitted to re-formulate their claim under the Employment Rights Act 1996 s 34 where proceedings commenced in respect of a claim which the tribunal decided in due course that it had no jurisdiction to determine and where a simple amendment would remove that difficulty).
10 Employment Rights Act 1996 s 34(3) (as amended: see note 5). As to the calculation of guarantee payments see PARA 263.

266.   Power to make exemption orders relating to guarantee payments.
Where:
> (1)   at any time there is in force a collective agreement[1], under which employees[2] to whom the agreement relates have a right to guaranteed remuneration[3]; and
> (2)   on the application of all the parties to the agreement, the Secretary of State[4], having regard to the provisions of the agreement, is satisfied that the statutory guarantee for payments to be made in respect of a workless day[5] should not apply to those employees[6],

he may make an order[7] excluding them from the operation of that statutory guarantee[8].

The Secretary of State must not, however, make such an order in respect of an agreement unless:
> (a)   the agreement provides for procedures to be followed, whether by arbitration or otherwise, in cases where an employee claims that his employer[9] has failed to pay the whole or any part of any guaranteed remuneration to which the employee is entitled under the agreement, and that those procedures include a right to arbitration or adjudication by an independent referee or body in cases where, by reason of an equality of votes or otherwise, a decision cannot otherwise be reached[10]; or
> (b)   the agreement indicates that an employee to whom the agreement relates may present a complaint[11] to an employment tribunal that his employer has failed to pay the whole or any part of any guaranteed remuneration to which the employee is entitled under the agreement[12].

1   As to the meaning of 'collective agreement' see PARA 119 note 21.
2   As to the meaning of 'employee' see PARA 2.
3   Employment Rights Act 1996 s 35(1)(a).

The text of s 35(1)(a) applies also to an agricultural wages order which is at any time in force but the reference that is made to the Agricultural Wages Act 1948 s 3 (power of Agricultural Wages Board to fix wages, holidays and other terms and conditions: see AGRICULTURAL PRODUCTION AND MARKETING vol 1 (2008) PARA 1231 et seq) in the definition of 'agricultural wages order' (see the Employment Rights Act 1996 s 35(2)(a)) has been repealed, along with most of the Agricultural Wages Act 1948 itself, as from a date to be appointed under the Enterprise and Regulatory Reform Act 2013 s 103(3), by s 72(4), Sch 20 para 2. That day has been appointed as 1 October 2013 in relation to England (see the Enterprise and Regulatory Reform Act 2013 (Commencement No 1, Transitional Provisions and Savings) Order 2013, SI 2013/1455, art 3(b), Sch 2 para 4 (art 3(b) amended by SI 2013/2271)), but such a day has not been appointed, at the date at which this volume states the law, in relation to Wales. As to the meanings of 'England' and 'Wales' see PARA 2 note 12.

4   The text of the Employment Rights Act 1996 s 35(1)(b) refers to the 'appropriate minister', which is defined for the purposes of s 35(1), in relation to a collective agreement or in relation to an order such as is referred to in s 35(2)(a), as meaning the Secretary of State: see s 35(3) (amended by the Enterprise and Regulatory Reform Act 2013 Sch 20 para 2; and by SI 2002/794). However, the reference to 'an order such as is referred to in [the Employment Rights Act 1996] s 35(2)(a)' falls: see note 3. As to the Secretary of State see PARA 5 note 21.

5   Ie the provisions of the Employment Rights Act 1996 s 28 (see PARA 261): see s 35(1)(b). As to the meaning of 'workless day' for these purposes see PARA 261 note 3.

6   Employment Rights Act 1996 s 35(1)(b).

7   Ie under the Employment Rights Act 1996 s 35: see s 35(1). As to the making of orders under the Employment Rights Act 1996 generally see PARA 162. An order under s 35 is not subject to annulment by Parliamentary resolution: see s 236(2)(b); and PARA 162. At the date at which this volume states the law, no such exemption orders had been made but, by virtue of s 241, Sch 2 para 2(1) (see PARA 162), the following orders have effect as if so made:

(1)   the Guarantee Payments (Exemption) (No 1) Order 1977, SI 1977/156 (Working Rule Agreement of the Civil Engineering Construction Conciliation Board for Great Britain);

(2)   the Guarantee Payments (Exemption) (No 2) Order 1977, SI 1977/157 (Working Rule Agreement for the Demolition and Dismantling Industry);

(3)   the Guarantee Payments (Exemption) (No 5) Order 1977, SI 1977/902 (National Conference (March 1974) Agreement of the Footwear Industry);

(4)   the Guarantee Payments (Exemption) (No 6) Order 1977, SI 1977/1096 (Working Rule Agreement of the National Joint Council for the Steeplejack and Lightning Conductor Engineering Industry);

(5)   the Guarantee Payments (Exemption) (No 7) Order 1977, SI 1977/1158 (National Agreements: (a) for Process and General Workers in the Papermaking and Boardmaking Industry; and (b) covering skilled craftsmen in that industry);

(6)   the Guarantee Payments (Exemption) (No 8) Order 1977, SI 1977/1322 (four agreements between Smiths Food Group (a division of Toms Food Ltd) and the Transport and General Workers' Union);

(7)   the Guarantee Payments (Exemption) (No 9) Order 1977, SI 1977/1349 (National Agreement between the Cut Sole Associates, British Leather Federation and the National Union of the Footwear, Leather and Allied Trades);

(8)   the Guarantee Payments (Exemption) (No 10) Order 1977, SI 1977/1522 (agreement between the Fibreboard Packing Case Employers' Association and the General and Municipal Workers' Union and the Society of Graphical and Allied Trades dated 14 October 1974);

(9)   the Guarantee Payments (Exemption) (No 11) Order 1977, SI 1977/1523 (agreement between Henry Wiggin & Co Ltd and the General and Municipal Workers' Union dated 30 October 1976; modified 4 July 1977);

(10)   the Guarantee Payments (Exemption) (No 12) Order 1977, SI 1977/1583 (agreements between the Refractory Users Federation and the General and Municipal Workers' Union, the Transport and General Workers' Union and the Union of Construction, Allied Trades and Technicians (Builders Section) and between the Refractory Users Federation and the Union of Construction, Allied Trades and Technicians (Builders Section));

(11)   the Guarantee Payments (Exemption) (No 13) Order 1977, SI 1977/1601 (agreement between the Multiwall Sack Manufacturers Employers' Association and the National Union of General and Municipal Workers, the Society of Graphical and Allied Trades and the Transport and General Workers' Union dated 29 March 1977);

(12) the Guarantee Payments (Exemption) (No 14) Order 1977, SI 1977/2032 (agreement as to short-time working or lay-off between Tudor Food Products and the General and Municipal Workers' Union);

(13) the Guarantee Payments (Exemption) (No 15) Order 1978, SI 1978/153 (agreement between the British Carton Association and the General and Municipal Workers' Union and the Society of Graphical and Allied Trades dated 30 July 1977);

(14) the Guarantee Payments (Exemption) (No 16) Order 1978, SI 1978/429 (agreement: (a) between Henry Wiggin & Co Ltd and the Electrical, Electronic and Telecommunications Union-Plumbing Trades Union dated 3 November 1977; (b) between Henry Wiggin & Co Ltd and the Amalgamated Union of Engineering Workers dated 14 November 1977);

(15) the Guarantee Payments (Exemption) (No 17) Order 1978, SI 1978/737 (Scheme of Conditions of Service of the National Joint Council for Workshops for the Blind);

(16) the Guarantee Payments (Exemption) (No 18) Order 1978, SI 1978/826 (Guaranteed Payments Agreements between the Employers' Federation of Card Clothing Manufacturers and: (a) the Card Dressers' Society; (b) the Amalgamated Society of Wiredrawers and Kindred Workers; and (c) the Card Setting Machine Tenters' Society);

(17) the Guarantee Payments (Exemption) (No 19) Order 1979, SI 1979/1403 (agreements of the National Joint Council for the Motor Vehicle Retail and Repair Industry as to pay and conditions and as to disputes);

(18) the Guarantee Payments (Exemption) (No 21) Order 1981, SI 1981/6 (Plant Hire Working Rule Agreement between the Contractors' Plant Association and the Transport and General Workers' Union (Construction and Crafts Section), the General and Municipal Workers' Union and the Union of Construction and Allied Trades and Technicians);

(19) the Guarantee Payments (Exemption) (No 23) Order 1987, SI 1987/1757 (National Agreements for the Wire and Wire Rope Industries);

(20) the Guarantee Payments (Exemption) (No 24) Order 1989, SI 1989/1326 (Substantive Agreement of the Joint Negotiating Council for Rowntree Mackintosh Confectionery Ltd);

(21) the Guarantee Payments (Exemption) (No 25) Order 1989, SI 1989/1575 (Working Rule Agreement of the Building and Allied Trades Joint Industrial Council dated 14 December 1988);

(22) the Guarantee Payments (Exemption) (No 26) Order 1989, SI 1989/2163 (Lay Off and Short-Time Working Scheme of Airflow Streamlines plc);

(23) the Guarantee Payments (Exemption) (No 27) Order 1990, SI 1990/927 (Lay Off and Short Time Agreement between G & G Kynoch plc and the Transport and General Workers' Union dated 12 January 1990);

(24) the Guarantee Payments (Exemption) (No 28) Order 1990, SI 1990/2330 (collective agreement between Bridon Ropes Ltd and the Transport and General Workers' Union, the General Municipal and Boilermakers' Union and the Wire Workers' Union dated 1 October 1990);

(25) the Guarantee Payments (Exemption) (No 30) Order 1996, SI 1996/2132 (collective agreement between the Building Employers Confederation and the National Federation of Roofing Contractors, and the Union of Construction, Allied Trades and Technicians, the Transport and General Workers Union and the General Municipal and Boilermakers' Union).

An order varying or revoking an earlier order under the Employment Rights Act 1996 s 35 may be made either in pursuance of an application by all or any of the parties to the agreement in question or in the absence of such an application: see s 35(6). The provision made by s 35(6) allows for an application to be made also by 'the [Agricultural Wages] Board which made the order in question', but the reference to such an order falls: see note 3.

8 See the Employment Rights Act 1996 s 35(1). The text refers to exclusion from the operation of s 28 (see PARA 261): see s 35(1).

9 As to the meaning of 'employer' see PARA 2.

10 Employment Rights Act 1996 s 35(4)(a).

11 Where an exemption order is in force in respect of such an agreement, an employment tribunal has jurisdiction over such a complaint as if it were a complaint falling within the Employment Rights Act 1996 s 34 (see PARA 265): s 35(5) (s 35(4)(b), (5) amended by the Employment Rights (Dispute Resolution) Act 1998 s 1(2)(a)). As to employment tribunals see PARA 1399 et seq; and as to the procedure on a complaint made to an employment tribunal see PARA 1453 et seq.

12 Employment Rights Act 1996 s 35(4)(b) (as amended: see note 11).

(7) WORKING TIME

(i) In general

267.   EU requirements concerning the organisation of working time. The purpose of the European Parliament and Council Directive of 4 November 2003 concerning certain aspects of the organisation of working time[1] is to lay down minimum safety and health requirements for the organisation of working time[2]; and it applies:

(1)   to minimum periods of daily rest, weekly rest and annual leave, to breaks and maximum weekly working time[3]; and

(2)   to certain aspects of night work, shift work and patterns of work[4].

Member states must take measures necessary to ensure that:

(a)   every worker is entitled to a minimum daily rest period[5] of 11 consecutive hours per 24-hour period[6];

(b)   where the working day is longer than six hours, every worker is entitled to a rest break, the details of which, including duration and the terms on which it is granted, must be laid down in collective agreements or agreements between the two sides of industry or, failing that, by national legislation[7];

(c)   per each seven-day period, every worker is entitled to a minimum uninterrupted rest period of 24 hours plus the 11 hours' daily rest referred to in head (a) above[8];

(d)   in keeping with the need to protect the safety and health of workers, the period of weekly working time is limited by means of laws, regulations or administrative provisions or by collective agreements or agreements between the two sides of industry[9], and the average working time for each seven-day period, including overtime, does not exceed 48 hours[10];

(e)   every worker is entitled to paid annual leave of at least four weeks in accordance with the conditions for entitlement to, and granting of, such leave laid down by national legislation and/or practice[11], and the minimum period of paid annual leave may not be replaced by an allowance in lieu, except where the employment relationship is terminated[12];

(f)   normal hours for night workers do not exceed an average of eight hours in any 24-hour period[13], and night workers whose work involves special hazards or heavy physical or mental strain do not work more than eight hours in any period of 24 hours during which they perform night work[14];

(g)   night workers are entitled to a free health assessment before their assignment and thereafter at regular intervals[15], and night workers suffering from health problems recognised as being connected with the fact that they perform night work are transferred whenever possible to day work to which they are suited[16];

(h)   an employer who regularly uses night workers brings this information to the attention of the competent authorities, if they so request[17];

(i)   night workers and shift workers have safety and health protection appropriate to the nature of their work[18], and appropriate protection and prevention services or facilities with regard to the safety and health of night workers and shift workers are equivalent to those applicable to other workers and are available at all times[19];

(j)   an employer who intends to organise work according to a certain pattern takes account of the general principle of adapting work to the worker, with a view, in particular, to alleviating monotonous work and work at a predetermined work-rate, depending on the type of activity, and of safety and health requirements, especially as regards breaks during working time[20],

but member states may derogate from the above in certain circumstances[21]. Subject to a requirement that adequate rest is taken[22], mobile workers[23] and workers on board a seagoing fishing vessel flying the flag of a member state are excepted from heads (a) to (c) and head (f) above[24]. The latter group is also excepted from head (d) above, but is subject to prescribed conditions regarding working hours, hours of rest and annual leave[25].

The special provision that is made for the purposes of protecting young people at work includes provision made in relation to working time, night work, rest periods, annual rest, and breaks[26].

1   Ie European Parliament and Council Directive (EC) 2003/88 of 4 November 2003 (OJ L299, 18.11.2003, p 9) concerning certain aspects of the organisation of working time (the 'Working Time Directive'), which entered into force on 2 August 2004 (see art 28) and codified the previous working time provisions contained in Council Directive (EC) 93/104 of 23 November 1993 (OJ L307, 13.12.93, p 18) concerning certain aspects of the organisation of working time (amended by European Parliament and Council Directive (EC) 2000/34 of 22 June 2000 (OJ L195, 1.8.2000, p 41) amending Council Directive (EC) 93/104 to cover sectors and activities excluded from that Directive). For the purpose of implementing Council Directive (EC) 93/104 of 23 November 1993 (OJ L307, 13.12.93, p 18), the Working Time Regulations 1998, SI 1998/1833 (see PARA 268 et seq) were made, and those regulations, which originally came into force on 1 October 1998 (see reg 1(1); and PARA 268 note 2), continue to apply for the purposes of European Parliament and Council Directive (EC) 2003/88 of 4 November 2003 (OJ L299, 18.11.2003, p 9). See also, specifically in relation to the organisation of working time for workers on the inland waterways, the Merchant Shipping (Working Time: Inland Waterways) Regulations 2003, SI 2003/3049 (cited in SHIPPING AND MARITIME LAW vol 94 (2008) PARA 625); and, specifically in relation to the organisation of working time for sea-fishermen, the Fishing Vessels (Working Time: Sea-fishermen) Regulations 2004, SI 2004/1713 (cited in SHIPPING AND MARITIME LAW vol 94 (2008) PARA 626). As to implementation see also *Gibson v East Riding of Yorkshire Council* [2000] ICR 890, [2000] IRLR 598, CA (employee not allowed to rely on the Working Time Directive to establish an entitlement to four weeks' paid annual leave in respect of the period during which the United Kingdom had failed to implement the Directive).

The Working Time Directive does not affect member states' right to apply or introduce laws, regulations or administrative provisions more favourable to the protection of the safety and health of workers or to facilitate or permit the application of collective agreements or agreements concluded between the two sides of industry (ie management and labour) which are more favourable to the protection of the safety and health of workers: Working Time Directive art 15. The Working Time Directive does not apply where other instruments of EU law contain more specific requirements relating to the organisation of working time concerning certain occupations or occupational services: art 14. Accordingly, see also:
   (1)   Council Directive (EC) 2000/79 of 27 November 2000 (OJ L302, 1.12.2000, p 56) concerning the European Agreement on the Organisation of Working Time of Mobile Workers in Civil Aviation concluded by the Association of European Airlines, the European Transport Workers' Federation, the European Cockpit Association, the European Regions Airline Association and the International Air Carrier Association (for the purpose of implementing which, the Civil Aviation (Working Time) Regulations 2004, SI 2004/756, were made: see AIR LAW vol 2 (2008) PARA 467 et seq);
   (2)   European Parliament and Council Directive (EC) 2002/15 of 11 March 2002 (OJ L80, 23.3.2002, p 35) concerning the organisation of the working time of persons performing mobile road transport activities (for the purpose of implementing which, the Road Transport (Working Time) Regulations 2005, SI 2005/639, were made: see ROAD TRAFFIC vol 90 (2011) PARA 1125 et seq); and
   (3)   Council Directive (EC) 2005/47 of 18 July 2005 (OJ L195, 27.7.2005, p 15) on the Agreement between the Community of European Railways (CER) and the European

Transport Workers' Federation (ETF) on certain aspects of the working conditions of mobile workers engaged in interoperable cross-border services in the railway sector (for the purpose of implementing which, the Cross-border Railway Services (Working Time) Regulations 2008, SI 2008/1660, were made: see RAILWAYS AND TRAMWAYS vol 86 (2013) PARAS 33, 328).

Consequently, the entitlement to paid annual leave guaranteed by the Working Time Directive (see head (e) in the text) is not available to office workers within the road transport sector: Case C-133/00 *Bowden v Tuffnells Parcels Express Ltd* [2001] All ER (EC) 865, [2001] IRLR 838, ECJ. As to other exceptions from the requirements of the Working Time Directive generally see also the text and notes 4, 21–25; and PARA 298.

2   Working Time Directive art 1(1). See also note 4. For these purposes, 'working time' means any period during which the worker is working, at the employer's disposal and carrying out his activity or duties, in accordance with national laws and/or practice: see art 2(1). This definition of 'working time' has been applied with some latitude by the CJEU, especially when 'on-call' time has been considered within the context of working time: see Case C-303/98 *Sindicato de Médicos de Asistencia Pública (SIMAP) v Conselleria de Sanidad y Consumo de la Generalidad Valenciana* [2001] All ER (EC) 609, [2001] ICR 1116, ECJ (time when doctors obliged to be present and available at health centre was 'working time' but only time linked to actual provision of primary care services was 'working time' for those periods during which they were available but not present); Case C-151/02 *Landeshauptstadt Kiel v Jaeger* [2004] All ER (EC) 604, [2004] ICR 1528, ECJ (periods spent by doctors on call, where they were required to be physically present in the hospital and were permitted to rest when their services were not required, was 'working time').

3   Working Time Directive art 1(2)(a).

4   Working Time Directive art 1(2)(b). For these purposes, 'shift work' means any method of organising work in shifts whereby workers succeed each other at the same work stations according to a certain pattern, including a rotating pattern, and which may be continuous or discontinuous, entailing the need for workers to work at different times over a given period of days or weeks: see art 2(5).

Without prejudice to art 14 (see note 1) and arts 17–19 (see the text and note 21), the Working Time Directive applies to all sectors of activity, both public and private, within the meaning of Council Directive (EC) 89/391 of 12 June 1989 (OJ L183, 29.6.89, p 1) on the introduction of measures to encourage improvements in the safety and health of workers at work (ie to all sectors of activity, both public and private (industrial, agricultural, commercial, administrative, service, educational, cultural, leisure, etc) but not where characteristics peculiar to certain specific public service activities (such as the armed forces or the police) or to certain specific activities in the civil protection services inevitably conflict with it: see art 2): see Working Time Directive art 1(3). The exceptions to the scope of the basic Working Time Directive thus adopted apply purely for the purpose of ensuring the proper operation of services essential for the protection of public health, safety and order in cases of exceptional gravity and scale that, by their nature, do not lend themselves to planning as regards the working time of teams of emergency workers (a civil protection service in the strict sense thus defined); the exceptions must be interpreted restrictively, accordingly: see Case C-303/98 *Sindicato de Médicos de Asistencia Pública (SIMAP) v Conselleria de Sanidad y Consumo de la Generalidad Valenciana* [2001] All ER (EC) 609, [2001] ICR 1116, ECJ (activity of doctors working in primary healthcare teams falls within the scope of the basic Working Time Directive); Joined Cases C-397/01 to C-403/01 *Pfeiffer v Deutsches Rotes Kreuz, Kreisverband Waldshut eV* [2005] ICR 1307, [2005] IRLR 137, ECJ (restriction did not apply to ambulance crews whose working time could be planned); Case C-52/04 *Personalrat der Feuerwehr Hamburg v Leiter der Feuerwehr Hamburg* [2005] ECR I-7111, ECJ (restriction does not apply to the activities of the fire service under normal circumstances, even when they are carried out by operational forces, even though the actions required may be inherently unforeseeable and liable to expose workers to certain safety and/or health risks); Case C-337/10 *Neidel v Stadt Frankfurt am Main* [2012] ICR 1201, [2012] IRLR 607, CJEU (public servant carrying out the activities of a fireman in normal circumstances not excluded).

The Working Time Directive does not apply, however, to seafarers as defined in the Agreement on the organisation of working time of seafarers concluded by the European Community Shipowners' Association (ECSA) and the Federation of Transport Workers' Unions in the European Union (FST) that is set out in Council Directive (EC) 1999/63 of 21 June 1999 (OJ L167, 2.7.99, p 33) (for the purpose of implementing which, the Merchant Shipping (Hours of Work) Regulations 2002, SI 2002/2125, were made: see SHIPPING AND MARITIME LAW vol 94 (2008) PARA 625): see Working Time Directive art 1(3); and see also PARA 297.

5   For these purposes, 'rest period' means any period which is not working time: see Working Time Directive art 2(2). See also *Russell v Transocean International Resources Ltd* [2011] UKSC 57, [2012] 2 All ER 166, [2012] ICR 185, [2012] IRLR 149 ('any period' includes every such period irrespective of where the worker is at that time and what he is doing, so long as it is a period when he is not working, such as any period when an oil rig worker is on field break onshore and free from all obligations to the employer (except that his contract remains in force), the requirement being that the time spent must constitute a 'rest period' of the requisite length); and PARA 293 note 3.

6   Working Time Directive art 3.

7   Working Time Directive art 4.

8   Working Time Directive art 5. If objective, technical or work organisation conditions so justify, a minimum rest period of 24 hours may be applied: see art 5. For the application of art 5, member states may lay down a reference period not exceeding 14 days: art 16(a).

9   Working Time Directive art 6(a).

10   Working Time Directive art 6(b). The obligation imposed by art 6(2) to restrict the average working week to 48 hours has horizontal direct effect: Cases C-397/01 to C-403/01 *Pfeiffer v Deutsches Rotes Kreuz, Kreisverband Waldshut eV* [2005] ICR 1307, [2005] IRLR 137, ECJ (considering the equivalent provision contained in Council Directive (EC) 93/104 of 23 November 1993 (OJ L307, 13.12.93, p 18) (see note 1)); Case C-243/09 *Fuß v Stadt Halle* [2010] ECR I-9849, [2011] 1 CMLR 1189, [2010] IRLR 1080, ECJ (national rules which provide for the working time of firemen employed in the public sector on operational duties to exceed the limit laid down by Working Time Directive art 6(b) infringe that provision without there being any need to establish, in addition, whether that worker has been subjected to a detriment, and such a worker could rely on EU law to obtain reparation from his employer for the breach). Consent given by trade union representatives in the context of a collective or other agreement to workers exceeding the maximum weekly working time of 48 hours is not equivalent to consent given by a worker himself: Case C-303/98 *Sindicato de Médicos de Asistencia Pública (SIMAP) v Conselleria de Sanidad y Consumo de la Generalidad Valenciana* [2001] All ER (EC) 609, [2001] ICR 1116, ECJ.

For the application of Working Time Directive art 6, member states may lay down a reference period not exceeding four months: see art 16(b). In the absence of national provisions transposing art 16(b) or expressly adopting one of the derogations provided for in art 17 (see the text and note 21), arts 16 and 17 could be interpreted as having direct effect with the result that the reference period could not exceed 12 months as allowed for in art 17: Case C-303/98 *Sindicato de Médicos de Asistencia Pública (SIMAP) v Conselleria de Sanidad y Consumo de la Generalidad Valenciana*. The periods of paid annual leave, granted in accordance with Working Time Directive art 7 (see head (e) in the text), and the periods of sick leave must not be included or must be neutral in the calculation of the average: art 16(b). Subject to compliance with the general principles relating to the protection of the safety and health of workers, and provided that there is consultation of representatives of the employer and employees concerned and efforts to encourage all relevant forms of social dialogue, including negotiation if the parties so wish, member states may, for objective or technical reasons or reasons concerning the organisation of work, extend the reference period referred to in art 16(b) to 12 months in respect of workers who mainly perform offshore work: art 20(2). For these purposes, 'offshore work' means work performed mainly on or from offshore installations (including drilling rigs), directly or indirectly in connection with the exploration, extraction or exploitation of mineral resources, including hydrocarbons, and diving in connection with such activities, whether performed from an offshore installation or a vessel: see art 2(8).

11   Working Time Directive art 7(1). This provision has direct effect: Case C-282/10 *Dominguez v Centre Informatique du Centre Ouest Atlantique* [2012] 2 CMLR 437, [2012] IRLR 321, CJEU (while member states are free to impose conditions on the exercise and implementation of the right to paid annual leave, the very existence of that right may not be made subject to any preconditions whatsoever); and see Case C-173/99 *R (on the application of the Broadcasting, Entertainment, Cinematographic and Theatre Union) v Secretary of State for Trade and Industry* [2001] ECR I-488, [2001] All ER (EC) 647, [2001] 3 CMLR 109, [2001] ICR 1152, [2001] IRLR 559, [2001] All ER (D) 272 (Jun), ECJ.

The term 'paid annual leave' in art 7(1) means that, for the duration of annual leave, remuneration must be maintained and workers must receive their normal remuneration for that period of rest: Joined Cases C-131/04 and C-257/04 *Robinson-Steele v RD Retail Services Ltd, Clarke v Frank Staddon Ltd* [2006] IRLR 386, ECJ (where sums have been paid as holiday pay, under a regime contrary to the Working Time Directive, in the form of part payments staggered over the corresponding annual period of work and paid together with remuneration for work done, the Working Time Directive art 7 does not preclude such sums from being offset against the entitlement to payment for a specific period during which the worker actually takes leave, provided the employer can prove that the sums have been paid transparently and comprehensibly). Where the remuneration received by the worker is composed of several components, the determination of that normal remuneration (and, consequently, of the amount to which that worker is entitled during his annual leave) requires a specific analysis to be conducted by the national court: Case C-155/10 *British Airways plc v Williams* [2011] IRLR 948, CJEU (an allowance, the amount of which is just sufficient to ensure that there is no serious risk that the worker will not take his leave, will not satisfy the requirements of EU law). Accordingly, the CJEU drew a distinction between: (1) remuneration (including remuneration based on personal or professional status) for all activities whether basic or 'inconvenient' undertaken during employment; and (2) payments intended exclusively to cover occasional or ancillary costs (which would not be incurred during holiday periods): see *British Airways plc v Williams* [2012] UKSC 43, [2013] 1 All ER 443, [2013] 1 CMLR 934, [2012] IRLR 1014. The UK Supreme Court held that the CJEU had made clear that it is for the national court to assess into which of the two categories any payment falls and that the 'assessment must be carried out on the basis of an average over a reference period which is judged to be representative' (ie judged by the national court to be representative of 'normal' working and remuneration, rather than a calculation based on what the employee might have earned during the holiday period had she or he then been working): *British Airways plc v Williams*. See also Case C-539/12 *ZJR Lock v British Gas Trading Ltd* [2014] ICR 813, [2014] IRLR 648, CJEU (worker's remuneration based on a basic salary plus commission requires commission to be taken into account in the calculation of the total remuneration to which he is entitled in respect of his annual leave); and see PARA 295 note 3.

The Working Time Directive art 7(1) makes no distinction between workers who are absent from work on sick leave (whether short-term or long-term) during the leave year, and those who have in fact worked in the course of that year, because the right to paid annual leave conferred by the Directive on all workers cannot be made subject to a condition concerning the obligation actually to have worked during the leave year laid down by that state; accordingly, the right to annual leave continues to accrue during sick leave, and any leave that a worker was unable to take because of being on sick leave can be taken on his or her return to work, notwithstanding that this may be in a later leave year: Joined Cases C-350/05 and C-520/06 *Schultz-Hoff v Deutsche Rentenversicherung Bund, Stringer v Revenue and Customs Comrs* [2009] ECR I-179, [2009] All ER (EC) 906, [2009] ICR 932, ECJ (entitlement to paid annual leave is to enable the worker to rest and to enjoy a period of relaxation and leisure, while the different purpose of the entitlement to sick leave is so that he can recover from being ill); and see Case C-282/10 *Dominguez v Centre Informatique du Centre Ouest Atlantique* (national law may, however, provide for leave in excess of four weeks to be subject to additional conditions, such as requiring the worker to have performed a minimum amount of actual work); Case C-277/08 *Pereda v Madrid Movilidad SA* [2009] ECR I-8405, [2010] 1 CMLR 103, [2009] IRLR 959, ECJ (worker who suffered an industrial injury and was unfit for work just before a period of previously-scheduled annual leave commenced, had the right, at his request, to take paid annual leave at a period outside sickness leave, even if it fell outside the corresponding reference period for annual leave, if he had not had an opportunity to exercise the right to take paid annual leave in the pay year); and Case C-78/11 *Asociacion Nacional de Grandes Empresas de Distribucion (ANGED) v Federacion de Asociaciones Sindicales (FASGA)* [2012] ICR 1211, [2012] IRLR 779, ECJ (it follows from *Pereda v Madrid Movilidad SA* that the point at which a temporary incapacity arose is irrelevant so that a worker who became unfit for work during a period of paid annual leave was entitled subsequently to take leave lost to sickness). Nevertheless, a worker who is unfit for work for several consecutive years, and who is prevented by national law from taking his paid annual leave during that period, cannot have the right to accumulate, without any limit, entitlements to paid annual leave acquired during that period: Case C-214/10 *KHS AG v Schulte* [2011] ECR I-11757, [2012] 1 CMLR 1352, [2012] IRLR 156, CJEU (collective agreement which provided that, if leave could not be taken because of illness, entitlement to that leave would lapse after 15 months after the end of the reference period, was not precluded by the Working Time Directive art 7 because the reference period was shorter than the carry over period). However, the period of carry-over must be 'substantially longer' than the reference period of a year, and it must take into account the specific circumstances of a worker who has been unfit for work for several consecutive reference periods, and it must allow for the worker to have rest periods that can be staggered, and planned in advance: Case C-337/10 *Neidel v Stadt Frankfurt Am Main* [2012] 3 CMLR 92, [2012] ICR 1201, [2012] IRLR 607, CJEU (nine months' carry forward of leave untaken because of ill health precluded by Working Time Directive, although only in relation to the minimum entitlement of four weeks a year); and see Cases C-229/11 and C-230/11 *Heimann v Kaiser GmbH* [2013] 1 CMLR 1425, [2013] ICR D11, [2013] IRLR 48, ECJ.

Where maternity leave coincides with a period of previously-scheduled annual leave, a worker maintains her entitlement to take paid annual leave during a period other than her maternity leave: Case C-342/01 *Merino Gómez v Continental Industrias del Caucho SA* [2005] ICR 1040, [2004] IRLR 407, ECJ (purpose of the entitlement to paid annual leave is different from that of the entitlement to maternity leave); and see PARA 355 et seq. As to the position where a worker changes from full-time to part-time working during the course of a leave year, without having been able to take all of her *pro rata* share of the year's leave allowance, see Case C-486/08 *Zentralbetriebsrat der Landeskrankenhauser Tirols v Land Tirol* [2010] ECR I-3527, [2010] IRLR 631, ECJ (a case arising under the 'Part-time Work Directive' which was answered in part by reference to the general principles of EU social law, whose implementation by the competent national authorities is confined within the limits expressly laid down by the Working Time Directive); and PARA 73 note 6.

The Working Time Directive art 7(1) does not require that the guaranteed weeks of annual leave have to be taken consecutively, or that those weeks could not be interrupted: see *Russell v Transocean International Resources Ltd* [2011] UKSC 57, [2012] 2 All ER 166, [2012] ICR 185, [2012] IRLR 149; and PARA 293 note 3.

12 Working Time Directive art 7(2). Accordingly, national legislation which allows leave not taken in a leave year to be carried forward to the following year, and further allows it either to be taken or commuted for payment in lieu, is incompatible with EU law (Case C-124/05 *Federatie Nederlandse Vakbeweging v Netherlands* [2006] All ER (EC) 913, [2006] ICR 962, ECJ), although it is permissible for national law to provide that payment in lieu of leave not taken, because it had not been possible to do so during the employment because of sickness, need not apply to leave in excess of the basic four weeks a year required by the Working Time Directive (Case C-337/10 *Neidel v Stadt Frankfurt am Main* [2012] 3 CMLR 92, [2012] ICR 1201, [2012] IRLR 607, CJEU).

As to the power of the Secretary of State to make provision about entitlement to annual leave in domestic legislation see PARA 270.

13 Working Time Directive art 8(a). For these purposes, 'night worker' means:
  (1) on the one hand, any worker who, during night time, works at least three hours of his daily working time as a normal course (art 2(4)(a)); and
  (2) on the other hand, any worker who is likely during night time to work a certain proportion of his annual working time, as defined at the choice of the member state concerned either by national legislation (following consultation with the two sides of industry) or by collective agreements or agreements concluded between the two sides of industry at national or regional level (see art 2(4)(b)).

'Night time' means any period of not less than seven hours, as defined by national law, and which must include in any case the period between midnight and 5 in the morning: see art 2(3). A worker may be a night worker for the purposes of art 2(4), notwithstanding that he spends only one week of each three-week shift cycle working from 9 pm to 7 am: *R v A-G for Northern Ireland, ex p Burns* [1999] IRLR 315.

14 Working Time Directive art 8(b). For the purposes of art 8(b), work involving special hazards or heavy physical or mental strain are to be defined by national legislation and/or practice or by collective agreements or agreements concluded between the two sides of industry, taking account of the specific effects and hazards of night work: see art 8. For the application of art 8 (length of night work), member states may lay down a reference period defined after consultation with the two sides of industry or by collective agreements or agreements concluded between the two sides of industry at national or regional level: see art 16(c). However, if the minimum weekly rest period of 24 hours required by art 5 (see head (c) in the text) falls within that reference period, it must not be included in the calculation of the average: see art 16(c). Member states may make the work of certain categories of night workers subject to certain guarantees, under conditions laid down by national legislation and/or practice, in the case of workers who incur risks to their safety or health linked to night-time working: art 10.

15 Working Time Directive art 9(1)(a). The free health assessment referred to in art 9(1)(a) must comply with medical confidentiality (see art 9(2)); and it may be conducted within the national health system (see art 9(3)).

16 Working Time Directive art 9(1)(b).

17 Working Time Directive art 11.

18 Working Time Directive art 12 para (a). For these purposes, 'shift worker' means any worker whose work schedule is part of shift work: see art 2(6).

19 Working Time Directive art 12 para (b).

20 Working Time Directive art 13.
21 As to derogations see Working Time Directive arts 17–19. In the absence of express measures transposing the Working Time Directive, a national court could apply its domestic law to the extent to which the activities of workers fell within the derogations mentioned in art 17: see Case C-303/98 *Sindicato de Médicos de Asistencia Pública (SIMAP) v Conselleria de Sanidad y Consumo de la Generalidad Valenciana* [2001] All ER (EC) 609, [2001] ICR 1116, ECJ; Joined Cases C-397 to 403/01 *Pfeiffer v Deutsches Rotes Kreuz, Kreisverband Waldshut eV* [2005] ICR 1307, [2005] IRLR 137, ECJ; and note 10. See also *Bridgeman v Associated British Ports* [2012] 2 CMLR 1317, [2012] ICR D26, [2012] IRLR 639, EAT (concerning proper construction of phrase 'activities involving the need for continuity of service or production' in Working Time Directive art 17(3)(c)); and PARA 301 note 8. The derogation under Working Time Directive art 18 (compensatory rest) serves to guarantee that each employee is to enjoy adequate rest periods which must not only be effective in enabling the persons concerned to recover from the fatigue engendered by their work but also are preventive in nature so as to reduce as much as possible the risk of affecting the safety or health of employees which successive periods of work without the necessary rest are likely to produce: Case C-151/02 *Landeshauptstadt Kiel v Jaeger* [2003] ECR I-8389, [2004] All ER (EC) 604, [2004] ICR 1528, [2003] IRLR 804, ECJ (rest must be capable of being taken away from working environment for a specific number of hours which must not only be consecutive but must also directly follow a period of work in order to enable worker to relax and dispel the fatigue caused by the performance of his duties); Case C-428/09 *Union Syndicale Solidaires Isère v Premier Ministre* [2010] ECR I-9961, [2011] IRLR 84, ECJ (during periods of compensatory rest, worker must not be subject to any obligation vis-a-vis his employer which may prevent him from pursuing freely and without interruption his own interests in order to neutralise the effects of work on his safety and health, and must follow on immediately from the working time which they are supposed to counteract).
22 For these purposes, 'adequate rest' means that workers have regular rest periods, the duration of which is expressed in units of time and which are sufficiently long and continuous to ensure that, as a result of fatigue or other irregular working patterns, they do not cause injury to themselves, to fellow workers or to others and that they do not damage their health, either in the short term or in the longer term: see Working Time Directive art 2(9).
23 For these purposes, 'mobile worker' means any worker employed as a member of travelling or flying personnel by an undertaking which operates transport services for passengers or goods by road, air or inland waterway: see Working Time Directive art 2(7). See also note 1.
24 Working Time Directive arts 20(1), 21(1). See also note 4.
25 Working Time Directive art 21(1)–(7).
26 See Council Directive (EC) 94/33 of 22 June 1994 (OJ L216, 20.8.94, p 12) on the protection of young people at work; and see especially Section III (arts 8–13). For the purposes of implementing Council Directive (EC) 94/33 of 22 June 1994 (OJ L216, 20.8.94, p 12), the Children (Protection at Work) Regulations 1998, SI 1998/276, were made, amending the Children and Young Persons Acts 1933 and 1963 (see CHILDREN AND YOUNG PERSONS vol 10 (2012) PARA 705 et seq).

268. Implementation in Great Britain of the Working Time Directive. For the purpose of implementing the European Parliament and Council Directive of 4 November 2003 concerning certain aspects of the organisation of working time (the 'Working Time Directive')[1], the Working Time Regulations 1998 were made[2], which (inter alia):

(1) impose obligations on employers[3], enforceable by the Health and Safety Executive, the Civil Aviation Authority, the Driver and Vehicle Standards Agency, the Office of Rail Regulation, and local authorities[4], where failure to comply with any of the relevant requirements is an offence[5];

(2) confer rights on workers[6], enforceable by proceedings before employment tribunals[7];

(3) provide for the application or, as the case may be, disapplication of particular obligations on employers, either in relation to workers engaged in certain kinds of work or where particular circumstances arise[8];

(4)   provide a general restriction on contracting out[9]; and

(5)   make provision for special classes of workers[10].

Workers have a right not to be subjected to any detriment for refusing to comply with a requirement contrary to the working time provisions or to forgo a right so conferred[11]; and the dismissal of a worker on account of any such refusal constitutes unfair dismissal[12].

1   Ie European Parliament and Council Directive (EC) 2003/88 of 4 November 2003 (OJ L299, 18.11.2003, p 9) concerning certain aspects of the organisation of working time (the 'Working Time Directive') (see PARA 267). See also note 2.

2   Ie the Working Time Regulations 1998, SI 1998/1833 (see also PARA 269 et seq), which came into force on 1 October 1998 (see reg 1(1)) and extend to Great Britain only (see reg 1(2)). As to the meaning of 'Great Britain' see PARA 2 note 12. As to the exclusions that operate under the Working Time Regulations 1998, SI 1998/1833, specifically, see head (3) in the text. As to the organisation of working time for sea-fishermen see specifically the Fishing Vessels (Working Time: Sea-fishermen) Regulations 2004, SI 2004/1713; and SHIPPING AND MARITIME LAW vol 94 (2008) PARA 626. As to the organisation of working time for workers on the inland waterways see specifically the Merchant Shipping (Working Time: Inland Waterways) Regulations 2003, SI 2003/3049; and SHIPPING AND MARITIME LAW vol 94 (2008) PARA 625.
     Special provision is made in EU law in relation to the working hours of mobile workers in civil aviation and persons performing mobile road and rail transport activities (see PARA 267 note 1) and seafarers (see PARA 267 note 4), and young people at work (see PARA 267 note 26), with separate arrangements for their implementation in domestic law being made accordingly.

3   See the Working Time Regulations 1998, SI 1998/1833, regs 4–9; and PARAS 280–281, 283–287.

4   See the Working Time Regulations 1998, SI 1998/1833, reg 28; and PARA 311.

5   See the Working Time Regulations 1998, SI 1998/1833, regs 29–29E; and PARAS 317–318.

6   See the Working Time Regulations 1998, SI 1998/1833, regs 10–17; and PARAS 288–296.

7   See the Working Time Regulations 1998, SI 1998/1833, regs 30–30B; and PARA 319.

8   See the Working Time Regulations 1998, SI 1998/1833, Pt III (regs 18–27A); and PARA 297 et seq.

9   See the Working Time Regulations 1998, SI 1998/1833, reg 35; and PARA 282. As to agreements to exclude the maximum number of working hours see reg 5; and PARA 283.

10   See the Working Time Regulations 1998, SI 1998/1833, Pt V (regs 36–43); and PARAS 273–279.

11   See the Employment Rights Act 1996 s 45A (protection from detriment (working time cases): see PARA 616), s 48(1ZA) (complaint to employment tribunal on grounds of detriment in contravention of s 45A: see PARA 625), s 49(5A) (compensation where complaint made under s 48(1ZA): see PARA 626).

12   See the Employment Rights Act 1996 s 101A; and PARA 788.

269. Publication of information and advice concerning the operation of the working time regulations. The Secretary of State[1] must, after consulting persons appearing to him to represent the two sides of industry[2], arrange for the publication, in such form and manner as he considers appropriate, of information and advice concerning the operation of the regulations[3] relating to working time[4].

The information and advice must be such as appear to him best calculated to enable employers and workers[5] affected by the working time regulations to understand their respective rights and obligations thereunder[6].

1   As to the Secretary of State see PARA 5 note 21.

2   In European Parliament and Council Directive (EC) 2003/88 of 4 November 2003 (OJ L299, 18.11.2003, p 9) concerning certain aspects of the organisation of working time (the 'Working Time Directive'), references to the two sides of industry are references to employers (management) and workers (labour): see PARA 267 note 1. As to the meanings of 'employer' and worker', for the purposes of the Working Time Regulations 1998, SI 1998/1833, see note 5.

3   Ie the Working Time Regulations 1998, SI 1998/1833 (see also PARAS 268, 271 et seq): see reg 35A(1) (reg 35A added by SI 1999/3372).

4   Working Time Regulations 1998, SI 1998/1833, reg 35A(1) (as added: see note 3).

5   For these purposes, in relation to a worker, 'employer' means the person by whom the worker is (or, where the employment has ceased, was) employed: see the Working Time Regulations 1998,

SI 1998/1833, reg 2(1). 'Employment', in relation to a worker, means employment under his contract; and 'employed' is to be construed accordingly: see reg 2(1). As to the meaning of 'worker' for these purposes see PARA 271. As to the meanings of 'employer', 'employment', and related expressions in relation to employment rights generally see PARA 2 et seq.
6   Working Time Regulations 1998, SI 1998/1833, reg 35A(2) (as added: see note 3).

270. Power of Secretary of State to prescribe amount of annual leave in each leave year. The Secretary of State[1] may by regulations[2] make provision conferring on workers the right, except in prescribed cases, to a prescribed amount of annual leave in each leave year, as defined for the purposes of the regulations[3]. The regulations may in particular:

(1)   make provision for determining the amount of annual leave to which workers are to be entitled[4];

(2)   make provision for determining the amount of pay in respect of any period of leave which is required by the regulations to be paid leave[5];

(3)   make provision enabling a worker to elect when to take leave to which he is entitled by virtue of the regulations, subject to any provision of the regulations enabling his employer to require him to take, or not to take, that leave at a particular time[6];

(4)   make provision for the payment of compensation in prescribed cases to a worker who has not taken leave to which he is entitled[7];

(5)   make provision as to the relationship between the rights conferred by the regulations and a worker's rights to leave, pay or compensation under any contract or under any Act or subordinate legislation[8];

(6)   enable a worker to present a complaint to an employment tribunal that his employer has refused to permit him to exercise any right he has under the regulations, or has failed to pay him any amount due to him under the regulations[9];

(7)   make, in connection with any right conferred by the regulations (including any right to payment), any other provision which is the same as or similar to any provision made, in connection with any right relating to annual leave conferred in pursuance of any EU obligation, by any regulations under the European Communities Act 1972[10] made at any time before the day on which the first regulations[11] are so made[12].

Such regulations may make provision as to:

(a)   who is to be treated as a worker for the purposes of the regulations[13]; and

(b)   who is to be treated as the worker's employer[14]; and

such regulations may in particular:

(i)   make provision applying to: (A) Crown employment[15] and persons in Crown employment[16]; (B) service as a member of the armed forces[17];

(ii)   make provision conferring rights to and in connection with annual leave on persons falling within any other categories of persons on whom any EU obligation of the United Kingdom[18] requires a right to annual leave to be conferred[19].

1   As to the Secretary of State see PARA 5 note 21.
2   Regulations under the Work and Families Act 2006 s 13:
    (1)   are to be made by statutory instrument (s 13(6)(a));
    (2)   may make different provision for different cases (s 13(6)(b)); and
    (3)   may contain incidental, supplemental, consequential, transitional or saving provision (including provision amending any Act or subordinate legislation) (s 13(6)(c)).
    No statutory instrument containing such regulations may be made, however, unless a draft of the instrument has been laid before, and approved by a resolution of, each House of Parliament:

s 13(7). For these purposes, 'subordinate legislation' has the same meaning as in the Interpretation Act 1978 (see STATUTES AND LEGISLATIVE PROCESS vol 96 (2012) PARA 609): see the Work and Families Act 2006 s 13(8). As to regulations so made see the Working Time (Amendment) Regulations 2007, SI 2007/2079 (and see eg PARAS 291, 292, 293, 294, 295, 298, 319).

3 Work and Families Act 2006 s 13(1). As to entitlement to annual leave see the Working Time Regulations 1998, SI 1998/1833, reg 13; and PARA 291. As to entitlement to additional annual leave see regs 13A, 26A; and PARA 292.

4 Work and Families Act 2006 s 13(2)(a).

5 Work and Families Act 2006 s 13(2)(b).

6 Work and Families Act 2006 s 13(2)(c).

7 Work and Families Act 2006 s 13(2)(d).

8 Work and Families Act 2006 s 13(2)(e).

9 Work and Families Act 2006 s 13(2)(f).

10 Ie under the European Communities Act 1972 s 2(2) (see CONSTITUTIONAL AND ADMINISTRATIVE LAW vol 20 (2014) PARA 156): see the Work and Families Act 2006 s 13(2)(g) (amended by SI 2011/1043).

11 Ie the first regulations under the Work and Families Act 2006 s 13: see s 13(2)(g) (as amended: see note 10).

12 Work and Families Act 2006 s 13(2)(g) (as amended: see note 10).

13 Work and Families Act 2006 s 13(3)(a).

14 Work and Families Act 2006 s 13(3)(b).

15 For these purposes, 'Crown employment' has the meaning given by the Employment Rights Act 1996 s 191(3) (see PARA 163): see the Work and Families Act 2006 s 13(8).

16 Work and Families Act 2006 s 13(4)(a)(i).

17 Work and Families Act 2006 s 13(4)(a)(ii). For these purposes, 'armed forces' means any of the naval, military or air forces of the Crown: see s 13(8).

18 As to the meaning of 'United Kingdom' see PARA 2 note 12.

19 Work and Families Act 2006 s 13(4)(b) (amended by SI 2011/1043).

(ii) Workers Entitled to Protection

271. Meaning of 'worker' for the purposes of the working time regulations.
For the purposes of the working time regulations[1], 'worker' means an individual who has entered into or works under (or, where the employment has ceased[2], worked under):

(1) a contract of employment[3]; or

(2) any other contract (whether express or implied and, if it is express, whether oral or in writing[4]) whereby the individual undertakes to do or perform personally any work or services for another party to the contract whose status is not, by virtue of the contract, that of a client or customer of any profession or business undertaking carried on by the individual[5],

and any reference to a worker's contract is to be construed accordingly[6].

1 Ie the Working Time Regulations 1998, SI 1998/1833 (see also PARAS 268, 269, 272 et seq): see reg 2(1).

2 As to the meaning of 'employment' see PARA 269 note 5.

3 See the Working Time Regulations 1998, SI 1998/1833, reg 2(1).

4 As to the meaning of 'writing' see PARA 2 note 8.

5 See the Working Time Regulations 1998, SI 1998/1833, reg 2(1). The intention behind reg 2(1) is plainly to create an intermediate class of protected worker who, on the one hand, is not an employee but, on the other hand, cannot in some narrower sense be regarded as carrying on a business: *Byrne Bros (Formwork) Ltd v Baird* [2002] ICR 667, [2002] IRLR 96, EAT (self-employed labour-only sub-contractors found to be workers under the Working Time Regulations 1998, SI 1998/1833, reg 2(1); and the purpose of the Regulations was said to be 'to extend protection to workers who are, substantively and economically, in the same position'); *Flynn v Torith Ltd* [2003] All ER (D) 45 (Jan), EAT (Sc) (joiner engaged by building contractor); *Cavil v Barratt Homes Ltd* [2003] All ER (D) 06 (Jul), EAT (joiner employed under labour-only sub-contract had contract for personal service); *JNJ Bricklaying Ltd v Stacey* [2003] All ER (D)

96 (Jul), EAT (labourers and bricklayers employed as gang); *Wright v Redrow Homes (Yorkshire) Ltd, Roberts v Redrow Homes (North West) Ltd* [2004] EWCA Civ 469, [2004] 3 All ER 98, sub nom *Redrow Homes (Yorkshire) Ltd v Wright, Roberts v Redrow Homes (North West) Ltd* [2004] ICR 1126 (intention of the parties when the contracts were made was that contract bricklayers were obliged personally to do the work). See also *Cotswold Developments Construction Ltd v Williams* [2006] IRLR 181, [2005] All ER (D) 355 (Dec), EAT; *Ashworth v Postworth (t/a Skyblue)* [2008] All ER (D) 21 (Sep), EAT; and *Redrow Homes (Yorkshire) Ltd v Buckborough* [2009] IRLR 34, [2008] All ER (D) 186 (Nov), EAT. As to the meaning of 'worker' in employment law generally see PARA 5. See also *Express and Echo Publications Ltd v Tanton* [1999] ICR 693, [1999] IRLR 367, CA; *Jozsa v Premier Groundworks Ltd* [2009] All ER (D) 22 (Apr), EAT; and PARA 4 note 14. As from 1 January 2010, the position of Church of England clergy has been put onto a statutory footing, including rights to paid annual leave and a weekly rest period of 24 hours: see the Ecclesiastical Offices (Terms of Service) Regulations 2009, SI 2009/2108; the Ecclesiastical Offices (Terms of Service) Directions 2010, SI 2010/1923; and ECCLESIASTICAL LAW vol 34 (2011) PARAS 407 et seq, 428. The position of clergy of other denominations, and their equivalents in other faiths, under the Working Time Regulations 1998, SI 1998/1833, however, remains dependent on whether they are held to be 'workers' (as so defined).

Because the Working Time Regulations 1998, SI 1998/1833, and the Working Time Directive (see PARA 267) apply only to adult workers (see PARA 285 note 2) and to young workers (see PARA 281 note 1), the expression 'worker' does not include children as defined in the Children and Young Persons Act 1933 s 30(1) (definition of the expression 'child': see CHILDREN AND YOUNG PERSONS vol 10 (2012) PARA 708), and their employment is governed by s 18(1) (restrictions on employment of children: see CHILDREN AND YOUNG PERSONS vol 10 (2012) PARA 708 et seq): *Ashby v Addison (t/a Brayton News)* [2003] ICR 667, [2003] IRLR 211, EAT.

6   See the Working Time Regulations 1998, SI 1998/1833, reg 2(1).

272.   Meaning of 'workforce agreement' for the purposes of the working time regulations. 'Workforce agreement' means an agreement between an employer[1] and workers[2] employed by him or their representatives in respect of which the following conditions are satisfied[3]:

(1)   the agreement is in writing[4];

(2)   it has effect for a specified period not exceeding five years[5];

(3)   it applies either: (a) to all of the relevant members of the workforce[6]; or (b) to all of the relevant members of the workforce who belong to a particular group[7];

(4)   the agreement is signed:

    (a)   in the case of an agreement of the kind referred to in head (3)(a) above, by the representatives of the workforce[8], and, in the case of an agreement of the kind referred to in head (3)(b) above, by the representatives of the group to which the agreement applies (excluding, in either case, any representative not a relevant member of the workforce on the date on which the agreement was first made available for signature)[9]; or

    (b)   if the employer employed 20 or fewer workers on the date referred to in head (4)(a) above, either by the appropriate representatives in accordance with that head or by the majority of the workers employed by him[10];

(5)   before the agreement was made available for signature, the employer provided all the workers to whom it was intended to apply on the date on which it came into effect with copies of the text of the agreement and such guidance as those workers might reasonably require in order to understand it fully[11].

1   As to the meaning of 'employer' see PARA 269 note 5.
2   As to the meaning of 'worker' for these purposes see PARA 271.

At the date at which this volume states the law, special provisions have effect in relation to workers employed in agriculture in Wales, where different provision may be made by a relevant agreement: see the Working Time Regulations 1998, SI 1998/1833, reg 43, Sch 2 (reg 43, Sch 2 amended by SI 2013/2228; the Working Time Regulations 1998, SI 1998/1833, Sch 2 further amended by SI 2007/2079). 'Relevant agreement', in relation to a worker, means a workforce agreement which applies to him, any provision of a collective agreement which forms part of a contract between him and his employer, or any other agreement in writing which is legally enforceable as between the worker and his employer: see the Working Time Regulations 1998, SI 1998/1833, reg 2(1). 'Collective agreement' means a collective agreement within the meaning of the Trade Union and Labour Relations (Consolidation) Act 1992 s 178 (see PARA 1093), the trade union parties to which are independent trade unions within the meaning of s 5 (see PARA 904): see the Working Time Regulations 1998, SI 1998/1833, reg 2(1). As to the meaning of 'Wales' see PARA 2 note 12.

3   See the Working Time Regulations 1998, SI 1998/1833, reg 2(1). The text refers to the conditions set out in reg 2(1), Sch 1 (see heads (1) to (5) in the text): see reg 2(1).

4   Working Time Regulations 1998, SI 1998/1833, Sch 1 para 1(a). As to the meaning of 'writing' see PARA 2 note 8.

5   Working Time Regulations 1998, SI 1998/1833, Sch 1 para 1(b).

6   Working Time Regulations 1998, SI 1998/1833, Sch 1 para 1(c)(i). For these purposes, 'relevant members of the workforce' are all of the workers employed by a particular employer, excluding any worker whose terms and conditions of employment are provided for, wholly or in part, in a collective agreement: see Sch 1 para 2.

7   Working Time Regulations 1998, SI 1998/1833, Sch 1 para 1(c)(ii). For these purposes, a 'particular group' is a group of the relevant members of a workforce who undertake a particular function, work at a particular workplace or belong to a particular department or unit within their employer's business: see Sch 1 para 2.

8   For these purposes, 'representatives of the workforce' are workers duly elected to represent the relevant members of the workforce: see the Working Time Regulations 1998, SI 1998/1833, Sch 1 para 2. Representatives are 'duly elected' if the election at which they were elected satisfied the following requirements (see Sch 1 para 2):

(1)   the number of representatives to be elected is determined by the employer (Sch 1 para 3(a));

(2)   the candidates for election as representatives of the workforce are relevant members of the workforce, and the candidates for election as representatives of a group are members of the group (Sch 1 para 3(b));

(3)   no worker who is eligible to be a candidate is unreasonably excluded from standing for election (Sch 1 para 3(c));

(4)   all the relevant members of the workforce are entitled to vote for representatives of the workforce, and all the members of a particular group are entitled to vote for representatives of the group (Sch 1 para 3(d));

(5)   the workers entitled to vote may vote for as many candidates as there are representatives to be elected (Sch 1 para 3(e));

(6)   the election is conducted so as to secure that: (a) so far as is reasonably practicable, those voting do so in secret (Sch 1 para 3(f)(i)); and (b) the votes given at the election are fairly and accurately counted (Sch 1 para 3(f)(ii)).

For these purposes, 'representatives of the group' are workers duly elected to represent the members of a particular group: see Sch 1 para 2.

9   Working Time Regulations 1998, SI 1998/1833, Sch 1 para 1(d)(i).

As to consent given by trade union representatives in the context of a collective or other agreement see Case C-303/98 *Sindicato de Médicos de Asistencia Pública (SIMAP) v Conselleria de Sanidad y Consumo de la Generalidad Valenciana* [2001] All ER (EC) 609, [2001] ICR 1116, ECJ (considering the position under the Working Time Directive: see PARA 267).

10   Working Time Regulations 1998, SI 1998/1833, Sch 1 para 1(d)(ii).

11   Working Time Regulations 1998, SI 1998/1833, Sch 1 para 1(e).

273.   Effect of working time regulations in relation to agency workers who are not otherwise 'workers'.

In any case where an individual (the 'agency worker')[1]:

(1)   is supplied by a person (the 'agent') to do work[2] for another (the 'principal') under a contract or other arrangements made between the agent and the principal[3]; but

(2)   is not, as respects that work, a worker, because of the absence of a worker's contract between the individual and the agent or the principal[4]; and

(3)   is not a party to a contract under which he undertakes to do the work for another party to the contract whose status is, by virtue of the contract, that of a client or customer of any profession or business undertaking carried on by the individual[5],

the working time regulations[6] have effect[7] as if there were a worker's contract for the doing of the work by the agency worker made between the agency worker[8], and:

(a)   whichever of the agent and the principal is responsible for paying the agency worker in respect of the work[9]; or

(b)   if neither the agent nor the principal is so responsible, whichever of them pays the agency worker in respect of the work[10],

and as if that person were the agency worker's employer[11].

1   See the Working Time Regulations 1998, SI 1998/1833, reg 36(1). As to the meaning of 'worker' generally for these purposes see PARA 271.
     The Agency Workers Regulations 2010, SI 2010/93, give agency workers a right to equal treatment with directly recruited counterpart employees after 12 weeks in the job but they do not affect either the statutory rules on the conduct of agencies or an agency worker's status at common law (see PARAS 11, 95 et seq).
2   As to the meaning of 'work' see PARA 280 note 4.
3   Working Time Regulations 1998, SI 1998/1833, reg 36(1)(a).
4   Working Time Regulations 1998, SI 1998/1833, reg 36(1)(b). As to the meaning of references to a worker's contract see PARA 271.
5   Working Time Regulations 1998, SI 1998/1833, reg 36(1)(c).
6   Ie the other provisions of the Working Time Regulations 1998, SI 1998/1833 (ie regs 1–35A, 37–43: see also PARAS 268 et seq, 274 et seq): see reg 36(2).
7   Ie where the Working Time Regulations 1998, SI 1998/1833, reg 36 applies (by virtue of reg 36(1): see the text and notes 1–5): see reg 36(2).
8   See the Working Time Regulations 1998, SI 1998/1833, reg 36(2).
9   Working Time Regulations 1998, SI 1998/1833, reg 36(2)(a).
10   Working Time Regulations 1998, SI 1998/1833, reg 36(2)(b).
11   See the Working Time Regulations 1998, SI 1998/1833, reg 36(2). As to the meaning of 'employer' see PARA 269 note 5.

274.   Effect of working time regulations in relation to Crown employment.
The working time regulations[1] have effect[2] in relation to Crown employment[3] and persons in Crown employment as they have effect in relation to other employment and other workers[4].

No act or omission by the Crown which constitutes an offence[5] makes the Crown criminally liable, but the High Court may, on the application of a person appearing to the court to have an interest, declare any such act or omission unlawful[6].

1   Ie the Working Time Regulations 1998, SI 1998/1833 (see also PARAS 268 et seq, 275 et seq): see reg 37(1).
2   Ie subject to the Working Time Regulations 1998, SI 1998/1833, reg 37(4) (treatment of offences: see the text and notes 5–6) and reg 38 (members of the armed forces: see PARA 275): see reg 37(1).
3   For this purpose, 'Crown employment' means employment under or for the purposes of a government department or any officer or body exercising on behalf of the Crown functions conferred by a statutory provision: see the Working Time Regulations 1998, SI 1998/1833, reg 37(2). As to the meaning of 'employment' see PARA 269 note 5.
4   Working Time Regulations 1998, SI 1998/1833, reg 37(1). For the purposes of the application of the provisions of the Working Time Regulations 1998, SI 1998/1833, in relation to Crown employment in accordance with reg 37(1):

(1)   references to a worker are to be construed as references to a person in Crown employment (reg 37(3)(a)); and
(2)   references to a worker's contract are to be construed as references to the terms of employment of a person in Crown employment (reg 37(3)(b)).

As to the meaning of 'worker' and as to the meaning of references to a worker's contract for these purposes see PARA 271.

5   Ie under the Working Time Regulations 1998, SI 1998/1833, reg 29 (see PARA 317): see reg 37(4).
6   Working Time Regulations 1998, SI 1998/1833, reg 37(4).

275.   Effect of working time regulations in relation to armed forces. The provisions that give effect to the working time regulations in relation to Crown employment[1] apply:

(1)   to service as a member of the armed forces[2]; and
(2)   to employment by an association established[3] for the purposes of Part XI of the Reserve Forces Act 1996[4];

However, no complaint under head (1) above may be presented to an employment tribunal[5] unless:

(a)   that person has made a complaint in respect of the same matter to an officer under the service redress procedures[6]; and
(b)   that complaint has not been withdrawn[7]; and

where such a complaint is presented to an employment tribunal, the service redress procedures may continue after the complaint is presented[8].

1   Ie the Working Time Regulations 1998, SI 1998/1833, reg 37 (see PARA 274): see reg 38(1).
2   See the Working Time Regulations 1998, SI 1998/1833, reg 38(1)(a). Head (1) in the text is subject to reg 38(2) (see the text and notes 5–7): see reg 38(1). For these purposes, 'armed forces' means any of the naval, military and air forces of the Crown: see reg 2(1).
3   Ie established for the purposes of the Reserve Forces Act 1996 Pt XI (ss 110–119) (reserve associations: see ARMED FORCES vol 3 (2011) PARA 473): see the Working Time Regulations 1998, SI 1998/1833, reg 38(1)(b).
4   See the Working Time Regulations 1998, SI 1998/1833, reg 38(1)(b).
5   Ie under the Working Time Regulations 1998, SI 1998/1833, reg 30 (see PARA 319): see reg 38(2). As to employment tribunals see PARA 1399 et seq; and as to the procedure on a complaint made to an employment tribunal see PARA 1453 et seq.
6   Working Time Regulations 1998, SI 1998/1833, reg 38(2)(a). For this purpose, 'service redress procedures' means the procedures, excluding those which relate to the making of a report on a complaint to Her Majesty, referred to in the Army Act 1955 s 180 (repealed), the Air Force Act 1955 s 180 (repealed), the Naval Discipline Act 1957 s 130 (repealed) or the Armed Forces Act 2006 s 334 (see ARMED FORCES vol 3 (2011) PARA 754): Working Time Regulations 1998, SI 1998/1833, reg 38(5) (amended by SI 2008/1696).
7   Working Time Regulations 1998, SI 1998/1833, reg 38(2)(b). For the purpose of head (b) in the text, a person is to be treated as having withdrawn his complaint if, having made a complaint to an officer under the service redress procedures:
(1)   where the service redress procedures are those referred to in the Armed Forces Act 2006 s 334 (see ARMED FORCES vol 3 (2011) PARA 754)), neither that officer nor a superior officer has decided to refer the complaint to the Defence Council, and the person who made the complaint fails to apply for such a reference to be made (Working Time Regulations 1998, SI 1998/1833, reg 38(3)(a) (reg 38(3) substituted by SI 2008/1696));
(2)   in any other case, the person who made the complaint fails to submit the complaint to the Defence Council under the service redress procedures (Working Time Regulations 1998, SI 1998/1833, reg 38(3)(b) (as so substituted)).
As to the Defence Council see ARMED FORCES vol 3 (2011) PARA 302.
8   Working Time Regulations 1998, SI 1998/1833, reg 38(4).

276.   Effect of working time regulations in relation to House of Lords staff. The working time regulations[1] have effect in relation to employment[2] as a relevant member of the House of Lords staff[3] as they have effect in relation to other employment[4].

Nothing in any rule of law or the law or practice of Parliament prevents a relevant member of the House of Lords staff from presenting a complaint[5] to an employment tribunal[6].

1   Ie the Working Time Regulations 1998, SI 1998/1833 (see also PARAS 268 et seq, 277 et seq): see reg 39(1).
2   As to the meaning of 'employment' see PARA 269 note 5.
3   For these purposes, 'relevant member of the House of Lords staff' means any person who is employed under a worker's contract with the Corporate Officer of the House of Lords: see the Working Time Regulations 1998, SI 1998/1833, reg 39(3). As to the meaning of 'worker' and as to the meaning of references to a worker's contract for these purposes see PARA 271. As to the Corporate Officer of the House of Lords see PARLIAMENT vol 78 (2010) PARA 990 et seq.
4   Working Time Regulations 1998, SI 1998/1833, reg 39(1).
5   Ie under the Working Time Regulations 1998, SI 1998/1833, reg 30 (see PARA 319): see reg 39(2).
6   Working Time Regulations 1998, SI 1998/1833, reg 39(2). As to employment tribunals see PARA 1399 et seq; and as to the procedure on a complaint made to an employment tribunal see PARA 1453 et seq.

277.   Effect of working time regulations in relation to House of Commons staff.   The working time regulations[1] have effect in relation to employment[2] as a relevant member of the House of Commons staff[3] as they have effect in relation to other employment[4].

Nothing in any rule of law or the law or practice of Parliament prevents a relevant member of the House of Commons staff from presenting a complaint[5] to an employment tribunal[6].

1   Ie the Working Time Regulations 1998, SI 1998/1833 (see also PARAS 268 et seq, 278 et seq): see reg 40(1).
2   As to the meaning of 'employment' see PARA 269 note 5.
3   For these purposes, 'relevant member of the House of Commons staff' means any person:
    (1)   who was appointed by the House of Commons Commission (Working Time Regulations 1998, SI 1998/1833, reg 40(4)(a)); or
    (2)   who is a member of the Speaker's personal staff (reg 40(4)(b)).
    As to the House of Commons Commission see PARLIAMENT vol 78 (2010) PARA 946. As to the Speaker of the House of Commons see PARLIAMENT vol 78 (2010) PARA 931 et seq.
4   Working Time Regulations 1998, SI 1998/1833, reg 40(1). For the purposes of the application of the provisions of the Working Time Regulations 1998, SI 1998/1833, in relation to a relevant member of the House of Commons staff:
    (1)   references to a worker are to be construed as references to a relevant member of the House of Commons staff (reg 40(2)(a)); and
    (2)   references to a worker's contract are to be construed as references to the terms of employment of a relevant member of the House of Commons staff (reg 40(2)(b)).
    As to the meaning of 'worker' and as to the meaning of references to a worker's contract for these purposes see PARA 271.
5   Ie under the Working Time Regulations 1998, SI 1998/1833, reg 30 (see PARA 319): see reg 40(3).
6   Working Time Regulations 1998, SI 1998/1833, reg 40(3). As to employment tribunals see PARA 1399 et seq; and as to the procedure on a complaint made to an employment tribunal see PARA 1453 et seq.

278.   Effect of working time regulations in relation to police service.   For the purposes of the working time regulations[1], the holding, otherwise than under a contract of employment, of the office of constable or an appointment as a police cadet is to be treated as employment[2], under a worker's contract[3], by the relevant officer[4].

Any matter relating to the employment of a worker which may be provided for the purposes of the working time regulations in a workforce agreement[5] may be provided for the same purposes in relation to the service of a person holding the office of constable or an appointment as a police cadet by an agreement between the relevant officer and a joint branch board[6].

1   Ie the Working Time Regulations 1998, SI 1998/1833 (see also PARAS 268 et seq, 279 et seq): see reg 41(1) (reg 41(1), (3) amended, reg 41(1A) added, by SI 2006/594).

2   The Working Time Regulations 1998, SI 1998/1833, reg 41(1) is subject to reg 41(1A): see reg 41(1) (as amended: see note 1). Accordingly, for these purposes, any constable who has been seconded to the National Crime Agency to serve as a member of its staff must be treated as employed by the National Crime Agency: reg 41(1A) (as added (see note 1); and amended by virtue of the Crime and Courts Act 2013 s 15(3), Sch 8 para 190). As to the meaning of 'employment' see PARA 269 note 5. As to the National Crime Agency see POLICE AND INVESTIGATORY POWERS vol 84 (2013) PARA 424.

3   As to the meaning of references to a worker's contract see PARA 271.

4   Working Time Regulations 1998, SI 1998/1833, reg 41(1) (as amended: see note 1). For these purposes, the 'relevant officer' means (in relation to a member of a police force or a special constable or police cadet appointed for a police area) the chief officer of police and (in relation to any other person holding the office of constable or an appointment as a police cadet) the person who has the direction and control of the body of constables or cadets in question: see reg 41(3) (as amended: see note 1). As to the meaning of 'chief officer of police' see POLICE AND INVESTIGATORY POWERS vol 84 (2013) PARA 5; and as to the meaning of 'police area' see POLICE AND INVESTIGATORY POWERS vol 84 (2013) PARA 52.

    The 'relevant officer' (as defined by the Working Time Regulations 1998, SI 1998/1833, reg 41(3)) is to be treated as a corporation sole for these purposes: reg 41(4) (reg 41(4)–(6) added by SI 2005/2241). Where, in a case in which the relevant officer is guilty of an offence under the Working Time Regulations 1998, SI 1998/1833, it is proved:

    (1)   that the office-holder personally consented to the commission of the offence (reg 41(5)(a) (as so added));

    (2)   that he personally connived in its commission (reg 41(5)(b) (as so added)); or

    (3)   that the commission of the offence was attributable to personal neglect on his part (reg 41(5)(c) (as so added)),

the office-holder (as well as the corporation sole) is guilty of an offence and is liable to be proceeded against and punished accordingly (see reg 41(5) (as so added)). In relation to the relevant officer, 'office-holder' means an individual who, at the time of the consent, connivance or neglect: (a) held the office or other position mentioned in reg 41(3) as the office or position of that officer (reg 41(6)(a) (as so added)); or (b) was for the time being responsible for exercising and performing the powers and duties of that office or position (reg 41(6)(b) (as so added)).

5   As to the meaning of 'workforce agreement' see PARA 272.

6   Working Time Regulations 1998, SI 1998/1833, reg 41(2). For these purposes, a 'joint branch board' means a joint branch board constituted in accordance with the Police Federation Regulations 1969, SI 1969/1787, reg 7(3) (see POLICE AND INVESTIGATORY POWERS vol 84 (2013) PARA 359): see the Working Time Regulations 1998, SI 1998/1833, reg 41(3).

279.   Non-employed trainees to be regarded as a 'worker' under the working time regulations. For the purposes of the working time regulations[1], a person receiving relevant training[2], otherwise than under a contract of employment[3], is to be regarded as a worker[4], and the person whose undertaking is providing the training is to be regarded as his employer[5].

1   Ie the Working Time Regulations 1998, SI 1998/1833 (see also PARAS 268 et seq, 280 note 4 et seq): see reg 42.

2   For the purposes of the Working Time Regulations 1998, SI 1998/1833, 'relevant training' means work experience provided pursuant to a training course or programme, training for employment, or both, other than work experience or training: (1) the immediate provider of which is an educational institution or a person whose main business is the provision of training; and (2) which is provided on a course run by that institution or person: see reg 2(1).

3   As to the meaning of 'employment' see PARA 269 note 5.

4   As to the meaning of 'worker' for these purposes see PARA 271.

5   Working Time Regulations 1998, SI 1998/1833, reg 42. As to the meaning of 'employer' see PARA 269 note 5.

(iii) Rights and Obligations concerning Working Time

280. Maximum weekly working time of a worker under the working time regulations. Unless his employer[1] has first obtained the worker's[2] agreement in writing[3] to perform such work, a worker's working time[4], including overtime, in any reference period[5] which is applicable in his case must not exceed an average of 48 hours for each seven days[6]. For these purposes, a worker's average working time for each seven days during a reference period is to be determined according to the statutory formula[7].

An employer must take all reasonable steps, in keeping with the need to protect the health and safety of workers[8], to ensure that the limit on working time so specified is complied with in the case of each worker employed by him in relation to whom that limit applies; and he must keep up-to-date records of all workers who carry out work to which it does not apply by reason of the fact that the employer has obtained[9] the worker's agreement[10].

1   As to the meaning of 'employer' see PARA 269 note 5.
2   As to the meaning of 'worker' for these purposes see PARA 271.
3   As to the meaning of 'writing' see PARA 2 note 8.
4   In relation to a worker, 'working time' means: (1) any period during which he is working, at his employer's disposal, and carrying out his activity or duties; (2) any period during which he is receiving relevant training; and (3) any additional period which is to be treated as working time for the purpose of the Working Time Regulations 1998, SI 1998/1833, under a relevant agreement; and 'work' is to be construed accordingly: see reg 2(1). As to the meaning of 'relevant training' see PARA 279 note 2; and as to the meaning of 'relevant agreement' for these purposes see PARA 272 note 2. A worker who lives on site and is required to be there to answer calls throughout a period of 24 hours is working for the whole 24 hours: *MacCartney v Oversley House Management* [2006] ICR 510, [2006] IRLR 514, EAT. See also *Hughes v Graham (t/a Graylyns Residential Home)* [2008] All ER (D) 137 (Oct), EAT (employee entitled to the benefit of the Working Time Regulations 1998, SI 1998/1833, and the National Minimum Wage Regulations 1999, SI 1999/584, in circumstances where she had actually worked eight hours a week and was required to be on call for 77, giving her a working week of 85 days). As to the maximum weekly working time for young workers see PARA 281. As to agreements to exclude the maximum weekly working time see PARA 283; and as to the employer's duty to keep and retain records see PARA 287.
5   Subject to the Working Time Regulations 1998, SI 1998/1833, reg 4(4), (5) and to any agreement under reg 23(b) (see PARA 303), the reference periods which apply in the case of a worker are:
    (1)   where a relevant agreement provides for the application of reg 4 in relation to successive periods of 17 weeks, each such period (reg 4(3)(a)); or
    (2)   in any other case, any period of 17 weeks in the course of his employment (reg 4(3)(b)).
    Where, however, a worker has worked for his employer for less than 17 weeks, the reference period applicable in his case is the period that has elapsed since he started work for his employer: see reg 4(4). Regulation 4(3), (4) applies to a worker who is excluded from the scope of certain provisions of the Working Time Regulations 1998, SI 1998/1833, by reg 21 (see PARA 301) as if for each reference to 17 weeks there were substituted a reference to 26 weeks: see reg 4(5). As to the modification of the application of reg 4(3), (4) by collective agreements and workforce agreements see PARA 303. As to the meaning of 'employment' see PARA 269 note 5.
    The provisions of the Working Time Regulations 1998, SI 1998/1833, Pt II (regs 3–17) (rights and obligations concerning working time: see also PARAS 281, 283 et seq) have effect subject to the exceptions provided for in Pt III (regs 18–27A) (exceptions: see PARA 297 et seq): see reg 3(1) (reg 3(1) renumbered, reg 3(2) added, by SI 2002/3128). Where, in the Working Time Regulations 1998, SI 1998/1833, Pt II, separate provision is made as respects the same matter in relation to workers generally and to young workers, the provision relating to workers generally applies only to adult workers and those young workers to whom, by virtue of any exception in Pt III, the provision relating to young workers does not apply: reg 3(2) (as so added). As to the meaning of 'young worker' see PARA 281 note 1; and as to the meaning of 'adult worker' see PARA 285 note 2.
6   Working Time Regulations 1998, SI 1998/1833, reg 4(1) (reg 4(1), (2) amended by SI 1999/3372). For these purposes, 'day' means a period of 24 hours beginning at midnight: see

the Working Time Regulations 1998, SI 1998/1833, reg 2(1). There is a mandatory requirement, applying to all contracts of employment, that an employee should work no more than the average of 48 hours in any week during the reference period; and the absence in, reg 4(1) of an express prohibition on an employer from requiring his employee to work longer hours does not prevent reg 4(1) from having the effect of placing such a mandatory obligation on an employer; reg 4(1) need not be read together with the qualified obligation in reg 4(2) (see the text and notes 8–10): *Barber v RJB Mining (UK) Ltd* [1999] 2 CMLR 833, [1999] ICR 679 (the Working Time Regulations 1998, SI 1998/1833, reg 4(1) confers a free-standing right, breach of which can be the subject of civil proceedings in the ordinary courts). As to the disapplication of the Working Time Regulations 1998, SI 1998/1833, reg 4(1) in relation to excluded sectors see PARA 298; as to its disapplication in relation to domestic service see PARA 299; and as to its disapplication in relation to unmeasured working time see PARA 300.

7   Working Time Regulations 1998, SI 1998/1833, reg 4(6). The text refers to a reference period to be determined according to the formula:

$$\frac{A + B}{C}$$

where A is the aggregate number of hours comprised in the worker's working time during the course of the reference period; B is the aggregate number of hours comprised in his working time during the course of the period beginning immediately after the end of the reference period and ending when the number of days in that subsequent period on which he has worked equals the number of excluded days during the reference period; and C is the number of weeks in the reference period: see reg 4(6). For these purposes, 'excluded days' means days comprised in:

(1)   any period of annual leave taken by the worker in exercise of his entitlement under reg 13 (see PARA 291) (reg 4(7)(a));

(2)   any period of sick leave taken by the worker (reg 4(7)(b));

(3)   any period of maternity, paternity, adoption or parental leave taken by the worker (reg 4(7)(c) (amended by SI 2002/3128)); and

(4)   any period in respect of which the limit specified in the Working Time Regulations 1998, SI 1998/1833, reg 4(1) (see the text and notes 1–6) did not apply in relation to the worker by reason of the fact that the employer has obtained the worker's agreement as mentioned in reg 4(1) (reg 4(7)(d) (amended by SI 1999/3372)).

8   This principle underlies European Parliament and Council Directive (EC) 2003/88 of 4 November 2003 (OJ L299, 18.11.2003, p 9) concerning certain aspects of the organisation of working time (the 'Working Time Directive'), for the purposes of implementing which the Working Time Regulations 1998, SI 1998/1833, were made: see PARA 267. In particular, reg 4 takes advantage of the continuing provision in the Working Time Directive art 22(1) which allows member states not to apply art 6 while respecting the general principles of the protection of the safety and health of workers: see PARA 267.

9   Ie as mentioned in the Working Time Regulations 1998, SI 1998/1833, reg 4(1) (see the text and notes 1–6): see reg 4(2) (as amended: see note 6).

10 Working Time Regulations 1998, SI 1998/1833, reg 4(2) (as amended: see note 6). As to the disapplication of reg 4(2) in relation to excluded sectors see PARA 298; as to its disapplication in relation to domestic service see PARA 299; and as to its disapplication in relation to unmeasured working time see PARA 300. As to the enforcement of reg 4(2) see PARA 311; and as to offences see PARA 317.

281.   Maximum weekly working time of a young worker under the working time regulations.   In the case of a young worker[1], working time[2] must not exceed eight hours a day[3], or 40 hours a week[4]. An employer[5] must take all reasonable steps, in keeping with the need to protect the health and safety of workers[6], to ensure that these limits are complied with in the case of each worker employed by him in relation to whom they apply[7].

If, on any day, or as the case may be, during any week[8], a young worker is employed by more than one employer, his working time must be determined for the purpose of limiting his working time by aggregating the number of hours worked by him for each employer[9].

1   For these purposes, 'young worker' means a worker who has attained the age of 15 but not the age of 18 and who, as respects England and Wales, is over compulsory school age (construed in

accordance with the Education Act 1996 s 8: see EDUCATION vol 35 (2011) PARA 18): see the Working Time Regulations 1998, SI 1998/1833, reg 2(1). As to the meanings of 'England' and 'Wales' see PARA 2 note 12. As to the meaning of 'worker' for these purposes see PARA 271. A person attains a particular age expressed in years at the commencement of the relevant anniversary of the date of his birth: see the Family Law Reform Act 1969 s 9; and CHILDREN AND YOUNG PERSONS vol 9 (2012) PARA 2.

  As to the application of the Working Time Regulations 1998, SI 1998/1833, Pt II (regs 3–17) (rights and obligations concerning working time: see also PARAS 280 note 4, 283 et seq) and Pt III (regs 18–27A) (exceptions: see PARA 297 et seq) to young workers see PARA 280 note 5.

2 As to the meaning of 'working time' see PARA 280 note 4.
3 See the Working Time Regulations 1998, SI 1998/1833, reg 5A(1)(a) (reg 5A added by SI 2002/3128). As to the meaning of 'day' for these purposes see PARA 280 note 6.
4 See the Working Time Regulations 1998, SI 1998/1833, reg 5A(1)(b) (as added: see note 3).
5 As to the meaning of 'employer' see PARA 269 note 5.
6 This principle underlies European Parliament and Council Directive (EC) 2003/88 of 4 November 2003 (OJ L299, 18.11.2003, p 9) concerning certain aspects of the organisation of working time (the 'Working Time Directive'), for the purposes of implementing which the Working Time Regulations 1998, SI 1998/1833, were made: see PARA 267.
7 Working Time Regulations 1998, SI 1998/1833, reg 5A(4) (as added: see note 3).
8 For these purposes, a week starts at midnight between Sunday and Monday: see the Working Time Regulations 1998, SI 1998/1833, reg 5A(3) (as added: see note 3).
9 Working Time Regulations 1998, SI 1998/1833, reg 5A(2) (as added: see note 3).

282. Restrictions on contracting out. Any provision in an agreement (whether a contract of employment or not) is void in so far as it purports[1]:

(1) to exclude or limit the operation of any of the working time regulations[2], save in so far as provision is made[3] for an agreement to have that effect[4]; or

(2) to preclude a person from bringing proceedings under the working time regulations before an employment tribunal[5].

However, this does not apply to:

(a) any agreement to refrain from instituting or continuing proceedings before an employment tribunal where a conciliation officer has taken action[6] under the Employment Tribunals Act 1996[7];

(b) any agreement to refrain from instituting or continuing proceedings falling within the jurisdiction of the Employment Tribunals Act 1996 where conciliation is available[8], being proceedings under the working time regulations[9], if the following conditions regulating settlement agreements under those regulations are satisfied in relation to that agreement[10], that is to say[11]:

 (i) the agreement is in writing[12];

 (ii) the agreement relates to the particular complaint[13];

 (iii) the worker[14] has received advice from a relevant independent adviser[15] as to the terms and effect of the proposed agreement and, in particular, its effect on his ability to pursue his rights before an employment tribunal[16];

 (iv) there is in force, when the adviser gives the advice, a contract of insurance, or an indemnity provided for members of a profession or a professional body, covering the risk of a claim by the worker in respect of loss arising in consequence of the advice[17];

 (v) the agreement identifies the adviser[18]; and

 (vi) the agreement states that the conditions regulating settlement agreements under the working time regulations are satisfied[19].

1 See the Working Time Regulations 1998, SI 1998/1833, reg 35(1).
2 Ie any provision of the Working Time Regulations 1998, SI 1998/1833 (see also PARAS 268 et seq, 283 et seq): see reg 35(1)(a).

3   Ie by the Working Time Regulations 1998, SI 1998/1833 (see also PARAS 268 et seq, 283 et seq): see reg 35(1)(a). See eg reg 5; and PARA 283.

4   Working Time Regulations 1998, SI 1998/1833, reg 35(1)(a). An agreement which provided for no sum to be paid in respect of outstanding leave entitlement in the event of termination of employment (see reg 14; and PARA 293) was rendered void by reg 35(1)(a) in *Witley and District Men's Club v Mackay* [2001] IRLR 595, EAT.

5   Working Time Regulations 1998, SI 1998/1833, reg 35(1)(b). As to employment tribunals see PARA 1399 et seq; and as to the procedure on a complaint made to an employment tribunal see PARA 1453 et seq.

6   Ie under any of the Employment Tribunals Act 1996 ss 18A–18C (requirement to contact ACAS before instituting proceedings: see PARAS 152, 153): see the Working Time Regulations 1998, SI 1998/1833, reg 35(2)(a) (amended by SI 2014/386). As to conciliation officers see PARA 1214. As to 'taking action' under equivalent provisions of the Employment Rights Act 1996 see PARA 150 note 16.

7   Working Time Regulations 1998, SI 1998/1833, reg 35(2)(a) (as amended: see note 6).

8   Ie proceedings within the Employment Tribunals Act 1996 s 18(1)(j) (employment tribunal proceedings under the Working Time Regulations 1998, SI 1988/1833: see PARA 152 note 1): see reg 35(2)(b) (amended by SI 2013/1956; and SI 2014/431).

9   Ie employment tribunal proceedings under the Working Time Regulations 1998, SI 1988/1833, reg 30 (see PARA 319): see reg 35(2)(b) (as amended: see note 8).

10   Working Time Regulations 1998, SI 1998/1833, reg 35(2)(b) (as amended: see note 8).
     Settlement agreements were formerly known as compromise agreements (ie before 29 July 2013: see the Enterprise and Regulatory Reform Act 2013 s 23 (renaming of 'compromise agreements', 'compromise contracts' and 'compromises'); and the Enterprise and Regulatory Reform Act 2013 (Commencement No 2) Order 2013, SI 2013/1648, art 2(c)).

11   For the purposes of head (b) in the text, the conditions regulating settlement agreements under the Working Time Regulations 1998, SI 1998/1833, are set out in reg 35(3)(a)–(f) (see heads (b)(i)–(b)(vi) in the text): see reg 35(3) (amended by SI 2013/1956).

12   Working Time Regulations 1998, SI 1998/1833, reg 35(3)(a).

13   Working Time Regulations 1998, SI 1998/1833, reg 35(3)(b).

14   As to the meaning of 'worker' for these purposes see PARA 271.

15   For the purposes of head (b)(iii) in the text, a person is a relevant independent adviser (see the Working Time Regulations 1998, SI 1998/1833, reg 35(4)):
     (1)   if he is a qualified lawyer (reg 35(4)(a));
     (2)   if he is an officer, official, employee or member of an independent trade union who has been certified in writing by the trade union as competent to give advice and as authorised to do so on behalf of the trade union (reg 35(4)(b)); or
     (3)   if he works at an advice centre, whether as an employee or a volunteer, and has been certified in writing by the centre as competent to give advice and as authorised to do so on behalf of the centre (reg 35(4)(c)).
     For the purposes of head (1) above, 'qualified lawyer' means, as respects England and Wales, a person who, for the purposes of the Legal Services Act 2007, is an authorised person in relation to an activity which constitutes the exercise of a right of audience or the conduct of litigation (within the meaning of that Act: see LEGAL PROFESSIONS vol 65 (2008) PARAS 497–498): Working Time Regulations 1998, SI 1998/1833, reg 35(6)(a) (amended by SI 2009/3348). A person is to be treated as being a qualified lawyer for the purposes of the Working Time Regulations 1998, SI 1998/1833, reg 35(6)(a) if he is a Fellow of the Institute of Legal Executives (see LEGAL PROFESSIONS vol 66 (2009) PARA 1463 et seq) practising in a solicitor's practice (including a body recognised under the Administration of Justice Act 1985 s 9: see LEGAL PROFESSIONS vol 65 (2008) PARA 515): Working Time Regulations 1998, SI 1998/1833, reg 35(6A) (added by SI 2004/2516; and amended by SI 2009/3348). A person is not, however, a relevant independent adviser for the purposes of head (b)(iii) in the text, in relation to the worker:
     (a)   if he is, is employed by or is acting in the matter for the employer or an associated employer (Working Time Regulations 1998, SI 1998/1833, reg 35(5)(a));
     (b)   in the case of a person within heads (2) or (3) above, if the trade union or advice centre is the employer or an associated employer (reg 35(5)(b)); or
     (c)   in the case of a person within head (3) above, if the worker makes a payment for the advice received from him (reg 35(5)(c)).
     Any two employers are to be treated as associated for these purposes if one is a company of which the other (directly or indirectly) has control, or if both are companies of which a third person (directly or indirectly) has control; and 'associated employer' is to be construed accordingly: see reg 35(7). As to the meaning of 'employer' see PARA 269 note 5.

16   Working Time Regulations 1998, SI 1998/1833, reg 35(3)(c).
17   Working Time Regulations 1998, SI 1998/1833, reg 35(3)(d).
18   Working Time Regulations 1998, SI 1998/1833, reg 35(3)(e).
19   Working Time Regulations 1998, SI 1998/1833, reg 35(3)(f) (amended by SI 2013/1956).

283.   Agreement to exclude the maximum weekly working time.   An agreement[1] to exclude the maximum weekly working time[2]:

(1)   may either relate to a specified period or apply indefinitely[3]; and

(2)   subject to any provision in the agreement for a different period of notice, must be terminable by the worker[4] by giving not less than seven days' notice[5] to his employer[6] in writing[7].

Where such an agreement makes provision for the termination of the agreement after a period of notice, the notice period provided for must not exceed three months[8].

1   Ie an agreement for the purposes of the Working Time Regulations 1998, SI 1998/1833, reg 4 (see PARA 280): see reg 5(2) (reg 5(2), (3) amended by SI 1999/3372).
        As to the application of the Working Time Regulations 1998, SI 1998/1833, Pt II (regs 3–17) (rights and obligations concerning working time: see also PARAS 280, 281, 284 et seq) and Pt III (regs 18–27A) (exceptions: see PARA 297 et seq) see PARA 280 note 5.
2   See the Working Time Regulations 1998, SI 1998/1833, reg 5(2) (as amended: see note 1). As to the meaning of 'working time' see PARA 280 note 4.
3   Working Time Regulations 1998, SI 1998/1833, reg 5(2)(a).
4   As to the meaning of 'worker' for these purposes see PARA 271.
5   As to the meaning of 'day' for these purposes see PARA 280 note 6.
6   As to the meaning of 'employer' for these purposes see PARA 269 note 5.
7   Working Time Regulations 1998, SI 1998/1833, reg 5(2)(b). As to the meaning of 'writing' see PARA 2 note 8.
8   Working Time Regulations 1998, SI 1998/1833, reg 5(3) (as amended: see note 1).

284.   Length of night work.   A night worker's[1] normal hours of work in any reference period[2] which is applicable in his case must not exceed an average of eight hours for each 24 hours[3]. For these purposes, a night worker's average normal hours of work for each 24 hours during a reference period are to be determined according to the statutory formula[4]. An employer must take all reasonable steps, in keeping with the need to protect the health and safety of workers[5], to ensure that the limit on working time so specified is complied with in the case of each night worker employed by him[6].

An employer must ensure that: (1) no night worker employed by him whose work involves special hazards or heavy physical or mental strain[7] works for more than eight hours in any 24-hour period during which the night worker performs night work[8]; and (2) no young worker[9] employed by him works during the restricted period[10].

1   For these purposes, 'night worker' means a worker: (1) who, as a normal course, works at least three hours of his daily working time during night time; or (2) who is likely, during night time, to work at least such proportion of his annual working time as may be specified for the purposes of the Working Time Regulations 1998, SI 1998/1833, in a collective agreement or a workforce agreement; and, for the purpose of head (1) above, a person works hours as a normal course, without prejudice to the generality of that expression, if he works such hours on the majority of days on which he works: see reg 2(1). 'Night time', in relation to a worker, means a period: (a) the duration of which is not less than seven hours; and (b) which includes the period between midnight and 5 am, which is determined for the purposes of the Working Time Regulations 1998, SI 1998/1833, by a relevant agreement, or, in default of such a determination, the period between 11 pm and 6 am: see reg 2(1). 'Night work' means work during night time: reg 2(1). As to the meaning of 'worker' for these purposes see PARA 271; as to the meanings of 'collective agreement' and 'relevant agreement' for these purposes see PARA 272 note 2; as to the

meaning of 'workforce agreement' see PARA 272; as to the meanings of 'work' and 'working time' see PARA 280 note 4; and as to the meaning of 'day' for these purposes see PARA 280 note 6.

A worker may be a night worker for the purposes of the Working Time Regulations 1998, SI 1998/1833, reg 2(1), notwithstanding that he spends only one week of each three-week shift cycle working from 9 pm to 7 am: *R v A-G for Northern Ireland, ex p Burns* [1999] IRLR 315.

2 For these purposes, the reference periods which apply in the case of a night worker are:
   (1) where a relevant agreement provides for the application of the Working Time Regulations 1998, SI 1998/1833, reg 6 in relation to successive periods of 17 weeks, each such period (reg 6(3)(a)); or
   (2) in any other case, any period of 17 weeks in the course of his employment (reg 6(3)(b)).
Where, however, a worker has worked for his employer for less than 17 weeks, the reference period applicable in his case is the period that has elapsed since he started work for his employer: reg 6(4). As to the meanings of 'employer' and 'employment' see PARA 269 note 5. As to the modification or exclusion of reg 6(3) by collective agreements or workforce agreements see PARA 303.

As to the application of Pt II (regs 3–17) (rights and obligations concerning working time: see also PARAS 280 et seq, 285 et seq) and Pt III (regs 18–27A) (exceptions: see PARA 297 et seq) see PARA 280 note 5.

3 Working Time Regulations 1998, SI 1998/1833, reg 6(1). As to the disapplication of reg 6(1) in relation to excluded sectors see PARA 298; as to its disapplication in relation to domestic service see PARA 299; as to its disapplication in relation to unmeasured working time see PARA 300; and as to its disapplication in relation to other special cases see PARA 301. As to the modification or exclusion of reg 6(1) by collective agreements or workforce agreements see PARA 303. As to the employer's duty to keep and retain records see PARA 287.

4 Working Time Regulations 1998, SI 1998/1833, reg 6(5). The text refers to a reference period to be determined according to the formula:

$$\frac{A}{B - C}$$

where A is the number of hours during the reference period which are normal working hours for that worker; B is the number of days during the reference period; and C is the total number of hours during the reference period comprised in rest periods spent by the worker in pursuance of his entitlement under reg 11 (see PARA 289) divided by 24: see reg 6(5). For these purposes, 'rest period', in relation to a worker, means a period which is not working time, other than a rest break or leave to which the worker is entitled under the Working Time Regulations 1998, SI 1998/1833: see reg 2(1). Guidelines issued in relation to the Working Time Regulations 1998, SI 1998/1833 (which were made for the purposes of implementing Council Directive (EC) 93/104) (see PARA 268), indicating that employers must ensure that workers are able to take rest breaks, but are not required to ensure that they do so, render the workers' rights meaningless: see Case C-484/04 *EC Commission v United Kingdom* [2007] ICR 592, [2006] IRLR 888, ECJ (the Working Time Regulations 1998, SI 1998/1833, reg 20(2) was revoked as a consequence of this decision: see generally PARA 300).

5 This principle underlies European Parliament and Council Directive (EC) 2003/88 of 4 November 2003 (OJ L299, 18.11.2003, p 9) concerning certain aspects of the organisation of working time (the 'Working Time Directive'), for the purposes of implementing which the Working Time Regulations 1998, SI 1998/1833, were made: see PARA 267.

6 Working Time Regulations 1998, SI 1998/1833, reg 6(2). As to the disapplication of reg 6(2) in relation to excluded sectors see PARA 298; as to its disapplication in relation to domestic service see PARA 299; as to its disapplication in relation to unmeasured working time see PARA 300; and as to its disapplication in relation to other special cases see PARA 301. As to the modification or exclusion of reg 6(2) by collective agreements or workforce agreements see PARA 303; as to enforcement of reg 6(2) see PARA 311; and as to offences see PARA 317.

7 For these purposes, the work of a night worker is to be regarded as involving special hazards or heavy physical or mental strain if:
   (1) it is identified as such in a collective agreement or in a workforce agreement which takes account of the specific effects and hazards of night work (Working Time Regulations 1998, SI 1998/1833, reg 6(8)(a)); or
   (2) it is recognised in a risk assessment made by the employer under the Management of Health and Safety at Work Regulations 1999, SI 1999/3242, reg 3 (see HEALTH AND

SAFETY AT WORK vol 52 (2014) PARA 394) as involving a significant risk to the health or safety of workers employed by him (Working Time Regulations 1998, SI 1998/1833, reg 6(8)(b) (amended by SI 1999/3242)).

8   See the Working Time Regulations 1998, SI 1998/1833, reg 6(7). As to the disapplication of reg 6(7) in relation to excluded sectors see PARA 298; as to its disapplication in relation to domestic service see PARA 299; as to its disapplication in relation to unmeasured working time see PARA 300; and as to its disapplication in relation to other special cases see PARA 301. As to the modification or exclusion of reg 6(7) by collective agreements or workforce agreements see PARA 303; as to enforcement of reg 6(7) see PARA 311; and as to offences see PARA 317.

9   As to the meaning of 'young worker' see PARA 281 note 1.

10 See the Working Time Regulations 1998, SI 1998/1833, reg 6A (added by SI 2002/3128). For these purposes, the 'restricted period', in relation to a worker, means the period between 10 pm and 6 am (or, where the worker's contract provides for him to work after 10 pm, the period between 11 pm and 7 am): see the Working Time Regulations 1998, SI 1998/1833, reg 2(1) (definition added by SI 2002/3128).

285.   Health assessment and transfer of night workers to day work.   An employer[1]:

(1)   must not assign an adult worker[2] to work[3] which is to be undertaken during periods such that the worker will become a night worker[4], unless:

(a)   the employer has ensured that the worker will have the opportunity of a free health assessment before he takes up the assignment[5]; or

(b)   the worker had a health assessment before being assigned to work to be undertaken during such periods on an earlier occasion, and the employer has no reason to believe that that assessment is no longer valid[6]; and

(2)   must ensure that each night worker employed by him has the opportunity of a free health assessment at regular intervals of whatever duration may be appropriate in his case[7].

Save in exceptional cases[8], an employer[9]:

(i)   must not assign a young worker to work during the restricted period[10], unless:

(A)   the employer has ensured that the young worker will have the opportunity of a free assessment[11] of his health and capacities before he takes up the assignment[12]; or

(B)   the young worker had an assessment of his health and capacities before being assigned to work during the restricted period on an earlier occasion, and the employer has no reason to believe that that assessment is no longer valid[13]; and

(ii)   must ensure that each young worker employed by him and assigned to work during the restricted period has the opportunity of a free assessment of his health and capacities at regular intervals of whatever duration may be appropriate in his case[14].

No person is to disclose an assessment made for these purposes to any person other than the worker to whom it relates, unless the worker has given his consent in writing to the disclosure[15], or unless the disclosure is confined to a statement that the assessment shows the worker to be fit either (in a case where head (1)(a) or head (i)(A) above applies) to take up an assignment[16], or (in a case where head (2) or head (ii) above applies) to continue to undertake an assignment[17].

Where a registered medical practitioner[18] has advised an employer that a worker employed by the employer is suffering from health problems which the practitioner considers to be connected with the fact that the worker performs night work[19], and where it is possible for the employer to transfer the worker to work to which the worker is suited, and which is to be undertaken during periods such that the worker will cease to be a night worker, the employer must transfer the worker accordingly[20].

1 See the Working Time Regulations 1998, SI 1998/1833, reg 7(1). As to the meaning of 'employer' see PARA 269 note 5.

   As to the application of Pt II (regs 3–17) (rights and obligations concerning working time: see also PARAS 280 et seq, 286 et seq) and Pt III (regs 18–27A) (exceptions: see PARA 297 et seq) see PARA 280 note 5. As to the disapplication of reg 7(1) in relation to excluded sectors see PARA 298; and as to its disapplication in relation to domestic service see PARA 299. As to enforcement of reg 7(1) see PARA 311; and as to offences see PARA 317. As to the employer's duty to keep and retain records see PARA 287.

2 For these purposes, 'adult worker' means a worker who has attained the age of 18: see the Working Time Regulations 1998, SI 1998/1833, reg 2(1). As to the meaning of 'worker' for these purposes see PARA 271. A person attains a particular age expressed in years at the commencement of the relevant anniversary of the date of his birth: see the Family Law Reform Act 1969 s 9; and CHILDREN AND YOUNG PERSONS vol 9 (2012) PARA 2.

3 As to the meaning of 'work' see PARA 280 note 4.

4 See the Working Time Regulations 1998, SI 1998/1833, reg 7(1)(a). See note 1. As to the meaning of 'night worker' see PARA 284 note 1.

5 Working Time Regulations 1998, SI 1998/1833, reg 7(1)(a)(i). See note 1. For these purposes, and for the purposes of reg 7(2) (see the text and notes 9–14), an assessment is free if it is at no cost to the worker to whom it relates: see reg 7(3).

6 Working Time Regulations 1998, SI 1998/1833, reg 7(1)(a)(ii). See note 1.

7 Working Time Regulations 1998, SI 1998/1833, reg 7(1)(b). See note 1.

8 Ie subject to the Working Time Regulations 1998, SI 1998/1833, reg 7(4): see reg 7(2). Accordingly, the requirements in reg 7(2) do not apply in a case where the work a young worker is assigned to do is of an exceptional nature: reg 7(4). As to the meaning of 'young worker' see PARA 281 note 1. As to the disapplication of reg 7(2) in relation to domestic service see PARA 299. As to enforcement of reg 7(2) see PARA 311; and as to offences see PARA 317.

9 See the Working Time Regulations 1998, SI 1998/1833, reg 7(2). See note 8.

10 See the Working Time Regulations 1998, SI 1998/1833, reg 7(2)(a) (amended by SI 2002/3128). See note 8. As to the meaning of 'restricted period' see PARA 284 note 10.

11 See note 5.

12 Working Time Regulations 1998, SI 1998/1833, reg 7(2)(a)(i). See note 8.

13 Working Time Regulations 1998, SI 1998/1833, reg 7(2)(a)(ii). See note 8.

14 Working Time Regulations 1998, SI 1998/1833, reg 7(2)(b). See note 8.

15 See the Working Time Regulations 1998, SI 1998/1833, reg 7(5)(a).

16 See the Working Time Regulations 1998, SI 1998/1833, reg 7(5)(b)(i).

17 See the Working Time Regulations 1998, SI 1998/1833, reg 7(5)(b)(ii).

18 As to the meaning of 'registered medical practitioner' see MEDICAL PROFESSIONS vol 74 (2011) PARA 176.

19 See the Working Time Regulations 1998, SI 1998/1833, reg 7(6)(a). As to the disapplication of reg 7(6) in relation to excluded sectors see PARA 298; and as to its disapplication in relation to domestic service see PARA 299. As to enforcement of reg 7(6) see PARA 311; and as to offences see PARA 317.

20 See the Working Time Regulations 1998, SI 1998/1833, reg 7(6)(b). See note 19.

286. Pattern of work. Where the pattern according to which an employer[1] organises work[2] is such as to put the health and safety of a worker employed by him at risk[3], in particular because the work is monotonous or the work-rate is predetermined, the employer must ensure that the worker is given adequate rest breaks[4].

1 As to the meaning of 'employer' see PARA 269 note 5.

2 As to the meaning of 'work' see PARA 280 note 4.

3 This principle underlies European Parliament and Council Directive (EC) 2003/88 of 4 November 2003 (OJ L299, 18.11.2003, p 9) concerning certain aspects of the organisation of

working time (the 'Working Time Directive'), for the purposes of implementing which the Working Time Regulations 1998, SI 1998/1833, were made: see PARA 267. As to the meaning of 'worker' for these purposes see PARA 271.

4 Working Time Regulations 1998, SI 1998/1833, reg 8.
   As to the application of Pt II (regs 3–17) (rights and obligations concerning working time: see also PARAS 280 et seq, 287 et seq) and Pt III (regs 18–27A) (exceptions: see PARA 297 et seq) see PARA 280 note 5. As to the disapplication of reg 8 in relation to excluded sectors see PARA 298; and as to its disapplication in relation to domestic service see PARA 299. As to enforcement of reg 8 see PARA 311; and as to offences see PARA 317.

287. Records to be kept by employer in relation to maximum weekly working time and night work. An employer[1] must:

(1) keep records which are adequate to show whether: (a) the limits specified in relation to the maximum weekly working time[2], and the length of night work[3]; and (b) the requirements relating to night work by young workers[4], and by night workers who are subject to transfer following a free health assessment[5], are being complied with in the case of each worker[6] employed by him in relation to whom those limits and requirements apply[7]; and

(2) retain such records for two years from the date on which they were made[8].

1 As to the meaning of 'employer' see PARA 269 note 5.
2 Ie the limits specified in the Working Time Regulations 1998, SI 1998/1833, reg 4(1) (see PARA 280), reg 5A(1) (see PARA 281): see reg 9(a) (amended by SI 2002/3128).
   As to the application of the Working Time Regulations 1998, SI 1998/1833, Pt II (regs 3–17) (rights and obligations concerning working time: see also PARAS 280 et seq, 288 et seq) and Pt III (regs 18–27A) (exceptions: see PARA 297 et seq) see PARA 280 note 5. As to the disapplication of reg 9 in relation to workers in the armed forces see PARA 306. As to enforcement of reg 9 see PARA 311; and as to offences see PARA 317.
3 Ie the limit specified in the Working Time Regulations 1998, SI 1998/1833, reg 6(1), (7) (see PARA 284): see reg 9(a) (as amended: see note 2). As to the meaning of 'night work' see PARA 284 note 1.
4 Ie the requirement in the Working Time Regulations 1998, SI 1998/1833, reg 6A (see PARA 284): see reg 9(a) (as amended: see note 2). As to the meaning of 'young worker' see PARA 281 note 1.
5 Ie the requirements in the Working Time Regulations 1998, SI 1998/1833, reg 7(1), (2) (see PARA 285): see reg 9(a) (as amended: see note 2). As to the meaning of 'night worker' see PARA 284 note 1.
6 As to the meaning of 'worker' for these purposes see PARA 271.
7 Working Time Regulations 1998, SI 1998/1833, reg 9(a) (as amended: see note 2).
8 Working Time Regulations 1998, SI 1998/1833, reg 9(b).

288. Daily rest. A worker[1] is entitled to a rest period[2] of not less than 11 consecutive hours in each 24-hour period during which he works for his employer[3].

A young worker[4], on the other hand, is entitled to a rest period of not less than 12 consecutive hours in each 24-hour period during which he works for his employer[5]; but that minimum rest period may be interrupted in the case of activities involving periods of work that are split up over the day or of short duration[6].

1 As to the meaning of 'worker' for these purposes see PARA 271.
2 As to the meaning of 'rest period' see PARA 284 note 4.
3 Working Time Regulations 1998, SI 1998/1833, reg 10(1) (amended by SI 2002/3128). As to the meaning of 'employer' see PARA 269 note 5.
   As to the application of the Working Time Regulations 1998, SI 1998/1833, Pt II (regs 3–17) (rights and obligations concerning working time: see also PARAS 280 et seq, 289 et seq) and Pt III (regs 18–27A) (exceptions: see PARA 297 et seq) see PARA 280 note 5. As to the disapplication of reg 10(1) in relation to excluded sectors see PARA 298; as to its disapplication in relation to

unmeasured working time see PARA 300; as to its disapplication in relation to other special cases see PARA 301; and as to its disapplication in relation to shift workers see PARA 302. As to the modification or exclusion of reg 10(1) by collective agreements and workforce agreements see PARA 303. As to the right to present a complaint to an employment tribunal see PARA 319. See also *MacCartney v Oversley House Management* [2006] ICR 510, [2006] IRLR 514, EAT; and PARA 280 note 4.

4   As to the meaning of 'young worker' see PARA 281 note 1.
5   Working Time Regulations 1998, SI 1998/1833, reg 10(2). As to the disapplication of reg 10(2) in relation to young workers in the armed forces see PARA 306; and as to its disapplication in relation to young workers and force majeure see PARA 309.
6   Working Time Regulations 1998, SI 1998/1833, reg 10(3).

289.   Weekly rest period. A worker[1] is entitled to an uninterrupted rest period[2] of not less than 24 hours in each seven-day period[3] during which he works for his employer[4]. However, if his employer so determines, a worker is entitled to either[5]:

(1)   two uninterrupted rest periods each of not less than 24 hours in each 14-day period during which he works for his employer[6]; or

(2)   one uninterrupted rest period of not less than 48 hours in each such 14-day period[7],

in place of the entitlement otherwise[8] provided for[9].

A young worker[10] is entitled[11] to a rest period of not less than 48 hours in each seven-day period during which he works for his employer[12]; but the minimum rest period to which a young worker is so entitled[13]:

(a)   may be interrupted in the case of activities involving periods of work that are split up over the day or are of short duration[14]; and

(b)   may be reduced where this is justified by technical or organisation reasons, but not to less than 36 consecutive hours[15].

1   As to the meaning of 'worker' for these purposes see PARA 271.
2   Ie subject to the Working Time Regulations 1998, SI 1998/1833, reg 11(2) (see the text and notes 5–9): see reg 11(1) (reg 11(1), (2), (7) amended by SI 2002/3128). As to the meaning of 'rest period' see PARA 284 note 4.
        As to the application of the Working Time Regulations 1998, SI 1998/1833, Pt II (regs 3–17) (rights and obligations concerning working time: see also PARAS 280 et seq, 290 et seq) and Pt III (regs 18–27A) (exceptions: see PARA 297 et seq) see PARA 280 note 5.
3   For the purposes of the Working Time Regulations 1998, SI 1998/1833, reg 11(1)–(3) (see also the text and notes 4–12), a seven-day period (or, as the case may be, 14-day period) is to be taken to begin:
        (1)   at such times on such days as may be provided for the purposes of reg 11 in a relevant agreement (reg 11(4)(a)); or
        (2)   where there are no provisions of a relevant agreement which apply, at the start of each week (or, as the case may be, every other week) (reg 11(4)(b)).
    In a case where, in accordance with reg 11(4), 14-day periods are to be taken to begin at the start of every other week, the first such period applicable in the case of a particular worker is to be taken to begin:
        (a)   if the worker's employment began on or before 1 October 1998 (ie the date on which the Working Time Regulations 1998, SI 1998/1833, came into force: see reg 1(1)), on 5 October 1998 (reg 11(5)(a)); or
        (b)   if the worker's employment begins after 1 October 1998, at the start of the week in which that employment begins (reg 11(5)(b)).
    For these purposes, a week starts at midnight between Sunday and Monday: reg 11(6). As to the meaning of 'worker' for these purposes see PARA 271; as to the meaning of 'relevant agreement' see PARA 272 note 2; and as to the meaning of 'day' see PARA 280 note 6.
4   Working Time Regulations 1998, SI 1998/1833, reg 11(1) (as amended: see note 2). As to the meaning of 'employer' see PARA 269 note 5. The minimum rest period to which a worker is entitled under the Working Time Regulations 1998, SI 1998/1833, reg 11(1) or reg 11(2) (see the text and notes 5–9) does not include any part of a rest period to which the worker is entitled

under reg 10(1) (daily rest period: see PARA 288), except where this is justified by objective or technical reasons or reasons concerning the organisation of work: reg 11(7) (as amended: see note 2).

As to the disapplication of reg 11(1) in relation to excluded sectors see PARA 298; as to its disapplication in relation to unmeasured working time see PARA 300; as to its disapplication in relation to other special cases see PARA 301; and as to its disapplication in relation to shift workers see PARA 302. As to the modification or exclusion of reg 11(1) by collective agreements and workforce agreements see PARA 303. As to the right to present a complaint to an employment tribunal see PARA 319.

5   See the Working Time Regulations 1998, SI 1998/1833, reg 11(2) (as amended: see note 2). As to the disapplication of reg 11(2) in relation to excluded sectors see PARA 298; as to its disapplication in relation to unmeasured working time see PARA 300; as to its disapplication in relation to other special cases see PARA 301; and as to its disapplication in relation to shift workers see PARA 302. As to the modification or exclusion of reg 11(2) by collective agreements and workforce agreements see PARA 303.
6   Working Time Regulations 1998, SI 1998/1833, reg 11(2)(a). See notes 3, 5.
7   Working Time Regulations 1998, SI 1998/1833, reg 11(2)(b). See notes 3, 5.
8   Ie in the Working Time Regulations 1998, SI 1998/1833, reg 11(1) (see the text and notes 1–4): see reg 11(2). See note 5.
9   See the Working Time Regulations 1998, SI 1998/1833, reg 11(2). See note 5.
10 As to the meaning of 'young worker' see PARA 281 note 1.
11 Ie subject to the Working Time Regulations 1998, SI 1998/1833, reg 11(8) (see the text and notes 13–15): see reg 11(3).
12 Working Time Regulations 1998, SI 1998/1833, reg 11(3). See note 3. As to the disapplication of reg 11(3) in relation to workers in the armed forces see PARA 306.
13 See the Working Time Regulations 1998, SI 1998/1833, reg 11(8).
14 Working Time Regulations 1998, SI 1998/1833, reg 11(8)(a).
15 Working Time Regulations 1998, SI 1998/1833, reg 11(8)(b).

290.   Rest breaks.   Where a worker's[1] daily working time[2] is more than six hours, he is entitled to a rest break[3]. The details of the rest break to which a worker is so entitled, including its duration and the terms on which it is granted, are to be in accordance with any provisions for these purposes which are contained in a collective agreement[4] or a workforce agreement[5]. Subject to the provisions of any applicable collective agreement or workforce agreement, the rest break so provided for is an uninterrupted period of not less than 20 minutes[6].

Where a young worker's[7] daily working time is more than four and a half hours, he is entitled to a rest break of at least 30 minutes (which must be consecutive, if possible)[8]. If, on any day, a young worker is employed by more than one employer[9], his daily working time is to be determined for that purpose by aggregating the number of hours worked by him for each employer[10].

1   As to the meaning of 'worker' for these purposes see PARA 271.
2   As to the meaning of 'working time' see PARA 280 note 4.
3   Working Time Regulations 1998, SI 1998/1833, reg 12(1) (reg 12(1), (2) amended by SI 2002/3128). Inactive time between tasks, but with the employee still at the call of the employer, is not a 'rest break' for these purposes: *Gallagher v Alpha Catering Services Ltd (t/a Alpha Flight Services)* [2004] EWCA Civ 1559, [2005] ICR 673, [2005] IRLR 102.
    As to the application of the Working Time Regulations 1998, SI 1998/1833, Pt II (regs 3–17) (rights and obligations concerning working time: see also PARAS 280 et seq, 291 et seq) and Pt III (regs 18–27A) (exceptions: see PARA 297 et seq) see PARA 280 note 5. As to the disapplication of reg 12(1) in relation to excluded sectors see PARA 298; as to its application in relation to unmeasured working time see PARA 300; and as to its application in relation to other special cases see PARA 301. As to the modification or exclusion of reg 12(1) by collective agreements and workforce agreements see PARA 303. As to the right to present a complaint to an employment tribunal see PARA 319.
4   As to the meaning of 'collective agreement' see PARA 272 note 2.
5   Working Time Regulations 1998, SI 1998/1833, reg 12(2) (as amended: see note 3). As to the meaning of 'workforce agreement' see PARA 272.

6   Working Time Regulations 1998, SI 1998/1833, reg 12(3). The worker is also entitled to spend the rest break so provided for away from his workstation, if he has one: see reg 12(3).
7   As to the meaning of 'young worker' see PARA 281 note 1.
8   Working Time Regulations 1998, SI 1998/1833, reg 12(4). The worker is also entitled to spend the rest break so provided for away from his workstation, if he has one: see reg 12(4). As to the disapplication of reg 12(4) in relation to young workers and force majeure see PARA 309.
9   As to the meaning of 'employer' see PARA 269 note 5.
10 Working Time Regulations 1998, SI 1998/1833, reg 12(5).

291. Entitlement to annual leave. A worker[1] is entitled[2] to four weeks' annual leave in each leave year[3]. A worker's leave year, for these purposes, begins[4]:

(1)   on such date during the calendar year[5] as may be provided for in a relevant agreement[6]; or

(2)   where there are no provisions of a relevant agreement which apply[7]: (a) if the worker's employment began on or before 1 October 1998[8], on that date and each subsequent anniversary of that date[9]; or (b) if the worker's employment begins after 1 October 1998[10], on the date on which that employment begins and each subsequent anniversary of that date[11].

Where the date on which a worker's employment[12] begins is later than the date on which, by virtue of a relevant agreement, his first leave year begins, the leave to which he is entitled in that leave year is a proportion of the period applicable[13] equal to the proportion of that leave year remaining on the date on which his employment begins[14].

1   As to the meaning of 'worker' for these purposes see PARA 271.
2   Ie subject to the Working Time Regulations 1998, SI 1998/1833, reg 13(5) (see the text and notes 12–14): see reg 13(1) (substituted by SI 2001/3256).
    As to the application of the Working Time Regulations 1998, SI 1998/1833, Pt II (regs 3–17) (rights and obligations concerning working time: see also PARAS 280 et seq, 292 et seq) and Pt III (regs 18–27A) (exceptions: see PARA 297 et seq) see PARA 280 note 5. As to the disapplication of reg 13 in relation to excluded sectors see PARA 298. As to the right to present a complaint to an employment tribunal see PARA 319.
3   Working Time Regulations 1998, SI 1998/1833, reg 13(1) (as substituted: see note 2). As to separate entitlement to additional annual leave (and protection of contractual entitlements) see regs 13A, 26A; and PARA 292. As to the power of the Secretary of State to make provision about entitlement to annual leave see PARA 270. As to the taking of leave and compensation associated with untaken leave see PARA 293; and as to the dates on which leave is to be taken see PARA 294.
    The former requirement (contained in reg 13(7), (8) as originally enacted) that reg 13 was to apply only to workers who had been continuously employed by the same employer for a minimum period of 13 weeks was revoked following the decision in Case C-173/99 *R (on the application of the Broadcasting, Entertainment, Cinematographic and Theatre Union) v Secretary of State for Trade and Industry* [2001] All ER (EC) 647, [2001] ECR I-4881, ECJ, which declared that such a condition was incompatible with European Parliament and Council Directive (EC) 2003/88 of 4 November 2003 (OJ L299, 18.11.2003, p 9) concerning certain aspects of the organisation of working time (the 'Working Time Directive': see PARA 267). See also *South Tyneside Metropolitan Borough Council v Toulson* [2003] 1 CMLR 867, EAT.
    The source provision that appears in the 'Working Time Directive', ie art 7, has generated much litigation, and CJEU case law, which is discussed in that context: see PARA 267. As with art 7 itself, however, the issue of whether entitlement to annual leave accrues during periods of sick leave has arisen specifically under the Working Time Regulations 1998, SI 1998/1833, reg 13, and has been answered partly by reference to the CJEU jurisprudence. Accordingly, failure to pay holiday pay under the Working Time Regulations 1998, SI 1998/1833, can constitute an unauthorised deduction from wages contrary to the Employment Rights Act 1996 s 13 (see PARA 255): *Revenue and Customs Comrs v Stringer* [2009] UKHL 31, [2009] 4 All ER 1205, [2009] ICR 985, a case whose substantive points were disposed of, by agreement of the parties, following a reference to the ECJ, sub nom Cases C-350/06, C-520/06 *Schultz-Hoff v Deutsche Rentenversicherung Bund, Stringer v Revenue and Customs Comrs* [2009] ECR I-179, [2009] All ER (EC) 906, [2009] ICR 932, [2009] IRLR 214, ECJ (see PARA 267 note 11). The decision of the ECJ in Cases C-350/06, C-520/06 *Schultz-Hoff v Deutsche Rentenversicherung*

Bund, Stringer v Revenue and Customs Comrs, and that of the House of Lords in *Revenue and Customs Comrs v Stringer*, not only restored the decision of the EAT in *Ainsworth v IRC* [2004] All ER (D) 147 (Mar), EAT, but also the decision in *Kigass Aero Components Ltd v Brown* [2002] ICR 697, [2002] IRLR 312, EAT (entitlement to annual leave derives from having the status of 'worker', which includes all individuals who have entered into or worked under a contract of a kind encompassed by the definition, and does not require the individual to have done any work for the entitlement to arise). Those two decisions of the EAT had been reversed and overruled respectively by the Court of Appeal in *Ainsworth v IRC* [2005] EWCA Civ 441, [2005] ICR 1149, [2005] IRLR 465 (on the basis that a worker who has been allowed to accrue annual leave requirement whilst on long-term sick leave would not be benefitting from the intended health and safety aspect of the Working Time Regulations 1998, SI 1998/1833, and that an arbitrary payment in relation to a period of notional holiday would be simply a windfall).

4   See the Working Time Regulations 1998, SI 1998/1833, reg 13(3). The provision made by reg 13(3) does not apply to workers to whom reg 13(4), Sch 2 applies (ie workers employed in agriculture in Wales: see PARA 272 note 2) except where, in the case of a worker partly employed in agriculture in Wales, a relevant agreement so provides: reg 13(4) (amended by SI 2013/2228). As to the meaning of 'relevant agreement' for these purposes see PARA 272 note 2. As to the meaning of 'Wales' see PARA 2 note 12.

5   For these purposes, 'calendar year' means the period of 12 months beginning with 1 January in any year: see the Working Time Regulations 1998, SI 1998/1833, reg 2(1).

6   Working Time Regulations 1998, SI 1998/1833, reg 13(3)(a).

7   Working Time Regulations 1998, SI 1998/1833, reg 13(3)(b).

8   Ie the date on which the Working Time Regulations 1998, SI 1998/1833, came into force: see reg 1(1).

9   Working Time Regulations 1998, SI 1998/1833, reg 13(3)(b)(i).

10   See note 8.

11   Working Time Regulations 1998, SI 1998/1833, reg 13(3)(b)(ii).

12   As to the meaning of 'employment' see PARA 269 note 5.

13   Ie the period applicable under the Working Time Regulations 1998, SI 1998/1833, reg 13(1) (see the text and notes 1–3): see reg 13(5) (amended by SI 2001/3256).

14   Working Time Regulations 1998, SI 1998/1833, reg 13(5) (as amended: see note 13).

292.   Entitlement to additional annual leave.   A worker[1] is entitled[2] to a period of additional leave[3], in any leave year beginning on or after 1 April 2009, of 1.6 weeks[4]; but the aggregate entitlement to leave provided for in relation to additional leave[5], and to paid annual leave[6], is subject to a maximum of 28 days[7]. For these purposes, a worker's leave year begins on the same date as the worker's leave year begins for the purposes of the annual leave provisions[8]. Where the date on which a worker's employment[9] begins is later than the date on which his first leave year begins, the additional leave to which he is entitled in that leave year is a proportion of the period applicable[10] that is equal to the proportion of that leave year remaining on the date on which his employment begins[11].

The entitlement to additional annual leave that is so provided for[12] does not apply in relation to a worker whose employer[13], as at 1 October 2007 and by virtue of a relevant agreement, provides each worker employed by him with an annual leave entitlement of 1.6 weeks or 8 days (whichever is the lesser) in addition to each worker's entitlement under the annual leave provisions[14], provided that such additional annual leave[15]:

(1)   may not be replaced by a payment in lieu except in relation to a worker whose employment is terminated[16];

(2)   may not be carried forward into a leave year other than that which immediately follows the leave year in respect of which the leave is due[17]; and

(3)   is leave for which the worker is entitled to be paid at not less than the

rate of a week's pay in respect of each week of leave, calculated in accordance with pay provisions of the Employment Rights Act 1996 as modified[18] for the purpose[19].

Notwithstanding this[20], any additional annual leave in excess of 1.6 weeks or 8 days (whichever is the lesser) to which a worker is entitled, is not subject to the conditions in heads (1) to (3) above[21]. The provisions that apply to a worker's entitlement to additional annual leave by virtue of a relevant agreement[22] cease to apply to a worker from the day when an employer ceases to provide additional annual leave in accordance with those conditions[23].

1 As to the meaning of 'worker' for these purposes see PARA 271.
2 Ie subject to the Working Time Regulations 1998, SI 1998/1833, reg 13A(3) (see the text and notes 5–7), reg 13A(5) (see the text and notes 9–11) and reg 26A (see the text and notes 12–23): see reg 13A(1) (regs 13A, 26A added by SI 2007/2079).
    As to the application of the Working Time Regulations 1998, SI 1998/1833, Pt II (regs 3–17) (rights and obligations concerning working time: see also PARAS 280 et seq, 293 et seq) and Pt III (regs 18–27A) (exceptions: see PARA 297 et seq) see PARA 280 note 5. As to the right to present a complaint to an employment tribunal see PARA 319.
    As to the power of the Secretary of State to make provision about entitlement to annual leave see PARA 270.
3 See the Working Time Regulations 1998, SI 1998/1833, reg 13A(1) (as added: see note 2). The period of additional leave to which a worker is entitled in each leave year, referred to in reg 13A(1), is determined in accordance with reg 13A(2): see reg 13A(1) (as so added). In addition to the provision made by reg 13A(2)(e) (see the text and note 4), the following transitional provision was made in relation to a worker's entitlement to a period of additional leave, being:
    (1) in any leave year beginning on or after 1 October 2007 but before 1 April 2008, 0.8 weeks (reg 13A(2)(a) (as so added));
    (2) in any leave year beginning before 1 October 2007, a proportion of 0.8 weeks equivalent to the proportion of the year beginning on 1 October 2007 which would have elapsed at the end of that leave year (reg 13A(2)(b) (as so added));
    (3) in any leave year beginning on 1 April 2008, 0.8 weeks (reg 13A(2)(c) (as so added));
    (4) in any leave year beginning after 1 April 2008 but before 1 April 2009, 0.8 weeks and a proportion of another 0.8 weeks equivalent to the proportion of the year beginning on 1 April 2009 which would have elapsed at the end of that leave year (reg 13A(2)(d) (as so added)).
4 Working Time Regulations 1998, SI 1998/1833, reg 13A(2)(e) (as added: see note 2). As to the taking of additional leave and compensation associated with untaken leave see PARA 293.
5 Ie provided for in the Working Time Regulations 1998, SI 1998/1833, reg 13A(2) (see the text and note 4): see reg 13A(3) (as added: see note 2).
6 Ie provided for in the Working Time Regulations 1998, SI 1998/1833, reg 13(1) (see PARA 291): see reg 13A(3) (as added: see note 2).
7 Working Time Regulations 1998, SI 1998/1833, reg 13A(3) (as added: see note 2).
8 Working Time Regulations 1998, SI 1998/1833, reg 13A(4) (as added: see note 2). The reference to the annual leave provisions is a reference to reg 13 (see PARA 291): see reg 13A(4) (as so added).
9 As to the meaning of 'employment' see PARA 269 note 5.
10 Ie applicable under the Working Time Regulations 1998, SI 1998/1833, reg 13A(2) (see the text and note 4): see reg 13A(5) (as added: see note 2).
11 Working Time Regulations 1998, SI 1998/1833, reg 13A(5) (as added: see note 2).
12 Ie the provision made by the Working Time Regulations 1998, SI 1998/1833, reg 13A (see the text and notes 1–11): see reg 26A(1) (as added: see note 2).
13 As to the meaning of 'employer' see PARA 269 note 5.
14 Ie under the Working Time Regulations 1998, SI 1998/1833, reg 13 (see PARA 291): see reg 26A(1) (as added: see note 2).
15 See the Working Time Regulations 1998, SI 1998/1833, reg 26A(1) (as added: see note 2).
16 Working Time Regulations 1998, SI 1998/1833, reg 26A(1)(a) (as added: see note 2).
17 Working Time Regulations 1998, SI 1998/1833, reg 26A(1)(b) (as added: see note 2).
18 Ie calculated in accordance with the Employment Rights Act 2006 ss 221–224 (see PARAS 144–145), modified (see the Working Time Regulations 1998, SI 1998/1833, reg 26A(1)(c) (as added: see note 2)), such that:

(1)   references to the employee are references to the worker (reg 26A(1)(c)(i) (as so added));
(2)   references to the employee's contract of employment are references to the worker's contract (reg 26A(1)(c)(ii) (as so added));
(3)   the calculation date is the first day of the period of leave in question (reg 26A(1)(c)(iii) (as so added)); and
(4)   the references to the Employment Rights Act 2006 ss 227, 228 (see PARAS 147, 148) do not apply (Working Time Regulations 1998, SI 1998/1833, reg 26A(1)(c)(iv) (as so added)).

19 Working Time Regulations 1998, SI 1998/1833, reg 26A(1)(c) (as added: see note 2).
20 Ie notwithstanding the Working Time Regulations 1998, SI 1998/1833, reg 26A(1) (see the text and notes 12–19): see reg 26A(3) (as added: see note 2).
21 Working Time Regulations 1998, SI 1998/1833, reg 26A(2) (as added: see note 2).
22 Ie the Working Time Regulations 1998, SI 1998/1833, reg 26A: see reg 26A(3) (as added: see note 2).
23 Working Time Regulations 1998, SI 1998/1833, reg 26A(3) (as added: see note 2).

293. Taking of leave and compensation associated with untaken leave. Paid annual leave to which a worker[1] is entitled[2] may be taken in instalments[3]. However:

(1)   it may only be taken in the leave year in respect of which it is due[4]; and
(2)   it may not be replaced by a payment in lieu except where the worker's employment is terminated[5].

The additional leave to which a worker is entitled[6] also may be taken in instalments[7]; and it may not be replaced by a payment in lieu, except where the worker's employment is terminated[8].

Accordingly, where:

(a)   a worker's employment is terminated during the course of his leave year[9]; and
(b)   on the date on which the termination takes effect (the 'termination date'), the proportion he has taken of the leave (including additional leave) to which he is entitled in the leave year[10] differs from the proportion of the leave year which has expired[11],

then, where the proportion of leave taken by the worker is less than the proportion of the leave year which has expired, his employer[12] must make him a payment in lieu of leave[13]; and such payment due must be:

(i)   such sum as may be provided[14] for these purposes in a relevant agreement[15]; or
(ii)   where there are no provisions of a relevant agreement which apply, a sum equal to the amount that would be due to the worker[16] in respect of a period of leave determined according to the statutory formula[17].

A relevant agreement may make the following provision:

(A)   that, where the proportion of paid annual leave taken by the worker exceeds the proportion of the leave year which has expired, the worker must compensate his employer (whether by a payment, by undertaking additional work or otherwise)[18]; and
(B)   for any additional leave to which a worker is entitled[19] to be carried forward into the leave year immediately following the leave year in respect of which it is due[20].

1 As to the meaning of 'worker' for these purposes see PARA 271.
2 Ie entitled under the Working Time Regulations 1998, SI 1998/1833, reg 13 (see PARA 291): see reg 13(9).
       As to the application of Pt II (regs 3–17) (rights and obligations concerning working time: see also PARAS 280 et seq, 294 et seq) and Pt III (regs 18–27A) (exceptions: see PARA 297 et seq) see PARA 280 note 5. As to the right to present a complaint to an employment tribunal see PARA 319.

As to the power of the Secretary of State to make provision about entitlement to annual leave see PARA 270.

3   See the Working Time Regulations 1998, SI 1998/1833, reg 13(9). See *Russell v Transocean International Resources Ltd* [2011] UKSC 57, [2012] 2 All ER 166, [2012] ICR 185, [2012] IRLR 149 (reading the Working Time Regulations 1998, SI 1998/1833, reg 13, in conjunction with the Working Time Directive art 7 (which, properly interpreted, did not require that the guaranteed weeks of annual leave had to be taken consecutively or that those weeks could not be interrupted), employers would be entitled to insist that employees who worked on offshore installations take their paid annual leave during periods when they were onshore on field break). As to European Parliament and Council Directive (EC) 2003/88 of 4 November 2003 (OJ L299, 18.11.2003, p 9) concerning certain aspects of the organisation of working time (the 'Working Time Directive'), for the purposes of implementing which the Working Time Regulations 1998, SI 1998/1833, were made, see PARA 267.

4   Working Time Regulations 1998, SI 1998/1833, reg 13(9)(a). The jurisprudence of the CJEU which sets out entitlement to annual leave accrued during periods of sickness absence (see PARA 291 note 3) does not make that entitlement conditional on the worker making positive attempts or formal requests to use it (or to preserve it) so that, if a worker chooses not to take leave during his or her sick leave, the accrued leave is preserved, and may be carried over to the following leave year: *Leeds NHS Primary Care Trust v Larner* [2012] EWCA Civ 1034, [2012] 4 All ER 1006, [2012] ICR 1389, [2012] IRLR 825; applied in *Lloyd v BCQ Ltd* [2013] 1 CMLR 1166, [2012] All ER (D) 343 (Nov), EAT; distinguished in *Sood Enterprises Ltd v Healy* [2013] ICR 1361, [2013] IRLR 865, EAT (additional leave not taken: see note 20). Accordingly, where the reason for leave not being taken during a leave year is that it was not possible for the worker to do so because of absence on sick leave, the prohibition contained in the Working Time Regulations 1998, SI 1998/1833, reg 13(9), on carrying forward the untaken leave, is incompatible with the requirements of the Working Time Directive, when read in conjunction with the relevant jurisprudence of the CJEU, and must be read down accordingly (ie so that head (1) in the text reads: 'it may only be taken in the leave year in respect of which it is due, save where the worker was unable or unwilling to take it because he was on sick leave and as a consequence did not exercise his right to annual leave'): *Leeds NHS Primary Care Trust v Larner*. Although the Working Time Directive art 7(1) has direct effect (see Case C-282/10 *Dominguez v Centre Informatique du Centre Ouest Atlantique* [2012] 2 CMLR 437, [2012] IRLR 321, CJEU; and PARA 267 note 11), the decision in *Leeds NHS Primary Care Trust v Larner* established that the provisions of the Working Time Regulations 1998, SI 1998/1833, reg 13, have to be read so as to be compatible with the Working Time Directive, even where litigants are private individuals or companies (*Sood Enterprises Ltd v Healy*).

5   Working Time Regulations 1998, SI 1998/1833, reg 13(9)(b). As to the meaning of 'employment' see PARA 269 note 5.
    Where a worker is entitled to carry over untaken paid annual leave to the next leave year, she is entitled to payment on termination for any paid annual leave that she had been prevented from taking because of her absence on sick leave: *Leeds NHS Primary Care Trust v Larner* [2012] EWCA Civ 1034, [2012] 4 All ER 1006, [2012] ICR 1389, [2012] IRLR 825. The wording of the Working Time Regulations 1998, SI 1998/1833, reg 13(9)(b) is clearly aimed at an employer's temptation to persuade employees not to take the leave to which they are entitled but to take more money instead, which would clearly be against the public policy of doing the best to ensure that employees take proper, refreshing periods of holiday in any given year: *List Design Group Ltd v Douglas* [2002] ICR 686, [2003] IRLR 14, EAT. A claim for unpaid holiday pay or pay in lieu of untaken holiday may be made either by way of the statutory remedy under the Working Time Regulations 1998, SI 1998/1833, reg 30 (see PARA 319) or by way of a complaint of unlawful deductions (see PARA 259): *List Design Group Ltd v Douglas*.

6   Ie entitled under the Working Time Regulations 1998, SI 1998/1833, reg 13A (see PARA 292): see reg 13A(6) (reg 13A added by SI 2007/2079).

7   See the Working Time Regulations 1998, SI 1998/1833, reg 13A(6) (as added: see note 6).

8   See the Working Time Regulations 1998, SI 1998/1833, reg 13A(6)(a) (as added: see note 6). Transitional provision provided further exceptions in relation to: (1) a worker's entitlement to a period of additional leave that was determined under reg 13A(2)(a)–(c) (see PARA 292 note 3) (see reg 13A(6)(b) (as so added)); or (2) where the leave is an entitlement to 0.8 weeks that arose under reg 13A(2)(d) (see PARA 292 note 3), that part of the leave year which would have elapsed before 1 April 2009 (see reg 13A(6)(c) (as so added)).

9   Working Time Regulations 1998, SI 1998/1833, reg 14(1)(a).

10 Ie under the Working Time Regulations 1998, SI 1998/1833, reg 13 (see PARA 291) and reg 13A (see PARA 292): see reg 14(1)(b) (amended by SI 2001/3256; and SI 2007/2079).

11 Working Time Regulations 1998, SI 1998/1833, reg 14(1)(b) (as amended: see note 10).

12 As to the meaning of 'employer' see PARA 269 note 5.

13 See the Working Time Regulations 1998, SI 1998/1833, reg 14(2). As to the time limits for bringing a claim see PARA 319.

14 The term 'such sum as may be provided' does not allow for no payment at all in respect of accrued holiday: *Witley and District Men's Club v Mackay* [2001] IRLR 595, EAT.

15 Working Time Regulations 1998, SI 1998/1833, reg 14(3)(a). As to the meaning of 'relevant agreement' for these purposes see PARA 272 note 2.

16 Ie under the Working Time Regulations 1998, SI 1998/1833, reg 16 (see PARA 295): see reg 14(3)(b) (amended by SI 2001/3256; and SI 2007/2079).

17 Working Time Regulations 1998, SI 1998/1833, reg 14(3)(b) (as amended: see note 16). The text refers to a period of leave to be determined according to the formula:

$$(A \times B) - C$$

where A is the period of leave to which the worker is entitled under reg 13 (see PARA 291) and reg 13A (see PARA 292); B is the proportion of the worker's leave year which expired before the termination date; and C is the period of leave taken by the worker between the start of the leave year and the termination date: see reg 14(3)(b) (as so amended).

    Where a worker's employment is terminated and on the termination date he remains entitled to leave in respect of any previous leave year which carried over under reg 13(9)(a) (as construed in accordance with *Leeds NHS Primary Care Trust v Larner* [2012] EWCA Civ 1034, [2012] 4 All ER 1006, [2012] ICR 1389, [2012] IRLR 825: see note 4) because of sick leave, the employer must make him a payment in lieu equal to the sum due under the Working Time Regulations 1998, SI 1998/1833, reg 16 (see PARA 295), for the period of untaken leave: *Leeds NHS Primary Care Trust v Larner*.

18 Working Time Regulations 1998, SI 1998/1833, reg 14(4). It is only where there is a relevant agreement providing for credit to be given to the employer for excess holiday taken that reg 14(4) permits the employer to recover the excess payment in accordance with the Employment Rights Act 1996 s 13(1) (see PARA 255), and a term of the contract cannot be implied allowing for the deduction of excess holiday pay in circumstances where such an implied term is inconsistent with the statutory scheme of the Working Time Regulations 1998, SI 1998/1833, and the Employment Rights Act 1996 Pt II (ss 13–27) (protection of wages: see PARA 254 et seq): *Hill v Chapell* [2003] IRLR 19, EAT.

19 Ie entitled under the Working Time Regulations 1998, SI 1998/1833, reg 13A (see PARA 292): see reg 13A(7) (as added: see note 6).

20 Working Time Regulations 1998, SI 1998/1833, reg 13A(7) (as added: see note 6).

    In the light of Case C-282/10 *Dominguez v Centre Informatique du Centre Ouest Atlantique* [2012] 2 CMLR 437, [2012] IRLR 321, CJEU, and Case C-337/10 *Neidel v Stadt Frankfurt Am Main* [2012] 3 CMLR 92, [2012] ICR 1201, [2012] IRLR 607, CJEU (see PARA 267 note 11), there is no necessity to strain at all the natural meaning of the Working Time Regulations 1998, SI 1998/1833, reg 13A(7), so there is no right to carry forward untaken additional leave unless a provision in a relevant agreement so provides: *Sood Enterprises Ltd v Healy* [2013] ICR 1361, [2013] IRLR 865, EAT (worker unable to take additional annual leave due to illness not entitled to carry it forward in the absence of a relevant agreement). Since there is no obligation on member states under European Parliament and Council Directive (EC) 2003/88 of 4 November 2003 (OJ L299, 18.11.2003, p 9) concerning certain aspects of the organisation of working time (the 'Working Time Directive': see PARA 267) to confer more than four weeks' leave a year, the Working Time Regulations 1998, SI 1998/1833, reg 13A, is not a measure implementing EU law, and it does not have to be interpreted as such: *Sood Enterprises Ltd v Healy*. Cf the provision for paid annual leave under the Working Time Regulations 1998, SI 1998/1833, reg 13 (see PARA 291).

294.   Dates on which leave is taken. A worker[1] may take leave (including additional leave) to which he is entitled[2] on such days[3] as he may elect by giving notice duly to his employer[4], subject to any requirement imposed on him[5] by his employer[6].

A worker's employer may require the worker[7]:

(1)   to take leave to which the worker is entitled[8]; or

(2)   not to take such leave[9],

on particular days, by giving notice duly to the worker[10].

A notice so given by a worker[11] or, as the case may be, an employer[12]:

(a)	may relate to all or part of the leave to which a worker is entitled in a leave year[13];

(b)	must specify the days on which leave is or, as the case may be, is not to be taken and, where the leave on a particular day is to be in respect of only part of the day, its duration[14]; and

(c)	must be given to the employer or, as the case may be, the worker before the relevant date[15].

Any right so conferred or obligation so imposed[16] may be varied or excluded by a relevant agreement[17].

During the first year of a worker's employment which began after 25 October 2001[18], the amount of leave (including additional leave) he may take at any time in exercise of his entitlement[19] is limited to the amount which is deemed to have accrued in his case at that time[20], less the amount of leave, if any, that he has already taken during that year[21].

1	As to the meaning of 'worker' for these purposes see PARA 271. The provision made by the Working Time Regulations 1998, SI 1998/1833, reg 15, does not apply to workers to whom reg 15(6), Sch 2 applies (ie workers employed in agriculture in Wales: see PARA 272 note 2) except where, in the case of a worker partly employed in agriculture in Wales, a relevant agreement so provides: reg 15(6) (amended by SI 2013/2228). As to the meaning of 'relevant agreement' for these purposes see PARA 272 note 2. As to the meaning of 'Wales' see PARA 2 note 12.

As to the application of the Working Time Regulations 1998, SI 1998/1833, Pt II (regs 3–17) (rights and obligations concerning working time: see also PARAS 280 et seq, 295 et seq) and Pt III (regs 18–27A) (exceptions: see PARA 297 et seq) see PARA 280 note 5. As to the right to present a complaint to an employment tribunal see PARA 319.

2	Ie under the Working Time Regulations 1998, SI 1998/1833, reg 13 (see PARA 291) and reg 13A (see PARA 292): see reg 15(1) (amended by SI 2001/3256; and SI 2007/2079).

As to the power of the Secretary of State to make provision about entitlement to annual leave see PARA 270.

3	As to the meaning of 'day' for these purposes see PARA 280 note 6.

4	Ie in accordance with the Working Time Regulations 1998, SI 1998/1833, reg 15(3) (see the text and notes 11–15): see reg 15(1) (as amended: see note 2). As to the meaning of 'employer' see PARA 269 note 5.

5	Ie under the Working Time Regulations 1998, SI 1998/1833, reg 15(2) (see the text and notes 7–10): see reg 15(1) (as amended: see note 2).

6	Working Time Regulations 1998, SI 1998/1833, reg 15(1) (as amended: see note 2).

A worker on long-term sick leave must give notice to his employer of his intention to take annual leave so that the employer can know whether to pay him sick leave or holiday pay (but an employer is not ordinarily obliged to inform a worker on sick leave that she was required to give notice in order to qualify for holiday pay): *Leeds NHS Primary Care Trust v Larner* [2012] EWCA Civ 1034, [2012] 4 All ER 1006, [2012] ICR 1389, [2012] IRLR 825; *Fraser v Southwest London St George's Mental Health Trust* [2012] ICR 403, [2012] IRLR 100, EAT. See also *Canada Life Ltd v Gray* [2004] ICR 673, EAT (requirement of notice by a worker is essential to the exercise of the right to paid holidays during employment but is not essential to a claim after termination that the worker was wrongfully denied paid holidays).

7	See the Working Time Regulations 1998, SI 1998/1833, reg 15(2).

8	Working Time Regulations 1998, SI 1998/1833, reg 15(2)(a) (amended by SI 2001/3256; and SI 2007/2079). Head (1) in the text refers to leave to which the worker is entitled under the Working Time Regulations 1998, SI 1998/1833, reg 13 (see PARA 291) or reg 13A (see PARA 292): see reg 15(2)(a) (as so amended).

9	Working Time Regulations 1998, SI 1998/1833, reg 15(2)(b).

10	See the Working Time Regulations 1998, SI 1998/1833, reg 15(2). The text refers to notice given in accordance with reg 15(3) (see the text and notes 11–15): see reg 15(2).

11	Ie a notice under the Working Time Regulations 1998, SI 1998/1833, reg 15(1) (see the text and notes 1–6): see reg 15(3).

12	Ie a notice under the Working Time Regulations 1998, SI 1998/1833, reg 15(2) (see the text and notes 7–10): see reg 15(3).

13	Working Time Regulations 1998, SI 1998/1833, reg 15(3)(a).

14	Working Time Regulations 1998, SI 1998/1833, reg 15(3)(b).

15 Working Time Regulations 1998, SI 1998/1833, reg 15(3)(c). For these purposes, the relevant date is the date: (1) in the case of a notice under reg 15(1) (see the text and notes 1–6) or reg 15(2)(a) (see head (1) in the text), twice as many days in advance of the earliest day specified in the notice as the number of days or part-days to which the notice relates (reg 15(4)(a)); and (2) in the case of a notice under reg 15(2)(b) (see head (2) in the text), as many days in advance of the earliest day so specified as the number of days or part-days to which the notice relates (reg 15(4)(b)).

16 Ie under the Working Time Regulations 1998, SI 1998/1833, reg 15(1)–(4) (see the text and notes 1–15): see reg 15(5).

17 Working Time Regulations 1998, SI 1998/1833, reg 15(5). By virtue of reg 15(5), entitlement to leave may be subject to any contractual variation, including provisions relating to notice, which, so long as it is not operated by an employer in an unreasonable, arbitrary or capricious way so as to deny any entitlement lawfully requested, may result in the loss of the right at the end of the leave year to leave in respect of leave not taken: *Lyons v Mitie Security Ltd* [2010] ICR 628, [2010] IRLR 288, EAT (tribunal had failed to consider whether there had been a breach of the contractual provisions in relation to holiday entitlement, in terms of four weeks' notice being required 'whenever possible', the merits of the employee's application for holiday at shorter notice and the employer's staffing requirements at the relevant time). See also *Briffa v Industrial & Commercial Maintenance Ltd* [2008] All ER (D) 105 (Sep), EAT (the variation of the employee's contract of employment was legally enforceable between the parties and constituted a relevant agreement within the meaning of the Working Time Regulations 1998, SI 1998/1833, and operated to vary the employer's obligations to give notice under reg 15).

18 The Working Time Regulations 1998, SI 1998/1833, reg 15A does not apply to a worker whose employment began on or before 25 October 2001: reg 15A(4) (reg 15A added by SI 2001/3256).

19 Ie under the Working Time Regulations 1998, SI 1998/1833, reg 13 (see PARA 291) or reg 13A (see PARA 292): see reg 15A(1) (reg 15A as added (see note 18); reg 15A(1) amended, reg 15(2A) added, by SI 2007/2079).

20 Ie under the Working Time Regulations 1998, SI 1998/1833, reg 15A(2A) (as modified under reg 15(3), where it applies): see reg 15A(1) (as added and amended: see note 19). Accordingly, for these purposes, leave is deemed to accrue over the course of the worker's first year of employment at the rate of one-twelfth of the amount specified in reg 13(1) (see PARA 291) and reg 13A(2) (see PARA 292), subject to the limit contained in reg 13A(3) (see PARA 292), on the first day of each month of that year: reg 15A(2A) (as added: see note 19). Where the amount of leave that has accrued in a particular case includes a fraction of a day other than a half day, the fraction must be treated as a half day if it is less than a half day and as a whole day if it is more than a half day: reg 15A(3) (as added: see note 18).

21 Working Time Regulations 1998, SI 1998/1833, reg 15A(1) (as added and amended: see note 19).

295. Payment in respect of periods of leave. A worker[1] is entitled to be paid in respect of any period of annual leave (including additional leave) to which he is entitled[2], at the rate of a week's pay[3] in respect of each week of leave[4]. A right to payment conferred in this way does not affect any right of a worker to remuneration under his contract ('contractual remuneration')[5]. Any contractual remuneration paid to a worker in respect of a period of leave goes towards discharging any liability of the employer[6] to make payments[7] in respect of that period; and, conversely, any payment of remuneration[8] in respect of a period goes towards discharging any liability of the employer to pay contractual remuneration in respect of that period[9].

1 As to the meaning of 'worker' for these purposes see PARA 271.
2 Ie under the Working Time Regulations 1998, SI 1998/1833, reg 13 (see PARA 291) and reg 13A (see PARA 292): see reg 16(1) (amended by SI 2007/2079).
   As to the application of the Working Time Regulations 1998, SI 1998/1833, Pt II (regs 3–17) (rights and obligations concerning working time: see also PARAS 280 et seq, 296) and Pt III (regs 18–27A) (exceptions: see PARA 297 et seq) see PARA 280 note 5. As to the disapplication of reg 16 in relation to excluded sectors see PARA 298. As to the right to present a complaint to an employment tribunal see PARA 319.
   As to the power of the Secretary of State to make provision about entitlement to annual leave see PARA 270.

3 The Employment Rights Act 1996 ss 221–224 (week's pay based on working hours: see PARAS 144–145) apply for the purpose of determining the amount of a week's pay for the purposes of the Working Time Regulations 1998, SI 1998/1833, reg 16 (see reg 16(2)), but as if:

(1) references to the employee were references to the worker (reg 16(3)(a));

(2) references to the employee's contract of employment were references to the worker's contract (reg 16(3)(b));

(3) the calculation date were the first day of the period of leave in question (reg 16(3)(c)); and

(4) the references to the Employment Rights Act 1996 s 227 (maximum amount: see PARA 147) and s 228 (week's pay where employee has not worked for long enough to average the most recent 12 weeks' pay: see PARA 148) did not apply (Working Time Regulations 1998, SI 1998/1833, reg 16(3)(d)).

The content and framework of the Working Time Regulations 1998, SI 1998/1833, show that the well-established definition of a 'week's pay' in the Employment Rights Act 1996 s 220 (see PARA 143) applies, save in the immaterial respects specifically provided for in the Working Time Regulations 1998, SI 1998/1833, reg 16(3), so that reg 16 clearly incorporates the interpretation of 'normal working hours' in the Employment Rights Act 1996 s 234 (see PARA 142): *Bamsey v Albon Engineering and Manufacturing plc* [2004] EWCA Civ 359, [2004] ICR 1083, [2004] IRLR 457 (entitlement to holiday pay calculated only on the basis of employees' contractual basic working week, notwithstanding that they regularly worked substantial hours of overtime which they were contractually obliged to do but which the employers were not obliged to provide). The question of whether *Bamsey v Albon Engineering and Manufacturing plc* can be harmonised with subsequent case law developed in the CJEU from consideration of the Working Time Directive (see PARA 267) was raised in *Neal v Freightliner Ltd* (12 July 2013, unreported), ET (the Working Time Regulations 1998, SI 1998/1833, reg 16(3) should be amended to exclude the Employment Rights Act 1996 s 223(3) (and s 234), in the case of entitlement under the Working Time Regulations 1998, SI 1998/1833, reg 13 (see PARA 291)).See also note 4.

As to statutory holiday pay for airline pilots, which is calculated under the Civil Aviation (Working Time) Regulations 2004 SI 2004/756 (where a different method of calculation applies: see AIR LAW vol 2 (2008) PARA 467), see Case C-155/10 *British Airways plc v Williams* [2011] ECR I-8409, [2012] 1 CMLR 591, [2012] ICR 847, [2011] IRLR 948, CJEU; and *British Airways plc v Williams* [2012] UKSC 43, [2013] 1 All ER 443, [2013] 1 CMLR 934, [2012] IRLR 1014 (EU law requires that holiday pay is the rate of average remuneration, taking a reasonable reference period to calculate the average, reasonableness being capable of assessment by the tribunal, not necessarily by reference to the Employment Rights Act 1996 ss 221–224, because of the particular factors affecting the civil aviation sector). See also Case C-539/12 *ZJR Lock v British Gas Trading Ltd* [2014] ICR 813, [2014] IRLR 648, CJEU (worker's commission payments to be considered in respect of periods of paid annual leave); and PARA 267 note 11.

4 Working Time Regulations 1998, SI 1998/1833, reg 16(1) (as amended: see note 2). As to the basis for calculating compensation in relation to unpaid leave that has accrued see PARA 293.

If a worker claims unpaid amounts of holiday pay which have accrued under the Working Time Regulations 1998, SI 1998/1833, and have to be ascertained, this can be done under the Apportionment Act 1870 s 2 (see PARA 22 note 5): *Leisure Leagues UK Ltd v Maconnachie* [2002] IRLR 600, EAT (in the light of industrial practice and the Working Time Regulations 1998, SI 1998/1833, whose approach is based upon the hours actually worked, the basis of calculating the payment of holiday entitlement on the basis of day to day accrual has to be by reference to actual working days and not to calendar days). *Leisure Leagues UK Ltd v Maconnachie* did not follow *Thames Water Utilities v Reynolds* [1996] IRLR 186, EAT (under the Apportionment Act 1870, wages and salaries are deemed apportionable and accrue from day to day on a calendar days basis rather than a working days basis); however, *Leisure Leagues UK Ltd v Maconnachie* was followed in *Yarrow v Edwards Chartered Accountants* [2007] All ER (D) 118 (Aug), EAT (in case of conflict, the most recent case of the EAT is followed in the interest of comity, and the approach found in the recent statutory employment provisions, ie the Working Time Regulations 1998, SI 1998/1833, is to be preferred to that found in the Victorian Apportionment Act).

5 Working Time Regulations 1998, SI 1998/1833, reg 16(4).

6 As to the meaning of 'employer' see PARA 269 note 5.

7 Ie under the Working Time Regulations 1998, SI 1998/1833, reg 16: see reg 16(5).

8 See note 7.

9 Working Time Regulations 1998, SI 1998/1833, reg 16(5). An employer may not unilaterally decide that a week's pay includes an element of holiday pay without the employee's agreement and reg 16(5) does not confer that right on an employer: *Blackburn v Gridquest Ltd (t/a Select Employment)* [2002] EWCA Civ 1037, [2002] ICR 1206, [2002] IRLR 604. The issue of

whether a contractually binding arrangement between an employer and a worker, which provides that a specific part of the wages paid to the worker represented that worker's holiday pay (an arrangement known as 'rolled-up holiday pay'), involves a violation of the worker's right to be paid for his annual leave under the Working Time Directive (see PARA 267) (transposed into domestic law by the Working Time Regulations 1998, SI 1998/1833, reg 16) was referred to the European Court of Justice for a preliminary ruling: see *Clarke v Frank Staddon Ltd, Caulfield v Marshalls Clay Products Ltd* [2004] All ER (D) 409 (May), CA. This followed the staying of proceedings in *Caulfield v Marshalls Clay Products Ltd, Clarke v Frank Staddon Ltd* [2004] EWCA Civ 422, [2004] 2 CMLR 1040, [2004] ICR 1502, after the Court of Appeal found that it could not agree with the decision in *MPB Structures Ltd v Munro* [2004] ICR 430, [2003] IRLR 350, IH, to the effect that payment for annual leave must be made 'in association with the taking of the leave' and that rolled-up holiday pay arrangements conflicted with the aims of the Working Time Directive and the Working Time Regulations 1998, SI 1998/1833, by discouraging workers from taking their holidays when they would otherwise have sought to do so. See *Smith v AJ Morrisroes & Sons Ltd, JJ Cafferkey & Co Ltd v Byrne* [2005] ICR 596, [2005] IRLR 72, EAT (where redrafted guidelines were given for the guidance of employment tribunals in order to avoid a breach of the Working Time Regulations 1998, SI 1998/1833, in respect of rolled-up holiday pay). However more recently rolled-up holiday pay arrangements were considered contrary to the Working Time Directive: see Cases C-131/04, C-257/04 *Robinson-Steele v RD Retail Services Ltd, Clarke v Frank Staddon Ltd, Caulfield v Hanson Clay Products Ltd* [2006] All ER (EC) 749, [2006] ICR 932, ECJ (distinguished in *British Airways plc v Noble* [2006] EWCA Civ 537, [2006] ICR 1227); and PARA 267 note 11. See also *Lyddon v Englefield Brickwork Ltd* [2008] IRLR 198, [2007] All ER (D) 198 (Nov), EAT (while rolled-up holiday pay should not have been used, the employer was entitled to set off the amounts it had paid to the employee against the employee's entitlement as the payments had been sufficiently transparent and comprehensible). See also *Taylor v East Midlands Offender Employment* [2000] IRLR 760, EAT (contractual entitlement to accrued holiday pay).

296.   Entitlements under other provisions. Where, during any period, a worker[1] is entitled to a rest period[2], rest break or annual leave, both under any provision of the working time regulations[3] and under a separate provision (including a provision of his contract), he may not exercise the two rights separately, but may, in taking a rest period, break or leave during that period, take advantage of whichever right is, in any particular respect, the more favourable[4].

1   As to the meaning of 'worker' for these purposes see PARA 271.
2   As to the meaning of 'rest period' see PARA 284 note 4.
3   Ie under any provision of the Working Time Regulations 1998, SI 1998/1833: see reg 17.
4   Working Time Regulations 1998, SI 1998/1833, reg 17.
    As to the application of Pt II (regs 3–17) (rights and obligations concerning working time: see also PARA 280 et seq) and Pt III (regs 18–27A) (exceptions: see PARA 297 et seq) see PARA 280 note 5.

(iv) Exclusions

297.   General scheme of exceptions to rights and obligations set out in the working time regulations. Part II of the working time regulations, setting out rights and obligations[1], has effect subject to the exceptions specified in Part III[2], which relate to:
(1)   excluded sectors[3];
(2)   domestic service[4];
(3)   unmeasured working time[5];
(4)   other special cases[6];
(5)   shift workers[7];
(6)   collective and workforce agreements[8];
(7)   compensatory rest[9];

(8)   mobile workers[10];

(9)   workers in the armed forces[11];

(10)   doctors in training[12];

(11)   workers employed in offshore work[13]; and

(12)   young workers[14] (including force majeure[15]).

Where, in Part II of the working time regulations[16], separate provision is made as respects the same matter in relation to workers generally and to young workers, the provision relating to workers generally applies only to adult workers[17] and those young workers to whom, by virtue of any exception in Part III[18], the provision relating to young workers does not apply[19].

Separate provision is made to implement the Working Time Directive[20] to the extent that it applies to the organisation of working time for workers on the inland waterways[21], or to the organisation of working time for sea-fishermen[22], and the Working Time Directive itself does not apply to seafarers, as defined in the Agreement on the organisation of working time of seafarers concluded by the European Community Shipowners' Association (ECSA) and the Federation of Transport Workers' Unions in the European Union (FST)[23], and separate provision is made to regulate hours of work in that sector accordingly[24].

1   Ie the Working Time Regulations 1998, SI 1998/1833, Pt II (regs 3–17) (see PARAS 280–281, 283–296): see reg 3(1); and PARA 280 note 5.

2   Ie subject to the exceptions provided for in the Working Time Regulations 1998, SI 1998/1833, Pt III (regs 18–27A) (see also PARA 298 et seq): see reg 3(1); and PARA 280 note 5.

3   See PARA 298.

4   See PARA 299.

5   See PARA 300.

6   See PARA 301.

7   See PARA 302.

8   See PARA 303.

9   See PARA 304.

10 See PARA 305. As to the meaning of 'mobile worker' see PARA 305 note 1. This category has been added to reflect the expanded scope of the Working Time Directive: see PARA 267.

11 See PARA 306.

12 See PARA 307. This category has been added to reflect the expanded scope of the Working Time Directive: see PARA 267.

13 See PARA 308. As to the meaning of 'offshore work' see PARA 301 note 2. This category has been added to reflect the expanded scope of the Working Time Directive: see PARA 267.

14 See PARA 310. As to the meaning of 'young worker' see PARA 281 note 1. This category has been added to reflect the expanded scope of the Working Time Directive: see PARA 267.

15 See PARA 309.

16 Ie in the Working Time Regulations 1998, SI 1998/1833, Pt II (see PARAS 280–281, 283–296): see reg 3(2); and PARA 280 note 5.

17 As to the meaning of 'adult worker' see PARA 285 note 2.

18 Ie by virtue of any exception in the Working Time Regulations 1998, SI 1998/1833, Pt III (see also PARA 298 et seq): see reg 3(2); and PARA 280 note 5.

19 See the Working Time Regulations 1998, SI 1998/1833, reg 3(2); and PARA 280 note 5.

20 Ie European Parliament and Council Directive (EC) 2003/88 of 4 November 2003 (OJ L299, 18.11.2003, p 9) concerning certain aspects of the organisation of working time (the 'Working Time Directive'), for the purposes of implementing which the Working Time Regulations 1998, SI 1998/1833, were made: see PARA 267.

21 As to the organisation of working time for workers on the inland waterways see specifically the Merchant Shipping (Working Time: Inland Waterways) Regulations 2003, SI 2003/3049; and SHIPPING AND MARITIME LAW vol 94 (2008) PARA 625. Accordingly, the Working Time Regulations 1998, SI 1998/1833, do not apply to workers to whom the Merchant Shipping (Working Time: Inland Waterways) Regulations 2003, SI 2003/3049, apply: Working Time Regulations 1998, SI 1998/1833, reg 18(1)(c) (reg 18 substituted by SI 2003/1684; the Working Time Regulations 1998, SI 1998/1833, reg 18(1)(c) further substituted by SI 2003/3049). The exclusion of workers on the inland waterways from the scope of the Working Time Directive

(ie Council Directive (EC) 93/104 (OJ L307, 13.12.93, p 18), as it was: see PARA 267 note 1) was removed by European Parliament and Council Directive (EC) 2000/34 (OJ L195, 1.8.2000, p 41): see PARA 267.

22   As to the organisation of working time for sea-fishermen see specifically the Fishing Vessels (Working Time: Sea-fishermen) Regulations 2004, SI 2004/1713; and SHIPPING AND MARITIME LAW vol 94 (2008) PARA 626. Accordingly, the Working Time Regulations 1998, SI 1998/1833, do not apply to workers to whom the Fishing Vessels (Working Time: Sea-fishermen) Regulations 2004, SI 2004/1713, apply: Working Time Regulations 1998, SI 1998/1833, reg 18(1)(b) (reg 18 as substituted (see note 21); reg 18(1)(b) further substituted by SI 2004/1713). The exclusion of sea-fishermen from the scope of the Working Time Directive (ie Council Directive (EC) 93/104 (OJ L307, 13.12.93, p 18), as it was: see PARA 267 note 1) was removed by European Parliament and Council Directive (EC) 2000/34 (OJ L195, 1.8.2000, p 41): see PARA 267.

23   Ie as defined in the Agreement on the organisation of working time of seafarers concluded by the European Community Shipowners' Association (ECSA) and the Federation of Transport Workers' Unions in the European Union (FST) that is set out in Council Directive (EC) 1999/63 of 21 June 1999 (OJ L167, 2.7.99, p 33): see Working Time Directive art 1(3); and PARA 267 note 4.

24   For the purpose of implementing Council Directive (EC) 1999/63 of 21 June 1999 (OJ L167, 2.7.99, p 33) (see note 23), the Merchant Shipping (Hours of Work) Regulations 2002, SI 2002/2125, were made: see SHIPPING AND MARITIME LAW vol 94 (2008) PARA 625. Accordingly, the Working Time Regulations 1998, SI 1998/1833, do not apply to workers to whom the Merchant Shipping (Hours of Work) Regulations 2002, SI 2002/2125, apply: Working Time Regulations 1998, SI 1998/1833, reg 18(1)(a) (reg 18 as substituted (see note 21); reg 18(1)(a) further substituted by SI 2014/308).

298. Specific exclusions allowed to certain sectors under the working time regulations. In relation to:

   (1)   cases where characteristics peculiar to certain services such as the armed forces[1] or the police, or to certain specific activities in the civil protection services[2], inevitably conflict with the provisions[3] of the working time regulations[4]; and

   (2)   workers[5] to whom the European Agreement on the organisation of working time of mobile staff in civil aviation[6] applies[7],

certain provisions of the working time regulations that relate to:

   (a)   a worker's maximum weekly working time (including overtime)[8];

   (b)   the average length of night work[9];

   (c)   a night worker's access to free health assessments and his transfer to other work where a registered medical practitioner has so advised[10];

   (d)   the pattern of work (especially where the work is monotonous or the work-rate is predetermined)[11];

   (e)   a worker's entitlement to a daily rest period[12], to a weekly rest period[13], and to a rest break[14];

   (f)   a worker's entitlement to annual leave (including additional leave)[15]; and

   (g)   a worker's entitlement to payment in respect of periods of leave[16],

do not apply[17].

Additionally, the provisions that are mentioned in heads (a), (b), (d) and (e) above do not apply to workers to whom the European Parliament and Council Directive on the organisation of the working time of persons performing mobile road transport activities[18] applies[19].

1   As to the meaning of 'armed forces' see PARA 275 note 2.

2   For these purposes, the 'civil protection services' includes the police, fire brigades and ambulance services, the security and intelligence services, customs and immigration officers, the prison service, the coastguard, and lifeboat crew and other voluntary rescue services: see the

Working Time Regulations 1998, SI 1998/1833, reg 2(1). As to such exclusions under the parent Working Time Directive see further art 1(3); and PARA 267 note 4.

3   Ie the Working Time Regulations 1998, SI 1998/1833: see reg 18(2)(a) (reg 18 substituted by SI 2003/1684).

4   Working Time Regulations 1998, SI 1998/1833, reg 18(2)(a) (as substituted: see note 3).

5   As to the meaning of 'worker' for these purposes see PARA 271.

6   Ie the European Agreement on the Organisation of Working Time of Mobile Workers in Civil Aviation concluded by the Association of European Airlines, the European Transport Workers' Federation, the European Cockpit Association, the European Regions Airline Association and the International Air Carrier Association, implemented by Council Directive (EC) 2000/79 of 27 November 2000 (OJ L302, 1.12.2000, p 56), and for the purposes of which the Civil Aviation (Working Time) Regulations 2004, SI 2004/756, were made (see AIR LAW vol 2 (2008) PARA 467 et seq): see the Working Time Regulations 1998, SI 1998/1833, reg 18(2)(b) (as substituted: see note 3). See also PARA 267 note 1.

7   Working Time Regulations 1998, SI 1998/1833, reg 18(2)(b) (as substituted: see note 3).

8   Ie the Working Time Regulations 1998, SI 1998/1833, reg 4(1), (2) (see PARA 280): see reg 18(2) (reg 18 as substituted (see note 3); reg 18(2) amended by SI 2007/2079). As to the meaning of 'working time' see PARA 280 note 4.

9   Ie the Working Time Regulations 1998, SI 1998/1833, reg 6(1), (2), (7) (see PARA 284): see reg 18(2) (as substituted and amended: see note 8). As to the meaning of 'work' see PARA 280 note 4; and as to the meaning of 'night work' see PARA 284 note 1.

10 Ie the Working Time Regulations 1998, SI 1998/1833, reg 7(1), (6) (see PARA 285): see reg 18(2) (as substituted and amended: see note 8). As to the meaning of 'night worker' see PARA 284 note 1.

11 Ie the Working Time Regulations 1998, SI 1998/1833, reg 8 (see PARA 286): see reg 18(2) (as substituted and amended: see note 8).

12 Ie the Working Time Regulations 1998, SI 1998/1833, reg 10(1) (see PARA 288): see reg 18(2) (as substituted and amended: see note 8). As to the meaning of 'adult worker' see PARA 285 note 2; and as to the meaning of 'rest period' see PARA 284 note 4.

13 Ie the Working Time Regulations 1998, SI 1998/1833, reg 11(1), (2) (see PARA 289): see reg 18(2) (as substituted and amended: see note 8).

14 Ie the Working Time Regulations 1998, SI 1998/1833, reg 12(1) (see PARA 290): see reg 18(2) (as substituted and amended: see note 8).

15 Ie the Working Time Regulations 1998, SI 1998/1833, reg 13 (see PARA 291) and reg 13A (see PARA 292): see reg 18(2) (as substituted and amended: see note 8).

16 Ie the Working Time Regulations 1998, SI 1998/1833, reg 16 (see PARA 295): see reg 18(2) (as substituted and amended: see note 8).

17 Working Time Regulations 1998, SI 1998/1833, reg 18(2) (as substituted and amended: see note 8). The exclusion of the transport sector effected by reg 18(2) affects all those employed within that sector, including 'non-mobile' workers: Case C-133/00 *Bowden v Tuffnells Parcels Express Ltd* [2001] All ER (EC) 865, [2001] IRLR 838, ECJ (entitlement to paid annual leave guaranteed by the Working Time Directive (see PARA 267) is not available to office workers within the road transport sector).

18 Ie European Parliament and Council Directive (EC) 2002/15 of 11 March 2002 (OJ L80, 23.3.2002, p 35) concerning the organisation of the working time of persons performing mobile road transport activities (for the purpose of implementing which, the Road Transport (Working Time) Regulations 2005, SI 2005/639, were made: see ROAD TRAFFIC vol 90 (2011) PARA 1125 et seq): see the Working Time Regulations 1998, SI 1998/1833, reg 18(4) (as substituted: see note 3). See also PARA 267 note 1.

19 Working Time Regulations 1998, SI 1998/1833, reg 18(4) (as substituted: see note 3). As to Council Directive (EC) 2005/47 of 18 July 2005 (OJ L195, 27.7.2005, p 15) on the Agreement between the Community of European Railways (CER) and the European Transport Workers' Federation (ETF) on certain aspects of the working conditions of mobile workers engaged in interoperable cross-border services in the railway sector (for the purpose of implementing which, the Cross-border Railway Services (Working Time) Regulations 2008, SI 2008/1660, were made: see RAILWAYS AND TRAMWAYS vol 86 (2013) PARAS 33, 328), see the Working Time Regulations 1998, SI 1998/1833, reg 18(5) see PARA 304 note 8. See also PARA 267 note 1.

299.   Domestic service. In relation to a worker[1] employed as a domestic servant in a private household, certain provisions of the working time regulations that relate to:

(1)   the maximum weekly working time for a worker[2];

(2)   the maximum weekly working time for young workers[3];

(3)   the average length of night work[4];

(4)   the restriction on night work by young workers[5];

(5)   a night worker's access to free health assessments and his transfer to other work where a registered medical practitioner has so advised[6]; and

(6)   the pattern of work (especially where the work is monotonous or the work-rate is predetermined)[7],

do not apply[8].

1   As to the meaning of 'worker' for these purposes see PARA 271.
2   Ie the Working Time Regulations 1998, SI 1998/1833, reg 4(1), (2) (see PARA 280): see reg 19 (amended by SI 2002/3128). As to the meaning of 'working time' see PARA 280 note 4.
3   Ie the Working Time Regulations 1998, SI 1998/1833, reg 5A(1), (4) (see PARA 281): see reg 19 (as amended: see note 2). As to the meaning of 'young worker' see PARA 281 note 1.
4   Ie the Working Time Regulations 1998, SI 1998/1833, reg 6(1), (2), (7) (see PARA 284): see reg 19 (as amended: see note 2). As to the meaning of 'night work' see PARA 284 note 1.
5   Ie the Working Time Regulations 1998, SI 1998/1833, reg 6A (see PARA 284): see reg 19 (as amended: see note 2).
6   Ie the Working Time Regulations 1998, SI 1998/1833, reg 7(1), (2), (6) (see PARA 285): see reg 19 (as amended: see note 2). As to the meaning of 'night worker' see PARA 284 note 1.
7   Ie the Working Time Regulations 1998, SI 1998/1833, reg 8 (see PARA 286): see reg 19 (as amended: see note 2).
8   Working Time Regulations 1998, SI 1998/1833, reg 19 (as amended: see note 2).

300.   Unmeasured working time. In relation to a worker[1] where, on account of the specific characteristics of the activity in which he is engaged, the duration of his working time[2] is not measured or predetermined, or can be determined by the worker himself, as may be the case for[3]:

(1)   managing executives or other persons with autonomous decision-taking powers[4];

(2)   family workers[5]; or

(3)   workers officiating at religious ceremonies in churches and religious communities[6],

certain provisions of the working time regulations that relate to:

(a)   the maximum weekly working time for a worker[7];

(b)   the average length of night work[8]; and

(c)   a worker's entitlement to a daily rest period[9], to a weekly rest period[10], and to a rest break[11],

do not apply[12].

1   As to the meaning of 'worker' for these purposes see PARA 271.
2   As to the meaning of 'working time' see PARA 280 note 4.
3   See the Working Time Regulations 1998, SI 1998/1833, reg 20(1) (reg 20(1) renumbered, reg 20(2) added, by SI 1999/3372).
4   Working Time Regulations 1998, SI 1998/1833, reg 20(1)(a) (as renumbered: see note 3).
5   Working Time Regulations 1998, SI 1998/1833, reg 20(1)(b) (as renumbered: see note 3).
6   Working Time Regulations 1998, SI 1998/1833, reg 20(1)(c) (as renumbered: see note 3).
7   Ie the Working Time Regulations 1998, SI 1998/1833, reg 4(1), (2) (see PARA 280): see reg 20(1) (as renumbered: see note 3).
8   Ie the Working Time Regulations 1998, SI 1998/1833, reg 6(1), (2), (7) (see PARA 284): see reg 20(1) (as renumbered: see note 3). As to the meaning of 'night work' see PARA 284 note 1.
9   Ie the Working Time Regulations 1998, SI 1998/1833, reg 10(1) (see PARA 288): see reg 20(1) (as renumbered: see note 3). As to the meaning of 'adult worker' see PARA 285 note 2; and as to the meaning of 'rest period' see PARA 284 note 4.
10   Ie the Working Time Regulations 1998, SI 1998/1833, reg 11(1), (2) (see PARA 289): see reg 20(1) (as renumbered: see note 3).
11   Ie the Working Time Regulations 1998, SI 1998/1833, reg 12(1) (see PARA 290): see reg 20(1) (as renumbered: see note 3).

Guidelines issued in relation to the Working Time Regulations 1998, SI 1998/1833 (which were made for the purposes of implementing Council Directive (EC) 93/104: see PARA 268), indicating that employers must ensure that workers are able to take rest breaks but are not required to ensure that they do so render the workers' rights meaningless: see Case C-484/04 *EC Commission v United Kingdom* [2007] ICR 592, [2006] IRLR 888, ECJ. The Working Time Regulations 1998, SI 1998/1833, reg 20(2) (as added: see note 3) was revoked by the Working Time (Amendment) Regulations 2006, SI 2006/99, reg 2, as a consequence of the decision in Case C-484/04 *EC Commission v United Kingdom*.

12 See the Working Time Regulations 1998, SI 1998/1833, reg 20(1) (as renumbered: see note 3).

301. Other special cases. In relation to a worker[1]:

(1) where the worker's activities are such that his place of work and place of residence are distant from one another (including cases where the worker is employed in offshore work[2]) or his different places of work are distant from one another[3];

(2) where the worker is engaged in security and surveillance activities requiring a permanent presence in order to protect property and persons (as may be the case for security guards and caretakers or security firms)[4];

(3) where the worker's activities involve the need for continuity of service or production[5], as may be the case in relation to:

    (a) services relating to the reception, treatment or care provided by hospitals or similar establishments (including the activities of doctors in training[6]), residential institutions and prisons[7];

    (b) work at docks or airports[8];

    (c) press, radio, television, cinematographic production, postal and telecommunications services and civil protection services[9];

    (d) gas, water and electricity production, transmission and distribution, household refuse collection and incineration[10];

    (e) industries in which work cannot be interrupted on technical grounds[11];

    (f) research and development activities[12];

    (g) agriculture[13];

    (h) the carriage of passengers on regular urban transport services[14];

(4) where there is a foreseeable surge of activity[15], as may be the case in relation to:

    (a) agriculture[16];

    (b) tourism[17]; and

    (c) postal services[18];

(5) where the worker's activities are affected by:

    (a) an occurrence due to unusual and unforeseeable circumstances, beyond the control of the worker's employer[19];

    (b) exceptional events, the consequences of which could not have been avoided despite the exercise of all due care by the employer[20]; or

    (c) an accident or the imminent risk of an accident[21];

(6) where the worker works in railway transport[22], and:

    (a) his activities are intermittent[23];

    (b) he spends his working time on board trains[24]; or

    (c) his activities are linked to transport timetables and to ensuring the continuity and regularity of traffic[25],

certain provisions of the working time regulations that relate to:

(i) the average length of night work[26]; and

(ii)   a worker's entitlement to a daily rest period[27], to a weekly rest period[28], and to a rest break[29],

do not apply[30].

1   As to the meaning of 'worker' for these purposes see PARA 271.
2   For these purposes, 'offshore work' means work performed mainly on or from offshore installations (including drilling rigs), directly or indirectly in connection with the exploration, extraction or exploitation of mineral resources, including hydrocarbons, and diving in connection with such activities, whether performed from an offshore installation or a vessel, including any such work performed in the territorial waters of the United Kingdom adjacent to Great Britain or in any area (except one or part of one in which the law of Northern Ireland applies) designated under the Continental Shelf Act 1964 s 1(7) (see ENERGY AND CLIMATE CHANGE vol 44 (2011) PARA 1040): see the Working Time Regulations 1998, SI 1998/1833, reg 2(1) (definition added by SI 2003/1684; and amended by SI 2006/2389). As to the meanings of 'United Kingdom' and 'Great Britain' see PARA 2 note 12. See also PARA 308.
3   Working Time Regulations 1998, SI 1998/1833, reg 21(a) (amended by SI 2003/1684).
4   Working Time Regulations 1998, SI 1998/1833, reg 21(b). See *Hughes v Corps of Commissionaires Management* [2011] EWCA Civ 1061, [2012] 1 CMLR 649, [2011] IRLR 915 (to demonstrate that the Working Time Regulations 1998, SI 1998/1833, reg 21 applies, employers need to show that there are objective reasons why a full break cannot be provided in accordance with *Gallagher v Alpha Catering Services Ltd (t/a Alpha Flight Services)* [2004] EWCA Civ 1559, [2005] ICR 673, [2005] IRLR 102 (see note 5)).
5   See the Working Time Regulations 1998, SI 1998/1833, reg 21(c). For this purpose, the test for continuity focuses on the activities and work patterns of the worker rather than the employer: *Gallagher v Alpha Catering Services Ltd (t/a Alpha Flight Services)* [2004] EWCA Civ 1559, [2005] ICR 673, [2005] IRLR 102 (no evidence to suggest that employee's working time could not be organised so as to have rest breaks that would not be interrupted; otherwise employers could avoid duty by not employing enough staff to cover for rest breaks). See also note 4.
6   As to exclusions relating to doctors in training see also PARA 307.
7   Working Time Regulations 1998, SI 1998/1833, reg 21(c)(i) (reg 21(c)(i) amended, reg 21(c)(viii), (f) added, by SI 2003/1684).
8   Working Time Regulations 1998, SI 1998/1833, reg 21(c)(ii). In order to determine the proper construction and application of the derogation authorised by head (3)(b) in the text, it is necessary to construe the phrase 'activities involving the need for continuity of service or production' in the Working Time Directive art 17(3)(c) (derogations: see PARA 267), to determine especially whether the requirement of continuity of service had to be established separately with regard to each right under the Working Time Directive from which derogation had been made, or whether continuity of service had to be addressed generally without consideration of the specific rights from which derogation had been made: *Bridgeman v Associated British Ports* [2012] 2 CMLR 1317, [2012] IRLR 639, EAT (requirement for ship's pilot to remain on duty for whole length of time taken to pilot a particular vessel into port potentially infringed rights to daily rest periods and to rest breaks (see head (ii) in the text)). Although *Bridgeman v Associated British Ports* was referred to the CJEU accordingly, the case was settled without further litigation, and the reference was withdrawn.
9   Working Time Regulations 1998, SI 1998/1833, reg 21(c)(iii). As to the meaning of 'civil protection services' see PARA 298 note 2.
10   Working Time Regulations 1998, SI 1998/1833, reg 21(c)(iv).
11   Working Time Regulations 1998, SI 1998/1833, reg 21(c)(v).
12   Working Time Regulations 1998, SI 1998/1833, reg 21(c)(vi).
13   Working Time Regulations 1998, SI 1998/1833, reg 21(c)(vii).
14   Working Time Regulations 1998, SI 1998/1833, reg 21(c)(viii) (as added: see note 7).
15   See the Working Time Regulations 1998, SI 1998/1833, reg 21(d). There is no definition of the word 'surge' given but as this provision is a derogation it should be construed narrowly: *Gallagher v Alpha Catering Services Ltd (t/a Alpha Flight Services)* [2004] EWCA Civ 1559, [2005] ICR 673, [2005] IRLR 102.
16   Working Time Regulations 1998, SI 1998/1833, reg 21(d)(i).
17   Working Time Regulations 1998, SI 1998/1833, reg 21(d)(ii).
18   Working Time Regulations 1998, SI 1998/1833, reg 21(d)(iii).
19   Working Time Regulations 1998, SI 1998/1833, reg 21(e)(i). As to the meaning of 'employer' see PARA 269 note 5.
20   Working Time Regulations 1998, SI 1998/1833, reg 21(e)(ii).
21   Working Time Regulations 1998, SI 1998/1833, reg 21(e)(iii).

22 See the Working Time Regulations 1998, SI 1998/1833, reg 21(f) (as added: see note 7).
23 Working Time Regulations 1998, SI 1998/1833, reg 21(f)(i) (as added: see note 7).
24 Working Time Regulations 1998, SI 1998/1833, reg 21(f)(ii) (as added: see note 7).
25 Working Time Regulations 1998, SI 1998/1833, reg 21(f)(iii) (as added: see note 7).
26 Ie the Working Time Regulations 1998, SI 1998/1833, reg 6(1), (2), (7) (see PARA 284): see reg 21. As to the meaning of 'night work' see PARA 284 note 1.
27 Ie the Working Time Regulations 1998, SI 1998/1833, reg 10(1) (see PARA 288): see reg 21. Regulation 21 is subject to reg 24 (compensatory rest: see PARA 304): see reg 21. As to the meaning of 'adult worker' see PARA 285 note 2; and as to the meaning of 'rest period' see PARA 284 note 4.
28 Ie the Working Time Regulations 1998, SI 1998/1833, reg 11(1), (2) (see PARA 289): see reg 21. See note 27.
29 Ie the Working Time Regulations 1998, SI 1998/1833, reg 12(1) (see PARA 290): see reg 21. See note 27.
30 See the Working Time Regulations 1998, SI 1998/1833, reg 21. See note 27.

302. Shift workers. In relation to a shift worker[1]:

(1) when he changes shift and cannot take a daily rest period[2] between the end of one shift and the start of the next one, the right to a daily rest period[3] does not apply[4];

(2) when he changes shift and cannot take a weekly rest period between the end of one shift and the start of the next one, the right to a weekly rest period[5] does not apply[6].

In relation to workers engaged in activities involving periods of work split up over the day (as may be the case for cleaning staff), neither the right to a daily rest period[7] nor the right to a weekly rest period[8] applies[9].

1 For these purposes, 'shift worker' means any worker whose work schedule is part of shift work; and 'shift work' means any method of organising work in shifts whereby workers succeed each other at the same workstations according to a certain pattern, including a rotating pattern, and which may be continuous or discontinuous, entailing the need for workers to work at different times over a given period of days or weeks: see the Working Time Regulations 1998, SI 1998/1833, reg 22(2). As to the meaning of 'worker' for these purposes see PARA 271.
2 As to the meaning of 'rest period' see PARA 284 note 4.
3 Ie the Working Time Regulations 1998, SI 1998/1833, reg 10(1) (see PARA 288): see reg 22(1)(a). Regulation 22 is subject to reg 24 (compensatory rest: see PARA 304): see reg 22(1).
4 Working Time Regulations 1998, SI 1998/1833, reg 22(1)(a). See note 3.
5 Ie the Working Time Regulations 1998, SI 1998/1833, reg 11(1), (2) (see PARA 289): see reg 22(1)(b). See note 3.
6 Working Time Regulations 1998, SI 1998/1833, reg 22(1)(b). See note 3.
7 Ie the Working Time Regulations 1998, SI 1998/1833, reg 10(1) (see PARA 288): see reg 22(1)(c). See note 3.
8 Ie the Working Time Regulations 1998, SI 1998/1833, reg 11(1), (2) (see PARA 289): see reg 22(1)(c). See note 3.
9 Working Time Regulations 1998, SI 1998/1833, reg 22(1)(c). See note 3.

303. Collective agreements and workforce agreements. A collective agreement[1] or a workforce agreement[2] may:

(1) modify or exclude the application of certain provisions of the working time regulations that relate to[3]:
(a) the average length of night work[4]; and
(b) a worker's entitlement to a daily rest period[5], to a weekly rest period[6], and to a rest break[7]; and

(2) for objective or technical reasons or reasons concerning the organisation of work, modify the application of certain provisions of the working time regulations that relate to the maximum weekly working time for a worker[8] by the substitution, for each reference to 17 weeks, of a different period (being a period not exceeding 52 weeks)[9],

in relation to particular workers or groups of workers[10].

1   As to the meaning of 'collective agreement' see PARA 272 note 2.
2   As to the meaning of 'workforce agreement' see PARA 272.
3   See the Working Time Regulations 1998, SI 1998/1833, reg 23(a).
4   Ie the Working Time Regulations 1998, SI 1998/1833, reg 6(1)–(3), (7) (see PARA 284): see reg 23(a). As to the meaning of 'night work' see PARA 284 note 1.
5   Ie the Working Time Regulations 1998, SI 1998/1833, reg 10(1) (see PARA 288): see reg 23(a). As to the meaning of 'adult worker' see PARA 285 note 2; and as to the meaning of 'rest period' see PARA 284 note 4.
6   Ie the Working Time Regulations 1998, SI 1998/1833, reg 11(1), (2) (see PARA 289): see reg 23(a).
7   Ie the Working Time Regulations 1998, SI 1998/1833, reg 12(1) (see PARA 290): see reg 23(a).
8   Ie the Working Time Regulations 1998, SI 1998/1833, reg 4(3), (4) (see PARA 280): see reg 23(b). As to the meaning of 'worker' for these purposes see PARA 271.
9   See the Working Time Regulations 1998, SI 1998/1833, reg 23(b).
10 See the Working Time Regulations 1998, SI 1998/1833, reg 23. Where parties enter into a collective agreement, which itself provides a mechanism for the final resolution of disputes between the parties in the form of arbitration, an arbitrator's award setting a term relevant to working time may constitute a collective agreement for the purposes of the Working Time Regulations 1998, SI 1998/1833, reg 23: *Bewley v HM Prison Service* [2004] ICR 422, EAT (award impliedly excluded or modified the entitlement to a daily rest period in the Working Time Regulations 1998, SI 1998/1833, reg 10 (see PARA 288)).

304.   Compensatory rest.   Where the application of any provision of the working time regulations[1] is excluded in relation to certain special cases of worker[2], or is modified or excluded[3] by means of a collective agreement[4] or a workforce agreement[5], and a worker is accordingly required by his employer[6] to work during a period which would otherwise be a rest period[7] or rest break[8]: (1) his employer must, wherever possible, allow him to take an equivalent period of compensatory rest[9]; and (2) in exceptional cases in which it is not possible, for objective reasons, to grant such a period of rest, his employer must afford him such protection as may be appropriate in order to safeguard the worker's health and safety[10].

1   Ie any provision of the Working Time Regulations 1998, SI 1998/1833: see reg 24.
2   Ie by the Working Time Regulations 1998, SI 1998/1833, reg 21 (other special cases: see PARA 301) or reg 22 (shift workers: see PARA 302): see reg 24. As to the meaning of 'worker' for these purposes see PARA 271. As to excluded sectors generally see PARA 298.
3   Ie under the Working Time Regulations 1998, SI 1998/1833, reg 23(a) (see PARA 303): see reg 24.
4   As to the meaning of 'collective agreement' see PARA 272 note 2.
5   As to the meaning of 'workforce agreement' see PARA 272.
6   As to the meaning of 'employer' see PARA 269 note 5.
7   As to the meaning of 'rest period' see PARA 284 note 4.
8   See the Working Time Regulations 1998, SI 1998/1833, reg 24. Regulation 24 does not apply to workers to whom the Cross-border Railways Services (Working Time) Regulations 2008, SI 2008/1660 apply (see RAILWAYS AND TRAMWAYS vol 86 (2013) PARAS 33, 328): Working Time Regulations 1998, SI 1998/1833, reg 18(5) (added by SI 2008/1660). See also PARA 267 note 1.
    As to enforcement of the Working Time Regulations 1998, SI 1998/1833, reg 24, in so far as it applies where reg 6(1), (2) or (7) (see PARA 284) is modified, see PARA 311. As to offences see PARA 317. As to the right to present a complaint to an employment tribunal, in so far as reg 24 applies where reg 10(1) (see PARA 288), reg 11(1) or (2) (see PARA 289) or reg 12(1) (see PARA 290) are modified or excluded, see PARA 319. As to the exception relating to mobile workers see PARA 305; and as to the exception relating to doctors in training see PARA 307.
9   Working Time Regulations 1998, SI 1998/1833, reg 24(a). See note 8.
    Although a 'rest break' under the Working Time Regulations 1998, SI 1998/1833, cannot occur within working hours (see PARA 290), an 'equivalent period of compensatory rest' under reg 24(a) may differ, so long as it has the characteristics of a rest in the sense of a break from work and so long as it ensures, so far as possible, that the period which is free from work is at least 20 minutes, so that it meets the criteria of equivalence and compensation: *Hughes v Corps*

of Commissionaires Management Ltd [2011] EWCA Civ 1061, [2012] 1 CMLR 649, [2011] IRLR 915 (rest afforded to security guard with option of choosing when to start his break and, if interrupted, allowing him to start his break again, amounted to an equivalent period of compensatory rest pursuant to the Working Time Regulations 1998, SI 1998/1833, reg 24(a)).

10 Working Time Regulations 1998, SI 1998/1833, reg 24(b). See note 8. The principle of safeguarding the worker's health and safety underlies European Parliament and Council Directive (EC) 2003/88 of 4 November 2003 (OJ L299, 18.11.2003, p 9) concerning certain aspects of the organisation of working time (the 'Working Time Directive', for the purposes of implementing which the Working Time Regulations 1998, SI 1998/1833, were made): see especially Case C-151/02 *Landeshauptstadt Kiel v Jaeger* [2003] ECR I-8389, [2004] All ER (EC) 604, [2004] ICR 1528, [2003] IRLR 804, ECJ; and Case C-428/09 *Union Syndicale Solidaires Isère v Premier Ministre* [2010] ECR I-9961, [2011] IRLR 84, ECJ (cited in PARA 267 note 21). The Working Time Regulations 1998, SI 1998/1833, reg 24(b) merely requires that there should be objective reasons why an equivalent period of compensatory rest cannot be provided and cases where the employer cannot provide either an appropriate rest break or a compensatory alternative will perforce be exceptional: *Hughes v Corps of Commissionaires Management Ltd* [2011] EWCA Civ 1061, [2012] 1 CMLR 649, [2011] IRLR 915.

305. Mobile workers. In relation to a mobile worker[1], certain provisions of the working time regulations that relate to:

(1)   the average length of night work[2]; and

(2)   a worker's entitlement to a daily rest period[3], to a weekly rest period[4], and to a rest break[5],

do not apply to the extent that the worker is one who is not already excluded[6] from the application of those regulations[7]; and he is entitled to adequate rest[8], except where his activities are affected by[9]: (a) an occurrence due to unusual and unforeseeable circumstances, beyond the control of the worker's employer[10]; (b) exceptional events, the consequences of which could not have been avoided despite the exercise of all due care by the employer[11]; or (c) an accident or the imminent risk of an accident[12].

1   For these purposes, 'mobile worker' means any worker employed as a member of travelling or flying personnel by an undertaking which operates transport services for passengers or goods by road or air: see the Working Time Regulations 1998, SI 1998/1833, reg 2(1) (definition added by SI 2003/1684). As to the meaning of 'worker' for these purposes see PARA 271.

Because European Parliament and Council Directive (EC) 2003/88 of 4 November 2003 (OJ L299, 18.11.2003, p 9) concerning certain aspects of the organisation of working time (the 'Working Time Directive': see PARA 267 note 1) does not apply where other instruments of EU law contain more specific requirements relating to the organisation of working time concerning certain occupations or occupational services (see art 14; and PARA 267 note 1), the following provision is made outwith that Directive (for the purposes of implementing which the Working Time Regulations 1998, SI 1998/1833, were made: see PARA 267 note 1):

(1)   Council Directive (EC) 2000/79 of 27 November 2000 (OJ L302, 1.12.2000, p 56) concerning the European Agreement on the Organisation of Working Time of Mobile Workers in Civil Aviation concluded by the Association of European Airlines, the European Transport Workers' Federation, the European Cockpit Association, the European Regions Airline Association and the International Air Carrier Association (for the purpose of implementing which, the Civil Aviation (Working Time) Regulations 2004, SI 2004/756, were made: see AIR LAW vol 2 (2008) PARA 467 et seq);

(2)   European Parliament and Council Directive (EC) 2002/15 of 11 March 2002 (OJ L80, 23.3.2002, p 35) concerning the organisation of the working time of persons performing mobile road transport activities (for the purpose of implementing which, the Road Transport (Working Time) Regulations 2005, SI 2005/639, were made: see ROAD TRAFFIC vol 90 (2011) PARA 1125 et seq); and

(3)   Council Directive (EC) 2005/47 of 18 July 2005 (OJ L195, 27.7.2005, p 15) on the Agreement between the Community of European Railways (CER) and the European Transport Workers' Federation (ETF) on certain aspects of the working conditions of mobile workers engaged in interoperable cross-border services in the railway sector (for the purpose of implementing which, the Cross-border Railway Services (Working Time) Regulations 2008, SI 2008/1660, were made: see RAILWAYS AND TRAMWAYS vol 86 (2013) PARAS 33, 328).

2   Ie the Working Time Regulations 1998, SI 1998/1833, reg 6(1), (2), (7) (see PARA 284): see
    reg 24A(1) (reg 24A added by SI 2003/1684). As to the meaning of 'night work' see PARA 284
    note 1.
3   Ie the Working Time Regulations 1998, SI 1998/1833, reg 10(1) (see PARA 288): see reg 24A(1)
    (as added: see note 2). As to the meaning of 'adult worker' see PARA 285 note 2; and as to the
    meaning of 'rest period' see PARA 284 note 4.
4   Ie the Working Time Regulations 1998, SI 1998/1833, reg 11(1), (2) (see PARA 289): see
    reg 24A(1) (as added: see note 2).
5   Ie the Working Time Regulations 1998, SI 1998/1833, reg 12(1) (see PARA 290): see reg 24A(1)
    (as added: see note 2).
6   Ie by any provision of the Working Time Regulations 1998, SI 1998/1833, reg 18 (excluded
    sectors: see PARAS 297, 298, 304 note 8): see reg 24A(1) (as added: see note 2).
7   See the Working Time Regulations 1998, SI 1998/1833, reg 24A(1) (as added: see note 2).
8   For these purposes, 'adequate rest' means that a worker has regular rest periods, the duration of
    which are expressed in units of time and which are sufficiently long and continuous to ensure
    that, as a result of fatigue or other irregular working patterns, he does not cause injury to
    himself, to fellow workers or to others and that he does not damage his health, either in the
    short term or in the longer term: Working Time Regulations 1998, SI 1998/1833, reg 24A(3) (as
    added: see note 2). See *Feist v First Hampshire & Dorset Ltd* [2007] All ER (D) 180 (Feb), EAT
    (bus drivers whose duties involved daily rest periods of fewer than 11 hours in 24 were entitled
    to 'adequate rest' under the Working Time Regulations 1998, SI 1998/1833, reg 24A, but not
    'compensatory rest' pursuant to reg 21 (see PARA 301) or reg 24 (see PARA 304)).
9   See the Working Time Regulations 1998, SI 1998/1833, reg 24A(2) (as added: see note 2). The
    exceptions referred to apply where the worker's activities are affected by any of the matters
    referred to in reg 21(e) (see PARA 301): see reg 24A(2) (as so added).
10 Working Time Regulations 1998, SI 1998/1833, reg 21(e)(i) (reg 21(e) applied by reg 24A(2) (as
    added: see note 2)). As to the meaning of 'employer' see PARA 269 note 5.
12 Working Time Regulations 1998, SI 1998/1833, reg 21(e)(ii) (as applied: see note 10).
13 Working Time Regulations 1998, SI 1998/1833, reg 21(e)(iii) (as applied: see note 10).

306.   Workers in the armed forces.   In relation to a worker[1] serving as a
member of the armed forces[2], the duty of the employer[3] under the working time
regulations to keep records[4] does not apply[5]; and, in relation to a young worker[6]
serving as a member of the armed forces, the provisions of those regulations that
relate to:

(1)   the maximum weekly working time for young workers[7];
(2)   the restriction on night work by young workers[8];
(3)   a young worker's entitlement to a daily rest period[9]; and
(4)   a young worker's entitlement to a weekly rest period[10],

do not apply[11].

In a case where a young worker is accordingly required to work during the
restricted period[12], or where he is not permitted the minimum daily rest period of
12 consecutive hours in each 24-hour period during which he works for his
employer[13], or the minimum weekly rest period of 48 hours in each seven-day
period[14], he must be allowed an appropriate period of compensatory rest[15].

1   As to the meaning of 'worker' for these purposes see PARA 271.
2   As to the meaning of 'armed forces' see PARA 275 note 2.
3   As to the meaning of 'employer' see PARA 269 note 5.
4   Ie under the Working Time Regulations 1998, SI 1998/1833, reg 9 (see PARA 287): see reg 25(1).
5   Working Time Regulations 1998, SI 1998/1833, reg 25(1).
6   As to the meaning of 'young worker' see PARA 281 note 1.
7   Ie the Working Time Regulations 1998, SI 1998/1833, reg 5A (see PARA 281): see reg 25(2)
    (reg 25(2), (3) amended by SI 2002/3128). As to the meaning of 'working time' see PARA 280
    note 4.
8   Ie the Working Time Regulations 1998, SI 1998/1833, reg 6A (see PARA 284): see reg 25(2) (as
    amended: see note 7). As to the meaning of 'night work' see PARA 284 note 1.
9   Ie the Working Time Regulations 1998, SI 1998/1833, reg 10(2) (see PARA 288): see reg 25(2)
    (as amended: see note 7). As to the meaning of 'rest period' see PARA 284 note 4.

10 Ie the Working Time Regulations 1998, SI 1998/1833, reg 11(3) (see PARA 289): see reg 25(2) (as amended: see note 7).
11 Working Time Regulations 1998, SI 1998/1833, reg 25(2) (as amended: see note 7).
12 As to the meaning of 'restricted period' see PARA 284 note 10.
13 Ie as provided for in the Working Time Regulations 1998, SI 1998/1833, reg 10(2) (daily rest periods: see PARA 288): see reg 25(3) (as amended: see note 7).
14 Ie as provided for in the Working Time Regulations 1998, SI 1998/1833, reg 11(3) (weekly rest periods: see PARA 289): see reg 25(3) (as amended: see note 7).
15 Working Time Regulations 1998, SI 1998/1833, reg 25(3) (as amended: see note 7). As to compensatory rest see PARA 304. As to the right to present a complaint to an employment tribunal see PARA 319.

307. Doctors in training. In the case of workers[1] who are doctors in training, in place of the usual provisions of the working time regulations that govern working time reference periods[2], the following reference periods apply instead[3]:

(1) where a relevant agreement[4] so provides[5] in relation to successive periods of 26 weeks, each such period[6]; and

(2) in any other case, any period of 26 weeks in the course of his employment[7],

except where a doctor in training has worked for his employer[8] for less than 26 weeks, in which case the reference period applicable is the period that has elapsed since he started work for his employer[9].

1 As to the meaning of 'worker' for these purposes see PARA 271.
2 Ie in place of the Working Time Regulations 1998, SI 1998/1833, reg 4(3)–(5) (see PARA 280): see reg 25A(2) (reg 25A added by SI 2003/1684). As to the meaning of 'working time' see PARA 280 note 4.
3 See the Working Time Regulations 1998, SI 1998/1833, reg 25A(2) (as added: see note 2). The reference periods set out in heads (1) and (2) in the text apply with effect from 1 August 2004: see reg 25A(2) (as so added).
4 As to the meaning of 'relevant agreement' for these purposes see PARA 272 note 2.
5 Ie where a relevant agreement provides for the application of the Working Time Regulations 1998, SI 1998/1833, reg 25A: see reg 25A(3)(a) (as added: see note 2). See further PARA 280 note 4.
6 Working Time Regulations 1998, SI 1998/1833, reg 25A(3)(a) (as added: see note 2).
7 Working Time Regulations 1998, SI 1998/1833, reg 25A(3)(b) (as added: see note 2). As to the meaning of 'employment' see PARA 269 note 5.
8 As to the meaning of 'employer' see PARA 269 note 5.
9 See the Working Time Regulations 1998, SI 1998/1833, reg 25A(4) (as added: see note 2).

308. Workers employed in offshore work. In the case of workers[1] employed in offshore work[2], in place of the usual provisions of the working time regulations that govern working time reference periods[3], the following reference periods apply instead[4]:

(1) where a relevant agreement[5] so provides[6] in relation to successive periods of 52 weeks, each such period[7]; and

(2) in any other case, any period of 52 weeks in the course of his employment[8],

except where a worker employed in offshore work has worked for his employer[9] for less than 52 weeks, in which case the reference period applicable is the period that has elapsed since he started work for his employer[10].

1 As to the meaning of 'worker' for these purposes see PARA 271.
2 As to the meaning of 'offshore work' see PARA 301 note 2.
3 Ie in place of the Working Time Regulations 1998, SI 1998/1833, reg 4(3)–(5) (see PARA 280): see reg 25B(1) (reg 25B added by SI 2003/1684). As to the meaning of 'working time' see PARA 280 note 4.
4 See the Working Time Regulations 1998, SI 1998/1833, reg 25B(1) (as added: see note 3).

5   As to the meaning of 'relevant agreement' for these purposes see PARA 272 note 2.
6   Ie where a relevant agreement provides for the application of the Working Time Regulations 1998, SI 1998/1833, reg 25B: see reg 25B(2)(a) (as added: see note 3). See further PARA 280 note 4.
7   Working Time Regulations 1998, SI 1998/1833, reg 25B(2)(a) (as added: see note 3).
8   Working Time Regulations 1998, SI 1998/1833, reg 25B(2)(b) (as added: see note 3). As to the meaning of 'employment' see PARA 269 note 5.
9   As to the meaning of 'employer' see PARA 269 note 5.
10 See the Working Time Regulations 1998, SI 1998/1833, reg 25B(3) (as added: see note 3).

309.   Young workers and force majeure.   In relation to a young worker[1] where his employer[2] requires him to undertake work[3] which no adult worker[4] is available to perform[5], and which:

(1)   is occasioned either by an occurrence due to unusual and unforeseeable circumstances beyond the employer's control[6], or by exceptional events, the consequences of which could not have been avoided despite the exercise of all due care by the employer[7];

(2)   is of a temporary nature[8]; and

(3)   must be performed immediately[9],

the provisions of the working time regulations that relate to:

(a)   the maximum weekly working time for young workers[10];

(b)   the restriction on night work by young workers[11];

(c)   a young worker's entitlement to a daily rest period[12]; and

(d)   a young worker's entitlement to rest breaks[13],

do not apply[14].

Where the application of the provisions referred to in heads (a) to (d) above is so excluded, and where a young worker is accordingly required to work during a period which would otherwise be a rest period or rest break, his employer must allow him to take an equivalent period of compensatory rest within the following three weeks[15].

1   As to the meaning of 'young worker' see PARA 281 note 1.
2   As to the meaning of 'employer' see PARA 269 note 5.
3   As to the meaning of 'work' see PARA 280 note 4.
4   As to the meaning of 'adult worker' see PARA 285 note 2.
5   See the Working Time Regulations 1998, SI 1998/1833, reg 27(1) (reg 27(1), (2) amended by SI 2002/3128).
6   Working Time Regulations 1998, SI 1998/1833, reg 27(1)(a)(i).
7   Working Time Regulations 1998, SI 1998/1833, reg 27(1)(a)(ii).
8   Working Time Regulations 1998, SI 1998/1833, reg 27(1)(b).
9   Working Time Regulations 1998, SI 1998/1833, reg 27(1)(c).
10 Ie the Working Time Regulations 1998, SI 1998/1833, reg 5A (see PARA 281): see reg 27(1) (as amended: see note 5). As to the meaning of 'working time' see PARA 280 note 4.
11 Ie the Working Time Regulations 1998, SI 1998/1833, reg 6A (see PARA 284): see reg 27(1) (as amended: see note 5). As to the meaning of 'night work' see PARA 284 note 1.
12 Ie the Working Time Regulations 1998, SI 1998/1833, reg 10(2) (see PARA 288): see reg 27(1) (as amended: see note 5). As to the meaning of 'rest period' see PARA 284 note 4.
13 Ie the Working Time Regulations 1998, SI 1998/1833, reg 12(4) (see PARA 290): see reg 27(1) (as amended: see note 5).
14 See the Working Time Regulations 1998, SI 1998/1833, reg 27(1) (as amended: see note 5).
15 Working Time Regulations 1998, SI 1998/1833, reg 27(2) (as amended: see note 5). As to compensatory rest see PARA 304. As to the right to present a complaint to an employment tribunal see PARA 319.

310.   Other exceptions relating to young workers.   The maximum weekly working time for young workers[1] does not apply in relation to a young worker where[2]:

(1)   his employer[3] requires him to undertake work[4] which is necessary either to maintain continuity of service or production or to respond to a surge in demand for a service or product[5];

(2)   no adult worker[6] is available to perform the work[7]; and

(3)   performing the work would not adversely affect the young worker's education or training[8].

The restriction on night work by young workers[9] does not apply:

(a)   in relation to a young worker who is employed: (i) in a hospital or similar establishment[10]; or (ii) in connection with cultural, artistic, sporting or advertising activities[11], in the circumstances set out in heads (1) to (3) above[12]; or

(b)   except in so far as it prohibits work between midnight and 4 am, in relation to a young worker employed in: (i) agriculture[13]; (ii) retail trading[14]; (iii) postal or newspaper deliveries[15]; (iv) a catering business[16]; (v) a hotel, public house, restaurant, bar or similar establishment[17]; or (vi) a bakery[18], in the circumstances set out in heads (1) to (3) above[19].

Where the application of the restriction on night work by young workers[20] is excluded in this way[21], and where a young worker is accordingly required to work during a period which would otherwise be a rest period[22] or rest break, he must be supervised by an adult worker (where such supervision is necessary for the young worker's protection), and he must be allowed an equivalent period of compensatory rest[23].

1   Ie as provided for in the Working Time Regulations 1998, SI 1998/1833, reg 5A (see PARA 281): see reg 27A(1) (reg 27A added by SI 2002/3128). As to the meaning of 'working time' see PARA 280 note 4; and as to the meaning of 'young worker' see PARA 281 note 1.
2   See the Working Time Regulations 1998, SI 1998/1833, reg 27A(1) (as added: see note 1).
3   As to the meaning of 'employer' see PARA 269 note 5.
4   As to the meaning of 'work' see PARA 280 note 4.
5   Working Time Regulations 1998, SI 1998/1833, reg 27A(1)(a) (as added: see note 1).
6   As to the meaning of 'adult worker' see PARA 285 note 2.
7   Working Time Regulations 1998, SI 1998/1833, reg 27A(1)(b) (as added: see note 1).
8   Working Time Regulations 1998, SI 1998/1833, reg 27A(1)(c) (as added: see note 1).
9   Ie the Working Time Regulations 1998, SI 1998/1833, reg 6A (see PARA 284): see reg 27A(2), (3) (as added: see note 1). As to the meaning of 'night work' see PARA 284 note 1.
10   Working Time Regulations 1998, SI 1998/1833, reg 27A(2)(a) (as added: see note 1).
11   Working Time Regulations 1998, SI 1998/1833, reg 27A(2)(b) (as added: see note 1).
12   See the Working Time Regulations 1998, SI 1998/1833, reg 27A(2) (as added: see note 1).
13   Working Time Regulations 1998, SI 1998/1833, reg 27A(3)(a) (as added: see note 1).
14   Working Time Regulations 1998, SI 1998/1833, reg 27A(3)(b) (as added: see note 1).
15   Working Time Regulations 1998, SI 1998/1833, reg 27A(3)(c) (as added: see note 1).
16   Working Time Regulations 1998, SI 1998/1833, reg 27A(3)(d) (as added: see note 1).
17   Working Time Regulations 1998, SI 1998/1833, reg 27A(3)(e) (as added: see note 1).
18   Working Time Regulations 1998, SI 1998/1833, reg 27A(3)(f) (as added: see note 1).
19   See the Working Time Regulations 1998, SI 1998/1833, reg 27A(3) (as added: see note 1).
20   Ie the Working Time Regulations 1998, SI 1998/1833, reg 6A (see PARA 284): see reg 27A(4) (as added: see note 1).
21   Ie by the Working Time Regulations 1998, SI 1998/1833, reg 27A(2) (see head (a) in the text) or by reg 27A(3) (see head (b) in the text): see reg 27A(4) (as added: see note 1).
22   As to the meaning of 'rest period' see PARA 284 note 4.
23   See the Working Time Regulations 1998, SI 1998/1833, reg 27A(4) (as added: see note 1). As to compensatory rest see PARA 304. As to the right to present a complaint to an employment tribunal see PARA 319.

(v) Enforcement

311. Responsibility for enforcement of relevant requirements under working time regulations. It is the duty of the Health and Safety Executive ('the Executive')[1] to make adequate arrangements for the enforcement of the relevant requirements[2], except to the extent that[3]:

(1)   a local authority[4] is made responsible[5] for their enforcement[6];
(2)   the Civil Aviation Authority[7] is made responsible[8] for their enforcement[9];
(3)   the Driver and Vehicle Standards Agency ('DVSA')[10] is made responsible[11] for their enforcement[12];
(4)   the Office of Rail Regulation[13] is made responsible[14] for their enforcement[15].

Where the relevant requirements apply in relation to workers[16] employed in premises[17] in respect of which a local authority is responsible[18] for enforcing any of the relevant statutory provisions[19], it is the duty of that authority to enforce those requirements[20] (and the duty so imposed on local authorities must be performed in accordance with such guidance as may be given to them by the Health and Safety Executive)[21].

1   For the purposes of the Working Time Regulations 1998, SI 1998/1833, regs 28–29E, Sch 3 (see also PARAS 312–318), 'the Executive' means the Health and Safety Executive referred to in the Health and Safety at Work etc Act 1974 s 10(1) (see HEALTH AND SAFETY AT WORK vol 52 (2014) PARA 326): see the Working Time Regulations 1998, SI 1998/1833, reg 28(1) (reg 28 substituted by SI 2003/1684; definition of 'the Executive' in the Working Time Regulations 1998, SI 1998/1833, reg 28(1) amended by SI 2008/960).
2   For the purposes of the Working Time Regulations 1998, SI 1998/1833, regs 28–29E, Sch 3 (see also PARAS 312–318), the 'relevant requirements' means the following provisions: (1) reg 4(2) (maximum weekly working time for workers: see PARA 280), reg 5A(4) (maximum weekly working time for young workers: see PARA 281), reg 6(2), (7) (average length of night work: see PARA 284), reg 6A (restriction on night work by young workers: see PARA 284), reg 7(1), (2), (6) (night worker's access to free health assessments and his transfer to other work where a registered medical practitioner has so advised: see PARA 285), reg 8 (pattern of work (especially where the work is monotonous or the work-rate is predetermined): see PARA 286), reg 9 (employer's duty to keep records: see PARA 287) and reg 27A(4)(a) (supervision of young workers: see PARA 310); (2) reg 24 (compensatory rest: see PARA 304), in so far as it applies where reg 6(1), (2) or (7) is modified or excluded; and (3) reg 27A(2) (disapplication of reg 6A: see PARA 310), in so far as it applies where reg 6(1), (2) or (7) is excluded: see reg 28(1) (as substituted: see note 1). The provisions of Sch 3 (see PARAS 312–316) apply in relation to the enforcement of the relevant requirements: reg 28(7) (as so substituted).
3   See the Working Time Regulations 1998, SI 1998/1833, reg 28(2) (as substituted: see note 1).
4   For the purposes of the Working Time Regulations 1998, SI 1998/1833, regs 28–29E, Sch 3 (see also PARAS 312–318), 'local authority' means: (1) in relation to England, a county council so far as it is the council for an area for which there are no district councils, a district council, a London borough council, the Common Council of the City of London, the Sub-Treasurer of the Inner Temple or the Under-Treasurer of the Middle Temple; and (2) in relation to Wales, a county council or a county borough council: see reg 28(1) (as substituted: see note 1). As to the meanings of 'England' and 'Wales' see PARA 2 note 12. As to local government areas and authorities in England see LOCAL GOVERNMENT vol 69 (2009) PARA 22 et seq. As to the London boroughs and their councils see LONDON GOVERNMENT vol 71 (2013) PARAS 15, 20–22, 55 et seq; as to the Common Council of the City of London see LONDON GOVERNMENT vol 71 (2013) PARAS 34–38; and as to the Temples see LONDON GOVERNMENT vol 71 (2013) PARA 77. As to local government areas and authorities in Wales see LOCAL GOVERNMENT vol 69 (2009) PARA 37 et seq.
5   Ie by the Working Time Regulations 1998, SI 1998/1833, reg 28(3) (see the text and notes 16–20): see reg 28(2)(a) (as substituted: see note 1).
6   Working Time Regulations 1998, SI 1998/1833, reg 28(2)(a) (as substituted: see note 1).
7   For the purposes of the Working Time Regulations 1998, SI 1998/1833, regs 28–29E, Sch 3 (see also PARAS 312–318), the 'Civil Aviation Authority' means the authority referred to in the Civil

Aviation Act 1982 s 2(1) (see AIR LAW vol 2 (2008) PARA 50): see the Working Time Regulations 1998, SI 1998/1833, reg 28(1) (as substituted: see note 1).

8   Ie by the Working Time Regulations 1998, SI 1998/1833, reg 28(5): see reg 28(2)(b) (reg 28 as substituted (see note 1); reg 28(2)(b) amended by SI 2006/557). Accordingly, it is the duty of the Civil Aviation Authority to enforce the relevant requirements in relation to relevant civil aviation workers: Working Time Regulations 1998, SI 1998/1833, reg 28(5) (reg 28 as so substituted). For the purposes of regs 28–29E, Sch 3 (see also PARAS 312–318), 'relevant civil aviation worker' means a mobile worker who works mainly on board civil aircraft, excluding any worker to whom reg 18(2)(b) applies (ie workers to whom the European Agreement on the organisation of working time of mobile staff in civil aviation applies: see PARA 298): see reg 28(1) (as so substituted). As to the meaning of 'mobile worker' see PARA 305 note 1.

9   Working Time Regulations 1998, SI 1998/1833, reg 28(2)(b) (reg 28 as substituted, reg 28(2)(b) as amended : see note 8). The Civil Aviation Authority also has responsibility for enforcing obligations imposed by the Civil Aviation (Working Time) Regulations 2004, SI 2004/756: see AIR LAW vol 2 (2008) PARA 467 et seq.

10   For the purposes of the Working Time Regulations 1998, SI 1998/1833, regs 28–29E, Sch 3 (see also PARAS 312–318), 'DVSA' means the Driver and Vehicle Standards Agency (see ROAD TRAFFIC): see reg 28(1) (reg 28 as substituted (see note 1); definition of 'DVSA' in reg 28(1) added by SI 2014/480).

11   Ie by the Working Time Regulations 1998, SI 1998/1833, reg 28(6): see reg 28(2)(c) (reg 28 as substituted (see note 1); reg 28(2)(c), (6) amended by SI 2014/480). Accordingly, it is the duty of DVSA to enforce the relevant requirements in relation to relevant road transport workers: Working Time Regulations 1998, SI 1998/1833, reg 28(6) (reg 28 as so substituted, reg 28(6) as so amended). For the purposes of regs 28–29E, Sch 3 (see also PARAS 312–318), 'relevant road transport worker' means a mobile worker to whom one or more of the following applies: (1) Council Regulation (EEC) 3820/85 (OJ L370, 31.12.85, p 1) (repealed: see now European Parliament and Council Regulation (EC) 561/2006 of 15 March 2006 (OJ L102, 11.4.2006, p 1) on the harmonisation of certain social legislation relating to road transport; and ROAD TRAFFIC vol 90 (2011) PARA 1125 et seq); (2) the European Agreement concerning the Work of Crews of Vehicles engaged in International Road Transport (AETR) (Geneva, 1 July 1970; TS 103 (1978); Cmnd 7401) (see ROAD TRAFFIC vol 90 (2011) PARA 1125); and (3) the United Kingdom domestic driver's hours code, which is set out in the Transport Act 1968 Pt VI (ss 95–103) (driver's hours: see ROAD TRAFFIC vol 90 (2011) PARA 1125): see the Working Time Regulations 1998, SI 1998/1833, reg 28(1) (as so substituted).

    See also European Parliament and Council Directive (EC) 2002/15 of 11 March 2002 (OJ L80, 23.3.2002, p 35) concerning the organisation of the working time of persons performing mobile road transport activities (for the purpose of implementing which, the Road Transport (Working Time) Regulations 2005, SI 2005/639, were made: see ROAD TRAFFIC vol 90 (2011) PARA 1125 et seq). The Secretary of State may appoint inspectors to enforce obligations imposed by the Road Transport (Working Time) Regulations 2005, SI 2005/639: see ROAD TRAFFIC vol 90 (2011) PARA 1125 et seq.

12   Working Time Regulations 1998, SI 1998/1833, reg 28(2)(c) (reg 28 as substituted, reg 28(2)(c) as amended: see note 11).

13   As to the Office of Rail Regulation see RAILWAYS AND TRAMWAYS vol 86 (2013) PARA 51 et seq.

14   Ie by the Working Time Regulations 1998, SI 1998/1833, reg 28(3A): see reg 28(2)(d) (reg 28 as substituted (see note 1); reg 28(2)(d), (3A) added by SI 2006/557). Accordingly, where the relevant requirements apply in relation to workers employed in the carrying out of any of the activities specified in the Health and Safety (Enforcing Authority for Railways and Other Guided Transport Systems) Regulations 2006, SI 2006/557, reg 3(2) (ie the operation of a railway, tramway, or any other system of guided transport: see RAILWAYS AND TRAMWAYS vol 86 (2013) PARA 194), it is the duty of the Office of Rail Regulation to enforce those requirements: Working Time Regulations 1998, SI 1998/1833, reg 28(3A) (reg 28 as so substituted, reg 28(3A) as so added).

15   Working Time Regulations 1998, SI 1998/1833, reg 28(2)(d) (reg 28 as substituted, reg 28(2)(d) as added: see note 14).

16   As to the meaning of 'worker' for these purposes see PARA 271.

17   For the purposes of the Working Time Regulations 1998, SI 1998/1833, regs 28–29E, Sch 3 (see also PARAS 312–318), 'premises' includes any place and, in particular, includes: (1) any vehicle, vessel, aircraft or hovercraft; (2) any installation on land (including the foreshore and other land intermittently covered by water), any offshore installation, and any other installation (whether floating, or resting on the seabed or the subsoil thereof, or resting on other land covered with water or the subsoil thereof); and (3) any tent or movable structure: see, reg 28(1) (as substituted: see note 1).

18 Ie under the under the Health and Safety (Enforcing Authority) Regulations 1998, SI 1998/494 (see HEALTH AND SAFETY AT WORK vol 52 (2014) PARA 332 et seq): see the Working Time Regulations 1998, SI 1998/1833, reg 28(3) (as substituted: see note 1).

19 For the purposes of the Working Time Regulations 1998, SI 1998/1833, regs 28–29E, Sch 3 (see also PARAS 312–318), 'relevant statutory provisions' means: (1) the provisions of the Health and Safety at Work etc Act 1974 and of any regulations made under powers contained in that Act (see HEALTH AND SAFETY AT WORK vol 52 (2014) PARA 384 et seq); and (2) while and to the extent that they remain in force, the provisions of the Acts mentioned and specified in the Health and Safety at Work etc Act 1974 ss 1, 53, Sch 1 (see HEALTH AND SAFETY AT WORK vol 52 (2014) PARA 302) and the regulations, orders or other instruments of a legislative character made or having effect under a provision so specified: see the Working Time Regulations 1998, SI 1998/1833, reg 28(1) (as substituted: see note 1).

20 Working Time Regulations 1998, SI 1998/1833, reg 28(3) (as substituted: see note 1).

21 Working Time Regulations 1998, SI 1998/1833, reg 28(4) (reg 28 as substituted (see note 1); reg 28(4) amended by SI 2008/960).

312.   Appointment of inspectors by enforcement authority under working time regulations and their powers.   Each enforcement authority[1] may appoint as inspectors, under whatever title it may from time to time determine, such persons having suitable qualifications as it thinks necessary for carrying into effect the Working Time Regulations 1998[2] within its field of responsibility, and each such authority may terminate any appointment so made[3]. Every such appointment must be made by an instrument in writing[4] specifying which of the powers conferred on inspectors by the Working Time Regulations 1998 are to be exercisable by the person appointed; and an inspector is in right of such appointment entitled to exercise only such of those powers as are so specified and is entitled to exercise the powers so specified only within the field of responsibility of the authority which appointed him[5]. So much of an inspector's instrument of appointment as specifies the powers which he is entitled to exercise may be varied by the enforcement authority which appointed him[6]. An inspector must, if so required when exercising or seeking to exercise any power conferred on him by the Working Time Regulations 1998, produce his instrument of appointment or a duly authenticated copy of it[7].

An inspector may, for the purpose of carrying into effect the Working Time Regulations 1998 within the field of responsibility of the enforcement authority which appointed him, exercise the following powers[8], namely:

(1)   at any reasonable time (or, in a situation which in his opinion is or may be dangerous, at any time) to enter any premises[9] which he has reason to believe it is necessary[10] for him to enter[11];

(2)   to take with him a constable if he has reasonable cause to apprehend any serious obstruction in the execution of his duty[12];

(3)   without prejudice to head (2) above, on entering any premises by virtue of head (1) above to take with him any other person duly authorised by the inspector's enforcement authority, and any equipment or materials required for any purpose for which the power of entry is being exercised[13];

(4)   to make such examination and investigation as may in any circumstances be necessary[14] for the purpose[15];

(5)   to require any person whom he has reasonable cause to believe to be able to give any information relevant to any examination or investigation under head (4) above to answer (in the absence of persons other than a person nominated by him to be present and any persons

whom the inspector may allow to be present) such questions as the inspector thinks fit to ask and to sign a declaration of the truth of his answers[16];

(6)   to require the production of, inspect, and take copies of or of any entry in:

(a)   any records which by virtue of the Working Time Regulations 1998 are required to be kept[17]; and

(b)   any other books, records or documents which it is necessary for him to see for the purposes of any examination or investigation under head (4) above[18];

(7)   to require any person to afford him such facilities and assistance with respect to any matters or things within that person's control or in relation to which that person has responsibilities as are necessary to enable the inspector to exercise any of the powers conferred[19] on him[20]; and

(8)   any other power which is necessary[21] for the purpose[22].

None of the powers so conferred[23] are to be taken to compel the production by any person of a document of which he would on grounds of legal professional privilege[24] be entitled to withhold production on an order for disclosure in a claim in the High Court[25].

Where a claim has been brought against an inspector in respect of an act done in the execution or purported execution of the Working Time Regulations 1998, and the circumstances are such that he is not legally entitled to require the enforcement authority to indemnify him, that authority may, nevertheless, indemnify him against the whole or part of any damages and costs or expenses which he may have been ordered to pay or may have incurred, if the authority is satisfied that the inspector honestly believed that the act complained of was within his powers and that his duty as an inspector required or entitled him to do it[26].

1   For the purposes of the Working Time Regulations 1998, SI 1998/1833, regs 28–29E, Sch 3 (see also PARAS 311, 313–318), 'enforcement authority' means the Health and Safety Executive (see HEALTH AND SAFETY AT WORK vol 52 (2014) PARA 326 et seq), a local authority (see PARA 311 note 4), the Civil Aviation Authority (see AIR LAW vol 2 (2008) PARA 50), the Driver and Vehicle Standards Agency (see ROAD TRAFFIC) or the Office of Rail Regulation (see RAILWAYS AND TRAMWAYS vol 86 (2013) PARA 51 et seq): see reg 28(1) (reg 28 substituted by SI 2003/1684; definition of 'enforcement authority' in the Working Time Regulations 1998, SI 1998/1833, reg 28(1) amended by SI 2006/557; SI 2014/480). As to the allocation of responsibility between enforcement authorities for the enforcement of relevant requirements under the Working Time Regulations 1998, SI 1998/1833, see PARA 311.

2   Ie the Working Time Regulations 1998, SI 1998/1833: see Sch 3 para 1(1) (Sch 3 added by SI 2003/1684).

3   Working Time Regulations 1998, SI 1998/1833, Sch 3 para 1(1) (as added: see note 2).

4   As to the meaning of 'writing' see PARA 2 note 8.

5   See the Working Time Regulations 1998, SI 1998/1833, Sch 3 para 1(2) (as added: see note 2).

6   Working Time Regulations 1998, SI 1998/1833, Sch 3 para 1(3) (as added: see note 2).

7   Working Time Regulations 1998, SI 1998/1833, Sch 3 para 1(4) (as added: see note 2).

8   Working Time Regulations 1998, SI 1998/1833, Sch 3 para 2(1) (as added: see note 2). The exercise of such powers is subject to the provisions of Sch 3 para 1 (see the text and notes 1–7) and Sch 3 para 2(1): see Sch 3 para 2(1) (as so added).

9   As to the meaning of 'premises' see PARA 311 note 17.

10   Ie for the purpose mentioned in the Working Time Regulations 1998, SI 1998/1833, Sch 3 para 2(1) (see the text and note 8): see Sch 3 para 2(2)(a) (as added: see note 2).

11   Working Time Regulations 1998, SI 1998/1833, Sch 3 para 2(2)(a) (as added: see note 2).

12   Working Time Regulations 1998, SI 1998/1833, Sch 3 para 2(2)(b) (as added: see note 2).

13   See the Working Time Regulations 1998, SI 1998/1833, Sch 3 para 2(2)(c) (as added: see note 2).

14 Ie for the purpose mentioned in the Working Time Regulations 1998, SI 1998/1833, Sch 3 para 2(1) (see the text and note 8): see Sch 3 para 2(2)(d) (as added: see note 2).

15 Working Time Regulations 1998, SI 1998/1833, Sch 3 para 2(2)(d) (as added: see note 2).

16 Working Time Regulations 1998, SI 1998/1833, Sch 3 para 2(2)(e) (as added: see note 2). No answer given by a person in pursuance of a requirement imposed under Sch 3 para 2(2)(e) is admissible in evidence against that person or the spouse or civil partner of that person in any proceedings: Sch 3 para 2(3) (Sch 3 as so added; Sch 3 para 2(3) amended by SI 2014/107). As to restrictions on the disclosure of information obtained under Sch 3 para 2(2)(e) see PARA 313.

17 Working Time Regulations 1998, SI 1998/1833, Sch 3 para 2(2)(f)(i) (as added: see note 2). As to the records that must be kept by an employer in relation to maximum weekly working time and night work by virtue of reg 9 see PARA 287. As to restrictions on the disclosure of information obtained under Sch 3 para 2(2)(f) see PARA 313.

18 Working Time Regulations 1998, SI 1998/1833, Sch 3 para 2(2)(f)(ii) (as added: see note 2). See note 17.

19 Ie conferred by the Working Time Regulations 1998, SI 1998/1833, Sch 3 para 2: see Sch 3 para 2(2)(g) (as added: see note 2).

20 Working Time Regulations 1998, SI 1998/1833, Sch 3 para 2(2)(g) (as added: see note 2).

21 Ie for the purpose mentioned in the Working Time Regulations 1998, SI 1998/1833, Sch 3 para 2(1) (see the text and note 8): see Sch 3 para 2(2)(h) (as added: see note 2).

22 Working Time Regulations 1998, SI 1998/1833, Sch 3 para 2(2)(h) (as added: see note 2).

23 Ie nothing in the Working Time Regulations 1998, SI 1998/1833, Sch 2 para 2: see Sch 3 para 2(4) (as added: see note 2).

24 As to legal professional privilege see CIVIL PROCEDURE vol 11 (2009) PARA 558 et seq, 972; CRIMINAL PROCEDURE vol 28 (2010) PARA 506. See also LEGAL PROFESSIONS vol 65 (2008) PARAS 740–741; LEGAL PROFESSIONS vol 66 (2009) PARA 1146.

25 Working Time Regulations 1998, SI 1998/1833, Sch 3 para 2(4) (as added: see note 2).

26 Working Time Regulations 1998, SI 1998/1833, Sch 3 para 7 (as added: see note 2).

313.   Restrictions on disclosure of information obtained by inspector in pursuance of requirement imposed under working time regulations. No relevant information[1] may be disclosed[2] without the consent of the person by whom it was furnished[3], except where such disclosure relates to:

(1)   disclosure of information to the Health and Safety Commission, a government department or any enforcement authority[4];

(2)   without prejudice to head (1) above, disclosure by the recipient[5] of information to any person for the purpose of any function conferred on the recipient by or under any of the relevant statutory provisions[6] or under the Working Time Regulations 1998[7];

(3)   without prejudice to head (1) above, disclosure by the recipient of information either to an officer of a local authority who is authorised by that authority to receive it, or to a constable authorised by a chief officer of police to receive it[8]; or

(4)   disclosure by the recipient of information in a form calculated to prevent it from being identified as relating to a particular person or case[9].

A person to whom information is disclosed in pursuance of heads (1) to (4) above must not use the information for a purpose other than:

(i)   in a case falling within head (1) above, a purpose of the Health and Safety Commission, of the government department, or of the enforcement authority, in question, in connection with the Working Time Regulations 1998 or with the relevant statutory provisions, as the case may be[10];

(ii)   in the case of information given to an officer of a body which is a local authority[11], the purposes of the body in connection with the relevant statutory provisions or any enactment whatsoever relating to working time[12], public health, public safety or the protection of the environment[13];

(iii) in the case of information given to a constable, the purposes of the police in connection with the Working Time Regulations 1998, the relevant statutory provisions or any enactment whatsoever relating to working time, public health, public safety or the safety of the state[14].

A person must not disclose any information obtained by him as a result of the exercise of any power conferred by the Working Time Regulations 1998[15] (including in particular any information with respect to any trade secret obtained by him in any premises[16] entered by him by virtue of any such power) except for the purposes of his functions, for the purposes of any legal proceedings, or with the relevant consent[17].

Notwithstanding this restriction, an inspector must, in circumstances in which it is necessary to do so for the purpose of assisting in keeping persons, or the representatives of persons[18], employed at any premises adequately informed about matters affecting their health, safety and welfare or working time, give to such persons or their representatives the following descriptions of information[19], that is to say:

(A) factual information so obtained by him which relates to those premises or anything which was or is therein or was or is being done therein[20]; and

(B) information with respect to any action which he has taken or proposes to take in or in connection with those premises in the performance of his functions[21],

and, where an inspector does so, he must give the like information to the employer[22] of the first-mentioned persons[23].

Also, notwithstanding the restriction mentioned above[24], a person who has obtained such information as is referred to therein may furnish to a person who appears to him to be likely to be a party to any civil proceedings arising out of any accident, occurrence, situation or other matter, a written[25] statement of the relevant facts observed by him in the course of exercising any of the powers referred to therein[26].

1 For the purposes of the Working Time Regulations 1998, SI 1998/1833, Sch 3 para 8(1)–(3), 'relevant information' means information obtained by an inspector in pursuance of a requirement imposed under Sch 3 para 2(2)(e) (see PARA 312) or Sch 3 para 2(2)(f) (see PARA 312): see Sch 3 para 8(1) (Sch 3 added by SI 2003/1684). As to the appointment and powers of inspectors under the Working Time Regulations 1998, SI 1998/1833, see PARA 312.

2 Ie subject to the Working Time Regulations 1998, SI 1998/1833, Sch 3 para 8(3) (see the text and notes 4–9): see Sch 3 para 8(2) (as added: see note 1).

3 Working Time Regulations 1998, SI 1998/1833, Sch 3 para 8(2) (as added: see note 1).

4 Working Time Regulations 1998, SI 1998/1833, Sch 3 para 8(3)(a) (as added: see note 1). As to the meaning of 'enforcement authority' see PARA 312 note 1. For these purposes, any reference to the Health and Safety Commission, a government department or an enforcement authority includes respectively a reference to an officer of that body or authority (including in the case of an enforcement authority, any inspector appointed by it); and, in the case of a reference to the Health and Safety Commission, it also includes a reference to: (1) a person performing any functions of the Health and Safety Commission or the Health and Safety Executive on its behalf by virtue of the Health and Safety at Work etc Act 1974 s 13(1)(a) (as originally enacted); (2) an officer of a body which is so performing any such functions; and (3) an adviser appointed in pursuance of s 13(1)(d) (as originally enacted): see the Working Time Regulations 1998, SI 1998/1833, Sch 3 para 8(4) (as so added). The Health and Safety Commission and the Health and Safety Executive, established under the Health and Safety at Work etc Act 1974 s 10 (as originally enacted), were abolished, and a single Health and Safety Executive, exercising the combined functions of those bodies, was established to replace them under s 10 (as substituted)

by the Legislative Reform (Health and Safety Executive) Order 2008, SI 2008/960: see HEALTH
AND SAFETY AT WORK vol 52 (2014) PARA 326 et seq.

5 For the purposes of the Working Time Regulations 1998, SI 1998/1833, Sch 3 para 8(1)–(3), the
'recipient', in relation to any relevant information, means the person by whom that information
was so obtained or to whom that information was so furnished, as the case may be: see Sch 3
para 8(1) (as added: see note 1).
6 As to the meaning of 'relevant statutory provisions' for these purposes see PARA 311 note 19.
7 Working Time Regulations 1998, SI 1998/1833, Sch 3 para 8(3)(b) (as added: see note 1).
8 See the Working Time Regulations 1998, SI 1998/1833, Sch 3 para 8(3)(c) (as added: see
note 1).
9 Working Time Regulations 1998, SI 1998/1833, Sch 3 para 8(3)(d) (as added: see note 1).
10 Working Time Regulations 1998, SI 1998/1833, Sch 3 para 8(5)(a) (as added: see note 1).
11 As to the meaning of 'local authority' see PARA 311 note 4.
12 As to the meaning of 'working time' see PARA 280 note 4.
13 Working Time Regulations 1998, SI 1998/1833, Sch 3 para 8(5)(b) (as added: see note 1).
14 Working Time Regulations 1998, SI 1998/1833, Sch 3 para 8(5)(c) (as added: see note 1).
15 Ie any power conferred by the Working Time Regulations 1998, SI 1998/1833, Sch 3 para 2 (see
PARA 312): see Sch 3 para 8(6) (as added: see note 1).
16 As to the meaning of 'premises' see PARA 311 note 17.
17 See the Working Time Regulations 1998, SI 1998/1833, Sch 3 para 8(6) (as added: see note 1).
For these purposes, 'relevant consent' means the consent of the person who furnished it, and, in
any other case, the consent of a person having responsibilities in relation to the premises where
the information was obtained: see Sch 3 para 8(6) (as so added).
18 As to the meaning of 'representatives of the workforce' see PARA 272 note 8.
19 See the Working Time Regulations 1998, SI 1998/1833, Sch 3 para 8(7) (as added: see note 1).
20 Working Time Regulations 1998, SI 1998/1833, Sch 3 para 8(7)(a) (as added: see note 1).
21 Working Time Regulations 1998, SI 1998/1833, Sch 3 para 8(7)(b) (as added: see note 1).
22 As to the meaning of 'employer' see PARA 269 note 5.
23 See the Working Time Regulations 1998, SI 1998/1833, Sch 3 para 8(7) (as added: see note 1).
24 Ie notwithstanding anything mentioned in the Working Time Regulations 1998, SI 1998/1833,
Sch 3 para 8(6) (see the text and notes 15–17): see Sch 3 para 8(8) (as added: see note 1).
25 As to the meaning of 'writing' see PARA 2 note 8.
26 Working Time Regulations 1998, SI 1998/1833, Sch 3 para 8(8) (as added: see note 1).

**314. Improvement notices for failure to comply with requirement imposed
under working time regulations.** If an inspector appointed under the Working
Time Regulations 1998[1] is of the opinion that a person is contravening one or
more of those Regulations[2], or that he has contravened one or more of those
Regulations in circumstances that make it likely that the contravention will
continue or be repeated[3], he may serve on him a notice (an 'improvement
notice')[4]:

(1)   stating that he is of that opinion[5];
(2)   specifying the provision or provisions as to which he is of that opinion[6];
(3)   giving particulars of the reasons why he is of that opinion[7]; and
(4)   requiring that person to remedy the contravention or, as the case may
        be, the matters occasioning it within such period (ending not earlier
        than the period within which an appeal against the notice can be
        brought[8]) as may be specified in the notice[9].

Such a notice may, but need not, include directions as to the measures to be
taken to remedy any contravention or matter to which the notice relates[10]; and
any such directions:

(a)   may be framed to any extent by reference to any approved code of
        practice[11]; and
(b)   may be framed so as to afford the person on whom the notice is served
        a choice between different ways of remedying the contravention or
        matter[12].

Where an improvement notice which is not to take immediate effect has been served: (i) the notice may be withdrawn by an inspector at any time before the end of the period specified[13] therein[14]; and (ii) the period so specified may be extended or further extended by an inspector at any time when an appeal against the notice is not pending[15].

1   As to the appointment of inspectors under the Working Time Regulations 1998, SI 1998/1833, and their powers, see PARA 312.
2   Working Time Regulations 1998, SI 1998/1833, Sch 3 para 3(a) (Sch 3 added by SI 2003/1684).
3   Working Time Regulations 1998, SI 1998/1833, Sch 3 para 3(b) (as added: see note 2).
4   See the Working Time Regulations 1998, SI 1998/1833, Sch 3 para 3 (as added: see note 2).
5   See the Working Time Regulations 1998, SI 1998/1833, Sch 3 para 3 (as added: see note 2).
6   See the Working Time Regulations 1998, SI 1998/1833, Sch 3 para 3 (as added: see note 2).
7   Ie under the Working Time Regulations 1998, SI 1998/1833, Sch 3 para 6 (see PARA 316): see Sch 3 para 3 (as added: see note 2).
8   See the Working Time Regulations 1998, SI 1998/1833, Sch 3 para 3 (as added: see note 2).
9   See the Working Time Regulations 1998, SI 1998/1833, Sch 3 para 3 (as added: see note 2).
10 See the Working Time Regulations 1998, SI 1998/1833, Sch 3 para 5(2) (as added: see note 2). For these purposes, 'notice' means an improvement notice: see Sch 3 para 5(1) (as so added).
11 Working Time Regulations 1998, SI 1998/1833, Sch 3 para 5(2)(a) (as added: see note 2). For the purposes of regs 28–29E, Sch 3 (see also PARAS 311–313, 315–318), 'code of practice' includes a standard, a specification and any other documentary form of practical guidance: see reg 28(1) (reg 28 substituted by SI 2003/1684).
12 Working Time Regulations 1998, SI 1998/1833, Sch 3 para 5(2)(b) (as added: see note 2).
13 Ie, in the case of an improvement notice, in pursuance of the Working Time Regulations 1998, SI 1998/1833, Sch 3 para 3 (see the text and notes 1–9): see Sch 3 para 5(3)(a) (as added: see note 2).
14 Working Time Regulations 1998, SI 1998/1833, Sch 3 para 5(3)(a) (as added: see note 2).
15 Working Time Regulations 1998, SI 1998/1833, Sch 3 para 5(3)(b) (as added: see note 2).

315.   Prohibition notices for failure to comply with requirement imposed under working time regulations. If, as regards any activities which are being or are likely to be carried on by or under the control of any person (being activities to or in relation to which any of the Working Time Regulations 1998[1] apply or, if the activities are so carried on, will apply), an inspector[2] is of the opinion that, as carried on or likely to be carried on by or under the control of the person in question, the activities involve or, as the case may be, will involve a risk of serious personal injury, the inspector may serve on that person a notice (a 'prohibition notice')[3]. A prohibition notice must:

(1)   state that the inspector is of the said opinion[4];
(2)   specify the matters which in his opinion give or, as the case may be, will give rise to the said risk[5];
(3)   where in his opinion any of those matters involves or, as the case may be, will involve a contravention of any of the Working Time Regulations 1998, state that he is of that opinion, specify the regulation or regulations as to which he is of that opinion, and give particulars of the reasons why he is of that opinion[6]; and
(4)   direct that the activities to which the notice relates are not to be carried on by or under the control of the person on whom the notice is served unless the matters specified in the notice in pursuance of head (2) above and any associated contraventions of provisions so specified in pursuance of head (3) above have been remedied[7].

Such a notice may, but need not, include directions as to the measures to be taken to remedy any contravention or matter to which the notice relates[8]; and any such directions:

(a)   may be framed to any extent by reference to any approved code of practice[9]; and

(b)   may be framed so as to afford the person on whom the notice is served a choice between different ways of remedying the contravention or matter[10].

Where an prohibition notice which is not to take immediate effect has been served: (i) the notice may be withdrawn by an inspector at any time before the end of the period specified[11] therein[12]; and (ii) the period so specified may be extended or further extended by an inspector at any time when an appeal against the notice is not pending[13].

1   Ie the Working Time Regulations 1998, SI 1998/1833: see Sch 3 para 4(1) (Sch 3 added by SI 2003/1684).

2   As to the appointment of inspectors under the Working Time Regulations 1998, SI 1998/1833, and their powers, see PARA 312.

3   See the Working Time Regulations 1998, SI 1998/1833, Sch 3 para 4(1), (2) (as added: see note 1).

4   Working Time Regulations 1998, SI 1998/1833, Sch 3 para 4(3)(a) (as added: see note 1).

5   Working Time Regulations 1998, SI 1998/1833, Sch 3 para 4(3)(b) (as added: see note 1).

6   Working Time Regulations 1998, SI 1998/1833, Sch 3 para 4(3)(c) (as added: see note 1).

7   Working Time Regulations 1998, SI 1998/1833, Sch 3 para 4(3)(d) (as added: see note 1). A direction contained in a prohibition notice in pursuance of Sch 3 para 4(3)(d) must take effect at the end of the period specified in the notice (or, if the notice so declares, immediately): see Sch 3 para 4(4) (as so added).

8   See the Working Time Regulations 1998, SI 1998/1833, Sch 3 para 5(2) (as added: see note 1). For these purposes, 'notice' means a prohibition notice: see Sch 3 para 5(1) (as so added).

9   Working Time Regulations 1998, SI 1998/1833, Sch 3 para 5(2)(a) (as added: see note 1). As to the meaning of 'code of practice' see PARA 314 note 11.

10   Working Time Regulations 1998, SI 1998/1833, Sch 3 para 5(2)(b) (as added: see note 1).

11   Ie, in the case of an prohibition notice, in pursuance of the Working Time Regulations 1998, SI 1998/1833, Sch 3 para 4(4) (see note 7): see Sch 3 para 5(3)(a) (as added: see note 1).

12   Working Time Regulations 1998, SI 1998/1833, Sch 3 para 5(3)(a) (as added: see note 1).

13   Working Time Regulations 1998, SI 1998/1833, Sch 3 para 5(3)(b) (as added: see note 1).

316.   Appeal against improvement or prohibition notice imposed under working time regulations.   A person on whom a notice[1] is served may within 21 days from the date of its service appeal to an employment tribunal[2]; and on such an appeal the tribunal may either cancel or affirm the notice and, if it affirms it, may do so either in its original form or with such modifications as the tribunal may in the circumstances think fit[3].

Where such an appeal is brought against a notice within the period so allowed, then:

(1)   in the case of an improvement notice, the bringing of the appeal has the effect of suspending the operation of the notice until the appeal is finally disposed of or, if the appeal is withdrawn, until the withdrawal of the appeal[4];

(2)   in the case of a prohibition notice, the bringing of the appeal has the like effect if, but only if, on the application of the appellant the tribunal so directs, and then only from the giving of the direction[5].

One or more assessors may be appointed for the purposes of any such proceedings brought before an employment tribunal[6].

1   For these purposes, 'notice' means an improvement or a prohibition notice: see the Working Time Regulations 1998, SI 1998/1833, Sch 3 para 6(1) (Sch 3 added by SI 2003/1684). As to improvement notices see PARA 314; and as to prohibition notices see PARA 315.

2   See the Working Time Regulations 1998, SI 1998/1833, Sch 3 para 6(2) (as added: see note 1). As to employment tribunals and the procedure before them see PARA 1399 et seq; and as to the procedure on a complaint made to an employment tribunal see PARA 1453 et seq.
3   See the Working Time Regulations 1998, SI 1998/1833, Sch 3 para 6(2) (as added: see note 1).
4   Working Time Regulations 1998, SI 1998/1833, Sch 3 para 6(3)(a) (as added: see note 1).
5   Working Time Regulations 1998, SI 1998/1833, Sch 3 para 6(3)(b) (as added: see note 1).
6   Working Time Regulations 1998, SI 1998/1833, Sch 3 para 6(4) (as added: see note 1).

317. Offences for failure to comply with requirement imposed under working time regulations. An employer[1] who fails to comply with any of the relevant requirements[2] is guilty of an offence[3], and liable to a penalty[4].

Where an inspector is exercising or has exercised any of the enforcement powers conferred[5] in relation to the relevant requirements[6], it is an offence for a person:

(1)   to contravene any requirement imposed[7] by the inspector in exercise of his powers[8];

(2)   to prevent or attempt to prevent any other person from appearing before the inspector, or from answering any question to which the inspector may[9] require an answer[10];

(3)   to contravene any requirement or prohibition imposed by an improvement notice[11] or a prohibition notice[12] (including any such notice as is modified on appeal)[13];

(4)   intentionally to obstruct the inspector in the exercise or performance of his powers or duties[14];

(5)   to use or disclose any information in contravention[15] of the restrictions on the disclosure of information[16];

(6)   to make a statement which he knows to be false or recklessly to make a statement which is false, where the statement is made in purported compliance with a requirement to furnish any information imposed by or under the Working Time Regulations 1998[17].

A person guilty of an offence under any of heads (1) to (6) above is liable to the prescribed penalty[18].

Where the commission by any person of an offence is due to the act or default of some other person, that other person is guilty of the offence, and a person may be charged with and convicted of the offence[19] whether or not proceedings are taken against the first-mentioned person[20].

Where an offence committed by a body corporate is proved to have been committed with the consent or connivance of, or to have been attributable to any neglect on the part of, any director, manager, secretary or other similar officer of the body corporate or a person who was purporting to act in any such capacity, he as well as the body corporate is guilty of that offence and is liable to be proceeded against and punished accordingly[21].

1   As to the meaning of 'employer' see PARA 269 note 5.
2   As to the meaning of 'relevant requirements' for these purposes see PARA 311 note 2.
3   Working Time Regulations 1998, SI 1998/1833, reg 29(1) (reg 29 substituted, regs 29A–29D added, by SI 2003/1684). The provisions set out in the Working Time Regulations 1998, SI 1998/1833, regs 29A–29E (see also PARA 318) apply in relation to the offences provided for in reg 29(1)–(3) (see also the text and notes 5–17): reg 29(9) (as so substituted).
    Accordingly, an inspector, if authorised in that behalf by an enforcement authority, may (although not of counsel or a solicitor) prosecute before a magistrate's court proceedings for an offence under the Working Time Regulations 1998, SI 1998/1833 (see reg 29D (as so added)); but proceedings for an offence must not, in England and Wales, be instituted except by an inspector or by or with the consent of the Director of Public Prosecutions (see reg 29C (as so added)). As to the meanings of 'England' and 'Wales' see PARA 2 note 12. As to the appointment

of inspectors under the Working Time Regulations 1998, SI 1998/1833, and their powers, see PARA 312. As to the meaning of 'enforcement authority' see PARA 312 note 1. As to the Director of Public Prosecutions see CRIMINAL PROCEDURE vol 27 (2010) PARAS 23, 33 et seq.

4   See the Working Time Regulations 1998, SI 1998/1833, reg 29(4) (as substituted: see note 3). An employer guilty of an offence under reg 29(1) is liable (on summary conviction) to a fine not exceeding the statutory maximum and (on conviction on indictment) to a fine: see reg 29(4) (as so substituted). As to the statutory maximum see SENTENCING AND DISPOSITION OF OFFENDERS vol 92 (2010) PARA 140.

5   Ie conferred by the Working Time Regulations 1998, SI 1998/1833, Sch 3 (see PARAS 311–316): see reg 29(2) (as substituted: see note 3).

6   See the Working Time Regulations 1998, SI 1998/1833, reg 29(2) (as substituted: see note 3).

7   Ie by the Working Time Regulations 1998, SI 1998/1833, Sch 3 para 2 (see PARA 312): see reg 29(3)(a) (as substituted: see note 3).

8   Working Time Regulations 1998, SI 1998/1833, reg 29(3)(a) (as substituted: see note 3).

9   Ie by virtue of the Working Time Regulations 1998, SI 1998/1833, Sch 3 para 2(2)(e) (information relevant to any examination or investigation under Sch 3 para 2(2)(d): see PARA 312): see reg 29(3)(b) (as substituted: see note 3).

10 Working Time Regulations 1998, SI 1998/1833, reg 29(3)(b) (as substituted: see note 3).

11 As to improvement notices see PARA 314.

12 As to prohibition notices see PARA 315.

13 Working Time Regulations 1998, SI 1998/1833, reg 29(3)(c) (as substituted: see note 3). As to appeals against improvement or prohibition notices see PARA 316.

14 Working Time Regulations 1998, SI 1998/1833, reg 29(3)(d) (as substituted: see note 3).

15 Ie in contravention of the Working Time Regulations 1998, SI 1998/1833, Sch 3 para 8 (see PARA 313): see reg 29(3)(e) (as substituted: see note 3).

16 Working Time Regulations 1998, SI 1998/1833, reg 29(3)(e) (as substituted: see note 3).

17 Working Time Regulations 1998, SI 1998/1833, reg 29(3)(f) (as substituted: see note 3).

18 See the Working Time Regulations 1998, SI 1998/1833, reg 29(5) (as substituted: see note 3). A person guilty of an offence under reg 29(3) (see the text and notes 7–17) is liable to the penalty so prescribed by reg 29(6), (7), (8), as the case may be: see reg 29(5) (as so substituted). Accordingly:

    (1)   a person guilty of an offence under head (1), (2) or (4) in the text is liable (on summary conviction) to a fine not exceeding level 5 on the standard scale (reg 29(6) (as so substituted));

    (2)   a person guilty of an offence under head (3) in the text is liable (on summary conviction) to imprisonment for a term not exceeding three months, or a fine not exceeding the statutory maximum (reg 29(7)(a) (as so substituted)); or (on conviction on indictment) to imprisonment for a term not exceeding two years, or a fine, or both (see reg 29(7)(b) (as so substituted));

    (3)   a person guilty of an offence under any of the heads in the text not falling within head (1) or (2) above is liable (on summary conviction) to a fine not exceeding the statutory maximum (reg 29(8)(a) (as so substituted)); or (on conviction on indictment): (a) if the offence is under head (5) in the text, to imprisonment for a term not exceeding two years, or a fine, or both (reg 29(8)(b)(i) (as so substituted)); (b) if the offence is not one to which head (a) above applies, to a fine (reg 29(8)(b)(ii) (as so substituted)).

    As to the standard scale see SENTENCING AND DISPOSITION OF OFFENDERS vol 92 (2010) PARA 142.

19 Ie by virtue of the Working Time Regulations 1998, SI 1998/1833, reg 29A: see reg 29A (as added: see note 3).

20 Working Time Regulations 1998, SI 1998/1833, reg 29A (as added: see note 3).

21 Working Time Regulations 1998, SI 1998/1833, reg 29B(1) (as added: see note 3). Where the affairs of a body corporate are managed by its members, reg 29B(1) applies in relation to the acts and defaults of a member in connection with his functions of management as if he were a director of the body corporate: reg 29B(2) (as so added).

318.   Power of court to order cause of offence under the working time regulations to be remedied.   Where a person is convicted of an offence under the working time regulations[1] in respect of any matters which appear to the court to be matters which it is in his power to remedy, the court may, in addition to or instead of imposing any punishment, order him, within such time as may be fixed by the order, to take such steps as may be specified in the order for remedying the said matters[2]. The time fixed by such an order may be extended or further extended by order of the court on an application made before the end of that time as originally fixed or as extended, as the case may be[3]. Where a person is ordered[4] to remedy any matters, that person is not liable under the working time regulations[5] in respect of those matters in so far as they continue during the time fixed by the order (or any further time so allowed)[6].

1 Ie under the Working Time Regulations 1998, SI 1998/1833: see reg 29; and PARA 317. The provisions set out in regs 29A–29E (see also PARA 317) apply in relation to the offences provided for in reg 29(1)–(3) (see PARA 317): reg 29(9) (reg 29 substituted, reg 29E added, by SI 2003/1684).
2 Working Time Regulations 1998, SI 1998/1833, reg 29E(1) (as added: see note 1).
3 Working Time Regulations 1998, SI 1998/1833, reg 29E(2) (as added: see note 1).
4 Ie under the Working Time Regulations 1998, SI 1998/1833, reg 29E(1) (see the text and notes 1–2): see reg 29E(3) (as added: see note 1).
5 Ie under the Working Time Regulations 1998, SI 1998/1833: see reg 29E(3) (as added: see note 1).
6 Working Time Regulations 1998, SI 1998/1833, reg 29E(3) (as added: see note 1).

319. Worker's remedies. A worker[1] may present a complaint to an employment tribunal[2] that his employer[3]:

(1) has refused to permit him to exercise certain of his statutory rights relating to working time[4];

(2) has failed to pay him the whole or any part of any amount due to him[5] in respect of leave to which he is entitled[6].

An employment tribunal must not consider such a complaint[7], however, unless it is presented[8]:

(a) before the end of the period of three months (or, in the case of a complaint concerning the service of any person as a member of the armed forces[9], six months) beginning with the date on which it is alleged that the exercise of the right should have been permitted (or in the case of a rest period[10] or leave extending over more than one day, the date on which it should have been permitted to begin) or, as the case may be, the payment should have been made[11];

(b) within such further period as the tribunal considers reasonable in a case where it is satisfied that it was not reasonably practicable for the complaint to be presented before the end of that period of three or, as the case may be, six months[12].

In working out when the time limit set under head (a) above[13] expires, the following period is not to be counted[14], namely the period that:

(i) begins with the day after the day on which the worker concerned complies with the requirement to contact ACAS before instituting proceedings[15] in relation to the matter in respect of which the proceedings are brought ('the day after Day A')[16]; and

(ii) ends with the day on which the worker concerned receives (or, if earlier, is treated as receiving[17]) the certificate issued by the conciliation officer[18] to the effect either that he has concluded that a settlement is not possible within the prescribed period or that the prescribed period has expired without a settlement having been reached ('Day B')[19].

If the unextended time limit set under head (a) above[20] would expire during the period beginning with Day A and ending one month after Day B, the time limit expires instead at the end of that period[21]. Furthermore, where: (A) a three-month time limit is set under head (a) above[22] in relation to the whole or part of a relevant cross-border dispute[23] (that is, a dispute to which European

Parliament and Council Directive (EC) 2008/52 of 21 May 2008 on certain aspects of mediation in civil and commercial matters applies[24]); (B) a mediation[25] in relation to the dispute starts[26] before the period expires[27]; and (C) the time limit would otherwise[28] expire before the mediation ends[29] or less than four weeks after it ends[30], the time limit expires instead at the end of four weeks after the mediation ends[31].

Where an employment tribunal finds a complaint under head (1) above well-founded, the tribunal must make a declaration to that effect[32], and it may make an award of compensation to be paid by the employer to the worker[33]. Where, on a complaint under head (2) above, an employment tribunal finds that an employer has failed to pay a worker in respect of leave to which he is entitled[34], it must order the employer to pay to the worker the amount which it finds to be due to him[35].

1   As to the meaning of 'worker' for these purposes see PARA 271.
2   As to employment tribunals see PARA 1399 et seq; and as to the procedure on a complaint made to an employment tribunal see PARA 1453 et seq.
3   See the Working Time Regulations 1998, SI 1998/1833, reg 30(1). As to the meaning of 'employer' see PARA 269 note 5.
      Before tribunal proceedings are instituted under the Working Time Regulations 1998, SI 1998/1833, reg 30, however, ACAS must be involved first in early conciliation to promote a settlement: see the Employment Tribunals Act 1996 s 18(1)(j); and PARA 152 note 1. As to the constitution and powers of ACAS see PARA 1213 et seq.
4   Working Time Regulations 1998, SI 1998/1833, reg 30(1)(a). See note 3. Head (1) in the text refers to any right a worker has under:
    (1)   reg 10(1) or (2) (worker's entitlement to a daily rest period: see PARA 288), reg 11(1), (2) or (3) (worker's entitlement to a weekly rest period: see PARA 289), reg 12(1) or (4) (worker's entitlement to a rest break: see PARA 290), reg 13 (worker's entitlement to paid annual leave: see PARA 291) or reg 13A (worker's entitlement to additional leave: see PARA 292) (reg 30(1)(a)(i) (substituted by SI 2007/2079));
    (2)   the Working Time Regulations 1998, SI 1998/1833, reg 24 (worker's entitlement to compensatory rest: see PARA 304), in so far as it applies where reg 10(1), reg 11(1) or (2) or reg 12(1) is modified or excluded (reg 30(1)(a)(ii) (amended by SI 2003/1684));
    (3)   the Working Time Regulations 1998, SI 1998/1833, reg 24A (mobile worker's entitlement to adequate rest: see PARA 305), in so far as it applies where reg 10(1), reg 11(1) or (2) or reg 12(1) is excluded (reg 30(1)(a)(iii) (substituted by SI 2003/1684)); or
    (4)   the Working Time Regulations 1998, SI 1998/1833, reg 25(3) (compensatory rest for young worker in the armed forces: see PARA 306), reg 27(2) (equivalent period of compensatory rest for young worker where force majeure applies: see PARA 309), or reg 27A(4)(b) (equivalent period of compensatory rest for young worker: see PARA 310) (reg 30(1)(a)(iv) (added by SI 2003/1684)).
    As to the right of a worker not to be subjected to any detriment for refusing to comply with a requirement contrary to the Working Time Regulations 1998, SI 1998/1833, or to forgo a right thereby conferred, see PARA 616; as to the right of a worker not to be unfairly dismissed on account of any such refusal see PARA 788; and as to the right of a worker not to be later selected for redundancy on account of any such refusal see the Employment Rights Act 1996 s 105(4A); and PARA 781.
5   Ie under the Working Time Regulations 1998, SI 1998/1833, reg 14(2) (see PARA 293) or reg 16(1) (see PARA 295): see reg 30(1)(b). See note 8.
6   Working Time Regulations 1998, SI 1998/1833, reg 30(1)(b). See note 3.
7   Ie subject to the Working Time Regulations 1998, SI 1998/1833, reg 30A (see the text and notes 12, 22–31) and reg 30B (see the text and notes 12–21): see reg 30(2) (amended by SI 2011/1133; SI 2014/386).
8   See the Working Time Regulations 1998, SI 1998/1833, reg 30(2) (as amended: see note 7).
      The principle of equivalence in EU law requires that a limitation period in respect of an action on a claim arising out of EU law must not be less favourable than for similar actions based on domestic law. Accordingly, because the Working Time Regulations 1998, SI 1998/1833, were made for the purposes of implementing European Parliament and Council Directive (EC) 2003/88 of 4 November 2003 (OJ L299, 18.11.2003, p 9) concerning certain

aspects of the organisation of working time (the 'Working Time Directive') (see PARA 267), and because payments due under the Working Time Regulations 1998, SI 1998/1833, reg 14(2) (see PARA 293) or reg 16(1) (see PARA 295), are similar to the many other types of payments described in, or covered by, the Employment Rights Act 1996 s 27(1) (meaning of 'wages' etc: see PARA 254), remedy for non-payment can be sought either under the Working Time Regulations 1998, SI 1998/1833, reg 30, or on the basis of unlawful deductions from wages under the Employment Rights Act 1996 Pt II (ss 13–27) (protection of wages: see PARA 254 et seq); and the more advantageous limitation periods afforded (especially in allowing a claim for a series of deductions to be brought within three months of the last deduction in the series) by s 23(2), (3), (4) (protection of wages (complaint to employment tribunal: see PARA 259) may be preferred over the limitation period given in the Working Time Regulations 1998, SI 1998/1833, reg 30: *Revenue and Customs Comrs v Stringer* [2009] UKHL 31, [2009] 4 All ER 1205, [2009] ICR 985, [2009] IRLR 677. See also *List Design Group Ltd v Douglas, List Design Group Ltd v Catley* [2002] ICR 686, [2003] IRLR 14, EAT (claim arising from employers' failure over two successive years to pay for annual leave could be framed as unlawful deduction from wages), and *Canada Life Ltd v Gray* [2004] ICR 673, EAT (self-employed consultants paid on commission-only basis were 'workers', and thus entitled to paid annual leave, and to recover pay in lieu of their annual leave entitlements for the whole period, not only for the leave year in the course of which the claimants' contracts terminated, but also for previous years as non-payment constituted unlawful deductions from wages). As to time limits generally see PARA 1453.

9   Ie in a case to which the Working Time Regulations 1998, SI 1998/1833, reg 38(2) applies (see PARA 275): see reg 30(2)(a). As to the meaning of 'armed forces' see PARA 275 note 2.

10   As to the meaning of 'rest period' see PARA 284 note 4.

11   Working Time Regulations 1998, SI 1998/1833, reg 30(2)(a).

12   Working Time Regulations 1998, SI 1998/1833, reg 30(2)(b). The power conferred on the employment tribunal by reg 30(2)(b) to extend the time limit set by reg 30(2)(a) (see head (a) in the text) is exercisable in relation to that time limit as it is extended by reg 30B (see also the text and notes 13–21): reg 30B(4) (reg 30B added by SI 2014/386). Where the employment tribunal has the power under the Working Time Regulations 1998, SI 1998/1833, reg 30(2)(b) to extend a period of limitation, the power is exercisable in relation to any period of limitation as it is extended by reg 30A (see also the text and notes 22–31): reg 30A(10) (reg 30A added by SI 2011/1133).

13   Ie the time limit set by the Working Time Regulations 1998, SI 1998/1833, reg 30(2)(a) (see head (a) in the text): see reg 30B(2) (as added: see note 12).

14   See the Working Time Regulations 1998, SI 1998/1833, reg 30B(2) (as added: see note 12).

15   Ie the requirement in the Employment Tribunals Act 1996 s 18A(1) (see PARA 152): see the Working Time Regulations 1998, SI 1998/1833, reg 30B(1)(a) (as added: see note 12).

16   Working Time Regulations 1998, SI 1998/1833, reg 30B(1)(a), (2) (as added: see note 12).

17   Ie by virtue of regulations made under the Employment Tribunals Act 1996 s 18A(11) (see PARA 152): see the Working Time Regulations 1998, SI 1998/1833, reg 30B(1)(b) (as added: see note 12).

18   Ie the certificate issued under the Employment Tribunals Act 1996 s 18A(4) (see PARA 152): see the Working Time Regulations 1998, SI 1998/1833, reg 30B(1)(b) (as added: see note 12).

19   See the Working Time Regulations 1998, SI 1998/1833, reg 30B(1)(b), (2) (as added: see note 12).

20   Ie the time limit set by the Working Time Regulations 1998, SI 1998/1833, reg 30(2)(a) (see head (a) in the text), if not extended by reg 30B(3): see reg 30B(3) (as added: see note 12).

21   See the Working Time Regulations 1998, SI 1998/1833, reg 30B(3) (as added: see note 12).

22   Ie the time limit set by the Working Time Regulations 1998, SI 1998/1833, reg 30(2) (see head (a) in the text): see reg 30A(2)(a) (as added: see note 12).

23   See the Working Time Regulations 1998, SI 1998/1833, reg 30A(2)(a) (as added: see note 12).

24   For these purposes, 'relevant dispute' means a dispute to which European Parliament and Council Directive (EC) 2008/52 of 21 May 2008 (OJ L136, 24.5.2008, p 3) on certain aspects of mediation in civil and commercial matters (the 'Mediation Directive': see CONFLICT OF LAWS vol 19 (2011) PARA 497) art 8(1) applies (certain cross-border disputes): see the Working Time Regulations 1998, SI 1998/1833, reg 30A(1)(a), (d) (as added: see note 12). It is submitted that a reference to the Mediation Directive art 2(1) (cross-border disputes) is meant instead of art 8(1) (effect of mediation on limitation and prescription periods). Accordingly, it is submitted that a 'relevant dispute' means a cross-border dispute in which at least one of the parties is domiciled or habitually resident in a member state other than that of any other party on the date on which: (1) the parties agree to use mediation after the dispute has arisen; (2) mediation is ordered by a court; (3) an obligation to use mediation arises under national law; or (4) an

invitation is made to the parties (for the purposes of art 5 (court offers recourse to mediation)) by a court before which an action is brought to use mediation in order to settle the dispute: see art 2(1); definition applied by the Working Time Regulations 1998, SI 1998/1833, reg 30A(1)(a), (d) (as so added). See also CONFLICT OF LAWS vol 19 (2011) PARA 497.

25 For these purposes, 'mediation' means a structured process, however named or referred to, whereby two or more parties to a dispute attempt by themselves, on a voluntary basis, to reach an agreement on the settlement of their dispute with the assistance of a mediator (which process may be initiated by the parties or suggested or ordered by a court or prescribed by the law of a member state); and it includes mediation conducted by a judge who is not responsible for any judicial proceedings concerning the dispute in question, but excludes attempts made by the court or the judge seised to settle a dispute in the course of judicial proceedings concerning the dispute in question: Mediation Directive art 3(a); definition applied by the Working Time Regulations 1998, SI 1998/1833, reg 30A(1)(b), (d) (as added: see note 12). See also CONFLICT OF LAWS vol 19 (2011) PARA 497. In the case of any relevant dispute, references in reg 30A to a mediation are references to the mediation so far as it relates to that dispute, and references to a party are to be read accordingly: see reg 30A(9) (as so added).

26 For these purposes, a mediation starts on the date of the agreement to mediate that is entered into by the parties and the mediator: see the Working Time Regulations 1998, SI 1998/1833, reg 30A(6) (as added: see note 12). 'Mediator' means any third person who is asked to conduct a mediation in an effective, impartial and competent way, regardless of the denomination or profession of that third person in the member state concerned and of the way in which the third person has been appointed or requested to conduct the mediation: Mediation Directive art 3(b); definition applied by the Working Time Regulations 1998, SI 1998/1833, reg 30A(1)(c), (d) (as so added). See also CONFLICT OF LAWS vol 19 (2011) PARA 497.

27 See the Working Time Regulations 1998, SI 1998/1833, reg 30A(2)(b) (as added: see note 12).

28 Ie if not extended by the Working Time Regulations 1998, SI 1998/1833, reg 30A: see reg 30A(2)(c) (as added: see note 12).

29 For these purposes, a mediation ends on the date of the first of these to occur (Working Time Regulations 1998, SI 1998/1833, reg 30A(7) (as added: see note 12)):
   (1)   the parties reach an agreement in resolution of the relevant dispute (reg 30A(7)(a) (as so added));
   (2)   a party completes the notification of the other parties that it has withdrawn from the mediation (reg 30A(7)(b) (as so added));
   (3)   a party to whom a qualifying request is made fails to give a response reaching the other parties within 14 days of the request (reg 30A(7)(c) (as so added));
   (4)   the parties, after being notified that the mediator's appointment has ended (by death, resignation or otherwise), fail to agree within 14 days to seek to appoint a replacement mediator (reg 30A(7)(d) (as so added)); or
   (5)   the mediation otherwise comes to an end pursuant to the terms of the agreement to mediate (reg 30A(7)(e) (as so added)).

For these purposes, a qualifying request is a request by a party that another ('A') confirm to all parties that A is continuing with the mediation: see reg 30A(8) (as so added).

30 See the Working Time Regulations 1998, SI 1998/1833, reg 30A(2)(c) (as added: see note 12).

31 See the Working Time Regulations 1998, SI 1998/1833, reg 30A(3) (as added: see note 12). The provision made by reg 30A(3) is subject to reg 30A(4): see reg 30A(3) (as so added). Accordingly, if a time limit mentioned in reg 30A(2)(a) (see head (A) in the text) has been extended by reg 30A, then reg 30A(2) (see the text and notes 22–30) and reg 30A(3) apply to the extended time limit as it applies to a time limit mentioned in reg 30A(2)(a): see reg 30A(4) (as so added).

     Where more than one time limit applies in relation to a relevant dispute, the extension by reg 30A(3) of one of those time limits does not affect the others: reg 30A(5) (as so added).

32 Working Time Regulations 1998, SI 1998/1833, reg 30(3)(a).

33 Working Time Regulations 1998, SI 1998/1833, reg 30(3)(b). The amount of the compensation is to be such as the tribunal considers just and equitable in all the circumstances having regard to: (1) the employer's default in refusing to permit the worker to exercise his right (reg 30(4)(a)); and (2) any loss sustained by the worker which is attributable to the matters complained of (reg 30(4)(b)). See *Miles v Linkage Community Trust Ltd* [2008] IRLR 602, EAT (tribunal entitled not to award compensation for breach).

34 Ie in accordance with the Working Time Regulations 1998, SI 1998/1833, reg 14(2) (see PARA 293) or reg 16(1) (see PARA 295): see reg 30(5).

35 Working Time Regulations 1998, SI 1998/1833, reg 30(5).

(8) SUNDAY WORKING FOR SHOP AND BETTING WORKERS

320. Scope of statutory protection given to shop workers and betting workers in relation to Sunday working. Special statutory protection is given[1] in relation to Sunday working for shop workers[2] and betting workers[3].

Workers qualifying as 'protected shop workers'[4] and 'protected betting workers'[5] are protected[6] from being required to work on Sundays[7]. In addition, all shop or betting workers are given an option not to work on Sundays[8].

Protected or opted-out[9] shop or betting workers have a right not to be discriminated against for refusal to work on Sundays[10]; and the dismissal of such a worker for such a refusal is automatically unfair[11], as is any later selection for redundancy on that ground[12].

1   Ie by the Employment Rights Act 1996 Pt IV (ss 36–43): see PARA 321 et seq.
2   As to the meaning of 'shop worker' see PARA 321 note 1.
3   As to the meaning of 'betting worker' see PARA 321 note 2.
4   As to the meaning of 'protected shop worker' see PARA 321.
5   As to the meaning of 'protected betting worker' see PARA 321.
6   For these purposes, in relation to either a shop worker or a betting worker, 'protected' must be construed in accordance with the Employment Rights Act 1996 s 36(1)–(5) (see PARA 321): see ss 232(8), 233(5) (s 233 substituted by the Gambling Act 2005 s 356(1), Sch 16 Pt 2 para 11).
7   See PARAS 321–322.
8   See PARA 323.
9   For these purposes, in relation to either a shop worker or a betting worker, 'opted-out' must be construed in accordance with the Employment Rights Act 1996 s 41(1), (2) (see PARA 323): see ss 232(8), 233(5) (s 233 as substituted: see note 6).
10 See the Employment Rights Act 1996 s 45; and PARA 615.
11 See the Employment Rights Act 1996 s 101; and PARA 787.
12 See the Employment Rights Act 1996 s 105(1), (4); and PARA 781. In addition, dismissal for asserting statutory rights by such a worker is automatically unfair: see s 104; and PARA 793.

321. Meaning of 'protected shop worker' and 'protected betting worker'. A shop worker[1] or betting worker[2] is to be regarded as 'protected'[3] if, and only if[4]:

(1)   he: (a) was employed as a shop worker or a betting worker on the day before the relevant commencement date, but not to work only on Sunday[5]; (b) has been continuously employed[6] during the period beginning with that day and ending with the day which, in relation to the statutory provision concerned, is the appropriate date[7]; and (c) was, throughout that period, or throughout every part of it during which his relations with his employer were governed by a contract of employment, a shop worker or a betting worker[8]; or

(2)   his contract of employment is such that under it he is not, and may not be, required to work on Sunday[9], and he could not be so required even if the statutory provisions protecting shop and betting workers were disregarded[10].

However, a shop worker is not a protected shop worker, and a betting worker is not a protected betting worker, if: (i) he has given his employer an opting-in notice[11] on or after the relevant commencement date[12]; and (ii) after giving the notice, he has expressly agreed with his employer to do shop work or betting work on Sunday or on a particular Sunday[13].

1   For the purposes of the Employment Rights Act 1996, 'shop worker' means an employee who, under his contract of employment, is or may be required to do shop work (see s 232(1)); and 'shop work' means work in or about a shop on a day on which the shop is open for the serving

of customers (see s 232(2) (amended by the Sunday Working (Scotland) Act 2003 s 1(1), (3)(a)). As to the meanings of 'employee' and 'contract of employment' see PARA 2.

Subject to the Employment Rights Act 1996 s 232(4), 'shop' includes any premises where any retail trade or business is carried on: see s 232(3). Accordingly, where premises are used mainly for purposes other than those of retail trade or business and would not (apart from s 232(3)) be regarded as a shop, only such part of the premises as:

(1)   is used wholly or mainly for the purposes of retail trade or business (s 232(4)(a)); or

(2)   is used both for the purposes of retail trade or business and for the purposes of wholesale trade and is used wholly or mainly for those two purposes considered together (s 232(4)(b)),

is to be regarded as a shop for the purposes of the Employment Rights Act 1996 (see s 232(4)). For the purposes of head (2) above, 'wholesale trade' means the sale of goods for use or resale in the course of a business or the hire of goods for use in the course of a business: see s 232(5). 'Retail trade or business' includes:

(a)   the business of a barber or hairdresser (s 232(6)(a));

(b)   the business of hiring goods, otherwise than for use in the course of a trade or business (s 232(6)(b)); and

(c)   retail sales by auction (s 232(6)(c)),

but does not include catering or the sale at theatres and places of amusement of programmes, catalogues and similar items (see s 232(6)). For these purposes, 'catering business' means:

(i)   the sale of meals, refreshments or alcohol for consumption on the premises on which they are sold (s 232(7)(a) (amended by the Licensing Act 2003 s 198(1), Sch 6 para 114(a))); or

(ii)   the sale of meals or refreshments prepared to order for immediate consumption off the premises (Employment Rights Act 1996 s 232(7)(b)).

As to the meaning of 'alcohol' for the purposes of head (i) above, see LICENSING AND GAMBLING vol 67 (2008) PARA 30; definition applied by the Employment Rights Act 1996 s 232(7) (amended by the Licensing Act 2003 Sch 6 para 114(b)). As to the meaning of 'business' see PARA 135 note 4.

2   For the purposes of the Employment Rights Act 1996, 'betting worker' means an employee who under his contract of employment is or may be required to do betting work: see s 233(1) (s 233 substituted by the Gambling Act 2005 s 356(1), Sch 16 Pt 2 para 11). 'Betting work' means:

(1)   work which consists of or includes dealing with betting transactions at a track in England or Wales and which is carried out for a person who holds a general betting operating licence, a pool betting operating licence or a horse-race pool betting operating licence (Employment Rights Act 1996 s 233(2)(a) (as so substituted)); and

(2)   work on premises in respect of which a betting premises licence has effect at a time when the premises are used for betting transactions (s 233(2)(b) (as so substituted)).

For these purposes, 'betting transactions' includes the collection or payment of winnings: see s 233(3) (as so substituted). Expressions used in s 233 and in the Gambling Act 2005 have the same meaning in the Employment Rights Act 1996 s 233 as in the Gambling Act 2005: see the Employment Rights Act 1996 s 233(4) (as so substituted). See LICENSING AND GAMBLING.

3   Ie for the purposes of any provision of the Employment Rights Act 1996, but subject to s 36(5) (see the text and notes 11–13): see s 36(1). As to the meaning of 'protected' for these purposes see PARA 320 note 6.

4   See the Employment Rights Act 1996 s 36(1).

5   Employment Rights Act 1996 s 36(2)(a). For these purposes, the 'relevant commencement date' means (in relation to a shop worker) 26 August 1994 and (in relation to a betting worker) 3 January 1995: see s 36(7) (amended by the Sunday Working (Scotland) Act 2003 s 1(1), (2)(a)). Where, on the day before the relevant commencement date, an employee's relations with his employer had ceased to be governed by a contract of employment, he is to be regarded as satisfying head (1)(a) in the text if:

(1)   that day fell in a week which counts as a period of employment with that employer under the Employment Rights Act 1996 s 212(2) (repealed) or s 212(3) (weeks of absence to be counted in computing employee's period of employment: see PARA 131) or under regulations made under s 219 (regulations made for preserving the continuity of a person's period of employment: see PARA 133) (s 36(4)(a)); and

(2)   on the last day before the relevant commencement date on which an employee's relations with his employer were governed by a contract of employment, the employee was employed as a shop worker or betting worker but not to work only on Sunday (s 36(4)(b)).

As to the meaning of 'employer' see PARA 2; and as to the meaning of 'week' see PARA 126 note 13.

6 As to continuity of employment see PARAS 130 et seq, 861 et seq.
7 Employment Rights Act 1996 s 36(2)(b). As to the appropriate date for these purposes generally see PARA 322 note 13. The appropriate date in relation to s 105 (dismissals unfair by reason of redundancy: see PARA 781) is the effective date of termination, however: see s 105(8); and PARA 781.
8 Employment Rights Act 1996 s 36(2)(c).
9 Employment Rights Act 1996 s 36(3)(a).
10 Employment Rights Act 1996 s 36(3)(b). The statutory provisions referred to in the text are those of Pt IV (ss 36–43) (Sunday working for shop and betting workers: see also PARAS 322–324): see s 36(3)(b).
11 For the purposes of the Employment Rights Act 1996, 'opting-in notice', in relation to either a shop worker or a betting worker, means written notice, signed and dated by the shop worker or betting worker, in which the shop worker or betting worker expressly states that he wishes to work on Sunday or that he does not object to Sunday working: see ss 36(6), 232(8), 233(5) (s 233 as substituted: see note 2). As to the meaning of 'written' see PARA 2 note 8.
12 Employment Rights Act 1996 s 36(5)(a).
13 Employment Rights Act 1996 s 36(5)(b).

322. Enforceability of contracts of employment relating to Sunday work. Any contract of employment[1] under which a worker was employed as a shop worker or as a betting worker[2] on the day before the relevant commencement date[3] (but not to work only on Sunday) is unenforceable to the extent that[4]:

(1) it requires the shop worker to do shop work[5], or the betting worker to do betting work[6], on Sunday on or after that date[7]; or

(2) it requires the employer[8] to provide the shop worker with shop work, or the betting worker with betting work, on Sunday on or after that date[9].

Any agreement entered into after the relevant commencement date, between a protected shop worker[10] or a protected betting worker[11], and his employer is unenforceable[12] to the extent that[13]:

(a) it requires the shop worker to do shop work, or the betting worker to do betting work, on Sunday[14]; or

(b) it requires the employer to provide the shop worker with shop work, or the betting worker with betting work, on Sunday[15].

Where, after giving an opting-in notice[16], a protected shop worker or a protected betting worker expressly agrees with his employer to do shop work or betting work on Sunday or on a particular Sunday (and so ceases to be protected), his contract of employment is taken to be varied to the extent necessary to give effect to the terms of the agreement[17].

1 As to the meaning of 'contract of employment' see PARA 2.
2 Ie a shop worker or betting worker who satisfies the Employment Rights Act 1996 s 36(2)(a) (see PARA 321): see s 37(1). As to the meaning of 'shop worker' see PARA 321 note 1; and as to the meaning of 'betting worker' see PARA 321 note 2.
3 As to the meaning of 'relevant commencement date' see PARA 321 note 5.
4 See the Employment Rights Act 1996 s 37(1).
5 As to the meaning of 'shop work' see PARA 321 note 1.
6 As to the meaning of 'betting work' see PARA 321 note 2.
7 Employment Rights Act 1996 s 37(1)(a).
8 As to the meaning of 'employer' see PARA 2.
9 Employment Rights Act 1996 s 37(1)(b).
10 As to the meaning of 'protected shop worker' see PARA 321.
11 As to the meaning of 'protected betting worker' see PARA 321.
12 Ie subject to the Employment Rights Act 1996 s 37(3) (see the text and notes 16–17): see s 37(2).
13 See the Employment Rights Act 1996 s 37(2). For the purposes of s 36(2)(b) (see PARA 321), the appropriate date, in relation to s 37(2) and s 37(3) (see the text and notes 16–17), is the day on which the agreement is entered into: see s 37(5) (amended by the Employment Relations Act 1999 ss 9, 44, Sch 4 Pt III paras 5, 6, Sch 9).

Where:
(1)   under the contract of employment under which a shop worker or betting worker who satisfies the Employment Rights Act 1996 s 36(2)(a) (see PARA 321) was employed on the day before the relevant commencement date, the employer is, or may be, required to provide him with shop work, or betting work, for a specified number of hours each week (s 38(1)(a));
(2)   under the contract, the shop worker or betting worker was, or might have been, required to work on Sunday before that date (s 38(1)(b)); and
(3)   the shop worker has done shop work, or the betting worker has done betting work, on Sunday in that employment (whether or not before that day) but has, on or after that date, ceased to do so (s 38(1)(c)),

then, so long as the shop worker remains a protected shop worker, or the betting worker remains a protected betting worker, the contract is not to be regarded as requiring the employer to provide him with shop work, or betting work, on weekdays in excess of the hours normally worked by the shop worker or betting worker on weekdays before he ceased to do shop work, or betting work, on Sunday (s 38(2)). For the purposes of s 36(2)(b), the appropriate date in relation to s 38 is any time in relation to which the contract is to be enforced: see s 38(3). As to the meaning of 'week' see PARA 126 note 13.

Where:
(a)   under the contract of employment under which a shop worker or betting worker who satisfies s 36(2)(a) was employed on the day before the relevant commencement date, the shop worker or betting worker was, or might have been, required to work on Sunday before the relevant commencement date (s 39(1)(a));
(b)   the shop worker has done shop work, or the betting worker has done betting work, on Sunday in that employment (whether or not before that date) but has, on or after that date, ceased to do so (s 39(1)(b)); and
(c)   it is not apparent from the contract what part of the remuneration payable, or of any other benefit accruing, to the shop worker or betting worker was intended to be attributable to shop work, or betting work, on Sunday (s 39(1)(c)),

then, so long as the shop worker remains a protected shop worker, or the betting worker remains a protected betting worker, the contract is to be regarded as enabling the employer to reduce the amount of remuneration paid, or the extent of the other benefit provided, to the shop worker or betting worker in respect of any period by the relevant proportion (s 39(2)). For these purposes, 'relevant proportion' means the proportion which the hours of shop work, or betting work, which, apart from Pt IV (ss 36–43) (Sunday working for shop and betting workers: see also PARAS 321, 323–324), the shop worker, or betting worker, could have been required to do on Sunday in the period (the 'contractual Sunday hours') bears to the aggregate of those hours and the hours of work actually done by the shop worker, or betting worker, in the period: see s 39(3). Where, under the contract of employment, the hours of work actually done on weekdays in any period would be taken into account in determining the contractual hours, they are to be taken into account in determining the contractual Sunday hours for the purposes of s 39(3): see s 39(4). For the purposes of s 36(2)(b), the appropriate date in relation to s 39 is the end of the period in respect of which the remuneration is paid or the benefit accrues: see s 39(5).

14 Employment Rights Act 1996 s 37(2)(a).
15 Employment Rights Act 1996 s 37(2)(b).
16 As to the meaning of 'opting-in notice', in relation to a shop worker or a betting worker, see PARA 321 note 11.
17 Employment Rights Act 1996 s 37(3).

323.   Opting-out of Sunday work.   Any shop worker[1] or betting worker[2] who under his contract of employment[3]:
(1)   is or may be required to work on Sunday (whether or not as a result of previously giving an opting-in notice)[4]; but
(2)   is not employed to work only on a Sunday[5],
may at any time give his employer[6] written notice[7], signed and dated by the shop worker or betting worker, to the effect that he objects to Sunday working[8] (an 'opting-out notice'[9]). Accordingly, a shop worker or betting worker is regarded as 'opted-out'[10] if, and only if[11]:
(a)   he has given his employer an opting-out notice[12];
(b)   he has been continuously employed[13] during the period beginning with

the day on which the notice was given and ending with the day which, in relation to the statutory provision concerned, is the appropriate date[14]; and

(c) throughout that period, or throughout every part of it during which his relations with his employer were governed by a contract of employment, he was a shop or betting worker[15].

A shop worker is not an opted-out shop worker, and a betting worker is not an opted-out betting worker, however, if[16]:

(i) after giving the opting-out notice concerned, he has given his employer an opting-in notice[17]; and

(ii) after giving the opting-in notice, he has expressly agreed with his employer to do shop work[18], or betting work[19], on Sunday or on a particular Sunday[20].

Where a shop worker or betting worker gives his employer an opting-out notice, the contract of employment under which he was employed immediately before he gave that notice becomes unenforceable to the extent that[21]:

(A) it requires the shop worker to do shop work, or the betting worker to do betting work, on Sunday after the end of the notice period[22]; or

(B) it requires the employer to provide the shop worker with shop work, or the betting worker with betting work, on Sunday after the end of that period[23].

Any agreement entered into between an opted-out shop worker, or an opted-out betting worker, and his employer is unenforceable[24] to the extent that[25]:

(aa) it requires the shop worker to do shop work, or the betting worker to do betting work, on Sunday after the end of the notice period[26]; or

(bb) it requires the employer to provide the shop worker with shop work, or the betting worker with betting work, on Sunday after the end of that period[27].

Where, after giving an opting-in notice, an opted-out shop worker or betting worker expressly agrees with his employer to do shop or betting work on Sunday or on a particular Sunday (and so ceases to be opted-out), his contract of employment is taken to be varied to the extent necessary to give effect to the terms of the agreement[28].

1 Ie a shop worker to whom the Employment Rights Act 1996 s 40 applies (ie as defined by s 40(3): see the text and notes 3–5): see s 40(1). As to the meaning of 'shop worker' see PARA 321 note 1.

2 Ie a betting worker to whom the Employment Rights Act 1996 s 40 applies (ie as defined by s 40(3): see the text and notes 3–5): see s 40(1). As to the meaning of 'betting worker' see PARA 321 note 2.

3 See the Employment Rights Act 1996 s 40(3). As to the meaning of 'contract of employment' see PARA 2.

4 Employment Rights Act 1996 s 40(3)(a). As to the meaning of 'opting-in notice' see PARA 321 note 11.

5 Employment Rights Act 1996 s 40(3)(b).

6 As to the meaning of 'employer' see PARA 2.

7 As to the meaning of 'written' see PARA 2 note 8.

8 See the Employment Rights Act 1996 s 40(1).

9 For the purposes of the Employment Rights Act 1996, 'opting-out notice' means a notice given under s 40(1) (see the text and notes 1–8) by a shop worker or betting worker to whom s 40 applies (see s 40(3); and the text and notes 3–5): see ss 40(2), 232(8), 233(5) (s 233 substituted by the Gambling Act 2005 s 356(1), Sch 16 Pt 2 para 11).

10 Ie for the purposes of any provision of the Employment Rights Act 1996, but subject to s 41(2) (see the text and notes 16–20): see s 41(1). As to the meaning of 'opted-out' see PARA 320 note 9.

11 See the Employment Rights Act 1996 s 41(1).
12 Employment Rights Act 1996 s 41(1)(a).
13 As to continuity of employment see PARAS 130 et seq, 861 et seq.
14 Employment Rights Act 1996 s 41(1)(b). For the purposes of s 41(1)(b), the appropriate date, in relation to s 43(2) (see the text and notes 24–27) and s 43(3) (see the text and note 28), is the day on which the agreement is entered into: see s 43(5) (amended by the Employment Relations Act 1999 ss 9, 44, Sch 4 Pt III paras 5, 7, Sch 9). The appropriate date for the purposes of the Employment Rights Act 1996 s 41(1)(b) in relation to s 105 (dismissals unfair by reason of redundancy: see PARA 781) is the effective date of termination, however: see s 105(8); and PARA 781.
15 Employment Rights Act 1996 s 41(1)(c).
16 See the Employment Rights Act 1996 s 41(2).
17 Employment Rights Act 1996 s 41(2)(a).
18 As to the meaning of 'shop work' see PARA 321 note 1.
19 As to the meaning of 'betting work' see PARA 321 note 2.
20 Employment Rights Act 1996 s 41(2)(b).
21 See the Employment Rights Act 1996 s 43(1).
22 Employment Rights Act 1996 s 43(1)(a). For the purposes of the Employment Rights Act 1996, 'notice period', in relation to an opted-out shop worker or an opted out betting worker, means, subject to s 42(2) (see PARA 324), the period of three months beginning with the day on which the opting-out notice concerned was given: see ss 41(3), 232(8), 233(5) (s 233 as substituted: see note 9).
23 Employment Rights Act 1996 s 43(1)(b).
24 Ie subject to the Employment Rights Act 1996 s 43(3) (see the text and note 28): see s 43(2).
25 See the Employment Rights Act 1996 s 43(2).
26 Employment Rights Act 1996 s 43(2)(a).
27 Employment Rights Act 1996 s 43(2)(b).
28 Employment Rights Act 1996 s 43(3).

324. Explanatory statements required to be given to shop workers and betting workers in relation to Sunday working. Where a person becomes a shop worker[1] or betting worker[2] who under his contract of employment[3] is or may be required to work on Sunday whether or not as a result of previously giving an opting-in notice[4] (but is not employed to work only on Sunday), his employer[5] must, before the end of the period of two months beginning with the day on which the person becomes such a worker, give him a written[6] statement in the prescribed form[7].

If:

(1)   an employer fails to comply with the requirement to give such a written statement in relation to any shop worker or betting worker[8]; and

(2)   the shop worker or betting worker, on giving an opting-out notice[9], becomes an opted-out shop worker[10] or an opted-out betting worker[11],

the notice period at the end of which the opting-out becomes effective[12] is reduced from three months to one month[13].

An employer is not to be regarded as failing to comply with the requirement to give such a written statement in any case where, before the end of the stipulated period[14], the shop worker or betting worker has given him an opting-out notice[15].

1   Ie a shop worker to whom the Employment Rights Act 1996 s 40 applies (see PARA 323): see s 42(1). As to the meaning of 'shop worker' see PARA 321 note 1.
2   Ie a betting worker to whom the Employment Rights Act 1996 s 40 applies (see PARA 323): see s 42(1). As to the meaning of 'betting worker' see PARA 321 note 2.
3   As to the meaning of 'contract of employment' see PARA 2.
4   As to the meaning of 'opting-in notice' see PARA 321 note 11.
5   As to the meaning of 'employer' see PARA 2.
6   As to the meaning of 'written' see PARA 2 note 8.
7   Employment Rights Act 1996 s 42(1). The prescribed form:
    (1)   in the case of a shop worker, is set out under the heading 'STATUTORY RIGHTS IN

RELATION TO SUNDAY SHOP WORK' (see s 42(4) (s 42(4), (5) amended by the Employment Rights (Dispute Resolution) Act 1998 s 1(2)(a))); and

(2) in the case of a betting worker, is set out under the heading 'STATUTORY RIGHTS IN RELATION TO SUNDAY BETTING WORK' (see the Employment Rights Act 1996 s 42(5) (as so amended)).

The Secretary of State may by order amend the prescribed forms set out under heads (1) and (2) above: s 42(6). As to the Secretary of State see PARA 5 note 21; and as to the making of orders under the Employment Rights Act 1996 generally see PARA 162. At the date at which this volume states the law, no such order had been made under s 42.

8   Employment Rights Act 1996 s 42(2)(a).
9   As to the meaning of 'opting-out notice' see PARA 323 note 9.
10 As to the meaning of 'opted-out', in relation to a shop worker, see PARA 323.
11 Employment Rights Act 1996 s 42(2)(b). As to the meaning of 'opted-out', in relation to a betting worker, see PARA 323.
12 Ie the notice period specified in the Employment Rights Act 1996 s 41(3) (see PARA 323 note 22): see s 42(2).
13 See the Employment Rights Act 1996 s 42(2).
14 Ie the period referred to in the Employment Rights Act 1996 s 42(1) (see the text and notes 1–7): see s 42(3).
15 Employment Rights Act 1996 s 42(3).

(9) RIGHT TO TIME OFF WORK

(i) In general

325. Guarantees for rights to time off work given by the Employment Rights Act 1996. The Employment Rights Act 1996 provides guarantees for rights to time off work[1] in relation to:

(1) public duties[2];
(2) looking for work or making arrangements for training[3];
(3) ante-natal care (including for agency workers)[4];
(4) adoption appointments (including for agency workers)[5];
(5) dependants[6];
(6) occupational pension scheme trustees[7];
(7) directly elected employee representatives (for the purposes specifically of consultations on collective redundancy or business transfers)[8]; and
(8) study and training[9].

Each of the rights set out under heads (1) to (8) above contains its own provisions allowing a complaint to an employment tribunal[10].

1   Ie under the Employment Rights Act 1996 Pts VI, VIA (ss 50–63K): see PARA 326 et seq.
2   See the Employment Rights Act 1996 ss 50–51; and PARAS 350, 351.
3   See the Employment Rights Act 1996 ss 52–54; and PARA 326.
4   See the Employment Rights Act 1996 ss 55–57ZD; and PARA 333 et seq.
5   See the Employment Rights Act 1996 ss 57ZJ–57ZS; and PARA 341 et seq.
6   See the Employment Rights Act 1996 ss 57A–57B; and PARA 347.
7   See the Employment Rights Act 1996 ss 58–60; and PARAS 352–353.
8   See the Employment Rights Act 1996 ss 61–63; and PARA 1209. There is also a right to time off work for trade union activities and duties: see the Trade Union and Labour Relations (Consolidation) Act 1992 ss 168–173; and PARAS 1020, 1065–1068.
9   As to the general right to request time for study or training which is available to employees who have qualifying service with certain employers in England see the Employment Rights Act 1996 Pt VIA (study and training) (ss 63D–63K); and PARA 328. As to the right to time off for employees in Wales in order to participate in education or training see ss 63A–63C; and PARAS 331, 332. As to rights to time off arising from an employer's duty to facilitate young employees' participation in education or training in England see the Education and Skills Act 2008 Pt 1 (ss 1–67); and EDUCATION vol 35 (2011) PARA 646 et seq.
10 As to complaints in relation to looking for work or arranging training see PARA 327; as to complaints in relation to an employee's right to study or training see PARAS 330, 332; as to

complaints in relation to ante-natal care see PARAS 334, 336, 338, 340; as to complaints in relation to adoption appointments see PARAS 343, 346; as to complaints in relation to time off work to make arrangements for dependants see PARA 348; as to complaints in relation to public duties see PARA 351; as to complaints in relation to occupational pension schemes see PARA 353.

(ii) Looking for Work; Making Arrangements for Training

326. Entitlement of employee given notice of dismissal by reason of redundancy to time off to look for work or make arrangements for training. An employee[1] who is given notice of dismissal by reason of redundancy[2] is entitled, before the end of his notice, to be permitted by his employer[3] to take reasonable time off during the employee's working hours[4] in order to[5]:

(1)   look for new employment[6]; or

(2)   make arrangements for training for future employment[7];

and he is entitled to be paid remuneration by his employer for the period of absence at the appropriate hourly rate[8].

An employee is not, however, entitled to time off in this way unless, on whichever is the later of[9]:

(a)   the date on which the notice is due to expire[10]; and

(b)   the date on which it would expire were it the notice required to be given[11] by an employer to terminate the contract of employment of a person who has been continuously employed for one month or more[12],

he will have been, or would have been, continuously employed for a period of two years or more[13].

If an employer unreasonably refuses so to permit an employee time off from work, the employee is entitled[14] to be paid an amount equal to the remuneration to which he would have been entitled[15] if he had been permitted to take the time off[16].

1   As to the meaning of 'employee' see PARA 2.

2   For the purposes of the Employment Rights Act 1996, references to dismissal by reason of redundancy and references to similar expressions are to be construed in accordance with the Employment Rights Act 1996 s 139 (see PARA 870): s 235(3). Thus this right may arise if the employee satisfies the statutory definition, even if for some other reason, eg unreasonable refusal of an offer of alternative employment, he does not actually qualify for a redundancy payment: *Dutton v Hawker Siddeley Aviation Ltd* [1978] ICR 1057, [1978] IRLR 390, EAT. As a general principle of redundancy law, a general warning of impending redundancy is not sufficient to constitute notice: see *Morton Sundour Fabrics Ltd v Shaw* (1966) 2 ITR 84; *Pritchard-Rhodes Ltd v Boon and Milton* [1979] IRLR 19, EAT; *International Computers Ltd v Kennedy* [1981] IRLR 28, EAT; *Doble v Firestone Tyre and Rubber Co Ltd* [1981] IRLR 300, EAT; and PARA 733 note 7.

3   As to the meaning of 'employer' see PARA 2.

4   For these purposes, the working hours of an employee must be taken to be any time when, in accordance with his contract of employment, the employee is required to be at work: Employment Rights Act 1996 s 52(3). As to the meaning of 'contract of employment' see PARA 2.

5   See the Employment Rights Act 1996 s 52(1). An employer is not liable under ss 88, 89 (see PARAS 738, 739) to make any payment in respect of a period of time so taken: see PARA 741. An employee is entitled to reasonable time off whether or not he can provide details of appointments or interviews, but failure to do so might be relevant in considering whether the employer had unreasonably refused time off: *Dutton v Hawker Siddeley Aviation Ltd* [1978] ICR 1057, [1978] IRLR 390, EAT. As to the right of complaint to an employment tribunal see PARA 327. The rights conferred by the Employment Rights Act 1996 s 52 (see the text and notes 9–13) and s 53 (see the text and notes 14–16) do not apply to a share fisherman (see s 199(2); and PARA 167) or to a police officer (see s 200(1); and PARA 168), and may also be lost for some other reason than statutory exclusion, in particular because the contract of employment is illegal (see PARA 18) or has terminated for some reason other than dismissal (see PARA 725 et seq).

6   Employment Rights Act 1996 s 52(1)(a).

7   Employment Rights Act 1996 s 52(1)(b).
8   Employment Rights Act 1996 s 53(1). The appropriate hourly rate, in relation to an employee, is the amount of one week's pay divided by the number of normal working hours in a week for that employee when employed under the contract of employment in force on the day when notice of dismissal was given: s 53(2). Where, however, the number of normal working hours differs from week to week or over a longer period, the amount of one week's pay must be divided instead by the average number of normal working hours calculated by dividing by 12 the total number of the employee's normal working hours during the period of 12 weeks ending with the last complete week before the day on which the notice was given: s 53(3). As to the calculation of a week's pay and normal working hours see PARA 142 et seq. As to the meaning of 'week' see PARA 126 note 13.
    A right to any amount under s 53(1) or s 53(4) (see the text and notes 14–16) does not affect any right of an employee in relation to remuneration under his contract of employment ('contractual remuneration'): s 53(6). Any contractual remuneration paid to an employee in respect of a period of time off under s 52 goes, however, towards discharging any liability of the employer to pay remuneration under s 53(1) in respect of that period; and, conversely, any payment of remuneration under s 53(1) in respect of a period goes towards discharging any liability of the employer to pay contractual remuneration in respect of that period: s 53(7).
    The amount of an employer's liability to pay remuneration under s 53(1) is not to exceed, in respect of the notice period of any employee, 40% of a week's pay of that employee: s 53(5).
9   See the Employment Rights Act 1996 s 52(2).
10 Employment Rights Act 1996 s 52(2)(a).
11 Ie by the Employment Rights Act 1996 s 86(1) (see PARA 736): see s 52(2)(b).
12 Employment Rights Act 1996 s 52(2)(b).
13 See the Employment Rights Act 1996 s 52(2). As to continuity of employment see PARAS 130 et seq, 861 et seq.
    In their application to a person who is prescribed by the Employment Protection (Continuity of Employment of National Health Service Employees) (Modification) Order 1996, SI 1996/1023 (ie a person who is employed in relevant employment for these purposes: see art 2), the Employment Rights Act 1996 s 52(2), s 65(1) (employee's entitlement to remuneration: see PARA 596), s 65(2) (repealed), s 86(1)–(4) (minimum notice of termination: see PARA 736), s 92(3) (written statement of reasons for dismissal: see PARA 755), s 108(1), (2) (right not to be unfairly dismissed: see PARA 758) and s 109(1) (repealed) have effect subject to the modification that, if a prescribed person employed in relevant employment by a health service employer is taken into relevant employment by another such employer, his period of employment at the time of the change of employer counts as a period of employment with the second-mentioned employer and the change of employer does not break the continuity of the period of employment: see the Employment Protection (Continuity of Employment of National Health Service Employees) (Modification) Order 1996, SI 1996/1023, arts 3, 4; and see the Employment Rights Act 1996 s 241, Sch 2 para 2(1). For these purposes, 'relevant employment' is employment by a health service employer as a medical practitioner or dental practitioner in the grade of registrar, senior registrar, specialist registrar, registrar (public health), senior registrar (public health) or specialist registrar (public health) while undergoing professional training which involves that person being employed successively by a number of different health service employers: see the Employment Protection (Continuity of Employment of National Health Service Employees) (Modification) Order 1996, SI 1996/1023, art 1(2)(a). As to the meaning of 'health service employers' for these purposes see art 1(2)(b) (amended by SI 2000/694; SI 2002/2469; SI 2004/696; SI 2005/1622; SI 2011/2581; SI 2013/235).
14 Ie subject to the Employment Rights Act 1996 s 53(5) (see note 8): see s 53(4).
15 Ie under Employment Rights Act 1996 s 53(1) (see the text and note 8): see s 53(4).
16 Employment Rights Act 1996 s 53(4).

327. Complaint to employment tribunal: employee's right to time off to look for work or make arrangements for training. An employee given notice of dismissal by reason of redundancy[1] may present a complaint to an employment tribunal[2] that his employer[3]:

(1)   has unreasonably refused to permit him to take time off[4] to look for work or make arrangements for training[5]; or

(2)   has failed to pay the whole or any part of any amount to which the employee is[6] entitled as remuneration for time so taken[7].

An employment tribunal must not consider such a complaint, however, unless it is presented[8]:

(a)   before the end of the period of three months beginning with the date on which it is alleged that the time off should have been permitted[9]; or

(b)   within such further period as the tribunal considers reasonable in a case where it is satisfied that it was not reasonably practicable for the complaint to be presented before the end of that period of three months[10].

Where an employment tribunal finds such a complaint well-founded[11], the tribunal must make a declaration to that effect[12], and it must order the employer to pay to the employee the amount[12] which it finds due to him[14].

1   Ie an employee to whom the Employment Rights Act 1996 s 52 applies: see PARA 326. As to the meaning of 'employee' see PARA 2.

2   As to employment tribunals see PARA 1399 et seq; and as to the procedure on a complaint made to an employment tribunal see PARA 1453 et seq.

3   See the Employment Rights Act 1996 s 54(1) (s 54(1), (2), (3) amended by the Employment Rights (Dispute Resolution) Act 1998 s 1(2)(a)). The remedy of an employee for infringement of any right conferred on him by the Employment Rights Act 1996 ss 52–53 is by way of complaint to an employment tribunal and not otherwise: see s 205(1); and PARA 1406. The right conferred by s 54 does not apply to a share fisherman (see s 199(2); and PARA 167) or to a police officer (see s 200(1); and PARA 168), and may also be lost for some other reason than statutory exclusion, in particular because the contract of employment is illegal (see PARA 18) or has terminated for some reason other than dismissal (see PARA 725 et seq). As to the meaning of 'employer' see PARA 2.

4   Ie as required by the Employment Rights Act 1996 s 52 (see PARA 326): see s 54(1)(a).

5   Employment Rights Act 1996 s 54(1)(a).

6   Ie under the Employment Rights Act 1996 s 53(1) or (4) (see PARA 326): see s 54(1)(b).

7   Employment Rights Act 1996 s 54(1)(b).

8   See the Employment Rights Act 1996 s 54(2) (as amended: see note 3).

9   Employment Rights Act 1996 s 54(2)(a). For the purposes of s 54(2)(a), s 207A(3) (extension because mediation in certain European cross-border disputes starts before the time limit expires: see PARA 1454) and s 207B (extension of time limits to facilitate conciliation before institution of proceedings: see PARA 1455) apply: s 54(2A) (added by SI 2011/1133; and amended by the Enterprise and Regulatory Reform Act 2013 s 8, Sch 2 paras 15, 21). As to time limits generally see PARA 1453.

10 Employment Rights Act 1996 s 54(2)(b).

11 See the Employment Rights Act 1996 s 54(3) (as amended: see note 3).

12 Employment Rights Act 1996 s 54(3)(a).

13 The amount which may be ordered by a tribunal to be so paid by an employer (or, where the employer is liable to pay remuneration under the Employment Rights Act 1996 s 53 (see PARA 326), the aggregate of that amount and the amount of that liability) is not to exceed, in respect of the notice period of any employee, 40% of a week's pay of that employee: s 54(4). As to the calculation of a week's pay and normal working hours see PARA 142 et seq. As to the meaning of 'week' see PARA 126 note 13.

14 Employment Rights Act 1996 s 54(3)(b).

(iii) Right to Request Time Off to Study or for Training

A.   RIGHT FOR QUALIFYING EMPLOYEES IN ENGLAND TO APPLY TO UNDERTAKE STUDY OR TRAINING

328.   Application pursuant to employee's right in England to request study or training.   A qualifying employee[1] may make an application[2] to his employer[3] which meets the following conditions[4]:

(1)   the application must be made for the purpose of enabling the employee to undertake study or training (or both)[5] whose purpose is to improve:

(a) the employee's effectiveness in the employer's business[6]; and (b) the performance of the employer's business[7]; and

(2)   the application must state that it is an application[8] relating to the statutory right to make a request for study or training[9],

as well as meeting any further conditions specified by the Secretary of State in regulations[10].

If:

(i)   an employer receives such an application[11] (the 'current application') from an employee[12]; and

(ii)   during the relevant 12 month period[13] the employer has not received another such application[14] (an 'earlier application') from the employee[15],

the employer must deal with the application in accordance with regulations made by the Secretary of State[16]. The employer may refuse an application[17] (or part of such an application) only if the employer thinks that one or more of the permissible grounds for refusal applies in relation to the application (or in relation to that part)[18]. The permissible grounds for refusal are:

(A)   that the proposed study or training to which the application, or the part in question, relates would not improve either the employee's effectiveness in the employer's business[19], or the performance of the employer's business[20];

(B)   the burden of additional costs[21];

(C)   detrimental effect on ability to meet customer demand[22];

(D)   inability to re-organise work among existing staff[23];

(E)   inability to recruit additional staff[24];

(F)   detrimental impact on quality[25];

(G)   detrimental impact on performance[26];

(H)   insufficiency of work during the periods the employee proposes to work[27];

(I)   planned structural changes[28];

(J)   any other grounds specified by the Secretary of State in regulations[29].

Accordingly, an employer to whom an application meeting the conditions given in heads (1) and (2) above[30] is submitted must hold a meeting to discuss the application within 28 days after the date on which the application is received[31], and the employer must give the employee notice[32] of his decision on the application within 14 days after the date of the meeting[33]. Such a meeting is not required, however, where the employer agrees to the application and notifies the employee accordingly in writing within the 28 days' period[34]. An employer and employee may agree to dispose of an application[35] (or part of such an application) by the employer granting a varied form of it[36].

If an employer has agreed to an application[37] (or part of such an application) made by an employee in relation to particular study or training (the 'agreed study or training')[38], the employee must inform the employer if the employee[39]:

(aa)   fails to start the agreed study or training[40];

(bb)   fails to complete the agreed study or training[41];

(cc)   undertakes, or proposes to undertake, study or training that differs from the agreed study or training in any respect[42].

The Secretary of State may make regulations about the way in which the employee is to comply with this duty[43] to inform[44].

1   For the purposes of the Employment Rights Act 1996 s 63D, an employee is a qualifying employee if he (see s 63D(6) (ss 63D–63K added by the Apprenticeships, Skills, Children and Learning Act 2009 s 40(1), (2))):

    (1)   satisfies any conditions about duration of employment specified by the Secretary of State in regulations (Employment Rights Act 1996 s 63D(6)(a) (as so added)); and

    (2)   is not a person within any of the following heads (s 63D(6)(b) (as so added)):

        (a)   a person of compulsory school age (s 63D(7)(a) (as so added));

        (b)   a person to whom the Education and Skills Act 2008 Pt 1 (ss 1–67) (duty to participate in education or training for 16 and 17 year olds in England: see EDUCATION vol 35 (2011) PARA 646 et seq) applies (Employment Rights Act 1996 s 63D(7)(b) (as so added));

        (c)   a person who, by virtue of the Education and Skills Act 2008 s 29, is treated as a person to whom Pt 1 applies for the purposes specified in s 29 (extension for person reaching 18: see EDUCATION vol 35 (2011) PARA 661) (Employment Rights Act 1996 s 63D(7)(c) (as so added));

        (d)   a person to whom s 63A (right to time off for young person in Wales for study or training: see PARA 331) applies (s 63D(7)(d) (as so added));

        (e)   an agency worker (s 63D(7)(e) (as so added));

        (f)   a person of a description specified by the Secretary of State in regulations (s 63D(7)(f) (as so added)).

As to the meaning of 'employee' see PARA 2. For these purposes, 'agency worker' means a worker supplied by a person (the 'agent') to do work for another person (the 'principal') under a contract or other arrangement between the agent and principal; and 'compulsory school age' has the meaning given in the Education Act 1996 s 8 (see EDUCATION vol 35 (2011) PARA 18): see the Employment Rights Act 1996 s 63D(9) (as so added). As to agency workers see PARAS 11, 95 et seq. As to the effect of the Education and Skills Act 2008 Pt 1 see further PARA 331 note 1. The time at which a person attains a particular age expressed in years is the commencement of the relevant anniversary of the date of his birth: see the Family Law Reform Act 1969 s 9; and CHILDREN AND YOUNG PERSONS vol 9 (2012) PARA 2. As to the Secretary of State see PARA 5 note 21. As to the making of regulations under the Employment Rights Act 1996 generally see PARA 162. Regulations under Pt VIA (ss 63D–63K) may make different provision for different cases: s 63K (as so added). In exercise of the powers conferred by s 63D(6)(a) (see head (1) above), the Secretary of State has made the Employee Study and Training (Qualifying Period of Employment) Regulations 2010, SI 2010/800. Accordingly, for the purposes of the Employment Rights Act 1996 s 63D(6), in order to be a qualifying employee, an employee must have been continuously employed for a period of not less than 26 weeks: Employee Study and Training (Qualifying Period of Employment) Regulations 2010, SI 2010/800, reg 2(1). For these purposes, a period of continuous employment is a period computed in accordance with the Employment Rights Act 1996 Pt XIV Ch I (ss 210–219) (continuous employment: see PARAS 130 et seq, 861 et seq), as if the Employee Study and Training (Qualifying Period of Employment) Regulations 2010, SI 2010/800, reg 2(1) were a provision of the Employment Rights Act 1996: see the Employee Study and Training (Qualifying Period of Employment) Regulations 2010, SI 2010/800, reg 2(2). As to persons to whom the Education and Skills Act 2008 Pt 1 does not apply see PARAS 331, 332.

    At the date at which this volume states the law, the Apprenticeships, Skills, Children and Learning Act 2009 s 40, Sch1 has come into force for all purposes except in relation to small employers and their employees: see the Apprenticeships, Skills, Children and Learning Act 2009 (Commencement No 2 and Transitional and Saving Provisions) Order 2010, SI 2010/303, art 4, Sch 3. 'Small employer' means an employer who employs fewer than 250 employees (Sch 3 col 2(1)); and, for these purposes, the number of employees employed by an employer at any time is determined by ascertaining the average number of employees employed by the employer in the previous 12 months, being calculated by determining the number of employees employed by the employer in each month in the 12 month period (whether they were employed throughout the month or not), adding together those monthly figures and dividing the number by 12 (Sch 3 col 2(2)). If the undertaking has been in existence for less than 12 months, the references to 12, and the divisor of 12, are to be replaced by the number of months the undertaking has been in existence: see Sch 3 col 2(3). The provision that was made in art 7, Sch 6 for the Apprenticeships, Skills, Children and Learning Act 2009 s 40, Sch1 to come into force to the extent that they had not already done so was revoked by the Apprenticeships, Skills, Children and Learning Act 2009 (Commencement No 2 and Transitional and Saving Provisions) Order 2010 (Amendment) Order 2011, SI 2011/882, art 2, with effect from 21 March 2011.

2   Ie an application under the Employment Rights Act 1996 s 63D (a 'section 63D application'): see s 63D(1), (2) (as added: see note 1). Accordingly, in the Employment Rights Act 1996,

'section 63D application' has the meaning given by s 63D(2): see s 235(1) (definition added by the Apprenticeships, Skills, Children and Learning Act 2009 s 40(5), Sch 1 paras 1, 10). See note 1.

3 See the Employment Rights Act 1996 s 63D(1) (as added: see note 1). As to the meaning of 'employer' see PARA 2. At the date at which this volume states the law, small employers are excluded: see note 1.

4 See the Employment Rights Act 1996 s 63D(2)(a) (as added: see note 1). The conditions referred to in the text are those in s 63D(3)–(5) (see also heads (1), (2) in the text): see s 63D(2)(a) (as so added).

5 See the Employment Rights Act 1996 s 63D(3) (as added: see note 1). The text refers to study or training (or both) within s 63D(4) (see heads (a), (b) in the text): see s 63D(3) (as so added).

A section 63D application may:

(1) be made in relation to study or training of any description (subject to s 63D(3), (4) and regulations under s 63D(2) (see the text and note 10)) (s 63E(1)(a) (as so added)); and

(2) relate to more than one description of study or training (s 63E(1)(b) (as so added)).

The study or training may (in particular) be study or training that (if undertaken):

(a) would be undertaken on the employer's premises or elsewhere (including at the employee's home) (s 63E(2)(a) (as so added));

(b) would be undertaken by the employee while performing the duties of the employee's employment or separately (s 63E(2)(b) (as so added));

(c) would be provided or supervised by the employer or by someone else (s 63E(2)(c) (as so added));

(d) would be undertaken without supervision (s 63E(2)(d) (as so added));

(e) would be undertaken within or outside the United Kingdom (s 63E(2)(e) (as so added)).

The study or training need not be intended to lead to the award of a qualification to the employee (see s 63E(3) (as so added)); and nothing in Pt VIA prevents an employee and an employer from making any other arrangements in relation to study or training (see s 63D(8) (as so added)). A section 63D application must:

(i) give the following details of the proposed study or training: its subject matter; where and when it would take place; who would provide or supervise it; what qualification (if any) it would lead to (see s 63E(4)(a) (as so added));

(ii) explain how the employee thinks the proposed study or training would improve the employee's effectiveness in the employer's business, and the performance of the employer's business (see s 63E(4)(b) (as so added));

(iii) contain information of any other description specified by the Secretary of State in regulations (see s 63E(4)(c) (as so added)).

The Secretary of State also may make regulations about: (A) the form of a section 63D application (see s 63E(5)(a) (as so added)); and (B) when a section 63D application is to be taken to be received for the purposes of Pt VIA (ss 63D–63K) (see s 63E(5)(b) (as so added)). In exercise of the powers conferred by s 63E(4)(c) (see head (iii) above), and s 63E(5)(a) (see head (A) above), the Secretary of State has made the Employee Study and Training (Eligibility, Complaints and Remedies) Regulations 2010, SI 2010/156. Accordingly, an employee must set out in the section 63D application the date on which the employee's last section 63D application (if any) was submitted to their employer, and the method by which that application was submitted: see reg 3(1). For these purposes, an employee submits a section 63D application by sending, delivering or otherwise transmitting it to their employer: see reg 3(2). A section 63D application must be made in writing, and it must be dated: see reg 4. As to the meaning of 'writing' see PARA 2 note 8. As to the meaning of 'United Kingdom' see PARA 2 note 12. As to the meaning of 'business' see PARA 135 note 4.

6 Employment Rights Act 1996 s 63D(4)(a) (as added: see note 1).

7 Employment Rights Act 1996 s 63D(4)(b) (as added: see note 1).

8 Ie that is an application under the Employment Rights Act 1996 s 63D: see s 63D(5) (as added: see note 1).

9 See the Employment Rights Act 1996 s 63D(5) (as added: see note 1).

10 See the Employment Rights Act 1996 s 63D(2)(b) (as added: see note 1). At the date at which this volume states the law, no regulations had been made for the purposes of s 63D(2)(b).

11 Ie a 'section 63D application' (see note 2): see the Employment Rights Act 1996 s 63F(1)(a) (as added: see note 1).

12 Employment Rights Act 1996 s 63F(1)(a) (as added: see note 1).

13 For these purposes, the 'relevant 12 month period' is the 12 month period ending with the day on which the employer receives the current application: see the Employment Rights Act 1996 s 63F(2) (as added: see note 1).

14 Ie another 'section 63D application' (see note 2): see the Employment Rights Act 1996
    s 63F(1)(b) (as added: see note 1).
15 Employment Rights Act 1996 s 63F(1)(b) (as added: see note 1).
16 See the Employment Rights Act 1996 s 63F(4) (as added: see note 1). Regulations under s 63F(4)
    may, in particular, include provision:
    (1)   for the employee to have a right to be accompanied by a person of a specified
           description when attending meetings held in relation to a section 63D application in
           accordance with any such regulations (s 63G(1)(a) (as so added));
    (2)   for the postponement of such a meeting if the employee's companion under head (1)
           above is not available to attend it (s 63G(1)(b) (as so added));
    (3)   in relation to companions under head (1) above, corresponding to the Employment
           Relations Act 1999 s 10(6), (7) (right to paid time off to act as companion, etc: see and
           PARA 717) (Employment Rights Act 1996 s 63G(1)(c) (as so added));
    (4)   in relation to the rights under heads (1) to (3) above, for rights to complain to an
           employment tribunal and not to be subjected to a detriment, and about unfair dismissal
           (s 63G(1)(d) (as so added));
    (5)   for section 63D applications to be treated as withdrawn in specified circumstances
           (s 63G(1)(e) (as so added)).
    For these purposes, 'specified' means specified in the regulations: s 63G(2) (as so added). The
    Secretary of State also may make regulations about circumstances in which, at an employee's
    request, an employer is to be required to ignore an earlier application for the purposes of
    s 63F(1) (see the text and notes 11–15): see s 63F(3) (as added: see note 1). In exercise of the
    powers conferred by s 63F(3), (4), the Secretary of State has made the Employee Study and
    Training (Procedural Requirements) Regulations 2010, SI 2010/155 (see also the text and notes
    30–36, 44; and PARAS 329, 330). Accordingly, for the purposes of the Employment Rights
    Act 1996 s 63F(1), at an employee's request, an employer must ignore an earlier application if
    head (a) or head (b) below applies (Employee Study and Training (Procedural Requirements)
    Regulations 2010, SI 2010/155, reg 3(1)), ie in circumstances where:
    (a)   the employee failed to start the agreed study or training due to: (i) an emergency or
           unforeseen circumstance beyond the employee's control (reg 3(2)(a)); or (ii) cancellation
           of the study or training by the employer, the institution at which the employee was due
           to undertake a course, the person whom it was agreed would supervise the training, or
           any other proposed provider or facilitator of the proposed study or training
           (reg 3(2)(b));
    (b)   the employee: (i) by mistake, submitted a section 63D application ('the earlier
           application') too soon after a previous section 63D application for the employer to be
           required to consider it under the Employment Rights Act 1996 s 63F (Employee Study
           and Training (Procedural Requirements) Regulations 2010, SI 2010/155, reg 3(4)(a));
           (ii) submits a further section 63D application ('the current application') which the
           employer would be required to consider but for the earlier application (reg 3(4)(b)); and
           (iii) at the time of making the current application, notifies the employer that the earlier
           application was submitted too early by mistake, and that the employee wishes to
           withdraw the earlier application (reg 3(4)(c)).
    Head (a)(ii) above does not apply where the cancellation of the study or training is attributable
    to the employee's own conduct in relation to the study or training, however: reg 3(3). For these
    purposes, 'employer' means the person by whom an employee is (or, where the employment has
    ceased, was) employed; and 'employee' means an individual who has entered into or works
    under (or, where the employment has ceased, worked under) a contract of employment: see
    reg 2(1). As to the meanings of 'employer', 'employee', 'contract of employment' and related
    expressions in relation to employment rights generally see PARA 2 et seq.
        As to the right not to be subjected to a detriment, or to dismissal which is deemed to be
    unfair, for exercising rights under the Employee Study and Training (Procedural Requirements)
    Regulations 2010, SI 2010/155, see reg 18; and PARA 618.
17 Ie a 'section 63D application' (see note 2): see the Employment Rights Act 1996 s 63F(5), (6) (as
    added: see note 1).
18 See the Employment Rights Act 1996 s 63F(5), (6) (as added: see note 1).
19 Employment Rights Act 1996 s 63F(7)(a)(i) (as added: see note 1).
20 Employment Rights Act 1996 s 63F(7)(a)(ii) (as added: see note 1).
21 Employment Rights Act 1996 s 63F(7)(b) (as added: see note 1).
22 Employment Rights Act 1996 s 63F(7)(c) (as added: see note 1).
23 Employment Rights Act 1996 s 63F(7)(d) (as added: see note 1).
24 Employment Rights Act 1996 s 63F(7)(e) (as added: see note 1).
25 Employment Rights Act 1996 s 63F(7)(f) (as added: see note 1).

26 Employment Rights Act 1996 s 63F(7)(g) (as added: see note 1).
27 Employment Rights Act 1996 s 63F(7)(h) (as added: see note 1).
28 Employment Rights Act 1996 s 63F(7)(i) (as added: see note 1).
29 Employment Rights Act 1996 s 63F(7)(j) (as added: see note 1). At the date at which this volume states the law, no regulations had been made for the purposes of s 63F(7)(j).
30 Ie a 'section 63D application' (see note 2): see the Employee Study and Training (Procedural Requirements) Regulations 2010, SI 2010/155, reg 4(1).
31 Employee Study and Training (Procedural Requirements) Regulations 2010, SI 2010/155, reg 4(1). A section 63D application is taken as having been received (in relation to an application transmitted by electronic communication) on the day on which it is transmitted, and (in relation to an application sent by post) on the day on which the application would be delivered in the ordinary course of post: see reg 2(2). For these purposes, 'electronic communication' means an electronic communication within the meaning of the Electronic Communications Act 2000 s 15(1) (see CIVIL PROCEDURE vol 11 (2009) PARA 947): see the Employee Study and Training (Procedural Requirements) Regulations 2010, SI 2010/155, reg 2(1). The time and place of a meeting under reg 4(1) must be convenient to the employer and the employee: see reg 13. The provision made by reg 4(1) is subject also to reg 4(2) (see the text and note 34) and reg 15: see reg 4(1). Accordingly, where the individual who would ordinarily consider a section 63D application is absent from work on annual leave or on sick leave on the day on which the application is received, the period referred to in reg 4(1) commences on the day the individual returns to work or 28 days after the application is received, whichever is the sooner: reg 15. An employer and employee may agree to an extension of either of the time periods referred to in regs 4, 15: see reg 14(1). An agreement under reg 14(1) must be recorded in writing by the employer (see reg 14(2)); and such a record must:
(1) specify what period the extension relates to (reg 14(3)(a));
(2) specify the date on which the extension is to end (reg 14(3)(b));
(3) be dated (reg 14(3)(c)); and
(4) be given to the employee (reg 14(3)(d)).
Where a meeting is held under reg 4(1) (see reg 16(1)(a)), and where the employee reasonably requests to be accompanied at the meeting (see reg 16(1)(b)), the employer must permit the employee to be accompanied at the meeting by a single companion who is chosen by the employee to attend the relevant meeting (see reg 16(2)(a)), and who is a worker employed by the same employer as the employee (see reg 16(2)(b)). For these purposes, 'companion' means a person who satisfies the requirements in reg 16(2): see reg 2(1). A companion may address the meeting (see reg 16(3)(a)) and may confer with the employee during the meeting (see reg 16(3)(b)); but, when addressing a meeting, a companion may not answer questions independently of the employee (see reg 16(4)). If:
(a) an employee has a right under reg 16 to be accompanied at a meeting (reg 16(5)(a));
(b) his chosen companion will not be available at the time proposed for the meeting by the employer (reg 16(5)(b)); and
(c) the employee proposes an alternative time which is not only convenient for employer, employee and companion (reg 16(5)(c), (6)(a)), but also falls before the end of the period of seven days beginning with the first day after the day proposed by the employer (reg 16(5)(c), (6)(b)),
the employer must postpone the meeting to the time proposed by the employee (see reg 16(5)). An employer must permit a worker to take time off during working hours for the purpose of accompanying an employee in accordance with a request under reg 16(1)(b) (see reg 16(7)); and the Trade Union and Labour Relations (Consolidation) Act 1992 ss 168(3), (4),169, and 171–173 (time off for carrying out trade union duties: see PARAS 1065, 1068) apply in relation to the Employee Study and Training (Procedural Requirements) Regulations 2010, SI 2010/155, reg 16(7) as they apply in relation to the Trade Union and Labour Relations (Consolidation) Act 1992 s 168(1) (see PARA 1065) (see the Employee Study and Training (Procedural Requirements) Regulations 2010, SI 2010/155, reg 16(8)). For these purposes, 'worker' means an individual who has entered into or works under (or where the employment has ceased, worked under) either a contract of employment, or any other contract, whether express or implied and (if it is express) whether oral or in writing, whereby the individual undertakes to do or perform personally any work or services for another party to the contract whose status is not by virtue of the contract that of a client or customer of any profession or business undertaking carried on by the individual: see reg 2(1).
   An employer must treat a section 63D application as withdrawn where the employee has (see reg 19(1)):
(i) notified the employer either orally or in writing that the employee is withdrawing the application (reg 19(1)(a));

    (ii)   without reasonable cause, failed to attend a meeting under reg 4(1) more than once (reg 19(1)(b)); or

    (iii)   without reasonable cause, refused to provide the employer with information the employer requires in order to assess whether the application should be agreed to (reg 19(1)(c)).

An employer must confirm the withdrawal of the section 63D application to the employee in writing unless the employee has provided him with written notice of the withdrawal under head (i) above: reg 19(2). For these purposes, 'writing' includes writing delivered by means of electronic communication: see reg 2(1).

32 For these purposes, a notice is taken as being given (in relation to a notice transmitted by electronic communication) on the day on which it is transmitted, and (in relation to a notice sent by post) on the day on which the section 63D application would be delivered in the ordinary course of post: see reg 2(3).

33 Employee Study and Training (Procedural Requirements) Regulations 2010, SI 2010/155, reg 5. A notice under reg 5 must be in writing, and must be dated: reg 6(1). An employer and employee may agree to an extension of the time period referred to in reg 5: see reg 14(1); and see reg 14(2), (3); and note 31.

    Where the employer's decision is to agree the section 63D application, a notice under reg 5 must (see reg 6(2)):

    (1)   give the following details of the agreed study or training: (a) the subject of the study or training (reg 6(2)(a)(i)); (b) where and when it is to take place (reg 6(2)(a)(ii)); (c) who is to provide or supervise it (reg 6(2)(a)(iii)); and (d) what qualification (if any) it is to lead to (reg 6(2)(a)(iv)); and

    (2)   make clear: (a) whether any remuneration under the employee's contract of employment is to be paid for the time spent undertaking the agreed study or training (reg 6(2)(b)(i)); (b) any changes to the employee's working hours in order to accommodate the agreed study or training (reg 6(2)(b)(ii)); and (c) how any tuition fees or other direct costs of the agreed study or training are to be met (reg 6(2)(b)(iii)).

    Where the decision is to refuse the section 63D application, a notice under reg 5 must (see reg 6(3)):

    (i)   state which of the grounds for refusal specified in the Employment Rights Act 1996 s 63F(7) (see heads (A) to (J) in the text) are considered by the employer to apply (Employee Study and Training (Procedural Requirements) Regulations 2010, SI 2010/155, reg 6(3)(a));

    (ii)   contain a sufficient explanation as to why those grounds apply (reg 6(3)(b)); and

    (iii) set out the appeal procedure (reg 6(3)(c)).

    Where the employer's decision is to agree part of a section 63D application and refuse part of a section 63D application, a notice under reg 5 must (see reg 6(4)):

    (A)   make clear which part of the application is agreed to (reg 6(4)(a));

    (B)   make clear which part of the application is refused (reg 6(4)(b));

    (C)   give, in respect of the part which is agreed to, the information required under reg 6(2) (reg 6(4)(c)); and

    (D)   include, in respect of the part which is refused, the details required under reg 6(3) (reg 6(4)(d)).

See also note 36. As to the procedure on appeal against an employer's decision to refuse an employee's application for study or training see PARA 329.

34 Employee Study and Training (Procedural Requirements) Regulations 2010, SI 2010/155, reg 4(2). The text refers to the 28 days' period referred to in reg 4(1) (see the text and notes 30–31): see reg 4(2).

35 Ie a section 63D application (see note 2): see the Employee Study and Training (Procedural Requirements) Regulations 2010, SI 2010/155, reg 7(1).

36 Employee Study and Training (Procedural Requirements) Regulations 2010, SI 2010/155, reg 7(1). Where agreement is reached by the employer and employee to a varied form of the application, the notice of the employer's decision under reg 5 (see note 33) must (see reg 7(2)):

    (1)   make clear the variation agreed to (reg 7(2)(a));

    (2)   be supported by written evidence of the employee's agreement to that variation (reg 7(2)(b)); and

    (3)   make clear: (a) whether any remuneration under the employee's contract of employment will be paid for the time spent undertaking the agreed study or training (reg 7(2)(c)(i)); (b) any changes to the employee's working hours in order to accommodate the agreed study or training (reg 7(2)(c)(ii)); and (c) how any tuition fees or other direct costs of the agreed study or training will be met (reg 7(2)(c)(iii)).

37 Ie a 'section 63D application' (see note 2): see the Employment Rights Act 1996 s 63H(1) (as added: see note 1).
38 See the Employment Rights Act 1996 s 63H(1) (as added: see note 1).
39 See the Employment Rights Act 1996 s 63H(2) (as added: see note 1).
40 Employment Rights Act 1996 s 63H(2)(a) (as added: see note 1).
41 Employment Rights Act 1996 s 63H(2)(b) (as added: see note 1).
42 Employment Rights Act 1996 s 63H(2)(c) (as added: see note 1). Head (cc) in the text includes reference to the study or training specified in s 63E(4)(a) (see note 5): see s 63H(2)(c) (as so added).
43 Ie the duty under the Employment Rights Act 1996 s 63H(2) (see the text and notes 39–42): see s 63H(3) (as added: see note 1).
44 See the Employment Rights Act 1996 s 63H(3) (as added: see note 1).In exercise of the powers conferred by s 63H(3), the Secretary of State has made the Employee Study and Training (Procedural Requirements) Regulations 2010, SI 2010/155. Accordingly, an employee must inform his employer within 14 days of an event listed in the Employment Rights Act 1996 s 63H(2) (see the text and notes 39–42) occurring: Employee Study and Training (Procedural Requirements) Regulations 2010, SI 2010/155, reg 20(1). Such notice must be in writing, and must be dated: see reg 20(2).

329.   Appeal against employer's decision to refuse employee's application for study or training. An employee[1] is entitled to appeal against the decision of an employer[2] to refuse an application relating to the statutory right to make a request for study or training[3] (or part of such an application) by giving notice[4] within 14 days after the date on which notice of the decision is given[5]. Within 14 days after the date on which such notice is given[6], the employer must hold a meeting with the employee to discuss the appeal[7], unless, within that 14 days limit[8], the employer[9]:

(1)   upholds the appeal[10]; and
(2)   notifies the employee in writing of the employer's decision[11], specifying[12]:
   (a)   the following details of the agreed study or training: (i) the subject of the study or training[13]; (ii) where and when it will take place[14]; (iii) who will provide or supervise it[15]; and (iv) what qualification (if any) it will lead to[16]; and
   (b)   by making clear: (i) whether any remuneration under the employee's contract of employment will be paid for the time spent undertaking the agreed study or training[17]; (ii) any changes to the employee's working hours in order to accommodate the agreed study or training[18]; and (iii) how any tuition fees or other direct costs of the agreed study or training will be met[19].

Where a meeting is held to discuss the appeal, the employer must notify the employee of the employer's decision on the appeal within 14 days after the date of the meeting[20].

1   As to the meaning of 'employee' for these purposes see PARA 328 note 16.
2   As to the meaning of 'employer' for these purposes see PARA 328 note 16.
3   Ie a 'section 63D application' (see PARA 328 note 2): see the Employee Study and Training (Procedural Requirements) Regulations 2010, SI 2010/155, reg 8.
4   Ie in accordance with the Employee Study and Training (Procedural Requirements) Regulations 2010, SI 2010/155, reg 9: see reg 8. Accordingly, a notice of appeal under reg 8 must be in writing, must set out the grounds of appeal, and it must be dated: see reg 9. For these purposes, a notice is taken as being given (in relation to a notice transmitted by electronic communication) on the day on which it is transmitted, and (in relation to a notice sent by post) on the day on which the section 63D application would be delivered in the ordinary course of post: see reg 2(3). As to the meanings of 'electronic communication' and 'writing' see PARA 328 note 31.

5   Employee Study and Training (Procedural Requirements) Regulations 2010, SI 2010/155, reg 8. An employer and employee may agree to an extension of the time period referred to in reg 8: see reg 14(1); and see reg 14(2), (3); and PARA 328 note 31.

6   An employer and employee may agree to an extension of the time period referred to in the Employee Study and Training (Procedural Requirements) Regulations 2010, SI 2010/155, reg 10: see reg 14(1); and see reg 14(2), (3); and PARA 328 note 31.

7   Employee Study and Training (Procedural Requirements) Regulations 2010, SI 2010/155, reg 10(1). The time and place of a meeting under reg 10(1) must be convenient to the employer and the employee: see reg 13.

    Where a meeting is held under reg 10(1) (see reg 16(1)(a)), and where the employee reasonably requests to be accompanied at the meeting (see reg 16(1)(b)), the employer must permit the employee to be accompanied at the meeting by a single companion who is chosen by the employee to attend the relevant meeting (see reg 16(2)(a)), and who is a worker employed by the same employer as the employee (see reg 16(2)(b)). A companion may address the meeting (see reg 16(3)(a)) and may confer with the employee during the meeting (see reg 16(3)(b)); but, when addressing a meeting, a companion may not answer questions independently of the employee (see reg 16(4)). As to the meanings of 'companion' and 'worker' for these purposes see PARA 328 note 31. If:

    (1)   an employee has a right under reg 16 to be accompanied at a meeting (reg 16(5)(a));

    (2)   his chosen companion will not be available at the time proposed for the meeting by the employer (reg 16(5)(b)); and

    (3)   the employee proposes an alternative time which is not only convenient for employer, employee and companion (reg 16(5)(c), (6)(a)), but also falls before the end of the period of seven days beginning with the first day after the day proposed by the employer (reg 16(5)(c), (6)(b)),

the employer must postpone the meeting to the time proposed by the employee (see reg 16(5)). An employer must permit a worker to take time off during working hours for the purpose of accompanying an employee in accordance with a request under reg 16(1)(b) (see reg 16(7)); and the Trade Union and Labour Relations (Consolidation) Act 1992 ss 168(3), (4), 169, and 171–173 (time off for carrying out trade union duties: see PARAS 1065, 1068) apply in relation to the Employee Study and Training (Procedural Requirements) Regulations 2010, SI 2010/155, reg 16(7) as they apply in relation to the Trade Union and Labour Relations (Consolidation) Act 1992 s 168(1) (see PARA 1065) (see the Employee Study and Training (Procedural Requirements) Regulations 2010, SI 2010/155, reg 16(8)).

    An employer must treat a section 63D application as withdrawn where the employee has (see reg 19(1)):

    (a)   notified the employer either orally or in writing that the employee is withdrawing the application (reg 19(1)(a));

    (b)   without reasonable cause, failed to attend a meeting under reg 10(1) more than once (reg 19(1)(b)); or

    (c)   without reasonable cause, refused to provide the employer with information the employer requires in order to assess whether the application should be agreed to (reg 19(1)(c)).

An employer must confirm the withdrawal of the section 63D application to the employee in writing unless the employee has provided him with written notice of the withdrawal under head (a) above: reg 19(2).

8   Ie within 14 days after the date on which such notice under the Employee Study and Training (Procedural Requirements) Regulations 2010, SI 2010/155, reg 8 is given (see the text and notes 1–5): see reg 10(2).

9   See the Employee Study and Training (Procedural Requirements) Regulations 2010, SI 2010/155, reg 10(2).

10   Employee Study and Training (Procedural Requirements) Regulations 2010, SI 2010/155, reg 10(2)(a).

11   See the Employee Study and Training (Procedural Requirements) Regulations 2010, SI 2010/155, reg 10(2)(b).

12   Ie specifying the information required by the Employee Study and Training (Procedural Requirements) Regulations 2010, SI 2010/155, reg 6(2) (see heads (a), (b) in the text): see reg 10(2)(b).

13   Employee Study and Training (Procedural Requirements) Regulations 2010, SI 2010/155, reg 6(2)(a)(i), 10(2)(b).

14   Employee Study and Training (Procedural Requirements) Regulations 2010, SI 2010/155, reg 6(2)(a)(ii), 10(2)(b).

15 Employee Study and Training (Procedural Requirements) Regulations 2010, SI 2010/155, reg 6(2)(a)(iii), 10(2)(b).

16 Employee Study and Training (Procedural Requirements) Regulations 2010, SI 2010/155, reg 6(2)(a)(iv), 10(2)(b).

17 Employee Study and Training (Procedural Requirements) Regulations 2010, SI 2010/155, reg 6(2)(b)(i), 10(2)(b).

18 Employee Study and Training (Procedural Requirements) Regulations 2010, SI 2010/155, reg 6(2)(b)(ii), 10(2)(b).

19 Employee Study and Training (Procedural Requirements) Regulations 2010, SI 2010/155, reg 6(2)(b)(iii), 10(2)(b).

20 Employee Study and Training (Procedural Requirements) Regulations 2010, SI 2010/155, reg 11. An employer and employee may agree to an extension of the time period referred to in reg 11: see reg 14(1); and see reg 14(2), (3); and PARA 328 note 31. Notice under reg 11 must be in writing, and must be dated: see reg 12(1). Where the employer upholds the appeal, notice under reg 11 must specify the information required by reg 6(2) (see heads (a), (b) in the text) (see reg 12(2)); but where the employer dismisses the appeal, notice under reg 11 must state the grounds for the decision, and it must contain a sufficient explanation as to why those grounds apply (see reg 12(3)).

330.   Complaint to employment tribunal: employee's application pursuant to right to make a request for study or training.   An employee[1] who makes an application relating to the statutory right to make a request for study or training[2] may present a complaint to an employment tribunal[3] that[4]:

(1)   the employer[5] has failed to deal with the application in accordance with the regulations made by the Secretary of State[6], or has refused such an application (or part of such an application) without reference to one or more of the permissible grounds[7] for refusal[8]; or

(2)   the employer's decision to refuse the application (or part of it) is based on incorrect facts[9].

No such complaint may be made, however, in respect of:

(a)   such an application[10] which has been disposed of by agreement or withdrawn[11]; or

(b)   failure to comply with provision included in regulations mentioned in head (1) above[12] relating to the employee's right to be accompanied at a meeting[13].

In the case of such an application[14] that has not been disposed of by agreement or withdrawn, such a complaint[15] may only be made if the employer[16]:

(i)   notifies the employee of a decision to refuse the application (or part of it) on appeal[17]; or

(ii)   commits a breach of regulations mentioned in head (1) above[18], where the breach is of a description specified by the Secretary of State in regulations[19].

An employment tribunal must not consider such a complaint, however, unless it is presented[20]:

(A)   before the end of the period of three months beginning with the relevant date[21]; or

(B)   within such further period as the tribunal considers reasonable in a case where it is satisfied that it was not reasonably practicable for the complaint to be presented before the end of that period of three months[22].

If an employment tribunal finds such a complaint well-founded, the tribunal must make a declaration to that effect[23]. It may also make either an order for reconsideration of the application[24], or an award of compensation to be paid by the employer to the employee[25].

An employee[26] also may present a complaint to an employment tribunal under regulations[27] on the basis that the employer has failed to comply with the employee's reasonable request to be accompanied at a meeting to discuss either such an application, or an appeal against the employer's decision to refuse such an application[28]. Where a tribunal finds that such a complaint is well-founded, it must order the employer to pay compensation to the worker of an amount not exceeding two weeks' pay[29].

1   As to the meaning of 'employee' see PARA 2. As to when an employee is a qualifying employee for the purposes of the Employment Rights Act 1996 s 63D, and as to the effect of Pt VIA (ss 63D–63K), see PARA 328 note 1.

2   Ie who makes a section 63D application: see the Employment Rights Act 1996 s 63I(1) (ss 63I, 63J added by the Apprenticeships, Skills, Children and Learning Act 2009 s 40(1), (2)). As to the meaning of 'section 63D application' for these purposes see PARA 328 note 2.

3   Ie subject to the Employment Rights Act 1996 s 63I(2)–(7) (see the text and notes 10–22): see s 63I(1) (as added: see note 2). As to employment tribunals see PARA 1399 et seq; and as to the procedure on a complaint made to an employment tribunal see PARA 1453 et seq. There is a requirement for early ACAS conciliation to be tried in order to promote a settlement before tribunal proceedings are instituted on a complaint under s 63I, however: see the Employment Tribunals Act 1996 s 18(1)(b); and PARA 152 note 1. As to the constitution and powers of ACAS see PARA 1213 et seq.

4   See the Employment Rights Act 1996 s 63I(1) (as added: see note 2).

5   As to the meaning of 'employer' see PARA 2.

6   Ie that the employer has failed to comply with the Employment Rights Act 1996 s 63F(4) (see PARA 328): see s 63I(1)(a) (as added: see note 2). As to the Secretary of State see PARA 5 note 21. As to the regulations that have been made in exercise of the powers conferred by s 63F(4) see the Employee Study and Training (Procedural Requirements) Regulations 2010, SI 2010/155; and PARAS 328, 329. See also note 19.

7   Ie that the employer has failed to comply with the Employment Rights Act 1996 s 63F(5), (6) (see PARA 328): see s 63I(1)(a) (as added: see note 2).

8   Employment Rights Act 1996 s 63I(1)(a) (as added: see note 2).

9   Employment Rights Act 1996 s 63I(1)(b) (as added: see note 2).

10 Ie a section 63D application: see the Employment Rights Act 1996 s 63I(2) (as added: see note 2).

11 See the Employment Rights Act 1996 s 63I(2) (as added: see note 2). As to disposal of an application by agreement or withdrawal see PARA 328.

12 Ie regulations under the Employment Rights Act 1996 s 63F(4) (see PARA 328): see s 63I(4) (as added: see note 2).

13 See the Employment Rights Act 1996 s 63I(4) (as added: see note 2). Head (b) in the text applies specifically in respect of failure to comply with provision included in regulations under s 63F(4) (see PARA 328) because of:
    (1)   s 63G(1)(a) or s 63G(1)(b) (see PARA 328 note 16), if provision is included in regulations under s 63F(4) by virtue of s 63G(1)(d) (see PARA 328 note 16) (s 63I(4)(a) (as so added)); or
    (2)   s 63G(1)(c) (see PARA 328 note 16) (s 63I(4)(b) (as so added)).
    See, however, the Employee Study and Training (Procedural Requirements) Regulations 2010, SI 2010/155, reg 17; and the text and notes 26–29.

14 Ie in the case of a section 63D application: see the Employment Rights Act 1996 s 63I(3) (as added: see note 2).

15 Ie a complaint under the Employment Rights Act 1996 s 63I: see s 63I(3) (as added: see note 2).

16 See the Employment Rights Act 1996 s 63I(3) (as added: see note 2).

17 Employment Rights Act 1996 s 63I(3)(a) (as added: see note 2).

18 Ie a breach of regulations under the Employment Rights Act 1996 s 63F(4) (see PARA 328): see s 63I(3)(b) (as added: see note 2).

19 Employment Rights Act 1996 s 63I(3)(b) (as added: see note 2). In exercise of the powers conferred by s 63I(3)(b), the Secretary of State has made the Employee Study and Training (Eligibility, Complaints and Remedies) Regulations 2010, SI 2010/156. Accordingly, the breaches of the Employee Study and Training (Procedural Requirements) Regulations 2010, SI 2010/155 (see note 6), which entitle an employee to make a complaint to an employment tribunal under the Employment Rights Act 1996 s 63I, notwithstanding the fact that the employee's section 63D application has not been disposed of by agreement or withdrawn are:

(1)　failure to hold a meeting in accordance with the Employee Study and Training (Procedural Requirements) Regulations 2010, SI 2010/155, reg 4(1) (see PARA 328) and reg 10(1) (see PARA 329) (Employee Study and Training (Eligibility, Complaints and Remedies) Regulations 2010, SI 2010/156, reg 5(a)); and

(2)　failure to notify a decision in accordance with the Employee Study and Training (Procedural Requirements) Regulations 2010, SI 2010/155, reg 5 (see PARA 328) and reg 11 (see PARA 329) (Employee Study and Training (Eligibility, Complaints and Remedies) Regulations 2010, SI 2010/156, reg 5(b)).

20　See the Employment Rights Act 1996 s 63I(5) (as added: see note 2).

21　Employment Rights Act 1996 s 63I(5)(a) (as added: see note 2). The relevant date is:

(1)　in the case of a complaint permitted by s 63I(3)(a) (see head (i) in the text), the date on which the employee is notified of the decision on the appeal (s 63I(6)(a) (as so added));

(2)　in the case of a complaint permitted by s 63I(3)(b) (see head (ii) in the text), the date on which the breach was committed (s 63I(6)(b) (as so added)).

For the purposes of s 63I(5)(a), s 207A(3) (extension because mediation in certain European cross-border disputes starts before the time limit expires: see PARA 1454) and s 207B (extension of time limits to facilitate conciliation before institution of proceedings: see PARA 1455) apply: s 63I(7) (s 63I as so added; s 63I(7) added by SI 2011/1133; and amended by the Enterprise and Regulatory Reform Act 2013 s 8, Sch 2 paras 15, 28). As to time limits generally see PARA 1453.

22　Employment Rights Act 1996 s 63I(5)(b) (as added: see note 2).

23　See the Employment Rights Act 1996 s 63J(1) (as added: see note 2).

24　Employment Rights Act 1996 s 63J(1)(a) (as added: see note 2). If an employment tribunal makes an order under s 63J(1)(a), then s 63F and regulations under s 63F (see PARA 328) apply as if the application had been received on the date of the order (instead of on the date it was actually received): s 63J(4) (as so added).

25　Employment Rights Act 1996 s 63J(1)(b) (as added: see note 2). The amount of any compensation must be the amount the tribunal considers just and equitable in all the circumstances, but must not exceed the permitted maximum: s 63J(2) (as so added). The permitted maximum for these purposes is the number of weeks' pay specified by the Secretary of State in regulations: s 63J(3) (as so added). In exercise of the powers conferred by s 63J(3), the Secretary of State has made the Employee Study and Training (Eligibility, Complaints and Remedies) Regulations 2010, SI 2010/156. Accordingly, the maximum amount of compensation that an employment tribunal may award under the Employment Rights Act 1996 s 63J where it finds a complaint by an employee under s 63I well-founded is 8 weeks' pay: Employee Study and Training (Eligibility, Complaints and Remedies) Regulations 2010, SI 2010/156, reg 6. As to the calculation of a week's pay and normal working hours see PARA 142 et seq. As to the meaning of 'week' see PARA 126 note 13.

26　As to the meaning of 'employee' for these purposes see PARA 328 note 16.

27　Ie under the Employee Study and Training (Procedural Requirements) Regulations 2010, SI 2010/155, reg 16(2), (3), (5) (see PARA 329 note 7): see reg 17(1). There is a requirement for early ACAS conciliation to be tried in order to promote a settlement before tribunal proceedings are instituted on a complaint under reg 17, however: see the Employment Tribunals Act 1996 s 18(1)(z1); and PARA 152 note 1.

28　See the Employee Study and Training (Procedural Requirements) Regulations 2010, SI 2010/155, reg 17(1). A tribunal must not consider a complaint under reg 17, however, in relation to a failure or threat unless the complaint is presented:

(1)　before the end of the period of three months beginning with the date of the failure or threat (reg 17(2)(a)); or

(2)　within such further period as the tribunal considers reasonable in a case where it is satisfied that it was not reasonably practicable for the complaint to be presented before the end of that period of three months (reg 17(2)(b)).

For the purposes of head (1) above, reg 17A (extension of time limits to facilitate conciliation before institution of proceedings) applies: reg 17(2A) (regs 17(2A), 17A added by SI 2014/431). Accordingly, in working out when the time limit set under head (1) above expires, the following period is not to be counted (see the Employee Study and Training (Procedural Requirements) Regulations 2010, SI 2010/155, reg 17A(2) (as so added)), namely the period that:

(a)　begins with the day after the day on which the worker concerned complies with the requirement in the Employment Tribunals Act 1996 s 18A(1) (requirement to contact ACAS before instituting proceedings: see PARA 152), in relation to the matter in respect of which the proceedings are brought ('the day after Day A') (Employee Study and Training (Procedural Requirements) Regulations 2010, SI 2010/155, reg 17A(1)(a), (2) (as so added)); and

(b)　ends with the day on which the worker concerned receives (or, if earlier, is treated as receiving by virtue of regulations made under the Employment Tribunals Act 1996 s 18A(11) (see PARA 152)) the certificate issued by the conciliation officer under s 18A(4) (see PARA 152) to the effect either that he has concluded that a settlement is not possible within the prescribed period or that the prescribed period has expired without a settlement having been reached ('Day B') (Employee Study and Training (Procedural Requirements) Regulations 2010, SI 2010/155, reg 17A(1)(b), (2) (as so added)).

If the time limit set under head (1) above would, if not extended by reg 17A(3), expire during the period beginning with Day A and ending one month after Day B, the time limit expires instead at the end of that period: reg 17A(3) (as so added). The power conferred on the employment tribunal by head (2) above to extend the time limit set by head (1) above is exercisable in relation to that time limit as extended reg 17A: reg 17A(4) (as so added). As to the meaning of 'worker' for these purposes see PARA 328 note 31.

29 Employee Study and Training (Procedural Requirements) Regulations 2010, SI 2010/155, reg 17(3). In applying the Employment Rights Act 1996 Pt XIV Ch II (ss 220–229) (calculation of a week's pay: see PARA 143 et seq) for the purposes of the Employee Study and Training (Procedural Requirements) Regulations 2010, SI 2010/155, reg 17(3), the calculation date must be taken to be the date on which the relevant meeting (ie under reg 4 or reg 10, as the case may be: see PARAS 328, 329) took place (or was to have taken place): reg 17(4). The limit in the Employment Rights Act 1996 s 227(1) (maximum amount of a week's pay: see PARA 147) also applies for the purposes of the Employee Study and Training (Procedural Requirements) Regulations 2010, SI 2010/155, reg 17(3): reg 17(5).

B.   COMPLEMENTARY RIGHT TO TIME OFF IN ORDER TO PARTICIPATE IN EDUCATION OR TRAINING

331.   Qualifying employees' right to time off in order to participate in education or training.   An employee[1] who:

(1)   is aged 16 or 17[2];

(2)   is not receiving full-time secondary[3] or further[4] education[5]; and

(3)   has not attained such standard of achievement as is prescribed by regulations made by the Secretary of State[6],

is entitled to be permitted by his employer to take time off during the employee's working hours[7] in order to undertake study or training[8] leading to a relevant qualification[9].

An employee who[10]:

(a)   satisfies the requirements of heads (1) to (3) above[11]; and

(b)   is for the time being supplied by his employer to another person (the 'principal') to perform work in accordance with a contract made between the employer and the principal[12],

also is entitled to be permitted by the principal to take time off during the employee's working hours in order to undertake study or training leading to a relevant qualification[13].

The amount of time off which an employee is to be permitted to take in this way, and the occasions on which and any conditions subject to which time off may be so taken, are those that are reasonable in all the circumstances having regard, in particular, to[14]:

(i)   the requirements of the employee's study or training[15]; and

(ii)   the circumstances of the business[16] of the employer or the principal and the effect of the employee's time off on the running of that business[17].

An employee who is permitted to take time off for these purposes[18] is entitled to be paid remuneration by his employer for the time taken off at the appropriate hourly rate[19]; and a right to any such amount[20] does not affect any right of an employee in relation to remuneration under his contract of employment ('contractual remuneration')[21].

1   As to the meaning of 'employee' see PARA 2. References in the Employment Rights Act 1996
     s 63A to an employee do not include a person to whom the Education and Skills Act 2008 Pt 1
     (ss 1–67) (duty to participate in education or training for 16 and 17 year olds in England: see
     EDUCATION vol 35 (2011) PARA 646 et seq) applies, or who is treated by s 29 (extension for
     person reaching 18: see EDUCATION vol 35 (2011) PARA 661) as applying: Employment Rights
     Act 1996 s 63A(5A) (s 63A added by the Teaching and Higher Education Act 1998 s 32;
     Employment Rights Act 1996 s 63A(5A) added by the Education and Skills Act 2008
     s 39(1), (2)). At the date at which this volume states the law, certain provisions of the Education
     and Skills Act 2008 Pt 1 came into force with effect from 28 June 2013 (and s 1 comes into force
     on 26 June 2015, to the extent that it is not already in force): see the Education and Skills
     Act 2008 (Commencement No 9 and Transitory Provision) Order 2013, SI 2013/1204, arts 1–3.
     Accordingly, from that latter date, the Employment Rights Act 1996 s 63A will apply only in
     Scotland and Wales. As to the meanings of 'England' and 'Wales' see PARA 2 note 12. As to the
     right to time off in order to participate in education or training for persons to whom the
     Education and Skills Act 2008 Pt 1 applies see PARAS 328–330.

2   Employment Rights Act 1996 s 63A(1)(a) (as added: see note 1). A person attains a particular
     age expressed in years at the commencement of the relevant anniversary of the date of his birth:
     see the Family Law Reform Act 1969 s 9; and CHILDREN AND YOUNG PERSONS vol 9 (2012)
     PARA 2.
         Where an employee:
     (1)   is aged 18 (Employment Rights Act 1996 s 63A(4)(a) (as so added));
     (2)   is undertaking study or training leading to a relevant qualification (s 63A(4)(b) (as so
            added)); and
     (3)   began such study or training before attaining that age (s 63A(4)(c) (as so added)),
     s 63A(1) (see also the text and notes 1, 3–9) and s 63A(3) (see the text and notes 10–13) apply
     to the employee, in relation to that study or training, as if s 63A(1)(a) referred to an employee
     aged 16, 17 or 18 (see s 63A(4) (as so added)). For these purposes, 'relevant qualification' means
     an external qualification, the attainment of which:
     (a)   would contribute to the attainment of the standard prescribed for the purposes of
            s 63A(1)(c) (see head (3) in the text) (s 63A(2)(c)(i) (as so added)); and
     (b)   would be likely to enhance the employee's employment prospects (whether with his
            employer or otherwise) (s 63A(2)(c)(ii) (as so added)).
     As to the meaning of 'employer' see PARA 2. For these purposes, 'external qualification' means
     an academic or vocational qualification awarded or authenticated by a person or body specified
     in or under regulations made by the Secretary of State: see s 63A(2)(c) (as so added). As to the
     Secretary of State see PARA 5 note 21. As to the making of regulations under the Employment
     Rights Act 1996 generally see PARA 162. Regulations made for the purposes of s 63A(2) and
     s 63A(1)(c) (see head (3) in the text) may make different provision for different cases and, in
     particular, may make different provision in relation to England and Wales respectively: s 63A(6)
     (as so added). In exercise of the power conferred by s 63A, the Secretary of State has made the
     Right to Time Off for Study or Training Regulations 2001, SI 2001/2801, which came into force
     on 1 September 2001 and applied in relation to any employee who ordinarily worked in
     England or Wales (now applicable in Wales only) (see reg 1(1), (2)). Accordingly, for the
     purposes of the Employment Rights Act 1996 s 63A(2)(c), the qualification-awarding bodies are
     those prescribed in the Right to Time Off for Study or Training Regulations 2001,
     SI 2001/2801, reg 4, Schedule (Schedule amended by SI 2010/1172). As to Scotland see the
     Right to Time Off for Study or Training (Scotland) Regulations 1999, SI 1999/1058.

3   For these purposes, 'secondary education' has the same meaning as in the Education Act 1996
     (see EDUCATION vol 35 (2011) PARA 20): see the Employment Rights Act 1996 s 63A(2)(a)(i) (as
     added: see note 1).

4   For these purposes, 'further education' has the same meaning as in the Education Act 1996 (see
     EDUCATION vol 35 (2011) PARA 22): see the Employment Rights Act 1996 s 63A(2)(b)(i) (s 63A
     as added (see note 1); s 63A(2)(b)(i) amended by the Learning and Skills Act 2000 s 149, Sch 9
     paras 1, 50).

5   Employment Rights Act 1996 s 63A(1)(b) (as added: see note 1).

6   Employment Rights Act 1996 s 63A(1)(c) (as added: see note 1). As to regulations made for the
     purposes of s 63A(1)(c) see note 2. Accordingly, for the purposes of s 63A(1), the standard of
     achievement is that prescribed in the Right to Time Off for Study or Training Regulations 2001,
     SI 2001/2801, reg 3.

7   For these purposes, the working hours of an employee are to be taken to be any time when, in
     accordance with his contract of employment, the employee is required to be at work: see the
     Employment Rights Act 1996 s 63A(8) (as added: see note 1). As to the meaning of 'contract of
     employment' see PARA 2.

8   For these purposes, references to study or training are references to study or training on the premises of the employer or, as the case may be, the principal or elsewhere: see the Employment Rights Act 1996 s 63A(7) (as added: see note 1).

9   See the Employment Rights Act 1996 s 63A(1) (as added: see note 1). An employer is not liable under ss 88, 89 (see PARAS 738, 739) to make any payment in respect of a period of time so taken: see PARA 741. As to the right of complaint to an employment tribunal see PARA 332.

10   See the Employment Rights Act 1996 s 63A(3) (as added: see note 1). See note 2. As to agency work relationships, where the status of the worker as against the agency is typically not that of employee, see PARA 95 et seq.

11   Employment Rights Act 1996 s 63A(3)(a) (as added: see note 1). See note 2.

12   Employment Rights Act 1996 s 63A(3)(b) (as added: see note 1). See note 2.

13   See the Employment Rights Act 1996 s 63A(3) (as added: see note 1). See note 2.

14   See the Employment Rights Act 1996 s 63A(5) (as added: see note 1).

15   Employment Rights Act 1996 s 63A(5)(a) (as added: see note 1).

16   As to the meaning of 'business' see PARA 135 note 4.

17   Employment Rights Act 1996 s 63A(5)(b) (as added: see note 1).

18   Ie under the Employment Rights Act 1996 s 63A (see the text and notes 1–17): see s 63B(1) (s 63B added by the Teaching and Higher Education Act 1998 s 33).

19   Employment Rights Act 1996 s 63B(1) (as added: see note 18). The appropriate hourly rate, in relation to an employee, is the amount of one week's pay divided by the number of normal working hours in a week for that employee when employed under the contract of employment in force on the day when the time off is taken: s 63B(2) (as so added). Where, however, the number of normal working hours differs from week to week or over a longer period, the amount of one week's pay is to be divided instead by:

    (1)   the average number of normal working hours calculated by dividing by 12 the total number of the employee's working hours during the period of 12 weeks ending with the last complete week before the day on which the time off is taken (s 63B(3)(a) (as so added)); or

    (2)   where the employee has not been employed for a sufficient period to enable the calculation to be made under head (1) above, a number which fairly represents the number of normal working hours in a week, having regard to such of the following considerations as are appropriate in the circumstances (see s 63B(3)(b) (as so added)): (a) the average number of normal working hours in a week which the employee could expect in accordance with the terms of his contract (s 63B(4)(a) (as so added)); and (b) the average number of normal working hours of other employees engaged in relevant comparable employment with the same employer (s 63B(4)(b) (as so added)).

As to the calculation of a week's pay and normal working hours see PARA 142 et seq. As to the meaning of 'week' see PARA 126 note 13.

20   Ie a right to any amount under the Employment Rights Act 1996 s 63B(1) (see the text and notes 18–19): see s 63B(5) (as added: see note 18).

21   Employment Rights Act 1996 s 63B(5) (as added: see note 18). However, any contractual remuneration paid to an employee in respect of a period of time off under s 63A (see the text and notes 1–17) goes towards discharging any liability of the employer to pay remuneration under s 63B(1) (see the text and notes 18–19) in respect of that period; and, conversely, any payment of remuneration under s 63B(1) in respect of a period goes towards discharging any liability of the employer to pay contractual remuneration in respect of that period: s 63B(6) (as so added).

332.   Complaint to employment tribunal: employee's right to time off for education or training.   An employee[1] may present a complaint to an employment tribunal[2] that[3]:

    (1)   his employer[4], or the principal[5], has unreasonably refused to permit him to take time off[6] for study or training[7]; or

    (2)   his employer has failed to pay the whole or any part of any amount to which the employee is[8] entitled as remuneration for time so taken[9].

An employment tribunal must not consider such a complaint, however, unless it is presented[10]:

    (a)   before the end of the period of three months beginning with the day on which the time off was taken or on which it is alleged the time off should have been permitted[11]; or

(b)   within such further period as the tribunal considers reasonable in a case where it is satisfied that it was not reasonably practicable for the complaint to be presented before the end of that period of three months[12].

Where an employment tribunal finds such a complaint well-founded, it must make a declaration to that effect[13]; and:

(i)   if the complaint is that the employer or principal has unreasonably refused to permit the employee to take time off, the tribunal must also order the employer or the principal, as the case may be, to pay to the employee an amount equal to the remuneration to which he would have been entitled[14] if the employer or principal had not refused[15];

(ii)   if the complaint is that the employer has failed to pay the employee the whole or part of any amount to which he is entitled[16], the tribunal must also order the employer to pay to the employee the amount which it finds due to him[17].

1   As to the meaning of 'employee' see PARA 2.
2   As to employment tribunals see PARA 1399 et seq; and as to the procedure on a complaint made to an employment tribunal see PARA 1453 et seq.
3   See the Employment Rights Act 1996 s 63C(1) (s 63C added by the Teaching and Higher Education Act 1998 s 33).
4   As to the meaning of 'employer' see PARA 2.
5   Ie the principal referred to in the Employment Rights Act 1996 s 63A(3) (see PARA 331): see s 63C(1)(a) (as added: see note 3).
6   Ie as required by the Employment Rights Act 1996 s 63A (see PARA 331): see s 63C(1)(a) (as added: see note 3).
7   Employment Rights Act 1996 s 63C(1)(a) (as added: see note 3).The remedy of an employee for infringement of any right conferred on him by s 63A is by way of complaint to an employment tribunal and not otherwise: see s 205(1); and PARA 1406.
8   Ie under the Employment Rights Act 1996 s 63B (see PARA 331): see s 63C(1)(b) (as added: see note 3).
9   Employment Rights Act 1996 s 63C(1)(b) (as added: see note 3).The remedy of an employee for infringement of any right conferred on him by s 63B is by way of complaint to an employment tribunal and not otherwise: see s 205(1); and PARA 1406.
10   See the Employment Rights Act 1996 s 63C(2) (as added: see note 3).
11   Employment Rights Act 1996 s 63C(2)(a) (as added: see note 3). For the purposes of s 63C(2)(a), s 207A(3) (extension because mediation in certain European cross-border disputes starts before the time limit expires: see PARA 1454) and s 207B (extension of time limits to facilitate conciliation before institution of proceedings: see PARA 1455) apply: s 63C(2A) (s 63C as so added; s 63C(2A) added by SI 2011/1133; and amended by the Enterprise and Regulatory Reform Act 2013 s 8, Sch 2 paras 15, 27). As to time limits generally see PARA 1453.
12   Employment Rights Act 1996 s 63C(2)(b) (as added: see note 3).
13   See the Employment Rights Act 1996 s 63C(3) (as added: see note 3).
14   Ie under the Employment Rights Act 1996 s 63B (see PARA 331): see s 63C(4) (as added: see note 3).
15   See the Employment Rights Act 1996 s 63C(4) (as added: see note 3).
16   Ie under the Employment Rights Act 1996 s 63B (see PARA 331): see s 63C(5) (as added: see note 3).
17   See the Employment Rights Act 1996 s 63C(5) (as added: see note 3).

(iv)   Ante-natal Care

A. EMPLOYEES

333.   Employee's right to time off work for ante-natal care.   An employee[1] who:

(1)   is pregnant[2]; and

(2)   has, on the advice of a registered medical practitioner[3], registered

midwife[4] or registered nurse[5], made an appointment to attend at any place for the purpose of receiving ante-natal care[6],

is entitled to be permitted by her employer[7] to take time off during her working hours[8] in order to enable her to keep the appointment[9].

An employee is not, however, entitled to take time off in this way to keep an appointment unless, if her employer requests her to do so, she produces for his inspection[10]:

(a)   a certificate from a registered medical practitioner, registered midwife or registered nurse stating that the employee is pregnant[11]; and

(b)   an appointment card or some other document showing that the appointment has been made[12].

However, these requirements to produce documentation[13] do not apply where the employee's appointment is the first appointment during her pregnancy for which she seeks permission to take[14] time off[15].

An employee who is permitted to take time off work for ante-natal care[16] is entitled to be paid remuneration by her employer for the period of absence at the appropriate hourly rate[17]; and a right to any such amount[18] does not affect any right of an employee in relation to remuneration under her contract of employment ('contractual remuneration')[19].

1   As to the meaning of 'employee' see PARA 2.
2   Employment Rights Act 1996 s 55(1)(a).
3   As to the meaning of 'registered medical practitioner' see MEDICAL PROFESSIONS vol 74 (2011) PARA 176.
4   As to the meaning of 'registered', in relation to midwives, see MEDICAL PROFESSIONS vol 74 (2011) PARA 713.
5   For these purposes, references to a registered nurse are references to such a nurse:
    (1)   who is also registered in the Specialist Community Public Health Nurses' part of the register maintained under the Nursing and Midwifery Order 2001, SI 2002/253, art 5 (see MEDICAL PROFESSIONS vol 74 (2011) PARA 713) (Employment Rights Act 1996 s 55(5)(a) (s 55(5) added by SI 2004/1771)); and
    (2)   whose entry in that part of the register is annotated to show that the nurse holds a qualification in health visiting (Employment Rights Act 1996 s 55(5)(b) (as so added)).
6   Employment Rights Act 1996 s 55(1)(b) (s 55(1)(b), (2)(a) amended by SI 2002/253).
7   As to the meaning of 'employer' see PARA 2.
8   For these purposes, the working hours of an employee are to be taken to be any time when, in accordance with her contract of employment, she is required to be at work: Employment Rights Act 1996 s 55(4). The rights conferred by s 55 and s 56 (see also the text and notes 1–7, 9–19) do not apply to a share fisherman (see s 199(2); and PARA 167) or to a police officer (see s 200(1); and PARA 168), and may also be lost for some other reason than statutory exclusion, in particular because the contract of employment is illegal (see PARA 18) or has terminated for some reason other than dismissal (see PARA 725 et seq). As to the meaning of 'contract of employment' see PARA 2.
9   Employment Rights Act 1996 s 55(1). An employer is not liable under ss 88, 89 (see PARAS 738, 739) to make any payment in respect of a period of time so taken: see PARA 741. There may be circumstances where it is reasonable to refuse time off, if the employee can reasonably be expected to make arrangements outside normal working hours: *Gregory v Tudsbury Ltd* [1982] IRLR 267. As to the right of complaint to an employment tribunal see PARA 334.
10 See the Employment Rights Act 1996 s 55(2).
11 Employment Rights Act 1996 s 55(2)(a) (as amended: see note 6).
12 Employment Rights Act 1996 s 55(2)(b).
13 Ie the provisions of the Employment Rights Act 1996 s 55(2) (see the text and notes 10–12): see s 55(3).
14 Ie in accordance with the Employment Rights Act 1996 s 55(1) (see the text and notes 1–9): see s 55(3).
15 Employment Rights Act 1996 s 55(3).
16 Ie under the Employment Rights Act 1996 s 55 (see the text and notes 1–15): see s 56(1).
17 Employment Rights Act 1996 s 56(1). The appropriate hourly rate, in relation to an employee, is the amount of one week's pay divided by the number of normal working hours in a week for

that employee when employed under the contract of employment in force on the day when the time off is taken: s 56(2). Where, however, the number of normal working hours differs from week to week or over a longer period, the amount of one week's pay is to be divided instead by:

(1) the average number of normal working hours calculated by dividing by 12 the total number of the employee's working hours during the period of 12 weeks ending with the last complete week before the day on which the time off is taken (s 56(3)(a)); or

(2) where the employee has not been employed for a sufficient period to enable the calculation to be made under head (1) above, a number which fairly represents the number of normal working hours in a week, having regard to such of the following considerations as are appropriate in the circumstances (see s 56(3)(b)): (a) the average number of normal working hours in a week which the employee could expect in accordance with the terms of her contract (s 56(4)(a)); and (b) the average number of normal working hours of other employees engaged in relevant comparable employment with the same employer (s 56(4)(b)).

As to the calculation of a week's pay and normal working hours see PARA 142 et seq. As to the meaning of 'week' see PARA 126 note 13. As to the right of complaint to an employment tribunal see PARA 334.

If an employer allows the employee time off in accordance with s 55, he thereby accepts that it was reasonable for her to have such time off and is, therefore, obliged to pay her for it: *Gregory v Tudsbury Ltd* [1982] IRLR 267.

18 Ie a right to any amount under the Employment Rights Act 1996 s 56(1) (see the text and notes 16–17): see s 56(5).

19 Employment Rights Act 1996 s 56(5). However, any contractual remuneration paid to an employee in respect of a period of time off under s 55 (see the text and notes 1–15) goes towards discharging any liability of the employer to pay remuneration under s 56(1) (see the text and notes 16–17) in respect of that period; and, conversely, any payment of remuneration under s 56(1) in respect of a period goes towards discharging any liability of the employer to pay contractual remuneration in respect of that period: s 56(6).

334. Complaint to employment tribunal: employee's right to time off work for ante-natal care. An employee[1] may present a complaint to an employment tribunal[2] that her employer[3]:

(1) has unreasonably refused to permit her to take time off[4] for ante-natal care[5]; or

(2) has failed to pay the whole or any part of any amount to which she is[6] entitled as remuneration for time so taken[7].

An employment tribunal must not consider such a complaint, however, unless it is presented[8]:

(a) before the end of the period of three months beginning with the date of the appointment concerned[9]; or

(b) within such further period as the tribunal considers reasonable in a case where it is satisfied that it was not reasonably practicable for the complaint to be presented before the end of that period of three months[10].

Where an employment tribunal finds such a complaint well-founded, it must make a declaration to that effect[11]; and:

(i) if the complaint is that the employer has unreasonably refused to permit the employee to take time off, the tribunal must also order the employer to pay to the employee an amount that is twice the amount of the remuneration to which she would have been entitled[12] if the employer had not refused[13];

(ii) if the complaint is that the employer has failed to pay the employee the whole or part of any amount to which she is entitled[14], the tribunal must also order the employer to pay to the employee the amount which it finds due to her[15].

1 As to the meaning of 'employee' see PARA 2.

2   As to employment tribunals see PARA 1399 et seq; and as to the procedure on a complaint made to an employment tribunal see PARA 1453 et seq.

3   See the Employment Rights Act 1996 s 57(1) (s 57(1), (2), (3) amended by the Employment Rights (Dispute Resolution) Act 1998 s 1(2)(a)). As to the meaning of 'employer' see PARA 2.

     The remedy of an employee for infringement of any right conferred on her by the Employment Rights Act 1996 ss 55–56 (see PARA 333) is by way of complaint to an employment tribunal and not otherwise: see s 205(1); and PARA 1406. The right conferred by s 57 does not apply to a share fisherman (see s 199(2); and PARA 167) or to a police officer (see s 200(1); and PARA 168), and may also be lost for some other reason than statutory exclusion, in particular because the contract of employment is illegal (see PARA 18) or has terminated for some reason other than dismissal (see PARA 725 et seq).

4   Ie as required by the Employment Rights Act 1996 s 55 (see PARA 333): see s 57(1)(a).

5   Employment Rights Act 1996 s 57(1)(a).

6   Ie under the Employment Rights Act 1996 s 56 (see PARA 333): see s 57(1)(b).

7   Employment Rights Act 1996 s 57(1)(b).

8   See the Employment Rights Act 1996 s 57(2) (as amended : see note 3).

9   Employment Rights Act 1996 s 57(2)(a). For the purposes of s 57(2)(a), s 207A(3) (extension because mediation in certain European cross-border disputes starts before the time limit expires: see PARA 1454) and s 207B (extension of time limits to facilitate conciliation before institution of proceedings: see PARA 1455) apply: s 57(2A) (added by SI 2011/1133; and amended by the Enterprise and Regulatory Reform Act 2013 s 8, Sch 2 paras 15, 22). As to time limits generally see PARA 1453.

10   Employment Rights Act 1996 s 57(2)(b).

11   See the Employment Rights Act 1996 s 57(3) (as amended: see note 3).

12   Ie under the Employment Rights Act 1996 s 56 (see PARA 333): see s 57(4).

13   See the Employment Rights Act 1996 s 57(4) (amended by the Children and Families Act 2014 s 130(1)).

14   Ie under the Employment Rights Act 1996 s 56 (see PARA 333): see s 57(5).

15   See the Employment Rights Act 1996 s 57(5).

335. Employee's right to time off work to accompany woman to ante-natal appointments.

An employee[1] who has a qualifying relationship with a pregnant woman or her expected child[2] is entitled to be permitted by his or her employer[3] to take time off during the employee's working hours[4] in order that he or she may accompany the woman when she attends by appointment at any place for the purpose of receiving ante-natal care[5].

An employee is not, however, entitled to take time off for the purpose of accompanying an woman to keep such an appointment unless the appointment is made on the advice of a registered medical practitioner[6], registered midwife[7] or registered nurse[8]; and, where the employer requests the employee to give the employer a declaration signed by the employee, the employee is not entitled to take time off for that purpose unless she gives that declaration (which may be given in electronic form)[9].

1   As to the meaning of 'employee' see PARA 2.

2   For these purposes, a person has a qualifying relationship with a pregnant woman or her expected child if:

     (1)   the person is the husband or civil partner of the pregnant woman (Employment Rights Act 1996 s 57ZE(7)(a) (s 57ZE added by the Children and Families Act 2014 s 127(1)));

     (2)   the person, being of a different sex or the same sex, lives with the woman in an enduring family relationship but is not a relative of the woman (Employment Rights Act 1996 s 57ZE(7)(b) (as so added));

     (3)   the person is the father of the expected child (s 57ZE(7)(c) (as so added));

     (4)   the person is a parent of the expected child by virtue of the Human Fertilisation and Embryology Act 2008 s 42 (cases in which woman to be other parent (woman in civil partnership or marriage to a woman at time of treatment): see CHILDREN AND YOUNG PERSONS vol 9 (2012) PARA 126) or s 43 (cases in which woman to be other parent

(treatment provided to woman who agrees that second woman to be parent): see CHILDREN AND YOUNG PERSONS vol 9 (2012) PARA 126) (Employment Rights Act 1996 s 57ZE(7)(d) (as so added)); or

(5) the person is a potential applicant for a parental order under the Human Fertilisation and Embryology Act 2008 s 54 (parental orders: see CHILDREN AND YOUNG PERSONS vol 9 (2012) PARA 129) in respect of the expected child (Employment Rights Act 1996 s 57ZE(7)(e) (as so added)).

For these purposes, a relative of a person is the person's parent, grandparent, sister, brother, aunt or uncle (s 57ZE(8) (as so added)); and references to such relationships are to relationships of the full blood or half blood or, in the case of an adopted person, such of those relationships as would exist but for the adoption, and they include the relationship of a child with the child's adoptive, or former adoptive, parents, but they do not include any other adoptive relationships (see s 57ZE(9) (as so added)). For the purposes of head (5) above, a person ('A') is a potential applicant for a parental order under the Human Fertilisation and Embryology Act 2008 s 54 in respect of an expected child only if:

(a) A intends to apply, jointly with another person ('B'), for such an order in respect of the expected child within the time allowed by s 54(3) (see CHILDREN AND YOUNG PERSONS vol 9 (2012) PARA 129) (Employment Rights Act 1996 s 57ZE(10)(a) (as so added));

(b) the expected child is being carried by the pregnant woman as a result of such procedure as is described in the Human Fertilisation and Embryology Act 2008 s 54(1)(a) (see CHILDREN AND YOUNG PERSONS vol 9 (2012) PARA 129) (Employment Rights Act 1996 s 57ZE(10)(b) (as so added));

(c) the requirement in the Human Fertilisation and Embryology Act 2008 s 54(1)(b) (see CHILDREN AND YOUNG PERSONS vol 9 (2012) PARA 129) is satisfied by reference to A or B (Employment Rights Act 1996 s 57ZE(10)(c) (as so added));

(d) A and B would satisfy the Human Fertilisation and Embryology Act 2008 s 54(2) (see CHILDREN AND YOUNG PERSONS vol 9 (2012) PARA 129) if they made an application under s 54 at the time that A seeks to exercise the right under the Employment Rights Act 1996 s 57E (see s 57ZE(10)(d) (as so added)); and

(e) A expects that A and B will satisfy the conditions in the Human Fertilisation and Embryology Act 2008 s 54(2), (4), (5), (8) (see CHILDREN AND YOUNG PERSONS vol 9 (2012) PARA 129) as regards the intended application (Employment Rights Act 1996 s 57ZE(10)(e) (as so added)).

3 As to the meaning of 'employer' see PARA 2.

4 For these purposes, the working hours of an employee are to be taken to be any time when, in accordance with her contract of employment, she is required to be at work: Employment Rights Act 1996 s 57ZE(12) (as added: see note 2). As to the meaning of 'contract of employment' see PARA 2.

5 Employment Rights Act 1996 s 57ZE(1) (as added: see note 2). In relation to any particular pregnancy, an employee is not entitled to take time off for the purpose specified in s 57ZE(1) on more than two occasions, however (s 57ZE(2) (as so added)); and, on each of those occasions, the maximum time off during working hours to which the employee is entitled is six and a half hours (s 57ZE(3) (as so added)). As to the right of complaint to an employment tribunal see PARA 336. An employee taking time off under s 57ZE is protected from suffering detriment in employment on that account (see PARA 620); and dismissal on that ground is automatically unfair (see PARA 784).

6 As to the meaning of 'registered medical practitioner' see MEDICAL PROFESSIONS vol 74 (2011) PARA 176.

7 As to the meaning of 'registered', in relation to midwives, see MEDICAL PROFESSIONS vol 74 (2011) PARA 713.

8 Employment Rights Act 1996 s 57ZE(4) (as added: see note 2). For these purposes, references to a registered nurse are references to such a nurse:

(1) who is also registered in the Specialist Community Public Health Nurses' part of the register maintained under the Nursing and Midwifery Order 2001, SI 2002/253, art 5 (see MEDICAL PROFESSIONS vol 74 (2011) PARA 713) (Employment Rights Act 1996 s 57ZE(11)(a) (as so added)); and

(2) whose entry in that part of the register is annotated to show that the nurse holds a qualification in health visiting (s 57ZE(11)(b) (as so added)).

9 Employment Rights Act 1996 s 57ZE(5) (as added: see note 2). The employee must state in the declaration: (1) that the employee has a qualifying relationship with a pregnant woman or her expected child (s 57ZE(6)(a) (as so added)); (2) that the employee's purpose in taking time off is the purpose specified in s 57E(1) (see the text and notes 1–5) (s 57ZE(6)(b) (as so added)); (3)

that the appointment in question is made on the advice of a registered medical practitioner, registered midwife or registered nurse (s 57ZE(6)(c) (as so added)); and (4) the date and time of the appointment (s 57ZE(6)(d) (as so added)).

336.   Complaint to employment tribunal: employee's right to time off work to accompany woman to ante-natal appointments.   An employee[1] may present a complaint to an employment tribunal[2] that his or her employer[3] has unreasonably refused to let him or her to take time off work[4] to accompany a woman to ante-natal appointments[5].

An employment tribunal must not consider such a complaint, however, unless it is presented[6]:

(1)   before the end of the period of three months beginning with the day of the appointment in question[7]; or

(2)   within such further period as the tribunal considers reasonable in a case where it is satisfied that it was not reasonably practicable for the complaint to be presented before the end of that period of three months[8].

Where an employment tribunal finds such a complaint well-founded, it must:

(a)   make a declaration to that effect[9]; and

(b)   order the employer to pay to the employee an amount determined in accordance with the statutory formula[10].

1   As to the meaning of 'employee' see PARA 2.
2   As to employment tribunals see PARA 1399 et seq; and as to the procedure on a complaint made to an employment tribunal see PARA 1453 et seq.
3   As to the meaning of 'employer' see PARA 2.
4   Ie as required by the Employment Rights Act 1996 s 57ZE (see PARA 335): see s 57ZF(1) (s 57ZF added by the Children and Families Act 2014 s 127(1)).
5   See the Employment Rights Act 1996 s 57ZF(1) (as added: see note 4). As to the meaning of 'employer' see PARA 2.
6   See the Employment Rights Act 1996 s 57ZF(2) (as added: see note 4).
7   Employment Rights Act 1996 s 57ZF(2)(a) (as added: see note 4). For the purposes of s 57ZF(2)(a), s 207A(3) (extension because mediation in certain European cross-border disputes starts before the time limit expires: see PARA 1454) and s 207B (extension of time limits to facilitate conciliation before institution of proceedings: see PARA 1455) apply: s 57ZF(3) (as so added). As to time limits generally see PARA 1453.
8   Employment Rights Act 1996 s 57ZF(2)(b) (as added: see note 4).
9   See the Employment Rights Act 1996 s 57ZF(4)(a) (as added: see note 4).
10 See the Employment Rights Act 1996 s 57ZF(4)(b) (as added: see note 4).The text refers to the amount payable to the employee to be determined according to the formula:

$$(A \times B) \times 2$$

where A is the appropriate hourly rate for the employee; and B is the number of working hours for which the employee would have been entitled under s 57ZE (see PARA 335) to be absent if the time off had not been refused: see s 57ZF(5) (as so added). The appropriate hourly rate, in relation to an employee, is the amount of one week's pay divided by the number of normal working hours in a week for that employee when employed under the contract of employment in force on the day when the time off would have been taken: s 57ZF(6) (as so added). Where, however, the number of normal working hours differs from week to week or over a longer period, the amount of one week's pay is to be divided instead by:

(1)   the average number of normal working hours calculated by dividing by 12 the total number of the employee's working hours during the period of 12 weeks ending with the last complete week before the day on which the time off would have been taken (s 56ZF(7)(a) (as so added)); or

(2)   where the employee has not been employed for a sufficient period to enable the calculation to be made under head (1) above, a number which fairly represents the number of normal working hours in a week, having regard to such of the following considerations as are appropriate in the circumstances (see s 56ZF(7)(b) (as so added)):

(a) the average number of normal working hours in a week which the employee could expect in accordance with the terms of his or her contract (s 56ZF(8)(a) (as so added)); and (b) the average number of normal working hours of other employees engaged in relevant comparable employment with the same employer (s 56ZF(8)(b) (as so added)).

As to the calculation of a week's pay and normal working hours see PARA 142 et seq. As to the meaning of 'week' see PARA 126 note 13.

B. AGENCY WORKERS

337. Agency worker's right to time off work for ante-natal care. An agency worker[1] who:

(1)   is pregnant[2]; and

(2)   has, on the advice of a registered medical practitioner[3], registered midwife[4] or registered nurse[5], made an appointment to attend at any place for the purpose of receiving ante-natal care[6],

is entitled to be permitted, by the temporary work agency and the hirer, to take time off during her working hours[7] in order to enable her to keep the appointment[8].

An agency worker is not, however, entitled to be permitted, by either the temporary work agency or the hirer, to take time off in this way to keep an appointment unless (if either the temporary work agency or the hirer requests her to do so) she produces for the inspection of either one[9]:

(a)   a certificate from a registered medical practitioner, registered midwife or registered nurse stating that the agency worker is pregnant[10]; and

(b)   an appointment card or some other document showing that the appointment has been made[11].

However, these requirements to produce documentation[12] do not apply where the agency worker's appointment is the first appointment during her pregnancy for which she seeks permission to take[13] time off[14].

An agency worker who is permitted to take time off work for ante-natal care[15] is entitled to be paid remuneration by the temporary work agency for the period of absence at the appropriate hourly rate[16]; and a right to any such amount[17] does not affect any right of an agency worker in relation to remuneration under her contract with the temporary work agency ('contractual remuneration')[18].

1   As to the meaning of 'agency worker' see PARA 97; definition in the Agency Workers Regulations 2010, SI 2010/93, reg 3, applied by the Employment Rights Act 1996 s 57ZD(4) (ss 57ZA, 57ZB, 57ZD added by SI 2010/93). The provision made by the Employment Rights Act 1996 ss 57ZA, 57ZB does not apply where ss 55, 56 apply (employee's right to time off work for ante-natal care: see PARA 333): see s 57ZD(3) (as so added). Nor, without prejudice to any other duties of the hirer or temporary work agency under any enactment or rule of law, does the provision made by ss 57ZA, 57ZB apply where the agency worker:

(1)   has not completed the qualifying period (s 57ZD(1)(a) (as so added)); or

(2)   is no longer entitled to the rights conferred by the Agency Workers Regulations 2010, SI 2010/93, reg 5 (basic working and employment conditions: see PARA 98), pursuant to reg 8(a), (b) (break between assignments: see PARA 99) (Employment Rights Act 1996 s 57ZD(1)(b) (as so added)).

Nor does anything in ss 57ZA, 57ZB impose a duty on the hirer or temporary work agency beyond the original intended duration, or likely duration of the assignment, whichever is the longer: s 57ZD(2) (as so added). As to the meaning of 'assignment' see PARA 99 note 4; definition in the Agency Workers Regulations 2010, SI 2010/93, reg 2, applied by the Employment Rights Act 1996 s 57ZD(4) (as so added). As to the meaning of 'hirer' see PARA 97 note 3; definition in the Agency Workers Regulations 2010, SI 2010/93, reg 2, applied by the Employment Rights Act 1996 s 57ZD(4) (as so added). As to the meaning of 'qualifying period' see PARA 99; definition in the Agency Workers Regulations 2010, SI 2010/93, reg 7, applied by the Employment Rights Act 1996 s 57ZD(4) (as so added). As to the meaning of 'temporary work agency' see PARA 97; definition in the Agency Workers Regulations 2010, SI 2010/93, reg 4, applied by the Employment Rights Act 1996 s 57ZD(4) (as so added).

2   Employment Rights Act 1996 s 57ZA(1)(a) (as added: see note 1).
3   As to the meaning of 'registered medical practitioner' see MEDICAL PROFESSIONS vol 74 (2011) PARA 176.
4   As to the meaning of 'registered', in relation to midwives, see MEDICAL PROFESSIONS vol 74 (2011) PARA 713.
5   As to the meaning of references to a registered nurse for these purposes see PARA 333 note 5; definition in the Employment Rights Act 1996 s 55(5) applied by the Employment Rights Act 1996 s 57ZA(5) (as added: see note 1).
6   Employment Rights Act 1996 s 57ZA(1)(b) (as added: see note 1).
7   For these purposes, the working hours of an agency worker are to be taken to be any time when, in accordance with the terms under which the agency worker works temporarily for and under the supervision and direction of the hirer, the agency worker is to be at work: Employment Rights Act 1996 s 57ZA(4) (as added: see note 1).
8   Employment Rights Act 1996 s 57ZA(1) (as added: see note 1). As to the right of complaint to an employment tribunal see PARA 334. An agency worker taking time off under s 57ZA is protected from suffering detriment in employment on that account: see PARA 620.
9   See the Employment Rights Act 1996 s 57ZA(2) (as added: see note 1).
10 Employment Rights Act 1996 s 57ZA(2)(a) (as added: see note 1).
11 Employment Rights Act 1996 s 57ZA(2)(b) (as added: see note 1).
12 Ie the provisions of the Employment Rights Act 1996 s 57ZA(2) (see the text and notes 9–11): see s 57ZA(3) (as added: see note 1).
13 Ie in accordance with the Employment Rights Act 1996 s 57ZA(1) (see the text and notes 1–8): see s 57ZA(3) (as added: see note 1).
14 Employment Rights Act 1996 s 57ZA(3) (as added: see note 1).
15 Ie under the Employment Rights Act 1996 s 57ZA (see the text and notes 1–14): see s 57ZB(1) (as added: see note 1).
16 Employment Rights Act 1996 s 57ZB(1) (as added: see note 1). The appropriate hourly rate, in relation to an agency worker, is the amount of one week's pay divided by the number of normal working hours in a week for that agency worker, in accordance with the terms under which the agency worker works temporarily for and under the supervision and direction of the hirer, that are in force on the day when the time off is taken: s 57ZB(2) (as so added). Where, however, the number of normal working hours during the assignment differs from week to week or over a longer period, the amount of one week's pay is to be divided instead by the average number of normal working hours calculated by dividing by 12 the total number of the agency worker's normal working hours during the period of 12 weeks ending with the last complete week before the day on which the time off is taken: s 57ZB(3) (as so added).
    As to the calculation of a week's pay and normal working hours see PARA 142 et seq. As to the meaning of 'week' see PARA 126 note 13.
17 Ie a right to any amount under the Employment Rights Act 1996 s 57ZB(1) (see the text and notes 15–16): see s 57ZB(4) (as added: see note 1).
18 Employment Rights Act 1996 s 57ZB(4) (as added: see note 1). However, any contractual remuneration paid to an agency worker in respect of a period of time off under s 57ZA (see the text and notes 1–14) goes towards discharging any liability of the temporary work agency to pay remuneration under s 57ZB(1) (see the text and notes 15–16) in respect of that period; and, conversely, any payment of remuneration under s 57ZB(1) in respect of a period goes towards discharging any liability of the temporary work agency to pay contractual remuneration in respect of that period: s 57ZB(5) (as so added). An agency worker receiving remuneration under s 57ZB is protected from suffering detriment in employment on that account: see PARA 620.

338.   Complaint to employment tribunal: agency worker's right to time off work for ante-natal care. An agency worker[1] may present a complaint to an employment tribunal[2] that:

(1)   the temporary work agency has unreasonably refused to permit her to take time off[4] for ante-natal care[5]; or

(2)   the temporary work agency has failed to pay the whole or any part of any amount to which she is[6] entitled as remuneration for time so taken[7]; or

(3)   the hirer has unreasonably refused to permit her to take time off[8] for ante-natal care[9].

An employment tribunal must not consider such complaint under any of heads (1) to (3) above, however, unless it is presented[10]:

(a)   before the end of the period of three months beginning with the date of the appointment concerned[11]; or

(b)   within such further period as the tribunal considers reasonable in a case where it is satisfied that it was not reasonably practicable for the complaint to be presented before the end of that period of three months[12].

Where an employment tribunal finds such a complaint well-founded, it must make a declaration to that effect[13]; and:

(i)   if the complaint is that the temporary work agency or the hirer has unreasonably refused to permit the agency worker to take time off, the tribunal must also order payment to the agency worker of an amount that is twice the amount of the remuneration to which she would have been entitled[14] if she had not been refused the time off[15];

(ii)   if the complaint is that the temporary work agency has failed to pay the agency worker the whole or part of any amount to which she is entitled[16], the tribunal must also order the temporary work agency to pay to the agency worker the amount which it finds due to her[17].

1   As to the meaning of 'agency worker' see PARA 97; definition in the Agency Workers Regulations 2010, SI 2010/93, reg 3, applied by the Employment Rights Act 1996 s 57ZD(4) (ss 57ZC, 57ZD added by SI 2010/93). The provision made by the Employment Rights Act 1996 s 57ZC does not apply where s 57 applies (complaint to employment tribunal (employee's right to time off work for ante-natal care): see PARA 334): see s 57ZD(3) (as so added). Nor, without prejudice to any other duties of the hirer or temporary work agency under any enactment or rule of law, does the provision made by s 57ZC apply where the agency worker:

    (1)   has not completed the qualifying period (s 57ZD(1)(a) (as so added)); or
    (2)   is no longer entitled to the rights conferred by the Agency Workers Regulations 2010, SI 2010/93, reg 5 (basic working and employment conditions: see PARA 98), pursuant to reg 8(a), (b) (break between assignments: see PARA 99) (Employment Rights Act 1996 s 57ZD(1)(b) (as so added)).

    Nor does anything in s 57ZC impose a duty on the hirer or temporary work agency beyond the original intended duration, or likely duration of the assignment, whichever is the longer: s 57ZD(2) (as so added). As to the meaning of 'assignment' see PARA 99 note 4; definition in the Agency Workers Regulations 2010, SI 2010/93, reg 2, applied by the Employment Rights Act 1996 s 57ZD(4) (as so added). As to the meaning of 'hirer' see PARA 97 note 3; definition in the Agency Workers Regulations 2010, SI 2010/93, reg 2, applied by the Employment Rights Act 1996 s 57ZD(4) (as so added). As to the meaning of 'qualifying period' see PARA 99; definition in the Agency Workers Regulations 2010, SI 2010/93, reg 7, applied by the Employment Rights Act 1996 s 57ZD(4) (as so added). As to the meaning of 'temporary work agency' see PARA 97; definition in the Agency Workers Regulations 2010, SI 2010/93, reg 4, applied by the Employment Rights Act 1996 s 57ZD(4) (as so added).

2   As to employment tribunals see PARA 1399 et seq; and as to the procedure on a complaint made to an employment tribunal see PARA 1453 et seq.

3   See the Employment Rights Act 1996 s 57ZC(1) (as added: see note 1). As to the meaning of 'employer' see PARA 2.

4   Ie as required by the Employment Rights Act 1996 s 57ZA (see PARA 337): see s 57ZC(1)(a) (as added: see note 1).

5   Employment Rights Act 1996 s 57ZC(1)(a) (as added: see note 1).

6   Ie under the Employment Rights Act 1996 s 57ZB (see PARA 337): see s 57ZC(1)(b) (as added: see note 1).

7   Employment Rights Act 1996 s 57ZC(1)(b) (as added: see note 1).

8   Ie under the Employment Rights Act 1996 s 57ZA (see PARA 337): see s 57ZC(2) (as added: see note 1).

9   Employment Rights Act 1996 s 57ZC(2) (as added: see note 1).

10   See the Employment Rights Act 1996 s 57ZC(3) (as added: see note 1).

11   Employment Rights Act 1996 s 57ZC(3)(a) (as added: see note 1). For the purposes of s 57ZC(3)(a), s 207A(3) (extension because mediation in certain European cross-border disputes starts before the time limit expires: see PARA 1454) and s 207B (extension of time limits to facilitate conciliation before institution of proceedings: see PARA 1455) apply: s 57ZC(3A) (s 57ZC as so added; s 57ZC(3A) added by the Enterprise and Regulatory Reform Act 2013 s 8, Sch 2 paras 15, 23). As to time limits generally see PARA 1453.

12   Employment Rights Act 1996 s 57ZC(3)(b) (as added: see note 1).

13   See the Employment Rights Act 1996 s 57ZC(4) (as added: see note 1).

14   Ie under the Employment Rights Act 1996 s 57ZB (see PARA 337): see s 57ZC(5) (as added: see note 1).

15   See the Employment Rights Act 1996 s 57ZC(5) (s 57ZC as added (see note 1); s 57ZC(5) amended by the Children and Families Act 2014 s 130(2)). Where the tribunal orders payment under the Employment Rights Act 1996 s 57ZC(5), the amount payable by each party is such as may be found by the tribunal to be just and equitable having regard to the extent of each respondent's responsibility for the infringement to which the complaint relates: s 57ZC(6) (as so added).

16   Ie under the Employment Rights Act 1996 s 57ZB (see PARA 337): see s 57ZC(7) (as added: see note 1).

17   See the Employment Rights Act 1996 s 57ZC(7) (as added: see note 1).

339. Agency worker's right to time off work to accompany woman to ante-natal appointments. An agency worker who has a qualifying relationship with a pregnant woman or her expected child[1] is entitled[2] to be permitted, by the temporary work agency and the hirer, to take time off during the agency worker's working hours[3] in order that he or she may accompany the woman when she attends by appointment at any place for the purpose of receiving ante-natal care[4].

An agency worker is not, however, entitled to take time off for the purpose of accompanying an woman to keep such an appointment unless the appointment is made on the advice of a registered medical practitioner[5], registered midwife[6] or registered nurse[7]; and, where either the temporary work agency or the hirer requests the agency worker to give to that person a declaration signed by the agency worker, the agency worker is not entitled to take time off for that purpose unless she gives that declaration (which may be given in electronic form)[8].

1   For these purposes, a person has a qualifying relationship with a pregnant woman or her expected child if:

    (1)   the person is the husband or civil partner of the pregnant woman (Employment Rights Act 1996 s 57ZG(7)(a) (ss 57ZG, 57ZI added by the Children and Families Act 2014 s 127(1)));

    (2)   the person, being of a different sex or the same sex, lives with the woman in an enduring family relationship but is not a relative of the woman (Employment Rights Act 1996 s 57ZG(7)(b) (as so added));

    (3)   the person is the father of the expected child (s 57ZG(7)(c) (as so added));

    (4)   the person is a parent of the expected child by virtue of the Human Fertilisation and Embryology Act 2008 s 42 (cases in which woman to be other parent (woman in civil partnership or marriage to a woman at time of treatment): see CHILDREN AND YOUNG PERSONS vol 9 (2012) PARA 126) or s 43 (cases in which woman to be other parent (treatment provided to woman who agrees that second woman to be parent): see CHILDREN AND YOUNG PERSONS vol 9 (2012) PARA 126) (Employment Rights Act 1996 s 57ZG(7)(d) (as so added)); or

    (5)   the person is a potential applicant for a parental order under the Human Fertilisation and Embryology Act 2008 s 54 (parental orders: see CHILDREN AND YOUNG PERSONS vol 9 (2012) PARA 129) in respect of the expected child (Employment Rights Act 1996 s 57ZG(7)(e) (as so added)).

For these purposes, a relative of a person is the person's parent, grandparent, sister, brother, aunt or uncle (s 57ZG(8) (as so added)); and references to such relationships are to relationships of the full blood or half blood or, in the case of an adopted person, such of those relationships as would exist but for the adoption, and they include the relationship of a child with the child's adoptive, or former adoptive, parents, but they do not include any other adoptive relationships (see s 57ZG(9) (as so added)). For the purposes of head (5) above, a person ('A') is a potential applicant for a parental order under the Human Fertilisation and Embryology Act 2008 s 54 in respect of an expected child only if:

    (a)   A intends to apply, jointly with another person ('B'), for such an order in respect of the expected child within the time allowed by s 54(3) (see CHILDREN AND YOUNG PERSONS vol 9 (2012) PARA 129) (Employment Rights Act 1996 s 57ZG(10)(a) (as so added));

    (b)   the expected child is being carried by the pregnant woman as a result of such procedure as is described in the Human Fertilisation and Embryology Act 2008 s 54(1)(a) (see CHILDREN AND YOUNG PERSONS vol 9 (2012) PARA 129) (Employment Rights Act 1996 s 57ZG(10)(b) (as so added));

    (c)   the requirement in the Human Fertilisation and Embryology Act 2008 s 54(1)(b) (see CHILDREN AND YOUNG PERSONS vol 9 (2012) PARA 129) is satisfied by reference to A or B (Employment Rights Act 1996 s 57ZG(10)(c) (as so added));

    (d)   A and B would satisfy the Human Fertilisation and Embryology Act 2008 s 54(2) (see CHILDREN AND YOUNG PERSONS vol 9 (2012) PARA 129) if they made an application under s 54 at the time that A seeks to exercise the right under the Employment Rights Act 1996 s 57ZG (see s 57ZG(10)(d) (as so added)); and

    (e)   A expects that A and B will satisfy the conditions in the Human Fertilisation and Embryology Act 2008 s 54(2), (4), (5), (8) (see CHILDREN AND YOUNG PERSONS vol 9 (2012) PARA 129) as regards the intended application (Employment Rights Act 1996 s 57ZG(10)(e) (as so added)).

2   The provision made by the Employment Rights Act 1996 s 57ZG does not apply where s 57ZE applies (employee's right to time off work to accompany woman to ante-natal appointments: see PARA 335): see s 57ZI(3) (as added: see note 1). Nor, without prejudice to any other duties of the hirer or temporary work agency under any enactment or rule of law, does the provision made by the Employment Rights Act 1996 s 57ZG apply where the agency worker:

    (1)   has not completed the qualifying period (s 57ZI(1)(a) (as so added)); or

    (2)   is no longer entitled to the rights conferred by the Agency Workers Regulations 2010, SI 2010/93, reg 5 (basic working and employment conditions: see PARA 98), pursuant to reg 8(a), (b) (break between assignments: see PARA 99) (Employment Rights Act 1996 s 57ZI(1)(b) (as so added)).

Nor does anything in s 57ZG impose a duty on the hirer or temporary work agency beyond the original intended duration, or likely duration of the assignment, whichever is the longer: s 57ZI(2) (as so added). As to the meaning of 'agency worker' see PARA 97; definition in the Agency Workers Regulations 2010, SI 2010/93, reg 3, applied by the Employment Rights Act 1996 s 57ZI(4) (as so added). As to the meaning of 'assignment' see PARA 99 note 4; definition in the Agency Workers Regulations 2010, SI 2010/93, reg 2, applied by the Employment Rights Act 1996 s 57ZI(4) (as so added). As to the meaning of 'hirer' see PARA 97 note 3; definition in the Agency Workers Regulations 2010, SI 2010/93, reg 2, applied by the Employment Rights Act 1996 s 57ZI(4) (as so added). As to the meaning of 'qualifying period' see PARA 99; definition in the Agency Workers Regulations 2010, SI 2010/93, reg 7, applied by the Employment Rights Act 1996 s 57ZI(4) (as so added). As to the meaning of 'temporary work agency' see PARA 97; definition in the Agency Workers Regulations 2010, SI 2010/93, reg 4, applied by the Employment Rights Act 1996 s 57ZI(4) (as so added).

3   For these purposes, the working hours of an agency worker are to be taken to be any time when, in accordance with the terms under which the agency worker works temporarily for and under the supervision and direction of the hirer, the agency worker is to be at work: Employment Rights Act 1996 s 57ZB(12) (as added: see note 1).

4   Employment Rights Act 1996 s 57ZG(1) (as added: see note 1). In relation to any particular pregnancy, an agency worker is not entitled to take time off for the purpose specified in s 57ZG(1) on more than two occasions, however (s 57ZG(2) (as so added)); and, on each of those occasions, the maximum time off during working hours to which the agency worker is entitled is six and a half hours (s 57ZG(3) (as so added)). An agency worker taking time off under s 57ZG is protected from suffering detriment in employment on that account: see PARA 620.

5   As to the meaning of 'registered medical practitioner' see MEDICAL PROFESSIONS vol 74 (2011) PARA 176.

6   As to the meaning of 'registered', in relation to midwives, see MEDICAL PROFESSIONS vol 74 (2011) PARA 713.

7   Employment Rights Act 1996 s 57ZG(4) (as added: see note 1). For these purposes, references to a registered nurse are references to such a nurse:

(1)   who is also registered in the Specialist Community Public Health Nurses' part of the register maintained under the Nursing and Midwifery Order 2001, SI 2002/253, art 5 (see MEDICAL PROFESSIONS vol 74 (2011) PARA 713) (Employment Rights Act 1996 s 57ZG(11)(a) (as so added)); and

(2)   whose entry in that part of the register is annotated to show that the nurse holds a qualification in health visiting (s 57ZG(11)(b) (as so added)).

8   Employment Rights Act 1996 s 57ZG(5) (as added: see note 1). The agency worker must state in the declaration: (1) that the agency worker has a qualifying relationship with a pregnant woman or her expected child (s 57ZG(6)(a) (as so added)); (2) that the agency worker's purpose in taking time off is the purpose specified in s 57ZG(1) (see the text and notes 1–4) (s 57ZG(6)(b) (as so added)); (3) that the appointment in question is made on the advice of a registered medical practitioner, registered midwife or registered nurse (s 57ZG(6)(c) (as so added)); and (4) the date and time of the appointment (s 57ZG(6)(d) (as so added)).

340.   Complaint to employment tribunal: agency worker's right to time off work to accompany woman to ante-natal appointments.   An agency worker may[1] present a complaint to an employment tribunal[2] that:

(1)   the temporary work agency has unreasonably refused to let him or her to take time off work[3] to accompany a woman to ante-natal appointments[4]; or

(2)   the hirer has unreasonably refused to let him or her to take time off work[5] to accompany a woman to ante-natal appointments[6].

An employment tribunal must not consider such a complaint under either head (1) or head (2) above, however, unless it is presented[7]:

(a)   before the end of the period of three months beginning with the day of the appointment in question[8]; or

(b)   within such further period as the tribunal considers reasonable in a case where it is satisfied that it was not reasonably practicable for the complaint to be presented before the end of that period of three months[9].

Where an employment tribunal finds such a complaint under either head (1) or head (2) above well-founded, it must:

(i)   make a declaration to that effect[10]; and

(ii)   order the payment to the agency worker of an amount determined in accordance with the statutory formula[11].

Where the tribunal orders that payment under head (ii) above be made by the temporary work agency and the hirer, the proportion of that amount payable by each respondent is to be such as may be found by the tribunal to be just and equitable having regard to the extent of each respondent's responsibility for the infringement to which the complaint relates[12].

1   The provision made by the Employment Rights Act 1996 s 57ZH does not apply where s 57ZF applies (complaint to employment tribunal (employee's right to time off work to accompany woman to ante-natal appointments): see PARA 336): see s 57ZI(3) (ss 57ZH, 57ZI added by the Children and Families Act 2014 s 127(1)). Nor, without prejudice to any other duties of the hirer or temporary work agency under any enactment or rule of law, does the provision made by the Employment Rights Act 1996 s 57ZH apply where the agency worker:

(1)   has not completed the qualifying period (s 57ZI(1)(a) (as so added)); or

(2)   is no longer entitled to the rights conferred by the Agency Workers Regulations 2010, SI 2010/93, reg 5 (basic working and employment conditions: see PARA 98), pursuant to reg 8(a), (b) (break between assignments: see PARA 99) (Employment Rights Act 1996 s 57ZI(1)(b) (as so added)).

Nor does anything in s 57ZH impose a duty on the hirer or temporary work agency beyond the original intended duration, or likely duration of the assignment, whichever is the longer: s 57ZI(2) (as so added). As to the meaning of 'agency worker' see PARA 97; definition in the Agency Workers Regulations 2010, SI 2010/93, reg 3, applied by the Employment Rights Act 1996 s 57ZI(4) (as so added). As to the meaning of 'assignment' see PARA 99 note 4;

definition in the Agency Workers Regulations 2010, SI 2010/93, reg 2, applied by the Employment Rights Act 1996 s 57ZI(4) (as so added). As to the meaning of 'hirer' see PARA 97 note 3; definition in the Agency Workers Regulations 2010, SI 2010/93, reg 2, applied by the Employment Rights Act 1996 s 57ZI(4) (as so added). As to the meaning of 'qualifying period' see PARA 99; definition in the Agency Workers Regulations 2010, SI 2010/93, reg 7, applied by the Employment Rights Act 1996 s 57ZI(4) (as so added). As to the meaning of 'temporary work agency' see PARA 97; definition in the Agency Workers Regulations 2010, SI 2010/93, reg 4, applied by the Employment Rights Act 1996 s 57ZI(4) (as so added).

2 As to employment tribunals see PARA 1399 et seq; and as to the procedure on a complaint made to an employment tribunal see PARA 1453 et seq.

3 Ie as required by the Employment Rights Act 1996 s 57ZG (see PARA 339): see s 57ZH(1) (as added: see note 1).

4 See the Employment Rights Act 1996 s 57ZH(1) (as added: see note 1).

5 Ie as required by the Employment Rights Act 1996 s 57ZG (see PARA 339): see s 57ZH(2) (as added: see note 1).

6 See the Employment Rights Act 1996 s 57ZH(2) (as added: see note 1).

7 See the Employment Rights Act 1996 s 57ZH(3) (as added: see note 1).

8 Employment Rights Act 1996 s 57ZH(3)(a) (as added: see note 1). For the purposes of s 57ZH(3)(a), s 207A(3) (extension because mediation in certain European cross-border disputes starts before the time limit expires: see PARA 1454) and s 207B (extension of time limits to facilitate conciliation before institution of proceedings: see PARA 1455) apply: s 57ZH(4) (as so added). As to time limits generally see PARA 1453.

9 Employment Rights Act 1996 s 57ZH(3)(b) (as added: see note 1).

10 See the Employment Rights Act 1996 s 57ZH(5)(a) (as added: see note 1).

11 See the Employment Rights Act 1996 s 57ZH(5)(b) (as added: see note 1).The text refers to the amount payable to the agency worker to be determined according to the formula:

$$(A \times B) \times 2$$

where A is the appropriate hourly rate for the agency worker; and B is the number of working hours for which the agency worker would have been entitled under s 57ZG (see PARA 339) to be absent if the time off had not been refused: see s 57ZH(7) (as so added). The appropriate hourly rate, in relation to an agency worker, is the amount of one week's pay divided by the number of normal working hours in a week for that agency worker in accordance with the terms under which the agency worker works temporarily for and under the supervision and direction of the hirer that are in force on the day when the time off would have been taken: s 57ZH(8) (as so added). However, where the number of normal working hours during the assignment differs from week to week or over a longer period, the amount of one week's pay must be divided instead by the average number of normal working hours calculated by dividing by 12 the total number of the agency worker's normal working hours during the period of 12 weeks ending with the last complete week before the day on which the time off would have been taken: s 57ZH(9) (as so added). As to the calculation of a week's pay and normal working hours see PARA 142 et seq. As to the meaning of 'week' see PARA 126 note 13.

12 Employment Rights Act 1996 s 57ZH(6) (as added: see note 1).

(v) Adoption Appointments

A. EMPLOYEES

341. Employee's right to paid time off work to attend adoption appointments. An employee[1] who has been notified by an adoption agency[2] that a child is to be, or is expected to be, placed for adoption with the employee alone[3] is entitled to be permitted by his or her employer[4] to take paid time off during the employee's working hours[5] in order that he or she may attend by appointment at any place for the purpose of having contact with the child or for any other purpose connected with the adoption[6]. An employee who:

(1) has been notified by an adoption agency that a child is to be, or is expected to be, placed for adoption with the employee and another person jointly[7]; and

(2)   has elected to exercise the right to take paid time off[8] in connection with
       the adoption[9],
is entitled to be permitted by his or her employer to take time off during the
employee's working hours in order that he or she may attend by appointment at
any place for the purpose of having contact with the child or for any other
purpose connected with the adoption[10].

An employee is not entitled to take time off for this purpose[11], however, on or
after the date of the child's placement for adoption with the employee[12]; and
unless:

(a)   the appointment has been arranged by or at the request of the adoption
       agency which made the notification[13]; and

(b)   in the case of a child that is to be, or is expected to be, placed for
       adoption with the employee alone[14], the employee gives the employer, if
       the employer requests it, a document showing the date and time of the
       appointment in question and that it has been arranged as described in
       head (a) above[15]; or

(c)   in the case of a child is to be, or is expected to be, placed for adoption
       with the employee and another person jointly[16], the employee gives the
       employer, if the employer requests it[17]:(i) a declaration signed by the
       employee stating that the employee has made an election for the
       purposes of head (2) above in connection with the adoption[18]; and (ii) a
       document showing the date and time of the appointment in question
       and that it has been arranged as described in head (a) above[19].

An employee who is permitted to take paid time off work to attend adoption
appointments[20] is entitled to be paid remuneration by his or her employer for the
number of working hours for which the employee is entitled to be absent at the
appropriate hourly rate[21]; and a right to any such amount[22] does not affect any
right of an employee in relation to remuneration under his or her contract of
employment ('contractual remuneration')[23].

1   As to the meaning of 'employee' see PARA 2.

2   For these purposes, 'adoption agency' means an adoption agency within the meaning of the
    Adoption and Children Act 2002 s 2 (see CHILDREN AND YOUNG PERSONS vol 9 (2012) PARAS
    432–433): see the Employment Rights Act 1996 s 57ZJ(13) (ss 57ZJ, 57ZK, 57ZS added by the
    Children and Families Act 2014 s 128(1)).

3   In cases where more than one child is to be, or is expected to be, placed for adoption with an
    employee as part of the same arrangement, the Employment Rights Act 1996 s 57ZJ has effect
    as if:
    (1)   the purposes specified in s 57ZJ(1) (see also the text and notes 1–2, 4–6) and s 57ZJ(2)
           (see the text and notes 7–10) were the purpose of having contact with any one or more
           of the children and any other purpose connected with any of the adoptions that are part
           of the arrangement (s 57ZJ(11)(a) (as added: see note 2));
    (2)   the references in s 57ZJ(2)(b) (see head (2) in the text) and s 57ZJ(9)(a) (see head (c)(i)
           in the text) to the adoption were references to all of the adoptions that are part of the
           arrangement (s 57ZJ(11)(b) (as so added));
    (3)   the references in s 57ZJ(3) (see note 9) to the adoption were references to any of the
           adoptions that are part of the arrangement (s 57ZJ(11)(c) (as so added));
    (4)   the reference in s 57ZJ(4) (see the text and notes 11–12) to the date of the child's
           placement for adoption were a reference to the date of placement of the first child to be
           placed as part of the arrangement (s 57ZJ(11)(d) (as so added));
    (5)   the reference in s 57ZJ(5) (see note 6) to a particular adoption were a reference to the
           adoptions that are part of a particular arrangement (s 57ZJ(11)(e) (as so added)).
    Where a local authority in England notifies a person:
    (a)   who is a local authority foster parent (s 57ZS(1)(a) (as so added)); and
    (b)   who has been approved as a prospective adopter (s 57ZS(1)(b) (as so added)),

that a child is to be, or is expected to be, placed with that person under the Children Act 1989 s 22C (local authority's duty to provide child is in its care with accommodation: see CHILDREN AND YOUNG PERSONS vol 10 (2012) PARA 858) (see the Employment Rights Act 1996 s 57ZS(1) (as so added)), s 57ZJ has effect as if:

    (i)   references to adoption or placement for adoption were references to placement of a child under the Children Act 1989 s 22C with a local authority foster parent who has been approved as a prospective adopter (Employment Rights Act 1996 s 57ZS(2)(a) (as so added));

    (ii)   references to placing for adoption were references to placing a child under the Children Act 1989 s 22C with a local authority foster parent who has been approved as a prospective adopter (Employment Rights Act 1996 s 57ZS(2)(b) (as so added));

    (iii)   references to an adoption agency were references to a local authority in England (s 57ZS(2)(c) (as so added)).

Where a child is placed under the Children Act 1989 s 22C with a local authority foster parent who has been approved as a prospective adopter, notification of that person by an adoption agency during that placement that the child is to be, or is expected to be, placed with that person for adoption is not to give rise to a right to time off under the Employment Rights Act 1996 s 57ZJ for that person or another person: s 57ZS(3) (as so added). As to the meaning of 'England' see PARA 2 note 12.

4   As to the meaning of 'employer' see PARA 2.

5   For these purposes, the working hours of an employee are to be taken to be any time when, in accordance with the employee's contract of employment, the employee is required to be at work: see the Employment Rights Act 1996 s 57ZJ(12) (as added: see note 2). As to the meaning of 'contract of employment' see PARA 2.

6   Employment Rights Act 1996 s 57ZJ(1) (as added: see note 2). In relation to any particular adoption, an employee is not entitled to take time off under s 57ZJ on more than five occasions (s 57ZJ(5) (as so added)); and, on each of those occasions, the maximum time off during working hours to which the employee is entitled is six and a half hours (s 57ZJ(6) (as so added)). An employee taking time off under s 57ZJ is protected from suffering detriment in employment on that account (see PARA 620); and dismissal on that ground is automatically unfair (see PARA 784).

7   Employment Rights Act 1996 s 57ZJ(2)(a) (as added: see note 2).

8   Ie under the Employment Rights Act 1996 s 57ZJ: see s 57ZJ(2)(b) (as added: see note 2).

9   Employment Rights Act 1996 s 57ZJ(2)(b) (as added: see note 2). An employee may not make an election for the purposes of s 57ZJ(2)(b), however, if:

    (1)   the employee has made an election for the purposes of s 57ZL(1)(b) (employee's right to unpaid time off work to attend adoption appointments: see PARA 342) in connection with the adoption (s 57ZJ(3)(a) (as so added)); or

    (2)   the other person with whom the child is to be, or is expected to be, placed for adoption has made an election for the purposes of 57ZJ(2)(b) or s 57ZN(2)(b) (agency worker's right to paid time off work to attend adoption appointments: see PARA 344) in connection with the adoption (s 57ZJ(3)(b) (as so added)).

10 See the Employment Rights Act 1996 s 57ZJ(2) (as added: see note 2). See note 6.

11 Ie under the Employment Rights Act 1996 s 57ZJ: see s 57ZJ(4) (as added: see note 2).

12 See the Employment Rights Act 1996 s 57ZJ(4) (as added: see note 2).

13 See the Employment Rights Act 1996 s 57ZJ(7) (as added: see note 2). The text refers to the notification that is described in s 57ZJ(1) (see the text and notes 1–6) or s 57ZJ(2)(a) (see head (1) in the text): see s 57ZJ(7) (as so added).

14 Ie under the Employment Rights Act 1996 s 57ZJ(1) (see the text and notes 1–6): see s 57ZJ(8) (as added: see note 2).

15 See the Employment Rights Act 1996 s 57ZJ(8) (as added: see note 2). A document requested under s 57ZJ(8) may be given in electronic form: see s 57ZJ(10) (as so added).

16 Ie under the Employment Rights Act 1996 s 57ZJ(2) (see the text and notes 7–10): see s 57ZJ(9) (as added: see note 2).

17 See the Employment Rights Act 1996 s 57ZJ(9) (as added: see note 2).

18 Employment Rights Act 1996 s 57ZJ(9)(a) (as added: see note 2). A declaration requested under s 57ZJ(9) may be given in electronic form: see s 57ZJ(10) (as so added).

19 Employment Rights Act 1996 s 57ZJ(9)(b) (as added: see note 2). A document requested under s 57ZJ(9) may be given in electronic form: see s 57ZJ(10) (as so added).

20 Ie under the Employment Rights Act 1996 s 57ZJ (see the text and notes 1–19): see s 57ZK(1) (as added: see note 2).

21 Employment Rights Act 1996 s 57ZK(1) (as added: see note 2). The appropriate hourly rate, in relation to an employee, is the amount of one week's pay divided by the number of normal

working hours in a week for that employee when employed under the contract of employment in force on the day when the time off is taken: s 57ZK(2) (as so added). Where, however, the number of normal working hours differs from week to week or over a longer period, the amount of one week's pay is to be divided instead by:

(1)   the average number of normal working hours calculated by dividing by 12 the total number of the employee's working hours during the period of 12 weeks ending with the last complete week before the day on which the time off is taken (s 57ZK(3)(a) (as so added)); or

(2)   where the employee has not been employed for a sufficient period to enable the calculation to be made under head (1) above, a number which fairly represents the number of normal working hours in a week, having regard to such of the following considerations as are appropriate in the circumstances (see s 57ZK(3)(b) (as so added)): (a) the average number of normal working hours in a week which the employee could expect in accordance with the terms of her contract (s 57ZK(4)(a) (as so added)); and (b) the average number of normal working hours of other employees engaged in relevant comparable employment with the same employer (s 57ZK(4)(b) (as so added)).

As to the calculation of a week's pay and normal working hours see PARA 142 et seq. As to the meaning of 'week' see PARA 126 note 13. As to the right of complaint to an employment tribunal see PARA 334.

22   Ie a right to any amount under the Employment Rights Act 1996 s 57ZK(1) (see the text and notes 20–21): see s 57ZK(5) (as added: see note 2).

23   Employment Rights Act 1996 s 57ZK(5) (as added: see note 2). However, any contractual remuneration paid to an employee in respect of a period of time off under s 57ZJ (see the text and notes 1–19) goes towards discharging any liability of the employer to pay remuneration under s 57ZK(1) (see the text and notes 20–21) in respect of that period (s 57ZK(6) (as so added)); and, conversely, any payment of remuneration under s 57ZK(1) in respect of a period of time off under s 57ZJ goes towards discharging any liability of the employer to pay contractual remuneration in respect of that period (s 57ZK(7) (as so added)).

342.   Employee's right to unpaid time off work to attend adoption appointments.

An employee[1] who:

(1)   has been notified by an adoption agency[2] that a child is to be, or is expected to be, placed for adoption with the employee[3] and another person jointly[4]; and

(2)   has elected to exercise the right to take unpaid time off[5] in connection with the adoption[6],

is entitled to be permitted by his or her employer[7] to take time off during the employee's working hours[8] in order that he or she may attend by appointment at any place for the purpose of having contact with the child or for any other purpose connected with the adoption[9].

An employee is not entitled to take time off for this purpose[10], however, on or after the date of the child's placement for adoption with the employee[11]; and unless:

(a)   the appointment has been arranged by or at the request of the adoption agency which made the notification described in head (1) above[12]; and

(b)   the employee gives the employer, if the employer requests it[13]:(i) a declaration signed by the employee stating that the employee has made an election for the purposes of head (2) above in connection with the adoption[14]; and (ii) a document showing the date and time of the appointment in question and that it has been arranged as described in head (a) above[15].

1   As to the meaning of 'employee' see PARA 2.
2   For these purposes, 'adoption agency' means an adoption agency within the meaning of the Adoption and Children Act 2002 s 2 (see CHILDREN AND YOUNG PERSONS vol 9 (2012) PARAS 432–433): see the Employment Rights Act 1996 s 57ZL(11) (ss 57ZL, 57ZS added by the Children and Families Act 2014 s 128(1)).

3   In cases where more than one child is to be, or is expected to be, placed for adoption with an
     employee and another person jointly as part of the same arrangement, the Employment Rights
     Act 1996 s 57ZL has effect as if:
     (1)   the purposes specified in s 57ZL(1) (see also the text and notes 1–2, 4–9) were the
            purpose of having contact with any one or more of the children and any other purpose
            connected with any of the adoptions that are part of the arrangement (s 57ZL(9)(a) (as
            added: see note 2));
     (2)   the references in s 57ZL(1)(b) (see head (2) in the text) and s 57ZL(7)(a) (see head (b)(i)
            in the text) to the adoption were references to all of the adoptions that are part of the
            arrangement (s 57ZL(9)(b) (as so added));
     (3)   the references in s 57ZL(2) (see note 6) to the adoption were references to any of the
            adoptions that are part of the arrangement (s 57ZL(9)(c) (as so added));
     (4)   the reference in s 57ZL(3) (see the text and notes 10–11) to the date of the child's
            placement for adoption were a reference to the date of placement of the first child to be
            placed as part of the arrangement (s 57ZL(9)(d) (as so added));
     (5)   the reference in s 57ZL(4) (see note 9) to a particular adoption were a reference to the
            adoptions that are part of a particular arrangement (s 57ZL(9)(e) (as so added)).
     Where a local authority in England notifies a person:
     (a)   who is a local authority foster parent (s 57ZS(1)(a) (as so added)); and
     (b)   who has been approved as a prospective adopter (s 57ZS(1)(b) (as so added)),
     that a child is to be, or is expected to be, placed with that person under the Children Act 1989
     s 22C (local authority's duty to provide child is in its care with accommodation: see CHILDREN
     AND YOUNG PERSONS vol 10 (2012) PARA 858) (see the Employment Rights Act 1996 s 57ZS(1)
     (as so added)), s 57ZL has effect as if:
     (i)   references to adoption or placement for adoption were references to placement of a
            child under the Children Act 1989 s 22C with a local authority foster parent who has
            been approved as a prospective adopter (Employment Rights Act 1996 s 57ZS(2)(a) (as
            so added));
     (ii)   references to placing for adoption were references to placing a child under the Children
            Act 1989 s 22C with a local authority foster parent who has been approved as a
            prospective adopter (Employment Rights Act 1996 s 57ZS(2)(b) (as so added));
     (iii) references to an adoption agency were references to a local authority in England
            (s 57ZS(2)(c) (as so added)).
     Where a child is placed under the Children Act 1989 s 22C with a local authority foster parent
     who has been approved as a prospective adopter, notification of that person by an adoption
     agency during that placement that the child is to be, or is expected to be, placed with that person
     for adoption is not to give rise to a right to time off under the Employment Rights Act 1996
     s 57ZL for that person or another person: s 57ZS(3) (as so added). As to the meaning of
     'England' see PARA 2 note 12.
4   Employment Rights Act 1996 s 57ZL(1)(a) (as added: see note 2).
5   Ie under the Employment Rights Act 1996 s 57ZL: see s 57ZL(1)(b) (as added: see note 2).
6   Employment Rights Act 1996 s 57ZL(1)(b) (as added: see note 2). An employee may not make
     an election for the purposes of s 57ZL(1)(b), however, if:
     (1)   the employee has made an election for the purposes of s 57ZJ(2)(b) (employee's right to
            paid time off work to attend adoption appointments: see PARA 341) in connection with
            the adoption (s 57ZL(2)(a) (as so added)); or
     (2)   the other person with whom the child is to be, or is expected to be, placed for adoption
            has made an election for the purposes of 57ZL(1)(b) or s 57ZP(1)(b) (agency worker's
            right to unpaid time off work to attend adoption appointments: see PARA 345) in
            connection with the adoption (s 57ZL(2)(b) (as so added)).
7   As to the meaning of 'employer' see PARA 2.
8   For these purposes, the working hours of an employee are to be taken to be any time when, in
     accordance with the employee's contract of employment, the employee is required to be at work:
     see the Employment Rights Act 1996 s 57ZL(10) (as added: see note 2). As to the meaning of
     'contract of employment' see PARA 2.
9   See the Employment Rights Act 1996 s 57ZL(1) (as added: see note 2). In relation to any
     particular adoption, an employee is not entitled to take time off under s 57ZL on more than two
     occasions (s 57ZL(4) (as so added)); and, on each of those occasions, the maximum time off
     during working hours to which the employee is entitled is six and a half hours (s 57ZL(5) (as so
     added)). An employee taking time off under s 57ZL is protected from suffering detriment in
     employment on that account (see PARA 620); and dismissal on that ground is automatically
     unfair (see PARA 784).
10   Ie under the Employment Rights Act 1996 s 57ZL: see s 57ZL(3) (as added: see note 2).

11 See the Employment Rights Act 1996 s 57ZL(3) (as added: see note 2).
12 See the Employment Rights Act 1996 s 57ZL(6) (as added: see note 2). The text refers to the
    notification that is described in s 57ZL(1)(a) (see head (1) in the text): see s 57ZL(6) (as so
    added).
13 See the Employment Rights Act 1996 s 57ZL(7) (as added: see note 2).
14 Employment Rights Act 1996 s 57ZL(7)(a) (as added: see note 2). A declaration requested under
    s 57ZL(7) may be given in electronic form: see s 57ZL(8) (as so added).
15 Employment Rights Act 1996 s 57ZL(7)(b) (as added: see note 2). A document requested under
    s 57ZL(7) may be given in electronic form: see s 57ZL(8) (as so added).

343. Complaint to employment tribunal: employee's right to paid and unpaid time off work to attend adoption appointments. An employee[1] may present a complaint to an employment tribunal[2] that his or her employer[3]:

(1)   has unreasonably refused to permit him or her to take time off work[4] (whether paid or unpaid) in order to attend adoption appointments[5]; or

(2)   has failed to pay the whole or any part of any amount to which he or she is[6] entitled[7].

An employment tribunal must not consider such a complaint, however, unless it is presented[8]:

(a)   before the end of the period of three months beginning with the day of the appointment in question[9]; or

(b)   within such further period as the tribunal considers reasonable in a case where it is satisfied that it was not reasonably practicable for the complaint to be presented before the end of that period of three months[10].

Where an employment tribunal finds such a complaint well-founded, it must make a declaration to that effect[11]; and:

(i)   if the complaint is that the employer has unreasonably refused to let the employee to take paid time off[12], the tribunal must also order the employer to pay to the employee an amount that is twice the amount of the remuneration to which he or she would have been entitled[13] if the employer had not refused[14];

(ii)   if the complaint is that the employer has failed to pay the employee the whole or part of any amount to which he or she is entitled as remuneration for time so taken[15], the tribunal must also order the employer to pay to the employee the amount which it finds due to him or her[16];

(iii)   if the complaint is that the employer has unreasonably refused to let the employee to take unpaid time off[17], the tribunal must also order the employer to pay to the employee an amount determined in accordance with the statutory formula[18].

1   As to the meaning of 'employee' see PARA 2.
2   As to employment tribunals see PARA 1399 et seq; and as to the procedure on a complaint made
    to an employment tribunal see PARA 1453 et seq.
3   See the Employment Rights Act 1996 s 57ZM(1) (s 57ZM added by the Children and Families
    Act 2014 s 128(1)). As to the meaning of 'employer' see PARA 2.
4   Ie as required by the Employment Rights Act 1996 s 57ZJ (employee's right to paid time off
    work to attend adoption appointments: see PARA 341) or s 57ZL (employee's right to unpaid
    time off work to attend adoption appointments: see PARA 342): see s 57ZM(1)(a) (as added: see
    note 3).
5   Employment Rights Act 1996 s 57ZM(1)(a) (as added: see note 3).
6   Ie under the Employment Rights Act 1996 s 57ZK (employee's right to remuneration for time
    off work to attend adoption appointments: see PARA 341): see s 57ZM(1)(b) (as added: see
    note 3).
7   Employment Rights Act 1996 s 57ZM(1)(b) (as added: see note 3).

8   See the Employment Rights Act 1996 s 57ZM(2) (as added: see note 3).
9   Employment Rights Act 1996 s 57ZM(2)(a) (as added: see note 3). For the purposes of
    s 57ZM(2)(a), s 207A(3) (extension because mediation in certain European cross-border
    disputes starts before the time limit expires: see PARA 1454) and s 207B (extension of time limits
    to facilitate conciliation before institution of proceedings: see PARA 1455) apply: s 57ZM(3) (as
    so added). As to time limits generally see PARA 1453.
10 Employment Rights Act 1996 s 57ZM(2)(b) (as added: see note 3).
11 See the Employment Rights Act 1996 s 57ZM(4) (as added: see note 3).
12 Ie as required by the Employment Rights Act 1996 s 57ZJ (employee's right to paid time off
    work to attend adoption appointments: see PARA 341): see s 57ZM(5) (as added: see note 3).
13 Ie under the Employment Rights Act 1996 s 57ZK (employee's right to remuneration for time
    off work to attend adoption appointments: see PARA 341): see s 57ZM(5) (as added: see note 3).
14 See the Employment Rights Act 1996 s 57ZM(5) (as added: see note 3).
15 Ie under the Employment Rights Act 1996 s 57ZK (employee's right to remuneration for time
    off work to attend adoption appointments: see PARA 341): see s 57ZM(6) (as added: see note 3).
16 See the Employment Rights Act 1996 s 57ZM(6) (as added: see note 3).
17 Ie as required by the Employment Rights Act 1996 s 57ZL (employee's right to unpaid time off
    work to attend adoption appointments: see PARA 342): see s 57ZM(7) (as added: see note 3).
18 See the Employment Rights Act 1996 s 57ZM(7) (as added: see note 3). The text refers to the
    amount payable to the employee to be determined in accordance with the formula:

$$(A \times B) \times 2$$

where A is the appropriate hourly rate for the employee determined in accordance with
s 57K(2)–(4) (see PARA 341 note 21); and B is the number of working hours for which the
employee would have been entitled under s 57ZL (see PARA 342) to be absent if the time off had
not been refused: see s 57ZM(8) (as so added). As to the calculation of a week's pay and normal
working hours see PARA 142 et seq. As to the meaning of 'week' see PARA 126 note 13.

B.   AGENCY WORKERS

**344.   Agency worker's right to paid time off work to attend adoption
appointments.**   An agency worker who has been notified by an adoption agency[1]
that a child is to be, or is expected to be, placed for adoption with the agency
worker alone[2] is entitled[3] to be permitted by the temporary work agency and the
hirer to take paid time off during the agency worker's working hours[4] in order
that he or she may attend by appointment at any place for the purpose of having
contact with the child or for any other purpose connected with the adoption[5]. An
agency worker who:

(1)   has been notified by an adoption agency that a child is to be, or is
      expected to be, placed for adoption with the agency worker and another
      person jointly[6]; and

(2)   has elected to exercise the right to take paid time off[7] in connection with
      the adoption[8],

is entitled to be permitted by the temporary work agency and the hirer to take
time off during the agency worker's working hours in order that he or she may
attend by appointment at any place for the purpose of having contact with the
child or for any other purpose connected with the adoption[9].

An agency worker is not entitled to take time off for this purpose[10], however,
on or after the date of the child's placement for adoption with the agency
worker[11]; and unless:

(a)   the appointment has been arranged by or at the request of the adoption
      agency which made the notification[12]; and

(b)   in the case of a child that is to be, or is expected to be, placed for
      adoption with the agency worker alone[13], the agency worker gives the
      temporary work agency or the hirer, if either one requests it, a document

showing the date and time of the appointment in question and that it has been arranged as described in head (a) above[14]; or

(c)   in the case of a child is to be, or is expected to be, placed for adoption with the agency worker and another person jointly[15], the agency worker gives the temporary work agency or the hirer, if either one requests it[16]: (i) a declaration signed by the agency worker stating that the agency worker has made an election for the purposes of head (2) above in connection with the adoption[17]; and (ii) a document showing the date and time of the appointment in question and that it has been arranged as described in head (a) above[18].

An agency worker who is permitted to take paid time off work to attend adoption appointments[19] is entitled to be paid remuneration by the temporary work agency for the number of working hours for which the agency worker is entitled to be absent at the appropriate hourly rate[20]; and a right to any such amount[21] does not affect any right of an agency worker in relation to remuneration under his or her contract with the temporary work agency ('contractual remuneration')[22].

1   For these purposes, 'adoption agency' means an adoption agency within the meaning of the Adoption and Children Act 2002 s 2 (see CHILDREN AND YOUNG PERSONS vol 9 (2012) PARAS 432–433): see the Employment Rights Act 1996 s 57ZN(13) (ss 57ZN, 57ZO, 57ZR, 57ZS added by the Children and Families Act 2014 s 128(1)).

2   In cases where more than one child is to be, or is expected to be, placed for adoption with an agency worker as part of the same arrangement, the Employment Rights Act 1996 s 57ZN has effect as if:
    (1)   the purposes specified in s 57ZN(1) (see also the text and notes 1, 3–5) and s 57ZN(2) (see the text and notes 6–9) were the purpose of having contact with any one or more of the children and any other purpose connected with any of the adoptions that are part of the arrangement (s 57ZN(11)(a) (as added: see note 1));
    (2)   the references in s 57ZN(2)(b) (see head (2) in the text) and s 57ZN(9)(a) (see head (c)(i) in the text) to the adoption were references to all of the adoptions that are part of the arrangement (s 57ZN(11)(b) (as so added));
    (3)   the references in s 57ZN(3) (see note 8) to the adoption were references to any of the adoptions that are part of the arrangement (s 57ZN(11)(c) (as so added));
    (4)   the reference in s 57ZN(4) (see the text and notes 10–11) to the date of the child's placement for adoption were a reference to the date of placement of the first child to be placed as part of the arrangement (s 57ZN(11)(d) (as so added));
    (5)   the reference in s 57ZN(5) (see note 5) to a particular adoption were a reference to the adoptions that are part of a particular arrangement (s 57ZN(11)(e) (as so added)).
    Where a local authority in England notifies a person:
    (a)   who is a local authority foster parent (s 57ZS(1)(a) (as so added)); and
    (b)   who has been approved as a prospective adopter (s 57ZS(1)(b) (as so added)),
    that a child is to be, or is expected to be, placed with that person under the Children Act 1989 s 22C (local authority's duty to provide child is in its care with accommodation: see CHILDREN AND YOUNG PERSONS vol 10 (2012) PARA 858) (see the Employment Rights Act 1996 s 57ZS(1) (as so added)), s 57ZN has effect as if:
    (i)   references to adoption or placement for adoption were references to placement of a child under the Children Act 1989 s 22C with a local authority foster parent who has been approved as a prospective adopter (Employment Rights Act 1996 s 57ZS(2)(a) (as so added));
    (ii)   references to placing for adoption were references to placing a child under the Children Act 1989 s 22C with a local authority foster parent who has been approved as a prospective adopter (Employment Rights Act 1996 s 57ZS(2)(b) (as so added));
    (iii) references to an adoption agency were references to a local authority in England (s 57ZS(2)(c) (as so added)).
    Where a child is placed under the Children Act 1989 s 22C with a local authority foster parent who has been approved as a prospective adopter, notification of that person by an adoption agency during that placement that the child is to be, or is expected to be, placed with that person

for adoption is not to give rise to a right to time off under the Employment Rights Act 1996 s 57ZN for that person or another person: s 57ZS(3) (as so added). As to the meaning of 'England' see PARA 2 note 12.

3   The provision made by the Employment Rights Act 1996 ss 57ZN, 57ZO does not apply where ss 57ZJ, 57ZK applies (employee's right to paid time off work to attend adoption appointments: see PARA 341): see s 57ZR(3) (as added: see note 1). Nor, without prejudice to any other duties of the hirer or temporary work agency under any enactment or rule of law, does the provision made by ss 57ZN, 57ZO apply where the agency worker:

   (1)   has not completed the qualifying period (s 57ZR(1)(a) (as so added)); or
   (2)   is no longer entitled to the rights conferred by the Agency Workers Regulations 2010, SI 2010/93, reg 5 (basic working and employment conditions: see PARA 98), pursuant to reg 8(a), (b) (break between assignments: see PARA 99) (Employment Rights Act 1996 s 57ZR(1)(b) (as so added)).

   Nor does anything in ss 57ZN, 57ZO impose a duty on the hirer or temporary work agency beyond the original intended duration, or likely duration of the assignment, whichever is the longer: s 57ZR(2) (as so added). As to the meaning of 'agency worker' see PARA 97; definition in the Agency Workers Regulations 2010, SI 2010/93, reg 3, applied by the Employment Rights Act 1996 s 57ZR(4) (as so added). As to the meaning of 'assignment' see PARA 99 note 4; definition in the Agency Workers Regulations 2010, SI 2010/93, reg 2, applied by the Employment Rights Act 1996 s 57ZR(4) (as so added). As to the meaning of 'hirer' see PARA 97 note 3; definition in the Agency Workers Regulations 2010, SI 2010/93, reg 2, applied by the Employment Rights Act 1996 s 57ZR(4) (as so added). As to the meaning of 'qualifying period' see PARA 99; definition in the Agency Workers Regulations 2010, SI 2010/93, reg 7, applied by the Employment Rights Act 1996 s 57ZR(4) (as so added). As to the meaning of 'temporary work agency' see PARA 97; definition in the Agency Workers Regulations 2010, SI 2010/93, reg 4, applied by the Employment Rights Act 1996 s 57ZR(4) (as so added).

4   For these purposes, the working hours of an agency worker are to be taken to be any time when, in accordance with the terms under which the agency worker works temporarily for and under the supervision and direction of the hirer, the agency worker is required to be at work: see the Employment Rights Act 1996 s 57ZN(12) (as added: see note 1).

5   Employment Rights Act 1996 s 57ZN(1) (as added: see note 1). In relation to any particular adoption, an agency worker is not entitled to take time off under s 57ZN on more than five occasions (s 57ZN(5) (as so added)); and, on each of those occasions, the maximum time off during working hours to which the agency worker is entitled is six and a half hours (s 57ZN(6) (as so added)). An agency worker taking time off under s 57ZN is protected from suffering detriment in employment on that account: see PARA 620.

6   Employment Rights Act 1996 s 57ZN(2)(a) (as added: see note 1).

7   Ie under the Employment Rights Act 1996 s 57ZN: see s 57ZN(2)(b) (as added: see note 1).

8   Employment Rights Act 1996 s 57ZN(2)(b) (as added: see note 1). An agency worker may not make an election for the purposes of s 57ZN(2)(b), however, if:

   (1)   the agency worker has made an election for the purposes of s 57ZP(1)(b) (agency worker's right to unpaid time off work to attend adoption appointments: see PARA 345) in connection with the adoption (s 57ZN(3)(a) (as so added)); or
   (2)   the other person with whom the child is to be, or is expected to be, placed for adoption has made an election for the purposes of s 57ZJ(2)(b) (employee's right to paid time off work to attend adoption appointments: see PARA 341) or s 57ZN(2)(b) in connection with the adoption (s 57ZN(3)(b) (as so added)).

9   See the Employment Rights Act 1996 s 57ZN(2) (as added: see note 1). See note 5.

10 Ie under the Employment Rights Act 1996 s 57ZN: see s 57ZN(4) (as added: see note 1).

11 See the Employment Rights Act 1996 s 57ZN(4) (as added: see note 1).

12 See the Employment Rights Act 1996 s 57ZN(7) (as added: see note 1). The text refers to the notification that is described in s 57ZN(1) (see the text and notes 1–5) or s 57ZN(2)(a) (see head (1) in the text): see s 57ZN(7) (as so added).

13 Ie under the Employment Rights Act 1996 s 57ZN(1) (see the text and notes 1–5): see s 57ZN(8) (as added: see note 1).

14 See the Employment Rights Act 1996 s 57ZN(8) (as added: see note 1). A document requested under s 57ZN(8) may be given in electronic form: see s 57ZN(10) (as so added).

15 Ie under the Employment Rights Act 1996 s 57ZN(2) (see the text and notes 6–9): see s 57ZN(9) (as added: see note 1).

16 See the Employment Rights Act 1996 s 57ZN(9) (as added: see note 1).

17 Employment Rights Act 1996 s 57ZN(9)(a) (as added: see note 1). A declaration requested under s 57ZN(9) may be given in electronic form: see s 57ZN(10) (as so added).

18   Employment Rights Act 1996 s 57ZN(9)(b) (as added: see note 1). A document requested under s 57ZN(9) may be given in electronic form: see s 57ZN(10) (as so added).

19   Ie under the Employment Rights Act 1996 s 57ZN (see the text and notes 1–18): see s 57ZO(1) (as added: see note 1).

20   Employment Rights Act 1996 s 57ZO(1) (as added: see note 1). The appropriate hourly rate, in relation to an agency worker, is the amount of one week's pay divided by the number of normal working hours in a week for that agency worker, in accordance with the terms under which the agency worker works temporarily for and under the supervision and direction of the hirer, that are in force on the day when the time off is taken: s 57ZO(2) (as so added). Where, however, the number of normal working hours during the assignment differs from week to week or over a longer period, the amount of one week's pay is to be divided instead by the average number of normal working hours calculated by dividing by 12 the total number of the agency worker's normal working hours during the period of 12 weeks ending with the last complete week before the day on which the time off is taken: s 57ZO(3) (as so added).

As to the calculation of a week's pay and normal working hours see PARA 142 et seq. As to the meaning of 'week' see PARA 126 note 13. As to the right of complaint to an employment tribunal see PARA 334.

21   Ie a right to any amount under the Employment Rights Act 1996 s 57ZO(1) (see the text and notes 19–20): see s 57ZO(4) (as added: see note 1).

22   Employment Rights Act 1996 s 57ZO(4) (as added: see note 1). However, any contractual remuneration paid to an agency worker in respect of a period of time off under s 57ZN (see the text and notes 1–18) goes towards discharging any liability of the temporary work agency to pay remuneration under s 57ZO(1) (see the text and notes 19–20) in respect of that period (s 57ZO(5) (as so added)); and, conversely, any payment of remuneration under s 57ZO(1) in respect of a period of time off under s 57ZN goes towards discharging any liability of the temporary work agency to pay contractual remuneration in respect of that period (s 57ZO(6) (as so added)). An agency worker receiving remuneration under s 57ZO is protected from suffering detriment in employment on that account: see PARA 620.

345. Agency worker's right to unpaid time off work to attend adoption appointments. An agency worker who[1]:

    (1)   has been notified by an adoption agency[2] that a child is to be, or is expected to be, placed for adoption with the agency worker[3] and another person jointly[4]; and

    (2)   has elected to exercise the right to take unpaid time off[5] in connection with the adoption[6],

is entitled to be permitted by the temporary work agency and the hirer to take time off during the agency worker's working hours[7] in order that he or she may attend by appointment at any place for the purpose of having contact with the child or for any other purpose connected with the adoption[8].

An agency worker is not entitled to take time off for this purpose[9], however, on or after the date of the child's placement for adoption with the agency worker[10]; and unless:

    (a)   the appointment has been arranged by or at the request of the adoption agency which made the notification described in head (1) above[11]; and

    (b)   the agency worker gives the temporary work agency or the hirer, if either one requests it[12]:(i) a declaration signed by the agency worker stating that the agency worker has made an election for the purposes of head (2) above in connection with the adoption[13]; and (ii) a document showing the date and time of the appointment in question and that it has been arranged as described in head (a) above[14].

1   The provision made by the Employment Rights Act 1996 s 57ZP does not apply where s 57ZL applies (employee's right to unpaid time off work to attend adoption appointments: see PARA 342): see s 57ZR(3) (ss 57ZP, 57ZR, 57ZS added by the Children and Families Act 2014 s 128(1)). Nor, without prejudice to any other duties of the hirer or temporary work agency under any enactment or rule of law, does the provision made by the Employment Rights Act 1996 s 57ZP apply where the agency worker:

(1)   has not completed the qualifying period (s 57ZR(1)(a) (as so added)); or

(2)   is no longer entitled to the rights conferred by the Agency Workers Regulations 2010, SI 2010/93, reg 5 (basic working and employment conditions: see PARA 98), pursuant to reg 8(a), (b) (break between assignments: see PARA 99) (Employment Rights Act 1996 s 57ZR(1)(b) (as so added)).

Nor does anything in s 57ZP impose a duty on the hirer or temporary work agency beyond the original intended duration, or likely duration of the assignment, whichever is the longer: s 57ZR(2) (as so added). As to the meaning of 'agency worker' see PARA 97; definition in the Agency Workers Regulations 2010, SI 2010/93, reg 3, applied by the Employment Rights Act 1996 s 57ZR(4) (as so added). As to the meaning of 'assignment' see PARA 99 note 4; definition in the Agency Workers Regulations 2010, SI 2010/93, reg 2, applied by the Employment Rights Act 1996 s 57ZR(4) (as so added). As to the meaning of 'hirer' see PARA 97 note 3; definition in the Agency Workers Regulations 2010, SI 2010/93, reg 2, applied by the Employment Rights Act 1996 s 57ZR(4) (as so added). As to the meaning of 'qualifying period' see PARA 99; definition in the Agency Workers Regulations 2010, SI 2010/93, reg 7, applied by the Employment Rights Act 1996 s 57ZR(4) (as so added). As to the meaning of 'temporary work agency' see PARA 97; definition in the Agency Workers Regulations 2010, SI 2010/93, reg 4, applied by the Employment Rights Act 1996 s 57ZR(4) (as so added).

2   For these purposes, 'adoption agency' means an adoption agency within the meaning of the Adoption and Children Act 2002 s 2 (see CHILDREN AND YOUNG PERSONS vol 9 (2012) PARAS 432–433): see the Employment Rights Act 1996 s 57ZP(11) (as added: see note 1)).

3   In cases where more than one child is to be, or is expected to be, placed for adoption with an agency worker and another person jointly as part of the same arrangement, the Employment Rights Act 1996 s 57ZP has effect as if:

(1)   the purposes specified in s 57ZP(1) (see also the text and notes 1–2, 4–8) were the purpose of having contact with any one or more of the children and any other purpose connected with any of the adoptions that are part of the arrangement (s 57ZP(9)(a) (as added: see note 1));

(2)   the references in s 57ZP(1)(b) (see head (2) in the text) and s 57ZP(7)(a) (see head (b)(i) in the text) to the adoption were references to all of the adoptions that are part of the arrangement (s 57ZP(9)(b) (as so added));

(3)   the references in s 57ZP(2) (see note 6) to the adoption were references to any of the adoptions that are part of the arrangement (s 57ZP(9)(c) (as so added));

(4)   the reference in s 57ZP(3) (see the text and notes 9–10) to the date of the child's placement for adoption were a reference to the date of placement of the first child to be placed as part of the arrangement (s 57ZP(9)(d) (as so added));

(5)   the reference in s 57ZP(4) (see note 8) to a particular adoption were a reference to the adoptions that are part of a particular arrangement (s 57ZP(9)(e) (as so added)).

Where a local authority in England notifies a person:

(a)   who is a local authority foster parent (s 57ZS(1)(a) (as so added)); and

(b)   who has been approved as a prospective adopter (s 57ZS(1)(b) (as so added)),

that a child is to be, or is expected to be, placed with that person under the Children Act 1989 s 22C (local authority's duty to provide child is in its care with accommodation: see CHILDREN AND YOUNG PERSONS vol 10 (2012) PARA 858) (see the Employment Rights Act 1996 s 57ZS(1) (as so added)), s 57ZP has effect as if:

(i)   references to adoption or placement for adoption were references to placement of a child under the Children Act 1989 s 22C with a local authority foster parent who has been approved as a prospective adopter (Employment Rights Act 1996 s 57ZS(2)(a) (as so added));

(ii)   references to placing for adoption were references to placing a child under the Children Act 1989 s 22C with a local authority foster parent who has been approved as a prospective adopter (Employment Rights Act 1996 s 57ZS(2)(b) (as so added));

(iii)   references to an adoption agency were references to a local authority in England (s 57ZS(2)(c) (as so added)).

Where a child is placed under the Children Act 1989 s 22C with a local authority foster parent who has been approved as a prospective adopter, notification of that person by an adoption agency during that placement that the child is to be, or is expected to be, placed with that person for adoption is not to give rise to a right to time off under the Employment Rights Act 1996 s 57ZP for that person or another person: s 57ZS(3) (as so added). As to the meaning of 'England' see PARA 2 note 12.

4   Employment Rights Act 1996 s 57ZP(1)(a) (as added: see note 1).

5   Ie under the Employment Rights Act 1996 s 57ZP: see s 57ZP(1)(b) (as added: see note 1).

6   Employment Rights Act 1996 s 57ZP(1)(b) (as added: see note 1). An agency worker may not make an election for the purposes of s 57ZP(1)(b), however, if:
    (1)   the agency worker has made an election for the purposes of s 57ZN(2)(b) (agency worker's right to paid time off work to attend adoption appointments: see PARA 344) in connection with the adoption (s 57ZP(2)(a) (as so added)); or
    (2)   the other person with whom the child is to be, or is expected to be, placed for adoption has made an election for the purposes of s 57ZL(1)(b) (employee's right to unpaid time off work to attend adoption appointments: see PARA 342) or s 57ZP(1)(b) in connection with the adoption (s 57ZP(2)(b) (as so added)).

7   For these purposes, the working hours of an agency worker are to be taken to be any time when, in accordance with the terms under which the agency worker works temporarily for and under the supervision and direction of the hirer, the agency worker is required to be at work: see the Employment Rights Act 1996 s 57ZN(10) (as added: see note 1).

8   See the Employment Rights Act 1996 s 57ZP(1) (as added: see note 1). In relation to any particular adoption, an agency worker is not entitled to take time off under s 57ZP on more than two occasions (s 57ZP(4) (as so added)); and, on each of those occasions, the maximum time off during working hours to which the agency worker is entitled is six and a half hours (s 57ZP(5) (as so added)). An agency worker taking time off under s 57ZP is protected from suffering detriment in employment on that account: see PARA 620.

9   Ie under the Employment Rights Act 1996 s 57ZP: see s 57ZP(3) (as added: see note 1).

10 See the Employment Rights Act 1996 s 57ZP(3) (as added: see note 1).

11 See the Employment Rights Act 1996 s 57ZP(6) (as added: see note 1). The text refers to the notification that is described in s 57ZP(1)(a) (see head (1) in the text): see s 57ZP(6) (as so added).

12 See the Employment Rights Act 1996 s 57ZP(7) (as added: see note 1).

13 Employment Rights Act 1996 s 57ZP(7)(a) (as added: see note 1). A declaration requested under s 57ZP(7) may be given in electronic form: see s 57ZP(8) (as so added).

14 Employment Rights Act 1996 s 57ZP(7)(b) (as added: see note 1). A document requested under s 57ZP(7) may be given in electronic form: see s 57ZP(8) (as so added).

346.   Complaint to employment tribunal: agency worker's right to paid and unpaid time off work to attend adoption appointments.

An agency worker may[1] present a complaint to an employment tribunal[2] that:

(1)   the temporary work agency has unreasonably refused to let him or her to take time off work[3] (whether paid or unpaid) in order to attend adoption appointments[4]; or

(2)   the temporary work agency has failed to pay the whole or any part of any amount to which he or she is[5] entitled[6]; or

(3)   the hirer has unreasonably refused to let him or her to take time off work[7] (whether paid or unpaid) in order to attend adoption appointments[8].

An employment tribunal must not consider such complaint under any of heads (1) to (3) above, however, unless it is presented[9]:

(a)   before the end of the period of three months beginning with the day of the appointment in question[10]; or

(b)   within such further period as the tribunal considers reasonable in a case where it is satisfied that it was not reasonably practicable for the complaint to be presented before the end of that period of three months[11].

Where an employment tribunal finds such complaint under any of heads (1) to (3) above well-founded, it must make a declaration to that effect[12]; and:

(i)   if the complaint is that the temporary work agency or hirer has unreasonably refused to let the agency worker to take paid time off work[13], the tribunal must also order payment to the agency worker of an amount that is twice the amount of the remuneration to which he or she would have been entitled[14] if he or she had not been refused the time off[15];

(ii)   if the complaint is that the temporary work agency has failed to pay the agency worker the whole or part of any amount to which he or she is entitled as remuneration for time so taken[16], the tribunal must also order the temporary work agency to pay to the agency worker the amount which it finds due to him or her[17];

(iii)   if the complaint is that the temporary work agency or hirer has unreasonably refused to let the agency worker to take unpaid time off work[18], the tribunal must also order payment to the agency worker of an amount determined in accordance with the statutory formula[19].

1 The provision made by the Employment Rights Act 1996 s 57ZQ does not apply where s 57ZM applies (complaint to employment tribunal (employee's right to paid and unpaid time off work to attend adoption appointments): see PARA 343): see s 57ZR(3) (ss 57ZQ, 57ZR are added by the Children and Families Act 2014 s 128(1)). Nor, without prejudice to any other duties of the hirer or temporary work agency under any enactment or rule of law, does the provision made by the Employment Rights Act 1996 s 57ZQ apply where the agency worker:

(1)   has not completed the qualifying period (s 57ZR(1)(a) (as so added)); or

(2)   is no longer entitled to the rights conferred by the Agency Workers Regulations 2010, SI 2010/93, reg 5 (basic working and employment conditions: see PARA 98), pursuant to reg 8(a), (b) (break between assignments: see PARA 99) (Employment Rights Act 1996 s 57ZR(1)(b) (as so added)).

Nor does anything in s 57ZQ impose a duty on the hirer or temporary work agency beyond the original intended duration, or likely duration of the assignment, whichever is the longer: s 57ZR(2) (as so added). As to the meaning of 'agency worker' see PARA 97; definition in the Agency Workers Regulations 2010, SI 2010/93, reg 3, applied by the Employment Rights Act 1996 s 57ZR(4) (as so added). As to the meaning of 'assignment' see PARA 99 note 4; definition in the Agency Workers Regulations 2010, SI 2010/93, reg 2, applied by the Employment Rights Act 1996 s 57ZR(4) (as so added). As to the meaning of 'hirer' see PARA 97 note 3; definition in the Agency Workers Regulations 2010, SI 2010/93, reg 2, applied by the Employment Rights Act 1996 s 57ZR(4) (as so added). As to the meaning of 'qualifying period' see PARA 99; definition in the Agency Workers Regulations 2010, SI 2010/93, reg 7, applied by the Employment Rights Act 1996 s 57ZR(4) (as so added). As to the meaning of 'temporary work agency' see PARA 97; definition in the Agency Workers Regulations 2010, SI 2010/93, reg 4, applied by the Employment Rights Act 1996 s 57ZR(4) (as so added).

2 As to employment tribunals see PARA 1399 et seq; and as to the procedure on a complaint made to an employment tribunal see PARA 1453 et seq.

3 Ie as required by the Employment Rights Act 1996 s 57ZN (agency worker's right to paid time off work to attend adoption appointments: see PARA 344) or s 57ZP (agency worker's right to unpaid time off work to attend adoption appointments: see PARA 345): see s 57ZQ(1)(a) (as added: see note 1).

4 Employment Rights Act 1996 s 57ZQ(1)(a) (as added: see note 1).

5 Ie under the Employment Rights Act 1996 s 57ZO (agency worker's right to remuneration for time off work to attend adoption appointments: see PARA 344): see s 57ZQ(1)(b) (as added: see note 1).

6 Employment Rights Act 1996 s 57ZQ(1)(b) (as added: see note 1).

7 Ie as required by the Employment Rights Act 1996 s 57ZN (agency worker's right to paid time off work to attend adoption appointments: see PARA 344) or s 57ZP (agency worker's right to unpaid time off work to attend adoption appointments: see PARA 345): see s 57ZQ(2) (as added: see note 1).

8 Employment Rights Act 1996 s 57ZQ(2) (as added: see note 1).

9 See the Employment Rights Act 1996 s 57ZQ(3) (as added: see note 1).

10 Employment Rights Act 1996 s 57ZQ(3)(a) (as added: see note 1). For the purposes of s 57ZQ(3)(a), s 207A(3) (extension because mediation in certain European cross-border disputes starts before the time limit expires: see PARA 1454) and s 207B (extension of time limits to facilitate conciliation before institution of proceedings: see PARA 1455) apply: s 57ZQ(4) (as so added). As to time limits generally see PARA 1453.

11 Employment Rights Act 1996 s 57ZQ(3)(b) (as added: see note 1).

12 See the Employment Rights Act 1996 s 57ZQ(5) (as added: see note 1).

13 Ie as required by the Employment Rights Act 1996 s 57ZN (agency worker's right to paid time off work to attend adoption appointments: see PARA 344): see s 57ZQ(6) (as added: see note 1).

14 Ie under the Employment Rights Act 1996 s 57ZO (agency worker's right to remuneration for time off work to attend adoption appointments: see PARA 344): see s 57ZQ(6) (as added: see note 1).

15 See the Employment Rights Act 1996 s 57ZQ(6) (as added: see note 1). Where the tribunal orders that payment under s 57ZQ(6) or s 57ZQ(8) (see head (iii) in the text) be made by the temporary work agency and the hirer, the proportion of that amount payable by each respondent is to be such as may be found by the tribunal to be just and equitable having regard to the extent of each respondent's responsibility for the infringement to which the complaint relates: s 57ZQ(10) (as so added).

16 Ie under the Employment Rights Act 1996 s 57ZO (agency worker's right to remuneration for time off work to attend adoption appointments: see PARA 344): see s 57ZQ(7) (as added: see note 1).

17 See the Employment Rights Act 1996 s 57ZQ(7) (as added: see note 1).

18 Ie as required by the Employment Rights Act 1996 s 57ZP (agency worker's right to unpaid time off work to attend adoption appointments: see PARA 345): see s 57ZQ(8) (as added: see note 1).

19 See the Employment Rights Act 1996 s 57ZQ(8) (as added: see note 1). The text refers to the amount payable to the agency worker to be determined in accordance with the formula:

$$(A \times B) \times 2$$

where A is the appropriate hourly rate for the agency worker determined in accordance with s 57O(2), (3) (see PARA 344 note 20); and B is the number of working hours for which the agency worker would have been entitled under s 57ZP (agency worker's right to unpaid time off work to attend adoption appointments: see PARA 345) to be absent if the time off had not been refused: see s 57ZQ(9) (as so added). See note 15. As to the calculation of a week's pay and normal working hours see PARA 142 et seq. As to the meaning of 'week' see PARA 126 note 13.

(vi) Dependants

347.   Employee's right to time off work to make arrangements for dependants.   An employee[1] is entitled to be permitted by his employer[2] to take a reasonable amount of time off during the employee's working hours[3] in order to take action which is necessary[4]:

(1)   to provide assistance on an occasion when a dependant[5] falls ill, gives birth or is injured or assaulted[6];

(2)   to make arrangements for the provision of care for a dependant who is ill or injured[7];

(3)   in consequence of the death of a dependant[8];

(4)   because of the unexpected disruption or termination of arrangements for the care of a dependant[9]; or

(5)   to deal with an incident which involves a child of the employee and which occurs unexpectedly in a period during which an educational establishment which the child attends is responsible for him[10].

An employee's right so conferred to time off to make arrangements for dependants does not apply, however, unless the employee[11]: (a) tells his employer the reason for his absence as soon as reasonably practicable[12]; and (b) except where head (a) above cannot be complied with until after the employee has returned to work, tells his employer for how long he expects to be absent[13].

1 As to the meaning of 'employee' see PARA 2.
2 As to the meaning of 'employer' see PARA 2.
3 As to the calculation of normal working hours see PARA 142.
   The right conferred by the Employment Rights Act 1996 s 57A does not apply to a share fisherman (see s 199(2); and PARA 167) or to a police officer (see s 200(1); and PARA 168), and may also be lost for some other reason than statutory exclusion, in particular because the contract of employment is illegal (see PARA 18) or has terminated for some reason other than dismissal (see PARA 725 et seq).
4 See the Employment Rights Act 1996 s 57A(1) (s 57A added by the Employment Relations Act 1999 s 8, Sch 4 Pt II).

An employer is not liable under the Employment Rights Act 1996 ss 88, 89 (see PARAS 738, 739) to make any payment in respect of a period of time so taken: see PARA 741. As to the right of complaint to an employment tribunal see PARA 348. As to the questions to be asked by an employment tribunal when determining whether an employee's dismissal comes within the Employment Rights Act 1996 s 57A see *Qua v John Ford Morrison*; applied in *Forster v Cartwright Black Solicitors* [2004] ICR 1728, [2004] IRLR 781, EAT; and see *O'Toole v Cortest Ltd* [2008] All ER (D) 220 (May), EAT.

5 For these purposes, 'dependant' means, in relation to an employee, a spouse or civil partner, a child, a parent or a person who lives in the same household as the employee, otherwise than by reason of being his employee, tenant, lodger or boarder: see the Employment Rights Act 1996 s 57A(3) (s 57A as added (see note 4); s 57A(3) amended by the Civil Partnership Act 2004 s 261(1), Sch 27 para 151). The Employment Rights Act 1996 s 57A(3) is subject to s 57A(4) (see note 6) and s 57A(5) (see note 9): see s 57A(3) (as so added and amended).

6 Employment Rights Act 1996 s 57A(1)(a) (as added: see note 4). For the purposes of s 57A(1)(a) or s 57A(1)(b) (see head (2) in the text), 'dependant' includes, in addition to the persons mentioned in s 57A(3) (see note 5), any person who reasonably relies on the employee: (1) for assistance on an occasion when the person falls ill or is injured or assaulted (s 57A(4)(a) (as so added)); or (2) to make arrangements for the provision of care in the event of illness or injury (s 57A(4)(b) (as so added)).

7 Employment Rights Act 1996 s 57A(1)(b) (as added: see note 4). See note 6. For these purposes, a reference to illness or injury includes a reference to mental illness or injury: s 57A(6) (as so added).The purpose of time off is to arrange for caring, not to do the caring personally: *Qua v John Ford Morrison* [2003] ICR 482, [2003] IRLR 184, EAT.

8 Employment Rights Act 1996 s 57A(1)(c) (as added: see note 4). The provision made by head (3) in the text does not introduce the right to compassionate leave as a result of a bereavement but rather is triggered by the need to take action which is necessary in consequence of the death, including registering the death and, if there was a will, applying for probate: *Forster v Cartwright Black Solicitors* [2004] ICR 1728, [2004] IRLR 781, EAT.

9 Employment Rights Act 1996 s 57A(1)(d) (as added: see note 4). For the purposes of s 57A(1)(d), 'dependant' includes, in addition to the persons mentioned in s 57A(3) (see note 5), any person who reasonably relies on the employee to make arrangements for the provision of care: s 57A(5) (as so added). See also *Harrison v Royal Bank of Scotland plc* [2009] ICR 116, [2009] IRLR 28, EAT (in deciding whether an employee was entitled to take time off under the Employment Rights Act 1996 s 57A(1)(d), the tribunal was entitled to take into account the time which had passed between the employee becoming aware of the risk of the relevant disruption and that risk becoming fact; but that element of time was primarily relevant to and would be considered as part of the question whether it had been necessary for the employee to take that time off).

10 Employment Rights Act 1996 s 57A(1)(e) (as added: see note 4).

11 See the Employment Rights Act 1996 s 57A(2) (as added: see note 4). Dismissal for time taken off work in order to care for a dependant is not automatically unfair where the employee has not complied with requirements of s 57A(2) (see heads (a), (b) in the text): *Qua v John Ford Morrison* [2003] ICR 482, [2003] IRLR 184, EAT. As to the employee's duty to inform the employer of relevant details including the urgent nature of a the need for time off see *Truelove v Safeway Stores plc* [2005] ICR 589, EAT.

12 Employment Rights Act 1996 s 57A(2)(a) (as added: see note 4). See note 11.

13 Employment Rights Act 1996 s 57A(2)(b) (as added: see note 4).See note 11.

348. Complaint to employment tribunal: employee's right to time off work to make arrangements for dependants. An employee[1] may present a complaint to an employment tribunal[2] that his employer[3] has unreasonably refused to permit him to take time off[4] in order to make arrangements for dependants[5]. The tribunal must not consider such a complaint, however, unless it is presented[6]:

(1) before the end of the period of three months beginning with the date when the refusal occurred[7]; or

(2) within such further period as the tribunal considers reasonable in a case where it is satisfied that it was not reasonably practicable for the complaint to be presented before the end of that period of three months[8].

Where an employment tribunal finds such a complaint well-founded, it must make a declaration to that effect[9]; and it may make an award of compensation to be paid by the employer to the employee[10]. The amount of compensation is to be such as the tribunal considers just and equitable in all the circumstances, having regard to[11]: (a) the employer's default in refusing to permit time off to be taken by the employee[12]; and (b) any loss sustained by the employee which is attributable to the matters complained of[13].

1   As to the meaning of 'employee' see PARA 2.
2   As to employment tribunals see PARA 1399 et seq; and as to the procedure on a complaint made to an employment tribunal see PARA 1453 et seq.
3   As to the meaning of 'employer' see PARA 2.
4   Ie as required by the Employment Rights Act 1996 s 57A (see PARA 347): see s 57B(1) (s 57B added by the Employment Relations Act 1999 s 8, Sch 4 Pt II). The remedy of an employee for infringement of any right conferred on him by the Employment Rights Act 1996 s 57A is by way of complaint to an employment tribunal and not otherwise: see s 205(1); and PARA 1406.
5   Employment Rights Act 1996 s 57B(1) (as added: see note 4). As to the meaning of 'dependant' for these purposes see PARA 347 notes 5, 6, 9.
    The right conferred by s 57B does not apply to a share fisherman (see s 199(2); and PARA 167) or to a police officer (see s 200(1); and PARA 168), and may also be lost for some other reason than statutory exclusion, in particular because the contract of employment is illegal (see PARA 18) or has terminated for some reason other than dismissal (see PARA 725 et seq).
6   See the Employment Rights Act 1996 s 57B(2) (as added: see note 4).
7   Employment Rights Act 1996 s 57B(2)(a) (as added: see note 4). For the purposes of s 57B(2)(a), s 207A(3) (extension because mediation in certain European cross-border disputes starts before the time limit expires: see PARA 1454) and s 207B (extension of time limits to facilitate conciliation before institution of proceedings: see PARA 1455) apply: s 57B(2A) (s 57B as so added; s 57B(2A) added by SI 2011/1133; and amended by the Enterprise and Regulatory Reform Act 2013 s 8, Sch 2 paras 15, 24). As to time limits generally see PARA 1453.
8   Employment Rights Act 1996 s 57B(2)(b) (as added: see note 4).
9   Employment Rights Act 1996 s 57B(3)(a) (as added: see note 4).
10 Employment Rights Act 1996 s 57B(3)(b) (as added: see note 4).
11 See the Employment Rights Act 1996 s 57B(4) (as added: see note 4).
12 Employment Rights Act 1996 s 57B(4)(a) (as added: see note 4).
13 Employment Rights Act 1996 s 57B(4)(b) (as added: see note 4).

(vii) Trade Union Activities and Duties

349.   Time off for trade union duties and activities.   Legal rights to time off work originated in the area of trade union law, and the rights to paid time off for trade union duties and unpaid time off for trade union activities are dealt with elsewhere in this title[1].

1   See the Trade Union and Labour Relations (Consolidation) Act 1992 ss 168–173; and PARAS 1065–1068. As to the right to time off for directly elected employee representatives (for the purposes of collective redundancy consultation under Pt IV Ch II (ss 188–198) and consultation on business transfers under the Transfer of Undertakings (Protection of Employment) Regulations 2006, SI 2006/246, regs 13–16: see PARAS 1196–1200) see the Employment Rights Act 1996 s 61–63; and PARA 1209.

(viii) Public Duties

350.   Employee's right to time off work for purposes connected with performing public duties.   An employer[1] must permit an employee[2] of his who is a justice of the peace[3] to take time off during the employee's working hours[4] for the purpose of performing any of the duties of his office[5].

An employer also must permit an employee of his who is a member of[6]:
(1)   a local authority[7];

(2)   a statutory tribunal[8];

(3)   an independent monitoring board for a prison[9];

(4)   a relevant health body[10];

(5)   a relevant education body[11]; or

(6)   the Environment Agency[12],

to take time off during the employee's working hours for the purposes of[13]:

(a)   attendance at a meeting of the body or any of its committees or sub-committees[14];

(b)   the doing of any other thing approved by the body, or anything of a class so approved, for the purpose of the discharge of the functions of the body or of any of its committees or sub-committees[15]; and

(c)   in the case of a local authority which is operating executive arrangements[16]: (i) attendance at a meeting of the executive[17] of that local authority or committee of that executive[18]; and (ii) the doing of any other thing, by an individual member of that executive, for the purposes of the discharge of any function which is to any extent the responsibility of that executive[19].

The amount of time off which an employee is to be permitted so to take, and the occasions on which and any conditions subject to which time off may be so taken, are those that are reasonable in all the circumstances, having regard, in particular, to[20]:

(A)   how much time off is required for the performance of the duties of the office or as a member of the body in question, and how much time off is required for the performance of the particular duty[21];

(B)   how much time off the employee has already been permitted[22] (under either the Trade Union and Labour Relations (Consolidation) Act 1992 or the Employment Rights Act 1996)[23]; and

(C)   the circumstances of the employer's business[24] and the effect of the employee's absence on the running of that business[25].

1   As to the meaning of 'employer' see PARA 2.

2   As to the meaning of 'employee' see PARA 2.

3   As to justices of the peace see MAGISTRATES vol 71 (2013) PARA 401 et seq.

4   For these purposes, the working hours of an employee are to be taken to be any time when, in accordance with his contract of employment, the employee is required to be at work: Employment Rights Act 1996 s 50(11). As to the meaning of 'contract of employment' see PARA 2. An employer is not liable under ss 88, 89 (see PARAS 738, 739) to make any payment in respect of a period of time so taken: see PARA 741. As to the right of complaint to an employment tribunal see PARA 351.

5   Employment Rights Act 1996 s 50(1). The Secretary of State may by order modify the provisions of:

(1)   s 50(1), s 50(2) (see the text and notes 6–13), s 50(5) (see note 7), s 50(7)–(9) (see notes 9–11) by adding any office or body, removing any office or body or altering the description of any office or body (s 50(10)(a)); or

(2)   s 50(3) (see the text and notes 14–19) (s 50(10)(b)).

As to the Secretary of State see PARA 5 note 21; and as to the making of orders under the Employment Rights Act 1996 generally see PARA 162. In exercise of the power conferred by s 50(10), the Secretary of State has made the Time Off for Public Duties Order 2000, SI 2000/1737; the Time Off for Public Duties (No 2) Order 2000, SI 2000/2463; and the Time Off for Public Duties (Parent Councils) Order 2007, SI 2007/1837.

6   See the Employment Rights Act 1996 s 50(2).

The right conferred by s 50 does not apply to a share fisherman (see s 199(2); and PARA 167) or to a police officer (see s 200(1); and PARA 168), and may also be lost for some other reason than statutory exclusion, in particular because the contract of employment is illegal (see PARA 18) or has terminated for some reason other than dismissal (see PARA 725 et seq). Where the terms of employment of a person in Crown employment, or a relevant member of the House of Lords staff, restrict his right to take part in:

(1)   certain political activities (see ss 191(5)(a), 194(5)(a); and PARAS 163, 164); or
(2)   activities which may conflict with his official functions (see ss 191(5)(b), 194(5)(b); and PARAS 163, 164),
nothing in s 50 requires him to be allowed time off work for public duties connected with any such activities (see ss 191(5), 194(5); and PARAS 163, 164). As to persons in Crown employment generally see PARA 6.

7   Employment Rights Act 1996 s 50(2)(a). For these purposes, 'local authority' means, in relation to England and Wales:
(1)   a local authority within the meaning of the Local Government Act 1972 (see LOCAL GOVERNMENT vol 69 (2009) PARA 22 et seq) (Employment Rights Act 1996 s 50(5)(a));
(2)   the Common Council of the City of London (see LONDON GOVERNMENT vol 71 (2013) PARAS 34–38) (s 50(5)(c));
(3)   a National Park authority (see OPEN SPACES AND COUNTRYSIDE vol 78 (2010) PARA 526 et seq) (s 50(5)(d)); or
(4)   the Broads Authority (see WATER AND WATERWAYS vol 101 (2009) PARA 734) (s 50(5)(e)).
See also note 5. As to the meanings of 'England' and 'Wales' see PARA 2 note 12.

8   Employment Rights Act 1996 s 50(2)(b). See also note 5. As to statutory tribunals see CONSTITUTIONAL AND ADMINISTRATIVE LAW vol 20 (2014) PARA 619 et seq; COURTS AND TRIBUNALS vol 24 (2010) PARA 864 et seq.

9   Employment Rights Act 1996 s 50(2)(d) (s 50(2)(d), (7)(a) amended by the Offender Management Act 2007 s 39, Sch 3 Pt 2 para 8). For these purposes, 'independent monitoring board' means a board appointed under the Prison Act 1952 s 6(2) (see PRISONS AND PRISONERS vol 85 (2012) PARA 413): Employment Rights Act 1996 s 50(7)(a) (as so amended). See also note 5.

10   Employment Rights Act 1996 s 50(2)(e). As to the meaning of 'relevant health body' see s 50(8) (amended by the Health and Social Care (Community Health and Standards) Act 2003 s 34, Sch 4 paras 99, 100; the National Health Service (Consequential Provisions) Act 2006 s 2, Sch 1 paras 177, 179; the Health and Social Care Act 2012 ss 55(2), 179(6), 249(1), 277, Sch 5 paras 72, 74, Sch 14 Pt 2 paras 68, 69, Sch 17 para 6(1), (2), Sch 19 para 6(1), (2); and SI 2000/90; SI 2002/2469; SI 2007/961). See also note 5.

11   Employment Rights Act 1996 s 50(2)(f). For these purposes, a 'relevant education body' means:
(1)   a managing or governing body of an educational establishment maintained by a local authority (as defined in the Education Act 1996 s 579(1): see EDUCATION vol 35 (2011) PARA 24) (Employment Rights Act 1996 s 50(9)(a) (amended by SI 2010/1158));
(2)   a further education corporation, sixth form college corporation or higher education corporation (Employment Rights Act 1996 s 50(9)(b) (s 50(9)(b) substituted, s 50(9B) added, by SI 2010/1080));
(3)   the General Teaching Council for Wales (Employment Rights Act 1996 s 50(9)(j) (added by SI 2000/2463)).
For these purposes, 'further education corporation', 'sixth form college corporation' and 'higher education corporation' have the same meanings as in the Further and Higher Education Act 1992: Employment Rights Act 1996 s 50(9B) (as so added). Accordingly, as to further education corporations see EDUCATION vol 36 (2011) PARA 733 et seq; as to sixth form college corporations see EDUCATION vol 36 (2011) PARA 758; and as to higher education corporations see EDUCATION vol 36 (2011) PARA 835 et seq. As to the General Teaching Council for Wales see EDUCATION vol 36 (2011) PARA 977 et seq. See also note 5.

12   Employment Rights Act 1996 s 50(2)(g). See also note 5. As to the Environment Agency see ENVIRONMENTAL QUALITY AND PUBLIC HEALTH vol 45 (2010) PARA 68 et seq.

13   See the Employment Rights Act 1996 s 50(2). The text refers to the purposes specified in s 50(3) (see heads (a)–(c) in the text): see s 50(2). See also note 5.
    An employer does not comply merely by allowing an employee to rearrange his time, so that time lost is made up elsewhere: *Ratcliffe v Dorset County Council* [1978] IRLR 191. Where an employee holds several offices, he may have to organise them so as to produce a reasonable amount of time off in aggregate: *Borders Regional Council v Maule* [1993] IRLR 199, EAT. In relation to the right to time off for trade union duties and activities (see PARA 349) it has been held that: (1) what is reasonable time off is a question of fact for a tribunal (*Thomas Scott & Sons (Bakers) Ltd v Allen* [1983] IRLR 329, CA); and (2) in so deciding, the tribunal should not set its own standard but should consider whether the employer's decision on the matter was within a band of reasonable conduct (*Ministry of Defence v Crook and Irving* [1982] IRLR 488, EAT).

14   Employment Rights Act 1996 s 50(3)(a).

15   Employment Rights Act 1996 s 50(3)(b).

16 See the Employment Rights Act 1996 s 50(3)(c) (s 50(3)(c), (9A) added, in relation to England, by SI 2001/2237 and, in relation to Wales, by SI 2002/808). For these purposes, 'executive arrangements' has the same meaning as in the Local Government Act 2000 Pt II (ss 10–48) (see LOCAL GOVERNMENT vol 69 (2009) PARA 303): see the Employment Rights Act 1996 s 50(9A) (as so added).

17 For these purposes, 'executive' has the same meaning as in the Local Government Act 2000 Pt II (see LOCAL GOVERNMENT vol 69 (2009) PARA 327 et seq): see the Employment Rights Act 1996 s 50(9A) (as added: see note 16).

18 Employment Rights Act 1996 s 50(3)(c)(i) (as added: see note 16).

19 Employment Rights Act 1996 s 50(3)(c)(ii) (as added: see note 16).

20 See the Employment Rights Act 1996 s 50(4).

21 Employment Rights Act 1996 s 50(4)(a).

22 Ie under the Trade Union and Labour Relations (Consolidation) Act 1992 s 168 (time off for trade union duties and activities: see PARA 1065) or s 170 (time off for trade union activities: see PARA 1066) or under the Employment Rights Act 1996 s 50: see s 50(4)(b).

23 Employment Rights Act 1996 s 50(4)(b).

24 As to the meaning of 'business' see PARA 135 note 4.

25 Employment Rights Act 1996 s 50(4)(c).

351. Complaint to employment tribunal: employee's right to time off work for purposes connected with performing public duties. An employee[1] may present a complaint to an employment tribunal[2] that his employer[3] has failed to permit him to take time off[4] for public duties[5]. An employment tribunal must not consider such a complaint, however, unless it is presented[6]:

(1) before the end of the period of three months beginning with the date on which the failure occurred[7]; or

(2) within such further period as the tribunal considers reasonable in a case where it is satisfied that it was not reasonably practicable for the complaint to be presented before the end of that period of three months[8].

Where an employment tribunal finds such a complaint well-founded, the tribunal[9]:

(a) must make a declaration to that effect[10]; and

(b) may make an award of compensation to be paid by the employer to the employee[11].

The amount of the compensation under head (b) above is to be such as the tribunal considers just and equitable in all the circumstances, having regard to[12]: (i) the employer's default in failing to permit time off to be taken by the employee[13]; and (ii) any loss sustained by the employee which is attributable to the matters to which the complaint relates[14].

1 As to the meaning of 'employee' see PARA 2.

2 As to employment tribunals see PARA 1399 et seq; and as to the procedure on a complaint made to an employment tribunal see PARA 1453 et seq.

3 As to the meaning of 'employer' see PARA 2.

4 Ie as required by the Employment Rights Act 1996 s 50 (see PARA 350): see s 51(1) (s 51(1), (2), (3) amended by the Employment Rights (Dispute Resolution) Act 1998 s 1(2)(a)).

5 Employment Rights Act 1996 s 51(1) (as amended: see note 4). In relation to the right to time off for trade union duties and activities (see PARA 349), it has been held that 'failure to permit' implies knowledge of the employee's request, so that, if the employer has simply not responded, and knowledge cannot be proved, there is no failure to permit: *Ryford Ltd v Drinkwater* [1996] IRLR 16, EAT.

The remedy of an employee for infringement of any right conferred on him by the Employment Rights Act 1996 s 50 is by way of complaint to an employment tribunal and not otherwise: see s 205(1); and PARA 1406. The right conferred by s 51 does not apply to a share fisherman (see s 199(2); and PARA 167) or to a police officer (see s 200(1); and PARA 168), and may also be lost for some other reason than statutory exclusion, in particular because the contract of employment is illegal (see PARA 18) or has terminated for some reason other than dismissal (see PARA 725 et seq).

6 See the Employment Rights Act 1996 s 51(2) (as amended: see note 4).
7 Employment Rights Act 1996 s 51(2)(a). For the purposes of s 51(2)(a), s 207A(3) (extension because mediation in certain European cross-border disputes starts before the time limit expires: see PARA 1454) and s 207B (extension of time limits to facilitate conciliation before institution of proceedings: see PARA 1455) apply: s 51(2A) (added by SI 2011/1133; and amended by the Enterprise and Regulatory Reform Act 2013 s 8, Sch 2 paras 15, 20). As to time limits generally see PARA 1453.
8 Employment Rights Act 1996 s 51(2)(b).
9 See the Employment Rights Act 1996 s 51(3) (as amended: see note 4).
    The tribunal's function is to adjudicate and, if necessary, award compensation; it has no power to attach conditions: *Corner v Buckinghamshire County Council* [1978] ICR 836, [1978] IRLR 320, EAT.
10 Employment Rights Act 1996 s 51(3)(a).
11 Employment Rights Act 1996 s 51(3)(b).
12 See the Employment Rights Act 1996 s 51(4).
13 Employment Rights Act 1996 s 51(4)(a).
14 Employment Rights Act 1996 s 51(4)(b).

(ix) Occupational Pension Scheme Trustees

352. Employee's right to time off work for purposes connected with his position as pension scheme trustee. In relation to a relevant occupational pension scheme[1], the employer[2] must permit an employee[3] of his who is a trustee of the scheme[4] to take time off during the employee's working hours[5] for the purpose of[6]:

(1)   performing any of his duties as such a trustee[7]; or
(2)   undergoing training[8] relevant to the performance of those duties[9].

The amount of time off which an employee is to be permitted so to take, and the purposes for which, the occasions on which, and any conditions subject to which, time off may be so taken are those that are reasonable in all the circumstances having regard, in particular, to[10]:

(a)   how much time off is required for the performance of the duties of a trustee of the scheme and the undergoing of relevant training, and how much time off is required for performing the particular duty or for undergoing the particular training[11]; and

(b)   the circumstances of the employer's business and the effect of the employee's absence on the running of that business[12].

An employer who permits an employee who is a trustee of an occupational pension scheme to take time off for these purposes[13] must pay the employee for the time taken off pursuant to that permission[14]; and a right to be paid any such amount[15] does not affect any right of an employee in relation to remuneration under his contract of employment ('contractual remuneration')[16].

1 For these purposes, 'relevant occupational pension scheme' means an occupational pension scheme as defined in the Pension Schemes Act 1993 s 1 (see PERSONAL AND OCCUPATIONAL PENSIONS vol 80 (2013) PARA 208) established under a trust: see the Employment Rights Act 1996 s 58(3)(a). As to personal and occupational pension provision generally see PERSONAL AND OCCUPATIONAL PENSIONS vol 80 (2013) PARA 201 et seq. See also PARA 115 note 1.
2 For these purposes, references to the employer, in relation to a relevant occupational pension scheme, are references to an employer of persons in the description or category of employment to which the scheme relates: see the Employment Rights Act 1996 s 58(3)(b). As to the meaning of 'employer' generally see PARA 2.
    As from a day to be appointed under the Pensions Act 2004 s 322(1), the Employment Rights Act 1996 s 58(3)(b) is amended so that references to the employer, in relation to a relevant occupational pension scheme, are references to an employer of persons in the

description of employment to which the scheme relates (see s 58(3)(b) (prospectively amended by the Pensions Act 2004 s 320, Sch 13 Pt 1)). However, at the date at which this volume states the law, no such day had been appointed.

3   As to the meaning of 'employee' see PARA 2.

4   The Employment Rights Act 1996 58 applies to an employee who is a director of a company which is a trustee of a relevant occupational pension scheme as it applies to an employee who is a trustee of such a scheme (references to such a trustee being read for this purpose as references to such a director): s 58(2A) (added by the Welfare Reform and Pensions Act 1999 s 18, Sch 2 para 19(1), (3)).

5   For these purposes, the working hours of an employee are to be taken to be any time when, in accordance with his contract of employment, the employee is required to be at work: see the Employment Rights Act 1996 s 58(4). See also note 4. As to the meaning of 'contract of employment' see PARA 2.

6   See the Employment Rights Act 1996 s 58(1).
    An employer is not liable under ss 88, 89 (see PARAS 738, 739) to make any payment in respect of a period of time so taken: see PARA 741. As to the right of complaint to an employment tribunal see PARA 353.

7   Employment Rights Act 1996 s 58(1)(a). See also note 4.

8   For these purposes, references to training are references to training on the employer's premises or elsewhere: see the Employment Rights Act 1996 s 58(3)(c) (added by the Teaching and Higher Education Act 1998 s 44(1), Sch 3 para 12). See also note 4.

9   Employment Rights Act 1996 s 58(1)(b).

10 See the Employment Rights Act 1996 s 58(2). See also note 4.

11 Employment Rights Act 1996 s 58(2)(a).

12 Employment Rights Act 1996 s 58(2)(b). See also note 4. As to the meaning of 'business' see PARA 135 note 4.

13 Ie under the Employment Rights Act 1996 s 58 (see the text and notes 1–12): see s 59(1).

14 Employment Rights Act 1996 s 59(1). Where the employee's remuneration for the work he would ordinarily have been doing during that time does not vary with the amount of work done, he must be paid as if he had worked at that work for the whole of that time: s 59(2). Where, however, the employee's remuneration for the work he would ordinarily have been doing during that time varies with the amount of work done, he must be paid an amount calculated by reference to the average hourly earnings for that work: s 59(3). The average hourly earnings mentioned in s 59(3) are:
    (1)   those of the employee concerned (s 59(4)(a)); or
    (2)   if no fair estimate can be made of those earnings, the average hourly earnings for work of that description of persons in comparable employment with the same employer or, if there are no such persons, a figure of average hourly earnings which is reasonable in the circumstances (s 59(4)(b)).

15 Ie under the Employment Rights Act 1996 s 59(1) (see the text and notes 13–14): see s 59(5).

16 Employment Rights Act 1996 s 59(5). However, any contractual remuneration paid to an employee in respect of a period of time off under s 58 (see the text and notes 1–12) goes towards discharging any liability of the employer under s 59(1) (see the text and notes 13–14) in respect of that period; and, conversely, any payment under s 59(1) in respect of a period goes towards discharging any liability of the employer to pay contractual remuneration in respect of that period: s 59(6).

353.   Complaint to employment tribunal: employee's right to time off work for purposes connected with his position as pension scheme trustee. An employee[1] may present a complaint to an employment tribunal[2] that his employer[3]:

   (1)   has failed to permit him to take time off work[4] for purposes connected with his position as a pension scheme trustee[5]; or

   (2)   has failed to pay the amount to which he is[6] entitled as remuneration for time so taken[7].

An employment tribunal must not consider such a complaint, however, unless it is presented[8]:

   (a)   before the end of the period of three months beginning with the date when the failure occurred[9]; or

   (b)   within such further period as the tribunal considers reasonable in a case where it is satisfied that it was not reasonably practicable for the complaint to be presented before the end of that period of three months[10].

Where an employment tribunal finds such a complaint under head (1) above well-founded, the tribunal[11]:

(i)   must make a declaration to that effect[12]; and

(ii)   may make an award of compensation to be paid by the employer to the employee[13].

The amount of the compensation under head (ii) above is to be such as the tribunal considers just and equitable in all the circumstances, having regard to[14]: (A) the employer's default in failing to permit time off to be taken by the employee[15]; and (B) any loss sustained by the employee which is attributable to the matters complained of[16].

Where, on a complaint under head (2) above, an employment tribunal finds that an employer has failed to pay an employee the amount to which he is[17] entitled as remuneration for time so taken, it must order the employer to pay the amount which it finds to be due[18].

1   As to the meaning of 'employee' see PARA 2. See also PARA 352 note 4.
2   As to employment tribunals see PARA 1399 et seq; and as to the procedure on a complaint made to an employment tribunal see PARA 1453 et seq.
3   See the Employment Rights Act 1996 s 60(1) (s 60(1), (2), (3), (5) amended by the Employment Rights (Dispute Resolution) Act 1998 s 1(2)(a)). As to the meaning of 'employer' see PARA 2.
4   Ie as required by the Employment Rights Act 1996 s 58 (see PARA 352): see s 60(1)(a).
        The remedy of an employee for infringement of any right conferred on him by s 58 is by way of complaint to an employment tribunal and not otherwise: see s 205(1); and PARA 1406.
5   Employment Rights Act 1996 s 60(1)(a).
6   Ie in accordance with the Employment Rights Act 1996 s 59 (see PARA 352): see s 60(1)(b).
        The remedy of an employee for infringement of any right conferred on him by s 59 is by way of complaint to an employment tribunal and not otherwise: see s 205(1); and PARA 1406.
7   Employment Rights Act 1996 s 60(1)(b).
8   See the Employment Rights Act 1996 s 60(2) (as amended: see note 3).
9   Employment Rights Act 1996 s 60(2)(a). For the purposes of s 60(2)(a), s 207A(3) (extension because mediation in certain European cross-border disputes starts before the time limit expires: see PARA 1454) and s 207B (extension of time limits to facilitate conciliation before institution of proceedings: see PARA 1455) apply: s 60(2A) (added by SI 2011/1133; and amended by the Enterprise and Regulatory Reform Act 2013 s 8, Sch 2 paras 15, 25). As to time limits generally see PARA 1453.
10   Employment Rights Act 1996 s 60(2)(b).
11   See the Employment Rights Act 1996 s 60(3) (as amended: see note 3).
12   Employment Rights Act 1996 s 60(3)(a).
13   Employment Rights Act 1996 s 60(3)(b).
14   See the Employment Rights Act 1996 s 60(4).
15   Employment Rights Act 1996 s 60(4)(a).
16   Employment Rights Act 1996 s 60(4)(b).
17   Ie in accordance with the Employment Rights Act 1996 s 59 (see PARA 352): see s 60(5) (as amended: see note 3).
18   Employment Rights Act 1996 s 60(5) (as amended: see note 3).

INDEX

Employment

References are to paragraph numbers; superior figures refer to notes

APPRENTICESHIP AGREEMENT
breach by apprentice, 747
consent requirements, 128
covenants in, 129
employee under, person treated as, 494
form of, 128
injunction against breach, restriction on
right to, 747
justification for quitting service, 748
non-performance, excuses for, 748
outside UK, whether apprentice obliged
to serve outside, 748
parties to, 128
specific performance, no right to, 747
termination—
at will, prohibition on, 128n[1]
bankruptcy of master, on, 752
change in composition of firm or
business, on, 753
death of master or apprentice, on,
751
minimum period of notice,
apprentice's right to, 750
minor's power to dissolve, 749
misconduct by apprentice, on, 754
mutual consent, by, 750
woman treated as employee, for
maternity pay purposes, 406
writing, need for, 128

ARBITRATION
ACAS involvement. *See* ADVISORY,
CONCILIATION AND ARBITRATION
SERVICE

ARBITRATION CLAUSE
minor, binding on, 15

ARMED FORCES, MEMBER
agency worker regulations, and, 107
continuous employment, following
reinstatement with former
employer, 419, 461, 507
industrial action, statutory restriction
on, 1391
national minimum wage, not qualifying
for, 192
part-time workers regulations—
application of, 82
employment tribunal, complaint to,
82n[11]
substitute labour, use as, 1398
working time protection—
exclusion from provisions, 306
generally, 275

ATTENDANCE ALLOWANCE
wages, as part of, 255n[2]

AUDIT
industrial training board accounts, of,
672
BAILMENT
employment relationship distinguished,
13
BANKRUPTCY
apprenticeship agreement, effect on,
752
contract of employment, effect on, 727
BETTING WORKER
meaning, 321n[2]
betting transactions: meaning, 321n[2]
betting work: meaning, 321n[2]
protected: meaning, 321
Sunday work—
detriment—
date of the act: meaning, 615n[7]
examples of no detriment suffered,
615n[6]
opted-out worker, 615n[8]
right not to suffer, 615
enforceability of employment
contract, 322
explanatory statements, requirement
for, 324
opting-in notice, effect, 321, 322
opting-out notice, 323
protected betting worker: meaning,
321
protected shop worker: meaning, 321
statutory protection, 320
unfair dismissal, 320, 787
BODY CORPORATE
national minimum wage offence by,
252
CADET FORCE
national minimum wage, member not
qualifying for, 190
CAREERS GUIDANCE
providers of, application of redundancy
payments legislation, 843
CAREERS SERVICES
ancillary goods and services, provision
of, 642
Her Majesty's Chief Inspector of
Education, Children's Services and
Skills, inspection by, 641
inspection, 641
local authority—
meaning, 640n[4]
ancillary goods and services, provision
of, 642
arrangements with, 640
control by Secretary of State, 643
directions to, 640

References are to paragraph numbers; superior figures refer to notes

COLLECTIVE BARGAINING—*continued*
bargaining unit—*continued*
changes affecting—*continued*
unit ceasing to exist. *See* ceasing to
exist, employer believing *above*
withdrawal of applications as to,
1147
demand to be recognised as, 1097
method of bargaining, negotiations as
to, 1123
new unit—
construction of references to
collective bargaining, 1132n[5]
decision as to—
procedure generally, 1141
relevant bargaining arrangements:
meaning, 1142n[5]
secret ballot, notice of, 1144
statutory outside unit, at least
one worker within, 1142
voluntary or statutory outside
unit, no worker within,
1144
voluntary outside unit, at least
one worker within, 1143
guidance from Secretary of State,
1144n[17]
method of bargaining in relation to,
effect, 1148
parties agreeing, 1134
residual workers, provisions as to,
1145
secret ballot as to, 1144
residual workers, provisions as to,
1145
specific performance for breach of
arrangements, 1148
statutory outside bargaining unit:
meaning, 1142n[4]
training for workers within—
consultation provisions—
complaint to tribunal, 1173
employer's failure to consult,
1173
generally, 1172
meeting. *See* meeting to discuss
below
meeting to discuss—
arrangements for, 1172
date for, 1172n[7]
subsequent meeting, employer
wishing to convene, 1172n[9]
voluntary outside bargaining unit:
meaning, 1143n[4]
'dynamic' interpretation of clauses,
139n[32]

COLLECTIVE BARGAINING—*continued*
information, disclosure of—
Central Arbitration Committee,
complaint to—
award, 1182
claim in addition to—
expiry of right to present,
1182n[16]
right to present, 1182
further complaint, 1182
hearing, 1182n[9, 12]
procedure on receipt, 1182
right to present, 1182
Code of Practice, 1180
employer's duty—
generally, 1179
restriction on, 1181
failure to disclose, complaint. *See*
Central Arbitration Committee,
complaint to *above*
restrictions on duty of, 1181
method of—
application to Central Arbitration
Committee to specify—
admissibility of, 1130
agreement, in absence of, 1129
failure to carry out agreement,
where, 1129
generally, 1129
procedure where application
made, 1130
response to application, 1131
withdrawal, restriction on, 1131
failure to carry out, 1124, 1129
negotiations as to, 1123
partnerships at work, encouraging,
1096
trade union recognition. *See* TRADE
UNION RECOGNITION

COMMISSIONER OF POLICE OF THE
METROPOLIS
redundancy payments legislation,
application of, 845

CONFIDENTIAL INFORMATION
disclosure in public interest, 68
European Works Council—
breach of duty not to disclose, 1273
withholding of information by central
management, 1274
information and consultation
representative—
breach of duty not to disclose, 1273,
1309
withholding of information by central
management, 1274

CONFIDENTIAL
  INFORMATION—*continued*
information and consultation
    representative—*continued*
  withholding of information by
    employer, 1310
misuse by employee—
  exceptions to duty, 68
  implied term, 67, 71
  intelligence and security services,
    71n[6]
  termination of employment,
    following, 7
  trade secret, 71
protected disclosure—
  meaning, 69
  detriment, employee's right not to
    suffer, 619
  forms of making, 69
  generally, 68
  qualifying disclosure for purposes of,
    70
  unfair dismissal for making, 792
  void term precluding the making of,
    69
whistleblowing—
  generally, 68
  protected disclosure, 68, 69

CONSTRUCTIVE DISMISSAL
  meaning, 763
  annual pay rise etc, failure to honour
    contractual entitlement, 763n[16]
  anticipatory repudiatory conduct, 763n[6]
  breaches of contract supporting findings
    of, 763
  generally, 763
  grievances not treated seriously, where,
    49
  illegal or dangerous orders, for refusing
    to obey, 63
  past waived breaches, effect, 763n[10]

CONTEMPT OF COURT
  acts giving rise to, 1442
  trade union, by, 1442

CONTINENTAL SHELF
  foreign sector of: meaning, 155n[5],
    156n[2], 184n[4]
  operations on, persons employed in—
    continental shelf operations:
      meaning, 407n[10]
    statutory adoption pay, 499
    statutory maternity pay, 411
    statutory paternity pay, 453
    statutory sick pay, 568
  United Kingdom sector of: meaning,
    155n[5], 184n[3]

CONTINUITY OF EMPLOYMENT
  change of employer, 135
  continuous employment, computation of
    period of—
    absence, weeks counting in case of,
      131
    beginning of period, 130
    determination of questions, 130
    generally, 130
    incapacity, weeks counting in case
      of, 131
    temporary cessations of work, 131n[5]
  dismissed employee, reinstatement or
    re-engagement, 133
  industrial disputes, effect of, 134
  lockout, in case of, 134
  military service, reinstatement after, 132
  redundancy payment, right to. *See under*
    REDUNDANCY PAYMENT
  statutory concept, as, 130n[10]
  strike, in case of, 134
  transfer of undertaking. *See* TRANSFER
    OF UNDERTAKING

CONTRACT
  unfair terms—
    consumer: meaning, 17
    contract of employment, in, 17
    legislation, applicability of, 17

CONTRACT OF EMPLOYMENT
  meaning. See under WORDS AND
    PHRASES *post*
  breach, employment tribunal's
    jurisdiction to hear complaint,
    1407
  capacity, 15
  certainty, need for, 16
  clarity, need for, 16
  collective agreement incorporated into,
    1176
  consideration, need for, 16
  constructive termination of, 867
  consumer, party to contract dealing as,
    17n[3]
  contracting out of rights, void provision
    as to, 150
  contrary to statute, effect, 18
  covenant in restraint of trade, 19
  Crown employment, 6
  effective date of termination: meaning,
    755n[11]
  employee's obligations—
    competing with employer, restriction
      on, 67
    confidential information. *See*
      CONFIDENTIAL INFORMATION
      (misuse by employee)

DATA PROTECTION
employees, information as to, 21
DATABASE
employee making, ownership, 72
DESIGN
employee creating, ownership, 72
DIRECTOR OF COMPANY
contract of service etc, company's duty
to keep, 8n[2]
employee, as, 8
employee involvement duties, 1235
office-holder, as, 8
one-man company, 8n[3]
DIRECTORS' REPORT
employee involvement, statement as to,
1235
DISABLED PERSON
sheltered employment. *See* SHELTERED
EMPLOYMENT
DISCIPLINARY PROCEDURE
ACAS code of practice—
generally, 698, 700
See also under revised system *below*
contractual basis for powers, 699
former dispute resolution procedures—
generally, 698
statutory—
ACAS code of practice, replacement
by, 700
application, 700
hearing, right to be accompanied at—
alternative time, where companion
not available, 717n[9]
detriment, right not to be subjected
to, 720
disciplinary hearing: meaning, 717n[3]
employment tribunal, complaint to,
719
generally, 717
participation of companion, 717n[7]
reasonable nature of request, 717n[5]
specified description of companion,
717n[6]
time off to accompany employee,
717n[11]
unfair dismissal, 721
worker: meaning, 718
powers—
contractual basis for, 699
examples, 699
revised system—
ACAS code of practice—
admissibility in evidence, 701
general principles, 702
guidance booklet, 701
helpline, 701

DISCIPLINARY
PROCEDURE—*continued*
revised system—*continued*
ACAS code of practice—*continued*
issue, 701
non-mandatory nature of, 701
appeal—
ad hoc procedure, arrangements
for, 708n[16]
generally, 708
internal, 708n[2]
no contractual right to, where,
708n[16]
time-limit for lodging, 708n[2]
appropriate action, decision on, 707
criminal offence involved, 709
disciplinary situations, examples of,
702n[2]
dismissal without notice, behaviour
warranting, 707
facts, establishing, 703
final written warning, 707
general principles, 702
generally, 698
hearing, right to be accompanied at.
See hearing, right to be
accompanied at *above*
informing employee of problem, 704
meeting—
companion accompanying employee
to, 706
inability or unwillingness to
attend, 707
procedure at, 705
time for holding, 705
special cases, 709
trade union representative action
against, 709
written warning, 707
written statement of, duty to provide,
120
DISCLOSURE OF INFORMATION
working time regulations, information
obtained by inspector, 313
DISCRIMINATION
employers' association, by, 1082
Equality Act 2010, under—
equal pay audit. *See* EQUAL PAY AUDIT
generally, 608
prohibited conduct, 51
protected characteristics, 51
sheltered employment. *See* SHELTERED
EMPLOYMENT
trade union, by, 1036
DISMISSAL
adoption leave, during, 386

EMPLOYMENT APPEAL TRIBUNAL
(EAT)—*continued*
  appeal to—*continued*
    notice of—*continued*
      consideration of, 1501
      contents, 1495n3
      institution of appeal by, 1495
      length of, 1495n3
      national security proceedings,
        procedure in case of, 1498
      prescribed form, 1495n3
      respondent's answer to—
        application to amend, 1501
        generally, 1499
        sealed copy, service of, 1498
        service, 1495, 1504
      settlement agreement, enforceable as
        contract, 1503
      striking out for non-payment of fee,
        1496
      time for, 1495
      time limits, extension, 1500
  authorities, citation of, 1508
  award, enforcement, 1529
  case management, 1501
  central office, 1426
  conciliation, promotion of, 1495
  constitution, 1422
  contempt, 1522
  costs order—
    meaning, 1525
    ability to pay, regard to, 1525
    application for, 1525
    assisted person, in case of, 1525
    costs: meaning, 1525n4
    determining amount of costs, 1525
    litigants in person, against, 1527
    power to make, 1525
    unreasonable conduct, in case of,
      1525n8
    wasted costs order, 1526
    written reasons request for, 1525
  Court of Appeal, appeal to, 1530
  decision—
    enforcement, 1529
    error in, correction of, 1528
    review of, 1528
    See also order *below*
  decisions binding on, 1445
  directions—
    application for, 1512
    automatic, prior to preliminary
      hearing, 1519
    full hearing, for, 1520
    further directions, 1512
    power to give, 1512

EMPLOYMENT APPEAL TRIBUNAL
(EAT)—*continued*
  disability cases, restriction of publicity,
    1433, 1518
  document—
    meaning, 1451n5
    appeal, to be served on institution
      of, 1495
    copies, right to request, 1505
    inspection, 1505
    production of, power to order, 1514
    register of cases, entry of details in,
      1505
    sealed with date of presentation,
      1505
    service of, 1504
  employment tribunal hearing, complaint
    about conduct of, 1497
  European Company, jurisdiction as to
    proceedings, 1336
  evidence before—
    application for admission, 1515
    'fishing expedition' to establish
      grounds, avoidance of, 1515
    fresh, putting in, 1516
    oath, on, 1522
  expenses order. *See* costs order *above*
  fact—
    perverse decision on, 1429
    questions of, examples, 1429
  fees—
    introduction of, unsuccessful
      application for judicial review,
      1496n17
    losing party, recovery from, 1496
    payment on making appeal, 1496
    power to prescribe, 1434
  fines, enforcement, 1529
  full hearing—
    agreeing bundle of papers, 1506
    directions, 1520
    fast-tracked, 1521
    listing for, 1520
    new point of law raised at, 1516
    time for, 1521
    unreserved judgment delivered at,
      1524
    website, judgments posted on, 1524
  guideline decisions, 1445
  hearing—
    citation of authorities at, co-operation
      as to, 1508
    contempt, 1522
    core bundle of papers, need to
      prepare, 1506

EMPLOYMENT TRIBUNAL—*continued*
  case management—*continued*
    other parties, power to add, 1466
    striking out of claim, 1466
    transfer of proceedings—
      court, from, 1469
      with the UK, 1469
  claim—
    meaning, 1457n^2
    commencement, 1461
    delivery, method of, 1461n^3, 1467
    employer's contract claim. *See*
      employer's contract claim *below*
    employment judge, reference to, 1461
    England and Wales, in, 1461
    equal value, for. *See* equal value claim
      below
    fees for. *See* fees *below*
    initial consideration of, 1464
    protected disclosure, allegation of,
      1461
    rejection, grounds for, 1461
    response to—
      application for reconsideration,
        1462
      case management order, making
        of, 1464
      consideration of documents
        following, 1464
      copies—
        national security case, procedure
          in, 1462
        right to, 1462
      employer's contract claim as part
        of, 1463
      extension of time to respond,
        application for, 1462
      generally, 1462
      hearing to consider, where
        necessary, 1464
      no reasonable prospect of success,
        judge deciding, 1464
      prescribed form, on, 1462
      rejection, 1462
      representations, judges' request
        for, 1464
      striking out, 1466
    single claimant: meaning, 1457n^5
    striking out, 1466
    time of receipt, 1461n^3
    to or more claimants, 1461
    withdrawal, 1475
    See also complaint to *below*
  common law claim, no inherent power
    to hear, 1399n^3

EMPLOYMENT TRIBUNAL—*continued*
  complaint to—
    adoption appointment—
      agency worker's right to attend,
        346
      employee's right to attend, 343
    agency worker, by—
      generally, 105
      supply ended on maternity
        grounds, 607
    ante-natal care, time off etc—
      agency worker, 338, 340
      refusal of right to accompany
        woman, 336
      refusal of time off etc, 334
    bankruptcy of either party before
      proceedings completed, 1409
    circumstances for making, 1406
    consultation duties, failure to fulfil,
      1200
    death of either party. *See* death of
      employee or employer *below*
    deduction from wages, as to—
      relief available, 260
      right to make, 259
    dependant, time off work to make
      arrangements for, 348
    detriment, employee or agency
      worker's right not to suffer—
      European Company employee etc,
        1334
      remedies available on, 626
      right to make, 625
      time for making, 625
    disciplinary hearing, as to
      companion's attendance at, 719
    education or training, young person's
      right to time off for, 332
    eligibility to make, 1406
    employee safety, as to infringed rights
      of representative of, 1210
    fixed-term work regulations, under,
      91
    flexible working application, as to,
      111
    grievance hearing, as to companion's
      attendance at, 719
    guarantee payment, as to, 265
    guaranteed debt, as to payment of,
      629
    information and consultation of
      employees regulations,
      proceedings under, 1316
    information duties, failure to fulfil,
      1200
    infringement of rights, for, 1406

EMPLOYMENT TRIBUNAL—*continued*
President—*continued*
Senior. *See* Senior President *below*
specialist panels, power to establish,
    1401
unable to carry out functions, where,
    1400
prohibition notice, appeal against, 316,
    1489
reasons for decision—
national security proceedings,
    modification of rules, 1476
procedural rules, 1476
reconsideration of judgment, 1479
recovery of sums awarded, 1484
reference to, to enforce statutory
    rights—
determination of, 126
employee requiring, 125
sanctions, 127
time limit for making, 125
regional employment judges, 1401
regulations—
conciliation procedure, as to, 1420
confidential information, as to
    hearing of, 1415
costs and expenses, as to, 1418
disability cases, restriction of publicity
    in, 1417
power to make, 1410
practice directions, as to. *See* practice
    directions *above*
pre-hearing reviews, 1414
preliminary matters, 1414
preparation time, payments for, 1419
scope, 1410
sexual misconduct cases, restriction of
    publicity, 1416
relevant decision day: meaning, 1483
reports, fees and allowances for
    preparation of, 1405
restricted reporting order, 1416n[4],
    1417n[4]
rules of procedure, 1421
Senior President—
directions as to procedure, power to
    make, 1412
members' panels, responsibility for,
    1401
sexual misconduct cases, restriction of
    publicity, 1416
time limits—
calculation, 1460
complaint, for presenting, 1409
trade union political fund contributions,
    objection to, 990

EMPLOYMENT TRIBUNAL—*continued*
transfer of proceedings—
court, from, 1469
with the UK, 1469
transfer of undertaking, complaint in
    connection with, 140
unlawful act notice—
meaning, 1490n[1]
appeal against, 1490
wasted costs order—
ability to pay, regard to, 1480
allowances for attendance at tribunal,
    payment of, 1480
application for, 1480
entitlement to, 1480
power to make, 1480
wasted costs: meaning, 1480
withdrawal of complaint, binding nature
    of, following consent order, 150n[4]
working time offences—
complaint to, 319
improvement notice, appeal against,
    316
prohibition notice, appeal against,
    316

EQUAL PAY
equal value claim. *See under*
    EMPLOYMENT TRIBUNAL

EQUAL PAY AUDIT
meaning, 609
not ordered, where, 609
power to order, 609
regulations as to, 609

EQUALITY
equal value claim. *See under*
    EMPLOYMENT TRIBUNAL

EUROPEAN COMPANY
employee involvement—
agreement—
meaning, 1320n[3]
content, 1325
disputes as to operation of, 1328
information and consultation
    procedures, establishment of,
    1325
negotiation in spirit of
    cooperation, 1325
participation, arrangements for,
    1325n[9]
parties charged with reaching,
    1320
representative body—
meaning, 1325n[7]
detriment, member's right not to
    be subjected to, 1334

EUROPEAN COMPANY—*continued*
employee involvement—*continued*
agreement—*continued*
representative body—*continued*
time off work for member of,
1332
unfair dismissal of member,
1333
standard rules on employee
involvement—
meaning, 1325n[15]
whether applicable, 1325
writing, need for, 1325
Central Arbitration Committee,
application to—
confidential information
requirements, as to, 1330,
1331
jurisdiction as to proceedings under
regulations, 1335
special negotiating body, as to
establishment of, 1320
Central Arbitration Committee,
complaint to—
employee involvement agreement,
as to operation of, 1328
failure to provide information, as
to, 1319
jurisdiction as to proceedings under
regulations, 1335
special negotiating body—
ballot arrangements, as to, 1321
consultative committee, as to
appointment of members
by, 1323
decisions taken by, as to, 1326
standard rules, as to
non-compliance with, 1328
confidential information—
breach of duty with regard to,
1330
withholding of information, 1331
consultative committee—
meaning, 1323n[4]
appointment of members by, 1323,
1324
information and consultation
function, 1323n[4]
Council Directive, implementation,
1317
detriment, employee's right not to be
subjected to, 1334
employees' representatives: meaning,
1319n[5]
participating company—
meaning, 1317n[6]

EUROPEAN COMPANY—*continued*
employee involvement—*continued*
participating company—*continued*
concerned subsidiary or
establishment: meaning,
1317n[13]
Great Britain, registered office in,
1317
information—
duty to provide, 1319
withholding, 1331
proceedings, jurisdiction as to, 1335–
1337
regulations—
application, 1317
contracting out, restrictions on,
1318
misuse of procedures under, 1329
special negotiating body—
ballot for election of UK
members—
arrangements, 1321
complaint as to arrangements,
1321
conduct of, 1322
ineffective ballot report, 1322
specified requirements, 1321
supervisor, 1322
composition, 1320
consultative committee,
appointment of members by,
1323, 1324
decisions of, 1326
detriment, member's right not to be
subjected to, 1334
eligible member: meaning, 1320n[11]
employees, member as representee
of, 1324
expenses incurred by, payment of,
1326
experts, use of, 1326
function, 1320
merger, European Company
established by, 1320
ordinary members, 1320
reduction of participation rights:
meaning, 1326n[5]
time off work for member, 1332
unfair dismissal of member, 1333
voting by members—
absolute majority vote, 1326n[4]
generally, 1326
two thirds majority vote, 1326n[6]
whether properly established,
application to CAC, 1320

References are to paragraph numbers; superior figures refer to notes

References are to paragraph numbers; superior figures refer to notes

PICKETING—_continued_
potential liability for—_continued_
tort, 1384
public, whether causing distress,
hardship etc to, 1386
statutory immunity, 1385
unlawful picketing, 1369
POLICE AND CRIME COMMISSIONER
redundancy payments legislation,
application of, 845
POLICE CADET
employment, nature of, 82, 93, 107,
278
working time protection, 278
POLICE CONSTABLE
employment, nature of, 82, 93, 107,
278
working time protection, 278
POLICE FORCE
redundancy payments legislation,
application of, 845
POLICE FORCE, MEMBER
industrial action, restriction on, 1392
POLICE OFFICER
dependants, no right to time off work to
make arrangements for, $347n^3$
employment protection legislation,
application of, 168
POSTAL WORKER
industrial action by, offences, 1394
PRISON OFFICER
industrial action by, restriction on, 1392
PRISONER
meaning, $190n^1$
national minimum wage, not qualifying
for, 190
PROFIT SHARING SCHEME
employee participating in, effect on
status, 11
PROHIBITION NOTICE
Energy Act notice, appeal against, 1489
health and safety notice, appeal
against, 1489
working time regulations, under. _See_
under WORKING TIME
PUBLIC TRANSPORT
redundancy payments legislation,
application of, 840
RECEIVER
termination of employment on
appointment of, 727
REDUNDANCY
meaning, 870
adoption leave, during, 386
'bumping', by, $870n^3$

REDUNDANCY—_continued_
changes in work, question of fact for
tribunal, $870n^9$
consultation with employees'
representatives—
adaptation of statutory procedure,
1195
appropriate representatives, where no
union involved, 1187
complete closure, $1185n^8$
duty to consult, 835, 1185
employee representative: meaning,
$1187n^{12}$
employment tribunal, complaint to—
declaration, 1189
failure to comply with
requirements, on, 1189
grounds for making, 1189
protective award. _See_ protective
award _below_
time limit for making, 1189
failure to consult. _See_ employment
tribunal, complaint to _above_
information to be given—
manner of giving, $1185n^{16}$
nature of, 1185
nature of consultation, $1185n^8$
pre-transfer consultation, 1186
sovereign nature, decision of,
$1185n^{10}$
special circumstances defence, 1188
time limit for starting, 1185
transfer of employees from another
undertaking, 1186
variation of statutory procedure,
1195
dismissal by reason of, whether fair. _See_
UNFAIR DISMISSAL (redundancy, on
grounds of)
employee representative—
consultation with. _See_ consultation
with employee representatives
above
detriment, right not to suffer, 1208
employment protection generally,
1207
time off work, 1209
maternity leave, during, 364
notification to Secretary of State—
adaptation of statutory procedure,
1195
employer's duty, 1192
failure to notify, offence and penalty,
1193
non-compliance, special
circumstances, 1192

References are to paragraph numbers; superior figures refer to notes

References are to paragraph numbers; superior figures refer to notes

TRADE UNION—*continued*
  amalgamation—*continued*
    ballot on resolution approving
      instrument—*continued*
      notice to members, 1002
      result, time for publication, 1006
      simple majority unless otherwise
        provided for, 1003
      storage and distribution of voting
        papers, 1005
      voting method, 1005
    certification after, 1008
    complaint by member—
      determination by certification
        officer, 1011
      procedure on, 1010
      right to make, 1010
      time limit for making, 1010
    election, certain positions, exemption
      from requirements, 968
    generally, 998
    instrument—
      approval by certification officer,
        998, 1001
      contents, 1001
      registration, 1007
    listing after, 1008
    Northern Ireland union, involving,
      1013
    political resolution, union treated as
      having passed, 995
    property, vesting of, 1012
    regulations, power to make, 1000
    supply of information after, 1008
  annual return—
    certification officer, to, 943
    contents, 943
    form of, 943
    offence and penalty as to, 956
    statement to members following, 944
  assurer—
    appointment, 932
    certification officer, duties in respect
      of, 932
    duties of, 932
    excluded persons, 932
    generally, 932
    qualified independent person as,
      932n[5]
    re-appointment, 932
  auditors—
    appointment, 946
    duty to appoint, 945
    eligibility for appointment, 945
    removal, 946
    report on accounts, 947

TRADE UNION—*continued*
  auditors—*continued*
    rights of, 948
  awards against, enforcement of, 928
  Bridlington Principles, 1017n[1]
  certificate of independence—
    application for, 905
    conclusive effect of certification
      officer's decision, 907
    refusal of, 905
    withdrawal or cancellation, 906
  certification officer. *See* CERTIFICATION
    OFFICER
  common law—
    legal status at, 896
    restraint of trade, validity of, 898
  contempt of court, liability for, 1442
  Crown employment, application of
    provisions, 893
  discrimination by, prohibition on, 1036
  disqualification from holding certain
    offices, 958
  dissolution, 1015
  documents, falsification etc, 956
  elections—
    access to records, 959
    addresses, 965
    ballot—
      conduct of, 962
      means of voting, 963
      method of voting, 962
      single transferable vote, use of, 962
      storage and distribution of voting
        papers, 962
      voting paper, format, 962
    cancellation, restriction on, 959
    candidacy, attempts to restrict, 964
    compliance with rules, need for, 959
    duty to hold, 960
    electable positions, 960
    entitlement to vote, 961
    exemption from requirements, 968
    federated union, exemption from
      requirements, 968
    independent scrutineer—
      appointment, 966
      interference with, prevention of,
        966
      powers, 966
      qualified independent person:
        meaning, 966
      report on election, 967
      supply of register to, 966
    means of voting, 963
    minor irregularity, whether rendering
      result void, 959

References are to paragraph numbers; superior figures refer to notes

TRADE UNION
  MEMBERSHIP—*continued*
  statutory rights—*continued*
    not to be unjustifiably
        disciplined—*continued*
      generally, 1029
      remedies, 1032
      unjustifiably disciplined: meaning,
        1030
    subscription deduction arrangements,
        as to. *See* unauthorised
        deductions, right not to suffer
        below
    termination of membership, 1033
    time off. *See* TIME OFF WORK (trade
        union duties and activities, for)
    unauthorised deductions, right not to
        suffer—
      employment tribunal, complaint
        to, 1035
      generally, 1034
      subscription deduction
        arrangements: meaning, 1034
      subscription deductions: meaning,
        $1034n^4$
  superannuation scheme. *See* members'
      superannuation scheme *above*
  termination, 1033
  time off. *See* TIME OFF WORK (trade
      union duties and activities, for)
  unauthorised deductions, right not to
      suffer. *See under* statutory rights
      above
  victimisation—
    complaint to employment tribunal—
      consideration of complaint, 1049
      remedies available to tribunal,
        1050
      right to make, 1048
    detriment, suffering, 1048
    remedies, 1050

TRADE UNION RECOGNITION
  meaning, 1094
  agreement for. *See* voluntary agreement
      below
  application for—
    acceptance—
      acceptance period: meaning,
        $1109n^{10, 21}$
      appropriate bargaining unit,
        deciding on, 1110
      CAC's role. *See* Central Arbitration
        Committee *below*
      notice of, 1109
      relevant bargaining unit: meaning,
        $1109n^8$

TRADE UNION
  RECOGNITION—*continued*
  application for—*continued*
    acceptance—*continued*
      ten per cent test, 1109
      union communications with
        workers after, 1111
    admissibility of—
      competing application, 1126
      further application, 1125
      generally, 1108
    Central Arbitration Committee—
      consideration of application by,
        1109
      declaration, issue of, 1115, 1117,
        1125
      duty to proceed with accepted
        application, 1116
      further applications to, admissibility
        of, 1125
      validity of application, approach to
        deciding on, 1115
    competing application—
      meaning, $1126n^2$
      inadmissibility or invalidity of,
        1126
    membership evidence as to support
        for, $1117n^{11}$
    notice to cease consideration of, 1113
    receipt, notice of, 1109
    relevant bargaining unit: meaning,
        $1108n^{12}$
    validity, 1114, 1115, 1126
    withdrawal, 1112
  ballot—
    cancellation, on failure of employer to
        fulfil duties, 1120
    conditions to be fulfilled prior to,
        1117
    conduct, 1118
    costs, responsibility for payment of,
        1121
    employer's duties, 1120
    holding of, 1118
    notice as to holding of, 1117, 1118
    of no effect, on failure of employer to
        fulfil duties, 1120
    outcome-specific offer, party making,
        $1119n^5$
    procedure following, 1122
    qualified independent person to
        conduct, $1118n^{15}$
    result, declaration following, 1122
    secret nature of, 1118
    special factors as to conduct, $1118n^{18}$
    unfair practices, 1119

References are to paragraph numbers; superior figures refer to notes

TRADE UNION
  RECOGNITION—*continued*
  derecognition—*continued*
  union not independent, where—
    application of provisions, 1162
    cessation of arrangements, 1165
    other unions recognised, where,
      1165
    workers' application to end
      arrangements—
      acceptance period: meaning,
        1163n[16]
      admissibility of application, 1163
      ballot on derecognition where
        application accepted, 1164
      CAC's response, 1163
      generally, 1163
      negotiation period: meaning,
        1163n[23]
      new negotiation period:
        meaning, 1163n[34]
    workers' application to end
      bargaining arrangements—
      acceptance, 1154
      acceptance period: meaning,
        1154n[18]
      admissibility of application, 1154
      generally, 1154
      negotiation period: meaning,
        1154n[25]
      notice of receipt, 1154
  detriment, right not to be subjected to—
    actions etc, examples, 1169
    employment tribunal, complaint to,
      1170
    generally, 1169
    unfair dismissal, 1171
  generally, 1094
  independence, union's loss of—
    application of provisions, 1166
    certificate of independence—
      reissue, effect, 1168
      withdrawal, effect, 1167
  membership evidence as to support for,
    1117n[11]
  recognised trade union: meaning,
    1206n[1]
  request for—
    agreement of parties, 1105
    collective bargaining to conduct,
      1103
    conditions, 1104
    failure of negotiations, 1107, 1108
    rejection by employer, 1106, 1108
    validity of, 1104
  right to. *See* statutory right to *below*

TRADE UNION
  RECOGNITION—*continued*
  statutory right to—
    amalgamations, power to make
      provision as to effect of, 1100
    application for recognition. *See*
      application for *above*
    bargaining unit, recognition as. *See*
      bargaining unit *above*
    Central Arbitration Committee—
      applications to—
        directions about, 1099
        failure of negotiations, 1107
        rejection by employer, following,
          1106
        See also Central Arbitration
          Committee *above*
      CAC case manager: meaning,
        1102n[5]
      general duty, 1098
      notice of declarations by, 1101
      supply of information to, 1102
    directions as to applications, 1099
    procedure, 1097
    request for recognition. *See* request
      for *above*
    transfer of engagements, power to
      make provision as to effect of,
      1100
  supply of goods or services—
    refusal to deal with on grounds of
      trade union exclusion, 1184
    void term in contract for, 1183
  training for workers within bargaining
    unit. *See under* bargaining unit
    above
  transfer of undertaking, before, 1095
  unfair dismissal due to, 1171
  unfair practices, Secretary of State's
    power to prohibit, 1174
  voluntary agreement as to—
    appropriate bargaining unit,
      determining. *See under* Central
      Arbitration Committee *above*
    collective bargaining methods,
      assistance in negotiating. *See*
      under Central Arbitration
      Committee *above*, 1129
    derecognition, effect on, 1094
    determining whether, 1127
    termination of agreement for, 1128
    unit ceasing to exist, employer
      believing. *See* bargaining unit
      (ceasing to exist, employer
      believing) *above*

UNFAIR DISMISSAL—*continued*
grounds for dismissal subsequently
discovered, 770
health and safety cases, in, 786
ill health, for—
importance of procedure involved,
775
misuse of medical certificates, 775
persistent intermittent absences, 775
sick pay term in contract as irrelevant
factor, 775
information and consultation
representative, of, 1277, 1312,
1333
internal appeal procedures, matters
coming to light during, 770
investigation of complaint against
employee, reasonableness of,
776n[15], 778
jury service, employee called for, 785
leave for family reasons, dismissal
related to, 784
national minimum wage, for attempting
to secure right to, 169, 794
national security, involving, 804
natural justice, effect of breach, 768
occupational pension scheme trustee,
of, 790
part-time worker applying regulations,
where, 78
Pensions Act 2008, for attempting to
enforce rights under, 797
pressure to dismiss unfairly, no account
to be taken of, 771
procedure, effect of failure to follow,
768
protected disclosure, for making, 792
reasonableness of employer's conduct,
767
redundancy, on grounds of—
examples of unfair dismissal, 781
general principles, unfair on, 782
generally, 780, 1063
objective criteria, application of,
782n[8]
procedure and effects, challenging,
780
safety committee, member of, 1077
safety representative, 1077
statute, unfair by reason of, 781
re-engagement, order for—
meaning, 811
compensation for failure to comply
with, 813
contributory fault, test for, 812n[8]
discretionary powers, exercise of, 812

UNFAIR DISMISSAL—*continued*
re-engagement, order for—*continued*
employer having already engaged
replacement, 813n[14]
enforcement, 813
generally, 811
low incidence of orders, 812n[7]
matters for consideration prior to
making of, 812
reasons for not making, 812n[7]
specified terms on making, 811
reinstatement, order for—
meaning, 811
compensation for failure to comply
with, 813
contributory fault, test for, 812n[8]
discretionary powers, exercise of, 812
employer having already engaged
replacement, 813n[14]
enforcement, 813
generally, 811
low incidence of orders, 812n[7]
matters for consideration prior to
making of, 812
reasons for not making, 812n[7]
specified terms on making, 811
remedies—
compensation. *See* compensation for
above
conciliation, binding nature of, 809
employment tribunal, complaint to.
See employment tribunal,
complaint to *above*
reorganisation of business, whether
justifying dismissal, 802
replacement, dismissal of, 801
representative body, of member of,
1333
'resign or be dismissed' case, 762n[16]
right not to be unfairly dismissed—
dismissals procedures agreement—
designation, 759
effect, 759
form and content, 760
revocation, 760
substitution of provisions for
statutory rights, 759
generally, 757
qualifying period, 758
remedy for infringement, 757n[4]
statutory nature of right, 757
teacher in foundation or voluntary
aided school, 757
safety committee, member of, 1077
safety representative, 1077

WELFARE BENEFITS
 industrial action, effect of—
  income support, on, 1356
  jobseeker's allowance, on, 1355
  statutory sick pay, on, 1358
  universal credit, on, 1357
WORK
 suspension from. *See* SUSPENSION FROM
  WORK
WORK EXPERIENCE
 course in, attendance at, exclusion from
  national minimum wage, 196
 government scheme, worker's exclusion
  from national minimum wage, 194
WORKER
 meaning. See under WORDS AND
  PHRASES *post*
 gangmaster, supplied by, 12
WORKING HOURS
 normal—
  meaning, 142
  express statement in contract, $142n^4$
  obligatory overtime, $142n^9$
  voluntary overtime, $142n^5$
  week's pay. *See* WEEK'S PAY
WORKING TIME
 meaning, $98n^6$, $267n^2$, $280n^4$
 adequate rest: meaning, $267n^{22}$, $305n^8$
 advice and information, publication,
  269
 annual leave—
  additional leave, $291n^3$, 292, 293
  airline pilot, statutory holiday pay
   for, $295n^3$
  carrying forward, 293
  compensation for untaken leave, 293
  contractual variation, subject to,
   $294n^{17}$
  dates for taking, 294
  entitlement to—
   other provisions, under, 296
   working time regulations, under,
    291
  exceeding entitlement, worker's duty
   to pay compensation, 293
  first year of employment, in, 294
  instalments, taken in, 293
  leave year, 291
  long-term sick leave, where worker
   on, $294n^6$
  payment in lieu where employment
   terminated, 293
  payment in respect of, right to, 295
  power to prescribe amount of, 270
  regulations as to, power to make,
   270

WORKING TIME—*continued*
 annual leave—*continued*
  termination of employment, payment
   for untaken leave, 293
  time for taking of, 293
 armed forces, exclusion of provisions,
  306
 civil protection services, exclusion of
  provisions, $298n^2$
 collective agreement, modification or
  exclusion of provisions by—
  compensatory rest, 304
  generally, 303
 contracting out, restrictions on, 282
 detriment, employee's right not to
  suffer, 616
 Directive—
  derogations, $267n^{21}$
  entry into force, $267n^1$
  horizontal direct effect of 48-hour
   week limit, $267n^{10}$
  implementation in Great Britain, 268
  measures to be taken under, 267
  purpose, 267
  seafarers, and, $267n^4$
  special hazards etc, work involving,
   $267n^{14}$
 doctor in training, exclusion of
  provisions, 307
 domestic service, exclusion of
  provisions, 299
 employment tribunal, complaint to, 319
 enforcement of provisions—
  enforcement authority: meaning,
   $312n^1$
  improvement notice. *See* improvement
   notice *below*
  inspection. *See* inspector *below*
  mediation. *See* mediation *below*
  offences. *See* offences *below*
  prohibition notice. *See* prohibition
   notice *below*
  remedies—
   generally, 319
   See also mediation *below*
  responsibility for, 311
 EU requirements, 267
 exclusions—
  armed forces, 306
  civil protection services: meaning,
   $298n^2$
  collective agreement, provided for
   by, 303
  doctor in training, 307
  domestic service, 299

WORKING TIME—*continued*
  exclusions—*continued*
    force majeure, and young worker,
      309
    generally, 297
    mobile worker, 305
    offshore work, employment in, 308
    seafarers, 297
    shift workers, 302
    special cases, 301
    specific exclusions, 298
    unmeasured working time, 300
    workforce agreement, provided for
      by, 303
    young workers, 309, 310
  improvement notice—
    meaning, 314
    appeal against, 316
    contents, 314
    directions in, 314
    power to serve, 314
    withdrawal, 314
  information and advice, publication,
    269
  inspector—
    appointment, 312
    claim against, 312
    improvement notice. *See* improvement
      notice *above*
    indemnification, 312
    information obtained by, restriction
      on disclosure, 313
    legal professional privilege, and, 312
    powers, 312
  maximum weekly—
    agreement to exclude, 283
    compliance with limit on, 280
    determining, 280
    excluded days: meaning, 280n^7
    records, need to keep, 287
    worker living on site, 280n^4
    young worker, 281
  mediation—
    meaning, 319n^{25}
    end of, 319n^{29}
    mediator: meaning, 319n^{26}
    start of, 319n^{26}
  mobile worker—
    meaning, 267n^{23}, 305n^1
    exclusion of provisions, 305
  night worker—
    meaning, 267n^{13}, 284n^1
    adult worker: meaning, 285n^2
    day work, transfer to, 285
    health assessment, 285
    length of night work, 284

WORKING TIME—*continued*
  night worker—*continued*
    records, need to keep, 287
    rest periods, 284n^4
    special hazards etc, having, 284n^7
    young worker, 285
  offences—
    act or default of another party, due
      to, 317
    body corporate, by, 317
    failure to comply with requirements,
      317
    inspector's powers, hindering, 317
    remedying cause of, 318
  offshore work—
    meaning, 267n^{10}, 301n^2
    exclusion of provisions, 301, 308
  pattern of work, risks presented by, 286
  prohibition notice—
    meaning, 315
    appeal against, 316
    contents, 315
    directions in, 315
    power to serve, 315
    withdrawal, 315
  records, need to keep, 287
  regulations—
    contracting out, restrictions on, 282
    generally, 268
    information and advice as to,
      publication of, 269
  rest breaks, 290, 296
  rest period—
    meaning, 267n^5
    daily, 288
    entitlement under other provisions,
      296
    night work, 284n^4
    pattern of work determining need
      for, 286
    shift worker, 302
    weekly, 289
  seafarers, exclusion of provisions, 297
  shift worker—
    meaning, 302n^1
    exclusion of provisions, 302
    rest periods, 302
    shift work: meaning, 267n^4
  transport sector, exclusion of
    provisions, 298
  unfair dismissal in cases of, 788
  unmeasured, exclusion of provisions,
    300
  workers entitled to protection—
    meaning, 271
    agency worker, 273

References are to paragraph numbers; superior figures refer to notes

Words and Phrases

Words in parentheses indicate the context in which the word or phrase is used

acceptance period—
  (application for trade union
    recognition), 1109n[10, 21]
  (trade union derecognition), 1161n[23],
    1163n[16]
accounting period (trade union), 945n[2]
acceptance theory (wrongful dismissal),
  826n[4]
act, 614n[3]
action, 614n[3]
additional maternity leave, 356n[2]
adequate rest (working time), 267n[22],
  305n[8]
adopter—
  (paternity leave), 370n[2], 374n[10],
    376n[15]
  (statutory adoption pay), 530n[17]
  (statutory paternity pay), 485n[21],
    487n[7]
adoption agency—
  (agency worker's time off work),
    344n[1], 345n[2]
  (employee's time off work), 341n[2],
    342n[2]
adoption from overseas—
  (paternity leave), 375n[6, 9], 376n[1, 15]
  (statutory adoption pay), 530n[18],
    532n[6]
  (statutory paternity pay), 484n[7], 485n[6],
    486n[6], 487n[6]
adoption pay period, 511
adult worker (night work), 285
advertisement (Trade Union and Labour
    Relations (Consolidation) Act 1992),
    1042n[7]
agency worker—
  (disciplinary or grievance hearing),
    718n[3]
  (fixed-term employee), 94n[5]
  (temporary), 97
  (time off to study or train), 328n[1]
agent, 13
agricultural work, 12n[3]
agriculture, 12n[3]
airman, 567n[1]
allowance (paid to worker), 221n[17]
annual value of the pension (redundancy
    payment), 860n[5]
appropriate representatives—
  (collective redundancies), 1187
  (transfer of undertaking), 1196

arrears of pay (insolvent employer),
  628n[12]
ascertained hours (unmeasured work),
  218n[10]
assessment (medical), 577n[24]
assigned employees (transfer of
    undertaking), 138n[13]
assignment (temporary agency worker),
  96n[3], 99n[4]
associated employer—
  (Employment Rights Act 1996), 3
  (Employment Tribunals Act 1996), 3
  (redundancy during adoption leave),
    386n[7]
  (redundancy during maternity leave),
    364n[8]
  (trade union legislation), 1026n[8]
associated fund-raising body (national
    minimum wage), 188n[5]
associated structure (offshore
    installation), 40n[8], 41n[4]
authorised insurer (liability insurance),
  40n[4]
authorised official (trade union), 1058n[6]
automatic theory (wrongful dismissal),
  826n[4]
basic hours (salaried hours work), 214n[5],
  215n[3]
basic working and employment
    conditions, 96n[3], 98
betting transactions, 321n[2]
betting work, 321n[2]
betting worker, 321n[2]
Bridlington Principles, 1017n[1]
British aircraft, 567n[4]
business—
  (change of employer), 135n[4]
  (liability insurance), 40n[1]
  (parental leave), 392n[19]
CAC case manager, 1102n[5]
calculation date (week's pay), 146
calculation year (salaried hours work),
  215n[1]
capability, 773
cash shortage, 257n[5]
catering business, 321n[1]
central management, 1240n[1]
certificate of independence (trade union),
  1008n[6]
changes in the workforce (transfer of
    undertaking), 139n[20], 803n[7]

References are to paragraph numbers; superior figures refer to notes

References are to paragraph numbers; superior figures refer to notes

References are to paragraph numbers; superior figures refer to notes

References are to paragraph numbers; superior figures refer to notes